STEPPING IT UP

foundations for success in **math**

MATH 1400
Conestoga College
Doon & Guelph Campus

PEARSON

Library and Archives Canada Cataloguing in Publication

Stepping it up : foundations for success in math / John Tobey ... [et al.].

Includes index.

ISBN 978-0-13-247418-4

1. Mathematics—Textbooks. I. Tobey, John, 1943–

QA37.3.S745 2010 510 C2010-901746-3

Cover Art: Courtesy of Veer, Inc.

This special edition published in cooperation with Pearson Learning Solutions.

ISBN: 978-0-13-247418-4

Printed in the United States of America.

Please visit our website at *www.pearsonlearningsolutions.com*.

Attention bookstores: For permission to return any unsold stock, contact us at *pe-uscustomreturns@pearson.com*.

ISBN 10: 1-256-61151-4
ISBN 13: 978-1-256-61151-6

STEPPING IT UP

foundations for success in math

U.S. Authors

John Tobey, North Shore Community College
Jeffrey Slater, North Shore Community College
Jamie Blair, Orange Coast College
Robert Blitzer, Miami Dade College

Canadian Authors

Michael Delgaty, Algonquin College
Lisa Hayden, Algonquin College
Michael Nauth, Algonquin College
Patricia Byers, Georgian College

Consultants

Patricia Byers, Georgian College
Lauren Fuentes, Durham College

Table of Contents

Preface

Welcome to *Stepping It Up*!

This text was adapted for Canadian college students, regardless of the trade or program they have chosen to pursue. We have revised the original U.S. text so that each module can be taught independently of the other modules. The result is a mathematics learning resource that can be tailored specifically to the needs of any class.

To ensure a more relevant learning experience for Canadian students, we have created nearly 100 new examples using actual Canadian data. The names of people and locations in the examples are as diverse as the population of Canada. We have converted most of the examples and questions to SI units; U.S. customary units are included where they are most commonly used by Canadians (for instance, in examples related to the trades). By using realistic Canadian examples, we hope to engage students and to help them understand the relevance of the material presented in each module.

As authors, we are committed to producing a textbook that emphasizes mathematical reasoning and problem-solving techniques. To this end, the problem sets are built on a wealth of real-life and real-data applications. Unique problems have been developed and incorporated into the exercise sets to help train students in data interpretation, mental mathematics, estimation, geometry and graphing, number sense, critical thinking, and decision making.

The **Mathematics Blueprint for Problem Solving** strengthens problem-solving skills by providing a consistent and interactive outline to help students organize their approach to problem solving. Once students fill in the blueprint, they can refer back to their plan as they do what is needed to solve the problem.

A dedicated **Study Skills** module opens the text, and **Developing Your Study Skills** boxes are integrated throughout the core modules to provide students with techniques for improving their study skills and succeeding in math courses.

Examples and exercises that incorporate a principle of geometry are marked with a triangle icon for easy identification. When students encounter mathematics in real-world publications, they often see data represented in a graph, chart, or table and are asked to make a reasonable conclusion based on the data presented. This emphasis on graphical interpretation is a continuing trend with today's expanding technology. In this text, students are asked to make simple interpretations, to solve medium-level problems, and to investigate challenging applied problems based on the data shown in a chart, graph, or table.

Students are given many opportunities to practise and review core concepts. Each module contains **Practice Problems**, **Quick Quizzes**, **Module Review Problems**, and two **How Am I Doing?** tests. The text is bookended by a **Diagnostic Pretest** and a **Practice Final Exam**.

We are confident that *Stepping It Up* offers Canadian college students the most effective mathematics learning resource available.

Diagnostic Pretest: Stepping It Up: Foundations for Success in Math

Whole Numbers

1. Add. $3846 + 527$

2. Divide. $58\overline{)1508}$

3. Subtract. $\begin{array}{r} 12\,807 \\ -11\,679 \\ \hline \end{array}$

4. The highway department used 115 truckloads of sand. Each truck held 8 tonnes of sand. How many tonnes of sand were used?

Fractions

5. Add. $\frac{3}{7} + \frac{2}{5}$

6. Multiply and simplify. $3\frac{3}{4} \times 2\frac{1}{5}$

7. Subtract. $2\frac{1}{6} - 1\frac{1}{3}$

8. Mike's car travelled 237 miles on $7\frac{9}{10}$ gallons of gas. How many miles per gallon did he achieve?

Decimals

9. Multiply. $\begin{array}{r} 51.06 \\ \times\ 0.307 \\ \hline \end{array}$

10. Divide. $0.026\overline{)0.0884}$

11. The copper pipe is 24.375 centimetres long. Paula has to shorten it by cutting off 1.75 centimetres. How long will the copper pipe be when it is shortened?

12. Russ bicycled 20.5 kilometres on Monday, 5.8 kilometres on Tuesday, and 14.9 kilometres on Wednesday. How many kilometres did he bicycle on those three days?

1. ________

2. ________

3. ________

4. ________

5. ________

6. ________

7. ________

8. ________

9. ________

10. ________

11. ________

12. ________

13. ______

14. ______

15. ______

16. ______

17. ______

18. ______

19. ______

20. ______

21. ______

22. ______

23. ______

24. ______

25. ______

26. ______

27. ______

28. ______

Ratio and Proportion

Solve each proportion problem. Round to the nearest tenth if necessary.

13. $\frac{3}{7} = \frac{n}{24}$

14. $\frac{0.5}{0.8} = \frac{220}{n}$

15. Wally earned \$600 for mowing lawns at 25 houses last week. At that rate, how much would he earn for doing 45 houses?

16. Two cities that are actually 300 miles apart appear to be 8 inches apart on the road map. How many miles apart are two cities that appear to be 6 inches apart on the map?

Percent

Round to the nearest tenth if necessary.

17. Change to a percent: $\frac{3}{8}$

18. 138% of 5600 is what number?

19. At Fanshawe College 53% of the students are women. There are 3267 women at the college. How many students are at the college?

20. At a manufacturing plant it was discovered that 9 out of every 3000 parts made were defective. What percent of the parts are defective?

Measurement

21. 150 cL = ______ L

22. 3 cm = ______ m

23. 1.56 tons = ______ lb

24. 4900 kg = ______ mg

Geometry

Round to the nearest hundredth when necessary. Use $\pi \approx 3.14$ *when necessary.*

▲ **25.** Find the area of a triangle with a base of 34 metres and an altitude of 23 metres.

▲ **26.** Find the cost to install carpet in a circular area with a radius of 5 metres at a cost of \$35 per square metre.

▲ **27.** In a right triangle the longest side is 15 metres and the shortest side is 9 metres. What is the length of the other side of the triangle?

▲ **28.** How many pounds of fertilizer can be placed in a cylindrical tank that is 4 feet tall and has a radius of 5 feet if one cubic foot of fertilizer weighs 70 pounds?

Statistics

The following double-bar graph indicates the sale of Dodge Calibers as reported by the district sales managers. Use this graph to answer questions 29–32.

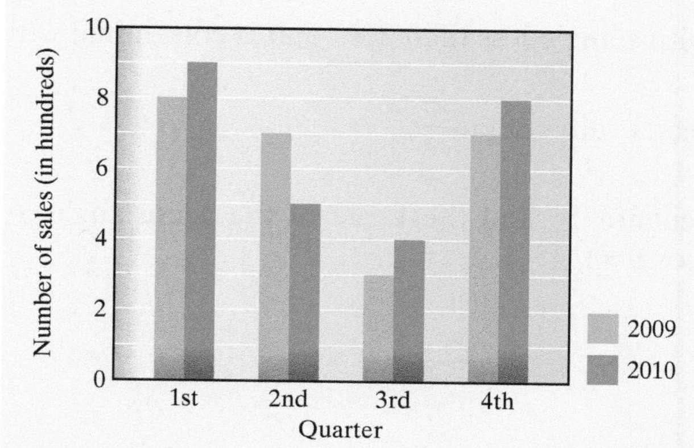

29. How many Dodge Calibers were sold in the second quarter of 2010?

30. How many more Dodge Calibers were sold in the fourth quarter of 2010 than were sold in the fourth quarter of 2009?

31. In which year were more Dodge Calibers sold, in 2009 or 2010?

32. What is the *mean* number of Dodge Calibers sold per quarter in 2009?

Signed Numbers

Perform the following operations.

33. $-5 + (-2) + (-8)$

34. $-8 - (-20)$

35. $\left(-\frac{3}{4}\right) \div \left(\frac{5}{6}\right)$

36. $(-3)(2)(-1)(-3)$

Introduction to Algebra

Simplify.

37. $9(x + y) - 3(2x - 5y)$

In exercises 38–39, solve for x.

38. $3x - 7 = 5x - 19$

39. $2(x - 3) + 4x = -2(3x + 1)$

▲ **40.** A rectangle has a perimeter of 134 metres. The length of the rectangle is 4 metres longer than double the width of the rectangle. What are the length and the width of the rectangle?

29. ____________

30. ____________

31. ____________

32. ____________

33. ____________

34. ____________

35. ____________

36. ____________

37. ____________

38. ____________

39. ____________

40. ____________

41. ______

42. ______

43. ______

44. ______

Trigonometry

41. $120° =$ ________ radians

42. Find a positive angle less than 360° that is coterminal with 410°.

43. Find the exact value of $\tan \frac{\pi}{4}$.

44. Use a calculator to find the value of the acute angle θ to the nearest degree if $\cos \theta = 0.4541$.

Study Skills

Study Skills 1 Your Brain Can Learn Mathematics

Student Learning Objectives

After studying this section, you will be able to:

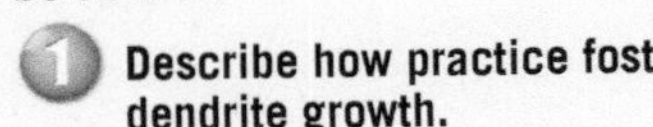 Describe how practice fosters dendrite growth.

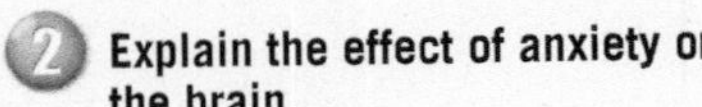 Explain the effect of anxiety on the brain.

Your brain knows how to learn, just as your lungs know how to breathe; however, there are important things you can do to maximize your brain's ability to do its work. This short introduction will help you choose effective strategies for learning mathematics. This is a simplified explanation of a complex process.

Your brain's outer layer is called the **neocortex**, which is where higher level thinking, language, reasoning, and purposeful behaviour occur. The neocortex has about 100 billion (100 000 000 000) brain cells called **neurons**.

Learning Something New

- As you learn something new, threadlike branches grow out of each neuron. These branches are called **dendrites**.
- A connection is made when the dendrite from one neuron grows close enough to the dendrite from another neuron. There is a small gap at the connection point called a **synapse**. One dendrite sends an electrical signal across the gap to another dendrite.
- ***Learning = growth and connecting of dendrites.***

Remembering New Skills

- When you practise a skill just once or twice, the connections between neurons are very weak. If you do not practise the skill again, the dendrites at the connection points wither and die back. You have forgotten the new skill!

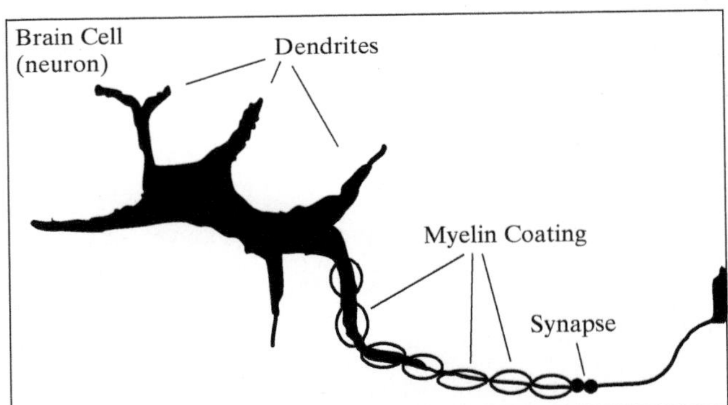

A neuron with several dendrites: one dendrite has developed a myelin coating through repeated practice.

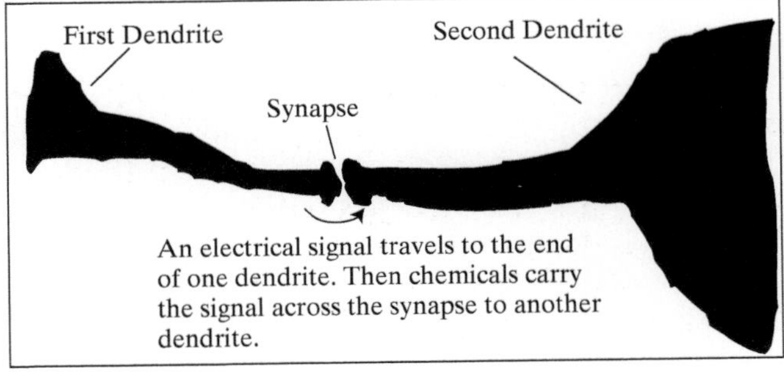

A close-up view of the connection (synapse) between two dendrites.

- If you practise a new skill many times, the dendrites for that skill become coated with a fatty protein called **myelin**. Each time one dendrite sends a signal to another dendrite, the myelin coating becomes thicker and smoother, allowing the signals to move faster and with less interference. Thinking can now occur more quickly and easily, and ***you will remember the skill for a long time*** because the dendrite connections are very strong.

Becoming An Effective Student

- You grow dendrites specifically for the thing you are studying. If you practise dividing fractions, you will grow specialized dendrites just for dividing fractions. If you ***watch other people*** solve fraction problems, **you will grow dendrites for watching, not for solving.** So, be sure you are actively learning and practising.
- If you practise something the wrong way, you will develop strong dendrite connections for doing it the wrong way! So, as you study, check frequently that you are getting correct answers.
- As you study a new topic that is related to things you already know, you will grow new dendrites, but your brain will also send signals throughout the network of dendrites for the related topics. In this way, you build a complex **neural network** that allows you to apply concepts, see differences and similarities between ideas, and understand relationships between concepts.

Throughout the modules, you will find "brain friendly" activities that are designed to help you grow and develop your own reliable neural networks for mathematics. Since you must grow your own dendrites (no one can grow them for you), these activities show you how to

- develop new dendrites,
- strengthen existing ones, and
- encourage the myelin coating to become thicker so signals are sent with less effort.

When you incorporate the activities into your regular study routine, you will discover that you understand better, remember longer, and forget less.

Also remember that it ***does take time for dendrites to grow.*** Trying to cram in several new concepts and skills at the last minute is not possible. Your dendrites simply can't grow that quickly. You can't expect to develop huge muscles by lifting weights for just one evening before a body building competition! In the same way, practise the study techniques ***throughout the course*** to facilitate strong growth of dendrites.

When Anxiety Strikes

If you are under stress or feeling anxious, such as during a test, your body secretes **adrenaline** into your system. Adrenaline in the brain blocks connections between neurons. In other words, you can't think! If you've ever experienced "blanking out" on a test, you know what adrenaline does. You'll learn several solutions to that problem in later activities.

Start Your Course Right!

- Attend all class sessions (especially the first one).
- Gather the necessary supplies.
- Carefully read the syllabus for the course, and ask questions if you don't understand.

STUDY SKILLS 2 USING YOUR TEXTBOOK

Student Learning Objectives

After studying this section, you will be able to:

1. **Explain the meaning of module features such as section numbering, objectives, Practice Problems.**
2. **Locate the Solutions, Glossary, and Index sections.**

Be sure to read ***Your Brain Can Learn Mathematics*** **before this activity.** You'll find out how your brain learns and remembers.

Your textbook can be very helpful. Find out what it has to offer. First, let's look at some general features that will help in all modules.

Table of Contents

Look in the very front of the book for the Table of Contents. Before you start the first module, you'll want to look at the Diagnostic Pretest, near the beginning of the book.

Section Numbering

Each module is divided into sections, and each section has a number, such as 3 or 5. Your instructor will use these numbers to assign homework.

Module Features

There are seven features to pay special attention to as you work in your book.

- **Student Learning Objectives.** Each section lists the objectives in the upper corner of the first page. The objectives are listed again as each one is introduced. An objective tells you what you will be able to do after you complete the section. An excellent way to check your learning is to go back to the list of objectives when you are finished with a section and ask yourself if you can do them all.
- **Examples and Practice Problems.** These examples apply the concepts just discussed. They include the worked out solutions for questions provided. The Practice Problems are similar questions. Fully worked out solutions can be found at the end of the module.
- **Important Definitions or Notes.** Look for specially marked purple boxes. They contain important definitions, formulas, mathematical processes, explanations, or interesting comments about a topic. They add to your understanding of the topic being discussed.
- **Developing Your Study Skills boxes.** These boxes are integrated throughout the modules. They provide tips and suggestions for improving your mathematics skills. These recommendations can be used in conjunction with this **Study Skills** section. There are 13 **Study Skills** provided for you to review and related exercises to work through. These Study Skills are designed to increase your ability to be organized in your studying, develop your test-taking skills, identify problem areas, and more.
- **Calculator boxes.** A small picture of a blue calculator with a blue box appears in several places. The calculator icon means that there is a calculator tip, which helps you learn more about using your calculator. A calculator in an Exercise section is a recommendation to use your calculator to work that exercise.

List a page number from Module 1 for three of these module features:

1. ____________________
2. ____________________
3. ____________________

- **End-of-Section Exercises and Quick Quizzes.** Each section ends with questions designed to provide you with practice of the concepts just learned. Answers to these questions are found at the end of the module. Short Quick Quizzes provide a re-cap of your knowledge by reinforcing key math ideas.
- **How Am I Doing?** Use these exercises as a way to check your understanding of all the concepts in the module. You can practise every type of problem. These questions are provided by module section. If you get stuck, you can go back to the appropriate section for more explanations.

End-of-Module Features

Go to the first page of a module. What features are listed at the end of each module?

- **Putting Your Skills to Work: Use Math to Save Money.** This section provides a real-life application of the mathematics just learned.
- **Module Organizer.** Find the Module Organizer for the first module. It lists in table format **Topics, Procedures,** and **Examples** found in this module.
- **Module Review Problems.** These are problems listed by module section. Again, you may go to the appropriate section for additional guidance if you find yourself having difficulty with a particular math idea.
- **How Am I Doing? Module Test.** Plan to take the test as a practice exam. That way you can be sure you really know how to work all types of problems without looking back at the module.

How will you make good use of the features at the end of each module?

____

____

____

Solutions

How do you find out if you've worked the exercises correctly? Solutions are provided to the Practice Problems in each module section.

Glossary

There is a glossary of terms used in mathematics that you can find at the end of each module. Each term is identified by the section in which it can be found.

Index

All of the topics, vocabulary, and concepts are listed in alphabetical order in the **Index**. Go to the page or pages listed and find each word. Write down the page that introduces or defines each one. There may be several subheadings listed under the main word, or several page numbers listed. Usually, the *first* place that a word appears in the textbook is where it is introduced and defined. So, the earliest page number is a good place to start.

Appendices

There are five appendices at the end of the textbook. These are:

- Appendix A: Consumer Finance Applications
- Appendix B: Tables
- Appendix C: Scientific Calculators
- Appendix D: Metric and U.S. Customary Measurements
- Appendix E: Useful Formulas from Geometry

Why Are These Features Brain Friendly?

The authors included features that make it easier for you to understand the mathematics. **Your brain naturally seeks organization and predictability.** When you pay attention to the regular features of the modules, you are allowing your brain to get familiar with all of the helpful tips, suggestions, and explanations that your book has to offer. You will make the best possible use of your textbook.

Other Features

A **Diagnostic Pretest** and **Practice Final Examination** are included. Results from the **Diagnostic Pretest** may indicate which mathematics skills you are strong in and those that require more understanding and practice. The **Practice Final Examination** prepares you for the final examination at your school. It provides an overview of all the content discussed in the modules.

Study Skills 3 Homework: How, Why, and When

It is best for your brain if you keep up with the reading and homework in your math class. Remember that the more times you work with the information, the more dendrites you grow! So, give yourself every opportunity to read, work problems, and review your mathematics.

You have two choices for reading your math textbook. Read the short descriptions below and decide which approach will be best for you.

Student Learning Objectives

After studying this section, you will be able to:

 **Select an appropriate strategy for homework.**

 **Use textbook features effectively.**

Preview Before Class; Read Carefully After Class

Maddy learns best by listening to her teacher explain things. She "gets it" when she sees the instructor work problems on the board. She likes to ask questions in class and put the information in her notes. She has learned that it helps if she has previewed the section before the lecture, so she knows generally what to expect in class. But after the class instruction, when Maddy gets home, she finds that she can understand the math material easily. She remembers what her teacher said, and she can double-check her notes if she gets confused. So, Maddy does her careful reading of the module section **after** hearing the classroom lecture on the topic.

Read Carefully Before Class

Pietre, on the other hand, feels he learns well by reading on his own. He prefers to read the section and try working the example problems before coming to class. That way, he already knows what the teacher is going to talk about. Then, he can follow the teacher's examples more easily. It is also easier for him to take notes in class. Pietre likes to have his questions answered right away, which he can do if he has already read the module section. So, Pietre **carefully** reads the section before he hears the classroom lecture on the topic.

Notice that there is no one right way to work with your textbook. You always must figure out what works best for you. Note also that both Maddy and Pietre work with one section at a time. The key is that you read the textbook regularly! The rest of this activity will give you some ideas of how to make the most of your reading.

Try the following steps as you read your math modules.

- Read slowly. Read only one section—or even part of a section—at a time.
- Do the Practice Problems **as you go.** Check them right away. The solutions are provided at the end of the module.
- If your mind wanders, work problems on separate paper and write explanations in your own words.
- Make study cards as you read each section. Pay special attention to the purple boxes in the book. Make cards for new vocabulary, rules, procedures, formulas, and sample problems.
- **NOW,** you are ready to do your homework assignment!

Why Are These Reading Techniques Brain Friendly?

The steps at the left encourage you to be **actively working with the material** in your textbook. Your brain **grows dendrites when it is doing something.**

These methods require you to **try several different techniques,** not just the same thing over and over. Your brain loves variety!

Also, the techniques allow you to take small breaks in your learning. Those **rest periods are crucial for good dendrite growth.**

Now Try This

Which steps for reading this book will be most helpful for you?

1. ______________________________
2. ______________________________
3. ______________________________

Homework

Teachers assign homework so you can grow your own dendrites (learn the material) and then coat the dendrites with myelin through practice (remember the material).

Really! In learning, you get good at what you practise. So, completing homework every day will strengthen your neural network and prepare you for exams.

If you have read each section in your textbook according to the steps above, you will probably encounter few difficulties with the exercises in the homework. Here are some additional suggestions that will help you succeed with the homework.

- If you **have trouble with a problem,** find a similar worked example in the section. Pay attention to every line of the worked example to see how to get from step to step. Work it yourself, too, on separate paper; don't just look at it.
- If it is **hard to remember the steps** to follow for certain procedures, write the steps on a separate card. Then write a short explanation of each step. Keep the card nearby while you do the exercises, but try not to look at it.
- If you **aren't sure you are working the assigned exercises correctly,** go back to the section in the module and review the examples and find out how to correct your errors. When you are sure you understand, try the assigned problems again.
- **Make sure you do some homework every day,** even if the math class does not meet each day!

Why Are These Homework Suggestions Brain Friendly?

Your brain will grow dendrites as you study the worked examples in the modules and try doing them yourself on separate paper. So, when you see similar problems in the homework, you will already have dendrites to work from.

Giving yourself a practice test by trying to remember the steps (without looking at your card) is an excellent way to reinforce what you are learning.

Correcting errors right away is how you learn and reinforce the correct procedures. It is hard to unlearn a mistake, so always check to see that you are on the right track!

Now Try This

What are your biggest homework concerns? List your two main concerns below. Then write a brain friendly solution for each one.

1. Concern: ________________ Solution: ________________
2. Concern: ________________ Solution: ________________

Study Skills 4 Taking Lecture Notes

Study the set of sample math notes in this section, and read the comments about them. Then try to incorporate the techniques into your own math note taking in class.

Student Learning Objectives

After studying this section, you will be able to:

 **Apply note taking strategies, such as writing problems as well as explanations.**

 **Use appropriate abbreviations in notes.**

- The **date and title** of the day's lecture topic are always at the top of every page. **Always begin a new day with a new page.**
- Note the **definitions** of base and exponent are written in parentheses—don't trust your memory!
- Skipping lines makes the notes easier to read.
- See how the **direction word** (*simplifying*) is emphasized and explained.

January 2

Exponents

Exponents used to show repeated multiplication.

$3 \cdot 3 \cdot 3 \cdot 3$ can be written 3^4 — *exponent (how many times it's multiplied)*; *base (the number being multiplied)*

Read 3^2 *as 3 to the 2nd power or 3 squared*
3^3 *as 3 to the 3rd power or 3 cubed*
3^4 *as 3 to the 4th power*
etc.

Simplifying an expresson with exponents → *actually do the repeated multiplication*

2^3 *means* $2 \cdot 2 \cdot 2$ *and* $2 \cdot 2 \cdot 2 = 8$

☆ *Careful!* 5^2 *means* $5 \cdot 5$ *NOT* $5 \cdot 2$
so $5^2 = 5 \cdot 5 = 25$ *BUT* $5^2 \neq 10$

Example	*Explanation*
Simplify $2^4 \cdot 3^2$	*Exponents mean multiplication.*
$2 \cdot 2 \cdot 2 \cdot 2 \cdot 3 \cdot 3$	*Use 2 as a factor 4 times. Use 3 as a factor 2 times.*
$16 \cdot 9$	$2 \cdot 2 \cdot 2 \cdot 2$ *is 16*, $3 \cdot 3$ *is 9* → $16 \cdot 9$ *is 144*
144	*Simplified result is 144 (no exponents left)*

- A **star marks an important concept.** This is a warning to avoid future mistakes. **Note the underlining,** too, which highlights the importance.
- Notice the two columns, which allow for the example and its explanation to be close together. **Whenever you know you'll be given a series of steps to follow, try the two-column method.**
- Note the **brackets and arrows,** which clearly show how the problem is set up to be simplified.

Why Are These Notes Brain Friendly?

The notes are **easy to look at,** and you know that the brain responds to things that are visually pleasing. Other techniques that are visually memorable are the use of spacing (the two columns), stars, underlining, and circling. All of these methods **allow your brain to take note of important concepts and steps.**

The notes are also **systematic,** which means that they use certain techniques regularly. This way, your brain easily recognizes the topic of the day, the signals that show an important point, and the steps to follow for procedures. When you develop a system that you always use in your notes, your notes are easy to understand later when you are reviewing for a test.

Now Try This

Find one or two people in your math class to work with. Compare lecture notes over a period of a week or so. Ask yourself the following questions as you examine the notes.

1. What are you doing in your notes to show the **main points** or larger concepts? (Such as underlining, boxing, using stars, capital letters, etc.)
2. In what ways do you **set off the explanations** for worked problems, examples, or smaller ideas (subpoints)? (Such as indenting, using arrows, circling or boxing)
3. What does **your instructor do** to show that he or she is moving from one idea to the next? (Such as saying "Next" or "Any questions," "Now," or erasing the board, etc.)
4. **How do you mark** that in your notes? (Such as skipping lines, using dashes or numbers, etc.)
5. What **explanations (in words) do you give yourself** in your notes, so when those new dendrites you grew in lecture are fading, you can read your notes and still remember the new concepts later when you try to do your homework?
6. What **did you learn** by examining your classmates' notes?
   - ______________________________
   - ______________________________
   - ______________________________
7. What **will you try** in your own note taking? List four techniques that you will use next time you take notes in math class.
   - ______________________________
   - ______________________________
   - ______________________________
   - ______________________________

Study Skills 5 Reviewing a Module

Student Learning Objectives

After studying this section, you will be able to:

1. **Use the Module Organizer to practise every type of problem.**
2. **Create study cards for vocabulary.**
3. **Practise by doing review and mixed review problems.**
4. **Take the Module Test as a practice test.**

This activity is really about **preparing for tests.** Some of the suggestions are ideas that you will learn to use a little later in the term, but get started trying them out now. Often, the first module in your math textbook will be review, so it is good to practise some of the study techniques on material that is not too challenging.

Use these **module reviewing techniques.**

Module Reviewing Techniques

- **Make a study card for each vocabulary word and concept.** Include a definition, an example, a sketch, and a page reference. Include the symbol or formula if there is one. See the Using Study Cards activity for a quick look at some sample study cards.
- **Go back to the section** to find more explanations or information about any new vocabulary, formulas, or symbols.
- **Use the Module Organizer** to practise each type of problem. Do not expect the Organizer to substitute for reading and working through the whole module! Work through the problems given using the Mathematics Blueprint for Problem Solving strategies.
- **Study your lecture notes** to see what your instructor has emphasized in class. Then review that material in your text.
- Do the **Review Exercises** and **Quick Quizzes.**
  - ✔ If you get stuck on a problem, **first** check the Module Organizer. If that doesn't clear up your confusion, then check the section and your lecture notes.
  - ✔ Pay attention to **direction words** for the problems, such as *simplify, round, solve,* and *estimate.*
  - ✔ Make **study cards for especially difficult problems.**
- **Do the Review Problems.** This is a good check to see if you can still do the problems when they are in mixed-up order. **Check your answers carefully** in the Answers section at the end of the module. Are your answers **exact** and **complete?** Make sure you are **labelling** answers correctly, using the right units. For example, does your answer need to include *\$*, cm^2, *ft,* and so on?
- **Take the How Am I Doing? Module Test as if it is a real test.** If your instructor has skipped sections in the module, figure out which problems to skip on the test before you start.
  - ✔ Time yourself just as you would for a real test.
  - ✔ Use a calculator or notes just as you would be permitted to (or not) on a real test.
  - ✔ Take the test in one sitting, just like a real test is given in one sitting.
  - ✔ Show all your work. Practise showing your work just the way your instructor has asked you to show it.
  - ✔ Practise neatness. Can someone else follow your steps?
  - ✔ Check your answers at the end of the module.

Why Are These Review Activities Brain Friendly?

You have already become familiar with the features of your textbook. This activity requires you to make good use of them. Your **brain needs repetition** to strengthen dendrites and the connections between them. By following the steps outlined here, you will be reinforcing the concepts, procedures, and skills you need to use for tests (and for the next modules).

This combination of techniques provides repetition in different ways. As a result, the brain develops **good branching of dendrites** instead of just relying on one branch or route to connect to the other dendrites. A thorough review of each module will **solidify your dendrite connections.** It will help you be sure that you understand the concepts **completely and accurately.** Also, taking the Module Test will **simulate the testing situation,** which gives you practice in test-taking conditions.

Notice that reviewing a module will take some time. Remember that it takes time for dendrites to grow! You cannot grow a good network of dendrites by rushing through a review in one night. But if you use the suggestions over a few days or evenings, you will notice that you understand the material more thoroughly and remember it longer.

Now Try This

Follow the reviewing techniques listed above for your next test. For each technique, write a comment about how it worked for you.

1. **Make a study card for each vocabulary word and concept.**
2. **Go back to the section** to find more explanations or information.
3. **Study your lecture notes** to see what your instructor has emphasized in class.
4. **Do the Exercises and Quick Quizzes,** following the specific suggestions on the previous page.
5. **Do the Review Problems exercises.**
6. **Take the How Am I Doing? Module Test** as if it is a real test.

Study Skills 6 Managing Your Time

Many college students find themselves juggling a difficult schedule and multiple responsibilities. Perhaps you are going to school, working part-time, and managing family demands. Here are some tips to help you develop good time management skills and habits.

- **Read the syllabus for each class.** Check on class policies, such as attendance, late homework, and make-up tests. Find out how you are graded. Keep the syllabus in your notebook.
- **Make a semester or quarter calendar.** Put test dates and major due dates for all your classes on the same calendar. In this way, you will see which weeks are the really busy ones. Try using a different colour pen for each class. Your brain responds well to the use of colour. A semester calendar is on the next page.
- **Make a weekly schedule.** After you fill in your classes and other regular responsibilities (such as work, picking up kids from school, etc.), block off some study periods during the day that you can guarantee you will use for studying. Aim for 2 hours of study for each 1 hour you are in class.
- **Make "To Do" lists.** Then use them by crossing off the tasks as you complete them. You might even number them in the order they need to be done (most important ones first).
- **Break big assignments into smaller chunks.** They won't seem so big that way. Make deadlines for each small part so you stay on schedule.
- **Give yourself small breaks in your studying.** Do not try to study for hours at a time! Your brain needs rest between periods of learning. Try to give yourself a 10-minute break each hour or so. You will learn more and remember it longer.
- **If you get off schedule, just try to get back on schedule tomorrow.** We all slip from time to time. All is not lost! Make a new "To Do" list and start doing the most important things first.
- **Get help when you need it.** Talk with your instructor during office hours. Also, most colleges have some kind of learning centre, tutoring centre, or counselling office. If you feel lost and overwhelmed, ask for help. Someone can help you decide what to do first and what to spend your time on right away.

Now Try This

What two or three of the suggestions above will you try this week? How do you think they will help you?

1. ______________________________
2. ______________________________
3. ______________________________

Student Learning Objectives

After studying this section, you will be able to:

 **Create a semester schedule.**

 **Create a "to do" list.**

Why Are These Techniques Brain Friendly?

Your brain appreciates some order. It enjoys a little routine, for example, choosing the same study time and place each day. You will find that you quickly settle in to your reading or homework.

Also, your brain **functions better when you are calm.** Too much rushing around at the last minute to get your homework and studying done sends hostile chemicals to your brain and makes it more difficult for you to learn and remember. So, a little planning can really pay off.

Building rest into your schedule is good for your brain. Remember, it takes time for dendrites to grow.

We've suggested using colour on your calendars. This, too, is brain friendly. Remember, your brain **likes pleasant colours and visual material** that is nice to look at. Messy and hard-to-read calendars will not be helpful, and you probably won't look at them often.

SEMESTER CALENDAR

WEEK	MON.	TUES.	WED.	THUR.	FRI.	SAT.	SUN.
1							
2							
3							
4							
5							
6							
7							
8							
9							
10							
11							
12							
13							
14							

Study Skills 7 Using Study Cards

You may have used "flash cards" in other classes before. In math, study cards can be helpful, too. However, they are different because the main things to remember in math are not necessarily terms and definitions; they are *sets of steps to follow* to solve problems (and how to know which set of steps to follow) and *concepts about how math works* (principles). So, the cards will look different but will be just as useful.

In this two-part activity, you will find four types of study cards to use in math. Look carefully at what kinds of information to put on them and where to put it. Then use them the way you would any flash card:

- to quickly review when you have a few minutes,
- to do daily reviews, and
- to review before a test.

Remember, the most helpful thing about study cards is making them. It is in the making of them that you have to do the kind of thinking that is most brain friendly and will improve your neural network of dendrites. After each card description you will find an assignment to try. It is marked **"Now Try This."**

Student Learning Objectives

After studying this section, you will be able to:

 **Create study cards for all new terms.**

 **Create study cards for new procedures.**

New Vocabulary Cards

For new vocabulary cards, put the word (spelled correctly) and the page number where it is found on the front of the card. On the back, write:

- the definition (in your own words if possible),
- an example, an exception (if there are any),
- any related words, and
- a sample problem (if appropriate).

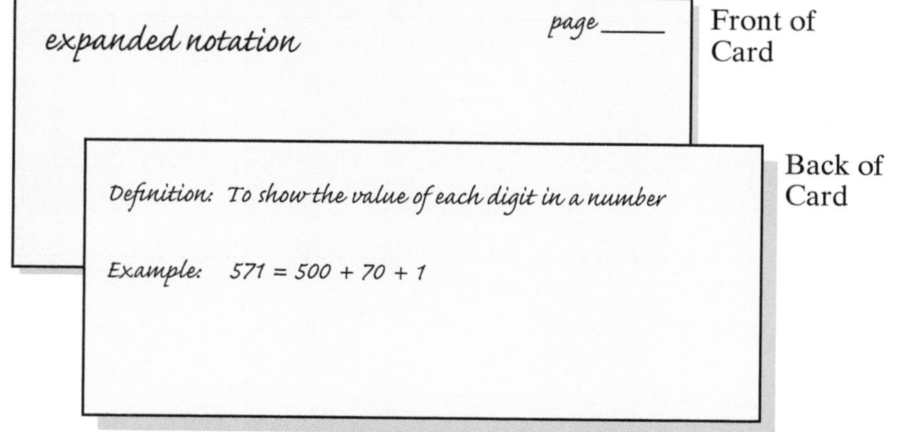

Why Are Study Cards Brain Friendly?

- Making cards is active.
- Cards are visually appealing.
- Repetition is good for your brain.

For details see "Using Study Cards Revisited."

Now Try This

List four new vocabulary words/concepts you need to learn right now. Make a card for each one.

1. ______________________ 2. ______________________

3. ______________________ 4. ______________________

Procedure ("Steps") Cards

For **procedure cards,** write the name of the procedure at the top on the front of the card. Then write each step in words. If you need to know abbreviations for some words, include them along with the whole words written out. On the back, put an example of the procedure, showing each step you need to take. You can review by looking at the front and practising a new worked example, or by looking at the back and remembering what the procedure is called and what the steps are.

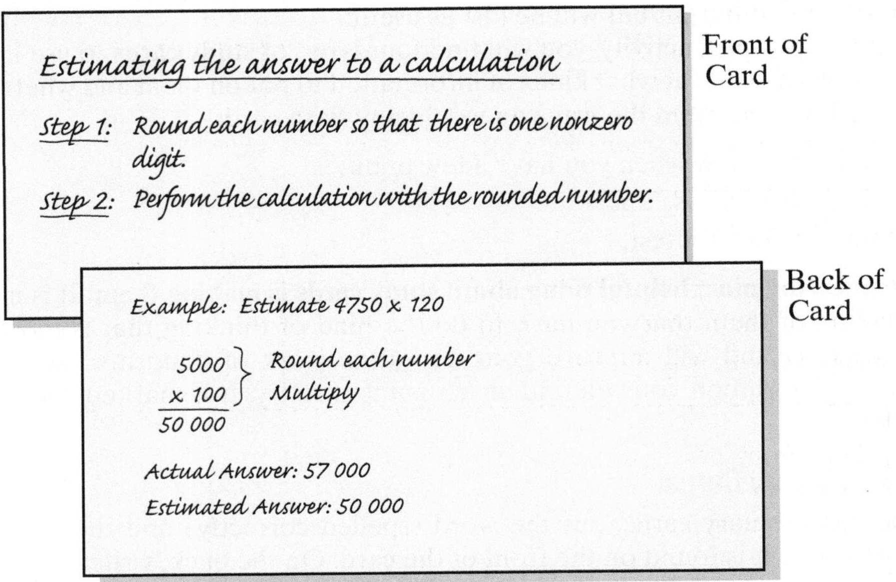

Estimating the answer to a calculation
Step 1: Round each number so that there is one nonzero digit.
Step 2: Perform the calculation with the rounded number.
Front of Card
Example: Estimate 4750 x 120
5000
x 100
50 000
Round each number
Multiply
Actual Answer: 57 000
Estimated Answer: 50 000
Back of Card

Now Try This

What procedure are you learning right now? Make a "steps" card for it.

Procedure: ____

Study Skills 8 Using Study Cards Revisited

This is the second part of the Study Cards activity. As you get further into a module, you can choose particular problems that will serve as a good test review. Here are two more types of study cards that will help you.

Student Learning Objectives

After studying this section, you will be able to:

 **Create study cards for difficult problems.**

 **Create study cards for quiz problems.**

Tough Problems Card

When you are doing your homework and find yourself saying, "This is really hard," or "I'm worried I'll make a mistake," make a **tough problem** study card! On the front, write out the procedure to work the type of problem in words. If there are special notes (like what not to do), include them. On the back, work at least one example; make sure you label what you are doing.

Adding fractions without a common denominator

1. Find the lowest common denominator (LCD) of each fraction.

2. Build each fraction to obtain the LCD in the denominator.

3. Add the numerators; keep the denominator the same. Reduce.

Front of Card

Example: $\frac{5}{12} + \frac{3}{5}$

1. LCD $2 \times 2 \times 3 \times 5 = 60$

2. $\frac{5 \times 5}{12 \times 5} = \frac{25}{60}$ *and* $\frac{3 \times 12}{5 \times 12} = \frac{36}{60}$

$= \frac{25}{60} + \frac{36}{60} = \frac{61}{60} = 1\frac{1}{60}$

Back of Card

Now Try This

Choose three types of difficult problems or problems that have given you trouble, and work them out on study cards. Be sure to put the words for solving the problem on one side and the worked problem on the other side.

Practice Quiz Cards

Make up a few quiz cards for each type of problem you learn, and use them to prepare for a test. Choose two or three problems from the different sections of the module. Be sure you don't just choose the easiest problems! Put the problem with the direction words (like *solve, simplify, evaluate*) on the front, and work the problem on the back. If you like, put the page number from the module there, too. When you review, you work the problem on a separate paper, and check it by looking at the back.

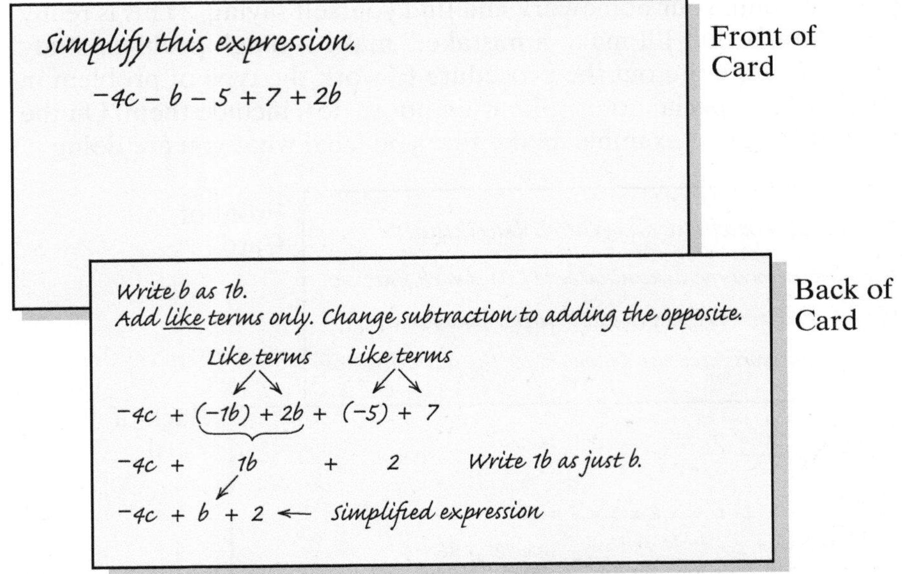

Why Are Study Cards Brain Friendly?

First, making the study cards is an **active technique** that really gets your dendrites growing. You have to make decisions about what is most important and how to put it on the card. This kind of thinking is more in-depth than just memorizing, and as a result, you will understand the concepts better and remember them longer.

Second, the cards are **visually appealing** (if you write neatly and try some colour). Your brain responds to pleasant visual images, and again, you will remember longer and may even be able to "picture in your mind" how your cards look. This will help you during tests.

Third, because study cards are small and portable, you can review them easily whenever you have a few minutes. Even while you're waiting for a bus or have a few minutes between classes you can take out your cards and read them to yourself. Your **brain really benefits from repetition;** each time you review your cards your dendrites are growing thicker and stronger. After a while, the information will become automatic and you will remember it for a long time.

Study Skills 9 Preparing for Tests

Many things besides studying can improve your test scores. You may not realize that eating the right foods, and getting enough exercise and sleep can also improve your scores. Your brain (and therefore your ability to think) is affected by the condition of your whole body. So, part of your preparation for tests includes keeping yourself in good physical shape as well as spending time on the actual course material. Try these suggestions and see the difference.

Student Learning Objectives

After studying this section, you will be able to:

 **Restate the importance of sleep and good nutrition as it affects learning.**

 **Explain the effect of anxiety and stress on learning.**

Performance Health Tips

Performance Health Tips to Improve Your Test Score	Explanation
Get ***seven to eight hours of sleep*** the night before the exam. (It's helpful to get that much sleep every night.)	***Fatigue and exhaustion*** reduce efficiency. They also cause poor memory and recall. If you didn't sleep much the night before a test, 20 minutes of relaxation or meditation can help. (Also see the comments below about eating carbohydrates to help you sleep.)
Eat a ***small, high-energy meal*** about two hours before the test. Start the meal with a small amount of protein such as fish, chicken, or non-fat yogurt. Include carbohydrates if you like, but no high-fat foods.	Just 85–115 grams of protein increases the amount of a chemical in the brain called tyrosine, which **improves your alertness, accuracy, and motivation.** High-fat foods dull your mind and slow down your brain.
Drink plenty of water. Don't wait until you feel thirsty; your body is already dehydrated by the time you feel it.	Research suggests that staying well hydrated improves the electrochemical communications in your brain.
Give your brain the time it needs to grow dendrites!	Cramming doesn't work; your brain cannot grow dendrites that quickly. ***Studying every day*** using these study skills techniques is the way to give your brain the time it needs.

Anxiety Prevention Tips

To Prevent Anxiety	Explanation
Practise slow, deep breathing for five minutes each day. Then do a minute or two of deep breathing right before the test. Also, if you feel your anxiety building during the test, stop for a minute, close your eyes, and do some deep breathing.	When test anxiety hits, you breathe more quickly and shallowly, which causes hyperventilation. Symptoms may be confusion, inability to concentrate, shaking, dizziness, and more. Slow, deep breathing will ***calm you and prevent panic.***
Do 15 to 20 minutes of ***moderate exercise*** (like walking) shortly before the test. Daily exercise is even better!	***Exercise reduces stress*** and will help prevent "blanking out" on a test. Exercise also increases your alertness, clear thinking, and energy.
To help you sleep the night before the test, or any time you need to calm down, eat high-carbohydrate foods such as popcorn, bread, rice, crackers, muffins, bagels, pasta, corn, baked potatoes (not fries or chips), and cereals.	Carbohydrates increase the level of a chemical in the brain called serotonin, which has a calming effect on the mind. It reduces feelings of tension and stress and improves your ability to concentrate. You only need to eat a small amount, like half a bagel, to get this effect.
Before the test, ***go easy on caffeinated beverages*** such as coffee, tea, and soft drinks. Do not eat candy bars or other sugary snacks.	Extra caffeine can make you jittery, "hyper," and shaky for the test. It can increase the tendency to panic. Too much sugar causes negative emotional reactions in some people.

Now Try This

What will you do to improve your next test score? List the three or four tips you think will help you the most.

1. ______________________________
2. ______________________________
3. ______________________________
4. ______________________________

What changes will you have to make in order to try the tips you chose?

____

____

____

See the Study Skills *Tips for Taking Math Tests* **and** *Preparing for Your Final Exam* **for more ideas about managing anxiety.**

Study Skills 10 Tips for Taking Math Tests

Improving Your Test Score

Student Learning Objectives

After studying this section, you will be able to:

 **Apply suggestions to tests and quizzes.**

 **Develop a set of "best practices" to apply while testing.**

To Improve Your Test Score	Comments
Come prepared with a pencil, eraser, and calculator, if allowed. If you are easily distracted, sit in the corner farthest from the door.	***Working in pencil lets you erase,*** keeping your work neat and readable.
Scan the entire test, note the point value of different problems, and plan your time accordingly. Allow at least five minutes to check your work at the end of the testing time.	If you have 50 minutes to do 20 problems, $50 \div 20 = 2.5$ minutes per problem. ***Spend less time on easy ones,*** more time on problems with higher point values.
Read directions carefully, and circle any significant words. When you finish a problem, read the directions again to make sure you did what was asked.	**Pay attention to announcements** written on the board or made by your instructor. Ask if you don't understand. You don't want to get problems wrong because you misread the directions!
Show your work. Most math teachers give partial credit if some of the steps in your work are correct, even if the final answer is wrong. ***Write neatly.*** If you like to scribble when first working or checking a problem, do it on scratch paper.	***If your teacher can't read your writing, you won't get credit for it.*** If you need more space to work, ask if you can use extra pieces of paper that you hand in with your test paper.
Check that the ***answer to an application problem is reasonable*** and makes sense. Read the problem again to make sure you've answered the question.	***Use common sense.*** Can the father really be seven years old? Would a month's rent be $32 140? Label your answer: $, years, metres, etc.
To check for careless errors, you need to ***rework the problem again, without looking at your previous work.*** Cover up your work with a piece of scratch paper, and pretend you are doing the problem for the first time. Then compare the two answers.	If you just "look over" your work, your mind can make the same mistake again without noticing it. Reworking the problem from the beginning ***forces you to rethink it.*** If possible, use a different method to solve the problem the second time.

Reducing Anxiety

To Reduce Anxiety	Comments
Do not try to review up until the last minute before the test. Instead, go for a walk, do some deep breathing, and arrive just in time for the test. Ignore other students.	Listening to anxious classmates before the test ***may cause you to panic.*** Moderate exercise and deep breathing will calm your mind.
Do a "knowledge dump" as soon as you get the test. Write important notes to yourself in a corner of the test paper: formulas, or common errors you want to watch out for.	Writing down tips and things that you've memorized ***lets you relax;*** you won't have to worry about forgetting those things and can refer to them as needed.
Do the easy problems first to build confidence. If you feel your anxiety starting to build, immediately stop for a minute, close your eyes, and take several slow, deep breaths.	Greater confidence helps you ***get the easier problems correct.*** Anxiety causes shallow breathing, which leads to confusion and reduced concentration. Deep breathing calms you.
As you work on more difficult problems, ***notice your "inner voice."*** You may have negative thoughts such as, "I can't do it," or "Who cares about this test anyway." In your mind, yell "STOP" and take several deep, slow breaths. Or, replace the negative thought with a positive one.	Here are ***examples of positive statements.*** Try writing one of them on the top of your test paper. • I know I can do it. • I can do this one step at a time. • I've studied hard, and I'll do the best I can.
If you still can't solve a difficult problem when you come back to it the second time, ***make a guess and do not change it.*** In this situation, your first guess is your best bet. Do not change the answer just because you're a little unsure. ***Change it only if you find an obvious mistake.***	If you are thinking about changing an answer, be sure you have a good reason for changing it. If you cannot find a specific error, leave your first answer alone. ***When the tests are returned, check to see if changing answers was an advantage or not.***
Read the harder problems twice. Write down anything that might help solve the problem: a formula, a picture, etc. If you still can't get it, circle the problem and ***come back to it later.*** Do not erase any of the things you wrote down.	If you know even a little bit about the problem, write it down. The ***answer may come to you*** as you work on it, or you may get partial credit. Don't spend too long on any one problem. Your subconscious mind will work on the tough problem while you go on with the test.
Ignore students who finish early. Use the entire test time. You do not get extra credit for finishing early. Use the extra time to rework problems and correct careless errors.	Students who leave early are often the ones who didn't study or who are too anxious to continue working. If they bother you, ***sit as far from the door as possible.***

Why Are These Suggestions Brain Friendly?

Several suggestions address anxiety. Reducing anxiety allows your brain to make the connections between dendrites; in other words, you can think clearly.

Remember that your brain continues to work on a difficult problem even if you skip it and go on to the next one. Your subconscious mind will come through for you if you are open to the idea!

Some of the suggestions ask you to use your common sense. Follow the directions, show your work, write neatly, and pay attention to whether your answers really make sense.

STUDY SKILLS 11 MAKING A MIND MAP

Mind mapping is a visual way to show information that you have learned. It is an excellent way to review. Mapping is flexible and can be personalized, which is helpful for your memory. Your brain likes to see things that are pleasing to look at, are colourful, and show connections between ideas. Take advantage of that by creating maps that

- are easy to read,
- use colour in a systematic way, and
- clearly show you how different concepts are related (using arrows or dotted lines, for example).

Directions for Making a Mind Map

Below are some general directions for making a map. After you read them, go to the next page and work on completing the map that has been started for you.

- To begin a mind map, write the concept in the centre of a piece of paper and either circle it or draw a box around it.
- Make a line out from the centre concept, and draw a box large enough to write the definition of the concept.
- Think of the other aspects (subpoints) of the concept that you have learned, such as procedures to follow or formulas. Make a separate line and box connecting each subpoint to the centre.
- From each of the new boxes, add the information you've learned. You can continue making new lines and boxes and circles, or you can list items below the new information.
- Use colour to highlight the major points. For example, everything related to one subpoint might be the same colour. That way you can easily see related ideas.
- You may also use arrows, underlining, or small drawings to help yourself remember.

Student Learning Objectives

After studying this section, you will be able to:

 **Create mind maps for appropriate concepts.**

 **Visually show how concepts relate to each other using arrows or lines.**

Why Is Mapping Brain Friendly?

Remember that your brain grows dendrites when you are **actively thinking** about and working with information. Making a map requires you to think hard about **how to place the information, how to show connections** between parts of the map, and **how colour will be useful.** It also takes a lot of thinking to fill in all related details and **show how those details connect to the larger concept.** All that thinking will let your brain grow a complex, many-branched neural network of interconnected dendrites. It is time well spent.

Try This Fractions Mind Map

On a separate paper, make a map that summarizes *Computations with Fractions.* Follow the directions below. Use the starter map below.

- The longest rectangles are instructions for all four operations. (The first one starts "Rewrite all numbers as fractions . . ." and the second one is at the bottom of the map.)
- Notice the wavy dividing lines that separate the map into two sides.
- Your job is to complete the map by writing the steps used in multiplying fractions and the steps used in adding and subtracting fractions.

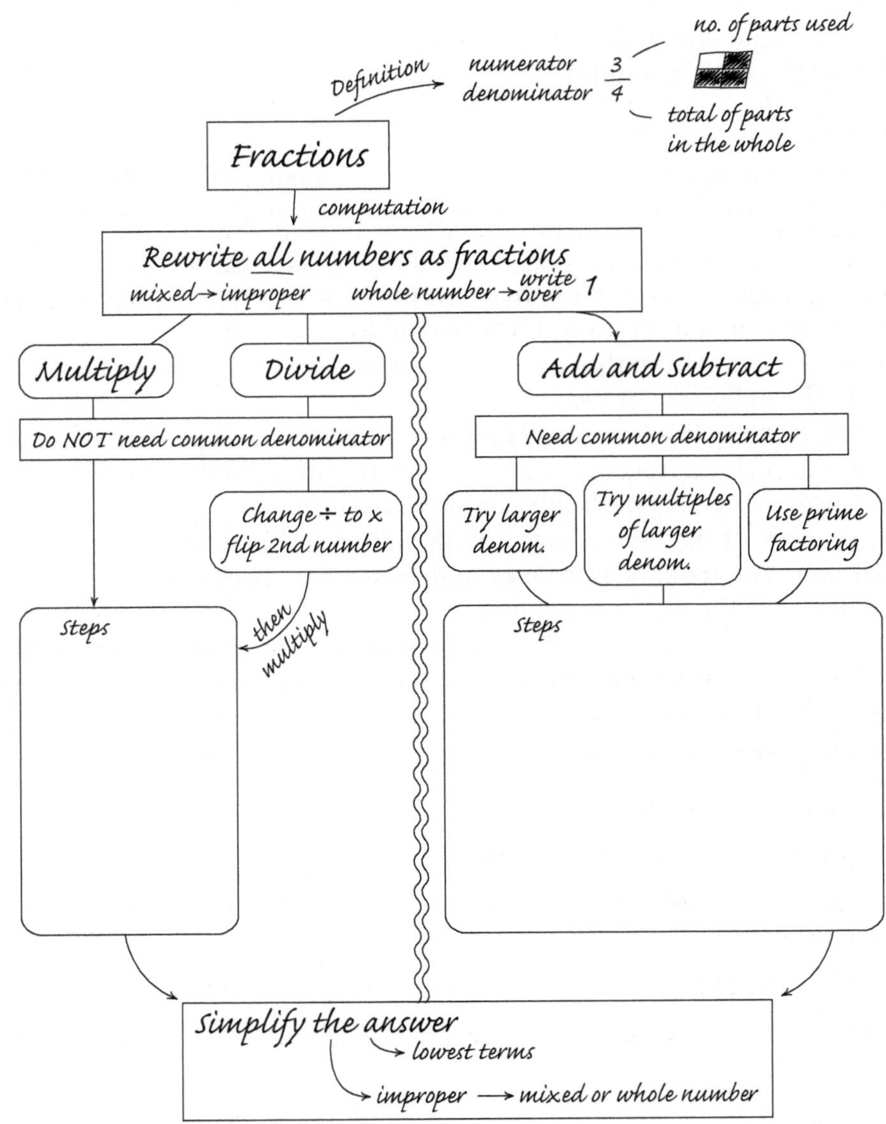

STUDY SKILLS 12 ANALYZING YOUR TEST RESULTS

After taking a test, many students heave a big sigh of relief and try to forget it ever happened. Don't fall into this trap! An exam is a learning opportunity. It gives you clues about what your instructor thinks is important, what concepts and skills are valued in mathematics, and if you are on the right track.

Student Learning Objectives

After studying this section, you will be able to:

 **Determine the reason for errors.**

 **Develop a plan to avoid test-taking errors.**

 **Review material to correct misunderstandings.**

Immediately After the Test

Jot down problems that caused you trouble. Find out how to solve them by checking your textbook, reviewing your notes, or asking your instructor or tutor (if available). You might see those same problems again on a final exam.

After the Test Is Returned

Find out what you got wrong and why you had points deducted. Write down the problem so you can learn how to do it correctly. Sometimes you only have a short time in class to review your test. If you need more time, ask your instructor if you can look at the test in his or her office.

Find Out Why You Made the Errors You Made

Here is a list of typical reasons for making errors on math tests.

1. You read the directions wrong.
2. You read the question wrong or skipped over something.
3. You made a computation error (maybe even an easy one).
4. Your answer is not accurate.
5. Your answer is not complete.
6. You labelled your answer wrong. For example, you labelled it "m" and it should have been "m^2."
7. You didn't show your work.
8. *You didn't understand the concept.
9. *You were unable to go from words (in a word problem) to setting up the problem.
10. *You were unable to apply a procedure to a new situation.
11. You were so anxious that you made errors even when you knew the material.

The first seven errors are test-taking errors. They are easy to correct if you decide to carefully read test questions and directions, proofread or rework your problems, show all your work, and double-check units and labels every time.

The three starred errors (*) are test-preparation errors. Remember that to grow a complex neural network, you need to practise the kinds of problems that you will see on the tests. So, for example, if application problems are difficult for you, you must do more application problems! If you have practised the study skills techniques, however, you are less likely to make these kinds of errors on tests because you will have a deeper understanding of course concepts and you will be able to remember them better.

The last error isn't really an error. **Anxiety** can play a big part in your test results. Go back to the Preparing for Tests activity and read the suggestions about exercise and deep breathing. Recall from the Your Brain Can Learn Mathematics activity that when you are anxious, your body produces adrenaline. The presence of adrenaline in the brain blocks connections between dendrites. If you can reduce the adrenaline in your system, you will be able to think more clearly during your test. Just five minutes of brisk walking right before your test can help do that. Also, practising a relaxation technique while you do your homework will make it more likely that you can benefit from using the technique during a test. Deep breathing is helpful because it gets oxygen into your brain. When you are anxious you tend to breathe more shallowly, which can make you feel confused and easily distracted.

Make a Plan for the Next Test

Make a plan for your next test based on your results from this test. You might review the Module Organizer and work the problems in the Module Review Problems or the How Am I Doing? Module Test. Ask your instructor or a tutor (if available) for more help if you are confused about any of the problems.

Now Try This

Below is a record sheet to track your progress in test taking. Use it to find out if you make particular kinds of errors. Then you can work specifically on correcting them. Just check in the box when you made one of the errors. If you take more than five tests, make your own grid on separate paper.

Test-taking Errors

Test #	Read directions wrong	Read questions wrong	Computation error	Not exact or accurate	Not complete	Labelled wrong	Didn't show work
1							
2							
3							
4							
5							

Test-preparation Errors

Test #	Didn't understand concept	Didn't set up problem correctly	Couldn't apply concept to new situation
1			
2			
3			
4			
5			

Anxiety

Test #	Felt anxious *before* the exam	Felt anxious *during* the exam	Blanked out on questions	Got questions wrong that I knew how to do
1				
2				
3				
4				
5				

What will you do to avoid test-taking errors?

____

____

____

What will you do to avoid test-preparation errors?

____

____

____

What will you do to reduce anxiety?

____

____

____

Study Skills 13 Preparing For Your Final Exam

Your math final exam is likely to be a **comprehensive exam.** This means that it will cover material from the **entire term.** The end of the term will be less stressful if you **make a plan** for how you will prepare for each of your exams.

Student Learning Objectives

After studying this section, you will be able to:

1. **Create a final exam week plan.**
2. **Break studying into chunks and study over several days.**
3. **Practise all types of problems.**

Set a Goal

First, figure out the **score you need to earn on the final exam** to get the course grade you are aiming for. Check your course syllabus for grading policies, or ask your instructor if you are not sure of them. This allows you to set a goal for yourself.

How many points do you need to earn on your mathematics final exam to get the grade you want? ____________________

____

Create a Plan

Second, create a **final exam week plan for your work and personal life.** If you need to make an adjustment in your work schedule, do it in advance, so you aren't scrambling at the last minute. If you have family members to care for, you might want to enlist some help from others so you can spend extra time studying. Try to plan in advance so you don't create additional stress for yourself. You will have to set some priorities, and studying has to be at the top of the list! Although life doesn't stop for finals, some things can be ignored for a short time. You don't want to "burn out" during final exam week; **get enough sleep and healthy food so you can perform your best.**

What adjustments in your personal life do you need to make for final exam week? ____________________

____

Study and Review

Third, use the following suggestions to guide your studying and reviewing.

- **Know exactly which modules and sections will be on the final exam.**
- **Divide up the modules,** and decide how much you will review each day.
- **Begin your reviewing several days before** the exam.
- **Use returned quizzes and tests** to review earlier material (if you have them).
- **Practise all types of problems,** but emphasize the types that are most difficult for you.
- **Complete the Practice Final Examination.**
- **Rewrite your notes or make mind maps** to create summaries.
- **Make study cards for all types of problems.** Be sure to use the same **direction words** (such as *simplify, solve, estimate*) that your exam will use. Carry the cards with you and review them whenever you have a few spare minutes.

Managing Stress

Of course, a week of final exams produces stress. **Students who develop skills for reducing and managing stress do better on their final exams and are less likely to "bomb" an exam.** You already know the damaging effect of adrenaline on your ability to think clearly. But several days (or weeks) of elevated stress is also harmful to your brain and your body. You will feel better if you make a conscious effort to reduce your stress level. Even if it takes you away from studying for a little while each day, the time will be well spent.

Reducing Physical Stress

Which techniques will you try?

____

____

____

Examples of ways to reduce **physical stress** are listed below. Can you add any of your own ideas to the list?

- *Laugh until your eyes water.* Watching your favourite funny movie, sharing a joke with a friend, and viewing a comedy bit on the Internet are all ways to generate a healthy laugh. Laughing raises the level of calming chemicals (endorphins) in your brain.
- *Exercise for 20 to 30 minutes.* If you normally exercise regularly, do NOT stop during final exam week! Exercising helps relax muscles, diffuses adrenaline, and raises the level of endorphins in your body. If you don't exercise much, get some gentle exercise, such as a daily walk, to help you relax.
- *Practise deep breathing.* Several minutes of deep, smooth breathing will calm you. Close your eyes too.
- *Visualize a relaxing scene.* Choose something that you find peaceful and picture it. Imagine what it feels like and sounds like. Try to put yourself in the picture.
- If you feel stress in your muscles, such as your shoulders or back, *slowly squeeze the muscles as much as you can, and then release them.* Sometimes we don't realize we are clenching our teeth or holding tension in our shoulders until we consciously work with them. Try to notice what it feels like when they are relaxed and loose. Squeezing and then releasing muscles is also something you can do during an exam if you feel yourself tightening up.

Reducing Mental Stress

Which techniques will you try?

____

____

____

Mental stress reduction is also a powerful tool both before and during an exam. In addition to these suggestions, do you have any of your own techniques?

- *Talk positively to yourself.* Tell yourself you will get through it.
- *Reward yourself.* Give yourself small breaks, a little treat—something that makes you happy—every day of final exam week.
- *Make a list of things to do* and feel the sense of accomplishment when you cross each item off.
- When you take time to relax or exercise, *make sure you are relaxing your mind too.* Use your mind for something *completely* different from the kind of thinking you do when you study. Plan your garden, play your favourite music, walk your dog, or read a good book.
- *Visualize.* Picture yourself completing exams and projects successfully. Picture yourself taking the test calmly and confidently.

For many years there were many more drivers in Canada than there were passenger cars. Over the years, that trend has changed. Now there are more passenger cars than there are drivers in Canada. When did that change occur? How many more cars are there than drivers? The mathematics you learn in this module will help you to answer these kinds of questions.

Shutterstock/Monkey Business Images

Whole Numbers

Student Learning Objectives

After studying this section, you will be able to:

1. Write numbers in expanded form.
2. Write whole numbers in standard notation.
3. Write a word name for a number and write a number for a word name.
4. Read numbers in tables.

 Writing Numbers in Expanded Form

To count a number of objects or to answer the question "How many?" we use a set of numbers called **whole numbers.** These whole numbers are as follows.

0, 1, 2, 3, 4, 5, 6, 7, 8, 9, 10, 11, 12, 13, 14, 15, . . .

There is no largest whole number. The three dots . . . indicate that the set of whole numbers goes on indefinitely. Our number system is based on tens and ones and is called the **decimal system** (or the **base 10 system**). The numbers 0, 1, 2, 3, 4, 5, 6, 7, 8, 9 are called **digits.** The position, or placement, of the digits in the number tells the value of the digits. For example, in the number 521, the "5" means 5 hundreds (500). In the number 54, the "5" means 5 tens (50).

521 — 5 means 5 hundreds or 500

54 — 5 means 5 tens or 50

For this reason, our number system is called a **place-value system.**

Consider the number 5643. We will use a place-value chart to illustrate the value of each digit in the number 5643.

Place-value Chart

Millions			Thousands			Ones		
					5	6	4	3
Hundred millions	Ten millions	Millions	Hundred thousands	Ten thousands	Thousands	Hundreds	Tens	Ones

The value of the number is 5 thousands, 6 hundreds, 4 tens, 3 ones.

The place-value chart shows the value of each place, from ones on the right to hundred millions on the left. When we write very large numbers, we place a space after every group of three digits, called a **period**, moving from right to left. This makes the number easier to read. It is usually agreed that a four-digit number does not have a space, but that numbers with five or more digits do. So 32 000 would be written with a space but 7000 would not. While financial disciplines still often utilize a comma instead of a space, we will use only spaces as it is both the SI standard and the standard in Canadian math classrooms.

To show the value of each digit in a number, we sometimes write the number in expanded notation. For example, 56 327 is 5 ten thousands, 6 thousands, 3 hundreds, 2 tens, and 7 ones. In **expanded notation,** this is

$$50\,000 + 6000 + 300 + 20 + 7.$$

EXAMPLE 1 Write each number in expanded notation.

(a) 2378 **(b)** 538 271 **(c)** 980 340 654

Solution

(a) Sometimes it helps to say the number to yourself.

	two thousand		three hundred		seventy		eight
2378 =	2000	+	300	+	70	+	8

(b)

Expanded notation

538 271 = 500 000 + 30 000 + 8000 + 200 + 70 + 1

(c) When 0 is used as a placeholder, you do not include it in the expanded form.

Expanded notation

980 340 654 = 900 000 000 + 80 000 000 + 300 000 + 40 000 + 600 + 50 + 4

Practice Problem 1 Write each number in expanded notation.

(a) 3182 **(b)** 520 890 **(c)** 709 680 059

NOTE TO STUDENT: *Fully worked-out solutions to all of the Practice Problems can be found at the end of the module.*

Writing Whole Numbers in Standard Notation

The way that you usually see numbers written is called **standard notation.** 980 340 654 is the standard notation for the number nine hundred eighty million, three hundred forty thousand, six hundred fifty-four.

EXAMPLE 2 Write each number in standard notation.

(a) 500 + 30 + 8

(b) 300 000 + 7000 + 40 + 7

Solution

(a) 538

(b) Be careful to keep track of the place value of each digit. You may need to use 0 as a placeholder.

3 hundred thousand

300 000 + 7000 + 40 + 7 = 307 047

7 thousand

We needed to use 0 in the ten thousands place and in the hundreds place.

Practice Problem 2 Write each number in standard notation.

(a) 400 + 90 + 2 **(b)** 80 000 + 400 + 20 + 7

EXAMPLE 3 Last year the population of Central City was 1 509 637. In the number 1 509 637

(a) How many ten thousands are there? **(b)** How many tens are there?
(c) What is the value of the digit 5? **(d)** In what place is the digit 6?

Solution A place-value chart will help you identify the value of each place.

(a) Look at the digit in the ten thousands place. There are 0 ten thousands.
(b) Look at the digit in the tens place. There are 3 tens.
(c) The digit 5 is in the hundred thousands place. The value of the digit is 5 hundred thousand or 500 000.
(d) The digit 6 is in the hundreds place.

NOTE TO STUDENT: *Fully worked-out solutions to all of the Practice Problems can be found at the end of the module.*

Practice Problem 3 The campus library has 904 759 books.

(a) What digit tells the number of hundreds?
(b) What digit tells the number of hundred thousands?
(c) What is the value of the digit 4?
(d) What is the value of the digit 9? Why does this question have two answers?

3 Writing Word Names for Numbers and Numbers for Word Names

A number has the same *value* no matter how we write it. For example, "a million dollars" means the same as "$1 000 000." In fact, any number in our number system can be written in several ways or forms:

- Standard notation — 521
- Expanded notation — 500 + 20 + 1
- Word name — five hundred twenty-one

You may want to write a number in any of these ways. To write a cheque, you need to use both standard notation and words.

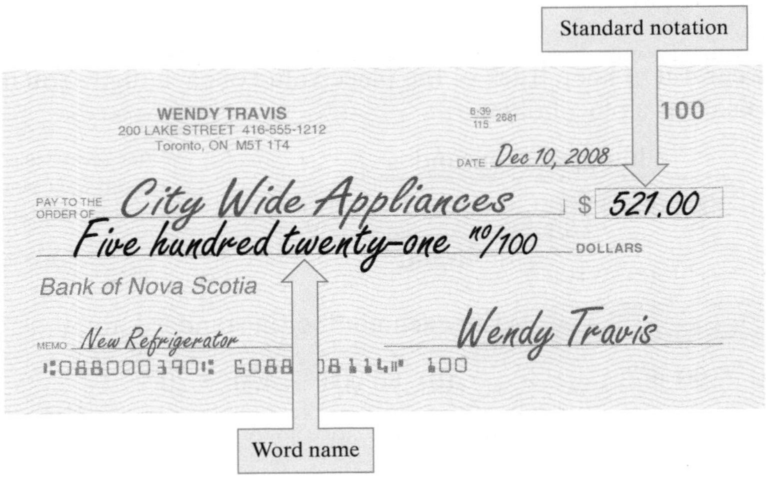

Standard notation
WENDY TRAVIS
200 LAKE STREET 416-555-1212
Toronto, ON M5T 1T4
100
DATE Dec 10, 2008
PAY TO THE ORDER OF City Wide Appliances
$ 521.00
Five hundred twenty-one no/100
DOLLARS
Bank of Nova Scotia
MEMO New Refrigerator
Wendy Travis
Word name

To write a word name, start from the left. Name the number in each period, followed by the name of the period, and a comma. The last period name, "ones," is not used.

EXAMPLE 4 Write a word name for 364 128 957.

Solution

Place-value Chart

Billions			Millions			Thousands			Ones		
			3	6	4	1	2	8	9	5	7
Hundreds	Tens	Ones	Hundreds	Tens	Ones	Hundreds	Tens	Ones	Hundreds	Tens	Ones

We want to write a word name for 364 128 957.

three hundred sixty-four million, → 364

one hundred twenty-eight thousand, → 128

nine hundred fifty-seven → 957

The answer is three hundred sixty-four million, one hundred twenty-eight thousand, nine hundred fifty-seven.

Practice Problem 4 Write a word name for 267 358 981.

EXAMPLE 5 Write the word name for each number.

(a) 1695 **(b)** 200 470 **(c)** 7 003 038

Solution Look at the place-value chart if you need help identifying the place for each digit.

(a) To help us, we will put in the optional space: 1 695.

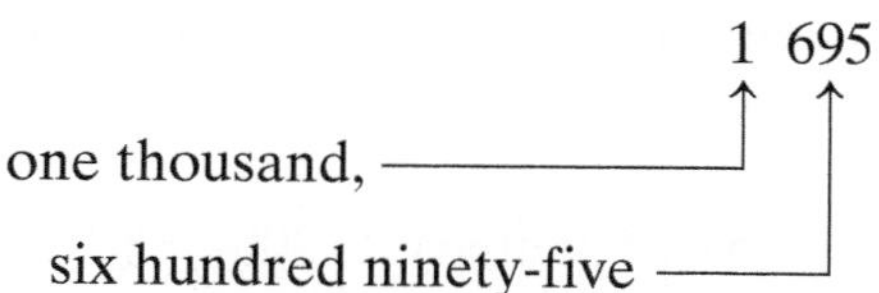

The word name is one thousand, six hundred ninety-five.

(b)

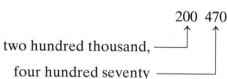

200 470

two hundred thousand, → 200

four hundred seventy → 470

The word name is two hundred thousand, four hundred seventy.

(c)

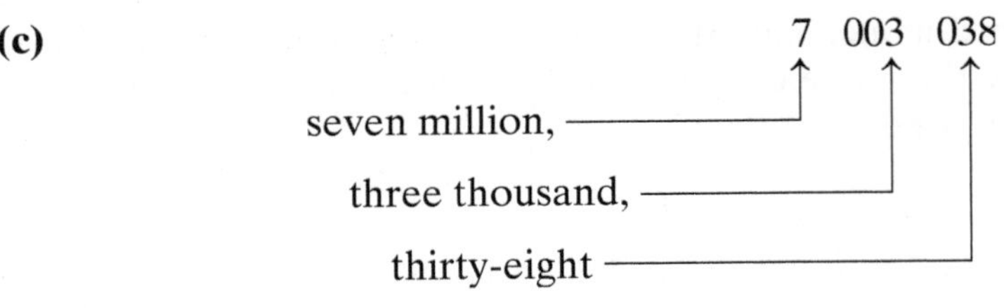

The word name is seven million, three thousand, thirty-eight.

NOTE TO STUDENT: Fully worked-out solutions to all of the Practice Problems can be found at the end of the module.

Practice Problem 5 Write the word name for each number.

(a) 2736 **(b)** 980 306 **(c)** 12 000 021

CAUTION: DO NOT USE THE WORD AND FOR WHOLE NUMBERS. Many people use the word *and* when giving the word name for a whole number. For example, you might hear someone say the number 34 507 as "thirty-four thousand, five hundred *and* seven." However, this is not technically correct. In mathematics we do NOT use the word *and* when writing word names for whole numbers. We use the word *and* to represent the decimal point. For example, 59.76 will have the word name "fifty-nine *and* seventy-six hundredths."

Very large numbers are used to measure quantities in some disciplines, such as distance in astronomy and the national debt in macroeconomics. We can extend the place-value chart to include these large numbers.

The national debt for Canada as of March 13, 2007, was $508 123 720 833. This number is indicated in the following place-value chart.

Place-value Chart

Trillions			Billions			Millions			Thousands			Ones		
			5	0	8	1	2	3	7	2	0	8	3	3

EXAMPLE 6 Write the number for the national debt for Canada as of March 13, 2007, in the amount of $508 123 720 833 using a word name.

Solution The national debt on March 13, 2007, was five hundred eight billion, one hundred twenty-three million, seven hundred twenty thousand, eight hundred thirty-three dollars.

Practice Problem 6 As of January 1, 2004, the estimated population of the world was 6 393 646 525. Write this world population using a word name.

Occasionally you may want to write a word name as a number.

EXAMPLE 7 Write each number in standard notation.

(a) twenty-six thousand, eight hundred sixty-four
(b) two billion, three hundred eighty-six million, five hundred forty-seven thousand, one hundred ninety

Solution

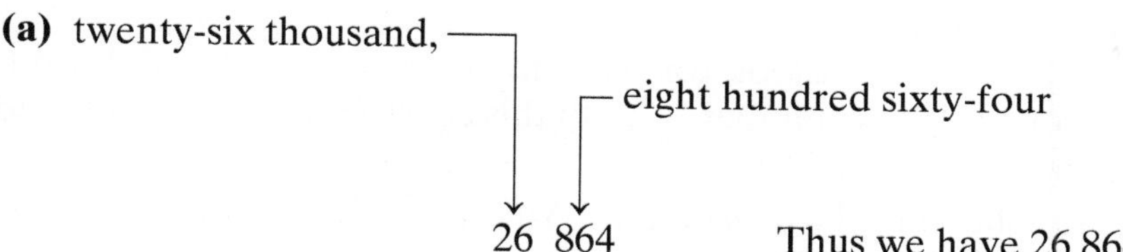

Thus we have 26 864.

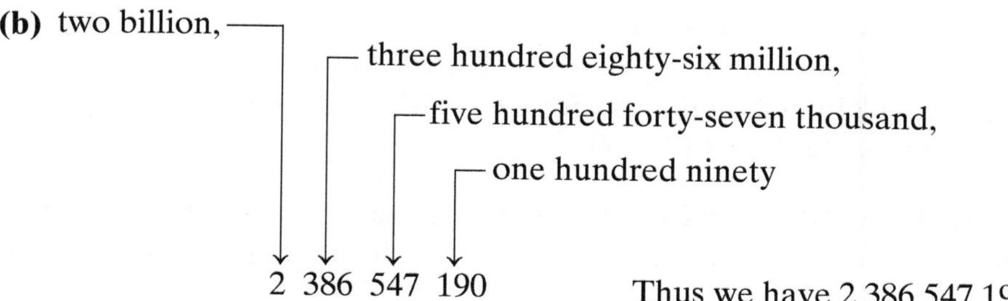

Thus we have 2 386 547 190.

Practice Problem 7 Write in standard notation.

(a) eight hundred three
(b) thirty thousand, two hundred twenty-nine

Reading Numbers in Tables

Sometimes numbers found in charts and tables are abbreviated. Look at the chart below from Statistics Canada. Notice that the numbers represent thousands. If the number 55 appears across from 1851 for British Columbia, the 55 represents 55 thousand. Note that census figures for some provinces and territories are not available for certain years.

Estimated Population of Canadian Provinces and Territories 1851–1931 (in thousands)

	British Columbia	Alberta	Saskatchewan	Manitoba	Prince Edward Island	Yukon	Nova Scotia
1851	55	*	*	*	63	*	277
1861	52	*	*	*	81	*	331
1871	36	*	*	25	94	*	388
1881	49	*	*	62	109	*	441
1891	98	*	*	153	109	*	450
1901	179	73	91	255	103	27	460
1911	392	374	492	461	94	9	492
1921	525	588	758	610	89	4	524
1931	694	732	922	700	88	4	513

Source: Adapted from Statistics Canada, www40.statcan.ca/l01/cst01/demo62k-eng.htm, Oct-09

EXAMPLE 8 Refer to the chart on the previous page to answer the following questions. Write each number in standard notation.

(a) What was the estimated population of Alberta in 1901?
(b) What was the estimated population of Yukon in 1931?
(c) What was the estimated population of British Columbia in 1901?

Solution

(a) To read the chart, first look for Alberta along the top. Read down to the row for 1901. The number is 73. In this chart 73 means 73 thousand. We will write this as 73 000.

(b) Read the column of the chart for the Yukon Territory. The number for the Yukon Territory in the row for 1931 is 4. This means 4 thousand. We will write this as 4000.

(c) Read the column of the chart for British Columbia. The number for British Columbia in the row for 1901 is 179. This means 179 thousand. We will write this as 179 000.

TO THINK ABOUT: Interpreting Data in a Table Why do you think Nova Scotia had the largest population for most of the years shown in the table?

NOTE TO STUDENT: Fully worked-out solutions to all of the Practice Problems can be found at the end of the module.

Practice Problem 8 Refer to the chart on the previous page to answer the following questions. Write each number in standard notation.

(a) What was the estimated population of Saskatchewan in 1921?
(b) What was the estimated population of Prince Edward Island in 1901?
(c) What was the estimated population of Manitoba in 1881?

Developing Your Study Skills

Class Participation

People learn mathematics through active participation, not through observation from the sidelines. If you want to do well in this course, get involved in all course activities. If you are in a traditional mathematics class, sit near the front where you can see and hear well, where your focus is on the material being covered in class. Ask questions, be ready to contribute toward solutions, and take part in all classroom activities. Your contributions are valuable to the class and to yourself. Class participation requires an investment of yourself in the learning process, which you will find pays huge dividends.

If you are in an online class or nontraditional class, be sure to e-mail the teacher or talk to the tutor on duty. Ask questions. Think about the concepts. Make your mind interact with the textbook. Be mentally involved. This active mental interaction is the key to your success.

Section 1 Exercises

Write each number in expanded notation.

1. 6731

2. 9519

3. 108 276

4. 701 285

5. 23 761 345

6. 46 198 253

7. 103 260 768

8. 820 310 574

Write each number in standard notation.

9. 600 + 70 + 1

10. 500 + 90 + 6

11. 9000 + 800 + 60 + 3

12. 7000 + 600 + 50 + 2

13. 40 000 + 800 + 80 + 5

14. 60 000 + 7000 + 200 + 4

15. 700 000 + 6000 + 200

16. 300 000 + 40 000 + 800

Verbal and Writing Skills

17. In the number 437 521

(a) What digit tells the number of thousands?
(b) What is the value of the digit 3?

18. In the number 805 712

(a) What digit tells the number of ten thousands?
(b) What is the value of the digit 8?

19. In the number 1 214 847

(a) What digit tells the number of hundred thousands?
(b) What is the value of the digit?

20. In the number 6 789 345

(a) What digit tells the number of thousands?
(b) What is the value of the digit?

Write a word name for each number.

21. 142

22. 376

23. 9304

24. 7606

25. 36 118

26. 55 742

27. 105 261

28. 370 258

29. 14 203 326

30. 68 089 213

31. 4 302 156 200

32. 7 436 210 400

Write each number in standard notation.

33. one thousand, five hundred sixty-one

34. three thousand, one hundred eighty-nine

35. thirty-three thousand, eight hundred nine

36. two hundred three thousand, three hundred seventy-four

37. one hundred million, seventy-nine thousand, eight hundred twenty-six

38. four hundred fifty million, three hundred thousand, two hundred forty-nine

Applications *When writing a cheque, a person must write the word name for the dollar amount of the cheque.*

ALEX J. WRITER
10 MAIN STREET 416-555-1212
Toronto, ON M5T 3S1
53-235 3254
113
6848
DATE April 1, 2010
PAY TO THE ORDER OF ______ $ 1965 00
______ DOLLARS
Last Chance Bank
Toronto, Ontario
MEMO ______
⑆01130234 7⑆ 01108114⑈ 6848

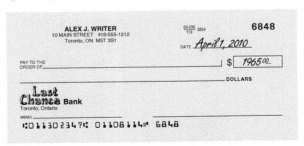

39. ***Personal Finance*** Alex bought new equipment for his laboratory for \$1965. What word name should he write on the cheque?

40. ***Personal Finance*** Alex later bought a new personal computer for \$1383. What word name should he write on the cheque?

In exercises 41–44, use the following chart prepared with data from Statistics Canada. Notice that the second line tells us that the numbers represent millions. These values are only approximate values representing numbers written to the nearest million. They are not exact census figures.

Estimated Population of Four Provinces from 1956 to 2008 (in millions)

	Québec	Ontario	Alberta	British Columbia
1956	5	5	1	1
1966	6	7	1	2
1971	6	8	2	2
1976	6	8	2	2
1981	6	9	2	3
1986	7	9	2	3
1991	7	10	3	3
1996	7	11	3	4
2001	7	11	3	4
2006	8	12	3	4
2008	8	13	4	4

Source: Adapted from Statistics Canada, www40.statcan.ca/l01/cst01/demo62k-eng.htm, and www40.statcan.ca/l01/cst01/demo02a-eng.htm, Oct-09

41. ***Historical Analysis*** What was the estimated population of British Columbia in 1991?

42. ***Historical Analysis*** What was the estimated population of Ontario in 1956?

43. ***Historical Analysis*** What was the estimated population of Québec in 2008?

44. ***Historical Analysis*** What was the estimated population of Alberta in 1971?

In exercises 45–48, use the following chart:

Number of Flights and Passengers for Selected Airlines in 1999, 2000, and 2005 (in thousands)

	1999		2000		2005	
Airline	**Flights***	**Passengers**	**Flights***	**Passengers**	**Flights**	**Passengers**
American	740	72 567	791	77 185	780	75 300
Continental	428	40 059	423	40 989	401	39 520
Delta	930	101 843	922	101 809	900	98 360
Northwest	552	50 441	565	52 566	448	49 690

*Includes passenger and freight flights
Source: Bureau of Transportation Statistics

45. ***Airline Travel*** How many flights did Delta have in 1999?

46. ***Airline Travel*** How many passengers flew on American flights in 2000?

47. ***Airline Travel*** How many passengers flew on Northwest flights in 2000?

48. ***Airline Travel*** How many flights did Continental have in 2005?

49. ***Physics*** The speed of light is approximately 29 979 250 000 centimetres per second.

(a) What digit tells the number of ten thousands?
(b) What digit tells the number of ten billions?

▲**50.** ***Earth Science*** The circumference of Earth at the equator is 40 075 020 metres.

(a) What digit tells the number of ten millions?
(b) What digit tells the number of hundred thousands?

51. ***Blood Vessels*** There are about 96 567 000 metres of blood vessels in an adult human body.

(a) What digit tells the number of ten thousands?
(b) What digit tells the number of ten millions?

52. ***Historical Analysis*** The world's population is expected to reach 7 900 000 000 by the year 2020, according to the U.S. Bureau of the Census.

(a) Which digit tells the number of hundred millions?
(b) Which digit tells the number of billions?

53. Write in standard notation: six hundred thirteen trillion, one billion, thirty-three million, two hundred eight thousand, three.

54. Write in standard notation: nine hundred fourteen trillion, two billion, fifty-two million, four hundred nine thousand, six.

To Think About

55. Write a word name for 3 682 968 009 931 960 747. (*Hint:* The digit 1 followed by 18 zeros represents the number *1 quintillion.* 1 followed by 15 zeros represents the number *1 quadrillion.*)

56. The number 50 000 000 000 000 000 000 is represented on some scientific calculators as 5 E 19. However, for the present we can see that this is a convenient notation that allows us to record very large whole numbers. Note that this number (50 quintillion) is a 5 followed by 19 zeros. Write in standard form the number that would be represented on a calculator as 6 E 22.

57. Think about the discussion in exercise 56. If the number 4 E 20 represented on a scientific calculator was divided by 2, what number would be the result? Write your answer in standard form.

58. Consider all the whole numbers between 200 and 800 that contain the digit 6. How many such numbers are there?

Quick Quiz 1

1. Write in expanded notation. 73 952

2. Write a word name. 8 932 475

3. Write in standard notation.

Nine hundred sixty-four thousand, two hundred fifty-seven

4. **Concept Check** Explain why the zeros are needed when writing the following number in standard notation: three hundred sixty-eight million, five hundred twenty-two.

Section 2 Adding Whole Numbers

Student Learning Objectives

After studying this section, you will be able to:

1. Master basic addition facts.
2. Add several single-digit numbers.
3. Add several-digit numbers when carrying is not needed.
4. Add several-digit numbers when carrying is needed.
5. Review the properties of addition.
6. Apply addition to real-life situations.

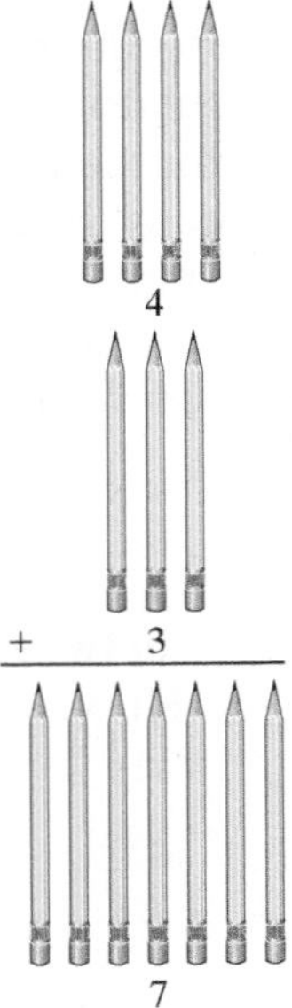

1 Mastering Basic Addition Facts

We see the addition process time and time again. Carpenters add to find the amount of lumber they need for a job. Auto mechanics add to make sure they have enough parts in the inventory. Bank tellers add to get cash totals.

What is addition? We do addition when we put sets of objects together.

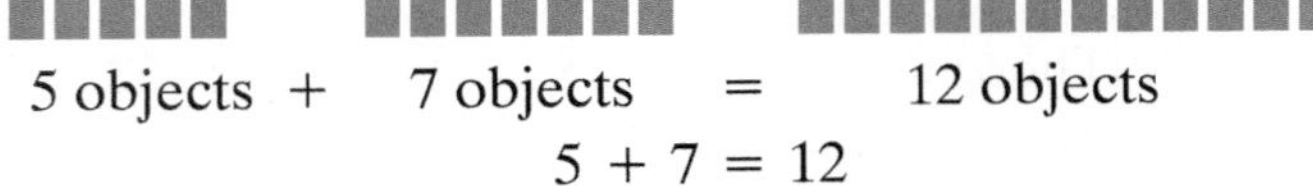

5 objects + 7 objects = 12 objects

$$5 + 7 = 12$$

Usually when we add numbers, we put one number under the other in a column. The numbers being added are called **addends.** The result is called the **sum.**

Suppose that we have four pencils in the car and we bring three more pencils from home. How many pencils do we have with us now? We add 4 and 3 to obtain a value of 7. In this case, the numbers 4 and 3 are the addends and the answer 7 is the sum.

$$\begin{array}{rl} 4 & \text{addend} \\ +3 & \text{addend} \\ \hline 7 & \text{sum} \end{array}$$

Think about what we do when we add 0 to another number. We are not making a change, so whenever we add zero to another number, that number will be the sum. Since this is always true, this is called a *property.* Since the sum is identical to the number added to zero, this is called the **identity property of zero.**

EXAMPLE 1 Add.

(a) $8 + 5$ **(b)** $3 + 7$ **(c)** $9 + 0$

Solution

(a) $\begin{array}{r} 8 \\ +5 \\ \hline 13 \end{array}$ **(b)** $\begin{array}{r} 3 \\ +7 \\ \hline 10 \end{array}$ **(c)** $\begin{array}{r} 9 \\ +0 \\ \hline 9 \end{array}$

Note: When we add zero to any other number, that number is the sum.

Practice Problem 1 Add.

(a) $\begin{array}{r} 7 \\ +5 \\ \hline \end{array}$ **(b)** $\begin{array}{r} 9 \\ +4 \\ \hline \end{array}$ **(c)** $\begin{array}{r} 3 \\ +0 \\ \hline \end{array}$

The following table shows the basic addition facts. You should know these facts. If any of the answers don't come to you quickly, now is the time to learn them. To check your knowledge try Section 2 Exercises, exercises 3 and 4.

Basic Addition Facts

+	0	1	2	3	4	5	6	7	8	9
0	0	1	2	3	4	5	6	7	8	9
1	1	2	3	4	5	6	7	8	9	10
2	2	3	4	5	6	7	8	9	10	11
3	3	4	5	6	7	8	9	10	11	12
4	4	5	6	7	8	9	10	11	12	13
5	5	6	7	8	9	10	11	12	13	14
6	6	7	8	9	10	11	12	13	14	15
7	7	8	9	10	11	12	13	14	15	16
8	8	9	10	11	12	13	14	15	16	17
9	9	10	11	12	13	14	15	16	17	18

To use the table to find the sum 4 + 7, read across the top of the table to the 4 column, and then read down the left to the 7 row. The box where the 4 and 7 meet is 11, which means that 4 + 7 = 11. Now read across the top to the 7 column and down the left to the 4 row. The box where these numbers meet is also 11. We can see that the order in which we add the numbers does not change the sum. 4 + 7 = 11, and 7 + 4 = 11. We call this the **commutative property of addition.**

This property does not hold true for everything in our lives. When you put on your socks and then your shoes, the result is not the same as if you put on your shoes first and then your socks! Can you think of any other examples where changing the order in which you add things would change the result?

Adding Several Single-Digit Numbers

If more than two numbers are to be added, we usually add from the first number to the next number and mentally note the sum. Then we add that sum to the next number, and so on.

EXAMPLE 2 Add. 3 + 4 + 8 + 2 + 5

Solution We rewrite the addition problem in a column format.

Mentally, we do these steps.

$$\begin{array}{r} 3 \\ 4 \\ 8 \\ 2 \\ +5 \\ \hline 22 \end{array}$$

3 + 4 = 7

7 + 8 = 15

15 + 2 = 17

17 + 5 = 22

Practice Problem 2 Add. 7 + 6 + 5 + 8 + 2

***NOTE TO STUDENT:** Fully worked-out solutions to all of the Practice Problems can be found at the end of the module.*

Because the order in which we add numbers doesn't matter, we can choose to add from the top down, from the bottom up, or in any other way. One shortcut is to add first any numbers that will give a sum of 10, or 20, or 30, and so on.

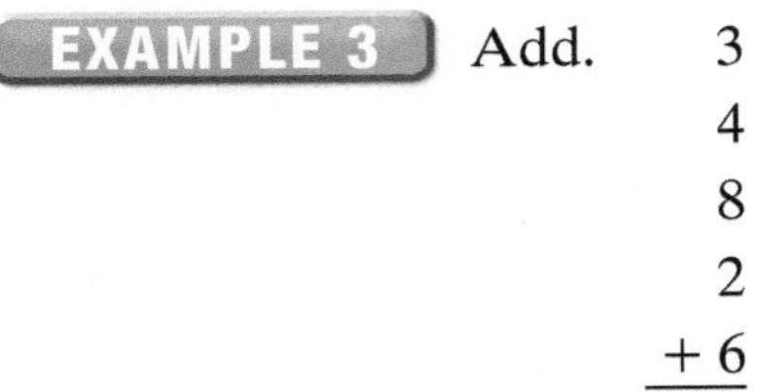

EXAMPLE 3 Add.

$$\begin{array}{r} 3 \\ 4 \\ 8 \\ 2 \\ +\,6 \\ \hline \end{array}$$

Solution We mentally group the numbers into tens.

3
4 ← (4 + 6 = 10)
8 ← (8 + 2 = 10)
2 ←
6 ←

$8 + 2 = 10$ → $4 + 6 = 10$

The sum is 10 + 10 + 3 or 23.

Practice Problem 3 Add. 1 + 7 + 2 + 9 + 3

3 Adding Several-Digit Numbers When Carrying Is Not Needed

Of course, many numbers that we need to add have more than one digit. In such cases, we must be careful to first add the digits in the ones column, then the digits in the tens column, then those in the hundreds column, and so on. Notice that we move from *right to left.*

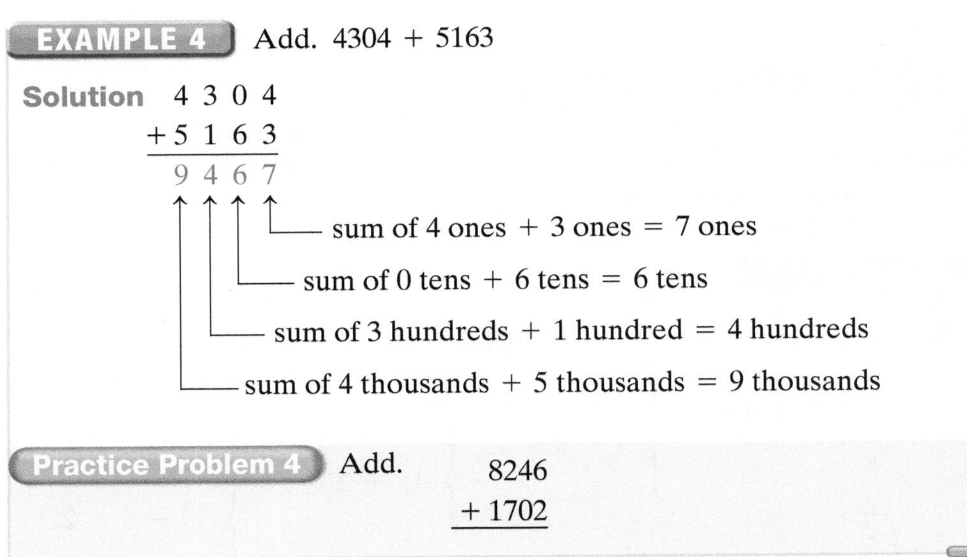

EXAMPLE 4 Add. 4304 + 5163

Solution

$$\begin{array}{r} 4\;3\;0\;4 \\ +\,5\;1\;6\;3 \\ \hline 9\;4\;6\;7 \end{array}$$

- 7: sum of 4 ones + 3 ones = 7 ones
- 6: sum of 0 tens + 6 tens = 6 tens
- 4: sum of 3 hundreds + 1 hundred = 4 hundreds
- 9: sum of 4 thousands + 5 thousands = 9 thousands

Practice Problem 4 Add.

$$\begin{array}{r} 8246 \\ +\,1702 \\ \hline \end{array}$$

4 Adding Several-Digit Numbers When Carrying Is Needed

When you add several whole numbers, often the sum in a column is greater than 9. However, we can only use *one* digit in any one place. What do we do with a two-digit sum? Look at the following example.

EXAMPLE 5 Add. 45 + 37

Solution

$$\begin{array}{r} \overset{1}{4}\,5 \\ +3\,7 \\ \hline 2 \end{array}$$

5 ones and 7 ones = 12.
We rename 12 in expanded notation: 1 ten + 2 ones.
We place the 2 ones in the ones column.
We carry the 1 ten over to the tens column.

Note: Placing the 1 in the next column is often called "carrying the one."

$$\begin{array}{r} \overset{1}{4}\,5 \\ +3\,7 \\ \hline 8\,2 \end{array}$$

Now we can add the digits in the tens column.

Thus, 45 + 37 = 82.

Practice Problem 5 Add.

$$\begin{array}{r} 56 \\ +36 \\ \hline \end{array}$$

NOTE TO STUDENT: Fully worked-out solutions to all of the Practice Problems can be found at the end of the module.

Often you must use carrying several times by bringing the left digit into the next column to the left.

EXAMPLE 6 Add. 257 + 688 + 94

Solution

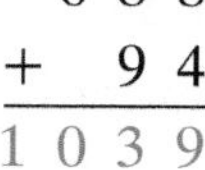

Thousands Column | Hundreds Column | Tens Column | Ones Column

$$\begin{array}{r} \overset{2}{2}\,\overset{1}{5}\,7 \\ 6\,8\,8 \\ +\ \ 9\,4 \\ \hline 1\,0\,3\,9 \end{array}$$

In the ones column we add 7 + 8 + 4 = 19. Because 19 is 1 ten and 9 ones, we place 9 in the ones column and carry 1 to the top of the tens column.

In the tens column we add 1 + 5 + 8 + 9 = 23. Because 23 tens is 2 hundreds and 3 tens, we place the 3 in the tens column and carry 2 to the top of the hundreds column.

In the hundreds column we add 2 + 2 + 6 = 10 hundreds. Because 10 hundreds is 1 thousand and 0 hundreds, we place the 0 in the hundreds column and place the 1 in the thousands column.

Practice Problem 6 Add. 789 + 63 + 297

We can add numbers in more than one way. To add $5 + 3 + 7$ we can first add the 5 and 3. We do this by using parentheses to show the first operation to be done. This shows us that $5 + 3$ is to be grouped together.

$$\begin{aligned} 5 + 3 + 7 &= (5 + 3) + 7 = 15 \\ &= \quad 8 \quad + 7 = 15 \end{aligned}$$

We could add the 3 and 7 first. We use parentheses to show that we group $3 + 7$ together and that we will add these two numbers first.

$$\begin{aligned} 5 + 3 + 7 &= 5 + (3 + 7) = 15 \\ &= 5 + \quad 10 \quad = 15 \end{aligned}$$

The way we group numbers to be added does not change the sum. This property is called the **associative property of addition.**

5 Reviewing the Properties of Addition

Look again at the three properties of addition we have discussed in this section.

1. **Associative Property of Addition** When we add three numbers, we can group them in any way.

   $(8 + 2) + 6 = 8 + (2 + 6)$
   $10 + 6 = 8 + 8$
   $16 = 16$

2. **Commutative Property of Addition** Two numbers can be added in either order with the same result.

   $5 + 12 = 12 + 5$
   $17 = 17$

3. **Identity Property of Zero** When zero is added to a number, the sum is that number.

   $8 + 0 = 8$
   $0 + 5 = 5$

Because of the commutative and associative properties of addition, we can check our addition by adding the numbers in the opposite order.

EXAMPLE 7 **(a)** Add the numbers. $39 + 7284 + 3132$
(b) Check by reversing the order of addition.

Solution

(a)
$$\begin{array}{r} \scriptstyle 1\,1 \\ 39 \\ 7284 \\ +3132 \\ \hline 10\,455 \end{array}$$
Addition

(b)
$$\begin{array}{r} \scriptstyle 1\,1\;\; \\ 3132 \\ 7284 \\ +\quad 39 \\ \hline 10\,455 \end{array}$$
Check by reversing the order.

The sum is the same in each case.

Practice Problem 7

(a) Add.
$$\begin{array}{r} 127 \\ 9876 \\ +\ 342 \\ \hline \end{array}$$

(b) Check by reversing the order.
$$\begin{array}{r} 342 \\ 9876 \\ +\ 127 \\ \hline \end{array}$$

 Applying Addition to Real-Life Situations

We use addition in all kinds of situations. There are several key words in word problems that imply addition. For example, it may be stated that there are 12 math books, 9 chemistry books, and 8 biology books on a book shelf. To find the *total* number of books implies that we add the numbers 12 + 9 + 8. Other key words are *how much, how many,* and *all.*

Sometimes a problem will have more information than you will need to answer the question. If you have too much information, to solve the problem you will need to separate out the facts that are not important. The following three steps are involved in the problem-solving process.

Step 1 Understand the problem.
Step 2 Calculate and state the answer.
Step 3 Check.

We may not write all of these steps down, but they are the steps we use to solve all problems.

EXAMPLE 8 The bookkeeper for Smithville Trucking was examining the following data for the company chequing account.

Monday:	\$23 416 was deposited and \$17 389 was debited.
Tuesday:	\$44 823 was deposited and \$34 089 was debited.
Wednesday:	\$16 213 was deposited and \$20 057 was debited.

What was the total of all deposits during this period?

Solution

Step 1 *Understand the problem.*
Total implies that we will use addition. Since we don't need to know about the debits to answer this question, we use only the *deposit* amounts.

Step 2 *Calculate and state the answer.*

Monday:	\$23 416 was deposited.	23 416 (carries: 1 1 1)
Tuesday:	\$44 823 was deposited.	44 823
Wednesday:	\$16 213 was deposited.	+ 16 213
		84 452

A total of \$84 452 was deposited on those three days.

Step 3 *Check.*
You may add the numbers in reverse order to check. We leave the check up to you.

Practice Problem 8 North University has 23 413 men and 18 316 women. South University has 19 316 men and 24 789 women. East University has 20 078 men and 22 965 women. What is the total enrolment of *women* at the three universities?

***NOTE TO STUDENT:** Fully worked-out solutions to all of the Practice Problems can be found at the end of the module.*

▲ **EXAMPLE 9** Mr. Ortiz has a rectangular field whose length is 400 metres and whose width is 200 metres. What is the total number of metres of fence that would be required to fence in the field?

Solution

1. *Understand the problem.*
To help us to get a picture of what the field looks like, we will draw a diagram.

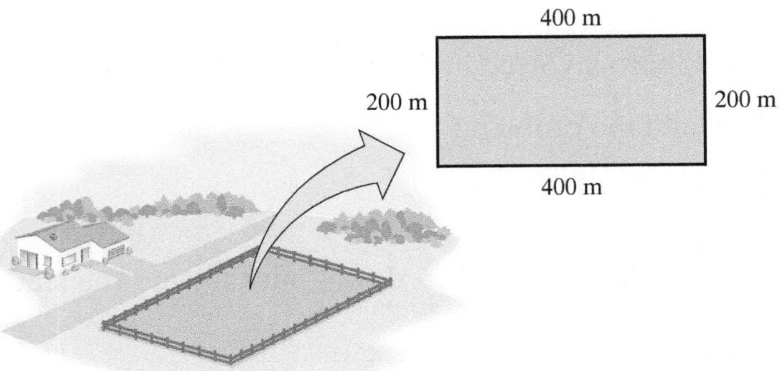

Note that m is the abbreviation for metres.

2. *Calculate and state the answer.*
Since the fence will be along each side of the field, we add the lengths all around the field.

$$\begin{array}{r} 200 \\ 400 \\ 200 \\ +\ 400 \\ \hline 1200 \end{array}$$

The amount of fence that would be required is 1200 metres.

3. *Check.*
Regroup the addends and add.

$$\begin{array}{r} 200 \\ 200 \\ 400 \\ +\ 400 \\ \hline 1200 \end{array} \checkmark$$

▲ **Practice Problem 9** In Manitoba, Gretchen fenced the rectangular field on which her sheep graze. The length of the field is 200 metres and the width of the field is 100 metres. What is the perimeter of the field? (*Hint:* The "distance around" an object [such as a field] is called the *perimeter.*)

Developing Your Study Skills

Getting Organized for an Exam

Studying adequately for an exam requires careful preparation. Begin early so that you will be able to spread your review over several days. Even though you may still be learning new material at this time, you can be reviewing concepts previously learned in the module. Giving yourself plenty of time for review will take the pressure off. You need this time to process what you have learned and to tie concepts together.

Adequate preparation enables you to feel confident and to think clearly with less tension and anxiety.

Section 2 Exercises

Verbal and Writing Skills

1. Explain in your own words.
   (a) the commutative property of addition
   (b) the associative property of addition

2. When zero is added to any number, it does not change that number. Why do you think this is called the identity property of zero?

Complete the addition facts for each table. Strive for total accuracy, but work quickly. Allow a maximum of five minutes for each table.

3.

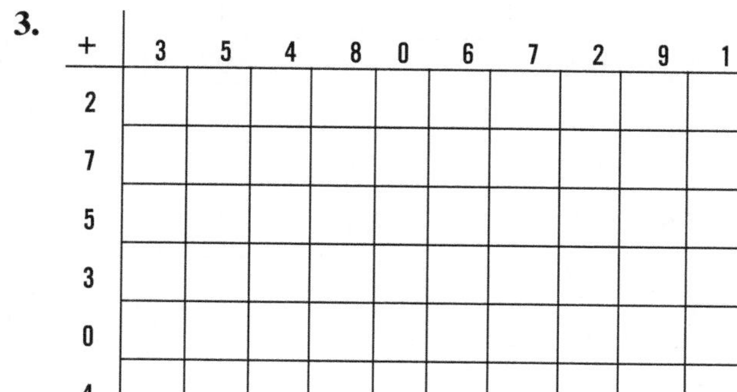

+	3	5	4	8	0	6	7	2	9	1
2										
7										
5										
3										
0										
4										
1										
8										
6										
9										

4.

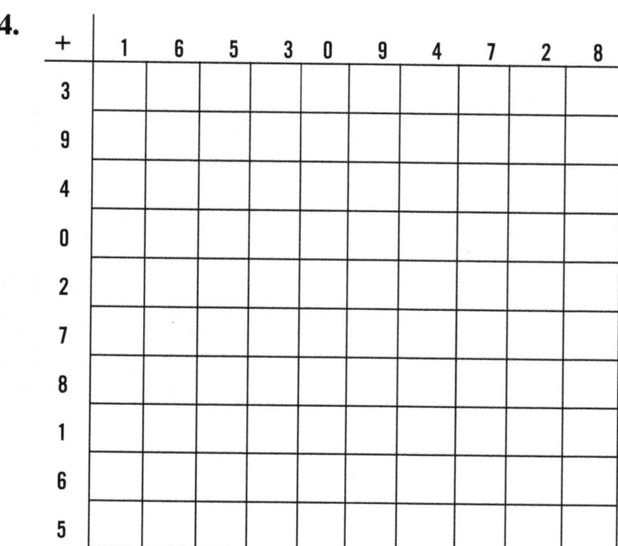

+	1	6	5	3	0	9	4	7	2	8
3										
9										
4										
0										
2										
7										
8										
1										
6										
5										

Add.

5. 4, 2, 8, + 9

6. 4, 6, 2, + 7

7. 2, 6, 7, 8, + 3

8. 1, 5, 5, 9, + 9

9. 18, 36, + 3

10. 63, 11, + 6

11. 63, 24, + 12

12. 54, 21, + 23

13. 3315, 726, + 84

14. 5773, 425, + 67

15. 5631, 2344, + 2019

16. 5017, 2984, + 1328

17. 8235 + 5626

18. 6753 + 3265

19. 62 504 + 54 736

20. 83 596 + 56 384

Add from the top. Then check by adding in the reverse order.

21. 36 + 41 + 25 + 6 + 13

22. 24 + 39 + 16 + 14 + 9

23. 207 + 15 + 3 + 57 + 861

24. 426 + 39 + 6 + 52 + 802

Add.

25. 85 + 256 + 55 + 9734

26. 582 + 1674 + 336 + 8458

27. 1 362 214 + 7 002 316 + 3 214 896

28. 4 002 983 + 2 134 702 + 3 592 001

29. 837 241 000 + 298 039 240

30. 982 306 000 + 583 215 320

31. 516 208 + 24 317 + 1 763 295

32. 32 500 + 763 420 + 2 837 667

33. 25 + 130 + 70 + 75

34. 125 + 60 + 140 + 75

35. 102 + 50 + 98 + 35 + 50

36. 20 + 205 + 95 + 42 + 80

Applications

37. ***Consumer Mathematics*** Vanessa took her children shopping for the new school year. She spent $455 on clothes, $186 on shoes, and $82 on supplies. What was the total amount of money Vanessa spent?

38. ***Consumer Mathematics*** Richy has a part-time job as a dog walker. He saves all of the money he earns for a vacation. He earned $235 in June, $198 in July, and $282 in August. What is the total amount of money Richy saved?

39. ***Personal Finance*** Sheila owns a studio where she teaches music classes to children. Two months ago she had earnings of $1875. Last month she made $1930 and this month she earned $1744. What is the total amount for the three months?

40. ***Consumer Mathematics*** Terrell flies to several cities each month for his job. During the past three months he has spent $2230, $2655, and $2570 on airline tickets. What is the total amount for the three months?

▲ **41.** ***Geometry*** Nate wants to put a fence around his backyard. The sketch below indicates the length of each side of the yard. What is the total number of metres of fence he needs for his backyard?

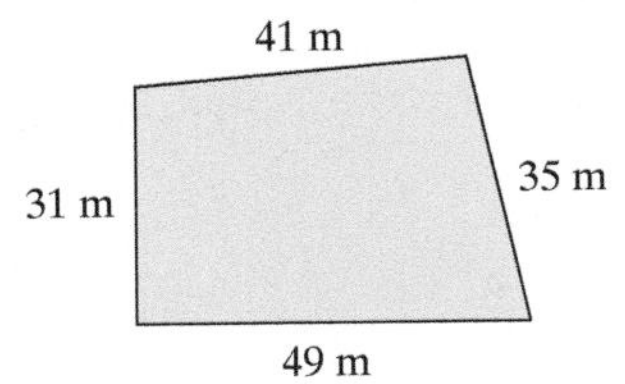

▲ **42.** ***Geometry*** Jessica has a field with the length of each side as labelled on the sketch. What is the total number of metres of fence that would be required to fence in the field? (Find the perimeter of the field.)

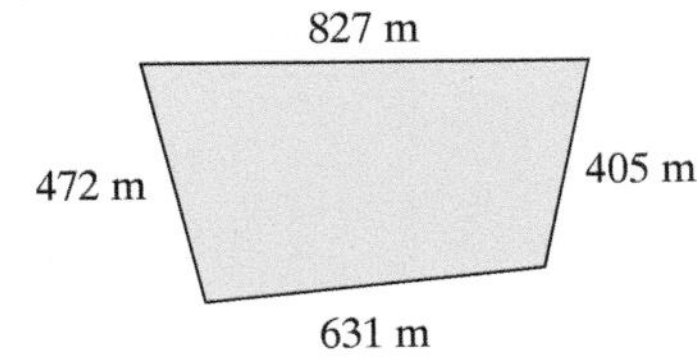

▲43. ***Geography*** The Pacific Ocean, the world's largest, has an area of 165 760 000 square kilometres. The Atlantic Ocean has an area of 82 362 000 square kilometres. The Indian Ocean has an area of 65 527 000 square kilometres. What is the total area of these oceans?

▲44. ***Geography*** The Arctic Ocean has an area of 13 986 000 square kilometres. The Mediterranean Sea has an area of 2 849 000 square kilometres. The Caribbean Sea has an area of 2 590 000 square kilometres. What is the total area of these bodies of water?

45. ***Geography*** The Nile River is Africa's longest river, measuring 6 649 809 metres. The second and third longest rivers in Africa are the Congo River, measuring 4 667 908 metres, and the Niger River, which measures 4 168 201 metres. What is the total length of these rivers?

▲46. ***Geography*** The world's three largest lakes are the Caspian Sea at 394 532 square kilometres, Lake Superior at 82 414 square kilometres, and Lake Victoria at 69 485 square kilometres. What is the total area of these three lakes?

In exercises 47–48, be sure you understand the problem and then choose the numbers you need in order to answer each question. Then solve the problem.

47. ***Education*** The admissions department of a competitive university is reviewing applications to see whether students are *eligible* or *ineligible* for student aid. On Monday, 415 were found eligible and 27 ineligible. On Tuesday, 364 were found eligible and 68 ineligible. On Wednesday, 159 were found eligible and 102 ineligible. On Thursday, 196 were found eligible and 61 ineligible.

(a) How many students were eligible for student aid over the four days?

(b) How many students were considered in all?

48. ***Manufacturing*** The quality control division of a motorcycle company classifies the final assembled bike as *passing* or *failing* final inspection. In January, 14 311 vehicles passed whereas 56 failed. In February, 11 077 passed and 158 failed. In March, 12 580 passed and 97 failed.

(a) How many motorcycles passed the inspection during the three months?

(b) How many motorcycles in all were assembled during the three months?

Use the following facts to solve exercises 49 and 50. It is 87 kilometres from Springfield to Weston. It is 17 kilometres from Weston to Kakula. Driving directly, it is 98 kilometres from Springfield to Kakula. It is 21 kilometres from Kakula to Manipo.

49. ***Geography*** If Melissa drives from Springfield to Weston, then from Weston to Kakula, and finally directly home to Springfield, how many kilometres does she drive?

50. ***Geography*** If Marcia drives from Manipo to Kakula, then from Kakula to Weston, and then from Weston to Springfield, how many kilometres does she drive?

▲51. ***Geometry*** Walter Swensen is examining the fences of a farm in Woodstock, Ontario. One field is in the shape of a four-sided figure with no sides equal. The field is enclosed with 2387 metres of wooden rail fence. The first side is 568 metres long, while the second side is 682 metres long. The third side is 703 metres long. How long is the fourth side?

▲52. ***Geometry*** Ivan is walking to examine the fences of a ranch in Calgary, Alberta. The field he is examining is in the shape of a rectangle. The perimeter of the rectangle is 1152 metres. One side of the rectangle is 310 metres long. How long are the other sides? (*Hint:* The opposite sides of a rectangle are equal.)

53. ***Personal Finance*** Answer using the information in the following Western University expense chart for the current academic year.

Western University Yearly Expenses	In-Province Student, Canadian Citizen	Out-of-Province Student, Canadian Citizen	Foreign Student
Tuition	$3640	$5276	$8352
Room	1926	2437	2855
Board	1753	1840	1840

How much is the total cost for tuition, room, and board for

(a) an out-of-province Canadian citizen?
(b) an in-province Canadian citizen?
(c) a foreign student?

To Think About *In exercises 54–55, add.*

54. 2 368 521 788 + 5 721 368 701 + 4 027 399 206

55. 89 + 166 + 23 + 45 + 72 + 190 + 203 + 77 + 18 + 93 + 46 + 73 + 66

56. What would happen if addition were not commutative?

57. What would happen if addition were not associative?

Quick Quiz 2 Add.

1.
$$\begin{array}{r} 56 \\ 38 \\ 92 \\ 17 \\ +\ 9 \\ \hline \end{array}$$

2.
$$\begin{array}{r} 831 \\ 276 \\ +508 \\ \hline \end{array}$$

3.
$$\begin{array}{r} 681\ 302 \\ 5\ 126 \\ 18\ 371 \\ +300\ 012 \\ \hline \end{array}$$

4. **Concept Check** Explain how you would use carrying when performing the calculation 4567 + 3189 + 895.

Section 3 Subtracting Whole Numbers

Mastering Basic Subtraction Facts

Subtraction is used day after day in the business world. The owner of a bakery placed an ad for his cakes in a local newspaper to see if this might increase his profits. To learn how many cakes had been sold, at closing time he subtracted the number of cakes remaining from the number of cakes the bakery had when it opened. To figure his profits, he subtracted his costs (including the cost of the ad) from his sales. Finally, to see if the ad paid off, he subtracted the profits he usually made in that period from the profits after advertising. He needed subtraction to see whether it paid to advertise.

What is subtraction? We do subtraction when we take objects away from a group. If you have 12 objects and take away 3 of them, 9 objects remain.

12 objects − 3 objects = 9 objects

$$12 - 3 = 9$$

If you earn \$400 per month, but have \$100 taken out for taxes, how much do you have left?

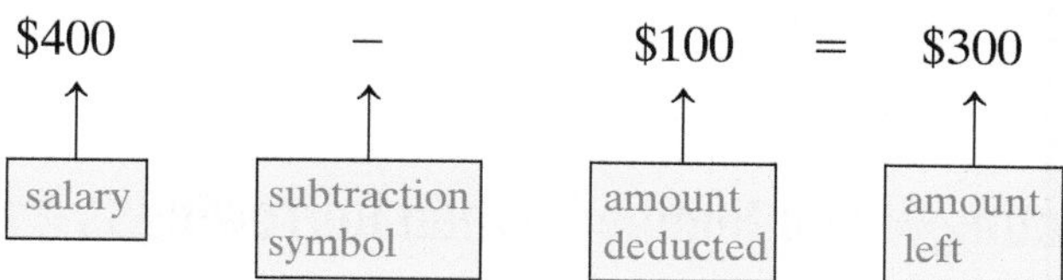

We can use addition to help with a subtraction problem.

To subtract: 200 − 196 = what number

We can think: 196 + what number = 200

Usually when we subtract numbers, we put one number under the other in a column. When we subtract one number from another, the answer is called the **difference.**

$$\begin{array}{r} 9 \\ -\,2 \\ \hline 7 \end{array} \qquad \begin{array}{r} 8 \\ -\,3 \\ \hline 5 \end{array} \qquad \begin{array}{r} 12 \\ -\,6 \\ \hline 6 \end{array} \qquad \begin{array}{r} 17 \\ -\,9 \\ \hline 8 \end{array}$$

Each of these is called the difference of the two numbers.

The other two parts of a subtraction problem have labels, although you will not often come across them. The number being subtracted is called the **subtrahend.** The number being subtracted from is called the **minuend.**

$$\begin{array}{rl} 17 & \text{minuend} \\ -\,9 & \text{subtrahend} \\ \hline 8 & \text{difference} \end{array}$$

In this case, the number 17 is called the *minuend.* The number 9 is called the *subtrahend.* The number 8 is called the *difference.*

Student Learning Objectives

After studying this section, you will be able to:

1. Master basic subtraction facts.
2. Subtract whole numbers when borrowing is not necessary.
3. Subtract whole numbers when borrowing is necessary.
4. Check the answer to a subtraction problem.
5. Apply subtraction to real-life situations.

QUICK RECALL OF SUBTRACTION FACTS It is helpful if you can subtract quickly. See if you can do Example 1 correctly in 15 seconds or less. Repeat again with Practice Problem 1. Strive to obtain all answers correctly in 15 seconds or less.

EXAMPLE 1 Subtract.

(a) $8 - 2$ **(b)** $13 - 5$ **(c)** $12 - 4$
(d) $15 - 8$ **(e)** $16 - 0$

Solution

(a) $\begin{array}{r} 8 \\ -2 \\ \hline 6 \end{array}$ **(b)** $\begin{array}{r} 13 \\ -5 \\ \hline 8 \end{array}$ **(c)** $\begin{array}{r} 12 \\ -4 \\ \hline 8 \end{array}$

(d) $\begin{array}{r} 15 \\ -8 \\ \hline 7 \end{array}$ **(e)** $\begin{array}{r} 16 \\ -0 \\ \hline 16 \end{array}$

NOTE TO STUDENT: Fully worked-out solutions to all of the Practice Problems can be found at the end of the module.

Practice Problem 1 Subtract.

(a) $\begin{array}{r} 9 \\ -6 \\ \hline \end{array}$ **(b)** $\begin{array}{r} 12 \\ -5 \\ \hline \end{array}$ **(c)** $\begin{array}{r} 17 \\ -8 \\ \hline \end{array}$ **(d)** $\begin{array}{r} 14 \\ -0 \\ \hline \end{array}$ **(e)** $\begin{array}{r} 18 \\ -9 \\ \hline \end{array}$

2 Subtracting Whole Numbers When Borrowing Is Not Necessary

When we subtract numbers with more than two digits, in order to keep track of our work, we line up the ones column, the tens column, the hundreds column, and so on. Note that we begin with the ones column, and move from right to left.

EXAMPLE 2 Subtract. $9867 - 3725$

Solution

$$\begin{array}{r} 9\,8\,6\,7 \\ -3\,7\,2\,5 \\ \hline 6\,1\,4\,2 \end{array}$$

7 ones − 5 ones = 2 ones
6 tens − 2 tens = 4 tens
8 hundreds − 7 hundreds = 1 hundred
9 thousands − 3 thousands = 6 thousands

Practice Problem 2 Subtract. $7695 - 3481$

 Subtracting Whole Numbers When Borrowing Is Necessary

In the subtraction that we have looked at so far, each digit in the upper number (the minuend) has been greater than the digit in the lower number (the subtrahend) for each place value. Many times, however, a digit in the lower number is greater than the digit in the upper number for that place value.

$$\begin{array}{r} 42 \\ -\ 28 \\ \hline \end{array}$$

The digit in the ones place in the lower number, the 8 of 28, is greater than the number in the ones place in the upper number, the 2 of 42. To subtract, we must *rename* 42, using place values. This is called **borrowing.**

EXAMPLE 3 Subtract. 42 − 28

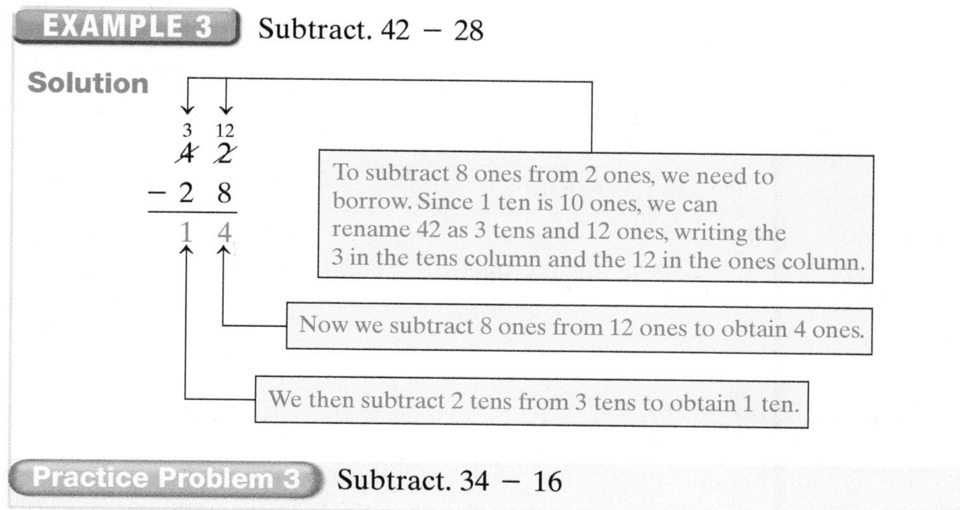

Solution
3 12
4 2
− 2 8
1 4
To subtract 8 ones from 2 ones, we need to borrow. Since 1 ten is 10 ones, we can rename 42 as 3 tens and 12 ones, writing the 3 in the tens column and the 12 in the ones column.
Now we subtract 8 ones from 12 ones to obtain 4 ones.
We then subtract 2 tens from 3 tens to obtain 1 ten.

Practice Problem 3 Subtract. 34 − 16

NOTE TO STUDENT: Fully worked-out solutions to all of the Practice Problems can be found at the end of the module.

EXAMPLE 4 Subtract. 864 − 548

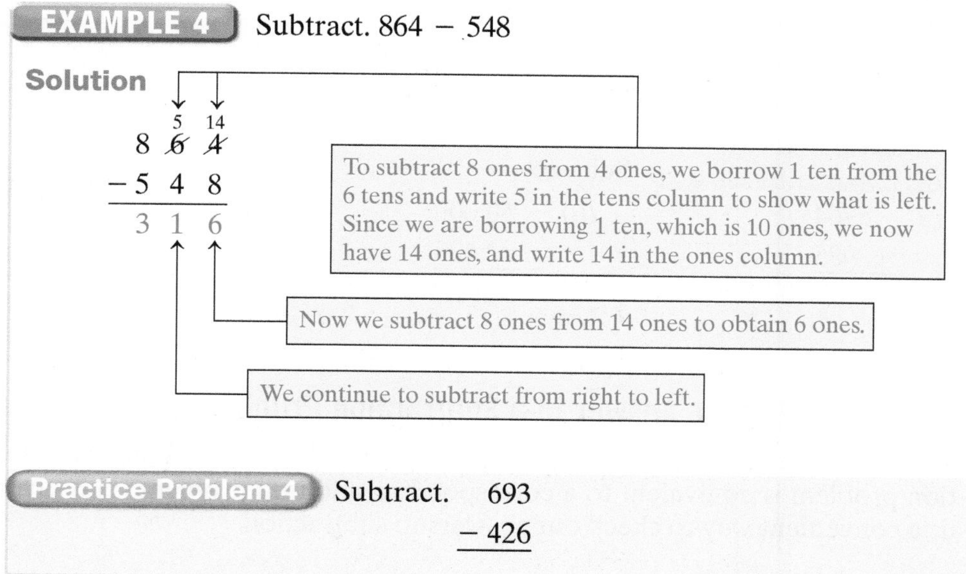

Solution
5 14
8 6 4
− 5 4 8
3 1 6
To subtract 8 ones from 4 ones, we borrow 1 ten from the 6 tens and write 5 in the tens column to show what is left. Since we are borrowing 1 ten, which is 10 ones, we now have 14 ones, and write 14 in the ones column.
Now we subtract 8 ones from 14 ones to obtain 6 ones.
We continue to subtract from right to left.

Practice Problem 4 Subtract.

$$\begin{array}{r} 693 \\ -\ 426 \\ \hline \end{array}$$

EXAMPLE 5 Subtract. 8040 − 6375

Solution

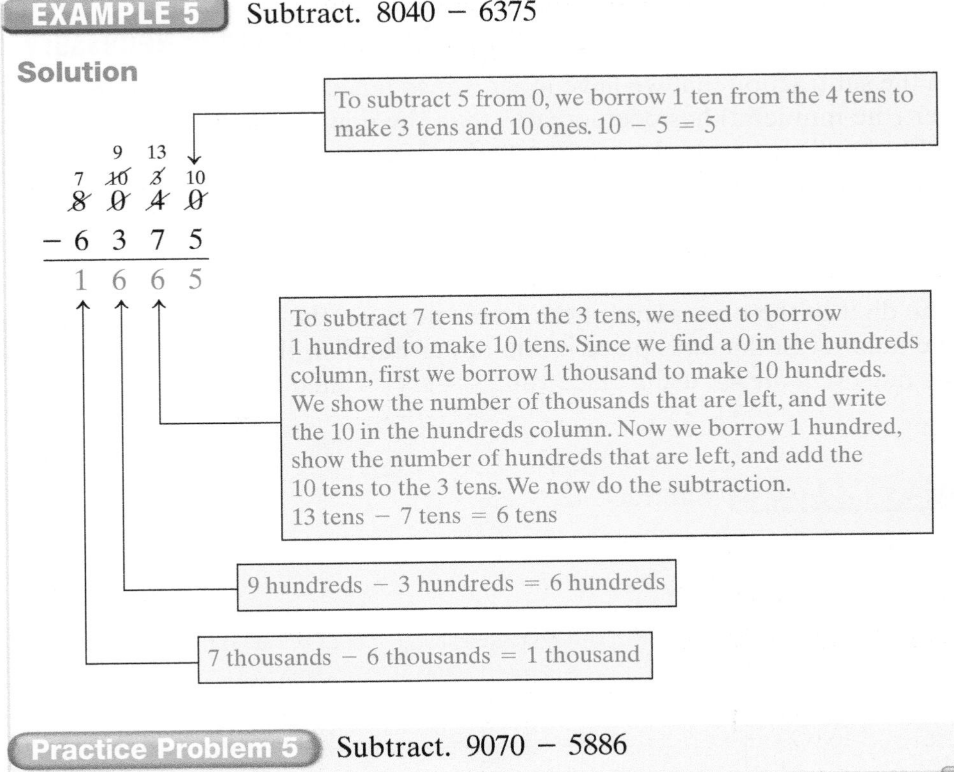

To subtract 5 from 0, we borrow 1 ten from the 4 tens to make 3 tens and 10 ones. 10 − 5 = 5
To subtract 7 tens from the 3 tens, we need to borrow 1 hundred to make 10 tens. Since we find a 0 in the hundreds column, first we borrow 1 thousand to make 10 hundreds. We show the number of thousands that are left, and write the 10 in the hundreds column. Now we borrow 1 hundred, show the number of hundreds that are left, and add the 10 tens to the 3 tens. We now do the subtraction. 13 tens − 7 tens = 6 tens
9 hundreds − 3 hundreds = 6 hundreds
7 thousands − 6 thousands = 1 thousand

Practice Problem 5 Subtract. 9070 − 5886

EXAMPLE 6 Subtract.

(a) 9521 − 943 **(b)** 40 000 − 29 056

Solution

(a)
$$\begin{array}{r} 9521 \\ -\ \ 943 \\ \hline 8578 \end{array}$$

(b)
$$\begin{array}{r} 40000 \\ -29056 \\ \hline 10944 \end{array}$$

Practice Problem 6 Subtract.

(a)
$$\begin{array}{r} 8964 \\ -\ \ 985 \\ \hline \end{array}$$

(b)
$$\begin{array}{r} 50\,000 \\ -\ 32\,508 \\ \hline \end{array}$$

4 Checking the Answer to a Subtraction Problem

We observe that when 9 − 7 = 2 it follows that 7 + 2 = 9. Each subtraction problem is equivalent to a corresponding addition problem. This gives us a convenient way to check our answers to subtraction.

EXAMPLE 7 Check this subtraction problem.

$$5829 - 3647 = 2182$$

Solution

$$\begin{array}{r} 5829 \\ -3647 \\ \hline 2182 \end{array} \quad \text{then} \quad \begin{array}{r} 3647 \\ +2182 \\ \hline 5829 \end{array}$$

The sum should equal 5829, which it does. We have checked our work, and it is correct.

Practice Problem 7 Check this subtraction problem.

$$9763 - 5732 = 4031$$

NOTE TO STUDENT: Fully worked-out solutions to all of the Practice Problems can be found at the end of the module.

EXAMPLE 8 Subtract and check your answers.

(a) 156 000 − 29 326 **(b)** 1 264 308 − 1 057 612

Solution

(a)

$$\begin{array}{r} 156\,000 \\ -\ 29\,326 \\ \hline 126\,674 \end{array} \qquad \begin{array}{r} 29\,326 \\ +\ 126\,674 \\ \hline 156\,000 \end{array}$$

It checks.

(b)

$$\begin{array}{r} 1\,264\,308 \\ -\ 1\,057\,612 \\ \hline 206\,696 \end{array} \qquad \begin{array}{r} 1\,057\,612 \\ +\ 206\,696 \\ \hline 1\,264\,308 \end{array}$$

It checks.

Practice Problem 8 Subtract and check your answers.

(a)
$$\begin{array}{r} 284\,000 \\ -\ 96\,327 \\ \hline \end{array}$$

(b)
$$\begin{array}{r} 8\,526\,024 \\ -\ 6\,397\,518 \\ \hline \end{array}$$

Subtraction can be used to solve word problems. Some problems can be expressed (and solved) with an **equation.** An equation is a number sentence with an equal sign, such as

$$10 = 4 + x$$

Here we use the letter x to represent a number we do not know. When we write $10 = 4 + x$, we are stating that 10 is equal to 4 added to some other number. Since $10 - 4 = 6$, we would assume that the number is 6. If we substitute 6 for x in the equation, we have two values that are the same.

$10 = 4 + x$

$10 = 4 + 6$ Substitute 6 for x.

$10 = 10$ Both sides of the equation are the same.

We can write an equation when one of the addends is not known, then use subtraction to solve for the unknown.

EXAMPLE 9 The librarian knows that he has eight world atlases and that five of them are in full colour. How many are not in full colour?

Solution We represent the number that we don't know as x and write an equation, or mathematical sentence.

$$8 = 5 + x$$

To solve an equation means to find those values that will make the equation true. We solve this equation by reasoning and by a knowledge of the relationship between addition and subtraction.

$$8 = 5 + x \text{ is equivalent to } 8 - 5 = x$$

We know that $8 - 5 = 3$. Then $x = 3$. We can check the answer by substituting 3 for x in the original equation.

$$8 = 5 + x$$
$$8 = 5 + 3 \quad \text{True} ✓$$

We see that $x = 3$ checks, so our answer is correct. There are three atlases not in full colour.

Practice Problem 9 Form an equation for each of the following problems. Solve the equation in order to answer the question.

(a) The Salem Harbourmaster's daily log noted that seventeen fishing vessels left the harbour yesterday during daylight hours. Walter was at the harbour all morning and saw twelve fishing vessels leave in the morning. How many vessels left in the afternoon? (Assume that sunset was at 6 P.M.)

(b) The Appalachian Mountain Club noted that twenty-two hikers left to climb Mount Washington during the morning. By 4 P.M., ten of them had returned. How many of the hikers were still on the mountain?

5 Applying Subtraction to Real-Life Situations

We use subtraction in all kinds of situations. There are several key words in word problems that imply subtraction. Words that involve comparison, such as *how much more, how much greater,* or how much a quantity *increased* or *decreased,* all imply subtraction. The *difference* between two numbers implies subtraction.

EXAMPLE 10 Look at the following population table.

Estimated Population of Four Regions from 1991 to 2008

	1991	1996	2001	2006	2008*
British Columbia	3 282 061	3 724 500	3 907 735	4 113 485	4 381 600
Nova Scotia	899 942	909 282	908 005	913 460	938 300
Newfoundland and Labrador	568 474	551 792	512 930	505 470	507 900
Yukon	27 797	30 766	28 670	30 375	33 100

*Rounded to nearest 100

Source: Adapted from Statistics Canada, www40.statcan.ca/l01/cst01/demo02a-eng.htm, and www12.statcan.ca/english/census01/products/highlight/AgeSex/Page.cfm?Lang=E&Geo=PR&View=1&Table=4a&StartRec=1&Sort=2&B1=Median&B2=Both, and www.statcan.gc.ca/c1996-r1996/4220363-eng.pdf, Oct-09

(a) In 1996, how much greater was the population of Nova Scotia than that of Newfoundland and Labrador?

(b) How much did the population of British Columbia increase from 1996 to 2006?

(c) How much greater was the population of British Columbia in 2001 than that of the other three regions combined?

Solution

(a)

909 282	1996 population of Nova Scotia
− 551 792	1996 population of Newfoundland and Labrador
357 490	difference

The population of Nova Scotia was greater by 357 490.

(b)

4 113 485	2006 population of British Columbia
− 3 724 500	1996 population of British Columbia
388 985	difference

The population of British Columbia increased by 388 985.

(c) First we need to find the total population in 2001 of Nova Scotia, Newfoundland and Labrador, and Yukon.

908 005	2001 population of Nova Scotia
512 930	2001 population of Newfoundland and Labrador
+ 28 670	2001 population of Yukon
1 449 605	

We use subtraction to compare this total with the population of British Columbia.

3 907 735	2001 population of British Columbia
− 1 449 605	
2 458 130	

The population of British Columbia in 2001 was 2 458 130 more than the population of the other three regions combined.

Practice Problem 10

(a) In 1996, how much greater was the population of British Columbia than the population of Nova Scotia?

(b) How much did the population of Nova Scotia increase from 1991 to 1996?

NOTE TO STUDENT: *Fully worked-out solutions to all of the Practice Problems can be found at the end of the module.*

EXAMPLE 11 The number of real estate transfers in several towns during the years 2007 to 2009 is given in the following bar graph.

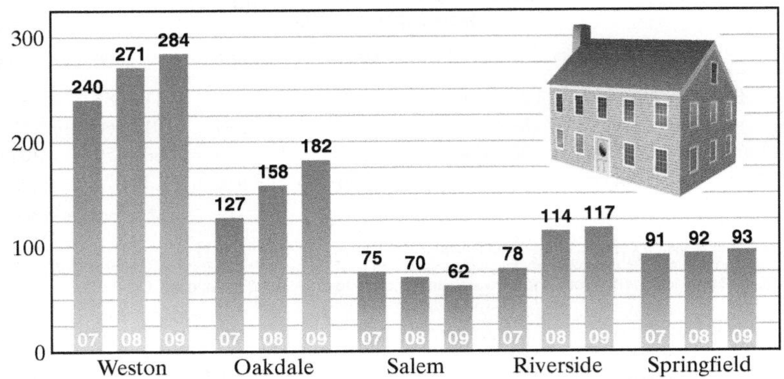

(a) What was the increase in homes sold in Weston from 2008 to 2009?

(b) What was the decrease in homes sold in Salem from 2007 to 2009?

(c) Between what two years did Oakdale have the greatest increase in sales?

Solution

(a) From the labels on the bar graph we see that 284 homes were sold in 2009 in Weston and 271 homes were sold in 2008. Thus the increase can be found by subtracting $284 - 271 = 13$. There was an increase of 13 homes sold in Weston from 2008 to 2009.

(b) In 2007, 75 homes were sold in Salem. In 2009, 62 homes were sold in Salem. The decrease in the number of homes sold is $75 - 62 = 13$. There was a decrease of 13 homes sold in Salem from 2007 to 2009.

(c) Here we will need to make two calculations in order to decide where the greatest increase occurred.

158	2008 sales	182	2009 sales
− 127	2007 sales	− 158	2008 sales
31	Sales increase from 2007 to 2008	24	Sales increase from 2008 to 2009

The greatest increase in sales in Oakdale occurred from 2007 to 2008.

Practice Problem 11 Based on the preceding bar graph, answer the following questions.

(a) What was the increase in homes sold in Riverside from 2007 to 2008?

(b) How many more homes were sold in Springfield in 2007 than in Riverside in 2007?

(c) Between what two years did Weston have the greatest increase in sales?

Section 3 Exercises

Verbal and Writing Skills

1. Explain how you can check a subtraction problem.

2. Explain how you use borrowing to calculate 107 − 88.

3. Explain what number should be used to replace the question mark in the subtraction equation 32?5 − 1683 = 1592.

4. Explain what number should be used to replace the question mark in the addition equation 1623 + 2?11 = 4334.

Try to do exercises 5–20 in one minute or less with no errors.

Subtract.

5. $8 - 3$

6. $17 - 8$

7. $15 - 9$

8. $14 - 5$

9. $16 - 0$

10. $17 - 9$

11. $18 - 9$

12. $12 - 7$

13. $11 - 4$

14. $15 - 8$

15. $13 - 7$

16. $16 - 9$

17. $11 - 8$

18. $10 - 7$

19. $15 - 6$

20. $12 - 5$

Subtract. Check your answers by adding.

21. $47 - 26$

22. $96 - 51$

23. $85 - 73$

24. $77 - 36$

25. $379 - 36$

26. $189 - 65$

27. $869 - 548$

28. $659 - 247$

29. $4799 - 596$

30. $5780 - 530$

31. $155\,835 - 12\,600$

32. $243\,951 - 12\,400$

33. $986\,302 - 433\,201$

34. $807\,965 - 304\,214$

Check each subtraction. If the problem has not been done correctly, find the correct answer.

35. $\begin{array}{r} 129 \\ -\ 19 \\ \hline 110 \end{array}$

36. $\begin{array}{r} 186 \\ -\ 45 \\ \hline 141 \end{array}$

37. $\begin{array}{r} 8596 \\ -3215 \\ \hline 5781 \end{array}$

38. $\begin{array}{r} 9956 \\ -7254 \\ \hline 2702 \end{array}$

39. $\begin{array}{r} 6030 \\ -5020 \\ \hline 1020 \end{array}$

40. $\begin{array}{r} 7890 \\ -3200 \\ \hline 7670 \end{array}$

41. $\begin{array}{r} 47\ 869 \\ -33\ 846 \\ \hline 13\ 023 \end{array}$

42. $\begin{array}{r} 99\ 583 \\ -41\ 181 \\ \hline 58\ 402 \end{array}$

Subtract. Use borrowing if necessary.

43. $\begin{array}{r} 98 \\ -52 \\ \hline \end{array}$

44. $\begin{array}{r} 86 \\ -33 \\ \hline \end{array}$

45. $\begin{array}{r} 174 \\ -\ 82 \\ \hline \end{array}$

46. $\begin{array}{r} 136 \\ -\ 95 \\ \hline \end{array}$

47. $\begin{array}{r} 647 \\ -263 \\ \hline \end{array}$

48. $\begin{array}{r} 706 \\ -435 \\ \hline \end{array}$

49. $\begin{array}{r} 955 \\ -237 \\ \hline \end{array}$

50. $\begin{array}{r} 861 \\ -345 \\ \hline \end{array}$

51. $\begin{array}{r} 20\ 000 \\ -\ 9\ 285 \\ \hline \end{array}$

52. $\begin{array}{r} 50\ 000 \\ -\ 7\ 338 \\ \hline \end{array}$

53. $\begin{array}{r} 152\ 000 \\ -117\ 908 \\ \hline \end{array}$

54. $\begin{array}{r} 361\ 000 \\ -121\ 520 \\ \hline \end{array}$

55. $\begin{array}{r} 45\ 312 \\ -37\ 865 \\ \hline \end{array}$

56. $\begin{array}{r} 64\ 381 \\ -29\ 997 \\ \hline \end{array}$

57. $\begin{array}{r} 2\ 378\ 862 \\ -1\ 469\ 932 \\ \hline \end{array}$

58. $\begin{array}{r} 3\ 554\ 830 \\ -1\ 710\ 913 \\ \hline \end{array}$

Solve.

59. $x + 14 = 19$

60. $x + 35 = 50$

61. $28 = x + 20$

62. $25 = x + 18$

63. $100 + x = 127$

64. $140 + x = 200$

Applications

65. ***Politics*** In the 2006 Federal Election in Ontario, the Liberal and Conservative parties combined to receive a total of 3 245 266 votes. If the Conservative Party received 1 985 242 of those votes, how many votes did the Liberal Party obtain? (*Source:* Elections Canada, http://www.elections.ca/scripts/OVR2006/default.html, Oct-09)

66. ***Politics*** In the 2006 Federal Election in Québec, the Bloc Québécois and Conservative parties combined to receive a total of 2 416 173 votes. If the Conservative Party received 907 972 of those votes, how many votes did the Bloc Québécois obtain? (*Source:* Elections Canada, http://www.elections.ca/scripts/OVR2006/default.html, Oct-09)

67. ***Population Trends*** In 2006, the population of Ireland was approximately 4 062 235. In the same year, the population of Portugal was approximately 10 605 870. How much less than the population of Portugal was the population of Ireland in 2006?

68. ***Geography*** The Nile River, the longest river in the world, is approximately 22 070 400 feet long. The Yangtze Kiang River, which is the longest river in China, is approximately 19 018 560 feet long. How much longer is the Nile River than the Yangtze Kiang River?

69. ***Personal Finance*** Michaela's gross pay on her last paycheque was \$1280. Her deductions totalled \$318 and she deposited \$200 into her savings account. She put the remaining amount into her chequing account to pay bills. How much did Michaela put into her chequing account?

70. ***Personal Finance*** Adam earned \$3450 last summer at his construction job. He owed his brother \$375 and saved \$2300 to pay for his college tuition. He used the remaining amount as a down payment for a car. How much did Adam have for the down payment?

Population Trends *In answering exercises 71–78, consider the following population table.*

	1991	1996	2001	2006	2008*
Ontario	10 084 885	10 753 573	11 410 045	12 028 895	12 929 000
Québec	6 895 963	7 138 795	7 237 480	7 435 905	7 750 500
Alberta	2 545 553	2 696 826	2 974 810	3 256 355	3 585 100
Manitoba	1 091 942	1 113 898	1 119 585	1 133 515	1 208 000

*Rounded to nearest 100

Source: Adapted from Statistics Canada, www40.statcan.ca/l01/cst01/demo02a-eng.htm, and www12.statcan.ca/english/census01/products/highlight/AgeSex/Page.cfm?Lang=E&Geo=PR&View=1&Table=4a&StartRec=1&Sort=2&B1=Median&B2=Both, and www.statcan.gc.ca/c1996-r1996/4220363-eng.pdf, Oct-09

71. How much did the population of Manitoba increase from 1991 to 2006?

72. How much did the population of Québec increase from 1991 to 2006?

73. In 1991, how much greater was the population of Ontario than the populations of Alberta and Manitoba combined?

74. In 2006, how much greater was the population of Ontario than the populations of Alberta and Manitoba combined?

75. How much did the population of Ontario increase from 1996 to 2001?

76. How much did the population of Québec increase from 1996 to 2001?

77. Compare your answers to exercises 75 and 76. How much greater was the population increase of Ontario than the population increase of Québec from 1996 to 2001?

78. In 2008, what was the difference in population between the province with the highest population and the province with the lowest population?

Real Estate *The number of real estate transfers in several towns during the years 2005 to 2007 is given in the following bar graph. Use the bar graph to answer exercises 79–86. The figures in the bar graph reflect sales of single-family detached homes only.*

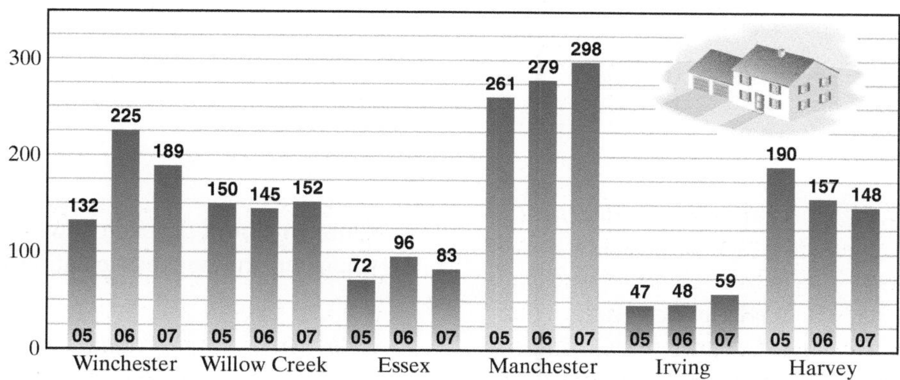

79. What was the increase in the number of homes sold in Winchester from 2005 to 2006?

80. What was the increase in the number of homes sold in Irving from 2006 to 2007?

81. What was the decrease in the number of homes sold in Essex from 2006 to 2007?

82. What was the decrease in the number of homes sold in Harvey from 2005 to 2006?

83. Between what two years did the greatest change occur in the number of homes sold in Willow Creek?

84. Between what two years did the greatest change occur in the number of homes sold in Manchester?

85. A real estate agent was trying to determine which two towns were closest to having the same number of sales in 2007. Which two towns should she select?

86. A real estate agent was trying to determine which two towns were closest to having the same number of sales in 2005. Which two towns should he select?

To Think About

87. In general, subtraction is not commutative. If a and b are whole numbers, $a - b \neq b - a$. For what types of numbers would it be true that $a - b = b - a$?

88. In general, subtraction is not associative. For example, $8 - (4 - 3) \neq (8 - 4) - 3$. In general, $a - (b - c) \neq (a - b) - c$. Can you find some numbers a, b, c for which $a - (b - c) = (a - b) - c$? (Remember, do operations inside the parentheses first.)

89. ***Consumer Mathematics*** Walter wants to replace some of the fences on a farm in Guelph, Ontario. The wooden rail fence costs about \$60 for wood and \$50 for labour to install a fence that is 12 metres long. His son estimated he would need 276 metres of new fence. However, when he measured it he realized he would only need 216 metres of new fence. What is the difference in cost of his son's estimate versus his estimate with regard to how many metres of fence are needed?

90. ***Consumer Mathematics*** Carlos is replacing some barbed-wire fence on a ranch in Moose Jaw, Saskatchewan. The barbed wire and poles for 12 metres of fence cost about \$80. The labour cost to install 12 metres of fence is about \$40. A ranch hand reported that 300 new metres of fence were needed. However, when Carlos actually rode out there and measured it, he found that only 228 metres of new fence were needed. What is the difference in cost of the ranch hand's estimate versus Carlos's estimate of how many metres of fence are needed?

Quick Quiz 3 Subtract.

1. $\begin{array}{r} 5392 \\ -\ 938 \\ \hline \end{array}$

2. $\begin{array}{r} 609\ 240 \\ -\ 386\ 307 \\ \hline \end{array}$

3. $\begin{array}{r} 17\ 200\ 300 \\ -\ 11\ 562\ 178 \\ \hline \end{array}$

4. Concept Check Explain how you would use borrowing when performing the calculation 12 345 − 11 976.

SECTION 4 MULTIPLYING WHOLE NUMBERS

 Mastering Basic Multiplication Facts

Like subtraction, multiplication is related to addition. Suppose that the pastry chef at the Gourmet Restaurant bakes croissants on a sheet that holds four croissants across, with room for three rows. How many croissants does the sheet hold?

We can add $4 + 4 + 4$ to get the total, or we can use a shortcut: three rows of four is the same as 3 times 4, which equals 12. This is **multiplication,** a shortcut for repeated addition.

The numbers that we multiply are called **factors.** The answer is called the **product.** For now, we will use $\times$ to show multiplication. 3×4 is read "three times four."

$$\underbrace{3}_{\text{factor}} \times \underbrace{4}_{\text{factor}} = \underbrace{12}_{\text{product}} \qquad \begin{array}{rl} 3 & \text{factor} \\ \times\ 4 & \text{factor} \\ \hline 12 & \text{product} \end{array}$$

Your skill in multiplication depends on how well you know the basic multiplication facts. Look at the table on the next page. You should learn these facts well enough to quickly and correctly give the products of any two factors in the table. To check your knowledge, try Section 4 Exercises, exercises 3 and 4.

Study the table to see if you can discover any properties of multiplication. What do you see as results when you multiply zero by any number? When you multiply any number times zero, the result is zero. That is the **multiplication property of zero.**

$$2 \times 0 = 0 \qquad 5 \times 0 = 0 \qquad 0 \times 6 = 0 \qquad 0 \times 0 = 0$$

You may recall that zero plays a special role in addition. Zero is the *identity element* for addition. When we add any number to zero, that number does not change. Is there an identity element for multiplication? Look at the table. What is the identity element for multiplication? Do you see that it is 1? The **identity element for multiplication** is 1.

$$5 \times 1 = 5 \qquad 1 \times 5 = 5$$

What other properties of addition hold for multiplication? Is multiplication commutative? Does the order in which you multiply two numbers change the results? Find the product of 3×4. Then find the product of 4×3.

$$3 \times 4 = 12$$
$$4 \times 3 = 12$$

The **commutative property of multiplication** tells us that when we multiply two numbers, changing the order of the numbers gives the same result.

Student Learning Objectives

After studying this section, you will be able to:

1. **Master basic multiplication facts.**
2. **Multiply a single-digit number by a several-digit number.**
3. **Multiply a whole number by a power of 10.**
4. **Multiply a several-digit number by a several-digit number.**
5. **Use the properties of multiplication to perform calculations.**
6. **Apply multiplication to real-life situations.**

Basic Multiplication Facts

×	0	1	2	3	4	5	6	7	8	9	10	11	12
0	0	0	0	0	0	0	0	0	0	0	0	0	0
1	0	1	2	3	4	5	6	7	8	9	10	11	12
2	0	2	4	6	8	10	12	14	16	18	20	22	24
3	0	3	6	9	12	15	18	21	24	27	30	33	36
4	0	4	8	12	16	20	24	28	32	36	40	44	48
5	0	5	10	15	20	25	30	35	40	45	50	55	60
6	0	6	12	18	24	30	36	42	48	54	60	66	72
7	0	7	14	21	28	35	42	49	56	63	70	77	84
8	0	8	16	24	32	40	48	56	64	72	80	88	96
9	0	9	18	27	36	45	54	63	72	81	90	99	108
10	0	10	20	30	40	50	60	70	80	90	100	110	120
11	0	11	22	33	44	55	66	77	88	99	110	121	132
12	0	12	24	36	48	60	72	84	96	108	120	132	144

QUICK RECALL OF MULTIPLICATION FACTS It is helpful if you can multiply quickly. See if you can do Example 1 correctly in 15 seconds or less. Repeat again with Practice Problem 1. Strive to obtain all answers correctly in 15 seconds or less.

EXAMPLE 1 Multiply.

(a) 5×7 **(b)** 8×9 **(c)** 6×8

(d) 9×3 **(e)** 7×8

Solution

(a) $\begin{array}{r} 5 \\ \times\ 7 \\ \hline 35 \end{array}$ **(b)** $\begin{array}{r} 8 \\ \times\ 9 \\ \hline 72 \end{array}$ **(c)** $\begin{array}{r} 6 \\ \times\ 8 \\ \hline 48 \end{array}$

(d) $\begin{array}{r} 9 \\ \times\ 3 \\ \hline 27 \end{array}$ **(e)** $\begin{array}{r} 7 \\ \times\ 8 \\ \hline 56 \end{array}$

Practice Problem 1 Multiply.

(a) $\begin{array}{r} 8 \\ \times\ 8 \\ \hline \end{array}$ **(b)** $\begin{array}{r} 7 \\ \times\ 6 \\ \hline \end{array}$ **(c)** $\begin{array}{r} 5 \\ \times\ 8 \\ \hline \end{array}$

(d) $\begin{array}{r} 9 \\ \times\ 7 \\ \hline \end{array}$ **(e)** $\begin{array}{r} 9 \\ \times\ 9 \\ \hline \end{array}$

***NOTE TO STUDENT:** Fully worked-out solutions to all of the Practice Problems can be found at the end of the module.*

 Multiplying a Single-Digit Number by a Several-Digit Number

EXAMPLE 2 Multiply. 4312 × 2

Solution We first multiply the ones column, then the tens column, and so on, moving right to left.

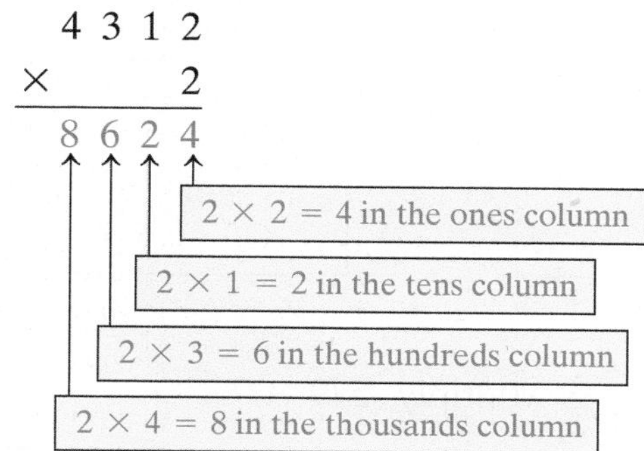

Practice Problem 2 Multiply. 3021 × 3

NOTE TO STUDENT: Fully worked-out solutions to all of the Practice Problems can be found at the end of the module.

Usually, we will have to carry one digit of the result of some of the multiplication into the next left-hand column.

EXAMPLE 3 Multiply. 36 × 7

Solution

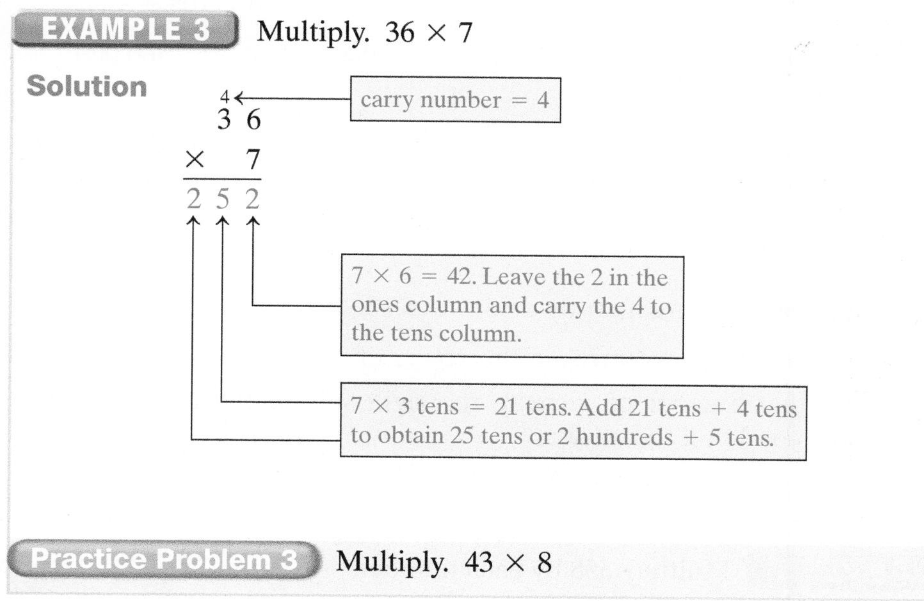

4
3 6
× 7
2 5 2
carry number = 4
7 × 6 = 42. Leave the 2 in the ones column and carry the 4 to the tens column.
7 × 3 tens = 21 tens. Add 21 tens + 4 tens to obtain 25 tens or 2 hundreds + 5 tens.

Practice Problem 3 Multiply. 43 × 8

EXAMPLE 4 Multiply. 359×9

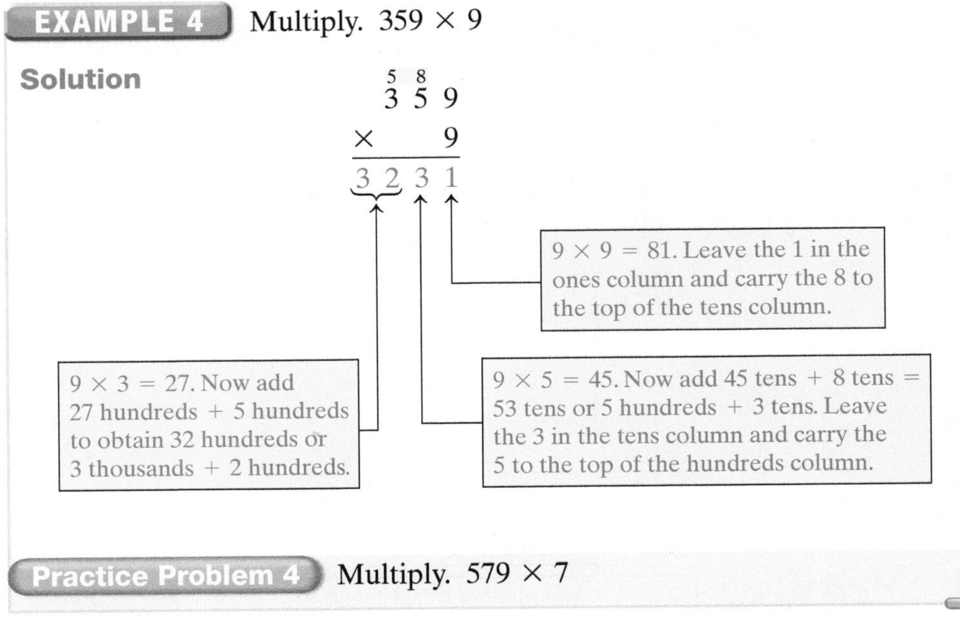

Solution
5 8
3 5 9
× 9
3 2 3 1
9 × 9 = 81. Leave the 1 in the ones column and carry the 8 to the top of the tens column.
9 × 3 = 27. Now add 27 hundreds + 5 hundreds to obtain 32 hundreds or 3 thousands + 2 hundreds.
9 × 5 = 45. Now add 45 tens + 8 tens = 53 tens or 5 hundreds + 3 tens. Leave the 3 in the tens column and carry the 5 to the top of the hundreds column.

Practice Problem 4 Multiply. 579×7

3 Multiplying a Whole Number by a Power of 10

Observe what happens when a number is multiplied by 10, 100, 1000, 10 000, and so on.

56 × 10 (one zero)	=	560
56 × 100 (two zeros)	=	5600
56 × 1000 (three zeros)	=	56 000
56 × 10 000 (four zeros)	=	560 000

A **power of 10** is a whole number that begins with 1 and ends in one or more zeros. The numbers 10, 100, 1000, 10 000, and so on are powers of 10.

> To multiply a whole number by a power of 10:
>
> **1.** Count the number of zeros in the power of 10.
>
> **2.** Attach that number of zeros to the right side of the other whole number to obtain the answer.

EXAMPLE 5 Multiply 358 by each number.

(a) 10 **(b)** 100 **(c)** 1000 **(d)** 100 000

Solution

(a) $358 \times 10 = 3580$ (one zero) **(b)** $358 \times 100 = 35\,800$ (two zeros)
(c) $358 \times 1000 = 358\,000$ (three zeros)
(d) $358 \times 100\,000 = 35\,800\,000$ (five zeros)

Practice Problem 5 Multiply 1267 by each number.

(a) 10 **(b)** 1000 **(c)** 10 000 **(d)** 1 000 000

NOTE TO STUDENT: Fully worked-out solutions to all of the Practice Problems can be found at the end of the module.

How can we handle zeros in multiplication involving a number that is not 10, 100, 1000, or any other power of 10? Consider 32 × 400. We can rewrite 400 as 4 × 100, which gives us 32 × 4 × 100. We can simply multiply 32 × 4 and then attach two zeros for the factor 100. We find that 32 × 4 = 128. Attaching two zeros gives us 12 800, or 32 × 400 = 12 800.

EXAMPLE 6 Multiply.

(a) 12 × 3000 **(b)** 25 × 600 **(c)** 430 × 260

Solution

(a) 12 × 3000 = 12 × 3 × 1000 = 36 × 1000 = 36 000

(b) 25 × 600 = 25 × 6 × 100 = 150 × 100 = 15 000

(c) 430 × 260 = 43 × 26 × 10 × 10 = 1118 × 100 = 111 800

Practice Problem 6 Multiply.

(a) 9 × 60 000 **(b)** 15 × 400 **(c)** 270 × 800

Multiplying a Several-Digit Number by a Several-Digit Number

EXAMPLE 7 Multiply. 234 × 21

Solution We can consider 21 as 2 tens (20) and 1 one (1). First we multiply 234 by 1.

We also multiply 234 × 20. This gives us two **partial products.**

$$\begin{array}{r} 234 \\ \times\ \ 1 \\ \hline 234 \end{array} \qquad \begin{array}{r} 234 \\ \times\ 20 \\ \hline 4680 \end{array}$$

Now we combine these two operations together by adding the two partial products to reach the final product, which is the solution.

$$\begin{array}{r} 2\ 3\ 4 \\ \times\ \ \ 2\ 1 \\ \hline 2\ 3\ 4 \\ 4\ 6\ 8\ 0 \\ \hline 4\ 9\ 1\ 4 \end{array} \begin{array}{l} \\ \\ \leftarrow \text{Multiply } 234 \times 1. \\ \leftarrow \text{Multiply } 234 \times 20. \\ \leftarrow \text{Add the two partial products.} \end{array}$$

Practice Problem 7 Multiply. 323 × 32

EXAMPLE 8 Multiply. 671×35

Solution

$$\begin{array}{r} 671 \\ \times \quad 35 \\ \hline 3355 \\ 20130 \\ \hline 23485 \end{array}$$

3355 ← First multiply 671×5.

20130 ← Now multiply 671×30.

23485 ← Now add the two partial products.

Note: We could omit zero on this line and leave the ones place blank.

Practice Problem 8 Multiply. 385×69

EXAMPLE 9 Multiply. 14×20

Solution

$$\begin{array}{r} 14 \\ \times 20 \\ \hline 0 \\ 280 \\ \hline 280 \end{array}$$

0 ← Multiply 14 by 0.

280 ← Multiply 14 by 2 tens.

Place 28 with the 8 in the tens column. To line up the digits for adding, we can insert a 0 in the ones column.

Now add the partial products. → 280

Notice that you will also get this result if you multiply $14 \times 2 = 28$ and then attach a zero to multiply it by 10: 280.

Practice Problem 9 Multiply. 34×20

EXAMPLE 10 Multiply. 120×40

Solution

$$\begin{array}{r} 120 \\ \times \quad 40 \\ \hline 0 \\ 4800 \\ \hline 4800 \end{array}$$

0 ← Multiply 120×0.

4800 ← Multiply 120 by 4 tens.

The answer is 480 tens. We place the 0 of the 480 in the tens column. To line up the digits for adding, we can insert a 0 in the ones column.

Now add the partial products. → 4800

Notice that this result is the same as $12 \times 4 = 48$ with two zeros attached: 4800.

Practice Problem 10 Multiply. 130×50

EXAMPLE 11 Multiply. 684×763

Solution

$$\begin{array}{r}
684 \\
\times\ 763 \\
\hline
2052 \\
4104 \\
4788 \\
\hline
521892
\end{array}$$

← Multiply 684×3.
← Multiply 684×60. Note that we omit the final zero.
← Multiply 684×700. Note that we omit the final two zeros.

Practice Problem 11 Multiply. 923×675

NOTE TO STUDENT: *Fully worked-out solutions to all of the Practice Problems can be found at the end of the module.*

5 Using the Properties of Multiplication to Perform Calculations

When we add three numbers, we use the associative property. Recall that the associative property allows us to group the three numbers in different ways. Thus to add $9 + 7 + 3$, we can group the numbers as $9 + (7 + 3)$ because it is easier to find the sum. $9 + (7 + 3) = 9 + 10 = 19$. We can demonstrate that multiplication is also associative.

Is this true? $2 \times (5 \times 3) = (2 \times 5) \times 3$

$$2 \times (15) = (10) \times 3$$
$$30 = 30$$

The final product is the same in both cases.

The way we group numbers to be multiplied does not change the product. This property is called the **associative property of multiplication.**

EXAMPLE 12 Multiply. $14 \times 2 \times 5$

Solution Since we can group any two numbers together, let's take advantage of the ease of multiplying by 10.

$$14 \times 2 \times 5 = 14 \times (2 \times 5) = 14 \times 10 = 140$$

Practice Problem 12 Multiply. $25 \times 4 \times 17$

For convenience, we list the properties of multiplication that we have discussed in this section.

1. Associative Property of Multiplication. When we multiply three numbers, the multiplication can be grouped in any way.

$$(7 \times 3) \times 2 = 7 \times (3 \times 2)$$
$$21 \times 2 = 7 \times 6$$
$$42 = 42$$

2. **Commutative Property of Multiplication.** Two numbers can be multiplied in either order with the same result.

$$9 \times 8 = 8 \times 9$$
$$72 = 72$$

3. **Identity Property of One.** When one is multiplied by a number, the result is that number.

$$7 \times 1 = 7$$
$$1 \times 15 = 15$$

4. **Multiplication Property of Zero.** The product of any number and zero yields zero as a result.

$$0 \times 14 = 0$$
$$2 \times 0 = 0$$

Sometimes you can use several properties in one problem to make the calculation easier.

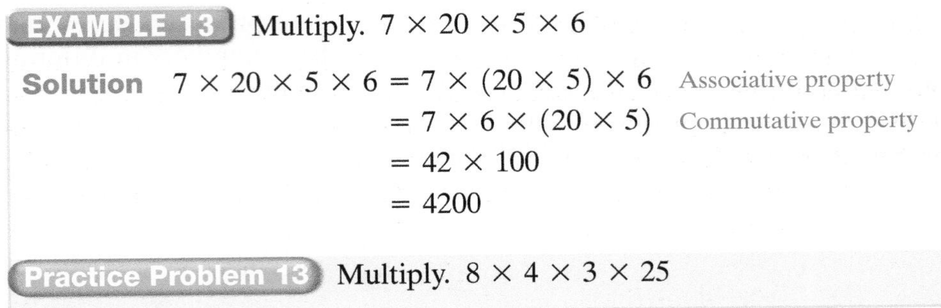

EXAMPLE 13 Multiply. $7 \times 20 \times 5 \times 6$

Solution $7 \times 20 \times 5 \times 6 = 7 \times (20 \times 5) \times 6$ Associative property

$= 7 \times 6 \times (20 \times 5)$ Commutative property

$= 42 \times 100$

$= 4200$

Practice Problem 13 Multiply. $8 \times 4 \times 3 \times 25$

Thus far we have discussed the properties of addition and the properties of multiplication. There is one more property that links both operations.

Before we discuss that property, we will illustrate several different ways of showing multiplication. The following are all the ways to show "3 times 4."

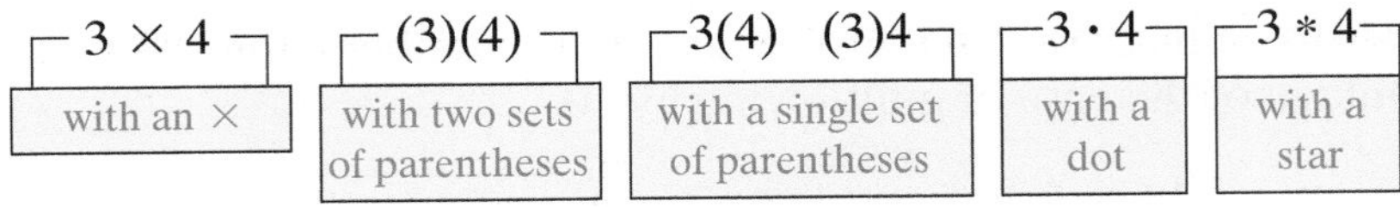

We will use parentheses to mean multiplication when we use the **distributive property.**

SIDELIGHT: The Distributive Property

Why does our method of multiplying several-digit numbers work? Why can we say that 234×21 is the same as $234 \times 1 + 234 \times 20$?

The *distributive property of multiplication over addition* allows us to distribute the multiplication and then add the results. To illustrate, 234×21 can be written as $234(20 + 1)$. By the distributive property

$$\begin{aligned} 234(20 + 1) &= (234 \times 20) + (234 \times 1) \\ &= 4680 + 234 \\ &= 4914 \end{aligned}$$

This is what we actually do when we multiply.

$$\begin{array}{r} 234 \\ \times \quad 21 \\ \hline 234 \\ 4680 \\ \hline 4914 \end{array}$$

DISTRIBUTIVE PROPERTY OF MULTIPLICATION OVER ADDITION

Multiplication can be distributed over addition without changing the result.

$$5 \times (10 + 2) = (5 \times 10) + (5 \times 2)$$

 Applying Multiplication to Real-Life Situations

To use multiplication in word problems, the number of items or the value of each item must be the same. Recall that multiplication is a quick way to do repeated addition where *each addend is the same.* In the beginning of the section we showed three rows of four croissants to illustrate 3×4. The number of croissants in each row was the same, 4. Look at another example. If we had six nickels, we could use multiplication to find the total value of the coins because the value of each nickel is the same, 5¢. Since $6 \times 5 = 30$, six nickels are worth 30¢.

In the following example the word *average* is used. The word *average* has several different meanings. In this example, we are told that the *average annual salary* of an employee at Software Associates is \$42 132. This means that we can calculate the total payroll as if each employee made \$42 132 even though we know that the president probably makes more than any other employee.

EXAMPLE 14 The average annual salary of an employee at Software Associates is \$42 132. There are 38 employees. What is the annual payroll?

Solution

$$\begin{array}{r} \$42\,132 \\ \times \qquad 38 \\ \hline 337\,056 \\ 1263\,96 \\ \hline 1\,601\,016 \end{array}$$

The total annual payroll is \$1 601 016.

Practice Problem 14 The average cost of a new car sold last year at Westover Chevrolet was \$17 348. The dealership sold 378 cars. What were the total sales of cars at the dealership last year?

NOTE TO STUDENT: *Fully worked-out solutions to all of the Practice Problems can be found at the end of the module.*

Another useful application of multiplication is area. The following example involves the area of a rectangle.

▲ **EXAMPLE 15** What is the area of a rectangular hallway that measures 1 metre wide and 3 metres long?

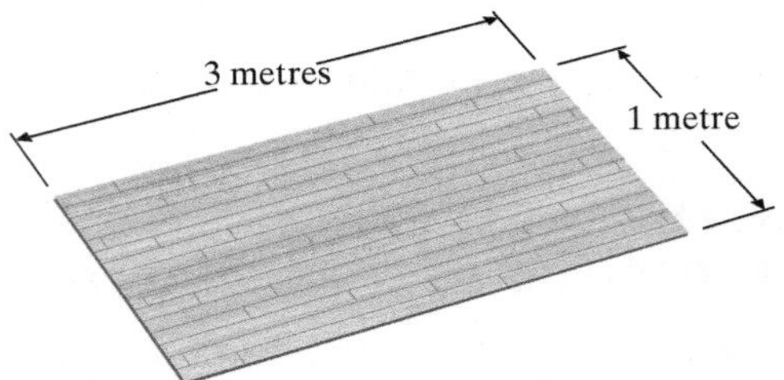

Solution The **area** of a rectangle is the product of the length times the width. Thus for this hallway

$$\text{Area} = 3 \text{ metres} \times 1 \text{ metre} = 3 \text{ square metres.}$$

The area of the hallway is 3 square metres.

Note: All measurements for area are given in square units such as square centimetres, square metres, and so on.

▲ **Practice Problem 15** What is the area of a rectangular rug that measures 5 yards by 7 yards?

Developing Your Study Skills

Why Is Homework Necessary?

Mathematics involves mastering a set of skills that you learn by practising, not by watching someone else do it. Your instructor may make solving a mathematics problem look very easy, but for you to learn the necessary skills, you must practise them over and over again, just as your instructor once had to. There is no other way. Learning mathematics is like learning to play a musical instrument, to type, or to play a sport. No matter how much you watch someone else do it, no matter how many books you read on "how to" do it, no matter how easy it seems to be, the key to success is practice on a regular basis.

Homework provides this practice. The amount of practice needed varies for each individual, but usually students need to do most or all of the exercises provided at the end of each section in the text. The more exercises you do, the better you get. Some exercises in a set are more difficult than others, and some stress different concepts. Only by working all the exercises will you cover the full range of skills.

Section 4 Exercises

Verbal and Writing Skills

1. Explain in your own words.

(a) the commutative property of multiplication

(b) the associative property of multiplication

2. How does the distributive property of multiplication over addition help us to multiply 4×13?

Complete the multiplication facts for each table. Strive for total accuracy, but work quickly. (Allow a maximum of six minutes for each table.)

3.

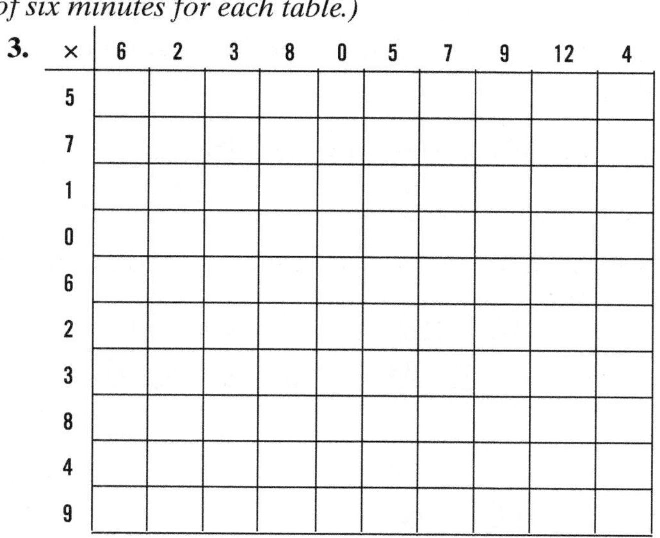

×	6	2	3	8	0	5	7	9	12	4
5										
7										
1										
0										
6										
2										
3										
8										
4										
9										

4.

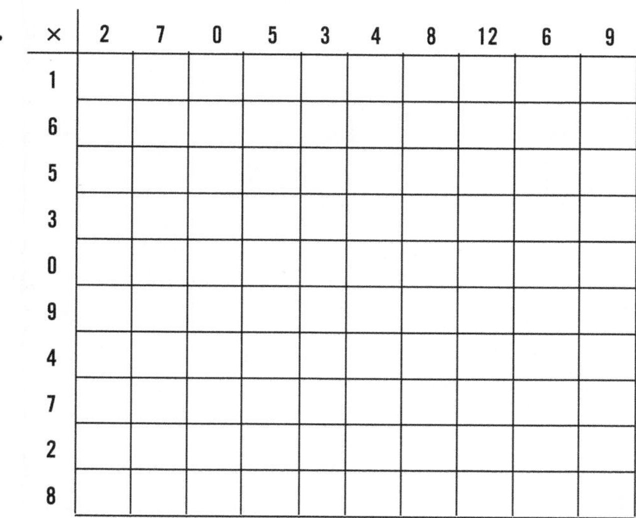

×	2	7	0	5	3	4	8	12	6	9
1										
6										
5										
3										
0										
9										
4										
7										
2										
8										

Multiply.

5. 32 × 3 **6.** 21 × 4 **7.** 14 × 5 **8.** 15 × 6 **9.** 87 × 6

10. 95 × 7 **11.** 231 × 3 **12.** 313 × 3 **13.** 276 × 7 **14.** 538 × 8

15. 6102 × 3 **16.** 5203 × 2 **17.** 12 203 × 3 **18.** 31 206 × 3 **19.** 5218 × 6

20. 3215 × 6 **21.** 12 526 × 8 **22.** 48 761 × 7 **23.** 344 601 × 9 **24.** 257 021 × 9

Multiply by powers of 10.

25. 156 × 10 **26.** 278 × 10 **27.** 27 158 × 100 **28.** 89 361 × 100

29. 482 × 1000 **30.** 579 × 1000 **31.** 37 256 × 10 000 **32.** 614 260 × 10 000

Multiply by multiples of 10.

33. $\begin{array}{r} 423 \\ \times\ 20 \\ \hline \end{array}$

34. $\begin{array}{r} 332 \\ \times\ 30 \\ \hline \end{array}$

35. $\begin{array}{r} 2120 \\ \times\ 30 \\ \hline \end{array}$

36. $\begin{array}{r} 4230 \\ \times\ 20 \\ \hline \end{array}$

37. $\begin{array}{r} 14\,000 \\ \times\ 4000 \\ \hline \end{array}$

38. $\begin{array}{r} 62\,000 \\ \times\ 3000 \\ \hline \end{array}$

Multiply.

39. $\begin{array}{r} 514 \\ \times\ 12 \\ \hline \end{array}$

40. $\begin{array}{r} 432 \\ \times\ 13 \\ \hline \end{array}$

41. $\begin{array}{r} 146 \\ \times\ 54 \\ \hline \end{array}$

42. $\begin{array}{r} 163 \\ \times\ 35 \\ \hline \end{array}$

43. $\begin{array}{r} 89 \\ \times 64 \\ \hline \end{array}$

44. $\begin{array}{r} 68 \\ \times 49 \\ \hline \end{array}$

45. $\begin{array}{r} 607 \\ \times\ 25 \\ \hline \end{array}$

46. $\begin{array}{r} 780 \\ \times\ 24 \\ \hline \end{array}$

47. $\begin{array}{r} 544 \\ \times\ 38 \\ \hline \end{array}$

48. $\begin{array}{r} 652 \\ \times\ 92 \\ \hline \end{array}$

49. $\begin{array}{r} 912 \\ \times\ 76 \\ \hline \end{array}$

50. $\begin{array}{r} 498 \\ \times\ 39 \\ \hline \end{array}$

51. $\begin{array}{r} 5123 \\ \times\ 29 \\ \hline \end{array}$

52. $\begin{array}{r} 1268 \\ \times\ 38 \\ \hline \end{array}$

53. $\begin{array}{r} 9053 \\ \times\ 91 \\ \hline \end{array}$

54. $\begin{array}{r} 3078 \\ \times\ 72 \\ \hline \end{array}$

55. $\begin{array}{r} 4326 \\ \times\ 435 \\ \hline \end{array}$

56. $\begin{array}{r} 3725 \\ \times\ 546 \\ \hline \end{array}$

57. $\begin{array}{r} 678 \\ \times 132 \\ \hline \end{array}$

58. $\begin{array}{r} 392 \\ \times 187 \\ \hline \end{array}$

Mixed Practice

59. $\begin{array}{r} 2076 \\ \times\ 105 \\ \hline \end{array}$

60. $\begin{array}{r} 5092 \\ \times\ 302 \\ \hline \end{array}$

61. $\begin{array}{r} 1324 \\ \times\ 2004 \\ \hline \end{array}$

62. $\begin{array}{r} 2074 \\ \times 1003 \\ \hline \end{array}$

63. $\begin{array}{r} 12\,000 \\ \times\ 60 \\ \hline \end{array}$

64. $\begin{array}{r} 15\,200 \\ \times\ 30 \\ \hline \end{array}$

65. $\begin{array}{r} 250 \\ \times\ 40 \\ \hline \end{array}$

66. $\begin{array}{r} 302 \\ \times\ 30 \\ \hline \end{array}$

67. $\begin{array}{r} 302 \\ \times 300 \\ \hline \end{array}$

68. $\begin{array}{r} 3000 \\ \times\ 302 \\ \hline \end{array}$

69. $7 \cdot 2 \cdot 5$

70. $8 \cdot 3 \cdot 2$

71. $11 \cdot 7 \cdot 4$

72. $15 \cdot 4 \cdot 4$

73. 412×33

74. 526×21

75. $5 \cdot 8 \cdot 4 \cdot 10$

76. $5 \cdot 10 \cdot 18 \cdot 2$

77. What is x if $x = 8 \cdot 7 \cdot 6 \cdot 0$?

78. What is x if $x = 3 \cdot 12 \cdot 0 \cdot 5$?

Applications

▲ **79.** ***Geometry*** Find the area of a patio that is 16 feet wide and 24 feet long.

▲ **80.** ***Geometry*** Find the area of a calculator screen that is 15 millimetres wide and 60 millimetres long.

▲ **81.** ***Consumer Mathematics*** Don Williams and his wife want to put down new carpet in the living room and the hallway of their house. The living room measures 4 metres by 5 metres. The hallway measures 3 metres by 1 metre. If the living room and the hallway are rectangular in shape, how many square metres of new carpet do Don and his wife need?

▲ **82.** ***Wildlife Management*** Abdul in Resolute, Nunavut, wants to put a field under helicopter surveillance because of a roving pack of wolves that are destroying other wildlife in the area. The field consists of two rectangular regions. The first one is 4 kilometres by 5 kilometres. The second one is 12 kilometres by 8 kilometres. How many square kilometres does he want to place under surveillance?

83. ***Business Decisions*** The student commons food supply needs to purchase espresso coffee. Find the cost of purchasing 240 kilograms of espresso coffee beans at $15 per kilogram.

84. ***Business Decisions*** The music department of Algonquin College wishes to purchase 345 sets of headphones at the music supply store at a cost of $8 each. What will be the total amount of the purchase?

85. ***Personal Finance*** Helen pays $266 per month for her car payment on her new Honda Civic. What is her automobile payment cost for a one-year period?

86. ***Personal Finance*** A company rents a compact car for a salesman at $276 per month for eight months. What is the cost for the car rental during this time?

87. ***Environmental Studies*** Marcos has a Toyota Corolla that gets 14 kilometres per litre during highway driving. Approximately how far can he travel if he has 18 litres of gas in the tank?

88. ***Environmental Studies*** Cheryl has a subcompact car that gets 18 kilometres per litre during highway driving. Approximately how far can she travel if she has 12 litres of gas in the tank?

89. ***Personal Finance*** Sylvia worked as a camp counsellor for twelve weeks during the summer. She earned $420 per week. What is the total amount Sylvia earned during the summer?

90. ***Personal Finance*** Each time Jorge receives a paycheque, $125 is put into his RRSP account. If he gets paid twice a month, how much does Jorge contribute to his RRSP in one year?

91. ***International Relations*** The country of Haiti has an average per capita (per person) income of $1070. If the approximate population of Haiti is 6 890 000, what is the approximate total yearly income of the entire country?

92. ***International Relations*** The country of the Netherlands (Holland) has an approximate population of 15 800 000. The average per capita (per person) income is $22 000. What is the approximate total yearly income of the entire country?

To Think About *Use the following information to answer exercises 93–96. There are 98 puppies in a room, with an assortment of black and white ears and paws. 18 puppies have totally black ears and 2 white paws; 26 puppies have 1 black ear and 4 white paws; and 54 puppies have no black ears and 1 white paw.*

93. How many black paws are in the room?

94. How many white paws are in the room?

95. How many black ears are in the room?

96. How many white ears are in the room?

In exercises 97–100, find the value of x in each equation.

97. $5(x) = 40$

98. $7(x) = 56$

99. $72 = 8(x)$

100. $63 = 9(x)$

101. Would the distributive property of multiplication be true for Roman numerals such as (XII) × (IV)? Why or why not?

102. We saw that multiplication is distributive over addition. Is it distributive over subtraction? Why or why not? Give examples.

Quick Quiz 4 Multiply.

1. $\begin{array}{r} 34\,986 \\ \times \quad 5 \\ \hline \end{array}$

2. $\begin{array}{r} 79 \\ \times 64 \\ \hline \end{array}$

3. $\begin{array}{r} 698 \\ \times 297 \\ \hline \end{array}$

4. Concept Check Explain what you do with the zeros when you multiply 3457 × 2008.

SECTION 5 DIVIDING WHOLE NUMBERS

Student Learning Objectives

After studying this section, you will be able to:

1. Master basic division facts.
2. Perform division by a one-digit number.
3. Perform division by a two- or three-digit number.
4. Apply division to real-life situations.

Mastering Basic Division Facts

Suppose that we have eight quarters and want to divide them into two equal piles. We would discover that each pile contains four quarters.

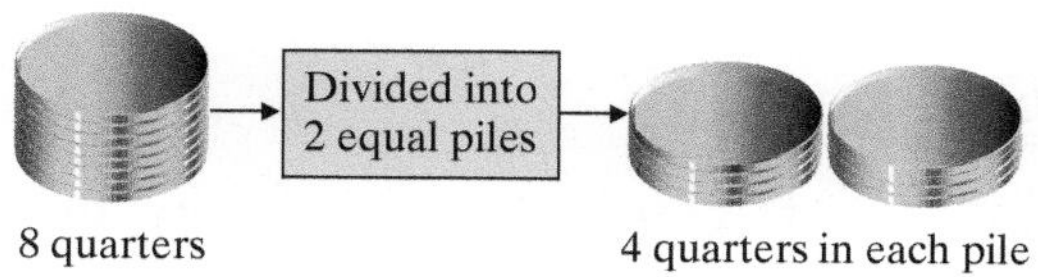

In mathematics we would express this thought by saying that

$$8 \div 2 = 4.$$

We know that this answer is right because two piles of four quarters is the same dollar amount as eight quarters. In other words, we know that $8 \div 2 = 4$ because $2 \times 4 = 8$. These two mathematical sentences are called **related sentences.** The division sentence $8 \div 2 = 4$ is related to the multiplication sentence $2 \times 4 = 8$.

In fact, in mathematics we usually define **division** in terms of multiplication. The answer to the division problem $12 \div 3$ is that number which when multiplied by 3 yields 12. Thus

$$12 \div 3 = 4 \quad \text{because } 3 \times 4 = 12.$$

Suppose that a surplus of \$30 in the French Club budget at the end of the year is to be equally divided among the five club members. We would want to divide the \$30 into five equal parts. We would write $30 \div 5 = 6$ because $5 \times 6 = 30$. Thus each of the five people would get \$6 in this situation.

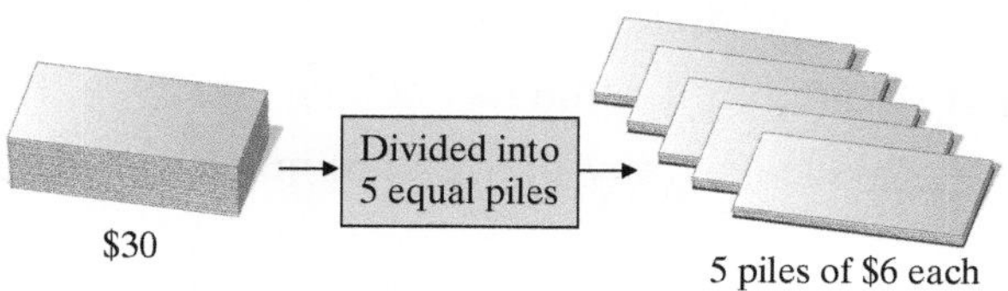

As a mathematical sentence, $30 \div 5 = 6$.
The division problem $30 \div 5 = 6$ could also be written $\frac{30}{5} = 6$ or $5\overline{)30}$ with quotient 6.

When referring to division, we sometimes use the words **divisor, dividend,** and **quotient** to identify the three parts.

$$\begin{array}{r} \text{quotient} \\ \text{divisor}\overline{)\text{dividend}} \end{array}$$

With $30 \div 5 = 6$, 30 is the dividend, 5 is the divisor, and 6 is the quotient.

$$\begin{array}{rl} 6 & \leftarrow \text{quotient} \\ \text{divisor} \rightarrow 5\overline{)30} & \leftarrow \text{dividend} \end{array}$$

So the quotient is the answer to a division problem. It is important that you be able to do short problems involving basic division facts quickly.

EXAMPLE 1 Divide.

(a) $12 \div 4$ **(b)** $81 \div 9$ **(c)** $56 \div 8$ **(d)** $54 \div 6$

Solution

(a) $4\overline{)12}$ = 3 **(b)** $9\overline{)81}$ = 9 **(c)** $8\overline{)56}$ = 7 **(d)** $6\overline{)54}$ = 9

NOTE TO STUDENT: Fully worked-out solutions to all of the Practice Problems can be found at the end of the module.

Practice Problem 1 Divide.

(a) $36 \div 4$ **(b)** $25 \div 5$ **(c)** $72 \div 9$ **(d)** $30 \div 6$

Zero can be divided by any nonzero number, but division by zero is not possible. Why is this?

Suppose that we could divide by zero. Then $7 \div 0 =$ some number. Let us represent "some number" by the letter a.

$$\text{If } 7 \div 0 = a, \text{ then } 7 = 0 \times a,$$

because every division problem has a related multiplication problem. But zero times any number is zero, $0 \times a = 0$. Thus

$$7 = 0 \times a = 0.$$

That is, $7 = 0$, which we know is not true. Therefore, our assumption that $7 \div 0 = a$ is wrong. Thus we conclude that we cannot divide by zero. Mathematicians state this by saying, "Division by zero is **undefined.**"

It is helpful to remember the following basic concepts:

DIVISION PROBLEMS INVOLVING THE NUMBER 1 AND THE NUMBER 0

1. Any nonzero number divided by itself is 1 ($7 \div 7 = 1$).
2. Any number divided by 1 remains unchanged ($29 \div 1 = 29$).
3. Zero may be divided by any nonzero number; the result is always zero ($0 \div 4 = 0$).
4. Zero can never be the divisor in a division problem ($3 \div 0$ is undefined).

EXAMPLE 2 Divide, if possible. If it is not possible, state why.

(a) $8 \div 8$ **(b)** $9 \div 1$ **(c)** $0 \div 6$ **(d)** $20 \div 0$

Solution

(a) $\frac{8}{8} = 1$ Any number divided by itself is 1.

(b) $\frac{9}{1} = 9$ Any number divided by 1 remains unchanged.

(c) $\frac{0}{6} = 0$ Zero divided by any nonzero number is zero.

(d) $\frac{20}{0}$ cannot be done Division by zero is undefined.

Practice Problem 2 Divide, if possible.

(a) $7 \div 1$ **(b)** $\frac{9}{9}$ **(c)** $\frac{0}{5}$ **(d)** $12 \div 0$

2 Performing Division by a One-Digit Number

Our accuracy with division is improved if we have a checking procedure. For each division fact, there is a related multiplication fact.

$$\text{If } 20 \div 4 = 5, \quad \text{then } 20 = 4 \times 5.$$
$$\text{If } 36 \div 9 = 4, \quad \text{then } 36 = 9 \times 4.$$

We will often use multiplication to check our answers.

When two numbers do not divide exactly, a number called the **remainder** is left over. For example, 13 cannot be divided exactly by 2. The number 1 is left over. We call this 1 the *remainder.*

$$\begin{array}{r} 6 \\ 2\overline{)13} \\ \underline{12} \\ 1 \end{array} \leftarrow \text{remainder}$$

Thus $13 \div 2 = 6$ with a remainder of 1. We can abbreviate this answer as

$$6 \text{ R } 1.$$

To check this division, we multiply $2 \times 6 = 12$ and add the remainder: $12 + 1 = 13$. That is, $(2 \times 6) + 1 = 13$. The result will be the dividend if the division was done correctly. The following box shows you how to check a division that has a remainder.

$$(\text{divisor} \times \text{quotient}) + \text{remainder} = \text{dividend}$$

EXAMPLE 3 Divide. $33 \div 4$. Check your answer.

Solution

$$\begin{array}{r} 8 \\ 4\overline{)33} \\ \underline{32} \\ 1 \end{array}$$

8 → How many times can 4 be divided into 33? 8.

32 ← What is 8×4? 32.

1 ← 32 subtracted from 33 is 1.

The answer is 8 with a remainder of 1. We abbreviate this as 8 R 1.

CHECK.

$$\begin{array}{r} 8 \\ \underline{\times\ 4} \\ 32 \\ \underline{+\ 1} \\ 33 \end{array}$$

32 Multiply. $8 \times 4 = 32$.

+ 1 Add the remainder. $32 + 1 = 33$.

33 Because the dividend is 33, the answer is correct.

Practice Problem 3 Divide. $45 \div 6$. Check your answer.

EXAMPLE 4 Divide. 158 ÷ 5. Check your answer.

Solution

```
   31
5)158        5 divided into 15?  3.
  15   ←  What is 3 × 5?  15.
  08 ←  15 subtract 15?  0.  Bring down 8.
   5 ←  5 divided into 8?  1.  What is 1 × 5?  5.
   3 ←  8 subtract 5?  3.
```

The answer is 31 R 3.

CHECK.

```
   31
 ×  5
  155    Multiply. 31 × 5 = 155.
 +  3    Add the remainder 3.
  158    Because the dividend is 158, the answer is correct.
```

***NOTE TO STUDENT:** Fully worked-out solutions to all of the Practice Problems can be found at the end of the module.*

Practice Problem 4 Divide. 129 ÷ 6. Check your answer.

EXAMPLE 5 Divide. 3672 ÷ 7

Solution

```
    524
 7)3672     How many times can 7 be divided into 36?  5.
   35    ← What is 5 × 7?  35.
    17   ← 36 subtract 35?  1.  Bring down 7.
    14   ← 7 divided into 17?  2.  What is 2 × 7?  14.
     32 ← 17 subtract 14?  3.  Bring down 2.
     28 ← 7 divided into 32?  4.  What is 4 × 7?  28.
      4 ← 32 subtract 28?  4.
```

The answer is 524 R 4.

Practice Problem 5 Divide. 4237 ÷ 8

3 Performing Division by a Two- or Three-Digit Number

When the divisor has more than one digit, an estimation technique may help. Figure how many times the first digit of the divisor goes into the first two digits of the dividend. Try this answer as the first number in the quotient.

EXAMPLE 6 Divide. 283 ÷ 41

Solution

First guess:

```
     7
41)283
   287   too large
```

How many times can the first digit of the divisor (4) be divided into the first two digits of the dividend (28)? 7. We try the answer 7 as the first number of the quotient. We multiply 7 × 41 = 287. We see that 287 is larger than 283.

Second guess:

```
      6
41)283      Because 7 is slightly too large, we try 6.
   246 ←    6 × 41?   246.
    37 ←    283 subtract 246?   37.
```

The answer is 6 R 37. (Note that the remainder must always be less than the divisor.)

Practice Problem 6 Divide. 243 ÷ 32

EXAMPLE 7 Divide. 33 897 ÷ 56

Solution

First guess:

```
       60
56)33 897    How many times can 33 be divided by 5?   6.
   33 6   ←  What is 6 × 56?   336.
      29     338 subtract 336?   2.   Bring down 9.
             56 cannot be divided into 29. Write 0 in quotient.
```

Second set of steps:

```
      605
56)33 897
   33 6      Bring down 7.
      297    How many times can 5 be divided into 29?   5.
      280 ←  What is 5 × 56?   280.   Subtract 297 − 280.
       17    Remainder is 17.
```

The answer is 605 R 17.

Practice Problem 7 Divide. 42 183 ÷ 33

EXAMPLE 8 Divide. 5629 ÷ 134

Solution

```
       42
134)5629    How many times does 134 divide into 562?
    536     We guess by saying that 1 divides into 5 five times, but
            this is too large. (5 × 134 = 670!)
     269    So we try 4. What is 4 × 134?   536.
     268    Subtract 562 − 536. We obtain 26. Bring down 9.
       1    How many times does 134 divide into 269?
            We guess by saying that 1 divided into 2 goes two times.
            What is 2 × 134?   268. Subtract 269 − 268.
            The remainder is 1.
```

The answer is 42 R 1.

Practice Problem 8 Divide. 3227 ÷ 128

 Applying Division to Real-Life Situations

When you solve a word problem that requires division, you will be given the total number and asked to calculate the number of items in each group or to calculate the number of groups. In the beginning of this section we showed eight quarters (the total number) and we divided them into two equal piles (the number of groups). Division was used to find how many quarters were in each pile (the number in each group). That is, $8 \div 2 = 4$. There were four quarters in each pile.

Let's look at another example. Suppose that $30 is to be divided equally among the members of a group. If each person receives $6, how many people are in the group? We use division, $30 \div 6 = 5$, to find that there are five people in the group.

You will find many real-world examples where you know the total cost of several identical items, and you need to find the cost per item. You will encounter this situation in the following example.

EXAMPLE 9 City Service Realty just purchased nine identical computers for the real estate agents in the office. The total cost for the nine computers was $25 848. What was the cost of one computer? Check your answer.

Solution To find the cost of one computer, we need to divide the total cost by 9. Thus we will calculate $25\,848 \div 9$.

$$\begin{array}{r} 2\,872 \\ 9\overline{)25\,848} \\ \underline{18} \\ 78 \\ \underline{72} \\ 64 \\ \underline{63} \\ 18 \\ \underline{18} \\ 0 \end{array}$$

Therefore, the cost of one computer is $2872. In order to check our work we will need to see if nine computers each costing $2872 will in fact result in a total of $25 848. We use multiplication to check division.

$$\begin{array}{r} 2872 \\ \times \quad 9 \\ \hline 25848 \end{array} \checkmark$$

We did obtain 25 848. Our answer is correct.

Practice Problem 9 The Vancouver police department purchased seven identical used police cars at a total cost of $117 964. Find the cost of one used car. Check your answer.

NOTE TO STUDENT: Fully worked-out solutions to all of the Practice Problems can be found at the end of the module.

In the following example you will see the word *average* used as it applies to division. The problem states that a car travelled 1144 kilometres in 11 hours. The problem asks you to find the average speed in kilometres per hour. This means that we will treat the problem as if the speed of the car were the same during each hour of the trip. We will use division to solve.

EXAMPLE 10 A car travelled from Georgina, Ontario, to Rimouski, Québec, a distance of 1144 kilometres, in 11 hours. What was the average speed in kilometres per hour?

Solution When doing distance problems, it is helpful to remember that distance ÷ time = rate. We need to divide 1144 kilometres by 11 hours to obtain the rate or speed in kilometres per hour.

$$\begin{array}{r} 104 \\ 11\overline{)1144} \\ \underline{11} \\ 44 \\ \underline{44} \\ 0 \end{array}$$

The car travelled an average of 104 kilometres per hour.

Practice Problem 10 An airplane travelled 5138 kilometres in 14 hours. What was the average speed in kilometres per hour?

Developing Your Study Skills

Taking Notes in Class

An important part of mathematics studying is taking notes. In order to take meaningful notes, you must be an active listener. Keep your mind on what the instructor is saying, and be ready with questions whenever you do not understand something.

If you have previewed the lesson material, you will be prepared to take good notes. The important concepts will seem somewhat familiar. You will have a better idea of what needs to be written down. If you frantically try to write all that the instructor says or copy all the examples done in class, you may find your notes nearly worthless when you look at them at home. You may find that you are unable to make sense of what you have written.

Write down *important* ideas and examples as the instructor lectures, making sure that you are listening and following the logic. Include any helpful hints or suggestions that your instructor gives you or refers to in your text. You will be amazed at how easily you will forget these if you do not write them down. Try to review your notes the *same day* sometime after class. You will find the material in your notes easier to understand if you have attended class within the last few hours.

Successful note taking requires active listening and processing. Stay alert in class. You will realize the advantages of taking your own notes over copying those of someone else.

Section 5 Exercises

Verbal and Writing Skills

1. Explain in your own words what happens when you

(a) divide a nonzero number by itself.

(b) divide a number by 1.

(c) divide zero by a nonzero number.

(d) divide a nonzero number by 0.

Divide. See if you can work exercises 2–30 in three minutes or less.

2. $5\overline{)35}$ **3.** $6\overline{)42}$ **4.** $4\overline{)32}$ **5.** $8\overline{)24}$ **6.** $9\overline{)27}$ **7.** $5\overline{)25}$

8. $7\overline{)49}$ **9.** $9\overline{)36}$ **10.** $4\overline{)16}$ **11.** $7\overline{)21}$ **12.** $9\overline{)81}$ **13.** $5\overline{)30}$

14. $6\overline{)54}$ **15.** $7\overline{)63}$ **16.** $4\overline{)28}$ **17.** $8\overline{)72}$ **18.** $8\overline{)64}$ **19.** $6\overline{)36}$

20. $9\overline{)72}$ **21.** $1\overline{)9}$ **22.** $1\overline{)8}$ **23.** $10\overline{)0}$ **24.** $7\overline{)0}$ **25.** $9 \div 0$

26. $12 \div 0$ **27.** $\frac{0}{8}$ **28.** $\frac{0}{7}$ **29.** $6 \div 6$ **30.** $5 \div 5$

Divide. In exercises 31–42, check your answer.

31. $29 \div 6$ **32.** $42 \div 8$ **33.** $76 \div 8$ **34.** $75 \div 9$ **35.** $128 \div 5$

36. $6\overline{)103}$ **37.** $9\overline{)196}$ **38.** $8\overline{)427}$ **39.** $9\overline{)288}$ **40.** $7\overline{)294}$

41. $5\overline{)185}$ **42.** $8\overline{)224}$ **43.** $4\overline{)1289}$ **44.** $3\overline{)758}$ **45.** $6\overline{)763}$

46. $7\overline{)403}$ **47.** $8\overline{)4504}$ **48.** $9\overline{)4095}$ **49.** $3\overline{)3367}$ **50.** $6\overline{)8086}$

51. $8\overline{)16\,450}$ **52.** $6\overline{)18\,127}$ **53.** $5\overline{)12\,813}$ **54.** $8\overline{)32\,223}$ **55.** $185 \div 6$

56. $202 \div 5$ **57.** $267 \div 52$ **58.** $324 \div 36$ **59.** $427 \div 61$

Mixed Practice

60. $72\overline{)432}$ **61.** $12\overline{)5024}$ **62.** $13\overline{)6810}$ **63.** $30\overline{)1452}$ **64.** $40\overline{)1125}$

65. $7\overline{)5915}$ **66.** $8\overline{)6144}$ **67.** $36\overline{)7568}$ **68.** $32\overline{)3527}$ **69.** $182\overline{)2550}$

70. $19\overline{)1982}$ **71.** $174\overline{)700}$ **72.** $128\overline{)896}$ **73.** $224\overline{)28\,000}$ **74.** $235\overline{)31\,490}$

Solve.

75. $518 \div 14 = x$. What is the value of x?

76. $1572 \div 131 = x$. What is the value of x?

Applications

77. ***Sports*** A *run* in skiing is going from the top of the ski lift to the bottom. If over seven days, 431 851 runs were made, what was the average number of ski runs per day?

78. ***Farming*** Western Saddle Stable uses 21 900 pounds of feed per year to feed its 30 horses. How much does each horse eat per year?

79. ***Sports*** Coach Deno Johnson purchased 9 pairs of cross-country skis for his team. He spent a total of \$2592. How much did each pair of skis cost?

80. ***Business Finances*** During the 2006–07 winter season, Manitoba's Ministry of Transportation spent \$9 120 000 on 76 new snowplows. How much did each snowplow cost?

81. ***Business Finances*** A horse and carriage company in New York City bought seven new carriages at exactly the same price each. The total bill was \$147 371. How much did each carriage cost?

82. ***Real Estate*** A group of eight friends invested the same amount each in a beach property that sold for \$369 432. How much did each friend pay?

83. ***Business Finances*** Appleton Community College spent \$10 290 to equip the math centre with 42 new flat-panel monitors. How much did each monitor cost?

84. ***Business Finances*** Fanshawe College spent \$13 020 on new bookcases for their faculty offices. If 70 faculty members received new bookcases, how much did each bookcase cost?

85. ***Business Planning*** The 2nd Avenue Delicatessen is making bagel sandwiches for an Ottawa Marathon party. The sandwich maker has 360 bagel halves, 340 slices of turkey, and 330 slices of Swiss cheese. If he needs to make sandwiches each consisting of two bagel halves, two slices of turkey, and two slices of Swiss cheese, what is the greatest number of sandwiches he can make?

▲ **86.** ***Geometry*** Ace Landscaping is mowing a rectangular lawn that has an area of 2652 square metres. The company keeps a record of all lawn mowed in terms of length, width, square metres, and number of minutes it takes to mow the lawn. The width of the lawn is 34 metres. However, the page that lists the length of the lawn is soiled and the number cannot be read. Determine the length of the lawn.

87. ***Business Management*** Dick Wightman is managing a company that is manufacturing and shipping modular homes in Canada. He has a truck that has made the trip from Toronto, Ontario, to Halifax, Nova Scotia, 12 times and has made the return run from Halifax to Toronto 12 times. The distance from Toronto to Halifax is 1742 kilometres.

(a) How many kilometres has the truck travelled on these 12 trips from Toronto to Halifax and back?

(b) If Dick wants to limit the truck to a total of 50 000 kilometres driven this year, how many more kilometres can the truck be driven?

88. ***Space Travel*** The space shuttle has recently gone through a number of repairs and improvements. NASA approved the use of a shuttle control panel that has an area of 3526 square centimetres. The control panel is rectangular. The width of the panel is 43 centimetres. What is the length of the panel?

To Think About

89. Division is not commutative. For example, $12 \div 4 \neq 4 \div 12$. If $a \div b = b \div a$, what must be true of the numbers a and b besides the fact that $b \neq 0$ and $a \neq 0$?

90. You can think of division as repeated subtraction. Show how $874 \div 138$ is related to repeated subtraction.

Quick Quiz 5

Divide. If there is a remainder, be sure to state it as part of your answer.

1. $9\overline{)4203}$

2. $8\overline{)26\,299}$

3. $76\overline{)24\,928}$

4. **Concept Check** When performing the division problem $2956 \div 43$, you need to decide how many times 43 goes into 295. Explain how you would decide this.

How Am I Doing? Sections 1–5

1. ____________
2. ____________
3. ____________
4. ____________
5. ____________
6. ____________
7. ____________
8. ____________
9. ____________
10. ____________
11. ____________
12. ____________
13. ____________
14. ____________
15. ____________
16. ____________
17. ____________
18. ____________
19. ____________
20. ____________

How are you doing with your homework assignments in Sections 1 to 5? Do you feel you have mastered the material so far? Do you understand the concepts you have covered? Before you go further, take some time to do each of the following problems.

1

1. Write in words. 78 310 436

2. Write in expanded notation. 38 247

3. Write in standard notation. five million, sixty-four thousand, one hundred twenty-two

Use the following table to answer questions 4 and 5.

Ontario Grade 12 High School Students (in thousands)

2000	228
2002	236
2004	197
2006	202
2008	217

Source: http://www.edu.gov.on.ca/

4. How many high school students were there in 2000?

5. How many high school students were there in 2008?

2 *Add.*

6. $\begin{array}{r} 13 \\ 31 \\ 88 \\ 43 \\ +69 \\ \hline \end{array}$

7. $\begin{array}{r} 28\,318 \\ 5\,039 \\ +17\,213 \\ \hline \end{array}$

8. $\begin{array}{r} 833\,576 \\ +517\,885 \\ \hline \end{array}$

3 *Subtract.*

9. $\begin{array}{r} 5728 \\ -1735 \\ \hline \end{array}$

10. $\begin{array}{r} 100\,450 \\ -\ \ 24\,139 \\ \hline \end{array}$

11. $\begin{array}{r} 45\,861\,413 \\ -43\,879\,761 \\ \hline \end{array}$

4 *Multiply.*

12. $9 \times 6 \times 1 \times 2$

13. $50 \times 10 \times 200$

14. $\begin{array}{r} 2658 \\ \times \quad 7 \\ \hline \end{array}$

15. $\begin{array}{r} 68 \\ \times 55 \\ \hline \end{array}$

16. $\begin{array}{r} 365 \\ \times 908 \\ \hline \end{array}$

5 *Divide. If there is a remainder, be sure to state it as part of the answer.*

17. $8\overline{)84\,840}$

18. $7\overline{)51\,633}$

19. $76\overline{)1984}$

20. $42\overline{)5838}$

Your institution may have included the Answers to Selected Exercises for this module, which contains the answers to these questions. Each answer also includes a reference to the objective in which the problem is first taught. If you missed any of these problems, you should stop and review the Examples and Practice Problems in the referenced objective. A little review now will help you master the material in the upcoming sections.

SECTION 6 EXPONENTS AND THE ORDER OF OPERATIONS

Evaluating Expressions with Whole-Number Exponents

Sometimes a simple math idea comes "disguised" in technical language. For example, an **exponent** is just a "shorthand" number that saves writing multiplication of the same numbers.

10^3 The exponent 3 means $10 \times 10 \times 10$ (which takes longer to write).

The product 5×5 can be written as 5^2. The small number 2 is called the *exponent.* The exponent tells us how many factors are in the multiplication. The number 5 is called the **base.** The base is the number that is multiplied.

$$3 \times 3 \times 3 \times 3 = 3^4$$

← exponent (the 4); ↑ base (the 3)

In 3^4 the base is 3 and the exponent is 4. (The 4 is sometimes called the *superscript.*) 3^4 is read as "three to the fourth power."

Student Learning Objectives

After studying this section, you will be able to:

Evaluate expressions with whole-number exponents.

Perform several arithmetic operations in the proper order.

EXAMPLE 1 Write each product in exponent form.

(a) $15 \times 15 \times 15$ **(b)** $7 \times 7 \times 7 \times 7 \times 7$

Solution

(a) $15 \times 15 \times 15 = 15^3$ **(b)** $7 \times 7 \times 7 \times 7 \times 7 = 7^5$

Practice Problem 1 Write each product in exponent form.

(a) $12 \times 12 \times 12 \times 12$ **(b)** $2 \times 2 \times 2 \times 2 \times 2 \times 2$

NOTE TO STUDENT: Fully worked-out solutions to all of the Practice Problems can be found at the end of the module.

EXAMPLE 2 Find the value of each expression.

(a) 3^3 **(b)** 7^2 **(c)** 2^5 **(d)** 1^8

Solution

(a) To find the value of 3^3, multiply the base 3 by itself 3 times.

$$3^3 = 3 \times 3 \times 3 = 27$$

(b) To find the value of 7^2, multiply the base 7 by itself 2 times.

$$7^2 = 7 \times 7 = 49$$

(c) $2^5 = 2 \times 2 \times 2 \times 2 \times 2 = 32$

(d) $1^8 = 1 \times 1 \times 1 \times 1 \times 1 \times 1 \times 1 \times 1 = 1$

Practice Problem 2 Find the value of each expression.

(a) 12^2 **(b)** 6^3 **(c)** 2^6 **(d)** 1^{10}

If a whole number does not have a visible exponent, the exponent is understood to be 1. Thus

$$3 = 3^1 \qquad \text{and} \qquad 10 = 10^1.$$

Large numbers are often expressed as a power of 10.

$10^1 = 10 = 1$ ten
$10^2 = 100 = 1$ hundred
$10^3 = 1000 = 1$ thousand
$10^4 = 10\,000 = 1$ ten thousand
$10^5 = 100\,000 = 1$ hundred thousand
$10^6 = 1\,000\,000 = 1$ million

What does it mean to have an exponent of zero? What is 10^0? Any whole number that is not zero can be raised to the zero power. The result is 1. Thus $10^0 = 1$, $3^0 = 1$, $5^0 = 1$, and so on. Why is this? Let's re-examine the powers of 10. As we go down one line at a time, notice the pattern that occurs.

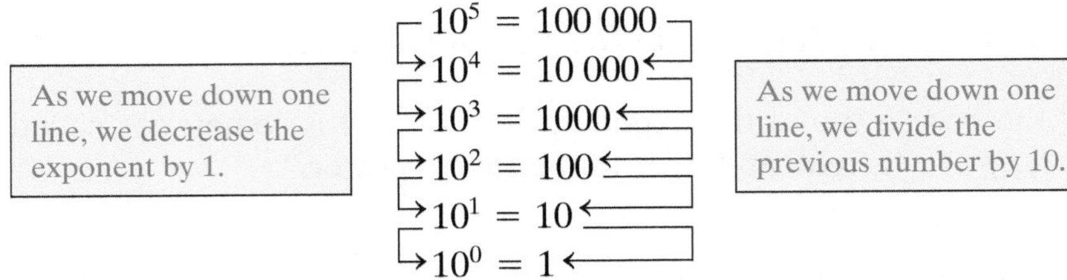

Therefore, we present the following definition.

For any whole number a other than zero, $a^0 = 1$.

If numbers with exponents are added to other numbers, it is first necessary to **evaluate,** or find the value of, the number that is raised to a power. Then we may combine the results with another number.

EXAMPLE 3 Find the value of each expression.

(a) $3^4 + 2^3$ **(b)** $5^3 + 7^0$ **(c)** $6^3 + 6$

Solution

(a) $3^4 + 2^3 = (3)(3)(3)(3) + (2)(2)(2) = 81 + 8 = 89$
(b) $5^3 + 7^0 = (5)(5)(5) + 1 = 125 + 1 = 126$
(c) $6^3 + 6 = (6)(6)(6) + 6 = 216 + 6 = 222$

NOTE TO STUDENT: Fully worked-out solutions to all of the Practice Problems can be found at the end of the module.

Practice Problem 3 Find the value of each expression.

(a) $7^3 + 8^2$ **(b)** $9^2 + 6^0$ **(c)** $5^4 + 5$

2 Performing Several Arithmetic Operations in the Proper Order

Sometimes the order in which we do things is not important. The order in which chefs hang up their pots and pans probably does not matter. The order in which they add and mix the elements in preparing food, however, makes all the difference in the world! If various cooks follow a recipe, though, they will get similar results. The recipe assures that the results will be consistent. It shows the **order of operations.**

In mathematics the order of operations is a list of priorities for working with the numbers in computational problems. This mathematical "recipe" tells how to handle certain indefinite computations. For example, how does a person find the value of $5 + 3 \times 2$?

A problem such as $5 + 3 \times 2$ sometimes causes students difficulty. Some people think $(5 + 3) \times 2 = 8 \times 2 = 16$. Some people think $5 + (3 \times 2) = 5 + 6 = 11$. Only one answer is right, 11. To obtain the right answer, follow the steps outlined in the following box.

ORDER OF OPERATIONS

In the absence of grouping symbols:

Do first	**1.** Simplify any expressions with exponents.
↓	**2.** Multiply or divide from left to right.
Do last	**3.** Add or subtract from left to right.

EXAMPLE 4 Evaluate. $3^2 + 5 - 4 \times 2$

Solution

$3^2 + 5 - 4 \times 2 = 9 + 5 - 4 \times 2$ Evaluate the expression with exponents.

$= 9 + 5 - 8$ Multiply from left to right.

$= 14 - 8$ Add from left to right.

$= 6$ Subtract.

Practice Problem 4 Evaluate. $7 + 4^3 \times 3$

EXAMPLE 5 Evaluate. $5 + 12 \div 2 - 4 + 3 \times 6$

Solution There are no numbers to raise to a power, so we first do any multiplication or division in order from *left to right.*

$5 + 12 \div 2 - 4 + 3 \times 6$ Multiply or divide from left to right.

$= 5 + 6 - 4 + 3 \times 6$ Divide.

$= 5 + 6 - 4 + 18$ Multiply. Add or subtract from left to right.

$= 11 - 4 + 18$ Add.

$= 7 + 18$ Subtract.

$= 25$ Add.

Practice Problem 5 Evaluate. $37 - 20 \div 5 + 2 - 3 \times 4$

EXAMPLE 6 Evaluate. $2^3 + 3^2 - 7 \times 2$

Solution

$2^3 + 3^2 - 7 \times 2 = 8 + 9 - 7 \times 2$ Evaluate exponent expressions $2^3 = 8$ and $3^2 = 9$.

$= 8 + 9 - 14$ Multiply.

$= 17 - 14$ Add.

$= 3$ Subtract.

Practice Problem 6 Evaluate. $4^3 - 2 + 3^2$

You can change the order in which you compute by using grouping symbols. Place the numbers you want to calculate first within parentheses. This tells you to do those calculations first. A common mnemonic device to help remember the order of operations is **PEDMAS** (when the word *brackets* is used instead of *parentheses* the mnemonic device would be **BEDMAS**).

ORDER OF OPERATIONS

With grouping symbols:

Do first	**P**	**1.** Perform operations inside parentheses.
↓	**E**	**2.** Simplify any expressions with exponents.
	D/M	**3.** Multiply or divide from left to right.
Do last	**A/S**	**4.** Add or subtract from left to right.

EXAMPLE 7 Evaluate. $2 \times (7 + 5) \div 4 + 3 - 6$

Solution First, we combine numbers inside the parentheses by adding the 7 to the 5. Next, because multiplication and division have equal priority, we work from left to right doing whichever of these operations comes first.

$$
\begin{aligned}
&2 \times (7 + 5) \div 4 + 3 - 6 \\
&= 2 \times 12 \div 4 + 3 - 6 && \text{Parentheses.} \\
&= 24 \div 4 + 3 - 6 && \text{Multiply.} \\
&= 6 + 3 - 6 && \text{Divide.} \\
&= 9 - 6 && \text{Add.} \\
&= 3 && \text{Subtract.}
\end{aligned}
$$

NOTE TO STUDENT: Fully worked-out solutions to all of the Practice Problems can be found at the end of the module.

Practice Problem 7 Evaluate. $(17 + 7) \div 6 \times 2 + 7 \times 3 - 4$

EXAMPLE 8 Evaluate. $4^3 + 18 \div 3 - 2^4 - 3 \times (8 - 6)$

Solution

$$
\begin{aligned}
&4^3 + 18 \div 3 - 2^4 - 3 \times (8 - 6) \\
&= 4^3 + 18 \div 3 - 2^4 - 3 \times 2 && \text{Work inside the parentheses.} \\
&= 64 + 18 \div 3 - 16 - 3 \times 2 && \text{Evaluate exponents.} \\
&= 64 + 6 - 16 - 3 \times 2 && \text{Divide.} \\
&= 64 + 6 - 16 - 6 && \text{Multiply.} \\
&= 70 - 16 - 6 && \text{Add.} \\
&= 54 - 6 && \text{Subtract.} \\
&= 48 && \text{Subtract.}
\end{aligned}
$$

Practice Problem 8 Evaluate. $5^2 - 6 \div 2 + 3^4 + 7 \times (12 - 10)$

Section 6 Exercises

Verbal and Writing Skills

1. Explain what the expression 5^3 means. Evaluate 5^3.

2. In exponent notation, the ___________ tells how many times to multiply the base.

3. In exponent notation, the ______ is the number that is multiplied.

4. 10^5 is read as _______________.

5. Explain the order in which we perform mathematical operations to ensure consistency.

6. Use the order of operations to solve $12 \times 5 + 3 \times 5 + 7 \times 5$. Is this the same as $5(12 + 3 + 7)$? Why or why not?

Write each number in exponent form.

7. $6 \times 6 \times 6 \times 6$

8. $2 \times 2 \times 2 \times 2 \times 2$

9. $5 \times 5 \times 5 \times 5 \times 5 \times 5$

10. $3 \times 3 \times 3 \times 3 \times 3 \times 3$

11. $9 \times 9 \times 9 \times 9$

12. $1 \times 1 \times 1 \times 1 \times 1 \times 1 \times 1$

13. 9

14. 27

Find the value of each expression.

15. 2^4

16. 3^3

17. 4^3

18. 5^2

19. 6^2

20. 10^3

21. 10^4

22. 1^{20}

23. 1^{17}

24. 2^5

25. 2^6

26. 4^2

27. 3^5

28. 12^2

29. 15^2

30. 3^4

31. 7^3

32. 5^4

33. 4^4

34. 7^2

35. 9^0

36. 8^0

37. 25^2

38. 20^3

39. 10^6

40. 8^1

41. 13^2

42. 11^2

43. 9^1

44. 14^2

45. 8^2

46. 5^3

47. $3^2 + 1^2$

48. $7^0 + 4^3$

49. $2^3 + 10^2$

50. $7^3 + 4^2$

51. $8^3 + 8$

52. $9^2 + 9$

Work each exercise, using the correct order of operations.

53. $9 \times 10 - 35$

54. $9 \times 7 + 42$

55. $3 \times 9 - 10 \div 2$

56. $4 \times 6 - 24 \div 4$

57. $48 \div 2^3 + 4$

58. $4^3 \div 4 - 11$

59. $3 \times 6^2 - 50$

60. $2 \times 12^2 - 80$

61. $10^2 + 3 \times (8 - 3)$

62. $4^3 - 5 \times (9 + 1)$

63. $(400 \div 20) \div 20$

64. $(600 \div 30) \div 20$

65. $950 \div (25 \div 5)$

66. $875 \div (35 \div 7)$

67. $(12)(5) - (12 + 5)$

68. $(3)(60) - (60 + 3)$

69. $3^2 + 4^2 \div 2^2$

70. $7^2 + 9^2 \div 3^2$

71. $(6)(7) - (12 - 8) \div 4$

72. $(8)(9) - (15 - 5) \div 5$

73. $100 - 3^2 \times 4$

74. $130 - 4^2 \times 5$

75. $5^2 + 2^2 + 3^3$

76. $2^3 + 3^2 + 4^3$

77. $72 \div 9 \times 3 \times 1 \div 2$

78. $120 \div 30 \times 2 \times 5 \div 8$

79. $12^2 - 2 \times 0 \times 5 \times 6$

80. $8^2 - 4 \times 3 \times 0 \times 7$

Mixed Practice *Work each exercise, using the correct order of operations.*

81. $4^2 \times 6 \div 3$

82. $7^2 \times 3 \div 3$

83. $60 - 2 \times 4 \times 5 + 10$

84. $75 - 3 \times 5 \times 2 + 15$

85. $3 + 3^2 \times 6 + 4$

86. $5 + 4^3 \times 2 + 7$

87. $32 \div 2 \times (3 - 1)^4$

88. $24 \div 3 \times (5 - 3)^2$

89. $3^2 \times 6 \div 9 + 4 \times 3$

90. $5^2 \times 3 \div 25 + 7 \times 6$

91. $6^2 + 5^0 + 2^3$

92. $8^0 + 7^2 + 3^3$

93. $1200 - 2^3(3) \div 6$

94. $2150 - 3^4(2) \div 9$

95. $120 \div (30 + 10) - 1$

96. $100 - 48 \div (2 \times 3)$

97. $120 \div 30 + 10 - 1$

98. $100 - 48 \div 2 \times 3$

99. $5 \times 2 + (7 - 4)^3 + 2^0$

100. $9 \times 8 + 5^0 - (8 - 4)^3$

To Think About

101. ***Astronomy*** Earth rotates once every 23 hours, 56 minutes, 4 seconds. How many seconds is that?

102. ***Astronomy*** The planet Saturn rotates once every 10 hours, 12 minutes. How many minutes is that? How many seconds?

Quick Quiz 6

1. Write in exponent form.
$12 \times 12 \times 12 \times 12 \times 12$

2. Evaluate. 6^4

3. Perform each operation in the proper order.
$42 - 2^5 + 3 \times (9 - 6)^3$

4. **Concept Check** Explain in what order you would do the steps to evaluate the expression $7 \times 6 \div 3 \times 4^2 - 2$.

Section 7 Rounding and Estimating

Student Learning Objectives

After studying this section, you will be able to:

 **Round whole numbers.**

 **Estimate the answer to a problem involving whole numbers.**

1 Rounding Whole Numbers

Large numbers are often expressed to the nearest hundred or to the nearest thousand, because an approximate number is "good enough" for certain uses.

Distances from Earth to other galaxies are measured in light-years. Although light really travels at 9 460 528 000 000 kilometres a year, we usually **round** this number to the nearest trillion and say it travels at 9 000 000 000 000 kilometres a year. To round a number, we first determine the place we are rounding to—in this case, trillion. Then we find which value is closest to the number that we are rounding. In this case, the number we want to round is closer to 9 trillion than to 10 trillion. How do we know the number is closer to 9 trillion than to 10 trillion?

To see which is the closest value, we may picture a **number line,** where whole numbers are represented by points on a line. To show how to use a number line in rounding, we will round 368 to the nearest hundred. 368 is between 300 and 400. When we round, we pick the hundred 368 is "closest to." We draw a number line to show 300 and 400. We also show the point midway between 300 and 400 to help us to determine which hundred 368 is closest to.

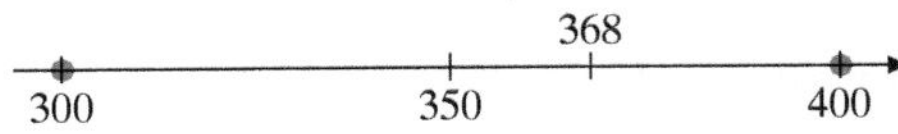

We find that the number 368 is closer to 400 than to 300, so we round 368 *up to* 400.

Let's look at another example. We will round 129 to the nearest hundred. 129 is between 100 and 200. We show this on the number line. We include the midpoint 150 as a guide.

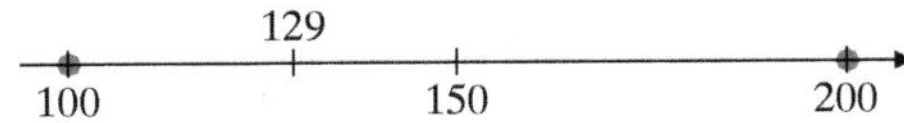

We find that the number 129 is closer to 100 than to 200, so we round 129 *down to* 100.

This leads us to the following simple rule for rounding.

ROUNDING A WHOLE NUMBER

1. If the first digit to the right of the round-off place is
   - **(a)** *less than 5,* we make no change to the digit in the round-off place. (We know it is closer to the smaller number, so we round down.)
   - **(b)** *5 or more,* we increase the digit in the round-off place by 1. (We know it is closer to the larger number, so we round up.)
2. Then we replace the digits to the right of the round-off place by zeros.

EXAMPLE 1 Round 37 843 to the nearest thousand.

Solution

3 7 8 4 3 — According to the directions, the thousands will be the round-off place. We locate the thousands place.

↓

3 7 ⑧4 3 — We see that the first digit to the right of the round-off place is 8, which is 5 or more. We increase the thousands digit by 1, and replace all digits to the right by zeros.

↓

3 8 0 0 0

We have rounded 37 843 to the nearest thousand: 38 000. This means that 37 843 is closer to 38 000 than to 37 000.

Practice Problem 1 Round 65 528 to the nearest thousand.

EXAMPLE 2 Round 2 445 360 to the nearest hundred thousand.

Solution

2 4 4 5 3 6 0 — Locate the hundred thousands round-off place.

↓

2 4 ④5 3 6 0 — The first digit to the right of this is less than 5, so round down. Do not change the hundred thousands digit.

↓

2 4 0 0 0 0 0 — Replace all digits to the right by zeros.

Practice Problem 2 Round 172 963 to the nearest ten thousand.

EXAMPLE 3 Round as indicated.

(a) 561 328 to the nearest ten **(b)** 3 798 152 to the nearest hundred
(c) 51 362 523 to the nearest million

Solution

(a) ↓ First locate the digit in the tens place.

561 328 The digit to the right of the tens place is greater than 5.

561 330 Round up.

561 328 rounded to the nearest ten is 561 330.

(b) 3 798 152 The digit to the right of the hundreds place is 5.

3 798 200 Round up.

3 798 152 rounded to the nearest hundred is 3 798 200.

(c) 51 362 523 The digit to the right of the millions place is less than 5.

51 000 000 Round down.

51 362 523 rounded to the nearest million is 51 000 000.

Practice Problem 3 Round as indicated.

(a) 53 282 to the nearest ten
(b) 164 485 to the nearest thousand
(c) 1 365 273 to the nearest hundred thousand

EXAMPLE 4 Round 763 571.

(a) To the nearest thousand
(b) To the nearest ten thousand
(c) To the nearest million

Solution

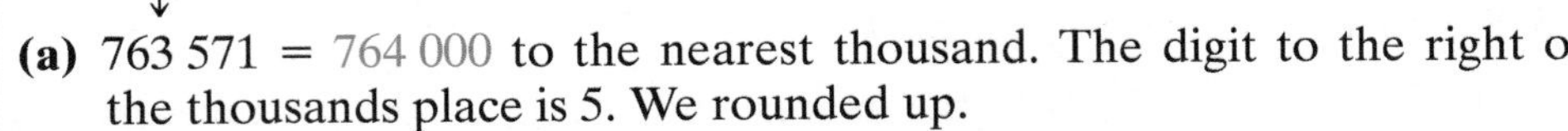

(a) 763 571 = 764 000 to the nearest thousand. The digit to the right of the thousands place is 5. We rounded up.

(b) 763 571 = 760 000 to the nearest ten thousand. The digit to the right of the ten thousands place is less than 5. We rounded down.

(c) 763 571 does not have any digits for millions. If it helps, you can think of this number as 0 763 571. Since the digit to the right of the millions place is 7, we round up to obtain one million or 1 000 000.

Practice Problem 4 Round 935 682 as indicated.

(a) To the nearest thousand
(b) To the nearest hundred thousand
(c) To the nearest million

EXAMPLE 5 Astronomers use the parsec as a measurement of distance. One parsec is approximately 30 900 000 000 000 kilometres. Round 1 parsec to the nearest trillion kilometres.

Solution 30 900 000 000 000 km is 31 000 000 000 000 km or 31 trillion km to the nearest trillion kilometres.

Practice Problem 5 One light-year is approximately 9 460 000 000 000 000 metres. Round to the nearest hundred trillion metres.

2 Estimating the Answer to a Problem Involving Whole Numbers

Often we need to quickly check the answer of a calculation to be reasonably assured that the answer is correct. If you expected your bill to be "around $40" for the groceries you had selected and the cashier's total came to $41.89, you would probably be confident that the bill is correct and pay it. If, however, the cashier rang up a bill of $367, you would not just assume that it is correct. You would know an error had been made. If the cashier's total came to $60, you might not be certain, but you would probably suspect an error and check the calculation.

In mathematics we often **estimate,** or determine the approximate value of a calculation, if we need to do a quick check. There are many ways to estimate, but in this book we will use one simple principle of estimation. We use the symbol $\approx$ to mean **is approximately equal to.**

PRINCIPLE OF ESTIMATION

1. Round the numbers so that there is one nonzero digit in each number.
2. Perform the calculation with the rounded numbers.

EXAMPLE 6 Estimate the sum. 163 + 237 + 846 + 922

Solution We first determine where to round each number in our problem to leave only one nonzero digit in each. In this case, we round all numbers to the nearest hundred. Then we perform the calculation with the rounded numbers.

Actual Sum	*Estimated Sum*
163	200
237	200
846	800
+922	+900
	2100

We estimate the answer to be 2100. We say the sum $\approx$2100. If we calculate using the exact numbers, we obtain a sum of 2168, so our estimate is quite close to the actual sum.

Practice Problem 6 Estimate the sum. 3456 + 9876 + 5421 + 1278

When we use the principle of estimation, we will not always round each number in a problem to the same place.

EXAMPLE 7 Phil and Melissa bought their first car last week. The selling price of this compact car was $8980. The dealer preparation charge was $289 and the sales tax was $449. Estimate the total cost that Phil and Melissa had to pay.

Solution We round each number to have only one nonzero digit, and add the rounded numbers.

8980	9000
289	300
+ 449	+ 400
	9700

The total cost $\approx$$9700. (The exact answer is $9718, so we see that our answer is quite close.)

Practice Problem 7 Greg and Marcia purchased a new sofa for $697, plus $35 sales tax. The store also charged them $19 to deliver the sofa. Estimate their total cost.

***NOTE TO STUDENT:** Fully worked-out solutions to all of the Practice Problems can be found at the end of the module.*

Now we turn to a case where an estimate can help us discover an error.

EXAMPLE 8 Roberto added together four numbers and obtained the following result. Estimate the sum and determine if the answer seems reasonable.

$$12\,456 + 17\,976 + 18\,452 + 32\,128 \stackrel{?}{=} 61\,012$$

Solution We round each number so that there is one nonzero digit. In this case, we round them all to the nearest ten thousand.

12 456	10 000
17 976	20 000
18 452	20 000
+ 32 128	+ 30 000
	80 000 Our estimate is 80 000.

This is significantly different from 61 012, so we would suspect that an error has been made. In fact, Roberto did make an error. The exact sum is actually 81 012!

Practice Problem 8 Ming did the following calculation. Estimate to see if her sum appears to be correct or incorrect.

$$11\,849 + 14\,376 + 16\,982 + 58\,151 = 81\,358$$

Next we look at a subtraction example where estimation is used.

EXAMPLE 9 The profit from Techno Industries for the first quarter of the year was \$642 987 000. The profit for the second quarter was \$238 890 000. Estimate how much less the profit was for the second quarter than for the first quarter.

Solution We round each number so that there is one nonzero digit. Then we subtract, using the two rounded numbers.

642 987 000	600 000 000
− 238 890 000	− 200 000 000
	400 000 000

We estimate that the profit was \$400 000 000 less for the second quarter.

Practice Problem 9 The 2008 population of Ontario was 12 891 800. The 2008 population of British Columbia was 4 428 400. Estimate how many more people lived in Ontario in 2008 than in British Columbia.

We also use this principle to estimate results of multiplication and division.

EXAMPLE 10 Estimate the product. $56\,789 \times 529$

Solution We round each number so that there is one nonzero digit. Then we multiply the rounded numbers to obtain our estimate.

$$\begin{array}{r} 56\,789 \\ \times \quad 529 \\ \hline \end{array} \qquad \begin{array}{r} 60\,000 \\ \times \quad 500 \\ \hline 30\,000\,000 \end{array}$$

Therefore the product $\approx$30 000 000. (This is reasonably close to the exact answer of 30 041 381.)

Practice Problem 10 Estimate the product. 8945×7317

EXAMPLE 11 Estimate the answer for the following division problem.

$$23\overline{)148\,902}$$

Solution We round each number to a number with one nonzero digit. Then we perform the division, using the two rounded numbers.

$$23\overline{)148\,902} \qquad \begin{array}{r} 5\,000 \\ 20\overline{)100\,000} \end{array}$$

Our estimate is 5000. (The exact answer is 6474. We see that our estimate is "in the ballpark" but is not very close to the exact answer. Remember, an estimate is just a rough approximation of the exact answer.)

Practice Problem 11 Estimate the answer for the following division problem.

$$39\overline{)75\,342}$$

Not all division estimates come out so easily. In some cases, you may need to carry out a long-division problem of several steps just to obtain the estimate. Do not be in a hurry. Students often want to rush the steps of division. It is better to take your time and carefully do each step. This approach will be very worthwhile in the long run.

EXAMPLE 12 John and Stephanie drove their car a distance of 478 kilometres. They used 25 litres of gas. Estimate how many kilometres they can travel on 1 litre of gas.

Solution In order to solve this problem, we need to divide 478 by 25 to obtain the number of kilometres John and Stephanie get with 1 litre of gas. We round each number to a number with one nonzero digit and then perform the division, using the rounded numbers.

$$25\overline{)478} \qquad \begin{array}{r} 16 \\ 30\overline{)500} \\ \underline{30} \\ 200 \\ \underline{180} \\ 20 \end{array} \text{ Remainder}$$

We obtain an answer of 16 with a remainder of 20. For our estimate we will use the whole number 17. Thus we estimate that the number of kilometres their car obtained on 1 litre of gas was 17 kilometres. (This is reasonably close to the exact answer, which is just slightly more than 19 kilometres per litre of gas.)

NOTE TO STUDENT: Fully worked-out solutions to all of the Practice Problems can be found at the end of the module.

Practice Problem 12 The highway department purchased 58 identical trucks at a total cost of $1 864 584. Estimate the cost for one truck.

Developing Your Study Skills

How To Do Homework

Set aside time each day for your homework assignments. Make a weekly schedule and write down the times each day you will devote to doing math homework. Two hours spent studying outside class for each hour in class is usual for college courses. You may need more than that for mathematics.

Before beginning to solve your homework exercises, read your textbook very carefully. Expect to spend much more time reading a few pages of a mathematics textbook than several pages of another text. Read for complete understanding, not just for the general idea.

As you begin your homework assignments, read the directions carefully. You need to understand what is being asked. Concentrate on each exercise, taking time to solve it accurately. Rushing through your work usually results in errors. Check your answers with those given. If your answer is incorrect, check to see that you are doing the right problem. Redo the problem, watching for errors. If it is still wrong, check with a friend. Perhaps the two of you can figure out where you are going wrong.

Also, check the examples in the textbook or in your notes for a similar exercise. Can this one be solved in the same way? Give it some thought. You may want to leave it for a while by taking a break or doing a different exercise. But come back later and try again. If you are still unable to figure it out, ask your instructor for help during office hours or in class.

Work on your assignments every day and do as many exercises as it takes for you to know what you are doing. Begin by doing all the exercises that have been assigned. If there are more available in that section of your text, then do more. When you think you have done enough exercises to fully understand the topic at hand, do a few more to be sure. This may mean that you do many more exercises than the instructor assigns, but you can never practise mathematics too much. Practice improves your skills and increases your accuracy, speed, competence, and confidence.

Section 7 Exercises

Verbal and Writing Skills

1. Explain the rule for rounding and provide examples.

2. What happens when you round 98 to the nearest ten?

Round to the nearest ten.

3. 83 **4.** 45 **5.** 65 **6.** 57 **7.** 168 **8.** 132

9. 7438 **10.** 2834 **11.** 2961 **12.** 4355

Round to the nearest hundred.

13. 247 **14.** 661 **15.** 2781 **16.** 1249 **17.** 7692 **18.** 1643

Round to the nearest thousand.

19. 7621 **20.** 3754 **21.** 1489 **22.** 515 **23.** 27 863 **24.** 94 489

Applications

25. ***History*** The worst death rate from an earthquake was in Shaanxi, China, in 1556. That earthquake killed an estimated 832 400 people. Round this number to the nearest hundred thousand.

26. ***Astronomy*** One light-year (the distance light travels in one year) measures 5 878 612 843 000 miles. Round this figure to the nearest hundred million.

27. ***Astronomy*** The Hubble Space Telescope's *Guide Star Catalogue* lists 15 169 873 stars. Round this figure to the nearest million.

28. ***Geography*** The point of highest elevation in the world is Mt. Everest in the country of Nepal. Mt. Everest is 8848 metres above sea level. Round this figure to the nearest thousand.

29. ***Native Studies*** In 2006, the total number of Aboriginal people living in Canada was estimated to be 1 172 790. Round this figure to

(a) the nearest hundred thousand.
(b) the nearest thousand.

30. ***Population Studies*** The population of Canada in 2030 is projected to be 36 095 100. Round this figure to

(a) the nearest ten thousand.
(b) the nearest ten million.

▲ **31.** ***Geography*** The total area of mainland China is 3 705 392 square miles, or 9 596 960 square kilometres. For *both* square miles and square kilometres, round this figure to

(a) the nearest hundred thousand.
(b) the nearest ten thousand.

▲ **32.** ***Geography*** The area of the Pacific Ocean is 165 384 000 square kilometres. Round this figure to

(a) the nearest hundred thousand.
(b) the nearest ten thousand.

Use the principle of estimation to find an estimate for each calculation.

33. 772 + 324 + 225 **34.** 186 + 509 + 872 **35.** 42 + 69 + 95 + 18

36. 62 + 27 + 54 + 98

37. 158 270 + 53 441 + 8701

38. 238 271 + 77 304 + 9551

39. 324 230 − 70 290

40. 975 935 − 593 228

41. 842 512 − 78 234

42. 382 140 − 56 117

43. 33 261 378 − 18 199 276

44. 89 263 000 − 54 198 635

45. 47 × 62

46. 43 × 95

47. 1324 × 8

48. 5926 × 3

49. 631 540 × 312

50. 374 193 × 193

51. 6368 ÷ 38

52. 7813 ÷ 22

53. 362 881 ÷ 39

54. 596 450 ÷ 64

55. 3 885 720 ÷ 831

56. 12 447 312 ÷ 497

Estimate the result of each calculation. Some results are correct and some are incorrect. Which results appear to be correct? Which results appear to be incorrect?

57.
$$\begin{array}{r} 361 \\ 522 \\ 873 \\ +\ 164 \\ \hline 1320 \end{array}$$

58.
$$\begin{array}{r} 476 \\ 124 \\ 516 \\ +\ 389 \\ \hline 1505 \end{array}$$

59.
$$\begin{array}{r} 97\,635 \\ 52\,123 \\ +\ 41\,986 \\ \hline 291\,744 \end{array}$$

60.
$$\begin{array}{r} 26\,181 \\ 47\,998 \\ +\ 63\,271 \\ \hline 137\,450 \end{array}$$

61.
$$\begin{array}{r} 302\,360 \\ -\ 89\,518 \\ \hline 212\,842 \end{array}$$

62.
$$\begin{array}{r} 735\,128 \\ -\ 116\,733 \\ \hline 518\,395 \end{array}$$

63. $\begin{array}{r} 78\,126\,345 \\ -\ 48\,972\,103 \\ \hline 19\,154\,242 \end{array}$

64. $\begin{array}{r} 42\,765\,317 \\ -\ 29\,318\,274 \\ \hline 23\,447\,043 \end{array}$

65. $\begin{array}{r} 378 \\ \times\ 32 \\ \hline 21\,096 \end{array}$

66. $\begin{array}{r} 512 \\ \times\ 46 \\ \hline 20\,552 \end{array}$

67. $\begin{array}{r} 5896 \\ \times\ 72 \\ \hline 424\,512 \end{array}$

68. $\begin{array}{r} 8076 \\ \times\ 89 \\ \hline 718\,764 \end{array}$

69. $36\overline{)82\,116}$ with quotient $2\,281$

70. $52\overline{)28\,912}$ with quotient 556

71. $423\overline{)161\,163}$ with quotient 381

72. $781\overline{)477\,972}$ with quotient 612

Applications

▲**73.** ***Geometry*** Victor and Shannon just purchased a new home with a two-car garage measuring 4 metres wide and 8 metres long. Estimate the number of square metres in the garage.

▲**74.** ***Geometry*** A huge restaurant in Toronto is 43 metres wide and 112 metres long. Estimate the number of square metres in the restaurant.

75. ***Population Studies*** In 2005, the populations of the three largest cities in Canada were Toronto with 5 304 600 people, Montréal with 3 635 842 people, and Vancouver with 2 208 312 people. Estimate the total population of the three cities.

76. ***Financial Management*** The highway departments in four towns in northwestern Ontario had the following budgets for snow removal for the year: \$329 560, \$672 940, \$199 734, and \$567 087. Estimate the total amount that the four towns spend for snow removal in one year.

77. ***Business Management*** The local pizzeria makes 267 pizzas on an average day. Estimate how many pizzas were made in the last 134 days.

78. ***Personal Finance*** Darcy makes \$68 for each shift she works. She is scheduled for 33 shifts during the next two months. Estimate how much she will earn in the next two months.

79. ***Transportation*** In 2004, Toronto's Pearson airport was the busiest with 404 736 flights (departures and arrivals). In the same year, the fourth busiest airport was in Montréal with 218 474 flights. Round each figure to the nearest ten thousand. Then estimate the difference.

80. ***Sports*** In 1980, the average attendance at a Toronto Blue Jays game was 17 288. In 2007, the average attendance at a Blue Jays game was 29 143. Estimate the increase in attendance over this time period.

▲ **81.** ***International Relations*** The largest state of the United States is Alaska, with a land area of 586 412 square miles. The second largest state is Texas, with an area of 267 339 square miles. Round each figure to the nearest ten thousand. Then estimate how many square miles larger Alaska is than Texas.

▲ **82.** ***International Relations*** The largest country in Africa is Sudan, measuring 2 505 810 square kilometres. South America's largest country is Brazil, measuring 8 514 877 square kilometres. Round each figure to the nearest hundred thousand, then estimate how many square kilometres larger Brazil is than Sudan.

To Think About

83. ***Space Travel*** A space probe travels at 23 560 kilometres per hour for a distance of 7 824 560 000 kilometres.

(a) How many *hours* will it take the space probe to travel that distance? (Estimate.)

(b) How many *days* will it take the space probe to travel that distance? (Estimate.)

84. ***Space Travel*** A space probe travels at 28 367 kilometres per hour for a distance of 9 348 487 000 kilometres.

(a) Estimate the number of *hours* it will take the space probe to travel that distance.

(b) Estimate the number of *days* it will take the space probe to travel that distance.

Quick Quiz 7

1. Round to the nearest hundred. 92 354

2. Round to the nearest ten thousand. 2 342 786

3. Use the principle of estimation to find an estimation for this calculation. $7862 \times 329\,182$

4. **Concept Check** Explain how to round 682 496 934 to the nearest million.

Section 8 Solving Applied Problems Involving Whole Numbers

Solving Problems Involving One Operation

When a builder constructs a new home or office building, he or she uses a *blueprint*. This accurate drawing shows the basic structure of the building. It also shows the dimensions of the structure to be built. This blueprint serves as a useful reference throughout the construction process.

Jean Miele/Corbis/Stock Market

Student Learning Objectives

After studying this section, you will be able to:

1. **Use the Mathematics Blueprint to solve problems involving one operation.**
2. **Use the Mathematics Blueprint to solve problems involving more than one operation.**

Similarly, when solving applied problems, it is helpful to have a "mathematics blueprint." This is a simple way to organize the information provided in the word problem. You record the facts you need to use and specify what you are solving for. You also record any other information that you feel will be helpful. We will use a Mathematics Blueprint for Problem Solving in this section.

Sometimes people feel totally lost when trying to solve a word problem. They sometimes say, "Where do I begin?" or "How in the world do you do this?" When you have this type of feeling, it sometimes helps to have a formal strategy or plan. Here is a plan you may find helpful:

1. *Understand the problem.*
   (a) Read the problem carefully.
   (b) Draw a picture if this helps you see the relationships more clearly.
   (c) Fill in the Mathematics Blueprint so that you have the facts and a method of proceeding in this situation.

2. *Solve and state the answer.*
   (a) Perform the calculations.
   (b) State the answer, including the unit of measure.

3. *Check.*
   (a) Estimate the answer.
   (b) Compare the exact answer with the estimate to see if your answer is reasonable.

Now exactly what does the Mathematics Blueprint for Problem Solving look like? It is a simple sheet of paper with four columns. Each column tells you something to do.

Gather the Facts—Find the numbers that you will need to use in your calculations.

What Am I Asked to Do?—Are you finding an area, a volume, a cost, the total number of people? What is it that you need to find?

How Do I Proceed?—Do you need to add items together? Do you need to multiply or divide? What types of calculations are required?

Key Points to Remember—Write down things you might forget. The length is in metres. The area is in square metres. We need the total number of something, not the intermediate totals. Whatever you need to help you, write it down in this column.

Mathematics Blueprint for Problem Solving

Gather the Facts	What Am I Asked to Do?	How Do I Proceed?	Key Points to Remember

EXAMPLE 1 Gerald made deposits of \$317, \$512, \$84, and \$161 into his chequing account. He also made out cheques for \$100 and \$125. What was the total of his deposits?

Solution

1. ***Understand the problem.*** First we read over the problem carefully and fill in the Mathematics Blueprint.

Mathematics Blueprint for Problem Solving

Gather the Facts	What Am I Asked to Do?	How Do I Proceed?	Key Points to Remember
We need only deposits—not cheques. The **deposits** are \$317, \$512, \$84, and \$161.	Find the total of Gerald's four deposits.	I must add the four deposits to obtain the total.	Watch out! Don't use the **cheques** of \$100 and \$125 in the calculation. We only want the total of the **deposits**.

2. ***Solve and state the answer.*** We need to *add* to find the sum of the deposits.

$$\begin{array}{r} 317 \\ 512 \\ 84 \\ +161 \\ \hline 1074 \end{array}$$

The total of the four deposits is $1074.

3. ***Check.*** Reread the problem. Be sure you have answered the question that was asked. Did it ask for the total of the deposits?
Yes. ✓

Is the calculation correct? You can use estimation to check. Here we round each of the deposits so that we have one nonzero digit.

$$\begin{array}{rr} 317 & 300 \\ 512 & 500 \\ 84 & 80 \\ +161 & +200 \\ \hline & 1080 \end{array}$$

Our estimate is $1080. $1074 is close to our estimated answer of $1080. Our answer is reasonable. ✓

Thus we conclude that the total of the four deposits is $1074.

Practice Problem 1 Use the Mathematics Blueprint to solve the following problem. Diane's paycheque shows deductions of $135 for federal taxes, $28 for provincial taxes, $13 for CPP, and $34 for health insurance. Her gross pay (amount before deductions) is $1352. What is the total amount that is taken out of Diane's paycheque?

NOTE TO STUDENT: *Fully worked-out solutions to all of the Practice Problems can be found at the end of the module.*

Mathematics Blueprint for Problem Solving

Gather the Facts	What Am I Asked to Do?	How Do I Proceed?	Key Points to Remember

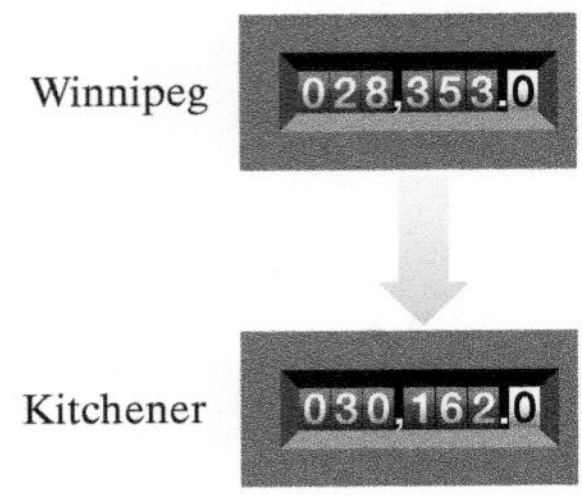

EXAMPLE 2 Theofilos looked at his odometer before he began his trip from Winnipeg, Manitoba, to Kitchener, Ontario. He checked his odometer again when he arrived in Kitchener. The two readings are shown in the figure. How many kilometres did Theofilos travel?

Solution

1. ***Understand the problem.*** Determine what information is given.
   The mileage reading before the trip began and when the trip was over.
   What do you need to find?
   The number of kilometres travelled.

Mathematics Blueprint for Problem Solving

Gather the Facts	What Am I Asked to Do?	How Do I Proceed?	Key Points to Remember
At the start of the trip, the odometer read 28 353 kilometres. At the end of the trip, the odometer read 30 162 kilometres.	Find out how many kilometres Theofilos travelled.	I must subtract the two mileage readings.	Subtract the mileage at the start of the trip from the mileage at the end of the trip.

2. ***Solve and state the answer.*** We need to subtract the two mileage readings to find the difference in the number of kilometres. This will give us the number of kilometres the car travelled on this trip alone.

   $30\ 162 - 28\ 353 = 1809$ The trip totalled 1809 kilometres.

3. ***Check.*** We estimate and compare the estimate with the preceding answer.

Kitchener	30 162 ⟶	30 000	We subtract
Winnipeg	28 353 ⟶	28 000	our rounded values.
		2 000	

   Our estimate is 2000 kilometres. We compare this estimate with our answer. Our answer is reasonable. ✓

2008 Federal Election

Party	Number of votes
Conservative	5 209 069
Liberal	3 633 185
NDP	2 515 288
BQ	1 379 991
Green	937 613

Source: Adapted From Elections Canada: www.elections.ca/scripts/OVR2008/default.html, Oct-09

Practice Problem 2 The table on the left shows the results of the 2008 Canadian Federal Election. By how many votes did the Conservative Party beat the Liberal Party in that year?

Mathematics Blueprint for Problem Solving

Gather the Facts	What Am I Asked to Do?	How Do I Proceed?	Key Points to Remember

NOTE TO STUDENT: *Fully worked-out solutions to all of the Practice Problems can be found at the end of the module.*

EXAMPLE 3 One horsepower is the power needed to lift 550 pounds a distance of 1 foot in 1 second. How many pounds can be lifted 1 foot in 1 second by 7 horsepower?

Solution

1. ***Understand the problem.*** Simplify the problem. If 1 horsepower can lift 550 pounds, how many pounds can be lifted by 7 horsepower? We draw and label a diagram.

We use the Mathematics Blueprint to organize the information.

Mathematics Blueprint for Problem Solving

Gather the Facts	What Am I Asked to Do?	How Do I Proceed?	Key Points to Remember
One horsepower will lift 550 pounds.	Find how many pounds can be lifted by 7 horsepower.	I need to multiply 550 by 7.	I do not use the information about moving 1 foot in 1 second.

2. ***Solve and state the answer.*** To solve the problem we multiply the 7 horsepower by 550 pounds for each horsepower.

$$\begin{array}{r} 550 \\ \times \quad 7 \\ \hline 3850 \end{array}$$

We find that 7 horsepower moves 3850 pounds 1 foot in 1 second. We include 1 foot in 1 second in our answer because it is part of the unit of measure.

3. ***Check.*** We estimate our answer. We round 550 to 600 pounds.

$$600 \times 7 = 4200 \text{ pounds}$$

Our estimate is 4200 pounds. Our calculations in step 2 gave us 3850. Is this reasonable? This answer is close to our estimate. Our answer is reasonable. ✓

Practice Problem 3 In a measure of liquid capacity, 1 litre is 1000 milli-litres. How many millilitres would be in 9 litres?

Mathematics Blueprint for Problem Solving

Gather the Facts	What Am I Asked to Do?	How Do I Proceed?	Key Points to Remember

EXAMPLE 4 Laura can type 35 words per minute. She has to type an English essay that has 5180 words. How many minutes will it take her to type the essay? How many hours and how many minutes will it take her to type the essay?

Solution

1. ***Understand the problem.*** We draw a picture. Each "package" of 1 minute is 35 words. We want to know how many packages make up 5180 words.

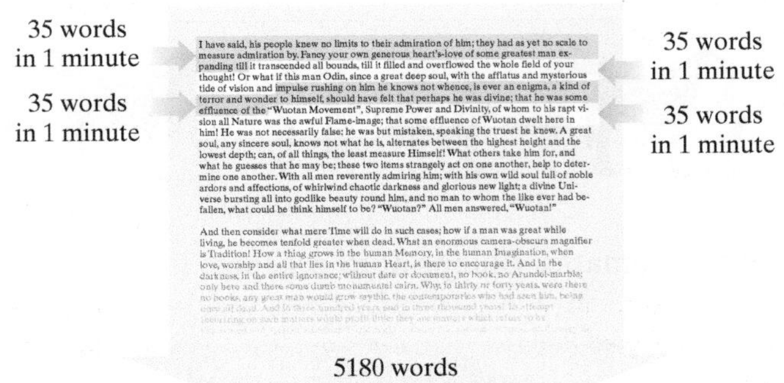

We use the Mathematics Blueprint to organize the information.

Mathematics Blueprint for Problem Solving

Gather the Facts	What Am I Asked to Do?	How Do I Proceed?	Key Points to Remember
Laura can type 35 words per minute. She must type a paper with 5180 words.	Find out how many 35-word units are in 5180 words.	I need to divide 5180 by 35.	In converting minutes to hours, I will use the fact that 1 hour = 60 minutes.

2. ***Solve and state the answer.***

$$\begin{array}{r} 148 \\ 35\overline{)5180} \\ \underline{35} \\ 168 \\ \underline{140} \\ 280 \\ \underline{280} \\ 0 \end{array}$$

It will take 148 minutes.
We will change this answer to hours and minutes. Since 60 minutes = 1 hour, we divide 148 by 60. The quotient will tell us how many hours. The remainder will tell us how many minutes.

$$\begin{array}{r} 2 \text{ R } 28 \\ 60\overline{)148} \\ \underline{-120} \\ 28 \end{array}$$

Laura can type the theme in 148 minutes or 2 hours, 28 minutes.

3. ***Check.*** The theme has 5180 words; she can type 35 words per minute. 5180 words is approximately 5000 words.

5180 words → 5000 words rounded to nearest thousand.

$$40\overline{)5000}\quad = 125$$

35 words per minute → 40 words per minute rounded to nearest ten.

We divide our estimated values.

Our estimate is 125 minutes. This is close to our calculated answer. Our answer is reasonable. ✓

Practice Problem 4 Donna bought 45 shares of stock for $1620. How much did the stock cost her per share?

Mathematics Blueprint for Problem Solving

Gather the Facts	What Am I Asked to Do?	How Do I Proceed?	Key Points to Remember

***NOTE TO STUDENT:** Fully worked-out solutions to all of the Practice Problems can be found at the end of the module.*

Solving Problems Involving More Than One Operation

Sometimes a chart, table, or bill of sale can be used to help us organize the data in an applied problem. In such cases, a blueprint may not be needed.

EXAMPLE 5 Cleanway Rent-A-Car bought four used luxury sedans at $21 000 each, three compact sedans at $14 000 each, and seven subcompact sedans at $8000 each. What was the total cost of the purchase?

Solution

1. ***Understand the problem.*** We will make an imaginary bill of sale to help us to visualize the problem.
2. ***Solve and state the answer.*** We do the calculations and enter the results in the bill of sale.

Car Fleet Sales, Inc., Hamilton, Ontario

Customer: *Cleanway Rent-A-Car*			
Quantity	**Type of Car**	**Cost per Car**	**Amount for This Type of Car**
4	Luxury sedans	$21 000	$84 000 (4 × $21 000 = $84 000)
3	Compact sedans	$14 000	$42 000 (3 × $14 000 = $42 000)
7	Subcompact sedans	$8000	$56 000 (7 × $8000 = $56 000)
		TOTAL	$182 000 (sum of the three amounts)

The total cost of all 14 cars is $182 000.

3. ***Check.*** You may use estimation to check. The check is left to the student.

NOTE TO STUDENT: Fully worked-out solutions to all of the Practice Problems can be found at the end of the module.

Practice Problem 5 Anderson Dining Commons purchased 50 tables at $200 each, 180 chairs at $40 each, and 6 moving carts at $65 each. What was the total cost of the purchase?

EXAMPLE 6 Dawn had a balance of $410 in her chequing account last month. She made deposits of $46, $18, $150, $379, and $22. She made out cheques for $316, $400, and $89. What is her balance?

Solution

1. ***Understand the problem.*** We want to *add* to get a total of all deposits and *add* to get a total of all cheques.

Old balance + total of deposits − total of cheques = new balance

Mathematics Blueprint for Problem Solving

Gather the Facts	What Am I Asked to Do?	How Do I Proceed?	Key Points to Remember
Old balance: $410. New deposits: $46, $18, $150, $379, and $22. New cheques: $316, $400, and $89.	Find the amount of money in the chequing account after deposits are made and cheques are withdrawn.	**(a)** I need to calculate the total of the deposits and the total of the cheques. **(b)** I add the total deposits to the old balance. **(c)** Then I subtract the total of the cheques from that result.	Deposits are added to a chequing account. Cheques are subtracted from a chequing account.

2. ***Solve and state the answer.***

First we find the total of deposits:

$$\begin{array}{r} 46 \\ 18 \\ 150 \\ 379 \\ +\ 22 \\ \hline \$615 \end{array}$$

Then the total of cheques:

$$\begin{array}{r} 316 \\ 400 \\ +\ 89 \\ \hline \$805 \end{array}$$

Add the deposits to the old balance and subtract the amount of the cheques.

$$\begin{array}{l|r} \text{Old balance} & 410 \\ +\text{ total deposits} & +\ 615 \\ \hline & 1025 \\ -\text{ total cheques} & -\ 805 \\ \hline \text{New balance} & 220 \end{array}$$

The new balance in the chequing account is $220.

3. ***Check.*** Work backward. You can add the total cheques to the new balance and then subtract the total deposits. The result should be the old balance. Try it.

$$\begin{array}{rl} 410 & \text{Old balance } \checkmark \\ -\ 615 & \uparrow \\ \hline 1025 & \\ +\ 805 & \\ \hline 220 & \text{Work backward.} \end{array}$$

Practice Problem 6 Last month Bridget had $498 in a savings account. She made two deposits: one for $607 and one for $163. The bank credited her with $36 interest. Since last month, she has made four withdrawals: $19, $158, $582, and $74. What is her balance this month?

Mathematics Blueprint for Problem Solving

Gather the Facts	What Am I Asked to Do?	How Do I Proceed?	Key Points to Remember

EXAMPLE 7 When Lorenzo began his car trip, his gas tank was full and the odometer read 76 368 kilometres. He ended his trip at 76 668 kilometres and filled the gas tank with 20 litres of gas. How many kilometres per litre did he get with his car?

Solution

1. ***Understand the problem.***

Mathematics Blueprint for Problem Solving

Gather the Facts	What Am I Asked to Do?	How Do I Proceed?	Key Points to Remember
Odometer reading at end of trip: 76 668 kilometres. Odometer reading at start of trip: 76 368 kilometres. Used on trip: 20 litres of gas.	Find the number of kilometres per litre that the car obtained on the trip.	**(a)** I need to subtract the two odometer readings to obtain the number of kilometres travelled. **(b)** I divide the number of kilometres driven by the number of litres of gas used to get the number of kilometres obtained per litre of gas.	The gas tank was full at the beginning of the trip. 20 litres fills the tank at the end of the trip.

2. ***Solve and state the answer.*** First we subtract the odometer readings to obtain the kilometres travelled.

$$\begin{array}{r} 76\,668 \\ -\ 76\,368 \\ \hline 300 \end{array}$$

The trip was 300 kilometres.
Next we divide the kilometres driven by the number of litres.

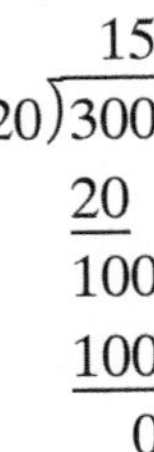

$$\begin{array}{r} 15 \\ 20\overline{)300} \\ \underline{20} \\ 100 \\ \underline{100} \\ 0 \end{array}$$

Thus Lorenzo obtained 15 kilometres per litre on the trip.

3. ***Check.*** We do not want to round to one nonzero digit here, because, if we do, the result will be zero when we subtract. Thus we will round to the nearest hundred for the values of mileage.

$$76\,668 \longrightarrow 76\,700$$
$$76\,368 \longrightarrow 76\,400$$

Now we subtract the estimated values.

$$\begin{array}{r} 76\,700 \\ -\ 76\,400 \\ \hline 300 \end{array}$$

Thus we estimate the trip to be 300 kilometres.
Then we divide.

$$\begin{array}{r} 15 \\ 20\overline{)300} \end{array}$$

We obtain 15 kilometres per litre for our estimate. This is the same as our calculated value of 15 kilometres per litre. ✓

NOTE TO STUDENT: *Fully worked-out solutions to all of the Practice Problems can be found at the end of the module.*

Practice Problem 7 Deidre took a car trip with a full tank of gas. Her trip began with the odometer at 50 698 and ended at 51 118 kilometres. She then filled the tank with 42 litres of gas. How many kilometres per litre did her car get on the trip?

Mathematics Blueprint for Problem Solving

Gather the Facts	What Am I Asked to Do?	How Do I Proceed?	Key Points to Remember

In general, most students find that they are more successful at solving applied problems if they take extra time to understand the problem. This requires careful reading and thinking about what the problem is asking you to do. Use a coloured pen or pencil and underline the most important facts. Draw a picture or sketch if it will help you visualize the situation. Remember, if you understand what you are solving for, your work will go much more quickly.

If you attend a traditional mathematics class that meets one or more times each week:

Developing Your Study Skills

Class Attendance

You will want to get started in the right direction by choosing to attend class every day, beginning with the first day of class. Statistics show that class attendance and good grades go together. Classroom activities are designed to enhance learning, and therefore you must be in class to benefit from them. Each day vital information and explanations are given that can help you understand concepts. Do not be deceived into thinking that you can just find out from a friend what went on in class. There is no good substitute for firsthand experience. Give yourself a push in the right direction by developing the habit of going to class every day.

If you are enrolled in an online mathematics class, a self-paced mathematics class taught in a math lab, or some other type of nontraditional class:

Developing Your Study Skills

Keeping Yourself on Schedule

In a class where you determine your own pace, you will need to commit yourself to keeping on a schedule. Follow the suggested pace provided in your course materials. Keep all your class materials organized and review them often to be sure you are doing everything that you should. If you discipline yourself to follow the suggested course schedule for the first six weeks, you will likely succeed in the class. Many professors have found that students usually succeed in the course as long as they do every suggested activity for the first six weeks. Make sure you succeed! Keep yourself on schedule!

Section 8 Exercises

Applications

You may want to use the Mathematics Blueprint for Problem Solving to help you to solve the word problems in exercises 1–34.

1. ***Real Estate*** Donna and Miguel want to buy a cabin for $31 500. After repairs, the total cost will be $40 300. How much will the repairs cost?

▲2. ***Geography*** China has a total area of 9 596 960 square kilometres. Bodies of water account for 270 550 square kilometres. How many square kilometres of land does China have?

3. ***Business Management*** Paula is organizing a large two-day convention. Bert's Bagels is providing the breakfast bagels. If Paula orders 120 baker's dozen, how many bagels is that? (There are 13 in a baker's dozen.)

4. ***Business Management*** There are 144 pencils in a gross. Jim Weston ordered 14 gross of pencils for the office. How many pencils did he order?

5. ***Consumer Affairs*** A 12-ounce can of Hunts tomato sauce costs 84¢. What is the unit cost of the tomato sauce? (How much does the tomato sauce cost per ounce?)

6. ***Consumer Affairs*** A 45 cL can of Del Monte pears costs 90¢. What is the unit cost of the pears? (How much do the pears cost per centilitre?)

7. ***Sports*** Kimberly began running 3 years ago. She has spent $832 on 13 pairs of running shoes during this time. How much on average did each pair of shoes cost?

8. ***Wildlife Management*** There are approximately 4500 bison living in Canada. If Northwest Trek, the animal preserve located in Wood Bison National Park, has 1300 bison, how many bison are living elsewhere?

9. ***Population Studies*** In October 2006, the population of Canada reached 33 098 932. In October 2005, there were 32 666 490 people in Canada. What was the increase in population from October 2005 to October 2006?

▲10. ***Geometry*** Valleyfair, an amusement park, covers 26 acres. If there are about 4047 square metres in 1 acre, how many square metres of land does Valleyfair cover?

11. ***Business Management*** A games arcade has recently opened in a Vancouver neighbourhood. The owners were nervous about whether it would be a success. Fortunately, the gross revenues over the last four weeks were $7356, $3257, $4777, and $4992. What was the gross revenue over these four weeks for the arcade?

12. ***International Relations*** The two largest cities in France are Paris, with 2 113 000 people, and Marseille, with 815 100 people. What is the difference in population between these two cities?

13. ***Wildlife Management*** The Federal Nigeria game preserve has 24 111 animals, 327 full-time staff, and 793 volunteers. What is the total of these three groups? How many more volunteers are there than full-time staff?

14. ***Geography*** The longest rivers in the world are the Nile River, the Amazon River, and the Mississippi River. Their lengths are 6650 kilometres, 6301 kilometres, and 6021 kilometres, respectively. How many total kilometres do these three rivers run? What is the difference in the lengths of the Nile and the Mississippi?

15. ***World History*** Every 60 minutes, the world population increases by 100 000 people. How many people will be born during the next 480 minutes?

16. ***Personal Finance*** Roberto had $2158 in his savings account six months ago. In the last six months he made four deposits: $156, $238, $1119, and $866. The bank deposited $136 in interest over the six-month period. How much does he have in the savings account at present?

In exercises 17–34, more than one type of operation is required.

17. ***Sports*** Carmen gives golf lessons every Saturday. She charges $15 for adults, $9 for children, and $5 for club rental. Last Saturday she taught six adults and eight children, and six people needed to rent clubs. How much money did Carmen make on that day?

18. ***Business Management*** Whale Watch Excursions charges $10 for adults, $6 for children, and $7 for senior citizens. On the last trip of the day, there were five adults, seven children, and three senior citizens. How much money did the company make on this trip?

19. ***Personal Finance*** Sue Li had a balance in her chequing account of $132. During the last two months she has deposited four paycheques of $715 each. She wrote two rent cheques for $575 each, and wrote cheques totalling $482 for other bills. When all the deposits are recorded and the cheques clear, what will be the balance in her chequing account?

20. ***Space Travel*** From 1957 to 2005, the number of successful space launches totalled 4361. Of these, 2746 were launched by the Soviet Union/Russia, and 1305 were launched by the United States. How many launches were completed by other countries?

21. ***Real Estate*** Diana owns 85 acres of forest land in Oregon. She rents it to a timber grower for $250 per acre per year. Her property taxes are $57 per acre. How much profit does she make on the land each year?

22. ***Real Estate*** Todd owns 13 acres of commercially zoned land in the city of Montréal, Québec. He rents it to a construction company for $12 350 per acre per year. His property taxes to the city are $7362 per acre per year. How much profit does he make on the land each year?

23. ***Environmental Studies*** Hanna wants to determine the kilometres-per-litre rating of her Chevrolet Cavalier. She filled the tank when the odometer read 14 926 kilometres. She then drove her car on a trip. At the end of the trip, the odometer read 15 276 kilometres. It took 25 litres to fill the tank. How many kilometres per litre does her car deliver?

24. ***Environmental Studies*** Gary wants to determine the kilometres-per-litre rating of his Geo Metro. He filled the tank when the odometer read 28 862 kilometres. After ten days, the odometer read 29 438 kilometres and the tank required 36 litres to be filled. How many kilometres per litre did Gary's car achieve?

25. ***Forestry*** A beautiful piece of land in the Wilmot Nature Preserve has three times as many oak trees as birches, two times as many maples as oaks, and seven times as many pine trees as maples. If there are 18 birches on the land, how many of each of the other trees are there? How many trees are there in all?

26. ***Business Management*** The Cool Coffee Lounge in Moosonee, Ontario, has 27 tables, and each table has either two or four chairs. If there are a total of 94 chairs accompanying the 27 tables, how many tables have four chairs? How many tables have two chairs?

Use the following list to answer exercises 27–30.

Education

The following table represents the primary language spoken at home of students attending a public school in Ottawa, Ontario, in the school year 2006–07.

Language	Number of Students
English	335
French	212
Mandarin	53
Cantonese	45
Spanish	44
Arabic	38
Hebrew	35
Chinese, other dialects	31
Russian	29
Korean	29
Italian	22
Hindi	15
Filipino	12
Romanian	8
Urdu	6
Albanian	5
Bulgarian	4
Gujarati	3

Ariel Skelley/Corbis/Stock Market

27. How many students speak Mandarin, Cantonese, or other Chinese dialects as the primary language in their homes?

28. How many students speak Korean, Hindi, or Filipino as the primary language in their homes?

29. How many more students speak English than speak Spanish or Russian as the primary language in their homes?

30. How many more students speak Gujarati or Bulgarian than speak Albanian as the primary language in their homes?

Use the following bar graph to answer exercises 31–34.

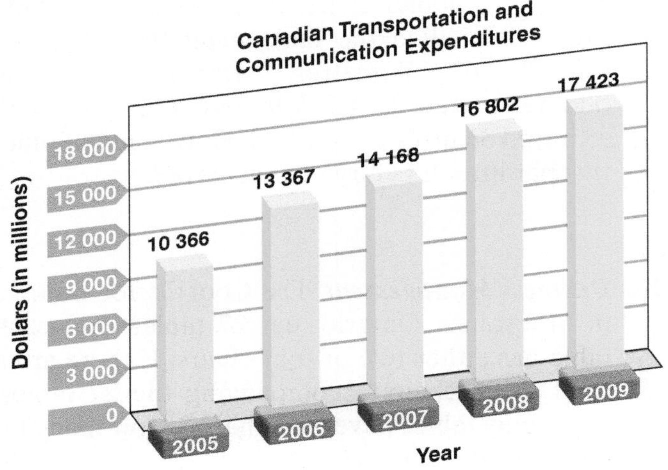

Source: Adapted from Statistics Canada, www40.statcan.gc.ca/l01/cst01/govt55a-eng.htm, Oct-09

Government Finances

31. How many more dollars were spent on Transportation and Communication in 2008 than in 2007?

32. How many more dollars were spent on Transportation and Communication in 2007 than in 2005?

33. If the exact same dollar increase occurs between 2008 and 2010 as occurred between 2005 and 2007, what will the expenditures be in 2010?

34. What were the total expenditures for Transportation and Communication over the five-year period?

Quick Quiz 8

1. Sixteen people in a travel club chartered a bus to go to Sault Ste. Marie to see the fall foliage. The bill for the bus charter was $4304. How much will each club member pay if the cost is shared equally?

2. Maria had a balance of $471 in her chequing account last month. She then deposited $198, $276, and $347. She made out cheques for $49, $227, and $158. What will her new balance be?

3. The entire Tobey family went on a fishing charter. The cost was $11 for people 60 or older, $14 for people age 12 to 59, and $5 for children under 12. The captain counted 2 people over 60, six people age 12 to 59, and four children under 12. What was the total cost for the Tobey family members to go on the fishing charter?

4. **Concept Check** A company has purchased 38 new cars for the sales department for $836 543. Assuming that each car cost the same, explain how you would estimate the cost of each car.

Putting Your Skills to Work: Use Math to Save Money

MANAGING DEBTS AND PAYMENTS

Can you imagine the joy of taking a great vacation without going into debt for it? Can you think about how great it would be to have all your debts paid off? It is a wonderful feeling! Paying off your debts and then being able to take a vacation is an excellent goal. But how is that done? Consider the story of Tracy and Max.

Facing Up to the Debt

Tracy and Max were overwhelmed with debt. Besides their ordinary living expenses, they had so much debt that they could barely make the money they earned last until the end of the month. They had little money left for extras and for having fun, and no money for a vacation. Each of their three credit cards was maxed out at \$8000; they had a line of credit debt of \$12 000; they still owed \$2000 on their car; and they had also borrowed money from friends in sums of \$100 and \$300.

Making a Plan

They decided to write down all of their debts, putting them in order from smallest to largest.

Then they made minimum payments on all the debts, but aimed at paying off the three smallest debts first.

1. Put the couple's debts in order from smallest to largest. Remember, there are three credit cards.

The minimum payment on each credit card averaged \$25 per month. They had arranged to pay the line of credit debt off at \$50 per month. Their car payment was \$200 per month, and they agreed to pay each of their friends \$20 per month.

2. What is the total amount of their minimum monthly payments?

What Tracy and Max Accomplished

Tracy and Max decided they would eliminate any extras and not spend money on fun activities so they could use this money to pay off their three smallest debts. As a result they were able to pay off the smallest debt in five months while making minimum payments on all other debts. Then each month they took the \$20 they would have used to pay the small debt and applied it towards he second smallest debt. Again, they made sure they made minimum payments on all other debts.

3. How many months will it take Tracy and Max to pay off the third smallest debt if they follow the plan stated above?

After eliminating the smaller debts, they took the money they would have spent on those debts and used it on the principal of the remaining debts. In other words, they paid more than the minimum payment on the remaining debts. Because they hated the way they felt when they were in debt, they stopped using credit cards for new purchases. Max also took a temporary part-time job so they could pay off their debts faster. Finally they paid off all the debts!

Applying It to Your Life

Many debt counsellors have a simple, practical suggestion for people in debt. Arrange debts in order, pay off the smallest first, and then let the consequences of that action help pay off the rest of the debts more quickly. Many people have been able to get out of debt in about two years by using this approach, other strategies for budgeting, and wise choices for living.

Module Organizer

Topic	Procedure	Examples
Place value of numbers.	Each digit has a value depending on location. millions | hundred thousands | ten thousands | thousands | hundreds | tens | ones	In the number 2 896 341, what place value does 9 have? ten thousands
Writing expanded notation.	Take the number of each digit and multiply it by one, ten, hundred, thousand, . . . according to its place.	Write in expanded notation. 46 235 40 000 + 6000 + 200 + 30 + 5
Writing whole numbers in words.	Take the number in each period and indicate if they are (millions) (thousands) (ones) xxx, xxx, xxx	Write in words. 134 718 216. one hundred thirty-four million, seven hundred eighteen thousand, two hundred sixteen
Adding whole numbers.	Starting with the right column, add each column separately. If a two-digit sum occurs, "carry" the left digit over to the next column to the left.	Add. $\begin{array}{r} \scriptstyle 2\,1 \\ 258 \\ 367 \\ 291 \\ +\,453 \\ \hline 1369 \end{array}$
Subtracting whole numbers.	Starting with the right column, subtract each column separately. If necessary, borrow a unit from the column to the left and bring it to the right as a "10."	Subtract. $\begin{array}{r} \scriptstyle 13 \\ \scriptstyle 6\ \not{3}\ 12 \\ 16\not{7}\not{4}\not{2} \\ -12395 \\ \hline 4347 \end{array}$
Multiplying several factors.	Keep multiplying from left to right. Take each product and multiply by the next factor to the right. Continue until all factors are used once. (Since multiplication is commutative and associative, the factors can be multiplied in any order.)	Multiply. $2 \times 9 \times 7 \times 6 \times 3 = 18 \times 7 \times 6 \times 3$ $= 126 \times 6 \times 3$ $= 756 \times 3$ $= 2268$
Multiplying several-digit numbers.	Multiply the top factor by the ones digit, then by the tens digit, then by the hundreds digit. Add the partial products together.	Multiply. $\begin{array}{r} 567 \\ \times\,238 \\ \hline 4536 \\ 1701 \\ 1134 \\ \hline 134\,946 \end{array}$
Dividing by a two- or three-digit number.	Figure how many times the first digit of the divisor goes into the first two digits of the dividend. To try this answer, multiply it back to see if it is too large or small. Continue each step of long division until finished.	Divide. $\begin{array}{r} 589 \\ 238\overline{)140\,182} \\ \underline{1190} \\ 2118 \\ \underline{1904} \\ 2142 \\ \underline{2142} \\ 0 \end{array}$

Topic	Procedure	Examples
Exponent form.	To show in short form the repeated multiplication of the same number, write the number being multiplied. (This is the base.) Write in smaller print above the line the number of times it appears as a factor. (This is the exponent.) To evaluate the exponent form, write the factor the number of times shown in the exponent. Then multiply.	Write in exponent form. $10 \times 10 \times 10 \times 10 \times 10 \times 10 \times 10 \times 10$ 10^8 Evaluate. 6^3 $6 \times 6 \times 6 = 216$
Order of operations.	**1.** Perform operations inside parentheses. **2.** Simplify exponents. **3.** Then do multiplication and division in order from left to right. **4.** Then do addition and subtraction in order from left to right.	Evaluate. $2^3 + 16 \div 4^2 \times 5 - 3$ Raise to a power first. $8 + 16 \div 16 \times 5 - 3$ Then do multiplication or division from left to right. $8 + 1 \times 5 - 3$ $8 + 5 - 3$ Then do addition and subtraction. $13 - 3 = 10$
Rounding.	**1.** If the first digit to the right of the round-off place is less than 5, the digit in the round-off place is unchanged. **2.** If the first digit to the right of the round-off place is 5 or more, the digit in the round-off place is increased by 1. **3.** Digits to the right of the round-off place are replaced by zeros.	Round to the nearest hundred. 56 743 ↓ 5 6 7 ④ 3 The digit 4 is less than 5. 56,700 Round to the nearest thousand. 128 517 ↓ 1 2 8 ⑤ 1 7 The digit 5 is obviously 5 or greater. We increase the thousands digit by 1. 129 000
Estimating the answer to a calculation.	**1.** Round each number so that there is one nonzero digit. **2.** Perform the calculation with the rounded numbers.	Estimate the answer. $45\,780 \times 9453$ First we round. $50\,000 \times 9000$ Then we multiply. $50\,000 \times 9\,000 = 450\,000\,000$ We estimate the answer to be 450 000 000.

Procedure for Solving Applied Problems

Using the Mathematics Blueprint for Problem Solving

In solving an applied problem, students may find it helpful to complete the following steps. You will not use all the steps all the time. Choose the steps that best fit the conditions of the problem.

1. Understand the problem.
  (a) Read the problem carefully.
  (b) Draw a picture if this helps you to visualize the situation. Think about what facts you are given and what you are asked to find.
  (c) Use the Mathematics Blueprint for Problem Solving to organize your work. Follow these four parts.
    1. Gather the facts. (Write down specific values given in the problem.)
    2. What am I asked to do? (Identify what you must obtain for an answer.)
    3. Decide what calculations need to be done.
    4. Key points to remember. (Record any facts, warnings, formulas, or concepts you think will be important as you solve the problem.)

2. Solve and state the answer.
  (a) Perform the necessary calculations.
  (b) State the answer, including the unit of measure.

3. Check.
  (a) Estimate the answer to the problem. Compare this estimate to the calculated value. Is your answer reasonable?
  (b) Repeat your calculations.
  (c) Work backward from your answer. Do you arrive at the original conditions of the problem?

EXAMPLE

The provincial highway department has just purchased two pickup trucks and three dump trucks. The cost of a pickup truck is $17 920. The cost of a dump truck is $48 670. What was the cost to purchase these five trucks?

1. ***Understand the problem.***

2. ***Solve and state the answer.***

Calculate cost of pickup trucks.

$$\begin{array}{r} \$17\,920 \\ \times \quad 2 \\ \hline \$35\,840 \end{array}$$

Calculate cost of dump trucks.

$$\begin{array}{r} \$48\,670 \\ \times \quad 3 \\ \hline \$146\,010 \end{array}$$

Find total cost. $35 840 + $146 010 = $181 850

The total cost of the five trucks is $181 850.

3. ***Check.***

Estimate cost of pickup trucks.

$$20\,000 \times 2 = 40\,000$$

Estimate cost of dump trucks.

$$50\,000 \times 3 = 150\,000$$

Total estimate.

$$40\,000 + 150\,000 = 190\,000$$

This is close to our calculated answer of $181 850. We determine that our answer is reasonable. ✓

Mathematics Blueprint for Problem Solving

Gather the Facts	What Am I Asked to Do?	How Do I Proceed?	Key Points to Remember
Buy 2 pickup trucks 3 dump trucks Cost Pickup: $17 920 Dump: $48 670	Find the total cost of the 5 trucks.	Find the cost of 2 pickup trucks. Find the cost of 3 dump trucks. Add to get final cost of all 5 trucks.	Multiply 2 times pickup truck cost. Multiply 3 times dump truck cost.

Module Review Problems

If you have trouble with a particular type of exercise, review the examples in the section indicated for that group of exercises.

Section 1

Write in words.

1. 892

2. 15 802

3. 109 276

4. 423 576 055

Write in expanded notation.

5. 4364

6. 35 414

7. 42 166 037

8. 1 305 128

Write in standard notation.

9. nine hundred twenty-four

10. five thousand three hundred two

11. one million, three hundred twenty-eight thousand, eight hundred twenty-eight

12. twenty-four million, seven hundred five thousand, one hundred twelve

Section 2

Add.

13. $76 + 39$

14. $148 + 152$

15. $235 + 165$

16. $12 + 28 + 34 + 76$

17. $\begin{array}{r} 123 \\ 61 \\ 9 \\ 84 \\ +123 \\ \hline \end{array}$

18. $\begin{array}{r} 546 \\ 254 \\ +153 \\ \hline \end{array}$

19. $\begin{array}{r} 226 \\ 134 \\ +647 \\ \hline \end{array}$

20. $\begin{array}{r} 52\,134 \\ +\ \ 7\,966 \\ \hline \end{array}$

21. $\begin{array}{r} 1356 \\ 2892 \\ 561 \\ 89 \\ +9805 \\ \hline \end{array}$

22. $\begin{array}{r} 26 \\ 503 \\ 935 \\ 1257 \\ +7861 \\ \hline \end{array}$

Section 3

Subtract.

23. $\begin{array}{r} 36 \\ -19 \\ \hline \end{array}$

24. $\begin{array}{r} 54 \\ -48 \\ \hline \end{array}$

25. $\begin{array}{r} 126 \\ -\ \ 99 \\ \hline \end{array}$

26. $\begin{array}{r} 543 \\ -372 \\ \hline \end{array}$

27. $\begin{array}{r} 7000 \\ -\ \ 845 \\ \hline \end{array}$

28. $\begin{array}{r} 9000 \\ -5833 \\ \hline \end{array}$

29. $\begin{array}{r} 201\,340 \\ -120\,618 \\ \hline \end{array}$

30. $\begin{array}{r} 320\,055 \\ -214\,237 \\ \hline \end{array}$

31. $\begin{array}{r} 6\,325\,034 \\ -\ \ \ \ 89\,023 \\ \hline \end{array}$

32. $\begin{array}{r} 5\,412\,022 \\ -\ \ \ \ 79\,031 \\ \hline \end{array}$

Section 4

Multiply.

33. $8 \times 1 \times 9 \times 2$ **34.** $7 \times 6 \times 0 \times 4$ **35.** $2 \cdot 5 \cdot 10 \cdot 8$ **36.** $4 \cdot 25 \cdot 1 \cdot 15$

37. 621×100 **38.** $84\,312 \times 1000$ **39.** $78 \times 10\,000$ **40.** $563 \times 1\,000\,000$

41. $\begin{array}{r} 58 \\ \times 32 \\ \hline \end{array}$ **42.** $\begin{array}{r} 73 \\ \times 24 \\ \hline \end{array}$ **43.** $\begin{array}{r} 150 \\ \times\ 27 \\ \hline \end{array}$ **44.** $\begin{array}{r} 360 \\ \times\ 38 \\ \hline \end{array}$

45. $\begin{array}{r} 709 \\ \times\ 36 \\ \hline \end{array}$ **46.** $\begin{array}{r} 502 \\ \times\ 48 \\ \hline \end{array}$ **47.** $\begin{array}{r} 123 \\ \times 714 \\ \hline \end{array}$ **48.** $\begin{array}{r} 431 \\ \times 623 \\ \hline \end{array}$

49. $\begin{array}{r} 1782 \\ \times\ 305 \\ \hline \end{array}$ **50.** $\begin{array}{r} 2057 \\ \times\ 124 \\ \hline \end{array}$ **51.** $\begin{array}{r} 3182 \\ \times\ \ 35 \\ \hline \end{array}$ **52.** $\begin{array}{r} 2713 \\ \times\ \ 42 \\ \hline \end{array}$

53. $\begin{array}{r} 1200 \\ \times 6000 \\ \hline \end{array}$ **54.** $\begin{array}{r} 2500 \\ \times 3000 \\ \hline \end{array}$ **55.** $\begin{array}{r} 100\,000 \\ \times\ 20\,000 \\ \hline \end{array}$ **56.** $\begin{array}{r} 300\,000 \\ \times\ 40\,000 \\ \hline \end{array}$

Section 5

Divide, if possible.

57. $20 \div 10$ **58.** $40 \div 8$ **59.** $0 \div 8$ **60.** $12 \div 1$

61. $7 \div 1$ **62.** $0 \div 5$ **63.** $\frac{81}{9}$ **64.** $\frac{42}{6}$

65. $\frac{5}{0}$ **66.** $\frac{24}{6}$ **67.** $\frac{56}{8}$ **68.** $\frac{63}{7}$

Divide. Be sure to indicate the remainder, if one exists.

69. $6\overline{)750}$ **70.** $7\overline{)875}$ **71.** $9\overline{)1863}$ **72.** $4\overline{)1236}$ **73.** $6\overline{)15\,024}$

74. $8\overline{)24\,512}$ **75.** $6\overline{)221\,748}$ **76.** $5\overline{)184\,605}$ **77.** $8\overline{)120\,371}$ **78.** $7\overline{)250\,485}$

79. $67\overline{)490}$ **80.** $72\overline{)325}$ **81.** $21\overline{)666}$ **82.** $22\overline{)319}$ **83.** $68\overline{)2614}$

84. $53\overline{)3202}$ **85.** $45\overline{)8775}$ **86.** $35\overline{)9030}$ **87.** $132\overline{)7128}$ **88.** $204\overline{)3876}$

Section 6

Write in exponent form.

89. 13×13

90. $21 \times 21 \times 21$

91. $8 \times 8 \times 8 \times 8 \times 8$

92. $10 \times 10 \times 10 \times 10 \times 10 \times 10$

Evaluate.

93. 2^6

94. 3^4

95. 2^7

96. 5^3

97. 7^2

98. 9^2

99. 6^3

100. 4^3

Perform each operation in proper order.

101. $7 + 2 \times 3 - 5$

102. $6 \times 2 - 4 + 3$

103. $2^5 + 4 - (5 + 3^2)$

104. $4^3 + 20 \div (2 + 2^3)$

105. $34 - 9 \div 9 \times 12$

106. $2 \times 7^2 - 20 \div 1$

107. $2^3 \times 5 \div 8 + 3 \times 4$

108. $2^3 + 4 \times 5 - 32 \div (1 + 3)^2$

109. $6 \times 3 + 3 \times 5^2 - 63 \div (5 - 2)^2$

Section 7

Round to the nearest ten.

110. 3364

111. 5895

112. 15 305

113. 42 644

In exercises 114–117, round to the nearest thousand.

114. 12 350

115. 22 986

116. 675 800

117. 202 498

118. Round to the nearest hundred thousand. 4 649 320

119. Round to the nearest ten thousand. 9 995 312

Use the principle of estimation to find an estimate for each calculation.

120. $324 + 655 + 187 + 245$

121. $18\,702 + 8331 + 36\,612$

122. $4\,326\,171 - 2\,916\,788$

123. $34\,950 - 15\,439$

124. 1463 × 5982

125. 2 965 372 × 893

126. 83 421 ÷ 24

127. 876 321 ÷ 335

Section 8

Solve.

128. ***Consumer Decisions*** Professor O'Shea bought 20 dozen doughnut holes for the faculty meeting. How many doughnut holes did he buy? (There are 12 in a dozen.)

129. ***Computer Applications*** Ward can type 25 words per minute on his computer. He typed for seven minutes at that speed. How many words did he type?

130. ***Travel*** In June, 2462 people visited the Renaissance Festival. There were 1997 visitors in July, and 2561 in August. How many people visited the festival during these three months?

131. ***Farming*** Applepickers, Inc. bought a truck for \$26 300, a car for \$14 520, and a minivan for \$18 650. What was the total purchase price?

132. ***Aviation*** A plane was flying at 14 630 feet. It flew over a mountain 4329 feet high. How many feet was it from the plane to the top of the mountain?

133. ***Personal Finance*** Gerardo was billed \$4330 for tuition, and he needs to spend \$268 on books. He received a \$1250 scholarship. How much will he have to pay for tuition and books after the scholarship is deducted?

134. ***Travel*** The expedition cost a total of \$32 544 for 24 paying passengers, who shared the cost equally. What was the cost per passenger?

135. ***Business Management*** Middlebury College ordered 112 dormitory beds for \$8288. What was the cost per bed?

136. ***Personal Finance*** Melissa's savings account balance last month was \$810. The bank added \$24 interest. Melissa deposited \$105, \$36, and \$177. She made withdrawals of \$18, \$145, \$250, and \$461. What will be her balance this month?

137. ***Environmental Studies*** Ali began a trip on a full tank of gas with the car odometer at 56 320 kilometres. He ended the trip at 56 720 kilometres and added 25 litres of gas to refill the tank. How many kilometres per litre did he get on the trip?

138. ***Business Management*** The maintenance group bought three lawn mowers at \$279, four power drills at \$61, and two riding tractors at \$1980. What was the total purchase price for these items?

139. ***Business Management*** Anita is opening a new café in town. She bought 15 tables at \$65 each, 60 chairs for \$12 each, and 8 ceiling fans for \$42 each. What was the total purchase price for these items?

Environmental Protection *Use the following bar graph to answer exercises 140–142.*

140. How many more tonnes of waste were disposed in 2002 than in 1996?

141. What was the greatest increase in tonnes of waste disposed in a two-year period?

142. If the exact same increase in the number of tonnes disposed occurs from 2004 to 2008 as occurred from 2000 to 2004, how many tonnes of waste will be disposed in 2008?

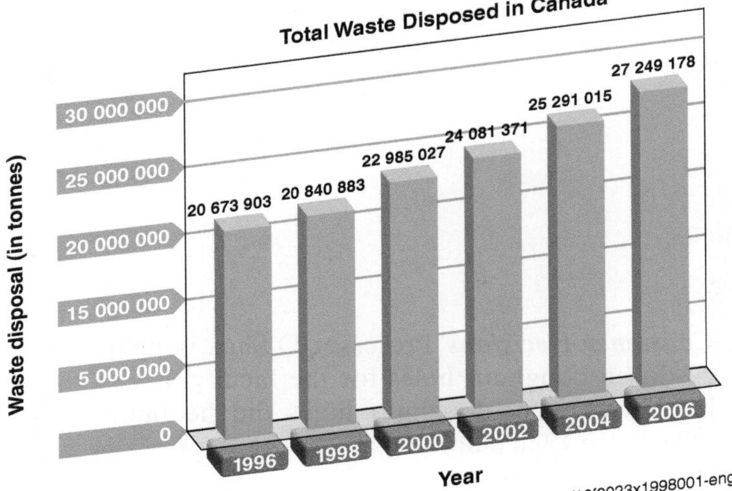

Source: Adapted from Statistics Canada, http://www.statcan.gc.ca/pub/16f0023x/16f0023x1998001-eng.pdf and http://www.statcan.gc.ca/pub/16f0023x/16f0023x2000001-eng.pdf and http://www.statcan.gc.ca/pub/16f0023x/16f0023x2004001-eng.pdf and http://www.statcan.gc.ca/pub/16f0023x/16f0023x2006001-eng.pdf, Oct-09

Mixed Practice

Perform each calculation.

143. $205 + 36 + 1983 + 60$

144. $\begin{array}{r} 56\,793 \\ -\,48\,926 \\ \hline \end{array}$

145. 396×28

146. $37\overline{)4773}$

147. Evaluate. $4 \times 12 - (12 + 9) + 2^3 \div 4$

148. ***Personal Finance*** Michael Evans has \$3000 in his chequing account. He buys 3 computers at \$699 each and 2 printers at \$78 each. How much does he have remaining after the purchases?

▲ **149.** ***Geometry*** Milton is building a rectangular patio in his backyard. The patio measures 7 metres by 5 metres.

(a) How many square metres is the patio?

(b) If Milton wanted to fence in the patio, how many metres of fence would he need?

How Am I Doing? Module Test

Write the answers.

1. Write in words. 44 007 635

2. Write in expanded notation. 26 859

3. Write in standard notation. three million, five hundred eighty-one thousand, seventy-six

Add.

4. $\begin{array}{r} 189 \\ 26 \\ 12 \\ 528 \\ +\ 76 \\ \hline \end{array}$

5. $\begin{array}{r} 763 \\ 220 \\ +508 \\ \hline \end{array}$

6. $\begin{array}{r} 135\,484 \\ 2\,376 \\ 81\,004 \\ +100\,113 \\ \hline \end{array}$

Subtract.

7. $\begin{array}{r} 8961 \\ -\ 894 \\ \hline \end{array}$

8. $\begin{array}{r} 501\,760 \\ -328\,902 \\ \hline \end{array}$

9. $\begin{array}{r} 18\,400\,100 \\ -13\,174\,332 \\ \hline \end{array}$

Multiply.

10. $1 \times 6 \times 9 \times 7$

11. $\begin{array}{r} 45 \\ \times 96 \\ \hline \end{array}$

12. $\begin{array}{r} 326 \\ \times 592 \\ \hline \end{array}$

13. $\begin{array}{r} 18{,}491 \\ \times \quad 7 \\ \hline \end{array}$

In problems 14–16, divide. If there is a remainder, be sure to state it as part of your answer.

14. $5\overline{)15\,071}$

15. $6\overline{)14\,148}$

16. $37\overline{)13\,024}$

17. Write in exponent form. $14 \times 14 \times 14$

18. Evaluate. 2^6

1. ______________________
2. ______________________
3. ______________________
4. ______________________
5. ______________________
6. ______________________
7. ______________________
8. ______________________
9. ______________________
10. ______________________
11. ______________________
12. ______________________
13. ______________________
14. ______________________
15. ______________________
16. ______________________
17. ______________________
18. ______________________

19. ____________

20. ____________

21. ____________

22. ____________

23. ____________

24. ____________

25. ____________

26. ____________

27. ____________

28. ____________

29. ____________

30. ____________

31. ____________

32. ____________

In problems 19–21, perform each operation in proper order.

19. $5 + 6^2 - 2 \times (9 - 6)^2$

20. $2^4 + 3^3 + 28 \div 4$

21. $4 \times 6 + 3^3 \times 2 + 23 \div 23$

22. Round to the nearest hundred. 94 768

23. Round to the nearest ten thousand. 6 462 431

24. Round to the nearest hundred thousand. 5 278 963

Estimate the answer.

25. $4\,867\,010 \times 27\,058$

26. $1423 + 3298 + 4103 + 7614$

Solve.

27. A cruise for 15 people costs $32 220. If each person paid the same amount, how much will it cost each individual?

28. The river is 201 metres wide at Big Bend Corner. A boy is in the shallow water, 35 metres from the shore. How far is the boy from the other side of the river?

29. At the bookstore, Hector bought three notebooks at $2 each, one textbook for $45, two lamps at $21 each, and two sweatshirts at $17 each. What was his total bill?

30. Patricia is looking at her chequebook. She had a balance last month of $31. She deposited $902 and $399. She made out cheques for $885, $103, $26, $17, and $9. What will be her new balance?

▲ **31.** The runway at Beverly Airport needs to be resurfaced. The rectangular runway is 2200 metres long and 30 metres wide. What is the area of the runway that needs to be resurfaced?

▲ **32.** Nancy Tobey planted a vegetable garden in the backyard. However, the deer and raccoons have been stealing all the vegetables. She asked John to fence in the garden. The rectangular garden measures 8 metres by 15 metres. How many metres of fence should John purchase if he wants to enclose the garden?

Solutions to Practice Problems

Section 1 Practice Problems

1. (a) $3182 = 3000 + 100 + 80 + 2$
   (b) $520\,890 = 500\,000 + 20\,000 + 800 + 90$
   (c) $709\,680\,059 = 700\,000\,000 + 9\,000\,000 + 600\,000 + 80\,000 + 50 + 9$
2. (a) 492 (b) 80 427
3. (a) 7 (b) 9 (c) 4000
   (d) 900 000 for the first 9; 9 for the last 9
4. two hundred sixty-seven million, three hundred fifty-eight thousand, nine hundred eighty-one
5. (a) two thousand, seven hundred thirty-six
   (b) nine hundred eighty thousand, three hundred six
   (c) twelve million, twenty-one
6. The world population on January 1, 2004, was six billion, three hundred ninety-three million, six hundred forty-six thousand, five hundred twenty-five.
7. (a) 803 (b) 30 229
8. (a) 758 000 (b) 103 000 (c) 62 000

Section 2 Practice Problems

1. (a) $7 + 5 = 12$ (b) $9 + 4 = 13$ (c) $3 + 0 = 3$
2. 7, 6, 5, 8, +2 = 28
   $7 + 6 = 13$
   $13 + 5 = 18$
   $18 + 8 = 26$
   $26 + 2 = 28$
3. 1, 7, 2, 9, +3 = 22
   (1 + 9 = 10; 7 + 3 = 10)
4. $8246 + 1702 = 9948$
5. $56 + 36 = 92$ (carry 1)
6. $789 + 63 + 297 = 1149$ (carries 2 1)
7. (a) $127 + 9\,876 + 342 = 10\,345$ (carries 1 1 1)
   (b) Check by adding in opposite order. $342 + 9\,876 + 127 = 10\,345$ — same
8. $18\,316 + 24\,789 + 22\,965 = 66\,070$ total women (carries 1 2 1 2)
9. $100 + 200 + 100 + 200 = 600$ m

Section 3 Practice Problems

1. (a) $9 - 6 = 3$ (b) $12 - 5 = 7$ (c) $17 - 8 = 9$ (d) $14 - 0 = 14$ (e) $18 - 9 = 9$
2. $7695 - 3481 = 4214$
3. $34 - 16 = 18$ (3 4 borrowed as 2 14)
4. $693 - 426 = 267$ (9 3 borrowed as 8 13)
5. $9078 - 5886 = 3184$ (9 0 7 8 borrowed as 8 9 16 10)
6. (a) $8964 - 985 = 7979$ (b) $50\,000 - 32\,508 = 17\,492$
7. Subtraction: $9763 - 5732 = 4031$
   Checking by addition: $5732 + 4031 = 9763$ IT CHECKS
8. (a) $284\,000 - 96\,327 = 187\,673$
   Checking by addition: $96\,327 + 187\,673 = 284\,000$ IT CHECKS
   (b) $8\,526\,024 - 6\,397\,518 = 2\,128\,506$
   Checking by addition: $6\,397\,518 + 2\,128\,506 = 8\,526\,024$ IT CHECKS
9. (a) $17 = 12 + x$
   $17 - 12 = x$
   $5 = x$
   5 vessels left in the afternoon.
   (b) $22 = 10 + x$
   $22 - 10 = x$
   $12 = x$
   12 hikers were still on the mountain.
10. (a) $3\,724\,500 - 909\,282 = 2\,815\,218$ (b) $909\,282 - 899\,942 = 9\,340$
11. (a) From the bar graph:
    2008 sales 114
    2007 sales − 78
    Sales increase 36
    (b) From the bar graph:
    Springfield 91
    Riverside − 78
    13 more homes
    (c) 2008 sales 271, 2007 sales − 240 = 31
    2009 sales 284, 2008 sales − 271 = 13
    Therefore, the greatest increase in sales occurred from 2007 to 2008.

Section 4 Practice Problems

1. (a) $\begin{array}{r} 8 \\ \times\ 8 \\ \hline 64 \end{array}$ **(b)** $\begin{array}{r} 7 \\ \times\ 6 \\ \hline 42 \end{array}$ **(c)** $\begin{array}{r} 5 \\ \times\ 8 \\ \hline 40 \end{array}$ **(d)** $\begin{array}{r} 9 \\ \times\ 7 \\ \hline 63 \end{array}$ **(e)** $\begin{array}{r} 9 \\ \times\ 9 \\ \hline 81 \end{array}$

2. $\begin{array}{r} 3021 \\ \times\ 3 \\ \hline 9063 \end{array}$

3. $\begin{array}{r} \overset{2}{4}3 \\ \times 8 \\ \hline 344 \end{array}$

4. $\begin{array}{r} \overset{5}{5}\overset{6}{7}9 \\ \times\ 7 \\ \hline 4053 \end{array}$

5. (a) $1267 \times 10 = 12\,670$ (one zero)
(b) $1267 \times 1000 = 1\,267\,000$ (three zeros)
(c) $1267 \times 10\,000 = 12\,670\,000$ (four zeros)
(d) $1267 \times 1\,000\,000 = 1\,267\,000\,000$ (six zeros)

6. (a) $9 \times 60\,000 = 9 \times 6 \times 10\,000 = 54 \times 10\,000 = 540\,000$
(b) $15 \times 400 = 15 \times 4 \times 100 = 60 \times 100 = 6000$
(c) $270 \times 800 = 27 \times 8 \times 10 \times 100 = 216 \times 1000 = 216\,000$

7. $\begin{array}{r} 323 \\ \times\ 32 \\ \hline 646 \\ 9690 \\ \hline 10\,336 \end{array}$

8. $\begin{array}{r} 385 \\ \times\ 69 \\ \hline 3465 \\ 23100 \\ \hline 26\,565 \end{array}$

9. $\begin{array}{r} 34 \\ \times\ 20 \\ \hline 0 \\ 680 \\ \hline 680 \end{array}$

10. $\begin{array}{r} 130 \\ \times\ 50 \\ \hline 0 \\ 6500 \\ \hline 6500 \end{array}$

11. $\begin{array}{r} 923 \\ \times\ 675 \\ \hline 4615 \\ 6461 \\ 5538 \\ \hline 623\,025 \end{array}$

12. $25 \times 4 \times 17 = (25 \times 4) \times 17 = 100 \times 17 = 1700$

13. $8 \times 4 \times 3 \times 25 = 8 \times 3 \times 4 \times 25$
$= 8 \times 3 \times (4 \times 25)$
$= 24 \times 100$
$= 2400$

14. $\begin{array}{r} 17\,348 \\ \times\ 378 \\ \hline 138\,784 \\ 1\,214\,36 \\ 5\,204\,4 \\ \hline 6\,557\,544 \end{array}$

The total sales of cars was \$6 557 544.

15. Area = 5 yards × 7 yards = 35 square yards.

Section 5 Practice Problems

1. (a) $4\overline{)36}$ with quotient 9 **(b)** $5\overline{)25}$ with quotient 5 **(c)** $9\overline{)72}$ with quotient 8 **(d)** $6\overline{)30}$ with quotient 5

2. (a) $\frac{7}{1} = 7$ **(b)** $\frac{9}{9} = 1$ **(c)** $\frac{0}{5} = 0$ **(d)** $\frac{12}{0}$ cannot be done

3. $\begin{array}{r} 7\text{ R }3 \\ 6\overline{)45} \\ 42 \\ \hline 3 \end{array}$ *Check* $\begin{array}{r} 6 \\ \times 7 \\ \hline 42 \\ +\ 3 \\ \hline 45 \end{array}$

4. $\begin{array}{r} 21\text{ R }3 \\ 6\overline{)129} \\ 12 \\ \hline 9 \\ 6 \\ \hline 3 \end{array}$ *Check* $\begin{array}{r} 21 \\ \times\ 6 \\ \hline 126 \\ +\ 3 \\ \hline 129 \end{array}$

5. $\begin{array}{r} 529\text{ R }5 \\ 8\overline{)4237} \\ 40 \\ \hline 23 \\ 16 \\ \hline 77 \\ 72 \\ \hline 5 \end{array}$

6. $\begin{array}{r} 7\text{ R }19 \\ 32\overline{)243} \\ 224 \\ \hline 19 \end{array}$

7. $\begin{array}{r} 1\,278\text{ R }9 \\ 33\overline{)42\,183} \\ 33 \\ \hline 91 \\ 66 \\ \hline 258 \\ 231 \\ \hline 273 \\ 264 \\ \hline 9 \end{array}$

8. $\begin{array}{r} 25\text{ R }27 \\ 128\overline{)3227} \\ 256 \\ \hline 667 \\ 640 \\ \hline 27 \end{array}$

9. $\begin{array}{r} 16\,852 \\ 7\overline{)117\,964} \end{array}$ *Check* $\begin{array}{r} 16\,852 \\ \times\quad 7 \\ \hline 117\,964 \end{array}$

The cost of one car is \$16 852.

10. $\begin{array}{r} 367 \\ 14\overline{)5138} \end{array}$ The average speed was 367 km/h.

Section 6 Practice Problems

1. (a) $12 \times 12 \times 12 \times 12 = 12^4$
(b) $2 \times 2 \times 2 \times 2 \times 2 \times 2 = 2^6$

2. (a) $12^2 = 12 \times 12 = 144$
(b) $6^3 = 6 \times 6 \times 6 = 216$
(c) $2^6 = 2 \times 2 \times 2 \times 2 \times 2 \times 2 = 64$
(d) $1^{10} = 1 \times 1 \times 1 \times 1 \times 1 \times 1 \times 1 \times 1 \times 1 \times 1 = 1$

3. **(a)** $7^3 + 8^2 = (7)(7)(7) + (8)(8) = 343 + 64 = 407$
(b) $9^2 + 6^0 = (9)(9) + 1 = 81 + 1 = 82$
(c) $5^4 + 5 = (5)(5)(5)(5) + 5 = 625 + 5 = 630$

4. $7 + 4^3 \times 3 = 7 + 64 \times 3$ Exponents
$= 7 + 192$ Multiply
$= 199$ Add

5. $37 - 20 \div 5 + 2 - 3 \times 4$
$= 37 - 4 + 2 - 3 \times 4$ Divide
$= 37 - 4 + 2 - 12$ Multiply
$= 33 + 2 - 12$ Subtract
$= 35 - 12$ Add
$= 23$ Subtract

6. $4^3 - 2 + 3^2$
$= 4 \times 4 \times 4 - 2 + 3 \times 3$ Evaluate exponents.
$= 64 - 2 + 9$ $4^3 = 64$ and $3^2 = 9$.
$= 62 + 9$ Subtract
$= 71$ Add

7. $(17 + 7) \div 6 \times 2 + 7 \times 3 - 4$
$= 24 \div 6 \times 2 + 7 \times 3 - 4$ Combine inside parentheses
$= 4 \times 2 + 7 \times 3 - 4$ Divide
$= 8 + 7 \times 3 - 4$ Multiply
$= 8 + 21 - 4$ Multiply
$= 29 - 4$ Add
$= 25$ Subtract

8. $5^2 - 6 \div 2 + 3^4 + 7 \times (12 - 10)$
$= 5^2 - 6 \div 2 + 3^4 + 7 \times 2$ Combine inside parentheses
$= 25 - 6 \div 2 + 81 + 7 \times 2$ Exponents
$= 25 - 3 + 81 + 7 \times 2$ Divide
$= 25 - 3 + 81 + 14$ Multiply
$= 22 + 81 + 14$ Subtract
$= 103 + 14$ Add
$= 117$ Add

Section 7 Practice Problems

1. 6↓5 528 — Locate the thousands round-off place.

6 5 ⑤2 8 — The first digit to the right is 5 or more. We will increase the thousands digit by 1.

66 000 — All digits to the right of the thousands place are replaced by zeros.

2. 17②963 = 170 000 to the nearest ten thousand.

3. **(a)** 53 282 = 53 280 to the nearest ten. The digit to the right of the tens place was less than 5.
(b) 164 485 = 164 000 to the nearest thousand. The digit to the right of the thousands place was less than 5.
(c) 1 365 273 = 1 400 000 to the nearest hundred thousand. The digit to the right of the hundred thousands place was greater than 5.

4. **(a)** 935 682 = 936 000 to the nearest thousand. The digit to the right of the thousands place is greater than 5.
(b) 935 682 = 900 000 to the nearest hundred thousand. The digit to the right of the hundred thousands place is less than 5.
(c) 935 682 = 1 000 000 to the nearest million. The digit to the right of the millions place is greater than 5.

5. 9 460 000 000 000 000 metres = 9 500 000 000 000 000 metres to the nearest hundred trillion metres.

6.

Actual Sum	Estimated Sum	
3 456	3 000	
9 876	10 000	
5 421	5 000	
+ 1 278	+ 1 000	
20 031	19 000	Close to the actual sum

7.

\$697	\$700
35	40
+ 19	+ 20
	\$760

We estimate that the total cost is \$760. (The exact answer is \$751, so we can see that our answer is quite close.)

8. Estimate: 10 000 + 10 000 + 20 000 + 60 000 = 100 000
This is significantly different from 81 358, so we would suspect that an error has been made. In fact, Ming did make an error. The exact sum is actually 101 358!

9. Estimate: 13 000 000 − 4 000 000 = 9 000 000
We estimate that 9 000 000 more people lived in Ontario than in British Columbia.

10. Estimate: 9000 × 7000 = 63 000 000
We estimate the product to be 63 000 000.

11. $40\overline{)80\,000}$ = 2000. Our estimate is 2000.

12. $60\overline{)2\,000\,000}$ = 33 333 R 20. Our estimate is \$33 333 for one truck.

Section 8 Practice Problems

Practice Problem 1

1. Understand the problem.

Mathematics Blueprint for Problem Solving

Gather the Facts	What Am I Asked to Do?	How Do I Proceed?	Key Points to Remember
The deductions are \$135, \$28, \$13, and \$34.	Find out the total amount of deductions.	I must add the four deductions to obtain the total.	Watch out! Gross pay of \$1352 is not needed to solve the problem.

2. Solve and state the answer:
135 + 28 + 13 + 34 = 210
The total amount taken out of Diane's paycheque is \$210.

3. ***Check.*** Estimate to see if the answer is reasonable.

Practice Problem 2

1. Understand the problem.

Mathematics Blueprint for Problem Solving			
Gather the Facts	**What Am I Asked to Do?**	**How Do I Proceed?**	**Key Points to Remember**
The Conservative Party had 5 209 069 votes. The Liberal Party had 3 633 185 votes.	Find out by how many votes the Conservative Party beat the Liberal Party.	I must subtract the amounts.	The other political party votes are not needed for this question.

2. Solve and state the answer:

$$\begin{array}{r} 5\,209\,069 \\ -\ 3\,633\,185 \\ \hline 1\,575\,884 \end{array}$$

The Conservative Party beat the Liberal Party by 1 575 884 votes..

3. ***Check.*** Estimate to see if the answer is reasonable.

Practice Problem 3

1. Understand the problem.

Mathematics Blueprint for Problem Solving			
Gather the Facts	**What Am I Asked to Do?**	**How Do I Proceed?**	**Key Points to Remember**
1 litre is 1000 millilitres.	Find out how many millilitres are in 9 litres.	I need to multiply 1000 by 9.	I must use millilitres as the measure in my answer.

2. Solve and state the answer:

$$\begin{array}{r} 1000 \\ \times\quad 9 \\ \hline 9000 \end{array}$$

There are 9000 millilitres in 9 litres.

3. ***Check.*** Estimate to see if the answer is reasonable.

Practice Problem 4

1. Understand the problem.

Mathematics Blueprint for Problem Solving			
Gather the Facts	**What Am I Asked to Do?**	**How Do I Proceed?**	**Key Points to Remember**
Donna bought 45 shares of stock. She paid $1620 for them.	Find out the cost per share of stock.	I need to divide 1620 by 45.	Use dollars as the unit in the answer.

2. Solve and state the answer:

$$\begin{array}{r} 36 \\ 45\overline{)1620} \\ \underline{135} \\ 270 \\ \underline{270} \\ 0 \end{array}$$

Donna paid $36 per share for the stock.

3. ***Check.*** Estimate to see if the answer is reasonable.

Practice Problem 5

1. Understand the problem. We will make an imaginary bill of sale.
2. Solve and state the answer. We do the calculation and enter the results in the bill of sale.

Customer: Anderson Dining Commons			
Quantity	**Item**	**Cost per Item**	**Amount for This Item**
50 180 6	Tables Chairs Moving Carts	\$200 \$ 40 \$ 65	\$10 000 (50 × \$200 = \$10 000) \$ 7200 (180 × \$40 = \$7200) \$ 390 (6 × \$65 = \$390)
		Total	\$17 590 (sum of the three amounts)

The total cost of purchase was \$17 590.

3. ***Check.*** Estimate to see if the answer is reasonable.

Practice Problem 6

1. Understand the problem.

Mathematics Blueprint for Problem Solving			
Gather the Facts	**What Am I Asked to Do?**	**How Do I Proceed?**	**Key Points to Remember**
Old balance: \$498 New deposits: \$607 \$163 Interest: \$36 Withdrawals: \$ 19 \$158 \$582 \$ 74	Find her new balance after the transactions.	**(a)** Add the new deposits and interest to the old balance. **(b)** Add the withdrawals. **(c)** Subtract the results from steps (a) and (b).	Deposits and interest are added and withdrawals are subtracted from savings accounts.

2. Solve and state the answer:

(a) $\begin{array}{r} 498 \\ 607 \\ 163 \\ +\ 36 \\ \hline 1304 \end{array}$ **(b)** $\begin{array}{r} 19 \\ 158 \\ 582 \\ +\ 74 \\ \hline 833 \end{array}$ **(c)** $\begin{array}{r} 1304 \\ -\ 833 \\ \hline 471 \end{array}$

Her balance this month is \$471.

3. ***Check.*** Estimate to see if the answer is reasonable.

Practice Problem 7

1. Understand the problem.

Mathematics Blueprint for Problem Solving			
Gather the Facts	**What Am I Asked to Do?**	**How Do I Proceed?**	**Key Points to Remember**
Odometer reading at end of trip: 51 118 kilometres Odometer reading at start of trip: 50 698 kilometres Used on trip: 42 litres of gas	Find the number of kilometres per litre that the car obtained on the trip.	**(a)** Subtract the two odometer readings. **(b)** Divide that number by 42.	The gas tank was full at the beginning of the trip. 42 litres fills the tank at the end of the trip.

2. Solve and state the answer:

$\begin{array}{rl} 51\,118 & \text{odometer at end of trip} \\ -\ 50\,698 & \text{odometer at start of trip} \\ \hline 420 & \text{kilometres travelled on trip} \end{array}$ $\dfrac{420 \text{ kilometres}}{42 \text{ litres of gas used}}$

$$\begin{array}{r} 10 \\ 42\overline{)420} \\ 42 \\ \hline 0 \end{array}$$

10 kilometres per litre on the trip

3. ***Check.*** Estimate to see if the answer is reasonable.

Glossary

Addends (Section 2) When two or more numbers are added, the numbers being added are called addends. In the problem $3 + 4 = 7$, the numbers 3 and 4 are both addends.

Associative property of addition (Section 2) The property that tells us that when three numbers are added, it does not matter which two numbers are added first. An example of the associative property is $5 + (1 + 2) = (5 + 1) + 2$. Whether we add $1 + 2$ first and then add 5 to that, or add $5 + 1$ first and then add that result to 2, we will obtain the same result.

Associative property of multiplication (Section 4) The property that tells us that when we multiply three numbers, it does not matter which two numbers we group together first to multiply; the result will be the same. An example of the associative property of multiplication follows: $2 \times (5 \times 3) = (2 \times 5) \times 3$.

Base (Section 6) The number that is to be repeatedly multiplied in exponent form. When we write $16 = 2^4$, the number 2 is the base.

Billion (Section 1) The number 1 000 000 000.

Borrowing (Section 3) The renaming of a number in order to facilitate subtraction. When we subtract $42 - 28$, we rename 42 as 3 tens plus 12. This represents 3 tens and 12 ones. This renaming is called borrowing.

Commutative property of addition (Section 2) The property that tells us that the order in which two numbers are added does not change the sum. An example of the commutative property of addition is $3 + 6 = 6 + 3$.

Commutative property of multiplication (Section 4) The property that tells us that the order in which two numbers are multiplied does not change the value of the answer. An example of the commutative property of multiplication is $7 \times 3 = 3 \times 7$.

Debit (Section 2) A debit in banking is a removal of money from an account. If you had a savings account and took $300 out of it on Wednesday, we would say that you had a debit of $300 from your account. Often a bank will add a service charge to your account and use the word *debit* to mean that it has removed money from your account to cover the charge.

Decimal system (Section 1) Our number system is called the decimal system or base 10 system because the value of numbers written in our system is based on tens and ones.

Deposit (Section 2) A deposit in banking is the placing of money in an account. If you had a chequing account and on Tuesday you placed $124 into that account, we would say that you made a deposit of $124.

Difference (Section 3) The result of performing a subtraction. In the problem $9 - 2 = 7$ the number 7 is the difference.

Digits (Section 1) The symbols 0, 1, 2, 3, 4, 5, 6, 7, 8, and 9 are called digits.

Distributive property of multiplication over addition (Section 4) The property illustrated by the following: $5 \times (4 + 3) = (5 \times 4) + (5 \times 3)$. In general, for any numbers a, b, and c, it is true that $a(b + c) = a \times b + a \times c$.

Dividend (Section 5) The number that is being divided by another. In the problem $14 \div 7 = 2$, the number 14 is the dividend.

Divisor (Section 5) The number that you divide into another number. In the problem $30 \div 5 = 6$, the number 5 is the divisor.

Expanded notation for a number (Section 1) A number is written in expanded notation if it is written as a sum of hundreds, tens, ones, etc. The expanded notation for 763 is $700 + 60 + 3$.

Exponent (Section 6) The number that indicates the number of times a factor occurs. When we write $8 = 2^3$, the number 3 is the exponent.

Factors (Section 4) Each of the numbers that are multiplied. In the problem $8 \times 9 = 72$, the numbers 8 and 9 are factors.

Million (Section 1) The number 1 000 000.

Minuend (Section 3) The number being subtracted from in a subtraction problem. In the problem $8 - 5 = 3$, the number 8 is the minuend.

Multiplicand (Section 4) The first factor in a multiplication problem. In the problem $7 \times 2 = 14$, the number 7 is the multiplicand.

Multiplier (Section 4) The second factor in a multiplication problem. In the problem $6 \times 3 = 18$, the number 3 is the multiplier.

Number line (Section 7) A line on which numbers are placed in order from smallest to largest.

Odometer (Section 8) A device on an automobile that displays how many kilometres the car has been driven since it was first put into operation.

Order of operations (Section 6) An agreed-upon procedure to do a problem with several arithmetic operations in the proper order.

Parentheses (Section 4) One of several symbols used in mathematics to indicate multiplication. For example, (3)(5) means 3 multiplied by 5. Parentheses are also used as a grouping symbol.

Placeholder (Section 1) The use of a digit to indicate a place. Zero is a placeholder in our number system. It holds a position and shows that there is no other digit in that place.

Place-value system (Section 1) Our number system is called a place-value system because the placement of the digits tells the value of the number. If we use the digits 5 and 4 to write the number 54, the result is different than if we placed them in opposite order and wrote 45.

Power of 10 (Section 4) Whole numbers that begin with 1 and end in one or more zeros are called powers of 10. The numbers 10, 100, 1000, etc., are all powers of 10.

Product (Section 4) The answer in a multiplication problem. In the problem $3 \times 4 = 12$ the number 12 is the product.

Quadrillion (Section 1) The number 1 000 000 000 000 000.

Quotient (Section 5) The answer after performing a division problem. In the problem $60 \div 6 = 10$ the number 10 is the quotient.

Remainder (Section 5) When two numbers do not divide exactly, a part is left over. This part is called the remainder. For example, $13 \div 2 = 6$ with 1 left over; the 1 is the remainder.

Rounding (Section 7) The process of writing a number in an approximate form for convenience. The number 9756 rounded to the nearest hundred is 9800.

Standard notation for a number (Section 1) A number written in ordinary terms. For example, $70 + 2$ in standard notation is 72.

Subtrahend (Section 3) The number being subtracted. In the problem $7 - 1 = 6$, the number 1 is the subtrahend.

Sum (Section 2) The result of an addition of two or more numbers. In the problem $7 + 3 + 5 = 15$, the number 15 is the sum.

Trillion (Section 1) The number 1 000 000 000 000.

Whole numbers (Section 1) The whole numbers are the set of numbers 0, 1, 2, 3, 4, 5, 6, 7, 8, 9, 10, 11, 12, ... The set goes on forever. There is no largest whole number.

Word names for whole numbers (Section 1) The notation for a number in which each digit is expressed by a word. To write 389 with a word name, we would write three hundred eighty-nine.

Zero (Section 1) The smallest whole number. It is normally written 0.

Answers to Selected Exercises for Whole Numbers

Answers to Selected Exercises for Whole Numbers

Section 1 Exercises **1.** 6000 + 700 + 30 + 1 **3.** 100 000 + 8000 + 200 + 70 + 6 **5.** 20 000 000 + 3 000 000 + 700 000 + 60 000 + 1000 + 300 + 40 + 5 **7.** 100 000 000 + 3 000 000 + 200 000 + 60 000 + 700 + 60 + 8 **9.** 671 **11.** 9863 **13.** 40 885 **15.** 706 200 **17.** **(a)** 7 **(b)** 30 000 **19.** **(a)** 2 **(b)** 200 000 **21.** one hundred forty-two **23.** nine thousand, three hundred four **25.** thirty-six thousand, one hundred eighteen **27.** one hundred five thousand, two hundred sixty-one **29.** fourteen million, two hundred three thousand, three hundred twenty-six **31.** four billion, three hundred two million, one hundred fifty-six thousand, two hundred **33.** 1561 **35.** 33 809 **37.** 100 079 826 **39.** one thousand, nine hundred sixty-five **41.** 3 million or 3 000 000 **43.** 8 million or 8 000 000 **45.** 930 000 **47.** 52 566 000 **49.** **(a)** 5 **(b)** 2 **51.** **(a)** 96 566 366 **(b)** 9 **53.** 613 001 033 208 003 **55.** three quintillion, six hundred eighty-two quadrillion, nine hundred sixty-eight trillion, nine billion, nine hundred thirty-one million, nine hundred sixty thousand, seven hundred forty-seven **57.** You would obtain 2 E 20. This is 200 000 000 000 000 000 000 in standard form.

Quick Quiz 1 **1.** 70 000 + 3000 + 900 + 50 + 2 **2.** eight million, nine hundred thirty-two thousand, four hundred seventy-five **3.** 964 257 **4.** See Instructor

Section 2 Exercises **1.** **(a)** You can change the order of the addends without changing the sum. **(b)** You can group the addends in any way without changing the sum.

3.

+	3	5	4	8	0	6	7	2	9	1
2	5	7	6	10	2	8	9	4	11	3
7	10	12	11	15	7	13	14	9	16	8
5	8	10	9	13	5	11	12	7	14	6
3	6	8	7	11	3	9	10	5	12	4
0	3	5	4	8	0	6	7	2	9	1
4	7	9	8	12	4	10	11	6	13	5
1	4	6	5	9	1	7	8	3	10	2
8	11	13	12	16	8	14	15	10	17	9
6	9	11	10	14	6	12	13	8	15	7
9	12	14	13	17	9	15	16	11	18	10

5. 23 **7.** 26 **9.** 57 **11.** 99 **13.** 4125 **15.** 9994 **17.** 13 861 **19.** 117 240 **21.** 121 **23.** 1143 **25.** 10 130 **27.** 11 579 426 **29.** 1 135 280 240 **31.** 2 303 820 **33.** 300 **35.** 335 **37.** $723 **39.** $5549 **41.** 156 metres **43.** 313 649 000 km^2 **45.** 15 485 918 m **47.** **(a)** 1134 students **(b)** 1392 students **49.** 202 kilometres **51.** 434 feet **53.** **(a)** $9553 **(b)** $7319 **(c)** $13 047 **55.** 1161 **57.** Answers may vary. A sample is: You could not group the addends in groups that sum to 10s to make column addition easier.

Quick Quiz 2 **1.** 212 **2.** 1615 **3.** 1 004 811 **4.** See Instructor

Section 3 Exercises **1.** In subtraction the minuend minus the subtrahead equals the difference. To check the problem, we add the subtrahead and the difference to see if we get the minuend. If we do, the answer is correct. **3.** We know that 1683 + 1592 = 32?5. Therefore if we add 8 tens and 9 tens we get 17 tens, which is 1 hundred and 7 tens. Thus the ? should be replaced by 7. **5.** 5 **7.** 6 **9.** 16 **11.** 9 **13.** 7 **15.** 6 **17.** 3 **19.** 9

21. 21; check: 26 + 21 = 47 **23.** 12; check: 73 + 12 = 85 **25.** 343; check: 36 + 343 = 379 **27.** 321; check: 548 + 321 = 869 **29.** 4203; check: 596 + 4203 = 4799 **31.** 143 235; check: 12 600 + 143 235 = 155 835 **33.** 553 101; check: 433 201 + 553 101 = 986 302

35. 19 + 110 = 129 Correct **37.** 3215 + 5781 = 8996 Incorrect Correct answer: 5381 **39.** 5020 + 1020 = 6040 Incorrect Correct answer: 1010 **41.** 33 846 + 13 023 = 46 869 Incorrect Correct answer: 14 023 **43.** 46 **45.** 92 **47.** 384

49. 718 **51.** 10 715 **53.** 34 092 **55.** 7447 **57.** 908 930 **59.** $x = 5$ **61.** $x = 8$ **63.** $x = 27$ **65.** 1 260 024 votes **67.** 6 543 635 **69.** $762 **71.** 41 573 people **73.** 6 447 390 people **75.** 656 472 people **77.** 557 787 people **79.** 93 homes **81.** 13 homes **83.** between 2006 and 2007 **85.** Willow Creek and Harvey **87.** It is true if a and b represent the same number, for example, if $a = 10$ and $b = 10$. **89.** $550

Quick Quiz 3 **1.** 4454 **2.** 222 933 **3.** 5 638 122 **4.** See Instructor

Section 4 Exercises **1. (a)** You can change the order of the factors without changing the product. **(b)** You can group the factors in any way without changing the product.

3.

×	6	2	3	8	0	5	7	9	12	4
5	30	10	15	40	0	25	35	45	60	20
7	42	14	21	56	0	35	49	63	84	28
1	6	2	3	8	0	5	7	9	12	4
0	0	0	0	0	0	0	0	0	0	0
6	36	12	18	48	0	30	42	54	72	24
2	12	4	6	16	0	10	14	18	24	8
3	18	6	9	24	0	15	21	27	36	12
8	48	16	24	64	0	40	56	72	96	32
4	24	8	12	32	0	20	28	36	48	16
9	54	18	27	72	0	45	63	81	108	36

5. 96 **7.** 70 **9.** 522 **11.** 693 **13.** 1932 **15.** 18 306 **17.** 36 609 **19.** 31 308 **21.** 100 208 **23.** 3 101 409 **25.** 1560 **27.** 2 715 800 **29.** 482 000 **31.** 372 560 000 **33.** 8460 **35.** 63 600 **37.** 56 000 000 **39.** 6168 **41.** 7884 **43.** 5696 **45.** 15 175 **47.** 20 672 **49.** 69 312 **51.** 148 567 **53.** 823 823 **55.** 1 881 810 **57.** 89 496 **59.** 217 980 **61.** 2 653 296 **63.** 720 000 **65.** 10 000 **67.** 90 600 **69.** 70 **71.** 308 **73.** 13 596 **75.** 1600 **77.** $x = 0$ **79.** 384 square feet **81.** 23 square metres **83.** \$3600 **85.** \$3192 **87.** 252 kilometres **89.** \$5040 **91.** \$7 372 300 000 **93.** 198 **95.** 62 **97.** $x = 8$ **99.** $x = 9$ **101.** No, it would not always be true. In our number system 62 = 60 + 2. But in Roman numerals IV ≠ I + V. The digit system in Roman numerals involves subtraction. Thus (XII) × (IV) ≠ (XII × I) + (XII × V).

Quick Quiz 4 **1.** 174 930 **2.** 5056 **3.** 207 306 **4.** See Instructor

Section 5 Exercises **1. (a)** When you divide a nonzero number by itself, the result is one. **(b)** When you divide a number by 1, the result is that number. **(c)** When you divide zero by a nonzero number, the result is zero. **(d)** You cannot divide a number by zero. Division by zero is undefined. **3.** 7 **5.** 3 **7.** 5 **9.** 4 **11.** 3 **13.** 6 **15.** 9 **17.** 9 **19.** 6 **21.** 9 **23.** 0 **25.** undefined **27.** 0 **29.** 1 **31.** 4 R 5 **33.** 9 R 4 **35.** 25 R 3 **37.** 21 R 7 **39.** 32 **41.** 37 **43.** 322 R 1 **45.** 127 R 1 **47.** 563 **49.** 1122 R 1 **51.** 2056 R 2 **53.** 2562 R 3 **55.** 30 R 5 **57.** 5 R 7 **59.** 7 **61.** 418 R 8 **63.** 48 R 12 **65.** 845 **67.** 210 R 8 **69.** 14 R 2 **71.** 4 R 4 **73.** 125 **75.** 37 **77.** 61 693 runs per day **79.** \$288 **81.** \$21 053 **83.** \$245 **85.** 165 sandwiches **87. (a)** 41 808 km **(b)** 8192 km **89.** a and b must represent the same number. For example, if $a = 12$, then $b = 12$.

Quick Quiz 5 **1.** 467 **2.** 3287 R 3 **3.** 328 **4.** See Instructor

How Am I Doing? Sections 1–5

1. seventy-eight million, three hundred ten thousand, four hundred thirty-six. (obj. 1.3) **2.** 30 000 + 8000 + 200 + 40 + 7 (obj. 1.1) **3.** 5 064 122 (obj. 1.2) **4.** 228 000 (obj. 1.4) **5.** 217 000 (obj. 1.4) **6.** 244 (obj. 2.4) **7.** 50 570 (obj. 2.4) **8.** 1 351 461 (obj. 2.4) **9.** 3993 (obj. 3.3) **10.** 76 311 (obj. 3.3) **11.** 1 981 652 (obj. 3.3) **12.** 108 (obj. 4.1) **13.** 100 000 (obj. 4.4) **14.** 18 606 (obj. 4.2) **15.** 3740 (obj. 4.4) **16.** 331 420 (obj. 4.4) **17.** 10 605 (obj. 5.2) **18.** 7376 R 1 (obj. 5.2) **19.** 26 R 8 (obj. 5.3) **20.** 139 (obj. 5.3)

Section 6 Exercises **1.** 5^3 means $5 \times 5 \times 5$. $5^3 = 125$. **3.** base
5. To ensure consistency we
  1. perform operations inside parentheses
  2. simplify any expressions with exponents
  3. multiply or divide from left to right
  4. add or subtract from left to right

7. 6^4 **9.** 5^6 **11.** 9^4 **13.** 9^1 **15.** 16 **17.** 64 **19.** 36 **21.** 10 000 **23.** 1 **25.** 64 **27.** 243 **29.** 225 **31.** 343 **33.** 256 **35.** 1 **37.** 625 **39.** 1 000 000 **41.** 169 **43.** 9 **45.** 64 **47.** 10 **49.** 108 **51.** 520 **53.** $90 - 35 = 55$ **55.** $27 - 5 = 22$ **57.** $48 \div 8 + 4 = 6 + 4 = 10$ **59.** $3 \times 36 - 50 = 108 - 50 = 58$ **61.** $100 + 3 \times 5 = 100 + 15 = 115$ **63.** $20 \div 20 = 1$ **65.** $950 \div 5 = 190$ **67.** $60 - 17 = 43$ **69.** $9 + 16 \div 4 = 9 + 4 = 13$ **71.** $42 - 4 \div 4 = 42 - 1 = 41$ **73.** $100 - 9 \times 4 = 100 - 36 = 64$ **75.** $25 + 4 + 27 = 56$ **77.** $8 \times 3 \times 1 \div 2 = 24 \div 2 = 12$ **79.** $144 - 0 = 144$ **81.** $16 \times 6 \div 3 = 96 \div 3 = 32$ **83.** $60 - 40 + 10 = 20 + 10 = 30$ **85.** $3 + 9 \times 6 + 4 = 3 + 54 + 4 = 61$ **87.** $32 \div 2 \times 16 = 16 \times 16 = 256$ **89.** $9 \times 6 \div 9 + 4 \times 3 = 6 + 12 = 18$ **91.** $36 + 1 + 8 = 45$ **93.** $1200 - 8(3) \div 6 = 1200 - 4 = 1196$ **95.** $120 \div 40 - 1 = 3 - 1 = 2$ **97.** $4 + 10 - 1 = 13$ **99.** $5 \times 2 + (3)^3 + 2^0 = 10 + 27 + 1 = 38$ **101.** 86 164 seconds

Quick Quiz 6 **1.** 12^5 **2.** 1296 **3.** 91 **4.** See Instructor

Section 7 Exercises **1.** Locate the rounding place. If the digit to the right of the rounding place is 5 or greater than 5, round up. If the digit to the right of the rounding place is less than 5, round down. **3.** 80 **5.** 70 **7.** 170 **9.** 7440 **11.** 2960 **13.** 200 **15.** 2800 **17.** 7700 **19.** 8000 **21.** 1000 **23.** 28 000 **25.** 800 000 **27.** 15 000 000 stars **29. (a)** 1 200 000 **(b)** 1 173 000 **31. (a)** 3 700 000 square miles; 9 600 000 square kilometres **(b)** 3 710 000 square miles; 9 600 000 square kilometres

33. $\begin{array}{r} 800 \\ 300 \\ +\ 200 \\ \hline 1300 \end{array}$ **35.** $\begin{array}{r} 40 \\ 70 \\ 100 \\ +\ 20 \\ \hline 230 \end{array}$ **37.** $\begin{array}{r} 200\,000 \\ 50\,000 \\ +\ 9\,000 \\ \hline 259\,000 \end{array}$ **39.** $\begin{array}{r} 300\,000 \\ -\ 70\,000 \\ \hline 230\,000 \end{array}$ **41.** $\begin{array}{r} 800\,000 \\ -\ 80\,000 \\ \hline 720\,000 \end{array}$ **43.** $\begin{array}{r} 30\,000\,000 \\ -\ 20\,000\,000 \\ \hline 10\,000\,000 \end{array}$ **45.** $\begin{array}{r} 50 \\ \times\ 60 \\ \hline 3000 \end{array}$ **47.** $\begin{array}{r} 1000 \\ \times\ 8 \\ \hline 8000 \end{array}$

49. $\begin{array}{r} 600\,000 \\ \times\ 300 \\ \hline 180\,000\,000 \end{array}$ **51.** $\begin{array}{r} 150 \\ 40\overline{)6000} \end{array}$ **53.** $\begin{array}{r} 10\,000 \\ 40\overline{)400\,000} \end{array}$ **55.** $\begin{array}{r} 5000 \\ 800\overline{)4\,000\,000} \end{array}$ **57.** Incorrect $\begin{array}{r} 400 \\ 500 \\ 900 \\ +\ 200 \\ \hline 2000 \end{array}$ **59.** Incorrect $\begin{array}{r} 100\,000 \\ 50\,000 \\ +\ 40\,000 \\ \hline 190\,000 \end{array}$

61. Correct $\begin{array}{r} 300\,000 \\ -\ 90\,000 \\ \hline 210\,000 \end{array}$ **63.** Incorrect $\begin{array}{r} 80\,000\,000 \\ -\ 50\,000\,000 \\ \hline 30\,000\,000 \end{array}$ **65.** Incorrect $\begin{array}{r} 400 \\ \times\ 30 \\ \hline 12\,000 \end{array}$ **67.** Correct $\begin{array}{r} 6000 \\ \times\ 70 \\ \hline 420\,000 \end{array}$ **69.** $\begin{array}{r} 2000 \\ 40\overline{)80\,000} \end{array}$ Correct **71.** $\begin{array}{r} 500 \\ 400\overline{)200\,000} \end{array}$ Correct

73. 32 square metres **75.** 11 000 000 people **77.** 30 000 pizzas **79.** 180 000 flights **81.** 590 000 − 270 000 = 320 000 square miles **83.** **(a)** 400 000 hours **(b)** 20 000 days

Quick Quiz 7 **1.** 92 400 **2.** 2 340 000 **3.** 2 400 000 000 **4.** See Instructor

Section 8 Exercises **1.** $8800 **3.** 1560 bagels **5.** 7¢ per ounce **7.** $64 **9.** 432 442 people **11.** $20 382 **13.** 25 231; 466 **15.** 800 000 people **17.** $192 **19.** $1360 **21.** $16 405 **23.** 14 kilometres per litre **25.** There are 54 oak trees, 108 maple trees, and 756 pine trees. In total there are 936 trees. **27.** 129 **29.** 262 **31.** $2 634 000 000 **33.** $20 604 000 000

Quick Quiz 8 **1.** $269 **2.** $858 **3.** $126 **4.** See Instructor

Putting Your Skills to Work

1. $100, $300, $2000, $8000, $8000, $8000, $12 000 **2.** $365 **3.** 10 months to pay off the lowest three debts

Module Review Problems

1. eight hundred ninety-two **2.** fifteen thousand, eight hundred two **3.** one hundred nine thousand, two hundred seventy-six **4.** four hundred twenty-three million, five hundred seventy-six thousand, fifty-five **5.** 4000 + 300 + 60 + 4 **6.** 30,000 + 5000 + 400 + 10 + 4 **7.** 40 000 000 + 2 000 000 + 100 000 + 60 000 + 6000 + 30 + 7 **8.** 1 000 000 + 300 000 + 5000 + 100 + 20 + 8 **9.** 924 **10.** 5302 **11.** 1 328 828 **12.** 24 705 112 **13.** 115 **14.** 300 **15.** 400 **16.** 150 **17.** 400 **18.** 953 **19.** 1007 **20.** 60 100 **21.** 14 703 **22.** 10 582 **23.** 17 **24.** 6 **25.** 27 **26.** 171 **27.** 6155 **28.** 3167 **29.** 80 722 **30.** 105 818 **31.** 6 236 011 **32.** 5 332 991 **33.** 144 **34.** 0 **35.** 800 **36.** 1500 **37.** 62 100 **38.** 84 312 000 **39.** 780 000 **40.** 536 000 000 **41.** 1856 **42.** 1752 **43.** 4050 **44.** 13 680 **45.** 25 524 **46.** 24 096 **47.** 87 822 **48.** 268 513 **49.** 543 510 **50.** 255 068 **51.** 111 370 **52.** 113 946 **53.** 7 200 000 **54.** 7 500 000 **55.** 2 000 000 000 **56.** 12 000 000 000 **57.** 2 **58.** 5 **59.** 0 **60.** 12 **61.** 7 **62.** 0 **63.** 9 **64.** 7 **65.** undefined **66.** 4 **67.** 7 **68.** 9 **69.** 125 **70.** 125 **71.** 207 **72.** 309 **73.** 2504 **74.** 3064 **75.** 36 958 **76.** 36 921 **77.** 15 046 R 3 **78.** 35 783 R 4 **79.** 7 R 21 **80.** 4 R 37 **81.** 31 R 15 **82.** 14 R 11 **83.** 38 R 30 **84.** 60 R 22 **85.** 195 **86.** 258 **87.** 54 **88.** 19 **89.** 13^2 **90.** 21^3 **91.** 8^5 **92.** 10^6 **93.** 64 **94.** 81 **95.** 128 **96.** 125 **97.** 49 **98.** 81 **99.** 216 **100.** 64 **101.** 8 **102.** 11 **103.** 22 **104.** 66 **105.** 22 **106.** 78 **107.** 17 **108.** 26 **109.** 86 **110.** 3360 **111.** 5900 **112.** 15 310 **113.** 42 640 **114.** 12 000 **115.** 23 000 **116.** 676 000 **117.** 202 000 **118.** 4 600 000 **119.** 10 000 000 **120.** $\begin{array}{r} 300 \\ 700 \\ 200 \\ +\ 200 \\ \hline 1400 \end{array}$ **121.** $\begin{array}{r} 20\,000 \\ 8\,000 \\ +\ 40\,000 \\ \hline 68\,000 \end{array}$ **122.** $\begin{array}{r} 4\,000\,000 \\ -\ 3\,000\,000 \\ \hline 1\,000\,000 \end{array}$ **123.** $\begin{array}{r} 30\,000 \\ -\ 20\,000 \\ \hline 10\,000 \end{array}$ **124.** $\begin{array}{r} 1000 \\ \times\ 6000 \\ \hline 6\,000\,000 \end{array}$ **125.** $\begin{array}{r} 3\,000\,000 \\ \times\ 900 \\ \hline 2\,700\,000\,000 \end{array}$

126. $\begin{array}{r} 4000 \\ 20\overline{)80\,000} \end{array}$ **127.** $\begin{array}{r} 3000 \\ 300\overline{)900\,000} \end{array}$ **128.** 240 doughnut holes **129.** 175 words **130.** 7020 people **131.** $59 470 **132.** 10 301 feet **133.** $3348 **134.** $1356 **135.** $74 **136.** $278 **137.** 16 kilometres per litre **138.** $5041 **139.** $2031 **140.** 3 407 468 tonnes **141.** 2 144 144 tonnes from 1998 to 2000 **142.** 27 597 003 tonnes **143.** 2284 **144.** 7867 **145.** 11 088 **146.** 129 **147.** 29 **148.** $747 **149.** **(a)** 35 square metres **(b)** 24 metres

How Am I Doing? Module Test

1. forty-four million, seven thousand, six hundred thirty-five (obj. 1.3) **2.** 20,000 + 6000 + 800 + 50 + 9 (obj. 1.1) **3.** 3 581 076 (obj. 1.2) **4.** 831 (obj. 2.4) **5.** 1491 (obj. 2.4) **6.** 318 977 (obj. 2.4) **7.** 8067 (obj. 3.3) **8.** 172 858 (obj. 3.3) **9.** 5 225 768 (obj. 3.3) **10.** 378 (obj. 4.1) **11.** 4320 (obj. 4.4) **12.** 192 992 (obj. 4.4) **13.** 129 437 (obj. 4.2) **14.** 3014 R 1 (obj. 5.2) **15.** 2358 (obj. 5.2) **16.** 352 (obj. 5.3) **17.** 14^3 (obj. 6.1) **18.** 64 (obj. 6.1) **19.** 23 (obj. 6.2) **20.** 50 (obj. 6.2) **21.** 79 (obj. 6.2) **22.** 94 800 (obj. 7.1) **23.** 6 460 000 (obj. 7.1) **24.** 5 300 000 (obj. 7.1) **25.** 150 000 000 000 (obj. 7.2) **26.** 16 000 (obj. 7.2) **27.** $2148 (obj. 8.1) **28.** 166 metres (obj. 8.1) **29.** $127 (obj. 8.2) **30.** $292 (obj. 8.2) **31.** 66 000 square metres (obj. 8.2) **32.** 46 metres (obj. 8.2)

All of us have seen pictures of the Pyramids of Egypt. These amazing structures were built very carefully. Measurements had to be made that were very precise. The ancient Egyptians used an elaborate system of fractions that allowed them to make highly accurate measurements. As you master the topics of this module, you will master the basic skills used by the designers of the Pyramids of Egypt.

Purestock/Superstock Royalty Free

Fractions

Section 1 Understanding Fractions

Student Learning Objectives

After studying this section, you will be able to:

1. **Use a fraction to represent part of a whole.**
2. **Draw a sketch to illustrate a fraction.**
3. **Use fractions to represent real-life situations.**

1 Using a Fraction to Represent Part of a Whole

In this module we will study a fractional part of a whole number. One way to represent parts of a whole is with **fractions.** The word *fraction* (like the word *fracture*) suggests that something is being broken. In mathematics, fractions represent the part that is "broken off" from a whole. The whole can be a single object (like a whole pie) or a group (the employees of a company). Here are some examples.

Single object

$\frac{1}{3}$

The whole is the pie on the left. The fraction $\frac{1}{3}$ represents the shaded part of the pie, 1 of 3 pieces. $\frac{1}{3}$ is read "one-third."

A group: ACE company employs 150 men, 200 women.

$\frac{150}{350}$

The whole is the company of 350 people (150 men plus 200 women). The fraction $\frac{150}{350}$ represents that part of the company consisting of men.

Recipe: Applesauce
4 apples
1/2 cup sugar
1 teaspoon cinnamon

The whole is 1 whole cup of sugar. This recipe calls for $\frac{1}{2}$ cup of sugar. Notice that in many real-life situations $\frac{1}{2}$ is written as 1/2.

When we say "$\frac{3}{8}$ of a pizza has been eaten," we mean 3 of 8 equal parts of a pizza have been eaten. (See the figure.) When we write the fraction $\frac{3}{8}$, the number on the top, 3, is the **numerator,** and the number on the bottom, 8, is the **denominator.**

The numerator specifies how many parts $\rightarrow$ 3
The denominator specifies the total number of parts $\rightarrow$ 8

When we say, "$\frac{2}{3}$ of the marbles are red," we mean 2 marbles out of a total of 3 are red marbles.

Part we are interested in $\rightarrow$ 2 numerator
Total number in the group $\rightarrow$ 3 denominator

EXAMPLE 1 Use a fraction to represent the shaded or completed part of the whole shown.

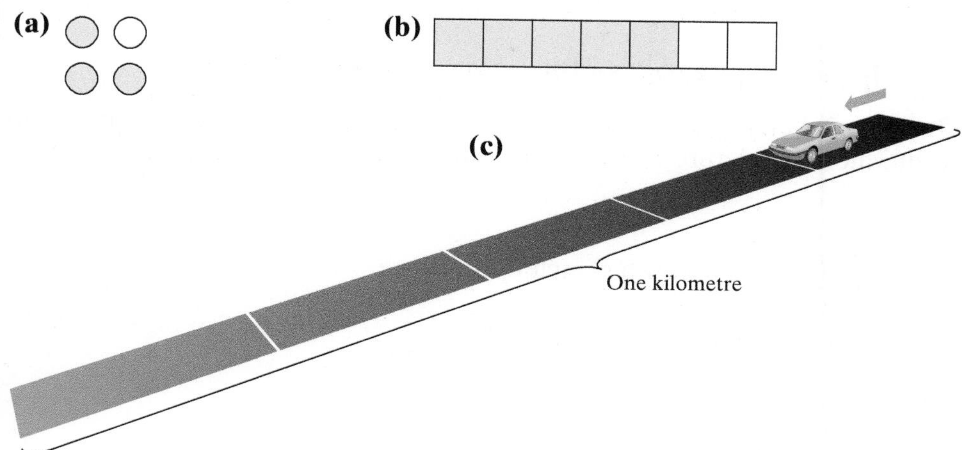

Solution

(a) Three out of four circles are shaded. The fraction is $\frac{3}{4}$.

(b) Five out of seven equal parts are shaded. The fraction is $\frac{5}{7}$.

(c) The kilometre is divided into five equal parts. The car has travelled 1 part out of 5 of the one-kilometre distance. The fraction is $\frac{1}{5}$.

Practice Problem 1 Use a fraction to represent the shaded part of the whole.

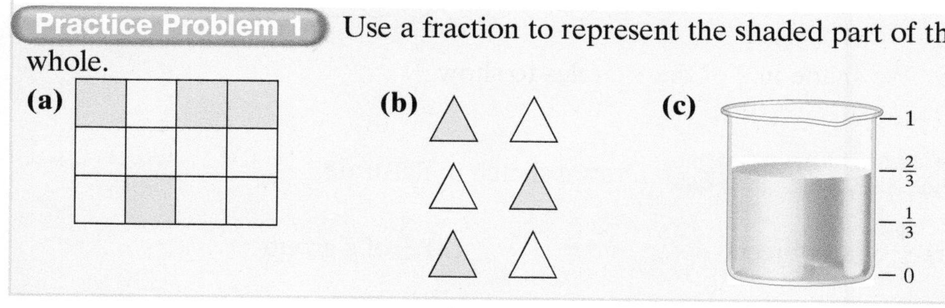

NOTE TO STUDENT: Fully worked-out solutions to all of the Practice Problems can be found at the end of the module.

We can also think of a fraction as a division problem.

$$\frac{1}{3} = 1 \div 3 \qquad \text{and} \qquad 1 \div 3 = \frac{1}{3}$$

The division way of looking at fractions asks the question:

What is the result of dividing one whole into three equal parts?

Thus we can say the fraction $\frac{a}{b}$ means the same as $a \div b$. However, special care must be taken with the number 0.

Suppose that we had four equal parts and we wanted to take none of them. We would want $\frac{0}{4}$ of the parts. Since $\frac{0}{4} = 0 \div 4 = 0$, we see that $\frac{0}{4} = 0$. Any fraction with a 0 numerator equals zero.

$$\frac{0}{8} = 0 \qquad \frac{0}{5} = 0 \qquad \frac{0}{13} = 0$$

What happens when zero is in the denominator? $\frac{4}{0}$ means 4 out of 0 parts. Taking 4 out of 0 does not make sense. We say $\frac{4}{0}$ is **undefined.**

$$\frac{3}{0}, \frac{7}{0}, \frac{4}{0} \quad \text{are } \textbf{undefined.}$$

We cannot have a fraction with 0 in the denominator. Since $\frac{4}{0} = 4 \div 0$, we say division by zero is *undefined*. We cannot divide by 0.

Drawing a Sketch to Illustrate a Fraction

Drawing a sketch of a mathematical situation is a powerful problem-solving technique. The picture often reveals information not always apparent in the words.

EXAMPLE 2 Draw a sketch to illustrate.

(a) $\frac{7}{11}$ of an object **(b)** $\frac{2}{9}$ of a group

Solution

(a) The easiest figure to draw is a rectangular bar.

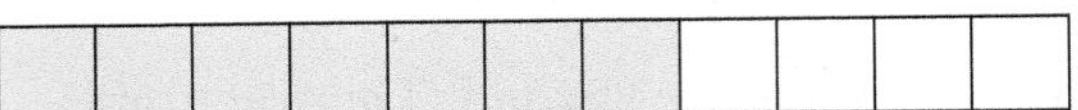

We divide the bar into 11 equal parts. We then shade in 7 parts to show $\frac{7}{11}$.

(b) We draw 9 circles of equal size to represent a group of 9.

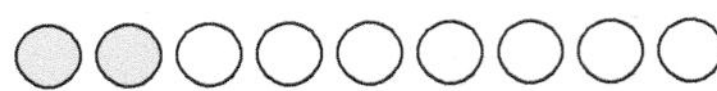

We shade in 2 of the 9 circles to show $\frac{2}{9}$.

NOTE TO STUDENT: Fully worked-out solutions to all of the Practice Problems can be found at the end of the module.

Practice Problem 2 Draw a sketch to illustrate.

(a) $\frac{4}{5}$ of an object **(b)** $\frac{3}{7}$ of a group

Recall these facts about division problems involving the number 1 and the number 0.

DIVISION INVOLVING THE NUMBER 1 AND THE NUMBER 0

1. Any nonzero number divided by itself is 1.

$$\frac{7}{7} = 1$$

2. Any number divided by 1 remains unchanged. $\frac{29}{1} = 29$

3. Zero may be divided by any nonzero number; the result is always zero.

$$\frac{0}{4} = 0$$

4. Division by zero is undefined. $\frac{3}{0}$ is undefined

3 Using Fractions to Represent Real-Life Situations

Many real-life situations can be described using fractions.

EXAMPLE 3 Use a fraction to describe each situation.

(a) A baseball player gets a hit 5 out of 12 times at bat.

(b) There are 156 men and 185 women taking psychology this semester. Describe the part of the class that consists of women.

(c) Marcel Jones found in the Northwest Territories moose count that five-eighths of the moose observed were female.

Solution

(a) The baseball player got a hit $\frac{5}{12}$ of his times at bat.

(b) The total class is $156 + 185 = 341$. The fractional part that is women is 185 out of 341. Thus $\frac{185}{341}$ of the class is women.

156 men	185 women

Total class 341 students

(c) Five-eighths of the moose observed were female. The fraction is $\frac{5}{8}$.

Practice Problem 3 Use a fraction to describe each situation.

(a) 9 out of the 17 players on the basketball team are on the dean's list.

(b) The senior class has 382 men and 351 women. Describe the part of the class consisting of men.

(c) John needed seven-eighths of a metre of material.

EXAMPLE 4 Wanda made 13 calls, out of which she made five sales. Albert made 17 calls, out of which he made six sales. Write a fraction that describes for both people together the number of calls in which a sale was made compared with the total number of calls.

Solution There are $5 + 6 = 11$ calls in which a sale was made.

There were $13 + 17 = 30$ total calls.

Thus $\dfrac{11}{30}$ of the calls resulted in a sale.

Practice Problem 4 An inspector found that one out of seven belts was defective. She also found that two out of nine shirts were defective. Write a fraction that describes what part of all the objects examined were defective.

Developing Your Study Skills

Previewing New Material

Part of your study time each day should consist of looking ahead to those sections in your text that are to be covered the following day. You do not necessarily have to study and learn the material on your own, but if you survey the concepts, terminology, diagrams, and examples, the new ideas will seem more familiar to you when the instructor presents them. You can take note of concepts that appear confusing or difficult and be ready to listen carefully for your instructor's explanations. You can be prepared to ask the questions that will increase your understanding. Previewing new material enables you to see what is coming and prepares you to be ready to absorb it.

Section 1 Exercises

Verbal and Writing Skills

1. A __________ can be used to represent part of a whole or part of a group.
2. In a fraction, the __________ tells the number of parts we are interested in.
3. In a fraction, the __________ tells the total number of parts in the whole or in the group.
4. Describe a real-life situation that involves fractions.

Name the numerator and the denominator in each fraction.

5. $\frac{3}{5}$

6. $\frac{9}{11}$

7. $\frac{7}{8}$

8. $\frac{9}{10}$

9. $\frac{1}{17}$

10. $\frac{1}{15}$

In exercises 11–30, use a fraction to represent the shaded part of the object or the shaded portion of the set of objects.

11.

12.

13.

14. 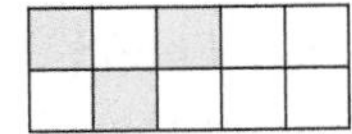

15. 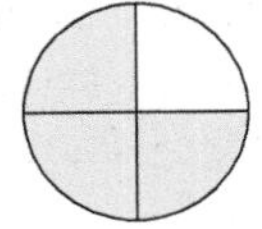

16. 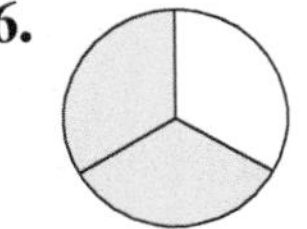

17. 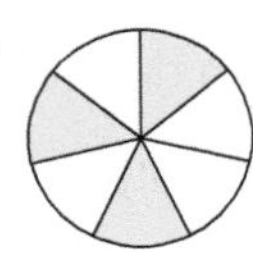

18. 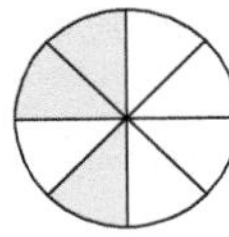

19. 

20. 

21. 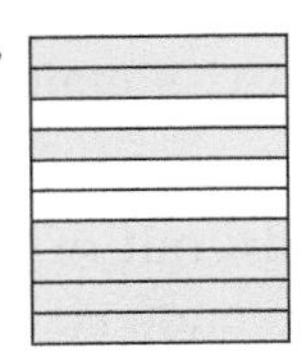

22. 

23. 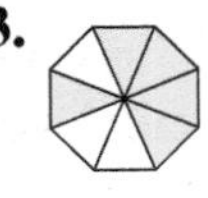

24. 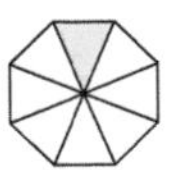

25.

26. 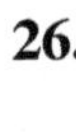 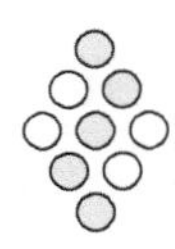

27. 

28. 

29. 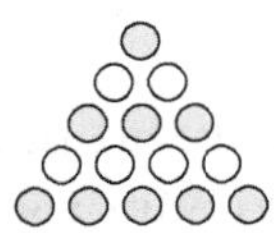

30. 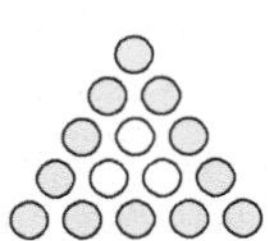

Draw a sketch to illustrate each fractional part.

31. $\frac{1}{5}$ of an object

32. $\frac{3}{7}$ of an object

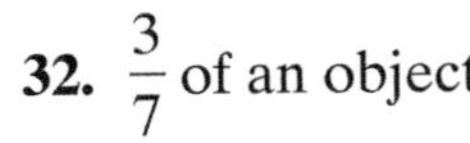

33. $\frac{3}{8}$ of an object

34. $\frac{5}{12}$ of an object

35. $\frac{7}{10}$ of an object

36. $\frac{5}{9}$ of an object

Applications

37. ***Anthropology Class*** Professor Sousa has 83 students in her anthropology lecture class. Forty-two of the students are sophomores and the others are juniors. What fraction of the class is sophomores?

38. ***Personal Finance*** Miguel bought a notebook with a total purchase price of 98¢. Of this amount, 7¢ was sales tax. What fractional part of the total purchase price was sales tax?

39. ***Personal Finance*** Lance bought a 100-CD jukebox for $750. Part of it was paid for with the $209 he earned parking cars for the valet service at a local wedding reception hall. What fractional part of the jukebox was paid for by his weekend earnings?

40. ***Personal Finance*** Jillian earned $165 over the weekend at her waitressing job. She used $48 of it to repay a loan to her sister. What fractional part of her earnings did Jillian use to repay her sister?

41. ***Political Campaigns*** The Conservative Party fundraising event served 122 chicken dinners and 89 roast beef dinners to its contributors. What fractional part of the guests ate roast beef?

42. ***Education*** George Brown College has 78 full-time instructors and 31 part-time instructors. What fractional part of the faculty are part-time?

43. ***Selling Trees*** Boy Scout Troop #33 had a Christmas tree sale to raise money for a summer camping trip. In one afternoon, they sold 9 balsam firs, 12 Norwegian pines, and 5 Douglas firs. What fractional part of the trees sold were balsam firs?

44. ***Animal Shelters*** At the local animal shelter there are 12 puppies, 25 adult dogs, 14 kittens, and 31 adult cats. What fractional part of the animals are either puppies or adult dogs?

45. ***Book Collection*** Marie has 9 novels, 4 biographies, 12 mysteries, and 15 magazines on her bookshelf. What fractional part of the reading material is either novels or magazines?

46. ***Music Collection*** A box of compact discs contains 5 classical CDs, 6 jazz CDs, 4 soundtracks, and 24 blues CDs. What fractional part of the total CDs is either jazz or blues?

47. ***Manufacturing*** The West Peabody Engine Company manufactured two items last week: 101 engines and 94 lawn mowers. It was discovered that 19 engines and 3 lawn mowers were defective. Of the engines that were not defective, 40 were properly constructed but 42 were not of the highest quality. Of the lawn mowers that were not defective, 50 were properly constructed but 41 were not of the highest quality.

(a) What fractional part of all items manufactured was of the highest quality?

(b) What fractional part of all items manufactured was defective?

48. ***Tour Bus*** A Chicago tour bus held 25 women and 33 men. 12 women wore jeans. 19 men wore jeans. In the group of 25 women, a subgroup of 8 women wore sandals. In the group of 19 men, a subgroup of 10 wore sandals.

(a) What fractional part of the people on the bus wore jeans?

(b) What fractional part of the women on the bus wore sandals?

To Think About

49. Illustrate a real-life example of the fraction $\frac{0}{6}$.

50. What happens when we try to illustrate a real-life example of the fraction $\frac{6}{0}$? Why?

Quick Quiz 1

1. Use a fraction to represent the shaded part of the object.

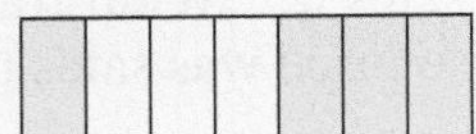

2. Fleming College has 371 students taking classes on Monday night. Of those students, 204 drive a car to campus. Write a fraction that describes the part of the Monday night students who drive a car to class.

3. At the YMCA at 10 P.M. last Friday, 8 men were lifting weights and 5 women were lifting weights. At the same time, 7 men were riding stationary bikes and 13 women were riding stationary bikes. No other people were in the gym at that time. What fractional part of the people in the gym were lifting weights?

4. **Concept Check** One hundred twenty new businesses have opened in Springfield in the last five years. Sixty-five of them were restaurants; the remaining ones were not. Thirty new restaurants went out of business; the other new restaurants did not. Of all the new businesses that were not restaurants, 25 of them went out of business; the others did not. Explain how you can find a fraction that represents the fractional part of the new businesses that did not go out of business.

SECTION 2 SIMPLIFYING FRACTIONS

 Writing a Number as a Product of Prime Factors

Student Learning Objectives

After studying this section, you will be able to:

 **Write a number as a product of prime factors.**

 **Reduce a fraction to lowest terms.**

3 **Determine whether two fractions are equal.**

A **prime number** is a whole number greater than 1 that cannot be evenly divided except by itself and 1. If you examine all the whole numbers from 1 to 50, you will find 15 prime numbers.

THE FIRST 15 PRIME NUMBERS

2, 3, 5, 7, 11, 13, 17, 19, 23, 29, 31, 37, 41, 43, 47

A **composite number** is a whole number greater than 1 that can be divided by whole numbers other than 1 and itself. The number 12 is a composite number.

$$12 = 2 \times 6 \qquad \text{and} \qquad 12 = 3 \times 4$$

The number 1 is neither a prime nor a composite number. The number 0 is neither a prime nor a composite number.

Recall that factors are numbers that are multiplied together. Prime factors are prime numbers. To check to see if a number is prime or composite, simply divide the smaller primes (such as 2, 3, 5, 7, 11, ...) into the given number. If the number can be divided exactly without a remainder by one of the smaller primes, it is a composite and not a prime.

Some students find the following rules helpful when deciding if a number can be divided by 2, 3, or 5.

DIVISIBILITY TESTS

1. A number is divisible by 2 if the last digit is 0, 2, 4, 6, or 8.
2. A number is divisible by 3 if the sum of the digits is divisible by 3.
3. A number is divisible by 5 if the last digit is 0 or 5.

To illustrate:

1. 478 is divisible by 2 since it ends in 8.
2. 531 is divisible by 3 since when we add the digits of 531 $(5 + 3 + 1)$ we get 9, which is divisible by 3.
3. 985 is divisible by 5 since it ends in 5.

EXAMPLE 1 Write each whole number as the product of prime factors.

(a) 12 **(b)** 60 **(c)** 168

Solution

(a) To start, write 12 as the product of any two factors. We will write 12 as 4×3.

$12 = 4 \times 3$ Now check whether the factors are prime. If not, factor these.

$2 \times 2 \times 3$

$12 = 2 \times 2 \times 3$ Now all factors are prime, so 12 is completely factored.

Instead of writing $2 \times 2 \times 3$, we can write $2^2 \times 3$.

Note: To start, we could write 12 as 2×6. Begin this way and follow the preceding steps. Is the product of prime factors the same? Will this always be true?

(b) We follow the same steps as in (a).

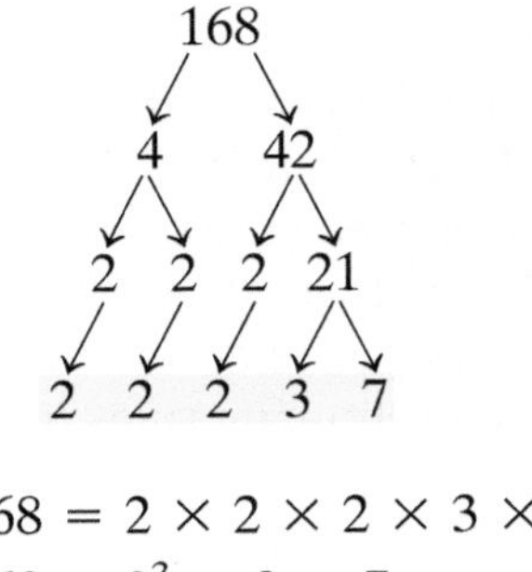

Check that all factors are prime.

Instead of writing $2 \times 2 \times 3 \times 5$, we can write $2^2 \times 3 \times 5$.

Note that in the final answer the prime factors are listed in order from least to greatest.

(c) Some students like to use a **factor tree** to help write a number as a product of prime factors as illustrated below.

168
4 42
2 2 2 21
2 2 2 3 7

$$168 = 2 \times 2 \times 2 \times 3 \times 7$$
or
$$168 = 2^3 \times 3 \times 7$$

Practice Problem 1 Write each whole number as a product of primes.

(a) 18 **(b)** 72 **(c)** 400

NOTE TO STUDENT: *Fully worked-out solutions to all of the Practice Problems can be found at the end of the module.*

Suppose we started Example 1(c) by writing $168 = 14 \times 12$. Would we get the same answer? Would our answer be correct? Let's compare.

Again we will use a factor tree.

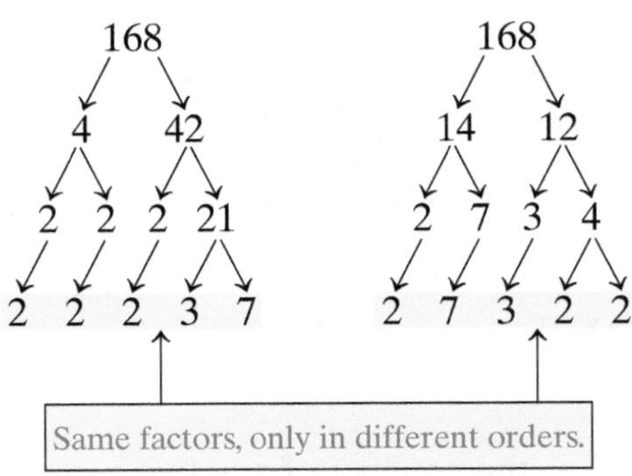

Thus $168 = 2 \times 2 \times 2 \times 3 \times 7$

or $\quad = 2^3 \times 3 \times 7$.

The order of prime factors is not important because multiplication is commutative. No matter how we start, when we factor a composite number, we always get exactly the same prime factors.

THE FUNDAMENTAL THEOREM OF ARITHMETIC

Every composite number can be written in exactly one way as a product of prime numbers.

We have seen this in our Solution to Example 1(c).

You will be able to check this theorem again in Section 2 Exercises, exercises 7–26. Writing a number as a product of prime factors is also called **prime factorization.**

Reducing a Fraction to Lowest Terms

You know that 5 + 2 and 3 + 4 are two ways to write the same number. We say they are *equivalent* because they are *equal* to the same *value.* They are both ways of writing the value 7.

Like whole numbers, fractions can be written in more than one way. For example, $\frac{2}{4}$ and $\frac{1}{2}$ are two ways to write the same number. The value of the fractions is the same. When we use fractions, we often need to write them in another form. If we make the numerator and denominator smaller, we *simplify* the fractions.

Compare the two fractions in the drawings on the right. In each picture the shaded part is the same size. The fractions $\frac{3}{4}$ and $\frac{6}{8}$ are called **equivalent fractions.** The fraction $\frac{3}{4}$ is in **simplest form.** To see how we can change $\frac{6}{8}$ to $\frac{3}{4}$, we look at a property of the number 1.

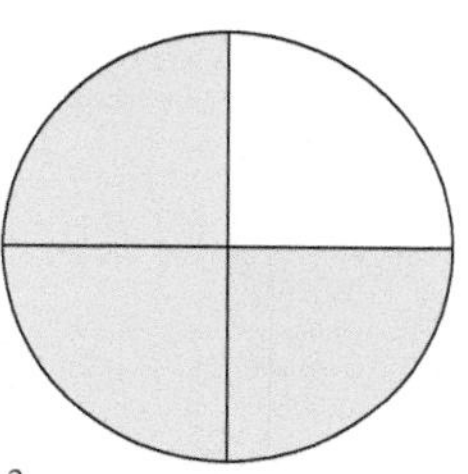

$\frac{3}{4}$ of the circle is shaded.

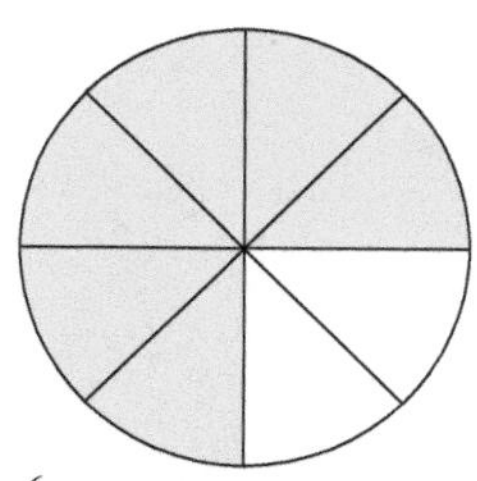

$\frac{6}{8}$ of the circle is shaded.

Any nonzero number divided by itself is 1.

$$\frac{5}{5} = \frac{17}{17} = \frac{c}{c} = 1$$

Thus, if we multiply a fraction by $\frac{5}{5}$ or $\frac{17}{17}$ or $\frac{c}{c}$ (remember, c cannot be zero), the value of the fraction is unchanged because we are multiplying by a form of 1. We can use this rule to show that $\frac{3}{4}$ and $\frac{6}{8}$ are equivalent.

$$\frac{3}{4} \times \frac{2}{2} = \frac{6}{8}$$

In general, if b and c are not zero,

$$\frac{a}{b} = \frac{a \times c}{b \times c}$$

To reduce a fraction, we find a **common factor** in the numerator and in the denominator and divide it out. In the fraction $\frac{6}{8}$, the common factor is 2.

$$\frac{6}{8} = \frac{3 \times \overset{1}{\cancel{2}}}{4 \times \underset{1}{\cancel{2}}} = \frac{3}{4}$$

$$\frac{6}{8} = \frac{3}{4}$$

For all fractions (where a, b, and c are not zero), if c is a common factor,

$$\frac{a}{b} = \frac{a \div c}{b \div c}$$

A fraction is called **simplified, reduced,** or **in lowest terms** if the numerator and the denominator have only 1 *as a common factor.*

EXAMPLE 2 Simplify (write in lowest terms).

(a) $\frac{15}{25}$ **(b)** $\frac{42}{56}$

Solution

(a) $\frac{15}{25} = \frac{15 \div 5}{25 \div 5} = \frac{3}{5}$ The greatest common factor is 5. Divide the numerator and the denominator by 5.

(b) $\frac{42}{56} = \frac{42 \div 14}{56 \div 14} = \frac{3}{4}$ The greatest common factor is 14. Divide the numerator and the denominator by 14.

Perhaps 14 was not the first common factor you thought of. Perhaps you did see the common factor 2. Divide out 2. Then look for another common factor, 7. Now divide out 7.

$$\frac{42}{56} = \frac{42 \div 2}{56 \div 2} = \frac{21}{28} = \frac{21 \div 7}{21 \div 7} = \frac{3}{4}$$

If we do not see large factors at first, sometimes we can simplify a fraction by dividing both numerator and denominator by a smaller common factor several times, until no common factors are left.

NOTE TO STUDENT: Fully worked-out solutions to all of the Practice Problems can be found at the end of the module.

Practice Problem 2 Simplify by dividing out common factors.

(a) $\frac{30}{42}$ **(b)** $\frac{60}{132}$

A second method to reduce or simplify fractions is called the *method of prime factors*. We factor the numerator and the denominator into prime numbers. We then divide the numerator and the denominator by any common prime factors.

EXAMPLE 3 Simplify the fractions by the method of prime factors.

(a) $\frac{35}{42}$ **(b)** $\frac{22}{110}$

Solution

(a) $\frac{35}{42} = \frac{5 \times 7}{2 \times 3 \times 7}$ We factor 35 and 42 into prime factors. The common prime factor is 7.

$= \frac{5 \times \overset{1}{\cancel{7}}}{2 \times 3 \times \underset{1}{\cancel{7}}}$ Now we divide out 7.

$= \frac{5 \times 1}{2 \times 3 \times 1} = \frac{5}{6}$ We multiply the factors in the numerator and denominator to write the reduced or simplified form.

Thus $\frac{35}{42} = \frac{5}{6}$, and $\frac{5}{6}$ is the simplified form.

(b) $\frac{22}{110} = \frac{2 \times 11}{2 \times 5 \times 11} = \frac{\overset{1}{\cancel{2}} \times \overset{1}{\cancel{11}}}{\underset{1}{\cancel{2}} \times 5 \times \underset{1}{\cancel{11}}} = \frac{1}{5}$

Practice Problem 3 Simplify the fractions by the method of prime factors.

(a) $\frac{120}{135}$ **(b)** $\frac{715}{880}$

NOTE TO STUDENT: Fully worked-out solutions to all of the Practice Problems can be found at the end of the module.

Determining Whether Two Fractions Are Equal

After we simplify, how can we check that a reduced fraction is *equivalent* to the original fraction? If two fractions are equal, their diagonal products or **cross products** are equal. This is called the **equality test for fractions.** If $\frac{3}{4} = \frac{6}{8}$, then

$$\frac{3}{4} \stackrel{?}{=} \frac{6}{8} \quad \begin{array}{l} \longrightarrow 4 \times 6 = 24 \\ \longrightarrow 3 \times 8 = 24 \end{array}$$

Products are equal.

If two fractions are unequal (we use the symbol $\neq$), their *cross* products are unequal. If $\frac{5}{6} \neq \frac{6}{7}$, then

$$\frac{5}{6} \stackrel{?}{=} \frac{6}{7} \quad \begin{array}{l} \longrightarrow 6 \times 6 = 36 \\ \longrightarrow 5 \times 7 = 35 \end{array}$$

Products are not equal.

Since $36 \neq 35$, we know that $\frac{5}{6} \neq \frac{6}{7}$. The test can be described in this way.

EQUALITY TEST FOR FRACTIONS

For any two fractions where a, b, c, and d are whole numbers and $b \neq 0, d \neq 0$, if $\frac{a}{b} = \frac{c}{d}$, then $a \times d = b \times c$.

EXAMPLE 4 Are these fractions equal? Use the equality test.

(a) $\frac{2}{11} \stackrel{?}{=} \frac{18}{99}$ **(b)** $\frac{3}{16} \stackrel{?}{=} \frac{12}{62}$

Solution

(a)

$$\frac{2}{11} \stackrel{?}{=} \frac{18}{99} \quad \begin{array}{l} \longrightarrow 11 \times 18 = 198 \\ \longrightarrow 2 \times 99 = 198 \end{array}$$

Products are equal.

Since $198 = 198$, we know that $\frac{2}{11} = \frac{18}{99}$.

(b)

$$\frac{3}{16} \stackrel{?}{=} \frac{12}{62} \quad \begin{array}{l} \longrightarrow 16 \times 12 = 192 \\ \longrightarrow 3 \times 62 = 186 \end{array}$$

Products are not equal.

Since $192 \neq 186$, we know that $\frac{3}{16} \neq \frac{12}{62}$.

Practice Problem 4 Test whether the following fractions are equal.

(a) $\frac{84}{108} \stackrel{?}{=} \frac{7}{9}$ **(b)** $\frac{3}{7} \stackrel{?}{=} \frac{79}{182}$

Section 2 Exercises

Verbal and Writing Skills

1. Which of these whole numbers are prime?
4, 12, 11, 15, 6, 19, 1, 41, 38, 24, 5, 46

2. A prime number is a whole number greater than 1 that cannot be evenly ________ except by itself and 1.

3. A ________ ________ is a whole number greater than 1 that can be divided by whole numbers other than itself and 1.

4. Every composite number can be written in exactly one way as a ________ of ________ numbers.

5. Give an example of a composite number written as a product of primes.

6. Give an example of equivalent (equal) fractions.

Write each number as a product of prime factors.

7. 15 **8.** 9 **9.** 35 **10.** 8 **11.** 49

12. 30 **13.** 16 **14.** 81 **15.** 55 **16.** 42

17. 63 **18.** 48 **19.** 84 **20.** 125 **21.** 54

22. 99 **23.** 120 **24.** 135 **25.** 184 **26.** 216

Determine which of these whole numbers are prime. If a number is composite, write it as the product of prime factors.

27. 47 **28.** 31 **29.** 57 **30.** 51

31. 67 **32.** 71 **33.** 62 **34.** 91

35. 89 **36.** 97 **37.** 127 **38.** 119

39. 121 **40.** 95 **41.** 129 **42.** 143

Reduce each fraction by finding a common factor in the numerator and in the denominator and dividing by the common factor.

43. $\frac{18}{27}$ **44.** $\frac{16}{24}$ **45.** $\frac{36}{48}$ **46.** $\frac{28}{49}$

47. $\frac{63}{90}$ **48.** $\frac{45}{75}$ **49.** $\frac{210}{310}$ **50.** $\frac{110}{140}$

Reduce each fraction by the method of prime factors.

51. $\frac{3}{15}$ **52.** $\frac{7}{21}$ **53.** $\frac{66}{88}$ **54.** $\frac{42}{56}$

55. $\frac{30}{45}$ **56.** $\frac{65}{91}$ **57.** $\frac{60}{75}$ **58.** $\frac{42}{70}$

Mixed Practice *Reduce each fraction by any method.*

59. $\frac{33}{36}$ **60.** $\frac{40}{96}$ **61.** $\frac{63}{108}$ **62.** $\frac{72}{132}$ **63.** $\frac{88}{121}$

64. $\frac{125}{200}$ **65.** $\frac{120}{200}$ **66.** $\frac{200}{300}$ **67.** $\frac{220}{260}$ **68.** $\frac{210}{390}$

Are these fractions equal? Why or why not?

69. $\frac{4}{16} \stackrel{?}{=} \frac{7}{28}$ **70.** $\frac{10}{65} \stackrel{?}{=} \frac{2}{13}$ **71.** $\frac{12}{40} \stackrel{?}{=} \frac{3}{13}$ **72.** $\frac{24}{72} \stackrel{?}{=} \frac{15}{45}$

73. $\frac{23}{27} \stackrel{?}{=} \frac{92}{107}$ **74.** $\frac{70}{120} \stackrel{?}{=} \frac{41}{73}$ **75.** $\frac{27}{57} \stackrel{?}{=} \frac{45}{95}$

76. $\frac{18}{24} \stackrel{?}{=} \frac{23}{28}$ **77.** $\frac{60}{95} \stackrel{?}{=} \frac{12}{19}$ **78.** $\frac{21}{27} \stackrel{?}{=} \frac{112}{144}$

Applications *Reduce the fractions in your answers.*

79. ***Pizza Delivery*** Pizza Palace made 128 deliveries on Saturday night. The manager found that 32 of the deliveries were of more than one pizza. He wanted to study the deliveries that consisted of just one pizza. What fractional part of the deliveries were of just one pizza?

80. ***Medical Students*** Medical students frequently work long hours. Susan worked a 16-hour shift, spending 12 hours in the emergency room and 4 hours in surgery. What fractional part of her shift was she in the emergency room? What fractional part of her shift was she in surgery?

81. ***Teaching*** Professor Nguyen found that 12 out of 96 students in his Aspects of Chemistry course failed the first exam. What fractional part of the class failed the exam? What fractional part of the class passed?

82. ***Wireless Communications*** William works for a wireless communications company that makes beepers and mobile phones. He inspected 315 beepers and found that 20 were defective. What fractional part of the beepers were not defective?

83. ***Personal Finance*** Amelia earned $8400 during her summer vacation. She saved $6000 of her earnings for a trip to New Zealand. What fractional part of her earnings did she save for her trip?

84. ***Real Estate*** Monique's sister and her husband have been working two jobs each to put a down payment on a plot of land where they plan to build their house. The purchase price is $42 500. They have saved $5500. What fractional part of the cost of the land have they saved?

Education *The following data was compiled on the students attending day classes at North Shore Community College.*

Number of Students	Daily Distance Travelled from Home to College (kilometres)	Length of Commute
1100	0–6	Very short
1700	7–12	Short
900	13–18	Medium
500	19–24	Long
300	More than 24	Very long

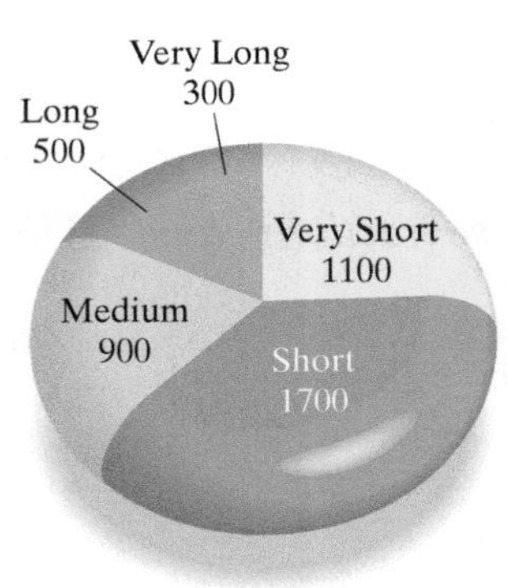

The number of students with each type of commute is displayed in the circle graph to the right.

Answer exercises 85–88 based on the preceding data. Reduce all fractions in your answers.

85. What fractional part of the student body has a short daily commute to the college?

86. What fractional part of the student body has a medium daily commute to the college?

87. What fractional part of the student body has a long or very long daily commute to the college?

88. What fractional part of the student body has a daily commute to the college that is considered less than long?

Quick Quiz 2 Reduce each fraction.

1. $\frac{25}{35}$

2. $\frac{14}{84}$

3. $\frac{105}{40}$

4. Concept Check Explain how you would determine if the fraction $\frac{195}{231}$ can be reduced.

SECTION 3 CONVERTING BETWEEN IMPROPER FRACTIONS AND MIXED NUMBERS

Changing a Mixed Number to an Improper Fraction

Student Learning Objectives

After studying this section, you will be able to:

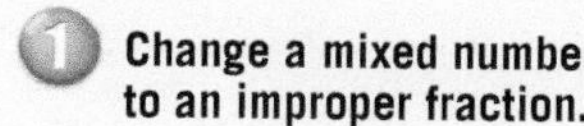

Change a mixed number to an improper fraction.

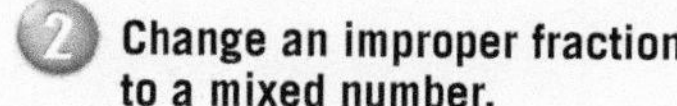

Change an improper fraction to a mixed number.

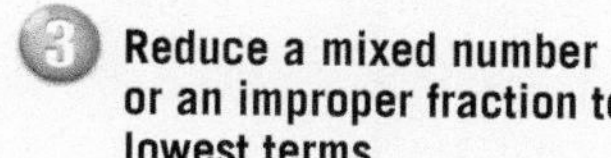

Reduce a mixed number or an improper fraction to lowest terms.

We have names for different kinds of fractions. If the value of a fraction is less than 1, we say the fraction is proper.

$$\frac{3}{5}, \frac{5}{7}, \frac{1}{8} \quad \text{are called } \textbf{proper fractions}.$$

Notice that the numerator is less than the denominator. If the numerator is less than the denominator, the fraction is a proper fraction.

If the value of a fraction is greater than or equal to 1, the quantity can be written as an improper fraction or as a mixed number.

Suppose that we have 1 whole pizza and $\frac{1}{6}$ of a pizza. We could write this as $1\frac{1}{6}$. $1\frac{1}{6}$ is called a mixed number. A **mixed number** is the sum of a whole number greater than zero and a proper fraction. The notation $1\frac{1}{6}$ actually means $1 + \frac{1}{6}$. The plus sign is not usually shown.

Another way of writing $1\frac{1}{6}$ pizza is to write $\frac{7}{6}$ pizza. $\frac{7}{6}$ is called an improper fraction. Notice that the numerator is greater than the denominator. If the numerator is greater than or equal to the denominator, the fraction is an improper fraction.

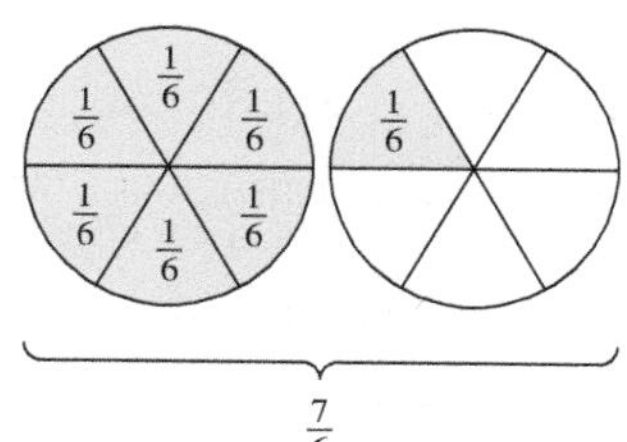

$$\frac{7}{6}, \frac{6}{6}, \frac{5}{4}, \frac{8}{3}, \frac{2}{2} \quad \text{are } \textbf{improper fractions}.$$

The following chart will help you visualize these different fractions and their names.

Because in some cases improper fractions are easier to add, subtract, multiply, and divide than mixed numbers, we often change mixed numbers to improper fractions when we perform calculations with them.

Value Less Than 1	Value Equal To 1	Value Greater Than 1
Proper Fraction	Improper Fraction	Improper Fraction or Mixed Number
$\frac{3}{4}$	$\frac{4}{4}$	$\frac{5}{4}$ or $1\frac{1}{4}$
$\frac{7}{8}$	$\frac{8}{8}$	$\frac{17}{8}$ or $2\frac{1}{8}$
$\frac{3}{100}$	$\frac{100}{100}$	$\frac{109}{100}$ or $1\frac{9}{100}$

CHANGING A MIXED NUMBER TO AN IMPROPER FRACTION

1. Multiply the whole number by the denominator of the fraction.
2. Add the numerator of the fraction to the product found in step 1.
3. Write the sum found in step 2 over the denominator of the fraction.

EXAMPLE 1 Change each mixed number to an improper fraction.

(a) $3\frac{2}{5}$ **(b)** $5\frac{4}{9}$ **(c)** $18\frac{3}{5}$

Solution

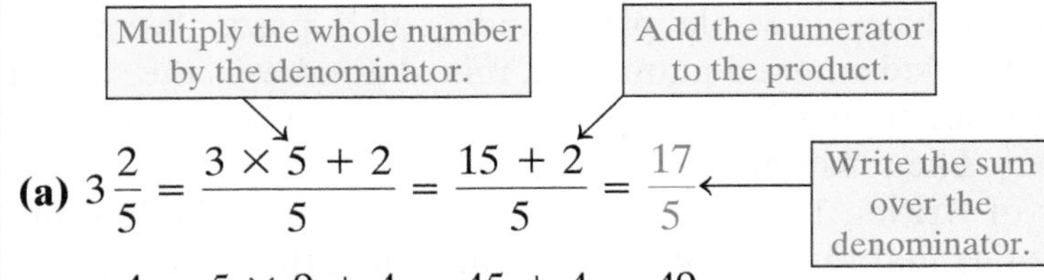

(a) $3\frac{2}{5} = \frac{3 \times 5 + 2}{5} = \frac{15 + 2}{5} = \frac{17}{5}$

(b) $5\frac{4}{9} = \frac{5 \times 9 + 4}{9} = \frac{45 + 4}{9} = \frac{49}{9}$

(c) $18\frac{3}{5} = \frac{18 \times 5 + 3}{5} = \frac{90 + 3}{5} = \frac{93}{5}$

NOTE TO STUDENT: Fully worked-out solutions to all of the Practice Problems can be found at the end of the module.

Practice Problem 1 Change the mixed numbers to improper fractions.

(a) $4\frac{3}{7}$ **(b)** $6\frac{2}{3}$ **(c)** $19\frac{4}{7}$

Changing an Improper Fraction to a Mixed Number

We often need to change an improper fraction to a mixed number.

CHANGING AN IMPROPER FRACTION TO A MIXED NUMBER

1. Divide the numerator by the denominator.
2. Write the quotient followed by the fraction with the remainder over the denominator.

$$\text{quotient}\,\frac{\text{remainder}}{\text{denominator}}$$

EXAMPLE 2 Write each improper fraction as a mixed number.

(a) $\frac{13}{5}$ **(b)** $\frac{29}{7}$ **(c)** $\frac{105}{31}$ **(d)** $\frac{85}{17}$

Solution

(a) We divide the denominator 5 into 13.

$$\begin{array}{r} 2 \\ 5\overline{)13} \\ \underline{10} \\ 3 \end{array} \quad \begin{array}{l} \longleftarrow \text{quotient} \\ \\ \\ \longleftarrow \text{remainder} \end{array}$$

The answer is in the form quotient$\dfrac{\text{remainder}}{\text{denominator}}$.

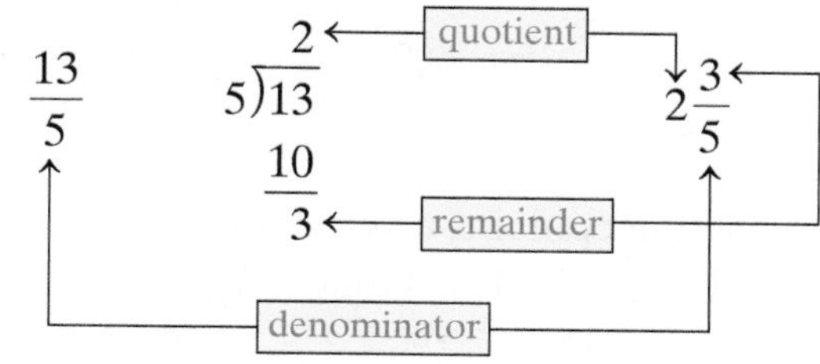

Thus $\dfrac{13}{5} = 2\dfrac{3}{5}$.

(b) $\begin{array}{r} 4 \\ 7\overline{)29} \\ \underline{28} \\ 1 \end{array}$ $\quad \dfrac{29}{7} = 4\dfrac{1}{7}$

(c) $\begin{array}{r} 3 \\ 31\overline{)105} \\ \underline{93} \\ 12 \end{array}$ $\quad \dfrac{105}{31} = 3\dfrac{12}{31}$

(d) $\begin{array}{r} 5 \\ 17\overline{)85} \\ \underline{85} \\ 0 \end{array}$ The remainder is 0, so $\dfrac{85}{17} = 5$, a whole number.

Practice Problem 2 Write as a mixed number or a whole number.

(a) $\dfrac{17}{4}$ **(b)** $\dfrac{36}{5}$ **(c)** $\dfrac{116}{27}$ **(d)** $\dfrac{91}{13}$

NOTE TO STUDENT: Fully worked-out solutions to all of the Practice Problems can be found at the end of the module.

3 Reducing a Mixed Number or an Improper Fraction to Lowest Terms

Mixed numbers and improper fractions may need to be reduced if they are not in simplest form. Recall that we write the fraction in terms of prime factors. Then we look for common factors in the numerator and the denominator of the fraction. Then we divide the numerator and the denominator by the common factor.

EXAMPLE 3 Reduce the improper fraction. $\dfrac{22}{8}$

Solution

$$\frac{22}{8} = \frac{\overset{1}{\cancel{2}} \times 11}{\underset{1}{\cancel{2}} \times 2 \times 2} = \frac{11}{4}$$

Practice Problem 3 Reduce the improper fraction.

$$\frac{51}{15}$$

EXAMPLE 4 Reduce the mixed number. $4\frac{21}{28}$

Solution We cannot reduce the whole number 4, only the fraction $\frac{21}{28}$.

$$\frac{21}{28} = \frac{3 \times \overset{1}{\cancel{7}}}{4 \times \underset{1}{\cancel{7}}} = \frac{3}{4}$$

Therefore, $4\frac{21}{28} = 4\frac{3}{4}$.

Practice Problem 4 Reduce the mixed number.

$$3\frac{16}{80}$$

If an improper fraction contains a very large numerator and denominator, it is best to change the fraction to a mixed number before reducing.

EXAMPLE 5 Reduce $\frac{945}{567}$ by first changing to a mixed number.

Solution

$$\begin{array}{r} 1 \\ 567\overline{)945} \\ \underline{567} \\ 378 \end{array} \qquad \text{so } \frac{945}{567} = 1\frac{378}{567}$$

To reduce the fraction we write

$$\frac{378}{567} = \frac{2 \times 3 \times 3 \times 3 \times 7}{3 \times 3 \times 3 \times 3 \times 7} = \frac{2 \times \overset{1}{\cancel{3}} \times \overset{1}{\cancel{3}} \times \overset{1}{\cancel{3}} \times \overset{1}{\cancel{7}}}{3 \times \underset{1}{\cancel{3}} \times \underset{1}{\cancel{3}} \times \underset{1}{\cancel{3}} \times \underset{1}{\cancel{7}}} = \frac{2}{3}$$

So $\frac{945}{567} = 1\frac{378}{567} = 1\frac{2}{3}$.

Problems like Example 5 can be done in several different ways. It is not necessary to follow these exact steps when reducing this fraction.

Practice Problem 5 Reduce $\frac{1001}{572}$ by first changing to a mixed number.

TO THINK ABOUT: When a Denominator Is Prime A student concluded that just by looking at the denominator he could tell that the fraction $\frac{1655}{97}$ cannot be reduced unless $1655 \div 97$ is a whole number. How did he come to that conclusion?

Note that 97 is a prime number. The only factors of 97 are 97 and 1. Therefore, *any* fraction with 97 in the denominator can be reduced only if 97 is a factor of the numerator. Since $1655 \div 97$ is not a whole number (see the following division), it is therefore impossible to reduce $\frac{1655}{97}$.

$$\begin{array}{r} 17 \\ 97\overline{)1655} \\ \underline{97} \\ 685 \\ \underline{679} \\ 6 \end{array}$$

You may explore this idea in Section 3 Exercises, exercises 83 and 84.

Section 3 Exercises

Verbal and Writing Skills

1. Describe in your own words how to change a mixed number to an improper fraction.

2. Describe in your own words how to change an improper fraction to a mixed number.

Change each mixed number to an improper fraction.

3. $2\frac{1}{3}$ 4. $2\frac{3}{4}$ 5. $2\frac{3}{7}$ 6. $3\frac{3}{8}$ 7. $9\frac{2}{9}$ 8. $8\frac{3}{8}$

9. $10\frac{2}{3}$ 10. $15\frac{3}{4}$ 11. $11\frac{3}{5}$ 12. $15\frac{4}{5}$ 13. $9\frac{1}{6}$ 14. $41\frac{1}{2}$

15. $20\frac{1}{6}$ 16. $6\frac{6}{7}$ 17. $10\frac{11}{12}$ 18. $13\frac{5}{7}$ 19. $7\frac{9}{10}$ 20. $4\frac{1}{50}$

21. $8\frac{1}{25}$ 22. $12\frac{5}{6}$ 23. $5\frac{5}{12}$ 24. $207\frac{2}{3}$ 25. $164\frac{2}{3}$ 26. $33\frac{1}{3}$

27. $8\frac{11}{15}$ 28. $5\frac{19}{20}$ 29. $4\frac{13}{25}$ 30. $5\frac{17}{20}$

Change each improper fraction to a mixed number or a whole number.

31. $\frac{4}{3}$ 32. $\frac{13}{4}$ 33. $\frac{11}{4}$ 34. $\frac{9}{5}$ 35. $\frac{15}{6}$ 36. $\frac{23}{6}$

37. $\frac{27}{8}$ 38. $\frac{80}{5}$ 39. $\frac{100}{4}$ 40. $\frac{42}{13}$ 41. $\frac{86}{9}$ 42. $\frac{47}{2}$

43. $\frac{70}{3}$ 44. $\frac{54}{17}$ 45. $\frac{25}{4}$ 46. $\frac{19}{3}$ 47. $\frac{57}{10}$ 48. $\frac{83}{10}$

49. $\frac{35}{2}$ 50. $\frac{132}{11}$ 51. $\frac{91}{7}$ 52. $\frac{183}{7}$ 53. $\frac{210}{15}$ 54. $\frac{196}{9}$

55. $\frac{102}{17}$ 56. $\frac{104}{8}$ 57. $\frac{175}{32}$ 58. $\frac{154}{25}$

Reduce each mixed number.

59. $5\frac{3}{6}$ 60. $4\frac{6}{8}$ 61. $4\frac{11}{66}$ 62. $3\frac{15}{90}$ 63. $15\frac{18}{72}$ 64. $10\frac{15}{75}$

Reduce each improper fraction.

65. $\frac{24}{6}$ 66. $\frac{36}{4}$ 67. $\frac{36}{15}$ 68. $\frac{63}{45}$ 69. $\frac{105}{28}$ 70. $\frac{112}{21}$

Change to a mixed number and reduce.

71. $\frac{340}{126}$ 72. $\frac{390}{360}$ 73. $\frac{580}{280}$

74. $\frac{764}{328}$ 75. $\frac{508}{296}$ 76. $\frac{2150}{1000}$

Applications

77. ***Banner Display*** The Science Museum is hanging banners all over the building to commemorate the Apollo astronauts. The art department is using $360\frac{2}{3}$ metres of starry-sky parachute fabric. Change this number to an improper fraction.

78. ***Sculpture*** For the Northwestern University alumni homecoming, the students studying sculpture have made a giant replica of the school using $244\frac{3}{4}$ kilograms of clay. Change this number to an improper fraction.

79. ***Environmental Studies*** A Cape Cod cranberry bog was contaminated by waste from abandoned oil storage tanks at Otis Air Force Base. Damage was done to $\frac{151}{3}$ acres of land. Write this as a mixed number.

80. ***Theatre*** Waite Auditorium needs new velvet stage curtains. The manufacturer took measurements and calculated he would need $\frac{331}{4}$ square metres of fabric. Write this as a mixed number.

81. ***Cooking*** The cafeteria workers at Ipswich High School used $\frac{1131}{8}$ kilograms of flour while cooking for the students last week. Write this as a mixed number.

82. ***Shelf Construction*** The new Centre for Construction Trades and Building Sciences at Algonquin College had several new offices for the faculty and staff. Shelving was constructed for these offices. A total of $\frac{1373}{8}$ metres of shelving was used in the construction. Write this as a mixed number.

To Think About

83. Can $\frac{5687}{101}$ be reduced? Why or why not?

84. Can $\frac{9810}{157}$ be reduced? Why or why not?

Quick Quiz 3

1. Change to an improper fraction.

$4\frac{7}{13}$

2. Change to a mixed number.

$\frac{89}{12}$

3. Reduce the improper fraction.

$\frac{42}{14}$

4. **Concept Check** Explain how you change the mixed number $5\frac{6}{13}$ to an improper fraction.

SECTION 4 MULTIPLYING FRACTIONS AND MIXED NUMBERS

Multiplying Two Fractions That Are Proper or Improper

Student Learning Objectives

After studying this section, you will be able to:

1. **Multiply two fractions that are proper or improper.**
2. **Multiply a whole number by a fraction.**
3. **Multiply mixed numbers.**

John Paul Endress/Corbis/Stock Market

FUDGE SQUARES

Ingredients:

2 cups sugar	1/4 teaspoon salt
4 oz chocolate	1 teaspoon vanilla
1/2 cup butter	1 cup all-purpose flour
4 eggs	1 cup nutmeats

Suppose you want to make an amount equal to half of what the recipe shown will produce. You would multiply the measure given for each ingredient by $\frac{1}{2}$.

$\frac{1}{2}$ of 2 cups sugar	$\frac{1}{2}$ of $\frac{1}{4}$ teaspoon salt
$\frac{1}{2}$ of 4 oz chocolate	$\frac{1}{2}$ of 1 teaspoon vanilla
$\frac{1}{2}$ of $\frac{1}{2}$ cup butter	$\frac{1}{2}$ of 1 cup all-purpose flour
$\frac{1}{2}$ of 4 eggs	$\frac{1}{2}$ of 1 cup nutmeats

We often use multiplication of fractions to describe taking a fractional part of something. To find $\frac{1}{2}$ of $\frac{3}{7}$, we multiply

$$\frac{1}{2} \times \frac{3}{7} = \frac{3}{14}.$$

We begin with a bar that is $\frac{3}{7}$ shaded. To find $\frac{1}{2}$ of $\frac{3}{7}$ we divide the bar in half and take $\frac{1}{2}$ of the shaded section. $\frac{1}{2}$ of $\frac{3}{7}$ yields 3 out of 14 squares.

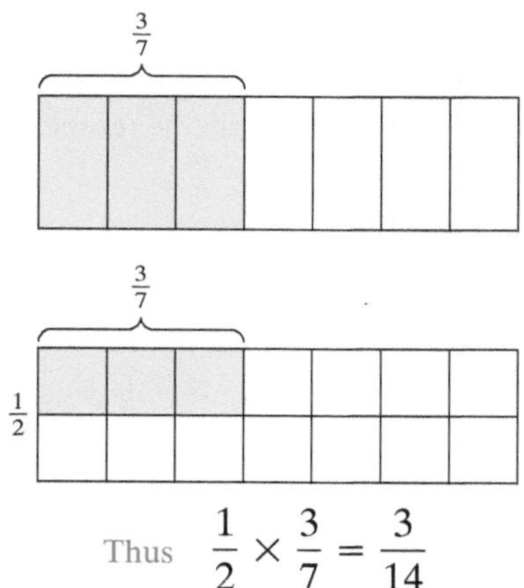

$$\text{Thus} \quad \frac{1}{2} \times \frac{3}{7} = \frac{3}{14}$$

When you multiply two proper fractions together, you get a smaller fraction.

To multiply two fractions, we multiply the numerators and multiply the denominators.

$$\frac{2}{3} \times \frac{5}{7} = \frac{10}{21} \begin{array}{l} \leftarrow 2 \times 5 = 10 \\ \leftarrow 3 \times 7 = 21 \end{array}$$

MULTIPLICATION OF FRACTIONS

In general, for all positive whole numbers a, b, c, and d,

$$\frac{a}{b} \times \frac{c}{d} = \frac{a \times c}{b \times d}.$$

EXAMPLE 1 Multiply.

(a) $\frac{3}{8} \times \frac{5}{7}$ **(b)** $\frac{1}{11} \times \frac{2}{13}$

Solution

(a) $\frac{3}{8} \times \frac{5}{7} = \frac{3 \times 5}{8 \times 7} = \frac{15}{56}$ **(b)** $\frac{1}{11} \times \frac{2}{13} = \frac{1 \times 2}{11 \times 13} = \frac{2}{143}$

NOTE TO STUDENT: Fully worked-out solutions to all of the Practice Problems can be found at the end of the module.

Practice Problem 1 Multiply.

(a) $\frac{6}{7} \times \frac{3}{13}$ **(b)** $\frac{1}{5} \times \frac{11}{12}$

Some products may be reduced. $\frac{12}{35} \times \frac{25}{18} = \frac{300}{630} = \frac{10}{21}$

By simplifying before multiplication, the reducing can be done more easily. For a multiplication problem, a factor in the numerator can be paired with a common factor in the denominator of the same or a different fraction. We can begin by finding the prime factors in the numerators and denominators. We then divide numerator and denominator by their common prime factors.

EXAMPLE 2 Simplify first and then multiply. $\frac{12}{35} \times \frac{25}{18}$

Solution

$\frac{12}{35} \times \frac{25}{18} = \frac{2 \cdot 2 \cdot 3}{5 \cdot 7} \times \frac{5 \cdot 5}{2 \cdot 3 \cdot 3}$ First we find the prime factors.

$= \frac{2 \cdot 2 \cdot 3 \cdot 5 \cdot 5}{5 \cdot 7 \cdot 2 \cdot 3 \cdot 3}$ Write the product as one fraction.

$= \frac{\overset{1}{\cancel{2}} \cdot 2 \cdot \overset{1}{\cancel{3}} \cdot \overset{1}{\cancel{5}} \cdot 5}{\underset{1}{\cancel{2}} \cdot \underset{1}{\cancel{3}} \cdot 3 \cdot \underset{1}{\cancel{5}} \cdot 7}$ Arrange the factors in order and divide the numerator and denominator by the common factors.

$= \frac{10}{21}$ Multiply the remaining factors.

Practice Problem 2 Simplify first and then multiply.

$$\frac{55}{72} \times \frac{16}{33}$$

Note: Although finding the prime factors of the numerators and denominators will help you avoid errors, you can also begin these problems by dividing the numerators and denominators by larger common factors. This method will be used for the remainder of the exercises in this section.

Multiplying a Whole Number by a Fraction

When multiplying a fraction by a whole number, it is more convenient to express the whole number as a fraction with a denominator of 1. We know that $5 = \frac{5}{1}$, $7 = \frac{7}{1}$, and so on.

EXAMPLE 3 Multiply.

(a) $5 \times \frac{3}{8}$ **(b)** $\frac{22}{7} \times 14$

Solution

(a) $5 \times \frac{3}{8} = \frac{5}{1} \times \frac{3}{8} = \frac{15}{8}$ or $1\frac{7}{8}$ **(b)** $\frac{22}{7} \times 14 = \frac{22}{\underset{1}{\cancel{7}}} \times \frac{\overset{2}{\cancel{14}}}{1} = \frac{44}{1} = 44$

Practice Problem 3 Multiply.

(a) $7 \times \frac{5}{13}$ **(b)** $\frac{13}{4} \times 8$

EXAMPLE 4 Mr. and Mrs. Jones found that $\frac{2}{7}$ of their income went to pay federal income taxes. Last year they earned \$37 100. How much did they pay in taxes?

Solution We need to find $\frac{2}{7}$ of \$37 100. So we must multiply $\frac{2}{7} \times 37\,100$.

$$\frac{2}{\underset{1}{\cancel{7}}} \times \overset{5300}{\cancel{37\,100}} = \frac{2}{1} \times 5300 = 10\,600$$

They paid \$10 600 in federal income taxes.

Practice Problem 4 Fred and Linda own 98 400 square metres of land. They found that $\frac{3}{8}$ of the land is in a wetland area and cannot be used for building. How many square metres of land are in the wetland area?

3 Multiplying Mixed Numbers

To multiply a fraction by a mixed number or to multiply two mixed numbers, first change each mixed number to an improper fraction.

EXAMPLE 5 Multiply.

(a) $\frac{5}{7} \times 3\frac{1}{4}$ **(b)** $20\frac{2}{5} \times 6\frac{2}{3}$ **(c)** $\frac{3}{4} \times 1\frac{1}{2} \times \frac{4}{7}$ **(d)** $4\frac{1}{3} \times 2\frac{1}{4}$

Solution

(a) $\frac{5}{7} \times 3\frac{1}{4} = \frac{5}{7} \times \frac{13}{4} = \frac{65}{28}$ or $2\frac{9}{28}$

(b) $20\frac{2}{5} \times 6\frac{2}{3} = \frac{\overset{34}{\cancel{102}}}{\underset{1}{\cancel{5}}} \times \frac{\overset{4}{\cancel{20}}}{\underset{1}{\cancel{3}}} = \frac{136}{1} = 136$

(c) $\frac{3}{4} \times 1\frac{1}{2} \times \frac{4}{7} = \frac{3}{\cancel{4}_1} \times \frac{3}{2} \times \frac{\overset{1}{\cancel{4}}}{7} = \frac{9}{14}$

(d) $4\frac{1}{3} \times 2\frac{1}{4} = \frac{13}{\cancel{3}_1} \times \frac{\overset{3}{\cancel{9}}}{4} = \frac{39}{4}$ or $9\frac{3}{4}$

NOTE TO STUDENT: Fully worked-out solutions to all of the Practice Problems can be found at the end of the module.

Practice Problem 5 Multiply.

(a) $2\frac{1}{6} \times \frac{4}{7}$

(b) $10\frac{2}{3} \times 13\frac{1}{2}$

(c) $\frac{3}{5} \times 1\frac{1}{3} \times \frac{5}{8}$

(d) $3\frac{1}{5} \times 2\frac{1}{2}$

▲ **EXAMPLE 6** Find the area in square kilometres of a rectangle with width $1\frac{1}{3}$ kilometres and length $12\frac{1}{4}$ kilometres.

Length = $12\frac{1}{4}$ kilometres

Width = $1\frac{1}{3}$ kilometres

Solution We find the area of a rectangle by multiplying the width times the length.

$$1\frac{1}{3} \times 12\frac{1}{4} = \frac{\overset{1}{\cancel{4}}}{3} \times \frac{49}{\cancel{4}_1} = \frac{49}{3} \quad \text{or} \quad 16\frac{1}{3}$$

The area is $16\frac{1}{3}$ square kilometres.

▲ **Practice Problem 6** Find the area in square metres of a rectangle with width $1\frac{1}{5}$ metres and length $4\frac{5}{6}$ metres.

EXAMPLE 7 Find the value of x if

$$\frac{3}{7} \cdot x = \frac{15}{42}.$$

Solution The variable x represents a fraction. We know that 3 times one number equals 15 and 7 times another equals 42.

Since $3 \cdot 5 = 15$
and $7 \cdot 6 = 42$ we know that $\frac{3}{7} \cdot \frac{5}{6} = \frac{15}{42}$.

Therefore, $x = \frac{5}{6}$.

Practice Problem 7 Find the value of x if $\frac{8}{9} \cdot x = \frac{80}{81}$.

Section 4 Exercises

Multiply. Make sure all fractions are simplified in the final answer.

1. $\frac{3}{5} \times \frac{7}{11}$

2. $\frac{1}{8} \times \frac{5}{11}$

3. $\frac{3}{4} \times \frac{5}{13}$

4. $\frac{4}{7} \times \frac{3}{5}$

5. $\frac{6}{5} \times \frac{10}{12}$

6. $\frac{7}{8} \times \frac{16}{21}$

7. $\frac{5}{36} \times \frac{9}{20}$

8. $\frac{22}{45} \times \frac{5}{11}$

9. $\frac{12}{25} \times \frac{5}{11}$

10. $\frac{9}{4} \times \frac{13}{27}$

11. $\frac{9}{10} \times \frac{35}{12}$

12. $\frac{12}{17} \times \frac{3}{24}$

13. $8 \times \frac{3}{7}$

14. $\frac{8}{9} \times 6$

15. $\frac{5}{12} \times 8$

16. $5 \times \frac{7}{25}$

17. $\frac{4}{9} \times \frac{3}{7} \times \frac{7}{8}$

18. $\frac{8}{7} \times \frac{5}{12} \times \frac{3}{10}$

19. $\frac{5}{4} \times \frac{9}{10} \times \frac{8}{3}$

20. $\frac{5}{7} \times \frac{15}{2} \times \frac{28}{15}$

Multiply. Change any mixed number to an improper fraction before multiplying.

21. $2\frac{5}{6} \times \frac{3}{17}$

22. $\frac{5}{6} \times 3\frac{3}{5}$

23. $10 \times 3\frac{1}{10}$

24. $12 \times 5\frac{7}{12}$

25. $1\frac{3}{16} \times 0$

26. $0 \times 6\frac{2}{3}$

27. $3\frac{7}{8} \times 1$

28. $\frac{5}{5} \times 11\frac{5}{7}$

29. $1\frac{1}{4} \times 3\frac{2}{3}$

30. $2\frac{3}{5} \times 1\frac{4}{7}$

31. $2\frac{3}{10} \times \frac{3}{5}$

32. $4\frac{3}{5} \times \frac{1}{10}$

33. $4\frac{1}{5} \times 8\frac{1}{3}$

34. $5\frac{1}{4} \times 4\frac{4}{7}$

35. $6\frac{2}{5} \times \frac{1}{4}$

36. $\frac{8}{9} \times 4\frac{1}{11}$

Mixed Practice *Multiply. Make sure all fractions are simplified in the final answer.*

37. $\frac{11}{15} \times \frac{35}{33}$

38. $\frac{14}{17} \times \frac{34}{42}$

39. $2\frac{3}{8} \times 5\frac{1}{3}$

40. $4\frac{3}{5} \times 3\frac{3}{4}$

Solve for x.

41. $\frac{4}{9} \cdot x = \frac{28}{81}$

42. $\frac{12}{17} \cdot x = \frac{144}{85}$

43. $\frac{7}{13} \cdot x = \frac{56}{117}$

44. $x \cdot \frac{11}{15} = \frac{77}{225}$

Applications

▲**45.** ***Geometry*** A spy is running from his captors in a forest that is $8\frac{3}{4}$ kilometres long and $4\frac{1}{3}$ kilometres wide. Find the area of the forest where he is hiding. (*Hint:* The area of a rectangle is the product of the length times the width.)

▲**46.** ***Geometry*** An area in the Midwest is a designated tornado danger zone. The land is $22\frac{5}{8}$ kilometres long and $16\frac{1}{2}$ kilometres wide. Find the area of the tornado danger zone. (*Hint:* The area of a rectangle is the product of the length times the width.)

47. ***Airplane Travel*** A Learjet airplane has 1360 litres of fuel. The plane averages $1\frac{3}{4}$ kilometres per litre. How far can the plane go?

48. ***Real Estate*** Mel and Sally Hauser bought their house in 1977 for a price of \$56 800. Thirty years later, in 2007, their house was worth $6\frac{1}{2}$ times what they paid for it. How much was Mel and Sally's house worth in 2007?

49. ***Cooking*** A recipe from Nanette's French cookbook for a scalloped potato tart requires $90\frac{1}{2}$ grams of grated cheese. How many grams of cheese would she need if she made one tart for each of her 18 cousins?

▲**50.** ***Geometry*** The dormitory rooms in Selkirk Hall are being carpeted. Each room requires $20\frac{1}{2}$ square metres of carpet. If there are 30 rooms, how much carpet is needed?

51. ***College Students*** Of the 7998 students at Normandale Community College, $\frac{2}{3}$ of them are under 25 years of age. How many students are under 25 years of age?

52. ***Health Care*** A nurse finds that of the 225 rooms at the Children's Hospital of Eastern Ontario, $\frac{1}{15}$ of them are occupied by surgery patients. How many rooms contain surgery patients?

53. ***Job Search*** Carlos has sent his resumé to 12 064 companies through an Internet job search service. If $\frac{1}{32}$ of the companies e-mail him with an invitation for an interview, how many companies will he have heard from?

54. ***Car Purchase*** Russ purchased a new Buick LeSabre for \$26 500. After one year the car was worth $\frac{4}{5}$ of the purchase price. What was the car worth after one year?

55. ***Jogging*** Mary jogged $4\frac{1}{4}$ kilometres per hour for $1\frac{1}{3}$ hours. During $\frac{1}{3}$ of her jogging time, she was jogging in the rain. How many kilometres did she jog in the rain?

56. ***College Students*** There were 1340 students at the Whitby campus of Durham College during the spring 2009 semester. The registrar discovered that $\frac{2}{5}$ of these students live in the city of Whitby. He further discovered that $\frac{1}{4}$ of the students living in Whitby attend classes only on Monday, Wednesday, and Friday. How many students at the Whitby campus live in the city of Whitby and attend classes only on Monday, Wednesday, and Friday?

To Think About

57. When we multiply two fractions, we look for opportunities to divide a numerator and a denominator by the same number. Why do we bother with that step? Why don't we just multiply the two numerators and the two denominators?

58. Suppose there is an unknown fraction that has *not* been simplified (it is not reduced). You multiply this unknown fraction by $\frac{2}{5}$ and you obtain a simplified answer of $\frac{6}{35}$. How many possible values could this unknown fraction be? Give at least three possible answers.

Quick Quiz 4 Multiply.

1. $32 \times \dfrac{5}{16}$

2. $\dfrac{11}{13} \times \dfrac{4}{5}$

3. $4\dfrac{1}{3} \times 2\dfrac{3}{4}$

4. **Concept Check** Explain how you would multiply the whole number 6 times the mixed number $4\frac{3}{5}$.

SECTION 5 DIVIDING FRACTIONS AND MIXED NUMBERS

Student Learning Objectives

After studying this section, you will be able to:

1. **Divide two proper or improper fractions.**
2. **Divide a whole number and a fraction.**
3. **Divide mixed numbers.**

Dividing Two Proper or Improper Fractions

Why would you divide fractions? Consider this problem.

- A copper pipe that is $\frac{3}{4}$ of a metre long is to be cut into $\frac{1}{4}$-metre pieces. How many pieces will there be?

To find how many $\frac{1}{4}$'s are in $\frac{3}{4}$, we divide $\frac{3}{4} \div \frac{1}{4}$. We draw a sketch.

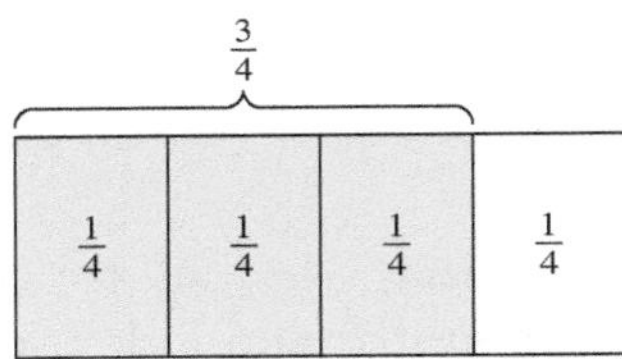

Notice that there are three $\frac{1}{4}$'s in $\frac{3}{4}$.

How do we divide two fractions? We **invert** the second fraction and multiply.

$$\frac{3}{4} \div \frac{1}{4} = \frac{3}{\cancel{4}_1} \times \frac{\cancel{4}^1}{1} = \frac{3}{1} = 3$$

When we invert a fraction, we interchange the numerator and the denominator. If we invert $\frac{5}{9}$, we obtain $\frac{9}{5}$. If we invert $\frac{6}{1}$, we obtain $\frac{1}{6}$. Numbers such as $\frac{5}{9}$ and $\frac{9}{5}$ are called **reciprocals** of each other.

RULE FOR DIVISION OF FRACTIONS

To divide two fractions, we invert the second fraction and multiply.

$$\frac{a}{b} \div \frac{c}{d} = \frac{a}{b} \times \frac{d}{c}$$

(when b, c, and d are not zero).

EXAMPLE 1 Divide.

(a) $\frac{3}{11} \div \frac{2}{5}$ **(b)** $\frac{5}{8} \div \frac{25}{16}$

Solution

(a) $\frac{3}{11} \div \frac{2}{5} = \frac{3}{11} \times \frac{5}{2} = \frac{15}{22}$

(b) $\frac{5}{8} \div \frac{25}{16} = \frac{\cancel{5}^1}{\cancel{8}_1} \times \frac{\cancel{16}^2}{\cancel{25}_5} = \frac{2}{5}$

Practice Problem 1 Divide.

(a) $\frac{7}{13} \div \frac{3}{4}$ **(b)** $\frac{16}{35} \div \frac{24}{25}$

NOTE TO STUDENT: Fully worked-out solutions to all of the Practice Problems can be found at the end of the module.

Dividing a Whole Number and a Fraction

When dividing with whole numbers, it is helpful to remember that for any whole number a, $a = \frac{a}{1}$.

EXAMPLE 2 Divide.

(a) $\frac{3}{7} \div 2$

(b) $5 \div \frac{10}{13}$

Solution

(a) $\frac{3}{7} \div 2 = \frac{3}{7} \div \frac{2}{1} = \frac{3}{7} \times \frac{1}{2} = \frac{3}{14}$

(b) $5 \div \frac{10}{13} = \frac{5}{1} \div \frac{10}{13} = \frac{\overset{1}{\cancel{5}}}{1} \times \frac{13}{\underset{2}{\cancel{10}}} = \frac{13}{2}$ or $6\frac{1}{2}$

Practice Problem 2 Divide.

(a) $\frac{3}{17} \div 6$

(b) $14 \div \frac{7}{15}$

EXAMPLE 3 Divide, if possible.

(a) $\frac{23}{25} \div 1$

(b) $1 \div \frac{7}{5}$

(c) $0 \div \frac{4}{9}$

(d) $\frac{3}{17} \div 0$

Solution

(a) $\frac{23}{25} \div 1 = \frac{23}{25} \times \frac{1}{1} = \frac{23}{25}$

(b) $1 \div \frac{7}{5} = \frac{1}{1} \times \frac{5}{7} = \frac{5}{7}$

(c) $0 \div \frac{4}{9} = \frac{0}{1} \times \frac{9}{4} = \frac{0}{4} = 0$ Zero divided by any nonzero number is zero.

(d) $\frac{3}{17} \div 0$ Division by zero is undefined.

Practice Problem 3 Divide, if possible.

(a) $1 \div \frac{11}{13}$

(b) $\frac{14}{17} \div 1$

(c) $\frac{3}{11} \div 0$

(d) $0 \div \frac{9}{16}$

SIDELIGHT: Invert and Multiply

Why do we divide by inverting the second fraction and multiplying? What is really going on when we do this? We are actually multiplying by 1. To see why, consider the following.

$$\frac{3}{7} \div \frac{2}{3} = \frac{\frac{3}{7}}{\frac{2}{3}}$$ We write the division by using another fraction bar.

$$= \frac{\frac{3}{7}}{\frac{2}{3}} \times 1$$ Any fraction can be multiplied by 1 without changing the value of the fraction. This is the fundamental rule of fractions.

$$= \frac{\frac{3}{7}}{\frac{2}{3}} \times \frac{\frac{3}{2}}{\frac{3}{2}}$$ Any nonzero number divided by itself equals 1.

$$= \frac{\frac{3}{7} \times \frac{3}{2}}{\frac{2}{3} \times \frac{3}{2}}$$ Definition of multiplication of fractions.

$$= \frac{\frac{3}{7} \times \frac{3}{2}}{1} = \frac{3}{7} \times \frac{3}{2}$$ Any number can be written as a fraction with a denominator of 1 without changing its value.

Thus

$$\frac{3}{7} \div \frac{2}{3} = \frac{3}{7} \times \frac{3}{2} = \frac{9}{14}.$$

3 Dividing Mixed Numbers

If one or more mixed numbers are involved in the division, they should be converted to improper fractions first.

EXAMPLE 4 Divide.

(a) $3\frac{7}{15} \div 1\frac{1}{25}$

(b) $\frac{3}{5} \div 2\frac{1}{7}$

Solution

(a) $3\frac{7}{15} \div 1\frac{1}{25} = \frac{52}{15} \div \frac{26}{25} = \frac{\overset{2}{\cancel{52}}}{\underset{3}{\cancel{15}}} \times \frac{\overset{5}{\cancel{25}}}{\underset{1}{\cancel{26}}} = \frac{10}{3}$ or $3\frac{1}{3}$

(b) $\frac{3}{5} \div 2\frac{1}{7} = \frac{3}{5} \div \frac{15}{7} = \frac{\overset{1}{\cancel{3}}}{5} \times \frac{7}{\underset{5}{\cancel{15}}} = \frac{7}{25}$

Practice Problem 4 Divide.

(a) $1\frac{1}{5} \div \frac{7}{10}$

(b) $2\frac{1}{4} \div 1\frac{7}{8}$

NOTE TO STUDENT: Fully worked-out solutions to all of the Practice Problems can be found at the end of the module.

The division of two fractions may be indicated by a wide fraction bar.

EXAMPLE 5 Divide.

(a) $\dfrac{10\frac{2}{9}}{2\frac{1}{3}}$ **(b)** $\dfrac{1\frac{1}{15}}{3\frac{1}{3}}$

Solution

(a) $\dfrac{10\frac{2}{9}}{2\frac{1}{3}} = 10\frac{2}{9} \div 2\frac{1}{3} = \frac{92}{9} \div \frac{7}{3} = \frac{92}{\cancelto{3}{9}} \times \frac{\cancelto{1}{3}}{7} = \frac{92}{21}$ or $4\frac{8}{21}$

(b) $\dfrac{1\frac{1}{15}}{3\frac{1}{3}} = 1\frac{1}{15} \div 3\frac{1}{3} = \frac{16}{15} \div \frac{10}{3} = \frac{\cancelto{8}{16}}{\cancelto{5}{15}} \times \frac{\cancelto{1}{3}}{\cancelto{5}{10}} = \frac{8}{25}$

Practice Problem 5 Divide.

(a) $\dfrac{5\frac{2}{3}}{7}$ **(b)** $\dfrac{1\frac{2}{5}}{2\frac{1}{3}}$

Some students may find Example 6 difficult at first. Read it slowly and carefully. It may be necessary to read it several times before it becomes clear.

EXAMPLE 6 Find the value of x if $x \div \frac{8}{7} = \frac{21}{40}$.

Solution First we will change the division problem to an equivalent multiplication problem.

$$x \div \frac{8}{7} = \frac{21}{40}$$

$$x \cdot \frac{7}{8} = \frac{21}{40}$$

x represents a fraction.

In the numerator, we want to know what times 7 equals 21. In the denominator, we want to know what times 8 equals 40.

$$\frac{3}{5} \cdot \frac{7}{8} = \frac{21}{40}$$

Thus $x = \frac{3}{5}$.

Practice Problem 6 Find the value of x if $x \div \frac{3}{2} = \frac{22}{36}$.

EXAMPLE 7 There are 117 milligrams of cholesterol in $4\frac{1}{3}$ cups of milk. How much cholesterol is in 1 cup of milk?

Solution We want to divide the 117 by $4\frac{1}{3}$ to find out how much is in 1 cup.

$$117 \div 4\frac{1}{3} = 117 \div \frac{13}{3} = \frac{\overset{9}{\cancel{117}}}{1} \times \frac{3}{\underset{1}{\cancel{13}}} = \frac{27}{1} = 27$$

Thus there are 27 milligrams of cholesterol in 1 cup of milk.

NOTE TO STUDENT: Fully worked-out solutions to all of the Practice Problems can be found at the end of the module.

Practice Problem 7 A copper pipe that is $19\frac{1}{4}$ metres long will be cut into 14 equal pieces. How long will each piece be?

Take a little time to review Examples 1–7 and Practice Problems 1–7. This is important material. It is crucial to understand how to do each of these problems. Some extra time spent reviewing here will make the homework exercises go much more quickly.

Developing Your Study Skills

Why Is Review Necessary?

You master a course in mathematics by learning the concepts one step at a time. There are basic concepts like addition, subtraction, multiplication, and division of whole numbers that are considered the foundation upon which all of mathematics is built. These must be mastered first. Then the study of mathematics is built step by step upon this foundation, each step supporting the next. The process is a carefully designed procedure, so no steps can be skipped. A student of mathematics needs to realize the importance of this building process to succeed.

Because learning new concepts depends on those previously learned, students often need to take time to review. The reviewing process will strengthen the understanding and application of concepts that are weak due to lack of mastery or passage of time. Review at the right time on the right concepts can strengthen previously learned skills and make progress possible.

Timely, periodic review of previously learned mathematical concepts is absolutely necessary in order to master new concepts. You may have forgotten a concept or grown a bit rusty in applying it. Reviewing is the answer. Make use of any review sections, whether they are assigned or not. Look back to previous material whenever you have forgotten how to do something. Study the examples and practise some exercises to refresh your understanding.

Be sure that you understand and can perform the computations of each new concept. This will enable you to move successfully on to the next ones.

Section 5 Exercises

Make sure all fractions are simplified in the final answer.

Verbal and Writing Skills

1. In your own words explain how to remember that when you divide two fractions you invert the *second* fraction and multiply by the first. How can you be sure that you don't invert the *first* fraction by mistake?

2. Explain why $2 \div \frac{1}{3}$ is a larger number than $2 \div \frac{1}{2}$.

Divide, if possible.

3. $\frac{7}{16} \div \frac{3}{4}$

4. $\frac{3}{13} \div \frac{9}{26}$

5. $\frac{2}{3} \div \frac{4}{27}$

6. $\frac{25}{49} \div \frac{5}{7}$

7. $\frac{7}{18} \div \frac{21}{6}$

8. $\frac{8}{15} \div \frac{24}{35}$

9. $\frac{5}{9} \div \frac{1}{5}$

10. $\frac{3}{4} \div \frac{2}{3}$

11. $\frac{4}{15} \div \frac{4}{15}$

12. $\frac{2}{7} \div \frac{2}{7}$

13. $\frac{3}{7} \div \frac{7}{3}$

14. $\frac{11}{12} \div \frac{1}{5}$

15. $\frac{4}{5} \div 1$

16. $1 \div \frac{3}{7}$

17. $\frac{3}{11} \div 4$

18. $2 \div \frac{7}{8}$

19. $1 \div \frac{7}{27}$

20. $\frac{9}{16} \div 1$

21. $0 \div \frac{3}{17}$

22. $0 \div \frac{5}{16}$

23. $\frac{18}{19} \div 0$

24. $\frac{24}{29} \div 0$

25. $8 \div \frac{4}{5}$

26. $16 \div \frac{8}{11}$

27. $\frac{7}{8} \div 4$

28. $\frac{5}{6} \div 12$

29. $\frac{9}{16} \div \frac{3}{4}$

30. $\frac{3}{4} \div \frac{9}{16}$

31. $3\frac{1}{4} \div 2\frac{1}{4}$

32. $2\frac{2}{3} \div 4\frac{1}{3}$

33. $6\frac{2}{5} \div 3\frac{1}{5}$

34. $9\frac{1}{3} \div 3\frac{1}{9}$

35. $6000 \div \frac{6}{5}$

36. $8000 \div \frac{4}{7}$

37. $\dfrac{\frac{4}{5}}{200}$

38. $\dfrac{\frac{5}{9}}{100}$

39. $\dfrac{\frac{5}{8}}{\frac{25}{7}}$

40. $\dfrac{\frac{3}{16}}{\frac{5}{8}}$

Mixed Practice *Multiply or divide.*

41. $3\frac{1}{5} \div \frac{1}{5}$

42. $4\frac{3}{4} \div \frac{1}{4}$

43. $2\frac{1}{3} \times \frac{1}{6}$

44. $6\frac{1}{2} \times \frac{1}{3}$

45. $5\frac{1}{4} \div 2\frac{5}{8}$

46. $1\frac{2}{9} \div 4\frac{1}{3}$

47. $5 \div 1\frac{1}{4}$

48. $7 \div 1\frac{2}{5}$

49. $5\frac{2}{3} \div 2\frac{1}{4}$

50. $14\frac{2}{3} \div 3\frac{1}{2}$

51. $\frac{7}{2} \div 3\frac{1}{2}$

52. $\frac{16}{3} \div 5\frac{1}{3}$

53. $\frac{13}{25} \times 2\frac{1}{3}$

54. $\frac{11}{20} \times 4\frac{1}{2}$

55. $3\frac{3}{4} \div 9$

56. $5\frac{5}{6} \div 7$

57. $\dfrac{5}{3\frac{1}{6}}$

58. $\dfrac{8}{2\frac{1}{2}}$

59. $\dfrac{0}{4\frac{3}{8}}$

60. $\dfrac{5\frac{2}{5}}{0}$

61. $\dfrac{\frac{7}{12}}{3\frac{2}{3}}$

62. $\dfrac{\frac{9}{10}}{3\frac{3}{5}}$

63. $4\frac{2}{5} \times 2\frac{8}{11}$

64. $4\frac{2}{3} \times 5\frac{1}{7}$

Review Example 6. Then find the value of x in each of the following.

65. $x \div \frac{4}{3} = \frac{21}{20}$

66. $x \div \frac{2}{5} = \frac{15}{16}$

67. $x \div \frac{10}{7} = \frac{21}{100}$

68. $x \div \frac{11}{6} = \frac{54}{121}$

Applications *Answer each question.*

69. ***Leather Factory*** A leather factory in Morocco tans leather. In order to make the leather soft, it has to soak in a vat of uric acid and other ingredients. The main holding tank holds $60\frac{3}{4}$ litres of the tanning mixture. If the mixture is distributed evenly into nine vats of equal size for the different coloured leathers, how much will each vat hold?

70. ***Marine Biology*** A specially protected stretch of beach bordering the Great Barrier Reef in Australia is used for marine biology and ecological research. The beach, which is $7\frac{1}{2}$ kilometres long, has been broken up into 20 equal segments for comparison purposes. How long is each segment of the beach?

71. ***Vehicle Travel*** Bruce drove in a snowstorm to get to his favourite mountain to do some snowboarding. He travelled 125 kilometres in $3\frac{1}{3}$ hours. What was his average speed (in kilometres per hour)?

72. ***Vehicle Travel*** Roberto drove his truck to Cedarville, a distance of 200 kilometres, in $4\frac{1}{6}$ hours. What was his average speed (in kilometres per hour)?

73. ***Cooking*** The school cafeteria is making hamburgers for the annual Senior Day Festival. The cooks have decided that because hamburger shrinks on the grill, they will allow $\frac{2}{3}$ pound of meat for each student. If the kitchen has $38\frac{2}{3}$ pounds of meat, how many students will be fed?

74. ***Making Costumes*** Costumes are needed for the junior high school's "Wizard of Oz" performance. Each costume requires $4\frac{1}{3}$ metres of fabric and $151\frac{2}{3}$ metres are available. How many costumes can be made?

75. ***Cooking*** A coffee pot that holds 150 cups of coffee is being used at a company meeting. Each large Styrofoam cup holds $1\frac{1}{2}$ cups of coffee. How many large Styrofoam cups can be filled?

76. ***Medicine Dosage*** A small bottle of eye drops contains 16 millilitres. If the recommended use is $\frac{2}{3}$ millilitre, how many times can a person use the drops before the bottle is empty?

77. ***Time Capsule*** In 1907, a time capsule was placed behind a steel wall measuring $4\frac{3}{4}$ inches thick. On December 22, 2007, a special drill was used to bore through the wall and extricate the time capsule. The drill could move only $\frac{5}{6}$ inch at a time. How many drill attempts did it take to reach the other side of the steel wall?

78. ***Ink Production*** Imagination Ink supplies different coloured inks for highlighter pens. Vat 1 has yellow ink, holds 150 litres, and is $\frac{4}{5}$ full. Vat 2 has green ink, holds 50 litres, and is $\frac{5}{8}$ full. One litre of ink will fill 300 pens. How many pens can be filled with the existing ink from Vats 1 and 2?

To Think About *When multiplying or dividing mixed numbers, it is wise to estimate your answer by rounding each mixed number to the nearest whole number.*

79. Estimate your answer to $14\frac{2}{3} \div 5\frac{1}{6}$ by rounding each mixed number to the nearest whole number. Then find the exact answer. How close was your estimate?

80. Estimate your answer to $18\frac{1}{4} \times 27\frac{1}{2}$ by rounding each mixed number to the nearest whole number. Then find the exact answer. How close was your estimate?

Quick Quiz 5 Divide.

1. $\frac{15}{24} \div \frac{5}{6}$

2. $6\frac{1}{3} \div 2\frac{5}{12}$

3. $7\frac{3}{4} \div 4$

4. **Concept Check** Explain how you would divide the whole number 7 by the mixed number $3\frac{3}{5}$.

How Am I Doing? Sections 1–5

1. ______

2. ______

3. ______

4. ______

5. ______

6. ______

7. ______

8. ______

9. ______

10. ______

11. ______

12. ______

13. ______

14. ______

15. ______

16. ______

17. ______

18. ______

19. ______

20. ______

How are you doing with your homework assignments in Sections 1 to 5? Do you feel you have mastered the material so far? Do you understand the concepts you have covered? Before you go further, take some time to do each of the following problems.

1

1. Use a fraction to represent the shaded part of the object.

2. Frederich University had 3500 students from inside the province, 2600 students from outside the province but inside the country, and 800 students from outside the country. Write a fraction that describes the part of the student body from outside the country. Reduce the fraction.

3. An inspector checked 124 CD players. Of these, 5 were defective. Write a fraction that describes the part that was defective.

2

Reduce each fraction.

4. $\frac{3}{18}$ **5.** $\frac{13}{39}$ **6.** $\frac{16}{112}$ **7.** $\frac{175}{200}$ **8.** $\frac{44}{121}$

3

Change to an improper fraction.

9. $3\frac{2}{3}$ **10.** $15\frac{1}{3}$

Change to a mixed number.

11. $\frac{81}{4}$ **12.** $\frac{29}{5}$ **13.** $\frac{36}{17}$

4

Multiply.

14. $\frac{5}{11} \times \frac{1}{4}$ **15.** $\frac{3}{7} \times \frac{14}{9}$ **16.** $3\frac{1}{3} \times 5\frac{1}{3}$

5

Divide.

17. $\frac{3}{7} \div \frac{3}{7}$ **18.** $\frac{7}{16} \div \frac{7}{8}$ **19.** $6\frac{4}{7} \div 1\frac{5}{21}$ **20.** $12 \div \frac{4}{7}$

Your institution may have included the Answers to Selected Exercises for this module, which contains the answers to these questions. Each answer also includes a reference to the objective in which the problem is first taught. If you missed any of these problems, you should stop and review the Examples and Practice Problems in the referenced objective. A little review now will help you master the material in the upcoming sections.

How Am I Doing? Test on Sections 1–5

Solve. Make sure all fractions are simplified in the final answer.

1. Norah answered 33 out of 40 questions correctly on her chemistry exam. Write a fraction that describes the part of the exam she answered correctly.

2. Carlos inspected the boxes that were shipped from the central warehouse. He found that 340 were the correct weight and 112 were not. Write a fraction that describes what part of the total number of the boxes were at the correct weight.

Reduce each fraction.

3. $\frac{19}{38}$ **4.** $\frac{40}{56}$ **5.** $\frac{24}{66}$

6. $\frac{125}{155}$ **7.** $\frac{50}{140}$ **8.** $\frac{84}{36}$

Change each mixed number to an improper fraction.

9. $12\frac{2}{3}$ **10.** $4\frac{1}{8}$

Change each improper fraction to a mixed number.

11. $\frac{45}{7}$ **12.** $\frac{75}{9}$

Multiply.

13. $\frac{3}{8} \times \frac{7}{11}$ **14.** $\frac{35}{16} \times \frac{4}{5}$

15. $18 \times \frac{5}{6}$ **16.** $\frac{3}{8} \times 44$

17. $2\frac{1}{3} \times 5\frac{3}{4}$ **18.** $24 \times 3\frac{1}{3}$

Divide.

19. $\frac{4}{7} \div \frac{3}{4}$ **20.** $\frac{8}{9} \div \frac{1}{6}$

21. $5\frac{1}{4} \div \frac{3}{4}$ **22.** $5\frac{3}{5} \div 2\frac{1}{3}$

1. ____________
2. ____________
3. ____________
4. ____________
5. ____________
6. ____________
7. ____________
8. ____________
9. ____________
10. ____________
11. ____________
12. ____________
13. ____________
14. ____________
15. ____________
16. ____________
17. ____________
18. ____________
19. ____________
20. ____________
21. ____________
22. ____________

23. ______

24. ______

25. ______

26. ______

27. ______

28. ______

29. ______

30. ______

31. ______

32. ______

33. ______

34. ______

35. ______

36. ______

37. ______

38. ______

39. ______

Mixed Practice

Perform the indicated operations. Simplify your answers.

23. $2\frac{1}{4} \times 3\frac{1}{2}$

24. $6 \times 2\frac{1}{3}$

25. $5 \div 1\frac{7}{8}$

26. $5\frac{3}{4} \div 2$

27. $\frac{13}{20} \div \frac{4}{5}$

28. $\frac{4}{7} \div 8$

29. $\frac{9}{22} \times \frac{11}{16}$

30. $\frac{14}{25} \times \frac{65}{42}$

Solve. Simplify your answer.

▲ **31.** A garden measures $5\frac{1}{4}$ metres by $8\frac{3}{4}$ metres. What is the area of the garden in square metres?

32. A recipe for two loaves of bread calls for $2\frac{2}{3}$ cups of flour. Lexi wants to make $1\frac{1}{2}$ times as much bread. How many cups of flour will she need?

33. Lisa drove $62\frac{1}{2}$ kilometres to visit a friend. Three-fourths of her trip was on the highway. How many kilometres did she drive on the highway?

34. The butcher prepared $12\frac{3}{8}$ kilograms of lean ground round. He placed it in packages that held $\frac{3}{4}$ of a kilogram. How many full packages did he have? How much lean ground round was left over?

35. The college computer centre has 136 computers. Samuel found that $\frac{3}{8}$ of them have Windows XP installed on them. How many computers have Windows XP installed on them?

36. The average household uses 310 000 litres of water each year. About $\frac{3}{10}$ of this amount is used for showers and baths. How many litres of water are used each year for showers and baths in an average household?

37. Yung Kim was paid \$132 last week at his part-time job. He was paid $\$8\frac{1}{4}$ per hour. How many hours did he work last week?

38. The Outdoor Shop is making some custom tents that are very light but totally waterproof. Each tent requires $8\frac{1}{4}$ metres of cloth. How many tents can be made from $56\frac{1}{2}$ metres of cloth? How much cloth will be left over?

39. A container of vanilla-flavoured syrup holds $32\frac{4}{5}$ centilitres. Nate uses $\frac{4}{5}$ centilitre every morning in his coffee. How many days will it take Nate to use up the container?

Section 6 The Least Common Denominator and Creating Equivalent Fractions

Finding the Least Common Multiple (LCM) of Two Numbers

The idea of a multiple of a number is fairly straightforward.

The **multiples** of a number are the products of that number and the numbers 1, 2, 3, 4, 5, 6, 7, ...

For example, the multiples of 4 are 4, 8, 12, 16, 20, 24, 28, ...
The multiples of 5 are 5, 10, 15, 20, 25, 30, 35, ...

The **least common multiple,** or **LCM,** of two natural numbers is the smallest number that is a multiple of both.

Student Learning Objectives

After studying this section, you will be able to:

1. **Find the least common multiple (LCM) of two numbers.**
2. **Find the least common denominator (LCD) given two or three fractions.**
3. **Create equivalent fractions with a least common denominator.**

EXAMPLE 1 Find the least common multiple of 10 and 12.

Solution

The multiples of 10 are 10, 20, 30, 40, 50, 60, 70, ...
The multiples of 12 are 12, 24, 36, 48, 60, 72, 84, ...

The first multiple that appears on both lists is the least common multiple. Thus the number 60 is the least common multiple of 10 and 12.

Practice Problem 1 Find the least common multiple of 14 and 21.

***NOTE TO STUDENT:** Fully worked-out solutions to all of the Practice Problems can be found at the end of the module.*

EXAMPLE 2 Find the least common multiple of 6 and 8.

Solution

The multiples of 6 are 6, 12, 18, 24, 30, 36, 42, ...
The multiples of 8 are 8, 16, 24, 32, 40, 48, 56, ...

The first multiple that appears on both lists is the least common multiple. Thus the number 24 is the least common multiple of 6 and 8.

Practice Problem 2 Find the least common multiple of 10 and 15.

Now, of course, we can do the problem immediately if the larger number is a multiple of the smaller number. In such cases the larger number is the least common multiple.

EXAMPLE 3 Find the least common multiple of 7 and 35.

Solution Because $7 \times 5 = 35$, 35 is a multiple of 7.

So we can state immediately that the least common multiple of 7 and 35 is 35.

Practice Problem 3 Find the least common multiple of 6 and 54.

Finding the Least Common Denominator (LCD) Given Two or Three Fractions

We need some way to determine which of two fractions is larger. Suppose that Marcia and Melissa each have some leftover pizza.

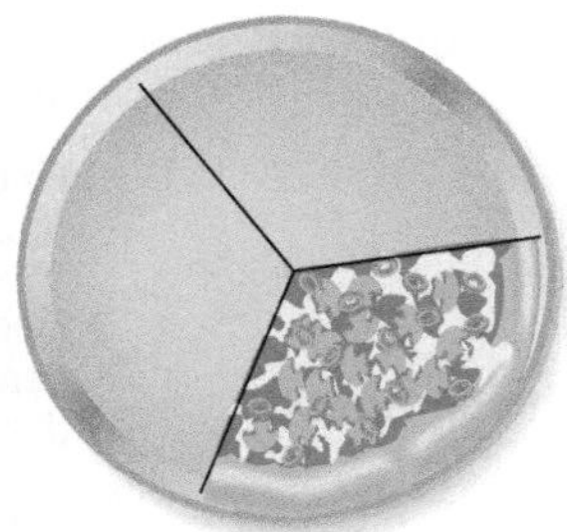

Marcia's Pizza

$\frac{1}{3}$ of a pizza left

Melissa's Pizza

$\frac{1}{4}$ of a pizza left

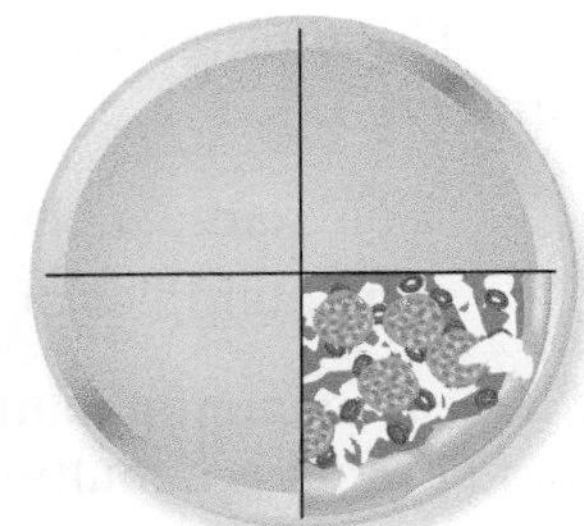

Who has more pizza left? How much more? Comparing the amounts of pizza left would be easy if each pizza had been cut into equal-sized pieces. If the original pizzas had each been cut into 12 pieces, we would be able to see that Marcia had $\frac{1}{12}$ of a pizza more than Melissa had.

Marcia's Pizza

(We know that $\frac{4}{12} = \frac{1}{3}$ by reducing.)

Melissa's Pizza

(We know that $\frac{3}{12} = \frac{1}{4}$ by reducing.)

The denominator 12 appears in the fractions $\frac{4}{12}$ and $\frac{3}{12}$. We call the smallest denominator that allows us to compare fractions directly the *least common denominator,* abbreviated LCD. The number 12 is the least common denominator for the fractions $\frac{1}{3}$ and $\frac{1}{4}$.

Notice that 12 is the least common multiple of 3 and 4.

LEAST COMMON DENOMINATOR

The **least common denominator (LCD)** of two or more fractions is the smallest number that can be divided evenly by each of the fractions' denominators.

How does this relate to least common multiples? The LCD of two fractions is the least common multiple of the two denominators.

In some problems you may be able to guess the LCD quite quickly. With practice, you can often find the LCD mentally. For example, you now know that if the denominators of two fractions are 3 and 4, the LCD is 12. For the fractions $\frac{1}{2}$ and $\frac{1}{4}$, the LCD is 4; for the fractions $\frac{1}{3}$ and $\frac{1}{6}$, the LCD is 6. We can see that if the denominator of one fraction divides without remainder into the denominator of another, the LCD of the two fractions is the larger of the denominators.

EXAMPLE 4 Determine the LCD for each pair of fractions.

(a) $\frac{7}{15}$ and $\frac{4}{5}$ **(b)** $\frac{2}{3}$ and $\frac{5}{27}$

Solution

(a) Since 5 can be divided into 15, the LCD of $\frac{7}{15}$ and $\frac{4}{5}$ is 15. (Notice that the least common multiple of 5 and 15 is 15.)

(b) Since 3 can be divided into 27, the LCD of $\frac{2}{3}$ and $\frac{5}{27}$ is 27. (Notice that the least common multiple of 3 and 27 is 27.)

Practice Problem 4 Determine the LCD for each pair of fractions.

(a) $\frac{3}{4}$ and $\frac{11}{12}$ **(b)** $\frac{1}{7}$ and $\frac{8}{35}$

***NOTE TO STUDENT:** Fully worked-out solutions to all of the Practice Problems can be found at the end of the module.*

In a few cases, the LCD is the product of the two denominators.

EXAMPLE 5 Find the LCD for $\frac{1}{4}$ and $\frac{3}{5}$.

Solution We see that $4 \times 5 = 20$. Also, 20 is the *smallest* number that can be divided without remainder by 4 and by 5. We know this because the least common multiple of 4 and 5 is 20. So the LCD $= 20$.

Practice Problem 5 Find the LCD for $\frac{3}{7}$ and $\frac{5}{6}$.

In cases where the LCD is not obvious, the following procedure will help us find the LCD.

THREE-STEP PROCEDURE FOR FINDING THE LEAST COMMON DENOMINATOR

1. Write each denominator as the product of prime factors.
2. List all the prime factors that appear in either product.
3. Form a product of those prime factors, using each factor the greatest number of times it appears in any one denominator.

EXAMPLE 6 Find the LCD by the three-step procedure.

(a) $\frac{5}{6}$ and $\frac{4}{15}$ **(b)** $\frac{7}{18}$ and $\frac{7}{30}$ **(c)** $\frac{10}{27}$ and $\frac{5}{18}$

Solution

(a) Step 1 Write each denominator as a product of prime factors.

$$6 = 2 \times 3 \qquad 15 = 5 \times 3$$

Step 2 The LCD will contain the factors 2, 3, and 5.

$$6 = 2 \times 3 \qquad 15 = 5 \times 3$$

Step 3 LCD $= 2 \times 3 \times 5$ We form a product.

$= 30$

(b) Step 1 Write each denominator as a product of prime factors.

$$18 = 2 \times 9 = 2 \times 3 \times 3$$
$$30 = 3 \times 10 = 2 \times 3 \times 5$$

Step 2 The LCD will be a product containing 2, 3, and 5.

Step 3 The LCD will contain the factor 3 twice since it occurs twice in the denominator 18.

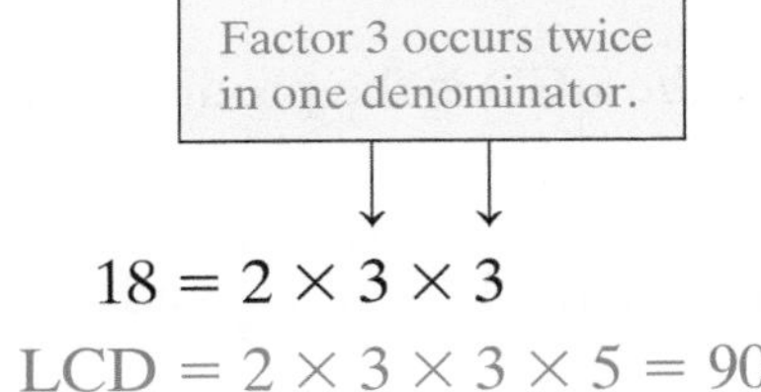
Factor 3 occurs twice
in one denominator.

$$18 = 2 \times 3 \times 3$$
$$\text{LCD} = 2 \times 3 \times 3 \times 5 = 90$$

(c) Write each denominator as a product of prime factors.

$$27 = 3 \times 3 \times 3 \qquad 18 = 3 \times 3 \times 2$$

Factor 3 occurs three times.

The LCD will contain the factor 2 once but the factor 3 three times.

$$\text{LCD} = 2 \times 3 \times 3 \times 3 = 54$$

Practice Problem 6 Find the LCD for each pair of fractions.

(a) $\frac{3}{14}$ and $\frac{1}{10}$ **(b)** $\frac{1}{15}$ and $\frac{7}{50}$ **(c)** $\frac{3}{16}$ and $\frac{5}{12}$

A similar procedure can be used for three fractions.

EXAMPLE 7 Find the LCD of $\frac{7}{12}$, $\frac{1}{15}$, and $\frac{11}{30}$.

Solution

$$12 = 2 \times 2 \times 3$$
$$15 = 3 \times 5$$
$$30 = 2 \times 3 \times 5$$
$$\text{LCD} = 2 \times 2 \times 3 \times 5$$
$$= 60$$

Practice Problem 7 Find the LCD of $\frac{3}{49}$, $\frac{5}{21}$, and $\frac{6}{7}$.

Creating Equivalent Fractions with a Least Common Denominator

In Section 7, we will discuss how to add fractions. We cannot add fractions that have different denominators. To change denominators, we must (1) find the LCD and (2) build up the addends—the fractions being added—into equivalent fractions that have the LCD as the denominator. We know now how to find the LCD. Let's look at how we build fractions. We know, for example, that

$$\frac{1}{2} = \frac{2}{4} = \frac{50}{100} \qquad \frac{1}{4} = \frac{25}{100} \qquad \text{and} \qquad \frac{3}{4} = \frac{75}{100}.$$

In these cases, we have mentally multiplied the given fraction by 1, in the form of a certain number, c, in the numerator and that same number, c, in the denominator.

$$\frac{1}{2} \times \boxed{\frac{c}{c}} = \frac{2}{4} \qquad \text{Here } c = 2, \frac{2}{2} = 1.$$

$$\frac{1}{2} \times \boxed{\frac{c}{c}} = \frac{50}{100} \qquad \text{Here } c = 50, \frac{50}{50} = 1.$$

This property is called the *building fraction property*.

BUILDING FRACTION PROPERTY

For whole numbers a, b, and c where $b \neq 0$, $c \neq 0$,

$$\frac{a}{b} = \frac{a}{b} \times 1 = \frac{a}{b} \times \boxed{\frac{c}{c}} = \frac{a \times c}{b \times c}.$$

EXAMPLE 8 Build each fraction to an equivalent fraction with the given LCD.

(a) $\frac{3}{4}$, LCD $= 28$ **(b)** $\frac{4}{5}$, LCD $= 45$ **(c)** $\frac{1}{3}$ and $\frac{4}{5}$, LCD $= 15$

Solution

(a) $\frac{3}{4} \times \boxed{\frac{c}{c}} = \frac{?}{28}$ We know that $4 \times 7 = 28$, so the value c that we multiply numerator and denominator by is 7.

$$\frac{3}{4} \times \frac{7}{7} = \frac{21}{28}$$

(b) $\frac{4}{5} \times \boxed{\frac{c}{c}} = \frac{?}{45}$ We know that $5 \times 9 = 45$, so $c = 9$.

$$\frac{4}{5} \times \frac{9}{9} = \frac{36}{45}$$

(c) $\dfrac{1}{3} = \dfrac{?}{15}$ We know that $3 \times 5 = 15$, so we multiply numerator and denominator by 5.

$$\frac{1}{3} \times \boxed{\frac{5}{5}} = \frac{5}{15}$$

$\dfrac{4}{5} = \dfrac{?}{15}$ We know that $5 \times 3 = 15$, so we multiply numerator and denominator by 3.

$$\frac{4}{5} \times \boxed{\frac{3}{3}} = \frac{12}{15}$$

$$\text{Thus } \frac{1}{3} = \frac{5}{15} \text{ and } \frac{4}{5} = \frac{12}{15}.$$

***NOTE TO STUDENT:** Fully worked-out solutions to all of the Practice Problems can be found at the end of the module.*

Practice Problem 8 Build each fraction to an equivalent fraction with the LCD.

(a) $\dfrac{3}{5}$, LCD = 40 **(b)** $\dfrac{7}{11}$, LCD = 44 **(c)** $\dfrac{2}{7}$ and $\dfrac{3}{4}$, LCD = 28

EXAMPLE 9

(a) Find the LCD of $\dfrac{1}{32}$ and $\dfrac{7}{48}$.

(b) Build the fractions to equivalent fractions that have the LCD as their denominators.

Solution

(a) First we find the prime factors of 32 and 48.

$$32 = 2 \times 2 \times 2 \times 2 \times 2$$
$$48 = 2 \times 2 \times 2 \times 2 \times 3$$

Thus the LCD will require a factor of 2 five times and a factor of 3 one time.

$$\text{LCD} = 2 \times 2 \times 2 \times 2 \times 2 \times 3 = 96$$

(b) $\dfrac{1}{32} = \dfrac{?}{96}$ Since $32 \times 3 = 96$ we multiply by the fraction $\dfrac{3}{3}$.

$$\frac{1}{32} = \frac{1}{32} \times \boxed{\frac{3}{3}} = \frac{3}{96}$$

$\dfrac{7}{48} = \dfrac{?}{96}$ Since $48 \times 2 = 96$, we multiply by the fraction $\dfrac{2}{2}$.

$$\frac{7}{48} = \frac{7}{48} \times \boxed{\frac{2}{2}} = \frac{14}{96}$$

Practice Problem 9

(a) Find the LCD of $\dfrac{3}{20}$ and $\dfrac{11}{15}$.

(b) Build the fractions to equivalent fractions that have the LCD as their denominators.

EXAMPLE 10

(a) Find the LCD of $\frac{2}{125}$ and $\frac{8}{75}$.

(b) Build the fractions to equivalent fractions that have the LCD as their denominators.

Solution

(a) First we find the prime factors of 125 and 75.

$$125 = 5 \times 5 \times 5$$
$$75 = 5 \times 5 \times 3$$

Thus the LCD will require a factor of 5 three times and a factor of 3 one time.

$$\text{LCD} = 5 \times 5 \times 5 \times 3 = 375$$

(b) $\frac{2}{125} = \frac{?}{375}$ Since $125 \times 3 = 375$, we multiply by the fraction $\frac{3}{3}$.

$$\frac{2}{125} = \frac{2}{125} \times \boxed{\frac{3}{3}} = \frac{6}{375}$$

$\frac{8}{75} = \frac{?}{375}$ Since $75 \times 5 = 375$, we multiply by the fraction $\frac{5}{5}$.

$$\frac{8}{75} = \frac{8}{75} \times \boxed{\frac{5}{5}} = \frac{40}{375}$$

Practice Problem 10

(a) Find the LCD of $\frac{5}{64}$ and $\frac{3}{80}$.

(b) Build the fractions to equivalent fractions that have the LCD as their denominators.

***NOTE TO STUDENT:** Fully worked-out solutions to all of the Practice Problems can be found at the end of the module.*

Section 6 Exercises

Find the least common multiple (LCM) for each pair of numbers.

1. 8 and 12 **2.** 6 and 9 **3.** 20 and 50 **4.** 22 and 55 **5.** 12 and 15

6. 18 and 30 **7.** 10 and 15 **8.** 8 and 60 **9.** 21 and 49 **10.** 25 and 35

Find the LCD for each pair of fractions.

11. $\frac{1}{5}$ and $\frac{3}{10}$ **12.** $\frac{3}{8}$ and $\frac{5}{16}$ **13.** $\frac{3}{7}$ and $\frac{1}{4}$ **14.** $\frac{5}{6}$ and $\frac{3}{5}$ **15.** $\frac{2}{5}$ and $\frac{3}{7}$

16. $\frac{1}{16}$ and $\frac{2}{3}$ **17.** $\frac{1}{6}$ and $\frac{5}{9}$ **18.** $\frac{1}{4}$ and $\frac{3}{14}$ **19.** $\frac{7}{12}$ and $\frac{14}{15}$ **20.** $\frac{7}{15}$ and $\frac{9}{25}$

21. $\frac{7}{32}$ and $\frac{3}{4}$ **22.** $\frac{2}{11}$ and $\frac{1}{44}$ **23.** $\frac{5}{10}$ and $\frac{11}{45}$ **24.** $\frac{13}{20}$ and $\frac{17}{30}$ **25.** $\frac{7}{16}$ and $\frac{17}{80}$

26. $\frac{5}{6}$ and $\frac{19}{30}$ **27.** $\frac{5}{21}$ and $\frac{8}{35}$ **28.** $\frac{1}{20}$ and $\frac{5}{70}$ **29.** $\frac{11}{24}$ and $\frac{7}{30}$ **30.** $\frac{23}{30}$ and $\frac{37}{50}$

Find the LCD for each set of three fractions.

31. $\frac{2}{3}, \frac{1}{2}, \frac{5}{6}$ **32.** $\frac{1}{5}, \frac{1}{3}, \frac{7}{10}$ **33.** $\frac{1}{4}, \frac{11}{12}, \frac{5}{6}$ **34.** $\frac{21}{48}, \frac{1}{12}, \frac{3}{8}$

35. $\frac{5}{11}, \frac{7}{12}, \frac{1}{6}$ **36.** $\frac{11}{16}, \frac{3}{20}, \frac{2}{5}$ **37.** $\frac{7}{12}, \frac{1}{21}, \frac{3}{14}$ **38.** $\frac{1}{30}, \frac{3}{40}, \frac{7}{8}$

39. $\frac{7}{15}, \frac{11}{12}, \frac{7}{8}$ **40.** $\frac{5}{36}, \frac{2}{48}, \frac{1}{24}$

Build each fraction to an equivalent fraction with the specified denominator. State the numerator.

41. $\frac{1}{3} = \frac{?}{9}$

42. $\frac{1}{5} = \frac{?}{35}$

43. $\frac{5}{7} = \frac{?}{49}$

44. $\frac{7}{9} = \frac{?}{81}$

45. $\frac{4}{11} = \frac{?}{55}$

46. $\frac{2}{13} = \frac{?}{39}$

47. $\frac{5}{12} = \frac{?}{96}$

48. $\frac{3}{50} = \frac{?}{100}$

49. $\frac{8}{9} = \frac{?}{108}$

50. $\frac{6}{7} = \frac{?}{147}$

51. $\frac{7}{20} = \frac{?}{180}$

52. $\frac{3}{25} = \frac{?}{175}$

The LCD of each pair of fractions is listed. Build each fraction to an equivalent fraction that has the LCD as the denominator.

53. LCD = 36, $\frac{7}{12}$ and $\frac{5}{9}$

54. LCD = 20, $\frac{9}{10}$ and $\frac{3}{4}$

55. LCD = 80, $\frac{5}{16}$ and $\frac{17}{20}$

56. LCD = 72, $\frac{5}{24}$ and $\frac{7}{36}$

57. LCD = 20, $\frac{9}{10}$ and $\frac{19}{20}$

58. LCD = 240, $\frac{13}{30}$ and $\frac{41}{80}$

Find the LCD. Build the fractions to equivalent fractions having the LCD as the denominator.

59. $\frac{2}{5}$ and $\frac{9}{35}$

60. $\frac{7}{9}$ and $\frac{35}{54}$

61. $\frac{5}{24}$ and $\frac{3}{8}$

62. $\frac{19}{42}$ and $\frac{6}{7}$

63. $\frac{8}{15}$ and $\frac{1}{6}$

64. $\frac{19}{20}$ and $\frac{7}{8}$

65. $\frac{4}{15}$ and $\frac{5}{12}$

66. $\frac{9}{10}$ and $\frac{3}{25}$

67. $\frac{5}{18}, \frac{11}{36}, \frac{7}{12}$

68. $\frac{1}{30}, \frac{7}{15}, \frac{1}{45}$

69. $\frac{3}{56}, \frac{7}{8}, \frac{5}{7}$

70. $\frac{5}{9}, \frac{1}{6}, \frac{3}{54}$

71. $\frac{5}{63}, \frac{4}{21}, \frac{8}{9}$

72. $\frac{3}{8}, \frac{5}{14}, \frac{13}{16}$

Applications

73. ***Door Repair*** Suppose that you wish to compare the lengths of the three portions of the given stainless steel bolt that came out of a door.

(a) What is the LCD for the three fractions?

(b) Build each fraction to an equivalent fraction that has the LCD as a denominator.

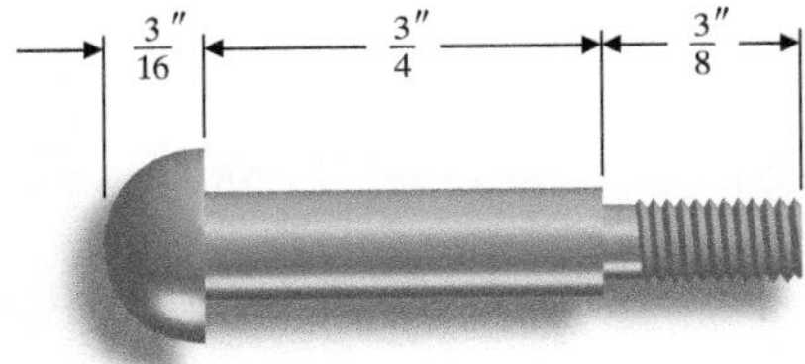

74. ***Plant Growth*** Suppose that you want to prepare a report on the growth of a plant. The total height of the plant in the pot is recorded for each week of a three-week experiment.

(a) What is the LCD for the three fractions?

(b) Build each fraction to an equivalent fraction that has the LCD for a denominator.

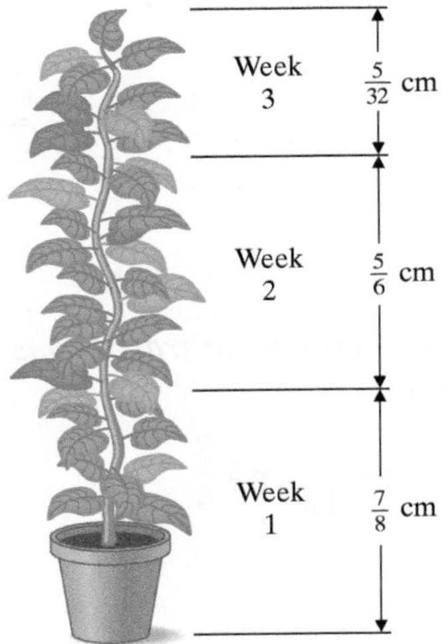

Quick Quiz 6

1. Find the least common denominator of

$\frac{5}{6}$ and $\frac{5}{21}$

2. Find the least common denominator of

$\frac{27}{28}, \frac{3}{4}, \frac{19}{20}$

3. Build the fraction to an equivalent fraction with the specified denominator.

$\frac{7}{26} = \frac{?}{78}$

4. Concept Check Explain how you would find the least common denominator of the fractions $\frac{5}{6}$, $\frac{11}{14}$, and $\frac{2}{15}$.

SECTION 7 ADDING AND SUBTRACTING FRACTIONS

Adding and Subtracting Fractions with a Common Denominator

You must have common denominators (denominators that are alike) to add or subtract fractions.

If your problem has fractions without a common denominator or if it has mixed numbers, you must use what you already know about changing the form of each fraction (how the fraction looks). Only after all the fractions have a common denominator can you add or subtract.

An important distinction: You must have common denominators to add or subtract fractions, but you need not have common denominators to multiply or divide fractions.

To add two fractions that have the same denominator, add the numerators and write the sum over the common denominator.

To illustrate we use $\frac{1}{5} + \frac{2}{5} = \frac{3}{5}$. The figure shows that $\frac{1}{5} + \frac{2}{5} = \frac{3}{5}$.

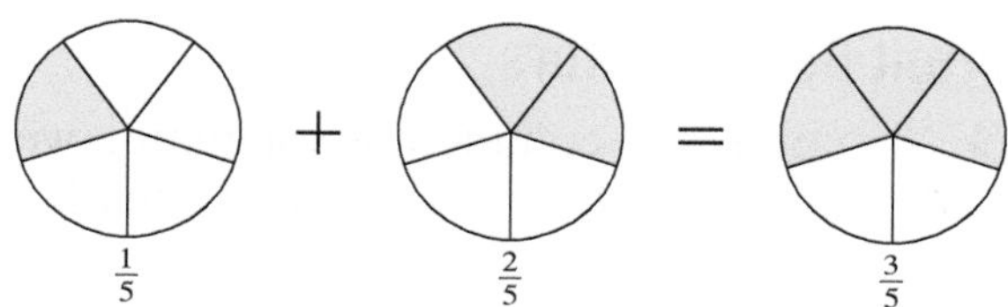

EXAMPLE 1 Add. $\frac{5}{13} + \frac{7}{13}$

Solution

$$\frac{5}{13} + \frac{7}{13} = \frac{12}{13}$$

Practice Problem 1 Add.

$$\frac{3}{17} + \frac{12}{17}$$

The answer may need to be reduced. Sometimes the answer may be written as a mixed number.

EXAMPLE 2 Add.

(a) $\frac{4}{9} + \frac{2}{9}$ **(b)** $\frac{5}{7} + \frac{6}{7}$

Solution

(a) $\frac{4}{9} + \frac{2}{9} = \frac{6}{9} = \frac{2}{3}$ **(b)** $\frac{5}{7} + \frac{6}{7} = \frac{11}{7}$ or $1\frac{4}{7}$

Practice Problem 2 Add.

(a) $\frac{1}{12} + \frac{5}{12}$ **(b)** $\frac{13}{15} + \frac{7}{15}$

Student Learning Objectives

After studying this section, you will be able to:

 **Add and subtract fractions with a common denominator.**

 **Add and subtract fractions with different denominators.**

NOTE TO STUDENT: Fully worked-out solutions to all of the Practice Problems can be found at the end of the module.

A similar rule is followed for subtraction, except that the numerators are subtracted and the result placed over the common denominator. Be sure to reduce all answers when possible.

EXAMPLE 3 Subtract.

(a) $\frac{5}{13} - \frac{4}{13}$ **(b)** $\frac{17}{20} - \frac{3}{20}$

Solution

(a) $\frac{5}{13} - \frac{4}{13} = \frac{1}{13}$ **(b)** $\frac{17}{20} - \frac{3}{20} = \frac{14}{20} = \frac{7}{10}$

Practice Problem 3 Subtract.

(a) $\frac{5}{19} - \frac{2}{19}$ **(b)** $\frac{21}{25} - \frac{6}{25}$

2 Adding and Subtracting Fractions with Different Denominators

If the two fractions do not have a common denominator, we follow the procedure in Section 6: Find the LCD and then build each fraction so that its denominator is the LCD.

EXAMPLE 4 Add. $\frac{7}{12} + \frac{1}{4}$

Solution The LCD is 12. The fraction $\frac{7}{12}$ already has the least common denominator.

$$\begin{array}{rcr} \frac{7}{12} & = & \boxed{\frac{7}{12}} \\ +\ \frac{1}{4} \times \frac{3}{3} & = & +\ \boxed{\frac{3}{12}} \\ \hline & & \boxed{\frac{10}{12}} \end{array}$$

We will need to reduce this fraction. Then we will have

$$\frac{7}{12} + \frac{1}{4} = \frac{7}{12} + \frac{3}{12} = \frac{10}{12} = \frac{5}{6}.$$

It is very important to remember to reduce our final answer.

Practice Problem 4 Add.

$$\frac{2}{15} + \frac{1}{5}$$

EXAMPLE 5 Add. $\frac{7}{20} + \frac{4}{15}$

Solution LCD = 60.

$$\frac{7}{20} \times \frac{3}{3} = \frac{21}{60} \qquad \frac{4}{15} \times \frac{4}{4} = \frac{16}{60}$$

Thus

$$\frac{7}{20} + \frac{4}{15} = \frac{21}{60} + \frac{16}{60} = \frac{37}{60}$$

Practice Problem 5 Add.

$$\frac{5}{12} + \frac{5}{16}$$

A similar procedure holds for the addition of three or more fractions.

EXAMPLE 6 Add. $\frac{3}{8} + \frac{5}{6} + \frac{1}{4}$

Solution LCD = 24.

$$\frac{3}{8} \times \frac{3}{3} = \frac{9}{24} \qquad \frac{5}{6} \times \frac{4}{4} = \frac{20}{24} \qquad \frac{1}{4} \times \frac{6}{6} = \frac{6}{24}$$

$$\frac{3}{8} + \frac{5}{6} + \frac{1}{4} = \frac{9}{24} + \frac{20}{24} + \frac{6}{24} = \frac{35}{24} \text{ or } 1\frac{11}{24}$$

Practice Problem 6 Add.

$$\frac{3}{16} + \frac{1}{8} + \frac{1}{12}$$

EXAMPLE 7 Subtract. $\frac{17}{25} - \frac{3}{35}$

Solution LCD = 175.

$$\frac{17}{25} \times \frac{7}{7} = \frac{119}{175} \qquad \frac{3}{35} \times \frac{5}{5} = \frac{15}{175}$$

Thus

$$\frac{17}{25} - \frac{3}{35} = \frac{119}{175} - \frac{15}{175} = \frac{104}{175}.$$

Practice Problem 7 Subtract.

$$\frac{9}{48} - \frac{5}{32}$$

▲ **EXAMPLE 8** John and Stephanie have a house on $\frac{7}{8}$ hectare of land. They have $\frac{1}{3}$ hectare of land planted with grass. How much of the land is not planted with grass?

Solution

1. ***Understand the problem.*** Draw a picture.

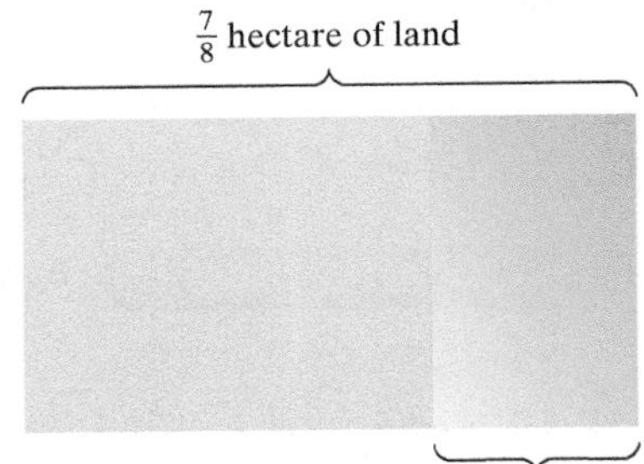

We need to subtract. $\frac{7}{8} - \frac{1}{3}$

2. ***Solve and state the answer.*** The LCD is 24.

$$\frac{7}{8} \times \frac{3}{3} = \frac{21}{24} \qquad \frac{1}{3} \times \frac{8}{8} = \frac{8}{24}$$

$$\frac{7}{8} - \frac{1}{3} = \frac{21}{24} - \frac{8}{24} = \frac{13}{24}$$

We conclude that $\frac{13}{24}$ hectare of land is not planted with grass.

3. ***Check.*** The check is left to the student.

Practice Problem 8 Leon had $\frac{9}{10}$ litre of cleaning fluid in the garage. He used $\frac{1}{4}$ litre to clean the garage floor. How much cleaning fluid is left?

Some students may find Example 9 difficult. Read it slowly and carefully.

EXAMPLE 9 Find the value of x in the equation $x + \frac{5}{6} = \frac{9}{10}$. Reduce your answer.

Solution The LCD for the two fractions $\frac{5}{6}$ and $\frac{9}{10}$ is 30.

$$\frac{5}{6} \times \frac{5}{5} = \frac{25}{30} \qquad \frac{9}{10} \times \frac{3}{3} = \frac{27}{30}$$

Thus we can write the equation in the equivalent form.

$$x + \frac{25}{30} = \frac{27}{30}$$

The denominators are the same. Look at the numerators. We must add 2 to 25 to get 27.

$$\frac{2}{30} + \frac{25}{30} = \frac{27}{30}$$

So $x = \frac{2}{30}$ and we reduce the fraction to obtain $x = \frac{1}{15}$.

Practice Problem 9 Find the value of x in the equation $x + \frac{3}{10} = \frac{23}{25}$.

ALTERNATIVE METHOD: Multiply the Denominators as a Common Denominator In all the problems in this section so far, we have combined two fractions by first finding the least common denominator. However, there is an alternative approach. You are only required to find a common denominator, not necessarily the least common denominator. One way to quickly find a common denominator of two fractions is to multiply the two denominators. However, if you use this method, the numbers will usually be larger and you will usually need to simplify the fraction in your final answer.

EXAMPLE 10 Add $\frac{11}{12} + \frac{13}{30}$ by using the product of the two denominators as a common denominator.

Solution Using this method we just multiply the numerator and denominator of each fraction by the denominator of the other fraction. Thus no steps are needed to determine what to multiply by.

$$\frac{11}{12} \times \frac{30}{30} = \frac{330}{360} \qquad \frac{13}{30} \times \frac{12}{12} = \frac{156}{360}$$

Thus $\frac{11}{12} + \frac{13}{30} = \frac{330}{360} + \frac{156}{360} = \frac{486}{360}$

We must reduce the fraction: $\frac{486}{360} = \frac{27}{20}$ or $1\frac{7}{20}$

Practice Problem 10 Add $\frac{15}{16} + \frac{3}{40}$ by using the product of the two denominators as a common denominator.

***NOTE TO STUDENT:** Fully worked-out solutions to all of the Practice Problems can be found at the end of the module.*

Some students find this alternative method helpful because you do not have to find the LCD or the number each fraction must be multiplied by. Other students find this alternative method more difficult because of errors encountered when working with large numbers or in reducing the final answer. You are encouraged to try a couple of the homework exercises by this method and make up your own mind.

Section 7 Exercises

Add or subtract. Simplify all answers.

1. $\frac{5}{9}+\frac{2}{9}$

2. $\frac{5}{8}+\frac{2}{8}$

3. $\frac{7}{18}+\frac{15}{18}$

4. $\frac{11}{25}+\frac{17}{25}$

5. $\frac{19}{20}-\frac{11}{20}$

6. $\frac{17}{30}-\frac{7}{30}$

7. $\frac{53}{88}-\frac{19}{88}$

8. $\frac{103}{110}-\frac{3}{110}$

Add or subtract. Simplify all answers.

9. $\frac{1}{3}+\frac{1}{2}$

10. $\frac{1}{4}+\frac{1}{3}$

11. $\frac{3}{10}+\frac{3}{20}$

12. $\frac{4}{9}+\frac{1}{6}$

13. $\frac{1}{8}+\frac{3}{4}$

14. $\frac{5}{16}+\frac{1}{2}$

15. $\frac{4}{5}+\frac{7}{20}$

16. $\frac{2}{3}+\frac{4}{7}$

17. $\frac{3}{10}+\frac{7}{100}$

18. $\frac{13}{100}+\frac{7}{10}$

19. $\frac{3}{10}+\frac{1}{6}$

20. $\frac{8}{15}+\frac{3}{10}$

21. $\frac{7}{8}+\frac{5}{12}$

22. $\frac{5}{6}+\frac{7}{8}$

23. $\frac{3}{8}+\frac{3}{10}$

24. $\frac{12}{35}+\frac{1}{10}$

25. $\frac{29}{18}-\frac{5}{9}$

26. $\frac{37}{20}-\frac{2}{5}$

27. $\frac{3}{7}-\frac{9}{21}$

28. $\frac{7}{8}-\frac{5}{6}$

29. $\frac{5}{9}-\frac{5}{36}$

30. $\frac{9}{10}-\frac{1}{15}$

31. $\frac{5}{12}-\frac{7}{30}$

32. $\frac{9}{24}-\frac{3}{8}$

33. $\frac{11}{12}-\frac{2}{3}$

34. $\frac{7}{10}-\frac{2}{5}$

35. $\frac{17}{21}-\frac{1}{7}$

36. $\frac{20}{25}-\frac{4}{5}$

37. $\frac{5}{12}-\frac{7}{18}$

38. $\frac{7}{8}-\frac{1}{12}$

39. $\frac{10}{16}-\frac{5}{8}$

40. $\frac{5}{6}-\frac{10}{12}$

41. $\frac{23}{36}-\frac{2}{9}$

42. $\frac{2}{3}-\frac{1}{16}$

43. $\frac{1}{2} + \frac{2}{7} + \frac{3}{14}$

44. $\frac{7}{8} + \frac{5}{6} + \frac{7}{24}$

45. $\frac{5}{30} + \frac{3}{40} + \frac{1}{8}$

46. $\frac{1}{12} + \frac{3}{14} + \frac{4}{21}$

47. $\frac{7}{30} + \frac{2}{5} + \frac{5}{6}$

48. $\frac{1}{12} + \frac{5}{36} + \frac{32}{36}$

Study Example 9 carefully. Then find the value of x in each equation.

49. $x + \frac{1}{7} = \frac{5}{14}$

50. $x + \frac{1}{8} = \frac{7}{16}$

51. $x + \frac{2}{3} = \frac{9}{11}$

52. $x + \frac{3}{4} = \frac{17}{18}$

53. $x - \frac{3}{10} = \frac{4}{15}$

54. $x - \frac{3}{14} = \frac{17}{28}$

Applications

55. ***Cooking*** Rita is baking a cake for a dinner party. The recipe calls for $\frac{2}{3}$ cup sugar for the frosting and $\frac{3}{4}$ cup sugar for the cake. How many total cups of sugar does she need?

56. ***Fitness Training*** Kia is training for a short triathlon. On Monday she swam $\frac{1}{4}$ kilometre and ran $\frac{5}{6}$ kilometre. On Tuesday she swam $\frac{1}{2}$ kilometre and ran $\frac{3}{4}$ kilometre. How many kilometres has she swum so far this week? How many kilometres has she run so far?

57. ***Food Purchase*** Yasmin wants to make a trail mix of nuts and dried fruit. She has $\frac{2}{3}$ kilogram peanuts and $\frac{1}{2}$ kilogram dried cranberries. She purchases $\frac{3}{4}$ kilogram almonds and $\frac{3}{8}$ kilogram raisins to mix with the peanuts and cranberries. After mixing the four ingredients, how many kilograms of nuts and how many kilograms of dried fruit will there be in the trail mix?

58. ***Automobile Maintenance*** Mandy purchased two new steel-belted all-weather radial tires for her car. The tread depth on the new tires measures $\frac{11}{32}$ of an inch. The dealer told her that when the tires have worn down and their tread depth measures $\frac{1}{8}$ of an inch, she should replace the worn tires with new ones. How much will the tread depth decrease over the useful life of the tire?

59. ***Power Outage*** Travis typed $\frac{11}{12}$ of his book report on his computer. Then he printed out $\frac{3}{5}$ of his book report on his computer printer. Suddenly, there was a power outage, and he discovered that he hadn't saved his book report before the power went off. What fractional part of the book report was lost when the power failed?

60. ***Childcare*** An infant's father knows that straight apple juice is too strong for his daughter. Her bottle is $\frac{1}{2}$ full, and he adds $\frac{1}{3}$ of a bottle of water to dilute the apple juice.

(a) How much is there to drink in the bottle after this addition?

(b) If she drinks $\frac{2}{5}$ of the bottle, how much is left?

61. ***Food Purchase*** While he was at the grocery store, Raymond purchased a box of candy for himself. On the way back to the dorm he ate $\frac{1}{4}$ of the candy. As he was putting away the groceries he ate $\frac{1}{2}$ of what was left. There are now six chocolates left in the box. How many chocolates were in the box to begin with?

62. ***Baking*** Peter has $\frac{3}{4}$ cup of cocoa. He needs $\frac{1}{8}$ cup to make brownies, and another $\frac{1}{4}$ cup to make fudge squares. After making the brownies and the fudge, how much cocoa will Peter have left?

63. ***Business Management*** The manager at Fit Factory Health Club was going through his files for 2009 and discovered that only $\frac{7}{10}$ of the members actually used the club. When he checked the numbers from the previous year of 2008, he found that $\frac{7}{8}$ of the members had used the club. What fractional part of the membership represents the decrease in club usage?

Quick Quiz 7 Simplify all answers.

1. Add. $\dfrac{7}{16} + \dfrac{3}{4}$

2. Add. $\dfrac{1}{3} + \dfrac{5}{7} + \dfrac{10}{21}$

3. Subtract. $\dfrac{8}{9} - \dfrac{7}{15}$

4. **Concept Check** Explain how you would subtract the fractions $\dfrac{8}{9} - \dfrac{3}{7}$.

SECTION 8 ADDING AND SUBTRACTING MIXED NUMBERS AND THE ORDER OF OPERATIONS

Adding Mixed Numbers

When adding mixed numbers, it is best to add the fractions together and then add the whole numbers together.

Student Learning Objectives

After studying this section, you will be able to:

1. **Add mixed numbers.**
2. **Subtract mixed numbers.**
3. **Evaluate fractional expressions using the order of operations.**

EXAMPLE 1 Add. $3\frac{1}{8} + 2\frac{5}{8}$

Solution

$$\begin{array}{r|c|} & 3 & \frac{1}{8} \\ & +2 & \frac{5}{8} \\ \hline \end{array}$$

Add the whole numbers. $3 + 2 = 5$ → $5\frac{6}{8}$ ← Add the fractions. $\frac{1}{8} + \frac{5}{8} = \frac{6}{8}$

$= 5\frac{3}{4}$ ← Reduce $\frac{6}{8} = \frac{3}{4}$

Practice Problem 1 Add. $5\frac{1}{12} + 9\frac{5}{12}$

NOTE TO STUDENT: Fully worked-out solutions to all of the Practice Problems can be found at the end of the module.

If the fraction portions of the mixed numbers do not have a common denominator, we must build the fraction parts to obtain a common denominator before adding.

EXAMPLE 2 Add. $1\frac{2}{7} + 5\frac{1}{3}$

Solution The LCD of $\frac{2}{7}$ and $\frac{1}{3}$ is 21.

$$\frac{2}{7} \times \frac{3}{3} = \frac{6}{21} \qquad \frac{1}{3} \times \frac{7}{7} = \frac{7}{21}$$

Thus $1\frac{2}{7} + 5\frac{1}{3} = 1\frac{6}{21} + 5\frac{7}{21}$.

$$1\frac{2}{7} = 1\frac{6}{21}$$
$$+\,5\frac{1}{3} = +\,5\frac{7}{21}$$

Add the whole numbers. $1 + 5$ → $6\frac{13}{21}$ ← Add the fractions. $\frac{6}{21} + \frac{7}{21}$

Practice Problem 2 Add. $6\frac{1}{4} + 2\frac{2}{5}$

If the sum of the fractions is an improper fraction, we convert it to a mixed number and add the whole numbers together.

EXAMPLE 3 Add. $6\frac{5}{6} + 4\frac{3}{8}$

Solution The LCD of $\frac{5}{6}$ and $\frac{3}{8}$ is 24.

$$\begin{aligned} 6\ \boxed{\frac{5}{6} \times \frac{4}{4}} &= \quad 6\ \frac{20}{24} \\ +4\ \boxed{\frac{3}{8} \times \frac{3}{3}} &= +4\ \frac{9}{24} \end{aligned}$$

Add the whole numbers. ⟶ $10\ \frac{29}{24}$ ← Add the fractions.

$= 10 + \boxed{1\frac{5}{24}}$ Since $\frac{29}{24} = 1\frac{5}{24}$

$= 11\frac{5}{24}$ We add the whole numbers $10 + 1 = 11$.

Practice Problem 3 Add. $7\frac{1}{4} + 3\frac{5}{6}$

2 Subtracting Mixed Numbers

Subtracting mixed numbers is like adding.

EXAMPLE 4 Subtract. $8\frac{5}{7} - 5\frac{5}{14}$

Solution The LCD of $\frac{5}{7}$ and $\frac{5}{14}$ is 14.

$$\begin{aligned} 8\ \boxed{\frac{5}{7} \times \frac{2}{2}} &= \quad 8\frac{10}{14} \\ -5\frac{5}{14} \qquad &= -5\frac{5}{14} \end{aligned}$$

Subtract the whole numbers. ⟶ $3\frac{5}{14}$ ⟵ Subtract the fractions.

Practice Problem 4 Subtract. $12\frac{5}{6} - 7\frac{5}{12}$

Sometimes we must borrow before we can subtract.

EXAMPLE 5 Subtract.

(a) $9\frac{1}{4} - 6\frac{5}{14}$ **(b)** $15 - 9\frac{3}{16}$

Solution This example is fairly challenging. Read through each step carefully. Be sure to have paper and pencil handy and see if you can verify each step.

(a) The LCD of $\frac{1}{4}$ and $\frac{5}{14}$ is 28.

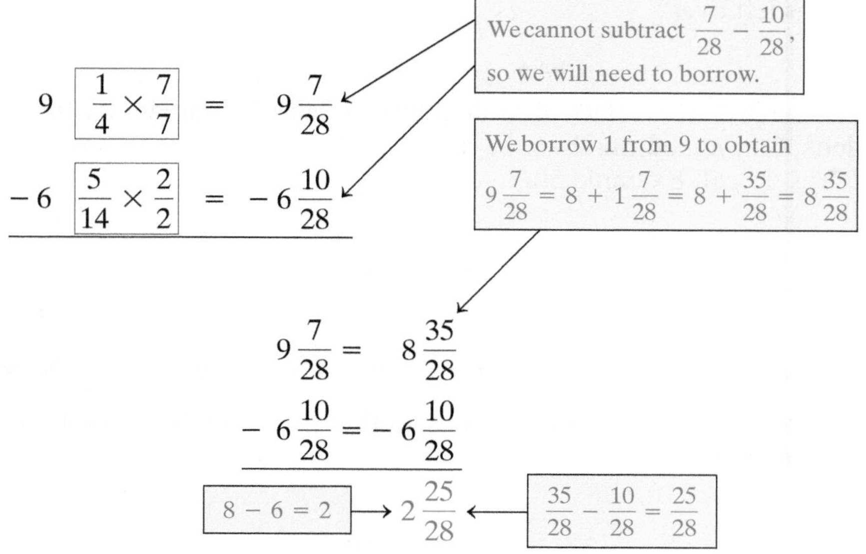
We cannot subtract $\frac{7}{28} - \frac{10}{28}$, so we will need to borrow.
$9\left[\frac{1}{4} \times \frac{7}{7}\right] = 9\frac{7}{28}$
$-6\left[\frac{5}{14} \times \frac{2}{2}\right] = -6\frac{10}{28}$
We borrow 1 from 9 to obtain
$9\frac{7}{28} = 8 + 1\frac{7}{28} = 8 + \frac{35}{28} = 8\frac{35}{28}$
$9\frac{7}{28} = 8\frac{35}{28}$
$-6\frac{10}{28} = -6\frac{10}{28}$
$8 - 6 = 2$
$2\frac{25}{28}$
$\frac{35}{28} - \frac{10}{28} = \frac{25}{28}$

(b) The LCD = 16.

$$\begin{aligned} 15 &= 14\frac{16}{16} \\ -9\frac{3}{16} &= -9\frac{3}{16} \\ \hline & 5\frac{13}{16} \end{aligned}$$

We borrow 1 from 15 to obtain

$$15 = 14 + 1 = 14 + \frac{16}{16} = 14\frac{16}{16}$$

$14 - 9 = 5$ → $5\frac{13}{16}$ ← $\frac{16}{16} - \frac{3}{16} = \frac{13}{16}$

Practice Problem 5 Subtract.

(a) $9\frac{1}{8} - 3\frac{2}{3}$ **(b)** $18 - 6\frac{7}{18}$

NOTE TO STUDENT: Fully worked-out solutions to all of the Practice Problems can be found at the end of the module.

EXAMPLE 6 A plumber had a pipe $5\frac{3}{16}$ inches long for a fitting under the sink. He needed a pipe that was $3\frac{7}{8}$ inches long, so he cut the pipe down. How much of the pipe did he cut off?

Solution We will need to subtract $5\frac{3}{16} - 3\frac{7}{8}$ to find the length that was cut off.

$$\begin{aligned} 5\frac{3}{16} &= 5\frac{3}{16} \\ -3\frac{7}{8} \times \frac{2}{2} &= -3\frac{14}{16} \end{aligned}$$

We borrow 1 from 5 to obtain

$$5\frac{3}{16} = 4 + 1\frac{3}{16} = 4 + \frac{19}{16}$$

$$\begin{aligned} & 4\frac{19}{16} \\ - & 3\frac{14}{16} \\ \hline & 1\frac{5}{16} \end{aligned}$$

$4 - 3 = 1$ → $1\frac{5}{16}$ ← $\frac{19}{16} - \frac{14}{16} = \frac{5}{16}$

The plumber had to cut off $1\frac{5}{16}$ inches of pipe.

Practice Problem 6 Hillary and Sam purchased $6\frac{1}{4}$ litres of paint to paint the first floor of their house. They used $4\frac{2}{3}$ litres of paint. How much paint was left over?

ALTERNATIVE METHOD: Add or Subtract Mixed Numbers as Improper Fractions Can mixed numbers be added and subtracted as improper fractions? Yes. Recall Example 5(a).

$$9\frac{1}{4} - 6\frac{5}{14} = 2\frac{25}{28}$$

If we write $9\frac{1}{4} - 6\frac{5}{14}$ using improper fractions, we have $\frac{37}{4} - \frac{89}{14}$. Now we build each of these improper fractions so that they both have the LCD for their denominators.

$$\begin{array}{rcrl} \frac{37}{4} & \boxed{\times\frac{7}{7}} & = & \frac{259}{28} \\ -\frac{89}{14} & \boxed{\times\frac{2}{2}} & = & -\frac{178}{28} \\ \hline & & & \frac{81}{28} = 2\frac{25}{28} \end{array}$$

The same result is obtained as in Example 5(a). This method does not require borrowing. However, you do work with larger numbers. For more practice, see exercises 53–54.

3 Evaluating Fractional Expressions Using the Order of Operations

The order of operations must be considered in problems involving fractions and mixed numbers.

ORDER OF OPERATIONS

With grouping symbols:

Do first	**1.** Perform operations inside parentheses.
↓	**2.** Simplify any expressions with exponents.
	3. Multiply or divide from left to right.
Do last	**4.** Add or subtract from left to right.

EXAMPLE 7 Evaluate. $\frac{3}{4} - \frac{2}{3} \times \frac{1}{8}$

Solution

$$\frac{3}{4} - \frac{2}{3} \times \frac{1}{8} = \frac{3}{4} - \frac{1}{12}$$ First we must multiply $\frac{2}{3} \times \frac{1}{8}$.

$$= \frac{9}{12} - \frac{1}{12}$$ Now we subtract, but first we need to build $\frac{3}{4}$ to an equivalent fraction with a common denominator of 12.

$$= \frac{8}{12}$$ Now we can subtract $\frac{9}{12} - \frac{1}{12}$.

$$= \frac{2}{3}$$ Finally we reduce the fraction.

Practice Problem 7 Evaluate.

$$\frac{3}{5} - \frac{1}{15} \times \frac{10}{13}$$

EXAMPLE 8 Evaluate. $\frac{2}{3} \times \frac{1}{4} + \frac{2}{5} \div \frac{14}{15}$

Solution

$$\frac{2}{3} \times \frac{1}{4} + \frac{2}{5} \div \frac{14}{15} = \frac{1}{6} + \frac{2}{5} \div \frac{14}{15}$$ First we multiply $\frac{2}{3} \times \frac{1}{4}$.

$$= \frac{1}{6} + \frac{2}{5} \times \frac{15}{14}$$ We express the division as a multiplication problem. We invert $\frac{14}{15}$ and multiply.

$$= \frac{1}{6} + \frac{3}{7}$$ Now we perform the multiplication.

$$= \frac{7}{42} + \frac{18}{42}$$ We obtain equivalent fractions with an LCD of 42.

$$= \frac{25}{42}$$ We add the two fractions.

Practice Problem 8 Evaluate.

$$\frac{1}{7} \times \frac{5}{6} + \frac{5}{3} \div \frac{7}{6}$$

***NOTE TO STUDENT:** Fully worked-out solutions to all of the Practice Problems can be found at the end of the module.*

Developing Your Study Skills

Problems with Accuracy

Strive for accuracy. Mistakes are often made because of human error rather than lack of understanding. Such mistakes are frustrating. A simple arithmetic or copying error can lead to an incorrect answer.

These five steps will help you cut down on errors.

1. Work carefully, and take your time. Do not rush through a problem just to get it done.
2. Concentrate on the problem. Sometimes problems become mechanical, and your mind begins to wander. You become careless and make a mistake.
3. Check your problem. Be sure that you copied it correctly from the book.
4. Check your computations from step to step. Check the solution to the problem. Does it work? Does it make sense?
5. Keep practising new skills. Remember the old saying, "Practice makes perfect." An increase in practice results in an increase in accuracy. Many errors are due simply to lack of practice.

There is no magic formula for eliminating all errors, but these five steps will be a tremendous help in reducing them.

SECTION 8 EXERCISES

Add or subtract. Express the answer as a mixed number. Simplify all answers.

1. $7\frac{1}{8} + 2\frac{5}{8}$

2. $6\frac{3}{10} + 4\frac{1}{10}$

3. $15\frac{3}{14} - 11\frac{1}{14}$

4. $8\frac{3}{4} - 3\frac{1}{4}$

5. $12\frac{1}{3} + 5\frac{1}{6}$

6. $20\frac{1}{4} + 3\frac{1}{8}$

7. $4\frac{3}{5} + 8\frac{2}{5}$

8. $8\frac{2}{9} + 7\frac{7}{9}$

9. $1 - \frac{3}{7}$

10. $1 - \frac{9}{11}$

11. $1\frac{3}{4} + \frac{5}{16}$

12. $1\frac{2}{3} + \frac{13}{18}$

13. $5\frac{1}{6} + 4\frac{5}{18}$

14. $6\frac{2}{5} + 7\frac{3}{20}$

15. $8\frac{1}{4} - 8\frac{4}{16}$

16. $8\frac{11}{15} - 3\frac{3}{10}$

17. $12\frac{1}{3} - 7\frac{2}{5}$

18. $10\frac{10}{15} - 10\frac{2}{3}$

19. $30 - 15\frac{3}{7}$

20. $25 - 14\frac{2}{11}$

21. $3 + 4\frac{2}{5}$

22. $8 + 2\frac{3}{4}$

23. $14 - 3\frac{7}{10}$

24. $19 - 5\frac{8}{9}$

Add or subtract. Express the answer as a mixed number. Simplify all answers.

25. $\begin{array}{r} 15\frac{4}{15} \\ +26\frac{8}{15} \\ \hline \end{array}$

26. $\begin{array}{r} 22\frac{1}{8} \\ +14\frac{3}{8} \\ \hline \end{array}$

27. $\begin{array}{r} 6\frac{1}{6} \\ +2\frac{1}{4} \\ \hline \end{array}$

28. $\begin{array}{r} 3\frac{2}{3} \\ +4\frac{1}{5} \\ \hline \end{array}$

29. $\begin{array}{r} 3\frac{3}{4} \\ +4\frac{5}{12} \\ \hline \end{array}$

30. $\begin{array}{r} 11\frac{5}{8} \\ +13\frac{1}{2} \\ \hline \end{array}$

31. $\begin{array}{r} 47\frac{3}{10} \\ +26\frac{5}{8} \\ \hline \end{array}$

32. $\begin{array}{r} 34\frac{1}{20} \\ +45\frac{8}{15} \\ \hline \end{array}$

33. $\begin{array}{r} 19\frac{5}{6} \\ -14\frac{1}{3} \\ \hline \end{array}$

34. $\begin{array}{r} 22\frac{7}{9} \\ -16\frac{1}{4} \\ \hline \end{array}$

35. $\begin{array}{r} 6\frac{1}{12} \\ -5\frac{10}{24} \\ \hline \end{array}$

36. $\begin{array}{r} 4\frac{1}{12} \\ -3\frac{7}{18} \\ \hline \end{array}$

37. $\begin{array}{r} 12\frac{3}{20} \\ -\ 7\frac{7}{15} \\ \hline \end{array}$

38. $\begin{array}{r} 8\frac{5}{12} \\ -5\frac{9}{10} \\ \hline \end{array}$

39. $\begin{array}{r} 12 \\ -\ 3\frac{7}{15} \\ \hline \end{array}$

40. $\begin{array}{r} 40 \\ -\ 6\frac{3}{7} \\ \hline \end{array}$

41. $\begin{array}{r} 120 \\ -\ 17\frac{3}{8} \\ \hline \end{array}$

42. $\begin{array}{r} 98 \\ -89\frac{15}{17} \\ \hline \end{array}$

43. $\begin{array}{r} 3\frac{5}{8} \\ 2\frac{2}{3} \\ +7\frac{3}{4} \\ \hline \end{array}$

44. $\begin{array}{r} 4\frac{2}{3} \\ 3\frac{4}{5} \\ +6\frac{3}{4} \\ \hline \end{array}$

Applications

45. ***Mountain Biking*** Lee Hong rode his mountain bike through part of Gatineau Park in Québec. On Wednesday he rode $20\frac{3}{4}$ kilometres. On Thursday he rode $22\frac{3}{8}$ kilometres. What was his total biking distance during those two days?

46. ***Hiking*** Ryan and Omar are planning an afternoon hike. Their map shows three loops measuring $2\frac{1}{8}$ kilometres, $1\frac{5}{6}$ kilometres, and $1\frac{2}{3}$ kilometres. If they hike all three loops, what will their total hiking distance be?

47. ***Bicycling*** Lake Harriet and Lake Calhoun have paved paths around them for runners, walkers, and bicyclists. The distance around Lake Harriet is $2\frac{4}{5}$ kilometres, and the distance around Lake Calhoun is $3\frac{1}{10}$ kilometres. The road connecting the two lakes is $\frac{1}{2}$ kilometre. If Lola rides her bike around both lakes, and uses the connecting road twice, how long is her bike ride?

48. ***Stock Market*** Shanna purchased stock in 1995 at $\$21\frac{3}{8}$ per share. When her son was ready for college, she sold the stock in 2009 at $\$93\frac{5}{8}$ per share. How much did she make per share for her son's tuition?

49. ***Basketball*** Nina and Julie are the two tallest basketball players on their high school team. Nina is $69\frac{3}{4}$ inches tall and Julie is $72\frac{1}{2}$ inches tall. How many inches taller is Julie than Nina?

50. ***Food Purchase*** Julio bought $3\frac{3}{4}$ kilograms of roast turkey and $1\frac{2}{3}$ kilograms of salami at the deli. How many more kilograms of turkey than salami did he buy?

51. ***Food Purchase*** Lara needs 8 kilograms of haddock for her dinner party. At the grocery store, haddock portions weighing $1\frac{3}{4}$ kilograms and $2\frac{1}{6}$ kilograms are placed on the scale.

(a) How many kilograms of haddock are on the scale?

(b) How many more kilograms of haddock does Lara need?

52. ***Medical Care*** A young man has been under a doctor's care to lose weight. His doctor wanted him to lose 46 pounds in the first three months. He lost $17\frac{5}{8}$ pounds the first month and $13\frac{1}{2}$ pounds the second month.

(a) How much did he lose during the first two months?

(b) How much would he need to lose in the third month to reach the goal?

To Think About

Use improper fractions and the Alternative Method as discussed in the text to perform each calculation.

53. $\dfrac{379}{8} + \dfrac{89}{5}$

54. $\dfrac{151}{6} - \dfrac{130}{7}$

When adding or subtracting mixed numbers, it is wise to estimate your answer by rounding each mixed number to the nearest whole number.

55. Estimate your answer to $35\frac{1}{6} + 24\frac{5}{12}$ by rounding each mixed number to the nearest whole number. Then find the exact answer. How close was your estimate?

56. Estimate your answer to $102\frac{5}{7} - 86\frac{2}{3}$ by rounding each mixed number to the nearest whole number. Then find the exact answer. How close was your estimate?

Evaluate using the correct order of operations.

57. $\frac{6}{7} - \frac{4}{7} \times \frac{1}{3}$

58. $\frac{3}{5} - \frac{1}{3} \times \frac{6}{5}$

59. $\frac{1}{2} + \frac{3}{8} \div \frac{3}{4}$

60. $\frac{3}{4} + \frac{1}{4} \div \frac{5}{3}$

61. $\frac{9}{10} \div \frac{3}{8} \times \frac{5}{8}$

62. $\frac{5}{12} \div \frac{3}{10} \times \frac{9}{5}$

63. $\frac{3}{5} \times \frac{1}{2} + \frac{1}{5} \div \frac{2}{3}$

64. $\frac{5}{6} \times \frac{1}{2} + \frac{2}{3} \div \frac{4}{3}$

65. $\left(\frac{3}{5} - \frac{3}{20}\right) \times \frac{4}{5}$

66. $\left(\frac{1}{3} + \frac{1}{6}\right) \times \frac{5}{11}$

67. $\left(\frac{1}{3}\right)^2 \div \frac{4}{9}$

68. $\left(\frac{1}{4}\right)^2 \div \frac{3}{4}$

69. $\frac{1}{4} \times \left(\frac{2}{3}\right)^2$

70. $\frac{5}{8} \times \left(\frac{2}{5}\right)^2$

71. $\frac{5}{6} \div \left(\frac{2}{3} + \frac{1}{6}\right)^2$

72. $\frac{4}{3} \div \left(\frac{3}{5} - \frac{3}{10}\right)^2$

Quick Quiz 8

1. Add. Express the answer as a mixed number.

$3\frac{4}{5} + 5\frac{3}{8}$

2. Subtract. Express the answer as a mixed number.

$6\frac{5}{12} - 4\frac{7}{10}$

3. Evaluate using the correct order of operations.

$\frac{1}{5} + \frac{3}{10} \div \frac{11}{20}$

4. Concept Check Explain how you would evaluate the following expression using the correct order of operations. $\frac{4}{5} - \frac{1}{4} \times \frac{2}{3}$

SECTION 9 SOLVING APPLIED PROBLEMS INVOLVING FRACTIONS

Solving Real-Life Problems with Fractions

Student Learning Objective

After studying this section, you will be able to:

 **Solve real-life problems with fractions.**

All problem solving requires the same kind of thinking. In this section we will combine problem-solving skills with our new computational skills with fractions. Sometimes the difficulty is in figuring out what must be done. Sometimes it is in doing the computation. Remember that *estimating* is important in problem solving. We may use the following steps.

1. ***Understand the problem.***
   (a) Read the problem carefully.
   (b) Draw a picture if this helps you.
   (c) Fill in the Mathematics Blueprint.

2. ***Solve.***
   (a) Perform the calculations.
   (b) State the answer, including the units of measure.

3. ***Check.***
   (a) Estimate the answer. Round fractions to the nearest whole number.
   (b) Compare the exact answer with the estimate to see if your answer is reasonable.

▲ **EXAMPLE 1** In designing a modern offshore speedboat, the design engineer has determined that one of the oak frames near the engine housing needs to be $26\frac{1}{8}$ centimetres long. At the end of the oak frame there will be $2\frac{5}{8}$ centimetres of insulation. Finally, there will be a steel mounting that is $3\frac{3}{4}$ centimetres long. When all three items are assembled, how long will the oak frame and insulation and steel mounting extend?

Solution

1. ***Understand the problem.***
We draw a picture to help us.

Then we fill in the Mathematics Blueprint.

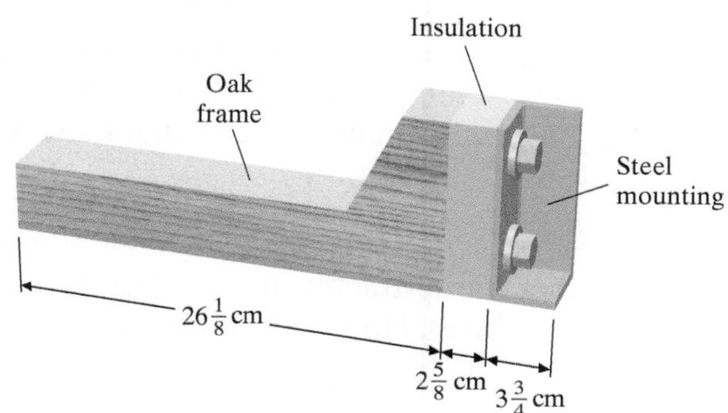

Mathematics Blueprint for Problem Solving

Gather the Facts	What Am I Asked to Do?	How Do I Proceed?	Key Points to Remember
Oak frame: $26\frac{1}{8}$ cm Insulation: $2\frac{5}{8}$ cm Steel mounting: $3\frac{3}{4}$ cm	Find the total length.	Add the lengths of the three items.	When adding mixed numbers, add the whole numbers first and then add the fractions.

2. *Solve and state the answer.*

Add the three amounts. $26\frac{1}{8} + 2\frac{5}{8} + 3\frac{3}{4}$

$$\text{LCD} = 8 \qquad \begin{aligned} 26\frac{1}{8} &= 26\frac{1}{8} \\ 2\frac{5}{8} &= 2\frac{5}{8} \\ +3\boxed{\frac{3}{4} \times \frac{2}{2}} &= +3\frac{6}{8} \\ \hline & \quad 31\frac{12}{8} = 32\frac{4}{8} = 32\frac{1}{2} \end{aligned}$$

The entire assembly will be $32\frac{1}{2}$ centimetres.

3. *Check.* Estimate the sum by rounding each fraction to the nearest whole number.

Thus $\quad 26\frac{1}{8} + 2\frac{5}{8} + 3\frac{3}{4}$

becomes $\quad 26 + 3 + 4 = 33$

This is close to our answer, $32\frac{1}{2}$. Our answer seems reasonable.

One of the most important uses of estimation in mathematics is in the calculation of problems involving fractions. People find it easier to detect significant errors when working with whole numbers. However, the extra steps involved in the calculations with fractions and mixed numbers often distract our attention from an error that we should have detected.

Thus it is particularly critical to take the time to check your answer by estimating the results of the calculation with whole numbers. Be sure to ask yourself, is this answer reasonable? Does this answer seem realistic? Only by estimating our results with whole numbers will we be able to answer that question. It is this estimating skill that you will find more useful in your own life as a consumer and as a citizen.

NOTE TO STUDENT: *Fully worked-out solutions to all of the Practice Problems can be found at the end of the module.*

Practice Problem 1 Nicole required the following amounts of gas for her farm tractor in the last three fill-ups: $18\frac{7}{10}$ litres, $15\frac{2}{5}$ litres, and $14\frac{1}{2}$ litres. How many litres did she need altogether?

The word *diameter* has two common meanings. First, it means a line segment that passes through the centre of and intersects a circle twice. It has its endpoints on the circle. Second, it means the *length* of this segment.

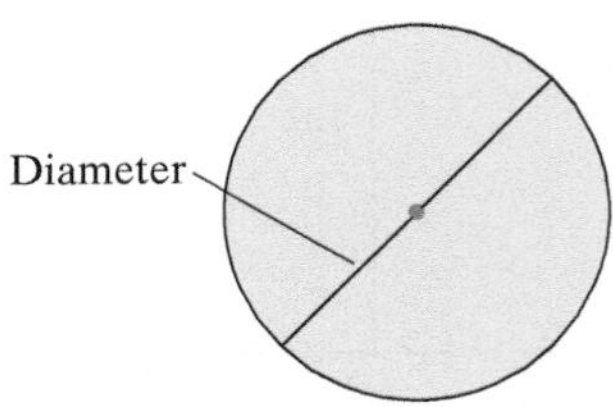

▲ **EXAMPLE 2** What is the inside diameter of (distance across) a cement storm drain pipe that has an outside diameter of $2\frac{1}{8}$ metres and is $\frac{1}{8}$ metre thick?

Solution

1. ***Understand the problem.*** Read the problem carefully. Draw a picture. The picture is in the margin on the right. Now fill in the Mathematics Blueprint.

Mathematics Blueprint for Problem Solving

Gather the Facts	What Am I Asked to Do?	How Do I Proceed?	Key Points to Remember
Outside diameter is $2\frac{1}{8}$ metres. Thickness is $\frac{1}{8}$ metre on both ends of the diameter.	Find the *inside* diameter of the pipe.	Add the two measures of thickness. Then subtract this total from the outside diameter.	Since the LCD = 8, all fractions must have this denominator.

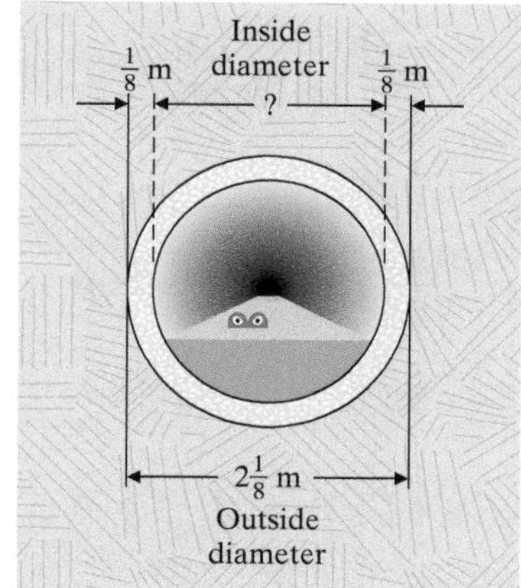

2. ***Solve and state the answer.*** Add the two thickness measurements together. Adding $\frac{1}{8} + \frac{1}{8} = \frac{2}{8}$ gives the total thickness of the pipe, $\frac{2}{8}$ metre. We will not reduce $\frac{2}{8}$ since the LCD is 8.

   We subtract the total of the two thickness measurements from the outside diameter.

$$\begin{array}{rcr} 2\frac{1}{8} & = & 1\frac{9}{8} \\ -\ \frac{2}{8} & = & -\ \frac{2}{8} \\ \hline & & 1\frac{7}{8} \end{array}$$

We borrow 1 from 2 to get $1 + 1\frac{1}{8}$ or $1\frac{9}{8}$.

   The inside diameter is $1\frac{7}{8}$ metres.

3. ***Check.*** We will work backward to check. We will use the exact values. If we have done our work correctly, $\frac{1}{8}$ metre + $1\frac{7}{8}$ metres + $\frac{1}{8}$ metre should add up to the outside diameter, $2\frac{1}{8}$ metres.

$$\frac{1}{8} + 1\frac{7}{8} + \frac{1}{8} \stackrel{?}{=} 2\frac{1}{8}$$

$$1\frac{9}{8} \stackrel{?}{=} 2\frac{1}{8}$$

$$2\frac{1}{8} = 2\frac{1}{8} \checkmark$$

   Our answer of $1\frac{7}{8}$ metres is correct.

▲ **Practice Problem 2** A postcard is $12\frac{1}{4}$ centimetres long. We want a $1\frac{3}{8}$-centimetre border on the top and a 2-centimetre border on the bottom. What is the length of the inside portion of the postcard?

***NOTE TO STUDENT:** Fully worked-out solutions to all of the Practice Problems can be found at the end of the module.*

EXAMPLE 3 On Tuesday, Michael earned $\$8\frac{1}{4}$ per hour working for eight hours. He also earned overtime pay, which is $1\frac{1}{2}$ times his regular rate of $\$8\frac{1}{4}$, for four hours on Tuesday. How much pay did he earn altogether on Tuesday?

Solution

1. ***Understand the problem.*** We draw a picture of the parts of Michael's pay on Tuesday.

   Michael's earnings on Tuesday are the sum of two parts:

   Pay at regular pay rate + Pay at overtime pay rate = Total pay for the day

   Now fill in the Mathematics Blueprint.

Mathematics Blueprint for Problem Solving

Gather the Facts	What Am I Asked to Do?	How Do I Proceed?	Key Points to Remember
He works eight hours at $\$8\frac{1}{4}$ per hour. He works four hours at the overtime rate, $1\frac{1}{2}$ times the regular rate.	Find his total pay for Tuesday.	Find out how much he is paid for regular time. Find out how much he is paid for overtime. Then add the two.	The overtime rate is $1\frac{1}{2}$ multiplied by the regular rate.

2. ***Solve and state the answer.*** Find his overtime pay rate.

$$1\frac{1}{2} \times 8\frac{1}{4} = \frac{3}{2} \times \frac{33}{4} = \frac{\$99}{8} \text{ per hour}$$

   We leave our answer as an improper fraction because we will need to multiply it by another fraction.

   How much was he paid for regular time? For overtime?

   For eight regular hours, he earned $8 \times 8\frac{1}{4} = \overset{2}{\cancel{8}} \times \frac{33}{\underset{1}{\cancel{4}}} = \$66.$

   For four overtime hours, he earned $\overset{1}{\cancel{4}} \times \frac{99}{\underset{2}{\cancel{8}}} = \frac{99}{2} = \$49\frac{1}{2}.$

   Now we add to find the total pay.

$$\begin{array}{rl} \$66 & \text{Pay at regular pay rate} \\ +\$49\frac{1}{2} & \text{Pay at overtime pay rate} \\ \hline \end{array}$$

   Michael earned $\$115\frac{1}{2}$ working on Tuesday. This is the same as \$115.50.

3. ***Check.*** We estimate his regular pay rate at \$8 per hour.

We estimate his overtime pay rate at $1\frac{1}{2} \times 8 = \frac{3}{2} \times 8 = 12$ or \$12 per hour.

$$8 \text{ hours} \times \$8 \text{ per hour} = \$64 \text{ regular pay}$$
$$4 \text{ hours} \times \$12 \text{ per hour} = \$48 \text{ overtime pay}$$

Estimated sum. $\$64 + \$48 \approx \$60 + \$50 = \$110$

\$110 is close to our calculated value, $\$115\frac{1}{2}$, so our answer is reasonable. ✓

Practice Problem 3 A tent manufacturer uses $8\frac{1}{4}$ metres of waterproof duck cloth to make a regular tent. She uses $1\frac{1}{2}$ times that amount to make a large tent. How many metres of cloth will she need to make 6 regular tents and 16 large tents?

▲ **EXAMPLE 4** Alicia is buying some 8-foot boards for shelving. She wishes to make two bookcases, each with three shelves. Each shelf will be $3\frac{1}{4}$ feet long.

(a) How many boards does she need to buy?

(b) How many linear feet of shelving are actually needed to build the bookcases?

(c) How many linear feet of shelving will be left over?

Solution

1. ***Understand the problem.*** Draw a sketch of a bookcase. Each bookcase will have three shelves. Alicia is making two such bookcases. (Alicia's boards are for the shelves, not the sides.)
Now fill in the Mathematics Blueprint.

Mathematics Blueprint for Problem Solving

Gather the Facts	What Am I Asked to Do?	How Do I Proceed?	Key Points to Remember
She needs three shelves for each bookcase. Each shelf is $3\frac{1}{4}$ feet long. She will make two bookcases. Shelves are cut from 8-foot boards.	Find out how many boards to buy. Find out how many feet of board are needed for shelves and how many feet will be left over.	First find out how many $3\frac{1}{4}$-foot shelves she can get from one board. Then see how many boards she needs to make all six shelves.	Each time she cuts up an 8-foot board, she will get some shelves and some leftover wood.

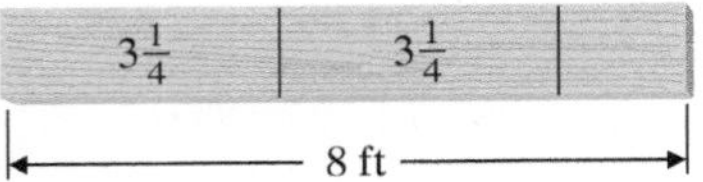

2. ***Solve and state the answer.*** We want to know how many $3\frac{1}{4}$-foot boards are in an 8-foot board. By drawing a rough sketch, we would probably guess the answer is 2. To find exactly how many $3\frac{1}{4}$-foot-long pieces are in 8 feet, we will use division.

$$8 \div 3\frac{1}{4} = \frac{8}{1} \div \frac{13}{4} = \frac{8}{1} \times \frac{4}{13} = \frac{32}{13} = 2\frac{6}{13}$$

She will get two shelves from each board, and some wood will be left over.

(a) How many boards does Alicia need to build two bookcases? For two bookcases, she needs six shelves. She will get two shelves out of each board. $6 \div 2 = 3$. She will need three 8-foot boards.

(b) How many linear feet of shelving are actually needed to build the bookcases?
She needs 6 shelves at $3\frac{1}{4}$ feet.

$$6 \times 3\frac{1}{4} = \overset{3}{\cancel{6}} \times \frac{13}{\underset{2}{\cancel{4}}} = \frac{39}{2} = 19\frac{1}{2}$$

A total of $19\frac{1}{2}$ linear feet of shelving is needed.

(c) How many linear feet of shelving will be left over?
Each time she uses one board she will have

$$8 - 3\frac{1}{4} - 3\frac{1}{4} = 8 - \left(3\frac{1}{4} + 3\frac{1}{4}\right) = 8 - 6\frac{1}{2} = 1\frac{1}{2}$$

feet left over. Each of the three boards will have $1\frac{1}{2}$ feet left over.

$$3 \times 1\frac{1}{2} = 3 \times \frac{3}{2} = \frac{9}{2} = 4\frac{1}{2}$$

A total of $4\frac{1}{2}$ linear feet of shelving will be left over.

3. ***Check.*** Work backward. See if you can check that with three 8-foot boards you

(a) can make the six shelves for the two bookcases.
(b) will use exactly $19\frac{1}{2}$ linear feet to make the shelves.
(c) will have exactly $4\frac{1}{2}$ linear feet left over.

The check is left to you.

Practice Problem 4 Michael is purchasing 4-metre boards for shelving. He wishes to make two bookcases, each with four shelves. Each shelf will be $1\frac{1}{4}$ metres long.

(a) How many boards does he need to buy?
(b) How many linear metres of shelving are actually needed to build the bookcases?
(c) How many linear metres of shelving will be left over?

Another useful method for solving applied problems is called "Do a similar, simpler problem." When a problem seems difficult to understand because of the fractions, change the problem to an easier but similar problem. Then decide how to solve the simpler problem and use the same steps to solve the original problem. For example:

> How many litres of water can a tank hold if its volume is $58\frac{2}{3}$ cubic metres? (1 cubic metre holds about 1000 litres.)

A similar, easier problem would be: "If 1 cubic metre holds 1000 litres and a tank holds 60 cubic metres, how many litres of water does the tank hold?"

The easier problem can be read more quickly and seems to make more sense. Probably we will see how to solve the easier problem right away: "I can find the number of litres by multiplying 1000×60." Therefore we can solve the first problem by multiplying $1000 \times 58\frac{2}{3}$ to obtain the number of litres of water. See the next example.

EXAMPLE 5 A fishing boat travelled $69\frac{3}{8}$ nautical miles in $3\frac{3}{4}$ hours. How many knots (nautical miles per hour) did the fishing boat average?

Solution

1. ***Understand the problem.*** Let us think of a simpler problem. If a boat travelled 70 nautical miles in 4 hours, how many knots did it average? We would divide distance by time.

$$70 \div 4 = \text{average speed}$$

Likewise in our original problem we need to divide distance by time.

$$69\frac{3}{8} \div 3\frac{3}{4} = \text{average speed}$$

Now fill in the Mathematics Blueprint.

Mathematics Blueprint for Problem Solving

Gather the Facts	What Am I Asked to Do?	How Do I Proceed?	Key Points to Remember
Distance is $69\frac{3}{8}$ nautical miles. Time is $3\frac{3}{4}$ hours.	Find the average speed of the boat.	Divide the distance in nautical miles by the time in hours.	You must change the mixed numbers to improper fractions before dividing.

2. ***Solve and state the answer.*** Divide distance by time to get speed in nautical miles per hour or knots.

$$69\frac{3}{8} \div 3\frac{3}{4} = \frac{555}{8} \div \frac{15}{4} = \frac{\overset{37}{\cancel{555}}}{\underset{2}{\cancel{8}}} \cdot \frac{\overset{1}{\cancel{4}}}{\underset{1}{\cancel{15}}}$$

$$= \frac{37}{2} \cdot \frac{1}{1} = \frac{37}{2} = 18\frac{1}{2}$$

The speed of the boat was $18\frac{1}{2}$ knots.

Bill Stanton/ImageState Media Partners Limited

3. *Check.*

We estimate $69\frac{3}{8} \div 3\frac{3}{4}$.

$$\text{Use } 70 \div 4 = 17\frac{1}{2} \text{ knots}$$

Our estimate is close to the calculated value.

Our answer is reasonable. ✓

NOTE TO STUDENT: *Fully worked-out solutions to all of the Practice Problems can be found at the end of the module.*

Practice Problem 5 Alfonso travelled $199\frac{3}{4}$ kilometres in his car and used $8\frac{1}{2}$ litres of gas. How many kilometres per litre did he get?

Be sure to allow extra time to read over Examples 1–5 and Practice Problems 1–5. Many students find it is helpful to study them on two different days. This allows you additional time to really understand the steps of reasoning involved.

Developing Your Study Skills

Why Study Mathematics?

Students often question the value of mathematics. They see little real use for it in their everyday lives. However, mathematics is often the key that opens the door to a better-paying job.

In our present-day technological world, many people use mathematics daily. Many vocational and professional areas—such as the fields of business, statistics, economics, psychology, finance, computer science, chemistry, physics, engineering, electronics, nuclear energy, banking, quality control, and teaching—require a certain level of expertise in mathematics. Those who want to work in these fields must be able to function at a given mathematical level. Those who cannot will not be able to enter these job areas.

So, whatever your field, be sure to realize the importance of mastering the basics of this course. It is very likely to help you advance to the career of your choice.

Section 9 Exercises

You may benefit from using the Mathematics Blueprint for Problem Solving when solving the following exercises.

Applications

▲**1.** ***Geometry*** A triangle has three sides that measure $8\frac{1}{3}$ cm, $5\frac{4}{5}$ cm, and $9\frac{3}{10}$ cm. What is the perimeter of (total distance around) the triangle?

2. ***Automobile Travel*** On Tuesday, Sally drove $10\frac{1}{2}$ kilometres while running errands. On Friday and Saturday, she had more errands to run and drove $6\frac{1}{3}$ kilometres and $12\frac{1}{4}$ kilometres, respectively. How many total kilometres did Sally drive this week while running errands?

3. ***Wildlife*** In 2006, only 700 mountain gorillas remained in the world. Of these, about $\frac{5}{9}$ of them were living in a mountain range along the borders of Congo, Rwanda, and Uganda. How many gorillas were living in this mountain range? Round your answer to the nearest whole number.

4. ***Consumer Decisions*** Between 2005 and 2006, prices on many electronic devices went down. The average price of a flat-panel television in 2005 was \$1190. In 2006, the average price was about $\frac{4}{5}$ as much. What was the average price of a flat-panel television in 2006?

5. ***Carpentry*** A bolt extends through $\frac{3}{4}$-inch-thick plywood, two washers that are each $\frac{1}{16}$ inch thick, and a nut that is $\frac{3}{16}$ inch thick. The main body of the bolt must be $\frac{1}{2}$ inch longer than the sum of the thicknesses of plywood, washers, and nut. What is the minimum length of the bolt?

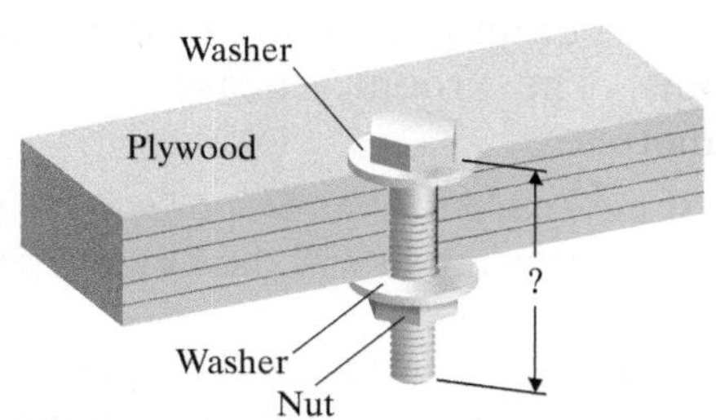

6. ***Carpentry*** A carpenter is using an 8-metre length of wood for a frame. The carpenter needs to cut a notch in the wood that is $4\frac{7}{8}$ metres from one end and $1\frac{2}{3}$ metres from the other end. How long does the notch need to be?

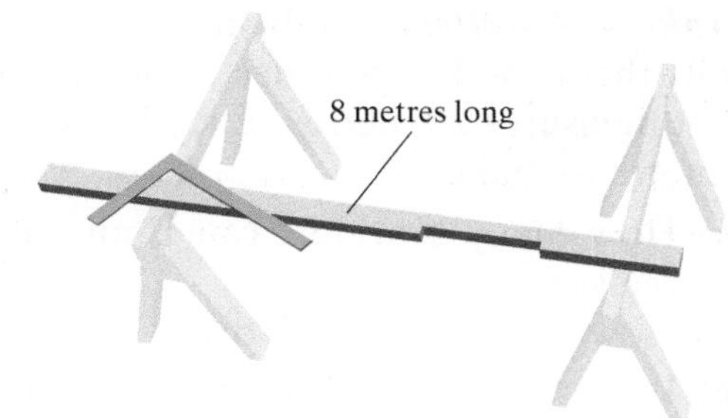

7. ***Running a Marathon*** Hank is running the Terry Fox Run, which is $26\frac{1}{5}$ kilometres long. At $6\frac{3}{4}$ kilometres from the start, he meets his wife, who is cheering him on. $9\frac{1}{2}$ kilometres farther down the course, he sees some friends from his running club volunteering at a water stop. Once he passes his friends, how many more kilometres does Hank have left to run?

8. ***Carpentry*** Norman Olerud makes birdhouses as a hobby. He has a long piece of lumber that measures $14\frac{1}{4}$ feet. He needs to cut it into pieces that are $\frac{3}{4}$ foot long for the birdhouse floors. How many floors will he be able to cut from the long piece?

9. ***Personal Finance*** Javier earned $\$10\frac{1}{2}$ per hour for 8 hours of work on Saturday. His manager asked him to stay for an additional 4 hours, for which he was paid $1\frac{1}{2}$ times the regular rate. How much did Javier earn on Saturday?

10. ***Food Purchase*** For a party of the British Literature Club using all "English foods," Nancy bought a $10\frac{2}{3}$-kilogram wheel of Stilton cheese, to go with the pears and the apples, at $\$8\frac{3}{4}$ per kilogram. How much did the wheel of Stilton cheese cost?

▲ **11.** ***Geometry*** How many litres can a tank hold that has a volume of $36\frac{3}{4}$ cubic metres? (Assume that 1 cubic metre holds 1000 litres.)

▲ **12.** ***Geometry*** A tank can hold a volume of $7\frac{1}{4}$ cubic metres. If it is filled with water, what is the mass of the water? (Assume that 1 cubic metre of water has a mass of 1000 kilograms.)

13. ***Titanic Disaster*** The night of the *Titanic* cruise ship disaster, the captain decided to run his ship at $22\frac{1}{2}$ knots (nautical miles per hour). The *Titanic* travelled at that speed for $4\frac{3}{4}$ hours before it met its tragic demise. How far did the *Titanic* travel at this excessive speed before the disaster?

14. ***Personal Finance*** William built a porch for his neighbour and got paid \$1200. He gave $\frac{1}{10}$ of this to his brother to pay back a debt. He used $\frac{1}{3}$ of it to pay bills and used $\frac{1}{6}$ to pay his helper. How much of the \$1200 did William have left?

15. ***Personal Finance*** Noriko earns \$660 per week. She has $\frac{1}{5}$ of her income deducted for federal taxes, $\frac{1}{15}$ of her income deducted for provincial taxes, and $\frac{1}{20}$ of her income deducted for medical coverage. How much per week is left for Noriko after these three deductions?

16. ***Real Estate*** Dan and Estella are saving for a down payment on a house. Their total take-home pay is \$960 per week. They have allotted $\frac{1}{4}$ of their weekly income for rent, $\frac{1}{10}$ for car insurance, and $\frac{1}{3}$ for all other expenses including groceries, clothing, entertainment, and monthly bills. How much is left per week to be saved for their down payment?

17. ***Making Jewellery*** Emily makes bracelets and sells them for $\$9\frac{1}{2}$. She has a long piece of wire that measures 20 metres. Each bracelet requires $\frac{3}{5}$ metre to make.

(a) How many bracelets can Emily make from the long piece of wire?

(b) How much wire is left over?

(c) If Emily sells all the bracelets, how much money will she make?

▲ **18.** ***Home Improvement*** The Costellos are having new carpet and moulding installed in their sunroom. The room measures $2\frac{1}{2}$ metres by $3\frac{2}{3}$ metres.

(a) If new carpet costs \$9 per square metre to install, how much will the new carpet cost?

(b) The new moulding will be placed around the room where the wall and ceiling meet. How many metres of moulding will they need?

19. ***Food Purchase*** Cecilia bought a loaf of sourdough bread that was made by a local gourmet bakery. The label said that the bread, plus its fancy box, weighed 1.85 kg, which is equivalent to $18\frac{1}{2}$ hg, in total. Of this, $1\frac{1}{4}$ hg turned out to be the weight of the ribbon. The box weighed $3\frac{1}{8}$ hg.

(a) How many hectograms of bread did she actually buy?

(b) The box stated its net weight as equivalent to $14\frac{3}{4}$ hg. (This means that she should have found $14\frac{3}{4}$ hg of gourmet sourdough bread in the box.) How much in error was this measurement?

20. ***Cooking*** Marnie has $12\frac{1}{2}$ cups of flour. She wants to make two pies, each requiring $1\frac{1}{4}$ cups of flour, and three cakes, each requiring $2\frac{1}{8}$ cups. How much flour will be left after Marnie makes the pies and cakes?

21. ***Coast Guard Boat Operation*** The largest Coast Guard boat stationed at Vancouver can travel $160\frac{1}{8}$ nautical miles in $5\frac{1}{4}$ hours.

(a) At how many knots is the boat travelling?

(b) At this speed, how long would it take the Coast Guard boat to travel $213\frac{1}{2}$ nautical miles?

22. ***Water Ski Boat*** Russ and Norma's Mariah water ski boat can travel $72\frac{7}{8}$ nautical miles in $2\frac{3}{4}$ hours.

(a) At how many knots is the boat travelling?

(b) At this speed, how long would it take their water ski boat to travel $92\frac{3}{4}$ nautical miles?

▲ 23. ***Farming*** A Saskatchewan wheat farmer has a storage bin with a capacity of $6856\frac{1}{4}$ cubic metres.

(a) If a bushel of wheat is $\frac{1}{30}$ cubic metre, how many bushels can the storage bin hold?

(b) If a farmer wants to make a new storage bin $1\frac{3}{4}$ times larger, how many cubic metres will it hold?

(c) How many bushels will the new bin hold?

▲ 24. ***Farming*** A wheat farmer from Manitoba has a storage bin with a capacity of $8693\frac{1}{3}$ cubic metres.

(a) If a bushel of wheat is $\frac{1}{25}$ cubic metre, how many bushels can the storage bin hold?

(b) If a farmer wants to make a new storage bin $1\frac{1}{3}$ times larger, how many cubic metres will it hold?

(c) How many bushels will the new bin hold?

Quick Quiz 9

1. Marcia wants to put wall-to-wall carpet in her rec-room. The room measures $15\frac{3}{4}$ metres by $10\frac{2}{3}$ metres. How many square metres of carpeting does she need?

2. Ken Thompson shipped out $41\frac{3}{5}$ kilograms of electrical supplies. The supplies are placed in individual packets that weigh $2\frac{3}{5}$ kilograms each. How many packets did he ship out?

3. Lexi bicycled $1\frac{1}{8}$ kilometres from Spruce St. to Fogg St. She then travelled $1\frac{1}{2}$ kilometres from Fogg St. to Westmount Blvd. Finally she travelled $2\frac{3}{4}$ kilometres from Westmount Blvd. to Spruce St. How far did she travel on her bicycle? Express your answer as a mixed number.

4. **Concept Check** A trail to a peak on Crowsnest Mountain is $3\frac{3}{5}$ kilometres long. Caleb started hiking on the trail and stopped after walking $1\frac{7}{8}$ kilometres to take a break. Explain how you would find how far he still has to go to get to the peak.

Putting Your Skills to Work: Use Math to Save Money

FINDING EXTRA MONEY EACH MONTH

Do you find yourself running short of money each month? Do you wish you could find a little extra cash for yourself? Is there some daily habit that costs money that maybe you could give up? Let's start with smoking cigarettes. (If you don't smoke, think of some other example, perhaps your daily cup of coffee, where you spend money.) Now consider the story of a young couple, Tricia and Jack.

Lim ChewHow/Shutterstock

Tricia and Jack both used to smoke cigarettes. Then Tricia experienced some health problems and had to go to the hospital for several days. Tricia and Jack both decided they were done with smoking. It was pretty hard to quit, and at first they just focused on how hard it was for them. But then Tricia and Jack noticed they were having more money left over at the end of the month.

They got to thinking. Where they live, cigarettes cost $6 a pack, and they were both pack-a-day smokers. How much had they spent together per month on cigarettes? (Figure 30 days for an average month.)

1. (a) Find out how much Tricia and Jack spent in a month (30 days) on cigarettes.

(b) Use your answer from (a) to find out how much they spent in 12 months on cigarettes.

Tricia and Jack enjoyed smoking but knew it was bad for their health. So they decided to put the money they saved by not smoking into a savings account for something they would really enjoy. They thought they could purchase a really nice plasma television for $2000. If they put the money they saved each month into the savings account, would there be enough money by Tricia's birthday (which is 7 months from now)?

2. (a) Find out if they would save enough money in 7 months for a television.

(b) Would there be extra money for a birthday celebration dinner for Tricia? If so, how much?

3. If Tricia and Jack found a plasma television on sale that only costs $\frac{3}{4}$ of what the television costs in problem 2 (above), how much money would be available for the birthday dinner?

Some cities and provinces across Canada are imposing taxes on the sale of cigarettes as a way to offset the cost of health care for people who suffer from smoking-related medical issues. These taxes make smoking cigarettes even more costly. For example, in July of 2008 in Toronto, a pack of cigarettes cost approximately $10.

If Tricia and Jack lived in Toronto and each smoked a pack of cigarettes per day, how much money would they spend on cigarettes for a month?

4. (a) Find out how much Tricia and Jack would spend in 30 days on cigarettes in Toronto.

(b) Use your answer from (a) to find out how much Tricia and Jack would spend on cigarettes in 12 months in Toronto.

(c) How much more is this amount than the amount you found in problem 1(b) above?

5. Can you think of one extra expense you could eliminate so you could save money to purchase a big ticket item? Calculate the savings.

Module Organizer

Topic	Procedure	Examples
Concept of a fractional part.	The numerator is the number of parts selected. The denominator is the number of total parts.	What part of this sketch is shaded? 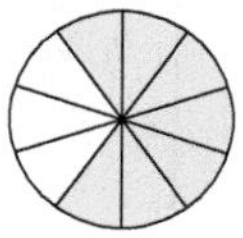 $\frac{7}{10}$
Prime factorization.	Prime factorization is the writing of a number as the product of prime numbers.	Write the prime factorization of 36. $36 = 4 \times 9$; $4 = 2 \times 2$, $9 = 3 \times 3$; $= 2 \times 2 \times 3 \times 3$
Reducing fractions.	**1.** Factor numerator and denominator into prime factors. **2.** Divide out factors common to numerator and denominator.	Reduce. $\frac{54}{90}$ $\frac{54}{90} = \frac{\cancel{2}^{1} \times \cancel{3}^{1} \times \cancel{3}^{1} \times 3}{\cancel{2}_{1} \times \cancel{3}_{1} \times \cancel{3}_{1} \times 5} = \frac{3}{5}$
Changing a mixed number to an improper fraction.	**1.** Multiply whole number by denominator. **2.** Add product to numerator. **3.** Place sum over denominator.	Write as an improper fraction. $7\frac{3}{4} = \frac{7 \times 4 + 3}{4} = \frac{28 + 3}{4} = \frac{31}{4}$
Changing an improper fraction to a mixed number.	**1.** Divide denominator into numerator. **2.** The quotient is the whole number. **3.** The fraction is the remainder over the divisor.	Change to a mixed number. $\frac{32}{5}$ $5\overline{)32}$ quotient 6; 30; remainder 2; $= 6\frac{2}{5}$
Multiplying fractions.	**1.** Divide out common factors from the numerators and denominators whenever possible. **2.** Multiply numerators. **3.** Multiply denominators.	Multiply. $\frac{3}{7} \times \frac{5}{13} = \frac{15}{91}$ Multiply. $\frac{\cancel{5}^{1}}{\cancel{8}_{1}} \times \frac{\cancel{16}^{2}}{\cancel{15}_{3}} = \frac{2}{3}$
Multiplying mixed and/or whole numbers.	**1.** Change any whole numbers to fractions with a denominator of 1. **2.** Change any mixed numbers to improper fractions. **3.** Use multiplication rule for fractions.	Multiply. $7 \times 3\frac{1}{4}$ $\frac{7}{1} \times \frac{13}{4} = \frac{91}{4}$ or $22\frac{3}{4}$
Dividing fractions.	To divide two fractions, we invert the second fraction and multiply.	Divide. $\frac{3}{7} \div \frac{2}{9} = \frac{3}{7} \times \frac{9}{2} = \frac{27}{14}$ or $1\frac{13}{14}$
Dividing mixed numbers and/or whole numbers.	**1.** Change any whole numbers to fractions with a denominator of 1. **2.** Change any mixed numbers to improper fractions. **3.** Use rule for division of fractions.	Divide. $8\frac{1}{3} \div 5\frac{5}{9} = \frac{25}{3} \div \frac{50}{9}$ $= \frac{\cancel{25}^{1}}{\cancel{3}_{1}} \times \frac{\cancel{9}^{3}}{\cancel{50}_{2}} = \frac{3}{2}$ or $1\frac{1}{2}$
Finding the least common denominator.	**1.** Write each denominator as the product of prime factors. **2.** List all the prime factors that appear in both products. **3.** Form a product of those factors, using each factor the greatest number of times it appears in any denominator.	Find LCD of $\frac{1}{10}, \frac{3}{8}$, and $\frac{7}{25}$. $10 = 2 \times 5$ $8 = 2 \times 2 \times 2$ $25 = 5 \times 5$ $\text{LCD} = 2 \times 2 \times 2 \times 5 \times 5 = 200$

(*Continued on next page*)

Topic	Procedure	Examples
Building fractions.	1. Find how many times the original denominator can be divided into the new denominator. 2. Multiply that value by numerator and denominator of original fraction.	Build $\frac{5}{7}$ to an equivalent fraction with a denominator of 42. First we find $7\overline{)42}$ = 6. Then we multiply the numerator and denominator by 6. $\frac{5}{7} \times \frac{6}{6} = \frac{30}{42}$
Adding or subtracting fractions with a common denominator.	1. Add or subtract the numerators. 2. Keep the common denominator.	Add. $\frac{3}{13} + \frac{5}{13} = \frac{8}{13}$ Subtract. $\frac{15}{17} - \frac{12}{17} = \frac{3}{17}$
Adding or subtracting fractions without a common denominator.	1. Find the LCD of the fractions. 2. Build each fraction, if needed, to obtain the LCD in the denominator. 3. Follow the steps for adding and subtracting fractions with the same denominator.	Add. $\frac{1}{4} + \frac{3}{7} + \frac{5}{8}$ LCD = 56 $\frac{1}{4} \times \frac{14}{14} + \frac{3}{7} \times \frac{8}{8} + \frac{5}{8} \times \frac{7}{7}$ $= \frac{14}{56} + \frac{24}{56} + \frac{35}{56} = \frac{73}{56}$ or $1\frac{17}{56}$
Adding mixed numbers.	1. Change fractional parts to equivalent fractions with LCD as a denominator, if needed. 2. Add whole numbers and fractions separately. 3. If improper fractions occur, change to mixed numbers and simplify.	Add. $6\frac{3}{4} + 2\frac{5}{8}$ $6\boxed{\frac{3}{4} \times \frac{2}{2}} = 6\frac{6}{8}$ $+2\frac{5}{8} = +2\frac{5}{8}$ $8\frac{11}{8} = 9\frac{3}{8}$
Subtracting mixed numbers.	1. Change fractional parts to equivalent fractions with LCD as a denominator, if needed. 2. If necessary, borrow from whole number to subtract fractions. 3. Subtract whole numbers and fractions separately.	Subtract. $8\frac{1}{5} - 4\frac{2}{3}$ $8\boxed{\frac{1}{5} \times \frac{3}{3}} = 8\frac{3}{15} = 7\frac{18}{15}$ $-4\boxed{\frac{2}{3} \times \frac{5}{5}} = -4\frac{10}{15} = -4\frac{10}{15}$ $3\frac{8}{15}$
Order of operations.	With grouping symbols: Do first 1. Perform operations inside parentheses. ↓ 2. Simplify any expressions with exponents. 3. Multiply or divide from left to right. Do last 4. Add or subtract from left to right.	$\frac{5}{6} \div \left(\frac{4}{5} - \frac{7}{15}\right)$ First combine numbers inside the parentheses. $\frac{5}{6} \div \left(\frac{12}{15} - \frac{7}{15}\right)$ Transform $\frac{4}{5}$ to equivalent fraction $\frac{12}{15}$. $\frac{5}{6} \div \frac{1}{3}$ Subtract the two fractions inside the parentheses and reduce. $\frac{5}{6} \times \frac{3}{1}$ Invert the second fraction and multiply. $\frac{5}{2}$ or $2\frac{1}{2}$ Simplify.

Procedure for Solving Applied Problems

Using the Mathematics Blueprint for Problem Solving

In solving an applied problem with fractions, students may find it helpful to complete the following steps. You will not use all the steps all of the time. Choose the steps that best fit the conditions of the problem.

1. Understand the problem.
   - (a) Read the problem carefully.
   - (b) Draw a picture if this helps you to visualize the situation. Think about what facts you are given and what you are asked to find.
   - (c) It may help to write a similar, simpler problem to get started and to determine what operation to use.
   - (d) Use the Mathematics Blueprint for Problem Solving to organize your work. Follow these four parts.
     1. Gather the facts. (Write down specific values given in the problem.)
     2. What am I asked to do? (Identify what you must obtain for an answer.)
     3. How do I proceed? (Decide what calculations need to be done.)
     4. Key points to remember. (Record any facts, warnings, formulas, or concepts you think will be important as you solve the problem.)
2. Solve and state the answer.
   - (a) Perform the necessary calculations.
   - (b) State the answer, including the unit of measure.
3. Check.
   - (a) Estimate the answer to the problem. Compare this estimate to the calculated value. Is your answer reasonable?
   - (b) Repeat your calculations.
   - (c) Work backward from your answer. Do you arrive at the original conditions of the problem?

EXAMPLE

A wire is $95\frac{1}{3}$ metres long. It is cut up into smaller, equal-sized pieces, each $4\frac{1}{3}$ metres long. How many pieces will there be?

1. ***Understand the problem.***
   Draw a picture of the situation.
   How will we find the number of pieces?
   Now we will use a simpler problem to clarify the idea. A wire 100 metres long is cut up into smaller pieces each 4 metres long. How many pieces will there be? We readily see that we would divide 100 by 4. Thus in our original problem we should divide $95\frac{1}{3}$ metres by $4\frac{1}{3}$ metres. This will tell us the number of pieces. Now we fill in the Mathematics Blueprint (see below).

2. ***Solve and state the answer.***
   We need to divide $95\frac{1}{3} \div 4\frac{1}{3}$.
   $$\frac{286}{3} \div \frac{13}{3} = \frac{\overset{22}{\cancel{286}}}{\underset{1}{\cancel{3}}} \times \frac{\overset{1}{\cancel{3}}}{\underset{1}{\cancel{13}}} = \frac{22}{1} = 22$$
   There will be 22 pieces of wire.

3. ***Check.***
   Estimate. Rounded to the nearest ten, $95\frac{1}{3} \approx 100$.
   Rounded to the nearest integer, $4\frac{1}{3} \approx 4$.
   $$100 \div 4 = 25$$
   This is close to our estimate. Our answer is reasonable. ✓

Mathematics Blueprint for Problem Solving

Gather the Facts	What Am I Asked to Do?	How Do I Proceed?	Key Points to Remember
Wire is $95\frac{1}{3}$ metres. It is cut into equal pieces $4\frac{1}{3}$ metres long.	Determine how many pieces of wire there will be.	Divide $95\frac{1}{3}$ by $4\frac{1}{3}$.	Change mixed numbers to improper fractions before carrying out the division.

Module Review Problems

If you have trouble with a particular type of exercise, review the examples in the section indicated for that group of exercises. Your institution may have included the Answers to Selected Exercises for this module, which contains the answers to these questions.

Section 1

Use a fraction to represent the shaded part of each object.

1. 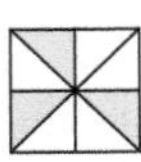

2. 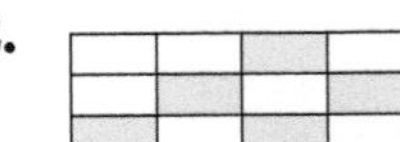

In exercises 3 and 4, draw a sketch to illustrate each fraction.

3. $\frac{4}{7}$ of an object

4. $\frac{7}{10}$ of a group

5. ***Quality Control*** An inspector looked at 80 semiconductors and found 9 of them defective. What fractional part of these items was defective?

6. ***Education*** The dean asked the 100 freshmen if they would be staying in the dorm over the holidays. A total of 87 said they would not. What fractional part of the freshmen said they would not?

Section 2

Express each number as a product of prime factors.

7. 54

8. 120

9. 168

Determine which of the following numbers are prime. If a number is composite, express it as the product of prime factors.

10. 59

11. 78

12. 167

Reduce each fraction.

13. $\frac{12}{42}$

14. $\frac{13}{52}$

15. $\frac{27}{72}$

16. $\frac{26}{34}$

17. $\frac{168}{192}$

18. $\frac{51}{105}$

Section 3

Change each mixed number to an improper fraction.

19. $4\frac{3}{8}$

20. $15\frac{3}{4}$

21. $5\frac{2}{7}$

22. $6\frac{3}{5}$

Change each improper fraction to a mixed number.

23. $\frac{45}{8}$

24. $\frac{100}{21}$

25. $\frac{53}{7}$

26. $\frac{74}{9}$

27. Reduce and leave your answer as a mixed number.
$3\frac{15}{55}$

28. Reduce and leave your answer as an improper fraction.
$\frac{234}{16}$

29. Change to a mixed number and then reduce.
$\frac{132}{32}$

Section 4

Multiply.

30. $\frac{4}{7} \times \frac{5}{11}$

31. $\frac{7}{9} \times \frac{21}{35}$

32. $12 \times \frac{3}{7} \times 0$

33. $\frac{3}{5} \times \frac{2}{7} \times \frac{10}{27}$

34. $12 \times 8\frac{1}{5}$

35. $5\frac{1}{4} \times 4\frac{6}{7}$

36. $5\frac{1}{8} \times 3\frac{1}{5}$

37. $36 \times \frac{4}{9}$

38. ***Stock Market*** In 1999, one share of stock cost $\$37\frac{5}{8}$. How much money did 18 shares cost?

▲ **39.** ***Geometry*** The O'Garas' new family room addition measures $4\frac{1}{2}$ metres long by $2\frac{2}{3}$ metres wide. Find the area of the addition.

Section 5

Divide, if possible.

40. $\frac{3}{7} \div \frac{2}{5}$

41. $\frac{3}{5} \div \frac{1}{10}$

42. $1200 \div \frac{5}{8}$

43. $900 \div \frac{3}{5}$

44. $5\frac{3}{4} \div 11\frac{1}{2}$

45. $\frac{20}{2\frac{1}{2}}$

46. $0 \div 3\frac{7}{5}$

47. $4\frac{2}{11} \div 3$

▲ **48.** ***Floor Carpeting*** Each roll of carpet covers $28\frac{1}{2}$ square metres. The community centre has 342 square metres of floor to carpet. How many rolls are needed?

49. There are 420 calories in $2\frac{1}{4}$ cans of grape pop. How many calories are in 1 can of pop?

Section 6

Find the LCD for each group of fractions.

50. $\frac{7}{14}$ and $\frac{3}{49}$

51. $\frac{13}{20}$ and $\frac{3}{25}$

52. $\frac{5}{18}, \frac{1}{6}, \frac{7}{45}$

Build each fraction to an equivalent fraction with the specified denominator.

53. $\frac{3}{7} = \frac{?}{56}$

54. $\frac{11}{24} = \frac{?}{72}$

55. $\frac{8}{15} = \frac{?}{150}$

56. $\frac{17}{18} = \frac{?}{198}$

Section 7

Add or subtract.

57. $\frac{9}{14} - \frac{5}{14}$

58. $\frac{1}{2} + \frac{1}{3} + \frac{1}{4}$

59. $\frac{4}{7} + \frac{7}{9}$

60. $\frac{7}{8} - \frac{3}{5}$

61. $\frac{7}{30} + \frac{2}{21}$

62. $\frac{5}{18} + \frac{7}{10}$

63. $\frac{15}{16} - \frac{13}{24}$

64. $\frac{14}{15} - \frac{3}{25}$

Section 8

Evaluate using the correct order of operations.

65. $8 - 2\frac{3}{4}$

66. $6 - \frac{5}{9}$

67. $3 + 5\frac{2}{3}$

68. $9\frac{3}{7} + 13$

69. $3\frac{3}{8} + 2\frac{3}{4}$

70. $5\frac{11}{16} - 2\frac{1}{5}$

71. $\frac{3}{5} \times \frac{1}{2} + \frac{2}{5} \div \frac{2}{3}$

72. $\left(\frac{4}{5} - \frac{1}{2}\right)^2 \times \frac{10}{3}$

73. ***Jogging*** Harminder jogged $1\frac{7}{8}$ kilometres on Monday, $2\frac{3}{4}$ kilometres on Tuesday, and $4\frac{1}{10}$ kilometres on Wednesday. How many kilometres did he jog on these three days?

74. ***Fuel Economy*** When it was new, Mariko's car got $18\frac{1}{6}$ kilometres per litre. It now gets $1\frac{5}{6}$ kilometres per litre less. How far can she drive now if the car has $10\frac{3}{4}$ litres in the tank?

Section 9

75. ***Cooking*** A recipe calls for $3\frac{1}{3}$ cups of sugar and $4\frac{1}{4}$ cups of flour. How much sugar and how much flour would be needed for $\frac{1}{2}$ of that recipe?

76. ***Fuel Economy*** Rafael travels in a car that gets $20\frac{1}{4}$ kilometres per litre. He has $8\frac{1}{2}$ litres of gas in the gas tank. Approximately how far can he drive?

77. ***Construction*** How many lengths of pipe $3\frac{1}{5}$ centimetres long can be cut from a pipe 48 centimetres long?

78. ***Automobile Maintenance*** A car radiator holds $15\frac{3}{4}$ litres. If it contains $6\frac{1}{8}$ litres of antifreeze and the rest is water, how much is water?

79. ***Reading Speed*** Tim found that he can read 5 pages of his biology book in $32\frac{1}{2}$ minutes. He has three chapters to read over the weekend. The first is 12 pages, the second is 9 pages, and the third is 14 pages. How long will it take him?

80. ***Personal Finance*** Tatiana earns $\$9\frac{1}{2}$ per hour for regular pay and $1\frac{1}{2}$ times that rate of pay for overtime. On Saturday she worked eight hours at regular pay and four hours at overtime pay. How much did she earn on Saturday?

81. ***Stock Market*** George bought 70 shares of stock in 2001 at $\$15\frac{3}{4}$ a share. He sold all the shares in 2003 for \$24 each. How much did George make when he sold his shares?

82. ***Carpentry*** A 3-inch bolt passes through $1\frac{1}{2}$ inches of pine board, a $\frac{1}{16}$-inch washer, and a $\frac{1}{8}$-inch nut. How many inches does the bolt extend beyond the board, washer, and nut if the head of the bolt is $\frac{1}{4}$ inch long?

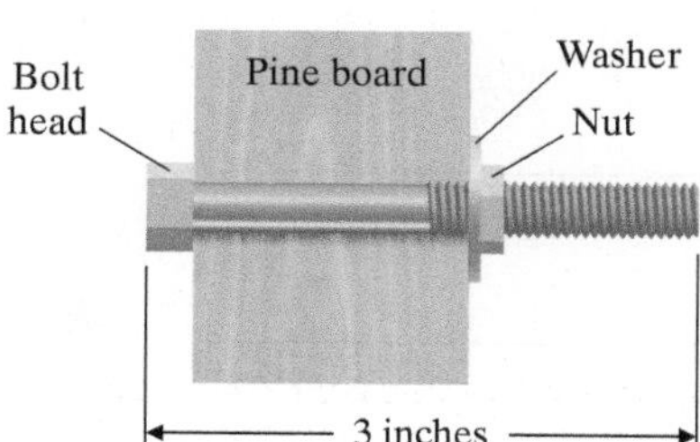

83. ***Budgeting*** Francine has a take-home pay of \$880 per month. She gives $\frac{1}{10}$ of it to her church, spends $\frac{1}{2}$ of it for rent and food, and spends $\frac{1}{8}$ of it on electricity, heat, and telephone. How many dollars per month does she have left for other things?

84. ***Cost of Auto Travel*** Manuel's new car used $18\frac{2}{5}$ litres of gas on a 368-kilometre trip.

(a) How many kilometres can his car travel on 1 litre of gas?

(b) How much did his trip cost him in gasoline expense if the average cost of gasoline was $\$1\frac{1}{5}$ per litre?

Mixed Practice

Perform each calculation or each requested operation.

85. Reduce. $\frac{27}{63}$

86. $\frac{7}{15} + \frac{11}{25}$

87. $4\frac{1}{3} - 2\frac{11}{12}$

88. $\frac{36}{49} \times \frac{14}{33}$

89. $4\frac{1}{4} \div \frac{3}{2}$

90. $\left(\frac{4}{7}\right)^3$

91. $\frac{3}{8} \div \frac{1}{10}$

92. $5\frac{1}{2} \times 18$

93. $150 \div 3\frac{1}{8}$

How Am I Doing? Module Test

Solve.

1. Use a fraction to represent the shaded part of the object.

2. A basketball star shot at the hoop 388 times. The ball went in 311 times. Write a fraction that describes the part of the time that his shots went in.

Reduce each fraction.

3. $\frac{18}{42}$ **4.** $\frac{15}{70}$ **5.** $\frac{225}{50}$

6. Change to an improper fraction. $6\frac{4}{5}$

7. Change to a mixed number. $\frac{145}{14}$

Multiply.

8. $42 \times \frac{2}{7}$ **9.** $\frac{7}{9} \times \frac{2}{5}$ **10.** $2\frac{2}{3} \times 5\frac{1}{4}$

Divide.

11. $\frac{7}{8} \div \frac{5}{11}$ **12.** $\frac{12}{31} \div \frac{8}{13}$

13. $7\frac{1}{5} \div 1\frac{1}{25}$ **14.** $5\frac{1}{7} \div 3$

Find the least common denominator of each set of fractions.

15. $\frac{5}{12}$ and $\frac{7}{18}$ **16.** $\frac{3}{16}$ and $\frac{1}{24}$ **17.** $\frac{1}{4}, \frac{3}{8}, \frac{5}{6}$

18. Build the fraction to an equivalent fraction with the specified denominator. $\frac{5}{12} = \frac{?}{72}$

1. ______
2. ______
3. ______
4. ______
5. ______
6. ______
7. ______
8. ______
9. ______
10. ______
11. ______
12. ______
13. ______
14. ______
15. ______
16. ______
17. ______
18. ______

Evaluate using the correct order of operations.

19. $\frac{7}{9} - \frac{5}{12}$

20. $\frac{2}{15} + \frac{5}{12}$

21. $\frac{1}{4} + \frac{3}{7} + \frac{3}{14}$

22. $8\frac{3}{5} + 5\frac{4}{7}$

23. $18\frac{6}{7} - 13\frac{13}{14}$

24. $\frac{2}{9} \div \frac{8}{3} \times \frac{1}{4}$

25. $\left(\frac{1}{2} + \frac{1}{3}\right) \times \frac{7}{5}$

Answer each question.

▲ **26.** Erin needs to find the area of her kitchen so she knows how much tile to purchase. The room measures $16\frac{1}{2}$ feet by $9\frac{1}{3}$ feet. How many square feet is the kitchen?

27. A butcher has $18\frac{2}{3}$ kilograms of steak that he wishes to place into packages that average $2\frac{1}{3}$ kilograms each. How many packages can he make?

28. From central parking it is $\frac{9}{10}$ of a kilometre to the science building. Bob started at central parking and walked $\frac{1}{5}$ of a kilometre toward the science building. He stopped for coffee. When he finished, how much farther did he have to walk to reach the science building?

29. Robin jogged $4\frac{1}{8}$ kilometres on Monday, $3\frac{1}{6}$ kilometres on Tuesday, and $6\frac{3}{4}$ kilometres on Wednesday. How far did she jog on those three days?

30. Mr. and Mrs. Samuel visited Florida and purchased 120 oranges. They gave $\frac{1}{4}$ of them to relatives, ate $\frac{1}{12}$ of them in the hotel, and gave $\frac{1}{3}$ of them to friends. They shipped the rest home to Ontario.

(a) How many oranges did they ship?

(b) If it costs 24¢ for each orange to be shipped to Ontario, what was the total shipping bill?

31. A candle company purchased $48\frac{1}{8}$ kilograms of wax to make specialty candles. It takes $\frac{5}{8}$ kilogram of wax to make one candle. The owners of the business plan to sell the candles for $12 each. The specialty wax cost them $2 per kilogram.

(a) How many candles can they make?

(b) How much does it cost to make one candle?

(c) How much profit will they make if they sell all of the candles?

19. ____________

20. ____________

21. ____________

22. ____________

23. ____________

24. ____________

25. ____________

26. ____________

27. ____________

28. ____________

29. ____________

30. (a) ____________

(b) ____________

31. (a) ____________

(b) ____________

(c) ____________

Solutions to Practice Problems

Section 1 Practice Problems

1. (a) Four parts of twelve are shaded. The fraction is $\frac{4}{12}$.

(b) Three parts out of six are shaded. The fraction is $\frac{3}{6}$.

(c) Two parts of three are shaded. The fraction is $\frac{2}{3}$.

2. (a) Shade $\frac{4}{5}$ of the object.

(b) Shade $\frac{3}{7}$ of the group.

3. (a) $\frac{9}{17}$ represents 9 players out of 17.

(b) The total class is $382 + 351 = 733$.

The fractional part that is men is $\frac{382}{733}$.

(c) $\frac{7}{8}$ of a metre of material.

4. Total number of defective items $1 + 2 = 3$. Total number of items $7 + 9 = 16$. A fraction that represents the portion of the items that were defective is $\frac{3}{16}$.

Section 2 Practice Problems

1. (a) $18 = 2 \times 9 = 2 \times 3 \times 3 = 2 \times 3^2$

(b) $72 = 8 \times 9 = 2 \times 2 \times 2 \times 3 \times 3 = 2^3 \times 3^2$

(c) $400 = 10 \times 40 = 5 \times 2 \times 5 \times 8 = 5 \times 2 \times 5 \times 2 \times 2 \times 2 = 2^4 \times 5^2$

2. (a) $\frac{30}{42} = \frac{30 \div 6}{42 \div 6} = \frac{5}{7}$

(b) $\frac{60}{132} = \frac{60 \div 12}{132 \div 12} = \frac{5}{11}$

3. (a) $\frac{120}{135} = \frac{2 \times 2 \times 2 \times \cancel{3} \times \cancel{5}}{3 \times 3 \times \cancel{3} \times \cancel{5}} = \frac{8}{9}$

(b) $\frac{715}{880} = \frac{\cancel{5} \times \cancel{11} \times 13}{2 \times 2 \times 2 \times 2 \times \cancel{5} \times \cancel{11}} = \frac{13}{16}$

4. (a) $\frac{84}{108} \stackrel{?}{=} \frac{7}{9}$

$84 \times 9 \stackrel{?}{=} 108 \times 7$

$756 = 756$ Yes

(b) $\frac{3}{7} \stackrel{?}{=} \frac{79}{182}$

$3 \times 182 \stackrel{?}{=} 7 \times 79$

$546 \neq 553$ No

Section 3 Practice Problems

1. (a) $4\frac{3}{7} = \frac{4 \times 7 + 3}{7} = \frac{28 + 3}{7} = \frac{31}{7}$

(b) $6\frac{2}{3} = \frac{6 \times 3 + 2}{3} = \frac{18 + 2}{3} = \frac{20}{3}$

(c) $19\frac{4}{7} = \frac{19 \times 7 + 4}{7} = \frac{133 + 4}{7} = \frac{137}{7}$

2. (a) $4\overline{)17}$ quotient 4, 16, remainder 1 so $\frac{17}{4} = 4\frac{1}{4}$

(b) $5\overline{)36}$ quotient 7, 35, remainder 1 so $\frac{36}{5} = 7\frac{1}{5}$

(c) $27\overline{)116}$ quotient 4, 108, remainder 8 so $\frac{116}{27} = 4\frac{8}{27}$

(d) $13\overline{)91}$ quotient 7, 91, remainder 0 so $\frac{91}{13} = 7$

3. $\frac{51}{15} = \frac{\cancel{3} \times 17}{\cancel{3} \times 5} = \frac{17}{5}$

4. $\frac{16}{80} = \frac{1}{5}$ so

$3\frac{16}{80} = 3\frac{1}{5}$.

5. $\frac{1001}{572} = 1\frac{429}{572}$

Now the fraction $\frac{429}{572} = \frac{3 \times \cancel{11} \times \cancel{13}}{2 \times 2 \times \cancel{11} \times \cancel{13}} = \frac{3}{4}$.

Thus $\frac{1001}{572} = 1\frac{429}{572} = 1\frac{3}{4}$.

Section 4 Practice Problems

1. (a) $\frac{6}{7} \times \frac{3}{13} = \frac{6 \times 3}{7 \times 13} = \frac{18}{91}$

(b) $\frac{1}{5} \times \frac{11}{12} = \frac{1 \times 11}{5 \times 12} = \frac{11}{60}$

2. $\frac{55}{72} \times \frac{16}{33} = \frac{5 \cdot 11}{2 \cdot 2 \cdot 2 \cdot 3 \cdot 3} \times \frac{2 \cdot 2 \cdot 2 \cdot 2}{3 \cdot 11}$

$= \frac{\cancel{2} \cdot \cancel{2} \cdot \cancel{2} \cdot 2 \cdot 5 \cdot \cancel{11}}{\cancel{2} \cdot \cancel{2} \cdot \cancel{2} \cdot 3 \cdot 3 \cdot 3 \cdot \cancel{11}}$

$= \frac{10}{27}$

3. (a) $7 \times \frac{5}{13} = \frac{7}{1} \times \frac{5}{13} = \frac{35}{13}$ or $2\frac{9}{13}$

(b) $\frac{13}{4} \times 8 = \frac{13}{\cancel{4}_1} \times \frac{\cancel{8}^2}{1} = \frac{26}{1} = 26$

4. $\frac{3}{\cancel{8}_1} \times \cancel{98\,400}^{12\,300} = \frac{3}{1} \times 12\,300 = 36\,900$

There are 36 900 square metres in the wetland area.

5. (a) $2\frac{1}{6} \times \frac{4}{7} = \frac{13}{\cancel{6}_3} \times \frac{\cancel{4}^2}{7} = \frac{26}{21}$ or $1\frac{5}{21}$

(b) $10\frac{2}{3} \times 13\frac{1}{2} = \frac{\cancel{32}^{16}}{\cancel{3}_1} \times \frac{\cancel{27}^{9}}{\cancel{2}_1} = \frac{144}{1} = 144$

(c) $\frac{3}{5} \times 1\frac{1}{3} \times \frac{5}{8} = \frac{\cancel{3}^1}{\cancel{5}_1} \times \frac{\cancel{4}^1}{\cancel{3}_1} \times \frac{\cancel{5}^1}{\cancel{8}_2} = \frac{1}{2}$

(d) $3\frac{1}{5} \times 2\frac{1}{2} = \frac{\cancel{16}^8}{\cancel{5}_1} \times \frac{\cancel{5}^1}{\cancel{2}_1} = \frac{8}{1} = 8$

6. Area $= 1\frac{1}{5} \times 4\frac{5}{6} = \frac{\cancel{6}^1}{5} \times \frac{29}{\cancel{6}_1} = \frac{29}{5} = 5\frac{4}{5}$

The area is $5\frac{4}{5}$ square metres.

7. Since $8 \cdot 10 = 80$ and $9 \cdot 9 = 81$,

we know that $\frac{8}{9} \cdot \frac{10}{9} = \frac{80}{81}$.

Therefore $x = \frac{10}{9}$.

Section 5 Practice Problems

1. (a) $\frac{7}{13} \div \frac{3}{4} = \frac{7}{13} \times \frac{4}{3} = \frac{28}{39}$

(b) $\frac{16}{35} \div \frac{24}{25} = \frac{\overset{2}{\cancel{16}}}{\underset{7}{\cancel{35}}} \times \frac{\overset{5}{\cancel{25}}}{\underset{3}{\cancel{24}}} = \frac{10}{21}$

2. (a) $\frac{3}{17} \div 6 = \frac{3}{17} \div \frac{6}{1} = \frac{\overset{1}{\cancel{3}}}{17} \times \frac{1}{\underset{2}{\cancel{6}}} = \frac{1}{34}$

(b) $14 \div \frac{7}{15} = \frac{14}{1} \div \frac{7}{15} = \frac{\overset{2}{\cancel{14}}}{1} \times \frac{15}{\underset{1}{\cancel{7}}} = 30$

3. (a) $1 \div \frac{11}{13} = \frac{1}{1} \times \frac{13}{11} = \frac{13}{11}$ or $1\frac{2}{11}$

(b) $\frac{14}{17} \div 1 = \frac{14}{17} \times \frac{1}{1} = \frac{14}{17}$

(c) $\frac{3}{11} \div 0$ Division by zero is undefined.

(d) $0 \div \frac{9}{16} = \frac{0}{1} \times \frac{16}{9} = \frac{0}{9} = 0$

4. (a) $1\frac{1}{5} \div \frac{7}{10} = \frac{6}{5} \div \frac{7}{10} = \frac{6}{\underset{1}{\cancel{5}}} \times \frac{\overset{2}{\cancel{10}}}{7} = \frac{12}{7}$ or $1\frac{5}{7}$

(b) $2\frac{1}{4} \div 1\frac{7}{8} = \frac{9}{4} \div \frac{15}{8} = \frac{\overset{3}{\cancel{9}}}{\underset{1}{\cancel{4}}} \times \frac{\overset{2}{\cancel{8}}}{\underset{5}{\cancel{15}}} = \frac{6}{5}$ or $1\frac{1}{5}$

5. (a) $\frac{5\frac{2}{3}}{7} = 5\frac{2}{3} \div 7 = \frac{17}{3} \times \frac{1}{7} = \frac{17}{21}$

(b) $\frac{1\frac{2}{5}}{2\frac{1}{3}} = 1\frac{2}{5} \div 2\frac{1}{3} = \frac{7}{5} \div \frac{7}{3} = \frac{\overset{1}{\cancel{7}}}{5} \times \frac{3}{\underset{1}{\cancel{7}}} = \frac{3}{5}$

6. $x \div \frac{3}{2} = \frac{22}{36}$

$x \cdot \frac{2}{3} = \frac{22}{36}$

$\frac{11}{12} \cdot \frac{2}{3} = \frac{22}{36}$ Thus $x = \frac{11}{12}$.

7. $19\frac{1}{4} \div 14 = \frac{\overset{11}{\cancel{77}}}{4} \times \frac{1}{\underset{2}{\cancel{14}}} = \frac{11}{8}$ or $1\frac{3}{8}$

Each piece will be $1\frac{3}{8}$ metres long.

Section 6 Practice Problems

1. The multiples of 14 are 14, 28, 42, 56, 70, 84, ...
The multiples of 21 are 21, 42, 63, 84, 105, 126, ...
42 is the least common multiple of 14 and 21.

2. The multiples of 10 are 10, 20, 30, 40 ...
The multiples of 15 are 15, 30, 45 ...
30 is the least common multiple of 10 and 15.

3. 54 is a multiple of 6. We know that $6 \times 9 = 54$.
The least common multiple of 6 and 54 is 54.

4. (a) The LCD of $\frac{3}{4}$ and $\frac{11}{12}$ is 12.
12 can be divided by 4 and 12.

(b) The LCD of $\frac{1}{7}$ and $\frac{8}{35}$ is 35.
35 can be divided by 7 and 35.

5. The LCD of $\frac{3}{7}$ and $\frac{5}{6}$ is 42.
42 can be divided by 7 and 6.

6. (a) $14 = 2 \times 7$
$10 = 2 \times 5$
$\text{LCD} = 2 \times 5 \times 7 = 70$

(b) $15 = 3 \times 5$
$50 = 2 \times 5 \times 5$
$\text{LCD} = 2 \times 3 \times 5 \times 5 = 150$

(c) $16 = 2 \times 2 \times 2 \times 2$
$12 = 2 \times 2 \times 3$
$\text{LCD} = 2 \times 2 \times 2 \times 2 \times 3 = 48$

7. $49 = 7 \times 7$
$21 = 7 \times 3$
$7 = 7 \times 1$
$\text{LCD} = 7 \times 7 \times 3 = 147$

8. (a) $\frac{3}{5} = \frac{3}{5} \times \frac{8}{8} = \frac{24}{40}$

(b) $\frac{7}{11} = \frac{7}{11} \times \frac{4}{4} = \frac{28}{44}$

(c) $\frac{2}{7} = \frac{2}{7} \times \frac{4}{4} = \frac{8}{28}$

$\frac{3}{4} = \frac{3}{4} \times \frac{7}{7} = \frac{21}{28}$

9. (a) $20 = 2 \times 2 \times 5$
$15 = 3 \times 5$
$\text{LCD} = 2 \times 2 \times 3 \times 5 = 60$

(b) $\frac{3}{20} = \frac{3}{20} \times \frac{3}{3} = \frac{9}{60}$ $\quad \frac{11}{15} = \frac{11}{15} \times \frac{4}{4} = \frac{44}{60}$

10. (a) $64 = 2 \times 2 \times 2 \times 2 \times 2 \times 2$
$80 = 2 \times 2 \times 2 \times 2 \times 5$
$\text{LCD} = 2 \times 2 \times 2 \times 2 \times 2 \times 2 \times 5 = 320$

(b) $\frac{5}{64} = \frac{5}{64} \times \frac{5}{5} = \frac{25}{320}$

$\frac{3}{80} = \frac{3}{80} \times \frac{4}{4} = \frac{12}{320}$

Section 7 Practice Problems

1. $\frac{3}{17} + \frac{12}{17} = \frac{15}{17}$

2. (a) $\frac{1}{12} + \frac{5}{12} = \frac{6}{12} = \frac{1}{2}$

(b) $\frac{13}{15} + \frac{7}{15} = \frac{20}{15} = \frac{4}{3}$ or $1\frac{1}{3}$

3. (a) $\frac{5}{19} - \frac{2}{19} = \frac{3}{19}$ $\quad$ **(b)** $\frac{21}{25} - \frac{6}{25} = \frac{15}{25} = \frac{3}{5}$

4.

$$\begin{array}{rcr} \frac{2}{15} & = & \frac{2}{15} \\ +\frac{1}{5} \times \frac{3}{3} & = & +\frac{3}{15} \\ \hline & & \frac{5}{15} = \frac{1}{3} \end{array}$$

5. $\text{LCD} = 48$ $\quad \frac{5}{12} \times \frac{4}{4} = \frac{20}{48}$ $\quad \frac{5}{16} \times \frac{3}{3} = \frac{15}{48}$

$\frac{5}{12} + \frac{5}{16} = \frac{20}{48} + \frac{15}{48} = \frac{35}{48}$

6. $\text{LCD} = 48$

$\frac{3}{16} \times \frac{3}{3} = \frac{9}{48}$ $\quad \frac{1}{8} \times \frac{6}{6} = \frac{6}{48}$ $\quad \frac{1}{12} \times \frac{4}{4} = \frac{4}{48}$

$\frac{3}{16} + \frac{1}{8} + \frac{1}{12} = \frac{9}{48} + \frac{6}{48} + \frac{4}{48} = \frac{19}{48}$

7. $\text{LCD} = 96$ $\quad \frac{9}{48} \times \frac{2}{2} = \frac{18}{96}$ $\quad \frac{5}{32} \times \frac{3}{3} = \frac{15}{96}$

$\frac{9}{48} - \frac{5}{32} = \frac{18}{96} - \frac{15}{96} = \frac{3}{96} = \frac{1}{32}$

8. $\frac{9}{10} \times \frac{2}{2} = \frac{18}{20}$ $\quad \frac{1}{4} \times \frac{5}{5} = \frac{5}{20}$

$\frac{9}{10} - \frac{1}{4} = \frac{18}{20} - \frac{5}{20} = \frac{13}{20}$

There is $\frac{13}{20}$ litre left.

9. The LCD of $\frac{3}{10}$ and $\frac{23}{25}$ is 50.

$\frac{3}{10} \times \frac{5}{5} = \frac{15}{50}$ Now rewriting: $x + \frac{15}{50} = \frac{46}{50}$

$\frac{23}{25} \times \frac{2}{2} = \frac{46}{50}$ $\frac{31}{50} + \frac{15}{50} = \frac{46}{50}$

So, $x = \frac{31}{50}$

10. $\frac{15}{16} + \frac{3}{40}$

$\frac{15}{16} \times \frac{40}{40} = \frac{600}{640}$ $\frac{3}{40} \times \frac{16}{16} = \frac{48}{640}$

Thus $\frac{15}{16} + \frac{3}{40} = \frac{600}{640} + \frac{48}{640} = \frac{648}{640} = \frac{81}{80}$ or $1\frac{1}{80}$

Section 8 Practice Problems

1.
$$\begin{array}{r} 5\frac{1}{12} \\ +\,9\frac{5}{12} \\ \hline 14\frac{6}{12} = 14\frac{1}{2} \end{array}$$

2. The LCD is 20.

$\frac{1}{4} \times \frac{5}{5} = \frac{5}{20}$ $\frac{2}{5} \times \frac{4}{4} = \frac{8}{20}$

$$\begin{array}{rcr} 6\frac{1}{4} & = & 6\frac{5}{20} \\ +\,2\frac{2}{5} & = & +2\frac{8}{20} \\ \hline & & 8\frac{13}{20} \end{array}$$

3. LCD = 12

$$\begin{array}{rcr} 7\boxed{\frac{1}{4} \times \frac{3}{3}} & = & 7\frac{3}{12} \\ +3\boxed{\frac{5}{6} \times \frac{2}{2}} & = & +3\frac{10}{12} \\ \hline & & 10\frac{13}{12} = 10 + 1\frac{1}{12} = 11\frac{1}{12} \end{array}$$

4. LCD = 12

$$\begin{array}{rcr} 12\frac{5}{6} & = & 12\frac{10}{12} \\ -\,7\frac{5}{12} & = & -7\frac{5}{12} \\ \hline & & 5\frac{5}{12} \end{array}$$

5. (a) LCD = 24

$$\begin{array}{rcrcr} 9\boxed{\frac{1}{8} \times \frac{3}{3}} & = & 9\frac{3}{24} & = & 8\frac{27}{24} \\ -3\boxed{\frac{2}{3} \times \frac{8}{8}} & = & -3\frac{16}{24} & = & -3\frac{16}{24} \\ \hline & & & & 5\frac{11}{24} \end{array}$$

Borrow 1 from 9:

$9\frac{3}{24} = 8 + 1\frac{3}{24} = 8\frac{27}{24}$

(b)
$$\begin{array}{rcr} 18 & = & 17\frac{18}{18} \\ -6\frac{7}{18} & = & -6\frac{7}{18} \\ \hline & & 11\frac{11}{18} \end{array}$$

6.
$$\begin{array}{rcrcr} 6\frac{1}{4} & = & 6\frac{3}{12} & = & 5\frac{15}{12} \\ -4\frac{2}{3} & = & -4\frac{8}{12} & = & -4\frac{8}{12} \\ \hline & & & & 1\frac{7}{12} \end{array}$$

They had $1\frac{7}{12}$ litres left over.

7. $\frac{3}{5} - \frac{1}{15} \times \frac{10}{13}$

$= \frac{3}{5} - \frac{2}{39}$ LCD $= 5 \cdot 39 = 195$

$= \frac{117}{195} - \frac{10}{195}$

$= \frac{107}{195}$

8. $\frac{1}{7} \times \frac{5}{6} + \frac{5}{3} \div \frac{7}{6} = \frac{1}{7} \times \frac{5}{6} + \frac{5}{3} \times \frac{6}{7}$

$= \frac{5}{42} + \frac{10}{7}$ LCD = 42

$= \frac{5}{42} + \frac{60}{42}$

$= \frac{65}{42}$ or $1\frac{23}{42}$

Section 9 Practice Problems

Practice Problem 1

1. Understand the problem.

Mathematics Blueprint for Problem Solving

Gather the Facts	What Am I Asked to Do?	How Do I Proceed?	Key Points to Remember
Gas amounts: $18\frac{7}{10}$ L, $15\frac{2}{5}$ L, $14\frac{1}{2}$ L	Find out how many litres of gas she bought altogether.	Add the three amounts.	When adding mixed numbers, the LCD is needed for the fractions.

2. Solve and state the answer:

LCD = 10

$$\begin{aligned} 18\frac{7}{10} &= 18\frac{7}{10} \\ 15\frac{2}{5} &= 15\frac{4}{10} \\ 14\frac{1}{2} &= +14\frac{5}{10} \\ & \quad 47\frac{16}{10} = 48\frac{6}{10} \\ & \quad = 48\frac{3}{5} \end{aligned}$$

The total is $48\frac{3}{5}$ litres.

3. ***Check.*** Estimate to see if the answer is reasonable.

Practice Problem 2

1. Understand the problem.

Mathematics Blueprint for Problem Solving			
Gather the Facts	**What Am I Asked to Do?**	**How Do I Proceed?**	**Key Points to Remember**
Postcard: $12\frac{1}{4}$ cm Top border: $1\frac{3}{8}$ cm Bottom border: 2 cm	Find the length of the inside portion of the postcard.	**(a)** Add the two border lengths. **(b)** Subtract this total from the postcard length.	When adding mixed numbers, the LCD is needed for the fractions.

2. Solve and state the answer:

(a) $\begin{array}{r} 1\frac{3}{8} \\ +2 \\ \hline 3\frac{3}{8} \end{array}$

(b) $\begin{array}{rcrcr} 12\frac{1}{4} & = & 12\frac{2}{8} & = & 11\frac{10}{8} \\ -3\frac{3}{8} & = & -3\frac{3}{8} & = & -3\frac{3}{8} \\ \hline & & & & 8\frac{7}{8} \end{array}$

The length of the inside portion is $8\frac{7}{8}$ centimetres.

3. ***Check.*** Estimate to see if the answer is reasonable or work backward to check.

Practice Problem 3

1. Understand the problem.

Mathematics Blueprint for Problem Solving			
Gather the Facts	**What Am I Asked to Do?**	**How Do I Proceed?**	**Key Points to Remember**
Regular tent uses $8\frac{1}{4}$ metres. Large tent uses $1\frac{1}{2}$ times the regular. She makes 6 regular and 16 large tents.	Find out how many metres of cloth will be needed to make the tents.	Find the amount used for regular tents, and the amount used for large tents. Then add the two.	Large tents use $1\frac{1}{2}$ times the regular amount.

2. Solve and state the answer:

We multiply $6 \times 8\frac{1}{4}$ for regular tents and $16 \times 1\frac{1}{2} \times 8\frac{1}{4}$ for large tents. Then add total metrage.

Regular tents: $6 \times 8\frac{1}{4} = \overset{3}{\cancel{6}} \times \frac{33}{\underset{2}{\cancel{4}}} = \frac{99}{2} = 49\frac{1}{2}$

Large tents: $16 \times 1\frac{1}{2} \times 8\frac{1}{4} = \overset{\overset{2}{\cancel{8}}}{\cancel{16}} \times \frac{3}{\underset{1}{\cancel{2}}} \times \frac{33}{\underset{1}{\cancel{4}}} = \frac{198}{1} = 198$

Total metrage for all tents is $198 + 49\frac{1}{2} = 247\frac{1}{2}$ metres.

3. ***Check.*** Estimate to see if the answer is reasonable.

Practice Problem 4

1. Understand the problem.

Mathematics Blueprint for Problem Solving			
Gather the Facts	**What Am I Asked to Do?**	**How Do I Proceed?**	**Key Points to Remember**
He purchases 4-metre boards. Each shelf is $1\frac{1}{4}$ m. He needs four shelves for each bookcase and he is making two bookcases.	**(a)** Find out how many boards he needs to buy. **(b)** Find out how many metres of shelving are actually needed. **(c)** Find out how many metres will be left over.	Find out how many $1\frac{1}{4}$-m shelves he can get from one board. Then see how many boards he needs to make all eight shelves.	There will be three answers to this problem. Don't forget to calculate the leftover wood.

2. Solve and state the answer:

We want to know how many $1\frac{1}{4}$-m shelves are in a 4-m board.

$4 \div 1\frac{1}{4} = \frac{4}{1} \div \frac{5}{4} = \frac{4}{1} \times \frac{4}{5} = \frac{16}{5} = 3\frac{1}{5}$

He will get 3 shelves from each board with some left over.

(a) For two bookcases, he needs eight shelves. He gets three shelves out of each board. $8 \div 3 = 2.67 \approx 3$. He will need three 4-m boards.

(b) He needs 8 shelves at $1\frac{1}{4}$ m.

$8 \times 1\frac{1}{4} = 8 \times \frac{5}{4} = 10$

He actually needs 10 metres of shelving.

(c)
```
   12 metres of shelving bought
 − 10 metres of shelving used
    2 metres of shelving left over.
```

3. ***Check.*** Work backward to check the answer.

Practice Problem 5

1. Understand the problem.

Mathematics Blueprint for Problem Solving			
Gather the Facts	**What Am I Asked to Do?**	**How Do I Proceed?**	**Key Points to Remember**
Distance is $199\frac{3}{4}$ kilometres. He uses $8\frac{1}{2}$ litres of gas.	Find out how many kilometres per litre he gets.	Divide the distance by the number of litres.	Change mixed numbers to improper fractions before dividing.

2. Solve and state the answer:

$$199\frac{3}{4} \div 8\frac{1}{2} = \frac{799}{4} \div \frac{17}{2}$$

$$= \frac{\overset{47}{\cancel{799}}}{\underset{2}{\cancel{4}}} \times \frac{\overset{1}{\cancel{2}}}{\underset{1}{\cancel{17}}}$$

$$= \frac{47}{2} = 23\frac{1}{2}$$

He gets $23\frac{1}{2}$ kilometres per litre.

3. ***Check.*** Estimate to see if the answer is reasonable.

Glossary

Building fraction property (Section 6) For whole numbers a, b, and c, where neither b nor c equals zero,

$$\frac{a}{b} = \frac{a}{b} \times 1 = \frac{a}{b} \times \frac{c}{c} = \frac{a \times c}{b \times c}.$$

Building up a fraction (Section 6) To make one fraction into an equivalent fraction by making the denominator and numerator larger numbers. For example, the fraction $\frac{3}{4}$ can be built up to the fraction $\frac{30}{40}$.

Common denominator (Section 7) Two fractions have a common denominator if the same number appears in the denominator of each fraction. $\frac{3}{7}$ and $\frac{1}{7}$ have a common denominator of 7.

Composite number (Section 2) A composite number is a whole number greater than 1 that can be divided by whole numbers other than itself. The number 6 is a composite number since it can be divided exactly by 2 and 3 (as well as by 1 and 6).

Denominator (Section 1) The number on the bottom of a fraction. In the fraction $\frac{2}{9}$ the denominator is 9.

Equal fractions (Section 2) Fractions that represent the same number. The fractions $\frac{3}{4}$ and $\frac{6}{8}$ are equal fractions.

Equality test of fractions (Section 2) Two fractions $\frac{a}{b}$ and $\frac{c}{d}$ are equal if the product $a \times d = b \times c$. In this case, a, b, c, and d are whole numbers and b and $d \neq 0$.

Equivalent fractions (Section 2) Two fractions that are equal.

Fundamental theorem of arithmetic (Section 2) Every composite number has a unique product of prime numbers.

Improper fraction (Section 3) A fraction in which the numerator is greater than or equal to the denominator. The fractions $\frac{34}{29}$, $\frac{8}{7}$, and $\frac{6}{6}$ are all improper fractions.

Invert a fraction (Section 5) To invert a fraction is to interchange the numerator and the denominator. If we invert $\frac{5}{9}$, we obtain the fraction $\frac{9}{5}$. To invert a fraction is sometimes referred to as *to take the reciprocal of a fraction*.

Irreducible (Section 2) A fraction that cannot be reduced (simplified) is called irreducible.

Least common denominator (LCD) (Section 6) The least common denominator (LCD) of two or more fractions is the smallest number that can be divided without remainder by each fraction's denominator. The LCD of $\frac{1}{3}$ and $\frac{1}{4}$ is 12. The LCD of $\frac{5}{6}$ and $\frac{4}{15}$ is 30.

Mixed number (Section 3) A number created by the sum of a whole number greater than 1 and a proper fraction. The numbers $4\frac{5}{6}$ and $1\frac{1}{8}$ are both mixed numbers. Mixed numbers are sometimes referred to as *mixed fractions*.

Numerator (Section 1) The number on the top of a fraction. In the fraction $\frac{3}{7}$ the numerator is 3.

Overtime (Section 9) The pay earned by a person if he or she works more than a certain number of hours per week. In most jobs that pay by the hour, a person will earn $1\frac{1}{2}$ times as much per hour for every hour beyond 40 hours worked in one workweek. For example, Carlos earns $6.00 per hour for the first 40 hours in a week and overtime for each additional hour. He would earn $9.00 per hour for all hours he worked in that week beyond 40 hours.

Prime factors (Section 2) Factors that are prime numbers. If we write 15 as a product of prime factors, we have $15 = 5 \times 3$.

Prime number (Section 2) A prime number is a whole number greater than 1 that can only be divided by 1 and itself. The first fifteen prime numbers are 2, 3, 5, 7, 11, 13, 17, 19, 23, 29, 31, 37, 41, 43, and 47. The list of prime numbers goes on forever.

Proper fraction (Section 3) A fraction in which the numerator is less than the denominator. The fractions $\frac{3}{4}$ and $\frac{15}{16}$ are proper fractions.

Reduced fraction (Section 2) A fraction for which the numerator and denominator have no common factor other than 1. The fraction $\frac{5}{7}$ is a reduced fraction. The fraction $\frac{15}{21}$ is not a reduced fraction because both numerator and denominator have a common factor of 3.

Answers to Selected Exercises for Fractions

Section 1 Exercises **1.** fraction **3.** denominator **5.** N: 3; D: 5 **7.** N: 7; D: 8 **9.** N: 1; D: 17 **11.** $\frac{1}{3}$ **13.** $\frac{7}{9}$ **15.** $\frac{3}{4}$ **17.** $\frac{3}{7}$ **19.** $\frac{2}{5}$ **21.** $\frac{7}{10}$ **23.** $\frac{5}{8}$ **25.** $\frac{4}{7}$ **27.** $\frac{7}{8}$ **29.** $\frac{9}{15}$ **31.** 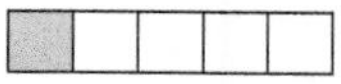 **33.** 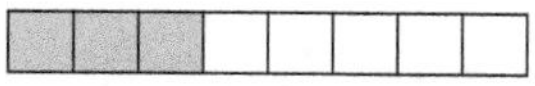 **35.**  **37.** $\frac{42}{83}$ **39.** $\frac{209}{750}$ **41.** $\frac{89}{211}$ **43.** $\frac{9}{26}$ **45.** $\frac{24}{40}$ **47. (a)** $\frac{90}{195}$ **(b)** $\frac{22}{195}$
49. The amount of money each of six business owners gets if the business has a profit of \$0.

Quick Quiz 1 **1.** $\frac{4}{7}$ **2.** $\frac{204}{371}$ **3.** $\frac{13}{33}$ **4.** See Instructor

Section 2 Exercises **1.** 11, 19, 41, 5 **3.** composite number **5.** $56 = 2 \times 2 \times 2 \times 7$ **7.** 3×5 **9.** 5×7 **11.** 7^2 **13.** 2^4 **15.** 5×11 **17.** $3^2 \times 7$ **19.** $2^2 \times 3 \times 7$ **21.** 2×3^3 **23.** $2^3 \times 3 \times 5$ **25.** $2^3 \times 23$ **27.** prime **29.** 3×19 **31.** prime **33.** 2×31 **35.** prime **37.** prime **39.** 11×11 **41.** 3×43 **43.** $\frac{18 \div 9}{27 \div 9} = \frac{2}{3}$ **45.** $\frac{36 \div 12}{48 \div 12} = \frac{3}{4}$ **47.** $\frac{63 \div 9}{90 \div 9} = \frac{7}{10}$ **49.** $\frac{210 \div 10}{310 \div 10} = \frac{21}{31}$ **51.** $\frac{3 \times 1}{3 \times 5} = \frac{1}{5}$ **53.** $\frac{2 \times 3 \times 11}{2 \times 2 \times 2 \times 11} = \frac{3}{4}$ **55.** $\frac{2 \times 3 \times 5}{3 \times 3 \times 5} = \frac{2}{3}$ **57.** $\frac{2 \times 2 \times 3 \times 5}{3 \times 5 \times 5} = \frac{4}{5}$ **59.** $\frac{3 \times 11}{3 \times 12} = \frac{11}{12}$ **61.** $\frac{9 \times 7}{9 \times 12} = \frac{7}{12}$ **63.** $\frac{11 \times 8}{11 \times 11} = \frac{8}{11}$ **65.** $\frac{40 \times 3}{40 \times 5} = \frac{3}{5}$ **67.** $\frac{11 \times 20}{13 \times 20} = \frac{11}{13}$ **69.** $4 \times 28 \stackrel{?}{=} 16 \times 7$
$112 = 112$
yes
71. no **73.** no **75.** yes **77.** yes **79.** $\frac{3}{4}$ **81.** $\frac{1}{8}$ failed; $\frac{7}{8}$ passed **83.** $\frac{5}{7}$ **85.** $\frac{17}{45}$ **87.** $\frac{8}{45}$

Quick Quiz 2 **1.** $\frac{5}{7}$ **2.** $\frac{1}{6}$ **3.** $\frac{21}{8}$ **4.** See Instructor

Section 3 Exercises **1. (a)** Multiply the whole number by the denominator of the fraction. **(b)** Add the numerator of the fraction to the product formed in step (a). **(c)** Write the sum found in step (b) over the denominator of the fraction. **3.** $\frac{7}{3}$ **5.** $\frac{17}{7}$ **7.** $\frac{83}{9}$ **9.** $\frac{32}{3}$ **11.** $\frac{58}{5}$ **13.** $\frac{55}{6}$ **15.** $\frac{121}{6}$ **17.** $\frac{131}{12}$ **19.** $\frac{79}{10}$ **21.** $\frac{201}{25}$ **23.** $\frac{65}{12}$ **25.** $\frac{494}{3}$ **27.** $\frac{131}{15}$ **29.** $\frac{113}{25}$ **31.** $1\frac{1}{3}$ **33.** $2\frac{3}{4}$ **35.** $2\frac{1}{2}$ **37.** $3\frac{3}{8}$ **39.** 25 **41.** $9\frac{5}{9}$ **43.** $23\frac{1}{3}$ **45.** $6\frac{1}{4}$ **47.** $5\frac{7}{10}$ **49.** $17\frac{1}{2}$ **51.** 13 **53.** 14 **55.** 6 **57.** $5\frac{15}{32}$ **59.** $5\frac{1}{2}$ **61.** $4\frac{1}{6}$ **63.** $15\frac{1}{4}$ **65.** 4 **67.** $\frac{12}{5}$ **69.** $\frac{15}{4}$ **71.** $2\frac{88}{126} = 2\frac{44}{63}$ **73.** $2\frac{20}{280} = 2\frac{1}{14}$ **75.** $1\frac{212}{296} = 1\frac{53}{74}$ **77.** $\frac{1082}{3}$ metres **79.** $50\frac{1}{3}$ acres **81.** $141\frac{3}{8}$ kilograms **83.** No, 101 is prime and is not a factor of 5687.

Quick Quiz 3 **1.** $\frac{59}{13}$ **2.** $7\frac{5}{12}$ **3.** 3 **4.** See Instructor

Section 4 Exercises **1.** $\frac{21}{55}$ **3.** $\frac{15}{52}$ **5.** 1 **7.** $\frac{1}{16}$ **9.** $\frac{12}{55}$ **11.** $\frac{21}{8}$ or $2\frac{5}{8}$ **13.** $\frac{24}{7}$ or $3\frac{3}{7}$ **15.** $\frac{10}{3}$ or $3\frac{1}{3}$ **17.** $\frac{1}{6}$ **19.** 3 **21.** $\frac{1}{2}$ **23.** 31 **25.** 0 **27.** $3\frac{7}{8}$ **29.** $\frac{55}{12}$ or $4\frac{7}{12}$ **31.** $\frac{69}{50}$ or $1\frac{19}{50}$ **33.** 35 **35.** $\frac{8}{5}$ or $1\frac{3}{5}$ **37.** $\frac{7}{9}$ **39.** $\frac{38}{3}$ or $12\frac{2}{3}$ **41.** $x = \frac{7}{9}$ **43.** $x = \frac{8}{9}$ **45.** $37\frac{11}{12}$ square kilometres **47.** 2380 kilometres **49.** 1629 grams **51.** 5332 students **53.** 377 companies **55.** $1\frac{8}{9}$ kilometres

57. The step of dividing the numerator and denominator by the same number allows us to work with smaller numbers when we do the multiplication. Also, this allows us to avoid the step of having to simplify the fraction in the final answer.

Quick Quiz 4 **1.** 10 **2.** $\frac{44}{65}$ **3.** $\frac{143}{12}$ or $11\frac{11}{12}$ **4.** See Instructor

Section 5 Exercises **1.** Think of a simple problem like $3 \div \frac{1}{2}$. One way to think of it is how many $\frac{1}{2}$'s can be placed in 3? For example, how many $\frac{1}{2}$-pound rocks could be put in a bag that holds 3 pounds of rocks? The answer is 6. If we inverted the first fraction by mistake, we would have $\frac{1}{3} \times \frac{1}{2} = \frac{1}{6}$. We know this is wrong since there are obviously several $\frac{1}{2}$-pound rocks in a bag that holds 3 pounds of rocks. The answer $\frac{1}{6}$ would make no sense. **3.** $\frac{7}{12}$ **5.** $\frac{9}{2}$ or $4\frac{1}{2}$ **7.** $\frac{1}{9}$ **9.** $\frac{25}{9}$ or $2\frac{7}{9}$ **11.** 1 **13.** $\frac{9}{49}$ **15.** $\frac{4}{5}$ **17.** $\frac{3}{44}$ **19.** $\frac{27}{7}$ or $3\frac{6}{7}$ **21.** 0 **23.** undefined **25.** 10 **27.** $\frac{7}{32}$ **29.** $\frac{3}{4}$ **31.** $\frac{13}{9}$ or $1\frac{4}{9}$ **33.** 2 **35.** 5000 **37.** $\frac{1}{250}$ **39.** $\frac{7}{40}$ **41.** 16 **43.** $\frac{7}{18}$ **45.** 2 **47.** 4

49. $\frac{68}{27}$ or $2\frac{14}{27}$ **51.** 1 **53.** $\frac{91}{75}$ or $1\frac{16}{75}$ **55.** $\frac{5}{12}$ **57.** $\frac{30}{19}$ or $1\frac{11}{19}$ **59.** 0 **61.** $\frac{7}{44}$ **63.** 12 **65.** $x = \frac{7}{5}$ **67.** $x = \frac{3}{10}$
69. $6\frac{3}{4}$ litres **71.** $37\frac{1}{2}$ kilometres per hour **73.** 58 students **75.** 100 large Styrofoam cups **77.** It took six drill attempts.
79. We estimate by dividing $15 \div 5$, which is 3. The exact value is $2\frac{26}{31}$, which is very close. Our answer is off by only $\frac{5}{31}$.

Quick Quiz 5 **1.** $\frac{3}{4}$ **2.** $\frac{76}{29}$ or $2\frac{18}{29}$ **3.** $\frac{31}{16}$ or $1\frac{15}{16}$ **4.** See Instructor

How Am I Doing? Sections 1–5 **1.** $\frac{3}{8}$ (obj. 1.1) **2.** $\frac{8}{69}$ (obj. 1.3) **3.** $\frac{5}{124}$ (obj. 1.3) **4.** $\frac{1}{6}$ (obj. 2.2) **5.** $\frac{1}{3}$ (obj. 2.2)
6. $\frac{1}{7}$ (obj. 2.2) **7.** $\frac{7}{8}$ (obj. 2.2) **8.** $\frac{4}{11}$ (obj. 2.2) **9.** $\frac{11}{3}$ (obj. 3.1) **10.** $\frac{46}{3}$ (obj. 3.1) **11.** $20\frac{1}{4}$ (obj. 3.2) **12.** $5\frac{4}{5}$ (obj. 3.2)
13. $2\frac{2}{17}$ (obj. 3.2) **14.** $\frac{5}{44}$ (obj. 4.1) **15.** $\frac{2}{3}$ (obj. 4.1) **16.** $\frac{160}{9}$ or $17\frac{7}{9}$ (obj. 4.3) **17.** 1 (obj. 5.1) **18.** $\frac{1}{2}$ (obj. 5.1)
19. $\frac{69}{13}$ or $5\frac{4}{13}$ (obj. 5.3) **20.** 21 (obj. 5.2)

How Am I Doing? Test on Sections 1–5 **1.** $\frac{33}{40}$ **2.** $\frac{85}{113}$ **3.** $\frac{1}{2}$ **4.** $\frac{5}{7}$ **5.** $\frac{4}{11}$ **6.** $\frac{25}{31}$ **7.** $\frac{5}{14}$ **8.** $\frac{7}{3}$ or $2\frac{1}{3}$ **9.** $\frac{38}{3}$
10. $\frac{33}{8}$ **11.** $6\frac{3}{7}$ **12.** $8\frac{1}{3}$ **13.** $\frac{21}{88}$ **14.** $\frac{7}{4}$ or $1\frac{3}{4}$ **15.** 15 **16.** $\frac{33}{2}$ or $16\frac{1}{2}$ **17.** $\frac{161}{12}$ or $13\frac{5}{12}$ **18.** 80 **19.** $\frac{16}{21}$ **20.** $\frac{16}{3}$ or $5\frac{1}{3}$
21. 7 **22.** $\frac{12}{5}$ or $2\frac{2}{5}$ **23.** $\frac{63}{8}$ or $7\frac{7}{8}$ **24.** 14 **25.** $\frac{8}{3}$ or $2\frac{2}{3}$ **26.** $\frac{23}{8}$ or $2\frac{7}{8}$ **27.** $\frac{13}{16}$ **28.** $\frac{1}{14}$ **29.** $\frac{9}{32}$ **30.** $\frac{13}{15}$
31. $45\frac{15}{16}$ square metres **32.** 4 cups **33.** $46\frac{7}{8}$ kilometres **34.** 16 full packages; $\frac{3}{8}$ kg left over **35.** 51 computers **36.** 93 000 litres
37. 16 hours **38.** 6 tents; 7 metres left over **39.** 41 days

Section 6 Exercises **1.** 24 **3.** 100 **5.** 60 **7.** 30 **9.** 147 **11.** 10 **13.** 28 **15.** 35 **17.** 18 **19.** 60 **21.** 32
23. 90 **25.** 80 **27.** 105 **29.** 120 **31.** 6 **33.** 12 **35.** 132 **37.** 84 **39.** 120 **41.** 3 **43.** 35 **45.** 20 **47.** 40
49. 96 **51.** 63 **53.** $\frac{21}{36}$ and $\frac{20}{36}$ **55.** $\frac{25}{80}$ and $\frac{68}{80}$ **57.** $\frac{18}{20}$ and $\frac{19}{20}$ **59.** LCD = 35; $\frac{14}{35}$ and $\frac{9}{35}$ **61.** LCD = 24; $\frac{5}{24}$ and $\frac{9}{24}$
63. LCD = 30; $\frac{16}{30}$ and $\frac{5}{30}$ **65.** LCD = 60; $\frac{16}{60}$ and $\frac{25}{60}$ **67.** LCD = 36; $\frac{10}{36}, \frac{11}{36}, \frac{21}{36}$ **69.** LCD = 56; $\frac{3}{56}, \frac{49}{56}, \frac{40}{56}$ **71.** LCD = 63; $\frac{5}{63}, \frac{12}{63}, \frac{56}{63}$
73. (a) LCD = 16 **(b)** $\frac{3}{16}, \frac{12}{16}, \frac{6}{16}$

Quick Quiz 6 **1.** 42 **2.** 140 **3.** $\frac{21}{78}$ **4.** See Instructor

Section 7 Exercises **1.** $\frac{7}{9}$ **3.** $\frac{11}{9}$ or $1\frac{2}{9}$ **5.** $\frac{2}{5}$ **7.** $\frac{17}{44}$ **9.** $\frac{5}{6}$ **11.** $\frac{9}{20}$ **13.** $\frac{7}{8}$ **15.** $\frac{23}{20}$ or $1\frac{3}{20}$ **17.** $\frac{37}{100}$ **19.** $\frac{7}{15}$
21. $\frac{31}{24}$ or $1\frac{7}{24}$ **23.** $\frac{27}{40}$ **25.** $\frac{19}{18}$ or $1\frac{1}{18}$ **27.** 0 **29.** $\frac{5}{12}$ **31.** $\frac{11}{60}$ **33.** $\frac{1}{4}$ **35.** $\frac{2}{3}$ **37.** $\frac{1}{36}$ **39.** 0 **41.** $\frac{5}{12}$ **43.** 1 **45.** $\frac{11}{30}$
47. $1\frac{7}{15}$ **49.** $x = \frac{3}{14}$ **51.** $x = \frac{5}{33}$ **53.** $x = \frac{17}{30}$ **55.** $1\frac{5}{12}$ cups **57.** $\frac{17}{12}$ or $1\frac{5}{12}$ kilograms of nuts; $\frac{7}{8}$ kilogram of dried fruit
59. $\frac{19}{60}$ of the book report **61.** 16 chocolates **63.** $\frac{7}{40}$ of the membership

Quick Quiz 7 **1.** $\frac{19}{16}$ or $1\frac{3}{16}$ **2.** $\frac{32}{21}$ or $1\frac{11}{21}$ **3.** $\frac{19}{45}$ **4.** See Instructor

Section 8 Exercises **1.** $9\frac{3}{4}$ **3.** $4\frac{1}{7}$ **5.** $17\frac{1}{2}$ **7.** 13 **9.** $\frac{4}{7}$ **11.** $2\frac{1}{16}$ **13.** $9\frac{4}{9}$ **15.** 0 **17.** $4\frac{14}{15}$ **19.** $14\frac{4}{7}$ **21.** $7\frac{2}{5}$
23. $10\frac{3}{10}$ **25.** $41\frac{4}{5}$ **27.** $8\frac{5}{12}$ **29.** $8\frac{1}{6}$ **31.** $73\frac{37}{40}$ **33.** $5\frac{1}{2}$ **35.** $\frac{2}{3}$ **37.** $4\frac{41}{60}$ **39.** $8\frac{8}{15}$ **41.** $102\frac{5}{8}$ **43.** $14\frac{1}{24}$
45. $43\frac{1}{8}$ kilometres **47.** $6\frac{9}{10}$ kilometres **49.** $2\frac{3}{4}$ inches **51. (a)** $3\frac{11}{12}$ kilograms **(b)** $4\frac{1}{12}$ kilograms **53.** $\frac{2607}{40}$ or $65\frac{7}{40}$
55. We estimate by adding 35 + 24 to obtain 59. The exact answer is $59\frac{7}{12}$. Our estimate is very close. We are off by only $\frac{7}{12}$. **57.** $\frac{2}{3}$
59. 1 **61.** $\frac{3}{2}$ or $1\frac{1}{2}$ **63.** $\frac{3}{5}$ **65.** $\frac{9}{25}$ **67.** $\frac{1}{4}$ **69.** $\frac{1}{9}$ **71.** $\frac{6}{5}$ or $1\frac{1}{5}$

Quick Quiz 8 **1.** $9\frac{7}{40}$ **2.** $1\frac{43}{60}$ **3.** $\frac{41}{55}$ **4.** See Instructor

Section 9 Exercises **1.** $23\frac{13}{30}$ centimetres **3.** 385 gorillas **5.** $1\frac{9}{16}$ inches **7.** $9\frac{19}{20}$ kilometres **9.** \$147 **11.** $275\frac{5}{8}$ litres **13.** $106\frac{7}{8}$ nautical miles **15.** \$451 per week **17. (a)** 33 bracelets **(b)** $\frac{1}{5}$ metre **(c)** $\$313\frac{1}{2}$ **19. (a)** $14\frac{1}{8}$ hg of bread **(b)** $\frac{5}{8}$ hg **21. (a)** $30\frac{1}{2}$ knots **(b)** 7 hours **23. (a)** $205\,687\frac{1}{2}$ bushels **(b)** $11\,998\frac{7}{16}$ cubic metres **(c)** $359\,953\frac{1}{8}$ bushels

Quick Quiz 9 **1.** 168 square metres **2.** 16 packets **3.** $5\frac{3}{8}$ kilometres **4.** See Instructor

Putting Your Skills to Work **1. (a)** \$360 **(b)** \$4320 **2. (a)** Yes **(b)** Yes, there would be \$520 left over for the celebration dinner. **3.** If the cost of the television is $\frac{3}{4}$ of \$2000, then the total would only be \$1500. Thus \$1020 would be left over for the birthday dinner. **4. (a)** \$600 **(b)** \$7200 **(c)** \$2880 **5.** Answers may vary

Module Review Problems **1.** $\frac{3}{8}$ **2.** $\frac{5}{12}$ **3.** Answers will vary **4.** Answers will vary **5.** $\frac{9}{80}$ **6.** $\frac{87}{100}$ **7.** 2×3^3 **8.** $2^3 \times 3 \times 5$ **9.** $2^3 \times 3 \times 7$ **10.** prime **11.** $2 \times 3 \times 13$ **12.** prime **13.** $\frac{2}{7}$ **14.** $\frac{1}{4}$ **15.** $\frac{3}{8}$ **16.** $\frac{13}{17}$ **17.** $\frac{7}{8}$ **18.** $\frac{17}{35}$ **19.** $\frac{35}{8}$ **20.** $\frac{63}{4}$ **21.** $\frac{37}{7}$ **22.** $\frac{33}{5}$ **23.** $5\frac{5}{8}$ **24.** $4\frac{16}{21}$ **25.** $7\frac{4}{7}$ **26.** $8\frac{2}{9}$ **27.** $3\frac{3}{11}$ **28.** $\frac{117}{8}$ **29.** $4\frac{1}{8}$ **30.** $\frac{20}{77}$ **31.** $\frac{7}{15}$ **32.** 0 **33.** $\frac{4}{63}$ **34.** $\frac{492}{5}$ or $98\frac{2}{5}$ **35.** $\frac{51}{2}$ or $25\frac{1}{2}$ **36.** $\frac{82}{5}$ or $16\frac{2}{5}$ **37.** 16 **38.** $\$677\frac{1}{4}$ **39.** 12 square metres **40.** $\frac{15}{14}$ or $1\frac{1}{14}$ **41.** 6 **42.** 1920 **43.** 1500 **44.** $\frac{1}{2}$ **45.** 8 **46.** 0 **47.** $\frac{46}{33}$ or $1\frac{13}{33}$ **48.** 12 rolls **49.** $\frac{560}{3}$ or $186\frac{2}{3}$ calories **50.** 98 **51.** 100 **52.** 90 **53.** $\frac{24}{56}$ **54.** $\frac{33}{72}$ **55.** $\frac{80}{150}$ **56.** $\frac{187}{198}$ **57.** $\frac{2}{7}$ **58.** $\frac{13}{12}$ or $1\frac{1}{12}$ **59.** $\frac{85}{63}$ or $1\frac{22}{63}$ **60.** $\frac{11}{40}$ **61.** $\frac{23}{70}$ **62.** $\frac{44}{45}$ **63.** $\frac{19}{48}$ **64.** $\frac{61}{75}$ **65.** $5\frac{1}{4}$ **66.** $\frac{49}{9}$ or $5\frac{4}{9}$ **67.** $8\frac{2}{3}$ **68.** $22\frac{3}{7}$ **69.** $\frac{49}{8}$ or $6\frac{1}{8}$ **70.** $\frac{279}{80}$ or $3\frac{39}{80}$ **71.** $\frac{9}{10}$ **72.** $\frac{3}{10}$ **73.** $8\frac{29}{40}$ kilometres **74.** $175\frac{7}{12}$ kilometres **75.** $1\frac{2}{3}$ cups sugar; $2\frac{1}{8}$ cups flour **76.** $172\frac{1}{8}$ kilometres **77.** 15 lengths **78.** $9\frac{5}{8}$ litres **79.** $227\frac{1}{2}$ minutes or 3 hours and $47\frac{1}{2}$ minutes **80.** \$133 **81.** $\$577\frac{1}{2}$ **82.** $1\frac{1}{16}$ inch **83.** \$242 **84. (a)** 20 kilometres per litre **(b)** $\$22\frac{2}{25}$ **85.** $\frac{3}{7}$ **86.** $\frac{68}{75}$ **87.** $1\frac{5}{12}$ **88.** $\frac{24}{77}$ **89.** $\frac{17}{6}$ or $2\frac{5}{6}$ **90.** $\frac{64}{343}$ **91.** $\frac{15}{4}$ or $3\frac{3}{4}$ **92.** 99 **93.** 48

How Am I Doing? Module Test **1.** $\frac{3}{5}$ (obj. 1.1) **2.** $\frac{311}{388}$ (obj. 1.3) **3.** $\frac{3}{7}$ (obj. 2.2) **4.** $\frac{3}{14}$ (obj. 2.2) **5.** $\frac{9}{2}$ (obj. 2.2) **6.** $\frac{34}{5}$ (obj. 3.1) **7.** $10\frac{5}{14}$ (obj. 3.2) **8.** 12 (obj. 4.2) **9.** $\frac{14}{45}$ (obj. 4.1) **10.** 14 (obj. 4.3) **11.** $\frac{77}{40}$ or $1\frac{37}{40}$ (obj. 5.1) **12.** $\frac{39}{62}$ (obj. 5.1) **13.** $\frac{90}{13}$ or $6\frac{12}{13}$ (obj. 5.3) **14.** $\frac{12}{7}$ or $1\frac{5}{7}$ (obj. 5.3) **15.** 36 (obj. 6.2) **16.** 48 (obj. 6.2) **17.** 24 (obj. 6.2) **18.** $\frac{30}{72}$ (obj. 6.3) **19.** $\frac{13}{36}$ (obj. 7.2) **20.** $\frac{11}{20}$ (obj. 7.2) **21.** $\frac{25}{28}$ (obj. 7.2) **22.** $14\frac{6}{35}$ (obj. 8.1) **23.** $4\frac{13}{14}$ (obj. 8.2) **24.** $\frac{1}{48}$ (obj. 8.3) **25.** $\frac{7}{6}$ or $1\frac{1}{6}$ (obj. 8.3) **26.** 154 square feet (obj. 9.1) **27.** 8 packages (obj. 9.1) **28.** $\frac{7}{10}$ kilometre (obj. 9.1) **29.** $14\frac{1}{24}$ kilometres (obj. 9.1) **30.** (obj. 9.1) **(a)** 40 oranges **(b)** $\$9\frac{3}{5}$ **31.** (obj. 9.1) **(a)** 77 candles **(b)** $\$1\frac{1}{4}$ **(c)** $\$827\frac{3}{4}$

Decimals

Shutterstock/Losevsky Pavel

The rising cost of gasoline is of great concern to every driver in the country. But what is the best bargain when you purchase gasoline? How can you use math to save you money at the pump? Should you always go to the station with the lowest price? This module's Putting Your Skills to Work section explores these questions, and you may be surprised at some of the answers.

Decimals

SECTION 1 USING DECIMAL NOTATION

 Writing a Word Name for a Decimal Fraction

In this module we will look at **decimal fractions**—that is, fractions with 10, 100, 1000, and so on, in the denominator, such as $\frac{1}{10}$, $\frac{18}{100}$, and $\frac{43}{1000}$.

Why, of all fractions, do we take special notice of these? Our hands have 10 digits. Our money system is based on the dollar, which has 100 equal parts, or cents. And the international system of measurement called the *metric system* is based on 10 and powers of 10.

As with other numbers, these decimal fractions can be written in different ways (forms). For example, the shaded part of the whole in the following drawing can be written:

in words (one-tenth)
in fractional form $\left(\frac{1}{10}\right)$
in decimal form (0.1)

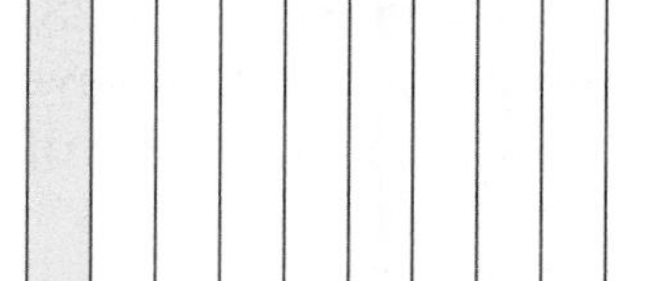

All mean the same quantity, namely 1 out of 10 equal parts of the whole. We'll see that when we use decimal notation, computations can be easily done based on the rules for whole numbers and a few rules about where to place the decimal point. In a world where calculators and computers are commonplace, many of the fractions we encounter are decimal fractions. A decimal fraction is a fraction whose denominator is a power of 10.

$\frac{7}{10}$ is a decimal fraction. $\quad \frac{89}{10^2} = \frac{89}{100}$ is a decimal fraction.

Decimal fractions can be written with numerals in two ways: fractional form or decimal form. Some decimal fractions are shown in decimal form below.

Fractional Form		**Decimal Form**
$\frac{3}{10}$	=	0.3
$\frac{59}{100}$	=	0.59
$\frac{171}{1000}$	=	0.171

The zero in front of the decimal point is not actually required. We place it there simply to make sure that we don't miss seeing the decimal point. A number written in decimal notation has three parts.

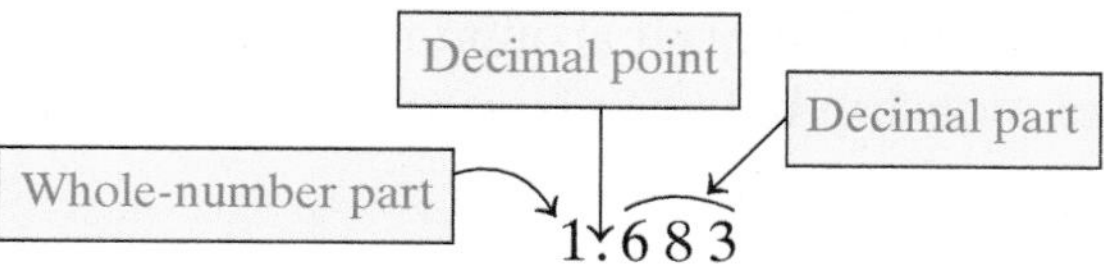

When a number is written in decimal form, the first digit to the right of the decimal point represents tenths, the next digit hundredths, the next digit thousandths, and so on. 0.9 means nine tenths and is equivalent to $\frac{9}{10}$. 0.51 means fifty-one hundredths and is equivalent to $\frac{51}{100}$. Some decimals

Student Learning Objectives

After studying this section, you will be able to:

1. Write a word name for a decimal fraction.
2. Change from fractional notation to decimal notation.
3. Change from decimal notation to fractional notation.

are larger than 1. For example, 1.683 means one and six hundred eighty-three thousandths. It is equivalent to $1\frac{683}{1000}$. Note that the word *and* is used to indicate the decimal point. A place-value chart is helpful.

Decimal Place Values

Hundreds	Tens	Ones	Decimal point	Tenths	Hundredths	Thousandths	Ten-thousandths
100	10	1	"and"	$\frac{1}{10}$	$\frac{1}{100}$	$\frac{1}{1000}$	$\frac{1}{10\,000}$
1	5	6	.	2	8	7	4

So, we can write 156.2874 in words as one hundred fifty-six and two thousand eight hundred seventy-four ten-thousandths. We say ten-thousandths because it is the name of the last decimal place on the right.

EXAMPLE 1 Write a word name for each decimal.

(a) 0.79 **(b)** 0.5308 **(c)** 1.6 **(d)** 23.765

Solution

(a) 0.79 = seventy-nine hundredths
(b) 0.5308 = five thousand three hundred eight ten-thousandths
(c) 1.6 = one and six tenths
(d) 23.765 = twenty-three and seven hundred sixty-five thousandths

NOTE TO STUDENT: Fully worked-out solutions to all of the Practice Problems can be found at the end of the module.

Practice Problem 1 Write a word name for each decimal.

(a) 0.073 **(b)** 4.68 **(c)** 0.0017 **(d)** 561.78

Sometimes, decimals are used where we would not expect them. For example, we commonly say that there are 365 days in a year, with 366 days in every fourth year (or leap year). However, this is not quite correct. In fact, from time to time further adjustments need to be made to the calendar to adjust for these inconsistencies. Astronomers know that a more accurate measure of a year is called a **tropical year** (measured from one equinox to the next). Rounded to the nearest hundred-thousandth, 1 tropical year = 365.241 22 days. This is read "three hundred sixty-five and twenty-four thousand, one hundred twenty-two hundred-thousandths." This approximate value is a more accurate measurement of the amount of time it takes Earth to complete one orbit around the sun.

Note the relationship between fractions and their equivalent numbers' decimal forms.

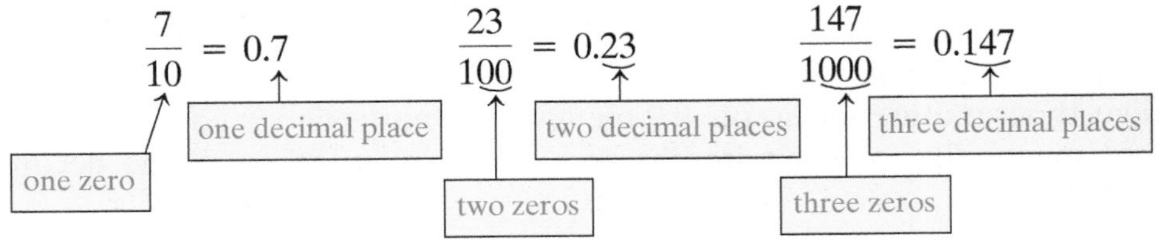

Decimal notation is commonly used with money. When writing a cheque, we often write the amount that is less than 1 dollar, such as 23¢, as $\frac{23}{100}$ dollar.

ALICE J. JENNINGTON
208 BARTON SPRINGS 519-555-1212
London, Ontario N6B 1T3

37-86/110 3680

DATE March 18, 2010

PAY TO THE ORDER OF Rosetta Ramirez $ 59.23

Fifty-nine and 23/100 DOLLARS

CIBC Canadian Imperial Bank of Commerce
Toronto, Ontario

MEMO textbooks

⑆06300042O⑆ 800⑈36492B⑈ 3680

EXAMPLE 2 Write a word name for the amount on a cheque made out for \$672.89.

Solution Six hundred seventy-two and $\frac{89}{100}$ dollars

Practice Problem 2 Write a word name for the amount of a cheque made out for \$7863.04.

2 Changing from Fractional Notation to Decimal Notation

It is helpful to be able to write decimals in both decimal notation and fractional notation. First we illustrate changing a fraction with a denominator of 10, 100, or 1000 into decimal form.

EXAMPLE 3 Write as a decimal.

(a) $\frac{8}{10}$ **(b)** $\frac{74}{100}$ **(c)** $1\frac{3}{10}$ **(d)** $2\frac{56}{1000}$

Solution

(a) $\frac{8}{10} = 0.8$ **(b)** $\frac{74}{100} = 0.74$ **(c)** $1\frac{3}{10} = 1.3$ **(d)** $2\frac{56}{1000} = 2.056$

Note: In part (d), we need to add a zero before the digits 56. Since there are three zeros in the denominator, we need three decimal places in the decimal number.

Practice Problem 3 Write as a decimal.

(a) $\frac{9}{10}$ **(b)** $\frac{136}{1000}$ **(c)** $2\frac{56}{100}$ **(d)** $34\frac{86}{1000}$

3 Changing from Decimal Notation to Fractional Notation

EXAMPLE 4 Write in fractional notation.

(a) 0.51 **(b)** 18.1 **(c)** 0.7611 **(d)** 1.363

Solution

(a) $0.51 = \frac{51}{100}$ **(b)** $18.1 = 18\frac{1}{10}$ **(c)** $0.7611 = \frac{7611}{10\,000}$ **(d)** $1.363 = 1\frac{363}{1000}$

Practice Problem 4 Write in fractional notation.

(a) 0.37 **(b)** 182.3 **(c)** 0.7131 **(d)** 42.019

When we convert from decimal form to fractional form, we reduce whenever possible.

EXAMPLE 5 Write in fractional notation. Reduce whenever possible.

(a) 2.6 **(b)** 0.38 **(c)** 0.525 **(d)** 361.007

Solution

(a) $2.6 = 2\frac{6}{10} = 2\frac{3}{5}$ **(b)** $0.38 = \frac{38}{100} = \frac{19}{50}$

(c) $0.525 = \frac{525}{1000} = \frac{105}{200} = \frac{21}{40}$

(d) $361.007 = 361\frac{7}{1000}$ (cannot be reduced)

Practice Problem 5 Write in fractional notation. Reduce whenever possible.

(a) 8.5 **(b)** 0.58 **(c)** 36.25 **(d)** 106.013

EXAMPLE 6 A chemist found that the concentration of lead in a water sample was 5 parts per million. What fraction would represent the concentration of lead?

Solution Five parts per million means 5 parts out of 1 000 000. As a fraction, this is $\frac{5}{1\,000\,000}$. We can reduce this by dividing numerator and denominator by 5. Thus

$$\frac{5}{1\,000\,000} = \frac{1}{200\,000}.$$

The concentration of lead in the water sample is $\frac{1}{200\,000}$.

Practice Problem 6 A chemist found that the concentration of PCBs in a water sample was 2 parts per billion. What fraction would represent the concentration of PCBs?

Developing Your Study Skills

Steps Toward Success in Mathematics

Mathematics is a building process, mastered one step at a time. The foundation of this process is formed by a few basic requirements. Those who are successful in mathematics realize the absolute necessity for building a study of mathematics on the firm foundation of these six minimum requirements.

1. Attend class every day.
2. Read the textbook.
3. Take notes in class.
4. Do assigned homework every day.
5. Get help immediately when needed.
6. Review regularly.

If you are in an online class or self-paced class, do some of your math assignment on five days during each week.

Section 1 Exercises

Verbal and Writing Skills

1. Describe a decimal fraction and provide examples.

2. What word is used to describe the decimal point when writing the word name for a decimal that is greater than 1?

3. What is the name of the last decimal place on the right for the decimal 132.456 78?

4. When writing \$82.75 on a cheque, we write 75¢ as ______________________.

Write a word name for each decimal.

5. 0.57

6. 0.78

7. 3.8

8. 12.4

9. 7.013

10. 2.056

11. 28.0037

12. 54.0013

Write a word name as you would on a cheque.

13. \$124.20

14. \$510.31

15. \$1236.08

16. \$5304.05

17. \$12 015.45

18. \$20 000.67

Write in decimal notation.

19. seven tenths

20. six tenths

21. ninety-six hundredths

22. eighteen hundredths

23. four hundred eighty-one thousandths

24. twenty-two thousandths

25. six thousand one hundred fourteen millionths

26. one thousand three hundred eighteen millionths

Write each fraction as a decimal.

27. $\frac{7}{10}$

28. $\frac{3}{10}$

29. $\frac{76}{100}$

30. $\frac{84}{100}$

31. $\frac{1}{100}$

32. $\frac{6}{100}$

33. $\frac{53}{1000}$

34. $\frac{328}{1000}$

35. $\frac{2403}{10\,000}$

36. $\frac{7794}{10\,000}$

37. $10\frac{9}{10}$

38. $5\frac{3}{10}$

39. $84\frac{13}{100}$

40. $52\frac{77}{100}$

41. $3\frac{529}{1000}$

42. $2\frac{23}{1000}$

43. $235\frac{104}{10\,000}$

44. $116\frac{312}{10\,000}$

Write in fractional notation. Reduce whenever possible.

45. 0.02

46. 0.05

47. 3.6

48. 8.9

49. 7.41

50. 15.75

51. 12.625

52. 29.875

53. 7.0615

54. 4.0016

55. 8.0108

56. 7.0605

57. 235.1254

58. 581.2406

59. 0.0125

60. 0.3375

Applications

61. ***Cigarette Use*** The highest use of cigarettes in Canada takes place in Nunavut. In 2005, 46 400 out of every 100 000 men age 15 or older who lived in Nunavut were smokers. That same year, 45 800 out of every 100 000 women age 15 or older who lived in Nunavut were smokers.

(a) What fractional part of the male population in Nunavut were smokers?

(b) What fractional part of the female population in Nunavut were smokers? Be sure to express these fractions in reduced form.
(*Source:* Statistics Canada, www40.statcan.gc.ca/l01/cst01/health74a-eng.htm)

62. ***Cigarette Use*** The lowest use of cigarettes in Canada takes place in British Columbia. In 2005, 13 900 out of every 100 000 men age 15 or older who lived in British Columbia were smokers. That same year, 11 400 out of every 100 000 women age 15 or older who lived in British Columbia were smokers.

(a) What fractional part of the male population in British Columbia were smokers?

(b) What fractional part of the female population in British Columbia were smokers? Be sure to express these fractions in reduced form.
(*Source:* Statistics Canada, www40.statcan.gc.ca/l01/cst01/health74a-eng.htm)

63. ***Bald Eagle Eggs*** American bald eagles have been fighting extinction due to environmental hazards such as DDT, PCBs, and dioxin. The problem is with the food chain. Fish or rodents consume contaminated food and/or water. Then the eagles ingest the poison, which in turn affects the durability of the eagles' eggs. It takes only 4 parts per million of certain chemicals to ruin an eagle egg; write this number as a fraction in lowest terms. (In 1994 the bald eagle was removed from the endangered species list.)

64. ***Turtle Eggs*** Every year turtles lay eggs on the islands of the 1000 Islands. Unfortunately, due to illegal polluting, a lot of the eggs are contaminated. If the turtle eggs contain more than 2 parts per one hundred million of chemical pollutants, they will not hatch and the population will continue to head toward extinction. Write the preceding amount of chemical pollutants as a fraction in the lowest terms.

Quick Quiz 1

1. Write a word name for the decimal. 5.367

2. Write as a decimal. $\frac{523}{10\,000}$

3. Write in fractional notation. Reduce your answer.
12.58

4. **Concept Check** Explain how you know how many zeros to put in your answer if you need to write $\frac{953}{100\,000}$ as a decimal.

SECTION 2 COMPARING, ORDERING, AND ROUNDING DECIMALS

Comparing Decimals

All of the numbers we have studied have a specific order. To illustrate this order, we can place the numbers on a **number line.** Look at the number line in the margin. Each number has a specific place on it. The arrow points in the direction of increasing value. Thus, if one number is to the right of a second number, it is larger, or greater, than that number. Since 5 is to the right of 2 on the number line, we say that 5 is greater than 2. We write $5 > 2$.

Since 4 is to the left of 6 on the number line, we say that 4 is less than 6. We write $4 < 6$. The symbols "$>$" and "$<$" are called **inequality symbols.**

$a < b$ is read "*a* is less than *b*."

$a > b$ is read "*a* is greater than *b*."

We can assign exactly one point on the number line to each decimal number. When two decimal numbers are placed on a number line, the one farther to the right is the larger. Thus we can say that $3.4 > 2.7$ and $4.3 > 4.0$. We can also say that $0.5 < 1.0$ and $1.8 < 2.2$. Why?

0.5 1.8 2.2 2.7 3.4 4.3

0 1.0 2.0 3.0 4.0 5.0

To compare or order decimals, we compare each digit.

COMPARING TWO NUMBERS IN DECIMAL NOTATION

1. Start at the left and compare corresponding digits. If the digits are the same, move one place to the right.
2. When two digits are different, the larger number is the one with the larger digit.

EXAMPLE 1 Write an inequality statement with 0.167 and 0.166.

Solution The numbers in the tenths place are the same. They are both 1.

0.1 6 7 0.1 6 6

The numbers in the hundredths place are the same. They are both 6.

0.1 6 7 0.1 6 6

The numbers in the thousandths place differ.

0.1 6 7 0.1 6 6

Since $7 > 6$, we know that $0.167 > 0.166$.

Practice Problem 1 Write an inequality statement with 5.74 and 5.75.

Student Learning Objectives

After studying this section, you will be able to:

1. Compare decimals.
2. Place decimals in order from smallest to largest.
3. Round decimals to a specified decimal place.

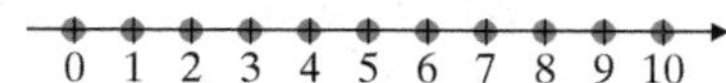

***NOTE TO STUDENT:** Fully worked-out solutions to all of the Practice Problems can be found at the end of the module.*

Whenever necessary, extra zeros can be written to the right of the last digit—that is, to the right of the decimal point—without changing the value of the decimal. Thus

$$0.56 = 0.56000 \qquad \text{and} \qquad 0.7768 = 0.77680.$$

The zero to the left of the decimal point is optional. Thus 0.56 = .56. Both notations are used. You are encouraged to place a zero to the left of the decimal point so that you don't miss the decimal point when you work with decimals.

EXAMPLE 2 Fill in the blank with one of the symbols <, =, or >.

0.77 ____ 0.777

Solution We begin by adding a zero to the first decimal.

$0.77\underline{0} \qquad 0.77\underline{7}$

We see that the tenths and hundredths digits are equal. But the thousandths digits differ. Since $0 < 7$, we have $0.770 < 0.777$.

Practice Problem 2 Fill in the blank with one of the symbols <, =, or >.

0.894 __ 0.89

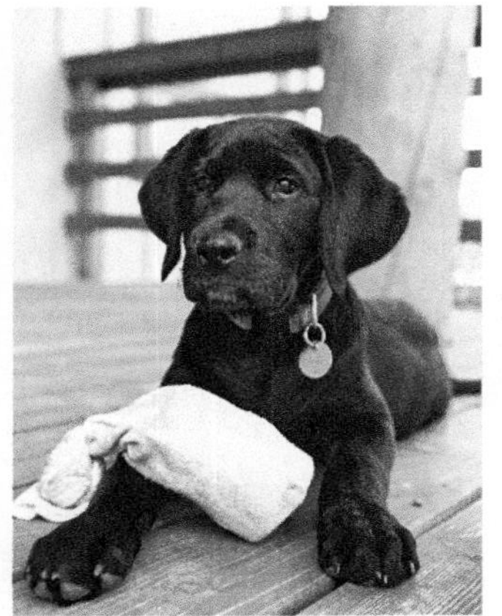
Dale C. Spartas/CORBIS

2 Placing Decimals in Order from Smallest to Largest

Which is the heaviest—a puppy that weighs 1.2 kg, a puppy that weighs 1.28 kg, or a puppy that weighs 1.028 kg? Did you choose the puppy that weighs 1.28 kg? You are correct.

You can place two or more decimals in order. If you are asked to order the decimals from smallest to largest, look for the smallest decimal and place it first.

EXAMPLE 3 Place the following five decimal numbers in order from smallest to largest.

1.834, 1.83, 1.381, 1.38, 1.8

Solution First we add zeros to make the comparison easier.

1.834, 1.830, 1.381, 1.380, 1.800

Now we rearrange with smallest first.

1.380, 1.381, 1.800, 1.830, 1.834

Practice Problem 3 Place the following five decimal numbers in order from smallest to largest.

2.45, 2.543, 2.46, 2.54, 2.5

 Rounding Decimals to a Specified Decimal Place

Sometimes in calculations involving money, we see numbers like \$386.432 and \$29.5986. To make these useful, we usually round them to the nearest cent. \$386.432 is rounded to \$386.43. \$29.5986 is rounded to \$29.60. A general rule for rounding decimals follows.

ROUNDING DECIMALS

1. Find the decimal place (units, tenths, hundredths, and so on) to which rounding is required.
2. If the first digit to the right of the given place value is less than 5, drop it and all digits to the right of it.
3. If the first digit to the right of the given place value is 5 or greater, increase the number in the given place value by 1. Drop all digits to the right of this place.

EXAMPLE 4 Round 156.37 to the nearest tenth.

Solution 156.3 7

↑ We find the tenths place.

Note that 7, the next place to the right, is greater than 5. We round up to 156.4 and drop the digits to the right. The answer is 156.4.

Practice Problem 4 Round 723.88 to the nearest tenth.

NOTE TO STUDENT: Fully worked-out solutions to all of the Practice Problems can be found at the end of the module.

EXAMPLE 5 Round to the nearest thousandth.

(a) 0.06358 **(b)** 128.37448

Solution

(a) 0.06 3 58

↑ We locate the thousandths place.

Note that the digit to the right of the thousandths place is 5. We round up to 0.064 and drop all the digits to the right.

(b) 128.37 4 48

↑ We locate the thousandths place.

Note that the digit to the right of the thousandths place is less than 5. We round to 128.374 and drop all the digits to the right.

Practice Problem 5 Round to the nearest thousandth.

(a) 12.92647 **(b)** 0.007892

Remember that rounding up to the next digit in a position may result in several digits being changed.

EXAMPLE 6 Round to the nearest hundredth. Fred and Linda used 203.9964 kilowatt-hours of electricity in their house in May.

203.9 9 64
↑ We locate the hundredths place.

Solution Since the digit to the right of the hundredths place is greater than 5, we round up. This affects the next two positions. Do you see why? The result is 204.00 kilowatt-hours. Notice that we have the two zeros to the right of the decimal place to show we have rounded to the nearest hundredth.

Practice Problem 6 Round to the nearest tenth. Last month the college gymnasium used 15 699.953 kilowatt-hours of electricity.

Sometimes we round a decimal to the nearest whole number. For example, when writing figures on income tax forms, a taxpayer may round all figures to the nearest dollar.

EXAMPLE 7 To complete her income tax return, Marge needs to round these figures to the nearest whole dollar.

Medical bills $779.86 Taxes $563.49
Retirement contributions $674.38 Contributions to charity $534.77

Solution Round the amounts.

	Original Figure	***Rounded to Nearest Dollar***
Medical bills	$779.86	$780
Taxes	$563.49	$563
Retirement	$674.38	$674
Charity	$534.77	$535

Practice Problem 7 Round the following figures to the nearest whole dollar.

Medical bills $375.50 Taxes $971.39
Retirement contributions $980.49 Contributions to charity $817.65

CAUTION: Why is it so important to consider only *one* digit to the right of the desired round-off position? What is wrong with rounding in steps? Suppose that Mark rounds 1.349 to the nearest tenth in steps. First he rounds 1.349 to 1.35 (nearest hundredth). Then he rounds 1.35 to 1.4 (nearest tenth). What is wrong with this reasoning?

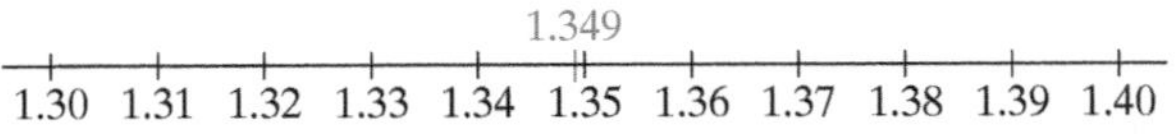

To round 1.349 to the nearest tenth, we ask if 1.349 is closer to 1.3 or to 1.4. It is closer to 1.3. Mark got 1.4, so he is not correct. He "rounded in steps" by first moving to 1.35, thus increasing the error and moving in the wrong direction. To control rounding errors, we consider *only* the first digit to the right of the decimal place to which we are rounding.

Section 2 Exercises

Fill in the blank with one of the symbols <, =, or >.

1. 1.3 ___ 1.29

2. 2.6 ___ 2.58

3. 0.34 ___ 0.340

4. 72.54 ___ 72.56

5. 18.92 ___ 8.93

6. 0.460 ___ 0.46

7. 0.00043 ___ 0.0004

8. 0.0037 ___ 0.036

9. 1.002 ___ 1.0021

10. 2.0056 ___ 2.006

11. 126.34 ___ 125.35

12. 406.78 ___ 407.75

13. 0.888 ___ 0.8888

14. 0.666 ___ 0.6666

15. 0.777 ___ 0.7077

16. 0.555 ___ 0.5505

17. $\frac{72}{1000}$ ___ 0.072

18. $\frac{54}{1000}$ ___ 0.054

19. $\frac{8}{10}$ ___ 0.08

20. $\frac{5}{100}$ ___ 0.005

Arrange each set of decimals from smallest to largest.

21. 12.6, 12.8, 12.65

22. 18.32, 18.038, 18.04

23. 0.0071, 0.05, 0.007

24. 0.0025, 0.0052, 0.002

25. 8.4, 8.39, 8.41, 8.31

26. 5.1, 5.01, 5.23, 5.02

27. 26.034, 26.003, 26.04, 26.033

28. 33.082, 33.02, 33.088, 33.079

29. 18.006, 18.060, 18.066, 18.606, 18.065

30. 15.020, 15.002, 15.001, 15.018, 15.0019

Round to the nearest tenth.

31. 6.92

32. 8.35

33. 28.98

34. 47.94

35. 578.064

36. 454.99

37. 2176.83

38. 4082.74

Round to the nearest hundredth.

39. 26.032

40. 47.071

41. 36.997

42. 24.999

43. 156.1749

44. 283.8441

45. 2786.706

46. 4609.285

Round to the nearest indicated place.

47. 7.8155; thousandths

48. 8.10263; thousandths

49. 0.05951; ten-thousandths

50. 0.063148; ten-thousandths

51. 12.0157823; hundred-thousandths

52. 15.4159266; hundred-thousandths

53. 135.564; nearest whole number

54. 389.645; nearest whole number

Round to the nearest dollar.

55. \$788.42

56. \$912.75

57. \$15 020.50

58. \$20 159.48

Round to the nearest cent.

59. \$96.3357

60. \$42.9261

61. \$5783.716

62. \$3928.649

Applications

63. ***Baseball*** During the 2006 baseball season, the winning percentages of the New York Yankees and the Seattle Mariners were 0.59876 and 0.48148, respectively. Round these values to the nearest thousandth.

64. ***Sales Tax*** Bryan purchased a CD for himself and a toy for his daughter. The sales tax calculated on the CD was \$1.2593 and the sales tax on the toy was \$1.7143. Round these values to the nearest cent.

65. ***Astronomy*** The number of days in a year is 365.241 22. Round this value to the nearest hundredth.

66. ***Mathematics History*** The numbers π and e are approximately equal to 3.141 59 and 2.718 28, respectively. You will encounter e in higher level mathematics courses. Round these values to the nearest hundredth.

To Think About

67. Arrange in order from smallest to largest.

$$0.61, 0.062, \frac{6}{10}, 0.006, 0.0059,$$
$$\frac{6}{100}, 0.0601, 0.0519, 0.0612$$

68. Arrange in order from smallest to largest.

$$1.05, 1.512, \frac{15}{10}, 1.0513, 0.049,$$
$$\frac{151}{100}, 0.0515, 0.052, 1.051$$

69. A person wants to round 86.234 98 to the nearest hundredth. He first rounds 86.234 98 to 86.2350. He then rounds to 86.235. Finally, he rounds to 86.24. What is wrong with his reasoning?

70. ***Personal Finance*** Mohammed is checking the calculations on his monthly bank statement. An interest charge of \$16.3724 was rounded to \$16.38. An interest charge of \$43.7214 was rounded to \$43.73. What rule does the bank use for rounding off to the nearest cent?

Quick Quiz 2

1. Arrange from smallest to largest:

   4.56, 4.6, 4.056, 4.559

2. Round to the nearest hundredth. 27.1782

3. Round to the nearest thousandth. 155.525 25

4. **Concept Check** Explain how you would round 34.958 365 to the nearest ten-thousandth.

Section 3 Adding and Subtracting Decimals

Adding Decimals

We often add decimals when we check the addition of our bill at a restaurant or at a store. We can relate addition of decimals to addition of fractions. For example,

$$\frac{3}{10} + \frac{6}{10} = \frac{9}{10} \quad \text{and} \quad 1\frac{1}{10} + 2\frac{8}{10} = 3\frac{9}{10}.$$

These same problems can be written more efficiently as decimals.

$$\begin{array}{r} 0.3 \\ +\ 0.6 \\ \hline 0.9 \end{array} \qquad \begin{array}{r} 1.1 \\ +\ 2.8 \\ \hline 3.9 \end{array}$$

The steps to follow when adding decimals are listed in the following box.

ADDING DECIMALS

1. Write the numbers to be added vertically and line up the decimal points. Extra zeros may be placed to the right of the decimal points if needed.
2. Add all the digits with the same place value, starting with the right column and moving to the left.
3. Place the decimal point of the sum in line with the decimal points of the numbers added.

Student Learning Objectives

After studying this section, you will be able to:

 **Add decimals.**

 **Subtract decimals.**

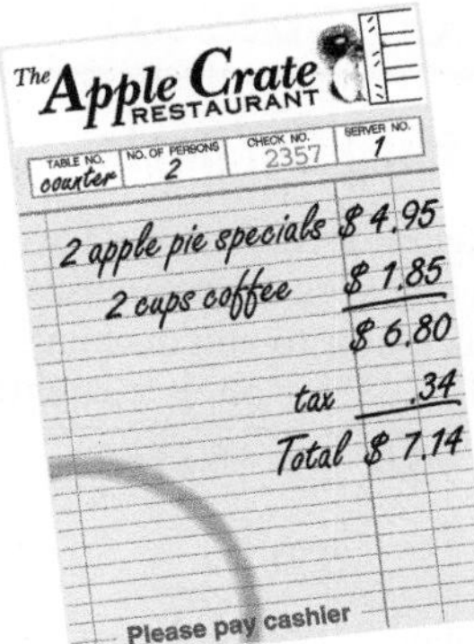

EXAMPLE 1 Add.

(a) 2.8 + 5.6 + 3.2 **(b)** 158.26 + 200.07 + 315.98

(c) 5.3 + 26.182 + 0.0007 + 624

Solution

(a) $\begin{array}{r} \overset{1}{2}.8 \\ 5.6 \\ +\ 3.2 \\ \hline 11.6 \end{array}$ **(b)** $\begin{array}{r} 1\overset{1}{5}\overset{1}{8}.\overset{2}{2}6 \\ 200.07 \\ +\ 315.98 \\ \hline 674.31 \end{array}$ **(c)** $\begin{array}{r} {}_{1}5.3000 \\ 26.1820 \\ 0.0007 \\ +\ 624.0000 \\ \hline 655.4827 \end{array}$

Extra zeros have been added to make the problem easier.
Note: The decimal point is understood to be to the right of the digit 4.

Practice Problem 1 Add.

(a) $\begin{array}{r} 9.8 \\ 3.6 \\ +\ 5.4 \\ \hline \end{array}$ **(b)** $\begin{array}{r} 300.72 \\ 163.75 \\ +\ 291.08 \\ \hline \end{array}$ **(c)** 8.9 + 37.056 + 0.0023 + 945

***NOTE TO STUDENT:** Fully worked-out solutions to all of the Practice Problems can be found at the end of the module.*

SIDELIGHT: Adding in Extra Zeros

When we add decimals like 3.1 + 2.16 + 4.007, we may write in zeros, as shown:

$$\begin{array}{r} 3.100 \\ 2.160 \\ +\ 4.007 \\ \hline 9.267 \end{array}$$

What are we really doing here? What is the advantage of adding these extra zeros?

"Decimals" means "decimal fractions." If we look at the numbers as fractions, we see that we are actually using the property of multiplying a fraction by 1 in order to obtain common denominators. Look at the problem this way:

$$\left.\begin{array}{l} 3.1 \quad = 3\frac{1}{10} \\ 2.16 \quad = 2\frac{16}{100} \\ 4.007 = 4\frac{7}{1000} \end{array}\right\}$$

The least common denominator is 1000. To obtain the common denominator for the first two fractions, we multiply.

$$\left.\begin{array}{l} 3\ \frac{1}{10} \times \frac{100}{100} = 3\frac{100}{1000} \\ 2\ \frac{16}{100} \times \frac{10}{10} = 2\frac{160}{1000} \\ +4\ \frac{7}{1000} \qquad = 4\frac{7}{1000} \end{array}\right\}$$

Once we obtain a common denominator, we can add the three fractions.

$$9\frac{267}{1000} = 9.267$$

This is the answer we arrived at earlier using the decimal form for each number. Thus writing in zeros in a decimal fraction is really an easy way to transform fractions to equivalent fractions with a common denominator. Working with decimal fractions is easier than working with other fractions.

The final digit of most odometers measures tenths of a kilometre.

EXAMPLE 2 Barbara checked her odometer before the summer began. It read 49 645.8 kilometres. She travelled 3852.6 kilometres that summer in her car. What was the odometer reading at the end of the summer?

Solution

$$\begin{array}{r} {}^{1\,1}\quad{}^{1}\ \ \\ 49\,645.8 \\ +\ \ 3\,852.6 \\ \hline 53\,498.4 \end{array}$$

The odometer read 53 498.4 kilometres.

Practice Problem 2 A car odometer read 93 521.8 kilometres before a trip of 1634.8 kilometres. What was the final odometer reading?

Calculator

Adding Decimals

The calculator can be used to verify your work. You can use your calculator to add decimals. To find 23.08 + 8.53 + 9.31 enter:

23.08 [+] 8.53 [+]

9.31 [=]

Display:

[40.92]

EXAMPLE 3 During his first semester at La Cité collégiale, Kelvey deposited cheques into his chequing account in the amounts of \$98.64, \$157.32, \$204.81, \$36.07, and \$229.89. What was the sum of his five cheques?

Solution

$$\begin{array}{r} {}^{2\,3\,2\;2} \\ \$\ \ 98.64 \\ 157.32 \\ 204.81 \\ 36.07 \\ +\ 229.89 \\ \hline \$726.73 \end{array}$$

Practice Problem 3 During the spring semester, Will deposited the following cheques into his account: \$80.95, \$133.91, \$256.47, \$53.08, and \$381.32. What was the sum of his five cheques?

Subtracting Decimals

It is important to see the relationship between the decimal form of a mixed number and the fractional form of a mixed number. This relationship helps us understand why calculations with decimals are done the way they are. Recall that when we subtract mixed numbers with common denominators, sometimes we must borrow from the whole number.

$$\begin{array}{rcr} 5\frac{1}{10} & = & 4\frac{11}{10} \\ -\ 2\frac{7}{10} & = & -\ 2\frac{7}{10} \\ \hline & & 2\frac{4}{10} \end{array}$$

We could write the same problem in decimal form:

$$\begin{array}{r} {}^{4\ 11} \\ \not{5}.\not{1} \\ -\ 2.7 \\ \hline 2.4 \end{array}$$

Subtraction of decimals is thus similar to subtraction of fractions (we get the same result), but it's usually easier to subtract with decimals than to subtract with fractions.

SUBTRACTING DECIMALS

1. Write the decimals to be subtracted vertically and line up the decimal points. Additional zeros may be placed to the right of the decimal point if not all numbers have the same number of decimal places.
2. Subtract all digits with the same place value, starting with the right column and moving to the left. Borrow when necessary.
3. Place the decimal point of the difference in line with the decimal point of the two numbers being subtracted.

EXAMPLE 4 Subtract.

(a)
$$\begin{array}{r} 84.8 \\ -\ 27.3 \\ \hline \end{array}$$

(b)
$$\begin{array}{r} 1076.320 \\ -\ 983.518 \\ \hline \end{array}$$

Solution

(a)
$$\begin{array}{r} \overset{7}{\cancel{8}}\ \overset{14}{\cancel{4}}\ .\ 8 \\ -\ 2\ 7\ .\ 3 \\ \hline 5\ 7\ .\ 5 \end{array}$$

(b)
$$\begin{array}{r} \overset{\overset{9}{\cancel{10}}}{\cancel{1}}\ \cancel{0}\ \overset{17}{\cancel{7}}\ \overset{5}{\cancel{6}}\ .\ \overset{13}{\cancel{3}}\ \overset{1}{\cancel{2}}\ \overset{10}{\cancel{0}} \\ -\ \ 9\ 8\ 3\ .\ 5\ 1\ 8 \\ \hline 9\ 2\ .\ 8\ 0\ 2 \end{array}$$

Practice Problem 4 Subtract.

(a)
$$\begin{array}{r} 38.8 \\ -\ 26.9 \\ \hline \end{array}$$

(b)
$$\begin{array}{r} 2034.908 \\ -\ 1986.325 \\ \hline \end{array}$$

When the two numbers being subtracted do not have the same number of decimal places, write in zeros as needed.

EXAMPLE 5 Subtract.

(a) 12 − 8.362 **(b)** 156.381 − 99.82

Solution

(a)
$$\begin{array}{r} \cancel{1}\ \overset{\overset{11}{\cancel{1}}}{\cancel{2}}\ .\ \overset{\overset{9}{\cancel{10}}}{\cancel{0}}\ \overset{\overset{9}{\cancel{10}}}{\cancel{0}}\ \overset{10}{\cancel{0}} \\ -\ \ \ 8\ .\ 3\ 6\ 2 \\ \hline 3\ .\ 6\ 3\ 8 \end{array}$$

(b)
$$\begin{array}{r} \cancel{1}\ \overset{\overset{14}{\cancel{4}}}{\cancel{5}}\ \overset{\overset{15}{\cancel{5}}}{\cancel{6}}\ .\ \overset{13}{\cancel{3}}\ 8\ 1 \\ -\ \ 9\ 9\ .\ 8\ 2\ 0 \\ \hline 5\ 6\ .\ 5\ 6\ 1 \end{array}$$

Practice Problem 5 Subtract.

(a) 19 − 12.579 **(b)** 283.076 − 96.38

EXAMPLE 6 On Tuesday, Don Ling filled the gas tank in his car. The odometer read 56 098.5. He drove for four days. The next time he filled the tank, the odometer read 56 420.2. How many kilometres had he driven?

Solution

$$\begin{array}{r} 5\ 6,\ \overset{3}{\cancel{4}}\ \overset{\overset{11}{\cancel{1}}}{\cancel{2}}\ \overset{\overset{9}{\cancel{10}}}{\cancel{0}}\ .\ \overset{12}{\cancel{2}} \\ -5\ 6,\ 0\ 9\ 8\ .\ 5 \\ \hline 3\ 2\ 1\ .\ 7 \end{array}$$

He had driven 321.7 kilometres.

Practice Problem 6 Abdul had his car's oil changed when the odometer read 82 370.9 kilometres. When he changed the oil again, the odometer read 87 160.1 kilometres. How many kilometres did he drive between oil changes?

EXAMPLE 7 Find the value of x if $x + 3.9 = 14.6$.

Solution Recall that the letter x is a variable. It represents a number that is added to 3.9 to obtain 14.6. We can find the number x if we calculate $14.6 - 3.9$.

$$\begin{array}{r} \overset{3\ 16}{1\not{4}.\not{6}} \\ -\ 3.9 \\ \hline 10.7 \end{array}$$

Thus $x = 10.7$.

Check. Is this true? If we replace x by 10.7, do we get a true statement?

$$x + 3.9 = 14.6$$
$$10.7 + 3.9 \stackrel{?}{=} 14.6$$
$$14.6 = 14.6 \quad \checkmark$$

Practice Problem 7 Find the value of x if $x + 10.8 = 15.3$.

NOTE TO STUDENT: Fully worked-out solutions to all of the Practice Problems can be found at the end of the module.

Adding and subtracting decimals is an important part of life. When you are recording deposits at the bank, reconciling your chequebook, or completing your income tax forms, you are adding and subtracting decimals. Be sure to learn to do it accurately. In the homework exercises, always check your answers with the Answers section at the end of the module. Making sure you have the correct answers is very important.

Developing Your Study Skills

Making a Friend in the Class

Attempt to make a friend in your class. You may find that you enjoy sitting together and drawing support and encouragement from each other. Exchange phone numbers so you can call each other whenever you get stuck in your work. Set up convenient times to study together on a regular basis, to do homework, and to review for exams.

You must not depend on a friend or fellow student to tutor you, do your work for you, or in any way be responsible for your learning. However, you will learn from each other as you seek to master the course. Studying with a friend and comparing notes, methods, and solutions can be very helpful. And it can make learning mathematics a lot more fun!

Section 3 Exercises

Add.

1. 57.1 + 19.7

2. 78.3 + 29.4

3. 384.25 + 209.65

4. 193.42 + 768.78

5.
```
   13.4
    7.6
+ 275.2
```

6.
```
  176.5
    8.4
+  22.5
```

7.
```
  4.71
+ 8.05
```

8.
```
  9.284
+ 5.77
```

9.
```
   4.9637
  28.12
+  3.645
```

10.
```
   7.0276
   3.451
+ 16.98
```

11.
```
  12
   3.62
+ 51.8
```

12.
```
  13
   4.52
+ 63.7
```

13. 108.36 + 14.3 + 85.12 + 28

14. 215.45 + 48 + 30.77 + 15.8

15. 753.61 + 28.75 + 162.3 + 100.5 + 67

16. 432.51 + 16.08 + 892.1 + 301.2 + 84

Applications *In exercises 17 and 18, calculate the perimeter of each triangle.*

17. 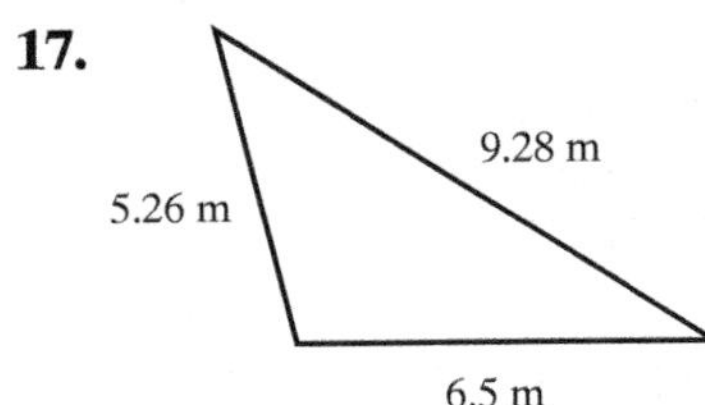

18. 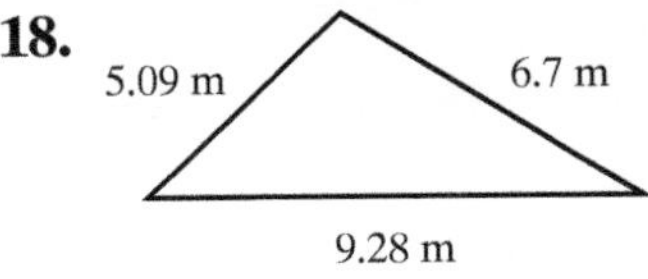

19. ***Weight Loss*** Lamar is losing weight by walking each evening after dinner. During the first week in February he lost 1.75 kilograms. During the second, third, and fourth weeks, he lost 2.5 kilograms, 1.55 kilograms, and 2.8 kilograms, respectively. How many total kilograms did Lamar lose in February?

20. ***Health*** Olivia knows she needs to drink more water while at work. One day during her morning break she drank 7.15 ounces. At lunch she drank 12.45 ounces and throughout the afternoon she drank 10.75 ounces. How many total ounces of water did she drink?

21. ***Beach Vacation*** Mick and Keith have arrived in Wasaga Beach and are going to the beach. They buy sunblock for \$4.99, beverages for \$12.50, sandwiches for \$11.85, towels for \$28.50, bottled water for \$3.29, and two novels for \$16.99. After they got what they needed, what was Mick and Keith's bill for their day at the beach?

22. ***Consumer Mathematics*** Anika bought school supplies at the campus bookstore. She purchased a calculator for \$37.25, pens for \$5.89, a T-shirt for \$13.95, and notebooks for \$10.49. The amount of sales tax was \$4.05. What was the total of Anika's bill including tax?

23. ***Truck Travel*** A truck odometer read 46 276.0 kilometres before a trip of 778.9 kilometres. What was the final odometer reading?

24. ***Car Travel*** Jane travelled 1723.1 kilometres. The car odometer at the beginning of the trip read 23 195.0 kilometres. What was the final odometer reading?

Personal Banking *In exercises 25 and 26, a portion of a bank chequing account deposit slip is shown. Add the numbers to determine the total deposit. The line drawn between the dollars and the cents column serves as the decimal point.*

25.

DEPOSIT SLIP
Foothills Bank
North Bay, Ontario

	DOLLARS	CENTS
CASH	18	42
CHEQUES	706	15
	21	03
	45	00
	621	37
LESS CASH RECEIVED		
TOTAL $		

26.

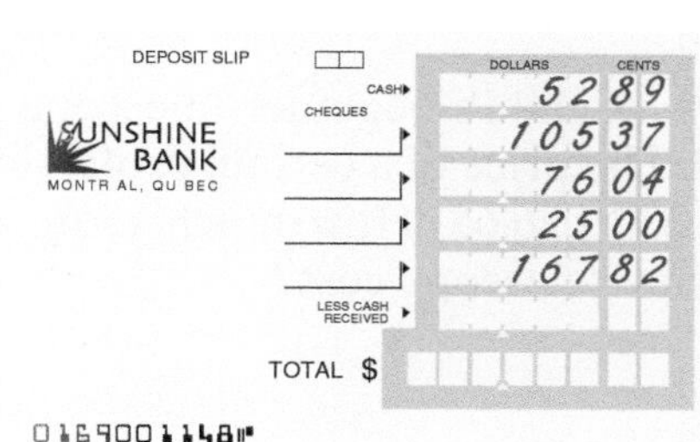
DEPOSIT SLIP
SUNSHINE BANK
MONTREAL, QUEBEC

	DOLLARS	CENTS
CASH	52	89
CHEQUES	105	37
	76	04
	25	00
	167	82
LESS CASH RECEIVED		
TOTAL $		

Subtract.

27. 12.8 − 9.3

28. 15.8 − 6.7

29. 35.75 − 9.82

30. 84.33 − 8.09

31. 126 − 76.22

32. 209 − 81.54

33. 586.513 − 78.2

34. 243.967 − 84.2

35. 220.9 − 85.47

36. 181.9 − 62.23

37. 24.0079 − 19.3614

38. 52.0708 − 41.9312

39. 8 − 1.263

40. 12 − 7.981

41. 7362.14 − 6173.07

42. 4986.71 − 3615.93

43. 1.5 − 0.0365

44. 2.8 − 0.077 63

Mixed Practice *Add or subtract.*

45. 123.621 + 52.96

46. 241.983 + 75.48

47. 98.3 − 56.71

48. 79.2 − 45.93

49. 0.0763 + 2 + 3.16

50. 18 − 2.75

51. 197.600 − 124.375

52. 382.700 − 291.927

Applications

53. ***World Records*** The heaviest apple on record was grown in Japan in 2005 and weighed 4.0678 pounds. The heaviest lemon was grown in Israel in 2003 and weighed 11.583 pounds. How much heavier was the lemon than the apple? (*Source:* www.guinessworldrecords.com)

54. ***Health*** At her 4-month checkup, baby Grace weighed 7.675 kilograms. When she was born, she weighed 3.7 kilograms. How much weight has Grace gained since she was born?

55. ***Telescope*** A child's beginner telescope is priced at $79.49. The price of a certain professional telescope is $37 026.65. How much more does the professional telescope cost?

56. ***Automobile Travel*** During their spring break vacation, Jeff and Manuel drove from their college in Halifax, Nova Scotia, to Ottawa, Ontario, and back. When they began the trip, the odometer of their rental car read 12 265.4 kilometres. When they returned the car, the odometer read 14 537.9 kilometres. How many kilometres did they drive?

57. ***Taxi Trip*** Malcolm took a taxi from Peterborough Airport to his hotel in the city. His fare was $47.70 and he tipped the driver $7.00. How much change did Malcolm get back if he gave the driver a $100 bill?

58. ***Personal Banking*** Nathan took $200 out of the ATM. He bought snow boots for $65.49, pet supplies for $27.75, and a bouquet of flowers for $18.95. How much money does he have left?

59. ***Electric Wire Construction*** An insulated wire measures 12.62 centimetres. The last 0.98 centimetre of the wire is exposed. How long is the part of the wire that is not exposed?

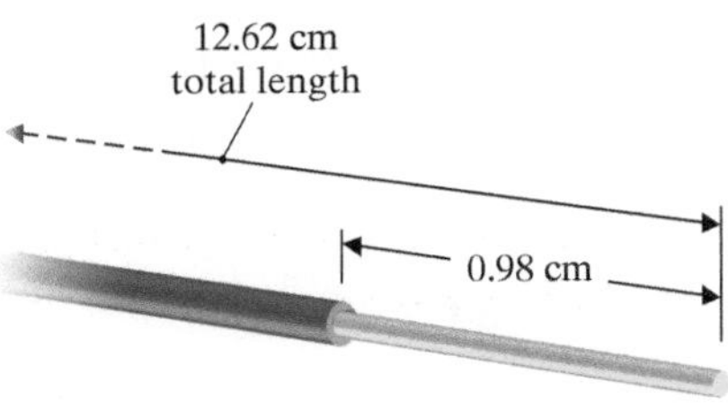

60. ***Plumbing*** The outside radius of a pipe is 9.39 centimetres. The inside radius is 7.93 centimetres. What is the thickness of the pipe?

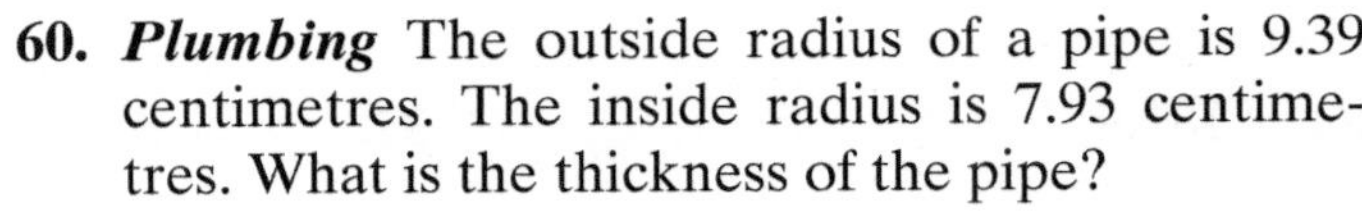

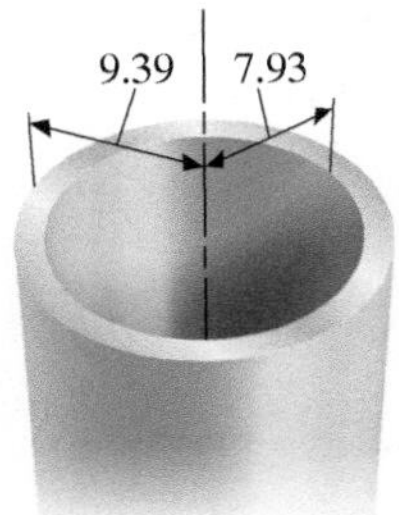

61. ***Medical Research*** A cancer researcher is involved in an important experiment. She is trying to determine how much of an anticancer drug is necessary for a Stage I (nonhuman or animal) test. She pours 2.45 litres of the experimental anticancer formula in one container and 1.35 litres of a reactive liquid in another. She then pours the contents of one container into the other. If 0.85 litre is expected to evaporate during the process, how much liquid will be left?

62. ***Rainforest Loss*** Everyone is becoming aware of the rapid loss of Earth's rainforests. Mexico's rainforests have one of the highest deforestation rates in the world. In 1997, there were 39.7 million hectares of rainforest in Mexico. By 2006, it had lost approximately 4.64 million hectares. How many hectares of rainforest did Mexico have in 2006? (A hectare is equal to 10 000 square metres.) (*Source:* www.geography.ndo.co.uk)

The U.S. federal water safety standard requires that drinking water contain no more than 0.015 milligram of lead per litre of water. (Source: Environmental Protection Agency)

63. ***Well Water Safety*** Carlos and Maria had the well that supplies their home analyzed for safety. A sample of well water contained 0.0089 milligram of lead per litre of water. What is the difference between their sample and the federal safety standard? Is it safe for them to drink the water?

64. ***City Water Safety*** Fred and Donna use water provided by the city for the drinking water in their home. A sample of their tap water contained 0.023 milligram of lead per litre of water. What is the difference between their sample and the federal safety standard? Is it safe for them to drink the water?

Income of Industries *The following table shows the number of employees in four industry sectors. Use this table for exercises 65–68. Write each answer as a decimal and as a whole number. The table values are recorded in thousands of employees.*

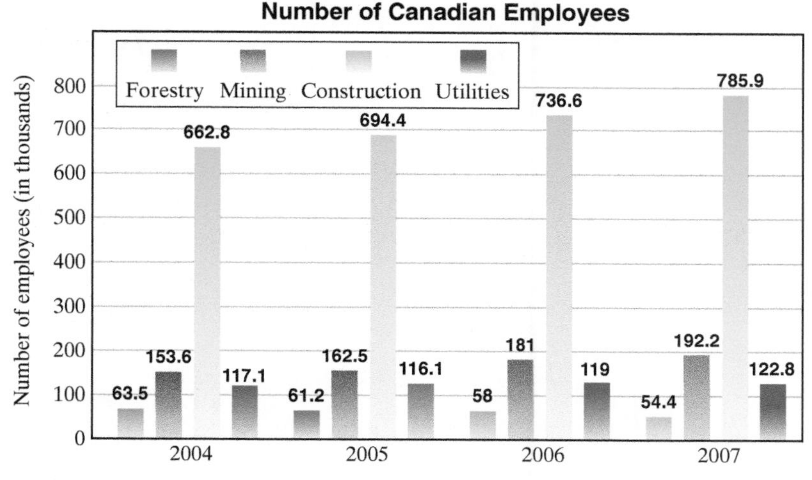

Source: Adapted from Statistics Canada, www40.statcan.gc.ca/l01/cst01/labr75a-eng.htm, Oct-09

65. How many more employees worked in mining in 2006 than in 2004?

66. How many more employees worked in construction in 2007 than in 2005?

67. How many more employees worked in construction than in forestry, mining, and utilities combined in 2007?

68. In 2005, how many more employees worked in mining than in utilities?

To Think About *Mr. Jensen made up the following shopping list of items he needs and the cost of each item. Use the list to answer exercises 69 and 70.*

69. ***Grocery Shopping*** Mr. Jensen goes to the store to buy the following items from his list: Raisin Bran, ranch salad dressing, sliced peaches, hot dog relish, and peanut butter. He has a ten-dollar bill. Estimate the cost of buying these items by first rounding the cost of each item to the nearest ten cents. Does he have enough money to buy all of them? Find the exact cost of these items. How close was your estimate?

70. ***Grocery Shopping*** The next day the Jensens' daughter, Brenda, goes to the store to buy the following items from the list: Cheerios, tomato sauce, peanut butter, white tuna, tomato soup, and cranberry sauce. She has fifteen dollars. Estimate the cost of buying these items by first rounding the cost of each item to the nearest ten cents. Does she have enough money to buy all of them? Find the exact cost of these items. How close was your estimate?

Find the value of x.

71. $x + 7.1 = 15.5$

72. $x + 4.8 = 23.1$

73. $156.9 + x = 200.6$

74. $210.3 + x = 301.2$

75. $4.162 = x + 2.053$

76. $7.076 = x + 5.602$

Quick Quiz 3

1. Add. $53.261 + 1.9 + 17.82$

2. Subtract. $5.2608 - 3.0791$

3. Subtract. $59.6 - 3.925$

4. **Concept Check** Explain how you perform the correct borrowing and correct use of the decimal point if you subtract $567.45 - 345.9872$.

SECTION 4 MULTIPLYING DECIMALS

 Multiplying a Decimal by a Decimal or a Whole Number

We learned previously that the product of two fractions is the product of the numerators over the product of the denominators. For example,

$$\frac{3}{10} \times \frac{7}{100} = \frac{21}{1000}$$

In decimal form this product would be written

$$\underbrace{0.3}_{\text{one decimal place}} \times \underbrace{0.07}_{\text{two decimal places}} = \underbrace{0.021}_{\text{three decimal places}}$$

MULTIPLICATION OF DECIMALS

1. Multiply the numbers just as you would multiply whole numbers.
2. Find the sum of the numbers of decimal places in the two factors.
3. Place the decimal point in the product so that the product has the same number of decimal places as the sum in step 2. You may need to write zeros to the left of the number found in step 1.

Now use these steps to do the preceding multiplication problem.

EXAMPLE 1 Multiply. 0.07×0.3

Solution

0.07	2 decimal places
× 0.3	1 decimal place
0.021	3 decimal places in product (2 + 1 = 3)

Practice Problem 1 Multiply. 0.09×0.6

When performing the calculation, it is usually easier to place the factor with the smallest number of nonzero digits underneath the other factor.

EXAMPLE 2 Multiply.

(a) 0.38×0.26 **(b)** 12.64×0.572

Solution

(a)

0.38	2 decimal places
× 0.26	2 decimal places
228	
76	
0.0988	4 decimal places (2 + 2 = 4)

Note that we need to insert a zero before the 988.

(b)

12.64	2 decimal places
×0.572	3 decimal places
25 28	
884 8	
6 320	
7.230 08	5 decimal places (2 + 3 = 5)

Student Learning Objectives

After studying this section, you will be able to:

1. Multiply a decimal by a decimal or a whole number.
2. Multiply a decimal by a power of 10.

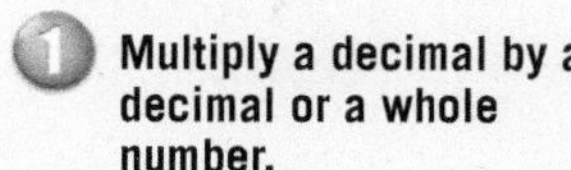

Calculator

Multiplying Decimals

You can use your calculator to multiply a decimal by a decimal. To find 0.08×1.53 enter:

0.08 [×] 1.53 [=]

Display: [0.1224]

Practice Problem 2 Multiply.

(a) 0.47×0.28 **(b)** 0.436×18.39

When multiplying decimal fractions by a whole number, you need to remember that a whole number has no decimal places.

EXAMPLE 3 Multiply. 5.261×45

Solution

$$\begin{array}{rl} 5.261 & \text{3 decimal places} \\ \times \quad 45 & \text{0 decimal places} \\ \hline 26\,305 & \\ 210\,44 & \\ \hline 236.745 & \text{3 decimal places } (3 + 0 = 3) \end{array}$$

Practice Problem 3 Multiply. 0.4264×38

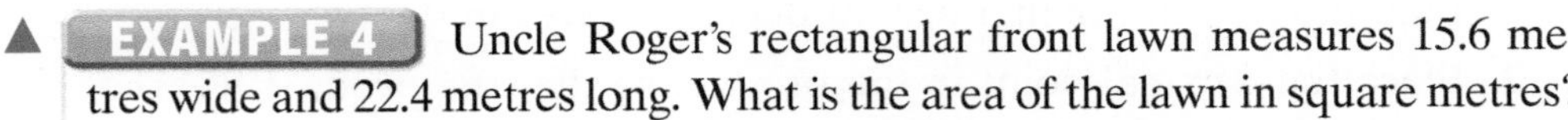

▲ **EXAMPLE 4** Uncle Roger's rectangular front lawn measures 15.6 metres wide and 22.4 metres long. What is the area of the lawn in square metres?

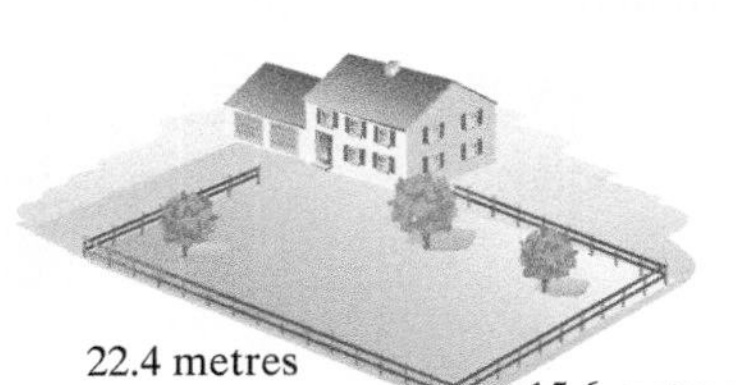

Solution Since the lawn is rectangular, we will use the fact that to find the area of a rectangle we multiply the length by the width.

$$\begin{array}{rl} 22.4 & \text{1 decimal place} \\ \times\ 15.6 & \text{1 decimal place} \\ \hline 13\,44 & \\ 112\,0 & \\ 224 & \\ \hline 349.44 & \text{2 decimal places} \end{array}$$

The area of the lawn is 349.44 square metres.

▲ **Practice Problem 4** A rectangular computer chip measures 1.26 millimetres wide and 2.3 millimetres long. What is the area of the chip in square millimetres?

2 Multiplying a Decimal by a Power of 10

Observe the following pattern.

one zero — Decimal point moved one place to the right.

$0.035 \times 10^1 = 0.035 \times 10 = 0.35$

two zeros — Decimal point moved two places to the right.

$0.035 \times 10^2 = 0.035 \times 100 = 3.5$

three zeros — Decimal point moved three places to the right.

$0.035 \times 10^3 = 0.035 \times 1000 = 35.$

MULTIPLICATION OF A DECIMAL BY A POWER OF 10

To multiply a decimal by a power of 10, move the decimal point to the right the same number of places as the number of zeros in the power of 10.

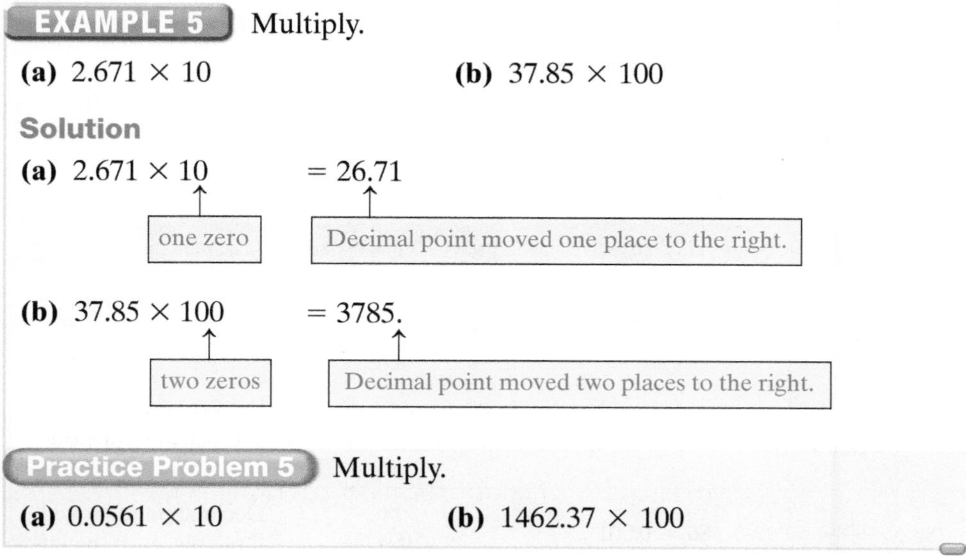

EXAMPLE 5 Multiply.

(a) 2.671×10 **(b)** 37.85×100

Solution

(a) $2.671 \times 10 = 26.71$

one zero
Decimal point moved one place to the right.

(b) $37.85 \times 100 = 3785.$

two zeros
Decimal point moved two places to the right.

Practice Problem 5 Multiply.

(a) 0.0561×10 **(b)** 1462.37×100

Sometimes it is necessary to add extra zeros before placing the decimal point in the answer.

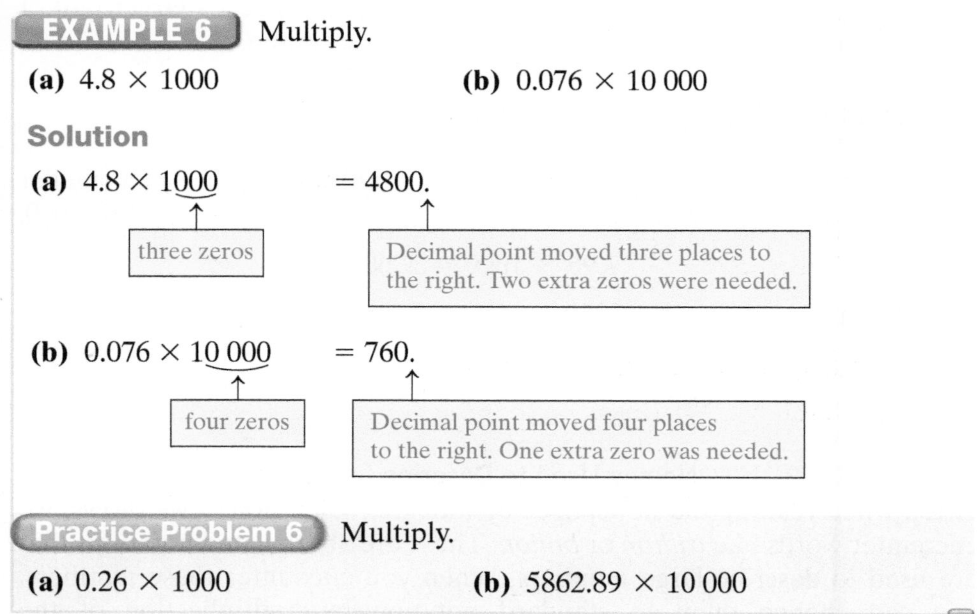

EXAMPLE 6 Multiply.

(a) 4.8×1000 **(b)** $0.076 \times 10\,000$

Solution

(a) $4.8 \times 1000 = 4800.$

three zeros
Decimal point moved three places to the right. Two extra zeros were needed.

(b) $0.076 \times 10\,000 = 760.$

four zeros
Decimal point moved four places to the right. One extra zero was needed.

Practice Problem 6 Multiply.

(a) 0.26×1000 **(b)** $5862.89 \times 10\,000$

If the number that is a power of 10 is in exponent form, move the decimal point to the right the same number of places as the number that is the exponent.

EXAMPLE 7 Multiply. 3.68×10^3

Solution

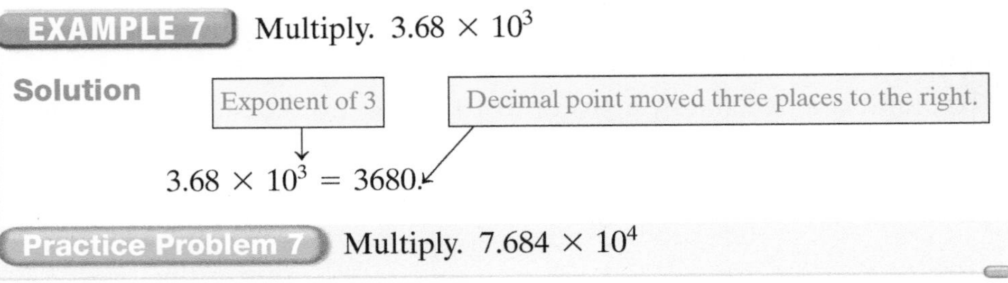
Exponent of 3
Decimal point moved three places to the right.
3.68 × 10³ = 3680.

$$3.68 \times 10^3 = 3680.$$

Practice Problem 7 Multiply. 7.684×10^4

SIDELIGHT: Moving the Decimal Point

Can you devise a quick rule to use when multiplying a decimal fraction by $\frac{1}{10}, \frac{1}{100}, \frac{1}{1000}$, and so on? How is it like the rules developed in this section? Consider a few examples:

Original Problem	Change Fraction to Decimal	Decimal Multiplication	Observation
$86 \times \frac{1}{10}$	86×0.1	$86 \times 0.1 = 8.6$	Decimal point moved one place to the left.
$86 \times \frac{1}{100}$	86×0.01	$86 \times 0.01 = 0.86$	Decimal point moved two places to the left.
$86 \times \frac{1}{1000}$	86×0.001	$86 \times 0.001 = 0.086$	Decimal point moved three places to the left.

Can you think of a way to describe a rule that you could use in solving this type of problem without going through all the foregoing steps?

You use multiplying by a power of 10 when you convert a larger unit of measure to a smaller unit of measure in the metric system.

1 kilometre

1000 metres

EXAMPLE 8 Change 2.96 kilometres to metres.

Solution Since we are going from a larger unit of measure to a smaller one, we multiply. There are 1000 metres in 1 kilometre. Multiply 2.96 by 1000.

$$2.96 \times 1000 = 2960$$

2.96 kilometres is equal to 2960 metres.

Practice Problem 8 Change 156.2 kilometres to metres.

TO THINK ABOUT: Names Used to Describe Large Numbers

Often when reading the newspaper or watching television news shows, we encounter words like *trillion* or *billion*. These are abbreviated notations that are used to describe large numbers. When you encounter these numbers, you can change them to standard notation by multiplication of the appropriate value.

For example, if someone says that the population of China is 1.31 billion people, we can write 1.31 billion = 1.31×1 billion = $1.31 \times 1\,000\,000\,000$ = 1 310 000 000. If someone says the population of Toronto is 2.48 million people, we can write

$$2.48 \text{ million} = 2.48 \times 1 \text{ million} = 2.48 \times 1\,000\,000 = 2\,480\,000.$$

SECTION 4 EXERCISES

Multiply.

Verbal and Writing Skills

1. Explain in your own words how to determine where to put the decimal point in the answer when you multiply 0.67×0.08.

2. Explain in your own words how to determine where to put the decimal point in the answer when you multiply 3.45×0.9.

3. Explain in your own words how to determine where to put the decimal point in the answer when you multiply 0.0078×100.

4. Explain in your own words how to determine where to put the decimal point in the answer when you multiply 5.0807 by 1000.

5. $\begin{array}{r} 0.6 \\ \times 0.2 \\ \hline \end{array}$

6. $\begin{array}{r} 0.9 \\ \times 0.3 \\ \hline \end{array}$

7. $\begin{array}{r} 0.12 \\ \times \ 0.5 \\ \hline \end{array}$

8. $\begin{array}{r} 0.17 \\ \times \ 0.4 \\ \hline \end{array}$

9. $\begin{array}{r} 0.0036 \\ \times \quad 0.8 \\ \hline \end{array}$

10. $\begin{array}{r} 0.067 \\ \times \ 0.07 \\ \hline \end{array}$

11. $\begin{array}{r} 452 \\ \times 0.12 \\ \hline \end{array}$

12. $\begin{array}{r} 316 \\ \times 0.24 \\ \hline \end{array}$

13. $\begin{array}{r} 0.043 \\ \times 0.012 \\ \hline \end{array}$

14. $\begin{array}{r} 0.037 \\ \times 0.011 \\ \hline \end{array}$

15. $\begin{array}{r} 10.97 \\ \times \ 0.06 \\ \hline \end{array}$

16. $\begin{array}{r} 18.07 \\ \times \ 0.05 \\ \hline \end{array}$

17. $\begin{array}{r} 3423 \\ \times \ 0.8 \\ \hline \end{array}$

18. $\begin{array}{r} 5119 \\ \times \ 0.7 \\ \hline \end{array}$

19. $\begin{array}{r} 2.163 \\ \times 0.008 \\ \hline \end{array}$

20. $\begin{array}{r} 1.892 \\ \times 0.007 \\ \hline \end{array}$

21. $\begin{array}{r} 0.7613 \\ \times \ 1009 \\ \hline \end{array}$

22. $\begin{array}{r} 0.6178 \\ \times \ 5004 \\ \hline \end{array}$

23. $\begin{array}{r} 2350 \\ \times \ 3.6 \\ \hline \end{array}$

24. $\begin{array}{r} 3720 \\ \times \ 8.1 \\ \hline \end{array}$

25. 4.57×11.8

26. 73.2×2.45

27. 0.001×6523.7

28. 0.01×826.75

Applications

29. ***Car Payments*** Kenny is making car payments of \$155.40 per month for the next 60 months. How much will he have spent in car payments after he sends in his final payment?

30. ***Food Purchase*** Each carton of ice cream contains 1.89 litres. Paul stocked his freezer with 25 cartons. How many total litres of ice cream did he buy?

31. ***Personal Income*** Mei Lee works for a forest and conservation company and earns \$12.35 per hour for a 40-hour week. How much does she earn in one week?

32. ***Personal Income*** Barry works as a fitness trainer and earns \$14.75 per hour for a 40-hour week. How much does he earn in one week?

▲**33.** ***Geometry*** Ralph and Darlene are getting new carpet in their bedroom and need to find how many square feet they need to purchase. The dimensions of their rectangular bedroom are 15.5 feet and 19.2 feet. What is the area of the room in square feet?

▲**34.** ***Geometry*** Sal is having his driveway paved by a company that charges by the square metre. Sal's driveway measures 8.6 metres by 17.5 metres. How many square metres is his driveway?

35. ***Student Loan*** Dwight is paying off a student loan at Westmont College with payments of $36.90 per month for the next 18 months. How much will he pay off during the next 18 months?

36. ***Car Payments*** Marcia is making car payments to Chevrolet West of $230.50 per month for 16 more months. How much will she pay for car payments in the next 16 months?

37. ***Fuel Efficiency*** Steve's car gets approximately 20.4 kilometres per litre. His gas tank holds 47.5 litres. Approximately how many kilometres can he travel on a full tank of gas?

38. ***Fuel Efficiency*** Caleb's 4 × 4 truck gets approximately 12.6 kilometres per litre. His gas tank holds 47.5 litres. Approximately how many kilometres can he travel on a full tank of gas? Compare this to your answer in exercise 37.

Multiply.

39. 2.86×10

40. 1.98×10

41. 52.125×100

42. 86.375×100

43. 22.615×1000

44. 34.105×1000

45. $5.609\,82 \times 10\,000$

46. $1.279\,86 \times 10\,000$

47. $17\,561.44 \times 10^2$

48. 7163.241×10^2

49. 816.32×10^3

50. 763.49×10^4

Applications

51. ***Metric Conversion*** To convert from metres to centimetres, multiply by 100. How many centimetres are in 5.932 metres?

52. ***Metric Conversion*** One metre is about 39.36 inches. About how many inches are in 100 metres?

53. ***Metric Conversion*** One metre is about 3.281 feet. How many feet are in 1000 metres?

54. ***Stock Market*** Jeremy bought 1000 shares of stock, each worth $1.45. How much did Jeremy spend on the stock?

55. ***Personal Finance*** In May, Ellen received a $925.75 tax refund. She decided to spend the money on some gifts. She spent $95.00 on her parents' anniversary gift, $47.50 on each of her two cousins' graduation gifts, and $39.25 on each of her three nieces' birthday gifts. How much money does she have left over?

56. ***Pet Cats*** Tomba is a beautiful orange tabby cat. When he was found by the side of the road, he was three weeks old and weighed 0.45 kg. At the age of three months, he weighed 1.85 kg. At the age of nine months, he weighed 3.30 kg; at one year, he weighed 5.7 kg. Today, Tomba the cat is $1\frac{1}{2}$ years old, and weighs 6.75 kg.

(a) How much weight did he gain?

(b) If the veterinarian wants him to lose 0.15 kg per week until he weighs 6 kg, how long will it take?

▲**57.** ***Geometry*** The college is purchasing new carpeting for the learning centre. What is the price of a carpet that is 19.6 yards wide and 254.2 yards long if the cost is $12.50 per square yard?

58. ***Jewellery Store Operations*** A jewellery store purchased long lengths of gold chain, which will be cut and made into necklaces and bracelets. The store purchased 3220 grams of gold chain at $3.50 per gram.

(a) How much did the jewellery store spend?

(b) If they sell a 28-gram gold necklace for $17.75 per gram, how much profit will they make on the necklace?

To Think About

59. State in your own words a rule for mental multiplication by 0.1, 0.01, 0.001, 0.0001, and so on.

60. State in your own words a rule for mental multiplication by 0.2, 0.02, 0.002, 0.0002, and so on.

Quick Quiz 4

1. Multiply. 0.76×0.04

2. Multiply. 25.6×0.128

3. Multiply. 5.162×10^4

4. **Concept Check** Explain how you know where to put the decimal point in the answer when you multiply 3.45×9.236.

How Am I Doing? Sections 1–4

1.
2.
3.
4.
5.
6.
7.
8.
9.
10.
11.
12.
13.
14.
15.
16.
17.
18.

How are you doing with your homework assignments in Sections 1 to 4? Do you feel you have mastered the material so far? Do you understand the concepts you have covered? Before you go further, take some time to do each of the following problems.

1

1. Write a word name for the decimal. 47.813

2. Express as a decimal. $\frac{567}{10\,000}$

Write as a fraction or a mixed number. Reduce whenever possible.

3. 4.09

4. 0.525

2

5. Place the set of numbers in the proper order from smallest to largest. 1.6, 1.59, 1.61, 1.601

6. Round to the nearest tenth. 123.492 68

7. Round to the nearest ten thousandth. 8.065 447

8. Round to the nearest hundredth. 17.985 23

3

Add.

9. $5.12 + 4.7 + 8.03 + 1.6$

10. $24.613 + 0.273 + 2.305$

Subtract.

11. $\begin{array}{r} 42.16 \\ -\ 31.57 \\ \hline \end{array}$

12. $26 - 18.329$

4

Multiply.

13. $\begin{array}{r} 11.67 \\ \times\ 0.03 \\ \hline \end{array}$

14. 4.7805×1000

15. $0.000\,379\,6 \times 10^5$

16. 3.14×2.5

17. 982×0.007

18. $0.000\,52 \times 0.006$

Your institution may have included the Answers to Selected Exercises for this module, which contains the answers to these questions. Each answer also includes a reference to the objective in which the problem is first taught. If you missed any of these problems, you should stop and review the Examples and Practice Problems in the referenced objective. A little review now will help you master the material in the upcoming sections.

SECTION 5 DIVIDING DECIMALS

 Dividing a Decimal by a Whole Number

When you divide a decimal by a whole number, place the decimal point for the quotient directly above the decimal point in the dividend. Then divide as if the numbers were whole numbers.

To divide 26.8 by 4, we place the decimal point of our answer (the quotient) directly *above* the decimal point in the dividend.

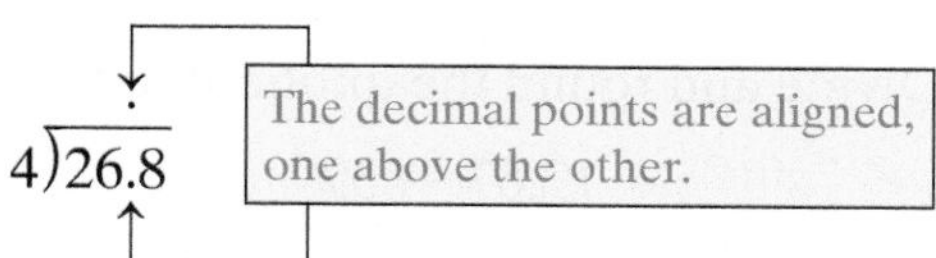

4)26.8
The decimal points are aligned, one above the other.

Then we divide as if we were dividing whole numbers.

```
   6.7   The quotient is 6.7.
4)26.8
  24
   2 8
   2 8
     0
```

The quotient to a problem may have all digits to the right of the decimal point. In some cases you will have to put a zero in the quotient as a "place holder." Let's divide 0.268 by 4.

```
  0.067
4)0.268
    24
     28
     28
      0
```

Note that we must have a zero after the decimal point in 0.067.

EXAMPLE 1 Divide.

(a) 9)0.3204 **(b)** 14)36.12

Solution

Note the zero *after* the decimal point.

```
(a)   0.0356            (b)    2.58
    9)0.3204               14)36.12
        27                    28
         50                    81
         45                    70
          54                   112
          54                   112
           0                     0
```

Practice Problem 1 Divide.

(a) 7)1.806 **(b)** 16)0.0928

NOTE TO STUDENT: Fully worked-out solutions to all of the Practice Problems can be found at the end of the module.

Student Learning Objectives

After studying this section, you will be able to:

 **Divide a decimal by a whole number.**

 **Divide a decimal by a decimal.**

Some division problems do not yield a remainder of zero. In such cases, we may be asked to round the answer to a specified place. To round when dividing, we carry out the division until our answer contains a digit that is one place to the right of that to which we intend to round. Then we round our answer to the specified place. For example, to round to the nearest thousandth, we carry out the division to the ten-thousandths place. In some division problems, you will need to write in zeros at the end of the dividend so that this division can be carried out.

EXAMPLE 2 Divide and round the quotient to the nearest thousandth.

$$12.67 \div 39$$

Solution We will carry out our division to the ten-thousandths place. Then we will round our answer to the nearest thousandth.

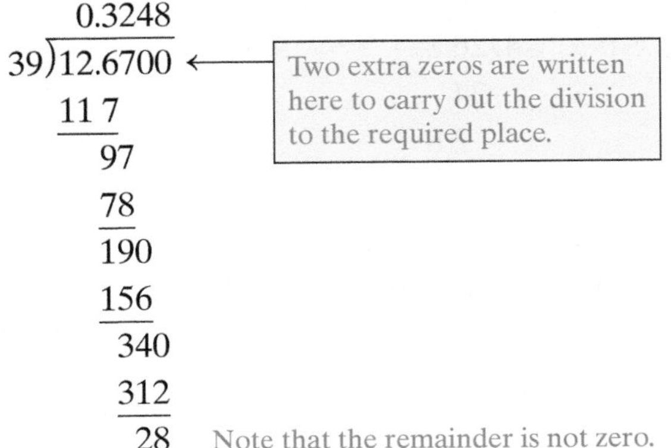

0.3248
39)12.6700
11 7
97
78
190
156
340
312
28
Two extra zeros are written here to carry out the division to the required place.
Note that the remainder is not zero.

Now we round 0.3248 to 0.325. The answer is rounded to the nearest thousandth.

Practice Problem 2 Divide and round the quotient to the nearest hundredth. $23.82 \div 46$

EXAMPLE 3 Maria paid $15.93 for 3 kilograms of tomatoes. How much did she pay per kilogram?

Solution The cost of one kilogram of tomatoes equals the total cost, $15.93, divided by 3 kilograms. Thus we will divide.

```
    5.31
 3)15.93
   15
    0 9
      9
     03
      3
      0
```

Maria paid $5.31 per kilogram for the tomatoes.

Practice Problem 3 Won Lin will pay off his auto loan for $3538.75 over 19 months. If the monthly payments are equal, how much will he pay each month?

 Dividing a Decimal by a Decimal

When the divisor is not a whole number, we can convert the division problem to an equivalent problem that has a whole number as a divisor. Think about the reasons why this procedure will work. We will ask you about it after you study Examples 4 and 5.

DIVIDING A DECIMAL BY A DECIMAL

1. Make the divisor a whole number by moving the decimal point to the right. Mark that position with a caret ($_\wedge$). Count the number of places the decimal point moved.
2. Move the decimal point in the dividend to the right the same number of places. Mark that position with a caret.
3. Place the decimal point of your answer directly above the caret marking the decimal point of the dividend.
4. Divide as with whole numbers.

EXAMPLE 4 **(a)** Divide. $0.08\overline{)1.632}$ **(b)** Divide. $1.352 \div 0.026$

Solution

(a) $0.08.\overline{)1.63.2}$ Move each decimal point two places to the right.

Place the decimal point of the answer directly above the caret.

$0.08_\wedge\overline{)1.63_\wedge 2}$ Mark the new position by a caret ($_\wedge$).

$$\begin{array}{r} 20.4 \\ 0.08_\wedge\overline{)1.63_\wedge 2} \\ \underline{16} \\ 3\ 2 \\ \underline{3\ 2} \\ 0 \end{array}$$

Perform the division.

The answer is 20.4.

(b)
$$\begin{array}{r} 52. \\ 0.026_\wedge\overline{)1.352_\wedge} \\ \underline{1\ 30} \\ 52 \\ \underline{52} \\ 0 \end{array}$$

Move each decimal point three places to the right and mark the new position by a caret.

The answer is 52.

Practice Problem 4 Divide.

(a) $0.09\overline{)0.1008}$ **(b)** $1.702 \div 0.037$

***NOTE TO STUDENT:** Fully worked-out solutions to all of the Practice Problems can be found at the end of the module.*

TO THINK ABOUT: The Multiplicative Identity Why do we move the decimal point to the right in the divisor and the dividend? What rule allows us to do this? How do we know the answer will be valid? We are actually using the property that multiplication of a fraction by 1 leaves the fraction unchanged. This is called the *multiplicative identity.* Let us examine Example 4(b) again. We will write $1.352 \div 0.026$ as a fraction.

$$\frac{1.352}{0.026} \times 1$$ Multiplication of a fraction by 1 does not change the value of the fraction.

$$= \frac{1.352}{0.026} \times \frac{1000}{1000}$$ We know that $\frac{1000}{1000} = 1$.

$$= \frac{1352}{26}$$ Multiplication by 1000 can be done by moving the decimal point three places to the right.

$$= 52$$ Divide the whole numbers.

Thus in Example 4(b) when we moved the decimal point three places to the right in the divisor and the dividend, we were actually creating an equivalent fraction where the numerator and the denominator of the original fraction were multiplied by 1000.

EXAMPLE 5 Divide.

(a) $1.7\overline{)0.0323}$

(b) $0.0032\overline{)7.68}$

Solution

(a)
$$\begin{array}{r} 0.019 \\ 1.7_\wedge\overline{)0.0_\wedge 323} \\ \underline{17} \\ 153 \\ \underline{153} \\ 0 \end{array}$$
Move the decimal point in the divisor and dividend one place to the right and mark that position with a caret.

(b)
$$\begin{array}{r} 2400. \\ 0.0032_\wedge\overline{)7.6800_\wedge} \\ \underline{6\,4} \\ 1\,28 \\ \underline{1\,28} \\ 000 \end{array}$$
Note that two extra zeros are needed in the dividend as we move the decimal point four places to the right.

Practice Problem 5 Divide.

(a) $1.8\overline{)0.0414}$

(b) $0.0036\overline{)8.316}$

EXAMPLE 6

(a) Find $2.9\overline{)431.2}$ rounded to the nearest tenth.

(b) Find $2.17\overline{)0.08}$ rounded to the nearest thousandth.

Solution

(a)
```
              14 8.68
     2.9^)431.2^00
          29
          141
          116
           25 2
           23 2
            2 0 0
            1 7 4
              2 60
              2 32
                28
```

Calculate to the hundredths place and round the answer to the nearest tenth.

The answer rounded to the nearest tenth is 148.7.

(b)
```
                 0.0368
     2.17^)0.08^0000
                6 51
                1 490
                1 302
                 1880
                 1736
                  144
```

Calculate to the ten-thousandths place and then round the answer. Rounding 0.0368 to the nearest thousandth, we obtain 0.037.

Calculator

Dividing Decimals

You can use your calculator to divide a decimal by a decimal. To find $21.38\overline{)54.53}$ rounded to the nearest hundredth, enter:

54.53 [÷] 21.38 [=]

Display:

[2.5505145]

This is an approximation. Some calculators will round to eight digits. The answer rounded to the nearest hundredth is 2.55.

Practice Problem 6

(a) Find $3.8\overline{)521.6}$ rounded to the nearest tenth.

(b) Find $8.05\overline{)0.17}$ rounded to the nearest thousandth.

EXAMPLE 7 John drove his 1997 Cavalier 210.25 kilometres to Sarnia. He used 14.5 litres of gas on the trip. How many kilometres per litre did his car get on the trip?

Solution To find kilometres per litre we need to divide the number of kilometres, 210.25, by the number of litres, 14.5.

```
            1 4.5
     14.5^)210.2^5
           145
            65 2
            58 0
             7 25
             7 25
                0
```

John's car achieved 14.5 kilometres per litre on the trip to Sarnia.

Practice Problem 7 Sarah rented a truck to move to Timmins. She drove 354.4 kilometres yesterday. She used 28.5 litres of gas on the trip. How many kilometres per litre did the rental truck get? Round to the nearest tenth.

EXAMPLE 8 Find the value of n if $0.8 \times n = 2.68$.

Solution Here 0.8 is multiplied by some number n to obtain 2.68. What is this number n? If we divide 2.68 by 0.8, we will find the value of n.

```
          3.35
     0.8^)2.6^80
          2 4
            2 8
            2 4
              40
              40
               0
```

Thus the value of n is 3.35.

Check. Is this true? Are we sure the value of $n = 3.35$?
We substitute the value of $n = 3.35$ into the equation to see if it makes the statement true.

$$0.8 \times n = 2.68$$
$$0.8 \times 3.35 \stackrel{?}{=} 2.68$$
$$2.68 = 2.68 \quad \checkmark \quad \text{Yes, it is true.}$$

Practice Problem 8 Find the value of n if $0.12 \times n = 0.696$.

EXAMPLE 9 The ground level ozone exposure in parts per billion is shown in the accompanying bar graph. Find the average amount of ozone at ground level over these four specific years.

Solution

First we take the sum of the four years.

$$\begin{array}{r} 35.6 \\ 35.8 \\ 34.9 \\ +\ 39.4 \\ \hline 145.7 \end{array}$$

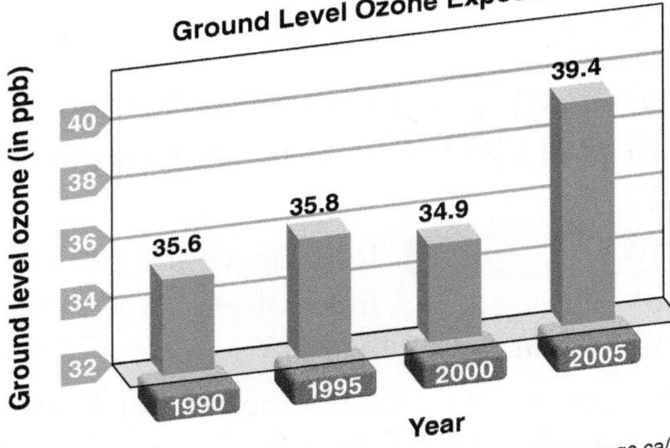

Source: Adapted from Statistics Canada, http://www41.statcan.gc.ca/2008/1762/grafx/htm/ceb1762_000_2-eng.htm#table, Oct-09

Then we divide by 4 to obtain the average.

$$\begin{array}{r} 36.425 \\ 4\overline{)145.700} \\ \underline{12} \\ 25 \\ \underline{24} \\ 17 \\ \underline{16} \\ 10 \\ \underline{8} \\ 20 \\ \underline{20} \\ 0 \end{array}$$

Thus the yearly average exposure is 36.425 parts per billion of ground level ozone.

Practice Problem 9 Use the accompanying bar graph to find the average level ozone exposure for the three years: 1990, 1995, and 2000. By how much does the three-year average differ from the four-year average?

Developing Your Study Skills

Exam Time: How To Review

Reviewing adequately for an exam enables you to bring together the concepts you have learned over several sections. For your review, you will need to do the following:

1. Reread your textbook. Make a list of any terms, rules, or formulas you need to know for the exam. Be sure you understand them all.
2. Reread your notes. Go over returned homework and quizzes. Redo the problems you missed.
3. Practise some of each type of problem covered in the module(s) you are to be tested on. In fact, it is a good idea to construct a practice test of your own and then discuss it with a friend from class.
4. Use the end-of-module materials provided. Read carefully through the Module Organizer. Do the Module Review Problems. Take the Module Test. When you are finished, check your answers. Redo any problems you missed.
5. Get help if any concepts give you difficulty.

Section 5 Exercises

Divide until there is a remainder of zero.

1. $6\overline{)12.6}$ **2.** $8\overline{)17.28}$ **3.** $4\overline{)71.32}$ **4.** $6\overline{)83.16}$

5. $7\overline{)73.64}$ **6.** $8\overline{)168.48}$ **7.** $0.6\overline{)81.9}$ **8.** $0.5\overline{)32.15}$

9. $0.2706 \div 0.05$ **10.** $0.6092 \div 0.08$ **11.** $153.7 \div 2.9$ **12.** $75.6 \div 3.6$

13. $68.4 \div 3.8$ **14.** $728 \div 5.6$ **15.** $40.30 \div 0.31$

Divide and round your answer to the nearest tenth.

16. $8\overline{)44}$ **17.** $9\overline{)47.31}$ **18.** $1.8\overline{)4.16}$

19. $1.9\overline{)2.36}$ **20.** $0.95\overline{)32.067}$ **21.** $0.85\overline{)41.901}$

Divide and round your answer to the nearest hundredth.

22. $4\overline{)263.82}$ **23.** $5\overline{)471.03}$ **24.** $1.7\overline{)20.8}$

25. $1.8\overline{)24.41}$ **26.** $24\overline{)3.126}$ **27.** $35\overline{)7.369}$

Divide and round your answer to the nearest thousandth.

28. $8\overline{)0.2019}$ **29.** $7\overline{)0.5681}$ **30.** $0.69\overline{)8.45}$ **31.** $0.87\overline{)79.40}$

Divide and round your answer to the nearest whole number.

32. $12\overline{)1396}$ **33.** $19\overline{)2341}$ **34.** $0.0024\overline{)0.2168}$ **35.** $0.0046\overline{)0.981}$

Applications

36. ***Travel in Mexico*** Americans Rhett and Liza are travelling in Mexico, where distances on the highway are given in kilometres. There are approximately 1.6 kilometres in one mile. They see a sign that reads "Mexico City: 342 km." How many miles is it to Mexico City?

37. ***Computer Payments*** The Millers want to use the latest technology to access the Internet from their home television system. The equipment needed to upgrade their existing equipment will cost $992.76. If the Millers make 12 equal monthly payments, how much will they pay per month?

38. ***Lasagna Dinner*** Four students sit down to their weekly lasagna dinner. At one end of the table, there is a bottle containing 67.6 centilitres of a popular soft drink. At the other end of the table is a bottle that contains 33.6 centilitres of water.

(a) If the students share the soft drink and water equally, how many centilitres of liquid will each student drink?

(b) At the last minute, another student is asked to join the group. How many centilitres of liquid will each of the five students share?

39. ***Fuel Efficiency*** Wally owns a car that travels 180 kilometres on 13.2 litres of gas. How many kilometres per litre does it achieve? (Round your answer to the nearest tenth.)

40. ***Costs of a Ski Trip*** The church youth group went on a ski trip. The ski resort charged the group \$1200 for 32 lift tickets. How much was each ticket?

41. ***Flower Sales*** Andrea makes Mother's Day bouquets each year for extra income. This year her goal is to make \$300. If she sells each bouquet for \$12.50, how many bouquets must she sell to reach her goal?

42. ***Outdoor Deck Payments*** Demitri had a contractor build an outdoor deck for his back porch. He now has \$1131.75 to pay off, and he agreed to pay \$125.75 per month. How many more payments on the outdoor deck must he make?

43. ***Wedding Reception Costs*** For their wedding reception, Sharon and Richard spent \$1865.50 on food and drinks. If the caterer charged them \$10.25 per person, how many guests did they have?

44. ***Record Rainfall***

(a) Using the chart below, find the average amount of precipitation for the months April, May, and June.

(b) On average, how much more precipitation does Mount Waialeale get per day in April than in March? (Use 30 days in a month, and round to the nearest thousandth.)

Month	Average Amount of Precipitation in Mount Waialeale, Hawaii, for January–June
January	24.78 in.
February	24.63 in.
March	27.24 in.
April	47.75 in.
May	28.34 in.
June	30.65 in.

Source: www.wrcc.dri.edu

45. ***Quality Inspection*** Yoshi is working as an inspector for a company that makes snowboards. A Mach 1 snowboard weighs 3.8 kilograms. How many of these snowboards are contained in a box in which the contents weigh 87.40 kilograms? If the box is labelled CONTENTS: 24 SNOWBOARDS, how great an error was made in packing the box?

Find the value of n.

46. $0.5 \times n = 3.55$

47. $0.3 \times n = 9.66$

48. $1.7 \times n = 129.2$

49. $1.3 \times n = 1267.5$

50. $n \times 0.063 = 2.835$

51. $n \times 0.098 = 4.312$

To Think About *Multiply the numerator and denominator of each fraction by 10 000. Then divide the numerator by the denominator. Is the result the same if we divide the original numerator by the original denominator? Why?*

52. $\dfrac{3.8702}{0.0523}$

53. $\dfrac{2.9356}{0.0716}$

Quick Quiz 5

1. Divide. $0.07\overline{)0.046\ 06}$

2. Divide. $0.52\overline{)1.694\ 16}$

3. Divide and round to the nearest hundredth.
$8\overline{)52.643}$

4. **Concept Check** Explain how you would know where to place the decimal point in the answer if you divided $0.173 \div 0.578$.

SECTION 6 CONVERTING FRACTIONS TO DECIMALS AND THE ORDER OF OPERATIONS

Student Learning Objectives

After studying this section, you will be able to:

 **Convert a fraction to a decimal.**

 **Use the order of operations with decimals.**

 Converting a Fraction to a Decimal

A number can be expressed in two equivalent forms: as a fraction or as a decimal.

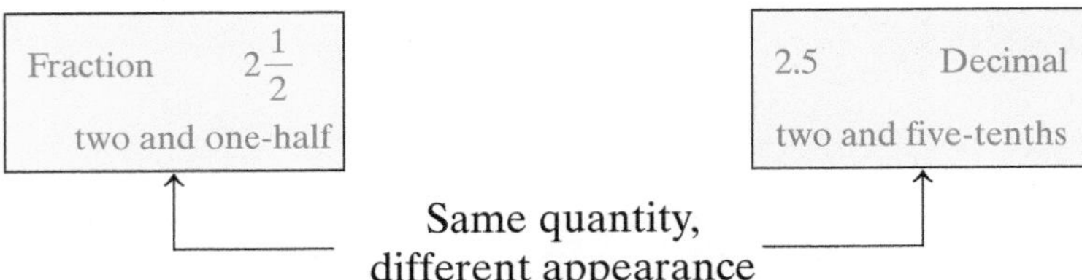

Every decimal in this module can be expressed as an equivalent fraction. For example,

Decimal form ⇒ fraction form

$$0.75 = \frac{75}{100} \quad \text{or} \quad \frac{3}{4}$$

$$0.5 = \frac{5}{10} \quad \text{or} \quad \frac{1}{2}$$

$$2.5 = 2\frac{5}{10} = 2\frac{1}{2} \quad \text{or} \quad \frac{5}{2}.$$

And every fraction can be expressed as an equivalent decimal, as we will learn in this section. For example,

Fraction form ⇒ decimal form

$$\frac{1}{5} = 0.20 \quad \text{or} \quad 0.2$$

$$\frac{3}{8} = 0.375$$

$$\frac{5}{11} = 0.4545\ldots \text{(The "45" keeps repeating.)}$$

Some of these decimal equivalents are so common that people find it helpful to memorize them. You would be wise to memorize the following equivalents:

$$\frac{1}{2} = 0.5 \qquad \frac{1}{4} = 0.25 \qquad \frac{1}{5} = 0.2 \qquad \frac{1}{10} = 0.1.$$

We previously studied how to convert some fractions with a denominator of 10, 100, 1000, and so on to decimal form. For example, $\frac{3}{10} = 0.3$ and $\frac{7}{100} = 0.07$. We need to develop a procedure to write other fractions, such as $\frac{3}{8}$ and $\frac{5}{16}$, in decimal form.

CONVERTING A FRACTION TO AN EQUIVALENT DECIMAL

Divide the denominator into the numerator until

(a) the remainder becomes zero, or

(b) the remainder repeats itself, or

(c) the desired number of decimal places is achieved.

EXAMPLE 1 Write as an equivalent decimal.

(a) $\frac{3}{8}$ **(b)** $\frac{31}{40}$ of a second

Divide the denominator into the numerator until the remainder becomes zero.

Solution

(a)
$$\begin{array}{r} 0.375 \\ 8\overline{)3.000} \\ \underline{2\ 4} \\ 60 \\ \underline{56} \\ 40 \\ \underline{40} \\ 0 \end{array}$$

Therefore, $\frac{3}{8} = 0.375$.

(b)
$$\begin{array}{r} 0.775 \\ 40\overline{)31.000} \\ \underline{28\ 0} \\ 3\ 00 \\ \underline{80} \\ 200 \\ \underline{200} \\ 0 \end{array}$$

Therefore, $\frac{31}{40} = 0.775$ of a second.

Practice Problem 1 Write as an equivalent decimal.

(a) $\frac{5}{16}$ **(b)** $\frac{11}{80}$

NOTE TO STUDENT: Fully worked-out solutions to all of the Practice Problems can be found at the end of the module.

Athletes' times in Olympic events, such as the 100-metre dash, are measured to the nearest hundredth of a second. Future Olympic athletes' times will be measured to the nearest thousandth of a second.

Decimals such as 0.375 and 0.775 are called **terminating decimals.** When converting $\frac{3}{8}$ to 0.375 or $\frac{31}{40}$ to 0.775, the division operation eventually yields a remainder of zero. Other fractions yield a repeating pattern. For example, $\frac{1}{3} = 0.3333\ldots$ and $\frac{2}{3} = 0.6666\ldots$ have a pattern of repeating digits. Decimals that have a digit or a group of digits that repeats are called **repeating decimals.** We often indicate the repeating pattern with a bar over the repeating group of digits:

$$0.3333\ldots = 0.\overline{3} \qquad 0.74\ 74\ 74\ \ldots = 0.\overline{74}$$
$$0.218\ 218\ 218\ \ldots = 0.\overline{218} \qquad 0.8942\ 8942\ \ldots = 0.\overline{8942}$$

If when converting fractions to decimal form the remainder repeats itself, we know that we have a repeating decimal.

EXAMPLE 2 Write as an equivalent decimal.

(a) $\frac{5}{11}$ **(b)** $\frac{13}{22}$ **(c)** $\frac{5}{37}$

Solution

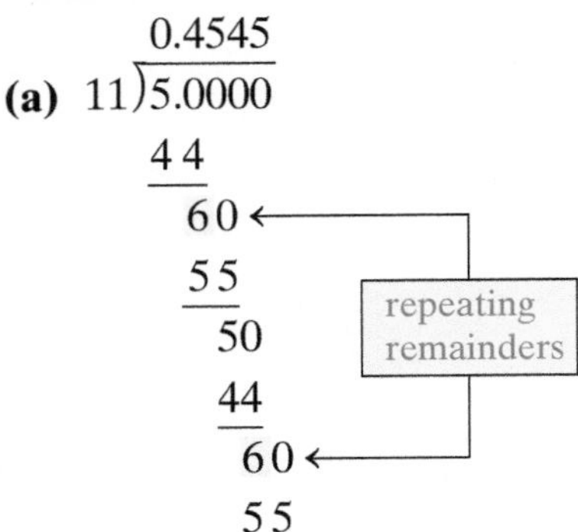

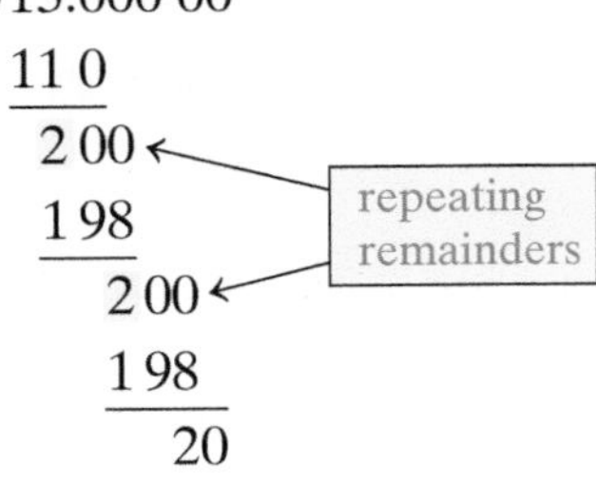

(c)

$$\begin{array}{r} 0.1351 \\ 37\overline{)5.0000} \\ \underline{37} \\ 130 \\ \underline{111} \\ 190 \\ \underline{185} \\ 50 \\ \underline{37} \\ 13 \end{array}$$

repeating remainders

Thus $\frac{5}{11} = 0.4545\ldots = 0.\overline{45}$.

Thus $\frac{13}{22} = 0.590\,909\,0\ \ldots = 0.5\overline{90}$.

Notice that the bar is over the digits 9 and 0 but *not* over the digit 5.

Thus $\frac{5}{37} = 0.135\,135\ldots = 0.\overline{135}$.

Practice Problem 2 Write as an equivalent decimal.

(a) $\frac{7}{11}$ **(b)** $\frac{8}{15}$ **(c)** $\frac{13}{44}$

EXAMPLE 3 Write as an equivalent decimal.

(a) $3\frac{7}{15}$ **(b)** $\frac{20}{11}$

Solution

(a) $3\frac{7}{15}$ means $3 + \frac{7}{15}$

$$\begin{array}{r} 0.466 \\ 15\overline{)7.000} \\ \underline{60} \\ 100 \\ \underline{90} \\ 100 \\ \underline{90} \\ 10 \end{array}$$

Thus $\frac{7}{15} = 0.4\overline{6}$ and $3\frac{7}{15} = 3.4\overline{6}$.

(b)

$$\begin{array}{r} 1.818 \\ 11\overline{)20.000} \\ \underline{11} \\ 90 \\ \underline{88} \\ 20 \\ \underline{11} \\ 90 \\ \underline{88} \\ 2 \end{array}$$

Thus $\frac{20}{11} = 1.818\,181\ldots = 1.\overline{81}$.

Practice Problem 3 Write as an equivalent decimal.

(a) $2\frac{11}{18}$ **(b)** $\frac{28}{27}$

Calculator

Fraction to Decimal

You can use a calculator to change $\frac{5}{8}$ to a decimal.

Enter:

5 [÷] 8 [=]

The display should read

[0.625]

Try the following.

(a) $\frac{17}{25}$ **(b)** $\frac{2}{9}$

(c) $\frac{13}{10}$ **(d)** $\frac{15}{19}$

Note: 0.789 473 68 is an approximation for $\frac{15}{19}$. Some calculators round to only eight places.

In some cases, the pattern of repeating is quite long. For example,

$$\frac{1}{7} = 0.142\,857\,142\,857\ldots = 0.\overline{142\,857}$$

Such problems are often rounded to a certain value.

EXAMPLE 4 Express $\frac{5}{7}$ as a decimal rounded to the nearest thousandth.

Solution

$$\begin{array}{r} 0.7142 \\ 7\overline{)5.0000} \\ \underline{4\,9} \\ 10 \\ \underline{7} \\ 30 \\ \underline{28} \\ 20 \\ \underline{14} \\ 6 \end{array}$$

Rounding to the nearest thousandth, we round 0.7142 to 0.714. (In repeating form, $\frac{5}{7} = 0.714\,285\,714\,285\ldots = 0.\overline{714\,285}$.)

Practice Problem 4 Express $\frac{19}{24}$ as a decimal rounded to the nearest thousandth.

NOTE TO STUDENT: Fully worked-out solutions to all of the Practice Problems can be found at the end of the module.

Recall that we studied placing two decimals in order in Section 2. If we are required to place a fraction and a decimal in order, it is usually easiest to change the fraction to decimal form and then compare the two decimals.

EXAMPLE 5 Fill in the blank with one of the symbols <, =, or >.

Solution

$$\frac{7}{16} \ \_\_\_ \ 0.43$$

Now we divide to find the decimal equivalent of $\frac{7}{16}$.

$$\begin{array}{r} 0.4375 \\ 16\overline{)7.0000} \\ \underline{6\,4} \\ 60 \\ \underline{48} \\ 120 \\ \underline{112} \\ 80 \\ \underline{80} \\ 0 \end{array}$$

Now in the thousandths place $7 > 0$, so we know

$$0.43\,7\,5 > 0.43\,0\,0.$$

Therefore, $\frac{7}{16} > 0.43$.

Practice Problem 5 Fill in the blank with one of the symbols $<$, $=$, or $>$.

$$\frac{5}{8} \_\_\_\_ 0.63$$

Using the Order of Operations with Decimals

The rules for order of operations apply to operations with decimals.

ORDER OF OPERATIONS

Do first ↓ Do last

1. Perform operations inside parentheses.
2. Simplify any expressions with exponents.
3. Multiply or divide from left to right.
4. Add or subtract from left to right.

Sometimes exponents are used with decimals. In such cases, we merely evaluate using repeated multiplication.

$$(0.2)^2 = 0.2 \times 0.2 = 0.04$$
$$(0.2)^3 = 0.2 \times 0.2 \times 0.2 = 0.008$$
$$(0.2)^4 = 0.2 \times 0.2 \times 0.2 \times 0.2 = 0.0016$$

EXAMPLE 6 Evaluate. $(0.3)^3 + 0.6 \times 0.2 + 0.013$

Solution First we need to evaluate $(0.3)^3 = 0.3 \times 0.3 \times 0.3 = 0.027$. Thus

$$(0.3)^3 + 0.6 \times 0.2 + 0.013$$
$$= 0.027 + 0.6 \times 0.2 + 0.013$$
$$= 0.027 + 0.12 + 0.013$$

⟵ When addends have a different number of decimal places, writing the problem in column form makes adding easier.

$$\begin{array}{r} 0.027 \\ 0.120 \\ +\ 0.013 \\ \hline 0.160 \end{array}$$

$$= 0.16$$

Practice Problem 6 Evaluate. $0.3 \times 0.5 + (0.4)^3 - 0.036$

In the next example, all four steps of the rules for order of operations will be used.

EXAMPLE 7 Evaluate. $(8 - 0.12) \div 2^3 + 5.68 \times 0.1$

Solution

$(8 - 0.12) \div 2^3 + 5.68 \times 0.1$

$= 7.88 \div 2^3 + 5.68 \times 0.1$ First do subtraction inside the parentheses.

$= 7.88 \div 8 + 5.68 \times 0.1$ Simplify the expression with an exponent.

$= 0.985 + 0.568$ From left to right do division and multiplication.

$= 1.553$ Add the final two numbers.

Practice Problem 7 Evaluate. $6.56 \div (2 - 0.36) + (8.5 - 8.3)^2$

***NOTE TO STUDENT:** Fully worked-out solutions to all of the Practice Problems can be found at the end of the module.*

Take the time to review these seven Examples and seven Practice Problems. This is an important skill to master. Some careful review will help you to work the homework exercises much more quickly and accurately.

Developing Your Study Skills

Keep Trying

We live in a highly technical world, and you cannot afford to give up on the study of mathematics. Dropping mathematics may prevent you from entering certain career fields that you may find interesting. You may not have to take math courses as high-level as calculus, but such courses as intermediate algebra, finite math, college algebra, and trigonometry may be necessary. Learning mathematics can open new doors for you.

Learning mathematics is a process that takes time and effort. You will find that regular study and daily practice are necessary to strengthen your skills and to help you grow academically. This process will lead you toward success in mathematics. Then, as you become more successful, your confidence in your ability to do mathematics will grow.

SECTION 6 EXERCISES

Verbal and Writing Skills

1. 0.75 and $\frac{3}{4}$ are different ways to express the ____________.

2. To convert a fraction to an equivalent decimal, divide the ____________ into the numerator.

3. Why is $0.\overline{8942}$ called a repeating decimal?

4. The order of operations for decimals is the same as the order of operations for whole numbers. Write the steps for the order of operations.

Write as an equivalent decimal. If a repeating decimal is obtained, use notation such as $0.\overline{7}$, $0.\overline{16}$, *or* $0.\overline{245}$.

5. $\frac{1}{4}$ **6.** $\frac{3}{4}$ **7.** $\frac{4}{5}$ **8.** $\frac{2}{5}$

9. $\frac{1}{8}$ **10.** $\frac{3}{8}$ **11.** $\frac{7}{20}$ **12.** $\frac{3}{40}$

13. $\frac{31}{50}$ **14.** $\frac{23}{25}$ **15.** $\frac{9}{4}$ **16.** $\frac{14}{5}$

17. $2\frac{7}{8}$ **18.** $3\frac{13}{16}$ **19.** $5\frac{3}{16}$ **20.** $2\frac{5}{12}$

21. $\frac{2}{3}$ **22.** $\frac{5}{6}$ **23.** $\frac{5}{11}$ **24.** $\frac{7}{11}$

25. $3\frac{7}{12}$ **26.** $7\frac{1}{3}$ **27.** $4\frac{2}{9}$ **28.** $8\frac{7}{9}$

Write as an equivalent decimal or a decimal approximation. Round your answer to the nearest thousandth if needed.

29. $\frac{4}{13}$ **30.** $\frac{8}{17}$ **31.** $\frac{19}{21}$ **32.** $\frac{20}{21}$

33. $\frac{7}{48}$ **34.** $\frac{5}{48}$ **35.** $\frac{57}{28}$ **36.** $\frac{15}{7}$

37. $\frac{21}{52}$ **38.** $\frac{1}{38}$ **39.** $\frac{17}{18}$ **40.** $\frac{5}{13}$

41. $\frac{22}{7}$ **42.** $\frac{17}{14}$ **43.** $3\frac{9}{19}$ **44.** $4\frac{11}{17}$

Fill in the blank with one of the symbols $<$, $=$, *or* $>$.

45. $\frac{7}{8}$ ___ 0.88 **46.** $\frac{10}{11}$ ___ 0.9 **47.** 0.07 ___ $\frac{1}{16}$ **48.** 0.9 ___ $\frac{15}{16}$

Applications

49. ***Toronto Stock Exchange*** One day in February 2007, the value of one share of Nortel stock decreased by $\frac{7}{25}$ of a dollar. Write the amount of decrease as a decimal.

50. ***Toronto Stock Exchange*** One day in January 2010, the value of one share of Bank of Nova Scotia stock increased by $\frac{39}{50}$ of a dollar. Write the amount of increase as a decimal.

51. ***Women's Shoe Sizes*** A size 7 women's shoe measures 23.6 cm and a size $7\frac{1}{2}$ measures 24.1 cm. What is the difference in length between a size 7 and a size $7\frac{1}{2}$ shoe?

52. ***Men's Shoe Sizes*** A size $9\frac{1}{2}$ men's shoe measures 26.7 cm and a size 10 measures 27.2 cm. What is the difference in length between a size $9\frac{1}{2}$ and a size 10 shoe?

53. ***Safety Regulations*** Federal safety regulations specify that the slots between the bars on a baby's crib must not be more than $2\frac{3}{8}$ inches. One crib's slots measured 2.4 inches apart. Is this too wide? If so, by how much?

54. ***Manufacturing*** To manufacture a circuit board, Rick must program a computer to place a piece of thin plastic atop a circuit board. For the current to flow through the circuit, the top plastic piece must form a border of exactly $\frac{1}{16}$ cm with the circuit board. A few circuit boards were made with a border of 0.055 cm by accident. Is this border too small or too large? By how much?

Evaluate.

55. $2.4 + (0.5)^2 - 0.35$

56. $9.6 + 3.6 - (0.4)^2$

57. $2.3 \times 3.2 - 5 \times 0.8$

58. $9.6 \div 3 + 0.21 \times 6$

59. $12 \div 0.03 - 50 \times (0.5 + 1.5)^3$

60. $61.95 \div 1.05 - 2 \times (1.7 + 1.3)^3$

61. $(1.1)^3 + 2.6 \div 0.13 + 0.083$

62. $(1.1)^3 + 8.6 \div 2.15 - 0.086$

63. $(14.73 - 14.61)^2 \div (1.18 + 0.82)$

64. $(32.16 - 32.02)^2 \div (2.24 + 1.76)$

65. $(0.5)^3 + (3 - 2.6) \times 0.5$

66. $(0.6)^3 + (7 - 6.3) \times 0.07$

67. $(0.76 + 4.24) \div 0.25 + 8.6$

68. $(2.4)^2 + 3.6 \div (1.2 - 0.7)$

Evaluate.

69. $(1.6)^3 + (2.4)^2 + 18.666 \div 3.05 + 4.86$

70. $5.9 \times 3.6 \times 2.4 - 0.1 \times 0.2 \times 0.3 \times 0.4$

Write as a decimal. Round your answer to six decimal places.

71. $\frac{5236}{8921}$

72. $\frac{17\,359}{19\,826}$

To Think About

73. Subtract. $0.\overline{16} - 0.00\overline{16}$

(a) What do you obtain?

(b) Now subtract $0.\overline{16} - 0.01\overline{6}$. What do you obtain?

(c) What is different about these results?

74. Subtract. $1.\overline{89} - 0.01\overline{89}$

(a) What do you obtain?

(b) Now subtract $1.\overline{89} - 0.18\overline{9}$. What do you obtain?

(c) What is different about these results?

Quick Quiz 6

1. Write as an equivalent decimal. $3\frac{9}{16}$

2. Write as an equivalent decimal. Round your answer to the nearest hundredth. $\frac{5}{17}$

3. Perform the operations in the proper order.
$(0.7)^2 + 1.92 \div 0.3 - 0.79$

4. **Concept Check** Explain how you would perform the operations in the calculation
$45.78 - (3.42 - 2.09)^2 \times 0.4$.

SECTION 7 ESTIMATING AND SOLVING APPLIED PROBLEMS INVOLVING DECIMALS

Estimating Sums, Differences, Products, and Quotients of Decimals

When we encounter real-life applied problems, it is important to know if an answer is reasonable. A car may get 21.8 kilometres per litre. However, a car will not get 218 kilometres per litre. Neither will a car get 2.18 kilometres per litre. To avoid making an error in solving applied problems, it is wise to make an estimate. The most useful time to make an estimate is at the end of solving the problem, in order to see if the answer is reasonable.

There are several different rules for estimating. Not all mathematicians agree on what is the best method for estimating in each case. Most students find that a very quick and simple method to estimate is to round each number so that there is one nonzero digit. Then perform the calculation. We will use that approach in this section. However, you should be aware that there are other valid approaches. Your instructor may wish you to use another method.

Student Learning Objectives

After studying this section, you will be able to:

 **Estimate sums, differences, products, and quotients of decimals.**

 **Solve applied problems using operations with decimals.**

EXAMPLE 1 Estimate.

(a) 184 987.09 + 676 393.95 **(b)** 0.007 82 − 0.003 58

(c) 145.87 × 78.323 **(d)** 138.85 ÷ 5.887

Solution In each case we will round to one nonzero digit to estimate.

(a) 184 987.09 + 676 393.95 ≈ 200 000 + 700 000 = 900 000

(b) 0.007 82 − 0.003 58 ≈ 0.008 − 0.004 = 0.004

(c) 145.87 × 78.323 ≈

$$\begin{array}{r} 100 \\ \times\ 80 \\ \hline 8000 \end{array}$$

Thus 145.87 × 78.323 ≈ 8000

(d) 138.85 ÷ 5.887 ≈

$$\begin{array}{r} 16 \\ 6\overline{)100} \\ \underline{6} \\ 40 \\ \underline{36} \\ 4 \end{array} = 16\frac{4}{6} \approx 17$$

Thus 138.85 ÷ 5.887 ≈ 17

Here we round the answer to the nearest whole number.

Practice Problem 1 Round to one nonzero digit. Then estimate the result of the indicated calculation.

(a) 385.98 + 875.34 **(b)** 0.0932 − 0.0579

(c) 5876.34 × 0.087 **(d)** 46 873 ÷ 8.456

NOTE TO STUDENT: Fully worked-out solutions to all of the Practice Problems can be found at the end of the module.

Take a few minutes to review Example 1. Be sure you can perform these estimation steps. We will use this type of estimation to check our work in the applied problems in this section.

 Solving Applied Problems Using Operations with Decimals

To analyze applied-problem situations, we must:

1. *Understand the problem.*
2. *Solve and state the answer.*
3. *Check.*

In Canada, for almost all jobs where you are paid an hourly wage, if you work more than 40 hours in one week, you should be paid overtime. The overtime rate is 1.5 times the normal hourly rate, for the extra hours worked in that week. The next problem deals with overtime wages.

EXAMPLE 2 A labourer is paid \$7.38 per hour for a 40-hour week and 1.5 times that wage for any hours worked beyond the standard 40. If he works 47 hours in a week, what will he earn?

Solution

1. ***Understand the problem.***

Mathematics Blueprint for Problem Solving

Gather the Facts	What Am I Asked to Do?	How Do I Proceed?	Key Points to Remember
He works 47 hours. He gets paid \$7.38 per hour for 40 hours. He gets paid 1.5 × \$7.38 per hour for 7 hours.	Find the earnings of the labourer if he works 47 hours in one week.	Add the earnings of 40 hours at \$7.38 per hour to the earnings of 7 hours at overtime pay.	Multiply 1.5 × \$7.38 to find the pay he earns for overtime.

2. ***Solve and state the answer.***

We want to compute his regular pay and his overtime pay and add the results.

Regular pay + Overtime pay = Total pay

Regular pay: Calculate his pay for 40 hours of work.

$$\begin{array}{r} 7.38 \\ \times\ \ 40 \\ \hline 295.20 \end{array}$$

He earns \$295.20 at \$7.38 per hour.

Overtime pay: Calculate his overtime pay rate. This is 7.38 × 1.5.

$$\begin{array}{r} 7.38 \\ \times\ 1.5 \\ \hline 3\ 690 \\ 7\ 38 \\ \hline 11.070 \end{array}$$

He earns \$11.07 per hour in overtime.

Calculate how much he earned doing 7 hours of overtime work.

$$\begin{array}{r} 11.07 \\ \times \quad 7 \\ \hline 77.49 \end{array}$$

For 7 overtime hours he earns \$77.49.

Total pay: Add the two amounts.

$$\begin{array}{rl} \$295.20 & \text{Regular 40-hour-week earnings} \\ +\quad 77.49 & \text{Overtime earnings} \\ \hline \$372.69 & \text{Total earnings} \end{array}$$

A. Ramey/Woodfin Camp & Associates, Inc.

The total earnings of the labourer for a 47-hour workweek will be \$372.69.

3. ***Check.***
Estimate his regular pay.

$$40 \times \$7 = \$280$$

Estimate his overtime rate of pay, and then his overtime pay.

$$2 \times \$7 = \$14$$
$$7 \times \$10 = \$70$$

Then add.

$$\begin{array}{r} \$280 \\ +\quad 70 \\ \hline \$350 \end{array}$$

Our estimate of \$350 is close to our answer of \$372.69. Our answer is reasonable. ✓

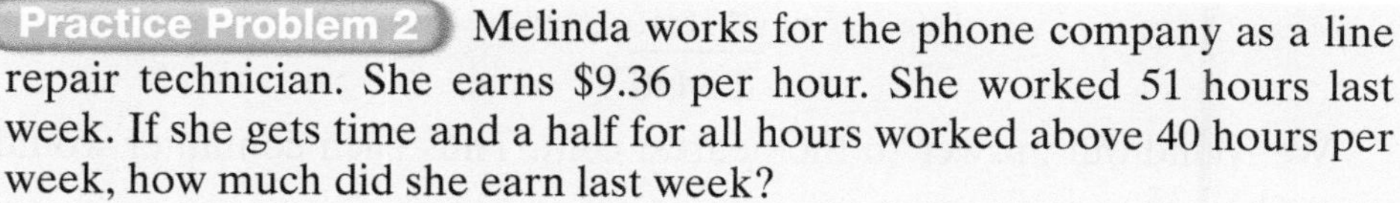
Practice Problem 2 Melinda works for the phone company as a line repair technician. She earns \$9.36 per hour. She worked 51 hours last week. If she gets time and a half for all hours worked above 40 hours per week, how much did she earn last week?

***NOTE TO STUDENT:** Fully worked-out solutions to all of the Practice Problems can be found at the end of the module.*

EXAMPLE 3 A chemist is testing 36.85 litres of cleaning fluid. She wishes to pour it into several smaller containers that each hold 0.67 litre of fluid. (a) How many containers will she need? (b) If each litre of this fluid costs \$3.50, how much does the cleaning fluid in one container cost? (Round your answer to the nearest cent.)

Mathematics Blueprint for Problem Solving

Gather the Facts	What Am I Asked to Do?	How Do I Proceed?	Key Points to Remember
The total amount of cleaning fluid is 36.85 litres. Each small container holds 0.67 litre. Each litre of fluid costs \$3.50.	**(a)** Find out how many containers the chemist needs. **(b)** Find the cost of cleaning fluid in each small container.	**(a)** Divide the total, 36.85 litres, by the amount in each small container, 0.67 litre, to find the number of containers. **(b)** Multiply the cost of one litre, \$3.50, by the amount of litres in one container, 0.67.	If you are not clear as to what to do at any stage of the problem, then do a similar, simpler problem.

Solution

(a) How many containers will the chemist need?

She has 36.85 litres of cleaning fluid and she wants to put it into several equal-sized containers each holding 0.67 litre. Suppose we are not sure what to do. Let's do a similar, simpler problem. If we had 40 litres of cleaning fluid and we wanted to put it into little containers each holding 2 litres, what would we do? Since the little containers would only hold 2 litres, we would need 20 containers. We know that $40 \div 2 = 20$. So we see that, in general, we divide the total number of litres by the amount in the small container. Thus $36.85 \div 0.67$ will give us the number of containers in this case.

$$
\begin{array}{r}
55. \\
0.67_\wedge\overline{)36.85_\wedge} \\
\underline{33\ 5} \\
3\ 35 \\
\underline{3\ 35} \\
0
\end{array}
$$

The chemist will need 55 containers to hold this amount of cleaning fluid.

(b) How much does the cleaning fluid in each container cost? Each container will hold only 0.67 litre. If one litre costs \$3.50, then to find the cost of one container we multiply $0.67 \times \$3.50$.

$$
\begin{array}{r}
3.50 \\
\underline{\times\ 0.67} \\
2450 \\
\underline{2100} \\
2.3450
\end{array}
$$

We round our answer to the nearest cent. Thus each container would cost \$2.35.

Check.

(a) Is it really true that 55 containers each holding 0.67 litre will hold a total of 36.85 litres? To check, we multiply.

$$
\begin{array}{r}
55 \\
\underline{\times\ 0.67} \\
385 \\
\underline{330} \\
36.85
\end{array}
\checkmark
$$

(b) One litre of cleaning fluid costs \$3.50. We would expect the cost of 0.67 litre to be less than \$3.50. \$2.35 is less than \$3.50. ✓

We use estimation to check more closely.

$$\begin{array}{rcr} \$3.50 & \longrightarrow & \$4.00 \\ \times \quad 0.67 & \longrightarrow & \times \quad 0.7 \\ \hline & & \$2.800 \end{array}$$

\$2.80 is fairly close to \$2.35. Our answer is reasonable. ✓

Practice Problem 3 A butcher divides 17.4 kilograms of prime steak into smaller equal-sized packages. Each package contains 1.45 kilograms of prime steak. (a) How many packages of steak will he have? (b) Prime steak sells for \$11.60 per kilogram. How much will each package of prime steak cost?

NOTE TO STUDENT: *Fully worked-out solutions to all of the Practice Problems can be found at the end of the module.*

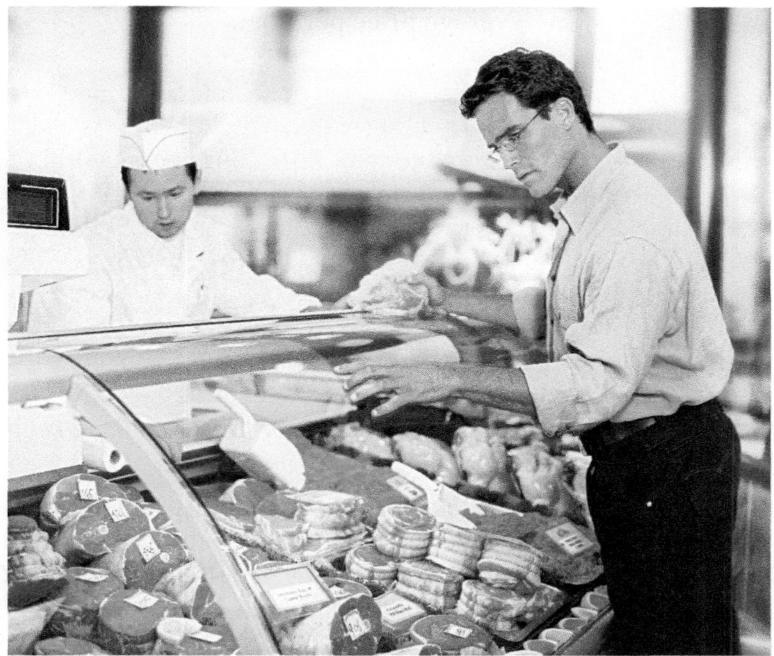

Getty Images-Stockbyte

Developing Your Study Skills

Applications or Word Problems

Applications or word problems are the very life of mathematics! They are the reason for doing mathematics, because they teach you how to put into use the mathematical skills you have developed.

The key to success is practice. Make yourself do as many problems as you can. You may not be able to do them all correctly at first, but keep trying. If you cannot solve a problem, try another one. Ask for help from your teacher or the tutoring lab. Ask other classmates how they solved the problem. Soon you will see great progress in your own problem-solving ability.

SECTION 7 EXERCISES

In exercises 1–10, first round each number to one nonzero digit. Then perform the calculation using the rounded numbers to obtain an estimate.

1. 238 598 980 + 487 903 870

2. 5 927 000 + 9 983 000

3. 56 789.345 − 33 875.125

4. 6949.45 − 1432.88

5. 12 638 × 0.7892

6. 47 225 × 0.463

7. 879.654 ÷ 56.82

8. 34.5684 ÷ 0.55

9. ***Car Sales*** Last year the sales of Honda Accords at Hopkins Honda totalled $11 760 770. If this represented a purchase of 483 Accords, estimate the average price per car.

10. ***Boat Sales*** Last year the sales of boats in Canada totalled $865 987 273.45. If this represented a purchase of 55 872 boats, estimate the average price per boat.

Catherine Ursillo/Photo Researchers, Inc.

Applications *Estimate an answer to each of the following by rounding each number first, then perform the actual calculation.*

11. ***Currency Conversion*** Kristy is taking a trip to Denmark. Before she leaves, she checks the newspaper and finds that every Canadian dollar is equal to 5.68 kroner (Danish currency). If Kristy takes $525 on her trip, how many kroner will she receive when she does the exchange?

▲ **12.** ***Football Field Dimensions*** The dimensions of a professional football field, including the end zones, are about 59.4 metres wide by 136.6 metres long. What is the area of a professional football field?

▲ **13.** ***Geometry*** Juan and Gloria are having their roof reshingled and need to determine its area in square metres. The dimensions of the roof are 16.3 metres by 18.9 metres. What is the area of the roof in square metres?

14. ***Baby Formula*** A large can of infant formula contains 808 grams of powder. To prepare a bottle, 35.2 grams are needed. How many bottles can be prepared from the can? Round to the nearest whole number.

15. ***Cooking*** Hans is making gourmet chocolate in Switzerland. He has 11.52 litres of liquid white chocolate that will be poured into moulds that hold 0.12 litre each. How many individual moulds can Hans make with his 11.52 litres of liquid white chocolate?

16. ***Food Purchase*** David bought McIntosh apples and Anjou pears at the grocery store for a fruit salad. At the checkout counter, the apples weighed 2.7 kilograms and the pears weighed 1.8 kilograms. If the apples cost $1.29 per kilogram and the pears cost $1.49 per kilogram, how much did David spend on fruit? (Round your answer to the nearest cent.)

17. ***Hawaii Rainfall*** One year in Mount Waialeale, Hawaii, considered the "rainiest place in the world," the yearly rainfall totalled 11.68 metres. The next year, the yearly rainfall on this mountain totalled 10.42 metres. The third year it was 12.67 metres. On average, how much rain fell on Mount Waialeale, Hawaii, per year?

David R. Frazier Photolibrary/Photo Researchers, Inc.

18. ***Auto Travel*** Emma and Jennie took a trip in their Ford Taurus from Saskatoon, Saskatchewan, to Calgary, Alberta, to check out the glacier lakes. When they left, their odometer read 54 089. When they returned home, the odometer read 55 401. They used 98.6 litres of gas. How many kilometres per litre did they get on the trip?

19. ***Food Portions*** A jumbo bag of potato chips contains 18 ounces of chips. The recommended serving is 0.75 ounce. How many servings are in the jumbo bag?

20. ***Telephone Costs*** Sylvia's telephone company offers a special rate of $0.23 per minute on calls made to the Philippines during certain parts of the day. If Sylvia makes a 28.5-minute call to the Philippines at this special rate, how much will it cost?

21. ***Consumer Mathematics*** The local Police Athletic League raised enough money to renovate the local youth hall and turn it into a coffeehouse/activity centre so that there is a safe place to hang out. The room that holds the Ping-Pong table needs 43.9 square metres of new carpeting. The entryway needs 11.3 square metres, and the stage/seating area needs 63.4 square metres. The carpeting will cost $10.65 per square metre. What will be the total bill for carpeting these three areas of the coffeehouse?

22. ***Painting Costs*** Kevin has a job as a house painter. On one job, the kitchen, family room, and hallway are to be painted. The respective amounts of paint needed are 2.7 litres, 3.3 litres, and 1.8 litres. If paint costs $7.40 per litre, how much will Kevin need to spend on paint to do the job?

23. ***Overtime Pay*** Lucy earns $8.50 per hour at the neighbourhood café. She earns time and a half (1.5 times the hourly wage) for each hour she works on a holiday. Lucy worked eight hours each day for six days, then worked eight hours on New Year's Day. How much did she earn for that week?

24. ***Electrician's Pay*** An electrician is paid $14.30 per hour for a 40-hour week. She is paid time and a half for overtime (1.5 times the hourly wage) for every hour more than 40 hours worked in the same week. If she works 48 hours in one week, what will she earn for that week?

25. ***Rainforest Loss*** In 1997, Brazil had 2.943 million square kilometres of rainforest. Each year, approximately 0.018 million square kilometres are lost to deforestation and development. By 2007, how many square kilometres of rainforest remained in Brazil? (*Source:* www.geography.ndo.co.uk)

26. ***Consumer Mathematics*** At the beginning of each month, Raul withdraws $100 for small daily purchases. This month he spent $18.50 on bus fares, $42.75 on coffee and snacks, and $21.25 on news magazines. How much did Raul have left at the end of the month?

27. ***Car Payments*** Charlie borrowed $11 500 to purchase a new car. His loan requires him to pay $288.65 each month over the next 60 months (five years). How much will he pay over the five years? How much more will he pay back than the amount of the loan?

28. ***House Payments*** Mel and Sally borrowed $140 000 to buy their new home. They make monthly payments to the bank of $764.35 to repay the loan. They will be making these payments for the next 30 years. How much money will they pay to the bank in the next 30 years? How much more will they pay back than they borrowed?

29. ***Drinking Water Safety*** The Health Canada standard for safe drinking water is a maximum of 1 milligram of copper per litre of water. A study was conducted on a sample of 7 litres of water drawn from Jeff Slater's house. The analysis revealed 8.06 milligrams of copper in the sample. Is the water safe or not? By how much?

30. ***Drinking Water Safety*** The Health Canada standard for safe drinking water is a maximum of 0.015 milligram of lead per litre of water. A study was conducted on 6 litres of water from West Towers Dormitory. The analysis revealed 0.0795 milligram of lead in the sample. Is the water safe or not? By how much?

31. ***Jet Travel*** A jet fuel tank containing 17 316.8 litres is being emptied at the rate of 126.4 litres per minute. How many minutes will it take to empty the tank?

32. ***Monopoly Game*** In a Hamilton mall, the average price of a Parker Brothers Monopoly game is $11.50. The Alfred Dunhill Company made a special commemorative set for $25 000 000.00. Instead of plastic houses and hotels, you can buy and trade gold houses and silver hotels! How many regular Monopoly games could you purchase for the price of one special commemorative set?

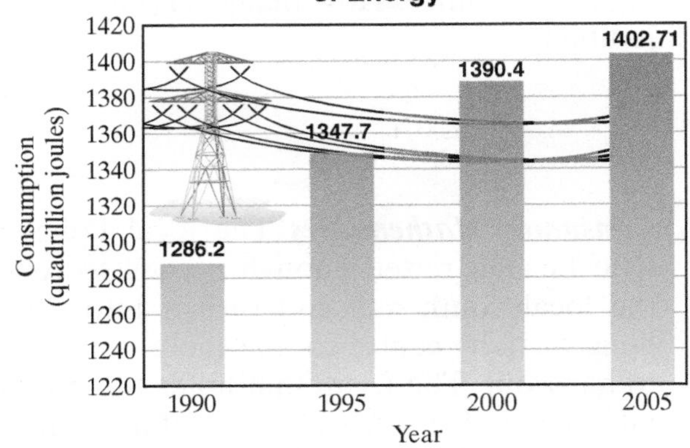

Source: Adapted from Natural Resources Canada, http://www.oee.nrcan.gc.ca/corporate/statistics/neud/dpa/tableshandbook2/res_00_1_e_3.cfm?attr=0, Oct-09

Energy Consumption *Use the bar graph to answer exercises 33–36.*

33. How many more joules were consumed in Canada during 2000 than in 1995?

34. What was the greatest increase in consumption of energy in a 5-year period? When did it occur?

35. What was the average consumption of energy per year in Canada for the years 1990 and 1995? Write your answer in quadrillion joules and then write your answer in joules. (Remember that a quadrillion is 1000 trillion.)

36. What was the average consumption of energy per year in Canada for the years 1995, 2000, and 2005? Write your answer in quadrillion joules and then write your answer in joules. (Remember that a quadrillion is 1000 trillion.)

Quick Quiz 7

1. The rainfall for North Bay last year was 1.23 inches in March, 2.58 inches in April, and 3.67 inches in May. Normally that city gets 8.5 inches during those three months. How much less rain was received during those three months compared to the normal rainfall amount?

2. Melissa and Phil started on a trip to the mountains with their Honda CRV. Their odometer read 87 569.2 kilometres at the start of the trip and 87 929.2 kilometres at the end of the trip. They used 25.5 litres of gas on the trip. How many kilometres per litre did they achieve with their car? (Round to the nearest tenth.)

3. Chris Smith is making car payments of $275.50 for the next 36 months to pay off a car loan for a new Saturn. He borrowed $8000 from a bank to purchase the car. How much will he make in car payments over the next three years? How much more will he pay back than the original amount of the loan?

4. **Concept Check** Explain how you would solve the following problem. The Classic Chocolate Company has 24.7 kilograms of chocolate. They wish to place them in individual boxes that each hold 1.3 kilograms of chocolate. How many boxes will they need?

Putting Your Skills to Work: Use Math to Save Money

GAS PRICES

It's July 2008 in Waterloo, Ontario, and Sam needs to put gas in his car. He is on a street that has an Petro-Canada gas station and a SHELL station. Sam will use his debit card to pay for the gas. The Petro-Canada station is charging $1.10 per litre of gas while the SHELL station is charging $1.16 per litre.

If Sam's goal is to save money, it would seem obvious that he should go to Petro-Canada, right? But Sam knows from experience it's not that simple. He knows that Petro-Canada will charge an extra $0.45 as an "ATM Transaction Fee" in addition to the gas he buys.

Javier Larrea/Pixtal/Superstock Royalty Free

1. If Sam plans on buying just **one litre** of gas, which gas station should he choose?
2. If Sam plans on buying **seven litres** of gas, which gas station should he choose?
3. If Sam plans on buying **eight litres** of gas, which gas station should he choose?
4. If Sam plans on buying **ten litres** of gas, which gas station should he choose?
5. How many litres of gas would Sam need to buy for the cost to be **exactly the same** at the two gas stations? Consider the results of Question 2 and Question 3 when formulating your answer.
6. Does the station where you normally get gas charge the same for cash/debit or credit?
7. Do you know if the station charges an "ATM transaction fee"?
8. Has the increase in gas prices caused you to change your driving habits? If so, please explain.

Module Organizer

Topic	Procedure	Examples
Word names for decimals.	3 Hundreds 4 Tens 1 Ones . Decimal point 6 Tenths 7 Hundredths 8 Thousandths 3 Ten-thousandths	The word name for 341.6783 is three hundred forty-one and six thousand seven hundred eighty-three ten-thousandths.
Writing a decimal as a fraction.	**1.** Read the decimal in words. **2.** Write it in fraction form. **3.** Reduce if possible.	Write 0.36 as a fraction. **1.** 0.36 is read "thirty-six hundredths." **2.** Write the fractional form. $\frac{36}{100}$ **3.** Reduce. $\frac{36}{100} = \frac{9}{25}$
Determining which of two decimals is larger.	**1.** Start at the left and compare corresponding digits. Write in extra zeros if needed. **2.** When two digits are different, the larger number is the one with the larger digit.	Which is larger? 0.138 or 0.13 0.138 ? 0.130 $8 > 0$ So $0.138 > 0.130$.
Rounding decimals.	**1.** Locate the place (units, tenths, hundredths, etc.) to which rounding is required. **2.** If the first digit to the right of the given place value is less than 5, drop it and all the digits to the right of it. **3.** If the first digit to the right of the given place value is 5 or greater, increase the number in the given place value by 1. Drop all digits to the right.	Round to the nearest hundredth: 0.8652 0.87 Round to the nearest thousandth: 0.21648 0.216
Adding and subtracting decimals.	**1.** Write the numbers vertically and line up the decimal points. Extra zeros may be written to the right of the decimal points after the nonzero digits if needed. **2.** Add or subtract all the digits with the same place value, starting with the right column, moving to the left. Use carrying or borrowing as needed. **3.** Place the decimal point of the result in line with the decimal points of all the numbers added or subtracted.	Add. 36.3 + 8.007 + 5.26 $\begin{array}{r} ^{1} \\ 36.300 \\ 8.007 \\ +\ 5.260 \\ \hline 49.567 \end{array}$ Subtract. 82.5 − 36.843 $\begin{array}{r} 82.500 \\ -\ 36.843 \\ \hline 45.657 \end{array}$ (borrowing marks: 7 11 . 4 14 9 10 10)
Multiplying decimals.	**1.** Multiply the numbers just as you would multiply whole numbers. **2.** Find the sum of the number of decimal places in the two factors. **3.** Place the decimal point in the product so that the product has the same number of decimal places as the sum in step 2. You may need to insert zeros to the left of the number found in step 1.	Multiply. $\begin{array}{r} 0.2 \\ \times\ 0.6 \\ \hline 0.12 \end{array}$ $\begin{array}{r} 0.3174 \\ \times\ 0.8 \\ \hline 0.253\,92 \end{array}$ $\begin{array}{r} 0.0064 \\ \times\ 0.21 \\ \hline 64 \\ 1\,28 \\ \hline 0.001\,344 \end{array}$ $\begin{array}{r} 1364 \\ \times\ 0.7 \\ \hline 954.8 \end{array}$
Multiplying a decimal by a power of 10.	Move the decimal point to the right the same number of places as there are zeros in the power of 10 or the same number of places as the exponent on the 10. (Sometimes it is necessary to write extra zeros before placing the decimal point in the answer.)	Multiply. $5.623 \times 10 = 56.23$ $0.0082 \times 1000 = 8.2$ $28.93 \times 10^2 = 2893$ $0.597 \times 10^4 = 5970$ $0.075 \times 10^6 = 75\,000$
Dividing by a decimal.	**1.** Make the divisor a whole number by moving the decimal point to the right. Mark that position with a caret (∧). **2.** Move the decimal point in the dividend to the right the same number of places. Mark that position with a caret. **3.** Place the decimal point of your answer directly above the caret in the dividend. **4.** Divide as with whole numbers.	Divide. **(a)** $0.06\overline{)0.162}$ **(b)** $0.003\overline{)85.8}$ **(a)** $0.06_\wedge\overline{)0.16_\wedge2}$ = 2.7 12 42 42 0 **(b)** $0.003_\wedge\overline{)85.800_\wedge}$ = 28 600. 6 25 24 18 18 0

Topic	Procedure	Examples
Converting a fraction to a decimal.	Divide the denominator into the numerator until **1.** the remainder is zero, or **2.** the decimal repeats itself, or **3.** the desired number of decimal places is achieved.	Find the decimal equivalent. **(a)** $\frac{13}{22}$ **(b)** $\frac{5}{7}$, rounded to the nearest ten-thousandth **(c)** $\frac{13}{22}$ **(a)** $22\overline{)13.0000}$ = 0.5909 110 200 198 200 198 2 **(b)** $7\overline{)5.000\ 00}$ = 0.714 28 49 10 7 30 28 20 14 60 56 4 0.71428 rounded to the nearest ten-thousandth is 0.7143. **(c)** $\frac{13}{22} = 0.5\overline{90}$ or 0.590 909 0 . . .
Order of operations with decimal numbers.	Same as order of operations of whole numbers. **1.** Perform operations inside parentheses. **2.** Simplify any expressions with exponents. **3.** Multiply or divide from left to right. **4.** Add or subtract from left to right.	Evaluate. $(0.4)^3 + 1.26 \div 0.12 - 0.12 \times (1.3 - 1.1)$ $= (0.4)^3 + 1.26 \div 0.12 - 0.12 \times 0.2$ $= 0.064 + 1.26 \div 0.12 - 0.12 \times 0.2$ $= 0.064 + 10.5 - 0.024$ $= 10.564 - 0.024$ $= 10.54$

Procedure for Solving Applied Problems

Using the Mathematics Blueprint for Problem Solving

In solving a real-life problem with decimals, students may find it helpful to complete the following steps. You will not use all the steps all of the time. Choose the steps that best fit the conditions of the problem.

1. Understand the problem.
   - **(a)** Read the problem carefully.
   - **(b)** Draw a picture if it helps you visualize the situation. Think about what facts you are given and what you are asked to find.
   - **(c)** It may help to write a similar, simpler problem to get started and to determine what operation to use.
   - **(d)** Use the Mathematics Blueprint for Problem Solving to organize your work. Follow these four parts.
     1. Gather the facts. (Write down specific values given in the problem.)
     2. What am I asked to do? (Identify what you must obtain for an answer.)
     3. How do I proceed? (Determine what calculations need to be done.)
     4. Key points to remember. (Record any facts, warnings, formulas, or concepts you think will be important as you solve the problem.)
2. Solve and state the answer.
   - **(a)** Perform the necessary calculations.
   - **(b)** State the answer, including the units of measure.
3. Check.
   - **(a)** Estimate the answer to the problem. Compare this estimate to the calculated value. Is your answer reasonable?
   - **(b)** Repeat your calculations.
   - **(c)** Work backward from your answer. Do you arrive at the original conditions of the problem?

EXAMPLE

▲ Fred has a rectangular living room that is 3.5 metres wide and 6.8 metres long. He has a hallway that is 1.8 metres wide and 3.5 metres long. He wants to carpet each area using carpeting that costs $12.50 per square metre. What will the carpeting cost him?

Understand the problem.

It is helpful to draw a sketch.

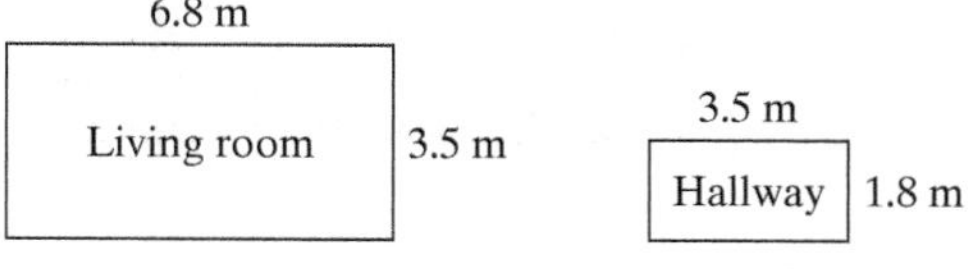

(continued on next page)

Procedure for Solving Applied Problems (*continued*)

Mathematics Blueprint for Problem Solving

Gather the Facts	What Am I Asked to Do?	How Do I Proceed?	Key Points to Remember
Living room: 6.8 metres by 3.5 metres Hallway: 3.5 metres by 1.8 metres Cost of carpet: \$12.50 per square metre	Find out what the carpeting will cost Fred.	Find the area of each room. Add the two areas. Multiply the total area by \$12.50.	Multiply the length by the width to get the area of the room. Remember, area is measured in square metres.

To find the area of each room, we multiply the dimensions for each room.

Living room $6.8 \times 3.5 = 23.80$ square metres

Hallway $3.5 \times 1.8 = 6.30$ square metres

Add the two areas.

$$\begin{array}{r} 23.80 \\ +\ 6.30 \\ \hline 30.10 \end{array}$$ square metres

Multiply the total area by the cost per square metre.

$30.1 \times 12.50 = \$376.25$

Estimate to check. You may be able to do some of this mentally.

$7 \times 4 = 28$ square metres $\quad 4 \times 2 = 8$ square metres

$$\begin{array}{r} 28 \\ +\ 8 \\ \hline 36 \end{array}$$ square metres

$36 \times 10 = \$360 \quad$ \$360 is close to \$376.25. ✓

Module Review Problems

If you have trouble with a particular type of exercise, review the examples in the section indicated for that group of exercises. Your institution may have included the Answers to Selected Exercises for this module, which contains the answers to these questions.

Section 1

Write a word name for each decimal.

1. 13.672 **2.** 0.000 84

Write as a decimal.

3. $\frac{7}{10}$ **4.** $\frac{81}{100}$ **5.** $1\frac{523}{1000}$ **6.** $\frac{79}{10\,000}$

Write as a fraction or a mixed number.

7. 0.17 **8.** 0.036 **9.** 34.24 **10.** 1.000 25

Section 2

Fill in the blank with <, =, or >.

11. $2\frac{9}{100}$ ___ 2.09 **12.** 0.716 ___ 0.706 **13.** $\frac{65}{100}$ ___ 0.655 **14.** 0.824 ___ 0.804

In exercises 15–18, arrange each set of decimal numbers from smallest to largest.

15. 0.981, 0.918, 0.98, 0.901 **16.** 5.62, 5.2, 5.6, 5.26, 5.59

17. 0.419, 0.49, 0.409, 0.491

18. 2.36, 2.3, 2.362, 2.302

19. Round to the nearest tenth. 0.613

20. Round to the nearest hundredth. 19.2076

21. Round to the nearest ten-thousandth. 9.852 15

22. Round to the nearest dollar. $156.48

Section 3

23. Add.
$$\begin{array}{r} 9.6 \\ 11.5 \\ 21.8 \\ +\ 34.7 \\ \hline \end{array}$$

24. Add.
$$\begin{array}{r} 2.5 \\ 32.7 \\ 116.94 \\ +\quad 0.67 \\ \hline \end{array}$$

25. Subtract.
$$\begin{array}{r} 17.03 \\ -\ 2.448 \\ \hline \end{array}$$

26. Subtract.
$$\begin{array}{r} 182.422 \\ -\quad 68.55 \\ \hline \end{array}$$

Section 4

In exercises 27–32, multiply.

27.
$$\begin{array}{r} 0.098 \\ \times\ 0.032 \\ \hline \end{array}$$

28.
$$\begin{array}{r} 126.83 \\ \times\qquad 7 \\ \hline \end{array}$$

29.
$$\begin{array}{r} 78 \\ \times\ 5.2 \\ \hline \end{array}$$

30.
$$\begin{array}{r} 7053 \\ \times\ 0.34 \\ \hline \end{array}$$

31. $0.000\,613 \times 10^3$

32. 1.2354×10^5

33. ***Food Cost*** Roast beef was on sale for $3.49 per kilogram. How much would 2.5 kilograms cost? Round to the nearest cent.

Section 5

In exercises 34–36, divide until there is a remainder of zero.

34. $0.07\overline{)0.000\,180\,6}$

35. $5.2\overline{)191.36}$

36. $8\overline{)1863.2}$

37. Divide and round your answer to the nearest tenth.

$$1.3\overline{)746.75}$$

38. Divide and round your answer to the nearest thousandth.

$$0.06\overline{)0.003\,539}$$

Section 6

Write as an equivalent decimal.

39. $\frac{11}{12}$

40. $\frac{17}{20}$

41. $1\frac{5}{6}$

42. $\frac{19}{16}$

Write as a decimal rounded to the nearest thousandth.

43. $\frac{11}{14}$

44. $\frac{10}{29}$

45. $2\frac{5}{17}$

46. $3\frac{9}{23}$

Evaluate by doing the operations in proper order.

47. $2.3 \times 1.82 + 3 \times 5.12$

48. $2.175 \div 0.15 \times 10 + 27.32$

49. $3.57 - (0.4)^3 \times 2.5 \div 5$

50. $2.4 \div (2 - 1.6)^2 + 8.13$

Mixed Practice

Calculate.

51. $2398.26 - 1959.07$

52. $32.15 \times 0.02 \times 10^2$

53. $1.809 - 0.62 + 3.27$

54. $2.0792 \div 2.3$

55. $8 \div 0.4 + 0.1 \times (0.2)^2$

56. $(3.8 - 2.8)^3 \div (0.5 + 0.3)$

Applications

Section 7

Solve each problem.

57. ***Football Tickets*** At a large football stadium there are 2600 people in line for tickets. In the first two minutes the computer is running slowly and tickets 228 people. Then the computer stops. For the next 2.5 minutes, the computer runs at medium speed and tickets 388 people per minute. For the next three minutes the computer runs at full speed and tickets 430 people per minute. Then the computer stops. How many people still have not received their tickets?

58. ***Fuel Efficiency*** Phil drove to the mountains. His odometer read 26 005.8 miles at the start, and 26 325.8 miles at the end of the trip. He used 12.9 gallons of gas on the trip. How many miles per gallon did his car get? (Round your answer to the nearest tenth.)

59. ***Car Payments*** Robert is considering buying a car and making instalment payments of $189.60 for 48 months. The cash price of the car is $6930.50. How much extra does he pay if he uses the instalment plan instead of buying the car with one payment?

60. ***Comparing Job Salaries*** Mr. Zeno has a choice of working as an assistant manager at ABC Company at $315.00 per week or receiving an hourly salary of $8.26 per hour at the XYZ company. He learned from several previous assistant managers at both companies that they usually worked 38 hours per week. At which company will he probably earn more money?

61. ***Drinking Water Safety*** The Health Canada standard for safe drinking water is a maximum of 0.001 milligram of mercury in one litre of water. The town wells at Winchester were tested. The test was done on 12 litres of water. The entire 12-litre sample contained 0.03 milligram of mercury. Is the water safe or not? By how much does it differ from the standard?

62. ***Infant Head Size*** It is common for infants to have their heads measured during the first year of life. At two months, Will's head measured 40 centimetres. There are 2.54 centimetres in one inch. How many inches was this measurement? Round to the nearest hundredth.

▲ **63.** ***Geometry*** Dick Wright's new rectangular garden measures 18.3 feet by 9.6 feet. He needs to install wire fence on all four sides.

(a) How many feet of fence does he need?

(b) The number of bags of wood chips Dick buys depends on the area of the garden. What is the area?

▲ **64.** ***Geometry*** Bill Tupper's rectangular driveway needs to be resurfaced. It is 25.5 metres long and 6.5 metres wide. How large is the area of the driveway?

65. ***International Distances*** The following strip map shows the distances in miles between several towns in Pennsylvania. How much longer is the distance from Coudersport to Gaines than the distance from Galeton to Wellsboro?

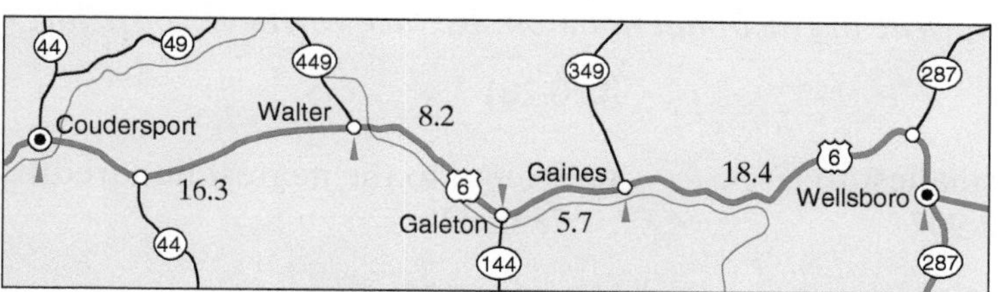

▲ **66.** ***Geometry*** A farmer in Woodstock has a field with an irregular shape. The distances are marked on the diagram. There is no fence but there is a path on the edge of the field. How long is the walking path around the field?

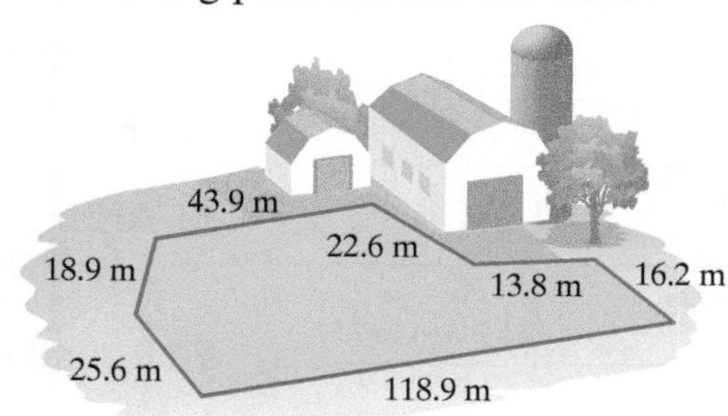

67. ***Car Payments*** Marcia and Greg purchased a new car. For the next five years they will be making monthly payments of $212.50. Their bank has offered to give them a loan at a lower interest rate so that they would make monthly payments of only $199.50. The bank would charge them $285.00 to reissue their car loan. How much would it cost them to keep their original loan? How much would it cost them if they took the new loan from the bank? Should they make the change or keep the original loan?

Pets in Canada *An estimate of the total number of pets owned in Canada for the year 2001 is given in the bar graph below. Use the following bar graph to answer exercises 68–73.*

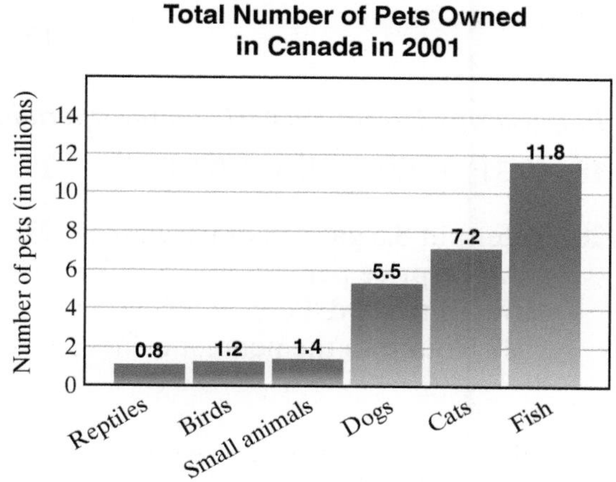

68. How many more pet cats are there in Canada than pet dogs?

69. How many more pet dogs are there in Canada than pet birds?

70. How many more pet fish are there in Canada than pet cats?

71. How many more pet fish are there in Canada than pet dogs, small animals, birds, and reptiles combined?

72. How many more pet fish are there in Canada than pet cats, small animals, birds, and reptiles combined?

73. How many more pet cats and dogs combined are there in Canada than pet fish?

How Am I Doing? Module Test

1. Write a word name for the decimal. 12.043

2. Write as a decimal. $\frac{3977}{10\,000}$

In questions 3 and 4, write in fractional notation. Reduce whenever possible.

3. 7.15

4. 0.261

5. Arrange from smallest to largest. 2.19, 2.91, 2.9, 2.907

6. Round to the nearest hundredth. 78.6562

7. Round to the nearest ten-thousandth. 0.034 175 2

Add.

8. $\begin{array}{r} 96.2 \\ 1.348 \\ +\ 2.15 \\ \hline \end{array}$

9. $17 + 2.1 + 16.8 + 0.04 + 1.59$

Subtract.

10. $\begin{array}{r} 1.0075 \\ -\ 0.9096 \\ \hline \end{array}$

11. $72.3 - 1.145$

Multiply.

12. $\begin{array}{r} 8.31 \\ \times\ 0.07 \\ \hline \end{array}$

13. 2.189×10^3

Divide.

14. $0.08\overline{)0.010\,28}$

15. $0.69\overline{)32.43}$

Write as a decimal.

16. $\frac{11}{9}$

17. $\frac{7}{8}$

In questions 18 and 19, perform the operations in the proper order.

18. $(0.3)^3 + 1.02 \div 0.5 - 0.58$

19. $19.36 \div (0.24 + 0.26) \times (0.4)^2$

20. Peter put 8.5 gallons of gas in his car. The price per gallon is $3.17. How much did Peter spend on gas? Round to the nearest cent.

21. Frank travelled from the city to the coast. His odometer read 42 620.5 kilometres at the start and 42 780.5 at the end of the trip. He used 8.5 litres of gas. How many kilometres per litre did his car achieve? Round to the nearest tenth.

22. The rainfall for March in Central City was 8.01 centimetres; for April, 5.03 centimetres; and for May, 8.53 centimetres. The normal rainfall for these three months is 25 centimetres. How much less rain fell during these three months than usual; that is, how does this year's figure compare with the figure for normal rainfall?

23. Wendy is earning $7.30 per hour in her new job as a teller trainee at the Springfield National Bank. She earns 1.5 times that amount for every hour over 40 hours she works in one week. She was asked to work 49 hours last week. How much did she earn last week?

1. __________
2. __________
3. __________
4. __________
5. __________
6. __________
7. __________
8. __________
9. __________
10. __________
11. __________
12. __________
13. __________
14. __________
15. __________
16. __________
17. __________
18. __________
19. __________
20. __________
21. __________
22. __________
23. __________

Solutions to Practice Problems

Section 1 Practice Problems

1. (a) 0.073 seventy-three thousandths
   (b) 4.68 four and sixty-eight hundredths
   (c) 0.0017 seventeen ten-thousandths
   (d) 561.78 five hundred sixty-one and seventy-eight hundredths
2. seven thousand, eight hundred sixty-three and $\frac{4}{100}$ dollars
3. (a) $\frac{9}{10} = 0.9$ (b) $\frac{136}{1000} = 0.136$
   (c) $2\frac{56}{100} = 2.56$ (d) $34\frac{86}{1000} = 34.086$
4. (a) $0.37 = \frac{37}{100}$ (b) $182.3 = 182\frac{3}{10}$
   (c) $0.7131 = \frac{7131}{10\,000}$ (d) $42.019 = 42\frac{19}{1000}$
5. (a) $8.5 = 8\frac{5}{10} = 8\frac{1}{2}$ (b) $0.58 = \frac{58}{100} = \frac{29}{50}$
   (c) $36.25 = 36\frac{25}{100} = 36\frac{1}{4}$ (d) $106.013 = 106\frac{13}{1000}$
6. $\frac{2}{1\,000\,000\,000} = \frac{1}{500\,000\,000}$

   The concentration of PCBs is $\frac{1}{500\,000\,000}$.

Section 2 Practice Problems

1. Since 4 < 5, therefore 5.74 < 5.75.

   5.74 5.75
2. 0.894 > 0.890, so 0.894 > 0.89
3. 2.45, 2.543, 2.46, 2.54, 2.5
   It is helpful to add extra zeros and to place the decimals that begin with 2.4 in a group and the decimals that begin with 2.5 in the other.
   2.450, 2.460, 2.543, 2.540, 2.500
   In order, we have from smallest to largest
   2.450, 2.460, 2.500, 2.540, 2.543.
   It is OK to leave the extra terminal zeros in the answer.
4. 723.88
   Since the digit to right of tenths is greater than 5, we round up.
   723.9
5. (a) 12.92 6 47
   Since the digit to right of thousandths is less than 5, we drop the digits 4 and 7.
   12.926
   (b) 0.00 7 892
   Since the digit to right of thousandths is greater than 5, we round up.
   0.008
6. 15 699.953
   Since the digit to right of tenths is five, we round up.
   15 700.0
7.

		Rounded to Nearest Dollar
Medical bills	375.50	376
Taxes	971.39	971
Retirement	980.49	980
Charity	817.65	818

Section 3 Practice Problems

1. (a)
```
    1
   9.8
   3.6
 + 5.4
  18.8
```
(b)
```
   1 1 1
  300.72
  163.75
+ 291.08
  755.55
```
(c)
```
   2
    8.9000
   37.0560
    0.0023
+ 945.0000
  990.9583
```
2.
```
  1    1
  93 521.8
+  1634.8
  95 156.6
```
The odometer reading was 95 156.6 kilometres.

3.
```
   3 1 2 2
  $ 80.95
   133.91
   256.47
    53.08
 + 381.32
  $905.73
```
4. (a)
```
   7 18
   38.8
 - 26.9
   11.9
```
(b)
```
   9 12
 1 10 2 14   8 10
 2 0 3 4 . 9 0 8
-1 9 8 6 . 3 2 5
       4 8 . 5 8 3
```
5. (a)
```
     9  9
  8 10 10 10
  19 . 0 0 0
- 12 . 5 7 9
   6 . 4 2 1
```
(b)
```
 17 12    9
 1 7 2   10 17
 2 8 3 . 0 7 6
-  9 6 . 3 8 0
 1 8 6 . 6 9 6
```
6.
```
   10 15 9
  6 0 8 10  11
  8 7, 1 6 0 . 1
- 8 2, 3 7 0 . 9
      4 7 8 9 . 2
```
He had driven 4789.2 kilometres.

7.
```
   4 13
   18.3
 - 10.8
    4.5
```
$x = 4.5$

Section 4 Practice Problems

1.
```
   0.09   2 decimal places
 × 0.6    1 decimal place
  0.054   3 decimal places in product
```
2. (a)
```
   0.47   2 decimal places
 × 0.28   2 decimal places
    376
    94
 0.1316   4 decimal places in product
```
(b)
```
    0.436   3 decimal places
  × 18.39   2 decimal places
     39 24
    130 8
   3488
   436
  8.018 04  5 decimal places in product
```

3.
0.4264 4 decimal places
× 38 0 decimal places
34112
12792
16.2032 4 decimal places in product

4. Area = length × width
1.26
× 2.3
378
252
2.898
The area is 2.898 square millimetres.

5. (a) 0.0561 × 10 = 0.561 Decimal point moved one place to the right.
(b) 1462.37 × 100 = 146,237. Decimal point moved two places to the right.

6. (a) 0.26 × 1000 = 260. Decimal point moved three places to the right. One extra zero needed.
(b) 5862.89 × 10 000 = 58 628 900. Decimal point moved four places to the right. Two extra zeros needed.

7. 7.684 × 10^4 = 76 840. Decimal point moved four places to the right. One extra zero needed.

8. 156.2 × 1000 = 156 200
156.2 kilometres is equal to 156 200 metres.

Section 5 Practice Problems

1. (a)
0.258
7)1.806
14
40
35
56
56
0

(b)
0.0058
16)0.0928
80
128
128
0

2.
0.517 = 0.52 to the nearest hundredth
46)23.820
230
82
46
360
322
38

3.
186.25
19)3538.75
19
163
152
118
114
47
38
95
95
0
He pays $186.25 per month.

4. (a)
1.12
0.09∧)0.10∧08
9
10
9
18
18
0

(b)
46.
0.037∧)1.702∧
1.48
222
222
0

5. (a)
0.023
1.8∧)0.0∧414
36
54
54
0

(b)
2310.
0.0036∧)8.3160∧
72
111
108
36
36
0

6. (a)
137.26
3.8∧)521.6∧00
38
141
114
27 6
26 6
1 0 0
7 6
2 40
2 28
12
The answer rounded to the nearest tenth is 137.3.

(b)
0.0211
8.05∧)0.17∧0000
16 10
900
805
950
805
145
The answer rounded to the nearest thousandth is 0.021.

7.
12.43
28.5∧)354.4∧00
285
69 4
57 0
12 4 0
11 4 0
1 0 00
8 55
1 45
The truck got approximately 12.4 kilometres per litre.

8.
5.8
0.12∧)0.69∧6
60
9 6
9 6
0
n is 5.8.

9. Find the sum of levels for the years 1990, 1995, and 2000.

$$\begin{array}{r} 35.6 \\ 35.8 \\ +\ 34.9 \\ \hline 106.3 \end{array}$$

Then divide by 3 to obtain the average.

$$\begin{array}{r} 35.433 \\ 3\overline{)106.3} \\ \underline{9} \\ 16 \\ \underline{15} \\ 13 \\ \underline{12} \\ 10 \\ \underline{9} \\ 1 \end{array}$$

The three-year average is 35.433 ppb. The four-year average was found to be 36.425 in Example 9. Find the difference between the averages.

$$\begin{array}{r} 36.425 \\ -\ 35.433 \\ \hline 0.992 \end{array}$$

The three-year average differs from the four-year average by 0.992 ppb.

Section 6 Practice Problems

1. (a)

$$\begin{array}{r} 0.3125 \\ 16\overline{)5.0000} \\ \underline{48} \\ 20 \\ \underline{16} \\ 40 \\ \underline{32} \\ 80 \\ \underline{80} \\ 0 \end{array}$$

$\frac{5}{16} = 0.3125$

(b)

$$\begin{array}{r} 0.1375 \\ 80\overline{)11.0000} \\ \underline{80} \\ 300 \\ \underline{240} \\ 600 \\ \underline{560} \\ 400 \\ \underline{400} \\ 0 \end{array}$$

$\frac{11}{80} = 0.1375$

2. (a)

$$\begin{array}{r} 0.6363 \\ 11\overline{)7.0000} \\ \underline{66} \\ 40 \\ \underline{33} \\ 70 \\ \underline{66} \\ 40 \\ \underline{33} \\ 7 \end{array}$$

$\frac{7}{11} = 0.\overline{63}$

(b)

$$\begin{array}{r} 0.533 \\ 15\overline{)8.000} \\ \underline{75} \\ 50 \\ \underline{45} \\ 50 \\ \underline{45} \\ 5 \end{array}$$

$\frac{8}{15} = 0.5\overline{3}$

(c)

$$\begin{array}{r} 0.295\ 45 \\ 44\overline{)13.000\ 000} \\ \underline{88} \\ 420 \\ \underline{396} \\ 240 \\ \underline{220} \\ 200 \\ \underline{176} \\ 240 \\ \underline{220} \\ 20 \end{array}$$

$\frac{13}{44} = 0.29\overline{54}$

3. (a) $2\frac{11}{18} = 2 + \frac{11}{18}$

$$\begin{array}{r} 0.611 = 0.6\overline{1} \\ 18\overline{)11.000} \\ \underline{108} \\ 20 \\ \underline{18} \\ 20 \\ \underline{18} \\ 2 \end{array}$$

$2\frac{11}{18} = 2.6\overline{1}$

(b)

$$\begin{array}{r} 1.037\ 03 \\ 27\overline{)28.000\ 00} \\ \underline{27} \\ 1\ 00 \\ \underline{81} \\ 190 \\ \underline{189} \\ 100 \\ \underline{81} \\ 19 \end{array}$$

$\frac{28}{27} = 1.\overline{037}$

4.

$$\begin{array}{r} 0.7916 \\ 24\overline{)19.0000} \\ \underline{168} \\ 220 \\ \underline{216} \\ 40 \\ \underline{24} \\ 160 \\ \underline{144} \\ 16 \end{array}$$

$\frac{19}{24} = 0.792$ rounded to the nearest thousandth.

5. Divide to find the decimal equivalent of $\frac{5}{8}$.

$$\begin{array}{r} 0.625 \\ 8\overline{)5.000} \\ \underline{48} \\ 20 \\ \underline{16} \\ 40 \\ \underline{40} \\ 0 \end{array}$$

In the hundredths place $2 < 3$, so we know $0.6\underline{2}5 < 0.6\underline{3}0$.

Therefore, $\frac{5}{8} < 0.63$.

6. $0.3 \times 0.5 + (0.4)^3 - 0.036 = 0.3 \times 0.5 + 0.064 - 0.036$
$= 0.15 + 0.064 - 0.036$
$= 0.214 - 0.036$
$= 0.178$

7. $6.56 \div (2 - 0.36) + (8.5 - 8.3)^2$

$= 6.56 \div (1.64) + (0.2)^2$	Parentheses
$= 6.56 \div 1.64 + 0.04$	Exponents
$= 4 + 0.04$	Divide
$= 4.04$	Add

Section 7 Practice Problems

Practice Problem 1

(a) $385.98 + 875.34 \approx 400 + 900 = 1300$
(b) $0.0932 - 0.0579 \approx 0.09 - 0.06 = 0.03$
(c) $5876.34 \times 0.087 \approx$

$$\begin{array}{r} 6000 \\ \times\ 0.09 \\ \hline 540.00 \end{array}$$

(d)

$$46\,873 \div 8.456 \approx 8\overline{)50\,000}$$

```
      6250
  8)50 000
    48
     2 0
     1 6
       40
       40
        0
```

Practice Problem 2

1. Understand the problem.

Mathematics Blueprint for Problem Solving

Gather the Facts	What Am I Asked to Do?	How Do I Proceed?	Key Points to Remember
She worked 51 hours. She gets paid \$9.36 per hour for 40 hours. She gets paid time-and-a-half for 11 hours.	Find the amount Melinda earned working 51 hours last week.	Add the earnings of 40 hours at \$9.36 per hour to the earnings of 11 hours at overtime pay.	Overtime pay is time-and-a-half, which is 1.5 × \$9.36.

2. Solve and state the answer:

(a) Calculate regular earnings for 40 hours.

```
   $9.36
 ×    40
 $374.40
```

(b) Calculate overtime pay rate.

```
   $9.36
 ×   1.5
    4680
    936
 $14.040
```

(c) Calculate overtime earnings for 11 hours.

```
  $14.04
 ×    11
    1404
   1404
 $154.44
```

(d) Add the two amounts.

```
   $374.40   Regular earnings
 +  154.44   Overtime earnings
   $528.84   Total earnings
```

Melinda earned \$528.84 last week.

3. ***Check.*** Regular pay: 40 × \$9 = \$360
Overtime pay: 2 × \$9 = \$18
10 × \$20 = \$200

```
  $360
 + 200
  $560
```

The answer is reasonable.

Practice Problem 3

1. Understand the problem.

Mathematics Blueprint for Problem Solving

Gather the Facts	What Am I Asked to Do?	How Do I Proceed?	Key Points to Remember
The total amount of steak is 17.4 kilograms. Each package contains 1.45 kilograms. Prime steak costs \$11.60 per kilogram.	**(a)** Find out how many packages of steak the butcher will have. **(b)** Find the cost of each package.	**(a)** Divide the total, 17.4 kilograms, by the amount in each package, 1.45 kilograms, to find the number of packages. **(b)** Multiply the cost of one kilogram, \$11.60, by the amount in one package, 1.45 kilograms.	There will be two answers to this problem.

2. Solve and state the answer.

(a)

```
            12.
 1.45^)17.40^
       14 5
        2 90
        2 90
           0
```

The butcher will have 12 packages of steak.

(b)

```
   $11.60
 ×   1.45
     5800
    4640
   1160
 $16.8200
```

Each package will cost \$16.82.

3. ***Check.***

(a)

```
   1.45
 ×   12
    290
   145
  17.40
```

(b) \$12 × 1 = \$12

The answers are reasonable.

Glossary

Caret (Section 5) A symbol $\wedge$ used to indicate the new location of a decimal point when performing division of decimal fractions.

Decimal fraction (Section 1) A fraction whose denominator is a power of 10.

Decimal places (Section 4) The number of digits to the right of the decimal point in a decimal fraction. The number 1.234 has three decimal places, while the number 0.129 845 has six decimal places. A whole number such as 42 is considered to have zero decimal places.

Decimal point (Section 1) The period that is used when writing a decimal fraction. In the number 5.346, the period between the 5 and the 3 is the decimal point. It separates the whole number from the fractional part that is less than 1.

Inequality symbol (Section 2) The symbol that is used to indicate whether a number is greater than another number or less than another number. Since 5 is greater than 3, we would write this with a "greater than" symbol as follows: $5 > 3$. The statement "7 is less than 12" would be written as follows: $7 < 12$.

Repeating decimals (Section 6) Decimals that have a digit or a group of digits that repeat. The decimals 0.333 333 333 33 . . . and 1.234 234 234 234 . . . are repeating decimals. The pattern of repeating continues forever. Repeating decimals can be written in a form with a bar over the repeating digit(s). Thus the preceding decimals could be written as $0.\overline{3}$ and $1.\overline{234}$.

Terminating decimals (Section 6) Every fraction can be written as a decimal. If the division process of dividing denominator into numerator ends with a remainder of zero, the decimal is a terminating decimal. Decimals such as 1.28, 0.007 856, and 5.123 are terminating decimals.

Answers to Selected Exercises for Decimals

Answers to Selected Exercises for Decimals

Section 1 Exercises **1.** A decimal fraction is a fraction whose denominator is a power of 10. $\frac{23}{100}$ and $\frac{563}{1000}$ are decimal fractions. **3.** hundred-thousandths **5.** fifty-seven hundredths **7.** three and eight tenths **9.** seven and thirteen thousandths **11.** twenty-eight and thirty-seven ten-thousandths **13.** one hundred twenty-four and $\frac{20}{100}$ dollars **15.** one thousand, two hundred thirty-six and $\frac{8}{100}$ dollars **17.** twelve thousand fifteen and $\frac{45}{100}$ dollars **19.** 0.7 **21.** 0.96 **23.** 0.481 **25.** 0.006 114 **27.** 0.7 **29.** 0.76 **31.** 0.01 **33.** 0.053 **35.** 0.2403 **37.** 10.9 **39.** 84.13 **41.** 3.529 **43.** 235.0104 **45.** $\frac{1}{50}$ **47.** $3\frac{3}{5}$ **49.** $7\frac{41}{100}$ **51.** $12\frac{5}{8}$ **53.** $7\frac{123}{2000}$ **55.** $8\frac{27}{2500}$ **57.** $235\frac{627}{5000}$ **59.** $\frac{1}{80}$ **61. (a)** $\frac{58}{125}$ **(b)** $\frac{229}{500}$ **63.** $\frac{1}{250\,000}$

Quick Quiz 1 **1.** five and three hundred sixty-seven thousandths **2.** 0.0523 **3.** $12\frac{29}{50}$ **4.** See Instructor

Section 2 Exercises **1.** > **3.** = **5.** < **7.** > **9.** < **11.** > **13.** < **15.** > **17.** = **19.** > **21.** 12.6, 12.65, 12.8 **23.** 0.007, 0.0071, 0.05 **25.** 8.31, 8.39, 8.4, 8.41 **27.** 26.003, 26.033, 26.034, 26.04 **29.** 18.006, 18.060, 18.065, 18.066, 18.606 **31.** 6.9 **33.** 29.0 **35.** 578.1 **37.** 2176.8 **39.** 26.03 **41.** 37.00 **43.** 156.17 **45.** 2786.71 **47.** 7.816 **49.** 0.0595 **51.** 12.015 78 **53.** 136 **55.** $788 **57.** $15 021 **59.** $96.34 **61.** $5783.72 **63.** 0.599; 0.481 **65.** 365.24 **67.** 0.0059, 0.006, 0.0519, $\frac{6}{100}$, 0.0601, 0.0612, 0.062, $\frac{6}{10}$, 0.61 **69.** You should consider only one digit to the right of the decimal place that you wish to round to. 86.234 98 is closer to 86.23 than to 86.24.

Quick Quiz 2 **1.** 4.056, 4.559, 4.56, 4.6 **2.** 27.18 **3.** 155.525 **4.** See Instructor

Section 3 Exercises **1.** 76.8 **3.** 593.9 **5.** 296.2 **7.** 12.76 **9.** 36.7287 **11.** 67.42 **13.** 235.78 **15.** 1112.16 **17.** 21.04 m **19.** 8.6 kilograms **21.** $78.12 **23.** 47 054.9 **25.** $1411.97 **27.** 3.5 **29.** 25.93 **31.** 49.78 **33.** 508.313 **35.** 135.43 **37.** 4.6465 **39.** 6.737 **41.** 1189.07 **43.** 1.4635 **45.** 176.581 **47.** 41.59 **49.** 5.2363 **51.** 73.225 **53.** 7.5152 pounds **55.** $36 947.16 **57.** $45.30 **59.** 11.64 centimetres **61.** 2.95 litres **63.** 0.0061 milligram; yes **65.** 27 400 **67.** 416 500 **69.** $8.40; yes; $8.34; very close: the estimate was off by 6¢. **71.** $x = 8.4$ **73.** $x = 43.7$ **75.** $x = 2.109$

Quick Quiz 3 **1.** 72.981 **2.** 2.1817 **3.** 55.675 **4.** See Instructor

Section 4 Exercises **1.** Each factor has two decimal places. You add the number of decimal places to get 4 decimal places. Multiply 67×8 to get 536. Place the decimal point 4 places to the left to obtain the result, 0.0536 **3.** When you multiply a number by 100, move the decimal point two places to the right. The answer is 0.78. **5.** 0.12 **7.** 0.06 **9.** 0.002 88 **11.** 54.24 **13.** 0.000 516 **15.** 0.6582 **17.** 2738.4 **19.** 0.017 304 **21.** 768.1517 **23.** 8460 **25.** 53.926 **27.** 6.5237 **29.** $9324 **31.** $494 **33.** 297.6 square feet **35.** $664.20 **37.** 969 kilometres **39.** 28.6 **41.** 5212.5 **43.** 22 615 **45.** 56 098.2 **47.** 1 756 144 **49.** 816 320 **51.** 593.2 centimetres **53.** 3281 feet **55.** $618.00 **57.** $62 279.00 **59.** To multiply by numbers such as 0.1, 0.01, 0.001, and 0.0001, count the number of decimal places in this first number. Then, in the other number, move the decimal point to the left from its present position the same number of decimal places as were in the first number.

Quick Quiz 4 **1.** 0.0304 **2.** 3.2768 **3.** 51 620 **4.** See Instructor

How Am I Doing? Sections 1–4 **1.** forty-seven and eight hundred thirteen thousandths (obj. 1.1) **2.** 0.0567 (obj. 1.2) **3.** $4\frac{9}{100}$ (obj. 1.3) **4.** $\frac{21}{40}$ (obj. 1.3) **5.** 1.59, 1.6, 1.601, 1.61 (obj. 2.2) **6.** 123.5 (obj. 2.3) **7.** 8.0654 (obj. 2.3) **8.** 17.99 (obj. 2.3) **9.** 19.45 (obj. 3.1) **10.** 27.191 (obj. 3.1) **11.** 10.59 (obj. 3.2) **12.** 7.671 (obj. 3.2) **13.** 0.3501 (obj. 4.1) **14.** 4780.5 (obj. 4.2) **15.** 37.96 (obj. 4.2) **16.** 7.85 (obj. 4.1) **17.** 6.874 (obj. 4.1) **18.** 0.000 003 12 (obj. 4.1)

Section 5 Exercises **1.** 2.1 **3.** 17.83 **5.** 10.52 **7.** 136.5 **9.** 5.412 **11.** 53 **13.** 18 **15.** 130 **17.** 5.3 **19.** 1.2 **21.** 49.3 **23.** 94.21 **25.** 13.56 **27.** 0.21 **29.** 0.081 **31.** 91.264 **33.** 123 **35.** 213 **37.** $82.73 **39.** approximately 13.6 kilometres per litre **41.** 24 bouquets **43.** 182 guests **45.** 23 snowboards. The error was in putting one fewer snowboard in the box than was required. **47.** $n = 32.2$ **49.** $n = 975$ **51.** $n = 44$ **53.** 41

Quick Quiz 5 **1.** 0.658 **2.** 3.258 **3.** 6.58 **4.** See Instructor

Section 6 Exercises **1.** same quantity **3.** The digits 8942 repeat. **5.** 0.25 **7.** 0.8 **9.** 0.125 **11.** 0.35 **13.** 0.62 **15.** 2.25 **17.** 2.875 **19.** 5.1875 **21.** $0.\overline{6}$ **23.** $0.\overline{45}$ **25.** $3.58\overline{3}$ **27.** $4.\overline{2}$ **29.** 0.308 **31.** 0.905 **33.** 0.146 **35.** 2.036 **37.** 0.404 **39.** 0.944 **41.** 3.143 **43.** 3.474 **45.** < **47.** > **49.** 0.28 **51.** 0.5 cm **53.** yes; it is 0.025 inch too wide. **55.** 2.3 **57.** 3.36 **59.** 0 **61.** 21.414 **63.** 0.0072 **65.** 0.325 **67.** 28.6 **69.** 20.836 **71.** 0.586 930 **73. (a)** 0.16 **(b)** $0.144\,9\overline{49}$ **(c)** b is a repeating decimal and a is a nonrepeating decimal

Quick Quiz 6 **1.** 3.5625 **2.** 0.29 **3.** 6.1 **4.** See Instructor

Section 7 Exercises **1.** 700 000 000 **3.** 30 000 **5.** 8000 **7.** 15 **9.** $20 000 **11.** 2982 kroner **13.** 308.07 square metres **15.** 96 moulds **17.** 11.59 metres **19.** 24 servings **21.** $1263.09 **23.** $510 **25.** 2.763 million or 2 763 000 square kilometres **27.** $17 319; $5819 **29.** yes; by 0.149 milligram per litre **31.** 137 minutes **33.** 42.7 quadrillion joules **35.** 61.5 quadrillion Joules or 61 500 000 000 000 000 Joules

Quick Quiz 7 **1.** 1.02 inches **2.** 14.1 kilometres per litre **3.** \$9918; \$1918 **4.** See Instructor

Putting Your Skills to Work **1.** SHELL **2.** SHELL **3.** Petro-Canada **4.** Petro-Canada **5.** 7.5 L **6.** Answers may vary **7.** Answers may vary **8.** Answers may vary

Module Review Problems **1.** thirteen and six hundred seventy-two thousandths **2.** eighty-four hundred-thousandths **3.** 0.7 **4.** 0.81 **5.** 1.523 **6.** 0.0079 **7.** $\frac{17}{100}$ **8.** $\frac{9}{250}$ **9.** $34\frac{6}{25}$ **10.** $1\frac{1}{4000}$ **11.** = **12.** > **13.** < **14.** > **15.** 0.901, 0.918, 0.98, 0.981 **16.** 5.2, 5.26, 5.59, 5.6, 5.62 **17.** 0.409, 0.419, 0.49, 0.491 **18.** 2.3, 2.302, 2.36, 2.362 **19.** 0.6 **20.** 19.21 **21.** 9.8522 **22.** \$156 **23.** 77.6 **24.** 152.81 **25.** 14.582 **26.** 113.872 **27.** 0.003 136 **28.** 887.81 **29.** 405.6 **30.** 2398.02 **31.** 0.613 **32.** 123 540 **33.** \$8.73 **34.** 0.00258 **35.** 36.8 **36.** 232.9 **37.** 574.4 **38.** 0.059 **39.** $0.91\overline{6}$ **40.** 0.85 **41.** $1.8\overline{3}$ **42.** 1.1875 **43.** 0.786 **44.** 0.345 **45.** 2.294 **46.** 3.391 **47.** 19.546 **48.** 172.32 **49.** 3.538 **50.** 23.13 **51.** 439.19 **52.** 64.3 **53.** 4.459 **54.** 0.904 **55.** 20.004 **56.** 1.25 **57.** 112 people **58.** 24.8 miles per gallon **59.** \$2170.30 **60.** ABC company **61.** no; by 0.0015 milligram per litre **62.** 15.75 inches **63. (a)** 55.8 feet **(b)** 175.68 square feet **64.** 165.75 square metres **65.** 6.1 miles **66.** 259.9 metres **67.** \$12 750.00; \$12 255.00; they should change to the new loan **68.** 1.7 million **69.** 4.3 million **70.** 4.6 million **71.** 2.9 million **72.** 1.2 million **73.** 0.9 million

How Am I Doing? Module Test **1.** twelve and forty-three thousandths (obj. 1.1) **2.** 0.3977 (obj. 1.2) **3.** $7\frac{3}{20}$ (obj. 1.3) **4.** $\frac{261}{1000}$ (obj. 1.3) **5.** 2.19, 2.9, 2.907, 2.91 (obj. 2.2) **6.** 78.66 (obj. 2.3) **7.** 0.0342 (obj. 2.3) **8.** 99.698 (obj. 3.1) **9.** 37.53 (obj. 3.1) **10.** 0.0979 (obj. 3.2) **11.** 71.155 (obj. 3.2) **12.** 0.5817 (obj. 4.1) **13.** 2189 (obj. 4.2) **14.** 0.1285 (obj. 5.2) **15.** 47 (obj. 5.2) **16.** $1.\overline{2}$ (obj. 6.1) **17.** 0.875 (obj. 6.1) **18.** 1.487 (obj. 6.2) **19.** 6.1952 (obj. 6.2) **20.** \$26.95 (obj. 7.2) **21.** 18.8 kilometres per litre (obj. 7.2) **22.** 3.43 centimetres (obj. 7.2) **23.** \$390.55 (obj. 7.2)

Ratio and Proportion

Kim Sayer © Dorling Kindersley

Ratio and Proportion

We all know that too much fast food is not good for us. Many people eat fast food nearly every day, but they may be unaware of just how many calories they are consuming. Do you know how many calories are in some common fast foods? How much exercise is necessary to burn off these calories? The mathematics you learn in this module will enable you to answer those questions.

SECTION 1 RATIOS AND RATES

Using a Ratio to Compare Two Quantities with the Same Units

Assume that you earn 13 dollars an hour and your friend earns 10 dollars per hour. The *ratio* 13 : 10 compares what you and your friend make. This ratio means that for every 13 dollars you earn, your friend earns 10. The *rate* you are paid is 13 dollars per hour, which compares 13 dollars to 1 hour. In this section we see how to use both ratios and rates to solve many everyday problems.

Suppose that we want to compare an object weighing 20 kilograms to an object weighing 23 kilograms. The ratio of their weights would be 20 to 23. We may also write this as $\frac{20}{23}$. A **ratio** is the comparison of two quantities that have the *same units*.

A commonly used video display for a computer has a horizontal dimension of 35 cm and a vertical dimension of 25 cm. The ratio of the horizontal dimension to the vertical dimension is 35 to 25. In reduced form we would write that as 7 to 5. We can express the ratio three ways.

We can write "the ratio of 7 to 5."
We can write 7 : 5 using a colon.
We can write $\frac{7}{5}$ using a fraction.

All three notations are valid ways to compare 7 to 5. Each is read as "7 to 5."

We always want to write a ratio in simplest form. A ratio is in **simplest form** when the two numbers do not have a common factor and both numbers are whole numbers.

EXAMPLE 1 Write in simplest form. Express your answer as a fraction.

(a) the ratio of 15 hours to 20 hours
(b) the ratio of 36 hours to 30 hours
(c) 125 : 150

Solution

(a) $\frac{15}{20} = \frac{3}{4}$ **(b)** $\frac{36}{30} = \frac{6}{5}$ **(c)** $\frac{125}{150} = \frac{5}{6}$

Notice that in each case the two numbers *do* have a common factor. When we form the fraction—that is, the ratio—we take the extra step of *reducing* the fraction. However, improper fractions *are not* changed to mixed numbers.

Practice Problem 1 Write in simplest form. Express your answer as a fraction.
(a) the ratio of 36 metres to 40 metres
(b) the ratio of 18 metres to 15 metres
(c) 220 : 270

Student Learning Objectives

After studying this section, you will be able to:

Use a ratio to compare two quantities with the same units.

Use a rate to compare two quantities with different units.

EXAMPLE 2 Martin earns $350 weekly. However, he takes home only $250 per week in his paycheque.

$350.00 gross pay (what Martin earns)

45.00	deducted for federal tax	(what is taken out of Martin's earnings)
20.00	deducted for provincial tax	
35.00	deducted for retirement	

$250.00 take-home pay (what Martin has left)

(a) What is the ratio of the amount deducted for federal tax to gross pay?
(b) What is the ratio of the amount deducted for provincial tax to the amount deducted for federal tax?

Solution

(a) The ratio of the amount deducted for provincial tax to gross pay is

$$\frac{45}{350} = \frac{9}{70}.$$

(b) The ratio of the amount deducted for provincial tax to the amount withheld for federal tax is

$$\frac{20}{45} = \frac{4}{9}.$$

Practice Problem 2 Recently President Burton conducted a survey of students at Niagara College who use the Internet. He wanted to determine how many of the students use the college Internet provider versus how many use AOL, MSN, or other commercial Internet providers. The results of his survey are shown in the circle graph.

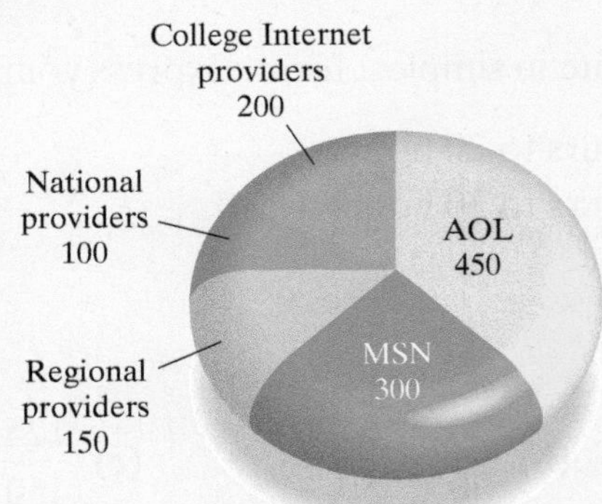

(a) Write the ratio of the number of students who use the college Internet provider to the number of students who use AOL.
(b) Write the ratio of the number of students who use MSN to the total number of students who use the Internet.

TO THINK ABOUT: Mach Numbers Perhaps you have heard statements like "a certain jet plane travels at Mach 2.2." What does that mean? A Mach number is a ratio that compares the velocity (speed) of an object to the velocity of sound. Sound travels at about 330 metres per second. The Mach number is written in decimal form.

What is the Mach number of a jet travelling at 690 metres per second?

$$\text{Mach number of jet} = \frac{690 \text{ metres per second}}{330 \text{ metres per second}} = \frac{69}{33} = \frac{23}{11}$$

Dividing this out, we obtain

$$2.090\,909\,09\ldots \text{ or } 2.\overline{09}$$

Rounded to the nearest tenth, the Mach number of the jet is 2.1.

Exercises 73 and 74 in Section 1 Exercises deal with Mach numbers.

Using a Rate to Compare Two Quantities with Different Units

A **rate** is a comparison of two quantities with *different units*. Usually, to avoid misunderstanding, we express a rate as a reduced or simplified fraction with the units included.

EXAMPLE 3 Recently an automobile manufacturer spent $946 000 for a 48-second television commercial shown on a national network. What is the rate of dollars spent to seconds of commercial time?

Solution The rate is $\dfrac{946\,000 \text{ dollars}}{48 \text{ seconds}} = \dfrac{59\,125 \text{ dollars}}{3 \text{ seconds}}$.

Practice Problem 3 A farmer is charged a $44 storage fee for every 900 tonnes of grain he stores. What is the rate of the storage fee in dollars to tonnes of grain?

Often we want to know the rate for a single unit, which is the unit rate. A **unit rate** is a rate in which the denominator is the number 1. Often we need to divide the numerator by the denominator to obtain this value.

EXAMPLE 4 A car travelled 301 kilometres in seven hours. Find the unit rate.

Solution $\frac{301}{7}$ can be simplified. We find $301 \div 7 = 43$.

Thus

$$\frac{301 \text{ kilometres}}{7 \text{ hours}} = \frac{43 \text{ kilometres}}{1 \text{ hour}}$$

The denominator is 1. We write our answer as 43 kilometres/hour. The fraction line is read as the word *per*, so our answer here is read "43 kilometres per hour." *Per* means "for every," so a rate of 43 kilometres per hour means 43 kilometres travelled for every hour spent.

Practice Problem 4 A car travelled 212 kilometres in four hours. Find the unit rate.

NOTE TO STUDENT: *Fully worked-out solutions to all of the Practice Problems can be found at the end of the module.*

EXAMPLE 5 A grocer purchased 80 kilograms of apples for $68. He sold the 80 kilograms of apples for $86. How much profit did he make per kilogram of apples?

Solution

$$\begin{array}{rl} \$86 & \text{selling price} \\ -\ \ 68 & \text{cost} \\ \hline \$18 & \text{profit} \end{array}$$

The rate that compares profit to kilograms of apples sold is $\frac{18 \text{ dollars}}{80 \text{ kilograms}}$. We will find 18 ÷ 80.

$$\begin{array}{r} 0.225 \\ 80\overline{)18.000} \\ \underline{16\ 0} \\ 2\ 00 \\ \underline{1\ 60} \\ 400 \\ \underline{400} \\ 0 \end{array}$$

The unit rate of profit is $0.23 per kilogram.

Practice Problem 5 A retailer purchased 120 nickel–cadmium batteries for flashlights for $129.60. She sold them for $170.40. What was her profit per battery?

EXAMPLE 6 Hamburger at a local butcher shop is packaged in large and extra-large packages. A large package costs $70.86 for 6 kilograms and an extra-large package is $90.08 for 8 kilograms.

(a) What is the unit rate in dollars per kilogram for each size package?

(b) How much per kilogram does a consumer save by buying the extra-large package?

Solution

(a) $\frac{70.86 \text{ dollars}}{6 \text{ kilograms}} = \$11.81/\text{kilogram}$ for the large package

$\frac{90.08 \text{ dollars}}{8 \text{ kilograms}} = \$11.26/\text{kilogram}$ for the extra-large package

(b)

$$\begin{array}{r} \$11.81 \\ -\ \ 11.26 \\ \hline \$\ \ 0.55 \end{array}$$

A person saves $0.55/kilogram by buying the extra-large package.

Practice Problem 6 A 400-gram package of Fred's favourite cereal costs $2.04. A 560-gram package of the same cereal costs $2.80.

(a) What is the unit rate in cost per gram of each size of cereal package?

(b) How much per gram would Fred save by buying the larger size?

SECTION 1 EXERCISES

Verbal and Writing Skills

1. A ________________ is a comparison of two quantities that have the same units.

2. A rate is a comparison of two quantities that have ________________ units.

3. The ratio 5 : 8 is read ________________ .

4. Marion compares the number of loaves of bread she bakes to the number of kilograms of flour she needs to make the bread. Is this a ratio or a rate? Why?

Write in simplest form. Express your answer as a fraction.

5. 6 : 18

6. 8 : 20

7. 21 : 18

8. 50 : 35

9. 150 : 225

10. 360 : 480

11. 165 to 90

12. 135 to 120

13. 60 to 72

14. 55 to 77

15. 28 to 42

16. 21 to 98

17. 32 to 20

18. 90 to 54

19. 8 grams to 12 grams

20. 50 years to 85 years

21. 39 kilograms to 26 kilograms

22. 255 metres to 15 metres

23. \$75 to \$95

24. \$54 to \$78

25. 312 yards to 24 yards

26. 91 tonnes to 133 tonnes

27. $2\frac{1}{2}$ pounds to $4\frac{1}{4}$ pounds

28. $4\frac{1}{3}$ metres to $5\frac{2}{3}$ metres

Personal Finance *Use the following table to answer exercises 29–32.*

ROBIN'S WEEKLY PAYCHEQUE

Total (Gross) Pay	Federal Deductions	Provincial Deductions	Retirement	Insurance	Savings Contribution	Take-Home Pay
\$285	\$35	\$20	\$28	\$16	\$21	\$165

29. What is the ratio of take-home pay to total (gross) pay?

30. What is the ratio of retirement to insurance?

31. What is the ratio of federal deductions to take-home pay?

32. What is the ratio of retirement to total (gross) pay?

Useful Life of an Automobile *An automobile insurance company prepared the following analysis for its clients. Use this table for exercises 33–36.*

33. What is the ratio of sedans that lasted two years or less to the total number of sedans?

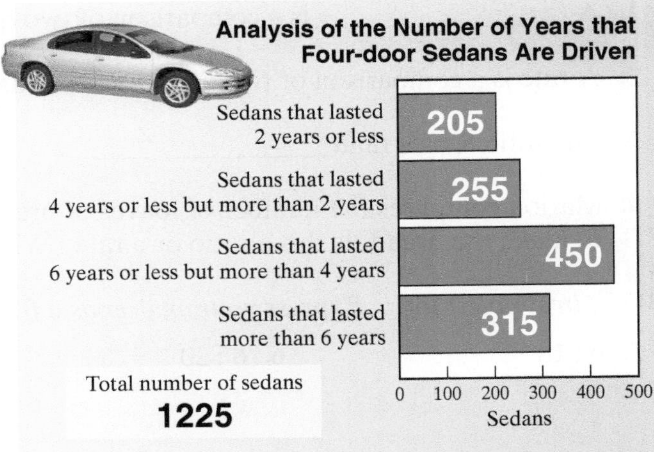

34. What is the ratio of sedans that lasted more than six years to the total number of sedans?

35. What is the ratio of the number of sedans that lasted six years or less but more than four years to the number of sedans that lasted two years or less?

36. What is the ratio of the number of sedans that lasted more than six years to the number of sedans that lasted four years or less but more than two years?

37. ***Basketball*** A basketball team scored a total of 704 points during one season. Of these, 44 points were scored by making one-point free throws. What is the ratio of free-throw points to total points?

38. ***Sales Tax*** When Michael bought his home theatre sound system, he paid \$34 in tax. The total cost was \$714. What is the ratio of tax to total cost?

Write as a rate in simplest form.

39. \$42 for 12 pairs of socks

40. \$50 for 15 deli sandwiches

41. \$170 for 12 bushes

42. 98 kilograms for 22 people

43. \$114 for 12 CDs

44. \$150 for 12 house plants

45. 6150 revolutions for every 15 kilometres

46. 9540 revolutions for every 18 kilometres

47. \$330 000 for 12 employees

48. \$156 000 for 24 people

Write as a unit rate.

49. Earn \$600 in 40 hours

50. Earn \$315 in 35 hours

51. Travel 192 kilometres on 12 litres of gas

52. Travel 222 kilometres on 14 litres of gas

▲**53.** 1120 people in 16 square kilometres

▲**54.** 3600 people in 24 square kilometres

55. 840 books for 12 libraries

56. 930 points in 15 games

57. Travel 297 kilometres in 4.5 hours

58. Travel 374 kilometres in 5.5 hours

59. 475 patients for 25 doctors

60. 375 trees planted on 15 acres

61. 60 eggs from 12 chickens

62. 78 children in 26 families

Applications

63. ***Stock Market*** $3870 was spent for 129 shares of Mattel stock. Find the cost per share.

64. ***Stock Market*** $6150 was spent for 150 shares of Polaroid stock. Find the cost per share.

65. ***Toy Store Profit*** A toy store owner purchased 90 puppets for $1080. She sold them for $1485. How much profit did she make per puppet?

66. ***Clothing Store Profit*** The manager of an outdoor clothing store ordered 40 pairs of hiking boots for $2400. The boots will sell for a total of $3560. How much profit will the store make per pair?

67. ***Food Cost*** A 16-ounce box of dry pasta costs $1.28. A 24-ounce box of the same pasta costs $1.68.

(a) What is the cost per ounce of each box of pasta?
(b) How much does the educated consumer save by buying the larger box?
(c) How much does the consumer save by buying 2 large boxes instead of 3 small boxes?

68. ***Food Cost*** A 500-mL can of beef stew costs $2.88. A 750-mL can of the same beef stew costs $4.16.

(a) What is the cost per millilitre of each can of stew?
(b) How much does the consumer save per millilitre by buying the larger can?

69. ***Moose Population Density*** Dr. Robert Tobey completed a count of two herds of moose in the central regions of Alaska. He recorded 3978 moose on the North Slope and 5520 moose on the South Slope. There are 306 acres on the North Slope and 460 acres on the South Slope.

(a) How many moose per acre were found on the North Slope?
(b) How many moose per acre were found on the South Slope?
(c) In which region are the moose more closely crowded together?

70. ***Australia Population Density*** In Melbourne, Australia, 27 900 people live in the suburb of St. Kilda and 38 700 live in the suburb of Caulfield. The area of St. Kilda is 2630 hectares. The area of Caulfield is 3720 hectares. Round your answers to the nearest tenth.

(a) How many people per hectare live in St. Kilda?
(b) How many people per hectare live in Caulfield?
(c) Which suburb is more crowded?

71. ***Stock Market***

(a) Ms. Handley bought 350 shares of Home Depot stock for \$14 332.50. How much did she pay per share?

(b) Mr. Johnston bought 210 shares of Office Max stock for \$11 088. How much did he pay per share?

(c) How much more per share did Mr. Johnston pay than Ms. Handley?

72. ***Baseball Statistics*** In 2006, Ryan Howard of the Philadelphia Phillies hit 58 home runs with 581 "at-bats." In the same year, David Ortiz of the Boston Red Sox hit 54 home runs with 558 at-bats.

(a) What are the rates of at-bats per home run for Ryan and David? Round to the nearest tenth.

(b) Which person hit home runs more often?

To Think About *For exercises 73 and 74, recall that the speed of sound is about 330 metres per second. (See the To Think About discussion.) Round your answers to the nearest tenth.*

73. ***Jet Speed*** A jet plane was originally designed to fly at 750 metres per second. It was modified to fly at 810 metres per second. By how much was its Mach number increased?

74. ***Rocket Speed*** A rocket was first flown at 1960 metres per second. It proved unstable and unreliable at that speed. It is now flown at a maximum of 1920 metres per second. By how much was its Mach number decreased?

Quick Quiz 1

1. Write as a ratio in simplest form.
51 to 85

2. Write as a rate in simplest form. Express your answer as a fraction.

1700 square metres for 55 kilograms

3. Write as a unit rate. Round to the nearest hundredth if necessary.
462 trees planted on 17 acres

4. **Concept Check** At a company picnic, there were 663 cans of pop for 231 people. Explain how you would write that as a rate in simplest form.

Section 2 The Concept of Proportions

1 Writing a Proportion

Student Learning Objectives

After studying this section, you will be able to:

1. **Write a proportion.**

2. **Determine whether a statement is a proportion.**

A **proportion** states that two ratios or two rates are equal. For example, $\frac{5}{8} = \frac{15}{24}$ is a proportion and $\frac{7 \text{ metres}}{8 \text{ dollars}} = \frac{35 \text{ metres}}{40 \text{ dollars}}$ is also a proportion. A proportion can be read two ways. The proportion $\frac{5}{8} = \frac{15}{24}$ can be read "five eighths equals fifteen twenty-fourths," or it can be read "five *is to* eight *as* fifteen *is to* twenty-four."

EXAMPLE 1 Write the proportion 5 is to 7 as 15 is to 21.

Solution

$$\frac{5}{7} = \frac{15}{21}$$

Practice Problem 1 Write the proportion 6 is to 8 as 9 is to 12.

EXAMPLE 2 Write a proportion to express the following: If four rolls of wallpaper measure 100 metres, then eight rolls of wallpaper will measure 200 metres.

Solution When you write a proportion, order is important. Be sure that the similar units for the rates are in the same position in the fractions.

$$\frac{4 \text{ rolls}}{100 \text{ metres}} = \frac{8 \text{ rolls}}{200 \text{ metres}}$$

Practice Problem 2 Write a proportion to express the following: If it takes two hours to drive 72 kilometres, then it will take three hours to drive 108 kilometres.

***NOTE TO STUDENT:** Fully worked-out solutions to all of the Practice Problems can be found at the end of the module.*

2 Determining Whether a Statement Is a Proportion

By definition, a proportion states that two ratios are equal. $\frac{2}{7} = \frac{4}{14}$ is a proportion because $\frac{2}{7}$ and $\frac{4}{14}$ are equivalent fractions. You might say that $\frac{2}{7} = \frac{4}{14}$ is a *true* statement. It is easy enough to see that $\frac{2}{7} = \frac{4}{14}$ is true. However, is $\frac{4}{14} = \frac{6}{21}$ true? Is $\frac{4}{14} = \frac{6}{21}$ a proportion? To determine whether a statement is a proportion, we use the equality test for fractions.

EQUALITY TEST FOR FRACTIONS

For any two fractions where $b \neq 0$ and $d \neq 0$,

$$\frac{a}{b} = \frac{c}{d} \text{ if and only if } a \times d = b \times c.$$

Thus, to see if $\frac{4}{14} = \frac{6}{21}$, we can multiply.

$$\frac{4}{14} \times \frac{6}{21} \qquad \begin{aligned} 14 \times 6 &= 84 \leftarrow \\ 4 \times 21 &= 84 \leftarrow \end{aligned}$$

The cross products are equal.

$\frac{4}{14} = \frac{6}{21}$ is true. $\frac{4}{14} = \frac{6}{21}$ is a proportion.

This method is called finding **cross products.**

EXAMPLE 3 Determine which equations are proportions.

(a) $\frac{14}{18} \stackrel{?}{=} \frac{35}{45}$ **(b)** $\frac{16}{21} \stackrel{?}{=} \frac{174}{231}$

Solution

(a) $\frac{14}{18} \stackrel{?}{=} \frac{35}{45}$

$18 \times 35 = 630$

$\frac{14}{18} \times \frac{35}{45}$ The cross products are equal. Thus $\frac{14}{18} = \frac{35}{45}$. This is a proportion.

$14 \times 45 = 630$

(b) $\frac{16}{21} \stackrel{?}{=} \frac{174}{231}$

$21 \times 174 = 3654$

$\frac{16}{21} \times \frac{174}{231}$ The cross products are not equal. Thus $\frac{16}{21} \neq \frac{174}{231}$. This is not a proportion.

$16 \times 231 = 3696$

Practice Problem 3 Determine which equations are proportions.

(a) $\frac{10}{18} \stackrel{?}{=} \frac{25}{45}$ **(b)** $\frac{42}{100} \stackrel{?}{=} \frac{22}{55}$

Proportions may involve fractions or decimals.

EXAMPLE 4 Determine which equations are proportions.

(a) $\frac{5.5}{7} \stackrel{?}{=} \frac{33}{42}$ **(b)** $\frac{5}{8\frac{3}{4}} \stackrel{?}{=} \frac{40}{72}$

Solution

(a) $\frac{5.5}{7} \stackrel{?}{=} \frac{33}{42}$

$7 \times 33 = 231$

$\frac{5.5}{7} \times \frac{33}{42}$ The cross products are equal. Thus $\frac{5.5}{7} = \frac{33}{42}$. This is a proportion.

$5.5 \times 42 = 231$

(b) $\dfrac{5}{8\frac{3}{4}} \stackrel{?}{=} \dfrac{40}{72}$

First we multiply $8\frac{3}{4} \times 40 = \dfrac{35}{\cancel{4}_1} \times \overset{10}{\cancel{40}} = 35 \times 10 = 350$

$8\frac{3}{4} \times 40 = 350$

$\dfrac{5}{8\frac{3}{4}} \times \dfrac{40}{72}$ — The cross products are not equal. Thus $\dfrac{5}{8\frac{3}{4}} \neq \dfrac{40}{72}$. This is not a proportion.

$5 \times 72 = 360$

Practice Problem 4 Determine which equations are proportions.

(a) $\dfrac{2.4}{3} \stackrel{?}{=} \dfrac{12}{15}$ **(b)** $\dfrac{2\frac{1}{3}}{6} \stackrel{?}{=} \dfrac{14}{38}$

***NOTE TO STUDENT:** Fully worked-out solutions to all of the Practice Problems can be found at the end of the module.*

EXAMPLE 5 **(a)** Is the rate $\dfrac{\$86}{\text{13 tonnes}}$ equal to the rate $\dfrac{\$79}{\text{12 tonnes}}$?

(b) Is the rate $\dfrac{\text{3 Canadian dollars}}{\text{2 British pounds}}$ equal to the rate $\dfrac{\text{27 Canadian dollars}}{\text{18 British pounds}}$?

Solution

(a) We want to know whether $\dfrac{86}{13} = \dfrac{79}{12}$.

$13 \times 79 = 1027$

$\dfrac{86}{13} \times \dfrac{79}{12}$ — The cross products are not equal.

$86 \times 12 = 1032$

Thus the two rates are not equal. This is not a proportion.

(b) We want to know whether $\dfrac{3}{2} = \dfrac{27}{18}$.

$2 \times 27 = 54$

$\dfrac{3}{2} \times \dfrac{27}{18}$ — The cross products are equal.

$3 \times 18 = 54$

Thus the two rates are equal. This is a proportion.

Practice Problem 5

(a) Is the rate $\dfrac{\text{1260 words}}{\text{7 pages}}$ equal to the rate $\dfrac{\text{3530 words}}{\text{20 pages}}$?

(b) Is the rate $\dfrac{\text{3 Canadian dollars}}{\text{2 euros}}$ equal to the rate $\dfrac{\text{5 Canadian dollars}}{\text{10 euros}}$?

SECTION 2 EXERCISES

Verbal and Writing Skills

1. A proportion states that two ratios or rates are ________.
2. Explain in your own words how we use the equality test for fractions to determine if a statement is a proportion. Give an example.

Write a proportion.

3. 6 is to 8 as 3 is to 4.
4. 12 is to 10 as 6 is to 5.
5. 20 is to 36 as 5 is to 9.
6. 120 is to 15 as 160 is to 20.
7. 220 is to 11 as 400 is to 20.
8. $2\frac{1}{2}$ is to 10 as $7\frac{1}{2}$ is to 30.
9. $4\frac{1}{3}$ is to 13 as $5\frac{2}{3}$ is to 17.
10. 5.5 is to 10 as 11 is to 20.
11. 6.5 is to 14 as 13 is to 28.

Applications *Write a proportion.*

12. ***Cooking*** When Jenny makes rice in her steamer, she mixes 2 cups of rice with 3 cups of water. If she uses 8 cups of rice, she needs 12 cups of water.
13. ***Cartography*** A cartographer (a person who makes maps) uses a scale of 3 centimetres to represent 40 kilometres. 27 centimetres would then represent 360 kilometres.
14. ***Reading Speed*** If Marcella can read 32 pages of her novel in 2 hours, she can read 80 pages in 5 hours.
15. ***Tips for Valets*** Stephen works as a valet parker. If he earns \$40 in tips for parking 12 cars, he should earn \$60 for parking 18 cars.
16. ***Food Cost*** If 20 kilograms of pistachio nuts cost \$75, then 30 kilograms will cost \$112.50.
17. ***Education*** If three credit hours at Centennial College cost \$525, then seven credit hours should cost \$1225.
18. ***Education*** When Humber College had 1200 students enrolled, 24 mathematics sections were offered. This year there are 1450 students enrolled, so 29 mathematics sections should be offered.
19. ***Teaching Ratio*** There are 3 teaching assistants for every 40 children in the elementary school. If we have 280 children, then we will have 21 teaching assistants.
20. ***Lawn Care*** If 16 pounds of fertilizer cover 1520 square feet of lawn, then 19 pounds of fertilizer should cover 1805 square feet of lawn.
21. ***Restaurants*** When New City had 4800 people, it had three restaurants. Now New City has 11 200 people, so it should have seven restaurants.

Determine which equations are proportions.

22. $\frac{8}{6} \stackrel{?}{=} \frac{20}{15}$

23. $\frac{10}{25} \stackrel{?}{=} \frac{6}{15}$

24. $\frac{14}{11} \stackrel{?}{=} \frac{12}{10}$

25. $\frac{8}{10} \stackrel{?}{=} \frac{13}{15}$

26. $\frac{99}{100} \stackrel{?}{=} \frac{49}{50}$

27. $\frac{17}{75} \stackrel{?}{=} \frac{22}{100}$

28. $\frac{315}{2100} \stackrel{?}{=} \frac{15}{100}$

29. $\frac{102}{120} \stackrel{?}{=} \frac{85}{100}$

30. $\frac{6}{14} \stackrel{?}{=} \frac{4.5}{10.5}$

31. $\frac{2.5}{4} \stackrel{?}{=} \frac{7.5}{12}$

32. $\frac{11}{12} \stackrel{?}{=} \frac{9.5}{10}$

33. $\frac{3}{17} \stackrel{?}{=} \frac{4.5}{24.5}$

34. $\frac{7}{1\frac{1}{2}} \stackrel{?}{=} \frac{14}{3}$

35. $\frac{6}{2\frac{1}{2}} \stackrel{?}{=} \frac{12}{5}$

36. $\frac{2\frac{1}{3}}{3} \stackrel{?}{=} \frac{7}{15}$

37. $\frac{7\frac{1}{3}}{3} \stackrel{?}{=} \frac{23}{9}$

38. $\frac{2.5}{\frac{1}{2}} \stackrel{?}{=} \frac{21}{5}$

39. $\frac{\frac{1}{4}}{2} \stackrel{?}{=} \frac{\frac{7}{20}}{2.8}$

40. $\frac{75 \text{ kilometres}}{5 \text{ hours}} \stackrel{?}{=} \frac{105 \text{ kilometres}}{7 \text{ hours}}$

41. $\frac{135 \text{ kilometres}}{3 \text{ hours}} \stackrel{?}{=} \frac{225 \text{ kilometres}}{5 \text{ hours}}$

42. $\frac{286 \text{ litres}}{12 \text{ hectares}} \stackrel{?}{=} \frac{429 \text{ litres}}{18 \text{ hectares}}$

43. $\frac{166 \text{ litres}}{14 \text{ kilograms}} \stackrel{?}{=} \frac{249 \text{ litres}}{21 \text{ kilograms}}$

44. $\frac{52 \text{ free throws}}{80 \text{ attempts}} \stackrel{?}{=} \frac{60 \text{ free throws}}{95 \text{ attempts}}$

45. $\frac{21 \text{ home runs}}{96 \text{ games}} \stackrel{?}{=} \frac{18 \text{ home runs}}{81 \text{ games}}$

46. ***Concert Audiences*** At the Michael W. Smith concert on Friday there were 9600 female fans and 8200 male fans. The concert on Saturday had 12 480 female fans and 10 660 male fans. Is the ratio of female fans to male fans the same for both nights of the concert?

47. ***Baseball Team Wins*** Since Harding High School opened, it has won 132 baseball games and lost 22. Derry High School has won 160 games and lost 32 since it opened. Is the ratio of lost games to won games the same for both schools?

48. ***Machine Operating Rate*** A machine folds 650 boxes in five hours. Another machine folds 580 boxes in four hours.

(a) Do they fold boxes at the same rate?
(b) Which machine folds more boxes in 24 hours?

49. ***Speed of Vehicle*** A bus travelled 675 kilometres in 18 hours. A passenger van travelled 820 kilometres in 20 hours.

(a) Did they travel at the same rate?
(b) Which vehicle travelled at a faster rate?

▲ **50.** ***Television Screen Size*** A common size for a television screen is 22 inches wide by 16 inches tall. Does a smaller television screen that is 11 inches wide by 8.5 inches tall have the same ratio of width to length?

▲ **51.** ***Driveway Size*** A common size for a driveway in suburban Wheaton, Illinois, is 75 feet long by 20 feet wide. Does a larger driveway that is 105 feet long by 28 feet wide have the same ratio of width to length?

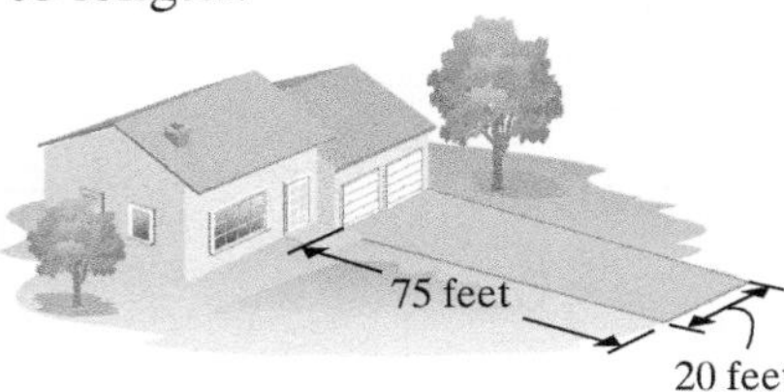

To Think About

52. Determine whether $\frac{63}{161} = \frac{171}{437}$

(a) by reducing each side to lowest terms.

(b) by using the equality test for fractions. (This is the cross-product method.)

(c) Which method was faster? Why?

53. Determine whether $\frac{169}{221} = \frac{247}{323}$

(a) by reducing each side to lowest terms.

(b) by using the equality test for fractions. (This is the cross-product method.)

(c) Which method was faster? Why?

Quick Quiz 2

1. Write as a proportion.
8 is to 18 as 28 is to 63.

2. Write as a proportion.

13 is to 32 as $3\frac{1}{4}$ is to 8.

3. Determine if this equation is a proportion.

$$\frac{15 \text{ shots}}{4 \text{ goals}} \stackrel{?}{=} \frac{75 \text{ shots}}{22 \text{ goals}}$$

4. Concept Check Explain how to determine if $\frac{33 \text{ chairs}}{45 \text{ employees}} \stackrel{?}{=} \frac{165 \text{ chairs}}{225 \text{ employees}}$ is a proportion.

How Am I Doing? Sections 1–2

How are you doing with your homework assignments in Sections 1 and 2? Do you feel you have mastered the material so far? Do you understand the concepts you have covered? Before you go further, take some time to do each of the following problems.

1 *In questions 1–4, write each ratio in simplest form.*

1. 13 to 18

2. 44 to 220

3. \$72 to \$16

4. 135 metres to 165 metres

5. Sam's take-home pay is \$240 per week. \$70 per week is deducted for federal taxes and \$22 per week is deducted for provincial taxes.

(a) Find the ratio of federal deductions to take-home pay.

(b) Find the ratio of provincial deductions to take-home pay.

Write each rate in simplest form.

6. 9 flight attendants for 300 passengers

7. 620 litres of water for 840 square metres of lawn

Write as a unit rate. Round to the nearest tenth if necessary.

8. A professional bicyclist travels 100 kilometres in 4 hours. What is the rate in kilometres per hour?

9. 15 CD players are purchased for \$435. What is the cost per CD player?

10. In a certain recipe, 2400 cookies are made with 15 pounds of cookie dough. How many cookies can be made with 1 pound of cookie dough?

2 *Write a proportion.*

11. 13 is to 40 as 39 is to 120

12. 116 is to 148 as 29 is to 37

13. If a speedboat can travel 33 nautical miles in 2 hours, then it can travel 49.5 nautical miles in 3 hours.

14. If the cost to manufacture 3000 athletic shoes is \$370, then the cost to manufacture 7500 athletic shoes is \$925.

Determine whether each equation is a proportion.

15. $\frac{14}{31} \stackrel{?}{=} \frac{42}{93}$

16. $\frac{17}{33} \stackrel{?}{=} \frac{19}{45}$

17. $\frac{6.5}{4.8} \stackrel{?}{=} \frac{120}{96}$

18. $\frac{15}{24} \stackrel{?}{=} \frac{1\frac{5}{8}}{2\frac{3}{5}}$

19. The Pine Street Inn can produce 670 servings of a chicken dinner for homeless people at a cost of \$1541. It will therefore cost \$1886 to produce 820 servings of the same chicken dinner.

20. For every 30 flights that arrive at London International Airport in December, approximately 4 of them are more than 15 minutes late. Therefore, for every 3000 flights that arrive at London International Airport in December, approximately 400 of them will be more than 15 minutes late.

Your institution may have included the Answers to Selected Exercises for this module, which contains the answers to these questions. Each answer also includes a reference to the objective in which the problem is first taught. If you missed any of these problems, you should stop and review the Examples and Practice Problems in the referenced objective. A little review now will help you master the material in the upcoming sections.

1. __________
2. __________
3. __________
4. __________
5.(a) _____ (b) _____
6. __________
7. __________
8. __________
9. __________
10. __________
11. __________
12. __________
13. __________
14. __________
15. __________
16. __________
17. __________
18. __________
19. __________
20. __________

SECTION 3 SOLVING PROPORTIONS

Student Learning Objectives

After studying this section, you will be able to:

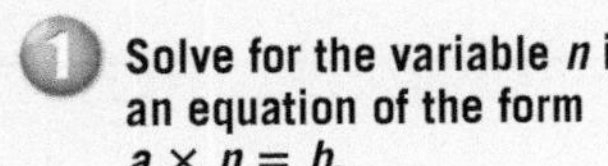

1. Solve for the variable n in an equation of the form $a \times n = b$.
2. Find the missing number in a proportion.

Solving for the Variable n in an Equation of the Form $a \times n = b$

Consider this expression: "3 times a number yields 15. What is the number?" We could write this as

$$3 \times \boxed{?} = 15$$

and guess that the number $\boxed{?} = 5$. There is a better way of solving this problem, a way that eliminates the guesswork. We will begin by using a **variable.** That is, we will use a letter to represent a number we do not yet know.

Let the letter n represent the unknown number. We write

$$3 \times n = 15.$$

This is called an **equation.** An equation has an equals sign. This indicates that the values on each side of it are equivalent. We want to find the number n in this equation without guessing. We will not change the value of n in the equation if we divide both sides of the equation by 3. Thus if

$$3 \times n = 15,$$

we can say $$\frac{3 \times n}{3} = \frac{15}{3},$$

which is $$\frac{3}{3} \times n = 5$$

or $$1 \times n = 5.$$

Since 1 multiplied by any number is the same number, we know that $n = 5$. Any equation of the form $a \times n = b$ can be solved in this way. We divide both sides of an equation of the form $a \times n = b$ by the number that is multiplied by n. (We do this because division is the inverse operation of multiplication. This method will not work for $3 + n = 15$, since here the 3 is added to n and not multiplied by n.)

EXAMPLE 1 Solve for n.

(a) $16 \times n = 80$ **(b)** $24 \times n = 240$

Solution

(a) $16 \times n = 80$

$$\frac{16 \times n}{16} = \frac{80}{16} \quad \text{Divide each side by 16.}$$

$$n = 5 \quad \text{because } 16 \div 16 = 1 \text{ and } 80 \div 16 = 5.$$

(b) $24 \times n = 240$

$$\frac{24 \times n}{24} = \frac{240}{24} \quad \text{Divide each side by 24.}$$

$$n = 10 \quad \text{because } 24 \div 24 = 1 \text{ and } 240 \div 24 = 10.$$

Practice Problem 1 Solve for n.

(a) $5 \times n = 45$ **(b)** $7 \times n = 84$

NOTE TO STUDENT: Fully worked-out solutions to all of the Practice Problems can be found at the end of the module.

The same procedure is followed if the variable n is on the right-hand side of the equation.

EXAMPLE 2 Solve for n.

(a) $66 = 11 \times n$ **(b)** $143 = 13 \times n$

Solution

(a) $66 = 11 \times n$

$$\frac{66}{11} = \frac{11 \times n}{11}$$ Divide each side by 11.

$$6 = n$$

(b) $143 = 13 \times n$

$$\frac{143}{13} = \frac{13 \times n}{13}$$ Divide each side by 13.

$$11 = n$$

Practice Problem 2 Solve for n.

(a) $108 = 9 \times n$ **(b)** $210 = 14 \times n$

The numbers in the equations are not always whole numbers, and the answer to an equation is not always a whole number.

EXAMPLE 3 Solve for n.

(a) $16 \times n = 56$ **(b)** $18.2 = 2.6 \times n$

Solution

(a) $16 \times n = 56$

$$\frac{16 \times n}{16} = \frac{56}{16}$$ Divide each side by 16.

$$n = 3.5$$

$$\begin{array}{r} 3.5 \\ 16\overline{)56.0} \\ \underline{48} \\ 8\,0 \\ \underline{8\,0} \\ 0 \end{array}$$

(b) $18.2 = 2.6 \times n$

$$\frac{18.2}{2.6} = \frac{2.6 \times n}{2.6}$$ Divide each side by 2.6

$$7 = n$$

$$\begin{array}{r} 7. \\ 2.6_{\wedge}\overline{)18.2_{\wedge}} \\ \underline{18\,2} \\ 0 \end{array}$$

Practice Problem 3 Solve for n.

(a) $15 \times n = 63$ **(b)** $39.2 = 5.6 \times n$

2 Finding the Missing Number in a Proportion

Sometimes one of the pieces of a proportion is unknown. We can use an equation such as $a \times n = b$ and solve for n to find the unknown quantity. Suppose we want to know the value of n in the proportion

$$\frac{5}{12} = \frac{n}{144}.$$

Since this is a proportion, we know that $5 \times 144 = 12 \times n$. Simplifying, we have

$$720 = 12 \times n.$$

Next we divide both sides by 12.

$$\frac{720}{12} = \frac{12 \times n}{12}$$

$$60 = n$$

We check to see if this is correct. Do we have a true proportion?

$$\frac{5}{12} \stackrel{?}{=} \frac{60}{144}$$

$$\frac{5}{12} \times \frac{60}{144} \quad \begin{array}{l} 12 \times 60 = 720 \\ 5 \times 144 = 720 \end{array}$$

The cross products are equal.

Thus $\frac{5}{12} = \frac{60}{144}$ is true. We have checked our answer.

TO SOLVE FOR A MISSING NUMBER IN A PROPORTION

1. Find the cross products.
2. Divide each side of the equation by the number multiplied by n.
3. Simplify the result.
4. Check your answer.

EXAMPLE 4 Find the value of n in $\frac{25}{4} = \frac{n}{12}$.

Solution

$$25 \times 12 = 4 \times n \quad \text{Find the cross products.}$$

$$300 = 4 \times n$$

$$\frac{300}{4} = \frac{4 \times n}{4} \quad \text{Divide each side by 4.}$$

$$75 = n$$

Check. Is this a proportion?

$$\frac{25}{4} \stackrel{?}{=} \frac{75}{12}$$

$$25 \times 12 \stackrel{?}{=} 4 \times 75$$

$$300 = 300 \quad ✓$$

It is a proportion. The answer $n = 75$ is correct.

Practice Problem 4 Find the value of n in

$$\frac{24}{n} = \frac{3}{7}.$$

The answer to the next problem is not a whole number.

EXAMPLE 5 Find the value of n in $\frac{125}{2} = \frac{150}{n}$.

Solution

$125 \times n = 2 \times 150$ Find the cross products.

$125 \times n = 300$

$\frac{125 \times n}{125} = \frac{300}{125}$ Divide each side by 125.

$n = 2.4$

Check. $\frac{125}{2} \stackrel{?}{=} \frac{150}{2.4}$

$125 \times 2.4 \stackrel{?}{=} 2 \times 150$

$300 = 300$ ✓

Practice Problem 5 Find the value of n in

$$\frac{176}{4} = \frac{286}{n}.$$

EXAMPLE 6 Find the value of n in

$$\frac{n}{20} = \frac{\frac{3}{4}}{5}.$$

Solution

$5 \times n = 20 \times \frac{3}{4}$ Find the cross products.

$5 \times n = 15$ Simplify.

$\frac{5 \times n}{5} = \frac{15}{5}$ Divide each side by 5.

$n = 3$

Check. Can you verify that this is a proportion?

Practice Problem 6 Find the value of n in

$$\frac{n}{30} = \frac{\frac{2}{3}}{4}.$$

In real-life situations it is helpful to write the units of measure in the proportion. Remember, order is important. The same units should be in the same position in the fractions.

EXAMPLE 7 If 5 grams of a non-icing additive are placed in 8 litres of diesel fuel, how many grams n should be added to 12 litres of diesel fuel?

Solution We need to find the value of n in $\frac{n \text{ grams}}{12 \text{ litres}} = \frac{5 \text{ grams}}{8 \text{ litres}}$.

$$8 \times n = 12 \times 5$$

$$8 \times n = 60$$

$$\frac{8 \times n}{8} = \frac{60}{8}$$

$$n = 7.5$$

The answer is 7.5 grams. 7.5 grams of the additive should be added to 12 litres of the diesel fuel.

Check.

$$\frac{7.5 \text{ grams}}{12 \text{ litres}} \stackrel{?}{=} \frac{5 \text{ grams}}{8 \text{ litres}}$$

$$7.5 \times 8 \stackrel{?}{=} 12 \times 5$$

$$60 = 60 \quad ✓$$

Practice Problem 7 If 25 millilitres of a lawn fertilizer is to be mixed with 3 litres of water, how many millilitres of fertilizer should be mixed with 24 litres of water?

Some answers will be exact values. In other cases we will obtain answers that are rounded to a certain decimal place. Recall that we sometimes use the $\approx$ symbol, which means "is approximately equal to."

EXAMPLE 8 Find the value of n in $\frac{141 \text{ kilometres}}{4.5 \text{ hours}} = \frac{67 \text{ kilometres}}{n \text{ hours}}$. Round to the nearest tenth.

Solution

$$141 \times n = 67 \times 4.5$$

$$141 \times n = 301.5$$

$$\frac{141 \times n}{141} = \frac{301.5}{141}$$

If we calculate to four decimal places, we have $n = 2.1382$. Rounding to the nearest tenth, $n \approx 2.1$.

The answer to the nearest tenth is $n = 2.1$. The check is up to you.

Practice Problem 8

Find the value of n in $\frac{264 \text{ metres}}{3.5 \text{ seconds}} = \frac{n \text{ metres}}{2 \text{ seconds}}$. Round to the nearest tenth.

TO THINK ABOUT: Proportions with Mixed Numbers or Fractions Suppose that the proportion contains many fractions or mixed numbers. Could you still follow all the steps? For example, find n when

$$\frac{n}{3\frac{1}{4}} = \frac{5\frac{1}{6}}{2\frac{1}{3}}$$

We have $2\frac{1}{3} \times n = 5\frac{1}{6} \times 3\frac{1}{4}$.

This can be written as

$$\frac{7}{3} \times n = \frac{31}{6} \times \frac{13}{4}$$

$$\boxed{\frac{7}{3} \times n = \frac{403}{24}} \qquad \text{equation (1)}$$

Now we divide each side of equation (1) by $\frac{7}{3}$. Why?

$$\frac{\frac{7}{3} \times n}{\frac{7}{3}} = \frac{\frac{403}{24}}{\frac{7}{3}}$$

Be careful here. The right-hand side means $\frac{403}{24} \div \frac{7}{3}$, which we evaluate by *inverting* the second fraction and multiplying.

$$\frac{403}{\underset{8}{\cancel{24}}} \times \frac{\overset{1}{\cancel{3}}}{7} = \frac{403}{56}$$

Thus $n = \frac{403}{56}$ or $7\frac{11}{56}$. Think about all the steps to solving this problem. Can you follow them? There is another way to do the problem. We could multiply each side of equation (1) by $\frac{3}{7}$.

$$\frac{7}{3} \times n = \frac{403}{24} \qquad \text{equation (1)}$$

$$\frac{3}{7} \times \frac{7}{3} \times n = \frac{3}{7} \times \frac{403}{24}$$

$$n = \frac{403}{56}$$

Why does this work? Now try exercises 56–59 in Section 3 Exercises.

Accuracy is especially important in this section. When you do the Section 3 Exercises, be sure to verify your answers at the end of the module. Take a little extra time with those problems that result in fraction or decimal answers. It is very important that you learn how to do this type of problem.

Section 3 Exercises

Verbal and Writing Skills

1. Suppose you have an equation of the form $a \times n = b$, where the letters a and b represent whole numbers and $a \neq 0$. Explain in your own words how you would solve the equation.

2. Suppose you have an equation of the form $\frac{n}{a} = \frac{b}{c}$, where a, b, and c represent whole numbers and $a, c \neq 0$. Explain in your own words how you would solve the equation.

Solve for n.

3. $8 \times n = 72$

4. $6 \times n = 72$

5. $3 \times n = 16.8$

6. $2 \times n = 19.6$

7. $n \times 6.7 = 134$

8. $n \times 3.8 = 95$

9. $50.4 = 6.3 \times n$

10. $40.6 = 5.8 \times n$

11. $\frac{4}{9} \times n = 22$ (*Hint:* Divide each side by $\frac{4}{9}$.)

12. $\frac{6}{7} \times n = 26$ (*Hint:* Divide each side by $\frac{6}{7}$.)

Find the value of n. Check your answer.

13. $\frac{n}{20} = \frac{3}{4}$

14. $\frac{n}{28} = \frac{3}{7}$

15. $\frac{6}{n} = \frac{3}{8}$

16. $\frac{4}{n} = \frac{2}{7}$

17. $\frac{12}{40} = \frac{n}{25}$

18. $\frac{13}{30} = \frac{n}{15}$

19. $\frac{50}{100} = \frac{2.5}{n}$

20. $\frac{40}{160} = \frac{1.5}{n}$

21. $\frac{n}{6} = \frac{150}{12}$

22. $\frac{n}{22} = \frac{25}{11}$

23. $\frac{15}{4} = \frac{n}{6}$

24. $\frac{16}{10} = \frac{n}{9}$

25. $\frac{240}{n} = \frac{5}{4}$

26. $\frac{180}{n} = \frac{4}{3}$

Find the value of n. Round your answer to the nearest tenth when necessary.

27. $\frac{21}{n} = \frac{2}{3}$

28. $\frac{62}{n} = \frac{5}{4}$

29. $\frac{9}{26} = \frac{n}{52}$

30. $\frac{12}{8} = \frac{21}{n}$

31. $\frac{15}{12} = \frac{10}{n}$

32. $\frac{n}{18} = \frac{3.5}{1}$

33. $\frac{n}{36} = \frac{4.5}{1}$

34. $\frac{2.5}{n} = \frac{0.5}{10}$

35. $\frac{1.8}{n} = \frac{0.7}{12}$

36. $\frac{7}{16} = \frac{n}{26.2}$

37. $\frac{11}{12} = \frac{n}{32.8}$

38. $\frac{12.5}{16} = \frac{n}{12}$

39. $\frac{13.8}{15} = \frac{n}{6}$

40. $\frac{5}{n} = \frac{12\frac{1}{2}}{100}$

41. $\frac{3}{n} = \frac{6\frac{1}{4}}{100}$

Applications *Find the value of n. Round to the nearest hundredth when necessary.*

42. $\frac{n \text{ grams}}{10 \text{ litres}} = \frac{7 \text{ grams}}{25 \text{ litres}}$

43. $\frac{n \text{ pounds}}{20 \text{ ounces}} = \frac{2 \text{ pounds}}{32 \text{ ounces}}$

44. $\frac{190 \text{ kilometres}}{3 \text{ hours}} = \frac{n \text{ kilometres}}{5 \text{ hours}}$

45. $\frac{145 \text{ kilometres}}{2 \text{ hours}} = \frac{220 \text{ kilometres}}{n \text{ hours}}$

46. $\frac{50 \text{ gallons}}{12 \text{ acres}} = \frac{36 \text{ gallons}}{n \text{ acres}}$

47. $\frac{32 \text{ metres}}{5 \text{ yards}} = \frac{24 \text{ metres}}{n \text{ yards}}$

48. $\frac{3 \text{ kilograms}}{6.6 \text{ pounds}} = \frac{n \text{ kilograms}}{10 \text{ pounds}}$

49. $\frac{36.4 \text{ feet}}{5 \text{ metres}} = \frac{n \text{ feet}}{12 \text{ metres}}$

50. $\frac{12 \text{ quarters}}{3 \text{ dollars}} = \frac{87 \text{ quarters}}{n \text{ dollars}}$

51. $\frac{35 \text{ dimes}}{3.5 \text{ dollars}} = \frac{n \text{ dimes}}{8 \text{ dollars}}$

52. $\frac{2\frac{1}{2} \text{ hectares}}{3 \text{ people}} = \frac{n \text{ hectares}}{5 \text{ people}}$

53. $\frac{3\frac{1}{4} \text{ feet}}{8 \text{ pounds}} = \frac{n \text{ feet}}{12 \text{ pounds}}$

▲**54.** ***Photography*** A photographic negative is 3.5 centimetres wide and 2.5 centimetres tall. If you want to make a colour print that is 6 centimetres tall, how wide will the print be?

▲**55.** ***Photography*** A colour photograph is 5 inches wide and 3 inches tall. If you want to make an enlargement of this photograph that is 6.6 inches tall, how wide will the enlargement be?

To Think About *Study the "To Think About" example in Section 3, after Practice Problem 8. Then solve for n in exercises 56–59. Express n as a mixed number.*

56. $\frac{n}{7\frac{1}{4}} = \frac{2\frac{1}{5}}{4\frac{1}{8}}$

57. $\frac{n}{2\frac{1}{3}} = \frac{4\frac{5}{6}}{3\frac{1}{9}}$

58. $\frac{9\frac{3}{4}}{n} = \frac{8\frac{1}{2}}{4\frac{1}{3}}$

59. $\frac{8\frac{1}{6}}{n} = \frac{5\frac{1}{2}}{7\frac{1}{3}}$

Quick Quiz 3

1. Solve.

$$\frac{n}{26} = \frac{9}{130}$$

2. Solve.

$$\frac{8}{6} = \frac{2\frac{2}{3}}{n}$$

3. Solve. Round to the nearest tenth.

$$\frac{17 \text{ hits}}{93 \text{ pitches}} = \frac{n \text{ hits}}{62 \text{ pitches}}$$

4. Concept Check Explain how you would solve the proportion.

$$\frac{2\frac{1}{2}}{3\frac{3}{4}} = \frac{16\frac{1}{2}}{n}$$

SECTION 4 SOLVING APPLIED PROBLEMS INVOLVING PROPORTIONS

Solving Applied Problems Using Proportions

Let us examine a variety of applied problems that can be solved by proportions.

Student Learning Objective

After studying this section, you will be able to:

1. **Solve applied problems using proportions.**

EXAMPLE 1 A company that makes eyeglasses conducted a recent survey using a quality control test. It was discovered that 37 pairs of eyeglasses in a sample of 120 pairs of eyeglasses were defective. If this rate remains the same each year, how many of the 36 000 pairs of eyeglasses made by this company each year are defective?

Solution

Mathematics Blueprint for Problem Solving

Gather the Facts	What Am I Asked to Do?	How Do I Proceed?	Key Points to Remember
Sample: 37 defective pairs in a total of 120 pairs 36 000 pairs were made by the company.	Find how many of the 36 000 pairs of eyeglasses are defective.	Set up a proportion comparing defective eyeglasses to total eyeglasses.	Make sure one fraction represents the sample and one fraction represents the total number of eyeglasses made by the company.

We will use the letter n to represent the number of defective eyeglasses in the total.

$$\underbrace{\frac{37 \text{ defective pairs}}{120 \text{ total pairs of eyeglasses}}}_{\text{We compare the sample}} \;\; \text{to} \;\; = \underbrace{\frac{n \text{ defective pairs}}{36\,000 \text{ total pairs of eyeglasses}}}_{\text{the total number}}$$

$$37 \times 36\,000 = 120 \times n \quad \text{Find the cross products.}$$

$$1\,332\,000 = 120 \times n \quad \text{Simplify.}$$

$$\frac{1\,332\,000}{120} = \frac{120 \times n}{120} \quad \text{Divide each side by 120.}$$

$$11\,100 = n$$

Thus, if the rate of defective eyeglasses holds steady, there are about 11 100 defective pairs of eyeglasses made by the company each year.

Practice Problem 1 Yesterday an automobile assembly line produced 243 engines, of which 27 were defective. If the same rate is true each day, how many of the 4131 engines produced this month are defective?

***NOTE TO STUDENT:** Fully worked-out solutions to all of the Practice Problems can be found at the end of the module.*

Looking back at Example 1, perhaps it occurred to you that the fractions in the proportion could be set up in an alternative way. **You can set up this problem in several different ways as long as the units are in correctly**

corresponding positions. It would be correct to set up the problem in the form

$$\frac{\text{defective pairs in sample}}{\text{total defective pairs}} = \frac{\text{total glasses in sample}}{\text{total glasses made by company}}$$

or

$$\frac{\text{total glasses in sample}}{\text{defective pairs in sample}} = \frac{\text{total glasses made by company}}{\text{total defective pairs}}$$

But we **cannot** set up the problem this way.

$$\frac{\text{defective pairs in sample}}{\text{total glasses made by company}} = \frac{\text{total defective pairs}}{\text{total glasses in sample}}$$

This is *not* correct. Do you see why?

EXAMPLE 2 Ted's car can go 245 kilometres on 21 litres of gas. Ted wants to take a trip of 455 kilometres. Approximately how many litres of gas will this take?

Solution Let n = the unknown number of litres.

$$\frac{245 \text{ kilometres}}{21 \text{ litres}} = \frac{455 \text{ kilometres}}{n \text{ litres}}$$

$245 \times n = 21 \times 455$ Find the cross products.

$245 \times n = 9555$ Simplify.

$\frac{245 \times n}{245} = \frac{9555}{245}$ Divide both sides by 245.

$n = 39$

Ted will need approximately 39 litres of gas for the trip.

Practice Problem 2 Cindy's car travels 234 kilometres on 18 litres of gas. How many litres of gas will Cindy need to take a 312-kilometre trip?

EXAMPLE 3 In a certain gear, Monique's 18-speed bicycle has a gear ratio of three revolutions of the pedal for every two revolutions of the bicycle wheel. If her bicycle wheel is turning at 65 revolutions per minute, how many times must she pedal per minute?

Peter Saloutos/Corbis/Bettman

Solution Let n = the number of revolutions of the pedal.

$$\frac{3 \text{ revolutions of the pedal}}{2 \text{ revolutions of the wheel}} = \frac{n \text{ revolutions of the pedal}}{65 \text{ revolutions of the wheel}}$$

$3 \times 65 = 2 \times n$ Cross-multiply.

$195 = 2 \times n$ Simplify.

$\frac{195}{2} = \frac{2 \times n}{2}$ Divide both sides by 2.

$97.5 = n$

Monique will pedal at the rate of 97.5 revolutions per 1 minute.

Practice Problem 3 Alicia must pedal at 80 revolutions per minute to ride her bicycle at 16 kilometres per hour. If she pedals at 90 revolutions per minute, how fast will she be riding?

EXAMPLE 4 Kie operates a bicycle rental centre during the summer months on the island of Martha's Vineyard. He discovered that when the ferryboats brought 8500 passengers a day to the island, his centre rented 340 bicycles a day. Next summer the ferryboats plan to bring 10 300 passengers a day to the island. How many bicycles a day should Kie plan to rent?

Solution Two important cautions are necessary before we solve the proportion. We need to be sure that the bicycle rentals are directly related to the number of people on the ferryboat. (Presumably, people who fly to the island or who take small pleasure boats to the island also rent bicycles.)

Next we need to be sure that the people who represent the increase in passengers per day would be as likely to rent bicycles as the present number of passengers do. For example, if the new visitors to the island are all senior citizens, they are not as likely to rent bicycles as younger people. If we assume those two conditions are satisfied, then we can solve the problem as follows.

$$\frac{8500 \text{ passengers per day now}}{340 \text{ bike rentals per day now}} = \frac{10\,300 \text{ passengers per day later}}{n \text{ bike rentals per day later}}$$

$$8500 \times n = 340 \times 10\,300$$

$$8500 \times n = 3\,502\,000$$

$$\frac{8500 \times n}{8500} = \frac{3\,502\,000}{8500}$$

$$n = 412$$

If the two conditions are satisfied, we would predict 412 bicycle rentals.

Practice Problem 4 For every 4050 people who walk into Tom's Souvenir Shop, 729 make a purchase. Assuming the same conditions, if 5500 people walk into Tom's Souvenir Shop, how many people may be expected to make a purchase?

Wildlife Population Counting Biologists and others who observe or protect wildlife sometimes use the capture-mark-recapture method to determine how many animals are in a certain region. In this approach some animals are caught and tagged in a way that does not harm them. They are then released into the wild, where they mix with their kind.

It is assumed (usually correctly) that the tagged animals will mix throughout the entire population in that region, so that when they are recaptured in a future sample, the biologists can use them to make reasonable estimates about the total population. We will employ the capture-mark-recapture method in the next example.

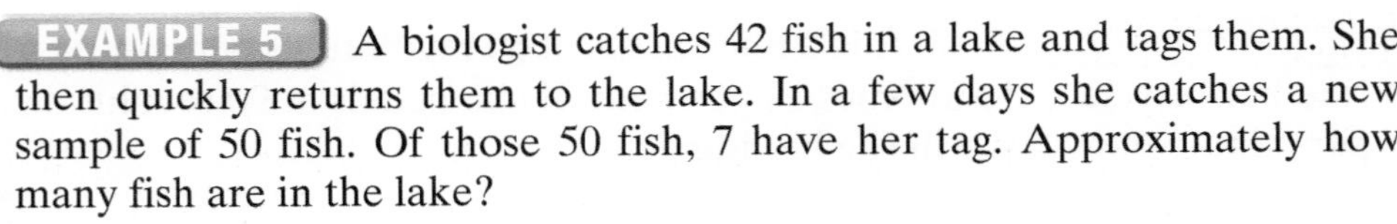

EXAMPLE 5 A biologist catches 42 fish in a lake and tags them. She then quickly returns them to the lake. In a few days she catches a new sample of 50 fish. Of those 50 fish, 7 have her tag. Approximately how many fish are in the lake?

Solution

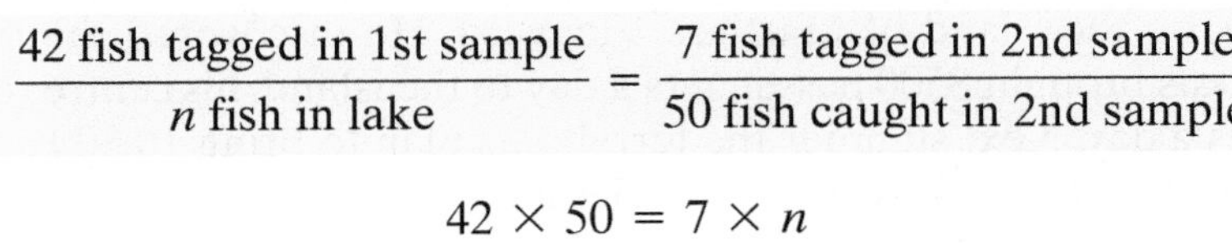

$$\frac{42 \text{ fish tagged in 1st sample}}{n \text{ fish in lake}} = \frac{7 \text{ fish tagged in 2nd sample}}{50 \text{ fish caught in 2nd sample}}$$

Photos.com

$$42 \times 50 = 7 \times n$$
$$2100 = 7 \times n$$
$$\frac{2100}{7} = \frac{7 \times n}{7}$$
$$300 = n$$

Assuming that no tagged fish died and that the tagged fish mixed throughout the population of fish in the lake, we estimate that there are 300 fish in the lake.

Practice Problem 5 A park ranger in Yukon captures and tags 50 bears. He then releases them to range through the forest. Sometime later he captures 50 bears. Of the 50, 4 have tags from the previous capture. Estimate the number of bears in the forest.

Developing Your Study Skills

Getting Help

Getting the right kind of help at the right time can be a key ingredient in being successful in mathematics. When you have gone to class on a regular basis, taken careful notes, methodically read your textbook, and diligently done your homework—in other words, when you have made every effort possible to learn the mathematics—you may still find that you are having difficulty. If this is the case, then you need to seek help. Make an appointment with your instructor to find out what help is available to you. The instructor, tutoring services, a mathematics lab, DVDs, and computer software may be among the resources you can draw on.

Section 4 Exercises

Verbal and Writing Skills

1. Dan saw 12 people on the beach on Friday night. He counted 5 dogs on the beach at that time. On Saturday night he saw 60 people on the same beach. He is trying to estimate how many dogs might be on the beach Saturday night. He started by writing the equation

$$\frac{12 \text{ people}}{5 \text{ dogs}} =$$

Explain how he should set up the rest of the proportion.

2. Lise drove to the top of Maple Mountain. As she drove up the roadway she observed 15 cars. On the same trip she observed 17 people walking. Later that afternoon she drove down the mountain. On that trip she observed 60 cars. She is trying to estimate how many people she might see walking. She started by writing the equation

$$\frac{15 \text{ cars}}{17 \text{ people}} =$$

Explain how she should set up the rest of the proportion.

Applications

3. ***Car Repairs*** An automobile dealership has found that for every 140 cars sold, 23 will be brought back to the dealer for major repairs. If the dealership sells 980 cars this year, approximately how many cars will be brought back for major repairs?

4. ***Hotel Management*** The policy at the Colonnade Hotel is to have 19 desserts for every 16 people if a buffet is being served. If the Saturday buffet has 320 people, how many desserts must be available?

5. ***Consumer Product Use*** The directions on a bottle of bleach say to use 75 millilitres of bleach for every 1 litre of soapy water. Ron needs a 4-litre mixture to mop his floors. How many millilitres of bleach will he need?

6. ***Food Preparation*** To make an 8-ounce serving of hot chocolate, $1\frac{1}{2}$ tablespoons of cocoa are needed. How much cocoa is needed to make 12 ounces of hot chocolate?

7. ***Measurement*** There are approximately $1\frac{1}{2}$ kilometres in one mile. Approximately how many kilometres are in 5 miles?

8. ***Measurement*** There are approximately $2\frac{1}{2}$ centimetres in 1 inch. Approximately how many centimetres are in 1 foot if there are 12 inches in 1 foot?

9. ***Exchange Rate*** When Julie flew to Hong Kong in 2009, the exchange rate was 39 Hong Kong dollars for every 5 Canadian dollars. If Julie brought 180 Canadian dollars for spending money, how many Hong Kong dollars did she receive?

10. ***Exchange Rate*** One day in February 2009, one Canadian dollar was worth 0.511 British pounds. Frederich exchanged 220 Canadian dollars when he arrived in London. How many British pounds did he receive?

Shadow Length *In exercises 11 and 12, two nearby objects cast shadows at the same time of day. The ratio of the height of one of the objects to the length of its shadow is equal to the ratio of the height of the other object to the length of its shadow.*

▲**11.** A pro football offensive tackle who stands 6.5 feet tall casts a 5-foot shadow. At the same time, the football stadium, which he is standing next to, casts a shadow of 152 feet. How tall is the stadium? Round your answer to the nearest tenth.

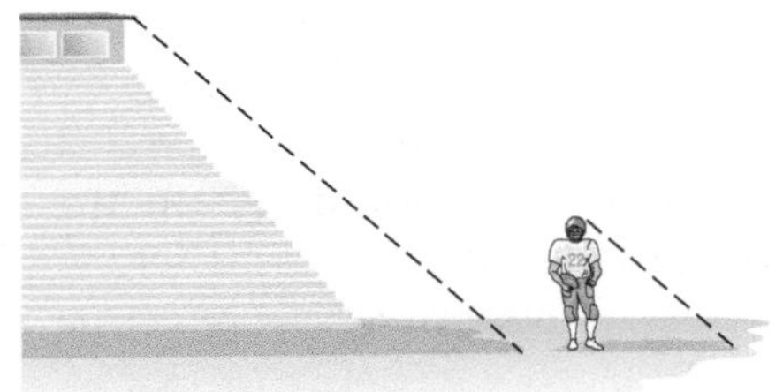

▲**12.** In Barrie, Ontario, at 2 P.M., a boulder that is 2 metres high casts a shadow that is 5.5 metres long. At that same time, Melinda is standing by a tree that is on the bank of the river. She measures the tree and finds it is exactly 10.5 metres tall. The tree has a shadow that crosses the entire width of the river. How wide is the river? Round your answer to the nearest tenth.

13. ***Map Scale*** On a tour guide map of Madagascar, the scale states that 3 centimetres represent 125 kilometres. Two beaches are 5.2 centimetres apart on the map. What is the approximate distance in kilometres between the two beaches? Round your answer to the nearest kilometre.

14. ***Map Scale*** On a map of Antarctica, the scale states that 4 centimetres represent 250 kilometres of actual distance. Two Antarctic mountains are 5.7 centimetres apart on the map. What is the approximate distance in kilometres between the two mountains? Round your answer to the nearest kilometre.

15. ***Food Preparation*** In his curry chicken recipe, Deepak uses 3 cups of curry sauce for every 8 people. How many cups of curry sauce will he need to make curry chicken for a dinner party of 34 people? Write your answer as a mixed number.

16. ***Food Preparation*** Bianca's chocolate fondue recipe uses 4 cups of chocolate chips to make fondue sauce for 6 people. How many cups of chocolate chips are needed to make fondue for 26 people? Write your answer as a mixed number.

17. ***Basketball*** During a basketball game against the Miami Heat, the Toronto Raptors made 17 out of 25 free throws attempted. If they attempt 150 free throws in the remaining games of the season, how many will they make if their success rate remains the same?

18. ***Baseball*** A baseball pitcher gave up 52 earned runs in 260 innings of pitching. At that rate, how many runs would he give up in a 9-inning game? (This decimal is called the pitcher's *earned run average*.)

19. ***Fuel Efficiency*** In her Dodge Neon, Claire can drive 192 kilometres on 12 litres of gas. During spring break, she plans to drive 600 kilometres. How many litres of gas will she use?

20. ***Fuel Efficiency*** In her car, Juanita can drive 75 kilometres on 5 litres of gas. She drove 318 kilometres for a business trip. How many litres of gas did she use?

21. ***Wildlife Population Counting*** An ornithologist is studying hawks in the Adirondack Mountains. She catches 24 hawks over a period of one month, tags them, and releases them back into the wild. The next month, she catches 20 hawks and finds that 12 are already tagged. Estimate the number of hawks in this part of the mountains.

22. ***Wildlife Population Counting*** In Kenya, a worker at the game preserve captures 26 giraffes, tags them, and then releases them back into the preserve. The next month, he captures 18 giraffes and finds that 6 of them have already been tagged. Estimate the number of giraffes on the preserve.

23. ***Farming*** Bill and Shirley Grant are raising tomatoes to sell at the local co-op. The farm has a yield of 425 kilograms of tomatoes for every 3 square kilometres. The farm has 14 square kilometres of good tomatoes. The crop this year should bring $1.80 per kilogram of tomatoes. How much will the Grants get from the sale of the tomato crop?

▲**24.** ***Painting*** A paint manufacturer suggests 2 litres of flat latex paint for every 11 square metres of wall. A painter is going to paint 875 square metres of wall in a Charlottetown office building with paint that costs $8.50 per litre. How much will the painter spend for the paint?

25. ***Manufacturing Quality*** A company that manufactures computer chips expects 5 out of every 100 made to be defective. In a shipment of 5400 chips, how many are expected to be defective?

26. ***Customer Satisfaction*** The editor of a small-town newspaper conducted a survey to find out how many customers are satisfied with their delivery service. Of the 100 people surveyed, 88 customers said they were satisfied. If 1700 people receive the newspaper, how many are satisfied?

To Think About

Cooking *The following chart is used for several brands of instant mashed potatoes. Use this chart in answering exercises 27–30.*

TO MAKE	WATER	MARGARINE OR BUTTER	SALT (optional)	MILK	FLAKES
2 servings	2/3 cup	1 tablespoon	1/8 teaspoon	1/4 cup	2/3 cup
4 servings	1-1/3 cups	2 tablespoons	1/4 teaspoon	1/2 cup	1-1/3 cups
6 servings	2 cups	3 tablespoons	1/2 teaspoon	3/4 cup	2 cups
Entire box	5 cups	1/2 cup	1 teaspoon	2-1/2 cups	Entire box

27. How many cups of water and how many cups of milk are needed to make enough mashed potatoes for three people?

28. How many cups of water and how many cups of milk are needed to make enough mashed potatoes for five people?

29. Phil and Melissa live in Banff. They found that the instructions on the box say that at high altitudes (above 1525 metres) the amount of water should be reduced by $\frac{1}{4}$. If you had to make enough mashed potatoes for eight people in a high-altitude city, how many cups of water and how many cups of milk would be needed?

30. Noah and Olivia live in Jasper. They found that the instructions on the box say that at high altitudes (above 1525 metres) the amount of water should be reduced by $\frac{1}{4}$.

(a) If you had to make two boxes of mashed potatoes at a high altitude, how many cups of water and how many cups of milk would be used?

(b) How many servings would be obtained?

Baseball Salaries *During the 2005–06 playing season, Albert Pujols of the St. Louis Cardinals hit 49 home runs and was paid an annual salary of $14 000 000. During the same season, Alfonso Soriano of the Washington Nationals hit 46 home runs and was paid an annual salary of $10 000 000. (Source:* www.usatoday.com*)*

31. Express the salary of each player as a unit rate in terms of dollars paid to home runs hit.

32. Which player hit more home runs per dollar?

Basketball Salaries *During the 2005–06 basketball season, Ray Allen of the Seattle Super Sonics made 269 three-point shots and was paid an annual salary of $13 220 000. During the same season, Gilbert Arenas of the Washington D.C. Wizards made 199 three-point shots and was paid an annual salary of $10 240 000. (Source:* www.usatoday.com*)*

33. Express the salary of each player as a unit rate in terms of dollars paid to three-point shots made.

34. Which player made more three-point shots per dollar?

Quick Quiz 4 Solve using a proportion. Round your answer to the nearest hundredth when necessary.

1. A copper cable 36 metres long weighs 160 kilograms. How much will 54 metres of this cable weigh?

2. If 11 centimetres on a map represent a distance of 64 kilometres, what distance does 5 centimetres represent?

3. During the first few games of the basketball season, Caleb shot 16 free throws and made 7 of them. If Caleb shoots free throws at the same rate as the first few games, he expects to shoot 100 more during the rest of the season. How many of these additional free throws should he expect to make? Round to the nearest whole number.

4. Concept Check When Fred went to France he discovered that 70 euros were worth 104 Canadian dollars. He brought 400 Canadian dollars on his trip. Explain how he would find what that is worth in euros.

Putting Your Skills to Work: Use Math to Save Money

CHOOSING A CELL PHONE PLAN

Everyone wants to comparison shop in order to save money. Finding the best cell phone plan is one place where comparison shopping can really help, especially when you're trying to work within a budget. Consider the story of Jake.

Comstock Complete

Jake is interested in purchasing a new cell phone plan. He would like to call his family, friends, and co-workers, as well as send/receive text and picture messages. He hopes he can afford to access the Internet, too, so he can check his e-mail with his phone. He wants to find a cell phone plan that would allow him to do these things for between $69 and $89 per month.

Analyzing the Options

He did some research and he is considering these cell phone plans:

Calling Plan A: 300 minutes per month, $0.20 each additional minute: **$39.99 per month**

Calling Plan B: 450 minutes per month, $0.45 each additional minute: **$39.99 per month**

Calling Plan C: 600 minutes per month, $0.20 each additional minute: **$49.99 per month**

Calling Plan D: 900 minutes per month, $0.40 each additional minute: **$59.99 per month**

Which calling plan is the best choice if. . .

1. Jake plans to talk for 100 minutes per month?

2. Jake plans to talk for 350 minutes per month?

3. Jake plans to talk for 470 minutes per month?

4. Jake plans to talk for 550 minutes per month?

5. Jake plans to talk for 11 hours per month?

6. Jake plans to talk for 16 hours, 40 minutes per month?

Making the Best Choice to Save Money

Jake expects he will talk between 500 and 750 minutes per month, and is therefore considering Calling Plan C or Calling Plan D. Remember, Jake would like to send/receive text and picture messages. He'd also like to check his e-mail on the Internet with his phone. Jake's research also shows that "message bundles" are available at an additional charge to the calling plans.

Bundle A: 200 messages (text, picture, video, and IM) per month, $0.10 each additional message: **$5.00 per month**

Bundle B: 1500 messages (text, picture, video, and IM) per month, $0.05 each additional message: **$15.00 per month**

Bundle C: Unlimited text, picture, video, and IM messages per month: **$20.00 per month**

Bundle D: Unlimited web access and unlimited text, picture, video, and IM messages per month: **$35.00 per month**

Bundle D is the only bundle that would provide Jake with web access to check his e-mail in addition to messaging. If Jake wants to keep the cost of his cell phone service between $69 and $89 per month, determine the following:

7. The cost of Calling Plan C and Bundle D per month.

8. The cost of Calling Plan D and Bundle D per month

Jake is excited that Calling Plan C and Bundle D fit his budget. However, he is nervous about what will happen if he goes over his minutes with Calling Plan C.

9. Determine the total cost for one month if Jake talks for 750 minutes with Calling Plan C and Bundle D.

10. If you were Jake, which calling plan and bundle would you choose? Why?

Module Organizer

Topic	Procedure	Examples
Forming a ratio.	A *ratio* is the comparison of two quantities that have the same units. A ratio is usually expressed as a fraction. The fraction should be in reduced form.	**1.** Find the ratio of 20 books to 35 books. $\frac{20}{35} = \frac{4}{7}$ **2.** Find the ratio in simplest form of 88 : 99. $\frac{88}{99} = \frac{8}{9}$ **3.** Bob earns \$250 each week, but \$15 is deducted for medical insurance. Find the ratio of medical insurance to total pay. $\frac{\$15}{\$250} = \frac{3}{50}$
Forming a rate.	A *rate* is a comparison of two quantities that have different units. A rate is usually expressed as a fraction in reduced form.	A college has 2520 students with 154 faculty. What is the rate of students to faculty? $\frac{2520 \text{ students}}{154 \text{ faculty}} = \frac{180 \text{ students}}{11 \text{ faculty}}$
Forming a unit rate.	A *unit rate* is a rate with a denominator of 1. Divide the denominator into the numerator to obtain the unit rate.	A car travelled 416 kilometres in 8 hours. Find the unit rate. $\frac{416 \text{ kilometres}}{8 \text{ hours}} = 52$ kilometres/hour Bob spread 50 kilograms of fertilizer over 1870 square metres of land. Find the unit rate of square metres per kilogram. $\frac{1870 \text{ square metres}}{50 \text{ kilograms}} = 37.4$ square metres/kilogram
Writing proportions.	A *proportion* is a statement that two rates or two ratios are equal. The proportion statement *a* is to *b* as *c* is to *d* can be written $\frac{a}{b} = \frac{c}{d}$.	Write a proportion for 17 is to 34 as 13 is to 26. $\frac{17}{34} = \frac{13}{26}$
Determining whether a relationship is a proportion.	For any two fractions where $b \neq 0$ and $d \neq 0$, $\frac{a}{b} = \frac{c}{d}$ if and only if $a \times d = b \times c$. A proportion is a statement that two rates or two ratios are equal.	**1.** Is this a proportion? $\frac{7}{56} \stackrel{?}{=} \frac{3}{24}$ $7 \times 24 \stackrel{?}{=} 56 \times 3$ $168 = 168$ ✓ It is a proportion. **2.** Is this a proportion? $\frac{64 \text{ litres}}{5 \text{ hectares}} \stackrel{?}{=} \frac{89 \text{ litres}}{7 \text{ hectares}}$ $64 \times 7 \stackrel{?}{=} 5 \times 89$ $448 \neq 445$ It is not a proportion.
Solving a proportion.	To solve a proportion where the value *n* is not known: **1.** Cross-multiply. **2.** Divide both sides of the equation by the number multiplied by *n*.	Solve for *n*. $\frac{17}{n} = \frac{51}{9}$ $17 \times 9 = 51 \times n$ Cross-multiply. $153 = 51 \times n$ Simplify. $\frac{153}{51} = \frac{51 \times n}{51}$ Divide by 51. $3 = n$

Topic	Procedure	Examples
Solving applied problems.	**1.** Write a proportion with n representing the unknown value. **2.** Solve the proportion.	Bob purchased eight notebooks for $19. How much would 14 notebooks cost? $\frac{8 \text{ notebooks}}{\$19} = \frac{14 \text{ notebooks}}{n}$ $8 \times n = 19 \times 14$ $8 \times n = 266$ $\frac{8 \times n}{8} = \frac{266}{8}$ $n = 33.25$ The 14 notebooks would cost $33.25.

Module Review Problems

If you have trouble with a particular type of exercise, review the examples in the section indicated for that group of exercises. Your institution may have included the Answers to Selected Exercises for this module, which contains the answers to these questions.

Section 1

Write in simplest form. Express your answer as a fraction.

1. 88 : 40

2. 65 : 39

3. 28 : 35

4. 250 : 475

5. $2\frac{1}{3}$ to $4\frac{1}{4}$

6. 27 to 81

7. 180 to 531

8. 168 to 300

9. 26 tons to 65 tons

Personal Finance *Bob earns $480 per week and has $60 deducted for federal taxes and $45 deducted for provincial taxes.*

10. Write the ratio of federal taxes deducted to earned income.

11. Write the ratio of total deductions to earned income.

Write as a rate in simplest form.

12. $75 donated by every 6 people

13. 44 revolutions every 121 minutes

14. 75 heartbeats every 60 seconds

15. 12 cups of flour for every 27 cakes

In exercises 16–21, write as a unit rate. Round to the nearest tenth when necessary.

16. $2125 was paid for 125 shares of stock. Find the cost per share.

17. ***Education*** $1344 was paid for 12 credit-hours. Find the cost per credit-hour.

▲ **18.** $742.50 was spent for 55 square metres of carpet. Find the cost per square metre.

19. ***DVD Cost*** Larry spent $600 on 48 DVDs. Find the cost per DVD.

20. ***Food Costs*** A 200-gram jar of instant coffee costs \$2.96. A 500-gram jar of the same brand of instant coffee costs \$5.22.

(a) What is the cost per gram of the 200-gram jar?

(b) What is the cost per gram of the 500-gram jar?

(c) How much per gram do you save by buying the larger jar?

21. ***Food Costs*** A 250-gram can of white tuna costs \$2.75. A 140-gram can of the same brand of white tuna costs \$1.75.

(a) What is the cost per gram of the large can?

(b) What is the cost per gram of the small can?

(c) How much per gram do you save by buying the larger can?

Section 2

Write as a proportion.

22. 12 is to 48 as 7 is to 28

23. $1\frac{1}{2}$ is to 5 as 4 is to $13\frac{1}{3}$

24. 7.5 is to 45 as 22.5 is to 135

25. ***Bus Capacity*** If three buses can transport 138 passengers, then five buses can transport 230 passengers.

26. ***Cost of Products*** If 15 litres cost \$4.50, then 27 litres will cost \$8.10.

Determine whether each equation is a proportion.

27. $\frac{16}{48} \stackrel{?}{=} \frac{2}{12}$

28. $\frac{20}{25} \stackrel{?}{=} \frac{8}{10}$

29. $\frac{36}{30} \stackrel{?}{=} \frac{60}{50}$

30. $\frac{28}{12} \stackrel{?}{=} \frac{84}{36}$

31. $\frac{37}{33} \stackrel{?}{=} \frac{22}{19}$

32. $\frac{15}{18} \stackrel{?}{=} \frac{18}{22}$

33. $\frac{84 \text{ kilometres}}{7 \text{ litres}} \stackrel{?}{=} \frac{108 \text{ kilometres}}{9 \text{ litres}}$

34. $\frac{156 \text{ revolutions}}{6 \text{ minutes}} \stackrel{?}{=} \frac{181 \text{ revolutions}}{7 \text{ minutes}}$

Section 3

Solve for n.

35. $9 \times n = 162$

36. $5 \times n = 38$

37. $442 = 20 \times n$

38. $663 = 39 \times n$

Solve. Round to the nearest tenth when necessary.

39. $\frac{3}{11} = \frac{9}{n}$

40. $\frac{2}{7} = \frac{12}{n}$

41. $\frac{n}{28} = \frac{6}{24}$

42. $\frac{n}{32} = \frac{15}{20}$

43. $\frac{2\frac{1}{4}}{9} = \frac{4\frac{3}{4}}{n}$

44. $\frac{3\frac{1}{3}}{2\frac{2}{3}} = \frac{7}{n}$

45. $\frac{42}{50} = \frac{n}{6}$

46. $\frac{38}{45} = \frac{n}{8}$

47. $\frac{2.25}{9} = \frac{4.75}{n}$

48. $\frac{3.5}{5} = \frac{10.5}{n}$

49. $\frac{20}{n} = \frac{43}{16}$

50. $\frac{36}{n} = \frac{109}{18}$

51. $\frac{35 \text{ kilometres}}{28 \text{ litres}} = \frac{15 \text{ kilometres}}{n \text{ litres}}$

52. $\frac{8 \text{ defective parts}}{100 \text{ perfect parts}} = \frac{44 \text{ defective parts}}{n \text{ perfect parts}}$

Section 4

Solve using a proportion. Round your answer to the nearest hundredth when necessary.

53. ***Painting*** The school volunteers used 9 litres of paint to paint two rooms. How many litres would they need to paint 10 rooms of the same size?

54. ***Coffee Consumption*** Several recent surveys show that 49 out of every 100 adults in Canada drink coffee. If a computer company employs 3450 people, how many of those employees would you expect would drink coffee? Round to the nearest whole number.

55. ***Exchange Rate*** When Marguerite travelled as a child, the rate of French francs to Canadian dollars was 24 francs to 5 dollars. How many francs did Marguerite receive for 420 dollars?

56. ***Exchange Rate*** When John and Nancy travelled to Switzerland in 2007, the rate of Swiss francs to Canadian dollars was 6 francs to 4.8 dollars. How many Swiss francs would they receive for 125 Canadian dollars?

57. ***Map Scale*** Two cities located 225 kilometres apart appear 3 centimetres apart on a map. If two other cities appear 8 centimetres apart on the map, how many kilometres apart are the cities?

58. ***Basketball*** In the first three games of the basketball season, Kyle made 8 rebounds. There are 15 games left in the season. How many rebounds would you expect Kyle to make in these 15 games?

▲ **59.** ***Shadow Length*** In the setting sun, a 6-foot man casts a shadow 16 feet long. At the same time a building casts a shadow of 320 feet. How tall is the building?

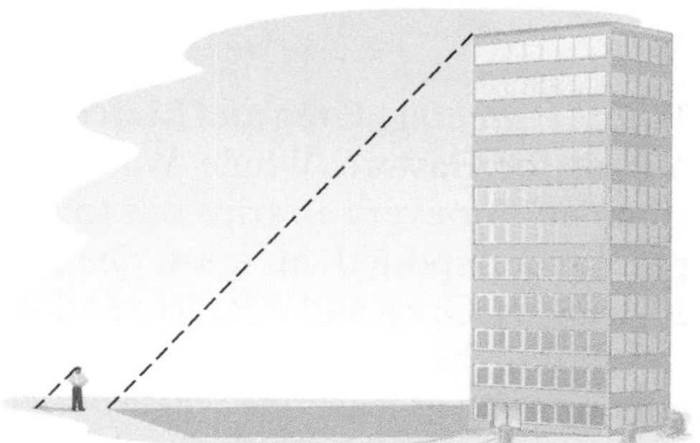

60. ***Gasoline Consumption*** During the first 380 kilometres of a trip, Johnny and Stephanie used 26 litres of gas. They need to travel 200 more kilometres. Assume that the car will have the same rate of gas consumption.

(a) How many more litres of gas will they need?

(b) If gas costs $1.20 per litre, what will fuel cost them for the last 200 kilometres?

▲ **61.** ***Photography*** A film negative is 3.5 centimetres wide and 2.5 centimetres tall. If you want to make a colour print that is 8 centimetres wide, how tall will the print be?

62. ***Medications*** The dosage of a certain medication is 3 grams for every 50 kilograms of body weight. If a person weighs 125 kilograms, how many grams of this medication should be taken?

63. ***Pool Walkway*** Carl is designing a walkway around his swimming pool. He will need 22 pavers for each 3-metre section of walkway. How many pavers will he need to buy to make a walkway that is 21 metres long?

64. ***Student Survey*** Greta did a study at her community college for her sociology class. Of the 35 students she interviewed, 21 of them said they eat in the campus cafeteria at least once a week. If there are a total of 2800 students at the college, how many of them eat at least once a week in the cafeteria?

▲ **65.** ***Painting*** When Carlos was painting his apartment, he found that he used 3 litres of paint to cover 140 square metres of wall space. He is planning to paint his sister's apartment. She said there are 1400 square metres of wall space that need to be painted. How many litres of paint will Carlos need?

66. ***Water Supplies*** From previous experience, the directors of a large running race know they need 2 litres of water for every 3 runners. This year 1250 runners will participate in the race. How many litres of water do they need?

▲ **67.** ***Scale Model*** A scale model of a new church sanctuary has a length of 14 centimetres. When the church is built, the actual length will be 145 feet. In the scale model, the width measures 11 centimetres. What will be the actual width of the church sanctuary?

68. ***Time Gain*** Jeff checked the time on his new watch. In 40 days his watch gained 3 minutes. How much time will the watch gain in a year? (Assume it is not a leap year.)

69. ***Soccer*** Jean, the top soccer player for the Springfield Comets, scored a total of 68 goals during the season. During the season the team played 32 games, but Jean played in only 27 of them due to a leg injury. The league has been expanded and next season the team will play 34 games. If Jean scores goals at the same rate and is able to play in every game, how many goals might she be expected to score? Round your answer to the nearest whole number.

70. ***Calories*** Hank found out there were 345 calories in the 10-ounce chocolate milkshake that he purchased yesterday. Today he decided to order the 16-ounce milkshake. How many calories would you expect to be in the 16-ounce milkshake?

71. ***Reader Survey*** A recent survey showed that 3 out of every 10 people in Ontario read the *Toronto Star*. In an Ontario town of 45 600 people, how many people would you expect to read the *Toronto Star?*

72. ***Whale Watching*** Greg and Marcia are managing a boat for Eastern Whale Watching Tours this summer. For every 16 trips out to the ocean, the passengers spotted at least one whale during 13 trips. If Greg and Marcia send out 240 trips this month, how many trips will have the passengers spotting at least one whale?

How Am I Doing? Module Test

Write as a ratio in simplest form.

1. 18 : 52

2. 70 to 185

Write as a rate in simplest form. Express your answer as a fraction.

3. 784 kilometres per 24 litres

4. 2100 square metres per 45 kilograms

Write as a unit rate. Round to the nearest hundredth when necessary.

5. 19 tonnes in five days

6. \$57.96 for seven hours

7. 5400 metres per 22 telephone poles

8. \$9373 for 110 shares of stock

Write as a proportion.

9. 17 is to 29 as 51 is to 87

10. $2\frac{1}{2}$ is to 10 as 6 is to 24

11. 490 miles is to 21 gallons as 280 miles is to 12 gallons

12. 3 hours is to 180 kilometres as 5 hours is to 300 kilometres

Determine whether each equation is a proportion.

13. $\frac{50}{24} \stackrel{?}{=} \frac{34}{16}$

14. $\frac{3\frac{1}{2}}{14} \stackrel{?}{=} \frac{5}{20}$

15. $\frac{32 \text{ smokers}}{46 \text{ nonsmokers}} \stackrel{?}{=} \frac{160 \text{ smokers}}{230 \text{ nonsmokers}}$

16. $\frac{\$0.74}{16 \text{ ounces}} \stackrel{?}{=} \frac{\$1.84}{40 \text{ ounces}}$

1. ______________

2. ______________

3. ______________

4. ______________

5. ______________

6. ______________

7. ______________

8. ______________

9. ______________

10. ______________

11. ______________

12. ______________

13. ______________

14. ______________

15. ______________

16. ______________

Solve. Round to the nearest tenth when necessary.

17. $\frac{n}{20} = \frac{4}{5}$

18. $\frac{8}{3} = \frac{60}{n}$

19. $\frac{2\frac{2}{3}}{8} = \frac{6\frac{1}{3}}{n}$

20. $\frac{4.2}{11} = \frac{n}{77}$

21. $\frac{\text{45 women}}{\text{15 men}} = \frac{n \text{ women}}{\text{40 men}}$

22. $\frac{\text{5 kilograms}}{\text{11 pounds}} = \frac{\text{32 kilograms}}{n \text{ pounds}}$

23. $\frac{n \text{ centimetres of snow}}{\text{14 centimetres of rain}} = \frac{\text{12 centimetres of snow}}{\text{1.4 centimetres of rain}}$

24. $\frac{\text{5 kilograms of coffee}}{\$n} = \frac{\text{1/2 kilogram of coffee}}{\$5.20}$

Solve using a proportion. Round your answer to the nearest hundredth when necessary.

25. Bob's recipe for pancakes calls for three eggs and will serve 11 people. If he wants to feed 22 people, how many eggs will he need?

26. A steel cable 42 metres long weighs 170 kilograms. How much will 20 metres of this cable weigh?

27. If 9 centimetres on a map represent 57 kilometres, what distance does 3 centimetres represent?

28. Dan and Oriana found it would cost $240 per year to fertilize their front lawn of 1000 square metres. How much would it cost to fertilize 1500 square metres?

29. Michael Delgaty knows that 1 mile is approximately 1.61 kilometres. He sees a sign that reads "Montréal 220 km." How many miles is Michael from Montréal? Round to the nearest tenth of a mile.

30. Rose travelled 570 kilometres in 9 hours. At this rate, how far could Rose go in 11 hours?

31. During the first few games of the basketball season, Tyler shot 15 free throws and made 11 of them. If Tyler shoots free throws at the same rate as the first few games, he expects to shoot 120 more during the rest of the season. How many of these free throws should he expect to make?

32. On the tri-city softball league, Lexi got seven hits in 34 times at bat last week. During the entire playing season, she was at bat 155 times. If she gets hits at the same rate all season as during last week's game, how many hits would she have for the entire season? Round to the nearest whole number.

17. ____________________

18. ____________________

19. ____________________

20. ____________________

21. ____________________

22. ____________________

23. ____________________

24. ____________________

25. ____________________

26. ____________________

27. ____________________

28. ____________________

29. ____________________

30. ____________________

31. ____________________

32. ____________________

Solutions to Practice Problems

Section 1 Practice Problems

1. (a) $\frac{36}{40} = \frac{9}{10}$ (b) $\frac{18}{15} = \frac{6}{5}$ (c) $\frac{220}{270} = \frac{22}{27}$

2. (a) $\frac{200}{450} = \frac{4}{9}$

   (b) The total number of students surveyed is $200 + 450 + 300 + 150 + 100 = 1200$. $\frac{300}{1200} = \frac{1}{4}$

3. $\frac{44 \text{ dollars}}{900 \text{ tonnes}} = \frac{11 \text{ dollars}}{225 \text{ tonnes}}$

4. $\frac{212 \text{ kilometres}}{4 \text{ hours}} = \frac{53 \text{ kilometres}}{1 \text{ hour}}$ 53 kilometres/hour

5.
selling price	\$170.40
− purchase price	− 129.60
profit	\$ 40.80

   She made a profit of \$40.80 on 120 batteries.

$$120\overline{)40.80} = 0.34$$
$$\begin{array}{r} 360 \\ \hline 480 \\ 480 \\ \hline 0 \end{array}$$

   Her profit was \$0.34 per battery.

6. (a) $\frac{\$2.04}{400 \text{ grams}} = 0.51 \text{ cent/gram}$ $\frac{\$2.80}{560 \text{ grams}} = 0.50 \text{ cent/gram}$

   (b) Fred saves 0.01 cent/gram by buying the larger size.

Section 2 Practice Problems

1. 6 is to 8 as 9 is to 12.
   $\frac{6}{8} = \frac{9}{12}$

2. $\frac{2 \text{ hours}}{72 \text{ kilometres}} = \frac{3 \text{ hours}}{108 \text{ kilometres}}$

3. (a) $\frac{10}{18} \stackrel{?}{=} \frac{25}{45}$

   $18 \times 25 = 450$

   $\frac{10}{18} \times \frac{25}{45}$ The cross products are equal.

   $10 \times 45 = 450$

   Thus $\frac{10}{18} = \frac{25}{45}$. This is a proportion.

   (b) $\frac{42}{100} \stackrel{?}{=} \frac{22}{55}$

   $100 \times 22 = 2200$

   $\frac{42}{100} \times \frac{22}{55}$ The cross products are not equal.

   $42 \times 55 = 2310$

   Thus $\frac{42}{100} \neq \frac{22}{55}$. This is not a proportion.

4. (a) $\frac{2.4}{3} \stackrel{?}{=} \frac{12}{15}$

   $3 \times 12 = 36$

   $\frac{2.4}{3} \times \frac{12}{15}$ The cross products are equal.

   $2.4 \times 15 = 36$

   Thus $\frac{2.4}{3} = \frac{12}{15}$. This is a proportion.

   (b) $\frac{2\frac{1}{3}}{6} \stackrel{?}{=} \frac{14}{38}$

   $2\frac{1}{3} \times 38 = \frac{7}{3} \times \frac{38}{1} = \frac{266}{3} = 88\frac{2}{3}$

   $\frac{2\frac{1}{3}}{6} \times \frac{14}{38}$

   $6 \times 14 = 84$

   The cross products are not equal.

   $2\frac{1}{3} \times 38 = 88\frac{2}{3}$

   Thus $\frac{2\frac{1}{3}}{6} \neq \frac{14}{38}$. This is not a proportion.

5. (a) $\frac{1260}{7} \stackrel{?}{=} \frac{3530}{20}$

   $7 \times 3530 = 24\,710$

   $\frac{1260}{7} \times \frac{3530}{20}$ The cross products are not equal.

   $1260 \times 20 = 25\,200$

   The rates are not equal. This is not a proportion.

   (b) $\frac{3}{2} \stackrel{?}{=} \frac{15}{10}$

   $2 \times 15 = 30$

   $\frac{3}{2} \times \frac{15}{10}$ The cross products are equal.

   $3 \times 10 = 30$

   The rates are equal. This is a proportion.

Section 3 Practice Problems

1. (a) $5 \times n = 45$
   $\frac{5 \times n}{5} = \frac{45}{5}$
   $n = 9$

   (b) $7 \times n = 84$
   $\frac{7 \times n}{7} = \frac{84}{7}$
   $n = 12$

2. (a) $108 = 9 \times n$
   $\frac{108}{9} = \frac{9 \times n}{9}$
   $12 = n$

   (b) $210 = 14 \times n$
   $\frac{210}{14} = \frac{14 \times n}{14}$
   $15 = n$

3. (a) $15 \times n = 63$
   $\frac{15 \times n}{15} = \frac{63}{15}$
   $n = 4.2$

$$15\overline{)63.0} = 4.2$$
$$\begin{array}{r} 60 \\ \hline 3\,0 \\ 3\,0 \\ \hline 0 \end{array}$$

(b) $39.2 = 5.6 \times n$

$$\frac{39.2}{5.6} = \frac{5.6 \times n}{5.6}$$

$$7 = n$$

$$5.6_{\wedge}\overline{)39.2_{\wedge}} \quad \text{quotient } 7. \quad 39\,2 \quad 0$$

4. $\dfrac{24}{n} = \dfrac{3}{7}$

$$24 \times 7 = n \times 3$$
$$168 = n \times 3$$
$$\frac{168}{3} = \frac{n \times 3}{3}$$
$$56 = n$$

5. $\dfrac{176}{4} = \dfrac{286}{n}$

$$176 \times n = 286 \times 4$$
$$176 \times n = 1144$$
$$\frac{176 \times n}{176} = \frac{1144}{176}$$
$$n = 6.5$$

$$176\overline{)1144.0} \quad \text{quotient } 6.5 \quad 1056 \quad 88\,0 \quad 88\,0 \quad 0$$

6. $\dfrac{n}{30} = \dfrac{\frac{2}{3}}{4}$

$$4 \times n = 30 \times \frac{2}{3}$$
$$4 \times n = 20$$
$$\frac{4 \times n}{4} = \frac{20}{4}$$
$$n = 5$$

7. $\dfrac{n \text{ tablespoons}}{24 \text{ litres}} = \dfrac{2.5 \text{ tablespoons}}{3 \text{ litres}}$

$$3 \times n = 24 \times 2.5$$
$$3 \times n = 60$$
$$\frac{3 \times n}{3} = \frac{60}{3}$$
$$n = 20$$

The answer is 20.

8. $264 \times 2 = 3.5 \times n$

$$528 = 3.5 \times n$$
$$\frac{528}{3.5} = \frac{3.5 \times n}{3.5}$$
$$150.9 \approx n$$

The answer to the nearest tenth is 150.9.

Section 4 Practice Problems

1. $\dfrac{27 \text{ defective engines}}{243 \text{ engines produced}} = \dfrac{n \text{ defective engines}}{4131 \text{ engines produced}}$

$$27 \times 4131 = 243 \times n$$
$$111\,537 = 243 \times n$$
$$\frac{111\,537}{243} = \frac{243 \times n}{243}$$
$$459 = n$$

Thus we estimate that 459 engines are defective.

2. $\dfrac{18 \text{ litres of gas}}{234 \text{ kilometres travelled}} = \dfrac{n \text{ litres of gas}}{312 \text{ kilometres travelled}}$

$$18 \times 312 = 234 \times n$$
$$5616 = 234 \times n$$
$$\frac{5616}{234} = \frac{234 \times n}{234}$$
$$24 = n$$

She will need 24 litres of gas.

3. $\dfrac{80 \text{ revolutions per minute}}{16 \text{ kilometres per hour}} = \dfrac{90 \text{ revolutions per minute}}{n \text{ kilometres per hour}}$

$$80 \times n = 16 \times 90$$
$$80 \times n = 1440$$
$$\frac{80 \times n}{80} = \frac{1440}{80}$$
$$n = 18$$

Alicia will be riding 18 kilometres per hour.

4. $\dfrac{4050 \text{ walk in}}{729 \text{ purchase}} = \dfrac{5500 \text{ walk in}}{n \text{ purchase}}$

$$4050 \times n = 729 \times 5500$$
$$4050 \times n = 4\,009\,500$$
$$\frac{4050 \times n}{4050} = \frac{4\,009\,500}{4050}$$
$$n = 990$$

Tom will expect 990 people to make a purchase in his store.

5. $\dfrac{50 \text{ bears tagged in 1st sample}}{n \text{ bears in forest}} = \dfrac{4 \text{ bears tagged in 2nd sample}}{50 \text{ bears caught in 2nd sample}}$

$$50 \times 50 = n \times 4$$
$$2500 = n \times 4$$
$$\frac{2500}{4} = \frac{n \times 4}{4}$$
$$625 = n$$

We estimate that there are 625 bears in the forest.

Glossary

Cross-multiplying (Section 3) If you have a proportion such as $\frac{n}{5} = \frac{12}{15}$, then to cross-multiply, you form products to obtain $n \times 15 = 5 \times 12$.

Earned run average (Section 4) A ratio formed by finding the number of runs a pitcher would give up in a nine-inning game. If a pitcher has an earned run average of 2, it means that, on the average, he gives up two runs for every nine innings he pitches.

Proportion (Section 2) A statement that two ratios or two rates are equal. The statement $\frac{3}{4} = \frac{15}{20}$ is a proportion. The statement $\frac{5}{7} = \frac{7}{9}$ is false, and is therefore not a proportion.

Rate (Section 1) A rate compares two quantities that have different units. Examples of rates are \$5.00 an hour and 13 kilograms for every 2 centimetres. In fraction form, these two rates would be written as $\frac{\$5.00}{1 \text{ hour}}$ and $\frac{13 \text{ kilograms}}{2 \text{ centimetres}}$.

Ratio (Section 1) A ratio is a comparison of two quantities that have the same units. To compare 2 to 3, we can express the ratio in three ways: the ratio of 2 to 3; 2 : 3; or the fraction $\frac{2}{3}$.

Ratio in simplest form (Section 1) A ratio is in simplest form when the two numbers do not have a common factor.

Answers to Selected Exercises for Ratio and Proportion

Answers to Selected Exercises for Ratio and Proportion

Section 1 Exercises **1.** ratio **3.** 5 to 8 **5.** $\frac{1}{3}$ **7.** $\frac{7}{6}$ **9.** $\frac{2}{3}$ **11.** $\frac{11}{6}$ **13.** $\frac{5}{6}$ **15.** $\frac{2}{3}$ **17.** $\frac{8}{5}$ **19.** $\frac{2}{3}$ **21.** $\frac{3}{2}$ **23.** $\frac{15}{19}$ **25.** $\frac{13}{1}$ **27.** $\frac{10}{17}$ **29.** $\frac{165}{285} = \frac{11}{19}$ **31.** $\frac{35}{165} = \frac{7}{33}$ **33.** $\frac{205}{1225} = \frac{41}{245}$ **35.** $\frac{450}{205} = \frac{90}{41}$ **37.** $\frac{1}{16}$ **39.** $\frac{\$7}{\text{2 pairs of socks}}$ **41.** $\frac{\$85}{\text{6 bushes}}$ **41.** $\frac{\$85}{\text{6 bushes}}$ **43.** $\frac{\$19}{\text{2 CDs}}$ **45.** $\frac{\text{410 revolutions}}{\text{1 kilometre}}$ or 410 revolutions/kilometre **47.** $\frac{\$27\ 500}{\text{1 employee}}$ or \$27 500/employee **49.** \$15/hour **51.** 16 kilometres/litre **53.** 70 people/square kilometre **55.** 70 books/library **57.** 66 km/h **59.** 19 patients/doctor **61.** 5 eggs/chicken **63.** \$30/share **65.** \$4.50 profit per puppet **67. (a)** \$0.08/oz small box; \$0.07/oz large box **(b)** 1¢ per ounce **(c)** The consumer saves \$0.48. **69. (a)** 13 moose **(b)** 12 moose **(c)** North Slope **71. (a)** \$40.95 **(b)** \$52.80 **(c)** \$11.85 **73.** increased by Mach 0.2

Quick Quiz 1 **1.** $\frac{3}{5}$ **2.** $\frac{\text{340 square metres}}{\text{11 kilograms}}$ **3.** 27.18 trees/acre **4.** See Instructor

Section 2 Exercises **1.** equal **3.** $\frac{6}{8} = \frac{3}{4}$ **5.** $\frac{20}{36} = \frac{5}{9}$ **7.** $\frac{220}{11} = \frac{400}{20}$ **9.** $\frac{4\frac{1}{3}}{13} = \frac{5\frac{2}{3}}{17}$ **11.** $\frac{6.5}{14} = \frac{13}{28}$ **13.** $\frac{\text{3 centimetres}}{\text{40 kilometres}} = \frac{\text{27 centimetres}}{\text{360 kilometres}}$ **15.** $\frac{\$40}{\text{12 cars}} = \frac{\$60}{\text{18 cars}}$ **17.** $\frac{\text{3 hours}}{\$525} = \frac{\text{7 hours}}{\$1225}$ **19.** $\frac{\text{3 teaching assistants}}{\text{40 children}} = \frac{\text{21 teaching assistants}}{\text{280 children}}$ **21.** $\frac{\text{4800 people}}{\text{3 restaurants}} = \frac{\text{11,200 people}}{\text{7 restaurants}}$ **23.** It is a proportion. **25.** It is not a proportion. **27.** It is not a proportion. **29.** It is a proportion. **31.** It is a proportion. **33.** It is not a proportion. **35.** It is a proportion. **37.** It is not a proportion. **39.** It is a proportion. **41.** It is a proportion.**43.** It is a proportion. **45.** It is not a proportion. **47.** no **49. (a)** no **(b)** The van travelled at a faster rate. **51.** yes **53. (a)** yes **(b)** yes **(c)** the equality test for fractions

Quick Quiz 2 **1.** $\frac{8}{18} = \frac{28}{63}$ **2.** $\frac{13}{32} = \frac{3\frac{1}{4}}{8}$ **3.** It is not a proportion. **4.** See Instructor

How Am I Doing? Sections 1–2 **1.** $\frac{13}{18}$ (obj. 1.1) **2.** $\frac{1}{5}$ (obj. 1.1) **3.** $\frac{9}{2}$ (obj. 1.1) **4.** $\frac{9}{11}$ (obj. 1.1) **5. (a)** $\frac{7}{24}$ **(b)** $\frac{11}{120}$ (obj. 1.2) **6.** $\frac{\text{3 flight attendants}}{\text{100 passengers}}$ (obj. 1.2) **7.** $\frac{\text{31 litres}}{\text{42 square metres}}$ (obj. 1.2) **8.** 25 kilometres per hour (obj. 1.2) **9.** \$29 per CD player (obj. 1.2) **10.** 160 cookies per pound of cookie dough (obj. 1.2) **11.** $\frac{13}{40} = \frac{39}{120}$ (obj. 2.1) **12.** $\frac{116}{148} = \frac{29}{37}$ (obj. 2.1) **13.** $\frac{\text{33 nautical miles}}{\text{2 hours}} = \frac{\text{49.5 nautical miles}}{\text{3 hours}}$ (obj. 2.1) **14.** $\frac{\text{3000 shoes}}{\$370} = \frac{\text{7500 shoes}}{\$925}$ (obj. 2.1) **15.** It is a proportion. (obj. 2.2) **16.** It is not a proportion. (obj. 2.2) **17.** It is not a proportion. (obj. 2.2) **18.** It is a proportion. (obj. 2.2) **19.** It is a proportion. (obj. 2.2) **20.** It is a proportion. (obj. 2.2)

Section 3 Exercises **1.** Divide each side of the equation by the number a. Calculate $\frac{b}{a}$. The value of n is $\frac{b}{a}$. **3.** $n = 9$ **5.** $n = 5.6$ **7.** $n = 20$ **9.** $n = 8$ **11.** $n = 49\frac{1}{2}$ **13.** $n = 15$ **15.** $n = 16$ **17.** $n = 7.5$ **19.** $n = 5$ **21.** $n = 75$ **23.** $n = 22.5$ **25.** $n = 192$ **27.** $n = 31.5$ **29.** $n = 18$ **31.** $n = 8$ **33.** $n = 162$ **35.** $n \approx 30.9$ **37.** $n \approx 30.1$ **39.** $n \approx 5.5$ **41.** $n = 48$ **43.** $n = 1.25$ **45.** $n \approx 3.03$ **47.** $n = 3.75$ **49.** $n = 87.36$ **51.** $n = 80$ **53.** $n = 4\frac{7}{8}$ **55.** 11 inches **57.** $n = 3\frac{5}{8}$ **59.** $n = 10\frac{8}{9}$

Quick Quiz 3 **1.** $n = 1.8$ **2.** $n = 2$ **3.** $n \approx 11.3$ **4.** See Instructor

Section 4 Exercises **1.** He should continue with people on the top of the fraction. That would be 60 people he observed on Saturday night. He does not know the number of dogs, so this would be n. The proportion would be:

$$\frac{\text{12 people}}{\text{5 dogs}} = \frac{\text{60 people}}{n \text{ dogs}}.$$

3. 161 cars **5.** 300 mL **7.** $7\frac{1}{2}$ kilometres **9.** 1404 Hong Kong dollars **11.** 197.6 feet **13.** 217 kilometres **15.** $12\frac{3}{4}$ cups **17.** 102 free throws **19.** 37.5 litres **21.** 40 hawks **23.** \$3570 **25.** 270 chips **27.** 1 cup of water and $\frac{3}{8}$ cup of milk **29.** 2 cups of water and 1 cup of milk **31.** Albert Pujols, approximately \$285 714 for each home run; Alfonso Soriano, approximately \$217 391 for each home run **33.** Ray Allen, approximately \$49 145 for each three-point shot; Gilbert Arenas, approximately \$51 457 for each three-point shot

Quick Quiz 4 **1.** 240 kilograms **2.** 29.09 kilometres **3.** 44 free throws **4.** See Instructor

Putting Your Skills to Work **1.** Either A or B **2.** B **3.** B **4.** C **5.** D **6.** D **7.** \$84.99 **8.** \$94.99 **9.** \$114.99 **10.** Answers may vary

Module Review Problems **1.** $\frac{11}{5}$ **2.** $\frac{5}{3}$ **3.** $\frac{4}{5}$ **4.** $\frac{10}{19}$ **5.** $\frac{28}{51}$ **6.** $\frac{1}{3}$ **7.** $\frac{20}{59}$ **8.** $\frac{14}{25}$ **9.** $\frac{2}{5}$ **10.** $\frac{1}{8}$ **11.** $\frac{7}{32}$ **12.** $\frac{\$25}{\text{2 people}}$ **13.** $\frac{\text{4 revolutions}}{\text{11 minutes}}$ **14.** $\frac{\text{5 heartbeats}}{\text{4 seconds}}$ **15.** $\frac{\text{4 cups}}{\text{9 cakes}}$ **16.** \$17/share **17.** \$112/credit-hour **18.** \$13.50/square metre **19.** \$12.50/DVD **20. (a)** 1.48 ¢/g **(b)** 1.044 ¢/g **(c)** 0.436 ¢/g **21. (a)** 1.1 ¢/g **(b)** 1.25 ¢/g **(c)** 0.15 ¢/g **22.** $\frac{12}{48} = \frac{7}{28}$ **23.** $\frac{1\frac{1}{2}}{5} = \frac{4}{13\frac{1}{3}}$ **24.** $\frac{7.5}{45} = \frac{22.5}{135}$ **25.** $\frac{\text{3 buses}}{\text{138 passengers}} = \frac{\text{5 buses}}{\text{230 passengers}}$ **26.** $\frac{\text{15 litres}}{\$4.50} = \frac{\text{27 litres}}{\$8.10}$ **27.** It is not a proportion. **28.** It is a proportion. **29.** It is a proportion. **30.** It is a proportion. **31.** It is not a proportion. **32.** It is not a proportion. **33.** It is a proportion. **34.** It is not a proportion. **35.** $n = 18$ **36.** $n = 7\frac{3}{5}$ or 7.6 **37.** $n = 22.1$ or $22\frac{1}{10}$ **38.** $n = 17$ **39.** $n = 33$ **40.** $n = 42$ **41.** $n = 7$ **42.** $n = 24$ **43.** $n = 19$ **44.** $n = 5\frac{3}{5}$ or 5.6 **45.** $n \approx 5.0$ **46.** $n \approx 6.8$ **47.** $n = 19$ **48.** $n = 15$ **49.** $n \approx 7.4$ **50.** $n \approx 5.9$ **51.** $n = 12$ **52.** $n = 550$ **53.** 45 litres **54.** 1691 employees **55.** 2016 francs **56.** 156.25 Swiss francs **57.** 600 kilometres **58.** 40 rebounds **59.** 120 feet **60. (a)** 13.68 litres **(b)** \$16.42 **61.** 5.71 centimetres tall **62.** 7.5 grams **63.** 154 pavers **64.** 1680 students **65.** 30 litres **66.** 834 litres **67.** approximately 113.93 feet **68.** approximately 27.38 minutes **69.** 86 goals **70.** 552 calories **71.** 13 680 people **72.** 195 trips

How Am I Doing? Module Test **1.** $\frac{9}{26}$ (obj. 1.1) **2.** $\frac{14}{37}$ (obj. 1.1) **3.** $\frac{\text{98 kilometres}}{\text{3 litres}}$ (obj. 1.2) **4.** $\frac{\text{140 square metres}}{\text{3 kilograms}}$ (obj. 1.2) **5.** 3.8 tonnes/day (obj. 1.2) **6.** \$8.28/hour (obj. 1.2) **7.** 245.45 metres/pole (obj. 1.2) **8.** \$85.21/share (obj. 1.2) **9.** $\frac{17}{29} = \frac{51}{87}$ (obj. 2.1) **10.** $\frac{2\frac{1}{2}}{10} = \frac{6}{24}$ (obj. 2.1) **11.** $\frac{\text{490 miles}}{\text{21 gallons}} = \frac{\text{280 miles}}{\text{12 gallons}}$ (obj. 2.1) **12.** $\frac{\text{3 hours}}{\text{180 kilometres}} = \frac{\text{5 hours}}{\text{300 kilometres}}$ (obj. 2.1) **13.** It is not a proportion. (obj. 2.2) **14.** It is a proportion. (obj. 2.2) **15.** It is a proportion. (obj. 2.2) **16.** It is not a proportion. (obj. 2.2) **17.** $n = 16$ (obj. 3.2) **18.** $n = 22.5$ (obj. 3.2) **19.** $n = 19$ (obj. 3.2) **20.** $n = 29.4$ (obj. 3.2) **21.** $n = 120$ (obj. 3.2) **22.** $n = 70.4$ (obj. 3.2) **23.** $n = 120$ (obj. 3.2) **24.** $n = 52$ (obj. 3.2) **25.** 6 eggs (obj. 4.1) **26.** 80.95 kilograms (obj. 4.1) **27.** 19 kilometres (obj. 4.1) **28.** \$360 (obj. 4.1) **29.** 136.6 miles (obj. 4.1) **30.** 696.67 kilometres (obj. 4.1) **31.** 88 free throws (obj. 4.1) **32.** 32 hits (obj. 4.1)

Percent

Hans Peter Merton/Robert Harding World Imagery

Percent

Compared to thirty years ago, today more high school students take a modern foreign language rather than an ancient language such as Latin.

This increase is partly due to a greater demand from businesses in our own country for more employees who are bilingual. However, there is a huge, growing need for companies that place employees overseas to have modern foreign language skills. Many companies require that a certain percent of their employees are bilingual. Many percent calculations require the knowledge of the mathematics of this module.

Section 1 Understanding Percent

Writing a Fraction with a Denominator of 100 as a Percent

Student Learning Objectives

After studying this section, you will be able to:

 Write a fraction with a denominator of 100 as a percent.

 Write a percent as a decimal.

 Write a decimal as a percent.

"My raise came through. I got a 6% increase!"

"The leading economic indicators show inflation rising at a rate of 1.3% per year."

"Mark McGwire and Babe Ruth each hit quite a few home runs. But I wonder who has the higher percentage of home runs per at-bat?"

We use percents often in our everyday lives. In business, in sports, in shopping, and in many areas of life, percentages play an important role. In this section we introduce the idea of percent, which means "*per centum*" or "per hundred." We then show how to use percentages.

When we describe parts of a whole, we use fractions or decimals. Using a percent is another way to describe a part of a whole. Percents can be described as ratios whose denominators are 100. The word **percent** means per 100. This sketch has 100 rectangles.

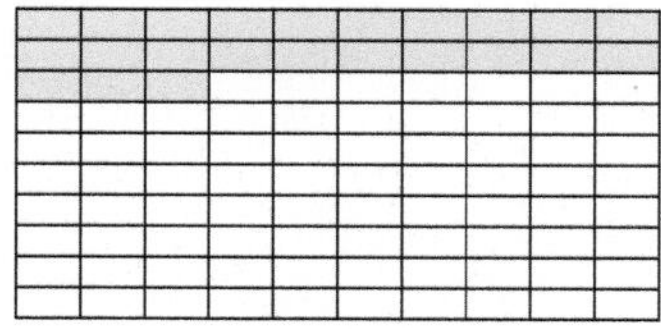

Of the 100 rectangles, 23 are shaded. We can say that 23 percent of the whole is shaded. We use the symbol % for percent. It means "parts per 100." When we write 23 percent as 23%, we understand that it means 23 parts per 100, or, as a fraction, $\frac{23}{100}$.

EXAMPLE 1 Recently 100 college students were surveyed about their intentions for voting in the next election. 39 students intended to vote for the Conservative Party, 28 students intended to vote for the Liberal Party, and 22 students intended to vote for the New Democratic Party. The remaining 11 students were undecided.

(a) What percent of the students intended to vote for the Liberal Party?

(b) What percent of the students intended to vote for the Conservative Party?

(c) What percent of the students intended to vote for the New Democratic Party?

(d) What percent of the students were undecided?

Solution

(a) $\frac{28}{100} = 28\%$ **(b)** $\frac{39}{100} = 39\%$

(c) $\frac{22}{100} = 22\%$ **(d)** $\frac{11}{100} = 11\%$

Percent notation is often used in circle graphs or pie charts.

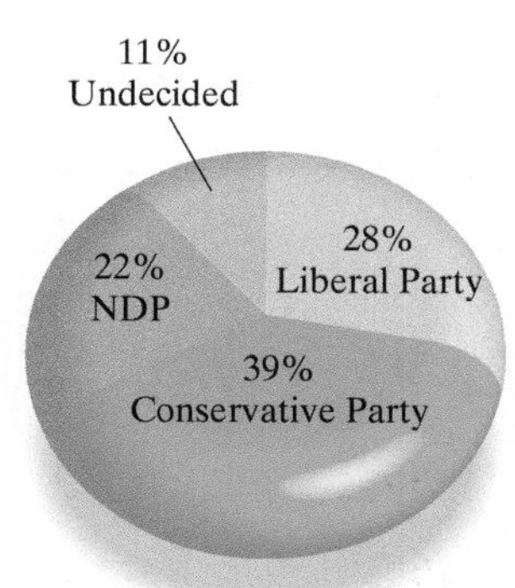

Practice Problem 1 Write as a percent.

(a) 51 out of 100 students in the class were women.

(b) 68 out of 100 cars in the parking lot have front-wheel drive.

(c) 7 out of 100 students in the dorm quit smoking.

(d) 26 out of 100 students did not vote in class elections.

NOTE TO STUDENT: Fully worked-out solutions to all of the Practice Problems can be found at the end of the module.

Some percents are larger than 100%. When you see expressions like 140% or 400%, you need to understand what they represent. Consider the following situations.

EXAMPLE 2

(a) Write $\frac{386}{100}$ as a percent.

(b) Twenty years ago, four car tires for a full-size car cost \$100. Now the average price for four car tires for a full-size car is \$270. Write the present cost as a percent of the cost 20 years ago.

Solution

(a) $\frac{386}{100} = 386\%$

(b) The ratio is $\frac{\$270 \text{ for four tires now}}{\$100 \text{ for four tires then}}$. $\frac{270}{100} = 270\%$

The present cost of four car tires for a full-size car is 270% of the cost 20 years ago.

Practice Problem 2

(a) Write $\frac{238}{100}$ as a percent.

(b) Last year, 100 students tried out for baseball. This year, 121 students tried out. Write this year's number as a percent of last year's number.

Some percents are smaller than 1%.

$\frac{0.7}{100}$ can be written as 0.7%. $\frac{0.3}{100}$ can be written as 0.3%.

$\frac{0.04}{100}$ can be written as 0.04%.

EXAMPLE 3 Write as a percent.

(a) $\frac{0.9}{100}$ **(b)** $\frac{0.002}{100}$ **(c)** $\frac{0.07}{100}$

Solution

(a) $\frac{0.9}{100} = 0.9\%$ **(b)** $\frac{0.002}{100} = 0.002\%$ **(c)** $\frac{0.07}{100} = 0.07\%$

Practice Problem 3 Write as a percent.

(a) $\frac{0.5}{100}$ **(b)** $\frac{0.06}{100}$ **(c)** $\frac{0.003}{100}$

Remember: Whenever the denominator of a fraction is 100, the numerator is the percent.

 Writing a Percent as a Decimal

Suppose we have a percent such as 59%. What would be the equivalent in decimal form? Using our definition of percent, $59\% = \frac{59}{100}$. This fraction could be written in decimal form as 0.59. In a similar way, we could write 21% as $\frac{21}{100} = 0.21$. This pattern allows us to quickly change the form of a number from a percent to a fraction whose denominator is 100, and then to a decimal.

EXAMPLE 4 Write as a decimal.

(a) 38% **(b)** 6%

Solution

(a) $38\% = \frac{38}{100} = 0.38$ **(b)** $6\% = \frac{6}{100} = 0.06$

Practice Problem 4 Write as a decimal.

(a) 47% **(b)** 2%

***NOTE TO STUDENT:** Fully worked-out solutions to all of the Practice Problems can be found at the end of the module.*

The results of Example 4 suggest that **when you remove a percent symbol (%) you are dividing by 100.** When we divide by 100 this moves the decimal point of a number two places to the left. Now that you understand this process, we can abbreviate it with the following rule.

CHANGING A PERCENT TO A DECIMAL

1. Drop the % symbol.
2. Move the decimal point two places to the left.

EXAMPLE 5 Write as a decimal.

(a) 26.9% **(b)** 7.2% **(c)** 0.13% **(d)** 158%

Solution In each case, we drop the percent symbol and move the decimal point two places to the left.

(a) 26.9% = 0.269 = 0.269

(b) 7.2% = 0.072 = 0.072 Note that we need to add an extra zero to the left of the 7.

(c) 0.13% = 0.0013 = 0.0013 Here we added zeros to the left of the 1.

(d) 158% = 1.58 = 1.58

Practice Problem 5 Write as a decimal.

(a) 80.6% **(b)** 2.5% **(c)** 0.29% **(d)** 231%

 Writing a Decimal as a Percent

In Example 4(a) we changed 38% to $\frac{38}{100}$ to 0.38. We can start with 0.38 and reverse the process. We obtain $0.38 = \frac{38}{100} = 38\%$. Study all the parts of Examples 4 and 5. You will see that the steps are reversible. Thus $0.38 = 38\%$, $0.06 = 6\%$, $0.70 = 70\%$, $0.269 = 26.9\%$, $0.072 = 7.2\%$, $0.0013 = 0.13\%$, and $1.58 = 158\%$.

In each part we are multiplying by 100. **To change a decimal number to a percent we are multiplying the number by 100.** In each part the decimal point is moved two places to the right. Then the percent symbol is written after the number.

CHANGING A DECIMAL TO A PERCENT

1. Move the decimal point two places to the right.
2. Then write the % symbol at the end of the number.

EXAMPLE 6 Write as a percent.

(a) 0.47 **(b)** 0.08 **(c)** 6.31

(d) 0.055 **(e)** 0.001

Solution In each part we move the decimal point two places to the right and write the percent symbol at the end of the number.

(a) $0.47 = 47\%$ **(b)** $0.08 = 8\%$ **(c)** $6.31 = 631\%$

(d) $0.055 = 5.5\%$ **(e)** $0.001 = 0.1\%$

Practice Problem 6 Write as a percent.

(a) 0.78 **(b)** 0.02 **(c)** 5.07

(d) 0.029 **(e)** 0.006

Calculator

Percent to Decimal

You can use a calculator to change 52% to a decimal.
Enter

52 [%]

The display should read

[0.52]

Try the following.

(a) 46% **(b)** 137%

(c) 9.3% **(d)** 6%

Note: The calculator divides by 100 when the percent key is pressed. If you do not have a [%] key then you can use the keystrokes [÷] 100 [=].

TO THINK ABOUT: The Meaning of Percent What is really happening when we change a decimal to a percent? Suppose that we wanted to change 0.59 to a percent.

$$0.59 = \frac{59}{100} \quad \text{Definition of a decimal.}$$

$$= 59 \times \frac{1}{100} \quad \text{Definition of multiplying fractions.}$$

$$= 59 \text{ percent} \quad \text{Because "per 100" means percent.}$$

$$= 59\% \quad \text{Writing the symbol for percent.}$$

Can you see why each step is valid? Since we know the reason behind each step, we know we can always move the decimal point two places to the right and write the percent symbol. See Section 1 Exercises, exercises 81 and 82.

Section 1 Exercises

Verbal and Writing Skills

1. In this section we introduced percent, which means *"per centum"* or "per ______________."

2. The number 1 written as a percent is __________.

3. To change a percent to a decimal, move the decimal point ________ places to the ________. ________ the % symbol.

4. To change a decimal to a percent, move the decimal point ________ places to the ________. ________ the % symbol at the end of the number.

Write as a percent.

5. $\frac{59}{100}$ **6.** $\frac{67}{100}$ **7.** $\frac{4}{100}$ **8.** $\frac{7}{100}$

9. $\frac{80}{100}$ **10.** $\frac{90}{100}$ **11.** $\frac{245}{100}$ **12.** $\frac{110}{100}$

13. $\frac{12.5}{100}$ **14.** $\frac{15.8}{100}$ **15.** $\frac{0.07}{100}$ **16.** $\frac{0.019}{100}$

Applications *Write a percent to express each of the following.*

17. 13 out of 100 loaves of bread had gone stale.

18. 54 out of 100 dog owners have attended an obedience class.

19. 9 out of 100 customers ordered black coffee.

20. 7 out of 100 students majored in exercise science.

Write as a decimal.

21. 51% **22.** 42% **23.** 7% **24.** 6%

25. 20% **26.** 40% **27.** 43.6% **28.** 81.5%

29. 0.03% **30.** 0.09% **31.** 0.72% **32.** 0.61%

33. 1.25% **34.** 9.6% **35.** 275% **36.** 189%

Write as a percent.

37. 0.74 **38.** 0.66 **39.** 0.50 **40.** 0.40

41. 0.08 **42.** 0.03 **43.** 0.563 **44.** 0.408

45. 0.002 **46.** 0.009 **47.** 0.0057 **48.** 0.0026

49. 1.35 **50.** 1.86 **51.** 5.16 **52.** 4.32

53. ***Income Taxes*** Robert Tansill paid $\frac{27}{100}$ of his income for federal income taxes. This means that 0.27 of his income was paid for federal taxes. Express this as a percent.

54. ***Housing Costs*** Sally LeBlanc spends $\frac{37}{100}$ of her income on housing. This means that 0.37 of her income was spent on housing. Express this as a percent.

55. ***Grade Distribution*** Professor Harlin gave $\frac{2}{10}$ of his students a grade of A for the semester. This means that 0.2 of his students got an A. Express this as a percent.

56. ***Chequing Account*** Michel Larocque puts $\frac{8}{10}$ of his income into his chequing account each month. This means that 0.8 of his income goes into his chequing account. Express this as a percent.

Mixed Practice *Write as a percent.*

57. 0.94

58. 0.25

59. 2.31

60. 1.48

61. $\frac{10}{100}$

62. $\frac{40}{100}$

63. 0.089

64. 0.055

Write as a decimal.

65. 62%

66. 49%

67. 138%

68. 210%

69. $\frac{0.3}{100}$

70. $\frac{0.8}{100}$

71. $\frac{75}{100}$

72. $\frac{35}{100}$

Applications *Write as a percent.*

73. ***Federal Elections*** For every 100 people in Ontario who voted in the 2006 Canadian election, 40 voted for the Liberals. (*Source:* Elections Canada, http://www.elections.ca/scripts/OVR2006/25/table8.html)

74. ***Federal Elections*** For every 100 people in Manitoba who voted in the 2006 Canadian election, 43 voted for the Conservative Party. (*Source:* Elections Canada, http://www.elections.ca/scripts/OVR2006/25/table8.html)

The following are statements found in newspapers. In each case write the percent as a decimal.

75. ***House Value*** The value of the Sanchez family's home increased by 115 percent during the last five years.

76. ***Charitable Donations*** According to a recent poll, 1 percent of Canadians receiving money from a GST rebate plan to donate the money.

77. ***Home Value*** 0.6 percent of homes in Canada are valued at more than $1 million.

78. ***Vitamins*** Canadians get 30 percent of their vitamin A from carrots.

79. ***Education*** In 1981, 60.9 percent of Canadians age 15 and older had not graduated high school. In 2001, that number had decreased to 45.4 percent. (*Source:* Statistics Canada, http://www40.statcan.ca/l01/cst01/educ45-eng.htm, Oct-09)

80. ***Vehicle Sales*** In February 2007, the number of vehicles sold by General Motors increased by 3.7 percent. The number of vehicles sold by Ford decreased by 13.4 percent. (*Source:* www.autodata.com)

To Think About

81. Suppose that we want to change 36% to 0.36 by moving the decimal point two places to the left and dropping the % symbol. Explain the steps to show what is really involved in changing 36% to 0.36. Why does the rule work?

82. Suppose that we want to change 10.65 to 1065%. Give a complete explanation of the steps.

Write the given value (a) as a decimal, (b) as a fraction with a denominator of 100, and (c) as a reduced fraction.

83. 1562%

84. 3724%

Quick Quiz 1 Write as a percent.

1. 0.007

2. $\frac{4.5}{100}$

3. Write as a decimal. 1.25%

4. **Concept Check** Explain how you would change 0.000 72% to a decimal.

SECTION 2 CHANGING BETWEEN PERCENTS, DECIMALS, AND FRACTIONS

Student Learning Objectives

After studying this section, you will be able to:

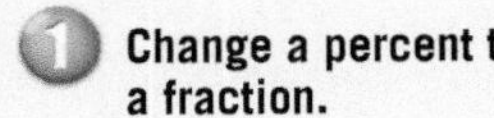

1. **Change a percent to a fraction.**
2. **Change a fraction to a percent.**
3. **Change a percent, a decimal, or a fraction to equivalent forms.**

1 Changing a Percent to a Fraction

By using the definition of percent, we can write any percent as a fraction whose denominator is 100. Thus when we change a percent to a fraction, we remove the percent symbol and write the number over 100. To write a number over 100 means that we are dividing by 100. If possible, we then simplify the fraction.

EXAMPLE 1 Write as a fraction in simplest form.

(a) 37% **(b)** 75% **(c)** 2%

Solution

(a) $37\% = \frac{37}{100}$ **(b)** $75\% = \frac{75}{100} = \frac{3}{4}$ **(c)** $2\% = \frac{2}{100} = \frac{1}{50}$

Practice Problem 1 Write as a fraction in simplest form.

(a) 71% **(b)** 25% **(c)** 8%

In some cases, it may be helpful to write the percent as a decimal before you write it as a fraction in simplest form.

EXAMPLE 2 Write as a fraction in simplest form.

(a) 43.5% **(b)** 36.75%

Solution

(a) $43.5\% = 0.435$ Change the percent to a decimal.

$= \frac{435}{1000}$ Change the decimal to a fraction.

$= \frac{87}{200}$ Reduce the fraction.

(b) $36.75\% = 0.3675 = \frac{3\,675}{10\,000} = \frac{147}{400}$

Practice Problem 2 Write as a fraction in simplest form.

(a) 8.4% **(b)** 28.5%

If the percent is greater than 100%, the simplified fraction is usually changed to a mixed number.

EXAMPLE 3 Write as a mixed number.

(a) 225% **(b)** 138%

Solution

(a) $225\% = 2.25 = 2\frac{25}{100} = 2\frac{1}{4}$ **(b)** $138\% = 1.38 = 1\frac{38}{100} = 1\frac{19}{50}$

Practice Problem 3 Write as a mixed number.

(a) 170% **(b)** 288%

Sometimes a percent is not a whole number, such as 9% or 10%. Instead, it contains a fraction, such as $9\frac{1}{12}\%$ or $9\frac{3}{8}\%$. Extra steps will be needed to write such a percent as a simplified fraction.

EXAMPLE 4 Convert $3\frac{3}{8}\%$ to a fraction in simplest form.

Solution

$$3\frac{3}{8}\% = \frac{3\frac{3}{8}}{100}$$ Change the percent to a fraction.

$$= 3\frac{3}{8} \div \frac{100}{1}$$ Write the division horizontally. $\frac{3\frac{3}{8}}{100}$ means $3\frac{3}{8}$ divided by 100.

$$= \frac{27}{8} \div \frac{100}{1}$$ Write $3\frac{3}{8}$ as an improper fraction.

$$= \frac{27}{8} \times \frac{1}{100}$$ Use the definition of division of fractions.

$$= \frac{27}{800}$$ Simplify.

Practice Problem 4 Convert $7\frac{5}{8}\%$ to a fraction in simplest form.

EXAMPLE 5 In Canada's fiscal year 2007, approximately $\frac{3}{40}\%$ of the federal budget was designated for defence. (*Source:* Department of Finance, http://budget.gc.ca/2007/pla/bpc6-eng.html, Oct-09) Write this percent as a fraction.

Solution

$$\frac{3}{40}\% = \frac{\frac{3}{40}}{100} = \frac{3}{40} \div 100 = \frac{3}{40} \times \frac{1}{100} = \frac{3}{4000}$$

Thus we could say that $\frac{3}{4000}$ of Canada's fiscal 2007 budget was designated for defence. That is, for every \$4000 in the budget, \$3 was spent for defence.

Practice Problem 5 In Canada's fiscal 2007 budget, approximately $1\frac{9}{10}\%$ was designated for the environment. (*Source:* Department of Finance, http://budget.gc.ca/2007/pla/bpc6-eng.html, Oct-09) Write this percent as a fraction.

Certain percents occur very often, especially in money matters. Here are some common equivalents that you may already know. If not, be sure to memorize them.

$$25\% = \frac{1}{4} \qquad 33\frac{1}{3}\% = \frac{1}{3} \qquad 10\% = \frac{1}{10}$$

$$50\% = \frac{1}{2} \qquad 66\frac{2}{3}\% = \frac{2}{3}$$

$$75\% = \frac{3}{4}$$

Changing a Fraction to a Percent

A convenient way to change a fraction to a percent is to write the fraction in decimal form first and then convert the decimal to a percent.

EXAMPLE 6 Write $\frac{3}{8}$ as a percent.

Solution We see that $\frac{3}{8} = 0.375$ by calculating $3 \div 8$.

$$\begin{array}{r} 0.375 \\ 8\overline{)3.000} \\ \underline{24} \\ 60 \\ \underline{56} \\ 40 \\ \underline{40} \\ 0 \end{array}$$

Thus $\frac{3}{8} = 0.375 = 37.5\%$.

Practice Problem 6 Write $\frac{5}{8}$ as a percent.

EXAMPLE 7 Write as a percent.

(a) $\frac{7}{40}$ **(b)** $\frac{39}{50}$

Solution

(a) $\frac{7}{40} = 0.175 = 17.5\%$ **(b)** $\frac{39}{50} = 0.78 = 78\%$

Practice Problem 7 Write as a percent.

(a) $\frac{21}{25}$ **(b)** $\frac{7}{16}$

Changing some fractions to decimal form results in infinitely repeating decimals. In such cases, we usually round to the nearest hundredth of a percent.

EXAMPLE 8 Write as a percent. Round to the nearest hundredth of a percent.

(a) $\frac{1}{6}$ **(b)** $\frac{15}{33}$

Solution

(a) We find that $\frac{1}{6} = 0.1666\ldots$ by calculating $1 \div 6$.

$$\begin{array}{r} 0.1666 \\ 6\overline{)1.0000} \\ \underline{6} \\ 40 \\ \underline{36} \\ 40 \\ \underline{36} \\ 40 \\ \underline{36} \\ 4 \end{array}$$

We will need a four-place decimal so that we will obtain a percent to the nearest hundredth. If we round the decimal to the nearest ten-thousandth, we have $\frac{1}{6} \approx 0.1667$. If we change this to a percent, we have

$$\frac{1}{6} \approx 16.67\%.$$

This is correct to the nearest hundredth of a percent.

(b) By calculating $15 \div 33$, we see that $\frac{15}{33} = 0.454\,545\,45\ldots$. We will need a four-place decimal so that we will obtain a percent to the nearest hundredth. If we round to the nearest ten-thousandth, we have

$$\frac{15}{33} \approx 0.4545 = 45.45\%.$$

This rounded value is correct to the nearest hundredth of a percent.

Practice Problem 8 Write as a percent. Round to the nearest hundredth of a percent.

(a) $\frac{7}{9}$ **(b)** $\frac{19}{30}$

NOTE TO STUDENT: Fully worked-out solutions to all of the Practice Problems can be found at the end of the module.

Recall that sometimes percents are written with fractions.

EXAMPLE 9 Express $\frac{11}{12}$ as a percent containing a fraction.

Solution We will stop the division after two steps and write the remainder in fraction form.

$$\begin{array}{r} 0.91 \\ 12\overline{)11.00} \\ \underline{108} \\ 20 \\ \underline{12} \\ 8 \end{array}$$

This division tells us that we can write

$$\frac{11}{12} \quad \text{as} \quad 0.91\frac{8}{12} \quad \text{or} \quad 0.91\frac{2}{3}.$$

We now have a decimal with a fraction. When we express this decimal as a percent, we move the decimal point two places to the right. We do not write the decimal point in front of the fraction.

$$0.91\frac{2}{3} = 91\frac{2}{3}\%$$

Note that our answer in Example 9 is an *exact answer*. We have not rounded off or approximated in any way.

Practice Problem 9 Express $\frac{7}{12}$ as a percent containing a fraction.

3 Changing a Percent, a Decimal, or a Fraction to Equivalent Forms

We have seen so far that a fraction, a decimal, and a percent are three different forms (notations) for the same number. We can illustrate this in a chart.

EXAMPLE 10 Complete the following table of equivalent notations. Round decimals to the nearest ten-thousandth. Round percents to the nearest hundredth of a percent.

Fraction	Decimal	Percent
$\frac{11}{16}$		
	0.265	
		$17\frac{1}{5}\%$

Solution Begin with the first row. The number is written as a fraction. We will change the fraction to a decimal and then to a percent.

The fraction is changed to a decimal is changed to a percent.

$$\frac{11}{16} \longrightarrow 16\overline{)11.0000}\ \ 0.6875 \longrightarrow 68.75\%$$

In the second row the number is written as a decimal. This can easily be written as a percent.

$$0.265 \longrightarrow 26.5\%$$

Now write 0.265 as a fraction and simplify.

$$0.265 \downarrow \quad \frac{265}{1000} \longrightarrow \frac{53}{200}$$

In the third row the number is written as a percent. Proceed from right to left—that is, write the number as a decimal and then as a fraction.

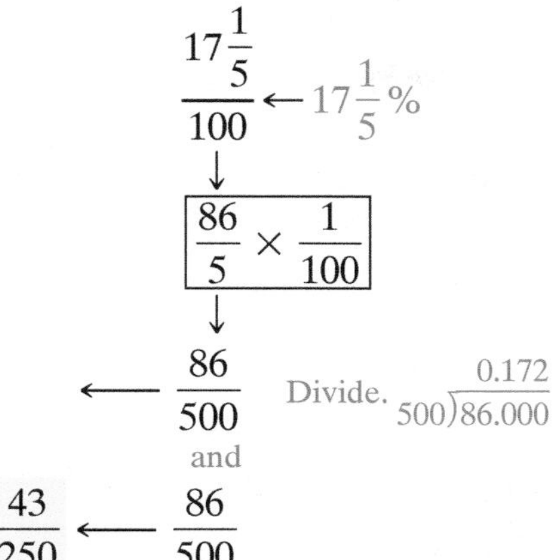

$$\frac{17\frac{1}{5}}{100} \leftarrow 17\frac{1}{5}\%$$

$$\downarrow$$

$$\boxed{\frac{86}{5} \times \frac{1}{100}}$$

$$\downarrow$$

$$\longleftarrow \frac{86}{500} \quad \text{Divide.} \quad 500\overline{)86.000} = 0.172$$

and

$$\frac{43}{250} \longleftarrow \frac{86}{500}$$

Thus the completed table is as follows.

Fraction	Decimal	Percent
$\frac{11}{16}$	0.6875	68.75%
$\frac{53}{200}$	0.265	26.5%
$\frac{43}{250}$	0.172	$17\frac{1}{5}\%$

Practice Problem 10 Complete the following table of equivalent notations. Round decimals to the nearest ten-thousandth. Round percents to the nearest hundredth of a percent.

Fraction	Decimal	Percent
$\frac{23}{99}$		
	0.516	
		$38\frac{4}{5}\%$

Calculator

Fraction to Decimal

You can use a calculator to change $\frac{3}{5}$ to a decimal. Enter

3 [÷] 5 [=]

The display should read

[0.6]

Try the following.

(a) $\frac{17}{25}$ **(b)** $\frac{2}{9}$

(c) $\frac{13}{10}$ **(d)** $\frac{15}{19}$

Note: 0.78947368 is an approximation for $\frac{15}{19}$. Some calculators round to only eight places.

***NOTE TO STUDENT:** Fully worked-out solutions to all of the Practice Problems can be found at the end of the module.*

ALTERNATIVE METHOD: Using Proportions to Convert from Fraction to Percent Another way to convert a fraction to a percent is to use a proportion. To change $\frac{7}{8}$ to a percent, write the proportion

$$\frac{7}{8} = \frac{n}{100}$$

$$7 \times 100 = 8 \times n \quad \text{Cross-multiply.}$$

$$700 = 8 \times n \quad \text{Simplify.}$$

$$\frac{700}{8} = \frac{8 \times n}{8} \quad \text{Divide each side by 8.}$$

$$87.5 = n \quad \text{Simplify.}$$

Thus $\frac{7}{8} = 87.5\%$. You will use this approach in Section 2 Exercises, exercises 85 and 86.

Section 2 Exercises

Verbal and Writing Skills

1. Explain in your own words how to change a percent to a fraction.

2. Explain in your own words how to change a fraction to a percent.

Write as a fraction or as a mixed number.

3. 6%	**4.** 8%	**5.** 33%	**6.** 47%	**7.** 55%
8. 35%	**9.** 75%	**10.** 25%	**11.** 20%	**12.** 40%
13. 9.5%	**14.** 6.5%	**15.** 22.5%	**16.** 92.5%	**17.** 64.8%
18. 12.2%	**19.** 71.25%	**20.** 38.75%	**21.** 168%	**22.** 256%
23. 340%	**24.** 420%	**25.** 1200%	**26.** 3600%	**27.** $3\frac{5}{8}\%$
28. $4\frac{3}{5}\%$	**29.** $12\frac{1}{2}\%$	**30.** $37\frac{1}{2}\%$	**31.** $8\frac{4}{5}\%$	**32.** $9\frac{3}{5}\%$

Applications

33. ***Crime Rates*** Between 2004 and 2008, the number of violent crimes in Canada decreased by 2.62%. Write the percent as a fraction. (*Source:* Statistics Canada, http://www40.statcan.ca/l01/cst01/legal02-eng.htm, Oct-09)

34. ***Crime Rates*** Between 2004 and 2008, the number of property crimes in Canada decreased by 22.6%. Write the percent as a fraction. (*Source:* Statistics Canada, http://www40.statcan.ca/l01/cst01/legal02-eng.htm, Oct-09)

35. ***Gasoline Prices*** On June 15, 2009, the average price in Canada for regular gasoline was \$0.93 per litre. This was a $6\frac{3}{5}\%$ decrease in the average price the previous week. Write this percent as a fraction. (*Source:* www.gasticker.com)

36. ***Gasoline Prices*** On July 22, 2009, the average price in Canada for premium gasoline was \$0.825 per litre. This was a $3\frac{18}{25}\%$ increase in the average price 4 months earlier. Write this percent as a fraction. (*Source:* www.gasticker.com)

Write as a percent. Round to the nearest hundredth of a percent when necessary.

37. $\frac{3}{4}$ **38.** $\frac{1}{4}$ **39.** $\frac{7}{10}$ **40.** $\frac{9}{10}$ **41.** $\frac{7}{20}$ **42.** $\frac{11}{20}$

43. $\frac{18}{25}$ **44.** $\frac{22}{25}$ **45.** $\frac{11}{40}$ **46.** $\frac{13}{40}$ **47.** $\frac{18}{5}$ **48.** $\frac{7}{4}$

49. $2\frac{1}{2}$ **50.** $3\frac{3}{4}$ **51.** $4\frac{1}{8}$ **52.** $2\frac{5}{8}$ **53.** $\frac{1}{3}$ **54.** $\frac{2}{3}$

55. $\frac{5}{12}$ **56.** $\frac{8}{15}$ **57.** $\frac{17}{4}$ **58.** $\frac{12}{5}$ **59.** $\frac{26}{50}$ **60.** $\frac{43}{50}$

Applications *Round to the nearest hundredth of a percent.*

61. ***Human Brain*** The brain represents approximately $\frac{1}{40}$ of an average person's weight. Express this fraction as a percent.

62. ***Monthly House Payments*** To calculate your maximum monthly house payment, a real estate agent multiplies your monthly income by $\frac{7}{25}$. Express this fraction as a percent.

63. ***Size of Africa*** Africa is the second largest continent on Earth, measuring 30 301 596 km^2. However, it comprises only $\frac{119}{2000}$ of Earth's total surface area. Express this fraction as a percent.

64. ***Size of Antarctica*** The continent of Antarctica takes up $\frac{11}{400}$ of Earth's total surface area. Express this fraction as a percent.

Express as a percent containing a fraction. (See Example 9.)

65. $\frac{3}{8}$ **66.** $\frac{5}{8}$ **67.** $\frac{3}{40}$ **68.** $\frac{11}{90}$

69. $\frac{4}{15}$ **70.** $\frac{11}{15}$ **71.** $\frac{2}{9}$ **72.** $\frac{8}{9}$

Mixed Practice *In exercises 73–82, complete the table of equivalents. Round decimals to the nearest ten-thousandth. Round percents to the nearest hundredth of a percent.*

	Fraction	Decimal	Percent
73.	$\frac{11}{12}$		
75.		0.56	
77.		0.005	
79.	$\frac{5}{9}$		
81.			$3\frac{1}{8}\%$

	Fraction	Decimal	Percent
74.	$\frac{1}{12}$		
76.		0.85	
78.		0.085	
80.	$\frac{7}{9}$		
82.			$2\frac{5}{8}\%$

83. Write $28\frac{15}{16}\%$ as a fraction.

84. Write $18\frac{7}{12}\%$ as a fraction.

Change each fraction to a percent by using a proportion.

85. $\frac{123}{800}$

86. $\frac{417}{600}$

Quick Quiz 2 Write as a fraction or as a mixed number in simplified form.

1. 45%

2. $7\frac{3}{5}\%$

3. Change to a percent. $\frac{23}{25}$

4. **Concept Check** Explain how you would change $8\frac{3}{8}\%$ to a decimal.

SECTION 3A SOLVING PERCENT PROBLEMS USING EQUATIONS

 Translating a Percent Problem Into an Equation

Student Learning Objectives

After studying this section, you will be able to:

 **Translate a percent problem into an equation.**

 **Solve a percent problem by solving an equation.**

In word problems like the ones in this section, we can translate from words to mathematical symbols and back again. After we have the mathematical symbols arranged in an *equation,* we solve the equation. When we find the values that make the equation true, we have also found the answer to our word problem.

To solve a percent problem, we express it as an equation with an unknown quantity. We use the letter n to represent the number we do not know. The following table is helpful when translating from a percent problem to an equation.

Word	Mathematical Symbol
of	Any multiplication symbol: $\times$ or ( ) or $\cdot$
is	$=$
what	Any letter; for example, n
find	$n =$

In Examples 1–5 we show how to translate words into an equation. Please do **not** solve the problem. Translate into an equation only.

EXAMPLE 1 Translate into an equation.

What is 5% of 19.00?

↓ ↓ ↓ ↓ ↓

Solution

$$n = 5\% \times 19.00$$

Practice Problem 1 Translate into an equation. What is 26% of 35?

NOTE TO STUDENT: Fully worked-out solutions to all of the Practice Problems can be found at the end of the module.

EXAMPLE 2 Translate into an equation.

Find 0.6% of 400.

Solution Notice here that the words *what is* are missing. The word *find* is equivalent to *what is.*

Find 0.6% of 400.

↓ ↓ ↓ ↓

$$n = 0.6\% \times 400$$

Practice Problem 2 Translate into an equation. Find 0.08% of 350.

The unknown quantity, n, does not always stand alone in an equation.

EXAMPLE 3 Translate into an equation.

(a) 35% of what is 60? **(b)** 7.2 is 120% of what?

Solution

(a) 35% of what is 60?

$$35\% \times n = 60$$

(b) 7.2 is 120% of what?

$$7.2 = 120\% \times n$$

Practice Problem 3 Translate into an equation.

(a) 58% of what is 400? **(b)** 9.1 is 135% of what?

EXAMPLE 4 Translate into an equation.

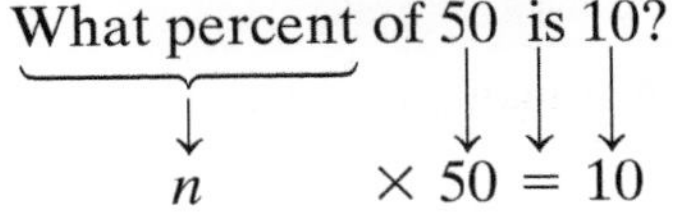

What percent of 50 is 10?
n
× 50 = 10

Solution

We see here that the words *what percent* are represented by the letter n.

Practice Problem 4 Translate into an equation. What percent of 250 is 36?

EXAMPLE 5 Translate into an equation.

(a) 30 is what percent of 16? **(b)** What percent of 3000 is 2.6?

Solution

(a) 30 is what percent of 16?

$$30 = n \times 16$$

(b) What percent of 3000 is 2.6?

$$n \times 3000 = 2.6$$

Practice Problem 5 Translate into an equation.

(a) 50 is what percent of 20? **(b)** What percent of 2000 is 4.5?

2 Solving a Percent Problem by Solving an Equation

The percent problems we have translated are of three types. Consider the equation $60 = 20\% \times 300$. This problem has the form

$$\text{amount} = \text{percent} \times \text{base}$$

Any one of these quantities—amount, percent, or base—may be unknown.

1. When *we do not know the amount,* we have an equation like
$$n = 20\% \times 300.$$
2. When *we do not know the base,* we have an equation like
$$60 = 20\% \times n.$$
3. When *we do not know the percent,* we have an equation like
$$60 = n \times 300.$$

We will study each type separately. It is not necessary to memorize the three types, but it is helpful to look carefully at the examples we give of each. In each example, do the computation in a way that is easiest for you. This may be using a pencil and paper, using a calculator, or, in some cases, doing the problem mentally.

Solving Percent Problems When the Amount Is Unknown In solving these equations we will need to change the percent number to decimal form.

EXAMPLE 6 What is 45% of 590?

↓ ↓ ↓ ↓ ↓

Solution

$n = 45\% \times 590$ Translate into an equation.

$n = (0.45)(590)$ Change the percent to decimal form.

$n = 265.5$ Multiply 0.45×590.

Practice Problem 6 What is 82% of 350?

EXAMPLE 7 Find 160% of 500.

Find 160% of 500. When you translate, remember that the word *find* is equivalent to *what is*.

↓ ↓ ↓ ↓

Solution

$n = 160\% \times 500$

$n = (1.60)(500)$ Change the percent to decimal form.

$n = 800$ Multiply 1.6 by 500.

Practice Problem 7 Find 230% of 400.

EXAMPLE 8 When Rick bought a new Toyota Yaris, he had to pay a sales tax of 5% on the cost of the car, which was \$12 000. What was the sales tax?

Solution This problem is asking

What is 5% of \$12 000?

↓ ↓ ↓ ↓ ↓

$n = 5\% \times \$12\,000$

$n = 0.05 \times 12\,000$

$n = \$600$

The sales tax was \$600.

Practice Problem 8 When Oprah bought an airplane ticket, she had to pay a tax of 8% on the cost of the ticket, which was \$350. What was the tax?

Solving Percent Problems When the Base Is Unknown If a number is multiplied by the letter n, this can be indicated by a multiplication sign, parentheses, a dot, or placing the number in front of the letter. Thus $3 \times n = 3(n) = 3 \cdot n = 3n$.

In this section we use equations like $3n = 9$ and $0.5n = 20$. To solve these equations we divide each side by the number multiplied by n.

Calculator

Percent of a Number

You can use a calculator to find 12% of 48.

Enter

12 [%] [×] 48 [=]

The display should read

[5.76]

If your calculator does not have a percent key, use the keystrokes

0.12 [×] 48 [=]

What is 54% of 450?

In solving these equations we will need to change the percent number to decimal form.

EXAMPLE 9 12 is 0.6% of what?

Solution

$12 = 0.6\% \times n$ — Translate into an equation.

$12 = 0.006n$ — Change 0.6% to a decimal.

$\dfrac{12}{0.006} = \dfrac{0.006n}{0.006}$ — Divide each side of the equation by 0.006.

$2000 = n$ — Divide $12 \div 0.006$.

Practice Problem 9 32 is 0.4% of what?

EXAMPLE 10 Demethir and Qing-Qing went out to dinner. They gave the waiter a tip that was 15% of the total bill. The tip the waiter received was $6. What was the total bill (not including the tip)?

Solution This problem is asking

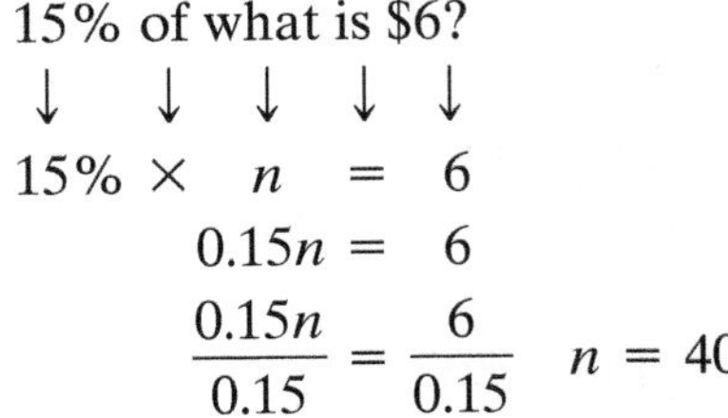

15% of what is $6?

$15\% \times n = 6$

$0.15n = 6$

$\dfrac{0.15n}{0.15} = \dfrac{6}{0.15} \quad n = 40$

The total bill for the meal (not including the tip) was $40.

Practice Problem 10 The coach of the university hockey team said that 30% of the players on his team are left-handed. Six people on the team are left-handed. How many people are on the team?

Calculator

Finding the Percent

You can use a calculator to find a missing percent. What percent of 95 is 19?

1. Enter as a fraction. Enter the number after "is," and then the division key. Then enter the number after the word "of."

   19 [÷] 95

2. Change to a percent.

   19 [÷] 95 [×] 100 [=]

   The display should read

   [20]

   This means 20%.

What percent of 625 is 250?

Solving Percent Problems When the Percent Is Unknown In solving these problems, we notice that there is no % symbol in the problem. The percent is what we are trying to find. Therefore, our answer for this type of problem will always have a percent symbol.

EXAMPLE 11 What percent of 5000 is 3.8?

Solution

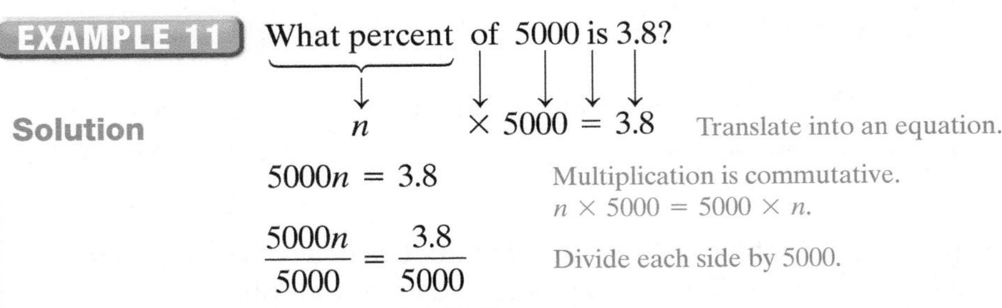

$n \times 5000 = 3.8$ — Translate into an equation.

$5000n = 3.8$ — Multiplication is commutative. $n \times 5000 = 5000 \times n$.

$\dfrac{5000n}{5000} = \dfrac{3.8}{5000}$ — Divide each side by 5000.

$n = 0.000\,76$ — Divide 3.8 by 5000.

$n = 0.076\%$ — Express the decimal as a percent.

Practice Problem 11 What percent of 9000 is 4.5?

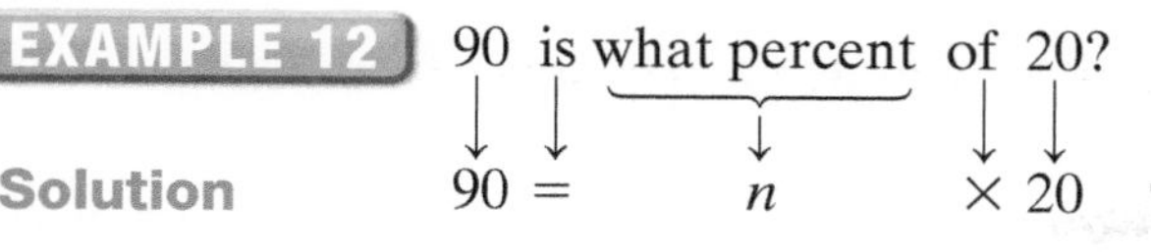

EXAMPLE 12 90 is what percent of 20?

Solution

$$90 = n \times 20 \quad \text{Translate into an equation.}$$

$$90 = 20n \quad \text{Multiplication is commutative. } n \times 20 = 20 \times n.$$

$$\frac{90}{20} = \frac{20n}{20} \quad \text{Divide each side by 20.}$$

$$4.5 = n \quad \text{Divide 90 by 20.}$$

$$450\% = n \quad \text{Express the decimal as a percent.}$$

Practice Problem 12 198 is what percent of 33?

EXAMPLE 13 In a basketball game for the New York Knicks, Jamal Crawford made 10 of his 24 shots. What percent of his shots did he make? (Round to the nearest tenth of a percent.)

Solution This is equivalent to

10 is what percent of 24?

$$10 = n \times 24$$

$$10 = 24n$$

$$\frac{10}{24} = \frac{24n}{24}$$

$$0.416\,66\ldots = n$$

To the nearest tenth of a percent we have

$$n = 41.7\%$$

Jamal Crawford made 41.7% of his shots in this game.

Practice Problem 13 In a basketball game for the Los Angeles Lakers, Kobe Bryant made 5 of his 16 shots. What percent of his shots did he make? (Round to the nearest tenth of a percent.)

Getty Images

Section 3A Exercises

Verbal and Writing Skills

1. Give an example of a percent problem when we do not know the amount.

2. Give an example of a percent problem when we do not know the base.

3. Give an example of a percent problem when we do not know the percent.

4. When you encounter a problem like "What is 65% of $600?" what type of percent problem is this? How would you solve such a problem?

5. When you encounter a problem like "108 is 18% of what number?" what type of percent problem is this? How would you solve such a problem?

6. When you encounter a problem like "What percent of 35 is 14?" what type of percent problem is this? How would you solve such a problem?

Translate into a mathematical equation in exercises 7–12. Use the letter n for the unknown quantity. Do ***not*** *solve, but rather just obtain the equation.*

7. What is 5% of 90?

8. What is 9% of 65?

9. 30% of what is 5?

10. 65% of what is 28?

11. 17 is what percent of 85?

12. 24 is what percent of 144?

Solve.

13. What is 20% of 140?

14. What is 30% of 210?

15. Find 40% of 140.

16. Find 60% of 210.

Applications

17. ***Sales Tax*** Malik bought a new flat-screen television. The price before the 6% sales tax was added on was $850. How much tax did Malik have to pay?

18. ***Coin-Counting Service*** At the local bank, coins can be placed into a machine to be counted. You can then receive bills for the amount the coins are worth. However, the bank charges a fee that is 8% of the coins' value. How much would the service fee be if someone put $215 worth of coins into the machine?

Solve.

19. 2% of what is 26?

20. 3% of what is 18?

21. 52 is 4% of what?

22. 36 is 6% of what?

Applications

23. ***Australia Tax*** In Australia, all general sales (except for food) have a hidden tax of 22% built into the final price. Walter is planning to purchase a camera while in Australia. He wants to know the before-tax price that the dealer is charging before he adds on the hidden tax of $33. Can you determine the amount of the before-tax price?

24. ***Opinion Poll*** A newspaper states that 522 of its residents are in favour of building a new high school. This is 12% of the town's population. What is the population of the town?

Solve.

25. What percent of 200 is 168?

26. What percent of 300 is 135?

27. 33 is what percent of 300?

28. 78 is what percent of 200?

Applications

29. ***Basketball*** The total number of points scored in a basketball game was 120. The winning team scored 78 of those points. What percent of the points were scored by the winning team?

30. ***Car Repairs*** Randy's bill for car repairs was $140. Of this amount, $28 was charged for labour and $112 was charged for parts. What percent of the bill was for labour?

Mixed Practice *Solve.*

31. 20% of 155 is what?

32. 60% of 215 is what?

33. 170% of what is 144.5?

34. 160% of what is 152?

35. 84 is what percent of 700?

36. 72 is what percent of 900?

37. Find 0.4% of 820.

38. Find 0.3% of 540.

39. What percent of 35 is 22.4?

40. What percent of 45 is 16.2?

41. 15 is 20% of what?

42. 10 is 25% of what?

43. 8 is what percent of 1000?

44. 6 is what percent of 800?

45. What is 10.5% of 180?

46. What is 17.5% of 260?

47. Scoring 44 problems out of 55 problems correctly on a test is what percent?

48. Scoring 27 problems out of 45 problems correctly on a test is what percent?

Applications

49. ***Computer Sales*** It was projected that in 2008, 283.2 million computers would be sold worldwide. Of these, 171.8 million would be for commercial use. What percent of all computers sold in 2008 would be for commercial use? Round your answer to the nearest hundredth of a percent. (*Source:* www.usatoday.com, March 2007)

50. ***Equestrian Rider*** An Olympic equestrian rider practised jumping over a water hazard. In 400 attempts, she and her horse touched the water 15 times. What percent of her jump attempts were not perfect?

51. ***College Courses*** At Conestoga College, 62% of the freshman class is enrolled in a composition course. There are 1070 freshmen this year. How many of them are taking a composition course? Round your answer to the nearest whole number.

52. ***Student Health*** A recent study indicates that 15% of all middle school students do not eat a proper breakfast. If Pineridge Middle School has 420 students, how many do not eat a proper breakfast?

53. ***Swim Team*** The swim team at Stonybrook College has gone on to the championships 24 times over the years. If that translates to 60% of the time in which the team has qualified for the finals, how many years has the swim team qualified for the finals?

54. ***Higher Education*** Loyalist College found that 60% of its graduates go on for further education. Last year 570 of the graduates went on for further education. How many students graduated from the college last year?

55. Find 12% of 30% of $1600.

56. Find 90% of 15% of 2700.

Quick Quiz 3A

1. What is 152% of 84?

2. 72 is 0.8% of what number?

3. 68 is what percent of 400?

4. **Concept Check** Explain how to solve the following problem using an equation. Jason found that 85% of all people who purchased a Mustang at Danvers Ford were previous Mustang owners. Last year 120 people purchased a Mustang at Danvers Ford. How many of them were previous Mustang owners?

SECTION 3B SOLVING PERCENT PROBLEMS USING PROPORTIONS

Student Learning Objectives

After studying this section, you will be able to:

1. Identify the parts of the percent proportion.
2. Use the percent proportion to solve percent problems.

Identifying the Parts of the Percent Proportion

In Section 3A we showed you how to use an equation to solve a percent problem. Some students find it easier to use proportions to solve percent problems. We will show you how to use proportions in this section. The two methods work equally well. Using percent proportions allows you to see one of the many uses of proportions.

Suppose your math class of 25 students has 19 right-handed students and 6 left-handed students. You could say that $\frac{19}{25}$ of the class or 76% is right-handed. Consider the following relationship.

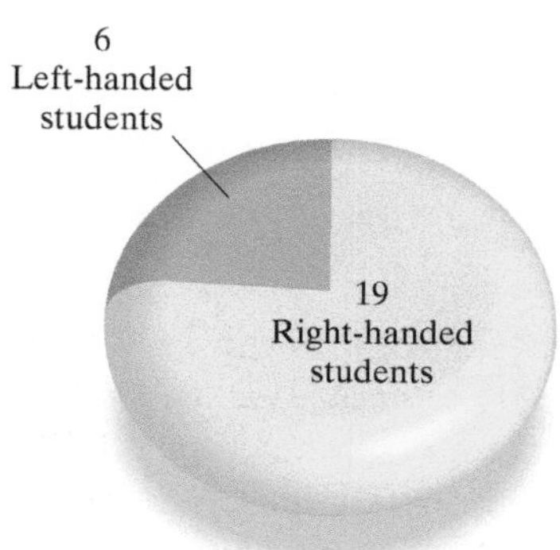

$$\frac{19}{25} = 76\%$$

This can be written as

$$\frac{19}{25} = \frac{76}{100}$$

As a rule, we can write this relationship using the **percent proportion**

$$\frac{\text{amount}}{\text{base}} = \frac{\text{percent number}}{100}.$$

To use this equation effectively, we need to find the amount, base, and percent number in a word problem. The easiest of these three parts to find is the percent number. We use the letter p (a variable) to represent the **percent number.**

EXAMPLE 1 Identify the percent number p.

(a) Find 16% of 370.
(b) 28% of what is 25?
(c) What percent of 18 is 4.5?

Solution

(a) Find 16% of 370.
The value of p is 16.

(b) 28% of what is 25?
The value of p is 28.

(c) $\underbrace{\text{What percent}}_{p}$ of 18 is 4.5?

We let p represent the unknown percent number.

Practice Problem 1 Identify the percent number p.

(a) Find 83% of 460.
(b) 18% of what number is 90?
(c) What percent of 64 is 8?

NOTE TO STUDENT: Fully worked-out solutions to all of the Practice Problems can be found at the end of the module.

We use the letter b to represent the base number. The **base** is the entire quantity or the total involved. The number that is the base usually appears after the word *of.* The **amount,** which we represent by the letter a, is the part being compared to the whole.

EXAMPLE 2 Identify the base b and the amount a.

(a) 20% of 320 is 64. **(b)** 12 is 60% of what?

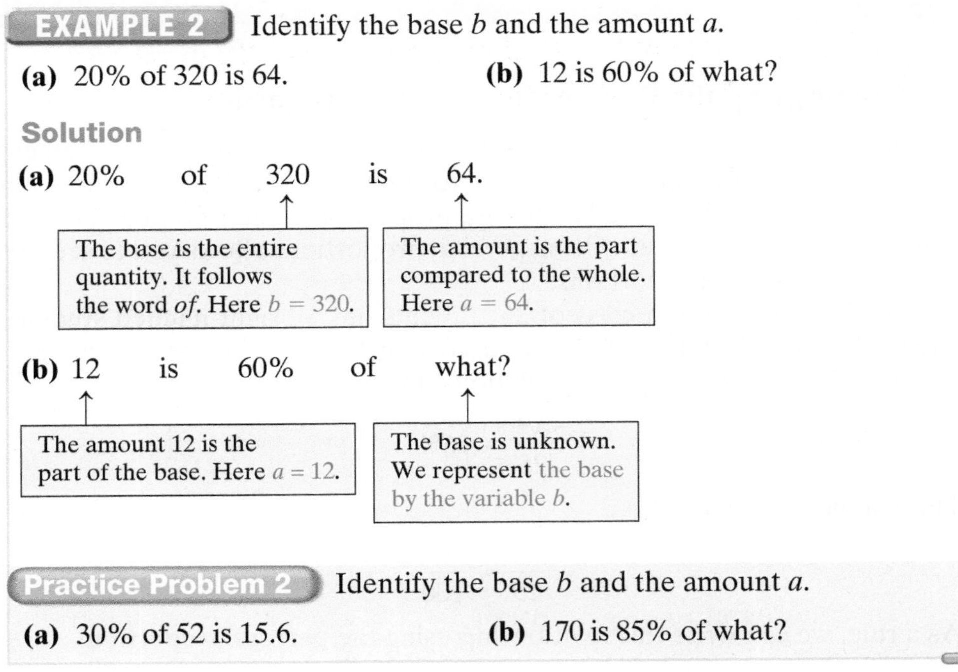

Solution
(a) 20% of 320 is 64.
The base is the entire quantity. It follows the word of. Here b = 320.
The amount is the part compared to the whole. Here a = 64.
(b) 12 is 60% of what?
The amount 12 is the part of the base. Here a = 12.
The base is unknown. We represent the base by the variable b.

Practice Problem 2 Identify the base b and the amount a.

(a) 30% of 52 is 15.6. **(b)** 170 is 85% of what?

When identifying p, b, and a in a problem, it is easiest to identify p and b first. The remaining quantity or variable is a.

EXAMPLE 3 Find p, b, and a.

(a) What is 52% of 300? **(b)** What percent of 30 is 18?

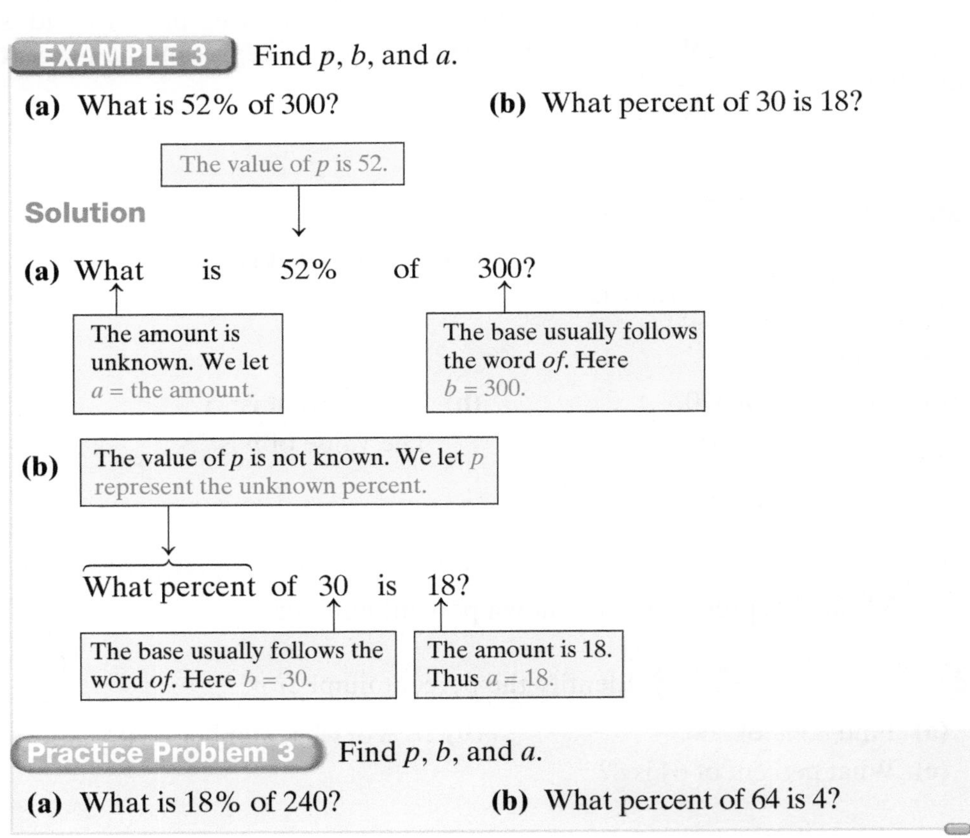

The value of p is 52.
Solution
(a) What is 52% of 300?
The amount is unknown. We let a = the amount.
The base usually follows the word of. Here b = 300.
(b) The value of p is not known. We let p represent the unknown percent.
What percent of 30 is 18?
The base usually follows the word of. Here b = 30.
The amount is 18. Thus a = 18.

Practice Problem 3 Find p, b, and a.

(a) What is 18% of 240? **(b)** What percent of 64 is 4?

 Using the Percent Proportion to Solve Percent Problems

When we solve the percent proportion, we will have enough information to state the numerical value for two of the three variables a, b, p in the equation

$$\frac{a}{b} = \frac{p}{100}$$

We first identify those two values, and then substitute those values into the equation. Then we solve proportions to find the value we do not know. Here and throughout the entire module we assume that $b \neq 0$.

When solving each problem it is a good idea to look at your answer and see if it is reasonable. Ask yourself, "Does my answer make sense?"

EXAMPLE 4 Find 260% of 40.

Solution The percent $p = 260$. The number that is the base usually appears after the word *of*. The base $b = 40$. The amount is unknown. We use the variable a. Thus

$$\frac{a}{b} = \frac{p}{100} \quad \text{becomes} \quad \frac{a}{40} = \frac{260}{100}.$$

If we reduce the fraction on the right-hand side, we have

$$\frac{a}{40} = \frac{13}{5}$$

$$5a = (40)(13) \quad \text{Cross-multiply.}$$

$$5a = 520 \quad \text{Simplify.}$$

$$\frac{5a}{5} = \frac{520}{5} \quad \text{Divide each side of the equation by 5.}$$

$$a = 104$$

Thus 260% of 40 is 104.

Practice Problem 4 Find 340% of 70.

EXAMPLE 5 85% of what is 221?

Solution The percent $p = 85$. The base is unknown. We use the variable b. The amount a is 221. Thus

$$\frac{a}{b} = \frac{p}{100} \quad \text{becomes} \quad \frac{221}{b} = \frac{85}{100}.$$

If we reduce the fraction on the right-hand side, we have

$$\frac{221}{b} = \frac{17}{20}$$

$$(221)(20) = 17b \quad \text{Cross-multiply.}$$

$$4420 = 17b \quad \text{Simplify.}$$

$$\frac{4420}{17} = \frac{17b}{17} \quad \text{Divide each side by 17.}$$

$$260 = b. \quad \text{Divide 4420 by 17.}$$

Thus 85% of 260 is 221.

***NOTE TO STUDENT:** Fully worked-out solutions to all of the Practice Problems can be found at the end of the module.*

Practice Problem 5 68% of what is 476?

EXAMPLE 6 George and Barbara purchased some no-load mutual funds. The account manager charged a service fee of 0.2% of the value of the mutual funds. George and Barbara paid this fee, which amounted to \$53. When they got home they could not find the receipt that showed the exact value of the mutual funds that they purchased. Can you find the value of the mutual funds that they purchased?

SuperStock, Inc.

Solution The basic situation here is that 0.2% of some number is \$53. This is equivalent to saying "\$53 is 0.2% of what?" If we want to answer the question "53 is 0.2% of what?", we need to identify a, b, and p.

The percent $p = 0.2$. The base is unknown. We use the variable b. The amount $a = 53$. Thus

$$\frac{a}{b} = \frac{p}{100} \quad \text{becomes} \quad \frac{53}{b} = \frac{0.2}{100}.$$

When we cross-multiply, we obtain

$$(53)(100) = 0.2b$$

$$5300 = 0.2b$$

$$\frac{5300}{0.2} = \frac{0.2b}{0.2}$$

$$26\,500 = b.$$

Thus \$53 is 0.2% of \$26 500. Therefore the value of the mutual funds was \$26 500.

Practice Problem 6 Everett Hatfield recently exchanged U.S. dollars for Canadian dollars for his company, Nova Scotia Central Trucking, Ltd. The bank charged a fee of 0.3% of the total U.S. dollars exchanged. The fee amounted to \$216 in U.S. money. How many U.S. dollars were exchanged?

EXAMPLE 7 What percent of 4000 is 160?

Solution The percent is unknown. We use the variable p. The base $b = 4000$. The amount $a = 160$. Thus

$$\frac{a}{b} = \frac{p}{100} \quad \text{becomes} \quad \frac{160}{4000} = \frac{p}{100}.$$

If we reduce the fraction on the left-hand side, we have

$$\frac{1}{25} = \frac{p}{100}$$

$$100 = 25p \quad \text{Cross-multiply.}$$

$$\frac{100}{25} = \frac{25p}{25} \quad \text{Divide each side by 25.}$$

$$4 = p \quad \text{Divide 100 by 25.}$$

Thus 4% of 4000 is 160.

Practice Problem 7 What percent of 3500 is 105?

Developing Your Study Skills

Reading the Textbook

Homework time each day should begin with the careful reading of the section(s) assigned in your textbook. Much time and effort have gone into the selection of a particular text, and your instructor has chosen a book that will help you become successful in this mathematics class. Expensive textbooks can be a wise investment if you take advantage of them by reading them.

Reading a mathematics textbook is unlike reading many other types of books that you may use in your literature, history, psychology, or sociology courses. Mathematics texts are technical books that provide you with exercises to practise on. Reading a mathematics text requires slow and careful reading of each word, which takes time and effort.

Begin reading your textbook with a paper and pencil in hand. As you come across a new definition, or concept, underline it in the text and/or write it down in your notebook. Whenever you encounter an unfamiliar term, look it up and make a note of it. When you come to an example, work through it step by step. Be sure to read each word and to follow directions carefully.

Notice the helpful hints the author provides to guide you to correct solutions and prevent you from making errors. Take advantage of these pieces of expert advice.

Be sure that you understand what you are reading. Make a note of any of those things that you do not understand and ask your instructor about them. Do not hurry through the material. Learning mathematics takes time.

SECTION 3B EXERCISES

Identify p, b, and a. Do not solve for the unknown.

	p	b	a
1. 75% of 660 is 495.	______	______	______
2. 65% of 820 is 532.	______	______	______
3. What is 22% of 60?	______	______	______
4. What is 35% of 95?	______	______	______
5. 49% of what is 2450?	______	______	______
6. 38% of what is 2280?	______	______	______
7. 30 is what percent of 50?	______	______	______
8. 50 is what percent of 250?	______	______	______

Solve using the percent proportion

$$\frac{a}{b} = \frac{p}{100}.$$

In exercises 9–14, the amount a is not known.

9. 40% of 70 is what?

10. 80% of 90 is what?

11. Find 210% of 40.

12. Find 150% of 80.

13. 0.7% of 8000 is what?

14. 0.8% of 9000 is what?

In exercises 15–20, the base b is not known.

15. 20 is 25% of what?

16. 45 is 60% of what?

17. 250% of what is 200?

18. 120% of what is 90?

19. 3000 is 0.5% of what?

20. 6000 is 0.4% of what?

In exercises 21–24, the percent p is not known.

21. 56 is what percent of 280?

22. 70 is what percent of 1400?

23. What percent of 90 is 18?

24. What percent of 120 is 18?

Mixed Practice

25. 25% of 88 is what?

26. 20% of 75 is what?

27. 300% of what is 120?

28. 200% of what is 120?

29. 82 is what percent of 500?

30. 75 is what percent of 600?

31. Find 0.7% of 520.

32. Find 0.4% of 650.

33. What percent of 66 is 16.5?

34. What percent of 49 is 34.3?

35. 68 is 40% of what?

36. 52 is 40% of what?

Applications *When solving each applied problem, examine your answer and see if it is reasonable. Ask yourself, "Does my answer make sense?"*

37. ***Paycheque Deposit*** Each time Lowell gets paid, 5% of his paycheque is deposited in his retirement account. Last week, $48 was put into his retirement account. What was the amount of Lowell's paycheque?

38. ***Income Tax*** Last year, Rachel had 24% of her salary deducted for taxes. If the total amount deducted was $6300 for the year, what was Rachel's annual salary?

39. ***Eating Out*** Ed and Suzie went out to eat at Pizzeria Uno. The dinner bill was $26.00. They left a tip of $3.90. What percent of the bill was the tip?

40. ***Baseball*** During the baseball season, Damon was up to bat 60 times. Of these at-bats, 12 were home runs. What percent of Damon's at-bats resulted in a home run?

41. ***Food Expiration Date*** The Super Shop and Save store had 120 litres of milk placed on the shelf one night. During the next morning's inspection, the manager found that 15% of the milk had passed the expiration date. How many litres of milk had passed the expiration date?

42. ***Police Arrests*** During June the Ajax police stopped 250 drivers for speed violations. It was found that 8% of the people who were stopped had outstanding warrants for their arrest. How many people had outstanding warrants for their arrest?

43. ***Car Purchase*** Victor purchased a used car for $9500. He made a down payment of 24% of the purchase price. How much was his down payment?

44. ***Education*** Trudy took a biology test with 40 problems. She got 8 of the problems wrong and 32 of the problems right. What percent of the test problems did she do incorrectly?

To Think About

Cost of Living *In 2005, Statistics Canada determined the average expenses for Canadian households. Some of the expenses are depicted in the pie chart below. Use the pie chart to answer questions 45–48. Round all answers to the nearest tenth.*

Average Expenditures (in dollars) per Household in 2005

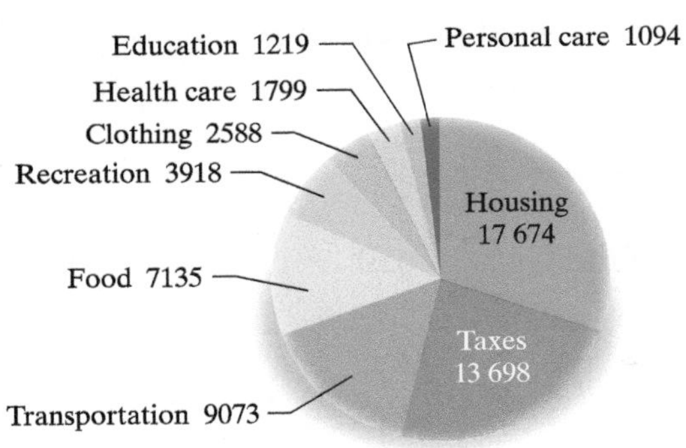

Source: Adapted from Statistics Canada, http://dsp-psd.pwgsc.gc.ca/Collection-R/Statcan/62-202-XIE/62-202-XIE2004000.pdf, Oct-09

45. What percent of the total expenditures in these nine categories was spent on housing?

46. What percent of the total expenditures in these nine categories was spent on clothing?

47. Suppose that compared to 2005, expenditures in 2010 for housing were 25% larger, expenditures for education were 10% larger, and the other seven categories remained at the same dollar amount. What percent of the total expenditures in 2010 in these nine categories would be used for food?

48. Suppose that compared to 2005, expenditures in 2015 for health care were 25% larger, expenditures for food were 15% larger, and the other seven categories remained at the same dollar amount. What percent of the total expenditures in 2015 in these nine categories would be used for personal care?

Quick Quiz 3B

1. What is 0.09% of 17 000?

2. 64.8 is 54% of what number?

3. 132 is what percent of 600?

Explain how to solve the following problem using a proportion.

4. Concept Check Alice purchased some stock and was charged a service fee of 0.7% of the value of the stock. The fee she paid was $140. What was the value of the stock that she purchased?

How Am I Doing?

How are you doing with your homework assignments in Sections 1 to 3? Do you feel you have mastered the material so far? Do you understand the concepts you have covered? Before you go further, take some time to do each of the following problems.

1

Write as a percent.

1. 0.17 **2.** 0.387 **3.** 7.95 **4.** 5.18

5. 0.006 **6.** 0.0004 **7.** $\frac{17}{100}$ **8.** $\frac{89}{100}$

9. $\frac{13.4}{100}$ **10.** $\frac{19.8}{100}$ **11.** $\frac{6\frac{1}{2}}{100}$ **12.** $\frac{1\frac{3}{8}}{100}$

2

Change to a percent. Round to the nearest hundredth of a percent when necessary.

13. $\frac{8}{10}$ **14.** $\frac{15}{30}$ **15.** $\frac{52}{20}$ **16.** $\frac{17}{16}$

17. $\frac{5}{7}$ **18.** $\frac{2}{7}$ **19.** $\frac{18}{24}$ **20.** $\frac{9}{36}$

21. $4\frac{2}{5}$ **22.** $2\frac{3}{4}$ **23.** $\frac{1}{300}$ **24.** $\frac{1}{400}$

Write as a fraction in simplified form.

25. 22% **26.** 53% **27.** 150% **28.** 160%

29. $6\frac{1}{3}\%$ **30.** $3\frac{1}{8}\%$ **31.** $51\frac{1}{4}\%$ **32.** $43\frac{3}{4}\%$

3

Solve. Round to the nearest hundredth when necessary.

33. What is 70% of 60? **34.** Find 12% of 200.

35. 68 is what percent of 72? **36.** What percent of 76 is 34?

37. 8% of what number is 240? **38.** 354 is 40% of what number?

Your institution may have included the Answers to Selected Exercises for this module, which contains the answers to these questions. Each answer also includes a reference to the objective in which the problem is first taught. If you missed any of these problems, you should stop and review the Examples and Practice Problems in the referenced objective. A little review now will help you master the material in the upcoming sections.

1. ____
2. ____
3. ____
4. ____
5. ____
6. ____
7. ____
8. ____
9. ____
10. ____
11. ____
12. ____
13. ____
14. ____
15. ____
16. ____
17. ____
18. ____
19. ____
20. ____
21. ____
22. ____
23. ____
24. ____
25. ____
26. ____
27. ____
28. ____
29. ____
30. ____
31. ____
32. ____
33. ____
34. ____
35. ____
36. ____
37. ____
38. ____

SECTION 4 SOLVING APPLIED PERCENT PROBLEMS

Student Learning Objectives

After studying this section, you will be able to:

 **Solve general applied percent problems.**

 **Solve applied problems when percents are added.**

 **Solve discount problems.**

1 Solving General Applied Percent Problems

In Sections 3A and 3B, we learned the three types of percent problems. Some problems ask you to find a percent of a number. Some problems give you an amount and a percent and ask you to find the base (or whole). Other problems give an amount and a base and ask you to find the percent. We will now see how the three types of percent problems occur in real life.

EXAMPLE 1 Of all the computers manufactured last month, an inspector found 18 that were defective. This is 2.5% of all the computers manufactured last month. How many computers were manufactured last month?

Solution

Method A Translate to an equation.

The problem is equivalent to: 2.5% of the number of computers is 18.

Let n = the number of computers.

$$\begin{array}{cccc} 2.5\% & \text{of} & \underbrace{\text{the number of computers}} & \text{is } 18 \\ \downarrow & \downarrow & \downarrow & \downarrow\ \downarrow \\ 2.5\% & \times & n & = 18 \end{array}$$

$$0.025n = 18$$

$$\frac{0.025n}{0.025} = \frac{18}{0.025}$$

$$n = 720$$

720 computers were manufactured last month.

Method B Use the percent proportion $\frac{a}{b} = \frac{p}{100}$.

The percent $p = 2.5$. The base is unknown. We will use the variable b. The amount $a = 18$. Thus

$$\frac{a}{b} = \frac{p}{100} \quad \text{becomes} \quad \frac{18}{b} = \frac{2.5}{100}.$$

Using cross multiplication, we have

$$(18)(100) = 2.5b$$

$$1800 = 2.5b$$

$$\frac{1800}{2.5} = \frac{2.5b}{2.5}$$

$$720 = b.$$

720 computers were manufactured last month.

By either Method A or Method B, we obtain the same number of computers, 720.

Substitute 720 into the original problem to check.

2.5% of 720 computers are defective.

$$(0.025)(720) = 18 \checkmark$$

Practice Problem 1 4800 people, or 12% of all passengers holding tickets for Air Canada flights in one month, did not show up for their flights. How many people held tickets that month?

NOTE TO STUDENT: Fully worked-out solutions to all of the Practice Problems can be found at the end of the module.

EXAMPLE 2 How much sales tax will you pay on a television priced at $299 if the sales tax is 5%?

Juice Images/Art Life Images

Solution

Method A Translate to an equation.

What is 5% of $299?

↓ ↓ ↓ ↓ ↓

$$n = 5\% \times 299$$
$$n = (0.05)(299)$$
$$n = 14.95 \qquad \text{The tax is \$14.95.}$$

Method B Use the percent proportion $\frac{a}{b} = \frac{p}{100}$.

The percent $p = 5$. The base $b = 299$. The amount is unknown. We use the variable a. Thus

$$\frac{a}{b} = \frac{p}{100} \quad \text{becomes} \quad \frac{a}{299} = \frac{5}{100}.$$

If we reduce the fraction on the right-hand side, we have

$$\frac{a}{299} = \frac{1}{20}.$$

We then cross-multiply to obtain

$$20a = 299$$
$$\frac{20a}{20} = \frac{299}{20}$$
$$a = 14.95 \qquad \text{The tax is \$14.95.}$$

Thus, by either method, the amount of the sales tax is $14.95.

Let's see if our answer is reasonable. Is 5% of $299 really $14.95? If we round $299 to one nonzero digit, we have $300. Thus we have 5% of 300 = 15. Since 15 is quite close to our value of $14.95, our answer seems reasonable.

Practice Problem 2 A salesperson rented a hotel room for $62.30 per night. The tax in her province is 8%. What tax does she pay for one night at the hotel? Round to the nearest cent.

EXAMPLE 3 A failing student attended class 39 times out of the 45 times the class met last semester. What percent of the classes did he attend? Round to the nearest tenth of a percent.

Solution

Method A Translate to an equation.

This problem is equivalent to:

$$\begin{array}{ccccc} 39 & \text{is} & \text{what percent} & \text{of} & 45? \\ \downarrow & \downarrow & \downarrow & \downarrow & \downarrow \\ 39 & = & n & \times & 45 \end{array}$$

$$39 = 45n$$

$$\frac{39}{45} = \frac{45n}{45}$$

$$0.8666\ldots = n.$$

To the nearest tenth of a percent we have $n = 86.7\%$.

Method B Use the percent proportion $\frac{a}{b} = \frac{p}{100}$.

The percent is unknown. We use the variable p. The base b is 45. The amount a is 39. Thus

$$\frac{a}{b} = \frac{p}{100} \quad \text{becomes} \quad \frac{39}{45} = \frac{p}{100}.$$

When we cross-multiply, we get

$$(39)(100) = 45p$$

$$3900 = 45p$$

$$\frac{3900}{45} = \frac{45p}{45}$$

$$86.666\ldots = p.$$

To the nearest tenth, the answer is 86.7%.

By using either method, we discover that the failing student attended approximately 86.7% of the classes.

Verify by estimating that the answer is reasonable.

NOTE TO STUDENT: Fully worked-out solutions to all of the Practice Problems can be found at the end of the module.

Practice Problem 3 Of the 130 flights at Jack Garland Airport yesterday, only 105 of them were on time. What percent of the flights were on time? (Round to the nearest tenth of a percent.)

Now you have some experience solving the three types of percent problems in real-life applications. You can use either Method A or Method B to solve applied percent problems. In the following pages we will present more percent applications. We will not list all the steps of Method A or Method B. Most students will find after a careful study of Examples 1–3 that they do not need to write out all the steps of Method A or Method B when solving applied percent problems.

 Solving Applied Problems When Percents Are Added

Percents can be added if the base (whole) is the same. For example, 50% of your salary added to 20% of your salary = 70% of your salary. 100% of your cost added to 15% of your cost = 115% of your cost. Problems like this are often called **markup problems.** If we add 15% of the cost of an item to the original cost, the markup is 15%. We will add percents in some applied situations.

The following example is interesting, but it is a little challenging. So please read it very carefully. A lot of students find it difficult at first.

EXAMPLE 4 Kolja and Helga are going out to a restaurant. They have a limit of $63.25 to spend for the evening. They want to tip the server 15% of the cost of the meal. How much money can they afford to spend on the meal itself? (Assume there is no tax.)

Solution In some of the problems in this section, it may help you to use the Mathematics Blueprint. We will use it here for Example 4.

Mathematics Blueprint for Problem Solving

Gather the Facts	What Am I Asked to Do?	How Do I Proceed?	Key Points to Remember
They have a spending limit of $63.25. They want to tip the server 15% of the cost of the meal.	Find the amount of money that the meal will cost.	Separate the $63.25 into two parts: the cost of the meal and the tip. Add these two parts to get $63.25.	We are not taking 15% of $63.25, but rather 15% of the cost of the meal.

Let n = the cost of the meal. 15% of the cost = the amount of the tip. We want to add the percents of the meal.

$$\boxed{\text{Cost of meal } n} + \boxed{\text{tip of 15\% of the cost}} = \boxed{\$63.25}$$

$$100\% \text{ of } n + 15\% \text{ of } n = \$63.25$$

Note that 100% of n added to 15% of n is 115% of n.

$$115\% \text{ of } n = \$63.25$$
$$1.15 \times n = 63.25$$
$$\frac{1.15 \times n}{1.15} = \frac{63.25}{1.15} \quad \text{Divide both sides by 1.15.}$$
$$n = 55$$

They can spend up to $55.00 on the meal itself.

Does this answer seem reasonable?

Practice Problem 4 Arash and Morgan have $46.00 to spend at a restaurant, including a 15% tip. How much can they spend on the meal itself? (Assume there is no tax.)

NOTE TO STUDENT: *Fully worked-out solutions to all of the Practice Problems can be found at the end of the module.*

3 Solving Discount Problems

Frequently, we see signs urging us to buy during a sale when the list price is discounted by a certain percent.

The amount of a **discount** is the product of the discount rate and the list price.

$$\text{Discount} = \text{discount rate} \times \text{list price}$$

EXAMPLE 5 Jeff purchased a large-screen TV on sale at a 35% discount. The list price was $430.00.

(a) What was the amount of the discount?

(b) How much did Jeff pay for the large-screen TV?

Solution

(a)
$$\begin{aligned} \text{Discount} &= \text{discount rate} \times \text{list price} \\ &= 35\% \times 430 \\ &= 0.35 \times 430 \\ &= 150.5 \end{aligned}$$

The discount was $150.50.

(b) We subtract the discount from the list price to get the selling price.

$$\begin{array}{rl} \$430.00 & \text{list price} \\ - \$150.50 & \text{discount} \\ \hline \$279.50 & \text{selling price} \end{array}$$

Jeff paid $279.50 for the large-screen TV.

Practice Problem 5 Kiera bought a car that lists for $13 600 at a 7% discount.

(a) What was the discount?

(b) What did she pay for the car?

Section 4 Exercises

Applications *Exercises 1–18 present the three types of percent problems. They are similar to Examples 1–3. Take the time to master exercises 1–18 before going on to the next ones. Round to the nearest hundredth when necessary.*

1. ***Education*** No graphite was found in 4500 pencils shipped to Sureway School Supplies. This was 2.5% of the total number of pencils received by Sureway. How many pencils in total were in the order?

2. ***Track and Field*** A high-jumper on the track and field team hit the bar 58 times last week. This means that he did not succeed in 29% of his jump attempts. How many total attempts did he make last week?

3. ***Cable Television Bill*** Under Todd's new cable television plan, his bill averages $63 per month. This is 140% of his average monthly bill last year when he had the basic cable package. What was his average monthly cable bill last year?

4. ***Salary Changes*** Renata now earns $9.50 per hour. This is 125% of what she earned last year. What did she earn per hour last year?

5. ***Square Footage of Home*** A 2100-square-foot home is for sale. The finished basement has an area of 432 square feet. The basement accounts for what percent of the total square footage?

6. ***Coffee Bar*** Every day this year, Sam ordered either cappuccino or espresso from the coffee bar downstairs. He had 85 espressos and 280 cappuccinos. What percent of the coffees were espressos?

7. ***Sales Tax*** Elizabeth bought new towels and sheets for $65. How much tax did she pay if the sales tax is 6%?

8. ***Sales Tax*** Leon bought new clothes for his office job. Before tax was added on, his total was $180. How much tax did he pay if the sales tax is 5%?

9. ***Mountain Bike*** Malia bought a new mountain bike. The sales tax in her province is 7%, and she paid $38.50 in tax. What was the price of the mountain bike before the tax?

10. ***Sales Tax*** Hiro bought some artwork and paid $10.75 in tax. The sales tax in his province is 5%. What was the price of the artwork?

11. ***Mortgage Payment*** Paul and Sue Yin together earn $4180 per month. Their mortgage payment is $1254 per month. What percent of their household income goes toward paying the mortgage?

12. ***Car Payment*** Cora puts aside $52.50 per week for her monthly car payment. She earns $350 per week. What percent of her income is set aside for car payments?

13. ***Charities*** The Children's Wish Charity raised 75% of its funds from sporting promotions. Last year the charity received $7 200 000 from its sporting promotions. What was the charity's total income last year?

14. ***Taxes*** Shannon paid $8400 in federal and provincial income taxes as a lab technician, which amounted to 28% of her annual income. What was her income last year?

15. ***Baseball*** 10 001 home runs have been hit in Boston's Fenway Park since it opened in 1912. Ted Williams of the Boston Red Sox hit 248 of these. What percent of the total home runs did Ted Williams hit?

16. ***Baseball*** During the 2006 baseball season, Nomar Garciaparra was up to bat 469 times. Of these, 20 resulted in a home run. What percent of Garciaparra's at-bats resulted in a home run?

17. ***Pediatrics*** In Sudbury, Ontario, 0.9% of all babies walk before they reach the age of 11 months. If 24 000 babies were born in Sudbury in the last 20 years, how many of them will have walked before they reached the age of 11 months?

18. ***Hockey*** At a Toronto Maple Leafs hockey game scheduled for 8:30 P.M., 0.8% of the spectators were children under age 12. If 28 000 people showed up for the game, how many children under age 12 were in the stands?

Exercises 19–30 include percents that are added and discounts. Solve. Round to the nearest hundredth when necessary.

19. ***Sales Tax*** Henry has $800 total to spend on a new dining room table and chairs. If the sales tax is 5%, how much can he afford to spend on the table and chairs?

20. ***Eating Out*** Belinda asked Martin out to dinner. She has $47.50 to spend. She wants to tip the server 15% of the cost of their meal. How much money can she afford to spend on the meal itself?

21. ***Building Costs*** John and Chris Maney are building a new house. When finished, the house will cost $163 500. The price of the house is 9% higher than the price when the original plans were made. What was the price of the house when the original plans were made?

22. ***SUV Purchase*** Dan and Connie Lacorazza purchased a new Honda Pilot. The purchase price was $25 440. The price was 6% higher than the price of a similar Honda Pilot three years ago. What was the price of the Honda Pilot three years ago?

23. ***Manufacturing*** When a new computer case is made, there is some waste of the plastic material used for the front of the computer case. Approximately 3% of the plastic that is delivered is of poor quality and is thrown away. Furthermore, 8% of the plastic that is delivered is waste material that is thrown away as the front pieces are created by a giant stamping machine. If 20 000 pounds of plastic are delivered to make the fronts of computer cases each month, how many pounds are thrown away?

24. ***Airport Operations*** In a recent survey of planes landing at Toronto's Pearson airport, it was observed that 12% of the flights were delayed less than an hour and 7% of the flights were delayed an hour or more but less than two hours. If 9000 flights arrive at Pearson airport in a day, how many flights are delayed less than two hours?

25. ***Political Parties*** Suppose the Conservative Party has a budget of $33 000 000 to spend on the swearing in of the new prime minister. 15% of the costs will be paid to personnel, 12% of the costs will go toward food, and 10% will go to decorations.

(a) How much money will go for personnel, food, and decorations?

(b) How much will be left over to cover security, facility rental, and all other expenses?

26. ***Medical Research*** A major research facility has developed an experimental drug to treat Alzheimer's disease. 20% of the research costs were paid to the staff. 16% of the research costs were paid to rent the building where the research was conducted. The rest of the money was used for research. The company has spent $6 000 000 in research on this new drug.

(a) How much was paid to cover the cost of staff and rental of the building?

(b) How much was left over for research?

27. ***Clothes Purchase*** Melinda purchased a new blouse, jeans, and a sweater in Moncton, New Brunswick. All of the clothes were discounted 35%. Before the sale, the total purchase price would have been $190 for these three items. How much did she pay for them with the discount?

28. ***Tire Purchase*** Juan went to purchase two new radial tires for his Honda Accord in Moose Jaw, Saskatchewan. The set of two tires normally costs $130. However, he bought them on sale at a discount of 30%. How much did he pay for the tires with the discount?

29. ***Snowmobile Purchase*** Jack bought his first Polaris snowmobile in Charlottetown, P.E.I. The price was $8800, but the dealer gave him a discount of 15%.

(a) What was the discount?

(b) How much did he pay for the snowmobile?

30. ***Appliance Purchase*** Charlotte bought a stainless steel refrigerator and stove that had been used as floor models at Home Depot. The list price of the set was $1150, but the store manager gave her a discount of 25%.

(a) What was the discount?

(b) How much did she pay for the refrigerator and stove?

Quick Quiz 4

1. Chris Smith bought a new laptop computer. The list price was $596. He got a 28% discount.

(a) What was the discount?

(b) How much did Chris pay for the laptop?

2. Laurie left on a trip for a week. When she returned she had 87 e-mail messages. 56 of these messages were "spam" junk mail. What percent of her e-mail was spam? Round your answer to the nearest tenth if necessary.

3. A total of 4500 people in the city bought take-out pizza at least once during the week. This was 30% of all the people who live in the city. How many people live in the city?

Explain how to solve the following problem.

4. Concept Check Sam works in sales for a pharmaceutical company. He can spend 23% of his budget for travel expenses. He can spend 14% for entertainment of clients. He can spend 17% of his budget for advertising. Last year he had a total budget of $80 000. Last year he spent a total of $48 000 for travel expenses, entertainment, and advertising. Did he stay within his budget allowance for those items?

Section 5 Solving Commission, Percent of Increase or Decrease, and Interest Problems

Student Learning Objectives

After studying this section, you will be able to:

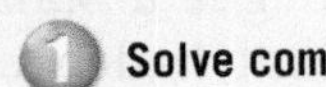 Solve commission problems.

 Solve percent-of-increase or percent-of-decrease problems.

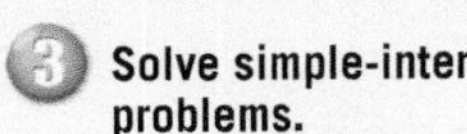 Solve simple-interest problems.

1 Solving Commission Problems

If you work as a salesperson, your earnings may be in part or in total a certain percentage of the sales you make. The amount of money you get that is a percentage of the value of your sales is called your **commission.** It is calculated by multiplying the percentage (called the **commission rate**) by the value of the sales.

$$\text{Commission} = \text{commission rate} \times \text{value of sales}$$

EXAMPLE 1 A salesperson has a commission rate of 17%. She sells \$32 500 worth of goods in a department store in two months. What is her commission?

Solution

$$\begin{aligned} \text{Commission} &= \text{commission rate} \times \text{value of sales} \\ \text{Commission} &= 17\% \times \$32\,500 \\ &= 0.17 \times 32\,500 \\ &= 5525 \end{aligned}$$

Her commission is \$5525.00.

Does this answer seem reasonable? Check by estimating.

Practice Problem 1 A real estate salesperson earns a commission rate of 6% when he sells a \$156 000 home. What is his commission?

In some problems, the unknown quantity will be the commission rate or the value of sales. However, the same equation is used:

$$\text{Commission} = \text{commission rate} \times \text{value of sales}$$

Solving Percent-of-Increase or Percent-of-Decrease Problems

We sometimes need to find the percent by which a number increases or decreases. If a car costs \$7000 and the price decreases \$1750, we say that the percent of decrease is $\frac{1750}{7000} = 0.25 = 25\%$.

$$\textbf{Percent of decrease} = \frac{\text{amount of decrease}}{\text{original amount}}$$

Similarly, if a population of 12 000 people increases by 1920 people, we say that the percent of increase is $\frac{1920}{12\,000} = 0.16 = 16\%$.

$$\textbf{Percent of increase} = \frac{\text{amount of increase}}{\text{original amount}}$$

Note that for these types of problems the base is always the *original amount.*

The most important thing to remember is that we must **first** find the amount of increase or decrease.

EXAMPLE 2 The population of Smallville increased from 50 000 to 59 500. What was the percent of increase?

Solution For this problem as well as others in this section, you may find it helpful to use the Mathematics Blueprint.

Mathematics Blueprint for Problem Solving

Gather the Facts	What Am I Asked to Do?	How Do I Proceed?	Key Points to Remember
The population increased from 50 000 to 59 500.	We must find the percent of increase.	First subtract to find the amount of increase. Then divide the amount of increase by the original amount.	Always divide by the original amount.

Amount of increase

$$\begin{array}{r} 59\,500 \\ -\,50\,000 \\ \hline 9\,500 \end{array}$$

$$\text{Percent of increase} = \frac{\text{amount of increase}}{\text{original amount}} = \frac{9500}{50\,000}$$

$$= 0.19 = 19\%$$

The percent of increase is 19%.

Practice Problem 2 A new car is sold for \$15 000. A year later its price has decreased to \$10 500. What is the percent of decrease?

3 Solving Simple Interest Problems

Interest is money paid for the use of money. If you deposit money in a bank, the bank uses that money and pays you interest. If you borrow money, you pay the bank interest for the use of that money.

The **principal** is the amount deposited or borrowed. Interest is usually expressed as a percent rate of the principal. The **interest rate** is assumed to be per year, unless otherwise stated. The formula used in business to compute simple interest is

$$\text{Interest} = \text{principal} \times \text{rate} \times \text{time}$$

$$I = P \times R \times T$$

If the interest rate is *per year,* the time *T must* be in *years.*

Calculator

Interest

You can use a calculator to find simple interest. Find the interest on \$450 invested at 6.5% for 15 months. Notice the time is in months. Since the interest formula $I = P \times R \times T$, is in years, you need to change 15 months to years by dividing 15 by 12.

Enter

15 [÷] 12 [=]

Display

[1.25]

Leave this on the display and multiply as follows:

1.25 [×] 450 [×]

6.5 [%] [=]

The display should read

[36.5625]

which would round to \$36.56.

Try the following.

(a) \$9516 invested at 12% for 30 months

(b) \$593 borrowed at 8% for 5 months

EXAMPLE 3 Find the simple interest on a loan of \$7500 borrowed at 13% for one year.

Solution

$$I = P \times R \times T$$

P = principal = \$7500 R = rate = 13% T = time = 1 year

$$I = 7500 \times 13\% \times 1 = 7500 \times 0.13 = 975$$

The interest is \$975.

NOTE TO STUDENT: Fully worked-out solutions to all of the Practice Problems can be found at the end of the module.

Practice Problem 3 Find the simple interest on a loan of \$5600 borrowed at 12% for one year.

Our formula is based on a yearly interest rate. Time periods of more than one year or a fractional part of a year are sometimes needed.

EXAMPLE 4 Find the simple interest on a loan of \$2500 that is borrowed at 9% for

(a) three years. **(b)** three months.

Solution

(a)

$$I = P \times R \times T$$

$P = \$2500$ $R = 9\%$ $T = 3$ years

$$I = 2500 \times 0.09 \times 3 = 225 \times 3 = 675$$

The interest for three years is \$675.

(b) Three months $= \frac{1}{4}$ year. The time period must be in years to use the formula.

Since $T = \frac{1}{4}$ year, we have

$$I = 2500 \times 0.09 \times \frac{1}{4}$$

$$= 225 \times \frac{1}{4}$$

$$= \frac{225}{4} = 56.25$$

The interest for three months is \$56.25.

Practice Problem 4 Find the simple interest on a loan of \$1800 that is borrowed at 11% for

(a) four years. **(b)** six months.

Many loans today are based on **compound interest.** This topic is covered in more advanced mathematics courses. The calculations for compound interest are tedious to do by hand. Usually people use a computer, a calculator, or a compound interest table to do compound interest problems.

SECTION 5 EXERCISES

Applications

Exercises 1–18 are problems involving commissions, percent of increase or decrease, and simple interest.

1. ***Appliance Sales*** Walter works as an appliance salesman in a department store. Last month he sold \$170 000 worth of appliances. His commission rate is 2%. How much money did he earn in commission last month?

2. ***Car Sales*** Susan works at the Acura dealership in Winchester. Last month she had car sales totalling \$230 000. Her commission rate is 3%. How much money did she earn in commission last month?

3. ***Mobile Phone Sales*** Allison works in the local Verizon office selling mobile phones. She is paid \$300 per month plus 4% of her total sales in mobile phones. Last month she sold \$96 000 worth of mobile phones. What was her total income for the month?

4. ***Stockbroker*** Tanvar is a stockbroker. He is paid \$500 per month plus 0.5% of the total sales of stocks that he sells. Last month he sold \$340 000 worth of stock. What was his total income for the month?

5. ***Airline Tickets*** Dawn is searching online for airline tickets. Two weeks ago the cost to fly from Kamloops to Halifax was \$275. The price now is \$330. What is the percent of increase?

6. ***Weight Loss*** Bohai weighed 133.5 kilograms before starting an exercise routine. Two years later, he weighed a healthy 91.5 kilograms. What was the percent of decrease in Bohai's weight? Round your answer to the nearest tenth of a percent.

7. ***Computer Prices*** In 2002, the average price for a notebook computer in Canada was \$1496. In 2006, the average price was \$948. What was the percent of decrease in average notebook computer price? Round your answer to the nearest tenth of a percent.

8. ***Computer Prices*** In 2002, the average price for a desktop computer in Canada was \$807. In 2006, the average price was \$635. What was the percent of decrease in average desktop computer price?

9. ***GIC Interest*** Phil placed \$2000 in a one-year GIC at the bank. The bank is paying simple interest of 7% for one year on the GIC. How much interest will Phil earn in one year?

10. ***Chequing Account Interest*** Charlotte has a chequing account that pays her simple interest of 1.2% on the average balance in her chequing account. Last year her average balance was \$450. How much interest did she earn in her chequing account?

11. ***Credit Card Expenses*** Melinda has a MasterCard account with CIBC. She has to pay a monthly interest rate of 1.5% on the average daily balance of the amount she owes on her credit card. Last month her average daily balance was \$500. How much interest was she charged last month? (*Hint:* The formula $I = P \times R \times T$ can be used if the interest rate is *per month* and the time is in *months.*)

12. ***Student Loan*** Ahmed borrowed \$3000 for a student loan to finish college this year. Next year he will need to pay 7% simple interest on the amount he borrowed. How much interest will he need to pay next year?

13. ***House Construction Loan*** James had to borrow \$26 000 for a house construction loan for four months. The interest rate was 12% per year. How much interest did he have to pay for borrowing the money for four months?

14. ***Small Business Loan*** Maya needed to borrow \$9200 for three months to finance some renovations to her gift shop. The interest rate was 15% per year. How much interest did she have to pay for borrowing the money for three months?

15. ***Life Insurance*** Robert sells life insurance for a major insurance company for a commission. Last year he sold \$12 000 000 worth of insurance. He earned \$72 000 in commissions. What was his commission rate?

16. ***Medical Supplies*** Hillary sells medical supplies to doctors' offices for a major medical supply company. Last year she sold \$9 000 000 worth of medical supplies. She works on a commission basis and last year she earned \$63 000 in commissions. What was her commission rate?

17. ***Furniture Sales*** Jennifer sells furniture for a major department store. Last year she was paid \$48 000 in commissions. If her commission rate is 3%, what was the sales total of the furniture that she sold last year?

18. ***Auto Sales*** Michael sells used cars for Madaglia Automotive. Last year he was paid \$42 000 in commissions. Madaglia Automotive pays the salespeople a commission rate of 6%. What was the sales total of the cars that Michael sold last year?

Mixed Applications *Exercises 19–36 are a variety of percent problems. They involve commissions, percent of increase or decrease, and simple interest. There are also some of each kind of percent problem encountered in the module. Unless otherwise directed, round to the nearest hundredth.*

19. ***Entertainment Expenses*** Ted is trying to decrease his spending on entertainment. He earns \$265 per week and is allowing himself to spend only 15% per week on movies, dining out, and so on. How much can Ted spend per week on entertainment?

20. ***Biology*** The maximum capacity of your lungs is 4.58 litres of air. In a typical breath, you breathe in 12% of the maximum capacity. How many litres of air do you breathe in a typical breath?

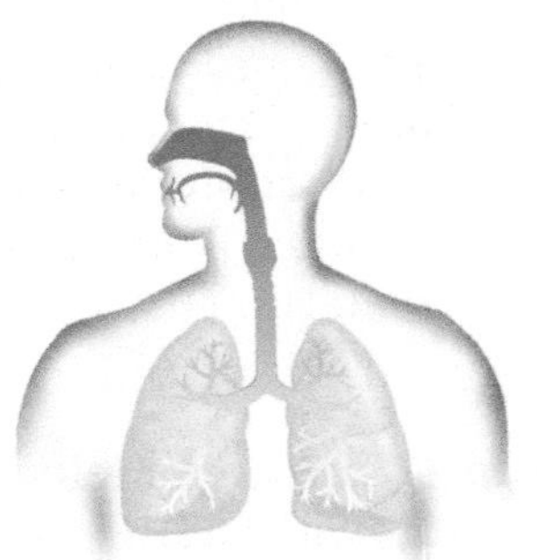

21. ***Girl Scout Cookies*** Of all the boxes of Girl Scout cookies sold, 25% are Thin Mints. If a Girl Scout troop sells 156 boxes of cookies, how many are Thin Mints?

22. ***Scotland*** 11% of the Scottish population have red hair. If the population of Scotland is 5 600 000, how many people have red hair?

23. ***Decrease in Crime*** In 1979, the number of fatal firearm incidents in Canada was 10.6 fatalities per population of 100 000. In 2002 that number had decreased to 4.9 fatalities per 100 000 people. What is the percent decrease in the number of fatal firearm incidents? Round your answer to the nearest hundredth of a percent. (*Source:* www.cbc.ca/canada.story.2005/06/28/gun-death05628.html, Oct-09)

24. ***Carbon Dioxide Emissions*** In 1990, the amount of energy-related carbon dioxide emissions in Canada was 473 million tonnes. In 2005, this number rose to 609 million tonnes. What is the percent of increase in carbon dioxide emissions? Round your answer to the nearest hundredth of a percent. (*Source:* www.statcan.gc.ca/pub/16-201-x/2007000/5212430-eng.htm)

25. ***Sporting Goods*** A sporting goods store buys cross-training shoes for $40, and sells them for $72. What is the percent of increase in the price of the shoes?

26. ***Jewellery Costs*** A gift store buys earrings from an artist for $20 and sells them for $29. What is the percent of increase in the price of the earrings?

27. ***Savings Account*** Adam deposited $3700 in his savings account for one year. His savings account earns 2.3% interest annually. He did not add any more money within the year, and at the end of that time, he withdrew all funds.

(a) How much interest did he earn?

(b) How much money did he withdraw from the bank?

28. ***Credit Card*** Nikki had $1258 outstanding on her MasterCard, which charges 2% monthly interest. At the end of this month Nikki paid off the loan.

(a) How much interest did Nikki pay for one month?

(b) How much did it cost to pay off the loan totally?

29. ***Shopping Trip*** Bryce went shopping and bought a pair of sandals for $52, swimming trunks for $38, and sunglasses for $26. The tax in Bryce's city is 6%.

(a) What is the total sales tax?

(b) What is the total of the purchases?

30. ***Automobile Purchase*** Jin bought a used Toyota Camry for $12 600. The tax in her province is 7%.

(a) What is the sales tax?

(b) What is the final price of the Camry?

31. ***Property Taxes*** Smithville Kitchen Cabinetry Inc. is late in paying $9500 in property taxes to the city of Sydney. It will be assessed 14% interest for being late in property tax payment. Find the one total amount it needs to pay off both the taxes and the interest charge.

32. ***Property Taxes*** Raymond and Elsie Ostram are late in paying $1600 in property taxes to the city of Kemptville. They will be assessed 12% interest for being late in property tax payment. Find the one total amount they need to pay off both the taxes and the interest charge.

33. ***Home Purchase*** Betty and Michael Bently purchased a new home for $349 000. They paid a down payment of 8% of the cost of the home. They took out a mortgage for the rest of the purchase price of the home.

(a) What was the amount of their down payment?

(b) What was the amount of their mortgage?

34. ***Home Purchase*** Marcia and Dan Perkins purchased a condominium for $188 000. They paid a down payment of 11% of the cost of the condominium. They took out a mortgage for the rest of the purchase price of the condominium.

(a) What was the amount of their down payment?

(b) What was the amount of their mortgage?

35. ***Interest Charges on a Mortgage*** Richard is making monthly mortgage payments of $840 for his home mortgage. He noticed on his monthly statement that $814 is used to pay off the interest charge. Only $26 is used to pay off the principal. What percent of his monthly mortgage payment is used to pay off the interest charge? Round to the nearest tenth of a percent.

36. ***Interest Charges on a Mortgage*** Alicia is making monthly mortgage payments of $960 for her home mortgage. She noticed on her monthly statement that $917 is used to pay off the interest charge. Only $43 is used to pay off the principal. What percent of her monthly mortgage payment is used to pay off the interest charge? Round to the nearest tenth of a percent.

Solve. Round to the nearest cent.

37. ***Sales Tax*** How much sales tax would you pay to purchase a new Honda Accord that costs $18 456.82 if the sales tax rate is 4.6%?

38. ***Living Room Set Purchase*** The Hartling family purchased a new living room set. The list price was $1249.95. However, they got a discount of 29%. How much did they pay for the new living room set?

Quick Quiz 5

1. A construction contractor working for a real estate developer builds a house that sells for $325 000. He gets a commission of 8% on the house. What is his commission?

2. Susanne runs a bakery. Five years ago the bakery sold 160 loaves of bread each day. Today it sells 275 loaves each day. What is the percent of increase of the number of loaves sold each day?

3. Find the simple interest on a loan of $4600 borrowed at 13% for six months.

4. **Concept Check** Explain how to find simple interest on a loan of $5800 borrowed at an annual rate of 16% for a period of three months.

Putting Your Skills to Work: Use Math to Save Money

AUTOMOBILE LEASING VS. PURCHASE

Louvy has his eye on a brand new car. He thinks he should lease the car because his best friend Tranh has a car lease and says he can get the same deal for Louvy. On the other hand, Louvy's girlfriend Allie says it is always better to buy the car and finance it by taking out a loan.

Louvy does some research and finds that it is not at all simple. While a lease offers lower monthly payments, at the end of the lease period you are left with nothing, except expenses.

Look at the following comparison for the lease vs. buy options for the car Louvy is considering.

	Lease	Purchase
Automobile price	\$23 000.00	\$23 000.00
Interest rate	6%	6%
Length of loan	36 months	36 months
Down payment	\$1000.00	\$1000.00
Residual (value of car you are turning in, amount you pay if you wish to purchase it)	\$11 000.00	Not applicable
Monthly payment	\$388.06	\$669.28

1. How much would Louvy pay over the entire length of the loan?
2. How much would Louvy pay over the entire length of the lease?
3. If Louvy decided to buy the car at the end of the lease, he would have to pay \$11 000.00 in addition to his lease cost. What would that bring the total cost of that car up to?

Making It Personal for You

4. How much can you afford per month for payments for a car? How much would you pay in insurance, taxes, and gas?
5. Would you prefer to lease or buy? Why?

Facts You Should Know

You may wish to lease a car if:

- You want a new vehicle every 2–3 years
- You don't drive an excessive number of kilometres each year

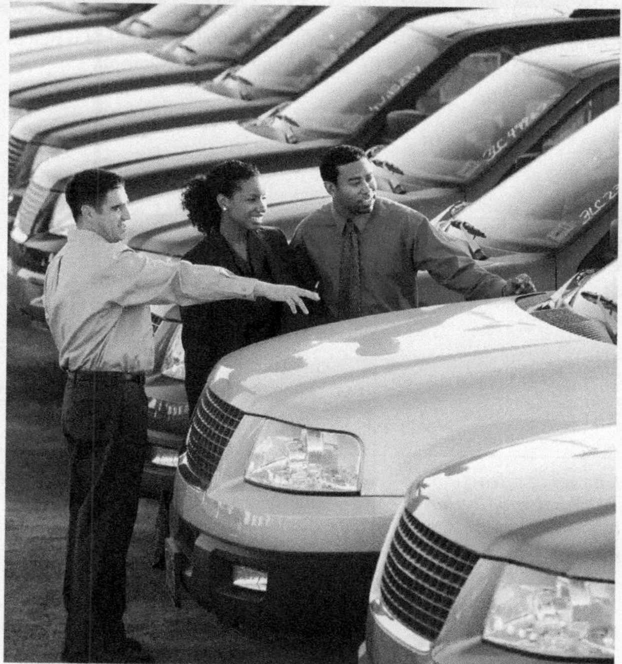

Comstock Complete

- You don't want major repairs risk
- You want a lower monthly payment

IF you lease a car:

- You pay only that portion of the vehicle you use
- There may be mileage restrictions, hidden fees, or security deposits
- You can sometimes find a lease with no down payment
- You pay sales tax only on monthly fees
- You usually must keep the car for the entire lease period, or pay a heavy penalty

You may wish to buy a car if:

- You intend to keep it a long time
- You want to be debt-free after a time
- You qualify for a very low interest rate
- The long-term cost is more important than the lower monthly payment

IF you buy a car:

- You pay for the entire vehicle
- You pay the sales tax on the entire price of the car
- There are no hidden mileage costs, except in wear and tear on the vehicle
- You can sell or trade the car during the period of the loan

Module Organizer

Topic	Procedure	Examples
Converting a decimal to a percent.	**1.** Move the decimal point two places to the right. **2.** Add the percent symbol.	$0.19 = 19\%$ $0.516 = 51.6\%$ $0.04 = 4\%$ $1.53 = 153\%$ $0.006 = 0.6\%$
Converting a fraction with a denominator of 100 to a percent.	**1.** Use the numerator only. **2.** Add the percent symbol.	$\frac{29}{100} = 29\%$ $\quad \frac{5.6}{100} = 5.6\%$ $\frac{3}{100} = 3\%$ $\quad \frac{7\frac{1}{3}}{100} = 7\frac{1}{3}\%$ $\frac{231}{100} = 231\%$
Changing a fraction (whose denominator is not 100) to a percent.	**1.** Divide the numerator by the denominator and obtain a decimal. **2.** Change the decimal to a percent.	$\frac{13}{50} = 0.26 = 26\%$ $\frac{1}{20} = 0.05 = 5\%$ $\frac{3}{800} = 0.003\,75 = 0.375\%$ $\frac{312}{200} = 1.56 = 156\%$
Changing a percent to a decimal.	**1.** Drop the percent symbol. **2.** Move the decimal point two places to the left.	$49\% = 0.49$ $2\% = 0.02$ $0.5\% = 0.005$ $196\% = 1.96$ $1.36\% = 0.0136$
Changing a percent to a fraction.	**1.** If the percent does not contain a decimal point, remove the % and write the number over a denominator of 100. Reduce the fraction if possible. **2.** If the percent contains a decimal point, change the percent to a decimal by removing the % and moving the decimal point two places to the left. Then write the decimal as a fraction and reduce if possible. **3.** If the percent contains a fraction, remove the % and write the number over a denominator of 100. If the numerator is a mixed number, change the numerator to an improper fraction. Next simplify by the "invert and multiply" rule. Then reduce the fraction if possible.	$25\% = \frac{25}{100} = \frac{1}{4}$ $38\% = \frac{38}{100} = \frac{19}{50}$ $130\% = \frac{130}{100} = \frac{13}{10}$ $5.8\% = 0.058$ $= \frac{58}{1000} = \frac{29}{500}$ $2.72\% = 0.0272$ $= \frac{272}{10\,000} = \frac{17}{625}$ $7\frac{1}{8}\% = \frac{7\frac{1}{8}}{100}$ $= 7\frac{1}{8} \div \frac{100}{1}$ $= \frac{57}{8} \times \frac{1}{100} = \frac{57}{800}$

Topic	Procedure	Examples
Changing a percent to a mixed number.	**1.** Drop the percent symbol and move the decimal point two places to the left. **2.** Write the decimal part of the number as a fraction. **3.** Reduce the fraction if possible.	$275\% = 2.75 = 2\frac{75}{100} = 2\frac{3}{4}$ $324\% = 3.24 = 3\frac{24}{100} = 3\frac{6}{25}$ $107\% = 1.07 = 1\frac{7}{100}$
Solving percent problems by translating to equations.	**1.** Translate by replacing "of" with × "is" with = "what" with n "find" with $n =$ **2.** Solve the resulting equation.	**(a)** What is 3% of 56? ↓ ↓ ↓ ↓ ↓ $n = 3\% \times 56$ $n = (0.03)(56)$ $n = 1.68$ **(b)** 16% of what is 208? ↓ ↓ ↓ ↓ ↓ $16\% \times n = 208$ $0.16n = 208$ $\frac{0.16n}{0.16} = \frac{208}{0.16}$ $n = 1300$ **(c)** What percent of 70 is 30? ↓ ↓ ↓ ↓ ↓ $n \times 70 = 30$ $70n = 30$ $\frac{70n}{70} = \frac{30}{70}$ $n = 0.428\ 571\ldots$ $n \approx 42.86\%$.
Solving percent problems by using proportions.	**1.** Identify the parts of the percent proportion. a = the amount b = the base (the whole; it usually appears after the word "of") p = the percent number **2.** Write the percent proportion $\frac{a}{b} = \frac{p}{100}$ using the values obtained in step 1 and solve.	**(a)** What is 28% of 420? The percent $p = 28$. The base $b = 420$. The amount a is unknown. We use the variable a. $\frac{a}{b} = \frac{p}{100}$ becomes $\frac{a}{420} = \frac{28}{100}$ If we reduce the fraction on the right-hand side, we have $\frac{a}{420} = \frac{7}{25}$ $25a = (7)(420)$ $25a = 2940$ $\frac{25a}{25} = \frac{2940}{25}$ $a = 117.6$ Thus, 28% of 420 is 117.6. **(b)** 64% of what is 320? The percent $p = 64$. The base is unknown. We use the variable b. The amount $a = 320$. $\frac{a}{b} = \frac{p}{100}$ becomes $\frac{320}{b} = \frac{64}{100}$ If we reduce the fraction on the right-hand side, we have $\frac{320}{b} = \frac{16}{25}$ $(320)(25) = 16b$ $8000 = 16b$ $\frac{8000}{16} = \frac{16b}{16}$ $500 = b$ Thus, 64% of 500 is 320.

(Continued on next page)

Topic	Procedure	Examples
Solving percent problems by using proportions.	**1.** Identify the parts of the percent proportion. a = the amount b = the base (the whole; it usually appears after the word "of") p = the percent number **2.** Write the percent proportion $\frac{a}{b} = \frac{p}{100}$ using the values obtained in step 1 and solve.	**(c)** What percent of 140 is 105? The percent is unknown. The base $b = 140$, the amount $a = 105$. $\frac{a}{b} = \frac{p}{100}$ becomes $\frac{105}{140} = \frac{p}{100}$ If we reduce the fraction on the left-hand side, we have $\frac{3}{4} = \frac{p}{100}$ $(100)(3) = 4p$ $300 = 4p$ $\frac{300}{4} = \frac{4p}{4}$ $75 = p$ Thus 105 is 75% of 140.
Solving discount problems.	Discount = discount rate × list price	Carla purchased a TV set that lists for \$350 at an 18% discount. **(a)** How much was the discount? **(b)** How much did she pay for the TV set? **(a)** Discount = (0.18)(350) = \$63 **(b)** 350 − 63 = 287 She paid \$287 for the TV set.
Solving commission problems.	Commission = commission rate × value of sales	A housewares salesperson gets a 16% commission on sales he makes. How much commission does he earn if he sells \$12 000 in housewares? Commission = (0.16)(12 000) = 1920 He earns a commission of \$1920.
Solving simple-interest problems.	Interest = principal × rate × time $I = P \times R \times T$ I = interest P = principal R = rate T = time	Hector borrowed \$3000 for 4 years at a simple interest rate of 12%. How much interest did he owe after 4 years? $I = P \times R \times T$ $I = (3000)(0.12)(4)$ $= (360)(4)$ $= 1440$ Hector owed \$1440 in interest.
Percent-of-increase or percent-of-decrease problems.	Percent of increase or decrease = amount of increase or decrease ÷ base	A car that costs \$16 500 now cost only \$15 000 last year. What is the percent of increase? 16 500 − 15 000 = 1 500 increase $\frac{1\,500}{15\,000} = 0.10$ Percent of increase = 10%

Module Review Problems

Section 1

Write as a percent. Round to the nearest hundredth of a percent when necessary.

1. 0.62 **2.** 0.43 **3.** 0.372 **4.** 0.529 **5.** 2.2 **6.** 1.8

7. 2.52 **8.** 4.37 **9.** 1.036 **10.** 1.052 **11.** 0.006 **12.** 0.002

13. $\frac{62.5}{100}$ **14.** $\frac{37.5}{100}$ **15.** $\frac{4\frac{1}{12}}{100}$ **16.** $\frac{3\frac{5}{12}}{100}$ **17.** $\frac{317}{100}$ **18.** $\frac{225}{100}$

Section 2

Change to a percent. Round to the nearest hundredth of a percent when necessary.

19. $\frac{19}{25}$ **20.** $\frac{13}{25}$ **21.** $\frac{11}{20}$ **22.** $\frac{9}{40}$ **23.** $\frac{7}{12}$

24. $\frac{14}{15}$ **25.** $2\frac{1}{4}$ **26.** $3\frac{3}{4}$ **27.** $2\frac{7}{9}$ **28.** $5\frac{5}{9}$

29. $\frac{152}{80}$ **30.** $\frac{200}{80}$ **31.** $\frac{3}{800}$ **32.** $\frac{5}{800}$

Change to decimal form.

33. 32% **34.** 68% **35.** 15.75% **36.** 12.35%

37. 236% **38.** 177% **39.** $32\frac{1}{8}\%$ **40.** $26\frac{3}{8}\%$

Change to fractional form.

41. 72% **42.** 92% **43.** 175% **44.** 260% **45.** 16.4%

46. 30.5% **47.** $31\frac{1}{4}\%$ **48.** $43\frac{3}{4}\%$ **49.** 0.08% **50.** 0.04%

Complete the following chart.

	Fraction	Decimal	Percent
51.	$\frac{3}{5}$		
52.	$\frac{7}{10}$		
53.			37.5%

	Fraction	Decimal	Percent
54.			56.25%
55.		0.008	
56.		0.45	

Section 3

Solve. Round to the nearest hundredth when necessary.

57. What is 20% of 85?

58. What is 25% of 92?

59. 15 is 25% of what number?

60. 30 is 75% of what number?

61. 50 is what percent of 130?

62. 70 is what percent of 180?

63. Find 162% of 60.

64. Find 124% of 80.

65. 92% of what number is 147.2?

66. 68% of what number is 95.2?

67. What percent of 70 is 14?

68. What percent of 60 is 6?

Sections 4 and 5

Solve. Round your answer to the nearest hundredth when necessary.

69. ***Education*** Professor Padron found that 35% of his World History course are sophomores. He has 140 students in his class. How many are sophomores?

70. ***Truck Dealer*** An Ontario truck dealer found that 64% of all the trucks he sold had four-wheel drive. If he sold 150 trucks, how many had four-wheel drive?

71. ***Car Depreciation*** Today Yvonne's car has 61% of the value that it had two years ago. Today it is worth $6832. What was it worth two years ago?

72. ***Administrative Expenses*** A charity organization spent 12% of its budget for administrative expenses. It spent $9624 on administrative expenses. What was the total budget?

73. ***Rain in Vancouver*** In Vancouver, it rained 20 days in February, 18 days in March, and 16 days in April. What percent of those three months did it rain? (Assume it was a leap year.)

74. ***Job Applications*** Moorehouse Industries received 600 applications and hired 45 of the applicants. What percent of the applicants obtained a job?

75. ***Appliance Purchase*** Nathan bought new appliances for $3670. The sales tax in his province is 5%. What did he pay in sales tax?

76. ***Boat Purchase*** Chris and Annette bought a boat for $12 600. The sales tax is 6% in their province. What did they pay in sales tax?

77. ***Budgets*** Joan and Michael budget 38% of their income for housing. They spend $684 per month for housing. What is their monthly income?

78. ***Real Estate Sales*** Waterfront property is very expensive. A real estate agent in Toronto earned $26 000 in commissions. The property she sold was worth $650 000. What was her commission rate?

79. ***Encyclopedia Sales*** Adam sold encyclopedias last summer to raise tuition money. He sold \$83 500 worth of encyclopedias and was paid \$5010 in commissions. What commission rate did he earn?

80. ***Commission Sales*** Roberta earns a commission at the rate of 7.5%. Last month she sold \$16 000 worth of goods. How much commission did she make last month?

81. ***Furniture Set*** Amy purchased a table and chairs set for her new patio at a 25% discount. The list price was \$1450.

(a) What was the discount?

(b) What did she pay for the set?

82. ***Laptop Computer*** A Dell laptop computer listed for \$2125. This week, Lisa heard that the manufacturer is offering a rebate of 12%.

(a) What is the rebate?

(b) How much will Lisa pay for the computer?

83. ***Medical School Applications*** In 2002, the number of students who applied to medical school in Canada was 1921. In 2006, the number who applied was 2380. What was the percent of increase in the number of medical school applications? (*Source:* http://www.afmc.ca/pdf/pdf_2007_cmes_trend_first_year_undergraduate_enrolment.pdf)

84. ***Cost of Education*** For the 1998–99 academic year, the average cost of tuition at a two-year public college in Canada was \$1592. By the 2008–09 academic year, the cost had risen to \$2539. Find the percent of increase. Round to the nearest whole percent. (*Source:* http://www.opseu.org/caat/parttime/pdf/collegetuitionfees.pdf)

85. ***Log Cabin*** Mark and Julie wanted to buy a prefabricated log cabin to put on their property in Jasper, Alberta. The price of the kit is listed at \$24 000. At the after-holiday cabin sale, a discount of 14% was offered.

(a) What was the discount?

(b) How much did they pay for the cabin?

86. ***Mutual Funds*** Sally invested \$6000 in mutual funds earning 11% simple interest in one year. How much interest will she earn in

(a) six months?

(b) two years?

87. ***College Loan*** Reed took out a college loan of \$3000. He will be charged 8% simple interest on the loan.

(a) How much interest will be due on the loan in three months?

(b) How much interest will be due on the loan in three years?

How Am I Doing? Module Test

Write as a percent. Round to the nearest hundredth of a percent when necessary.

1. 0.57

2. 0.01

3. 0.008

4. 12.8

5. 3.56

6. $\frac{71}{100}$

7. $\frac{1.8}{100}$

8. $\frac{3\frac{1}{7}}{100}$

Change to a percent. Round to the nearest hundredth of a percent when necessary.

9. $\frac{19}{40}$

10. $\frac{27}{36}$

11. $\frac{225}{75}$

12. $1\frac{3}{4}$

Write as a percent.

13. 0.0825

14. 3.024

Write as a fraction in simplified form.

15. 152%

16. $7\frac{3}{4}\%$

Solve. Round to the nearest hundredth if necessary.

17. What is 40% of 50?

18. 33.8 is 26% of what number?

19. What percent of 72 is 40?

20. Find 0.8% of 25 000.

1. ______
2. ______
3. ______
4. ______
5. ______
6. ______
7. ______
8. ______
9. ______
10. ______
11. ______
12. ______
13. ______
14. ______
15. ______
16. ______
17. ______
18. ______
19. ______
20. ______

21. 16% of what number is 800?

21. ______

22. 92 is what percent of 200?

22. ______

23. 132% of 530 is what number?

23. ______

24. What percent is 15 of 75?

24. ______

Solve. Round to the nearest hundredth if necessary.

25. A real estate agent sells a house for $152 300. She gets a commission of 4% on the sale. What is her commission?

25. ______

26. (a) ______

26. Julia and Charles bought a new dishwasher at a 33% discount. The list price was $457.

(a) What was the discount?

(b) How much did they pay for the dishwasher?

(b) ______

27. An inspector found that 75 out of 84 parts were not defective. What percent of the parts were not defective?

27. ______

28. Last year Shawna was the top player on the basketball team, scoring 185 points. This year, she scored 228 points. What is the percentage of increase in the number of points?

28. ______

29. ______

29. A total of 5160 people voted in the city election. This was 43% of the registered voters. How many registered voters are in the city?

30. (a) ______

30. Tanisha borrowed $3000 at a simple interest rate of 16%.

(a) How much interest did she pay in six months?

(b) How much interest did she pay in two years?

(b) ______

Solutions to Practice Problems

Section 1 Practice Problems

1. (a) $\frac{51}{100} = 51\%$ **(b)** $\frac{68}{100} = 68\%$

(c) $\frac{7}{100} = 7\%$ **(d)** $\frac{26}{100} = 26\%$

2. (a) $\frac{238}{100} = 238\%$ **(b)** $\frac{121}{100} = 121\%$

3. (a) $\frac{0.5}{100} = 0.5\%$ **(b)** $\frac{0.06}{100} = 0.06\%$

(c) $\frac{0.003}{100} = 0.003\%$

4. (a) $47\% = \frac{47}{100} = 0.47$ **(b)** $2\% = \frac{2}{100} = 0.02$

5. (a) $80.6\% = 0.806$ **(b)** $2.5\% = 0.025$

(c) $0.29\% = 0.0029$ **(d)** $231\% = 2.31$

6. (a) $0.78 = 78\%$ **(b)** $0.02 = 2\%$

(c) $5.07 = 507\%$ **(d)** $0.029 = 2.9\%$

(e) $0.006 = 0.6\%$

Section 2 Practice Problems

1. (a) $71\% = \frac{71}{100}$ **(b)** $25\% = \frac{25}{100} = \frac{1}{4}$

(c) $8\% = \frac{8}{100} = \frac{2}{25}$

2. (a) $8.4\% = 0.084 = \frac{84}{1000} = \frac{21}{250}$

(b) $28.5\% = 0.285 = \frac{285}{1000} = \frac{57}{200}$

3. (a) $170\% = 1.70 = 1\frac{7}{10}$ **(b)** $288\% = 2.88 = 2\frac{88}{100} = 2\frac{22}{25}$

4.
$$7\frac{5}{8}\% = 7\frac{5}{8} \div 100$$
$$= \frac{61}{8} \times \frac{1}{100}$$
$$= \frac{61}{800}$$

5.
$$1\frac{9}{10}\% = 1\frac{9}{10} \div 100$$
$$= 1\frac{9}{10} \times \frac{1}{100}$$
$$= \frac{19}{10} \times \frac{1}{100}$$
$$= \frac{19}{1000}$$

6. $\frac{5}{8} = 8\overline{)5.000}$ with quotient 0.625; $= 62.5\%$

7. (a) $\frac{21}{25} = 0.84 = 84\%$ **(b)** $\frac{7}{16} = 0.4375 = 43.75\%$

8. (a) $\frac{7}{9} = 0.777\,7\overline{7} \approx 0.7778 = 77.78\%$

(b) $\frac{19}{30} = 0.633\,3\overline{3} \approx 0.6333 = 63.33\%$

9. $\frac{7}{12}$ If we divide

$$\begin{array}{r} 0.58 \\ 12\overline{)7.00} \\ \underline{60} \\ 100 \\ \underline{96} \\ 4 \end{array}$$

Thus $\frac{7}{12} = 0.58\frac{4}{12} = 58\frac{1}{3}\%$.

10.

Fraction	Decimal	Percent
$\frac{23}{99}$	0.2323	23.23%
$\frac{129}{250}$	0.516	51.6%
$\frac{97}{250}$	0.388	$38\frac{4}{5}\%$

Section 3A Practice Problems

1. What is 26% of 35?

↓ ↓ ↓ ↓ ↓

$n = 26\% \times 35$

2. Find 0.08% of 350.

↓ ↓ ↓ ↓

$n = 0.08\% \times 350$

3. (a) 58% of what is 400?

↓ ↓ ↓ ↓ ↓

$58\% \times n = 400$

(b) 9.1 is 135% of what?

↓ ↓ ↓ ↓ ↓

$9.1 = 135\% \times n$

4. What percent of 250 is 36?

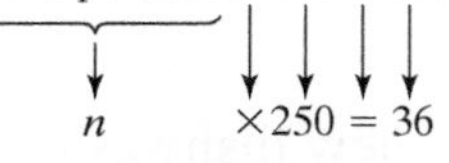

$n \times 250 = 36$

5. (a) 50 is what percent of 20?

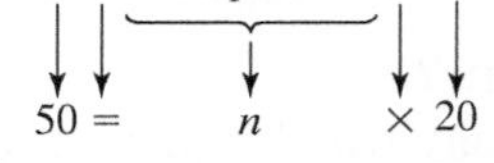

$50 = n \times 20$

(b) What percent of 2000 is 4.5?

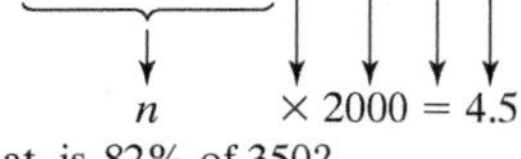

$n \times 2000 = 4.5$

6. What is 82% of 350?

↓ ↓ ↓ ↓ ↓

$n = 82\% \times 350$

$n = 0.82(350)$

$n = 287$

7. $n = 230\% \times 400$

$n = (2.30)(400)$

$n = 920$

8. The problem asks: What is 8% of $350?

$n = 8\% \times \$350$

$n = \$28$

The tax was $28.

9.
$$32 = 0.4\% \times n$$
$$32 = 0.004n$$
$$\frac{32}{0.004} = \frac{0.004n}{0.004}$$
$$8000 = n$$

10. The problem asks: 30% of what is 6?

$$30\% \times n = 6$$
$$0.30n = 6$$
$$\frac{0.30n}{0.30} = \frac{6}{0.30}$$
$$n = 20$$

There are 20 people on the team.

11. What percent of 9000 is 4.5?

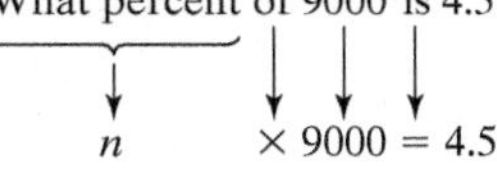

$n \quad \times 9000 = 4.5$

$9000n = 4.5$

$\frac{9000n}{9000} = \frac{4.5}{9000}$

$n = 0.0005$

$n = 0.05\%$

12. $198 = n \times 33$

$\frac{198}{33} = \frac{33n}{33}$

$6 = n$

Now express n as a percent: 600%

13. The problem asks: 5 is what percent of 16?

$5 = n \times 16$

$\frac{5}{16} = \frac{16n}{16}$

$0.3125 = n$

Now express n as a percent rounded to the nearest tenth: 31.3%

Section 3B Practice Problems

1. (a) Find 83% of 460.
$p = 83$

(b) 18% of what number is 90?
$p = 18$

(c) What percent of 64 is 8?
The percent is unknown. Use the variable p.

2. (a) 30% of 52 is 15.6
$b = 52, a = 15.6$

(b) 170 is 85% of what? Base $= b, a = 170$

3. (a) What is 18% of 240?
Percent $p = 18$
Base $b = 240$
Amount is unknown; use the variable a.

(b) What percent of 64 is 4?
Percent is unknown; use the variable p.
Base $b = 64$
Amount $a = 4$

4. Find 340% of 70.
Percent $p = 340$
Base $b = 70$
Amount is unknown; use amount $= a$.

$\frac{a}{b} = \frac{p}{100}$ becomes $\frac{a}{70} = \frac{340}{100}$

$\frac{a}{70} = \frac{17}{5}$

$5a = (70)(17)$

$5a = 1190$

$\frac{5a}{5} = \frac{1190}{5}$

$a = 238$

Thus 340% of 70 is 238.

5. 68% of what is 476?
Percent $p = 68$
Base is unknown; use base $= b$.
Amount $a = 476$

$\frac{a}{b} = \frac{p}{100}$ becomes $\frac{476}{b} = \frac{68}{100}$

$\frac{476}{b} = \frac{17}{25}$

$(476)(25) = 17b$

$11\,900 = 17b$

$\frac{11\,900}{17} = \frac{17b}{17}$

$700 = b$

Thus 68% of 700 is 476.

6. 216 is 0.3% of what?
Percent $p = 0.3$
Base is unknown; use base $= b$.
Amount $a = 216$

$\frac{a}{b} = \frac{p}{100}$ becomes $\frac{216}{b} = \frac{0.3}{100}$

$(216)(100) = 0.3b$

$21\,600 = 0.3b$

$\frac{21\,600}{0.3} = \frac{0.3b}{0.3}$

$72\,000 = b$

Thus \$72 000 was exchanged.

7. What percent of 3500 is 105?
Percent is unknown; use percent $= p$.
Base $b = 3500$
Amount $a = 105$

$\frac{a}{b} = \frac{p}{100}$ becomes $\frac{105}{3500} = \frac{p}{100}$

$\frac{3}{100} = \frac{p}{100}$

$300 = 100p$

$\frac{300}{100} = \frac{100p}{100}$

$3 = p$

Thus 3% of 3500 is 105.

Section 4 Practice Problems

1. Method A Let $n =$ number of people with reserved airline tickets.

12% of $n = 4800$

$0.12 \times n = 4800$

$\frac{0.12 \times n}{0.12} = \frac{4800}{0.12}$

$n = 40{,}000$

Method B The percent $p = 12$. Use b for the unknown base. The amount $a = 4800$.

$\frac{a}{b} = \frac{p}{100}$ becomes $\frac{4800}{b} = \frac{12}{100}$.

$(4800)(100) = 12b$

$480\,000 = 12b$

$\frac{480\,000}{12} = b$

$40\,000 = b$

40 000 people held airline tickets that month.

2. Method A The problem asks: What is 8% of \$62.30?

$n = 0.08 \times 62.30$

$n = 4.984$

Method B The percent $p = 8$. The base $b = 62.30$. Use a for the unknown amount.

$\frac{a}{b} = \frac{p}{100}$ becomes $\frac{a}{62.30} = \frac{8}{100}$.

$\frac{a}{62.3} = \frac{2}{25}$

$25a = (2)(62.3)$

$25a = 124.60$

$\frac{25a}{25} = \frac{124.60}{25}$

$a = 4.984$

The tax is \$4.98.

3. Method A The problem asks: 105 is what percent of 130?

$105 = n \times 130$

$\frac{105}{130} = n$

$0.8077 \approx n$

Method B Use p for the unknown percent. The base $b = 130$. The amount $a = 105$.

$$\frac{a}{b} = \frac{p}{100} \quad \text{becomes} \quad \frac{105}{130} = \frac{p}{100}.$$

$$\frac{21}{26} = \frac{p}{100}$$

$$(21)(100) = 26p$$

$$2100 = 26p$$

$$\frac{2100}{26} = \frac{26p}{26}$$

$$80.769\,230\ldots = p$$

Thus 80.8% of the flights were on time.

4. 100% Cost of meal + tip of 15% = \$46.00
Let n = Cost of meal
100% of n + 15% of n = \$46.00
115% of n = 46.00
$1.15 \times n = 46.00$

$$\frac{1.15 \times n}{1.15} = \frac{46.00}{1.15}$$

$$n = 40.00$$

They can spend \$40.00 on the meal itself.

5. (a) 7% of \$13 600 is the discount.
$0.07 \times 13\,600$ = the discount
\$952 is the discount.

(b)
\$13 600 list price
− 952 discount
\$12 648 Amount Kiera paid for the car.

Section 5 Practice Problems

1. Commission = commission rate × value of sales
Commission = 6% × \$156 000
= 0.06 × 156 000
= 9360
His commission is \$9360.

2.
15 000
−10 500
4 500 the amount of decrease

$$\text{Percent of decrease} = \frac{\text{amount of decrease}}{\text{original amount}} = \frac{4\,500}{15\,000}$$

$$= 0.30 = 30\%$$

The percent of decrease is 30%.

3. $I = P \times R \times T$
$P = \$5600 \qquad R = 12\% \qquad T = 1 \text{ year}$
$I = 5600 \times 12\% \times 1$
$= 5600 \times 0.12$
$= 672$
The interest is \$672.

4. (a) $I = P \times R \times T$
$= 1800 \times 0.11 \times 4$
$= 198 \times 4$
$= 792$
The interest for four years is \$792.

(b) $I = P \times R \times T$

$$= 1800 \times 0.11 \times \frac{1}{2}$$

$$= 198 \times \frac{1}{2}$$

$$= 99$$

The interest for six months is \$99.

Glossary

Amount of a percent equation (Section 3A) The product we obtain when we multiply a percent times a number. In the equation $75 = 50\% \times 150$, the amount is 75.

Base of a percent equation (Section 3A) The quantity we take a percent of. In the equation $8 = 20\% \times 400$, the base is 400.

Commission (Section 5) The amount of money a salesperson is paid that is a percentage of the value of the sales made by that salesperson. The commission is obtained by multiplying the commission rate times the value of the sales. If a salesman sells \$120 000 of insurance and his commission rate is 0.5%, then his commission is $0.5\% \times \$120\,000 = \$600.00$.

Discount (Section 4) The amount of reduction in a price. The discount is a product of the discount rate times the list price. If the list price of a television is \$430.00 and it has a discount rate of 35%, then the amount of discount is $35\% \times \$430.00 = \$150.50$. The price would be reduced by \$150.50.

Interest (Section 4) The money that is paid for the use of money. If you deposit money in a bank, the bank uses that money and pays you interest. If you borrow money, you pay the bank interest for the use of that money. Simple interest is determined by the formula $I = P \times R \times T$. Compound interest is usually determined by a table, a calculator, or a computer.

Percent (Section 1) The word *percent* means per one hundred. For example, 14 percent means $\frac{14}{100}$.

Percent of decrease (Section 5) The percent that something decreases is determined by dividing the amount of decrease by the original amount. If a DVD player sold for \$300 and its price was decreased by \$60, the percent of decrease would be $\frac{60}{300} = 0.20 = 20\%$.

Percent of increase (Section 5) The percent that something increases is determined by dividing the amount of increase by the original amount. If the population of a town was 5000 people and the population increased by 500 people, the percent of increase would be $\frac{500}{5000} = 0.10 = 10\%$.

Percent proportion (Section 3B) The percent proportion is the equation $\frac{a}{b} = \frac{p}{100}$ where a is the amount, b is the base, and p is the percent number.

Percent symbol (Section 1) A symbol that is used to indicate percent. To indicate 23 percent, we write 23%.

Principal (Section 4) The amount of money deposited or borrowed on which interest is computed. In the simple interest formula $I = P \times R \times T$, the P stands for the principal. (The other letters are I = interest, R = interest rate, and T = amount of time.)

Sales tax (Section 4) The amount of tax on a purchase. The sales tax for any item is a product of the sales tax rate times the purchase price. If an item is purchased for \$12.00 and the sales tax rate is 5%, the sales tax is $5\% \times \$12.00 = \$0.60$.

Simple interest (Section 4) The interest determined by the formula $I = P \times R \times T$ where I = the interest obtained, P = the principal or the amount borrowed or invested, R = the interest rate (usually on an annual basis), and T = the number of time periods (usually years).

Answers to Selected Exercises for Percent

Answers to Selected Exercises for Percent

Section 1 Exercises **1.** hundred **3.** two; left; Drop **5.** 59% **7.** 4% **9.** 80% **11.** 245% **13.** 12.5% **15.** 0.07% **17.** 13% **19.** 9% **21.** 0.51 **23.** 0.07 **25.** 0.2 **27.** 0.436 **29.** 0.0003 **31.** 0.0072 **33.** 0.0125 **35.** 2.75 **37.** 74% **39.** 50% **41.** 8% **43.** 56.3% **45.** 0.2% **47.** 0.57% **49.** 135% **51.** 516% **53.** 27% **55.** 20% **57.** 94% **59.** 231% **61.** 10% **63.** 8.9% **65.** 0.62 **67.** 1.38 **69.** 0.003 **71.** 0.75 **73.** 40% **75.** 1.15 **77.** 0.006 **79.** 0.609; 0.454

81. $36\% = 36 \text{ percent} = 36 \text{ "per one hundred"} = 36 \times \frac{1}{100} = \frac{36}{100} = 0.36$. The rule is using the fact that 36% means 36 per one hundred.

83. **(a)** 15.62 **(b)** $\frac{1562}{100}$ **(c)** $\frac{781}{50}$

Quick Quiz 1 **1.** 0.7% **2.** 4.5% **3.** 0.0125 **4.** See Instructor

Section 2 Exercises **1.** Write the number in front of the percent symbol as the numerator of a fraction. Write the number 100 as the denominator of the fraction. Reduce the fraction if possible. **3.** $\frac{3}{50}$ **5.** $\frac{33}{100}$ **7.** $\frac{11}{20}$ **9.** $\frac{3}{4}$ **11.** $\frac{1}{5}$ **13.** $\frac{19}{200}$ **15.** $\frac{9}{40}$ **17.** $\frac{81}{125}$ **19.** $\frac{57}{80}$ **21.** $1\frac{17}{25}$ **23.** $3\frac{2}{5}$ **25.** 12 **27.** $\frac{29}{800}$ **29.** $\frac{1}{8}$ **31.** $\frac{11}{125}$ **33.** $\frac{131}{5000}$ **35.** $\frac{33}{500}$ **37.** 75% **39.** 70% **41.** 35% **43.** 72% **45.** 27.5% **47.** 360% **49.** 250% **51.** 412.5% **53.** 33.33% **55.** 41.67% **57.** 425% **59.** 52% **61.** 2.5% **63.** 5.95% **65.** $37\frac{1}{2}\%$ **67.** $7\frac{1}{2}\%$ **69.** $26\frac{2}{3}\%$ **71.** $22\frac{2}{9}\%$

	Fraction	Decimal	Percent
73.	$\frac{11}{12}$	0.9167	91.67%
75.	$\frac{14}{25}$	0.56	56%
77.	$\frac{1}{200}$	0.005	0.5%
79.	$\frac{5}{9}$	0.5556	55.56%
81.	$\frac{1}{32}$	0.0313	$3\frac{1}{8}\%$

83. $\frac{463}{1600}$ **85.** 15.375%

Quick Quiz 2 **1.** $\frac{9}{20}$ **2.** $\frac{19}{250}$ **3.** 92% **4.** See Instructor

Section 3A Exercises **1.** What is 20% of \$300? **3.** 20 baskets out of 25 shots is what percent?
5. This is "a percent problem when we do not know the base."
Translated into an equation:

$$108 = 18\% \times n$$
$$108 = 0.18n$$
$$\frac{108}{0.18} = \frac{0.18n}{0.18}$$
$$600 = n$$

7. $n = 5\% \times 90$ **9.** $30\% \times n = 5$ **11.** $17 = n \times 85$ **13.** 28 **15.** 56 **17.** \$51 **19.** 1300 **21.** 1300 **23.** \$150 **25.** 84% **27.** 11% **29.** 65% **31.** 31 **33.** 85 **35.** 12% **37.** 3.28 **39.** 64% **41.** 75 **43.** 0.8% **45.** 18.9 **47.** 80% **49.** 60.66% **51.** 663 students **53.** 40 years **55.** \$57.60

Quick Quiz 3A **1.** 127.68 **2.** 9000 **3.** 17% **4.** See Instructor

Section 3B Exercises

	p	b	a
1.	75	660	495
3.	22	60	a
5.	49	b	2450
7.	p	50	30

9. 28 **11.** 84 **13.** 56 **15.** 80 **17.** 80 **19.** 600 000 **21.** 20 **23.** 20 **25.** 22 **27.** 40 **29.** 16.4% **31.** 3.64 **33.** 25% **35.** 170 **37.** \$960 **39.** 15% **41.** 18 litres **43.** \$2280 **45.** 30.37% **47.** 11.37%

Quick Quiz 3B **1.** 1.53 **2.** 120 **3.** 22% **4.** See Instructor

How Am I Doing? Sections 1–3 **1.** 17% (obj. 1.3) **2.** 38.7% (obj. 1.3) **3.** 795% (obj. 1.3) **4.** 518% (obj. 1.3) **5.** 0.6% (obj. 1.3) **6.** 0.04% (obj. 1.3) **7.** 17% (obj. 1.1) **8.** 89% (obj. 1.1) **9.** 13.4% (obj. 1.1) **10.** 19.8% (obj. 1.1) **11.** $6\frac{1}{2}\%$ (obj. 1.1) **12.** $1\frac{3}{8}\%$ (obj. 1.1) **13.** 80% (obj. 2.2) **14.** 50% (obj. 2.2) **1** 260% (obj. 2.2) **16.** 106.25% (obj. 2.2) **17.** 71.43% (obj. 2.2) **18.** 28.57% (obj. 2.2) **19.** 75% (obj. 2.2) **20.** 25% (obj. 2.2) **21.** 440% (obj. 2.2) **22.** 275% (obj. 2.2) **23.** 0.33% (obj. 2.2) **24.** 0.25% (obj. 2.2) **2** $\frac{11}{50}$ (obj. 2.1) **26.** $\frac{53}{100}$ (obj. 2.1) **27.** $\frac{3}{2}$ or $1\frac{1}{2}$ (obj. 2.1) **28.** $\frac{8}{5}$ or $1\frac{3}{5}$ (obj. 2.1) **29.** $\frac{19}{300}$ (obj. 2.1) **30.** $\frac{1}{32}$ (obj. 2.1) **31.** $\frac{41}{80}$ (obj. 2.1) **32.** $\frac{7}{16}$ (obj. 2.1) **33.** 42 (obj. 3.2) **34.** 24 (obj. 3.2) **35.** 94.44% (obj. 3.2) **36.** 44.74% (obj. 3.2) **37.** 3000 (obj. 3.2) **38.** 885 (obj. 3.2)

Section 4 Exercises **1.** 180 000 pencils **3.** $45 **5.** 20.57% **7.** $3.90 **9.** $550 **11.** 30% **13.** $9 600 000 **15.** 2.48% **17.** 216 babies **19.** $761.90 **21.** $150 000 **23.** 2200 pounds **25.** $12 210 000 for personnel, food, and decorations; $20 790 000 for security, facility rental, and all other expenses **27.** $123.50 **29.** **(a)** $1320 **(b)** $7480

Quick Quiz 4 **1.** **(a)** $166.88 **(b)** $429.12 **2.** 64.4% **3.** 15 000 people **4.** See Instructor

Section 5 Exercises **1.** $3400 **3.** $4140 **5.** 20% **7.** 36.6% **9.** $140 **11.** $7.50 **13.** $1040 **15.** 0.6% **17.** $1 600 000 **19.** $39.75 **21.** 39 boxes **23.** 53.77% **25.** 80% **27.** **(a)** $85.10 **(b)** $3785.10 **29.** **(a)** $6.96 **(b)** $122.96 **31.** $10 830 **33.** **(a)** $27 920 **(b)** $321 080 **35.** 96.9% **37.** $849.01

Quick Quiz 5 **1.** $26 000 **2.** 71.875% **3.** $299 **4.** See Instructor

Putting Your Skills to Work **1.** $25 094.08 **2.** $14 970.16 **3.** $25 970.16 **4.** Answers will vary **5.** Answers will vary **6.** Answers will vary.

Module Review Problems **1.** 62% **2.** 43% **3.** 37.2% **4.** 52.9% **5.** 220% **6.** 180% **7.** 252% **8.** 437% **9.** 103.6% **10.** 105.2% **11.** 0.6% **12.** 0.2% **13.** 62.5% **14.** 37.5% **15.** $4\frac{1}{12}\%$ **16.** $3\frac{5}{12}\%$ **17.** 317% **18.** 225% **19.** 76% **20.** 52% **21.** 55% **22.** 22.5% **23.** 58.33% **24.** 93.33% **25.** 225% **26.** 375% **27.** 277.78% **28.** 555.56% **29.** 190% **30.** 250% **31.** 0.38% **32.** 0.63% **33.** 0.32 **34.** 0.68 **35.** 0.1575 **36.** 0.1235 **37.** 2.36 **38.** 1.77 **39.** 0.321 25 **40.** 0.263 75 **41.** $\frac{18}{25}$ **42.** $\frac{23}{25}$ **43.** $\frac{7}{4}$ **44.** $\frac{13}{5}$ **45.** $\frac{41}{250}$ **46.** $\frac{61}{200}$ **47.** $\frac{5}{16}$ **48.** $\frac{7}{16}$ **49.** $\frac{1}{1250}$ **50.** $\frac{1}{2500}$

	Fraction	Decimal	Percent
51.		0.6	60%
52.		0.7	70%
53.	$\frac{3}{8}$	0.375	
54.	$\frac{9}{16}$	0.5625	
55.	$\frac{1}{125}$		0.8%
56.	$\frac{9}{20}$		45%

57. 17 **58.** 23 **59.** 60 **60.** 40 **61.** 38.46% **62.** 38.89% **63.** 97.2 **64.** 99.2 **65.** 160 **66.** 140 **67.** 20% **68.** 10% **69.** 49 students **70.** 96 trucks **71.** $11 200 **72.** $80 200 **73.** 60% **74.** 7.5% **75.** $183.50 **76.** $756 **77.** $1800 **78.** 4% **79.** 6% **80.** $1200 **81.** **(a)** $362.50 **(b)** $1087.50 **82.** **(a)** $255 **(b)** $1870 **83.** 23.89% **84.** 59.48% **85.** **(a)** $3360 **(b)** $20 640 **86.** **(a)** $330 **(b)** $1320 **87.** **(a)** $60 **(b)** $720

How Am I Doing? Module Test **1.** 57% (obj. 1.3) **2.** 1% (obj. 1.3) **3.** 0.8% (obj. 1.3) **4.** 1280% (obj. 1.3) **5.** 356% (obj. 1.3) **6.** 71% (obj. 1.1) **7.** 1.8% (obj. 1.1) **8.** $3\frac{1}{7}\%$ (obj. 1.1) **9.** 47.5% (obj. 2.2) **10.** 75% (obj. 2.2) **11.** 300% (obj. 2.2) **12.** 175% (obj. 2.2) **13.** 8.25% (obj. 2.3) **14.** 302.4% (obj. 2.3) **15.** $1\frac{13}{25}$ (obj. 2.3) **16.** $\frac{31}{400}$ (obj. 2.3) **17.** 20 (obj. 3.2) **18.** 130 (obj. 3.2) **19.** 55.56% (obj. 3.2) **20.** 200 (obj. 3.2) **21.** 5000 (obj. 3.2) **22.** 46% (obj. 3.2) **23.** 699.6 (obj. 3.2) **24.** 20% (obj. 3.2) **25.** $6092 (obj. 5.1) **26.** **(a)** $150.81 (obj. 4.3) **(b)** $306.19 **27.** 89.29% (obj. 4.1) **28.** 23.24% (obj. 4.1) **29.** 12 000 registered voters (obj. 4.1) **30.** **(a)** $240 **(b)** $960 (obj. 5.3)

Measurement

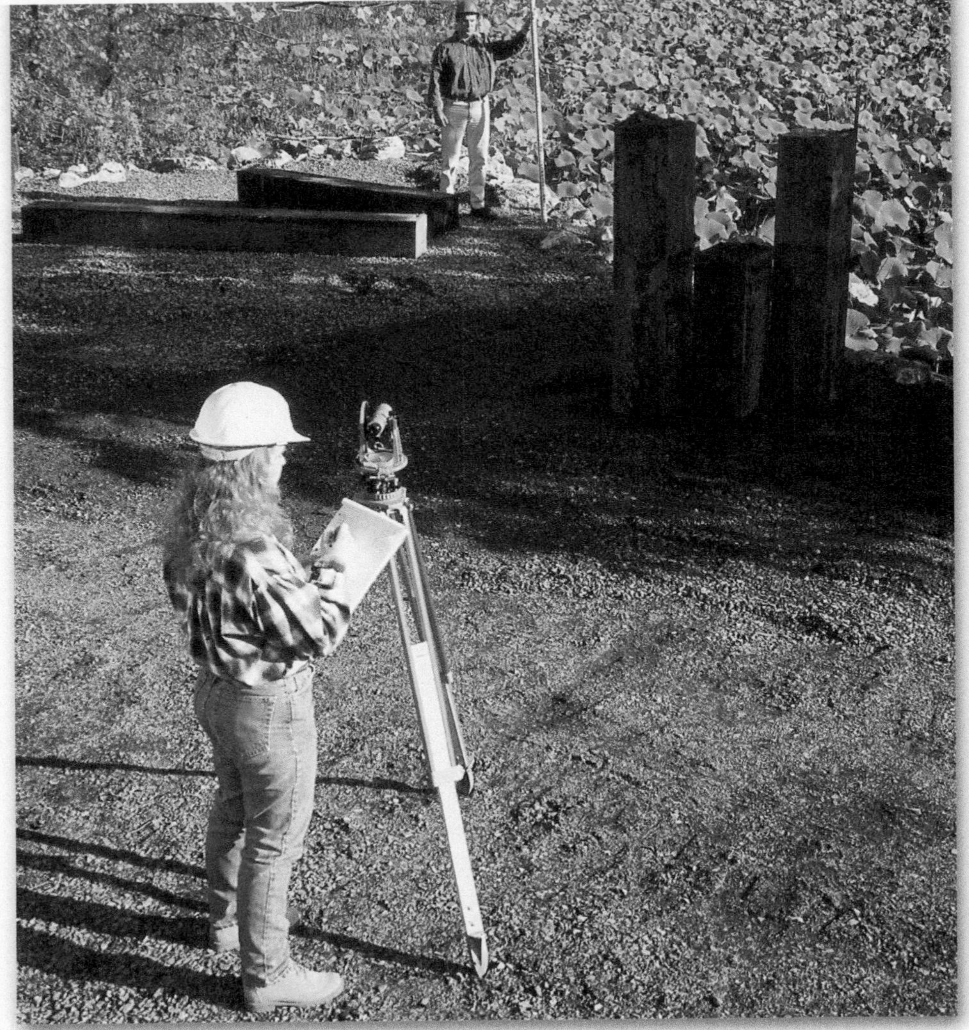

Blair Seitz/Photo Researchers, Inc.

Measurement

About fifty years ago a major change occurred in the way land is measured in Canada. All new deeds recording the amount of land area had to be changed from recording the area in acres to recording the area in hectares. Farmers, forestry personnel, and all landowners had to do some extensive calculations. When you have mastered the content of this module you will be able to do these types of calculations.

SECTION 1 U.S. CUSTOMARY UNITS

Student Learning Objectives

After studying this section, you will be able to:

 **Identify the basic unit equivalencies in the U.S. customary system.**

 **Convert from one unit of measure to another.**

 Identifying the Basic Unit Equivalencies in the U.S. Customary System

We often ask questions about measurements. How far is it to work? How much does this bottle hold? What is the weight of this box? How long will it be until exams? To answer these questions, we need to agree on a unit of measure for each type of measurement.

In Canada, we use the International System of Units, the standard **metric system** used around the world. During the 1970s, Canada replaced the imperial measurement system with the metric system. The United States uses **U.S. customary units**, a system of measurement that was derived from an old version of the imperial system. Although lengths and distances in the two systems are equal in size, liquid volume measurements differ (1 U.S. gallon is equal to approximately 0.8 imperial gallon). Due to commerce with the United States, many of Canada's trades continue to work in the American system as a matter of convenience; therefore, we need to be familiar with both countries' systems. This section explores U.S. customary units.

One of the most familiar measuring devices is a ruler that measures lengths as great as 30 centimetres, which is about equal to 1 foot. One foot equals 30.54 centimetres. Many rulers show both measurement systems. A foot is divided into 12 inches; that is,

1 foot = 12 inches.

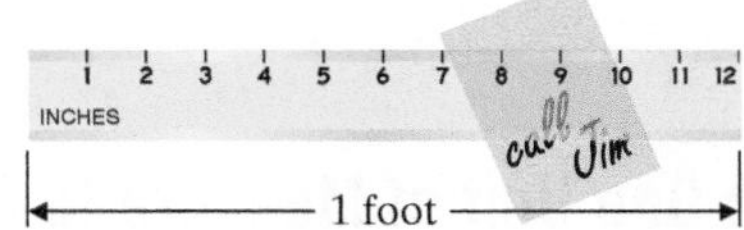

There are several other important relationships you need to know. Your instructor may require you to memorize the following facts.

Length
12 inches = 1 foot
36 inches = 1 yard
3 feet = 1 yard
5280 feet = 1 mile
1760 yards = 1 mile

Time
60 seconds = 1 minute
60 minutes = 1 hour
24 hours = 1 day
7 days = 1 week

Note that time is measured in the same units in both the metric and the U.S. customary systems.

Weight
16 ounces = 1 pound
2000 pounds = 1 ton

Volume
8 fluid ounces = 1 cup
2 cups = 1 pint
2 pints = 1 quart
4 quarts = 1 gallon

We can choose to measure an object—say, a bridge—using a small unit (an inch), a larger unit (a foot), or a still larger unit (a mile). We may say that the bridge spans 7920 inches, 660 feet, or an eighth of a mile. Although we probably would not choose to express our measurement in inches because this is not a convenient measurement to work with for an object as long as a bridge, the bridge length is the same whatever unit of measurement we use.

Notice that the smaller the measuring unit, the larger the number of those units in the final measurement. The inch is the smallest unit in our example, and the inch measurement has the greatest number of units (7920). The mile is the largest unit, and it has the smallest number of units (an eighth equals 0.125). Whatever measuring system you use, and whatever you measure (length, volume, and so on), the smaller the unit of measurement you use, the greater the number of those units.

After studying the values in the length, time, weight, and volume tables, see if you can quickly do Example 1.

EXAMPLE 1 Answer the following questions.

(a) How many inches are in a foot? **(b)** How many yards are in a mile?
(c) How many seconds are in a minute? **(d)** How many hours are in a day?
(e) How many pounds are in a ton? **(f)** How many cups are in a pint?

Solution

(a) 12 **(b)** 1760 **(c)** 60 **(d)** 24 **(e)** 2000 **(f)** 2

Practice Problem 1 Answer the following questions.

(a) How many feet are in a yard? **(b)** How many feet are in a mile?
(c) How many minutes are in an hour? **(d)** How many days are in a week?
(e) How many ounces are in a pound? **(f)** How many pints are in a quart?
(g) How many quarts are in a gallon?

2 Converting from One Unit of Measure to Another

To convert or change one measurement to another, we simply multiply by 1 since multiplying by 1 does not change the value of a quantity. For example, to convert 180 inches to feet, we look for a name for 1 that has inches and feet.

$$1 = \frac{1 \text{ foot}}{12 \text{ inches}}$$

A ratio of measurements for which the measurement in the numerator is equivalent to the measurement in the denominator is called a **unit fraction.**

We now use the unit fraction $\frac{1 \text{ foot}}{12 \text{ inches}}$ to convert 180 inches to feet.

$$180 \cancel{\text{inches}} \times \frac{1 \text{ foot}}{12 \cancel{\text{inches}}} = \frac{180 \text{ feet}}{12} = 15 \text{ feet}$$

Notice that when we multiplied, the inches divided out. We are left with the unit feet.

What name for 1 (that is, unit fraction) should we choose if we want to change from feet to inches? Convert 4 feet to inches.

$$1 = \frac{12 \text{ inches}}{1 \text{ foot}}$$

$$4 \cancel{\text{feet}} \times \frac{12 \text{ inches}}{1 \cancel{\text{foot}}} = \frac{48 \text{ inches}}{1} = 48 \text{ inches}$$

When multiplying by a unit fraction, the unit we want to change to should be in the *numerator*. The unit we start with should be in the *denominator*. This unit will divide out.

EXAMPLE 2 Convert. 8800 yards to miles

Solution $8800 \text{ yards} \times \dfrac{1 \text{ mile}}{1760 \text{ yards}} = \dfrac{8800 \text{ miles}}{1760} = 5 \text{ miles}$

Practice Problem 2 Convert. 15 840 feet to miles

William Taufic/Corbis/Stock Market

Some conversions involve fractions or decimals. Whether you want to measure the area of a living room or the dimensions of a piece of property, it is helpful to be able to make conversions like these.

EXAMPLE 3 Convert.

(a) 26.48 miles to yards **(b)** $3\frac{2}{3}$ feet to yards

Solution

(a) $26.48 \text{ miles} \times \dfrac{1760 \text{ yards}}{1 \text{ mile}} = 46\,604.8 \text{ yards}$

(b) $3\frac{2}{3} \text{ feet} \times \dfrac{1 \text{ yard}}{3 \text{ feet}} = \dfrac{11}{3} \times \dfrac{1}{3} \text{ yard} = \dfrac{11}{9} \text{ yards} = 1\frac{2}{9} \text{ yards}$

Practice Problem 3 Convert.

(a) 18.93 miles to feet **(b)** $16\frac{1}{2}$ inches to yards

EXAMPLE 4 Lynda's new car weighs 2.43 tons. How many pounds is that?

Solution $2.43 \text{ tons} \times \dfrac{2000 \text{ pounds}}{1 \text{ ton}} = 4860 \text{ pounds}$

Practice Problem 4 A package weighs 760.5 pounds. How many ounces does it weigh?

EXAMPLE 5 The chemistry lab has 34 quarts of weak hydrochloric acid. How many gallons of this acid are in the lab? (Express your answer as a decimal.)

Solution $34 \text{ quarts} \times \dfrac{1 \text{ gallon}}{4 \text{ quarts}} = \dfrac{34 \text{ gallons}}{4} = 8.5 \text{ gallons}$

Practice Problem 5 19 pints of milk is the same as how many quarts? (Express your answer as a decimal.)

EXAMPLE 6 A window is 4 feet 5 inches wide. How many inches is that? 4 feet 5 inches means 4 feet and 5 inches. Change the 4 feet to inches and add the 5 inches.

Solution

$$4\ \cancel{\text{feet}} \times \frac{12\ \text{inches}}{1\ \cancel{\text{foot}}} = 48\ \text{inches}$$

$$48\ \text{inches} + 5\ \text{inches} = 53\ \text{inches}$$

The window is 53 inches wide.

Practice Problem 6 A path through Dr. Sherf's property measures 26 yards 2 feet in length. How many feet long is the path?

EXAMPLE 7 The Great White North all-night garage charges \$1.50 per hour for parking both day and night. A businessman left his car there for $2\frac{1}{4}$ days. How much was he charged?

Solution

1. ***Understand the problem.*** Here it might help to look at a simpler problem. If the businessman had left his car for two hours, we would multiply.

   The fraction bar means "per." →
   $$\frac{1.50\ \text{dollars}}{1\ \cancel{\text{hour}}} \times 2\ \cancel{\text{hours}} = 3.00\ \text{dollars or } \$3.00$$

   Thus, if the businessman had left his car for two hours, he would have been charged \$3. We see that we need to multiply \$1.50 by the number of hours the car was in the garage to solve the problem.

   Since the original problem gave the time in days, not hours, we will need to change the days to hours.

2. ***Solve and state the answer.*** Now that we know that the way to solve the problem is to multiply by hours, we will begin. To make our calculations easier we will write $2\frac{1}{4}$ as 2.25. Change days to hours. Then multiply by \$1.50 per hour.

   $$2.25\ \cancel{\text{days}} \times \frac{24\ \cancel{\text{hours}}}{1\ \cancel{\text{day}}} \times \frac{1.50\ \text{dollars}}{1\ \cancel{\text{hour}}} = 81\ \text{dollars or } \$81$$

   The businessman was charged \$81.

3. ***Check.*** Is our answer in the desired unit? Yes. The answer is in dollars and we would expect it to be in dollars. ✓

   The check is up to you.

Practice Problem 7 A businesswoman parked her car at a garage for $1\frac{3}{4}$ days. The garage charges \$1.50 per hour. How much did she pay to park the car?

ALTERNATIVE METHOD: Using Proportions How did people first come up with the idea of multiplying by a unit fraction? What mathematical principles are involved here? Actually, this is the same as solving a proportion. Consider Example 5, where we changed 34 quarts to 8.5 gallons by multiplying.

$$34 \cancel{\text{quarts}} \times \frac{1 \text{ gallon}}{4 \cancel{\text{quarts}}} = \frac{34 \text{ gallons}}{4} = 8.5 \text{ gallons}$$

What we were actually doing is setting up the proportion:

1 gallon is to 4 quarts as n gallons is to 34 quarts.

$$\frac{1 \text{ gallon}}{4 \text{ quarts}} = \frac{n \text{ gallons}}{34 \text{ quarts}}$$

$$1 \text{ gallon} \times 34 \text{ quarts} = 4 \text{ quarts} \times n \text{ gallons} \quad \text{Cross-multiply}$$

$$\frac{1 \text{ gallon} \times 34 \cancel{\text{quarts}}}{4 \cancel{\text{quarts}}} = \frac{\cancel{4} \cancel{\text{quarts}} \times n \text{ gallons}}{\cancel{4} \cancel{\text{quarts}}} \quad \text{Divide both sides of the equation by 4 quarts}$$

$$1 \text{ gallon} \times \frac{34}{4} = n \text{ gallons} \quad \text{Simplify}$$

$$8.5 \text{ gallons} = n \text{ gallons}$$

Thus the number of gallons is 8.5. Using proportions takes a little longer, so multiplying by a fractional name for 1 is the more popular method.

You will find the methods covered in Section 1 to be quite useful in everyday life, so the topic is worth a little extra study. Take a few minutes to read over Examples 1–7. Think about the steps that are shown. Now work out each of the Practice Problems 1–7. Turn to the end of the module and make sure you have done them correctly. You will find this review to be very worthwhile.

Section 1 Exercises

Verbal and Writing Skills

1. Explain in your own words how you would use a unit fraction to change 23 miles to inches.

2. Explain in your own words how you would use a unit fraction to change 27 days to minutes.

From memory, write the equivalent value.

3. ________ yards = 1 mile

4. ________ feet = 1 mile

5. 1 ton = ________ pounds

6. 1 pound = ________ ounces

7. ________ quarts = 1 gallon

8. ________ cups = 1 pint

9. 1 quart = ________ pints

10. ________ minutes = 1 hour

Convert. When necessary, express your answer as a decimal.

11. 21 feet = ________ yards

12. 63 feet = ________ yards

13. 108 inches = ________ feet

14. 180 inches = ________ feet

15. 9 feet = ________ inches

16. 11 feet = ________ inches

17. 10 560 feet = ________ miles

18. 5 miles = ________ feet

19. 7 miles = ________ yards

20. 21 120 feet = ________ miles

21. 12 gallons = ________ quarts

22. 15 gallons = ________ quarts

23. 48 quarts = ________ gallons

24. 24 pints = ________ quarts

25. 16 cups = ________ fluid ounces

26. 40 fluid ounces = ________ cups

27. $8\frac{1}{2}$ gallons = ________ pints

28. $6\frac{1}{2}$ gallons = ________ pints

29. 77 days = ________ weeks

30. 56 days = ________ weeks

31. 960 seconds = ________ minutes

32. 1500 seconds = ________ minutes

33. 8 ounces = ________ pound

34. 12 ounces = ________ pounds

35. 12 500 pounds = ________ tons

36. $4\frac{3}{4}$ tons = ________ pounds

37. 15 pints = ________ cups

38. 23 pints = ________ cups

39. 2.25 pounds = ________ ounces

40. 4.25 pounds = ________ ounces

41. 66 inches = ________ feet

42. 90 inches = ________ feet

Applications

43. ***Wheelchair Racer*** Candace Cable is a champion wheelchair racer. In Grandma's Marathon, she covered the 26.2-mile course in 1:46 (1 hour and 46 minutes). How many feet did she travel in the race?

44. ***Marathon Record*** In September 2003, Paul Tergat of Kenya set the men's world record for the marathon, winning the Berlin Marathon with a time of 2:04:55 (hours:minutes:seconds). How many seconds is that?

45. ***Ocean Depth*** The deepest part of the Pacific Ocean, known as the Mariana Trench, is 35 840 feet deep. How many miles is that? Round your answer to the nearest hundredth.

46. ***Shot Put*** Fatima threw the shot put $36\frac{1}{4}$ feet at a college track meet. How many inches is that?

47. ***Food Purchase*** Judy is making a wild mushroom sauce for pasta tonight with a large group of friends. She bought 26 ounces of wild mushrooms at $6.00 per pound. How much were the mushrooms?

48. ***Food Purchase*** Ming is trying to eat a low-fat diet. He finds a store that sells 1% fat ground white-meat turkey breast at $6.00 per pound. He buys one packet weighing 18 ounces and another weighing 22 ounces. How much does he pay?

▲49. ***Geometry*** A window in Lynn and Jorge's house needs to be replaced. The rectangular window is 3 feet 6 inches tall and 2 feet 5 inches wide. Change each of the measurements to inches.

(a) Find the perimeter of the window in inches.

(b) If the perimeter needs to be sealed with insulation that is $0.60 per inch, how much will it cost to insulate the perimeter?

▲50. ***Geometry*** The cellar in Jeff and Shelley's house needs to be sealed along the edge of the concrete floor. The rectangular floor measures 7 yards 2 feet wide and 12 yards 1 foot long. Change each of the measurements to feet.

(a) Find the perimeter of the cellar in feet.

(b) If the perimeter (edge) of the cellar floor needs to be sealed with waterproof sealer that costs $1.75 per foot, how much will it cost to seal the perimeter?

51. ***Heart Capacity*** Every day, your heart pumps 7200 quarts of blood through your body. How many cups is that?

52. ***Peach Tree Growth*** A seedling peach tree grew for seven years until it produced its first fruit. How many hours was that if you assume that there are 365 days in a year?

Estimating and Rounding

53. ***Boating Map*** A local boater's map shows a marker buoy 6 miles out in the ocean from the harbour at Woods Hole. Estimate the number of yards this distance is. (*Hint:* First round the number of yards in one mile to the nearest thousand yards. Then finish the calculation.)

54. ***Plant Growth*** Igor Brigham is examining a new experimental type of wheat in his laboratory at St. Lawrence College. The plant is 618 days old. Estimate the age of the plant in months. (*Hint:* First round 618 to the nearest hundred. Then finish the calculation.)

55. ***Altitude of a Plane*** Greg Salzman is flying from Chicago. The pilot announces that the plane is flying at an altitude of 33 000 feet. The man seated next to Greg asks him to estimate how many miles high the plane is at that point. How should Greg answer the man? (*Hint:* First round the altitude to the nearest ten thousand feet. Then round the conversion equivalent for the number of feet in a mile to the nearest thousand feet. Then perform the calculation.)

56. ***Plane Flight Time*** Melissa LaBelle is flying from Paris. The pilot announces that the plane has 3170 miles to go to complete the flight. Earlier he said that the plane is flying at 640 miles per hour. Estimate the number of hours left in the flight. (*Hint:* First round the distance to the nearest thousand miles. Then round the speed to the nearest hundred miles per hour. Then perform the calculation.) The pilot then announces that it will take 318 minutes to complete the flight. How close was our estimate?

Quick Quiz 1 Convert. Express your answer as a decimal rounded to the nearest hundredth when necessary.

1. Convert 3.5 tons to pounds.

2. Convert 4.5 yards to feet.

3. Convert 24 ounces to pounds.

4. **Concept Check** Explain how you would convert 250 pints to quarts.

SECTION 2 METRIC MEASUREMENTS: LENGTH

Understanding Prefixes in Metric Units

Student Learning Objectives

After studying this section, you will be able to:

Understand prefixes in metric units.

Convert from one metric unit of length to another.

The **metric system** of measurement is used in most industrialized nations of the world. The metric system is designed for ease in calculating and in converting from one unit to another.

In the metric system, the basic unit of length measurement is the **metre.** A metre is about equal in length to 3.3 of those 30-centimetre long rulers. This is just slightly longer than a yard. To be more precise, the metre is approximately 39.37 inches long.

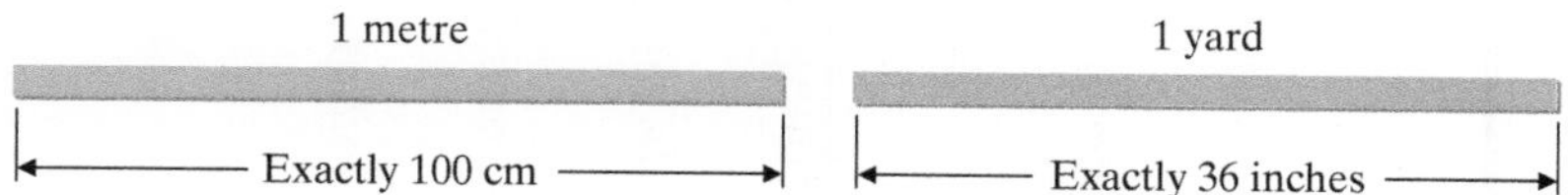

Units that are larger or smaller than the metre are based on the metre and powers of 10. For example, the unit *deca*metre is *ten* metres. The unit *deci*metre is *one-tenth* of a metre. The prefix *deca* means 10. What does the prefix *deci* mean? All the prefixes in the metric system are names for multiples of 10. A list of metric prefixes and their meanings follows.

Prefix	Meaning
kilo-	thousand
hecto-	hundred
deca-	ten
deci-	tenth
centi-	hundredth
milli-	thousandth

The most commonly used prefixes are *kilo-*, *centi-*, and *milli-*. *Kilo-* means thousand, so a *kilo*metre is a thousand metres. Similarly, *centi-* means one hundredth, so a *centi*metre is one hundredth of a metre. And *milli-* means one thousandth, so a *milli*metre is one thousandth of a metre.

The kilometre is used to measure distances much larger than the metre. How far did you travel in a car? The centimetre is used to measure shorter lengths. What are the dimensions of a DVD case? The millimetre is used to measure very small lengths. What is the width of the lead in a pencil?

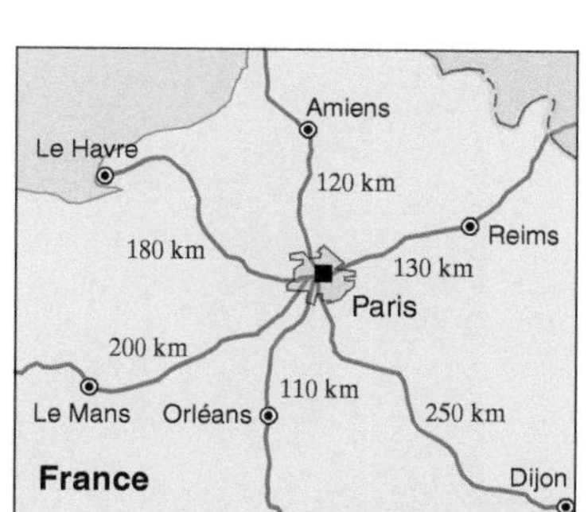

EXAMPLE 1 Write the prefixes that mean **(a)** thousand and **(b)** tenth.

Solution

(a) The prefix *kilo-* is used for thousand.

(b) The prefix *deci-* is used for tenth.

Practice Problem 1 Write the prefixes that mean **(a)** ten and **(b)** thousandth.

Converting from One Metric Unit of Length to Another

How do we convert from one metric unit to another? For example, how do we change 5 kilometres into an equivalent number of metres?

When we multiply by 10 we move the decimal point one place to the right. When we divide by 10 we move the decimal point one place to the left. Let's see how we use this idea to change from one metric unit to another.

Changing from Larger Metric Units to Smaller Ones

When you change from one metric prefix to another by moving to the **right** on this prefix chart, move the decimal point to the **right** the same number of places.

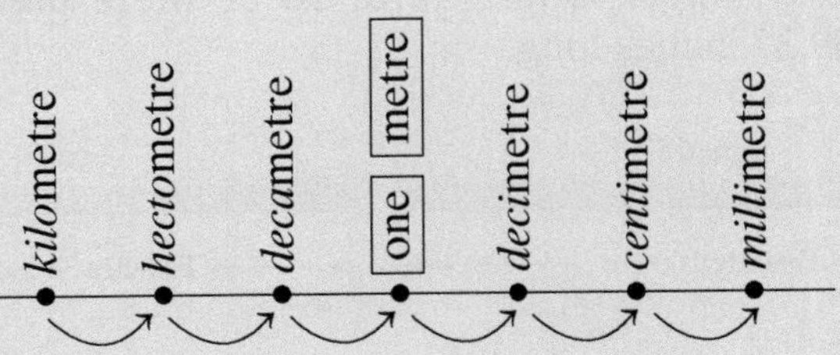

Thus 1 metre = 100 centimetres because we move two places to the right on the chart of prefixes and we also move the decimal point (1.00) two places to the right.

Now let us examine the four most commonly used metric measurements of length and their abbreviations.

COMMONLY USED METRIC LENGTHS

1 kilometre (km) = 1000 metres
1 metre (m) (the basic unit of length in the metric system)
1 centimetre (cm) = 0.01 metre
1 millimetre (mm) = 0.001 metre

Now let us see how we can change a measurement stated in a larger unit to an equivalent measurement stated in smaller units.

EXAMPLE 2

(a) Change 5 kilometres to metres. **(b)** Change 20 metres to centimetres.

Solution

(a) To go from *kilometres* to metres, we move three places to the right on the prefix chart. So we move the decimal point three places to the right.

5 kilometres = 5.000. metres (move three places) = 5000 metres

(b) To go from metres to *centimetres,* we move two places to the right on the prefix chart. Thus we move the decimal point two places to the right.

20 metres = 20.00. centimetres (move two places) = 2000 centimetres

Practice Problem 2

(a) Change 4 metres to centimetres.
(b) Change 30 centimetres to millimetres.

Changing from Smaller Metric Units to Larger Ones

When you change from one metric prefix to another by moving to the **left** on this prefix chart, move the decimal point to the **left** the same number of places.

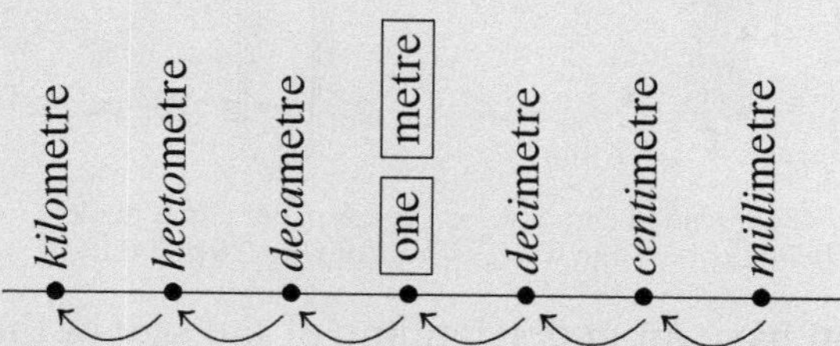

EXAMPLE 3

(a) Change 163 centimetres to metres.
(b) Change 56 millimetres to kilometres.

Solution

(a) To go from *centi*metres to metres, we move *two* places to the left on the prefix chart. Thus we move the decimal point two places to the left.

163 centimetres = 1.63. metres (move two places to the left)
= 1.63 metres

(b) To go from *milli*metres to *kilo*metres, we move six places to the left on the prefix chart. Thus we move the decimal point six places to the left.

56 millimetres = 0.000056. kilometre (move six places to the left)
= 0.000 056 kilometre

Practice Problem 3

(a) Change 3 millimetres to metres.
(b) Change 47 centimetres to kilometres.

NOTE TO STUDENT: Fully worked-out solutions to all of the Practice Problems can be found at the end of the module.

Thinking Metric Long distances are customarily measured in kilometres. A kilometre is about 0.62 mile. It takes about 1.6 kilometres to make a mile. The following drawing shows the relationship between the kilometre and the mile.

1 kilometre

1 mile (about 1.6 kilometres)

Many small distances are measured in centimetres. A centimetre is about 0.394 inch. It takes 2.54 centimetres to make an inch. You can get a good idea of their size by looking at a ruler marked in both inches and centimetres.

1 centimetre

1 inch (2.54 centimetres)

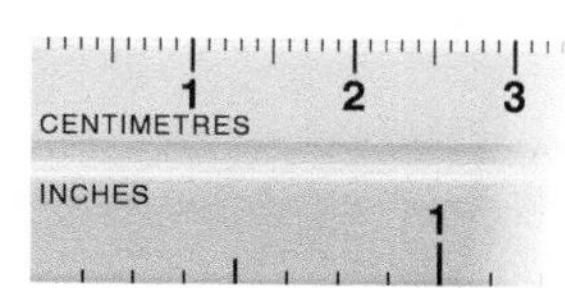

Try to visualize how many centimetres long or wide a DVD case is. It is 12.4 centimetres wide and 14.2 centimetres long.

A millimetre is a very small unit of measurement, often used in manufacturing.

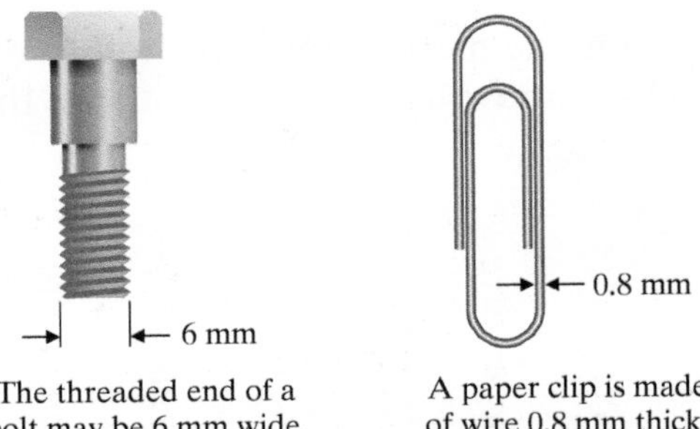

The threaded end of a bolt may be 6 mm wide.

A paper clip is made of wire 0.8 mm thick.

Now that you have an understanding of the size of these metric units, let's try to select the most convenient metric unit for measuring the length of an object.

EXAMPLE 4 Bob measured the width of a doorway in his house. He wrote down "73." What unit of measurement did he use?

(a) 73 kilometres **(b)** 73 metres **(c)** 73 centimetres

Solution The most reasonable choice is (c), 73 centimetres. The other two units would be much too long. A metre is about half the height of a man, and a doorway would not be as wide as the height of 36 men! A kilometre is much larger than a metre.

Practice Problem 4 Joan measured the length of her car. She wrote down 3.8. Which unit of measurement did she use?

(a) 3.8 kilometres **(b)** 3.8 metres **(c)** 3.8 centimetres

The most frequent metric conversions in length are done between kilometres (km), metres (m), centimetres (cm), and millimetres (mm).

EXAMPLE 5 Convert. **(a)** 982 cm to metres **(b)** 5.2 m to millimetres

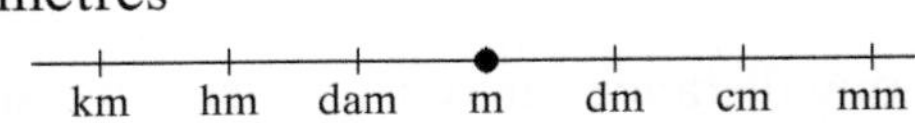

Solution

(a) In the first case, we move the decimal point to the left because we are going from a smaller unit to a larger unit.

$$982 \text{ cm} = 9.82 \text{ m} \quad \text{(two places to left)}$$
$$= 9.82 \text{ m}$$

(b) In the next case, we need to move the decimal point to the right because we are going from a larger unit to a smaller unit.

$$5.2 \text{ m} = 5200. \text{ mm} \quad \text{(three places to right)}$$
$$= 5200 \text{ mm}$$

Practice Problem 5 Convert.

(a) 375 cm to metres **(b)** 46 m to millimetres

The other metric units of length are the hectometre, the decametre, and the decimetre. These are not used very frequently, but it is good to understand how their lengths relate to the basic unit, the metre. A complete list of the metric lengths we have discussed appears in the following table.

METRIC LENGTHS WITH ABBREVIATIONS

1 kilometre (km) = 1000 metres
1 hectometre (hm) = 100 metres
1 decametre (dam) = 10 metres
1 metre (m)
1 decimetre (dm) = 0.1 metre
1 centimetre (cm) = 0.01 metre
1 millimetre (mm) = 0.001 metre

EXAMPLE 6 Convert.

(a) 426 decimetres to kilometres
(b) 9.47 hectometres to metres

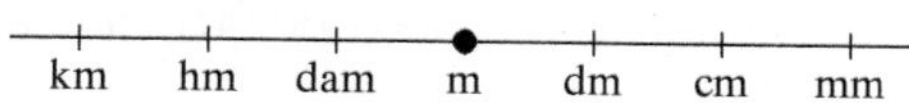

Solution

(a) We are converting from a smaller unit, decimetres, to a larger one, kilometres. Therefore, there will be fewer kilometres than decimetres. (The number we get will be smaller than 426.) We move the decimal point four places to the left.

426 dm = 0.0426. km (four places to left)
= 0.0426 km

(b) We are converting from a larger unit, hectometres, to a smaller one, metres.Therefore, there will be more metres than hectometres. (The number will be larger than 9.47.) We move the decimal point two places to the right.

9.47 hm = 9.47. m (two places to right)
= 947 m

Practice Problem 6 Convert.

(a) 389 millimetres to decametres
(b) 0.48 hectometre to centimetres

When several metric measurements are to be added, we change them to a convenient common unit.

EXAMPLE 7 Add. 125 m + 1.8 km + 793 m

Solution First we change the kilometre measurement to a measurement in metres.

1.8 km = 1800 m

Then we add.

$$\begin{array}{r} 125\text{ m} \\ 1800\text{ m} \\ +\ \ 793\text{ m} \\ \hline 2718\text{ m} \end{array}$$

Practice Problem 7 Add. 782 cm + 2 m + 537 m

SIDELIGHT: Extremely Large Metric Distances
Is the biggest length in the metric system a kilometre? Is the smallest length a millimetre? No. The system extends to very large units and very small ones. Usually, only scientists use these units.

1 gigametre = 1 000 000 000 metres
1 megametre = 1 000 000 metres
1 kilometre = 1000 metres
1 metre
1 millimetre = 0.001 metre
1 micrometre = 0.000 001 metre
1 nanometre = 0.000 000 001 metre

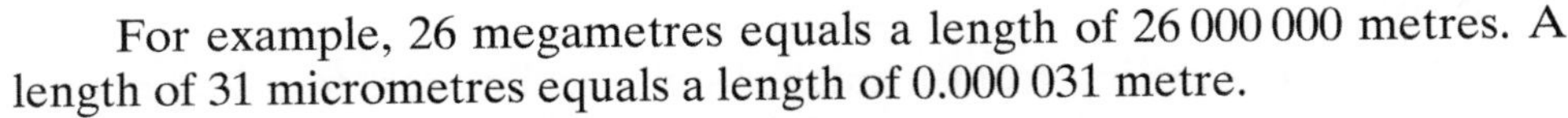

For example, 26 megametres equals a length of 26 000 000 metres. A length of 31 micrometres equals a length of 0.000 031 metre.

SIDELIGHT: Metric Measurements for Computers
A **byte** is the amount of computer memory needed to store one alphanumeric character. When referring to computers you may hear the following words: **kilobytes, megabytes, gigabytes,** and **terabytes.** The following chart may help you.

1 terabyte (TB) = one trillion bytes = 1 000 000 000 000 bytes
1 gigabyte (GB) = one billion bytes = 1 000 000 000 bytes
1 megabyte (MB) = one million bytes = 1 000 000 bytes
1 kilobyte (KB) = one thousand bytes* = 1000 bytes

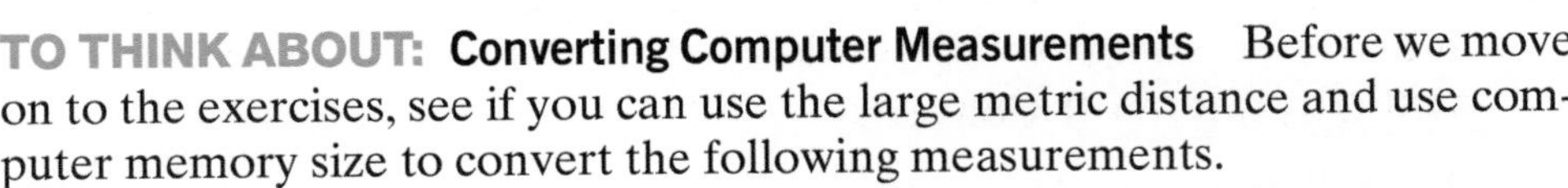

TO THINK ABOUT: Converting Computer Measurements Before we move on to the exercises, see if you can use the large metric distance and use computer memory size to convert the following measurements.

1. 18 megametres = __________ kilometres
2. 26 millimetres = __________ micrometres
3. 17 nanometres = __________ millimetre
4. 38 metres = __________ megametre
5. 1.2 gigabytes = __________ bytes
6. 528 megabytes = __________ bytes
7. 78.9 kilobytes = __________ bytes
8. 24.9 gigabytes = __________ bytes

*In computer science, sometimes 1 kilobyte is considered to be 1024 bytes, in which case 1 megabyte would be considered to be 1024 kilobytes or 1 048 576 bytes.

SECTION 2 EXERCISES

Verbal and Writing Skills

Write the prefix for each of the following.

1. Hundred

2. Hundredth

3. Tenth

4. Thousandth

5. Thousand

6. Ten

The following conversions involve metric units that are very commonly used. You should be able to perform each conversion without any notes and without consulting your text.

7. 46 centimetres = ____________ millimetres

8. 79 centimetres = ____________ millimetres

9. 2.61 kilometres = ____________ metres

10. 8.3 kilometres = ____________ metres

11. 12 500 millimetres = ____________ metres

12. 10 600 millimetres = ____________ metres

13. 7.32 centimetres = ____________ metres

14. 9.14 centimetres = ____________ metres

15. 2 kilometres = ____________ centimetres

16. 7 kilometres = ____________ centimetres

17. 78 000 millimetres = ____________ kilometre

18. 840 millimetres = ____________ kilometre

Abbreviations are used in the following. Fill in the blanks with the correct values.

19. 35 mm = ____________ cm = ____________ m

20. 6300 mm = ____________ cm = ____________ m

21. 4.5 km = ____________ m = ____________ cm

22. 6.8 km = ____________ m = ____________ cm

Applications

23. ***Driving in Spain*** Amanda is driving in Spain and sees a road sign that gives the distance to the next city. Choose the most reasonable measurement.

(a) 24 m **(b)** 24 km **(c)** 24 cm

24. ***Picture Frame Construction*** Estelle is making a picture frame. She needs to measure the length to know how much decorative border to buy. Choose the most reasonable measurement.

(a) 20 m **(b)** 20 cm **(c)** 20 mm

25. ***Compact Disc Case*** Eddie measured the width of a compact disc case. Choose the most appropriate measurement.

(a) 80.5 km **(b)** 80.5 m **(c)** 80.5 mm

26. ***Botanical Gardens*** The Botanical Gardens are located in the centre of the city. If it takes approximately 10 minutes to walk directly from the east entrance to the west entrance, which would be the most likely measurement of the width of the Gardens?

(a) 1.4 km **(b)** 1.4 m **(c)** 1.4 mm

27. ***Computer Monitor*** Julie measured her monitor to see if it would fit under a shelf on her computer desk. Choose the most reasonable measurement.

(a) 45 cm **(b)** 45 m **(c)** 45 mm

28. ***Jewellery Box Construction*** Rich is making a jewellery box and must use very small screws. Which would be the most likely measurement of the screws?

(a) 8 cm **(b)** 8 m **(c)** 8 mm

29. ***Street Length*** Brenda and Stanley live on Brookwood Street. It is a dead end street with about 12 houses on it. Which would be the most likely measurement of the length of the street?

(a) 0.5 km **(b)** 0.5 m **(c)** 0.5 cm

30. ***Bookcase*** Gabe has a bookcase for all of his college textbooks. It is fairly full but one shelf has room for about 5 or 6 more textbooks. Which would be the most likely measurement of the available space on his bookcase?

(a) 32 km **(b)** 32 cm **(c)** 32 mm

31. ***House Insulation*** Bob and Debbie found that one corner of their townhouse is chilly in the winter. They examined the wall and found that one portion of the wall does not have insulation. They needed to install insulation between the wall board and the outer wall. What would be the most likely measurement of the thickness of the insulation?

(a) 11.9 mm **(b)** 11.9 cm **(c)** 11.9 m

32. ***Hockey*** Kanisha and Rashawn got excellent tickets to see a Toronto Maple Leafs hockey game. Which would be the most likely measurement of the distance from their seats to centre ice?

(a) 320 cm **(b)** 320 km **(c)** 320 m

The following conversions involve metric units that are not used extensively. You should be able to perform each conversion, but it is not necessary to do it from memory.

33. 390 decimetres = ___________ metres

34. 270 decimetres = ___________ metres

35. 800 decametres = ___________ metres

36. 530 decametres = ___________ metres

37. 48.2 metres = ___________ hectometre

38. 435 hectometres = ___________ kilometres

Change to a convenient unit of measure and add.

39. 243 m + 2.7 km + 312 m

40. 845 m + 5.79 km + 701 m

41. 225 mm + 12.7 cm + 148 cm

42. 305 mm + 45.4 cm + 318 cm

43. 15 mm + 2 dm + 42 cm

44. 8 dm + 21 mm + 38 cm

45. ***Stereo Cabinet*** The outside casing of a stereo cabinet is built of plywood 0.95 centimetre thick attached to plastic 1.35 centimetres thick and a piece of mahogany veneer 2.464 millimetres thick. How thick is the stereo casing?

46. ***House Construction*** A plywood board is 2.2 centimetres thick. A layer of tar paper is 3.42 millimetres thick. A layer of false brick siding is 2.7 centimetres thick. A house wall consists of these three layers. How thick is the wall?

Mixed Practice

47. 65 cm + 80 mm + 2.5 m

48. 82 m + 471 cm + 0.32 km

49. 46 m + 986 cm + 0.884 km

50. 56.3 centimetres = __________ metre

51. 96.4 centimetres = __________ metre

Write true *or* false *for each statement.*

52. 0.001 kilometre = 1 metre

53. 1 kilometre = 0.001 metre

54. 1000 metres = 1 kilometre

55. 10 millimetres = 1 centimetre

56. An airport runway might be 2 kilometres long.

57. A man might be 2 metres tall.

58. A kilometre is longer than a mile.

59. A yard is longer than a metre.

Applications

60. ***Trans-Siberian Train*** The world's longest train run is on the Trans-Siberian line in Russia, from Moscow to Nakhodka, a city on the Sea of Japan. The length of the run, which has 97 stops, measures 94 380 000 centimetres. The run takes 8 days, 4 hours, and 25 minutes to travel.

(a) How many metres is the run?

(b) How many kilometres is the run?

61. ***Peruvian Train*** The highest railroad line in the world is a track on the Morococha branch of the Peruvian State Railways at La Cima. The track is 4818 metres high.

(a) How many centimetres high is the track?

(b) How many kilometres high is the track?

62. ***Dam Construction*** The world's highest dam, the Rogun dam in Tajikistan, is 335 metres high.

(a) How many kilometres high is the dam?

(b) How many centimetres high is the dam?

63. ***Virus Size*** A typical virus of the human body measures just 0.000 000 254 centimetre in diameter. How many metres in diameter is a typical virus?

To Think About

World's Longest Subway Systems *The lengths of some of the world's longest subway systems are given in the following bar graph. Use the graph to answer exercises 64–69.*

64. How many metres longer is the subway system in Seoul, South Korea, than that in Paris, France?

65. How many metres longer is the London, England, subway system than that of Tokyo, Japan?

66. How many megametres long is the subway system in New York City?

67. How many megametres long is the subway system in Seoul?

To convert from kilometres to miles, multiply the number of kilometres by 0.62.

68. How many miles long is London's subway system?

69. How many miles long is Moscow's subway system?

Quick Quiz 2

1. Convert 45.9 metres to centimetres.

2. Convert 0.0283 centimetre to millimetres.

3. Convert 5160 metres to kilometres.

4. **Concept Check** Explain how you would convert 5643 centimetres to kilometres.

 SECTION 3 METRIC MEASUREMENTS: VOLUME AND WEIGHT

Converting Between Metric Units of Volume

As products are distributed worldwide, more and more of them are being sold in metric units. Soft drinks come in 1-, 2-, or 3-litre bottles. Labels often contain these amounts in both U.S. customary units and metric units. Try looking at these labels to gain a sense of the size of metric units of volume.

The basic metric unit for volume is the litre. A **litre** is defined as the volume of a box 10 cm × 10 cm × 10 cm, or 1000 cm^3. A cubic centimetre may be written as cc, so we sometimes see 1000 cc = 1 litre. A litre is slightly larger than a quart; 1 litre of liquid is 1.057 quarts of that liquid.

The most common metric units of volume are the millilitre, the litre, and the kilolitre. The capital letter L is used as an abbreviation for *litre*.

Student Learning Objectives

After studying this section, you will be able to:

 **Convert between metric units of volume.**

 **Convert between metric units of weight.**

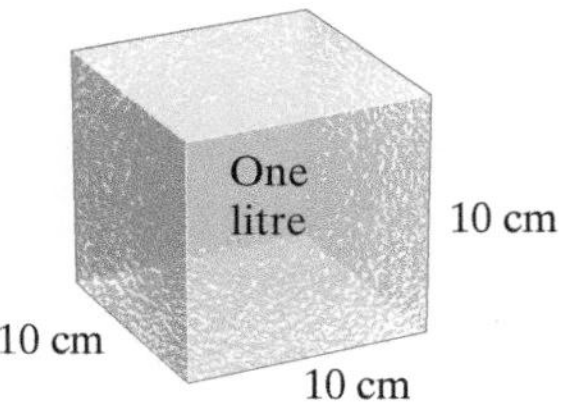

COMMON METRIC VOLUME MEASUREMENTS

1 kilolitre (kL) = 1000 litres
1 litre (L)
1 millilitre (mL) = 0.001 litre

We know that 1000 cc = 1 litre. Dividing each side of that equation by 1000, we get 1 cc = 1 mL.

1 litre 2 litres

Use this prefix chart as a guide when you change one metric prefix to another. Move the decimal point in the same direction and the same number of places.

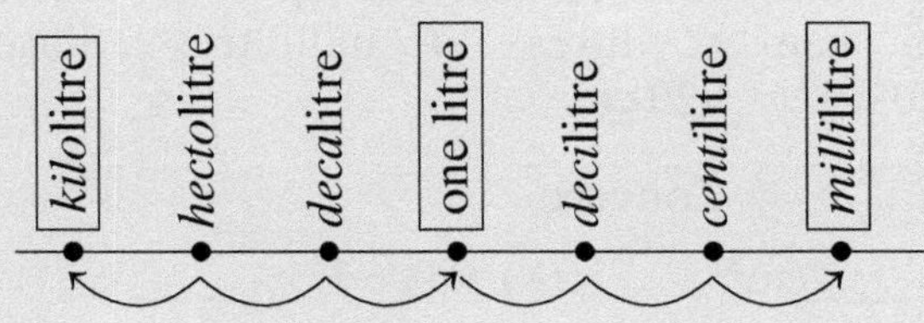

The prefixes for litres follow the pattern we have seen for metres. Note that *kilo-* is three places to the left of the litre and *milli-* is three places to the right. Because the kilolitre, the litre, and the millilitre are the most commonly used units of volume, we will focus on them in this text.

EXAMPLE 1 Convert.

(a) 3 L = _____ mL **(b)** 24 kL = _____ L **(c)** 0.084 L = _____ mL

Solution

(a) The prefix *milli-* is three places to the right. We move the decimal point three places to the right.

3 L = 3.000 = 3000 mL

(b) 24 kL = 24.000 = 24 000 L **(c)** 0.084 L = 0.084 = 84 mL

Practice Problem 1 Convert.

(a) 5 L = _____ mL **(b)** 84 kL = _____ L **(c)** 0.732 L = _____ mL

EXAMPLE 2 Convert.

(a) 26.4 mL = ____ L **(b)** 5982 mL = ____ L **(c)** 6.7 L = ____ kL

Solution

(a) The unit L is three places to the left of the unit mL. We move the decimal three places to the left. 26.4 mL = 0.0264 L

(b) 5982 mL = 5.982 L

(c) 6.7 L = 0.0067 kL

Practice Problem 2 Convert.

(a) 15.8 mL = ___________ L **(b)** 12 340 mL = ___________ L

(c) 86.3 L = ___________ kL

The cubic centimetre is often used in medicine. Recall that 1 mL = 1 cm^3 or 1 cc.

EXAMPLE 3 Convert.

(a) 26 mL = _____ cm^3 **(b)** 0.82 L = _____ cc

Solution

(a) A millilitre and a cubic centimetre are equivalent. 26 mL = 26 cm^3

(b) We use the same rule to convert litres to cubic centimetres as we do to convert litres to millilitres. Since 1 cm^3 = 1 cc, 0.82 L = 820 cm^3 = 820 cc.

Practice Problem 3 Convert.

(a) 396 mL = ____ cm^3 **(b)** 0.096 L = ____ cc

2 Converting Between Metric Units of Weight

In a science class we make a distinction between weight and **mass.** Mass is the amount of material in an object. Weight is a measure of the pull of gravity on an object. The farther you are from the centre of the earth, the less you weigh. If you were an astronaut floating in outer space you would be weightless. The mass of your body, however, would not change. The U.S. customary units of weight used in the first section are true weight measurements, specific to Earth. The metric system measures units of mass. In everyday language, we say that someone weighs 70 kilograms, although strictly speaking we should say they have a mass of 70 kilograms. We will continue to use the terms *weight* and *mass* interchangeably.

In the metric system the basic unit of weight is the gram. A **gram** is the weight of the water in a box that is 1 centimetre on each side. To get an idea of how small a gram is, we note that two small paper clips weigh about 1 gram. A gram is only about 0.035 ounce.

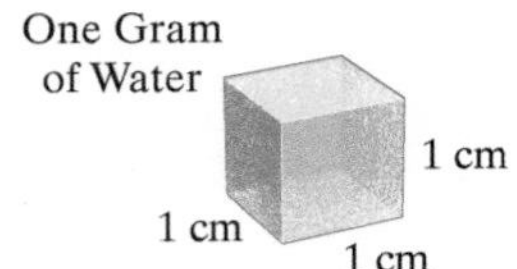

One kilogram is 1000 times larger than a gram. A kilogram is about 2.2 pounds. Some of the measures of weight in the metric system are shown in the following chart. Note that the tonne (sometimes referred to as a metric ton) is spelled differently than the U.S. customary ton, allowing an easy way to make the distinction without reference to which measurement system is being used.

COMMON METRIC WEIGHT MEASUREMENTS

1 tonne (t) = 1 000 000 grams
1 kilogram (kg) = 1000 grams
1 gram (g)
1 milligram (mg) = 0.001 gram

Use this prefix chart as a guide when you change one metric prefix to another. Move the decimal point in the same direction and the same number of places.

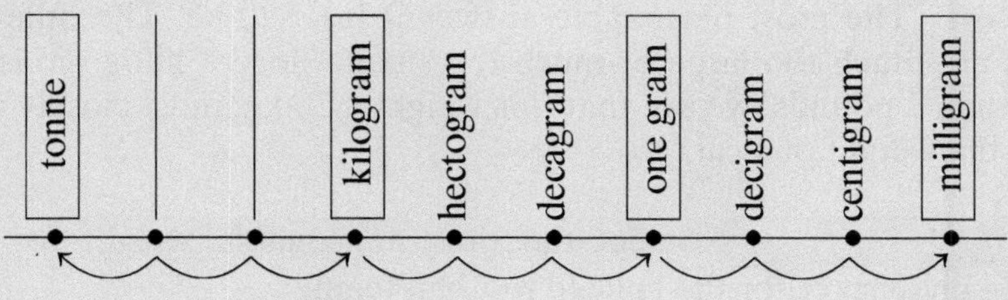

We will focus exclusively on the tonne, kilogram, gram, and milligram. We convert weight measurements the same way we convert volume and length measurements. The tonne is also called a **megagram.** *Mega* means "million" so a megagram is 1 000 000 grams.

EXAMPLE 4 Convert.

(a) 2 t = _____ kg **(b)** 0.42 kg = _____ g

Solution **(a)** 2 t = 2000 kg **(b)** 0.42 kg = 420 g

Practice Problem 4 Convert.

(a) 3.2 t = ________ kg **(b)** 7.08 kg = ________ g

EXAMPLE 5 Convert.

(a) 283 kg = _____ t **(b)** 7.98 mg = _____ g

Solution

(a) 283 kg = 0.283 t **(b)** 7.98 mg = 0.007 98 g

Practice Problem 5 Convert.

(a) 59 kg = _________ t **(b)** 28.3 mg = _________ g

EXAMPLE 6 If a chemical costs \$0.03 per gram, what will it cost per kilogram?

Solution Since there are 1000 grams in a kilogram, a chemical that costs \$0.03 per gram would cost 1000 times as much per kilogram.

$$1000 \times \$0.03 = \$30.00$$

The chemical would cost \$30.00 per kilogram.

Practice Problem 6 If coffee costs \$10.00 per kilogram, what will it cost per gram?

Gerard Lacz/Peter Arnold, Inc.

A kilogram is slightly more than 2 pounds. A 3-week-old miniature pinscher weighs about 1 kilogram.

EXAMPLE 7 Select the most reasonable weight for Tammy's Toyota.

(a) 820 t **(b)** 820 g **(c)** 820 kg **(d)** 820 mg

Solution The most reasonable answer is **(c)**, 820 kg. The other weight values are much too large or much too small. Since a kilogram is slightly more than 2 pounds, we see that this weight, 820 kg, most closely approximates the weight of a car.

Practice Problem 7 Select the most reasonable weight for Hank, starting linebacker for the college football team.

(a) 120 kg **(b)** 120 g **(c)** 120 mg

SIDELIGHT: Using Very Small Units

When dealing with very small particles or atomic elements, scientists sometimes use units smaller than a gram.

SMALL WEIGHT MEASUREMENTS

1 milligram = 0.001 gram
1 microgram = 0.000 001 gram
1 nanogram = 0.000 000 001 gram
1 picogram = 0.000 000 000 001 gram

We could make the following conversions.

2.6 picograms = 0.0026 nanogram
29.7 micrograms = 0.0297 milligram
58 nanograms = 58 000 picograms
58 nanograms = 0.058 microgram

SECTION 3 EXERCISES

Verbal and Writing Skills

Write the metric unit that best represents each measurement.

1. one thousand litres

2. one thousandth of a litre

3. one thousandth of a gram

4. one thousand grams

5. one thousandth of a kilogram

6. one thousand millilitres

Perform each conversion.

7. 9 kL = ________ L

8. 5 kL = ________ L

9. 12 L = ________ mL

10. 25 L = ________ mL

11. 18.9 mL = ________ L

12. 31.5 mL = ________ L

13. 752 L = _______ kL

14. 368 L = _______ kL

15. 5.652 kL = ________ mL

16. 14.3 kL = _________ mL

17. 82 mL = _____ cc

18. 152 mL = _______ cm^3

19. 24 418 mL = ________ kL

20. 8835 mL = ________ kL

21. 74 L = ________ cm^3

22. 122 L = ________ cm^3

23. 216 g = ________ kg

24. 2940 g = ________ kg

25. 35 mg = ________ g

26. 13 mg = ________ g

27. 6328 mg = ________ g

28. 986 mg = ________ g

29. 2.92 kg = ________ g

30. 14.6 kg = ________ g

31. 2.4 t = ________ kg

32. 9500 kg = _____ t

Fill in the blanks with the correct values.

33. 7 mL = ______ L = ________ kL

34. 18 mL = ______ L = ________ kL

35. 84 cm^3 = _______ L = ________ kL

36. 0.315 kL = ______ L = ________ cc

37. 0.033 kg = _____ g = ________ mg

38. 0.098 kg = ____ g = _______ mg

39. 2.58 tonnes = _______ kg = ___________ g

40. 7183 g = _______ kg = ___________ t

41. ***Bottle Size*** Alice bought a bottle of apple juice at the store. Choose the most reasonable measurement for its contents.

(a) 0.32 kL **(b)** 0.32 L **(c)** 0.32 mL

42. ***Injection Dosage*** A nurse gave an injection of insulin to a diabetic patient. Choose the most reasonable measurement for the dose.

(a) 4 kL **(b)** 4 L **(c)** 4 mL

43. ***Dinosaurs*** One of the heaviest dinosaurs was the Argentinosaurus. Choose the most reasonable measurement for its weight.

(a) 100 t **(b)** 100 kg **(c)** 100 g

44. ***College Textbooks*** Robert bought a new psychology textbook. Choose the most reasonable measurement for its weight.

(a) 0.49 t **(b)** 0.49 kg **(c)** 0.49 g

Find a convenient unit of measure and add.

45. 83 L + 822 mL + 30.1 L

46. 152 L + 473 mL + 77.3 L

47. 20 g + 52 mg + 1.5 kg

48. 2 kg + 42 mg + 120 g

Mixed Practice

Write true *or* false *for each statement.*

49. 1 millilitre = 0.001 litre

50. 1 tonne = 1000 grams

51. Orange juice can be purchased in millilitre containers at the grocery store.

52. Small amounts of medicine are often measured in litres.

53. A reasonable weight for an adult man is 500 000 grams.

54. A bottle of pop might contain 1000 mL.

55. A nickel weighs about 5 grams.

56. A convenient size for a family purchase is 2 kilograms of ground beef.

Applications

57. ***Food Costs*** Starbucks sells 453-gram bags of ground coffee for $8.99. Rhonda bought 3.624 kg. How much did she spend on coffee?

58. ***Food Cost*** Randy's Premier Pizza needs to order tomato sauce from the distributor. The sauce comes in 4000-gram jars for $6.80. If Randy orders 56 kg, how much will he pay for the tomato sauce?

59. ***Biogenetic Research*** A very rare essence of an almost extinct flower found in the Amazon jungle of South America is extracted by a biogenetic company trying to copy and synthesize it. The company estimates that if the procedure is successful, the product will cost the company $850 per millilitre to produce. How much will it cost the company to produce 0.4 litre of the engineered essence?

60. ***Price of Gold*** One day in May 2007, the price of gold was $21.06 per gram. At that price, how much would a kilogram of gold cost?

To Think About

Carbon Dioxide Emissions *Very heavy items are measured in terms of **tonnes.** A tonne is defined as 1000 kilograms (or 2205 pounds).*

*Carbon dioxide being released into the air fuels the greenhouse effect and warms Earth's atmosphere. Consider the bar graph, which displays the billions of tonnes of carbon dioxide emitted by two categories: countries such as Canada, the United States, Japan, Australia, New Zealand, and the countries in Western Europe, considered industrialized countries; the countries in Asia, the Middle East, Africa, Central America, and South America, considered to be developing countries.**

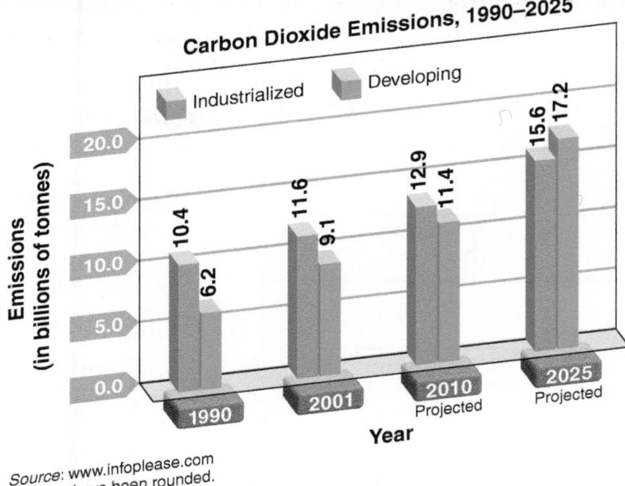

Source: www.infoplease.com
*Figures have been rounded.

61. By how many tonnes did carbon dioxide emissions by industrialized countries increase from 1990 to 2001?

62. By how many tonnes did carbon dioxide emissions by developing countries increase from 1990 to 2001?

63. How many kilograms of carbon dioxide are expected to be emitted by developing countries in 2025?

64. How many kilograms of carbon dioxide are expected to be emitted by industrialized countries in 2025?

65. If the same *percent of increase* that is expected to occur from 2001 to 2010 also occurs from 2025 to 2034, how many tonnes of carbon dioxide will be emitted by industrialized countries in 2034?

66. If the same *percent of increase* that is expected to occur from 2001 to 2010 also occurs from 2025 to 2034, how many tonnes of carbon dioxide will be emitted by developing countries in 2034?

Quick Quiz 3

1. Convert 671 grams to kilograms.

2. Convert 8.52 litres to millilitres.

3. Convert 45.62 milligrams to grams.

4. Concept Check Explain how you would convert 54 kilograms to milligrams.

How Am I Doing? Sections 1–3

1. __________
2. __________
3. __________
4. __________
5. __________
6. __________
7. __________
8. __________
9. __________
10. __________
11. __________
12. __________
13. __________
14. __________
15. __________
16. __________
17. __________
18. __________
19. __________
20. __________
21. __________
22. __________
23. __________
24. __________
25. __________
26. __________

How are you doing with your homework assignments in Sections 1 to 3? Do you feel you have mastered the material so far? Do you understand the concepts you have covered? Before you go further, take some time to do each of the following problems.

1 *Convert. When necessary, express your answer as a decimal rounded to the nearest hundredth.*

1. 48 feet = ____ yards

2. 24 quarts = ____ gallons

3. 3 miles = ____ yards

4. 6400 pounds = ____ tons

5. 22 minutes = ____ seconds

6. 5 gallons = ____ pints

7. Isabel is making a fish dinner for her roommates. She purchases 2 pounds 4 ounces of haddock for $6.80 per pound. How much did Isabel spend on the haddock?

2 *Perform each conversion.*

8. 6.75 km = ____ m

9. 73.9 m = ____ cm

10. 34 cm = ____ mm

11. 27 mm = ____ m

12. 5296 mm = ____ cm

13. 482 m = ____ km

Convert to metres and add.

14. 1.2 km + 192 m + 984 m

15. 305 cm + 82.5 m + 6150 mm

16. The wire that connects a motor to a control panel is 3.4 metres long. One portion of the wire measuring 78 centimetres has double insulation. Another portion of the wire measuring 128 centimetres has triple insulation. The remaining part of the wire has single insulation. How long is the portion of the wire that has single insulation?

3 *Perform each conversion.*

17. 5.66 L = ____ mL

18. 535 g = ____ kg

19. 56.3 kg = ____ t

20. 4.8 kL = ____ L

21. 568 mg = ____ g

22. 8.9 L = ____ cm^3

23. A wholesaler sells peanut butter in canisters of 5000 g for $7.75. The Rescue Mission needs to buy 75 kg to restock its pantry. How much will the mission spend on peanut butter from this wholesaler?

24. Old Italy Foods receives a special shipment of olive oil in 5000-gram cans. Old Italy Foods sells these cans for $32.50. If Ricardo's Restaurant needs 35 kg of olive oil and purchases it from Old Italy Foods, how much will it cost?

25. An antibacterial spray costs $36 per litre to produce. The Smiths purchased 200 millilitres of the spray. They know the owner of the company that produces the spray and he sold it to them at cost. How much did they pay for 200 millilitres?

26. Last year gold cost $21.20 per gram. Samuel purchased 0.5 kilogram of gold at that price. How much did he pay?

Your institution may have included the Answers to Selected Exercises for this module, which contains the answers to these questions. Each answer also includes a reference to the objective in which the problem is first taught. If you missed any of these problems, you should stop and review the Examples and Practice Problems in the referenced objective. A little review now will help you master the material in the upcoming sections.

SECTION 4 CONVERTING UNITS

Converting Units of Length, Volume, or Weight Between the Metric and U.S. Customary Systems

So far we've seen how to convert units when working *within* either the U.S. customary or the metric system. Many people, however, work in *both* the metric and the U.S. customary systems. If you study such fields as chemistry, electromechanical technology, business, X-ray technology, nursing, or computers, you will probably need to convert measurements between the two systems.

To convert between U.S. customary units and metric units, it is helpful to have equivalent values. The most commonly used equivalents are listed in the following table. Most of these are approximate.

Equivalent Measures

	U.S. Customary to Metric	Metric to U.S. Customary
Units of length	1 mile ≈ 1.61 kilometres 1 yard ≈ 0.914 metre 1 foot ≈ 0.305 metre 1 inch = 2.54 centimetres*	1 kilometre ≈ 0.62 mile 1 metre ≈ 1.09 yards 1 metre ≈ 3.28 feet 1 centimetre ≈ 0.394 inch
Units of volume	1 gallon ≈ 3.79 litres 1 quart ≈ 0.946 litre	1 litre ≈ 0.264 gallon 1 litre ≈ 1.06 quarts
Units of weight	1 pound ≈ 0.454 kilogram 1 ounce ≈ 28.35 grams	1 kilogram ≈ 2.2 pounds 1 gram ≈ 0.0353 ounce

*exact value

Remember that to convert from one unit to another you multiply by a fraction that is equivalent to 1. Create a fraction from the equivalent measures table so that the unit in the denominator cancels the unit you are changing.

To change 5 miles to kilometres, we look in the table and find that 1 mile ≈ 1.61 kilometres. We will use the unit fraction

$$\frac{1.61 \text{ kilometres}}{1 \text{ mile}}$$

because we want to have miles in the denominator.

$$5 \cancel{\text{miles}} \times \frac{1.61 \text{ kilometres}}{1 \cancel{\text{mile}}} = 5 \times 1.61 \text{ kilometres} = 8.05 \text{ kilometres}$$

Thus 5 miles ≈ 8.05 kilometres.

Is this the only way to do the problem? No. To make the previous conversion, we also could have used the relationship that 1 kilometre ≈ 0.62 mile. Again, we want to have miles in the denominator, so we use

$$\frac{1 \text{ kilometre}}{0.62 \text{ mile}}$$

$$5 \cancel{\text{miles}} \times \frac{1 \text{ kilometres}}{0.62 \cancel{\text{mile}}} = \frac{5}{0.62} = 8.06 \text{ kilometres.}$$

Using this approach, we find that 5 miles ≈ 8.06 kilometres. This is not the same result we obtained before. The discrepancy between the results of

Student Learning Objectives

After studying this section, you will be able to:

 **Convert units of length, volume, or weight between the metric and U.S. customary systems.**

 **Convert between Fahrenheit and Celsius degrees of temperature.**

Tom McHugh/Photo Researchers, Inc.

the two conversions has occurred because the numbers given in the equivalent measures table are approximations.

Often we have to make conversions in order to make comparisons. For example, is the 6 inches of attic insulation commonly used in the northeastern United States more or less than the 16 centimetres of attic insulation commonly used in Sweden? In order to find out we would have to convert 6 inches to centimetres. What unit fraction would we use? What result would we get?

EXAMPLE 1 Convert 6 inches to centimetres.

Solution

$$6 \cancel{\text{inches}} \times \frac{2.54 \text{ centimetres}}{1 \cancel{\text{inch}}} = 15.24 \text{ centimetres}$$

Practice Problem 1 Convert 7 feet to metres.

Unit abbreviations are quite common, so we will use them for the remainder of this section. We list them here for your reference.

U.S. Customary Measure (Alphabetical Order)	Standard Abbreviation
feet	ft
gallon	gal
inch	in.
mile	mi
ounce	oz
pound	lb
quart	qt
yard	yd

Metric Measure	Standard Abbreviation
centimetre	cm
gram	g
kilogram	kg
kilometre	km
litre	L
metre	m
millimetre	mm

EXAMPLE 2

(a) Convert 26 m to yards.

(b) Convert 1.9 km to miles.

(c) Convert 14 gal to litres.

(d) Convert 2.5 L to quarts.

Solution

(a) $26 \cancel{\text{m}} \times \frac{1.09 \text{ yd}}{1 \cancel{\text{m}}} = 28.34 \text{ yd}$

(b) $1.9 \cancel{\text{km}} \times \frac{0.62 \text{ mi}}{1 \cancel{\text{km}}} = 1.178 \text{ mi}$

(c) $14 \cancel{\text{gal}} \times \frac{3.79 \text{ L}}{1 \cancel{\text{gal}}} = 53.06 \text{ L}$

(d) $2.5 \cancel{\text{L}} \times \frac{1.06 \text{ qt}}{1 \cancel{\text{L}}} = 2.65 \text{ qt}$

Practice Problem 2

(a) Convert 17 m to yards.

(b) Convert 29.6 km to miles.

(c) Convert 26 gal to litres.

(d) Convert 6.2 L to quarts.

Some conversions require more than one step.

EXAMPLE 3 Convert 235 cm to feet. Round to the nearest hundredth of a foot.

Solution Our first fraction converts centimetres to inches. Our second fraction converts inches to feet.

$$235 \cancel{\text{cm}} \times \frac{0.394 \cancel{\text{in.}}}{1 \cancel{\text{cm}}} \times \frac{1 \text{ ft}}{12 \cancel{\text{in.}}} = \frac{92.59}{12} \text{ ft}$$

$$\approx 7.72 \text{ ft (rounded to the nearest hundredth)}$$

Practice Problem 3 Convert 180 cm to feet.

The same rules can be followed for a rate such as 50 miles per hour.

If the unit to be converted is in the numerator, be sure to express that unit in the denominator of the unit fraction. If the unit to be converted is in the denominator, be sure to express that unit in the numerator of the unit fraction.

EXAMPLE 4 Convert 100 km/h to mi/h.

Solution We need to multiply by a unit fraction. The fraction we multiply by must have kilometres in the denominator.

$$\frac{100 \cancel{\text{km}}}{1 \text{ h}} \times \frac{0.62 \text{ mi}}{1 \cancel{\text{km}}} = 62 \text{ mi/h}$$

Thus 100 km/h is approximately equal to 62 mi/h.

Practice Problem 4 Convert 88 km/h to miles per hour.

Sometimes we need more than one unit fraction to make the conversion of two rates. We will see how this is accomplished in Example 5.

EXAMPLE 5 A rocket carrying a communication satellite is launched from a rocket launch pad. It is travelling at 700 miles per hour. How many feet per second is the rocket travelling? Round to the nearest whole number.

Solution

$$\frac{700 \cancel{\text{miles}}}{1 \cancel{\text{h}}} \times \frac{5280 \text{ ft}}{1 \cancel{\text{mile}}} \times \frac{1 \cancel{\text{h}}}{60 \cancel{\text{min}}} \times \frac{1 \cancel{\text{min}}}{60 \text{ s}}$$

$$= \frac{700 \times 5280 \text{ ft}}{60 \times 60 \text{ s}} = \frac{3\,696\,000 \text{ ft}}{3600 \text{ s}} \approx 1027 \text{ ft/s}$$

The missile is travelling at approximately 1027 feet per second.

Practice Problem 5 A Concorde jet in a 2003 flight from Boston to Paris flew at 900 miles per hour. What was the speed of the Concorde jet in feet per second?

▲SIDELIGHT: From Square Yards to Square Metres

Suppose we consider a rectangle that measures 2 yards wide by 4 yards long. The area would be 2 yards × 4 yards = 8 square yards. How could you change 8 square yards to square metres? Suppose that we look at 1 square yard. Each side is 1 yard long, which is equivalent to 0.914 metre.

$$\text{Area} = 1 \text{ yard} \times 1 \text{ yard} \approx 0.914 \text{ metre} \times 0.914 \text{ metre}$$
$$\text{Area} = 1 \text{ square yard} \approx 0.8354 \text{ square metre}$$

Thus 1 $\text{yd}^2 \approx 0.8354 \text{ m}^2$. Therefore

$$8 \cancel{\text{yd}^2} \times \frac{0.8354 \text{ m}^2}{1 \cancel{\text{yd}^2}} = 6.6832 \text{ m}^2.$$

8 square yards ≈ 6.6832 square metres.

2 Converting Between Fahrenheit and Celsius Degrees of Temperature

In the metric system, temperature is measured on the **Celsius scale.** Water boils at 100° (100 °C) and freezes at 0° (0 °C) on the Celsius scale. In the **Fahrenheit system,** water boils at 212° (212 °F) and freezes at 32° (32 °F).

Calculator

Converting Temperatures

You can use your calculator to convert temperature readings between Fahrenheit and Celsius. To convert 30 °C to Fahrenheit temperature, enter

1.8 [×] 30 [+] 32 [=]

Display

[86]

The temperature is 86 °F.

To convert 82.4 °F to Celsius temperature, enter

5 [×] 82.4 [−] 160

[=] [÷] 9 [=]

Display

[28]

The temperature is 28 °C.

To convert Celsius to Fahrenheit, we can use the formula

$$F = 1.8 \times C + 32,$$

where C is the number of Celsius degrees and F is the number of Fahrenheit degrees.

EXAMPLE 6 When the temperature is 35 °C, what is the Fahrenheit reading?

Solution

$$\begin{aligned} F &= 1.8 \times C + 32 \\ &= 1.8 \times 35 + 32 \\ &= 63 + 32 \\ &= 95 \end{aligned}$$

The temperature is 95 °F.

Practice Problem 6 Convert 20 °C to Fahrenheit temperature.

To convert Fahrenheit temperature to Celsius, we can use the formula

$$C = \frac{5 \times F - 160}{9},$$

where F is the number of Fahrenheit degrees and C is the number of Celsius degrees.

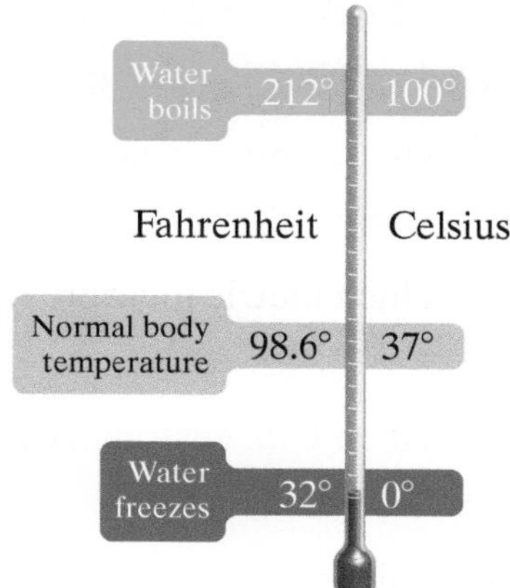

EXAMPLE 7 When the temperature is 50 °F, what is the Celsius reading?

Solution

$$\begin{aligned} C &= \frac{5 \times F - 160}{9} \\ &= \frac{5 \times 50 - 160}{9} \\ &= \frac{250 - 160}{9} \\ &= \frac{90}{9} \\ &= 10 \end{aligned}$$

The temperature is 10 °C.

Practice Problem 7 When the temperature is 86 °F, what is the Celsius reading?

NOTE TO STUDENT: Fully worked-out solutions to all of the Practice Problems can be found at the end of the module.

You may find it helpful to refer to this conversion chart.

Celsius	30°	25°	20°	10°	0°	−10°	−20°
Fahrenheit	86°	77°	68°	50°	32°	14°	−4°

Section 4 Exercises

Verbal and Writing Skills

1. Which metric measure is approximately the same length as a yard? Which unit is larger?

2. Which metric measure of volume is approximately the same as a quart? Which unit is larger?

3. Which U.S. customary measure is approximately twice the length of a centimetre?

4. Which metric measure is approximately double a pound?

Perform each conversion. Round to the nearest hundredth when necessary.

5. 7 ft to metres

6. 11 ft to metres

7. 9 in. to centimetres

8. 13 in. to centimetres

9. 32 m to yards

10. 115 m to yards

11. 30.8 yd to metres

12. 42.5 yd to metres

13. 82 mi to kilometres

14. 68 mi to kilometres

15. 9.25 m to yards

16. 12.75 m to yards

17. 17.5 cm to inches

18. 19.6 cm to inches

19. 200 m to feet

20. 400 m to feet

21. 5 km to miles

22. 16 km to miles

23. 48 gal to litres

24. 63 gal to litres

25. 23 qt to litres

26. 28 qt to litres

27. 19 L to gallons

28. 15 L to gallons

29. 4.5 L to quarts

30. 6.5 L to quarts

31. 82 kg to pounds

32. 45 kg to pounds

33. 130 lb to kilograms

34. 155 lb to kilograms

35. 26 oz to grams

36. 34 oz to grams

37. 152 kg to pounds

38. 188 kg to pounds

Mixed Practice *Perform each conversion. Round to the nearest hundredth if necessary.*

39. 158 g to ounces

40. 105 g to ounces

41. 35 ft to centimetres

42. 14 ft to centimetres

43. 55 km/h to miles per hour

44. 120 km/h to miles per hour

45. 400 ft/s to miles per hour (Round to the nearest whole number.)

46. 300 ft/s to miles per hour (Round to the nearest whole number.)

47. A wire that is 13 mm wide is how many inches wide?

48. A bolt that is 7 mm wide is how many inches wide?

49. 85 °C to Fahrenheit

50. 105 °C to Fahrenheit

51. 12 °C to Fahrenheit

52. 21 °C to Fahrenheit

53. 140 °F to Celsius

54. 131 °F to Celsius

55. 95 °F to Celsius

56. 88 °F to Celsius

Applications *Solve. Round to the nearest hundredth when necessary.*

57. ***Speed Limit*** The speed limit on a New Zealand highway is 90 km/h. Molly is driving at 65 mi/h. Is Molly speeding?

58. ***Spain Bike Trip*** John and Sandy Westphal travelled to Spain for a bike tour. The woman leading the tour told the participants they would be biking 75 km the first day, 83 km the second day, and 78 km the third day. How many miles did John and Sandy bike in those three days?

59. ***Fuel Consumption*** Pierre had a Jeep imported into France. During a trip from Paris to Lyon, he used 38 litres of gas. The tank, which he had filled before starting the trip, holds 15 gallons of gas. How many litres of gas were left in the tank when he arrived?

60. ***Drinking Water*** It is recommended that each visitor to Death Valley, California, have 2 gallons of drinking water available. Rachel brought six 1-litre bottles of water. Does she have the recommended amount? Why?

61. ***Weight Records*** One of the heaviest males documented in medical records weighed 635 kg in 1978. What would have been his weight in pounds?

62. ***Weight of a Child*** The average weight for a 7-year-old girl is 22.2 kilograms. What is the average weight in pounds?

63. ***Male Height Record*** According to the Guinness Book of World Records, the tallest male reached a height of 2.72 m. What would his height be in feet?

64. ***Female Height Record*** According to the Guinness Book of World Records, the tallest female reached a height of 2.31 m. What would her height be in feet?

65. ***Australia Rock Climbing*** Tourists who visit Ayers Rock in central Australia in the summer begin climbing at 4 A.M., when the temperature is 19° Celsius. They do this because after 7 A.M., the temperature can reach 45 °C and can cause climbers to die of dehydration. What are equivalent Fahrenheit temperatures?

66. ***Medication*** A prescription label says that a medication should be stored at room temperature, which is between 15 °C and 30 °C. What is this temperature range in Fahrenheit?

67. ***Biology*** There are 96 550 km of blood vessels in the human body. How many miles of blood vessels is this?

68. ***Earth Science*** The distance around the Earth at the equator (the circumference) is approximately 40 325 km. How many miles is this?

Round to four decimal places.

▲**69.** 28 square inches = ? square centimetres

▲**70.** 36 square metres = ? square yards

To Think About

▲**71.** ***Geometry*** Frederick Himlein is planning to carpet his rectangular living room, which measures 8 metres by 4 metres. He has found some carpet in Toronto that he likes that costs \$28 per square metre. While visiting family friends in New York City, his wife Gertrude found some carpet that costs \$30 per square yard. The company has a Toronto office and can sell it in Canada for the same price. Frederick says that the American carpet is much too expensive. How much would it cost to carpet the living room with the Canadian carpet? How much would it cost to carpet the living room with the American carpet? How much difference in cost is there between these two choices? (Round to the nearest dollar.)

▲**72.** ***Geometry*** Phillipe Bertoude is planning to carpet his rectangular family room, which measures 7 metres by 5 metres. His wife found some carpet in Ottawa that she likes, and it costs \$28 per square metre. While Phillipe was visiting his father in Baltimore, he found some carpet that costs \$26 per square yard. The company has an Ottawa office and can sell it in Canada for the same price. Phillipe told his wife that the carpet from Baltimore was a better buy. She does not agree. How much would it cost to carpet the family room with the Canadian carpet? How much would it cost to carpet the family room with the American carpet? How much difference in cost is there between these two choices? (Round to the nearest dollar.)

Quick Quiz 4 Round to the nearest hundredth when necessary.

1. Convert 5 ounces to grams.

2. Convert 24 kilometres to miles.

3. Convert 6 litres to quarts.

4. Concept Check Explain how you would convert a speed of 65 miles per hour to a speed in kilometres per hour.

Section 5 Solving Applied Measurement Problems

Student Learning Objective

After studying this section, you will be able to:

 **Solve applied problems involving metric and U.S. customary units.**

 Solving Applied Problems Involving Metric and U.S. Customary Units

Once again, we will be using the Mathematics Blueprint for solving applied problems that we used previously.

EXAMPLE 1 A triangular support piece holds a solar panel. The sketch shows the dimensions of the triangle. Find the perimeter of this triangle. Express the answer in *feet*.

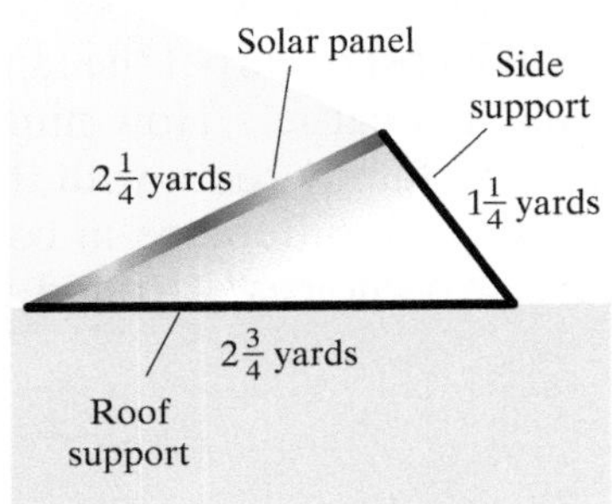

Solution

Mathematics Blueprint for Problem Solving

Gather the Facts	What Am I Asked to Do?	How Do I Proceed?	Key Points to Remember
The triangle has three sides: $2\frac{1}{4}$ yd, $1\frac{1}{4}$ yd, and $2\frac{3}{4}$ yd.	Find the perimeter.	Add the lengths of the three sides. Then change the answer from yards to feet.	Be sure to change the number of yards to an improper fraction before multiplying by 3 to obtain feet.

1. ***Understand the problem.*** The perimeter is the sum of the lengths of the sides. Remember to convert the yards to feet.
2. ***Solve and state the answer.***
   Add the three sides.

$$\begin{array}{r} 2\frac{1}{4}\text{ yards} \\ 1\frac{1}{4}\text{ yards} \\ +\ 2\frac{3}{4}\text{ yards} \\ \hline 5\frac{5}{4}\text{ yards} \end{array} = 6\frac{1}{4}\text{ yards}$$

   Convert $6\frac{1}{4}$ yards to feet using the fact that 1 yard = 3 feet. To make the calculation easier, we will change $6\frac{1}{4}$ to $\frac{25}{4}$.

$$6\frac{1}{4}\,\cancel{\text{yards}} \times \frac{3\text{ feet}}{1\,\cancel{\text{yard}}} = \frac{25}{4}\,\cancel{\text{yards}} \times \frac{3\text{ feet}}{1\,\cancel{\text{yard}}} = \frac{75}{4}\text{ feet} = 18\frac{3}{4}\text{ feet}$$

   The perimeter of the triangle is $18\frac{3}{4}$ feet.
3. ***Check.*** We will check by estimating the answer.

$$2\frac{1}{4}\text{ yd} \approx 2\text{ yd} \qquad 1\frac{1}{4}\text{ yd} \approx 1\text{ yd} \qquad 2\frac{3}{4}\text{ yd} \approx 3\text{ yd}$$

   Now we add the three sides, using our estimated values.

$$2 + 1 + 3 = 6\text{ yards} \qquad 6\text{ yards} = 18\text{ feet}$$

   Our estimated answer, 18 feet, is close to our calculated answer, $18\frac{3}{4}$ feet. Thus our answer seems reasonable. ✓

▲ **Practice Problem 1** Find the perimeter of the rectangle on the right. Express the answer in *feet*.

$2\frac{2}{3}$ yd

$8\frac{1}{3}$ yd $8\frac{1}{3}$ yd

$2\frac{2}{3}$ yd

EXAMPLE 2 How many 210-*litre* gasoline barrels can be filled from a tank of 5.04 *kilolitres* of gasoline?

Solution

1. *Understand the problem.*

Mathematics Blueprint for Problem Solving

Gather the Facts	What Am I Asked to Do?	How Do I Proceed?	Key Points to Remember
We have 5.04 kilolitres of gasoline. We are going to divide the gasoline into smaller barrels that hold 210 litres each.	Find out how many of these smaller 210-litre barrels can be filled.	We need to get all measurements in the same units. We choose to convert 5.04 kilolitres to litres. Then we divide that result by 210 to find out how many barrels can be filled.	To convert 5.04 kilolitres to litres, we move the decimal point three places to the right.

2. *Solve and state the answer.* First we convert 5.04 kilolitres to litres.

$$5.04 \text{ kilolitres} = 5040 \text{ litres}$$

Now we find out how many barrels can be filled. How many 210-litre barrels will 5040 litres fill? Visualize fitting 210-litre barrels into a big barrel that holds 5040 litres. (Use rectangular barrels.)

We need to divide

$$\frac{5040 \text{ litres}}{210 \text{ litres}} = 24.$$

Thus we can fill 24 of the 210-litre barrels.

3. *Check.* Estimate each value. First 5.04 kilolitres is approximately 5 kilolitres or 5000 litres. 210-litre barrels hold approximately 200 litres. How many times does 200 fit into 5000?

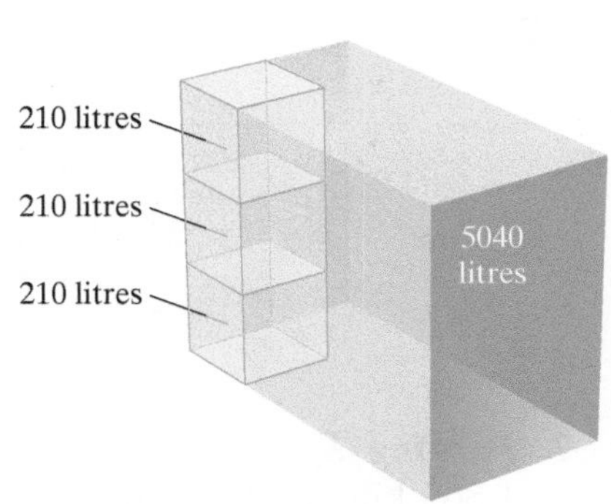

$$\frac{5000}{200} = 25$$

We estimate that 25 barrels can be filled. This is very close to our calculated value of 24 barrels. Thus our answer is reasonable. ✓

Practice Problem 2 A lab assistant must use 18.06 litres of solution to fill 42 jars. How many millilitres of the solution will go into each jar?

Section 5 Exercises

Applications *Solve. Round to the nearest hundredth when necessary.*

▲ **1.** Find the perimeter of the triangle. Express your answer in feet.

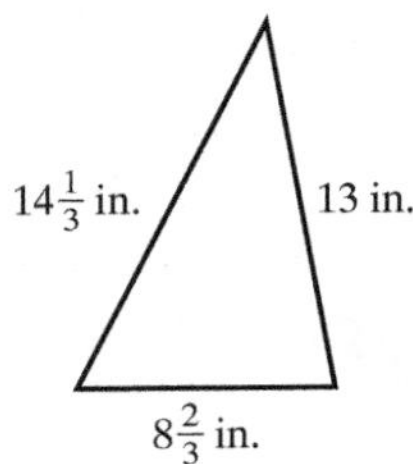

▲ **2.** Find the perimeter of the triangle. Express your answer in feet.

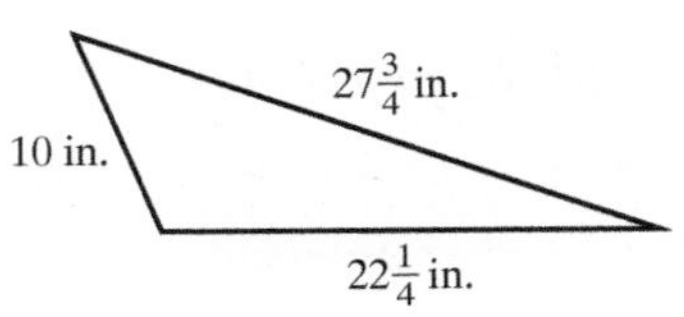

▲ **3.** ***Petting Zoo Fence*** At the county fair, a triangular area is being fenced for a petting zoo. One side is 42 yards long and a second side is 65 yards long. If there are 480 feet of fencing available, how much is left for the third side? Express your answer in yards.

▲ **4.** ***Farm Fencing*** A farmer has 630 feet of fencing to fence in a triangular area for his pigs. One side will be 85 yards and a second side will be 70 yards. How much fencing will the farmer have left for the third side? Express your answer in yards.

▲ **5.** ***Doorway Insulation*** A rectangular doorway measures 90 centimetres × 200 centimetres. Weatherstripping is applied on the top and the two sides. The weatherstripping costs \$6.00 per metre. What did it cost to weatherstrip the door?

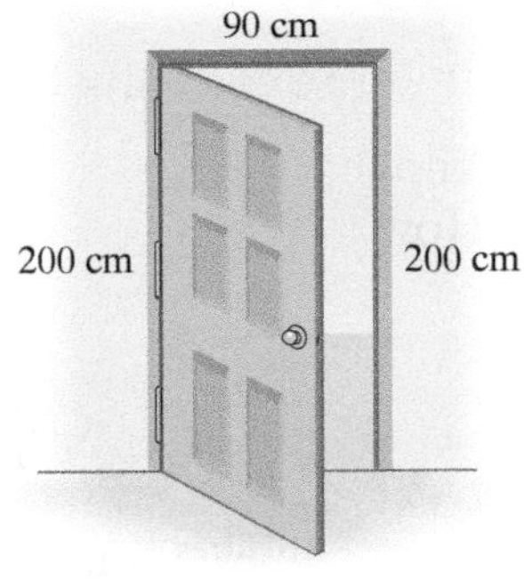

▲ **6.** ***Window Insulation*** A rectangular picture window measures 87 centimetres × 152 centimetres. Window insulation is applied along all four sides. The insulation costs \$7.00 per metre. What will it cost to insulate the window?

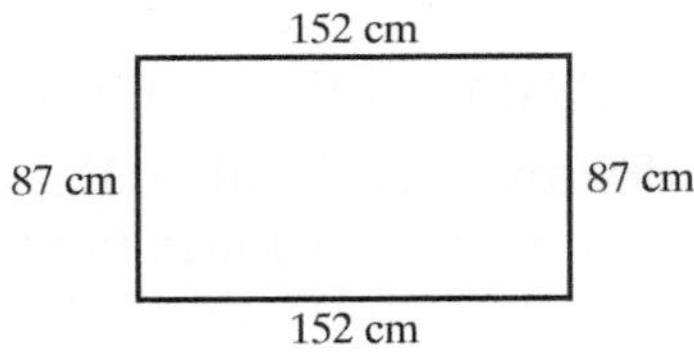

7. ***Parking Space Dimensions*** A stretch of road 1.863 kilometres long has 230 parking spaces of equal length painted in white on the pavement. How many metres long is each parking space?

8. ***Leather Horse Equipment*** A tack supply company, which makes saddles, fittings, bridles, and other equipment for horses and riders, has a length of braided leather 12.4 metres long. The leather must be cut into 4 equal pieces. How many centimetres long will each piece be?

9. ***Track and Field*** When Gary's father was in high school, he ran the 880 yd run. Gary is on the high school track team and is training for the 800 m race. Which distance is longer? By how much?

10. ***Hair Length*** The world record for the longest hair is about 18.5 ft. How many metres is this?

11. ***Gasoline Prices*** Don drove his car from Winnipeg, Manitoba, to Detroit, Michigan. The price of gasoline in Michigan is $3.20 per gallon. In Manitoba, the price is $0.89 per litre. Where is gasoline more expensive?

12. ***Food Costs*** Kimberly lives in New Zealand, where bananas sell for $0.80 per kilogram. While visiting her sister in Texas, she noticed that bananas were $0.39 per pound. Where are bananas more expensive?

13. ***Temperature*** While travelling in Scotland, Jenny noticed a high temperature one day of 25 °C. What is the equivalent temperature in the Fahrenheit system? Jenny called her husband in Boston and found that the high temperature in Boston the same day was 86 °F. How much hotter was Boston than Scotland that day?

14. ***Temperature*** The temperature in Baghdad, Iraq, today is 39 °C. The temperature on this date last year was 95 °F. What is the difference in degrees Fahrenheit between the temperature in Baghdad today and the temperature one year ago?

15. ***Cooking*** A Swedish flight attendant is heating passenger meals for the new American airline he is working for. He is used to heating meals at 180 °C. His co-worker tells him that the food must be heated at 350 °F. What is the difference in temperature in degrees Fahrenheit between the two temperatures? Which temperature is hotter?

16. ***Temperature*** The weather page in an American newspaper listed 111 °F as the temperature one day in New Delhi, India. This country uses the Celsius scale. How would an Indian report the temperature? That same day, the high temperature in Oslo, Norway, was 14 °C. How much cooler was Oslo than New Delhi on that day?

17. ***Car Travel*** Sharon and James Hanson travelled from Pittsburgh, U.S., to Nova Scotia. The last day of their trip, they travelled 520 miles and it took them eight hours. The maximum speed limit is 110 kilometres per hour.

(a) How many kilometres per hour did they average on the last day of the trip?

(b) Did they break the speed limit?

18. ***Jet Travel*** A small corporate jet travels at 600 kilometres per hour for 1.5 hours. The pilot says the plane will be on time if it travels at 350 miles per hour.

(a) What is the jet's speed in miles per hour?

(b) Will it arrive on time?

19. ***U.S. Concession Stand Sales*** The concession stand at an American high school sells large 1-pint sodas. On an average night, two sodas are sold each minute. How many gallons of soda are sold per hour?

20. ***Leaky Faucet*** On May 1, Frank placed an empty bucket under his dripping faucet. After one day, a quart of water had dripped into the bucket. If Frank doesn't fix the faucet until June 1, how many gallons of water will have dripped out?

21. ***U.S. Tax on Trucks*** Trucks in Sam's home state are taxed each year at $0.03 per pound. Sam's empty truck weighs 1.8 tons. What is his annual tax?

22. ***Banana Shipment*** 3.4 tons of bananas are off-loaded from a ship that has just arrived from Costa Rica. The port taxes imported fruit at $0.015 per pound. What is the tax on the entire shipment?

23. ***Raisin Bran*** There are 708 g of cereal in a family-size box of Raisin Bran. The box contains 12 servings. How many ounces is one serving?

24. ***Canned Fruit*** A can of peaches contains 16 ounces. Fred discovered that 5 ounces were syrup and the rest was fruit. How many grams of fruit were in the can?

25. ***Tree Insecticide*** Carlos is mixing a fruit tree spray to retard the damage caused by beetles. He has 16 quarts of spray concentrate available. The old recipe he used in Mexico called for 11 litres of spray concentrate.

(a) How many extra quarts of spray concentrate does he have?

(b) If the spray costs $2.89 per quart, how much will it cost him to prepare the old recipe?

26. ***Motor Oil Consumption*** Maria bought 18 litres of motor oil for $2.75 per litre. Her uncle from the U.S. will be visiting this summer. He said he will use 12 quarts of the oil while driving his car this summer.

(a) How many extra litres of oil did Maria buy?

(b) How much did this extra oil cost her?

27. ***Fuel Efficiency*** Jackson's small motorcycle gets 56 kilometres per litre. He drives 392 kilometres to Québec City and gas is $1.09 per litre.

(a) How much does the gas used for the trip cost?

(b) How many miles per gallon does Jackson's motorcycle get?

28. ***Fuel Efficiency*** Ryan's Volvo station wagon runs on diesel fuel. He gets 25 miles per gallon on the highway.

(a) If he drives 275 kilometres to Mexico City, and diesel fuel costs $4.90 per gallon, how much does the fuel used for the trip cost him? Round to the nearest cent.

(b) How many kilometres per litre does he get?

29. ***Discharge Rate at a Dam*** The flow rate of a safety discharge pipe at a dam in Lowell, Massachusetts, is rated for a maximum of 240 000 gallons per hour. The inspector asked if this flow rate could have handled the floods of 1927. During the floods of 1927 the flow rate at the dam was measured as 440 pints per second. Could the safety discharge pipe safely handle a flow rate of 440 pints per second? Why?

30. ***Water Reservoir*** The old main lines that run water from the Glenmore Reservoir to Calgary have some leaks. It is estimated that the lines leak approximately 36 000 litres per hour. A U.S. newspaper said that the lines leak 20 pints per second. Did the newspaper have the correct information? Why?

Quick Quiz 5 Round each answer to the nearest tenth if necessary.

1. In Switzerland, John and Nancy Tobey rode the mountain train to the top of the Jungfrau. The guide said it would be 28 °F at the top of the mountain. The outdoor thermometer actually read 2 °C. How close was the guide's prediction to the actual temperature? Indicate your answer in Fahrenheit.

2. A rectangular box measures 4 cm by 8 cm. What is the perimeter of the box in inches?

3. The speed limit on a Mexican road is 100 km/h. Maria is driving a distance of 45 miles. How long will it take her if she drives at the speed limit? Indicate your answer in minutes.

4. **Concept Check** Suppose you are reading a map that has a scale showing that 3 inches represents 6.5 miles on the ground. Explain how you would find out how many miles there are between two cities that are 5 inches apart on the map.

Putting Your Skills to Work: Use Math to Save Money

BALANCE YOUR FINANCES

A Personal Question for You

How often do you balance your chequebook? Once a day, once a week, never? One of the first steps in saving money is to determine your current spending trends. The first step in that process is learning to balance your finances. Consider the story of Teresa.

Keeping a Record of Deposits

Teresa balances her chequebook once a month when she receives her bank statement. Below is a table that records the deposits Teresa made for the month of May. The beginning balance for May was $300.50.

Date	Deposits
May 1	$200.00
May 3	$150.50
May 10	$120.25
May 25	$50.00
May 28	$25.00

Purestock/Superstock Royalty Free

Keeping a Record of Cheques

Below is a table that records each cheque that Teresa wrote for the month of May.

Date	Cheque Number	Cheques
May 2	102	$238.50
May 6	103	$75.00
May 12	104	$200.00
May 28	105	$28.56
May 30	106	$36.00

Finding the Facts

1. What is the total amount of her deposits?
2. What is the total amount of her cheques?
3. Based on the given information, will Teresa be able to cover all her cheques?
4. All cheques written before or on May 25 have cleared. What was her balance on May 25?
5. What should Teresa assume her balance to be at the beginning of June? (Hint: She should assume all the cheques and deposits for May will clear.)
6. If Teresa continues her current spending habits, what will happen?

Applying This Lesson to Your Life

Do you know your monthly income and how much you spend each month? Take that first step toward using math to help you save. Balance your chequebook and organize your deposits and expenses. Find out how much you earn and spend each month.

Module Organizer

Topic	Procedure	Examples
Changing from one U.S. customary unit to another.	**1.** Find the equality statement that relates what you want to find and what you know. **2.** Form a unit fraction. The denominator will contain the units of the original measurement. **3.** Multiply by the unit fraction and simplify.	Convert 210 inches to feet. **1.** Use 12 inches = 1 foot. **2.** Unit fraction $= \dfrac{1 \text{ foot}}{12 \text{ inches}}$ **3.** $210 \cancel{\text{in.}} \times \dfrac{1 \text{ ft}}{12 \cancel{\text{in.}}} = \dfrac{210}{12} \text{ ft}$ $= 17.5 \text{ ft}$ Convert 86 yards to feet. **1.** Use 1 yard = 3 feet. **2.** Unit fraction $= \dfrac{3 \text{ feet}}{1 \text{ yard}}$ **3.** $86 \cancel{\text{yd}} \times \dfrac{3 \text{ ft}}{1 \cancel{\text{yd}}} = 86 \times 3 \text{ ft} = 258 \text{ ft}$
Changing from one metric unit to another.	When you change from one prefix to another by moving to the *left* in the prefix guide, move the decimal point to the *left* the same number of places. kilo- = 1000, hecto- = 100, deca- = 10, one unit = 1, deci- = 0.1, centi- = 0.01, milli- = 0.001 When you change from one prefix to another by moving to the *right* in the prefix guide, move the decimal point to the *right* the same number of places.	Change 7.2 metres to kilometres. **1.** Move three decimal places to the left. 0.007.2 **2.** 7.2 m = 0.0072 km Change 196 centimetres to metres. **1.** Move two places to the left. 196. **2.** 196 cm = 1.96 m Change 17.3 litres to millilitres. **1.** Move three decimal places to the right. 17.300 **2.** 17.3 L = 17 300 mL
Changing from U.S. customary units to metric units.	**1.** From the list of approximate equivalent measures, pick an equality statement that begins with the unit in the original measurement. 1 mi ≈ 1.61 km 1 yd ≈ 0.914 m 1 ft ≈ 0.305 m 1 in. = 2.54 cm (exact) 1 gal ≈ 3.79 L 1 qt ≈ 0.946 L 1 lb ≈ 0.454 kg 1 oz ≈ 28.35 g **2.** Multiply by a unit fraction.	Convert 7 gallons to litres. **1.** 1 gal ≈ 3.79 L **2.** $7 \cancel{\text{gal}} \times \dfrac{3.79 \text{ L}}{1 \cancel{\text{gal}}} = 26.53 \text{ L}$ Convert 18 pounds to kilograms. **1.** 1 lb ≈ 0.454 kg **2.** $18 \cancel{\text{lb}} \times \dfrac{0.454 \text{ kg}}{1 \cancel{\text{lb}}} = 8.172 \text{ kg}$
Changing from metric units to U.S. customary units.	**1.** From the list of approximate equivalent measures, pick an equality statement that begins with the unit in the original measurement and ends with the unit you want. 1 km ≈ 0.62 mi 1 m ≈ 3.28 ft 1 m ≈ 1.09 yd 1 cm ≈ 0.394 in. 1 L ≈ 0.264 gal 1 L ≈ 1.06 qt 1 kg ≈ 2.2 lb 1 g ≈ 0.0353 oz **2.** Multiply by a unit fraction.	Convert 605 grams to ounces. **1.** 1 g ≈ 0.0353 oz **2.** $605 \cancel{\text{g}} \times \dfrac{0.0353 \text{ oz}}{1 \cancel{\text{g}}} = 21.3565 \text{ oz}$ Convert 80 km/h to miles per hour. **1.** 1 km ≈ 0.62 mi **2.** $80 \dfrac{\cancel{\text{km}}}{\text{h}} \times \dfrac{0.62 \text{ mi}}{1 \cancel{\text{km}}} = 49.6 \text{ mi/h}$

(*Continued on next page*)

Topic	Procedure	Examples
Changing from Celsius to Fahrenheit temperature.	**1.** To convert Celsius to Fahrenheit, we use the formula $F = 1.8 \times C + 32.$ **2.** We replace C by the Celsius temperature. **3.** We calculate to find the Fahrenheit temperature.	Convert 65 °C to Fahrenheit. **1.** $F = 1.8 \times C + 32$ **2.** $F = 1.8 \times 65 + 32$ **3.** $F = 117 + 32 = 149$ 65 °C is 149 °F.
Changing from Fahrenheit to Celsius temperature.	**1.** To convert Fahrenheit to Celsius, we use the formula $C = \dfrac{5 \times F - 160}{9}.$ **2.** We replace F by the Fahrenheit temperature. **3.** We calculate to find the Celsius temperature.	Convert 50 °F to Celsius. **1.** $C = \dfrac{5 \times F - 160}{9}$ **2.** $C = \dfrac{5 \times 50 - 160}{9}$ **3.** $C = \dfrac{250 - 160}{9} = \dfrac{90}{9} = 10$ 50 °F is 10 °C.

Module Review Problems

Section 1

Convert. When necessary, express your answer as a decimal. Round to the nearest hundredth.

1. 33 ft = ____ yd

2. 27 ft = ____ yd

3. 5 mi = ______ yd

4. 6 mi = _______ yd

5. 126 in. = _____ ft

6. 150 in. = _____ ft

7. 2.5 mi = _________ ft

8. 4 mi = __________ ft

9. 7 tons = _________ lb

10. 4 tons = _____ lb

11. 8 oz = _____ lb

12. 12 oz = _____ lb

13. 15 gal = ____ qt

14. 21 gal = _____ qt

15. 31 pt = _____ qt

16. 27 pt = _____ qt

Section 2

Convert. Do not round.

17. 56 cm = _____ mm

18. 29 cm = _____ mm

19. 1763 mm = _____ cm

20. 2598 mm = _______ cm

21. 13.25 m = _______ cm

22. 16.75 m = _______ cm

23. 10 000 m = _____ km

24. 8200 m = _____ km

Change all units to metres and add.

25. 6.2 m + 121 cm + 0.52 m

26. 9.8 m + 673 cm + 0.48 m

27. 0.024 km + 1.8 m + 983 cm

28. 0.078 km + 5.5 m + 609 cm

Section 3

Convert. Do not round.

29. 17 kL = ______ L

30. 23 kL = ______ L

31. 196 kg = ______ g

32. 721 kg = ______ g

33. 95 mg = ______ g

34. 78 mg = ______ g

35. 3500 g = _____ kg

36. 12 750 g = _____ kg

37. 765 cc = _____ mL

38. 423 cm^3 = _____ mL

39. 0.256 L = _____ cm^3

40. 0.922 L = _____ cc

Section 4

Perform each conversion. Round to the nearest hundredth.

41. 42 kg = _____ lb

42. 9 ft = _____ m

43. 45 mi = ______ km

44. 88 mi = ______ km

45. 14 cm = _____ in.

46. 18 cm = _____ in.

47. 20 lb = _____ kg

48. 30 lb = _____ kg

49. 50 yd = _____ m

50. 100 yd = _____ m

51. 80 km/h = _____ mi/h

52. 70 km/h = _____ mi/h

53. 12 °C = _____ F

54. 32 °C = _____ F

55. 221 °F = _____ C

56. 185 °F = _____ C

57. 32 °F = _____ C

58. 212 °F = _____ C

59. 13 L = _____ gallons

60. 27 quarts = _____ L

Section 5

Solve. Round to the nearest hundredth when necessary.

▲ **61.** ***Geometry*** Allison's living room measures 5 yd by 18 ft. What is the area of her living room in square feet? What is the area in square yards?

▲ **62.** Find the perimeter of the triangle.
(a) Express your answer in feet.
(b) Express your answer in inches.

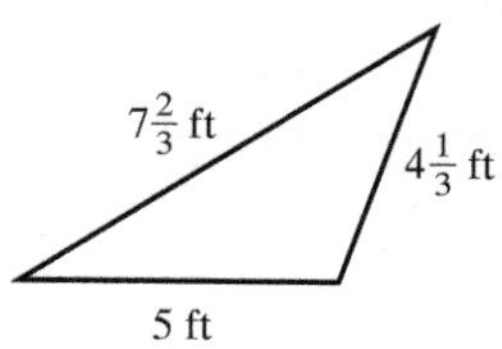

63. Find the perimeter of the rectangle.
(a) Express your answer in metres.
(b) Express your answer in kilometres

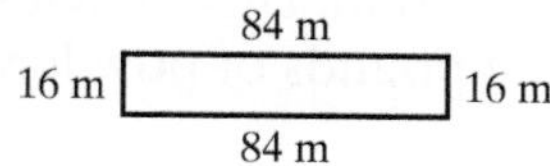

64. ***Food Cost*** The unit price on a box of Rice Krispies was $0.16 per ounce. The net weight was 510 grams. How much did the cereal cost?

65. ***Metric Conversion*** Lisa and Ray moved from Canada to the United States. For their new home, they need 15 metres of lumber to repair some stairs. They bought 45 feet at the lumberyard. Did they purchase enough lumber? How many feet extra or how short was this amount?

66. ***Metric Conversion*** Lucia is from Mexico, where distances are measured in kilometres. While in San Diego, she rented a car and drove 70 mi/h on the highway. In Mexico, she never drives faster than 100 km/h. Was she driving faster than this in San Diego?

67. ***Cooking*** A German cook wishes to bake a cake at 185° Celsius. The oven is set at 390° Fahrenheit. By how many degrees Fahrenheit is the oven temperature different from what is desired? Is the oven too hot or not hot enough?

68. ***Flagpole*** A flagpole is 19 metres long. The bottom $\frac{1}{5}$ of it is coated with a special water sealant before being placed in the ground. How many centimetres long is the portion that has the water sealant?

69. ***Horse Racing*** In January 2005, a horse named Mr. Light set a record time for the mile, finishing in 91.41 seconds. What was the horse's speed in miles per hour?

70. ***Horse Racing*** In July 1969, a horse named Petrone set a record time for two miles, finishing in 198 seconds. What was the horse's speed in miles per hour?

71. ***Mountain Hike*** Marcia and Melissa went up the Gatineau Park hiking trail each carrying a backpack tent that weighed 2.2 kg, a canteen with water that weighed 1.4 kg, and some supplies that weighed 3.8 kg. They were told to carry less than 16 pounds while hiking. How close were they to the limit? Did they succeed in carrying less than the weight limit?

72. ***Gasoline Cost*** When buying gas in Canada, Greg Salzman was told by the attendant that in U.S. currency he was paying $1.05 per litre. How much did the gas cost per gallon?

73. ***Car Interior Measurements*** The Dodge Caravan that is made in Canada is built to accommodate a person who is 1.88 metres tall. A person who is taller than this will not be comfortable. Would a person who is 6 feet 2 inches tall be comfortable in this car?

▲ **74.** ***Geometry*** The driveway of Sir Arthur Jensen in London is 4 metres wide and 12 metres long. How many square feet of sealer does he need to cover his driveway?

75. ***Food Cost*** While travelling through Berlin, Al Dundtreim purchased some powdered milk for $1.23 per kilogram. How much would it have cost him to buy 4 pounds of powdered milk?

How Am I Doing? Module Test

Convert. *Express your answer as a decimal rounded to the nearest hundredth when necessary.*

1. 1.6 tons = ____ lb

2. 19 ft = ____ in.

3. 21 gal = ____ qt

4. 36 960 ft = ____ mi

5. 1800 sec = ____ min

6. 3 cups = ____ qt

7. 8 oz = ____ lb

8. 5.5 yd = ____ ft

Perform each conversion. *Do not round.*

9. 9.2 km = ____ m

10. 9.88 cm = ____ m

11. 46 mm = ____ cm

12. 12.7 m = ____ cm

13. 0.936 cm = ____ mm

14. 46 L = ____ kL

15. 28.9 mg = ____ g

16. 983 g = ____ kg

17. 0.92 L = ____ mL

18. 9.42 g = ____ mg

Perform each conversion. *Round to the nearest hundredth when necessary.*

19. 42 mi = ____ km

20. 1.78 yd = ____ m

21. 9 cm = ____ in.

22. 30 km = ____ mi

23. 7.3 kg = ____ lb

24. 3 oz = ____ g

1. ____________
2. ____________
3. ____________
4. ____________
5. ____________
6. ____________
7. ____________
8. ____________
9. ____________
10. ____________
11. ____________
12. ____________
13. ____________
14. ____________
15. ____________
16. ____________
17. ____________
18. ____________
19. ____________
20. ____________
21. ____________
22. ____________
23. ____________
24. ____________

25. ______

26. ______

27. (a) ______

(b) ______

28. (a) ______

(b) ______

29. ______

30. (a) ______

(b) ______

31. ______

32. ______

Solve. *Round to the nearest hundredth when necessary.*

25. 15 gallons = ____ L

26. 3 L = ____ quarts

▲**27.** A rectangular picture frame measures 3 m × 7 m.

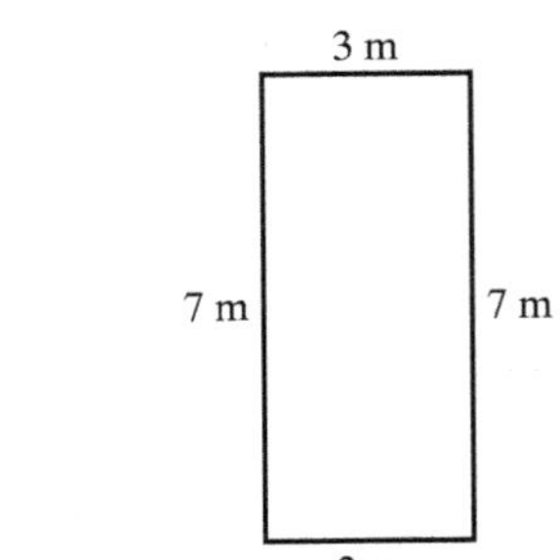

(a) What is the perimeter of the picture frame in metres?

(b) What is the perimeter of the picture frame in yards?

28. The temperature is 80 °F today. Kristen's computer has a warning not to operate above 35 °C.

(a) How many degrees Fahrenheit are there between the two temperatures?

(b) Can she use her computer today?

29. A pump is running at 5.5 quarts per minute. How many gallons per hour is this?

30. The speed limit on a Canadian road is 100 km/h.

(a) How far can Samuel travel at this speed limit in three hours?

(b) If Samuel has to travel 200 miles, how much farther will he need to go after three hours of driving at 100 km/h?

31. Rick bought 1 lb 6 oz of bananas, 2 lb 2 oz of grapes, and 1 lb 12 oz of plums. How many pounds of fruit did he buy?

32. The warmest day this year in Acapulco, Mexico, was 40 °C. What was the Fahrenheit temperature?

Solutions to Practice Problems

Section 1 Practice Problems

1. (a) 3 **(b)** 5280 **(c)** 60 **(d)** 7 **(e)** 16 **(f)** 2 **(g)** 4

2. $15\,840 \text{ feet} \times \dfrac{1 \text{ mile}}{5280 \text{ feet}} = \dfrac{15\,840 \text{ miles}}{5280} = 3 \text{ miles}$

3. (a) $18.93 \text{ miles} \times \dfrac{5280 \text{ feet}}{1 \text{ mile}} = 99\,950.4 \text{ feet}$

(b) $16\frac{1}{2} \text{ inches} \times \dfrac{1 \text{ yard}}{36 \text{ inches}} = \dfrac{33}{2} \times \dfrac{1}{36} \text{ yard}$

$= \dfrac{\overset{11}{\cancel{33}}}{2} \times \dfrac{1}{\underset{12}{\cancel{36}}} \text{ yard} = \dfrac{11}{24} \text{ yard}$

4. $760.5 \text{ pounds} \times \dfrac{16 \text{ ounces}}{1 \text{ pound}} = 760.5 \times 16 \text{ ounces} = 12\,168 \text{ ounces}$

5. $19 \text{ pints} \times \dfrac{1 \text{ quart}}{2 \text{ pints}} = \dfrac{19}{2} \text{ quarts} = 9.5 \text{ quarts}$

6. Step 1: $26 \text{ yards} \times \dfrac{3 \text{ feet}}{1 \text{ yard}} = 26 \times 3 \text{ feet} = 78 \text{ feet}$

Step 2: 78 feet + 2 feet = 80 feet
The path is 80 feet long.

7. Step 1: $1\frac{3}{4} \text{ days} \times \dfrac{24 \text{ hours}}{1 \text{ day}} = \dfrac{7}{4} \times \dfrac{24}{1} \text{ hours} = 42 \text{ hours parked}$

Step 2: $42 \text{ hours} \times \dfrac{1.50 \text{ dollars}}{1 \text{ hour}} = 63 \text{ dollars}$

She paid $63.

Section 2 Practice Problems

1. (a) deca- means ten **(b)** milli- means thousandth

2. (a) 4 metres = 4.00‸ centimetres = 400 cm

(b) 30 centimetres = 30.0‸ millimetres = 300 mm

3. (a) 3 millimetres = 0‸003. metre = 0.003 metre

(b) 47 centimetres = 0‸00047. kilometre = 0.000 47 kilometre

4. The car length would logically be choice **(b)** 3.8 metres.

5. (a) 375 cm = 3‸75 m = 3.75 m

(b) 46 m = 46.000‸ mm = 46 000 mm

6. (a) 389 mm = 0.0389 dam (four places to left)
(b) 0.48 hm = 4800 cm (four places to right)

7.

782 cm	=	7.82 m
2 m	=	2.00 m
537 m	=	537.00 m
		546.82 m

Section 3 Practice Problems

1. (a) 5 L = 5.000‸ mL = 5000 mL

(b) 84 kL = 84.000‸ L = 84 000 L

(c) 0.732 L = 0.732‸ mL = 732 mL

2. (a) 15.8 mL = 0.0158 L **(b)** 12 340 mL = 12.34 L
(c) 86.3 L = 0.0863 kL

3. (a) 396 mL = 396 cm^3
(because 1 millilitre = 1 cubic centimetre)
(b) 0.096 L = 96 cm^3 = 96 cc

4. (a) 3.2 t = 3200 kg **(b)** 7.08 kg = 7080 g

5. (a) 59 kg = 0.059 t **(b)** 28.3 mg = 0.0283 g

6. A gram is $\frac{1}{1000}$ of a kilogram. If the coffee costs $10.00 per kilogram, then 1 gram would cost $\frac{1}{1000}$ of $10.

$\dfrac{1}{1000} \times \$10 = \dfrac{\$10.00}{1000} = \$0.01$

The coffee costs $0.01 per gram.

7. (a) 120 kg (A kilogram is slightly more than 2 pounds.)

Section 4 Practice Problems

1. $7 \text{ feet} \times \dfrac{0.305 \text{ metre}}{1 \text{ foot}} \approx 2.135 \text{ metres}$

2. (a) $17 \text{ m} \times \dfrac{1.09 \text{ yd}}{1 \text{ m}} \approx 18.53 \text{ yd}$

(b) $29.6 \text{ km} \times \dfrac{0.62 \text{ mi}}{1 \text{ km}} \approx 18.352 \text{ mi}$

(c) $26 \text{ gal} \times \dfrac{3.79 \text{ L}}{1 \text{ gal}} \approx 98.54 \text{ L}$

(d) $6.2 \text{ L} \times \dfrac{1.06 \text{ qt}}{1 \text{ L}} \approx 6.572 \text{ qt}$

3. $180 \text{ cm} \times \dfrac{0.394 \text{ in.}}{1 \text{ cm}} \times \dfrac{1 \text{ ft}}{12 \text{ in.}} = 5.91 \text{ ft}$

4. $\dfrac{88 \text{ km}}{1 \text{ h}} \times \dfrac{0.62 \text{ mi}}{1 \text{ km}} = 54.56 \text{ mi/h}$

5. $\dfrac{900 \text{ miles}}{1 \text{ h}} \times \dfrac{5280 \text{ ft}}{1 \text{ mile}} \times \dfrac{1 \text{ h}}{60 \text{ min}} \times \dfrac{1 \text{ min}}{60 \text{ s}}$

$= \dfrac{900 \times 5280 \text{ ft}}{60 \times 60 \text{ s}} = \dfrac{4\,752\,000 \text{ ft}}{3600 \text{ s}}$

$= 1320 \text{ ft/s}$

The jet is travelling at 1320 feet per second.

6. $F = 1.8 \times C + 32$
$= 1.8 \times 20 + 32$
$= 36 + 32$
$= 68$

The temperature is 68 °F.

7. $C = \dfrac{5 \times F - 160}{9}$

$= \dfrac{5 \times 86 - 160}{9}$

$= \dfrac{430 - 160}{9}$

$= \dfrac{270}{9}$

$= 30$

The temperature is 30 °C.

Section 5 Practice Problems

Practice Problem 1

Step 1:

$2\frac{2}{3}$ yd
$8\frac{1}{3}$ yd
$2\frac{2}{3}$ yd
$+\ 8\frac{1}{3}$ yd
22 yd

Step 2: $22 \text{ yd} \times \dfrac{3 \text{ ft}}{1 \text{ yd}} = 66 \text{ ft}$

The perimeter is 66 ft.

Practice Problem 2

1. ***Understand the problem.***

Mathematics Blueprint for Problem Solving			
Gather the Facts	**What Am I Asked to Do?**	**How Do I Proceed?**	**Key Points to Remember**
He must use 18.06 litres of solution. He has 42 jars to fill.	Find out how many millilitres of solution will go into each jar.	We need to convert 18.06 litres to millilitres, and then divide that result by 42.	To convert 18.06 litres to millilitres, we move the decimal point three places to the right.

2. ***Solve and state the answer:***

(a) 18.06 L = 18 060 mL

(b) $\frac{18\,060 \text{ mL}}{42 \text{ jars}} = 430 \text{ mL/jar}$

Thus, 430 mL of solution will go into each jar.

3. ***Check.*** 18.06 L is approximately 18 L, or 18 000 mL.

$\frac{18\,000}{40} = 450$

The answer is reasonable.

Glossary

Celsius temperature (Section 4) A temperature scale in which water boils at 100 degrees (100 °C) and freezes at 0 degrees (0 °C). To convert Celsius temperature to Fahrenheit, we use the helpful formula $F = 1.8 \times C + 32$.

Centimetre (Section 2) A unit of length commonly used in the metric system to measure small distances. 1 centimetre = 0.01 metre.

Cubic centimetre (Section 3) A metric measurement of volume equal to 1 millilitre.

Cup (Section 1) One of the smallest units of volume in the U.S. customary system. 2 cups = 1 pint.

Decametre (Section 2) A unit of length not commonly used in the metric system. 1 decametre = 10 metres.

Decimetre (Section 2) A unit of length not commonly used in the metric system. 1 decimetre = 0.1 metre.

Fahrenheit temperature (Section 4) A temperature scale in which water boils at 212 degrees (212 °F) and freezes at 32 degrees (32 °F). To convert Fahrenheit temperature to Celsius, we use the formula $C = \dfrac{5 \times F - 160}{9}$.

Foot (Section 1) U.S. customary system unit of length. 3 feet = 1 yard. 12 inches = 1 foot.

Gallon (Section 1) A unit of volume in the U.S. customary system. 4 quarts = 1 gallon.

Gigametre (Section 2) A metric unit of length equal to 1 000 000 000 metres.

Gram (Section 3) The basic unit of weight in the metric system. A gram is defined as the weight of the water in a box that is 1 centimetre on each side. 1 gram = 1000 milligrams. 1 gram = 0.001 kilogram.

Hectometre (Section 2) A unit of length not commonly used in the metric system. 1 hectometre = 100 metres.

Inch (Section 1) The smallest unit of length in the U.S. customary system. 12 inches = 1 foot.

Kilogram (Section 3) The most commonly used metric unit of weight. 1 kilogram = 1000 grams. 1000 kilograms = 1 tonne.

Kilolitre (Section 3) The metric unit of volume normally used to measure large volumes. 1 kilolitre = 1000 litres.

Kilometre (Section 2) The unit of length commonly used in the metric system to measure large distances. 1 kilometre = 1000 metres.

Litre (Section 3) The standard metric measurement of volume. 1 litre = 1000 millilitres. 1 litre = 0.001 kilolitre.

Megametre (Section 2) A metric unit of length equal to 1 000 000 metres.

Metre (Section 2) The basic unit of length in the metric system. 1 metre = 1000 millimetres. 1 metre = 0.001 kilometre.

Microgram (Section 3) A metric unit of weight equal to 0.000 001 gram.

Micrometre (Section 2) A metric unit of length equal to 0.000 001 metre.

Mile (Section 1) Largest unit of length in the U.S. customary system. 5280 feet = 1 mile. 1760 yards = 1 mile.

Milligram (Section 3) A metric unit of weight used for very, very small objects. 1 milligram = 0.001 gram.

Millilitre (Section 3) The metric unit of volume normally used to measure small volumes. 1 millilitre = 0.001 litre.

Millimetre (Section 2) A unit of length commonly used in the metric system to measure very small distances. 1 millimetre = 0.001 metre.

Nanogram (Section 3) A unit of weight equal to 0.000 000 001 gram.

Nanometre (Section 2) A metric unit of length equal to 0.000 000 001 metre.

Ounce (Section 1) Smallest unit of weight in the U.S. customary system. 16 ounces = 1 pound.

Picogram (Section 3) A unit of weight equal to 0.000 000 000 001 gram.

Pint (Section 1) Unit of volume in the U.S. customary system. 2 pints = 1 quart.

Pound (Section 1) Basic unit of weight in the U.S. customary system. 2000 pounds = 1 ton. 16 ounces = 1 pound.

Quart (Section 1) Unit of volume in the U.S. customary system. 4 quarts = 1 gallon.

Ton (Section 1) A U.S. customary unit used to measure heavy weights. 1 ton = 2000 pounds.

Tonne (Section 3) A metric unit of measurement for very heavy weights. 1 tonne = 1 000 000 grams.

Unit fraction (Section 1) A fraction used to change one unit to another. For example, to change 180 centimetres to metres, we multiply by the unit fraction $\dfrac{1 \text{ metre}}{100 \text{ centimetres}}$. Thus we have

$$180 \text{ centimetres} \times \frac{1 \text{ metre}}{100 \text{ centimetres}} = 1.8 \text{ metres}.$$

Answers to Selected Exercises for Measurement

Answers to Selected Exercises for Measurement

Section 1 Exercises **1.** We know that each mile is 5280 feet. Each foot is 12 inches. So we know that one mile is $5280 \times 12 = 63\,360$ inches. The unit fraction we want is $\frac{63\,360 \text{ inches}}{1 \text{ mile}}$. So we multiply 23 miles $\times \frac{63\,360 \text{ inches}}{1 \text{ mile}}$. The mile unit divides out. We obtain 1 457 280 inches. Thus 23 miles = 1 457 280 inches. **3.** 1760 **5.** 2000 **7.** 4 **9.** 2 **11.** 7 **13.** 9 **15.** 108 **17.** 2 **19.** 12 320 **21.** 48 **23.** 12 **25.** 128 **27.** 68 **29.** 11 **31.** 16 **33.** 0.5 **35.** 6.25 **37.** 30 **39.** 36 **41.** 5.5 **43.** 138 336 feet **45.** 6.79 miles **47.** $9.75 **49.** **(a)** 142 inches **(b)** $85.20 **51.** 28 800 cups **53.** ≈ 12 000 yards **55.** ≈ 6 miles

Quick Quiz 1 **1.** 7000 pounds **2.** 13.5 feet **3.** 1.5 pounds **4.** See Instructor

To Think About **1.** 18 000 **2.** 26 000 **3.** 0.000 017 **4.** 0.000 038 **5.** 1 200 000 000 **6.** 528 000 000 **7.** 78 900 **8.** 24 900 000 000

Section 2 Exercises **1.** hecto- **3.** deci- **5.** kilo- **7.** 460 **9.** 2610 **11.** 12.5 **13.** 0.0732 **15.** 200 000 **17.** 0.078 **19.** 3.5; 0.035 **21.** 4500; 450 000 **23.** b **25.** c **27.** a **29.** a **31.** b **33.** 39 **35.** 8000 **37.** 0.482 **39.** 3255 m **41.** 183.2 cm **43.** 63.5 cm **45.** 2.5464 cm or 25.464 mm **47.** 3.23 m **49.** 939.86 m **51.** 0.964 **53.** false **55.** true **57.** true **59.** false **61.** **(a)** 481 800 cm **(b)** 4.818 km **63.** 0.000 000 002 54 **65.** 134 000 m **67.** 0.278 megametre **69.** 210.8 mi

Quick Quiz 2 **1.** 4590 cm **2.** 0.283 mm **3.** 5.16 km **4.** See Instructor

Section 3 Exercises **1.** 1 kL **3.** 1 mg **5.** 1 g **7.** 9000 **9.** 12 000 **11.** 0.0189 **13.** 0.752 **15.** 5 652 000 **17.** 82 **19.** 0.024 418 **21.** 74 000 **23.** 0.216 **25.** 0.035 **27.** 6.328 **29.** 2920 **31.** 2400 **33.** 0.007; 0.000 007 **35.** 0.084; 0.000 084 **37.** 33; 33 000 **39.** 2580; 2 580 000 **41.** b **43.** a **45.** 83 L + 0.822 L + 30.1 L = 113.922 L or 113 922 mL **47.** 20 g + 0.052 g + 1500 g = 1520.052 g or 1 520 052 mg **49.** true **51.** false **53.** false **55.** true **57.** $71.92 **59.** $340 000 **61.** 1 200 000 000 tonnes **63.** 17 200 000 000 000 kg **65.** about 17 300 000 000 tonnes

Quick Quiz 3 **1.** 0.671 kg **2.** 8520 mL **3.** 0.045 62 g **4.** See Instructor

How Am I Doing? Sections 1–3 **1.** 16 (obj. 1.2) **2.** 6 (obj. 1.2) **3.** 5280 (obj. 1.2) **4.** 3.2 (obj. 1.2) **5.** 1320 (obj. 1.2) **6.** 40 (obj. 1.2) **7.** $15.30 (obj. 1.2) **8.** 6750 (obj. 2.2) **9.** 7390 (obj. 2.2) **10.** 340 (obj. 2.2) **11.** 0.027 (obj. 2.2) **12.** 529.6 (obj. 2.2) **13.** 0.482 (obj. 2.2) **14.** 2376 m (obj. 2.2) **15.** 91.7 m (obj. 2.2) **16.** 1.34 m or 134 cm (obj. 2.2) **17.** 5660 (obj. 3.1) **18.** 0.535 (obj. 3.2) **19.** 0.0563 (obj. 3.2) **20.** 4800 (obj. 3.1) **21.** 0.568 (obj. 3.2) **22.** 8900 (obj. 3.1) **23.** $116.25 (obj. 3.2) **24.** $227.50 (obj. 3.2) **25.** $7.20 (obj. 3.1) **26.** $10 600 (obj. 3.2)

Section 4 Exercises **1.** The metre is approximately the same length as a yard. The metre is slightly longer. **3.** The inch is approximately twice the length of a centimetre. **5.** 2.14 m **7.** 22.86 cm **9.** 34.88 yd **11.** 28.15 m **13.** 132.02 km **15.** 10.08 yd **17.** 6.90 in **19.** 656 ft **21.** 3.1 mi **23.** 181.92 L **25.** 21.76 L **27.** 5.02 gal **29.** 4.77 qt **31.** 180.4 lb **33.** 59.02 kg **35.** 737.1 g **37.** 334.4 lb **39.** 5.58 oz **41.** 1066.8 cm **43.** 34.1 mi/h **45.** 273 mi/h **47.** 0.51 in. **49.** 185 °F **51.** 53.6 °F **53.** 60 °C **55.** 35 °C **57.** yes **59.** 18.85 litres **61.** 1397 lb **63.** 8.92 ft **65.** 66.2 °F at 4 A.M. 113 °F after 7 A.M. **67.** 59 861 miles **69.** 180.6448 sq cm **71.** $896 for the Canadian carpet; $1149 for the American carpet; the Canadian carpet is $253 cheaper.

Quick Quiz 4 **1.** 141.75 g **2.** 14.88 mi **3.** 6.36 qt **4.** See Instructor

Section 5 Exercises **1.** 3 ft **3.** 53 yd **5.** $29.40 **7.** 8.1 m **9.** 880 yd is 4.32 m longer than 880 m. **11.** $3.37/gal gasoline is more expensive in Manitoba. **13.** 77 °F; 9 °F **15.** The difference is 6 °F. The temperature reading of 180 °C is hotter. **17.** **(a)** about 105 km/h **(b)** Probably not. We cannot be sure, but we have no evidence to indicate that they broke the speed limit. **19.** 15 gallons **21.** $108 **23.** 2.08 oz **25.** **(a)** 4.34 quarts extra **(b)** $33.70 **27.** **(a)** $7.63 **(b)** about 132 mi/gal **29.** yes; 240 000 gal/h is equivalent to $533\frac{1}{3}$ pt/s

Quick Quiz 5 **1.** The prediction was 7.6 °F cooler than the actual temperature. **2.** 9.5 in. **3.** 43.5 min **4.** See Instructor

Putting Your Skills to Work **1.** $545.75 **2.** $578.06 **3.** She spent more than she deposited, but the $300.50 would help her to cover her expenses. **4.** $307.75 **5.** $268.19 **6.** Eventually she will be in debt.

Module Review Problems **1.** 11 **2.** 9 **3.** 8800 **4.** 10 560 **5.** 10.5 **6.** 12.5 **7.** 13 200 **8.** 21 120 **9.** 14 000 **10.** 8000 **11.** 0.5 **12.** 0.75 **13.** 60 **14.** 84 **15.** 15.5 **16.** 13.5 **17.** 560 **18.** 290 **19.** 176.3 **20.** 259.8 **21.** 1325 **22.** 1675 **23.** 10 **24.** 8.2 **25.** 7.93 m **26.** 17.01 m **27.** 35.63 m **28.** 89.59 m **29.** 17 000 **30.** 23 000 **31.** 196 000 **32.** 721 000 **33.** 0.095 **34.** 0.078 **35.** 3.5 **36.** 12.75 **37.** 765 **38.** 423 **39.** 256 **40.** 922 **41.** 92.4 **42.** 2.75 **43.** 72.45 **44.** 141.68 **45.** 5.52 **46.** 7.09 **47.** 9.08 **48.** 13.62 **49.** 45.7 **50.** 91.4 **51.** 49.6 **52.** 43.4 **53.** 53.6° **54.** 89.6° **55.** 105° **56.** 85° **57.** 0° **58.** 100° **59.** 3.43 **60.** 25.54 **61.** 270 sq ft; 30 sq yd **62.** **(a)** 17 ft **(b)** 204 in. **63.** **(a)** 200 m **(b)** 0.2 km **64.** $2.88 **65.** no; 4.2 ft short **66.** yes; 112.7 km/h **67.** 25 °F. Too hot **68.** 380 cm **69.** 39.38 mi/h **70.** 36.36 mi/h **71.** They are carrying 16.28 pounds. They are slightly over the weight limit. **72.** about $3.98 **73.** yes **74.** approximately 516.4 square feet **75.** approximately $2.23

How Am I Doing? Module Test **1.** 3200 (obj. 1.2) **2.** 228 (obj. 1.2) **3.** 84 (obj. 1.2) **4.** 7 (obj. 1.2) **5.** 30 (obj. 1.2) **6.** 0.75 (obj. 1.2) **7.** 0.5 (obj. 1.2) **8.** 16.5 (obj. 1.2) **9.** 9200 (obj. 2.2) **10.** 0.0988 (obj. 2.2) **11.** 4.6 (obj. 2.2) **12.** 1270 (obj. 2.2) **13.** 9.36 (obj. 2.2) **14.** 0.046 (obj. 3.1) **15.** 0.0289 (obj. 3.2) **16.** 0.983 (obj. 3.2) **17.** 920 (obj. 3.1) **18.** 9420 (obj. 3.2) **19.** 67.62 (obj. 4.1) **20.** 1.63 (obj. 4.1) **21.** 3.55 (obj. 4.1) **22.** 18.6 (obj. 4.1) **23.** 16.06 (obj. 4.1) **24.** 85.05 (obj. 4.1) **25.** 56.85 (obj. 4.1) **26.** 3.18 (obj. 4.1) **27.** **(a)** 20 m (obj. 5.1) **(b)** 21.8 yd **28.** **(a)** 15 °F (obj. 5.1) **(b)** yes (obj. 4.2)

28. **(a)** 15 °F (obj. 5.1) **(b)** yes (obj. 4.2) **29.** 82.5 gal/h (obj. 5.1) **30.** **(a)** 300 km (obj. 5.1) **(b)** 14 mi **31.** $5\frac{1}{4}$ lb (obj. 5.1) **32.** 104 °F (obj. 4.2) (obj. 5.1)

Tourists from all over the world come to see the Great Pyramid of Giza. The construction of this pyramid required a substantial amount of mathematics. You will learn most of these mathematics skills in this module.

Shutterstock

Geometry

SECTION 1 ANGLES

Student Learning Objective

After studying this section, you will be able to:

 **Understand and use angles.**

 Understanding and Using Angles

Geometry is a branch of mathematics that deals with the properties of and relationships between figures in space. One of the simplest figures is a *line*. A **line** extends indefinitely, but a portion of a line, called a **line segment,** has a beginning and an end. A **ray** is a part of a line that has only one endpoint and goes on forever in one direction. An **angle** is made up of two rays that start at a common endpoint. The two rays are called the **sides** of the angle. The point at which they meet is called the **vertex** of the angle.

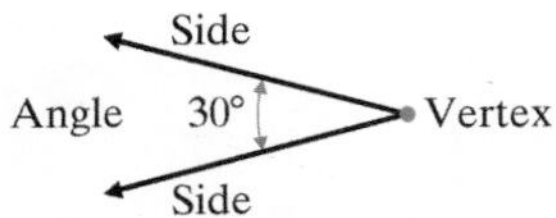

The "amount of opening" of an angle can be measured. Angles are commonly measured in **degrees.** In the preceding sketch the angle measures 30 degrees, or 30°. The symbol ° indicates degrees. If you fix one side of an angle and keep moving the other side, the angle measure will get larger and larger until eventually you have gone around in one complete revolution.

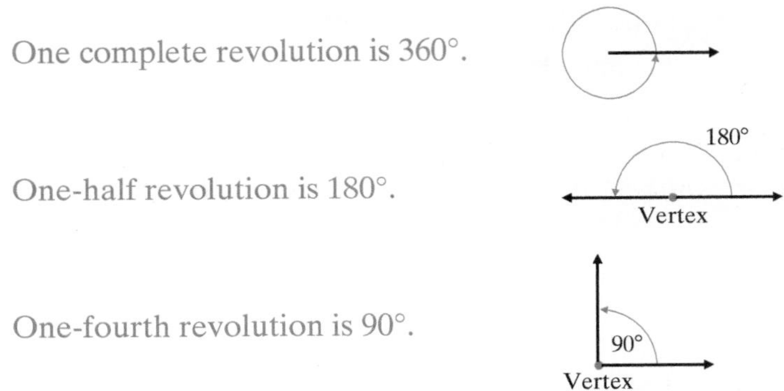

We call two lines **perpendicular** when they meet at an angle of 90°. A 90° angle is called a **right angle.** A 90° angle is often indicated by a small □ at the vertex. Thus when you see ⦜ you know that the angle measures 90° and also that the sides are perpendicular to each other. The following three angles are right angles.

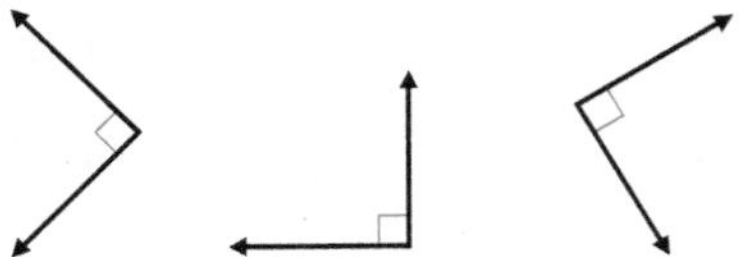

Often, to avoid confusion, angles are labelled with letters. Suppose we consider the angle with a vertex at point B. This angle can be called $\angle ABC$

or $\angle CBA$. Notice that when three letters are used, the middle letter is the vertex. This angle can also be called $\angle B$ or $\angle x$.

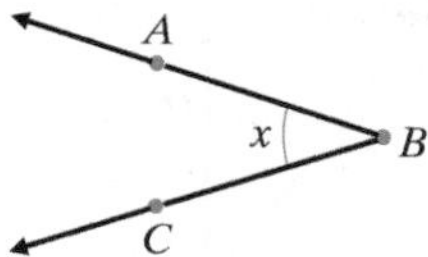

Now consider the following angles. We could label angle y as $\angle DEF$ or angle FED. However, we could not label it as $\angle E$ because this would be unclear. If we referred to $\angle E$, people would not know for sure whether we meant $\angle DEF$, $\angle FEG$, or $\angle DEG$. In cases where there might be some confusion, the use of the three-letter label is always preferred.

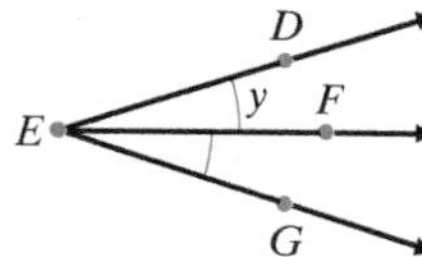

Certain types of angles are commonly encountered. It is important to learn their names. An angle that measures 180° is called a **straight angle.** Angle ABC in the following figure is a straight angle. As we mentioned previously, this is one-half of a revolution.

Wally Stemberger/Shutterstock

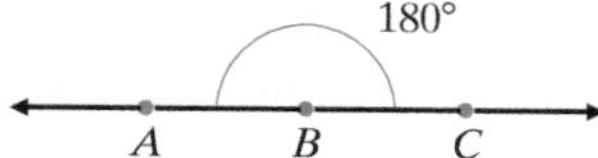

An angle whose measure is between but does not include 0° and 90° is called an **acute angle.** $\angle DEF$ and $\angle GHJ$ are both acute angles.

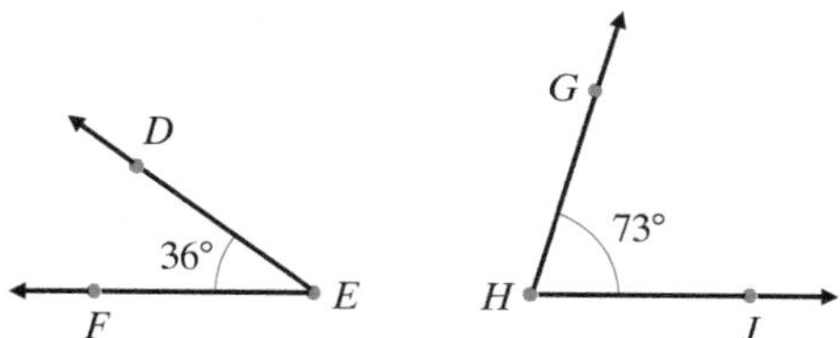

An angle whose measure is between but does not include 90° and 180° is called an **obtuse angle.** $\angle ABC$ and $\angle JKL$ are both obtuse angles.

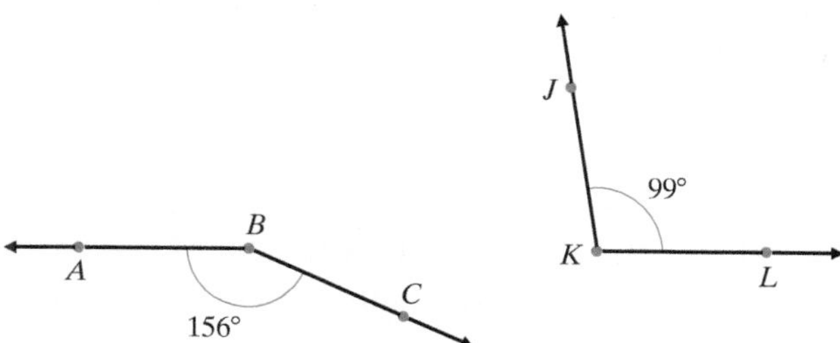

Surveyors make accurate measurements of angles so that reliable maps of land regions and buildings can be made.

EXAMPLE 1 In the following sketch, determine which angles are acute, obtuse, right, or straight angles.

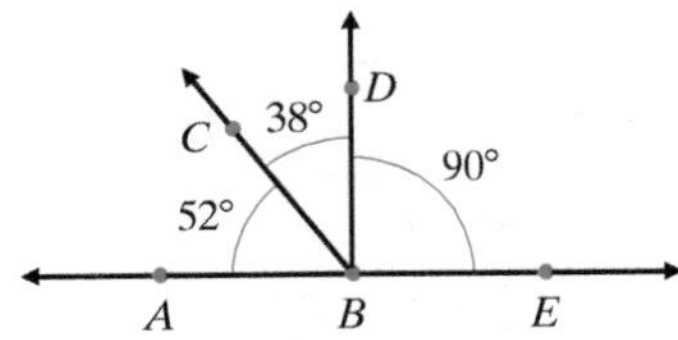

Solution $\angle ABC$ and $\angle CBD$ are acute angles, $\angle CBE$ is an obtuse angle, $\angle ABD$ and $\angle DBE$ are right angles, and $\angle ABE$ is a straight angle.

Practice Problem 1 In the following sketch, determine which angles are acute, obtuse, right, or straight angles.

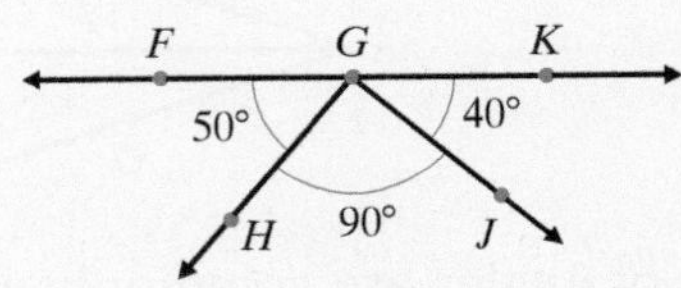

NOTE TO STUDENT: Fully worked-out solutions to all of the Practice Problems can be found at the end of the module.

Two angles whose measures have a sum of 90° are called **complementary angles.** We can therefore say that each angle is the **complement** of the other. Two angles whose measures have a sum of 180° are called **supplementary angles.** In this case we say that each angle is the **supplement** of the other.

EXAMPLE 2 Angle A measures 39°.

(a) Find the complement of angle A.
(b) Find the supplement of angle A.

Solution

(a) Complementary angles have a sum of 90°. So the complement of angle A measures $90° - 39° = 51°$.
(b) Supplementary angles have a sum of 180°. So the supplement of angle A measures $180° - 39° = 141°$.

Practice Problem 2 Angle B measures 83°.

(a) Find the complement of angle B.
(b) Find the supplement of angle B.

Four angles are formed when two lines intersect. Think of how you have four angles if two straight streets intersect. The two angles that are opposite each other are called **vertical angles.** Vertical angles have the same measure. In the following sketch, angle x and angle z are vertical angles, and they have the same measure. Also, angle w and angle y are vertical angles, so they have the same measure.

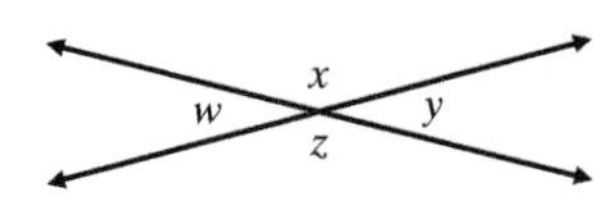

Now suppose we consider two angles that have a common side and a common vertex, such as angle w and angle x. Two angles that share a common side are called **adjacent angles.** Adjacent angles of intersecting lines are supplementary. If we know that the measure of angle x is 120°, then we also know that the measure of angle w is 60°.

EXAMPLE 3 In the following sketch, two lines intersect, forming four angles. The measure of angle a is 55°. Find the measure of all the other angles.

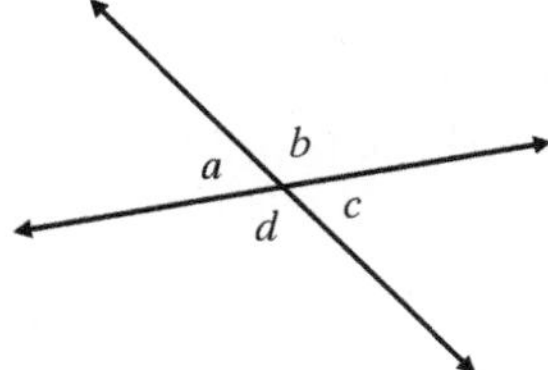

Solution Since $\angle a$ and $\angle c$ are vertical angles, we know that they have the same measure. Thus we know that $\angle c$ measures 55°.

Since $\angle a$ and $\angle b$ are adjacent angles of intersecting lines, we know that they are supplementary angles. Thus we know that $\angle b$ measures $180° - 55° = 125°$.

Finally, $\angle b$ and $\angle d$ are vertical angles, so we know that they have the same measure. Thus we know that $\angle d$ measures 125°.

Practice Problem 3 In the following sketch, two lines intersect, forming four angles. The measure of angle y is 133°. Find the measure of all the other angles.

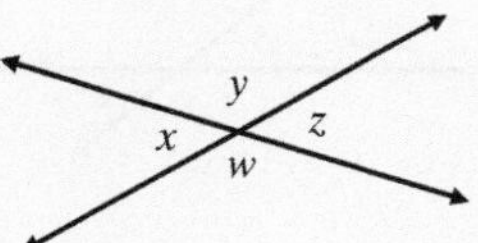

In mathematics there is a common notation for perpendicular lines. If line m is perpendicular to line n, we write $m \perp n$. **Parallel lines** never meet. If line p is parallel to line q, we write $p \| q$.

One more situation that is very important in geometry involves lines and angles. A line that intersects two or more lines at different points is called a **transversal.** In the following figure, line m is a transversal that intersects line n and line p. **Alternate interior angles** are two angles that are on opposite sides of the transversal and between the other two lines. In the figure, $\angle c$ and $\angle w$ are alternate interior angles.

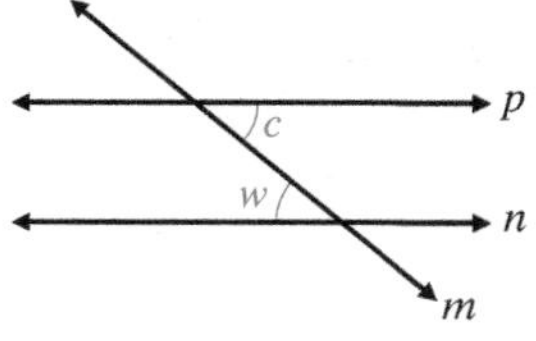

Corresponding angles are two angles that are on the same side of the transversal and are both above (or both below) the other two lines. In the following figure, angle a and angle b are corresponding angles.

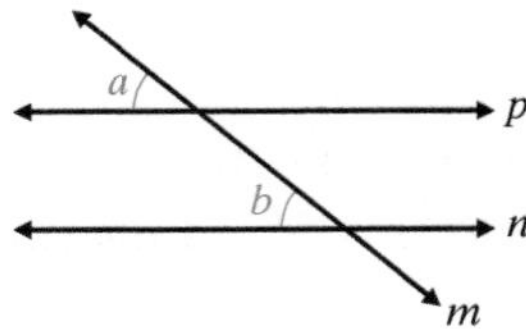

The most important case occurs when the two lines cut by the transversal are parallel. We will state this as follows:

PARALLEL LINES CUT BY A TRANSVERSAL

If two parallel lines are cut by a transversal, then the measures of **corresponding angles are equal** and the measures of **alternate interior angles** are equal.

EXAMPLE 4 In the following figure, $m \parallel n$ and the measure of $\angle a$ is $64°$. Find the measures of $\angle b$, $\angle c$, $\angle d$, and $\angle e$.

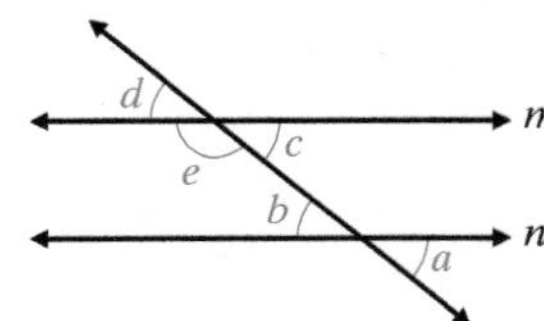

Solution

$\angle a = \angle b = 64°$. — $\angle a$ and $\angle b$ are vertical angles.

$\angle b = \angle c = 64°$. — $\angle b$ and $\angle c$ are alternate interior angles.

$\angle b = \angle d = 64°$. — $\angle b$ and $\angle d$ are corresponding angles.

$\angle e = 180° - 64° = 116°$. — $\angle e$ and $\angle d$ are adjacent angles of intersecting lines.

NOTE TO STUDENT: Fully worked-out solutions to all of the Practice Problems can be found at the end of the module.

Practice Problem 4 In the following figure, $p \parallel q$ and the measure of $\angle x$ is $105°$. Find the measures of $\angle w$, $\angle y$, $\angle z$, and $\angle v$.

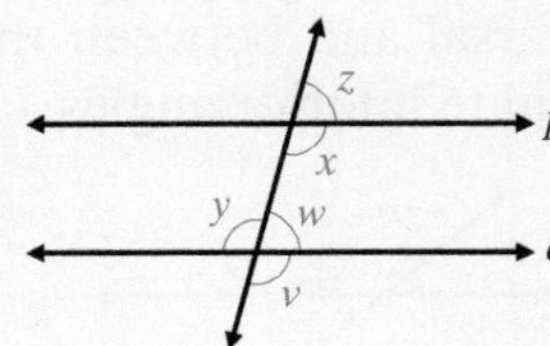

Section 1 Exercises

Verbal and Writing Skills *In your own words, give a definition for each term.*

1. acute angle

2. obtuse angle

3. complementary angles

4. supplementary angles

5. vertical angles

6. adjacent angles

7. transversal

8. alternate interior angles

In exercises 9–14, two straight lines intersect at B, as shown in the following sketch.

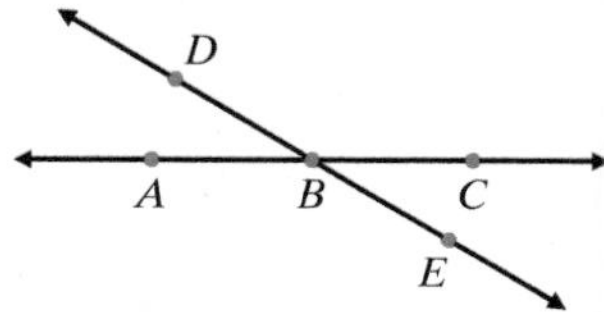

9. Name all the acute angles.

10. Name all the obtuse angles.

11. Name two pairs of angles that have the same measure.

12. Name two pairs of angles that are supplementary.

13. Name two pairs of angles that are complementary, if any exist.

14. Name a pair of vertical angles.

In exercises 15–22, find the measure of each angle, as shown in the following sketch. Assume that angle LOK is a right angle, and angle JOK is a straight angle.

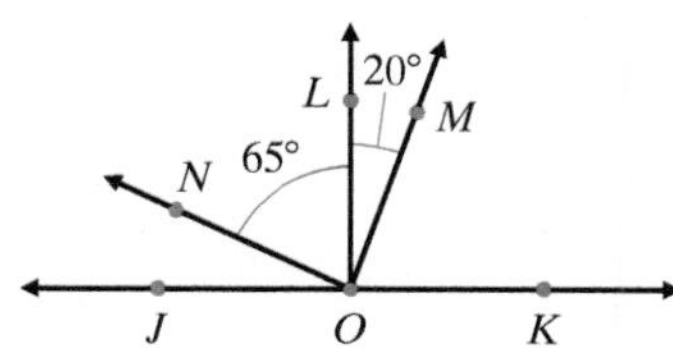

15. $\angle LOJ$

16. $\angle NOL$

17. $\angle JON$

18. $\angle NOM$

19. $\angle JOM$

20. $\angle MOK$

21. $\angle NOK$

22. $\angle KOJ$

23. Find the complement of an angle that measures 31°.

24. Find the complement of an angle that measures 5°.

25. Find the supplement of an angle that measures 127°.

26. Find the supplement of an angle that measures 18°.

Find the measure of $\angle a$.

27.

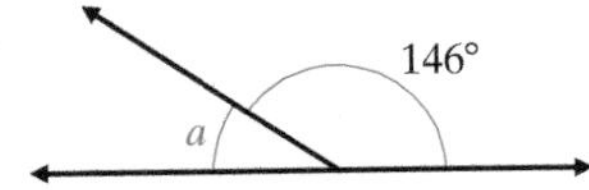

28.

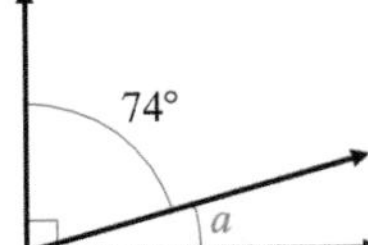

29.

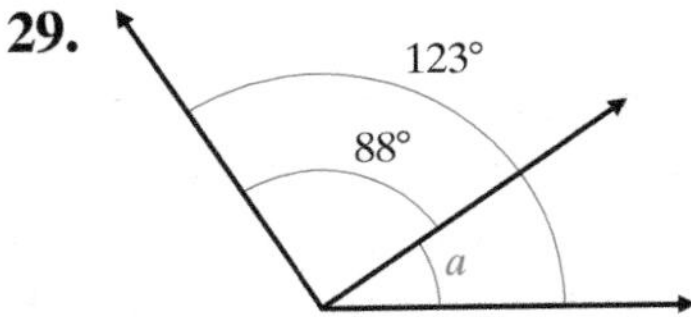

30.

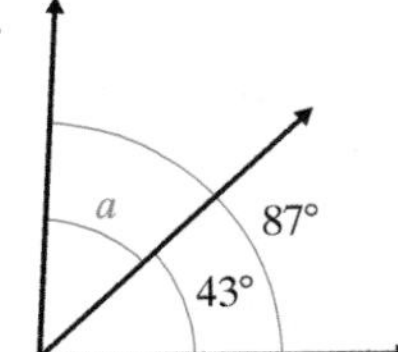

31.

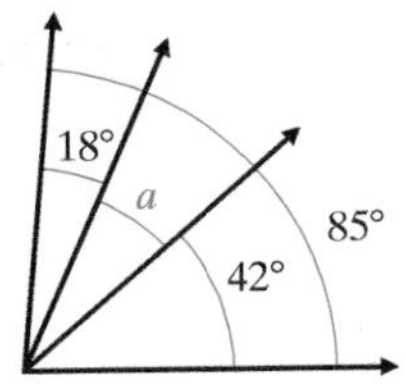

32.

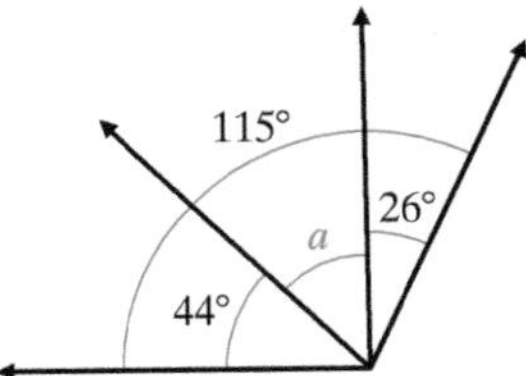

Find the measures of $\angle a$, $\angle b$, and $\angle c$.

33.

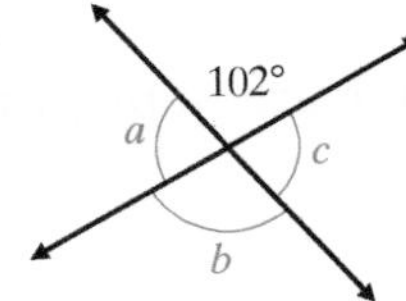

34.

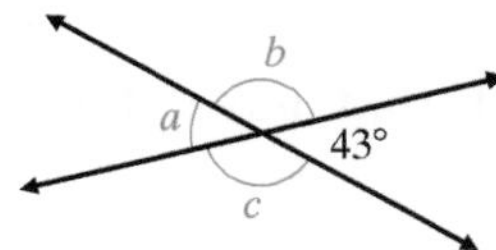

35.

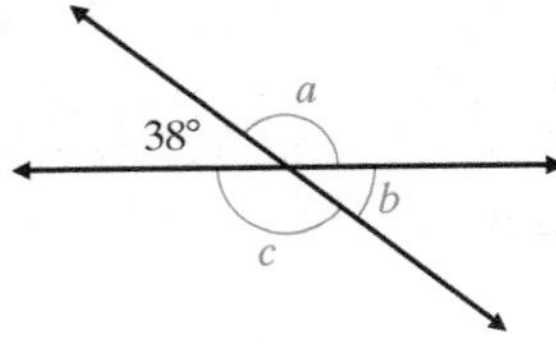

36.

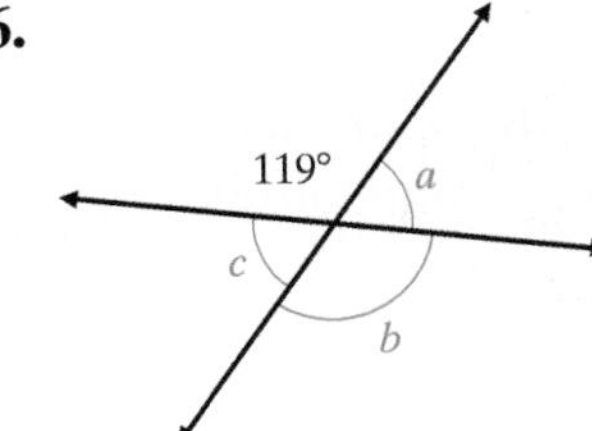

Find the measures of $\angle a$, $\angle b$, and $\angle c$ if we know that $p \| q$.

37.

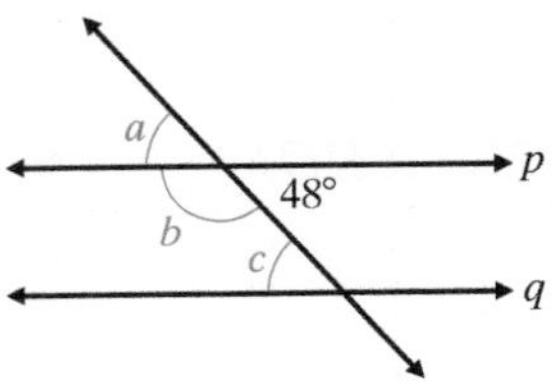

38.

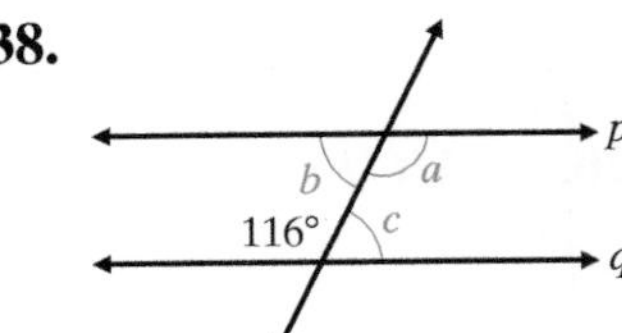

Find the measures of $\angle a$, $\angle b$, $\angle c$, $\angle d$, $\angle e$, $\angle f$, and $\angle g$ if we know that $p \parallel q$.

39.

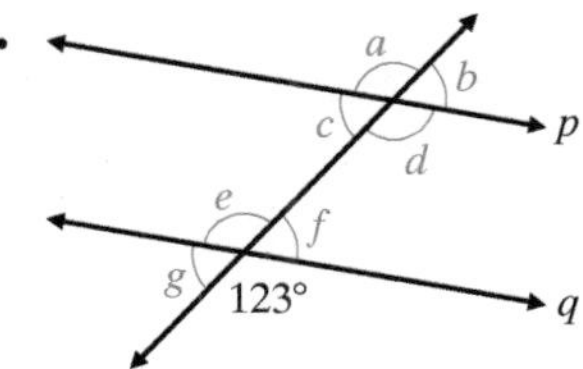

40.

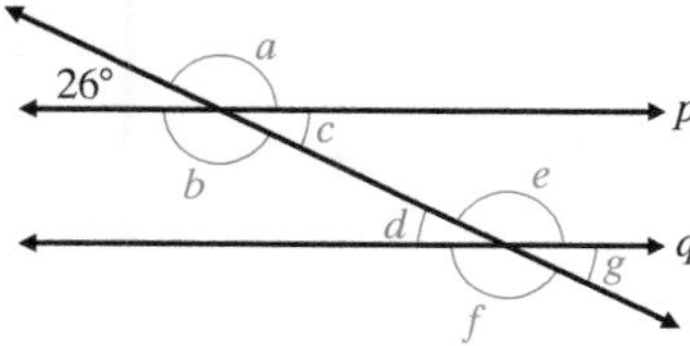

Applications

41. ***Leaning Tower of Pisa*** The famous Leaning Tower of Pisa has an angle of inclination of 84°. Scientists are working now to move the tower slightly so that it does not lean so much. Find the angle x, at which the tower deviates from the normal upright position.

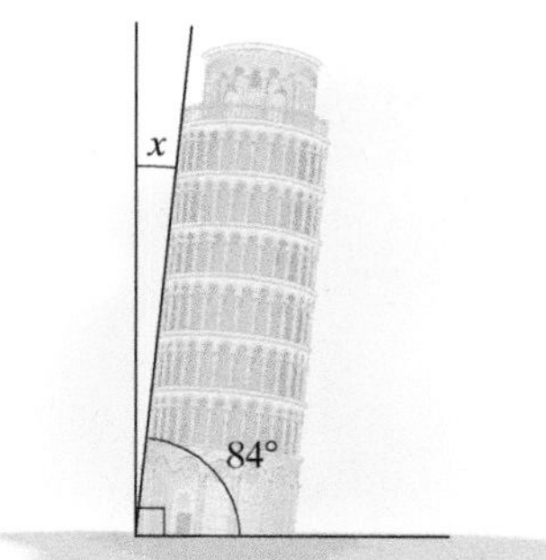

42. ***Pyramids of Monte Albán*** In Mexico the famous pyramids of Monte Albán are visited by thousands of tourists each month. The one most often climbed by tourists is steeper than the pyramids of Egypt and tourists find the climb very challenging. Find the angle x, which indicates the angle of inclination of the pyramid, based on the following sketch.

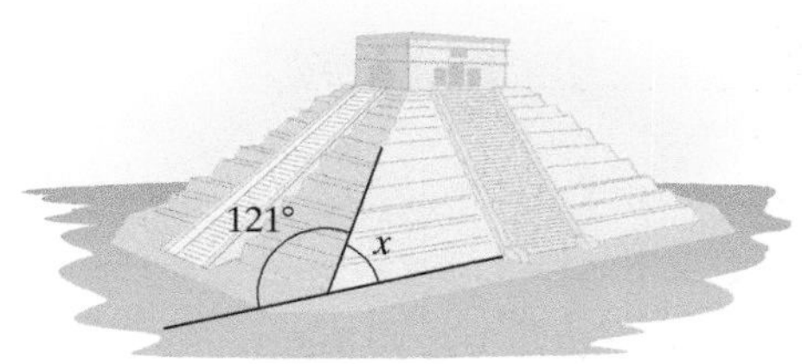

43. ***Course of Jet Plane*** A jetliner is flying 62° north of east when it leaves the airport in St. John's. The control tower orders the plane to change course by turning to the right 9°. Describe the new course in terms of how many degrees north of east the plane is flying.

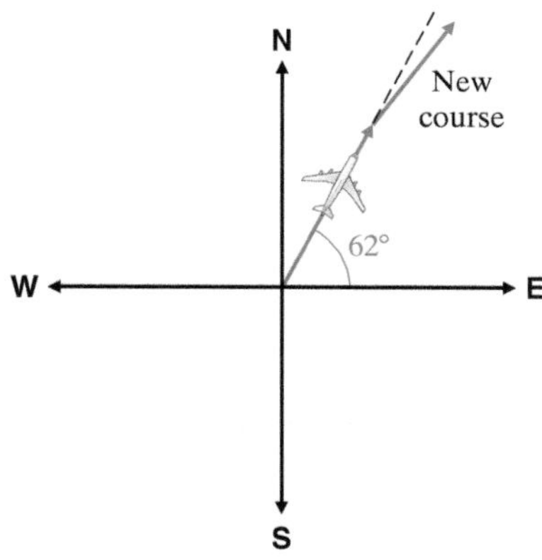

44. ***Course of Cruise Ship*** A cruise ship is leaving Vancouver and is heading on a course 72° north of west. The captain orders that the ship be turned to the left 9°. Describe the new course in terms of how many degrees north of west the ship is heading.

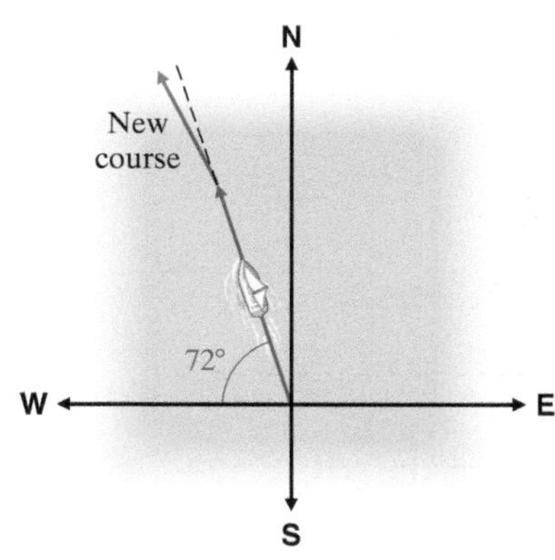

Quick Quiz 1 In the figure below, lines m and n are parallel. The measure of angle a is 124°.

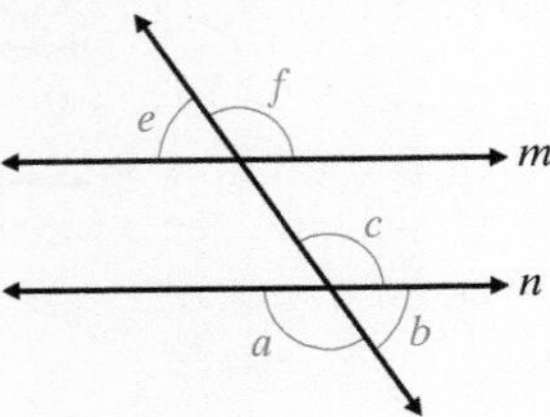

1. Find the measure of $\angle c$.

2. Find the measure of $\angle b$.

3. Find the measure of $\angle e$.

4. **Concept Check** In the figure shown, explain what the relationship is between $\angle e$ and $\angle a$. If you know the measure of $\angle e$, how can you find the measure of $\angle a$?

SECTION 2 RECTANGLES AND SQUARES

 Finding the Perimeters of Rectangles and Squares

Student Learning Objectives

After studying this section, you will be able to:

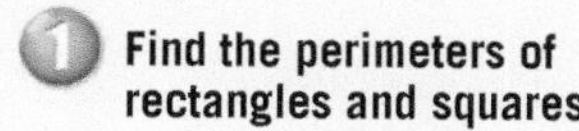

1. **Find the perimeters of rectangles and squares.**
2. **Find the perimeters of shapes made up of rectangles and squares.**
3. **Find the areas of rectangles and squares.**
4. **Find the areas of shapes made up of rectangles and squares.**

Geometry has a visual aspect that numbers and abstract ideas do not have. We can take pen in hand and draw a picture of a rectangle that represents a room with certain dimensions. We can easily visualize problems such as "What is the distance around the outside edges of the room (perimeter)?" or "How much carpeting will be needed for the room (area)?"

A rectangle is a four-sided figure like those shown here.

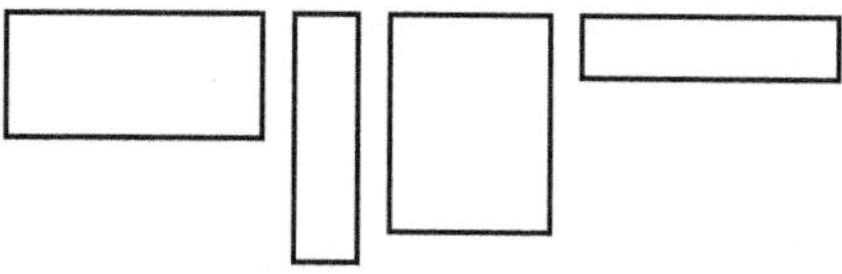

A rectangle has two interesting properties: (1) Any two adjoining sides are perpendicular and (2) the lengths of the opposite sides of a rectangle are equal. By "any two adjoining sides are perpendicular," we mean that any two sides that meet form an angle that measures 90°. We indicate the 90° angle with a small red box □ at each corner. When we say that "the lengths of the opposite sides of a rectangle are equal," we mean that the measure of one side is equal to the measure of the side opposite to it. Thus, we define a **rectangle** as a four-sided figure that has four right angles. If all four sides have the same length, then the rectangle is called a **square.**

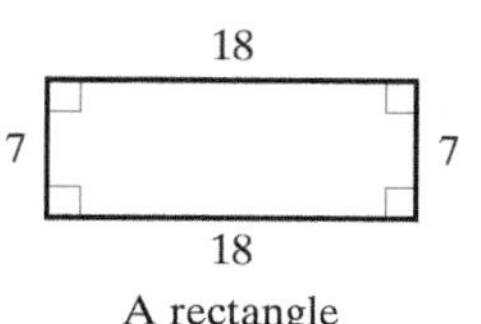

A rectangle

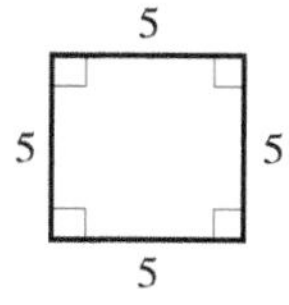

This rectangle is also a square.

A farmer owns some land in Manitoba. It is in the shape of a rectangle. The **perimeter** of a rectangle is the sum of the lengths of all its sides. To find the perimeter of the rectangular field shown in the following figure, we add up the lengths of all the sides of the field.

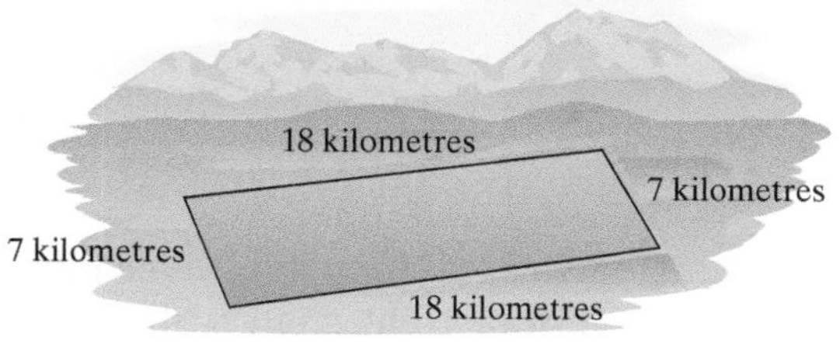

Perimeter = 7 kilometres + 18 kilometres + 7 kilometres + 18 kilometres
= 50 kilometres

Thus the perimeter of the field is 50 kilometres.

We could also use a formula to find the perimeter of a rectangle. In the formula we use letters to represent the measurements of the length and width of the rectangle. Let l represent the length, w represent the width, and P represent the perimeter. Note that the length is the longer side and the width is the shorter side. Since the perimeter is found by adding up the measurements all around the rectangle, we see that

$$P = w + l + w + l$$
$$= 2l + 2w.$$

When we write $2l$ and $2w$, we mean 2 times l and 2 times w. We can use the formula to find the perimeter of the rectangle.

$$P = 2l + 2w$$
$$= (2)(18 \text{ km}) + (2)(7 \text{ km})$$
$$= 36 \text{ km} + 14 \text{ km}$$
$$= 50 \text{ km}$$

Notice that we use parentheses ( ) here to indicate multiplication of 2×18 and 2×7.

Thus the perimeter can be found quickly by using the following formula.

The **perimeter (*P*) of a rectangle** is twice the length plus twice the width.

$$P = 2l + 2w$$

EXAMPLE 1 A helicopter has a 3-cm by 5.5-cm insulation pad near the control panel that is rectangular. Find the perimeter of the rectangle.

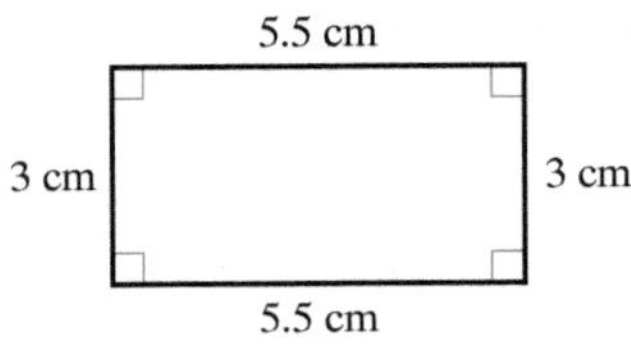

Solution

$$\text{Length} = l = 5.5 \text{ cm}$$
$$\text{Width} = w = 3 \text{ cm}$$

In the formula for the perimeter of a rectangle, we substitute 5.5 cm for l and 3 cm for w. Remember, $2l$ means 2 times l and $2w$ means 2 times w. Thus

$$P = 2l + 2w$$
$$= (2)(5.5 \text{ cm}) + (2)(3 \text{ cm})$$
$$= 11 \text{ cm} + 6 \text{ cm} = 17 \text{ cm}.$$

NOTE TO STUDENT: *Fully worked-out solutions to all of the Practice Problems can be found at the end of the module.*

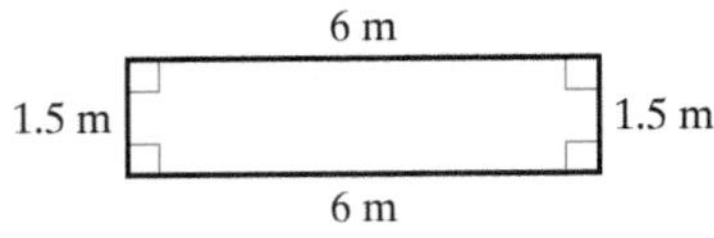

Practice Problem 1 Find the perimeter of the rectangle in the margin.

A square is a rectangle where all four sides have the same length. Since a rectangle is defined to have four right angles, all squares have four right angles. Some examples of squares are shown in the following figure.

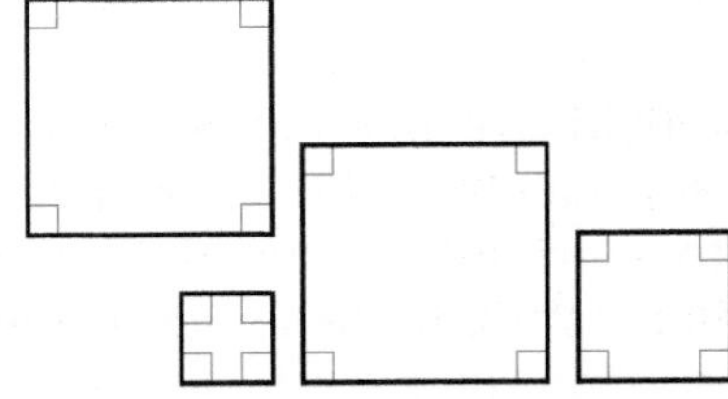

A square, then, is only a special type of rectangle. We can find the perimeter of a square just as we found the perimeter of a rectangle—by adding the measurements of all the sides of the square. Because the lengths of all sides are the same, the formula for the perimeter of a square is very simple. Let s represent the length of one side and P represent the perimeter. To find the perimeter, we multiply the length of a side by 4.

The **perimeter of a square** is four times the length of a side.

$$P = 4s$$

EXAMPLE 2 High Ridge Stables has a new sign at the highway entrance that is in the shape of a square, with each side measuring 8.6 metres. Find the perimeter of the sign.

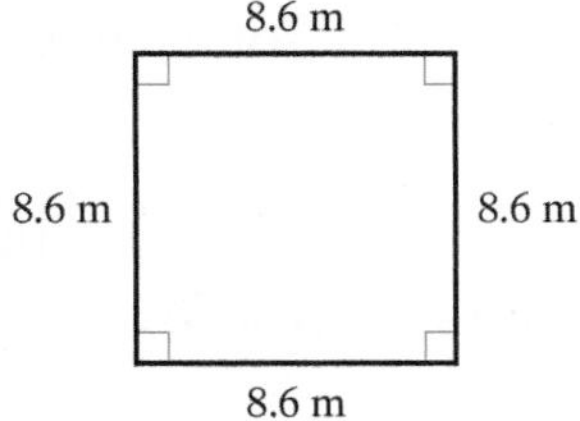

Solution

$$\begin{aligned} \text{Side} &= s = 8.6 \text{ m} \\ P &= 4s \\ &= (4)(8.6 \text{ m}) \\ &= 34.4 \text{ m} \end{aligned}$$

Practice Problem 2 Find the perimeter of the square in the margin.

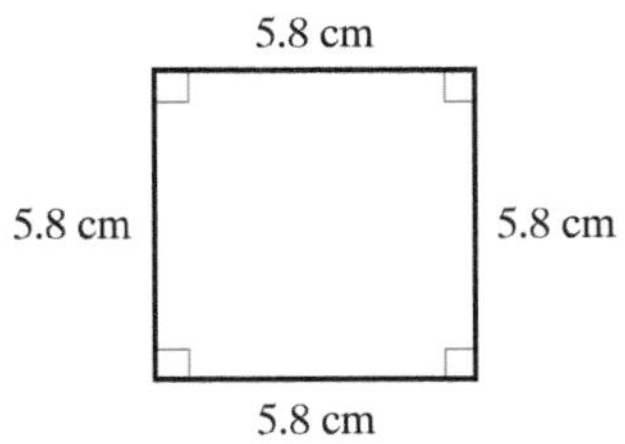

Since drawing the small red boxes sometimes makes drawings overly complicated, we will assume that all drawings in this module that appear to be rectangles and squares do in fact have four 90° angles.

 Finding the Perimeters of Shapes Made Up of Rectangles and Squares

Some figures are a combination of rectangles and squares. To find the perimeter of the total figure, look only at the outside edges.

We can apply our knowledge to everyday problems. For example, by knowing how to find the perimeter of a rectangle, we can find out how many centimetres of picture framing a painting will need or how many metres of weather stripping will be needed to seal a doorway. Consider the following problem.

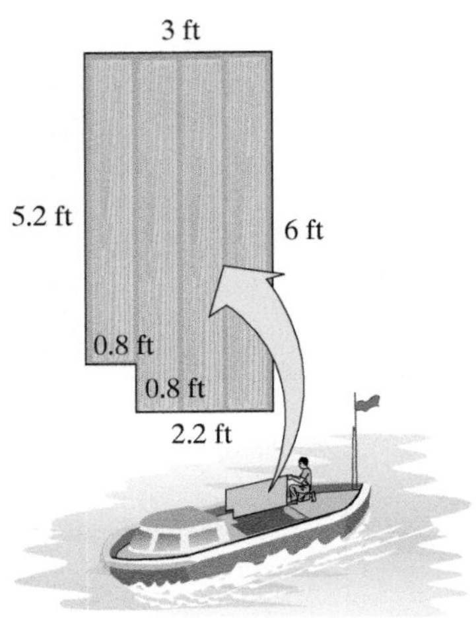

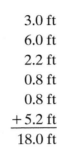

EXAMPLE 3 Find the cost of weather stripping needed to seal the edges of the hatch of a boat pictured at left. Weather stripping costs \$0.12 per foot.

Solution First we need to find the perimeter of the hatch. The perimeter is the sum of all the edges. We use the sketch at the right.

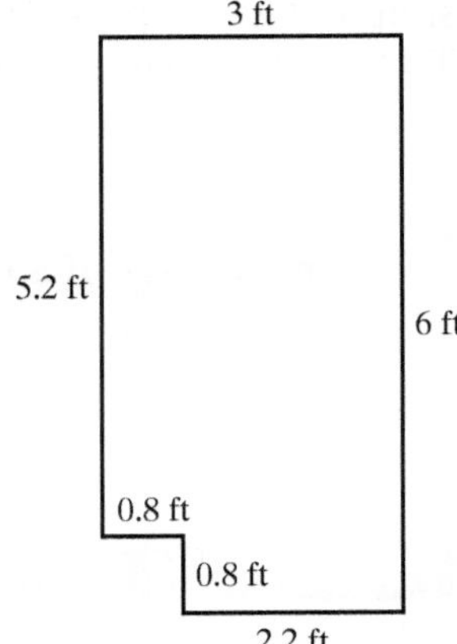

$$\begin{array}{r} 3.0 \text{ ft} \\ 6.0 \text{ ft} \\ 2.2 \text{ ft} \\ 0.8 \text{ ft} \\ 0.8 \text{ ft} \\ +5.2 \text{ ft} \\ \hline 18.0 \text{ ft} \end{array}$$

The perimeter is 18 ft. Now we calculate the cost.

$$18.0 \cancel{\text{ft}} \times \frac{0.12 \text{ dollar}}{\cancel{\text{ft}}} = \$2.16 \text{ for weather stripping materials}$$

Practice Problem 3 Find the cost of weather stripping required to seal the edges of the hatch shown below. Weather stripping costs \$0.48 per metre.

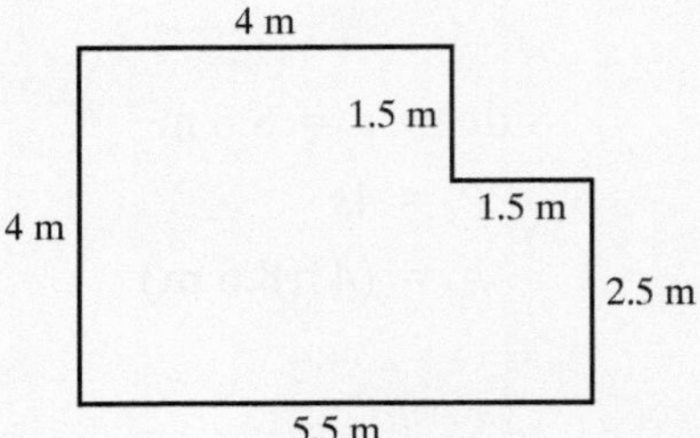

3 Finding the Areas of Rectangles and Squares

What do we mean by **area?** Area is the measure of the *surface inside* a geometric figure. For example, for a rectangular room, the area is the amount of floor in that room.

One *square metre* is the measure of a square that is 1 m on each side.

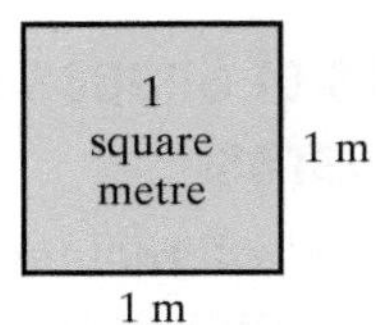

We can abbreviate *square metre* as m^2. In fact, all areas are measured in square metres, square feet, square inches, and so on (written as m^2, ft^2, $in.^2$, and so on).

We can calculate the area of a rectangular region if we know its length and its width. To find the area, *multiply* the length by the width.

The **area (A) of a rectangle** is the length times the width.

$$A = lw$$

EXAMPLE 4 Find the area of the rectangle shown below.

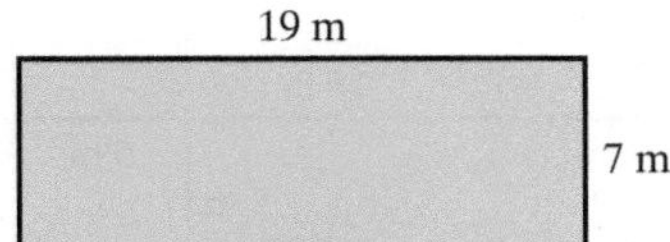

Solution Our answer must be in square metres because the measures of the length and width are in metres.

$$l = 19 \text{ m} \qquad w = 7 \text{ m}$$
$$A = (l)(w) = (19 \text{ m})(7 \text{ m}) = 133 \text{ m}^2$$

The area is 133 square metres.

Practice Problem 4 Find the area of the rectangle shown below.

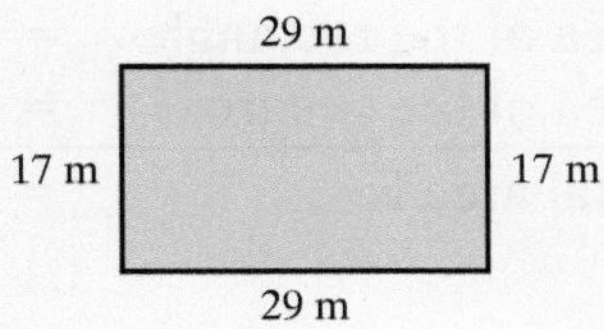

To find the area of a square, we multiply the length of one side by itself.

The **area of a square** is the square of the length of one side.

$$A = s^2$$

EXAMPLE 5 A square measures 9.6 in. on each side. Find its area.

Solution We know our answer will be measured in square inches. We will write this as in.^{2}.

$$\begin{aligned} A &= s^2 \\ &= (9.6 \text{ in.})^2 \\ &= (9.6 \text{ in.})(9.6 \text{ in.}) \\ &= 92.16 \text{ in.}^2 \end{aligned}$$

Practice Problem 5 Find the area of a square computer chip that measures 11.8 mm on each side.

4 Finding the Areas of Shapes Made Up of Rectangles and Squares

EXAMPLE 6 Consider the shape shown below, which is made up of a rectangle and a square. Find the area of the shaded region.

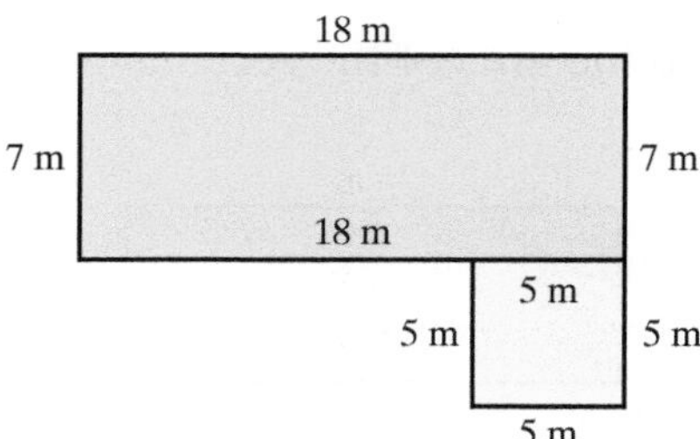

Solution The shaded region is made up of two separate regions. You can think of each separately, and calculate the area of each one. The total area is just the sum of the two separate areas.

$$\text{Area of rectangle} = (7\text{ m})(18\text{ m}) = 126\text{ m}^2$$

$$\text{Area of square} = (5\text{ m})^2 = 25\text{ m}^2$$

$$\begin{array}{lr} \text{The area of the rectangle} & = 126\text{ m}^2 \\ + \text{The area of the square} & = 25\text{ m}^2 \\ \hline \text{The total area is} & = 151\text{ m}^2 \end{array}$$

NOTE TO STUDENT: Fully worked-out solutions to all of the Practice Problems can be found at the end of the module.

Practice Problem 6 Find the area of the shaded region shown in the figure below.

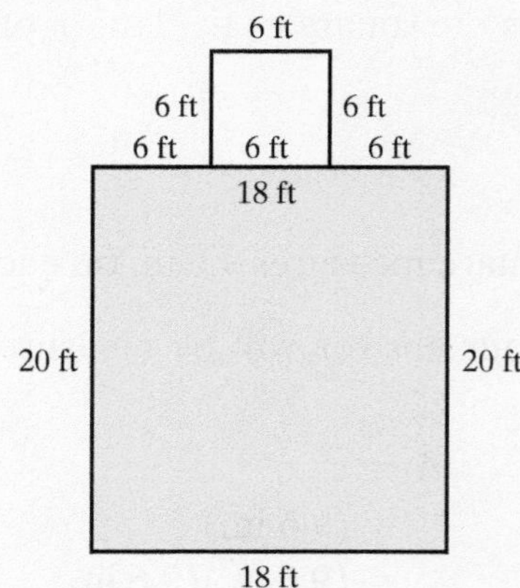

Section 2 Exercises

Verbal and Writing Skills

1. A rectangle has two properties: (1) any two adjoining sides are ____________ and (2) the lengths of opposite sides are ____________.

2. To find the perimeter of a figure, we ____________ the lengths of all of the sides.

3. To find the area of a rectangle, we ____________ the length by the width.

4. All area is measured in ____________ units.

Find the perimeter of the rectangle or square.

5.

5.5 km
2 km
2 km
5.5 km

6.

9 cm
1.5 cm
1.5 cm
9 cm

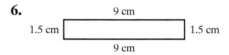

7.

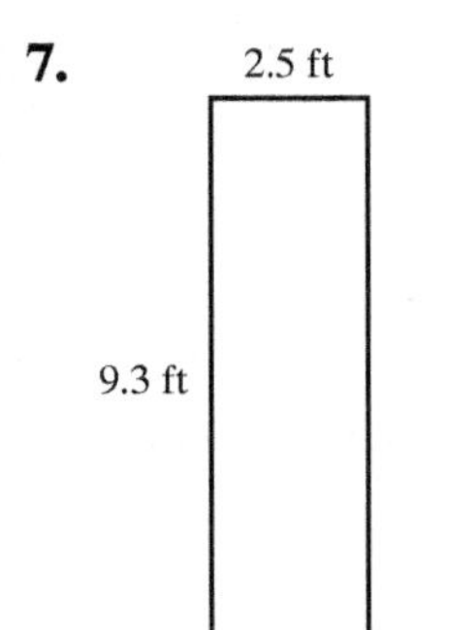

8.

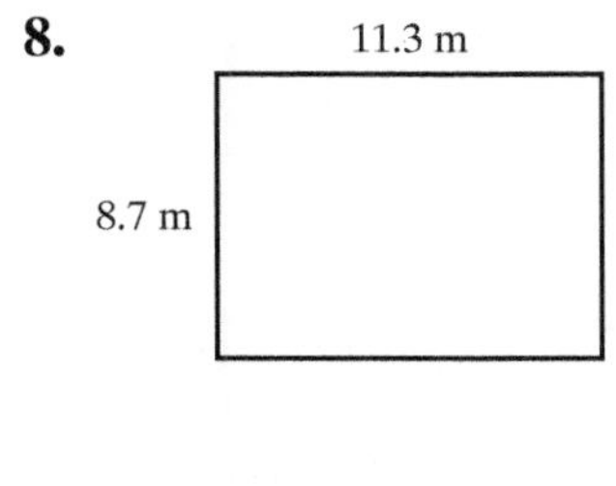

9.

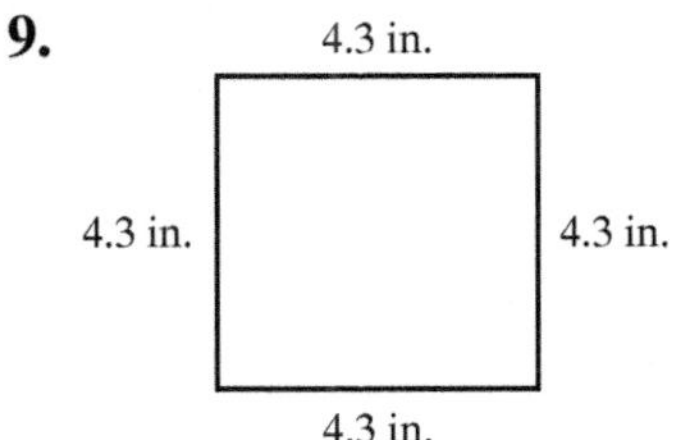

10.

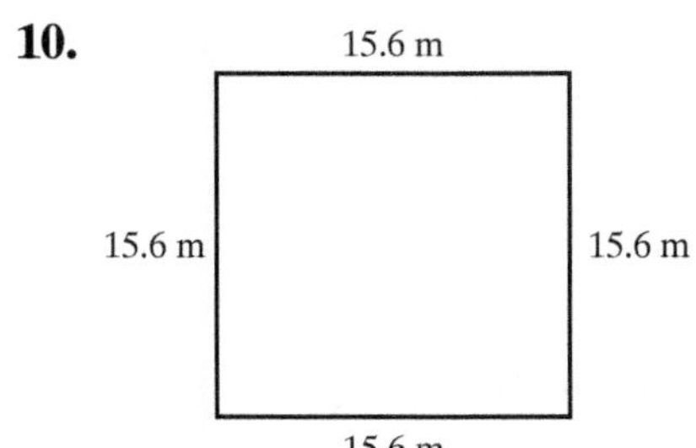

11. Length = 0.84 mm, width = 0.12 mm

12. Length = 9.4 m, width = 4.3 m

13. Length = width = 4.28 km

14. Length = width = 9.63 cm

15. Length = 3.2 ft, width = 48 in. (*Hint:* Make the units of length the same.)

16. Length = 8.5 m, width = 30 cm. (*Hint:* Make the units of length the same.)

Find the perimeter of the square. The length of the side is given.

17. 0.068 mm

18. 0.097 mm

19. $3\frac{1}{2}$ cm

20. $5\frac{3}{4}$ cm

Find the perimeter of each shape made up of rectangles and squares.

21.

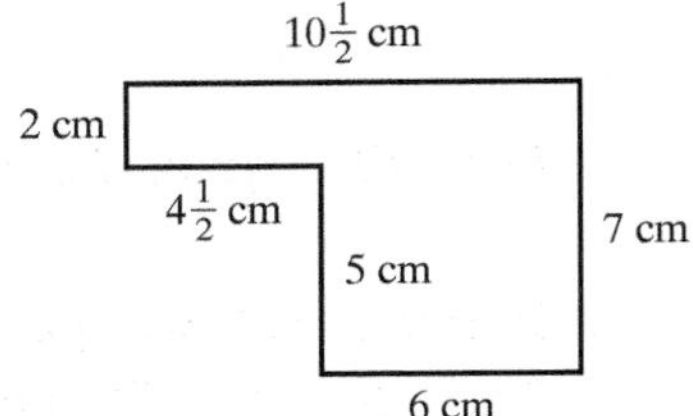

22.

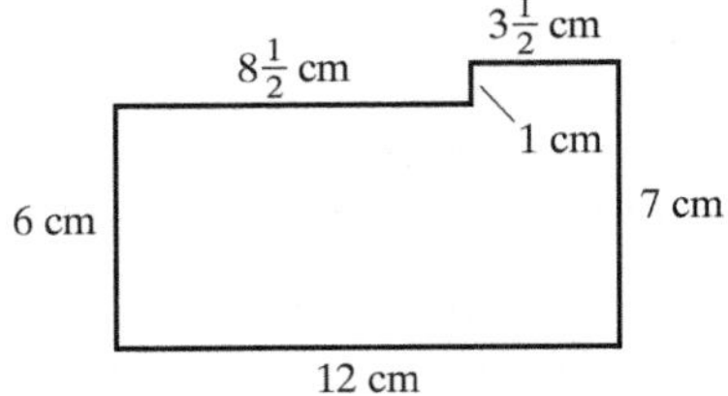

23.

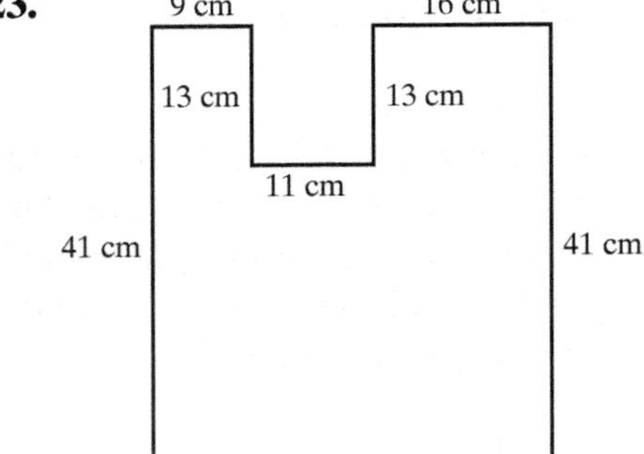

24.

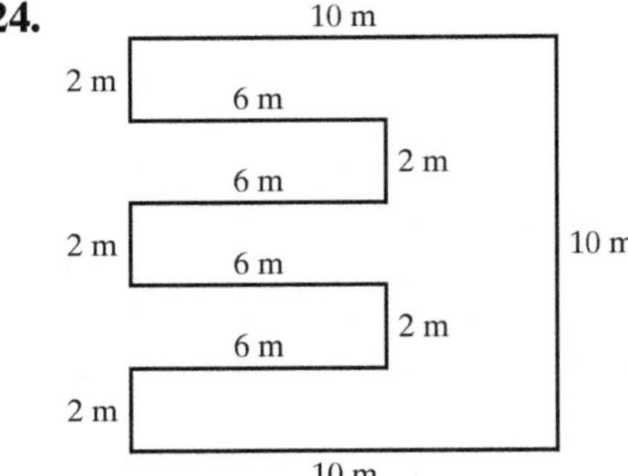

Find the area of the rectangle or square.

25. Length = width = 2.5 m

26. Length = width = 5.1 m

27. Length = 8 mi, width = 1.5 mi

28. Length = 12.4 km, width = 8 km

29. Length = 39 yd, width = 9 ft (*Hint:* Make the units of length the same.)

30. Length = 57 m, width = 15 dm (*Hint:* Make the units of length the same.)

Mixed Practice

31.

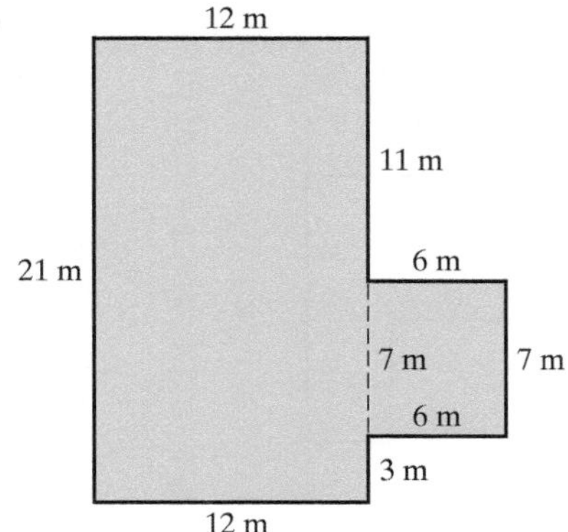

(a) Find the shaded area.

(b) Find the perimeter indicated by the black lines.

32.

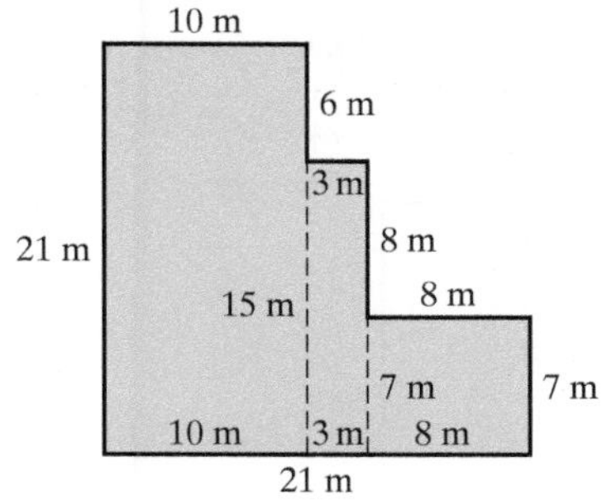

(a) Find the shaded area.

(b) Find the perimeter indicated by the black lines.

Applications

Some of the following exercises will require that you find a perimeter. Others will require that you find an area. Read each problem carefully to determine which you are to find.

33. ***Indoor Fitness Area*** A hotel conference centre is building an indoor fitness area measuring 220 m × 50 m. The flooring to cover the space is made of a special three-layered cushioned tile and costs $12.00 per square metre. How much will the new flooring cost?

34. ***Soccer Team Warm-Up*** In 1995, a rule was passed that no soccer field can be larger than 80 metres wide by 120 metres long. Merivale High School has a field with these dimensions. The team is running the perimeter of the field to warm up for a game. If they run around the field 4 times, how many metres will they run? How many metres more would they need to run to make two kilometres?

35. ***California King Blanket*** Caroline is making a fleece blanket for her bed. Her mattress is a California king size, measuring 72 in. wide by 84 in. long. She wants the blanket to be the same length as the mattress, but the width she wants increased by 12 in.

(a) Find how many square feet the blanket will be.

(b) If Caroline sews a border on all four sides of the blanket, how many feet of border should she buy?

36. ***Scuba Shop Sign*** Sammy's Scuba Shop is installing a new sign measuring 5.4 m × 8.1 m. The sign will be framed in purple neon light, which will cost $32.50 per metre. How much will it cost to frame the sign in purple neon light?

37. A farmer has 16 metres of fencing. He constructs a rectangular garden whose sides are whole numbers. He uses all the fence to enclose the garden.

(a) How many possible shapes can the garden have?

(b) What is the area of each possible garden?

(c) Which shape has the largest area?

38. A farmer has 18 metres of fencing. She constructs a rectangular garden whose sides are whole numbers. She uses all the fence to enclose the garden.

(a) How many possible shapes can the garden have?

(b) What is the area of each possible garden?

(c) Which shape has the largest area?

Installation of Carpeting *A family decides to have custom carpeting installed. It will cost $14.50 per square yard. The binding, which runs along the outside edges of the carpet, will cost $1.50 per yard. Find the cost of carpeting and binding for each room. Note that dimensions are given in feet. (Remember, 1 square yard equals 9 square feet.)*

39.

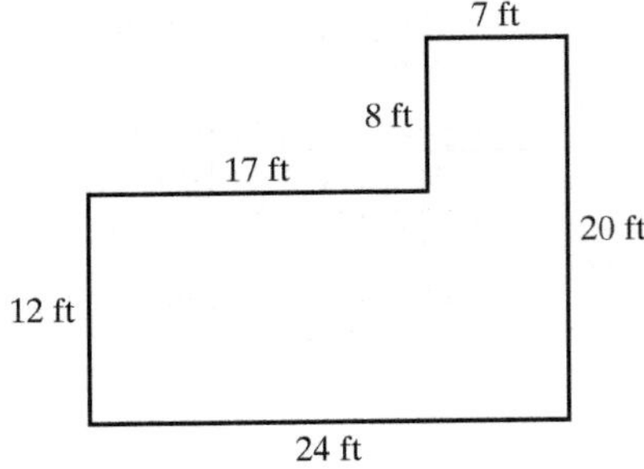

40.

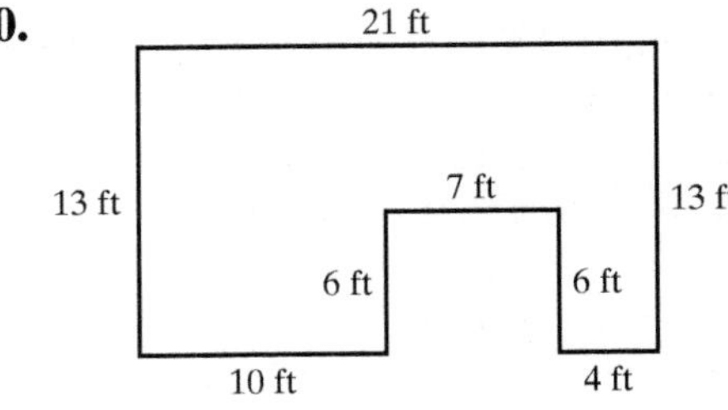

Quick Quiz 2

1. Find the perimeter of a rectangle that measures 2.3 centimetres by 1.5 centimetres.

2. Find the area of a square that measures 11 kilometres on each side.

3. Find the cost of carpeting a rectangular room that measures 11 metres by 16 metres if the carpeting costs $6 per square metre.

4. Concept Check If a rectangle that measures 12 metres by 15 metres is attached to a square that measures 15 metres on a side, explain how you would find the area of the entire region.

SECTION 3 PARALLELOGRAMS, TRAPEZOIDS, AND RHOMBUSES

 Finding the Perimeter and Area of a Parallelogram or a Rhombus

Parallelograms, rhombuses, and trapezoids are figures related to rectangles. Actually, they are in the same "family," the **quadrilaterals** (four-sided figures). For all these figures, the perimeter is the distance around the figure. But there is a different formula for finding the area of each.

A **parallelogram** is a four-sided figure in which both pairs of opposite sides are parallel. The opposite sides of a parallelogram are equal in length.

The following figures are parallelograms. Notice that the adjoining sides need not be perpendicular as in a rectangle.

Student Learning Objectives

After studying this section, you will be able to:

 **Find the perimeter and area of a parallelogram or a rhombus.**

 **Find the perimeter and area of a trapezoid.**

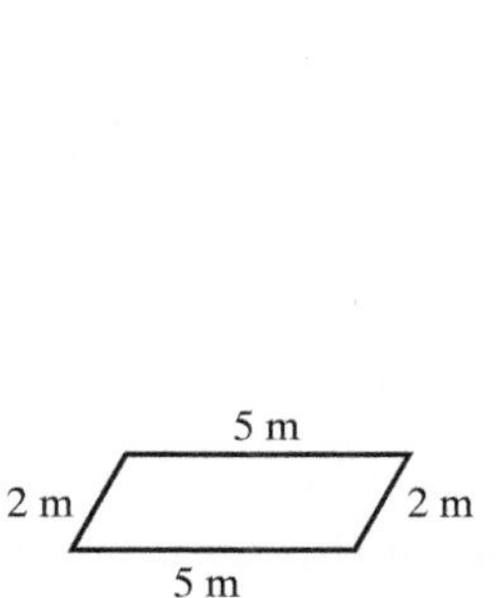

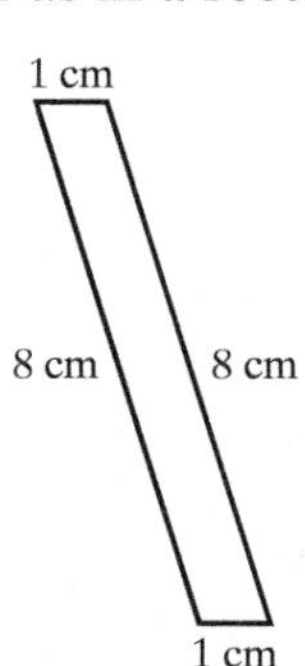

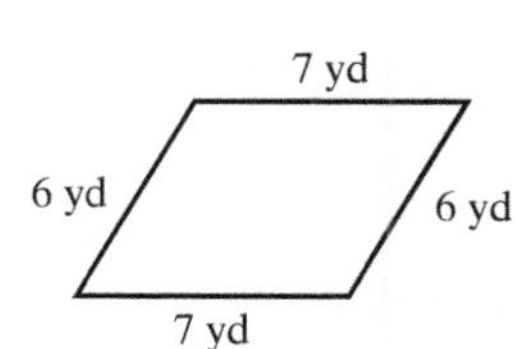

The **perimeter** of a parallelogram is the distance around the parallelogram. It is found by adding the lengths of all the sides of the figure.

EXAMPLE 1 Find the perimeter.

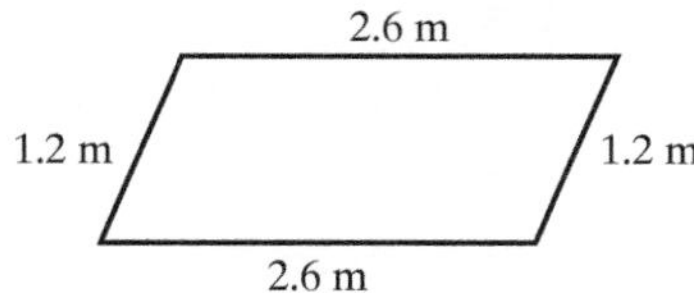

Solution $P = (2)(1.2 \text{ metres}) + (2)(2.6 \text{ metres})$
$= 2.4 \text{ metres} + 5.2 \text{ metres} = 7.6 \text{ metres}$

Practice Problem 1 Find the perimeter of the parallelogram in the margin.

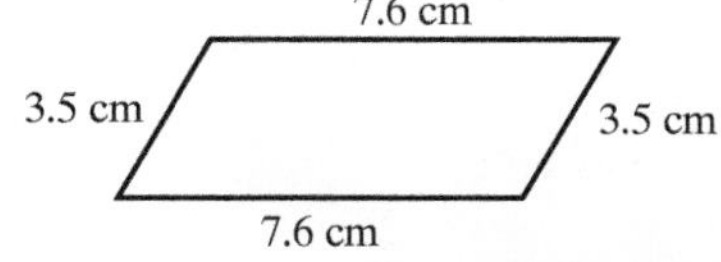

To find the **area** of a parallelogram, we multiply the base times the height. Any side of a parallelogram can be considered the **base.** The **height** is the shortest distance between the base and the side opposite the base. The height is a line segment that is perpendicular to the base. When we write the formula for area, we use the lengths of the base (b) and the height (h).

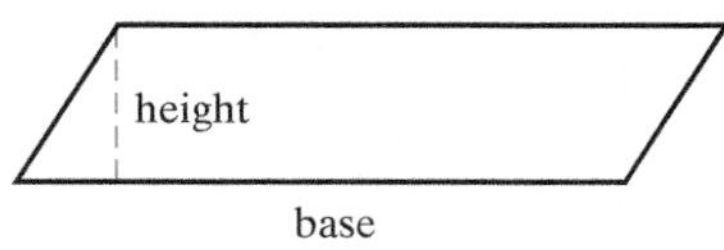

> The **area of a parallelogram** is the base (b) times the height (h).
>
> $$A = bh$$

Why is the area of a parallelogram equal to the base times the height? What reasoning leads us to that formula? Suppose that we cut off the triangular region on one side of the parallelogram and move it to the other side.

We now have a rectangle.

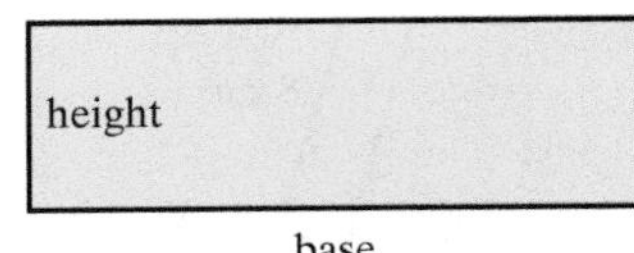

To find the area, we multiply the width by the length. In this case, $A = bh$. Thus finding the area of a parallelogram is like finding the area of a rectangle of length b and width h: $A = bh$.

EXAMPLE 2 Find the area of a parallelogram with base 7.5 m and height 3.2 m.

Solution

$$\begin{aligned} A &= bh \\ &= (7.5 \text{ m})(3.2 \text{ m}) \\ &= 24 \text{ m}^2 \end{aligned}$$

Practice Problem 2 Find the area of a parallelogram with base 10.3 km and height 1.5 km.

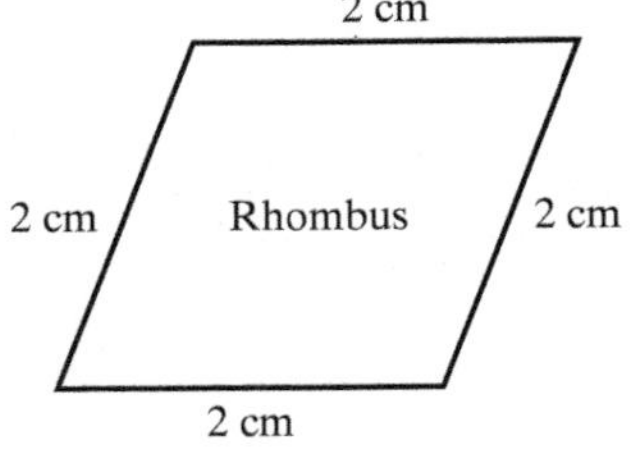

A **rhombus** is a parallelogram with all four sides equal. The figure to the left, with each side of length 2 centimetres, is a rhombus. We will solve a problem involving a rhombus in Example 3.

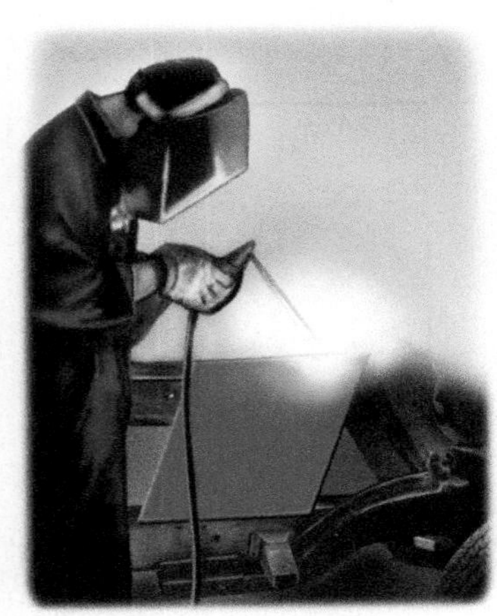

EXAMPLE 3 A truck is manufactured with an iron brace welded to the truck frame. The brace is shaped like a rhombus. The brace has a base of 9 inches and a height of 5 inches. Find the perimeter and the area of this iron brace.

Solution Since all four sides are equal, we merely multiply

$$P = 4(9 \text{ in.}) = 36 \text{ in.}$$

The perimeter of this brace is 36 inches.

Since the rhombus is a special type of parallelogram, we can use the area formula for a parallelogram. In this case the base is 9 inches and the height is 5 inches.

$$A = bh = (9 \text{ in.})(5 \text{ in.}) = 45 \text{ in.}^2$$

Thus the area of the brace is 45 square inches.

Practice Problem 3 An inlaid piece of cherry wood on the front of a hope chest is shaped like a rhombus. This piece has a base of 6 centimetres and a height of 4 centimetres. Find the perimeter and the area of this inlaid piece of cherry wood.

Finding the Perimeter and Area of a Trapezoid

A **trapezoid** is a four-sided figure with two parallel sides. The parallel sides are called **bases.** The lengths of the bases do not have to be equal. The adjoining sides do not have to be perpendicular.

Sometimes the trapezoid is sitting on a base. Then both bases are horizontal. But be careful. Sometimes the bases are vertical. You can recognize the bases because they are the two parallel sides. This becomes important when you use the formula for finding the area of a trapezoid.

Look at the following trapezoids. See if you can recognize the bases.

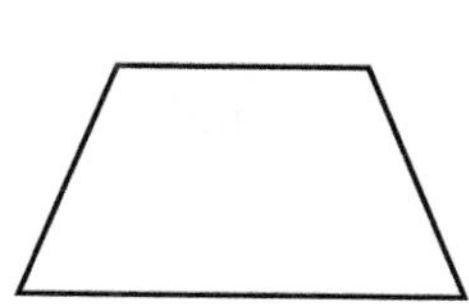

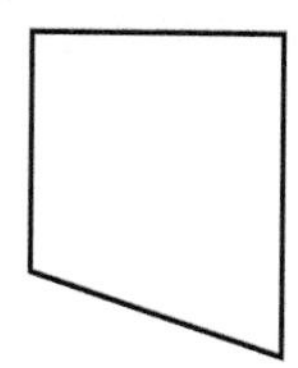

The perimeter of a trapezoid is the sum of the lengths of all of its sides.

EXAMPLE 4 Find the perimeter of the trapezoid on the right.

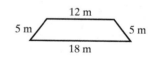

Solution

$$P = 18 \text{ m} + 5 \text{ m} + 12 \text{ m} + 5 \text{ m}$$
$$= 40 \text{ m}$$

12 m, 5 m, 5 m, 18 m

Practice Problem 4 Find the perimeter of a trapezoid with sides of 7 km, 15 km, 21 km, and 13 km.

Remember, we often use parentheses as a way to group numbers together. The numbers inside parentheses should be combined first.

$(5)(7 + 2) = (5)(9)$ First we add numbers inside the parentheses.

$= 45$ Then we multiply.

The formula for the area of a trapezoid uses parentheses in this way.

The **height** of a trapezoid is the distance between the two parallel sides. The area of a trapezoid is one-half the height times the sum of the bases. (This means you add the bases *first*.)

Now this can be written $\frac{h}{2} \cdot (b + B)$ or $h\left(\frac{b + B}{2}\right)$ or $\frac{h(b + B)}{2}$.

Some students like to remember $h\left(\frac{b + B}{2}\right)$ because it is the height times the average of the bases.

The **area of a trapezoid** with a shorter base b, a longer base B, and height h is

$$A = \frac{h(b + B)}{2}.$$

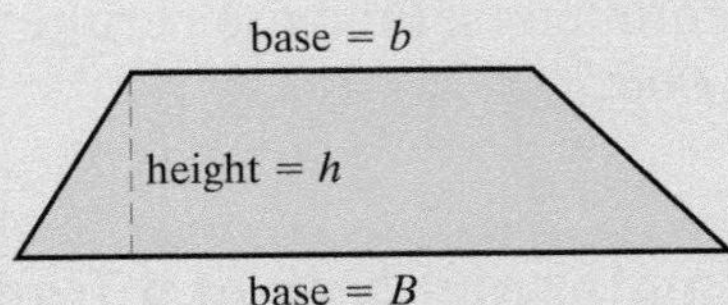

EXAMPLE 5 A roadside sign is in the shape of a trapezoid. It has a height of 8 m, and the bases are 15 m and 20 m.

(a) What is the area of the sign?

(b) If 1 litre of paint covers 7 m^2, how many litres of paint will be needed to paint the sign?

Solution

(a) We use the trapezoid formula with $h = 8$, $b = 15$, and $B = 20$.

$$A = \frac{h(b + B)}{2}$$

$$= \frac{(8\text{ m})(15\text{ m} + 20\text{ m})}{2}$$

$$= \frac{(8\text{ m})(35\text{ m})}{2} = \frac{280}{2}\text{ m}^2 = 140\text{ m}^2$$

(b) Each litre covers 7 m^2, so we multiply the area by the fraction $\frac{1\text{ L}}{7\text{ m}^2}$. This fraction is equivalent to 1.

$$140\ \cancel{\text{m}^2} \times \frac{1\text{ L}}{7\ \cancel{\text{m}^2}} = \frac{140}{7}\text{ L}$$

$$= 20\text{ L}$$

Thus 20 litres of paint would be needed.

Practice Problem 5 A corner parking lot is shaped like a trapezoid. The trapezoid has a height of 140 m. The bases measure 180 m and 130 m.

(a) Find the area of the parking lot.

(b) If 3 litres of sealant will cover 100 square metres of the parking lot, how many litres are needed to cover the entire parking lot?

Some area problems involve two or more separate regions. Remember, areas can be added or subtracted.

EXAMPLE 6 Find the area of the following piece of inlaid woodwork made by a master carpenter. Since this shape is hard to cut, it is made of one trapezoid and one rectangle laid together.

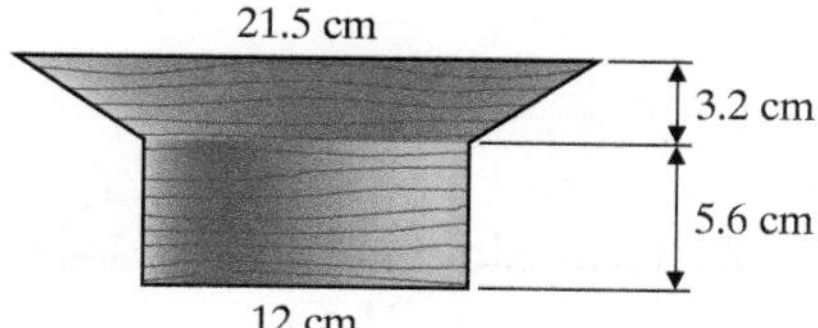

Rosenthal/SuperStock, Inc.

Solution We separate the area into two portions and find the area of each portion separately.

21.5 cm

3.2 cm

12 cm

The area of the trapezoid is

$$
\begin{aligned}
A &= \frac{h(b + B)}{2} \\
&= \frac{(3.2\text{ cm})(12\text{ cm} + 21.5\text{ cm})}{2} \\
&= \frac{(3.2\text{ cm})(33.5\text{ cm})}{2} \\
&= \frac{107.2}{2}\text{ cm}^2 \\
&= 53.6\text{ cm}^2.
\end{aligned}
$$

The area of the rectangle is

$$
\begin{aligned}
A &= lw \\
&= (12\text{ cm})(5.6\text{ cm}) \\
&= 67.2\text{ cm}^2.
\end{aligned}
$$

We now add the areas.

$$
\begin{array}{r}
67.2\text{ cm}^2 \\
+\,53.6\text{ cm}^2 \\
\hline
120.8\text{ cm}^2
\end{array}
$$

The total area of the piece of inlaid woodwork is 120.8 cm^2.

Practice Problem 6 Find the area of the piece of inlaid woodwork shown in the margin. The shape is made of one trapezoid and one rectangle.

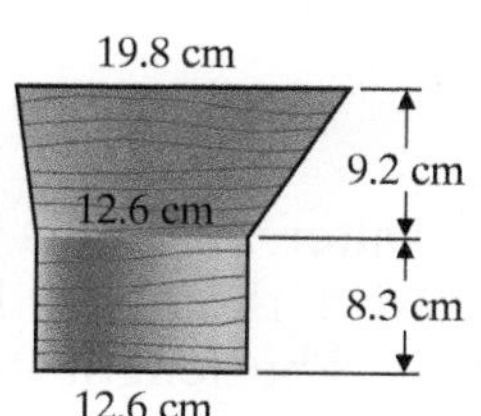

Section 3 Exercises

Verbal and Writing Skills

1. The perimeter of a parallelogram is found by ____________ the lengths of all the sides of the figure.

2. To find the area of a parallelogram, multiply the base times the ____________.

3. The height of a parallelogram is a line segment that is ____________ to the base.

4. The area of a trapezoid is one-half the height times the ____________ of the bases.

Find the perimeter of the parallelogram.

5. One side measures 2.8 m and a second side measures 17.3 m.

6. One side measures 14.7 m and a second side measures 21.5 m.

7.

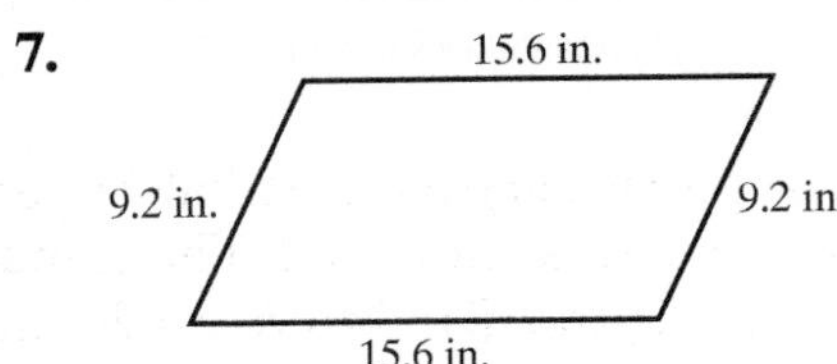

8.

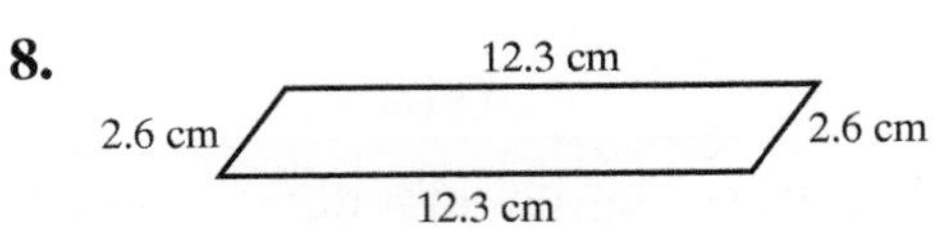

Find the area of the parallelogram.

9. The base is 17.6 m and the height is 20.15 m.

10. The base is 9.5 m and the height is 24.8 m.

11. ***Music Theatre Seating*** The preferred seating area at the Orpheus Theatre is in the shape of a parallelogram. Its base is 28 m and its height is 21.5 m. Find the area.

12. ***Courtyard*** A courtyard is shaped like a parallelogram. Its base is 126 yd and its height is 28 yd. Find its area.

13. Find the perimeter and the area of a rhombus with height 6 metres and base 12 metres.

14. Find the perimeter and the area of a rhombus with height 9 metres and base 14 metres.

15. ***Kite*** Walter made his son Daniel a kite in the shape of a rhombus. The height of the kite is 1.5 feet. The length of the base of the kite is 2.4 feet. Find the perimeter and the area of the kite.

16. ***Provincial Park*** The lawn in front of Mississagi Park is constructed in the shape of a rhombus. The height of the lawn region is 17 metres. The length of the base is 25 metres. Find the perimeter and the area of this lawn.

Find the perimeter of the trapezoid.

17.

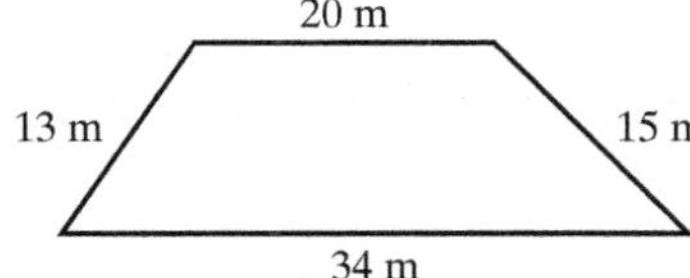

18.

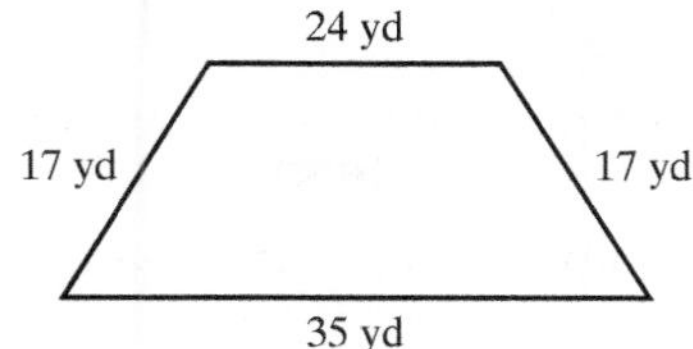

19. The two bases are 55 m and 135 m. The other two sides are 80.5 m and 75.5 m.

20. The two bases are 18.5 m and 23 m. The other two sides are 43.5 m and 48 m.

Find the area of the trapezoid.

21. The height is 12 m and the bases are 9.6 m and 10.2 m.

22. The height is 15 cm and the bases are 18.3 cm and 9.8 cm.

23. ***Diving in Key West*** An underwater diving area for snorkelers and scuba divers in Key West, Florida, is designated by buoys and ropes, making the diving section into the shape of a trapezoid on the surface of the water. The trapezoid has a height of 265 metres. The bases are 300 metres and 280 metres. Find the area of the designated diving area.

24. ***Provincial Park*** A provincial park in Saskatchewan is laid out in the shape of a trapezoid. The trapezoid has a height of 20 km. The bases are 24 km and 31 km. Find the area of the park.

Mixed Practice

(a) *Find the area of the entire shape made of trapezoids, parallelograms, squares, and rectangles.*

(b) *Name the object that is shaded in orange.*

(c) *Name the object that is shaded in yellow.*

25.

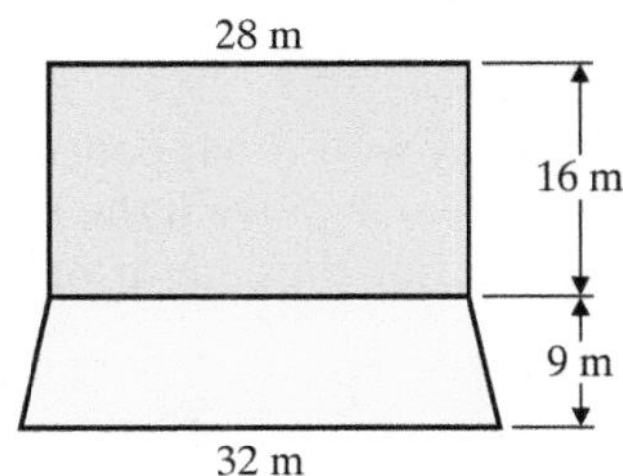

26.

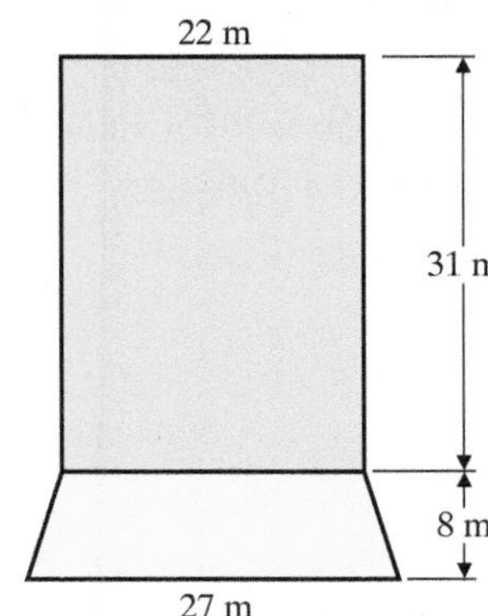

27.

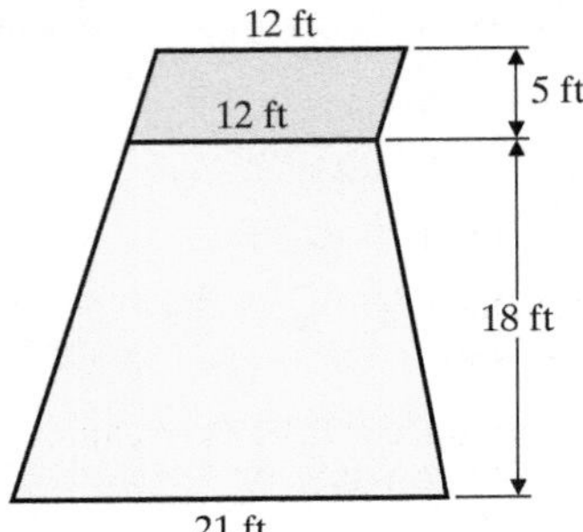

28.

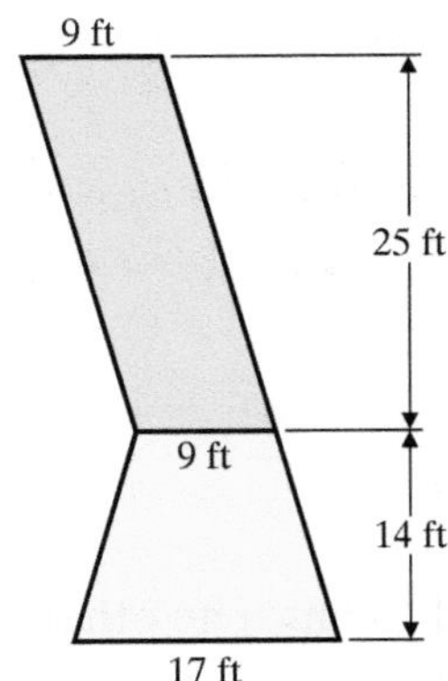

Applications

Carpeting in Conference Centre *Each of the following shapes represents the lobby of a conference centre. The lobby will be carpeted at a cost of $22 per square metre. How much will the carpeting cost?*

29.

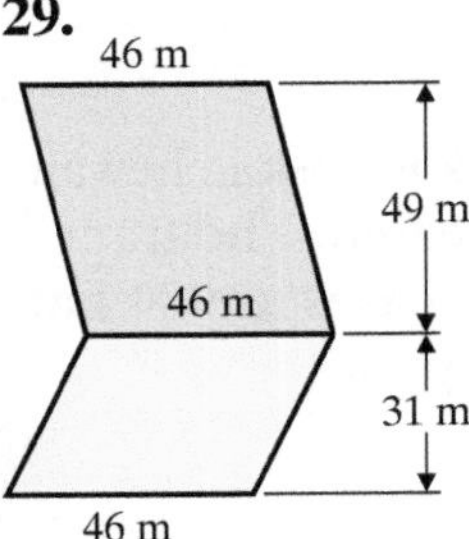

30.

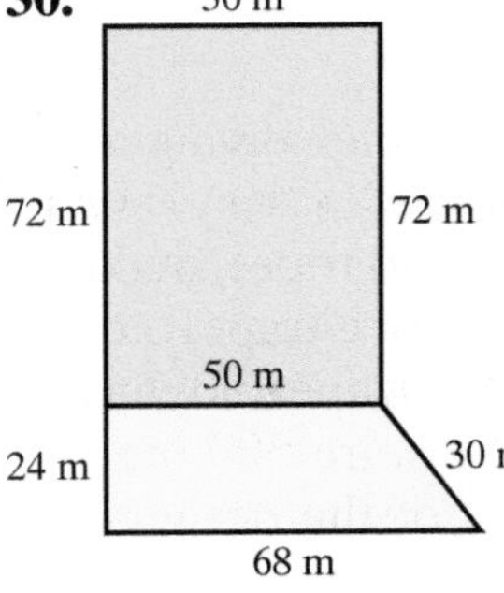

Quick Quiz 3

1. Find the perimeter of a trapezoid with sides measuring 9 metres, 15 metres, 9 metres, and 17 metres.

2. Find the area of a trapezoid with a height of 9 metres and bases of 30 metres and 34 metres.

3. Find the area of a parallelogram with a height of 2.5 centimetres and a base of 4.8 centimetres.

4. **Concept Check** Explain what would happen to the area of the trapezoid in problem 2 above if the height were increased to 16 metres but the length of each base remained the same.

SECTION 4 TRIANGLES

 Finding the Measures of Angles in a Triangle

Student Learning Objectives

After studying this section, you will be able to:

 **Find the measures of angles in a triangle.**

 **Find the perimeter and the area of a triangle.**

A **triangle** is a three-sided figure with three angles. The prefix *tri-* means "three." Some triangles are shown.

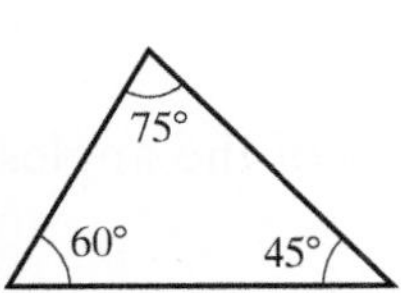

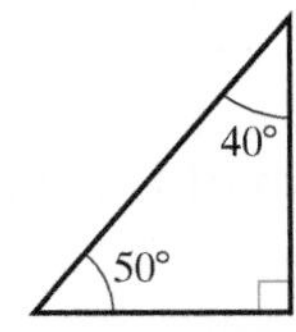

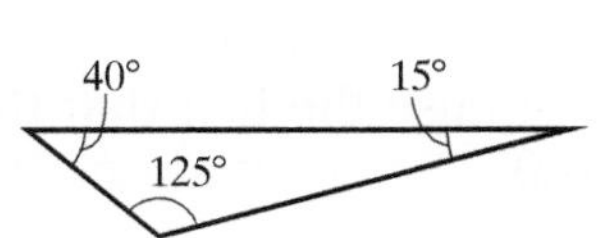

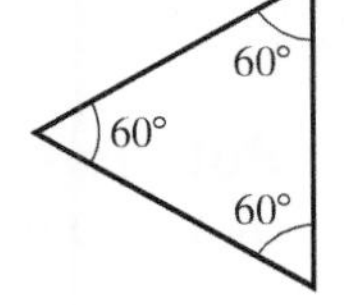

Although all triangles have three sides, not all triangles have the same shape. The shape of a triangle depends on the sizes of the angles and the lengths of the sides.

We will begin our study of triangles by looking at the angles. Although the sizes of the angles in triangles may be different, the sum of the angle measures of any triangle is always 180°.

The sum of the measures of the angles in a triangle is 180°.

Why is this? Perhaps you are wondering why all the angles of a triangle have measures that add up to 180°.

Remember, a straight angle is 180°.

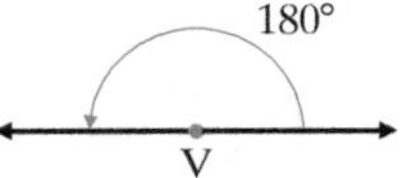

Suppose you take any triangle with $\angle A$, $\angle B$, and $\angle C$. Now cut off each corner of the triangle.

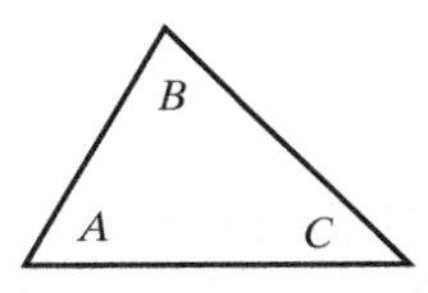

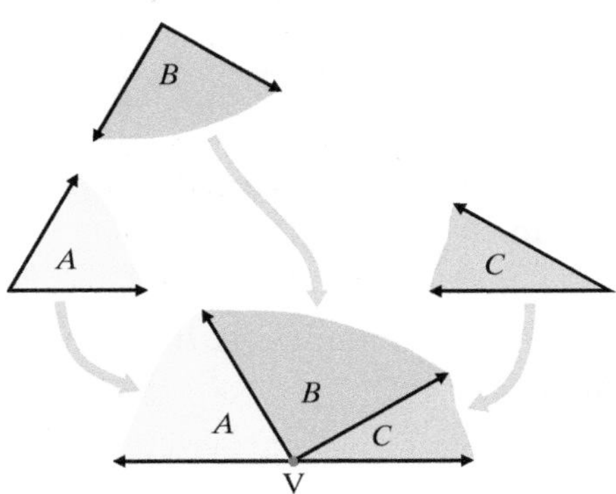

Now move the three angles so that they all have the same vertex and the middle angle shares an adjacent side with each of the other two angles. The three angles form a straight angle. Thus, the sum of the measures in a triangle is 180°.

We can use this fact to find the measure of an unknown angle in a triangle if we know the measures of the other two angles.

EXAMPLE 1 In the triangle below, angle A measures 35° and angle B measures 95°. Find the measure of angle C.

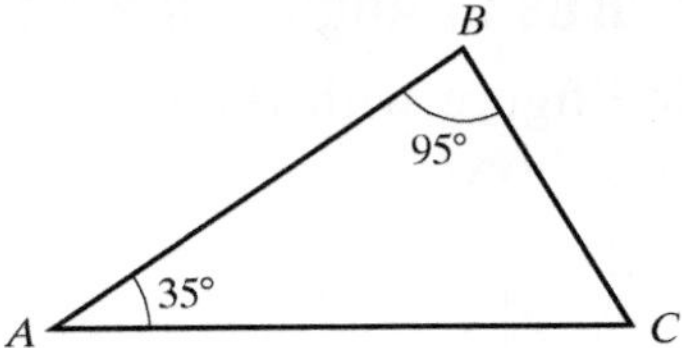

Solution We will use the fact that the sum of the measures of the angles of a triangle is 180°.

$$35 + 95 + x = 180$$
$$130 + x = 180$$

What number x when added to 130 equals 180? Since $130 + 50 = 180$, x must equal 50.

Angle C must measure 50°.

Practice Problem 1 In a triangle, angle B measures 125° and angle C measures 15°. What is the measure of angle A?

2 Finding the Perimeter and the Area of a Triangle

Recall that the perimeter of any figure is the sum of the lengths of its sides. Thus the perimeter of a triangle is the sum of the lengths of its three sides.

EXAMPLE 2 Find the perimeter of a triangular sail whose sides are 12 m, 14 m, and 17 m.

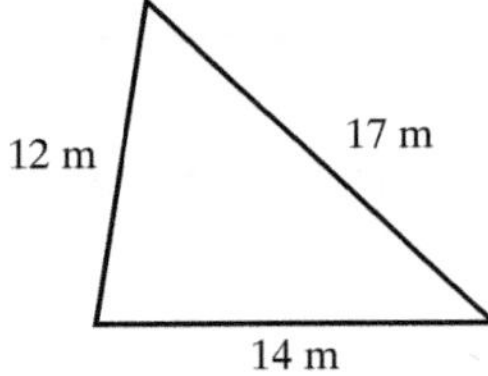

Solution $P = 12 \text{ m} + 14 \text{ m} + 17 \text{ m} = 43 \text{ m}$

Practice Problem 2 Find the perimeter of a triangle whose sides are 10.5 m, 10.5 m, and 8.5 m.

Some triangles have special names. A triangle with two equal sides is called an **isosceles triangle.**

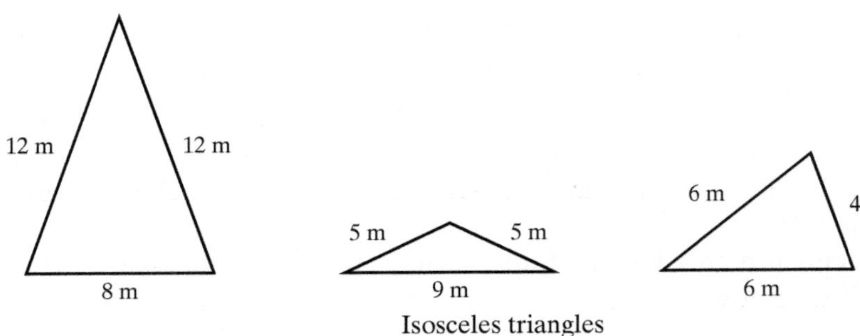

Isosceles triangles

A triangle with three equal sides is called an **equilateral triangle.** All angles in an equilateral triangle are exactly 60°.

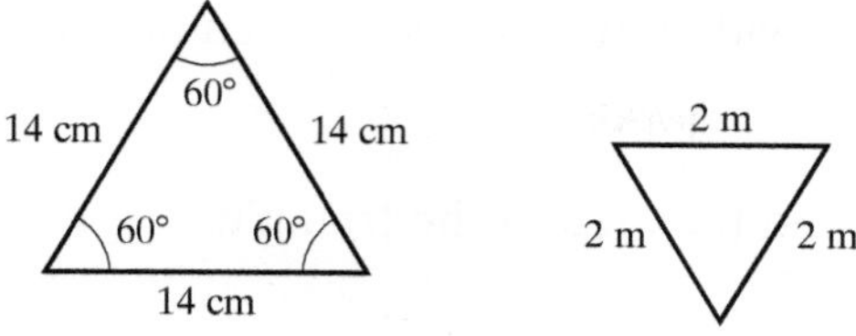

Equilateral triangles

A **scalene triangle** has no two sides of equal lengths and no two angles of equal measure.

A triangle with one 90° angle is called a **right triangle.**

The **height** of any triangle is the distance of a line drawn from a vertex perpendicular to the opposite side or an extension of the opposite side. The height may be one of the sides in a right triangle. The **base** of a triangle is perpendicular to the height.

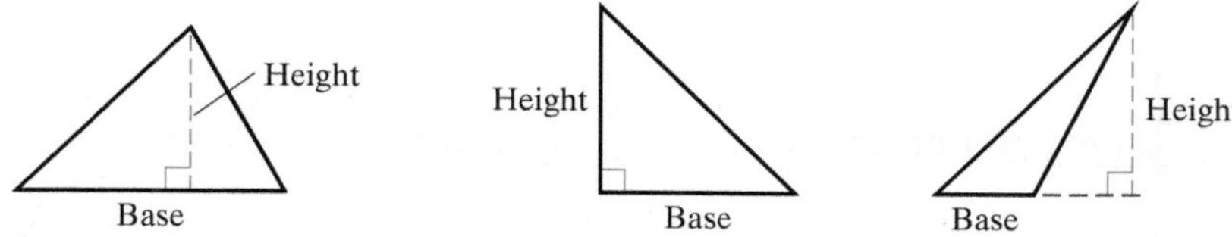

To find the area of a triangle, we need to be able to identify its height and base. The area of any triangle is half of the product of the base times the height of the triangle. The height is measured from the vertex above the base to that base.

The **area of a triangle** is the base times the height divided by 2.

$$A = \frac{bh}{2}$$

h = height

b = base

Where does the 2 come from in the formula $A = \frac{bh}{2}$? Why does this formula for the area of a triangle work? Suppose that we construct a triangle with base b and height h.

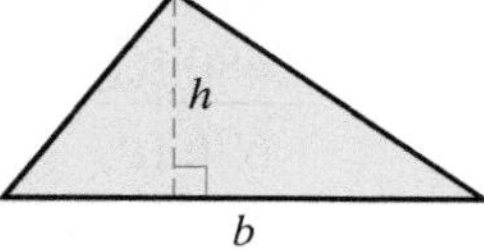

Now let us make an exact copy of the triangle and turn the copy around to the right exactly 180°. Carefully place the two triangles together. We now have a parallelogram of base b and height h. The area of a parallelogram is $A = bh$.

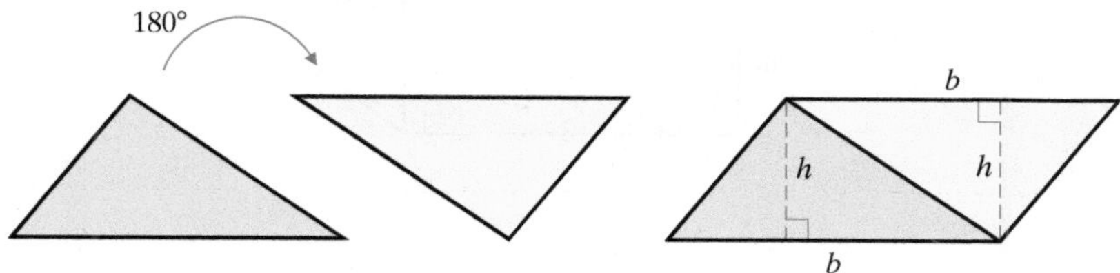

Because the parallelogram has area $A = bh$ and is made up of two triangles of identical shape and area, the area of one of the triangles is the area of the parallelogram divided by 2. Thus the area of a triangle is $A = \frac{bh}{2}$.

EXAMPLE 3 Find the area of the triangle.

Solution

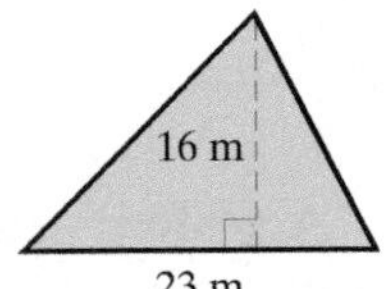

$$A = \frac{bh}{2} = \frac{(23\text{ m})(16\text{ m})}{2} = \frac{368\text{ m}^2}{2} = 184\text{ m}^2$$

Practice Problem 3 Find the area of the triangle in the margin.

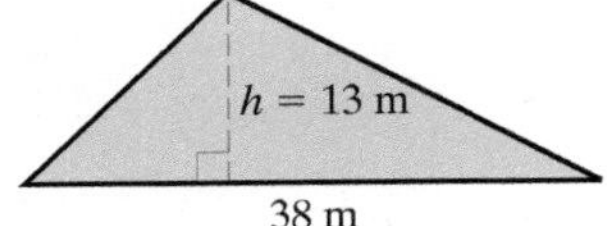

In some geometric shapes, a triangle is combined with rectangles, squares, parallelograms, and trapezoids.

EXAMPLE 4 Find the area of the side of the house shown in the margin.

Solution Because the lengths of opposite sides of a rectangle are equal, the triangle has a base of 24 ft. Thus we can calculate its area.

$$A = \frac{bh}{2} = \frac{(24\text{ ft})(18\text{ ft})}{2} = \frac{432\text{ ft}^2}{2} = 216\text{ ft}^2$$

The area of the rectangle is $A = lw = (24\text{ ft})(20\text{ ft}) = 480\text{ ft}^2$.

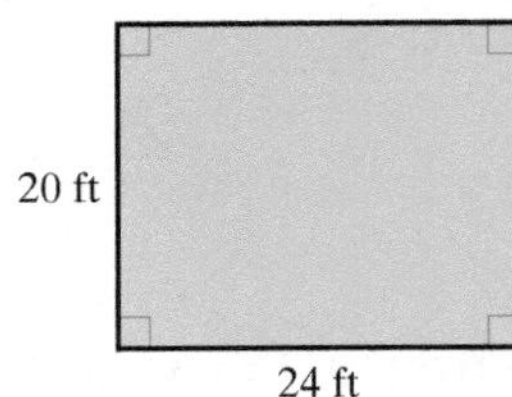

Now we find the sum of the two areas.

$$\begin{array}{r} 216\text{ ft}^2 \\ +480\text{ ft}^2 \\ \hline 696\text{ ft}^2 \end{array}$$

Thus the area of the side of the house is 696 square feet.

Practice Problem 4 Find the area of the figure.

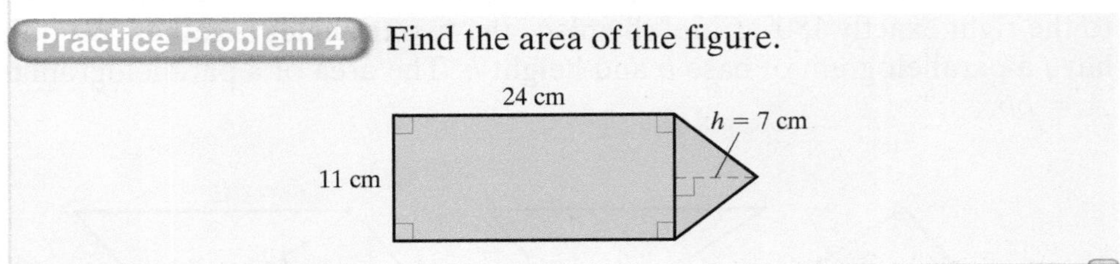

Section 4 Exercises

Verbal and Writing Skills

1. A 90° angle is called a ____________ angle.

2. The sum of the angle measures of a triangle is ____________.

3. Explain in your own words how you would find the measure of an unknown angle in a triangle if you knew the measures of the other two angles.

4. If you were told that a triangle was an isosceles triangle, what could you conclude about the sides of that triangle?

5. If you were told that a triangle was an equilateral triangle, what could you conclude about the sides of the triangle?

6. How do you find the area of a triangle?

Write true *or* false *for each statement.*

7. Two lines that meet at a 90° angle are perpendicular.

8. A right triangle has two angles of 90°.

9. The sum of the angles of a triangle is 180°.

10. The three sides of an isosceles triangle are all different lengths.

11. An equilateral triangle has one angle greater than 90°.

12. A scalene triangle has two angles of equal measures.

13. To find the area of a triangle, multiply its base by its height.

14. To find the perimeter of an equilateral triangle, you can multiply the length of one of the sides by 3.

Find the missing angle in the triangle.

15. Two angles are 36° and 74°.

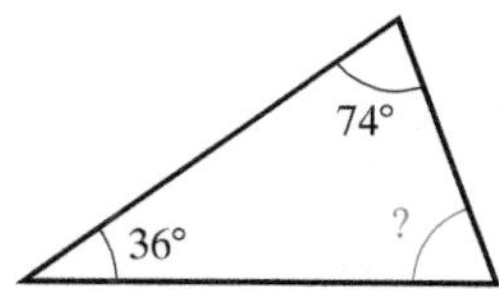

16. Two angles are 23° and 95°.

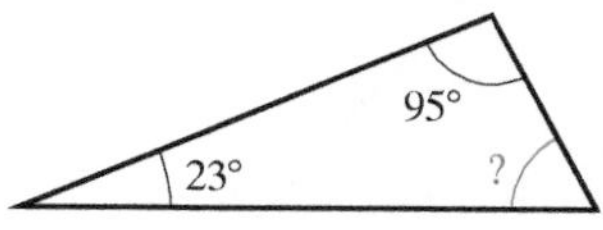

17. Two angles are 44.6° and 52.5°.

18. Two angles are 94.5° and 68.2°.

Find the perimeter of the triangle.

19. A scalene triangle whose sides are 18 m, 45 m, and 55 m.

20. A scalene triangle whose sides are 27 m, 44 m, and 23 m.

21. An isosceles triangle whose sides are 45.25 cm, 35.75 cm, and 35.75 cm.

22. An isosceles triangle whose sides are 36.2 cm, 47.65 cm, and 47.65 cm.

23. An equilateral triangle whose side measures $3\frac{1}{3}$ mi.

24. An equilateral triangle whose side measures $12\frac{2}{3}$ ft.

Find the area of the triangle.

25.

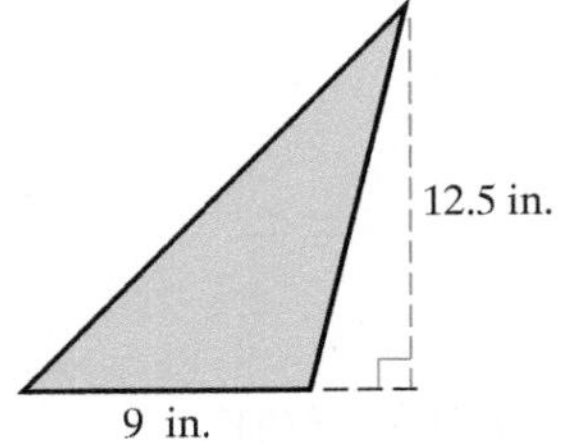

26.

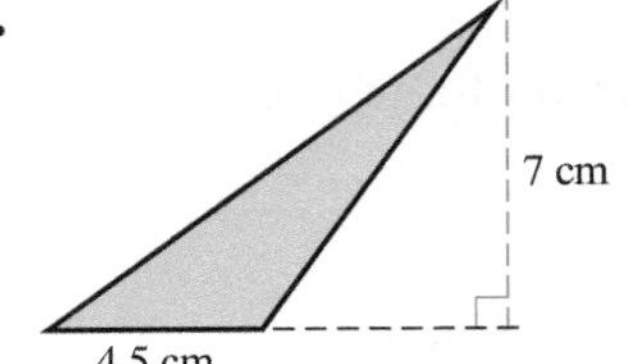

27. The base is 17.5 cm and the height is 9.5 cm.

28. The base is 3.6 cm and the height is 11.2 cm.

29. The base is $3\frac{1}{2}$ m and the height is $4\frac{1}{3}$ m.

30. The base is $11\frac{1}{4}$ ft and the height is $4\frac{2}{3}$ ft.

Mixed Practice *Find the area of the shaded region.*

31.

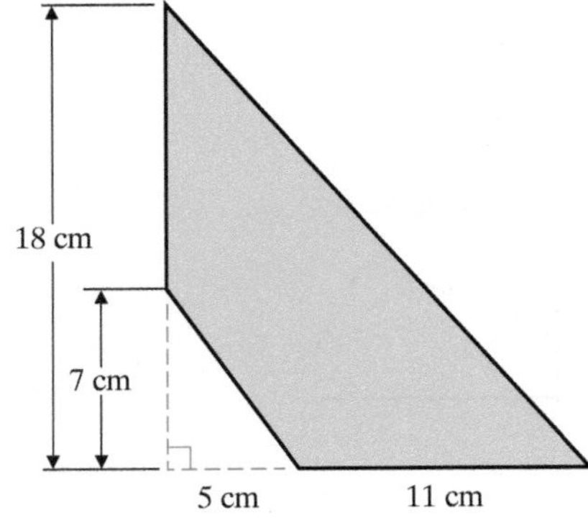

32.

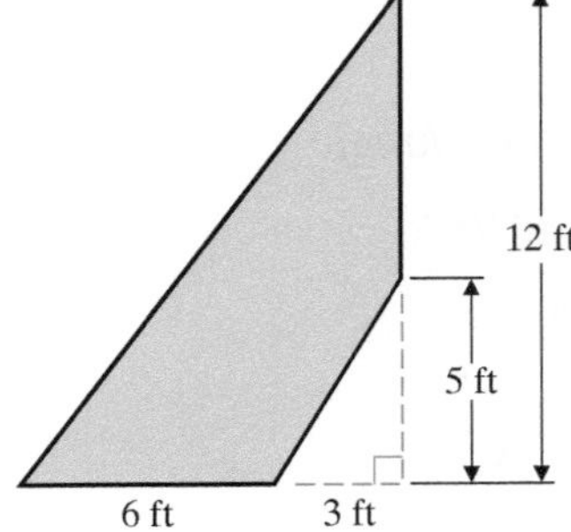

33.

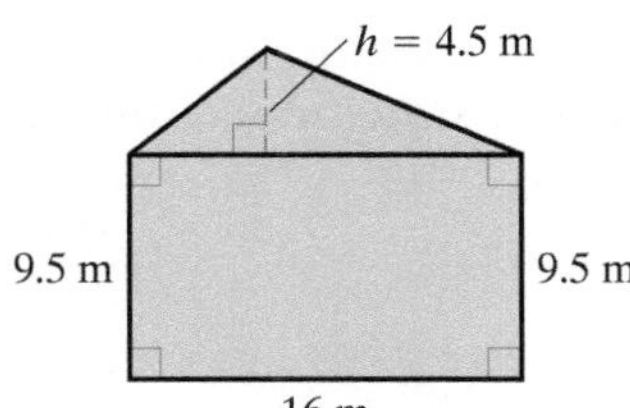

34.

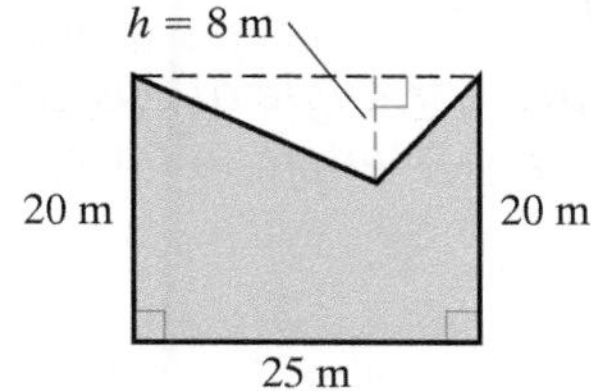

Applications

Area of Siding on a Building *Find the total area of all four vertical sides of the building.*

35.

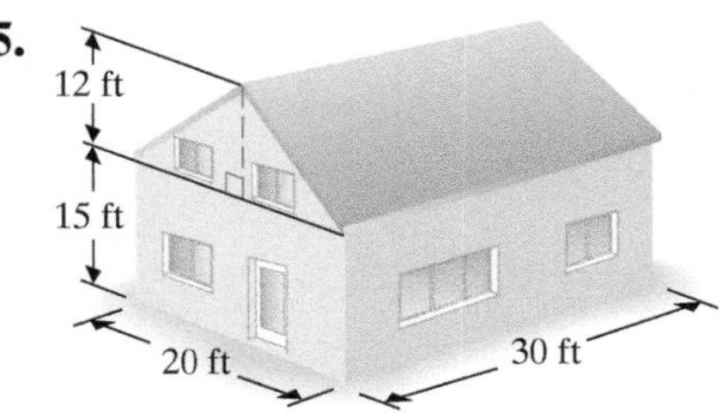

36.

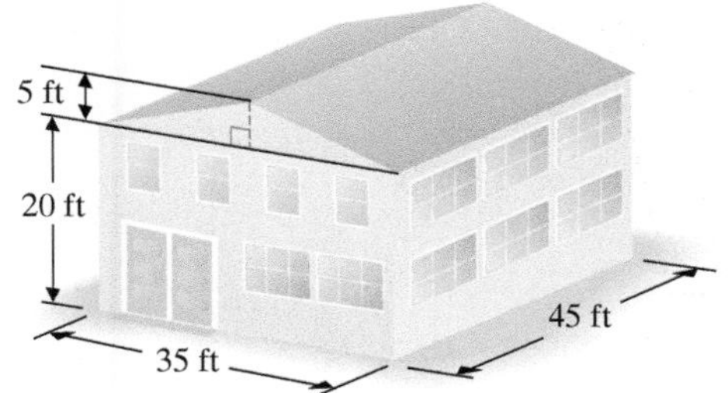

Coating on Test Plane Wings *The top surface of the wings of a test plane must be coated with a special lacquer that costs $90 per square metre. Find the cost to coat the shaded wing surface of the plane.*

37.

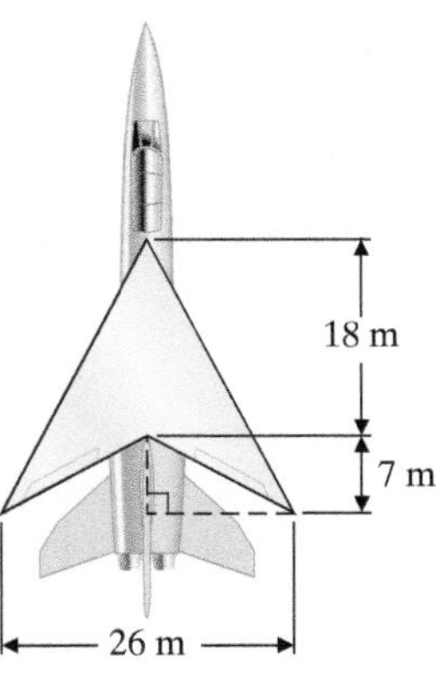

38.

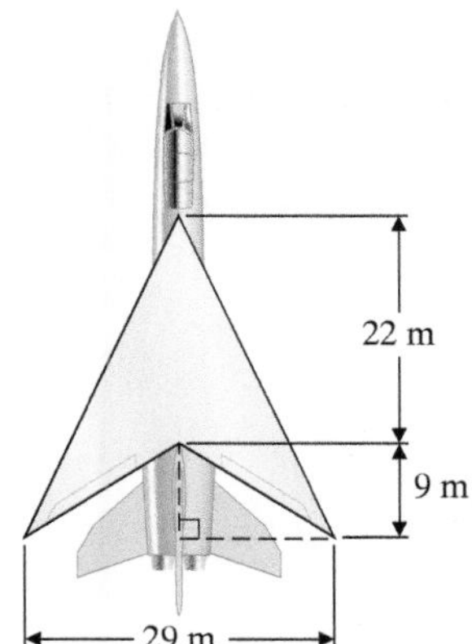

To Think About *An equilateral triangle has a base of 20 metres and a height of h metres. Inside that triangle is constructed a second equilateral triangle of base 10 metres and a height of 0.5 h metres. Inside the second triangle is constructed a third equilateral triangle of base 5 metres and a height of 0.25 h metres.*

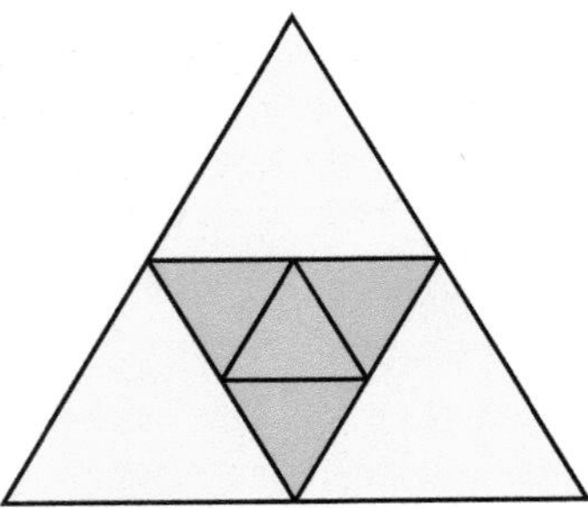

39. What percent of the area of the largest triangle is the area of the smallest triangle?

40. What percent of the perimeter of the largest triangle is the perimeter of the smallest triangle?

Quick Quiz 4

1. Find the perimeter of a triangle that has sides measuring 22.8 metres, 21.9 metres, and 36.7 metres.

2. Find the area of a triangle that has a base of 17 centimetres and a height of 12 centimetres.

3. A triangle has an angle that measures 75.4° and another that measures 53.7°. What is the measure of the third angle?

4. Concept Check A triangle has a base of 20 yards and an altitude of 20 yards. The triangle is attached to a rectangle that measures 20 yards by 15 yards. Explain how you would find the combined area of the triangle and the rectangle.

SECTION 5 SQUARE ROOTS

Evaluating the Square Root of a Perfect Square

Student Learning Objectives

After studying this section, you will be able to:

Evaluate the square root of a perfect square.

Approximate the square root of a number that is not a perfect square.

We know that by using the formula $A = s^2$ we can quickly find the area of a square with a side of 3 cm. We simply square 3 cm. That is, $A = (3\text{ cm})(3\text{ cm}) = 9\text{ cm}^2$ for an answer. Sometimes we want to ask another kind of question. If a square has an area of 64 cm^2, what is the length of its sides?

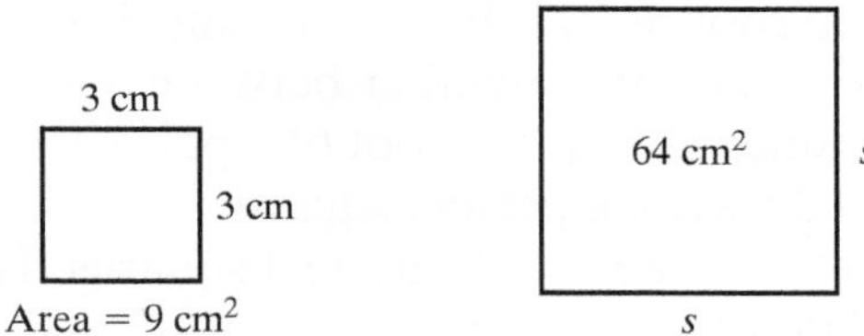

The answer is 8 cm. Why? The skill we need to find a number when we are given the square of that number is called *finding the square root.* The square root of 64 is 8.

If a number is a product of two identical factors, then either factor is called a **square root.**

The square root of 64 is 8 because $(8)(8) = 64$.
The square root of 9 is 3 because $(3)(3) = 9$.

The symbol for finding the square root of a number is $\sqrt{\ }$. To write the square root of 64, we write $\sqrt{64} = 8$. Sometimes we speak of finding the square root of a number as *taking* the square root of the number, or we can say that we will *evaluate* the square root of the number. Thus to take the square root of 9, we write $\sqrt{9} = 3$; to evaluate the square root of 9, we write $\sqrt{9} = 3$.

EXAMPLE 1 Find.

(a) $\sqrt{25}$ **(b)** $\sqrt{121}$

Solution

(a) $\sqrt{25} = 5$ because $(5)(5) = 25$.

(b) $\sqrt{121} = 11$ because $(11)(11) = 121$.

Practice Problem 1 Find.

(a) $\sqrt{49}$ **(b)** $\sqrt{169}$

If square roots are added or subtracted, they must be evaluated *first*, then added or subtracted.

EXAMPLE 2 Find. $\sqrt{25} + \sqrt{36}$

Solution

$\sqrt{25} = 5$ because $(5)(5) = 25$.
$\sqrt{36} = 6$ because $(6)(6) = 36$.

Thus $\sqrt{25} + \sqrt{36} = 5 + 6 = 11$.

Practice Problem 2 Find. $\sqrt{49} - \sqrt{4}$

When a whole number is multiplied by itself, the number that is obtained is called a **perfect square.**

36 is a perfect square because $(6)(6) = 36$.
49 is a perfect square because $(7)(7) = 49$.

The numbers 20 or 48 are *not* perfect squares. There is no *whole number* that when squared—multiplied by itself—yields 20 or 48. Consider 20. $4^2 = 16$, which is less than 20. $5^2 = 25$, which is more than 20. We realize, then, that the square root of 20 is between 4 and 5 because 20 is between 16 and 25. Since there is no whole number between 4 and 5, no whole number squared equals 20. Since the square root of a perfect square is a whole number, we can say that 20 is *not* a perfect square.

It is helpful to know the first 15 perfect squares. Take a minute to complete the following table.

Number, n	1	2	3	4	5	6	7	8	9	10	11	12	13	14	15
Number Squared, n^2	1	4	9	16										196	225

EXAMPLE 3

(a) Is 81 a perfect square? **(b)** If so, find $\sqrt{81}$.

Solution

(a) Yes. 81 is a perfect square because $(9)(9) = 81$.
(b) $\sqrt{81} = 9$

Practice Problem 3

(a) Is 144 a perfect square? **(b)** If so, find $\sqrt{144}$.

Approximating the Square Root of a Number That Is Not a Perfect Square

If a number is not a perfect square, we can only approximate its square root. This can be done by using a square root table such as the one that follows. Except for exact values such as $\sqrt{4} = 2.000$, all values are rounded to the nearest thousandth.

Number, n	Square Root of the Number, $\sqrt{n}$	Number, n	Square Root of the Number, $\sqrt{n}$
1	1.000	8	2.828
2	1.414	9	3.000
3	1.732	10	3.162
4	2.000	11	3.317
5	2.236	12	3.464
6	2.449	13	3.606
7	2.646	14	3.742

A square root table is located in Appendix: Tables. It gives you the square root of whole numbers up to 200. Square roots can also be found with any calculator that has a square root key. Usually the key looks like this $\boxed{\sqrt{\ }}$ or this $\boxed{\sqrt{x}}$. To find the square root of 8 on most calculators, ber 8 and press $\boxed{\sqrt{\ }}$ or $\boxed{\sqrt{x}}$. You will see displayed 2.8284271. On some enter the numcalculators, you must enter the square root key first followed by the number. (Your calculator may display fewer or more digits.) Remember, no matter how many digits your calculator displays, when we find $\sqrt{8}$, we have only an **approximation.** It is not an exact answer. To emphasize this we use the $\approx$ notation to mean "is approximately equal to." Thus $\sqrt{8} \approx 2.828$.

EXAMPLE 4 Find approximate values using the square root table or a calculator. Round to the nearest thousandth.

(a) $\sqrt{2}$ **(b)** $\sqrt{12}$ **(c)** $\sqrt{7}$

Solution

(a) $\sqrt{2} \approx 1.414$ **(b)** $\sqrt{12} \approx 3.464$ **(c)** $\sqrt{7} \approx 2.646$

Practice Problem 4 Approximate to the nearest thousandth.

(a) $\sqrt{3}$ **(b)** $\sqrt{13}$ **(c)** $\sqrt{5}$

EXAMPLE 5 Approximate to the nearest thousandth of a centimetre the length of the side of a square that has an area of 6 cm^2.

Solution $\sqrt{6 \text{ cm}^2} \approx 2.449$ cm

Thus, to the nearest thousandth of a centimetre, the side measures 2.449 cm.

Practice Problem 5 Approximate to the nearest thousandth of a metre the length of the side of a square that has an area of 22 m^2.

Calculator

Square Roots

Locate the square root key $\boxed{\sqrt{\ }}$ on your calculator.

1. To find $\sqrt{289}$, enter

289 $\boxed{\sqrt{\ }}$

The display should read

$\boxed{17}$

2. To find $\sqrt{194}$, enter

194 $\boxed{\sqrt{\ }}$

The display should read

$\boxed{13.928388}$

This is just an approximation of the actual square root. We will round the answer to the nearest thousandth.

$\sqrt{194} \approx 13.928$

Your calculator may require you to enter the square root key first and then the number.

Section 5 Exercises

Verbal and Writing Skills

1. Why is $\sqrt{25} = 5$?

2. $\sqrt{49}$ is read "the ____________ of 49."

3. 25 is a perfect square because its square root, 5, is a ____________ number.

4. Is 32 a perfect square? Why or why not?

5. How can you approximate the square root of a number that is not a perfect square?

6. How would you find $\sqrt{0.04}$?

Find each square root. Do not use a calculator. Do not refer to a table of square roots.

7. $\sqrt{9}$
8. $\sqrt{16}$
9. $\sqrt{64}$
10. $\sqrt{81}$
11. $\sqrt{144}$
12. $\sqrt{196}$
13. $\sqrt{0}$
14. $\sqrt{225}$
15. $\sqrt{169}$
16. $\sqrt{121}$
17. $\sqrt{100}$
18. $\sqrt{324}$

In exercises 19–28, evaluate the square roots first, then add, subtract, or multiply the results. Do not use a calculator or a square root table.

19. $\sqrt{49} + \sqrt{9}$
20. $\sqrt{25} + \sqrt{64}$
21. $\sqrt{81} + \sqrt{1}$
22. $\sqrt{0} + \sqrt{121}$
23. $\sqrt{225} - \sqrt{144}$
24. $\sqrt{169} - \sqrt{64}$
25. $\sqrt{169} - \sqrt{121} + \sqrt{36}$
26. $\sqrt{196} + \sqrt{36} - \sqrt{16}$
27. $\sqrt{4} \times \sqrt{121}$
28. $\sqrt{225} \times \sqrt{9}$
29. **(a)** Is 256 a perfect square?
    (b) If so, find $\sqrt{256}$.
30. **(a)** Is 289 a perfect square?
    (b) If so, find $\sqrt{289}$.

Use a table of square roots or a calculator with a square root key to approximate to the nearest thousandth.

31. $\sqrt{18}$
32. $\sqrt{45}$
33. $\sqrt{76}$
34. $\sqrt{82}$
35. $\sqrt{200}$
36. $\sqrt{194}$

Find the length of the side of the square. If the area is not a perfect square, approximate by using a square root table or a calculator with a square root key. Round to the nearest thousandth.

37. A square with area 34 m^2.
38. A square with area 62 m^2.
39. A square with area 136 m^2.
40. A square with area 250 m^2.

Mixed Practice *Evaluate the square roots first. Then combine the results. Use a calculator or square root table when needed. Round to the nearest thousandth.*

41. $\sqrt{36} + \sqrt{20}$

42. $\sqrt{20} + \sqrt{81}$

43. $\sqrt{198} - \sqrt{49}$

44. $\sqrt{154} - \sqrt{36}$

Applications

Basketball Court *High school basketball is played on a standard rectangular court that measures 92 feet in length and 50 feet in width. Some middle schools have smaller basketball courts that measure 80 feet in length and 42 feet in width.*

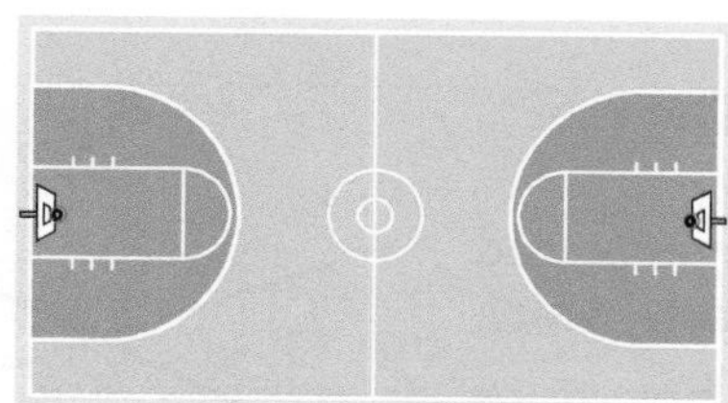

45. The diagonal of a standard high school basketball court measures $\sqrt{10\,964}$ feet in length. Find the length of this diagonal to the nearest tenth of a foot.

46. The diagonal of the smaller basketball court found in some middle schools measures $\sqrt{8164}$ feet in length. Find the length of this diagonal to the nearest tenth of a foot.

47. ***Baseball*** The distance from second base to home plate on a professional baseball field is $\sqrt{1505}$ m. Find this distance to the nearest tenth of a metre.

48. ***Television Measurements*** Television screens are measured diagonally. The screen of a Sony TV has a diagonal measurement of about $\sqrt{23\,154.5}$ cm. Find the length of this diagonal to the nearest whole centimetre.

Using a calculator with a square root key, evaluate and round to the nearest thousandth.

 **49.** $\sqrt{456} + \sqrt{322}$

50. $\sqrt{578} + \sqrt{984}$

Quick Quiz 5 Evaluate the following without the use of a calculator or a table of square roots.

1. $\sqrt{64}$

2. $\sqrt{36} + \sqrt{144}$

3. Find the length of the side of a square with area $196\ \text{ft}^2$.

4. **Concept Check** Explain how you would find the length of the side of a tiny square with an area of $0.81\ \text{cm}^2$ without using a calculator.

How Am I Doing? Sections 1–5

1. ____________

2. ____________

3. ____________

4. ____________

5. ____________

6. ____________

7. ____________

8. ____________

9. ____________

10. ____________

11. ____________

12. ____________

How are you doing with your homework assignments in Sections 1 to 5? Do you feel you have mastered the material so far? Do you understand the concepts you have covered? Before you go further, take some time to do each of the following problems.

1

1. Find the complement of an angle that is 72°.

2. Find the supplement of an angle that is 63°.

3. Find the measures of angle a, angle b, and angle c in the sketch to the right, which shows two intersecting straight lines.

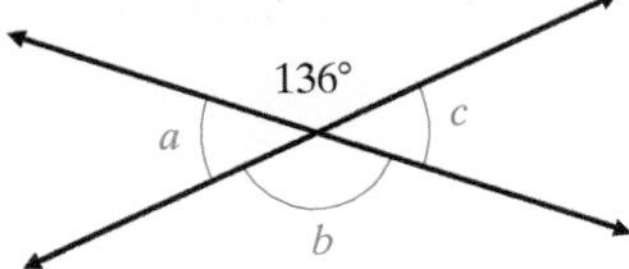

2

Find the perimeter of each rectangle or square.

4. Length = 6.5 m, width = 2.5 m

5. Length = width = 3.5 m

Find the area of each square or rectangle.

6. Length = width = 4.8 cm

7. Length = 5.8 yd, width = 3.9 yd

3

Find the perimeter.

8. A parallelogram with one side measuring 9.2 m and another side measuring 3.6 m.

9. A trapezoid with sides measuring 17 ft, 15 ft, $25\frac{1}{2}$ ft, and $21\frac{1}{2}$ ft.

Find the area.

10. A parallelogram with a base of 27 cm and a height of 13 cm.

11. A trapezoid with a height of 9 cm and bases of 16 cm and 22 cm.

12.

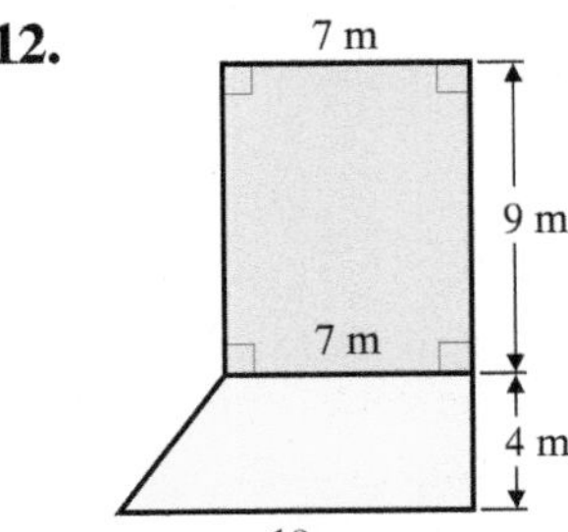

4

13. A triangle has two angles measuring 43° and 81°. Find the measure of the third angle.

13. ______

14. Find the perimeter of a triangle whose sides measure $9\frac{1}{2}$ in., 4 in., and $6\frac{1}{2}$ in.

14. ______

15. Find the area of a triangle with a base of 16 m and a height of 9 m.

15. ______

Applications of 1 to 4

16. A college entrance has a sign shaped like this figure.

(a) How many square feet of painted surface will the front of the sign have?

(b) How many feet of trim are needed to cover the edge (perimeter) of the sign?

30 ft
20 ft
16 ft
20 ft
44 ft

16. (a) ______

(b) ______

5

Evaluate exactly.

17. $\sqrt{64}$

18. $\sqrt{225} + \sqrt{16}$

19. $\sqrt{169}$

20. $\sqrt{256}$

17. ______

18. ______

19. ______

20. ______

21. Approximate $\sqrt{46}$ using a square root table or a calculator with a square root key. Round to the nearest thousandth.

21. ______

Your institution may have included the Answers to Selected Exercises for this module, which contains the answers to these questions. Each answer also includes a reference to the objective in which the problem is first taught. If you missed any of these problems, you should stop and review the Examples and Practice Problems in the referenced objective. A little review now will help you master the material in the upcoming sections.

Section 6 The Pythagorean Theorem

Student Learning Objectives

After studying this section, you will be able to:

1. Find the hypotenuse of a right triangle given the length of each leg.
2. Find the length of a leg of a right triangle given the lengths of the hypotenuse and the other leg.
3. Solve applied problems using the Pythagorean Theorem.
4. Solve for the missing sides of special right triangles.

1 Finding the Hypotenuse of a Right Triangle Given the Length of Each Leg

The Pythagorean Theorem is a mathematical idea formulated long ago. It is as useful today as it was when it was discovered. The Pythagoreans lived in Italy about 2500 years ago. They studied various mathematical properties. They discovered that for any right triangle, the square of the hypotenuse equals the sum of the squares of the two legs of the triangle. This relationship is known as the **Pythagorean Theorem.** The side opposite the right angle is called the **hypotenuse;** the other two sides are called the legs of the right triangle.

The Pythagoreans discovered that this theorem could be used to find the length of the third side of any right triangle if the lengths of two of the sides were known. We still use this theorem today for the very same reason.

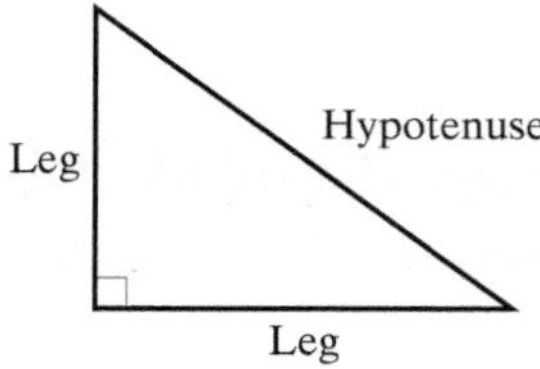

$$(\text{hypotenuse})^2 = (\text{leg})^2 + (\text{leg})^2$$

Note how the Pythagorean Theorem applies to the right triangle shown here.

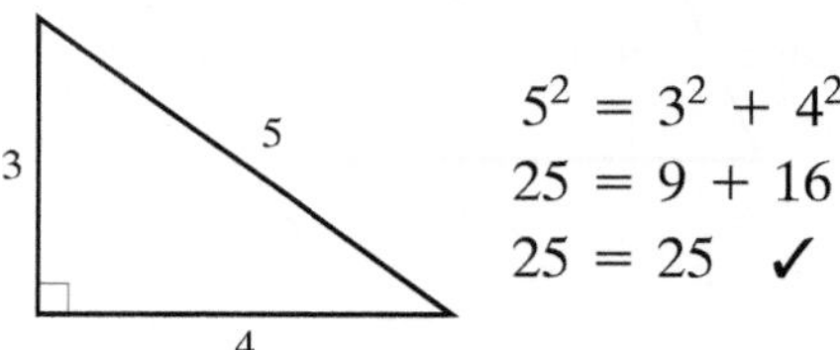

$$5^2 = 3^2 + 4^2$$
$$25 = 9 + 16$$
$$25 = 25 \quad ✓$$

In a right triangle, the hypotenuse is the longest side. It is always opposite the largest angle, the right angle. The legs are the two shorter sides. When we know each leg of a right triangle, we use the following property.

$$\text{Hypotenuse} = \sqrt{(\text{leg})^2 + (\text{leg})^2}$$

EXAMPLE 1 Find the hypotenuse of a right triangle with legs of 5 cm and 12 cm.

Solution

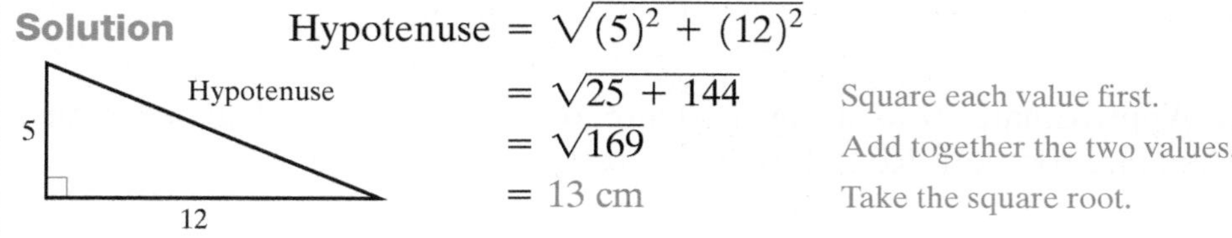

$$\begin{aligned} \text{Hypotenuse} &= \sqrt{(5)^2 + (12)^2} \\ &= \sqrt{25 + 144} && \text{Square each value first.} \\ &= \sqrt{169} && \text{Add together the two values.} \\ &= 13 \text{ cm} && \text{Take the square root.} \end{aligned}$$

Practice Problem 1 Find the hypotenuse of a right triangle with legs of 8 m and 6 m.

Sometimes we cannot find the hypotenuse exactly. In those cases, we often approximate the square root by using a calculator or a square root table.

EXAMPLE 2 Find the hypotenuse of a right triangle with legs of 4 m and 5 m. Round to the nearest thousandth.

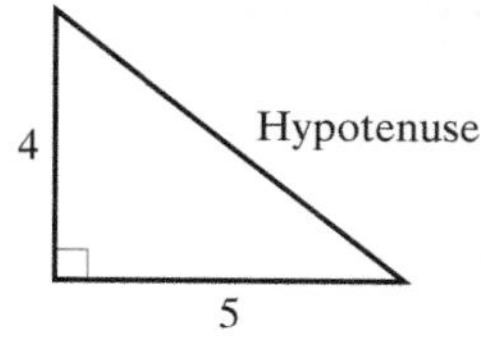

Solution

$$\begin{aligned} \text{Hypotenuse} &= \sqrt{(4)^2 + (5)^2} \\ &= \sqrt{16 + 25} && \text{Square each value first.} \\ &= \sqrt{41} \text{ m} && \text{Add the two values together.} \end{aligned}$$

Using the square root table or a calculator, we have the hypotenuse $\approx$ 6.403 m.

Practice Problem 2 Find to the nearest thousandth the hypotenuse of a right triangle with legs of 3 cm and 7 cm.

2 Finding the Length of a Leg of a Right Triangle Given the Lengths of the Hypotenuse and the Other Leg

When we know the hypotenuse and one leg of a right triangle, we find the length of the other leg by using the following property.

$$\text{Leg} = \sqrt{(\text{hypotenuse})^2 - (\text{leg})^2}$$

EXAMPLE 3 A right triangle has a hypotenuse of 15 cm and a leg of 12 cm. Find the length of the other leg.

Leg
15
12

Solution

$$\begin{aligned} \text{Leg} &= \sqrt{(15)^2 - (12)^2} \\ &= \sqrt{225 - 144} && \text{Square each value first.} \\ &= \sqrt{81} && \text{Subtract.} \\ &= 9 \text{ cm} && \text{Find the square root.} \end{aligned}$$

Practice Problem 3 A right triangle has a hypotenuse of 17 m and a leg of 15 m. Find the length of the other leg.

EXAMPLE 4 A sail for a sailboat is in the shape of a right triangle. The right triangle has a hypotenuse of 14 feet and a leg of 8 feet. Find the length of the other leg. Round to the nearest thousandth.

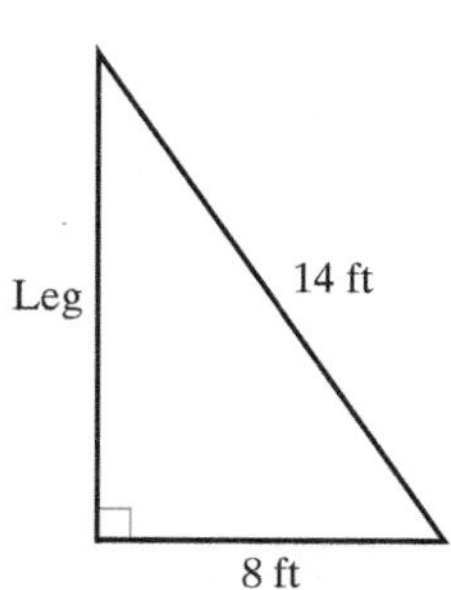

Solution

$$\begin{aligned} \text{Leg} &= \sqrt{(14)^2 - (8)^2} \\ &= \sqrt{196 - 64} && \text{Square each value first.} \\ &= \sqrt{132} \text{ feet} && \text{Subtract the two numbers.} \end{aligned}$$

Using a calculator or the square root table, we find that the leg $\approx$ 11.489 feet.

Practice Problem 4 A right triangle has a hypotenuse of 10 m and a leg of 5 m. Find the length of the other leg. Round to the nearest thousandth.

 Solving Applied Problems Using the Pythagorean Theorem

Certain applied problems call for the use of the Pythagorean Theorem in the solution.

EXAMPLE 5 A pilot flies 18 km east from Marmora to Madoc. She then flies 11 km south from Madoc to Centre Hastings. What is the straight-line distance from Marmora to Centre Hastings? Round to the nearest tenth of a kilometre.

Solution

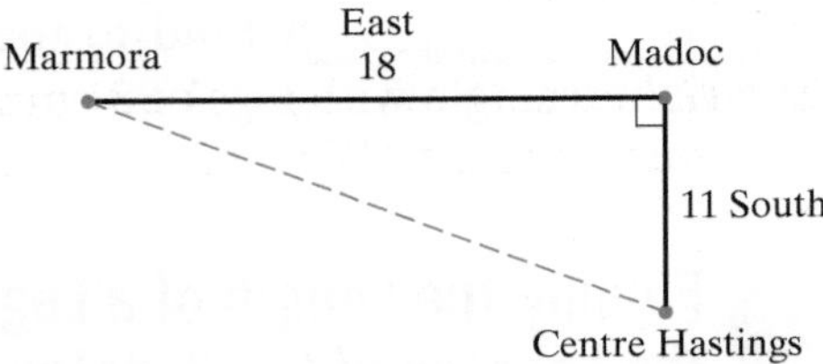

1. ***Understand the problem.*** It might help to draw a picture.

   The distance from Marmora to Centre Hastings is the hypotenuse of the triangle.

2. ***Solve and state the answer.***

$$\begin{aligned} \text{Hypotenuse} &= \sqrt{(\text{leg})^2 + (\text{leg})^2} \\ &= \sqrt{(18)^2 + (11)^2} \\ &= \sqrt{324 + 121} \\ &= \sqrt{445} \\ \sqrt{445} &\approx 21.095 \end{aligned}$$

   Rounded to the nearest tenth, the distance is 21.1 km.

3. ***Check.*** Work backward to check. Use the Pythagorean Theorem.

$$21.1^2 \stackrel{?}{\approx} 18^2 + 11^2 \quad \text{(We use } \approx \text{ because 21.1 is an approximate answer.)}$$
$$445.21 \stackrel{?}{\approx} 324 + 121$$
$$445.21 \approx 445 \ \checkmark$$

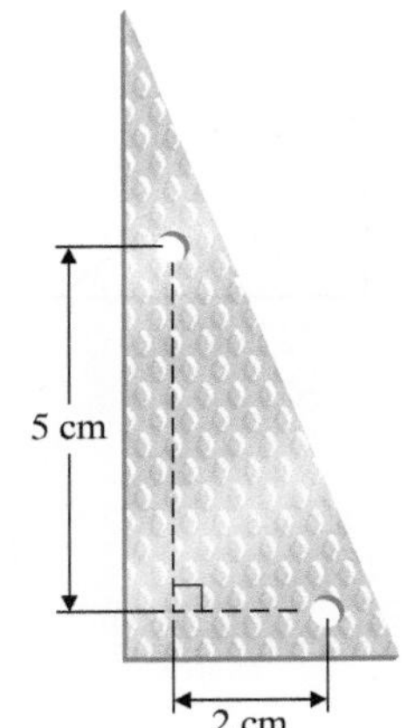

Practice Problem 5 Find the distance to the nearest thousandth between the centres of the holes in the triangular metal plate in the margin.

EXAMPLE 6 A 25-ft ladder is placed against a building at a point 22 ft from the ground. What is the distance of the base of the ladder from the building? Round to the nearest tenth.

Solution

1. ***Understand the problem.*** Draw a picture.

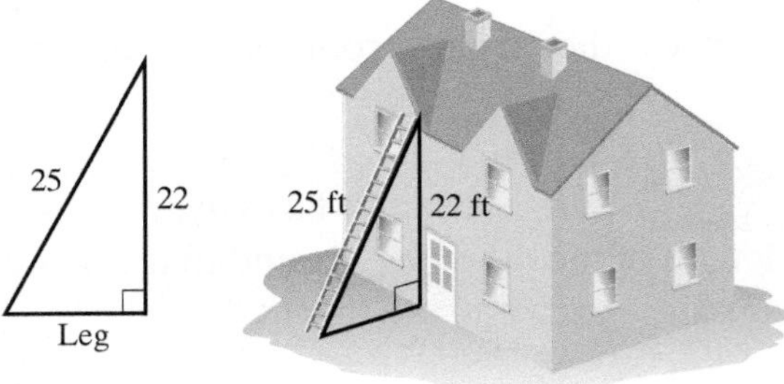

2. *Solve and state the answer.*

$$\begin{aligned}\text{Leg} &= \sqrt{(\text{hypotenuse})^2 - (\text{leg})^2}\\ &= \sqrt{(25)^2 - (22)^2}\\ &= \sqrt{625 - 484}\\ &= \sqrt{141}\end{aligned}$$

$$\sqrt{141} \approx 11.874$$

If we round to the nearest tenth, the base of the ladder is 11.9 ft from the house.

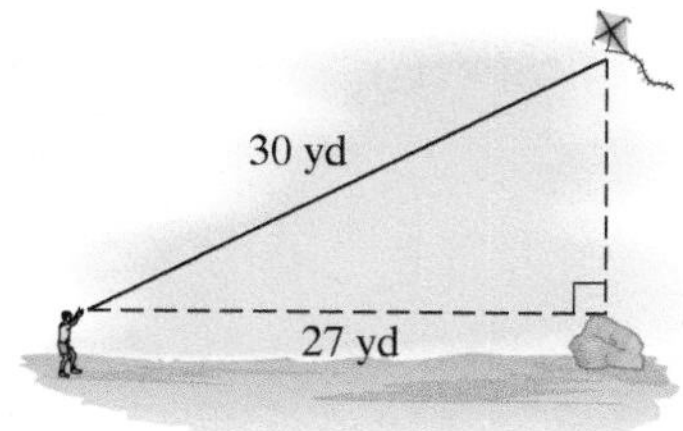

Practice Problem 6 A kite is out on 30 yd of string. The kite is directly above a rock. The rock is 27 yd from the boy flying the kite. How far above the rock is the kite? Round to the nearest tenth.

4 Solving for the Missing Sides of Special Right Triangles

If we use the Pythagorean Theorem and some other facts from geometry, we can find a relationship among the sides of two special right triangles. The first special right triangle is one that contains an angle that measures 30° and one that measures 60°. We call this the 30°–60°–90° right triangle.

> In a 30°–60°–90° triangle the length of the leg opposite the 30° angle is $\frac{1}{2}$ the length of the hypotenuse.

Notice that the hypotenuse of the first triangle is 10 m and the side opposite the 30° angle is exactly $\frac{1}{2}$ of that, or 5 m. The second triangle has a hypotenuse of 15 yd. The side opposite the 30° angle is exactly $\frac{1}{2}$ of that, or 7.5 yd.

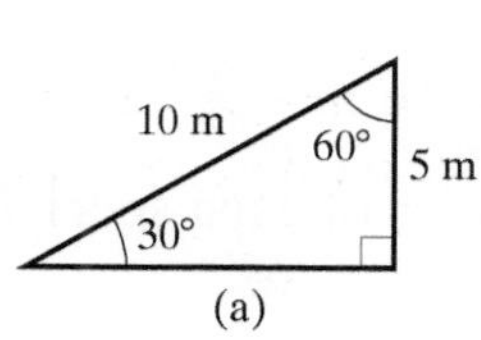

(a)

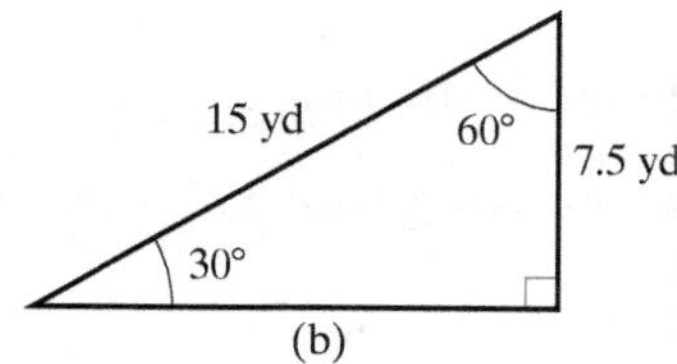

(b)

The second special right triangle is one that contains exactly two angles that each measure 45°. We call this the 45°–45°–90° right triangle.

> In a 45°–45°–90° triangle the lengths of the sides opposite the 45° angles are equal. The length of the hypotenuse is equal to $\sqrt{2} \times$ the length of either leg.

We will use the decimal approximation $\sqrt{2} \approx 1.414$ with this property.

$$\begin{aligned}\text{Hypotenuse} &= \sqrt{2} \times 7\\ &\approx 1.414 \times 7\\ &\approx 9.898 \text{ cm}\end{aligned}$$

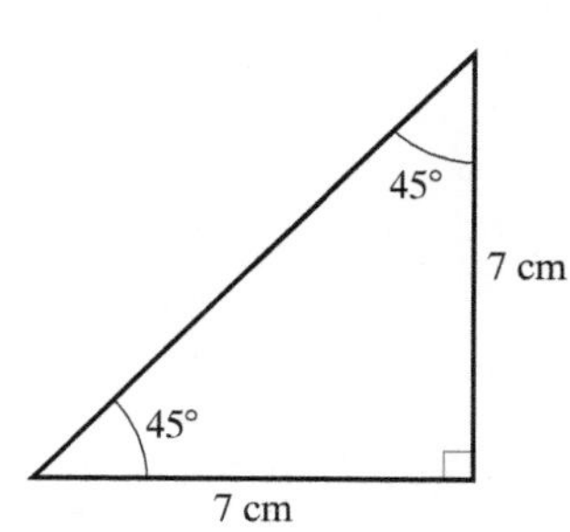

EXAMPLE 7 Find the requested sides of each special triangle. Round to the nearest tenth.

(a) Find the lengths of sides y and x. **(b)** Find the length of hypotenuse z.

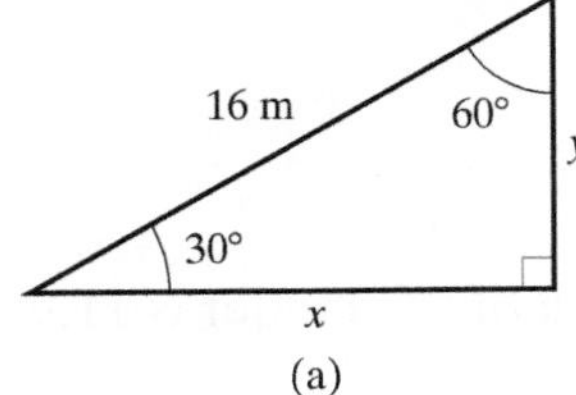

(a)

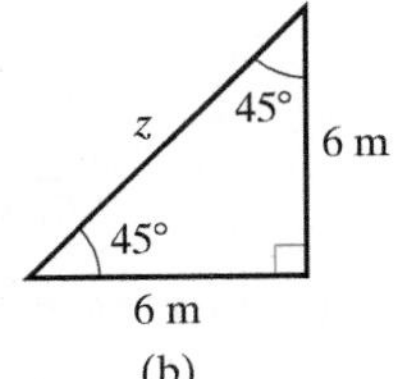

(b)

Solution

(a) In a 30°–60°–90° triangle the side opposite the 30° angle is $\frac{1}{2}$ of the hypotenuse.

$$\frac{1}{2} \times 16 = 8$$

Therefore, $y = 8$ m.

When we know two sides of a right triangle, we find the third side using the Pythagorean Theorem.

$$\begin{aligned} \text{Leg} &= \sqrt{(\text{hypotenuse})^2 - (\text{leg})^2} \\ &= \sqrt{16^2 - 8^2} = \sqrt{256 - 64} \\ &= \sqrt{192} \approx 13.856 \end{aligned}$$

Thus $x = 13.9$ m rounded to the nearest tenth.

(b) In a 45°–45°–90° triangle we have the following.

$$\begin{aligned} \text{Hypotenuse} &= \sqrt{2} \times \text{leg} \\ &\approx 1.414(6) \\ &= 8.484 \end{aligned}$$

Rounded to the nearest tenth, the hypotenuse = 8.5 m.

***NOTE TO STUDENT:** Fully worked-out solutions to all of the Practice Problems can be found at the end of the module.*

Practice Problem 7 Find the requested sides of each special triangle. Round to the nearest tenth.

(a) Find the lengths of sides y and x. **(b)** Find the length of hypotenuse z.

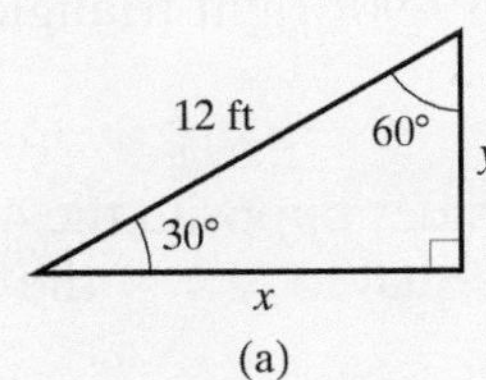

(a)

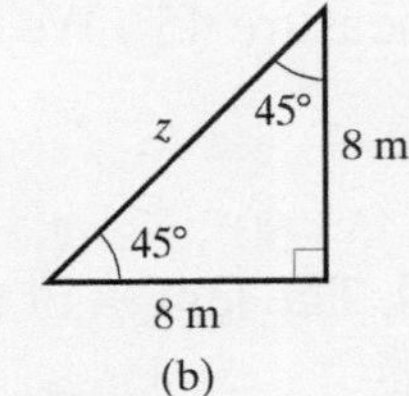

(b)

Section 6 Exercises

Verbal and Writing Skills

1. Explain in your own words how to obtain the length of the hypotenuse of a right triangle if you know the length of each of the legs of the triangle.

2. Explain in your own words how to obtain the length of one leg of a right triangle if you know the length of the hypotenuse and the length of the other leg.

Find the unknown side of the right triangle. Use a calculator or square root table when necessary and round to the nearest thousandth.

3. 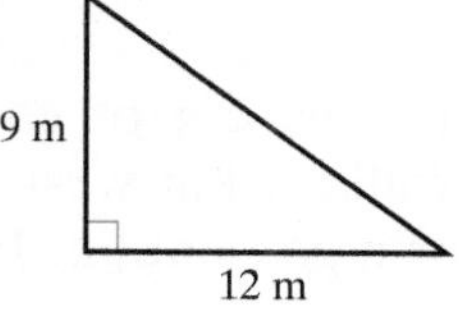

4. 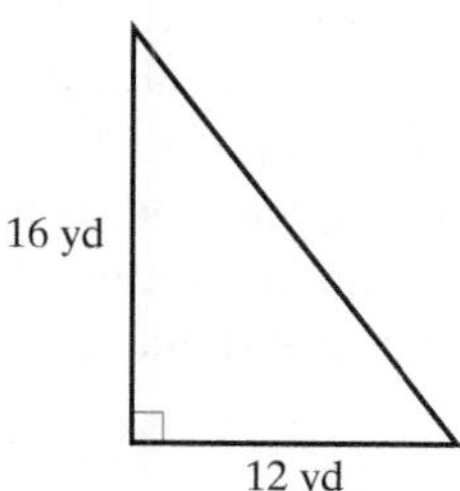

5. 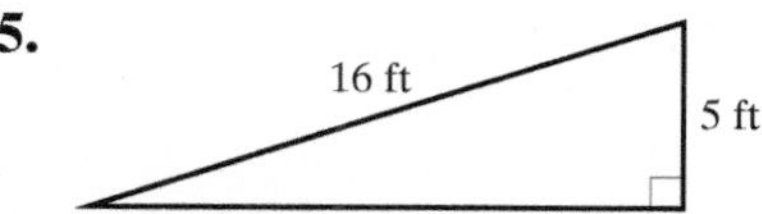

6. 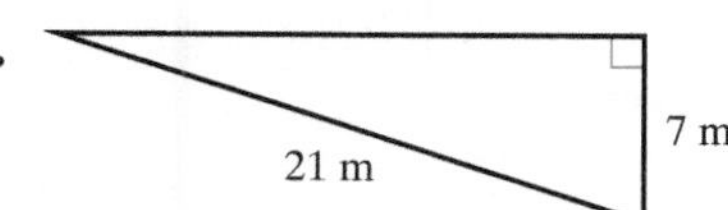

Using the information given, find the unknown side of the right triangle to the nearest thousandth.

7. leg = 11 m, leg = 3 m

8. leg = 8 m, leg = 2 m

9. leg = 10 m, leg = 10 m

10. leg = 7 m, leg = 7 m

11. hypotenuse = 10 ft, leg = 5 ft

12. hypotenuse = 13 cm, leg = 11 cm

13. hypotenuse = 14 yd, leg = 10 yd

14. hypotenuse = 20 km, leg = 14 km

15. leg = 12 m, leg = 9 m

16. leg = 6 m, leg = 8 m

17. hypotenuse = 16 cm, leg = 11 cm

18. hypotenuse = 23 mm, leg = 9 mm

Applications *Solve. Round to the nearest tenth.*

19. ***Loading Ramp*** Find the length of this ramp to the back of a truck.

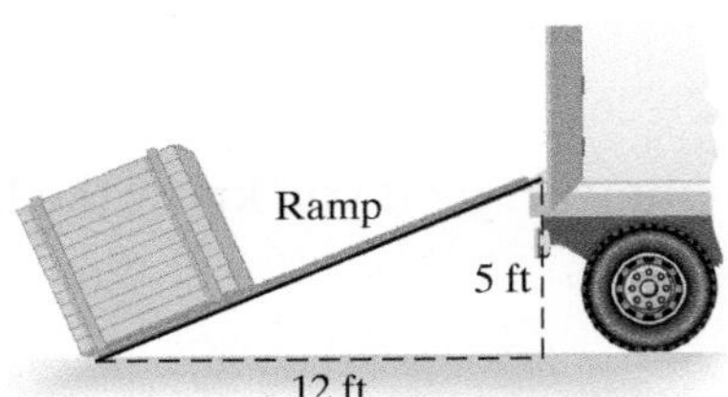

20. ***Telephone Pole*** Find the length of the guy wire supporting the telephone pole.

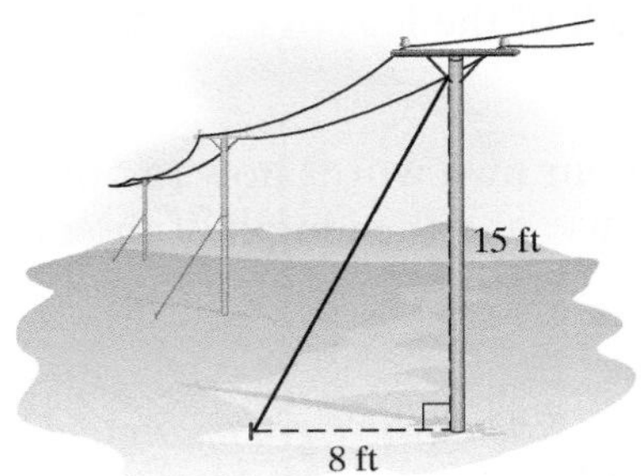

21. ***Construction of a Steel Plate*** A construction project requires a stainless steel plate with holes drilled as shown. Find the distance between the centres of the holes in this triangular plate.

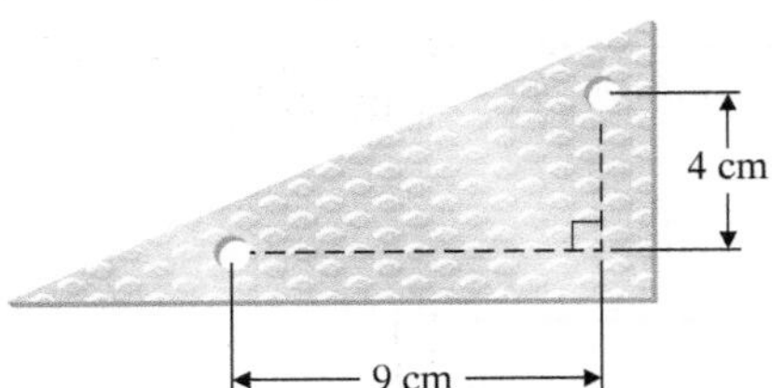

22. ***Running Out of Gas*** Juan runs out of gas in Smiths Falls, Ontario. He walks 4 km west and then 3 km south looking for a gas station. How far is he from his starting point?

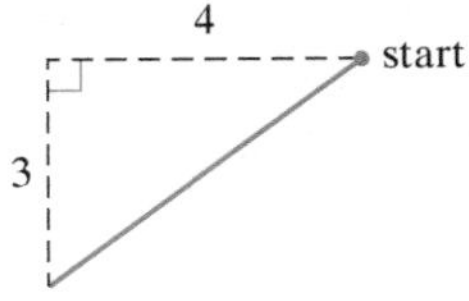

23. ***Kite Flying*** Barbara is flying her dragon kite on 32 yd of string. The kite is directly above the edge of a pond. The edge of the pond is 30 yd from where the kite is tied to the ground. How far is the kite above the pond?

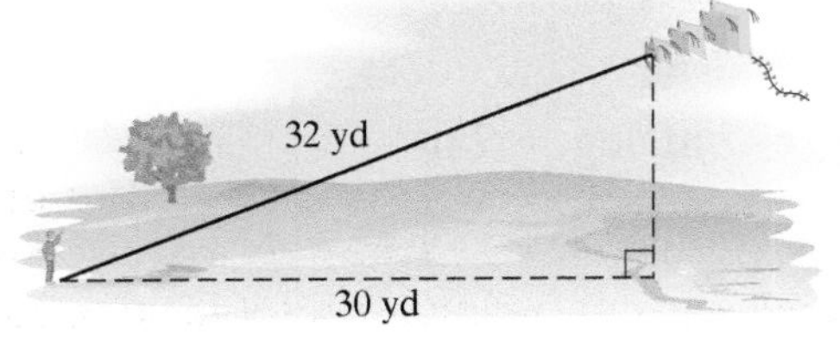

24. ***Ladder Distance*** A 20-ft ladder is placed against a college classroom building at a point 18 ft above the ground. What is the distance from the base of the ladder to the building?

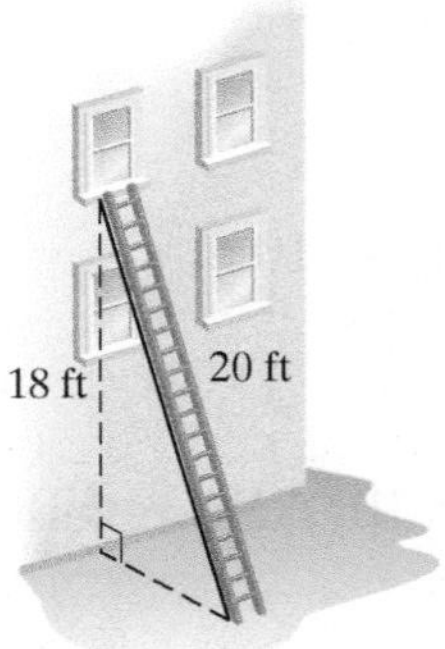

Using your knowledge of special right triangles, find the length of each leg. Round to the nearest tenth.

25.

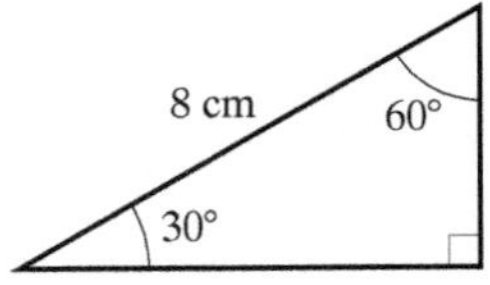

26.

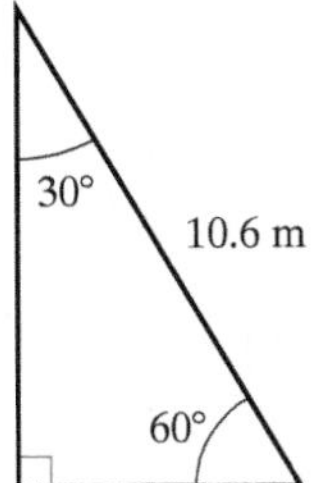

Using your knowledge of special right triangles, find the length of the hypotenuse. Round to the nearest tenth.

27.

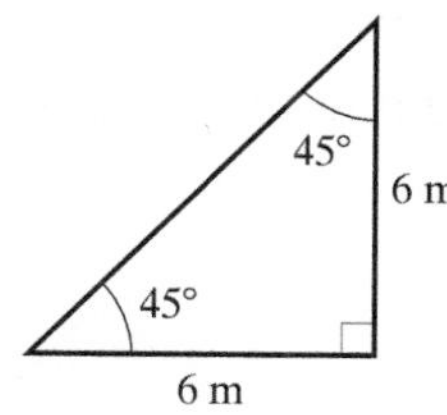

28.

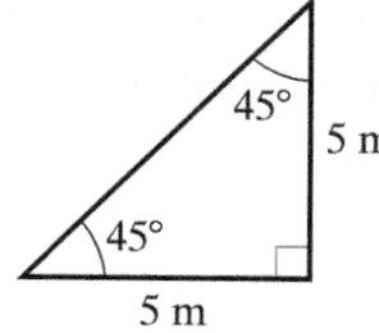

29.

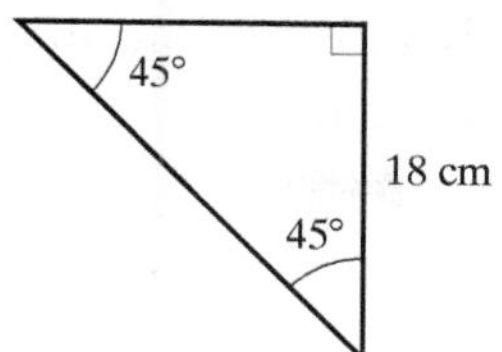

30.

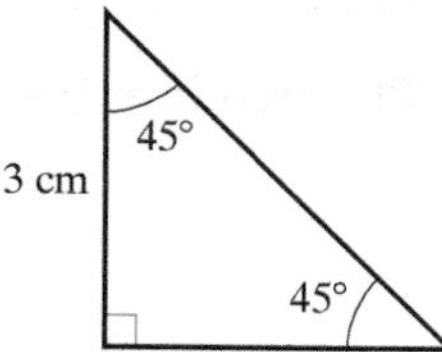

To Think About

31. ***Flagpole Construction*** A carpenter is going to use a wooden flagpole 10 in. in diameter, from which he will shape a rectangular base. The base will be 7 in. wide. The carpenter wishes to make the base as tall as possible, minimizing any waste. How tall will the rectangular base be? (Round to the nearest tenth.)

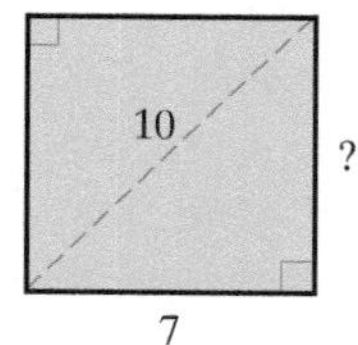

32. ***Shortwave Antenna*** A 4-m shortwave antenna is placed on a garage roof that is 2 m above the lower part of the roof. The base of the garage roof is 16 m wide. How long is an antenna support from point A to point B?

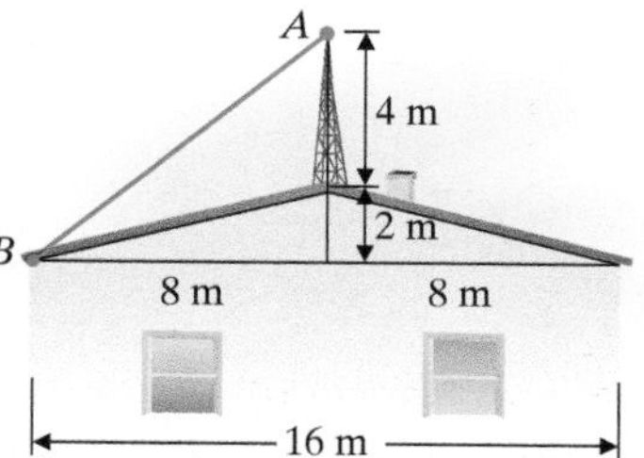

33. ***Campus Walkway*** Natasha needs to walk from the campus library to her dormitory. The library is 0.4 mi directly east of the student common, and her dormitory is 0.25 mi directly south of the common. There is a straight walkway from her dormitory to the library. How long is this walkway? Round to the nearest hundredth.

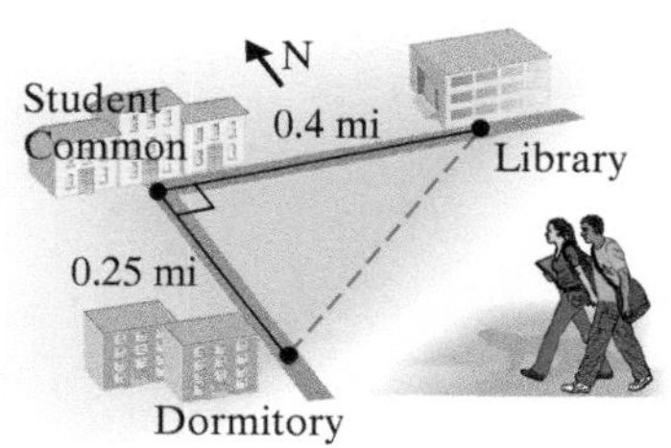

34. ***Picture Frame Construction*** Charini makes picture frames from strips of wood, plastic, and metal. She often measures the lengths of each frame's diagonals to be sure the corners are true right angles. If the dimensions of a frame are 17.78 cm by 22.86 cm, how long would the diagonal measures be? (Round to the nearest hundredth.)

Mixed Practice *Find the approximate value of the unknown side of the right triangle. Round to the nearest thousandth.*

35. The two legs are 14 cm and 5 cm.

36. The hypotenuse is 45 yd and one leg is 43 yd.

Quick Quiz 6 You may use a calculator or a square root table to complete the following problems. Round your answers to the nearest hundredth.

1. One leg of a triangle measures 10 metres. Another leg measures 5 metres. Find the length of the hypotenuse.

2. The hypotenuse of a triangle is 26 centimetres. One leg of the triangle is 24 centimetres. What is the length of the other leg of the triangle?

3. Stephanie is hiking at the Grand Canyon. She walks north for exactly 3 miles. Then she walks east for exactly 8 miles. If you draw a straight line from her finishing point to her starting point, how many miles is she from where she started?

4. Concept Check You look up at a plane that is flying at a distance of exactly 2 kilometres from your position. The plane is flying at an altitude of exactly 1.5 kilometres above the land and drops a package of supplies. Explain how you would find the distance from your position to the supplies.

SECTION 7 CIRCLES

Finding the Area and Circumference of a Circle

Student Learning Objectives

After studying this section, you will be able to:

 **Find the area and circumference of a circle.**

 **Solve area problems containing circles and other geometric shapes.**

Every point on a circle is the same distance from the centre of the circle, so the circle looks the same all around. In geometry we study the relationship between the parts of a circle and learn how to calculate the distance around a circle as well as the area of a circle.

A **circle** is a two-dimensional flat figure for which all points are at an equal distance from a given point. This given point is called the **centre** of the circle.

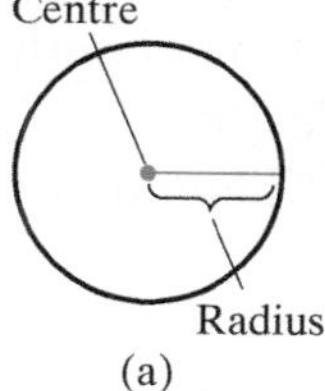

(a)

A **radius** is a line segment from the centre to a point on the circle.

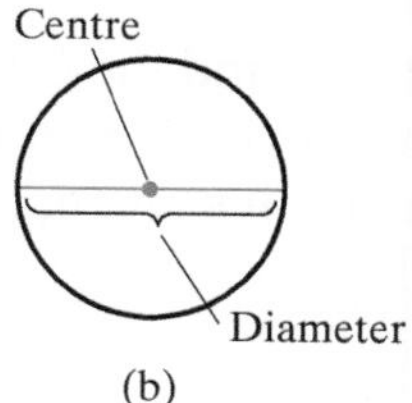

(b)

A **diameter** is a line segment across the circle that passes through the centre with end-points on the circle.

We often use the words **radius** and **diameter** to mean the length of those segments. Note that the plural of radius is radii. Clearly, then,

$$\text{diameter} = 2 \times \text{radius} \quad \text{or} \quad d = 2r.$$

We could also say that

$$\text{radius} = \text{diameter} \div 2 \quad \text{or} \quad r = \frac{d}{2}.$$

The distance around the circle is called the **circumference.**

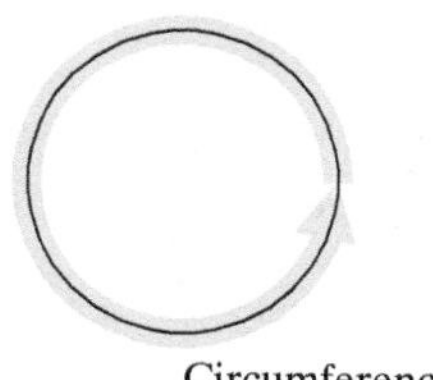

There is a special number called **pi,** which we denote by the symbol π. π is the number we get when we divide the circumference of a circle by the diameter: $\frac{C}{d} = \pi$. The value of π is approximately 3.141 592 653 59. We can approximate π to any number of digits. For all work in this book we will use the following.

> π is approximately 3.14, rounded to the nearest hundredth.

When we approximate π with 3.14 in this section, the answers are *approximate values.*

> We find the **circumference** C of a circle by multiplying the length of the diameter d times π.
>
> $$C = \pi d$$

EXAMPLE 1 Find the circumference of a quarter if we know the diameter is 2.4 cm. Use $\pi \approx 3.14$. Round to the nearest tenth.

Solution

$$C = \pi d = (3.14)(2.4 \text{ cm})$$
$$= 7.536 \text{ cm} \approx 7.5 \text{ cm (rounded to the nearest tenth)}$$

Practice Problem 1 Find the circumference of a circle when the diameter is 9 m. Use $\pi \approx 3.14$. Round to the nearest tenth.

An alternative formula is $C = 2\pi r$. Remember, $d = 2r$. We can use this formula to find the circumference if we are given the length of the radius.

When solving word problems involving circles, be careful. Ask yourself, "Is the radius given, or is the diameter given?" Then do the calculations accordingly.

EXAMPLE 2 A bicycle tire has a diameter of 60 cm. How many metres does the bicycle travel if the wheel makes one revolution?

Solution

1. ***Understand the problem.*** The distance the wheel travels when it makes one revolution is the circumference of the tire. Think of the tire unwinding.

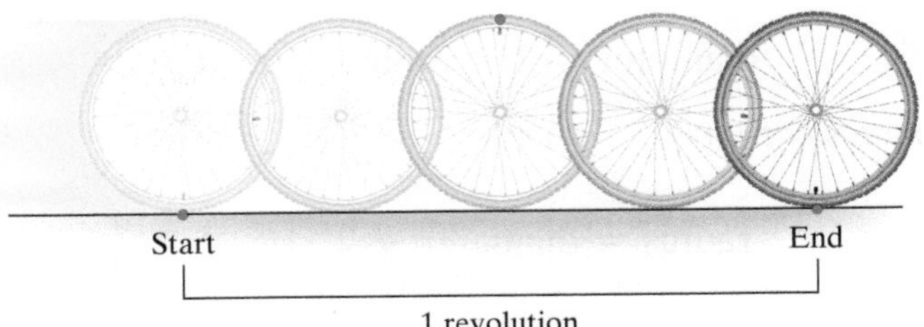

We are given the *diameter*. The diameter is given in *centimetres*. The answer should be in *metres*.

2. ***Solve and state the answer.*** Since we are given the diameter, we will use $C = \pi d$. We use 3.14 for π.

$$C = \pi d$$
$$= (3.14)(60 \text{ cm}) = 188.4 \text{ cm}$$

We will change 188.4 centimetres to metres.

$$188.4 \cancel{\text{cm}} \times \frac{1 \text{ m}}{100 \cancel{\text{cm}}} = 1.88 \text{ m}$$

When the wheel makes one revolution, the bicycle travels 1.88 m.

3. ***Check.*** We estimate to check. Since $\pi \approx 3.14$, we will use 3 for π.

$$C \approx (3)(60 \text{ cm}) \times \frac{1 \text{ m}}{100 \text{ cm}} \approx 1.8 \text{ m} \quad ✓$$

Practice Problem 2 A bicycle tire has a diameter of 30 in. How many feet does the bicycle travel if the wheel makes two revolutions?

The **area of a circle** is the product of π times the radius squared.

$$A = \pi r^2$$

EXAMPLE 3

(a) Estimate the area of a circle whose radius is 6 cm.
(b) Find a more exact area of a circle whose radius is 6 cm. Use $\pi \approx 3.14$. Round to the nearest tenth.

Solution

(a) Since π is approximately equal to 3.14, we will use 3 for π to estimate the area.

$$\begin{aligned} A &= \pi r^2 \\ &\approx (3)(6 \text{ cm})^2 \\ &\approx (3)(6 \text{ cm})(6 \text{ cm}) \\ &\approx (3)(36 \text{ cm}^2) \\ &\approx 108 \text{ cm}^2 \end{aligned}$$

Thus our *estimated* area is 108 cm^2.

(b) Now let's compute a more exact area.

$$\begin{aligned} A &= \pi r^2 \\ &= (3.14)(6 \text{ cm})^2 \\ &= 3.14(6 \text{ cm})(6 \text{ cm}) \\ &= (3.14)(36 \text{ cm}^2) \\ &= 113.04 \text{ cm}^2 \\ &\approx 113.0 \text{ cm}^2 \text{ (rounded to the nearest tenth)} \end{aligned}$$

We *must* square the radius first before multiplying by 3.14.

Our exact answer is close to the value 108 that we found in part (a).

Practice Problem 3 Find the area of a circle whose radius is 5 km. Use $\pi \approx 3.14$. Round to the nearest tenth. Estimate to check.

The formula for the area of a circle uses the length of the radius. If we are given the diameter, we can use the property that $r = \frac{d}{2}$.

EXAMPLE 4 Lexie Hatfield wants to buy a circular braided rug that is 8 ft in diameter. Find the cost of the rug at $35 a square yard.

Solution

1. ***Understand the problem.*** We are given the *diameter in feet*. We will need to find the radius. The cost of the rug is in *square yards*. We will need to change square feet to square yards.
2. ***Solve and state the answer.*** Find the radius.

$$\begin{aligned} r &= \frac{d}{2} \\ &= \frac{8\text{ ft}}{2} \\ &= 4\text{ ft} \end{aligned}$$

Use 3.14 for π.

$$\begin{aligned} A &= \pi r^2 \\ &= (3.14)(4\text{ ft})^2 \\ &= (3.14)(4\text{ ft})(4\text{ ft}) \\ &= (3.14)(16\text{ ft}^2) \\ &= 50.24\text{ ft}^2 \end{aligned}$$

Change square feet to square yards. Since 1 yd = 3 ft, $(1\text{ yd})^2 = (3\text{ ft})^2$. That is, $1\text{ yd}^2 = 9\text{ ft}^2$.

$$50.24\ \cancel{\text{ft}^2} \times \frac{1\text{ yd}^2}{9\ \cancel{\text{ft}^2}} \approx 5.58\text{ yd}^2$$

Find the cost.

$$\frac{\$35}{1\ \cancel{\text{yd}^2}} \times 5.58\ \cancel{\text{yd}^2} = \$195.30$$

3. ***Check.*** You may use a calculator to check.

NOTE TO STUDENT: Fully worked-out solutions to all of the Practice Problems can be found at the end of the module.

Practice Problem 4 Dorrington Little wants to buy a circular pool cover that is 10 ft in diameter. Find the cost of the pool cover at $12 a square yard.

2 Solving Area Problems Containing Circles and Other Geometric Shapes

Several applied area problems have a circular region combined with another region.

EXAMPLE 5 Find the area of the shaded region. Use $\pi \approx 3.14$. Round to the nearest tenth.

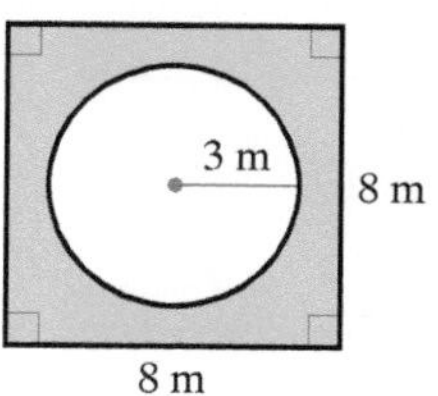

Solution We will subtract two areas to find the shaded region.

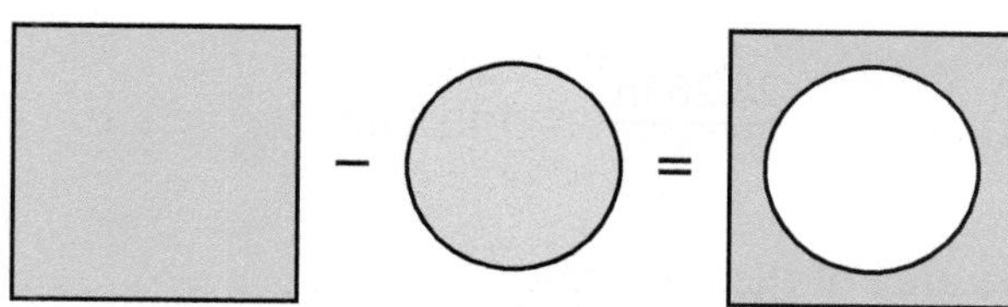

Area of the square − area of the circle = area of the shaded region

$$A = s^2 \qquad\qquad A = \pi r^2$$
$$= (8\text{ m})^2 \qquad\qquad = (3.14)(3\text{ m})^2$$
$$= 64\text{ m}^2 \qquad\qquad = (3.14)(9\text{ m}^2)$$
$$= 28.26\text{ m}^2$$

Area of the square		area of the circle		area of the shaded region
64 m^2	−	28.26 m^2	=	35.74 m^2
				$\approx 35.7\text{ m}^2$
				(rounded to nearest tenth)

Practice Problem 5 Find the area of the shaded region in the margin. Use $\pi \approx 3.14$. Round to the nearest tenth.

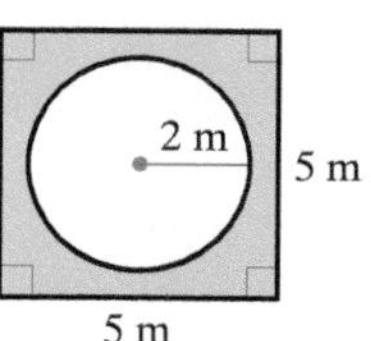

Many geometric shapes involve the semicircle. A **semicircle** is one-half of a circle. The area of a semicircle is therefore one-half of the area of a circle.

EXAMPLE 6 Find the area of the shaded region. Use $\pi \approx 3.14$. Round to the nearest tenth.

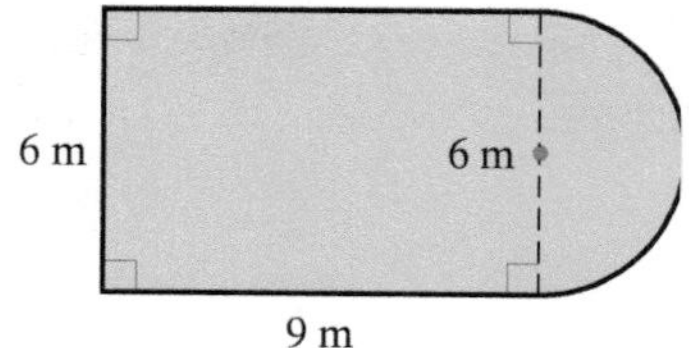

Solution First we will find the area of the semicircle with diameter 6 m.

$$r = \frac{d}{2} = \frac{6\text{ m}}{2} = 3\text{ m}$$

The radius is 3 m. The area of a semicircle with radius 3 m is

$$A_{\text{semicircle}} = \frac{\pi r^2}{2} = \frac{(3.14)(3\text{ m})^2}{2} = \frac{(3.14)(9\text{ m}^2)}{2}$$

$$= \frac{28.26\text{ m}^2}{2} = 14.13\text{ m}^2.$$

Now we add the area of the rectangle.

$$A = lw = (9\text{ m})(6\text{ m}) = 54\text{ m}^2$$

54.00 m^2	area of rectangle
$+\ 14.13\text{ m}^2$	area of semicircle
68.13 m^2	total area

Rounded to the nearest tenth, area $= 68.1\text{ m}^2$.

NOTE TO STUDENT: Fully worked-out solutions to all of the Practice Problems can be found at the end of the module.

Practice Problem 6 Find the area of the shaded region below. Use $\pi \approx 3.14$. Round to the nearest tenth.

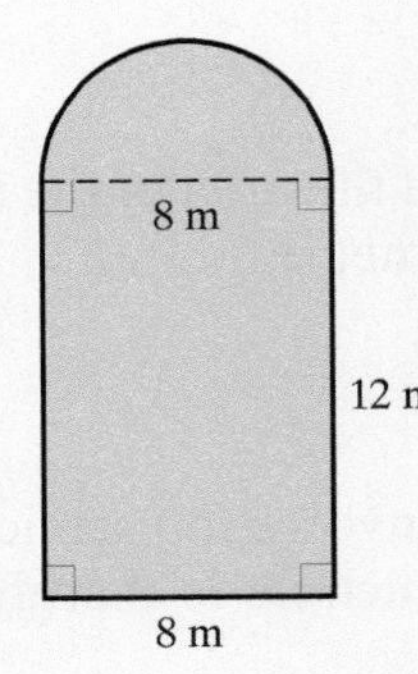

Section 7 Exercises

Verbal and Writing Skills

1. The distance around a circle is called the ______________.

2. The radius is a line segment from the __________ to a point on the circle.

3. The diameter is two times the ______________ of the circle.

4. Explain in your own words how to *estimate* the area of a circle if you are given the diameter.

5. Explain in your own words how to find the circumference of a circle if you are given the radius.

6. Explain in your own words how to find the area of a semicircle if you are given the radius.

In all exercises, use $\pi \approx 3.14$. Round to the nearest hundredth.

Find the diameter of a circle if the radius has the value given.

7. $r = 29$ cm

8. $r = 33$ in.

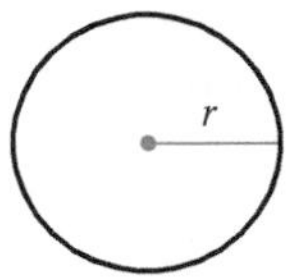

9. $r = 8\frac{1}{2}$ mm

10. $r = 12\frac{3}{8}$ yd

Find the radius of a circle if the diameter has the value given.

11. $d = 45$ m

12. $d = 65$ m

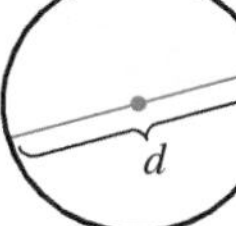

13. $d = 32.18$ ft

14. $d = 27.06$ cm

Find the circumference of the circle.

15. diameter = 32 cm

16. diameter = 17 cm

17. radius = 18.5 mm

18. radius = 24.5 mm

Travel Distance on a Bicycle *A bicycle wheel makes five revolutions. Determine how far the bicycle travels in feet.*

19. The diameter of the wheel is 32 in.

20. The diameter of the wheel is 24 in.

Find the area of each circle.

21. radius = 5 m

22. radius = 7 m

23. radius = 8.5 in.

24. radius = 12.5 mm

25. diameter = 32 cm

26. diameter = 52 cm

Water Sprinkler Distribution *A water sprinkler sends water out in a circular pattern. Determine how large an area is watered.*

27. The radius of watering is 12 ft.

28. The radius of watering is 8 m.

Radio Signal Distribution *A radio station sends out radio waves in all directions from a tower at the centre of the circle of broadcast range. Determine how large an area is reached.*

29. The diameter is 90 mi.

30. The diameter is 120 km.

Find the area of the shaded region.

31.

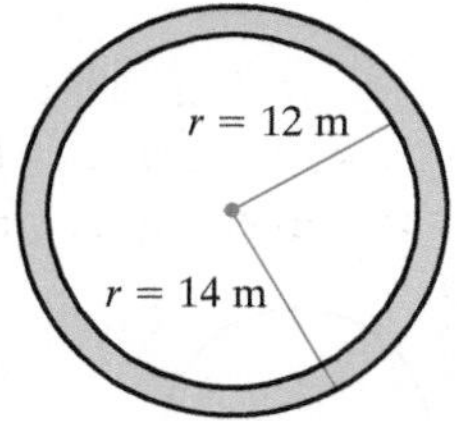

32.

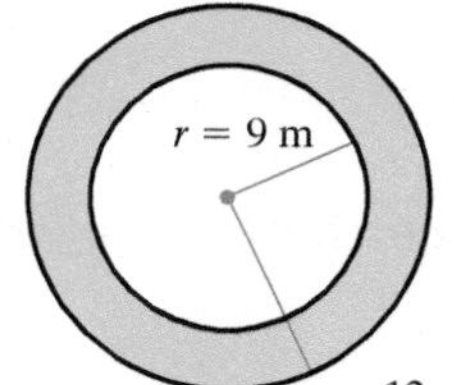

33.

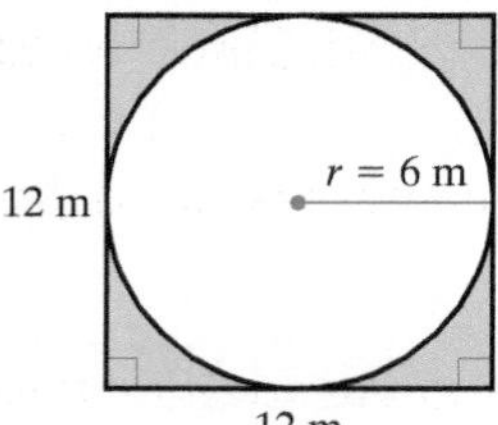

34.

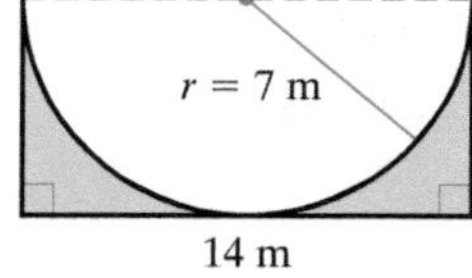

35.

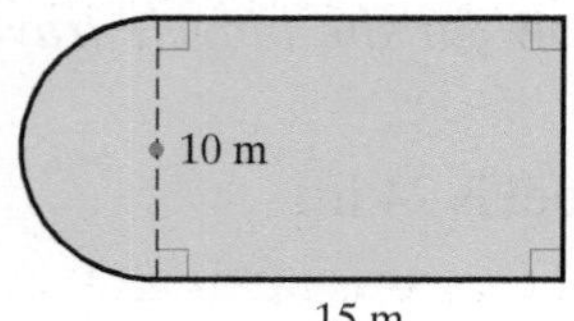

36.

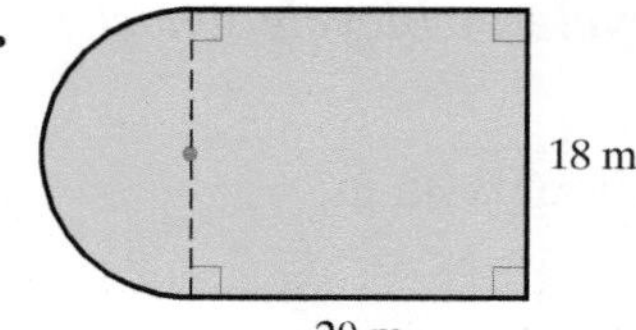

Fertilizing a Playing Field *Find the cost of fertilizing a playing field at $0.20 per square yard for the conditions stated.*

37. The rectangular part of the field is 120 yd long and the diameter of each semicircle is 40 yd.

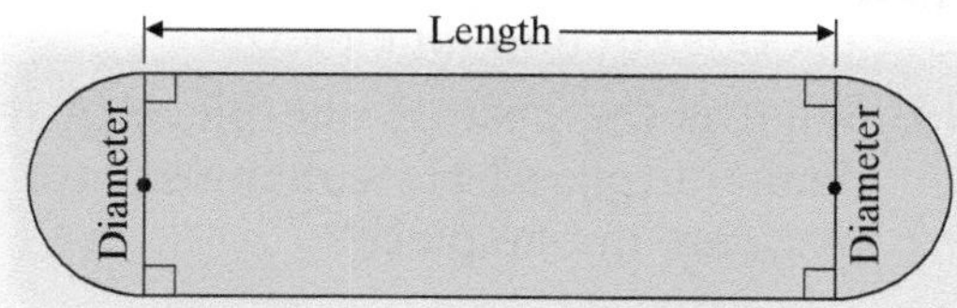

38. The rectangular part of the field is 110 yd long and the diameter of each semicircle is 50 yd.

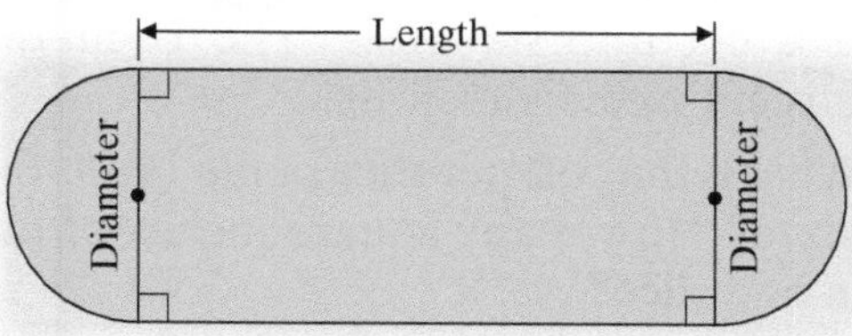

Applications *Use* $\pi \approx 3.14$ *in exercises 39–48. Round to the nearest hundredth.*

39. ***Manhole Cover*** A manhole cover has a diameter of 1 m. What is the length of the brass grip-strip that encircles the cover, making it easier to manage?

40. ***Ship Porthole*** A porthole window on a freighter ship has a diameter of 0.6 m. What is the length of the insulating strip that encircles the window and keeps out wind and moisture?

41. ***Truck Travel*** Jimmy's truck has tires with a radius of 30 inches. How many feet does his truck travel if the wheel makes nine revolutions?

42. ***Car Travel*** Elena's car has tires with a radius of 14 in. How many feet does her car travel if the wheel makes 35 revolutions?

43. ***Car Travel*** Lucy's car has tires with a radius of 16 in. How many complete revolutions do her wheels make in 1 mile? (*Hint:* First determine how many inches are in 1 mile.)

44. ***Car Travel*** Mickey's car has tires with a radius of 15 in. How many complete revolutions do his wheels make in 1 mile? (*Hint:* First determine how many inches are in 1 mile.)

45. ***Basketball Court*** In the centre of a new basketball court, a circle with a diameter of 8 ft must be marked with tape before it is painted.

(a) How long will the tape be?

(b) The circle is then painted. How large an area must be painted?

46. ***Food Delivery*** Great Wall Chinese Restaurant will make deliveries within a 1.5-kilometre radius of the restaurant.

(a) How many square kilometres is the delivery area?

(b) Jiang has one delivery 1.5 km straight west of the restaurant, and another 1.5 km directly east of the restaurant. If he is able to drive around the edge of the delivery area, how many kilometres will he drive between the two deliveries?

47. ***Mountain Radio Station Broadcast*** A radio station broadcasts from the top of a mountain. The signal can be heard 200 kilometres away in every direction. How many square kilometres are in the receiving range of the radio station?

48. ***Distance of Sound Travel*** The sound of an explosion at a fireworks factory was heard 300 kilometres away in every direction. How many square kilometres are in the area where people heard the explosion?

To Think About

49. ***Value of Pizza Slice*** Noah discovered that a 16-in.-diameter pizza costs \$12.00. A 12-in.-diameter pizza costs \$8.00. The 12-in.-diameter pizza is cut into six slices. The 16-in.-diameter pizza is cut into eight slices.

(a) What is the cost per slice of the 16-in.-diameter pizza? How many square inches of pizza are in one slice?

(b) What is the cost per slice of the 12-in.-diameter pizza? How many square inches of pizza are in one slice?

(c) If you want more value for your money, which slice of pizza should you buy?

50. ***Value of Pizza Slice*** Olivia discovered that a 14-in.-diameter pizza costs \$10.00. It is cut into eight pieces. A 12.5 in. $\times$ 12.5 in. square pizza costs \$12.00. It is cut into nine pieces.

(a) What is the cost of one piece of the 14-in.-diameter pizza? How many square inches of pizza are in one piece?

(b) What is the cost of one piece of the 12.5 in. $\times$ 12.5 in. square pizza? How many square inches of pizza are in one piece?

(c) If you want more value for your money, which piece of pizza should you buy?

Quick Quiz 7

In the following problems, use $\pi \approx 3.14$. Round to the nearest hundredth.

1. What is the circumference of a circle with a diameter of 9 inches?

2. What is the area of a circle with a radius of 11 metres?

3. An engineer constructs a rectangular steel plate that measures 3.5 centimetres by 3.1 centimetres. In the centre of the plate he drills a hole with a radius of 1.5 centimetres. What is the area of the rectangular plate AFTER he drills the hole in it? (*Hint:* Draw a sketch of the circle inside the rectangle.)

4. **Concept Check** A carpenter makes a semicircle with a radius of 3 metres. Explain how you would find the area of the semicircle.

Section 8 Volume

Student Learning Objectives

After studying this section, you will be able to:

1. Find the volume of a rectangular solid (box).
2. Find the volume of a cylinder.
3. Find the volume of a sphere.
4. Find the volume of a cone.
5. Find the volume of a pyramid.

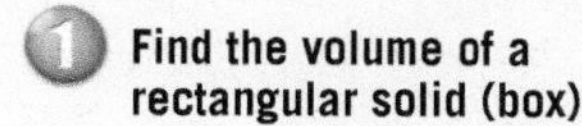

 Finding the Volume of a Rectangular Solid (Box)

How much grain can that shed hold? How much water is in the polluted lake? How much air is inside a basketball? These are questions of **volume.** In this section we compute the volume of several three-dimensional geometric figures: the rectangular solid (box), cylinder, sphere, cone, and pyramid.

We can start with a box 1 cm × 1 cm × 1 cm.

This is a **cube** with a side of 1 centimetre.

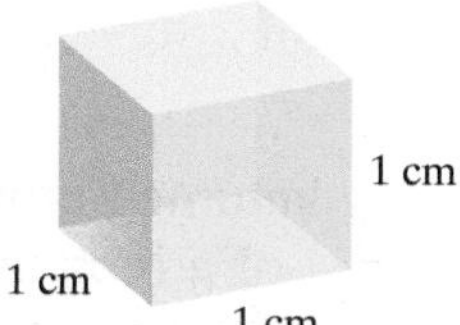

This box has a volume of 1 cubic centimetre (written 1 cm^3). We can use this as a **unit of volume.** Volume is measured in cubic units such as cubic metres (abbreviated m^3) or cubic feet (abbreviated ft^3). When we measure volume, we are measuring the space inside an object.

> The **volume of a rectangular solid** (box) is the length times the width times the height.
>
> $$V = lwh$$
>
> 
>

EXAMPLE 1 Find the volume of a box of width 2 m, length 3 m, and height 4 m.

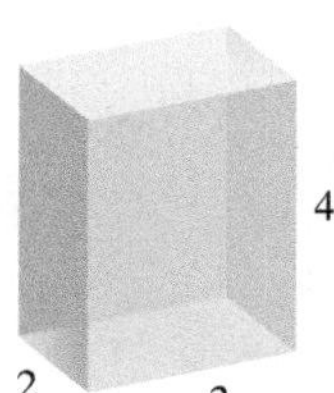

Solution $V = lwh = (3\text{ m})(2\text{ m})(4\text{ m}) = (6)(4)\text{ m}^3 = 24\text{ m}^3$

Practice Problem 1 Find the volume of a box of width 5 m, length 6 m, and height 2 m.

If all sides of the box are equal, then the formula is $V = s^3$ where s is the side of the cube.

 Finding the Volume of a Cylinder

Cylinders are the shape we observe when we see a tin can or a tube.

> The **volume of a cylinder** is the area of its circular base, πr^2, times the height h.
>
> $$V = \pi r^2 h$$
>
> 
>

We will continue to use 3.14 as an approximation for π, as we did in Section 7, in all volume problems requiring the use of π.

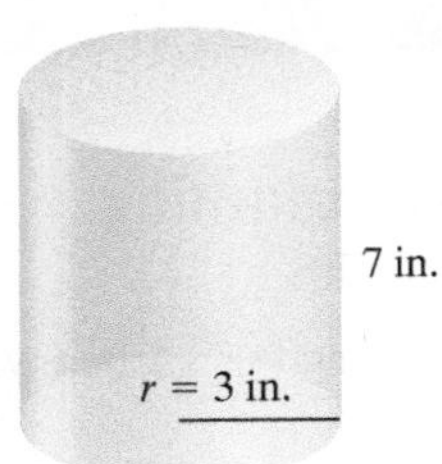

EXAMPLE 2 Find the volume of a cylinder of radius 3 in. and height 7 in. Round to the nearest tenth.

Solution $V = \pi r^2 h = (3.14)(3\text{ in.})^2(7\text{ in.}) = (3.14)(3\text{ in.})(3\text{ in.})(7\text{ in.})$

Be sure to square the radius before doing any other multiplication.

$$V = (3.14)(9\text{ in.}^2)(7\text{ in.}) = (28.26\text{ in.}^2)(7\text{ in.})$$
$$= 197.82\text{ in.}^3 \approx 197.8\text{ in.}^3 \text{ rounded to the nearest tenth}$$

Practice Problem 2 Find the volume of a cylinder of radius 2 in. and height 5 in. Round to the nearest tenth.

TO THINK ABOUT: Comparing Volume Formulas Take a minute to compare the formulas for the volumes of a rectangular solid and a cylinder. Do you see how they are similar? Consider the area of the base of each figure. In each case, what must you multiply the base area by to obtain the volume of the solid?

3 Finding the Volume of a Sphere

Have you ever considered how you would find the volume of the inside of a ball? How many cubic centimetres of air are inside a basketball? To answer these questions we need a volume formula for a *sphere.*

The **volume of a sphere** is 4 times π times the radius cubed divided by 3.

$$V = \frac{4\pi r^3}{3}$$

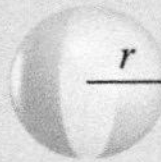

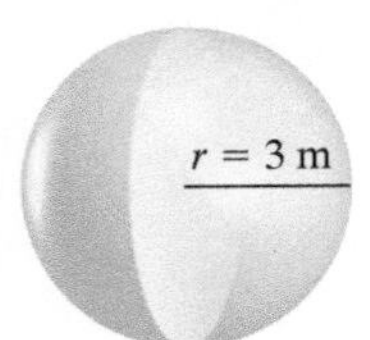

EXAMPLE 3 Find the volume of a sphere with radius 3 m. Round to the nearest tenth.

Solution
$$V = \frac{4\pi r^3}{3} = \frac{(4)(3.14)(3\text{ m})^3}{3}$$
$$= \frac{(4)(3.14)(27)\text{ m}^3}{3}$$
$$= (12.56)(9)\text{ m}^3 = 113.04\text{ m}^3$$
$$\approx 113.0\text{ m}^3 \text{ rounded to the nearest tenth}$$

Practice Problem 3 Find the volume of a sphere with radius 6 m. Round to the nearest tenth.

4 Finding the Volume of a Cone

We see the shape of a cone when we look at the sharpened end of a pencil or at an ice cream cone. To find the volume of a cone we use the following formula.

The **volume of a cone** is π times the radius of the base squared times the height divided by 3.

$$V = \frac{\pi r^2 h}{3}$$

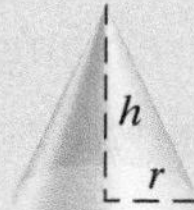

EXAMPLE 4 Find the volume of a cone of radius 7 m and height 9 m. Round to the nearest tenth.

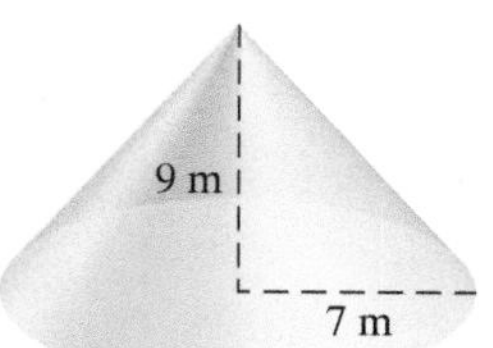

Solution

$$\begin{aligned} V &= \frac{\pi r^2 h}{3} \\ &= \frac{(3.14)(7\text{ m})^2(9\text{ m})}{3} \\ &= \frac{(3.14)(49\text{ m}^2)(9\text{ m})}{3} \\ &= (3.14)(49)(3)\text{ m}^3 \\ &= (153.86)(3)\text{ m}^3 \\ &= 461.58\text{ m}^3 \\ &\approx 461.6\text{ m}^3 \text{ rounded to the nearest tenth} \end{aligned}$$

Practice Problem 4 Find the volume of a cone of radius 5 m and height 12 m. Round to the nearest tenth.

5 Finding the Volume of a Pyramid

You have seen pictures of the great pyramids of Egypt. These amazing stone structures are over 4000 years old.

Photos.com

The **volume of a pyramid** is obtained by multiplying the area B of the base of the pyramid by the height h and dividing by 3.

$$V = \frac{Bh}{3}$$

EXAMPLE 5 Find the volume of a pyramid with height 6 m, length of base 7 m, and width of base 5 m.

Solution The base is a rectangle.

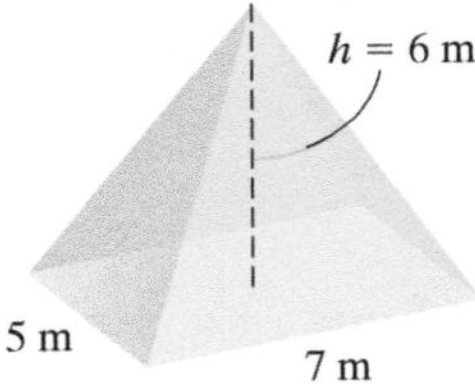

$$\text{Area of base} = (7\text{ m})(5\text{ m}) = 35\text{ m}^2$$

Substituting the area of the base 35 m^2 and the height of 6 m, we have

$$V = \frac{Bh}{3} = \frac{(35\text{ m}^2)(6\text{ m})}{3}$$
$$= (35)(2)\text{ m}^3$$
$$= 70\text{ m}^3$$

Practice Problem 5 Find the volume of a pyramid with the dimensions given.

(a) height 10 m, width of base 6 m, length of base 6 m

(b) height 15 m, width of base 7 m, length of base 8 m

NOTE TO STUDENT: Fully worked-out solutions to all of the Practice Problems can be found at the end of the module.

Section 8 Exercises

Verbal and Writing Skills

In this section, we have studied six volume formulas. They are $V = lwh$, $V = \pi r^2 h$, $V = \frac{4\pi r^3}{3}$, $V = s^3$, $V = \frac{\pi r^2 h}{3}$, *and* $V = \frac{Bh}{3}$.

*For each of the following figures, state **(a)** the name of the figure and **(b)** the correct formula for its volume.*

1. 

2. 

3. 

4. 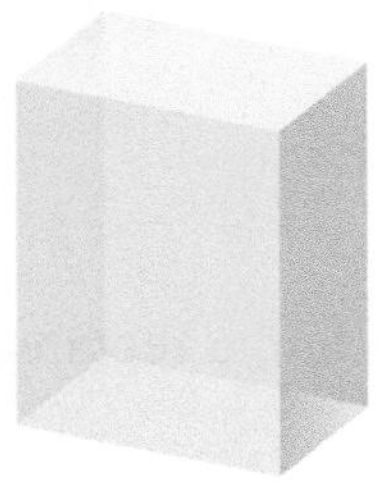

5. 

6. 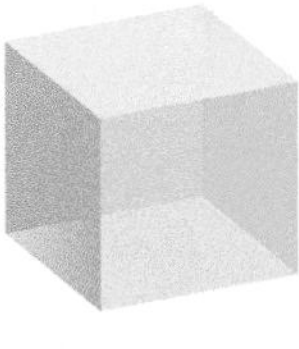

Find the volume. Use $\pi \approx 3.14$. *Round to the nearest tenth unless otherwise directed.*

7. a rectangular solid with width = 12 mm, length = 30 mm, height = 1.5 mm

8. a rectangular solid with width = 14 mm, length = 20 mm, height = 2.5 mm

9. a cylinder with radius 3 m and height 8 m

10. a cylinder with radius 2 m and height 7 m

11. a cylinder with diameter 22 m and height 17 m

12. a cylinder with diameter 30 m and height 9 m

13. a sphere with radius 9 m

14. a sphere with radius 12 m

15. a pyramid with a base of 18 ft^2 and a height of 35 feet

16. a pyramid with a base of 24 ft^2 and a height of 55 feet

17. a cube with side 0.6 cm (Round to the nearest thousandth.)

18. a cube with side 0.8 cm (Round to the nearest thousandth.)

19. a cone with a radius of 3 yd and a height of 7 yd (Round to the nearest hundredth.)

20. a cone with a radius of 6 yd and a height of 4 yd (Round to the nearest hundredth.)

Exercises 21 and 22 involve hemispheres. A hemisphere is exactly one half of a sphere.

21. Find the volume of a hemisphere with radius = 7 m.

22. Find the volume of a hemisphere with radius = 6 m.

Mixed Practice *Find the volume. Use $\pi \approx 3.14$. Round to the nearest tenth.*

23. a cone with a height of 14 cm and a radius of 8 cm

24. a cone with a height of 12 cm and a radius of 9 cm

25. a cone with a height of 12.5 ft and a radius of 7 ft

26. a cone with a height of 14.2 ft and a radius of 9 ft

27. a pyramid with a height of 10 m and a square base of 7 m on a side

28. a pyramid with a height of 7 m and a square base of 3 m on a side

29. a pyramid with a height of 10 m and a rectangular base measuring 8 m by 14 m

30. a pyramid with a height of 5 m and a rectangular base measuring 6 m by 12 m

Applications *Use $\pi \approx 3.14$ when necessary.*

31. ***Garden Mulch*** Lexi Salzman has a large rectangular vegetable garden measuring 9 ft by 16 ft. An employee at the local nursery recommended putting down mulch 3 in. thick to prevent weeds from growing. Each bag of mulch covers 3 cubic feet. How many bags should Lexi purchase for her vegetable garden?

32. ***Driveway Construction*** Caleb Salzman wants to put down a crushed-stone driveway to his summer camp. The driveway is 7 m wide and 120 m long. The crushed stone is to be $\frac{1}{9}$ m thick. How-many cubic metres of stone will he need?

Pipe Insulation *A collar of Styrofoam is made to insulate a pipe. Find the volume of the collar surrounding a pipe of radius r. The large radius R is to the outer rim of the collar. Use the small radius r as the inner edge of the insulation.*

33. $r = 3$ in.
$R = 5$ in.
$h = 20$ in.

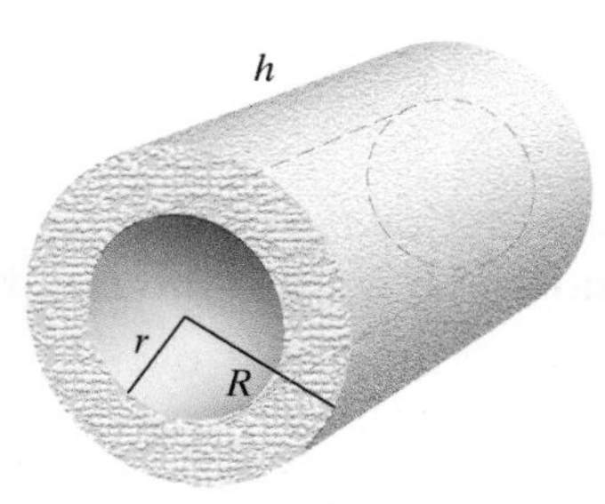

34. $r = 4$ in.
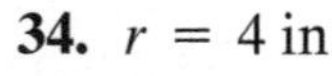
$R = 6$ in.
$h = 25$ in.

35. ***Astronomy*** Jupiter has a radius of approximately 45 000 mi. Earth has a radius of approximately 3950 mi. Assuming both planets are spheres, what is the difference in volume between Earth and Jupiter?

36. ***Softballs and Golf Balls*** A softball has a diameter of about 3.8 in. Most golf balls are about 1.7 in. in diameter. What is the difference in volume between the softball and golf ball? Round your answer to the nearest tenth.

37. ***Shipping a Fragile Object*** Lora Connelly has a fragile glass box in the shape of a rectangular solid of width 6 cm, length 18 cm, and height 12 cm. It is being shipped in a larger box of width 12 cm, length 22 cm, and height 16 cm. All of the space between the glass box and shipping box will be packed with Styrofoam packing "peanuts." How many cubic centimetres of the shipping box will be Styrofoam peanuts?

38. ***Cereal Box*** A large box of cereal is 3 in. wide, 14 in. high, and 8 in. long. The cereal inside fills $\frac{3}{4}$ of the box. How many cubic inches of cereal are in the box?

39. ***Television Antenna Cone*** A special stainless steel cone sits on top of a cable television antenna. The cost of the stainless steel is \$3.00 per cubic centimetre. The cone has a radius of 6 cm and a height of 10 cm. What is the cost of the stainless steel needed to make this *solid* steel cone?

40. ***Radar Nose Cone*** The nose cone of a passenger jet is used to receive and send radar. It is made of a special aluminum alloy that costs \$4.00 per cubic centimetre. The cone has a radius of 5 cm and a height of 9 cm. What is the cost of the aluminum needed to make this *solid* nose cone?

41. ***Root Beer Can*** The old Smith Root Beer can was 13.5 cm high. The new can is 1.4 cm shorter. The new can has a diameter of 6.6 cm. What is the volume of the new can?

42. ***Swimming Pool*** Dan and Connie are installing a new circular in-ground swimming pool. The pool will measure 9 feet deep and 20 feet in diameter. How many cubic feet of earth will need to be removed for the pool to be installed?

43. ***Stone Pyramid*** Suppose that a stone pyramid has a rectangular base that measures 87 m by 130 m. Also suppose that the pyramid has a height of 70 m. Find the volume.

44. ***Stone Pyramid*** Suppose the pyramid in exercise 43 is made of solid stone. It is not hollow like the pyramids of Egypt. It is composed of layer after layer of cut stone. The stone weighs 422 kg per cubic metre. How many kilograms does the pyramid weigh? How many tonnes does the pyramid weigh?

Quick Quiz 8 Use $\pi \approx 3.14$ in the following problems. Round all answers to the nearest hundredth.

1. Find the volume of a sphere with a radius of 4 centimetres.

2. Find the volume of a pyramid with a height of 8 yards and a rectangular base of 7 yards on one side and 6 yards on the other side.

3. Find the volume of a cylinder with a radius of 3 metres and a height of 13 metres.

4. **Concept Check** Suppose a new cylinder is formed similar to the cylinder described in problem 3 but the new radius is 4 metres while the height is unchanged. Explain how to determine how much larger the volume of the new cylinder is compared to the original cylinder.

SECTION 9 SIMILAR GEOMETRIC FIGURES

Student Learning Objectives

After studying this section, you will be able to:

 **Find the corresponding parts of similar triangles.**

 **Find the corresponding parts of similar geometric figures.**

 Finding the Corresponding Parts of Similar Triangles

In English, "similar" means that the things being compared are, in general, alike. But in mathematics, "similar" means that the things being compared are alike in a special way—they are *alike in shape,* even though they may be different in size. So photographs that are enlarged produce images *similar* to the original; a floor plan of a building is *similar* to the actual building; a model car is *similar* to the actual vehicle.

Two triangles with the same shape but not necessarily the same size are called **similar triangles.** Here are two pairs of similar triangles.

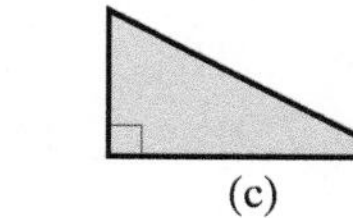

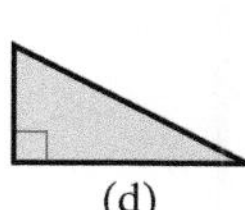

The two triangles at right are similar. The smallest angle in the first triangle is angle A. The smallest angle in the second triangle is angle D. Both angles measure 36°. We say that angle A and angle D are **corresponding angles** in these similar triangles.

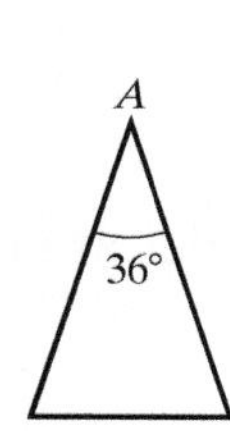

First triangle

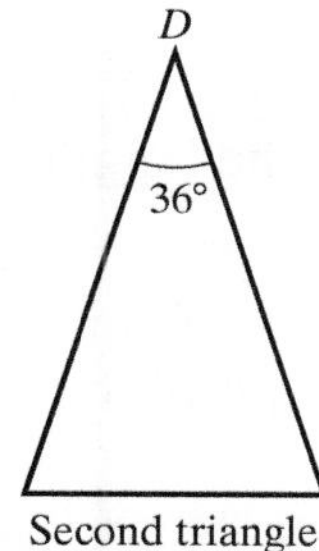

Second triangle

The **corresponding angles** of similar triangles are equal.

The following two triangles are similar. Notice the **corresponding sides.**

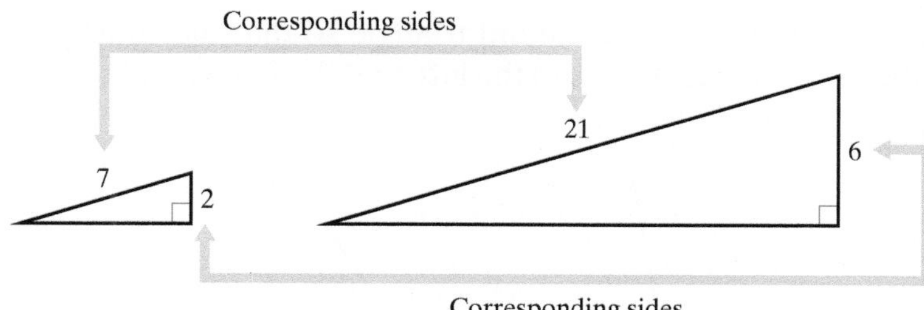

We see that the ratio of 7 to 21 is the same as the ratio of 2 to 6.

$$\frac{7}{21} = \frac{2}{6} \text{ is obviously true since } \frac{1}{3} = \frac{1}{3}.$$

The corresponding sides of similar triangles have the same ratio.

We can use the fact that corresponding sides of similar triangles have the same ratio to find the lengths of the missing sides of triangles.

EXAMPLE 1 These two triangles are similar. Find the length of side n. Round to the nearest tenth.

Solution The ratio of 12 to 19 is the same as the ratio of 5 to n.

$$\frac{12}{19} = \frac{5}{n}$$

$$12n = (5)(19) \quad \text{Cross-multiply.}$$

$$12n = 95 \quad \text{Simplify.}$$

$$\frac{12n}{12} = \frac{95}{12} \quad \text{Divide each side by 12.}$$

$$n = 7.91\overline{6}$$

$$\approx 7.9 \quad \text{Round to the nearest tenth.}$$

Side n is of length 7.9.

Practice Problem 1 The two triangles in the margin are similar. Find the length of side n. Round to the nearest tenth.

Similar triangles are not always oriented the same way. You may find it helpful to rotate one of the triangles so that the similarity is more apparent.

EXAMPLE 2 These two triangles are similar. Name the sides that correspond.

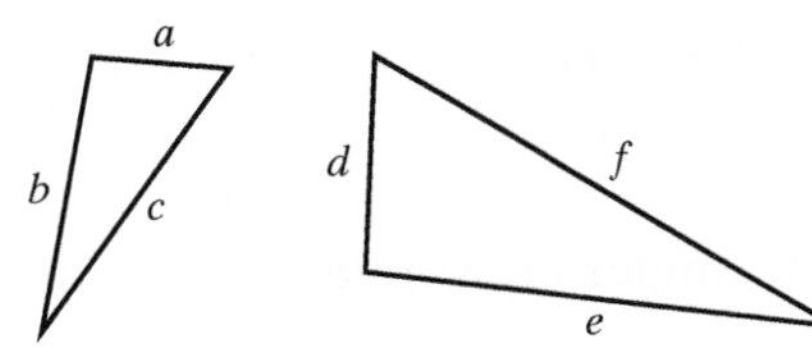

Solution First we turn the second triangle so that the shortest side is on the top, the intermediate side is to the left, and the longest side is on the right.

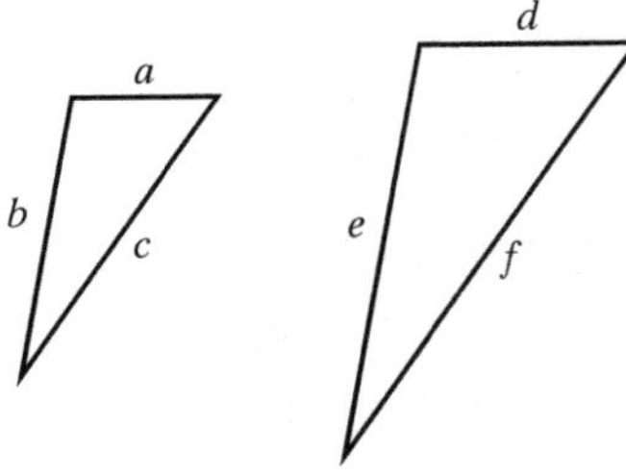

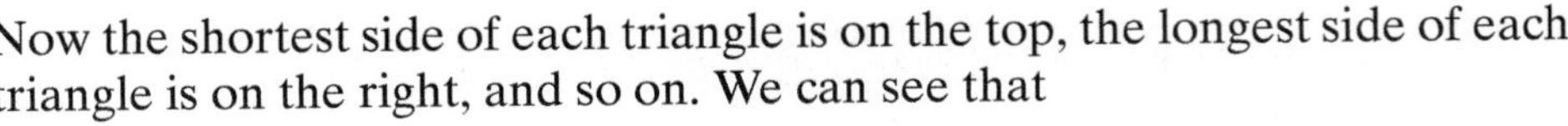

Now the shortest side of each triangle is on the top, the longest side of each triangle is on the right, and so on. We can see that

a corresponds to d.
b corresponds to e.
c corresponds to f.

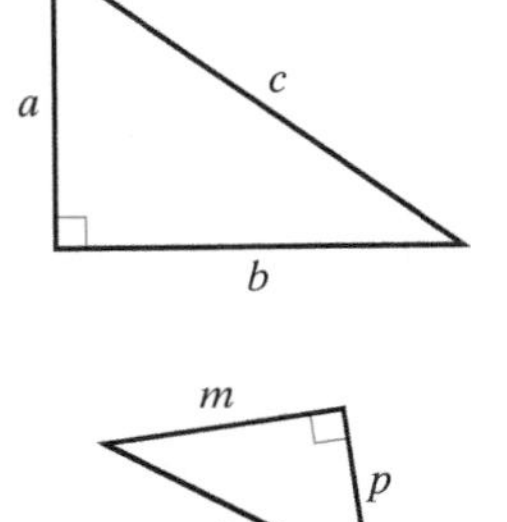

Practice Problem 2 The two triangles in the margin are similar. Name the sides that correspond.

The perimeters of similar triangles have the same ratio as the corresponding sides.

Similar triangles can be used to find distances or lengths that are difficult to measure.

EXAMPLE 3 A flagpole casts a shadow of 12 m. At the same time, a nearby tree that is 1 m tall has a shadow of $\frac{5}{3}$ m. How tall is the flagpole?

Solution

1. ***Understand the problem.*** The shadows cast by the sun shining on vertical objects at the same time of day form similar triangles. We draw a picture.

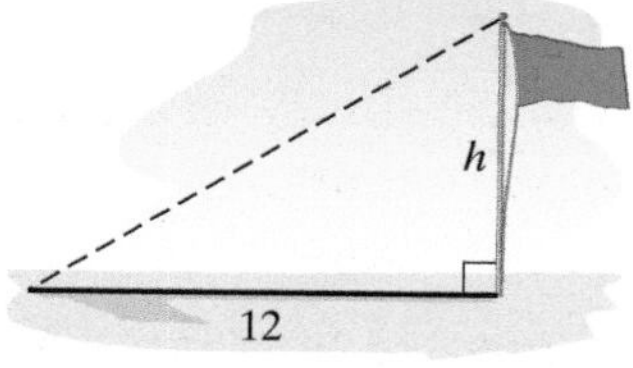

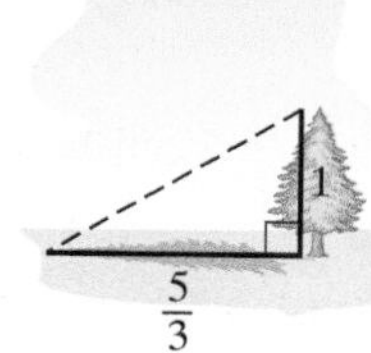

2. ***Solve and state the answer.*** Let h = the height of the flagpole. Thus we can say h is to 1 as 12 is to $\frac{5}{3}$.

$$\frac{h}{1} = \frac{12}{\frac{5}{3}}$$

$$5h = (3)(12)$$

$$5h = 36$$

$$\frac{5h}{5} = \frac{36}{5}$$

$$h = 7.2$$

The flagpole is about 7.2 metres tall.

3. ***Check.*** The check is up to you.

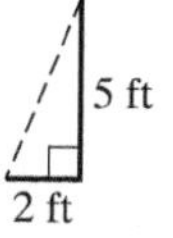

Practice Problem 3 What is the height (h) of the side wall of the building in the margin if the two triangles are similar?

2 Finding the Corresponding Parts of Similar Geometric Figures

Geometric figures such as rectangles, trapezoids, and circles can also be similar figures.

The corresponding sides of similar geometric figures have the same ratio.

EXAMPLE 4 The two rectangles shown here are similar because the corresponding sides of the two rectangles have the same ratio. Find the width of the larger rectangle.

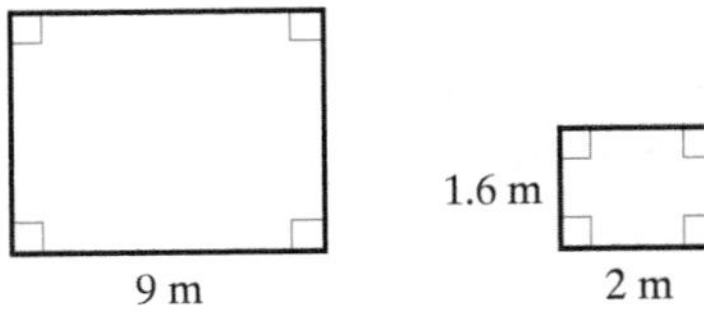

Solution Let w = the width of the larger rectangle.

$$\frac{w}{1.6} = \frac{9}{2}$$
$$2w = (1.6)(9)$$
$$2w = 14.4$$
$$\frac{2w}{2} = \frac{14.4}{2}$$
$$w = 7.2$$

The width of the larger rectangle is 7.2 metres.

3 m
1.8 m
29 m
w

Practice Problem 4 The two rectangles in the margin are similar. Find the width of the larger rectangle.

NOTE TO STUDENT: *Fully worked-out solutions to all of the Practice Problems can be found at the end of the module.*

The perimeters of similar figures—whatever the figures—have the same ratio as their corresponding sides. Circles are a special case. *All* circles are similar. The circumferences of two circles have the same ratio as their radii.

TO THINK ABOUT: Comparing Two Areas How would you find the relationship between the areas of two similar geometric figures? Consider the following two similar rectangles.

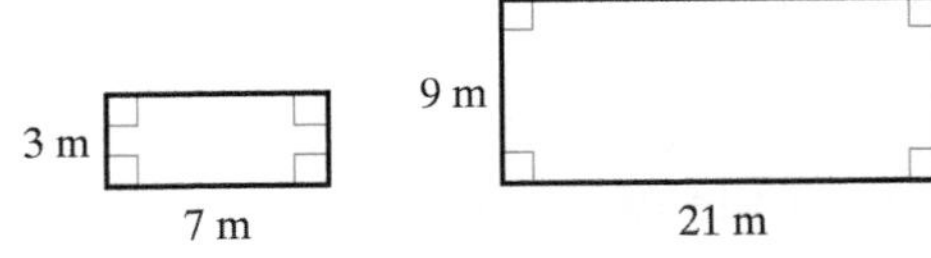

The area of the smaller rectangle is $(3\text{ m})(7\text{ m}) = 21\text{ m}^2$. The area of the larger rectangle is $(9\text{ m})(21\text{ m}) = 189\text{ m}^2$. How could you have predicted this result?

The ratio of small width to large width is $\frac{3}{9} = \frac{1}{3}$. The small rectangle has sides that are $\frac{1}{3}$ as large as the large rectangle. The ratio of the area of the small rectangle to the area of the large rectangle is $\frac{21}{189} = \frac{1}{9}$. Note that $\left(\frac{1}{3}\right)^2 = \frac{1}{9}$.

Thus we can develop the following principle: The areas of two similar figures are in the same ratio as the square of the ratio of two corresponding sides.

Section 9 Exercises

Verbal and Writing Skills

1. Similar figures may be different in ____________ but they are alike in ____________.

2. The corresponding sides of similar triangles have the same ____________.

3. The perimeters of similar figures have the same ratio as their corresponding ____________.

4. You are given the lengths of the sides of a large triangle and the length of a corresponding side of a smaller, similar triangle. Explain in your own words how to find the perimeter of the smaller triangle.

For each pair of similar triangles, find the missing side n. Round to the nearest tenth when necessary.

5.

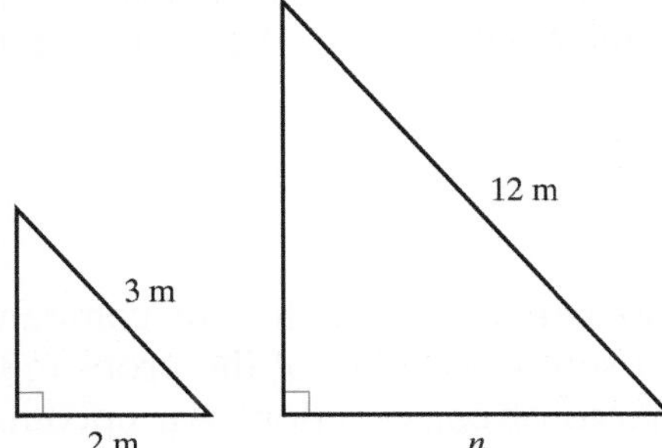

6.

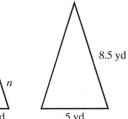

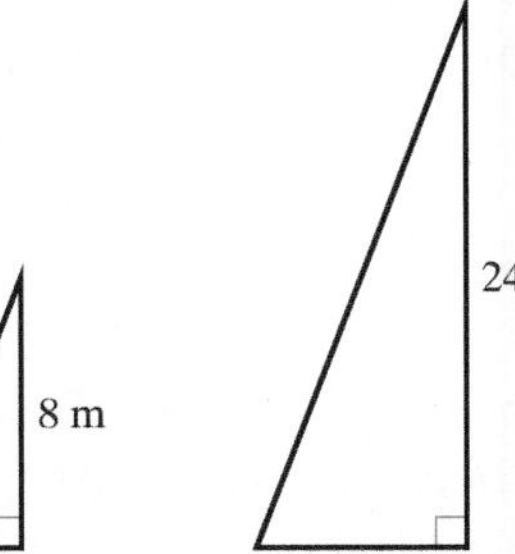

7.

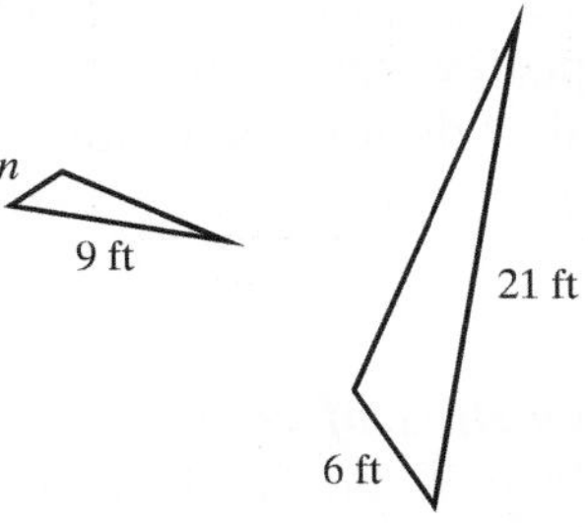

8.

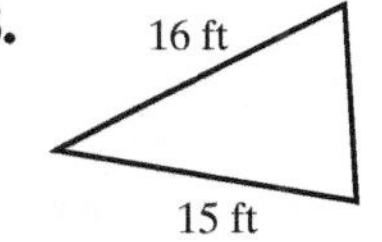

7 ft

n

9.

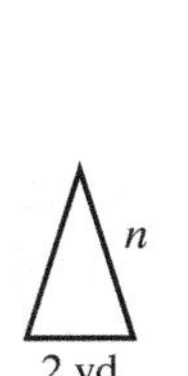

10.

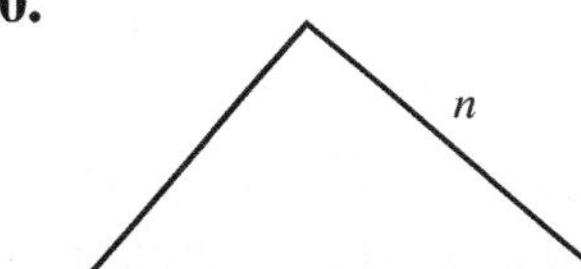

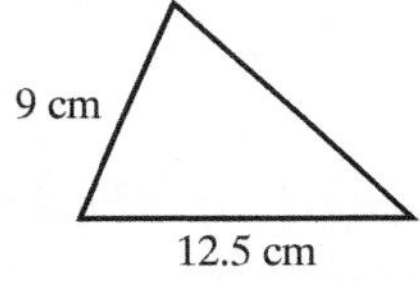

Each pair of triangles is similar. Determine the three pairs of corresponding sides in each case.

11.

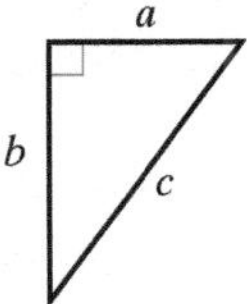

d e f

12.

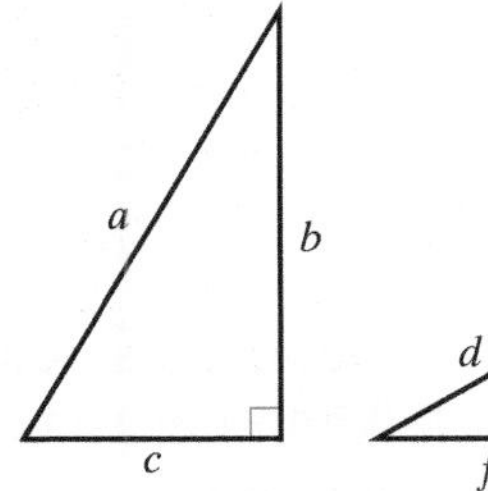

d e f

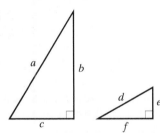

Applications

13. ***Sculptor*** A sculptor is designing her new triangular masterpiece. In her scale drawing, the shortest side of the triangular piece to be made measures 8 cm. The longest side of the drawing measures 25 cm. The longest side of the actual triangular piece to be sculpted must be 10.5 m long. How long will the shortest side of this piece be? Round to the nearest tenth.

14. ***Landscape Architect*** The zoo has hired a landscape architect to design the triangular lobby of the children's petting zoo. In his scale drawing, the longest side of the lobby is 9 cm. The shortest side of the lobby is 5 cm. The longest side of the actual lobby will be 30 m. How long will the shortest side of the actual lobby be? Round to the nearest tenth.

15. ***Photography*** Cora took a great photo of the entire family at this year's reunion. She brought it to a professional photography studio and asked that the 4-in.-by-6-in. photo be enlarged to poster size, which is 3.75 ft tall. What is the smaller dimension (width) of the poster?

16. ***Porch Addition*** Greg and Marcia are adding a new back porch onto their home. On the blueprints, the room measures 2 cm wide by 5 cm long. The actual room is similar in shape with a length of 6 m. What will be the width of the porch?

17. ***Blueprints of New House*** On the blueprints of their new home, Ben and Heather notice the bathtub measures 2 cm by 5 cm. They know that the actual bathtub will be 167.6 cm long. How wide will the tub be?

18. ***Theatre Company Props*** A theatre company's prop designer sends drawings of the props to the person in charge of construction. An upcoming play will require a large brick wall to stretch across the stage floor. In the designer's drawing, the wall measures $\frac{1}{4}$ ft by $\frac{3}{4}$ ft. If the length of the stage is 36 ft, how tall will the wall be?

Length of Shadows *In exercises 19 and 20, a flagpole casts a shadow. At the same time, a nearby tree casts a shadow. Use the sketch to find the height n of each flagpole.*

19.

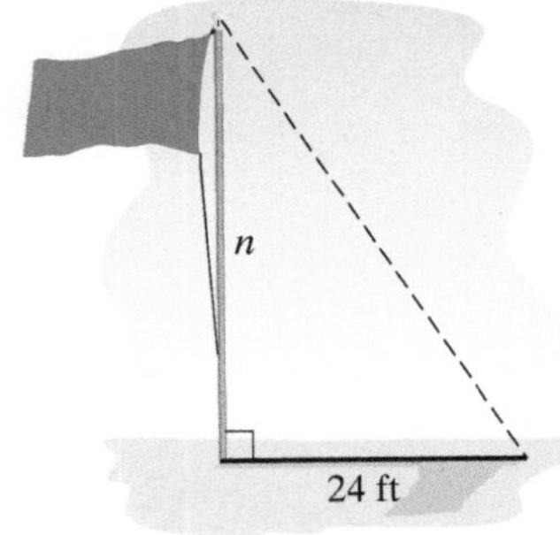

20.

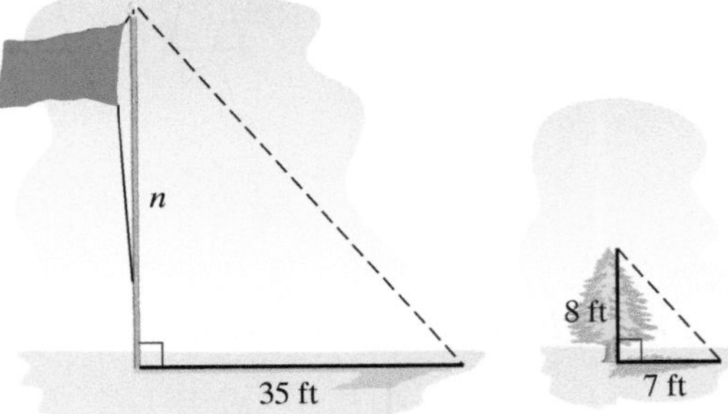

21. ***Length of Shadows*** Lola is standing outside the shopping mall. She is 5.5 ft tall and her shadow measures 6.5 ft long. The outside of the department store casts a shadow of 96 ft. How tall is the store? Round to the nearest foot.

22. ***Length of Shadows*** Thomas is rock climbing in British Columbia. He is 2 m tall and his shadow measures 2.33 m long. The rock he wants to climb casts a shadow of 203.33 m. How tall is the rock he is about to climb?

Each pair of figures is similar. Find the missing side. Round to the nearest tenth when necessary.

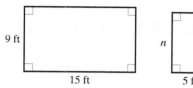

23.

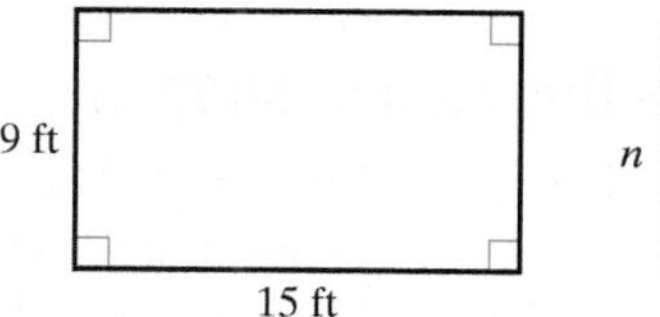

24.

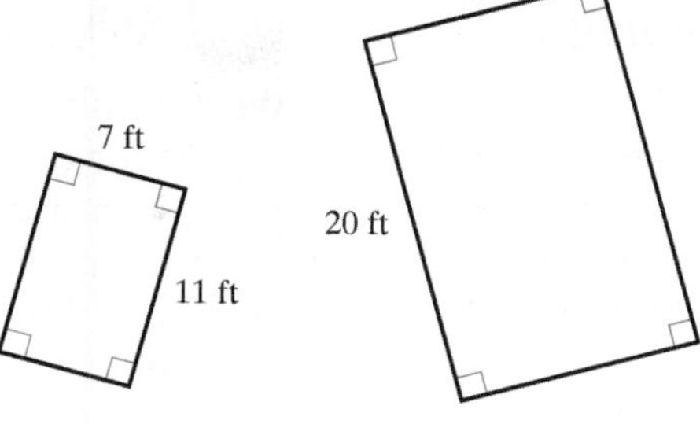

25.

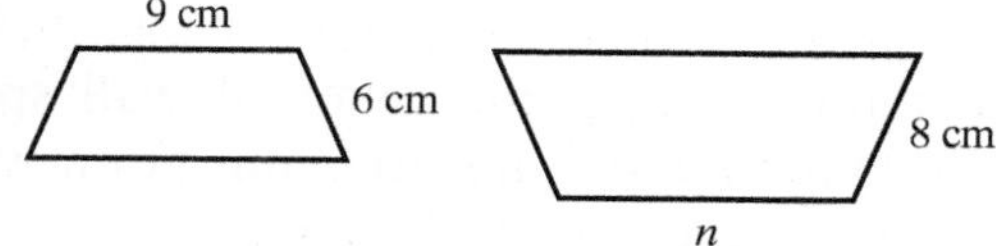

26.

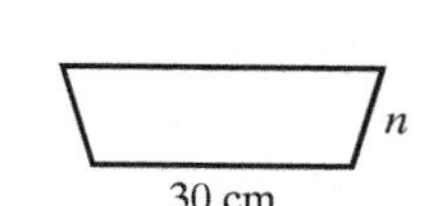

Quick Quiz 9 Round all answers to the nearest hundredth.

1. John is 6 feet tall. At 3 P.M. his shadow is 7 feet long. He is climbing a mountain cliff in Jasper, Alberta. The top of the cliff casts a shadow in the valley of 100 feet. How tall is the cliff? (*Hint:* Assume they are similar triangles.)

2. Two triangles are similar. The larger triangle has one side of 14 metres and one side of 15 metres. The longest side of the larger triangle is not known. The shortest side of the smallest triangle is 3 metres long. What is the length of the next-largest side?

3. Olivia has an architect's plan for her new house. The plan is drawn to scale. The plan measures 7 inches by 12 inches. Her new house will be 36 feet long. (This is the longest side.) How wide will her new house be?

4. **Concept Check** A safari guide conducts tours in a rectangular park in Zambia that measures 5 kilometres by 9 kilometres. The drawing in the guide's office is drawn to scale. The smallest side of the rectangle in the scale drawing is 6 centimetres. Explain how you would find the largest side in the scale drawing.

Section 10 Solving Applied Problems Involving Geometry

Student Learning Objective

After studying this section, you will be able to:

 **Solve applied problems involving geometric shapes.**

Solving Applied Problems Involving Geometric Shapes

We can solve many real-life problems with the geometric knowledge we now have. Our everyday world is filled with objects that are geometric in shape, so we can use our knowledge of geometry to find length, area, or volume. How far is the automobile trip? How much framing, edging, or fencing is required? How much paint, siding, or roofing is required? How much can we store? All of these questions can be answered with geometry.

If it is helpful to you, use the Mathematics Blueprint for Problem Solving to organize a plan to solve these applied problems.

Jens Stolt/Shutterstock

EXAMPLE 1 A professional painter can paint 15 m^2 of wall space in 20 minutes. How long will it take the painter to paint four walls with the following dimensions: $5\text{ m} \times 3\text{ m}$, $4\text{ m} \times 3\text{ m}$, $3\text{ m} \times 3\text{ m}$, and $3\text{ m} \times 2\text{ m}$?

Solution

1. ***Understand the problem.***

Mathematics Blueprint for Problem Solving

Gather the Facts	What Am I Asked to Do?	How Do I Proceed?	Key Points to Remember
Painter paints four walls: $5\text{ m} \times 3\text{ m}$ $4\text{ m} \times 3\text{ m}$ $3\text{ m} \times 3\text{ m}$ $3\text{ m} \times 2\text{ m}$ Painter can paint 15 m^2 in 20 minutes.	Find out how long it will take the painter to paint the four walls.	**(a)** Find the total area to be painted. **(b)** Then find how long it will take to paint the total area.	The area of each rectangular wall is length $\times$ width. To get the time, we set up a proportion.

2. ***Solve and state the answer.***

(a) Find the total area of the four walls.

Each wall is a rectangle. The first one is 3 m wide and 5 m long.

$$A = lw$$
$$= (5\text{ m})(3\text{ m}) = 15\text{ m}^2$$

We find the areas of the other three walls.

$$(4\text{ m})(3\text{ m}) = 12\text{ m}^2 \quad (3\text{ m})(3\text{ m}) = 9\text{ m}^2 \quad (3\text{ m})(2\text{ m}) = 6\text{ m}^2$$

The total area is obtained by adding.

$$\begin{array}{r} 15\text{ m}^2 \\ 12\text{ m}^2 \\ 9\text{ m}^2 \\ +\quad 6\text{ m}^2 \\ \hline 42\text{ m}^2 \end{array}$$

(b) Determine how long it will take to paint the four walls.
Now we set up a proportion. If 15 m^2 can be done in 20 minutes, then 42 m^2 can be done in t minutes.

$$\begin{aligned} \frac{15\text{ m}^2}{20\text{ minutes}} &= \frac{42\text{ m}^2}{t\text{ minutes}} \\ \frac{15}{20} &= \frac{42}{t} \\ 15(t) &= 42(20) \\ 15t &= 840 \\ \frac{15t}{15} &= \frac{840}{15} \\ t &= 56 \end{aligned}$$

Thus the work can be done in 56 minutes.

3. *Check.* Estimate the answer.

$$\begin{aligned} 5 \times 3 &= 15\text{ m}^2 \\ 4 \times 3 &= 12\text{ m}^2 \\ 3 \times 3 &= 9\text{ m}^2 \\ 3 \times 2 &= 6\text{ m}^2 \end{aligned}$$

If we estimate the sum of the number of square metres, we will have

$$15 + 12 + 9 + 6 = 42\text{ m}^2.$$

Now since 60 minutes = 1 hour, we know that if you can paint 15 m^2 in 20 minutes, you can paint 45 m^2 in one hour. Our estimate of 42 m^2 is slightly less than 45 m^2, so we would expect that the answer would be slightly less than one hour.

Thus our calculated value of 56 minutes seems reasonable. ✓

Practice Problem 1 Dharmesh rented an electric floor sander. It will sand 80 ft^2 of hardwood floor in 15 minutes. He needs to sand the floors in three rooms. The floor dimensions are 24 ft × 13 ft, 12 ft × 9 ft, and 16 ft × 3 ft. How long will it take him to sand the floors in all three rooms?

NOTE TO STUDENT: *Fully worked-out solutions to all of the Practice Problems can be found at the end of the module.*

EXAMPLE 2 Carlos and Rosetta want to put vinyl siding on the front of their home in Charlottetown. The house dimensions are shown in the figure at right. The door dimensions are 6 ft × 3 ft. The windows measure 2 ft × 4 ft.

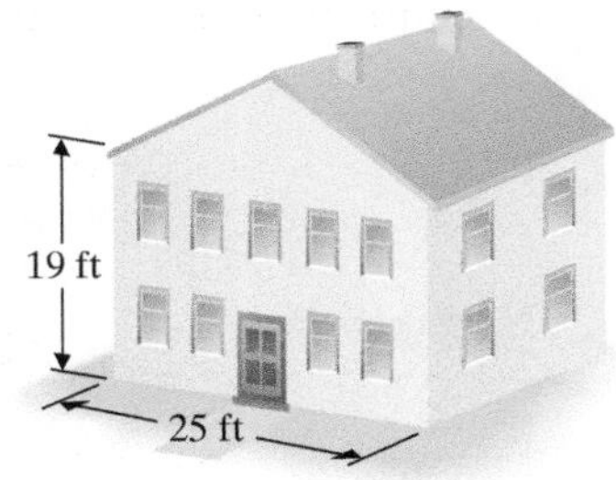

(a) Excluding windows and doors, how many square feet of siding will be needed?

(b) If the siding costs $2.25 per square foot, how much will it cost to side the front of the house?

Solution

1. ***Understand the problem.***

Mathematics Blueprint for Problem Solving

Gather the Facts	What Am I Asked to Do?	How Do I Proceed?	Key Points to Remember
House measures 19 ft × 25 ft. Windows measure 2 ft × 4 ft. Door measures 6 ft × 3 ft. Siding costs $2.25 per square foot.	Find the cost to put siding on the front of the house.	**(a)** Find the area of the entire front of the house by multiplying 19 ft by 25 ft. Find the area of one window by multiplying 2 ft by 4 ft. Find the area of the door by multiplying 6 ft by 3 ft. **(b)** Multiply desired area by $2.25.	**(a)** To obtain the desired area we must subtract the area of nine windows and one door from the area of the entire front. **(b)** We must multiply the resulting area by the cost of the siding per foot.

2. ***Solve and state the answer.***

(a) Find the area of the front of the house.

We will find the area of the large rectangle representing the front of the house. Then we will subtract the area of the windows and the door.

$$\begin{aligned}\text{Area of each window} &= (2\text{ ft})(4\text{ ft}) = 8\text{ ft}^2\\ \text{Area of 9 windows} &= (9)(8\text{ ft}^2) = 72\text{ ft}^2\\ \text{Area of 1 door} &= (6\text{ ft})(3\text{ ft}) = 18\text{ ft}^2\\ \text{Area of 9 windows} + 1\text{ door} &= 90\text{ ft}^2\\ \text{Area of large rectangle} &= (19\text{ ft})(25\text{ ft}) = 475\text{ ft}^2\end{aligned}$$

$$\begin{array}{lr}\text{Total area of front of house} & 475\text{ ft}^2\\ \underline{-\ \text{Area of 9 windows and 1 door}} & \underline{-\ 90\text{ ft}^2}\\ =\text{Total area to be covered} & 385\text{ ft}^2\end{array}$$

We see that 385 ft² of siding will be needed.

(b) Find the cost of the siding.

$$\text{Cost} = 385\ \cancel{\text{ft}^2} \times \frac{\$2.25}{1\ \cancel{\text{ft}^2}} = \$866.25$$

The cost to put up siding on the front of the house will be $866.25.

3. ***Check.*** We leave the check up to you.

Practice Problem 2 Below is the sketch of the roof of a commercial building.

NOTE TO STUDENT: Fully worked-out solutions to all of the Practice Problems can be found at the end of the module.

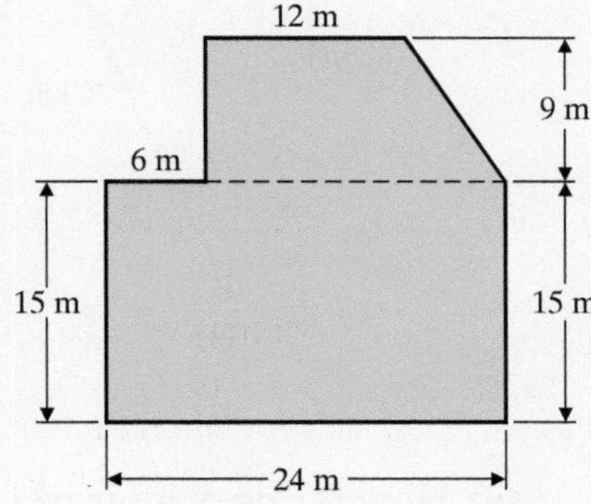

(a) What is the area of the roof?

(b) How much would it cost to install new roofing on the roof area shown if the roofing costs $24.75 per square metre?

Section 10 Exercises

Applications *Round to the nearest tenth unless otherwise directed.*

1. ***Driving Distances*** Monica drives to work each day from Bethel to Bridgeton. The following sketch shows the two possible routes.

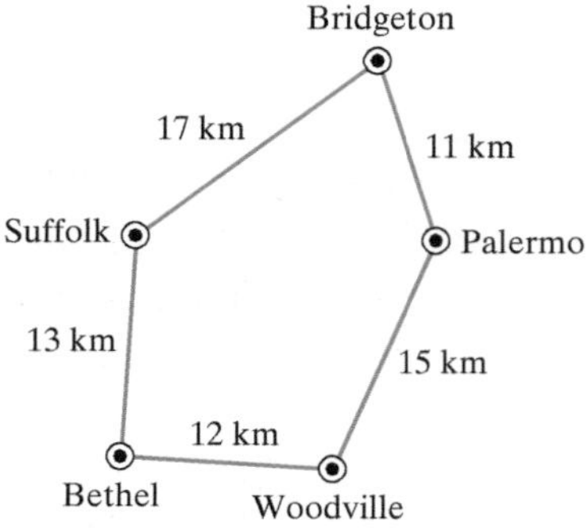

   (a) How many kilometres is the trip if she drives through Suffolk? What is her average speed if this trip takes her 0.4 hour?

   (b) How many kilometres is the trip if she drives through Woodville and Palermo? What is her average speed if this trip takes her 0.5 hour?

   (c) Over which route does she travel at a more rapid rate?

2. ***Driving Distances*** Robert drives from work either to a convenience store and then home or to a supermarket and then home. The sketch shows the distances.

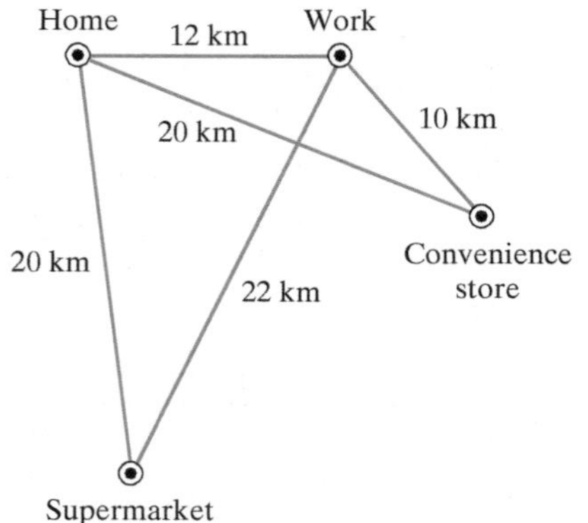

   (a) How far does he travel if he goes from work to the supermarket and then home? How fast does he travel if the trip takes 0.6 hour?

   (b) How far does he travel if he goes from work to the convenience store and then home? How fast does he travel if the trip takes 0.5 hour?

   (c) Over which route does he travel at a more rapid rate?

3. ***Hanging Wallpaper*** A professional wallpaper hanger can wallpaper 12 m^2 in 15 minutes. She will be papering four walls in a house. They measure 2 m × 3 m, 2 m × 4 m, 3 m × 3 m, and 3 m × 3.5 m. How many minutes will it take her to paper all four walls?

4. ***Painting an Apartment*** Mirek and Sarka are painting the walls of their apartment in Perth. When they worked together at Sarka's mother's house, they were able to paint 18 m^2 in 25 minutes. The living room they wish to paint has one wall that measures 5 metres by 2 metres, one wall that measures 4.5 metres by 2.5 metres, and two walls that measure 4 metres by 2.5 metres. How long will it take Mirek and Sarka together to paint the living room of their apartment? Round to the nearest minute.

5. ***Painting Exterior of House*** The Crawfords need to paint the outside of their house. The front and back each measure 55 ft by 24 ft, and each side measures 32 ft by 24 ft. There are sixteen windows and two doors, measuring 4 ft by 2 ft and 7 ft by 3 ft, respectively. They need to calculate the total area to be painted so they know how much paint to purchase. What is the total area to be painted?

6. ***Tiling a Kitchen*** A new restaurant is ordering tile for a large wall in the kitchen. The wall measures 19 feet long by 8 feet high, and will be tiled the entire length, but only to three-fourths of the wall height. The tile costs $4 per square foot. How much will the tile cost?

7. ***Carpeting a Recreation Room*** The floor area of the recreation room at Yvonne's house is shown in the following drawing. How much will it cost to carpet the room if the carpet costs $15 per square yard?

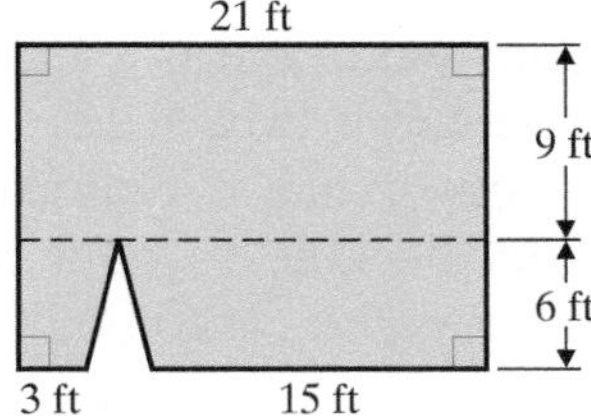

8. ***Aluminum Siding on a Barn*** The side view of a barn is shown in the following diagram. The cost of aluminum siding is $18 per square yard. How much will it cost to put siding on this side of the barn?

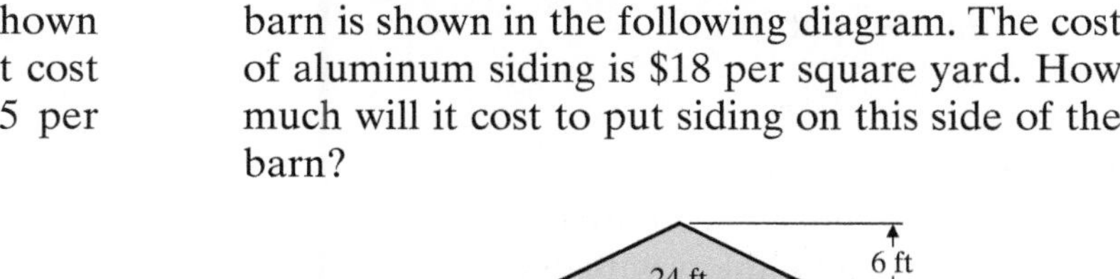

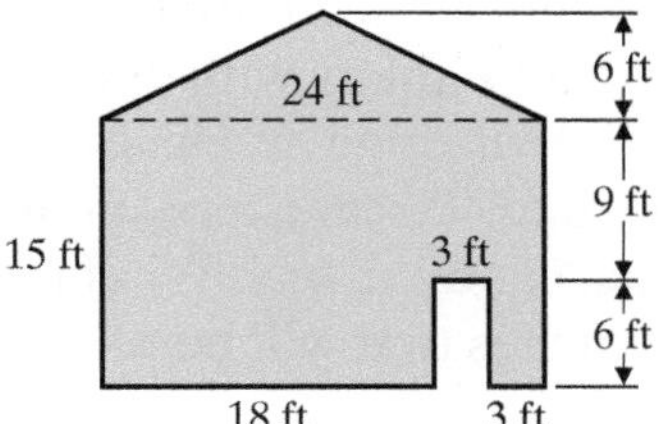

9. ***Gold Filling for a Tooth*** A dentist places a gold filling in the shape of a cylinder with a hemispherical top in a patient's tooth. The radius r of the filling is 1 mm. The height of the cylinder is 2 mm. Find the volume of the filling. If dental gold costs $95 per cubic millimetre, how much did the gold cost for the filling?

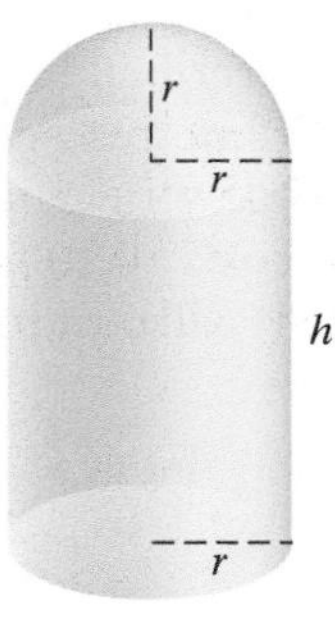

10. ***City Sewer System*** Find the volume of a concrete connector for the city sewer system. A diagram of the connector is shown. It is shaped like a box with a hole of diameter 2 m. If it is formed using concrete that costs $1.20 per cubic metre, how much will the necessary concrete cost?

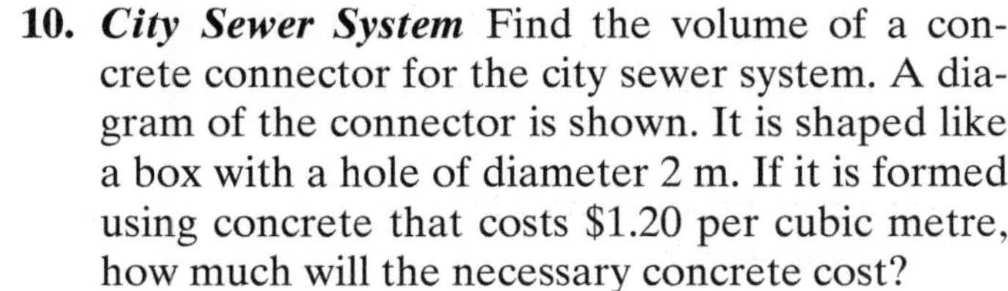

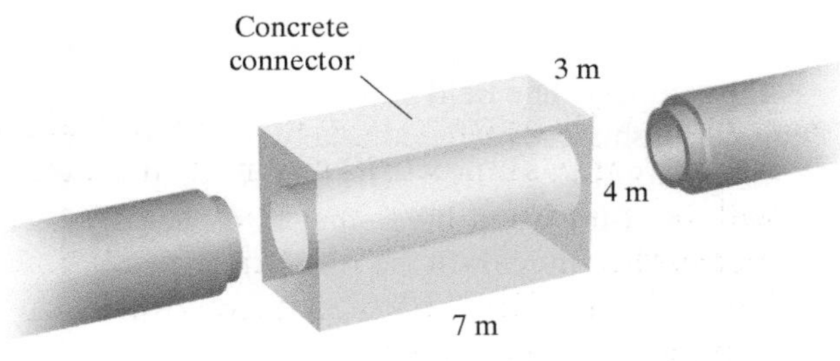

11. ***Satellite Orbit*** The Landsat satellite orbits Earth in an almost circular pattern. Assume that the radius of orbit (distance from centre of Earth to the satellite) is 6500 km.

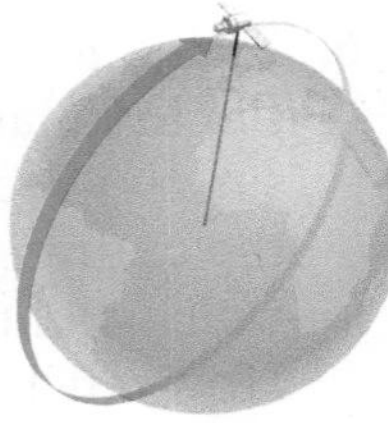

(a) How many kilometres long is one orbit of the satellite? (That is, what is the circumference of the orbit path?)

(b) If the satellite goes through one orbit around Earth in two hours, what is its speed in kilometres per hour?

12. ***City Park*** The North City Park is constructed in a shape that includes the region outside one-fourth of a circle. It is shaded in this sketch.

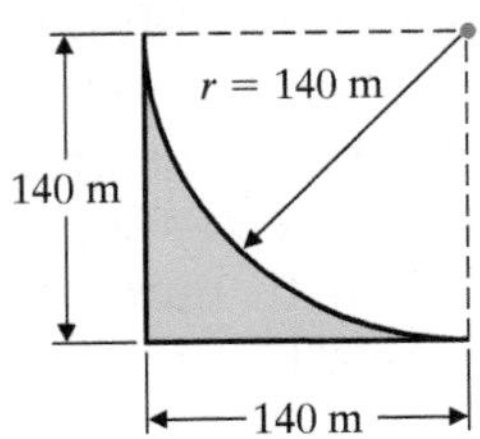

(a) What is the perimeter of the park?

(b) How much will it cost to place a fence around the park at $15 per metre?

13. ***Valentine's Day Candy*** For Valentine's Day, a company makes decorative cylinder-shaped canisters and fills them with red hot candies. Each canister is 10 in. high and has a radius of 2 in. They want to make 400 canisters and need to determine how much candy to buy. What is the total number of cubic inches that will be filled with candy?

14. ***Cargo Box of Ford F-150*** Manuel has two large gardens each measuring 15 feet by 11 feet. He wants to put wood chips 2 inches deep in each garden. The cargo box of his Ford F-150, when he uses the cover, has a volume of 55.5 cubic feet. Will Manuel be able to haul the load of wood chips in his covered cargo box?

Quick Quiz 10

Use $\pi \approx 3.14$. Round all answers to the nearest hundredth.

1. What is the area of a circular lawn with radius 7.25 m?

2. Michael wants to paint the side of his house. The side is a rectangle 20 feet high and 34 feet long. There are 7 windows on that side of the house. Each window measures 3 feet by 2 feet. Assuming he does not want to paint over the windows, how many square feet of area will he need to cover with paint?

3. Camp Cherith has built a new rope-obstacle course for the campers. The field that contains the course is triangular in shape. The field has a base of 200 metres and a height of 140 metres. The entire field needs to be sprayed with weed killer that costs $0.05 per square metre. How much will the weed killer cost?

4. **Concept Check** Suppose there is a second field at Camp Cherith, described in problem 3. The new field has a base of 300 metres and the same height as the other field. The new field needs to be sprayed with weed killer that costs $0.20 per square metre. Explain how much more it will cost to spray the new field than the other field.

Putting Your Skills to Work: Use Math to Save Money

GAS MONEY AND KILOMETRES PER LITRE (km/L)

How many litres of gas do you purchase for your car in one year? With the sharp increase in the price of gasoline, people are thinking about questions like this more than ever before. Michelle drives a 2003 SUV because she likes the room and comfort it provides. However, it has a gas-guzzling engine that only gets 8 kilometres per litre.

Michelle has spent more and more money on gas each month, so she is thinking about buying another car that will get better gas mileage. She is even thinking about a hybrid model (a car with a combined gas and electric engine) so she can get the best possible mileage.

Analyzing the Options

Michelle wants to make a smart choice, so she is going to determine the cost and potential savings she would enjoy from three different types of cars:

Option A: A small SUV that gets 10 kilometres per litre (km/L) and sells for $21 540

Option B: A hybrid model of the same SUV that gets 18 km/L and sells for $28 150

Option C: The most fuel-efficient hybrid car that gets 23 km/L and sells for $23 770

During her research Michelle learned that she drives her car 20 000 kilometres in a year. In the following questions, round to the nearest hundredth when necessary.

1. Determine the number of litres of gasoline that each car (Options A, B, and C) would need if they are driven 20 000 kilometres in one year.

2. If the average price of gasoline is $0.95 per litre, how much would it cost to fuel each car for 20 000 kilometres?

Making the Best Choice to Save Money

The hybrid model SUV in Option B would cost Michelle $6610 more to purchase than the SUV in Option A.

3. How much gas money would Michelle save in one year with Option B compared to Option A?
4. How many years would it take for Michelle to save $6610 in gas money with Option B compared to Option A?
5. How much gas money would Michelle save after 5 years with Option B compared to Option A? after 10 years?

The incredibly fuel-efficient hybrid car in Option C would cost Michelle $2230 more to purchase than the SUV in Option A.

6. How much gas money will Michelle save in one year with Option C compared to Option A?
7. How many years would it take for Michelle to save $2230 in gas money with Option C compared to Option A?
8. How much gas money would Michelle save after 5 years with Option C compared to Option A? after 10 years?

Even though Michelle enjoyed the comfort of her SUV, she could not ignore the potential savings in gas money she saw with Option C. She decided it was time to make a smart financial decision instead of one based on comfort. She expected to have her new car for at least 5 years. At that point, Option C will have saved her over $5000 in gas money!

9. Do you drive more than 20 000 kilometres per year or fewer? How would more kilometres or fewer kilometres per year affect this analysis?
10. How much do you pay for a litre of gas? How would higher or lower prices for a litre of gas affect this analysis?

Module Organizer

Topic	Procedure	Examples
Perimeter of a rectangle.	$P = 2l + 2w$	Find the perimeter of a rectangle with width = 3 m and length = 8 m. $P = (2)(8\text{ m}) + (2)(3\text{ m})$ $= 16\text{ m} + 6\text{ m} = 22\text{ m}$
Perimeter of a square.	$P = 4s$	Find the perimeter of a square with side $s = 6$ m. $P = (4)(6\text{ m}) = 24\text{ m}$
Area of a rectangle.	$A = lw$	Find the area of a rectangle with width = 2 m and length = 7 m. $A = (7\text{ m})(2\text{ m}) = 14\text{ m}^2$
Area of a square.	$A = s^2$	Find the area of a square with a side of 4 m. $A = s^2 = (4\text{ m})^2 = 16\text{ m}^2$
Perimeter of parallelograms, trapezoids, and triangles.	Add up the lengths of all sides.	Find the perimeter of a triangle with sides of 3 m, 6 m, and 4 m. $3\text{ m} + 6\text{ m} + 4\text{ m} = 13\text{ m}$
Area of a parallelogram.	$A = bh$ b = length of base h = height h b	Find the area of a parallelogram with a base of 12 m and a height of 7 m. $A = bh = (12\text{ m})(7\text{ m}) = 84\text{ m}^2$
Area of a trapezoid.	$A = \frac{h(b + B)}{2}$ b = length of shorter base B = length of longer base h = height b h B	Find the area of a trapezoid whose height is 12 m and whose bases are 17 m and 25 m. $A = \frac{(12\text{ m})(17\text{ m} + 25\text{ m})}{2} = \frac{(12\text{ m})(42\text{ m})}{2}$ $= \frac{504\text{ m}^2}{2} = 252\text{ m}^2$
The sum of the measures of the three interior angles of a triangle is 180°.	In a triangle, to find one missing angle if two are given: **1.** Add up the two known angles. **2.** Subtract the sum from 180°.	Find the missing angle if two known angles in a triangle are 60° and 70°. **1.** 60° + 70° = 130° **2.** 180° − 130° = 50° The missing angle is 50°.
Area of a triangle.	$A = \frac{bh}{2}$ b = base h = height h b	Find the area of a triangle whose base is 1.5 m and whose height is 3 m. $A = \frac{bh}{2} = \frac{(1.5\text{ m})(3\text{ m})}{2} = \frac{4.5\text{ m}^2}{2} = 2.25\text{ m}^2$
Evaluating square roots of numbers that are perfect squares.	If a number is a product of two identical factors, then either factor is called a square root.	$\sqrt{0} = 0$ because $(0)(0) = 0$ $\sqrt{4} = 2$ because $(2)(2) = 4$ $\sqrt{100} = 10$ because $(10)(10) = 100$ $\sqrt{169} = 13$ because $(13)(13) = 169$

<table>
<tr><th>Topic</th><th>Procedure</th><th>Examples</th></tr>
<tr><td>Approximating the square root of a number that is not a perfect square.</td><td>

1. If a calculator with a square root key is available, enter the number and then press the $\boxed{\sqrt{x}}$ or $\boxed{\sqrt{\ }}$ key. The approximate value will be displayed.
2. If using a square root table, find the number n, then look for the square root of that number. The approximate value will be rounded to the nearest thousandth.

<table>
<tr><th>Number, n</th><th>Square Root of That Number, $\sqrt{n}$</th></tr>
<tr><td>31</td><td>5.568</td></tr>
<tr><td>32</td><td>5.657</td></tr>
<tr><td>33</td><td>5.745</td></tr>
<tr><td>34</td><td>5.831</td></tr>
</table>

</td><td>

1. Find on a calculator.
(a) $\sqrt{13}$ **(b)** $\sqrt{182}$
Round to the nearest thousandth.
(a) 13 $\boxed{\sqrt{x}}$ 3.60555128 rounds to 3.606.
(b) 182 $\boxed{\sqrt{x}}$ 13.49073756 rounds to 13.491.
2. Find from a square root table.
(a) $\sqrt{31}$ **(b)** $\sqrt{33}$ **(c)** $\sqrt{34}$
To the nearest thousandth, the approximate values are as follows.
(a) $\sqrt{31} \approx 5.568$ **(b)** $\sqrt{33} \approx 5.745$
(c) $\sqrt{34} \approx 5.831$

</td></tr>
<tr><td>Finding the hypotenuse of a right triangle when given the length of each leg.</td><td>

$\text{hypotenuse} = \sqrt{(\text{leg})^2 + (\text{leg})^2}$

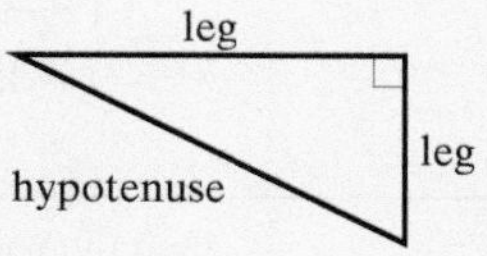

</td><td>

Find the hypotenuse of a triangle with legs of 9 m and 12 m.

$$\begin{aligned}\text{hypotenuse} &= \sqrt{(12)^2 + (9)^2}\\ &= \sqrt{144 + 81} = \sqrt{225}\\ &= 15 \text{ m}\end{aligned}$$

</td></tr>
<tr><td>Finding the leg of a right triangle when given the length of the other leg and the hypotenuse.</td><td>

$\text{leg} = \sqrt{(\text{hypotenuse})^2 - (\text{leg})^2}$

</td><td>

Find the leg of a right triangle. The hypotenuse is 14 in. and the other leg is 12 in.

Round to nearest thousandth.

$$\text{leg} = \sqrt{(14)^2 - (12)^2} = \sqrt{196 - 144} = \sqrt{52}$$

Using a calculator or a square root table, the leg $\approx$ 7.211 in.

</td></tr>
<tr><td>Solving applied problems involving the Pythagorean Theorem.</td><td>

1. Read the problem carefully.
2. Draw a sketch.
3. Label the two sides that are given.
4. If the hypotenuse is unknown, use
$\text{hypotenuse} = \sqrt{(\text{leg})^2 + (\text{leg})^2}$.
5. If one leg is unknown, use
$\text{leg} = \sqrt{(\text{hypotenuse})^2 - (\text{leg})^2}$.

</td><td>

A boat travels 5 mi south and then 3 mi east. How far is it from the starting point? Round to the nearest tenth.

$$\begin{aligned}\text{hypotenuse} &= \sqrt{(5)^2 + (3)^2}\\ &= \sqrt{25 + 9} = \sqrt{34}\end{aligned}$$

Using a calculator or a square root table, the distance is approximately 5.8 mi.

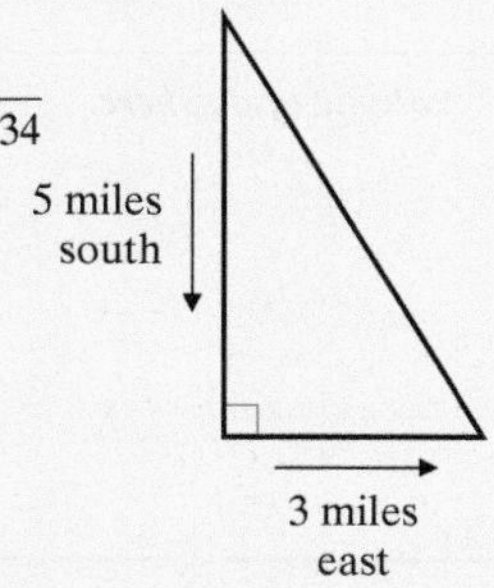

</td></tr>
<tr><td>The special 30°–60°–90° right triangle.</td><td>

The length of the leg opposite the 30° angle is $\frac{1}{2} \times$ the length of the hypotenuse.

</td><td>

Find y.

$$y = \frac{1}{2}(26 \text{ m}) = 13 \text{ m}$$

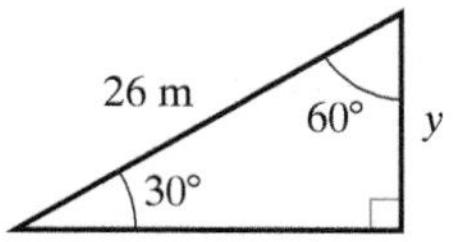

</td></tr>
<tr><td>The special 45°–45°–90° right triangle.</td><td>

The sides opposite the 45° angles are equal. The hypotenuse is $\sqrt{2} \times$ the length of either leg.

</td><td>

Find z.

$$z = \sqrt{2}(13 \text{ m}) \approx (1.414)(13 \text{ m}) = 18.382 \text{ m}$$

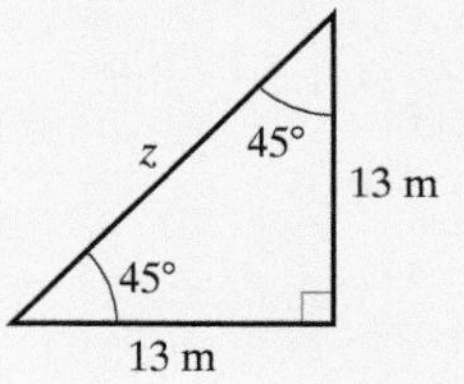

</td></tr>
</table>

(*Continued on next page*)

Topic	Procedure	Examples
Radius and diameter of a circle.	r = radius d = diameter $r = \frac{d}{2}$ $d = 2r$	What is the radius of a circle with diameter 50 in.? $r = \frac{50 \text{ in.}}{2} = 25 \text{ in.}$ What is the diameter of a circle with radius 16 in.? $d = (2)(16 \text{ in.}) = 32 \text{ in.}$
Pi.	Pi is a decimal that goes on forever. It can be approximated by as many decimal places as needed. $\pi = \frac{\text{circumference of a circle}}{\text{diameter of same circle}}$	Use $\pi \approx 3.14$ for all calculations. Unless otherwise directed, round your final answer to the nearest tenth when any calculation involves π.
Circumference of a circle.	$C = \pi d$	Find the circumference of a circle with diameter 12 ft. $C = \pi d = (3.14)(12 \text{ ft}) = 37.68 \text{ ft}$ $\approx 37.7 \text{ ft}$ (rounded to the nearest tenth)
Area of a circle.	$A = \pi r^2$ **1.** Square the radius first. **2.** Then multiply the result by 3.14.	Find the area of a circle with radius 7 ft. $A = \pi r^2 = (3.14)(7 \text{ ft})^2 = (3.14)(49 \text{ ft}^2)$ $= 153.86 \text{ ft}^2$ $\approx 153.9 \text{ ft}^2$ (rounded to the nearest tenth)
Volume of a rectangular solid (box).	$V = lwh$	Find the volume of a box whose dimensions are 5 m by 8 m by 2 m. $V = (5 \text{ m})(8 \text{ m})(2 \text{ m}) = (40)(2) \text{ m}^3 = 80 \text{ m}^3$
Volume of a cylinder.	r = radius h = height $V = \pi r^2 h$ **1.** Square the radius first. **2.** Then multiply the result by 3.14 and by the height.	Find the volume of a cylinder with radius 7 m and height 3 m. $V = \pi r^2 h = (3.14)(7 \text{ m})^2(3 \text{ m})$ $= (3.14)(49)(3) \text{ m}^3$ $= (153.86)(3) \text{ m}^3 = 461.58 \text{ m}^3$ $\approx 461.6 \text{ m}^3$ (rounded to the nearest tenth)
Volume of a sphere.	$V = \frac{4\pi r^3}{3}$ r = radius	Find the volume of a sphere of radius 3 m. $V = \frac{4\pi r^3}{3} = \frac{(4)(3.14)(3 \text{ m})^3}{3}$ $= \frac{(4)(3.14)\overset{9}{\cancel{(27)}} \text{ m}^3}{\underset{1}{\cancel{3}}}$ $= (12.56)(9) \text{ m}^3 = 113.04 \text{ m}^3$ $\approx 113.0 \text{ m}^3$ (rounded to the nearest tenth)
Volume of a cone.	$V = \frac{\pi r^2 h}{3}$ r = radius h = height	Find the volume of a cone of height 9 m and radius 7 m. $V = \frac{\pi r^2 h}{3} = \frac{(3.14)(7 \text{ m})^2(9 \text{ m})}{3}$ $= \frac{(3.14)(7^2)\overset{3}{\cancel{(9)}} \text{ m}^3}{\underset{1}{\cancel{3}}} = (3.14)(49)(3) \text{ m}^3$ $= (153.86)(3) \text{ m}^3 = 461.58 \text{ m}^3$ $\approx 461.6 \text{ m}^3$ (rounded to the nearest tenth)

Topic	Procedure	Examples
Volume of a pyramid.	$V = \frac{Bh}{3}$ B = area of the base h = height 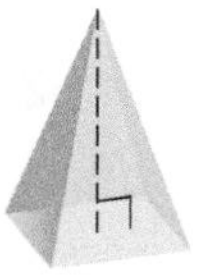 **1.** Find the area of the base. **2.** Multiply this area by the height and divide the result by 3.	Find the volume of a pyramid whose height is 6 m and whose rectangular base is 10 m by 12 m. **1.** $B = (12\text{ m})(10\text{ m}) = 120\text{ m}^2$ **2.** $V = \frac{(120)(\overset{2}{\cancel{6}})\text{ m}^3}{\underset{1}{\cancel{3}}} = (120)(2)\text{ m}^3 = 240\text{ m}^3$
Similar figures, corresponding sides.	The corresponding sides of similar figures have the same ratio.	Find n in the following similar figures. $\frac{n}{4} = \frac{9}{3}$ $3n = 36$ $n = 12\text{ m}$ 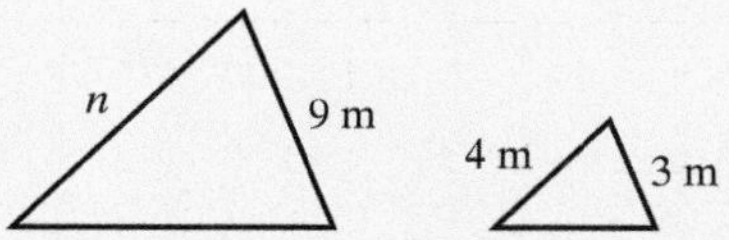 n 9 m 4 m 3 m
Similar figures, corresponding perimeters.	The perimeters of similar figures have the same ratio as the corresponding sides.	The following two figures are similar. Find the perimeter of the larger figure. $\frac{6}{12} = \frac{29}{p}$ $6p = (12)(29)$ $6p = 348$ $\frac{6p}{6} = \frac{348}{6}$ $p = 58$ The perimeter of the larger figure is 58 m. 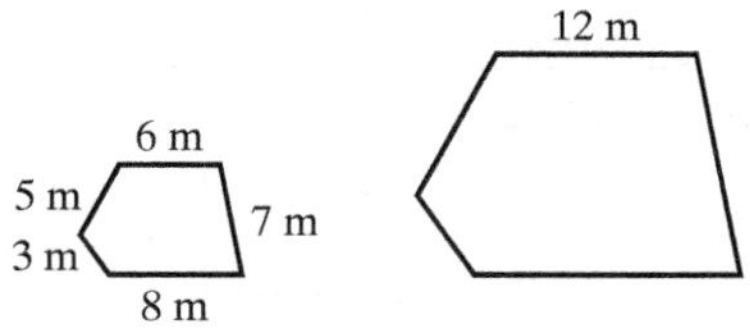 12 m 6 m 5 m 3 m 7 m 8 m

Module Review Problems

Round to the nearest tenth when necessary. Use $\pi \approx 3.14$ in all calculations requiring the use of π.

Section 1

1. Find the complement of an angle of 76°.

2. Find the supplement of an angle of 76°.

3. Find the measures of $\angle a$, $\angle b$, and $\angle c$ in the following sketch.

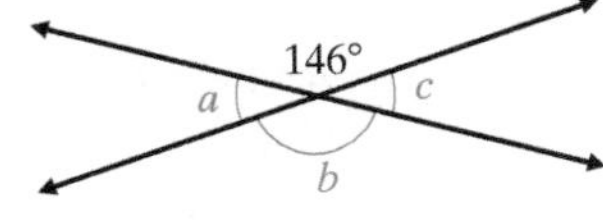

4. Find $\angle s$, $\angle t$, $\angle u$, $\angle w$, $\angle x$, $\angle y$, and $\angle z$ in the following sketch if we know that line p is parallel to line q.

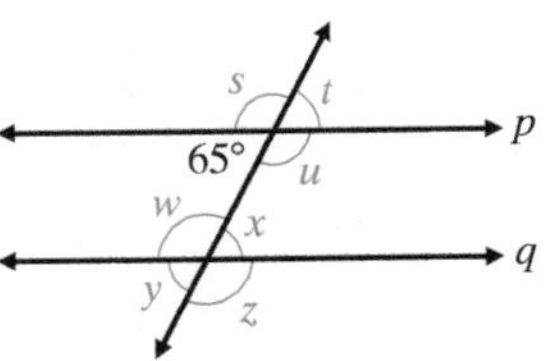

Section 2

Find the perimeter of the square or rectangle.

5. length = 9.5 m, width = 2.3 m

6. length = width = 12.7 yd

Find the area of the square or rectangle.

7. length = 5.9 cm, width = 2.8 cm

8. length = width = 7.2 in.

Find the perimeter of each object made up of rectangles and squares.

9.

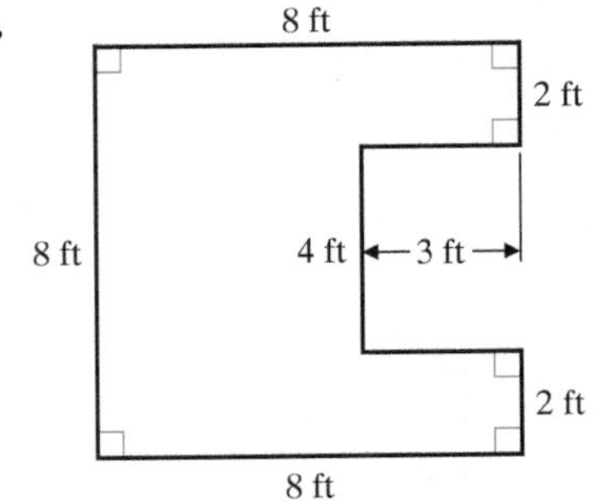

10.

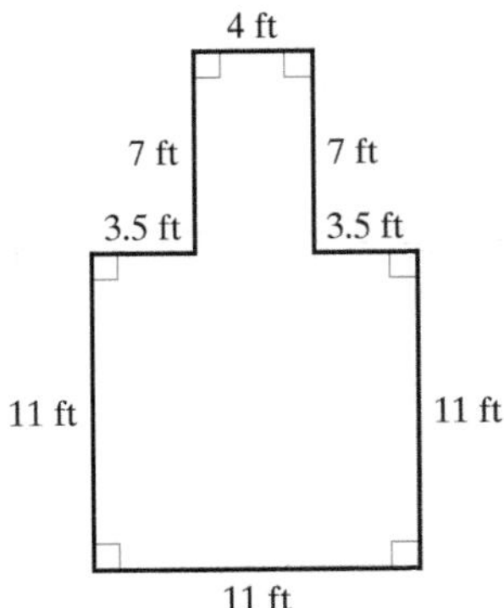

Find the area of each shaded region made up of rectangles and squares.

11.

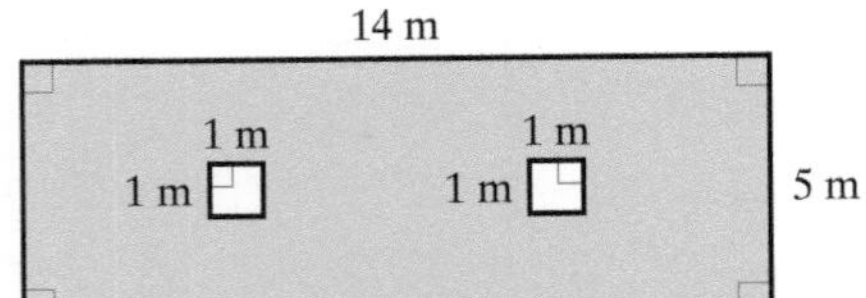

12.

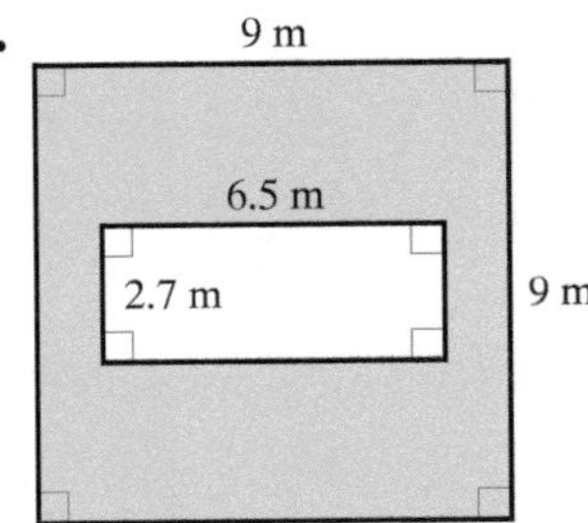

Section 3

Find the perimeter of the parallelogram or trapezoid.

13. Two sides of the parallelogram are 38.5 m and 14 m.

14. The sides of the trapezoid are 5 km, 22 km, 5 km, and 30 km.

Find the area of the parallelogram or trapezoid.

15. A parallelogram has a base of 70 m and a height of 50 m.

16. A trapezoid has a height of 18 m and bases of 21 m and 19 m.

Find the total area of each region made up of parallelograms, trapezoids, and rectangles.

17.

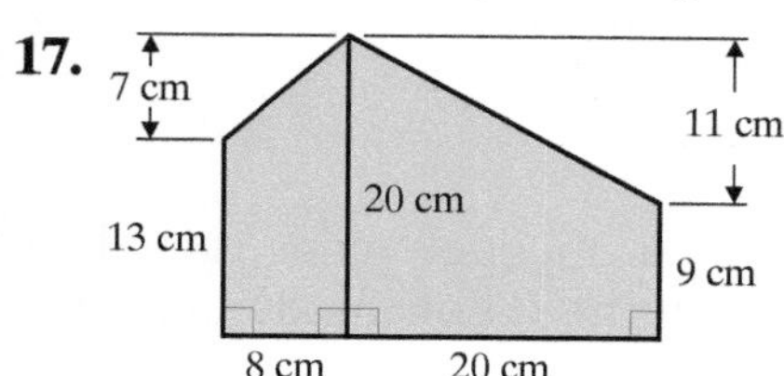

18.

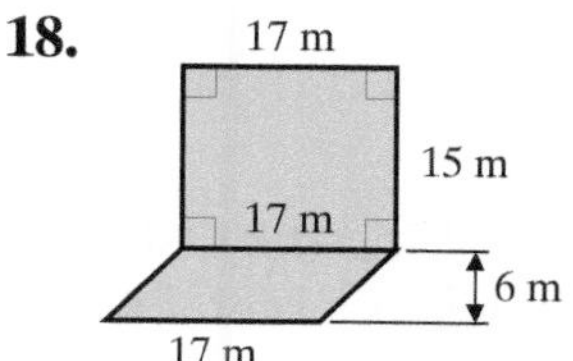

Section 4

Find the perimeter of the triangle.

19. An isosceles triangle with one side 18 ft and each of the other two sides 21 ft.

20. An equilateral triangle with each side 15.5 ft.

Find the measure of the third angle in the triangle.

21. Two known angles are 28° and 45°.

22. A right triangle with one angle of 35°.

Find the area of the triangle.

23. base = 8.5 m, height = 12.3 m

24. base = 12.5 m, height = 9.5 m

Find the total area of each region made up of triangles and rectangles.

25.

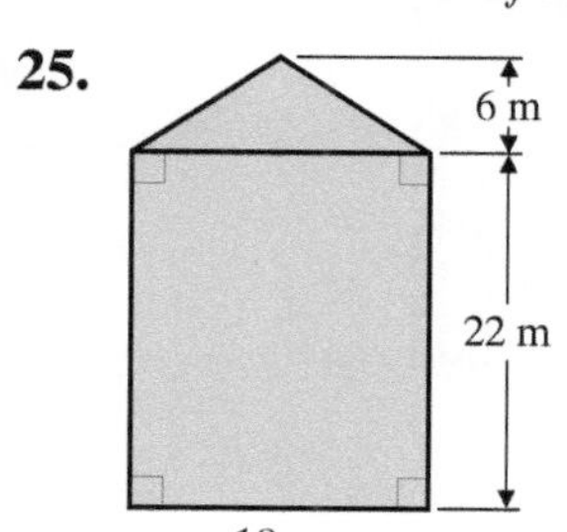

26.

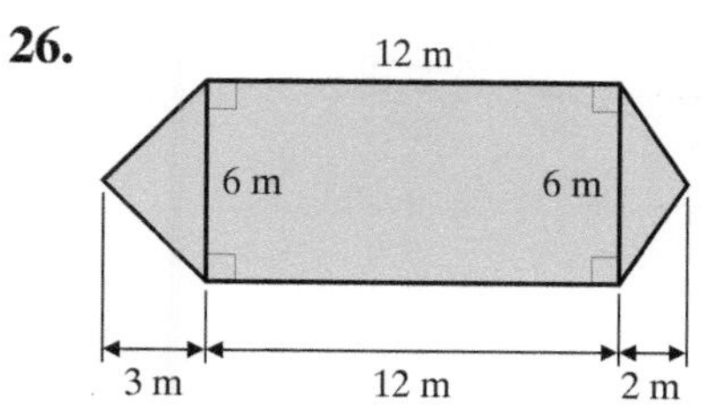

Section 5

Evaluate exactly.

27. $\sqrt{81}$

28. $\sqrt{64}$

29. $\sqrt{121}$

30. $\sqrt{144} + \sqrt{16}$

31. $\sqrt{100} - \sqrt{36} + \sqrt{196}$

Approximate using a square root table or a calculator with a square root key. Round to the nearest thousandth when necessary.

32. $\sqrt{45}$ **33.** $\sqrt{62}$ **34.** $\sqrt{165}$ **35.** $\sqrt{180}$

Section 6

Find the unknown side. If the answer cannot be obtained exactly, use a square root table or a calculator with a square root key. Round to the nearest hundredth when necessary.

36.

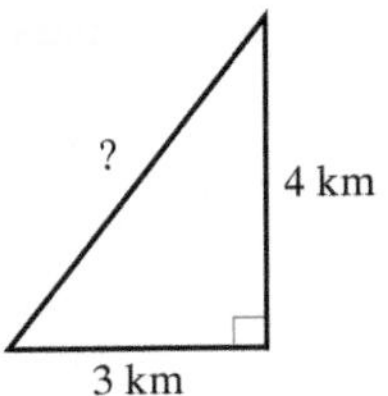

37.

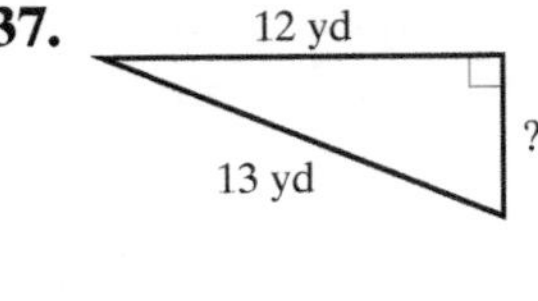

38.

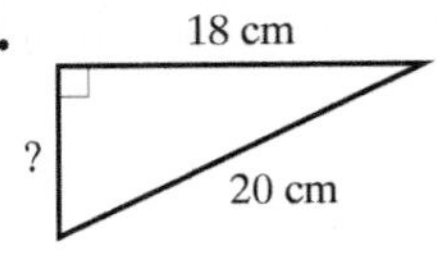

39.

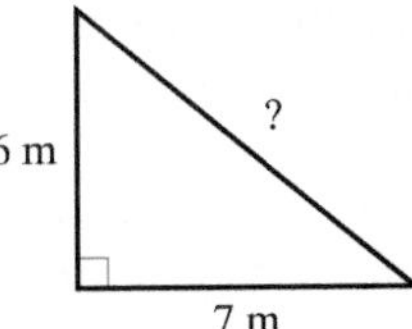

Round to the nearest tenth.

40. ***Construction of a Metal Plate*** Find the distance between the centres of the holes of a metal plate with the dimensions labelled in the following sketch.

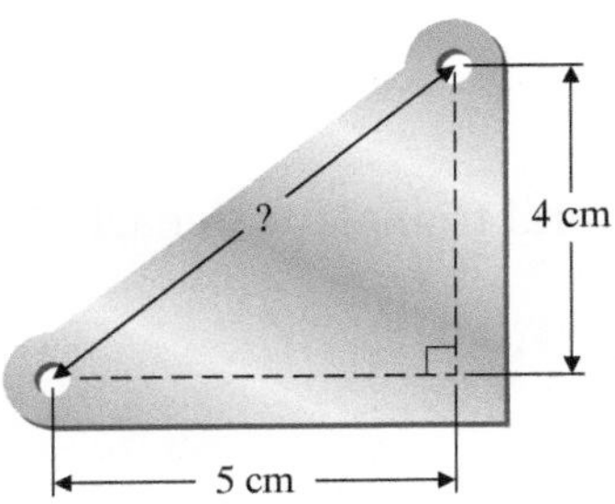

41. ***Wheelchair Ramp*** A builder constructed a wheelchair ramp with the following dimensions. Find the length of the ramp.

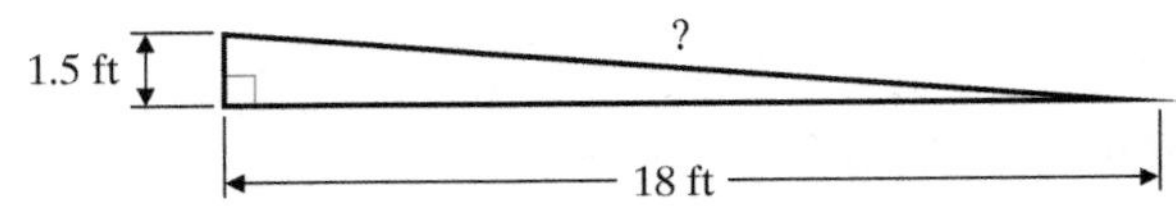

42. ***Shed Construction*** A shed is built with the following dimensions. Find the distance from the peak of the roof to the horizontal support brace.

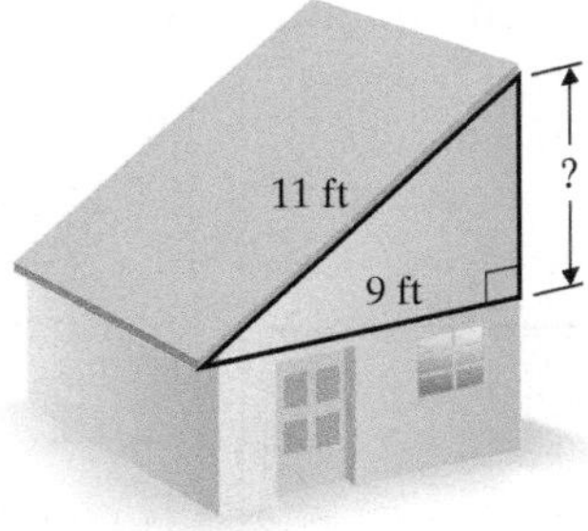

43. ***Replacing a Door*** Find the width of a replacement door if it is 6 ft tall and the diagonal measures 7 ft.

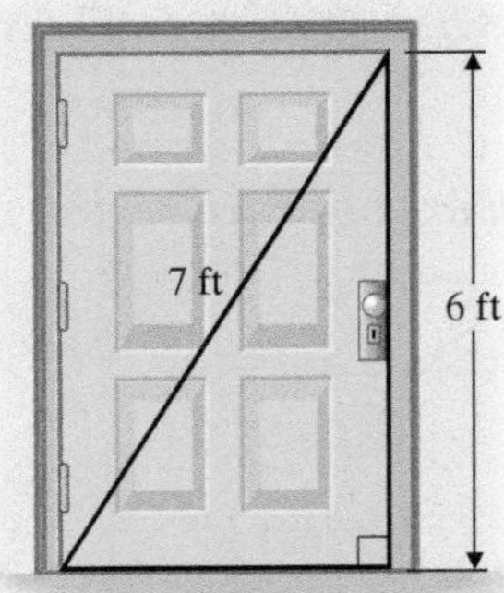

Section 7

44. What is the diameter of a circle whose radius is 53 cm?

45. What is the radius of a circle whose diameter is 126 cm?

46. Find the circumference of a circle with diameter 20 m.

47. Find the circumference of a circle with radius 9 cm.

Find the area of each circle.

48. radius = 9 m

49. diameter = 8.6 km

Find the area of each shaded region made up of circles, semicircles, rectangles, trapezoids, and parallelograms. Round your answer to the nearest tenth.

50.

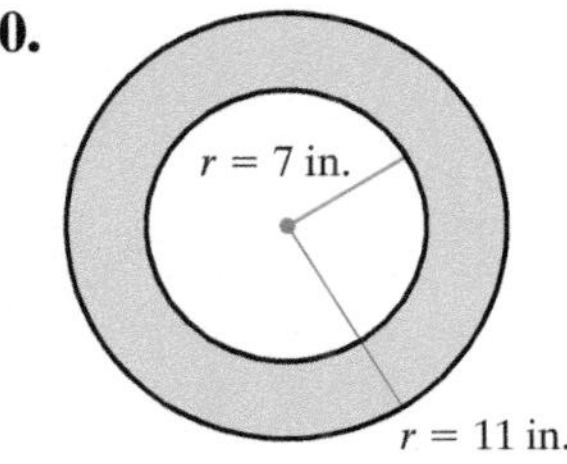

51.

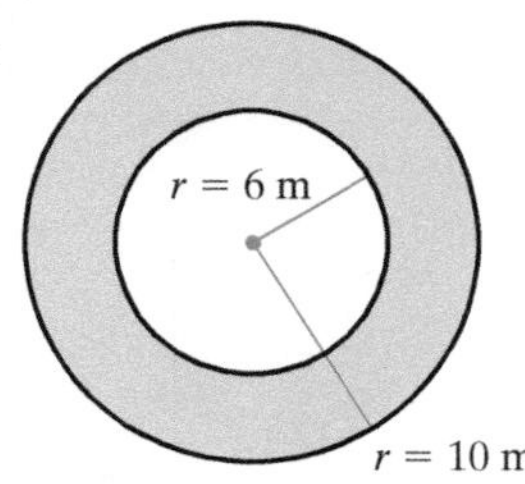

52.

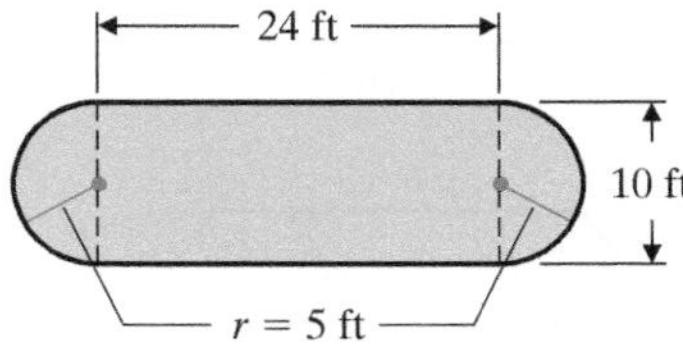

53.

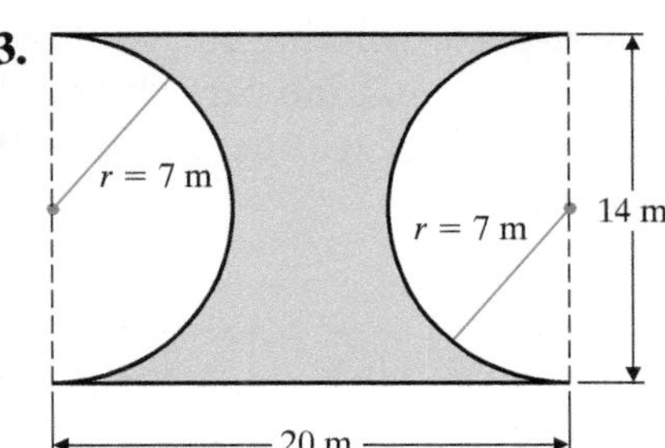

54.

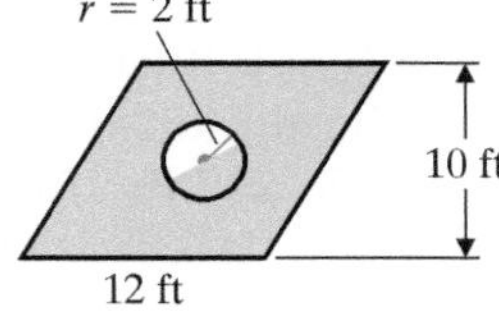

55.

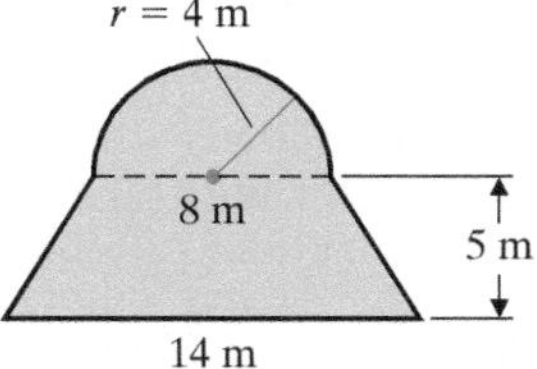

Section 8

In exercises 56–62, find the volume. Round answers to the nearest tenth.

56. ***U-Haul Truck*** U-Haul advertises a moving truck with a storage area measuring 20.8 ft by 7.5 ft by 8.1 ft. Find the volume of the storage area.

57. ***Soccer Ball*** Find the volume of a soccer ball with radius 11.43 cm.

58. ***Garbage Can*** Find the volume of a garbage can that is 3 ft high and has a radius of 1.5 ft.

59. ***Cup of Coffee*** Find the volume of a medium cup of coffee with a height of 12.7 cm and radius of 3.8 cm.

60. ***Sculpture*** Find the volume of a sculpture in the shape of a pyramid that is 15 m high and whose square base measures 7 m by 7 m.

61. ***Sand Construction at the Beach*** Greg and Marcia took Lexi to play in the sand at the beach. Find the volume of a cone of sand Greg made that is 9 ft tall with a radius of 20 ft.

62. ***Chemical Pollution*** A chemical has polluted a volume of ground in a cone shape. The depth of the cone is 30 m. The radius of the cone is 17 m. Find the volume of polluted ground.

Section 9

Find n in each set of similar triangles.

63.

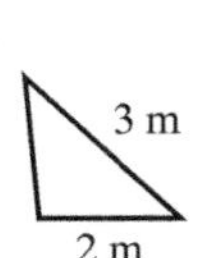

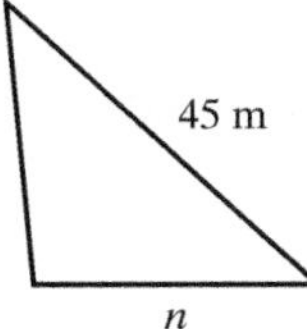

64.

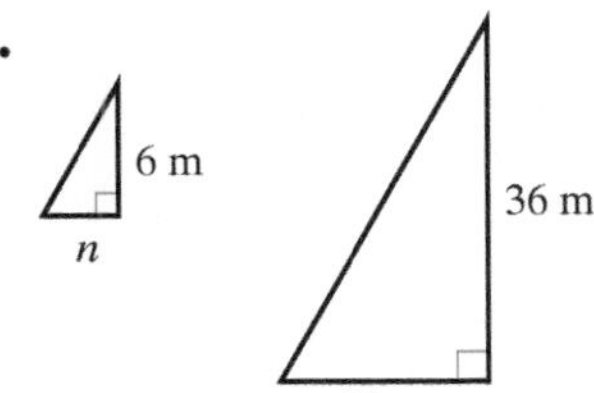

Determine the perimeter of the unlabelled figure.

65.

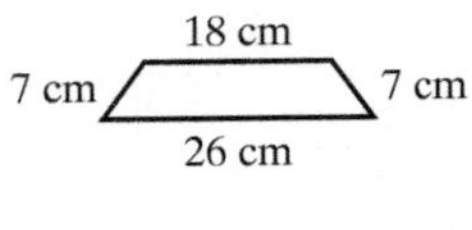

66.

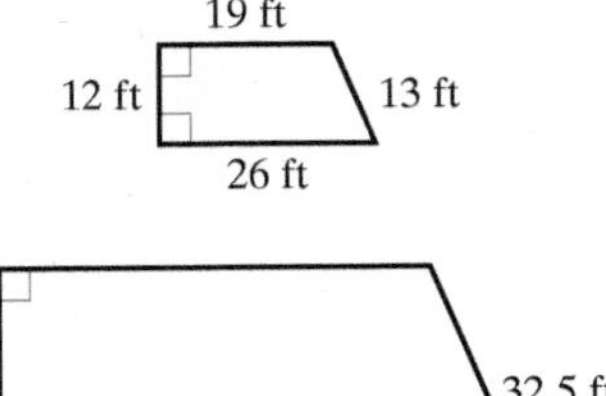

67. ***Banner Construction*** Anastasio is in charge of decorations for the "International Cars of the Future" show. He has designed a rectangular banner that will hang in front of the first-prize-winning car, so that all he has to do is push a button and the banner will fly up into the ceiling space to reveal the car. The model of the banner used 12 square metres of fabric. The dimensions of the actual banner will be $3\frac{1}{2}$ times the length and the width of the model. How much fabric will the finished banner need?

Section 10

68. ***Chemistry Lab Tank*** A conical tank holds acid in a chemistry lab. The tank has a radius of 9 cm and a height of 24 cm. How many cubic centimetres does the tank hold? The acid weighs 16 grams per cubic centimetre. What is the weight of the acid if the tank is full?

69. ***Carpeting a Recreation Room*** The Wilsons are carpeting a recreation room with the dimensions shown. Carpeting costs \$8 per square yard. How much will the carpeting cost?

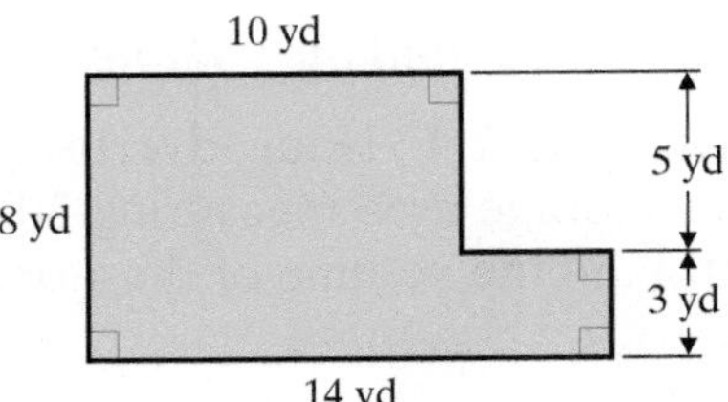

70. ***Driving Distances***

(a) In the following diagram, how many kilometres is it from Homeville to Seaview if you drive through Ipswich? How fast do you travel if it takes 0.5 hour to travel that way?

(b) How many kilometres is it from Homeville to Seaview if you drive through Acton and Westville? How fast do you travel if it takes 0.8 hour to travel that way?

(c) Over which route do you travel at a more rapid rate?

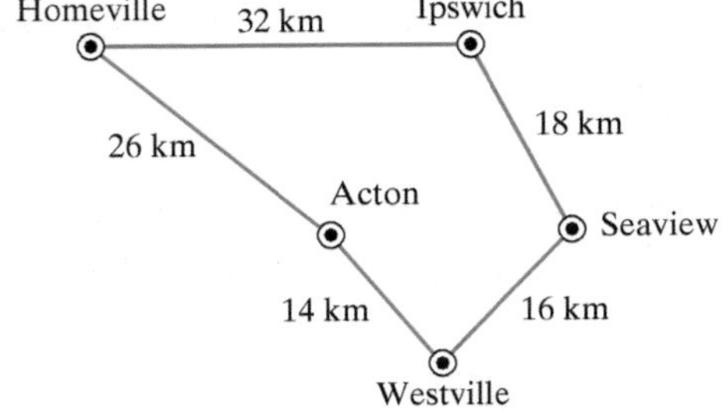

71. ***Silo Capacity*** A silo has a cylindrical shape with a hemispherical dome. It has dimensions as shown in the following figure.

(a) What is its volume in cubic feet?

(b) If 1 cubic foot $\approx$ 0.8 bushel, how many bushels of grain will it hold?

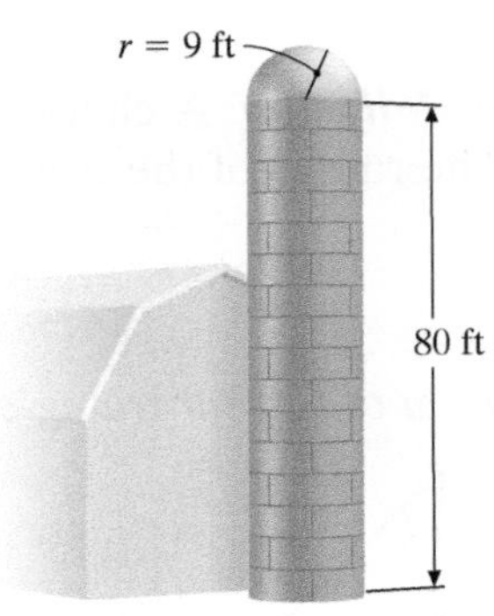

72. ***Farm Production*** In 1996, Canada produced an estimated 30 million tonnes of wheat. If one cubic metre of wheat weighs 196.78 kg, how many cubic metres of wheat were produced? (*Source:* www.statcan.gc.ca/kits-trousses/agric/edu04_0152a-eng.htm)

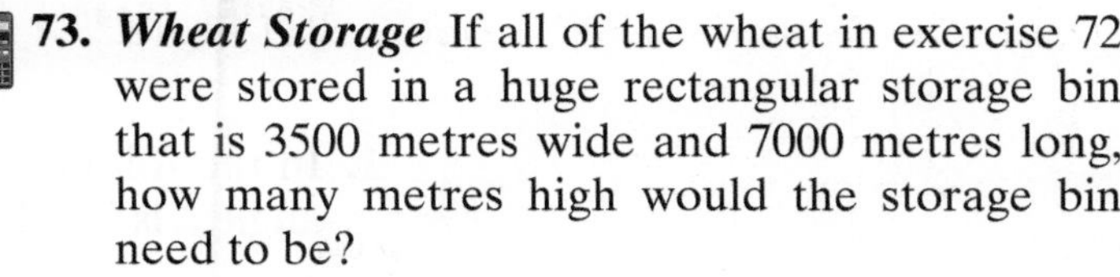

73. ***Wheat Storage*** If all of the wheat in exercise 72 were stored in a huge rectangular storage bin that is 3500 metres wide and 7000 metres long, how many metres high would the storage bin need to be?

74. ***Pet Aquarium*** The largest aquarium at Pets-Mart measures 2.25 m by 4 m by 2 m. Water weighs 1000 kilograms per cubic metre. How many kilograms of water does the aquarium hold? There is one kilogram for every litre. How many litres of water does this aquarium hold?

75. ***Pet Aquarium*** It is recommended that 4 centimetres of gravel be placed in the bottom of the aquarium in exercise 74. How many cubic centimetres of gravel are needed? Assume the base of the aquarium is 4 m by 2 m.

76. ***Pony Rides*** At the county fair a pony is tied to a 10-m rope. The pony gives children rides by walking in a circle 5 times with the rope pulled taut. How many metres does the pony walk for each ride?

77. ***Art Exhibit Hall*** Nikolai manages an art exhibit hall in Elmer. The floor of the hall consists of a large rectangle with a semicircle at each end. The rectangular part measures 18 metres by 25 metres. Each semicircle has a diameter of 18 metres. What is the perimeter of the floor?

78. ***Rope Lighting*** Nikolai has decided to install a special rope lighting along the perimeter of the art exhibit hall in exercise 77. He can order the lighting in 50-metre spools. How many spools does he need to order?

79. ***Flying a Kite*** A kite is flying exactly 10 metres above the edge of a pond. The person flying the kite is using exactly 11 metres of string. Assuming that the string is so tight that it forms a straight line, how far is the person standing from the edge of the pond? Round to the nearest tenth.

80. ***Gas Tank Storage*** The Suburban Gas Company has a spherical gas tank. The diameter of the tank is 90 metres. Find the volume of the spherical tank.

81. ***Hot Water Tank*** Charlie and Ginny have a cylindrical hot water tank that is 5 feet high and has a diameter of 18 inches. How many cubic feet does the tank hold?

82. ***Hot Water Tank*** The tank in exercise 81 is filled with water. One cubic foot of water is about 7.5 gallons. How many gallons does the tank hold?

83. ***Field of a High School*** A field at St. Patrick's High School in Sarnia is in the shape of a trapezoid. The bases of the trapezoid are 45 metres and 50 metres. The height of the trapezoid is 35 metres. What is the area of the field?

84. ***Fertilizer Cost*** The principal of the high school in exercise 83 has stated that the field needs to be fertilized three times a year. The lawn company charges $0.50 per square metre to apply fertilizer. How much will it cost to have the field fertilized three times a year?

How Am I Doing? Module Test

1. In the following figure, lines m and n are parallel, and the measure of angle a is 52°. Find the measure of angle b, angle c, and angle e.

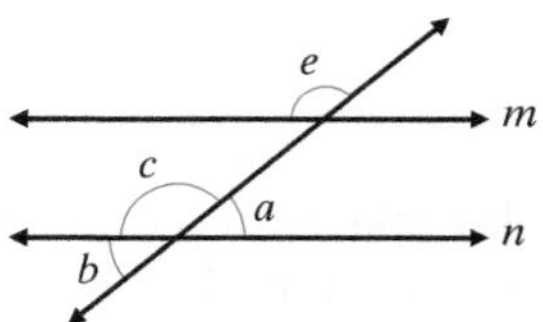

Find the perimeter.

2. a rectangle that measures 9 yd × 11 yd

3. a square with side 6.3 ft

4. a parallelogram with sides measuring 6.5 m and 3.5 m

5. a trapezoid with sides measuring 22 m, 13 m, 32 m, and 13 m

6. a triangle with sides measuring 58.6 m, 32.9 m, and 45.5 m

Find the area. Round to the nearest tenth.

7. a rectangle that measures 10 yd × 18 yd

8. a square 10.2 m on a side

9. a parallelogram with a height of 6 m and a base of 13 m

10. a trapezoid with a height of 9 m and bases of 7 m and 25 m

11. a triangle with a base of 4 cm and a height of 6 cm

Evaluate exactly.

12. $\sqrt{144}$

13. $\sqrt{169}$

14. Find the complement of an angle that measures 63°.

15. Find the supplement of an angle that measures 107°.

16. A triangle has an angle that measures 12.5° and another that measures 83.5°. What is the measure of the third angle?

1. ______
2. ______
3. ______
4. ______
5. ______
6. ______
7. ______
8. ______
9. ______
10. ______
11. ______
12. ______
13. ______
14. ______
15. ______
16. ______

Approximate using a square root table or a calculator with a square root key. Round to the nearest thousandth when necessary.

17. $\sqrt{54}$ **18.** $\sqrt{135}$

In exercises 19 and 20, find the unknown side. Use a calculator or a square root table to approximate square roots to the nearest thousandth.

19.

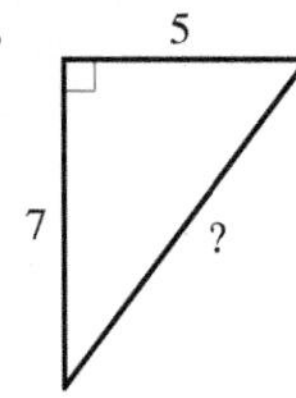

20.

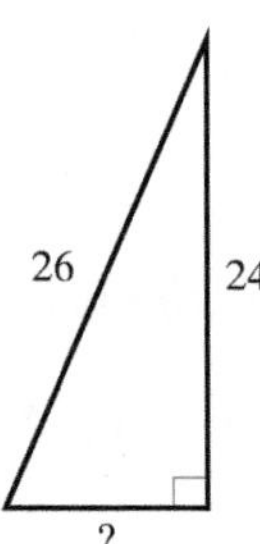

In exercises 21–24, round to the nearest hundredth.

21. Find the distance between the centres of the holes drilled in a rectangular metal plate with the dimensions labelled in the following sketch.

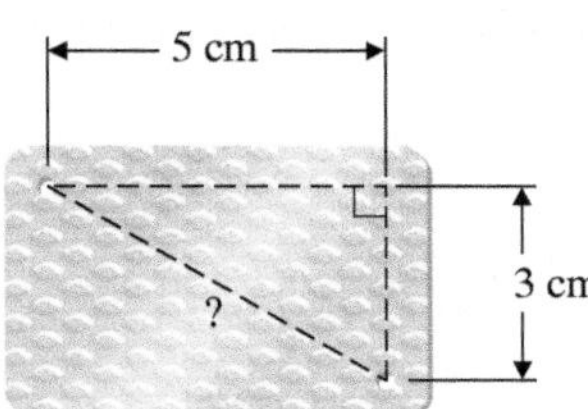

22. A 15-ft-tall ladder is placed so that it reaches 12 ft up on the wall of a house. How far is the base of the ladder from the wall of the house?

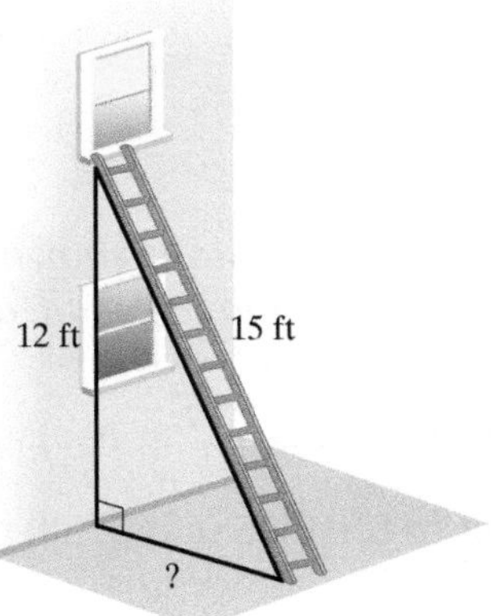

23. Find the circumference of a circle with diameter 18 m.

24. Find the area of a circle with diameter 12 ft.

17. ______

18. ______

19. ______

20. ______

21. ______

22. ______

23. ______

24. ______

25. ______________________

26. ______________________

27. ______________________

28. ______________________

29. ______________________

30. ______________________

31. ______________________

32. ______________________

33. ______________________

34. ______________________

35. ______________________

Find the shaded area of each region made up of circles, semicircles, rectangles, squares, trapezoids, and parallelograms. Round to the nearest tenth.

25.

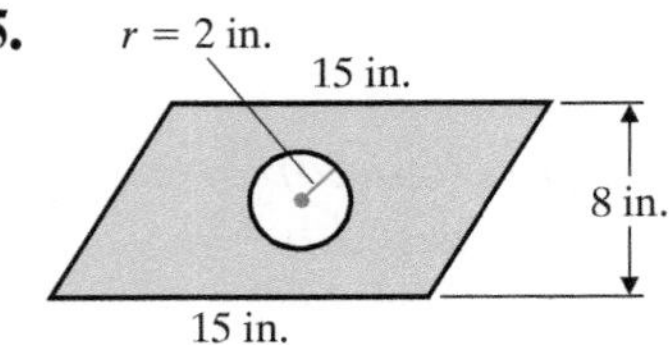

26.

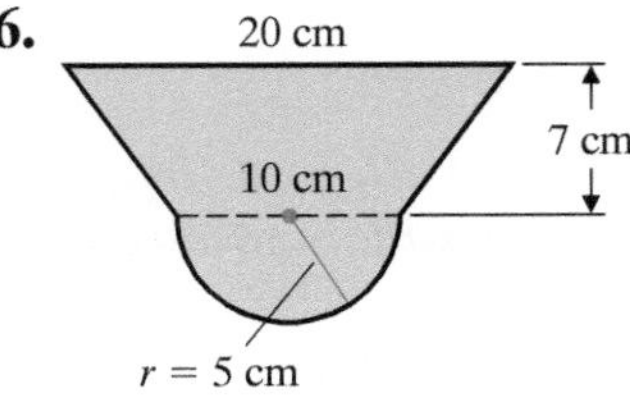

Find the volume. Round to the nearest tenth.

27. a rectangular box measuring 3.5 m by 20 m by 10 m

28. a cone with height 12 m and radius 8 m

29. a sphere of radius 3 m

30. a cylinder of height 2 ft and radius 9 ft

31. a pyramid of height 14 m and whose rectangular base measures 4 m by 3 m

Each pair of triangles is similar. Find the missing side n.

32.

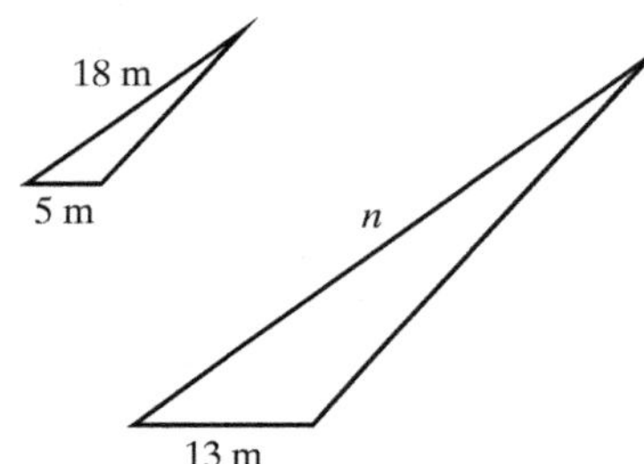

33.

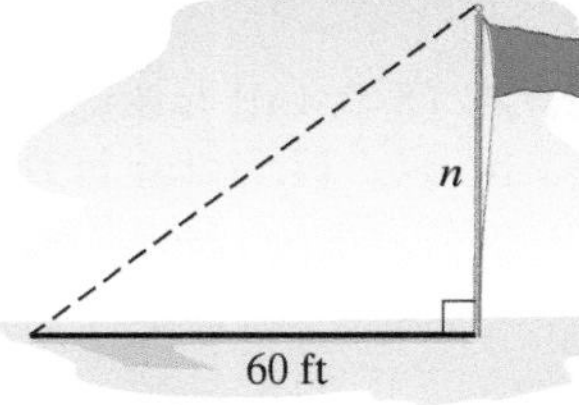

Solve. An athletic field has the dimensions shown in the figure below. Assume you are considering only the darker green shaded area. Use $\pi \approx 3.14$.

34. What is the area of the athletic field?

35. How much will it cost to fertilize it at $3.40 per square metre?

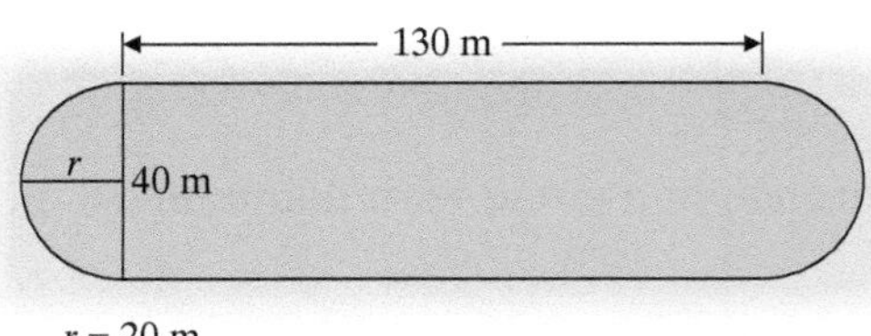

r = 20 m

Solutions to Practice Problems

Section 1 Practice Problems

1. $\angle FGH$ and $\angle KGJ$ are acute angles, $\angle HGK$ and $\angle FGJ$ are obtuse angles, $\angle HGJ$ is a right angle, and $\angle FGK$ is a straight angle.
2. **(a)** The complement of angle B measures $90° - 83° = 7°$.
   (b) The supplement of angle B measures $180° - 83° = 97°$.
3. $\angle y$ and $\angle w$ are vertical angles and so have the same measure. Thus $\angle w = 133°$. $\angle y$ and $\angle z$ are adjacent angles, so we know they are supplementary. Thus $\angle z$ measures $180° - 133° = 47°$. Finally, $\angle x$ and $\angle z$ are vertical angles, so we know they have the same measure. Thus $\angle x$ measures $47°$.
4. $\angle z = 180° - 105° = 75°$ ($\angle x$ and $\angle z$ are adjacent angles).
   $\angle x = \angle y = 105°$ ($\angle x$ and $\angle y$ are alternate interior angles).
   $\angle v = \angle x = 105°$ ($\angle v$ and $\angle x$ are corresponding angles).
   $\angle w = 180° - 105° = 75°$ ($\angle w$ and $\angle v$ are adjacent angles).

Section 2 Practice Problems

1. $P = 2l + 2w$
   $= (2)(6\text{ m}) + 2(1.5\text{m})$
   $= 12\text{ m} + 3\text{ m} = 15\text{ m}$
2. $P = 4s$
   $= (4)(5.8\text{ cm}) = 23.2\text{ cm}$
3. $P = 4 + 4 + 5.5 + 2.5 + 1.5 + 1.5 = 19\text{ m}$
   $\text{Cost} = 19\text{ m} \times \dfrac{0.48\text{ dollar}}{1\text{ m}} = \$9.12$
4. $A = lw = (29\text{ m})(17\text{ m}) = 493\text{ m}^2$
5. $A = s^2$
   $= (11.8\text{ mm})^2$
   $= (11.8\text{ mm})(11.8\text{ mm})$
   $= 139.24\text{ mm}^2$
6. Area of rectangle $= (18\text{ ft})(20\text{ ft}) = 360\text{ ft}^2$
   Area of square $= (6\text{ ft})^2 = 36\text{ ft}^2$
   Total area $= 396\text{ ft}^2$

Section 3 Practice Problems

1. $P = (2)(7.6\text{ cm}) + (2)(3.5\text{ cm})$
   $= 15.2\text{ cm} + 7.0\text{ cm} = 22.2\text{ cm}$
2. $A = bh$
   $= (10.3\text{ km})(1.5\text{ km})$
   $= 15.45\text{ km}^2$
3. $P = 4(6\text{ cm}) = 24\text{ cm}$
   $A = bh$
   $= (4\text{ cm})(6\text{ cm}) = 24\text{ cm}^2$
4. $P = 7\text{ km} + 15\text{ km} + 21\text{ km} + 13\text{ km} = 56\text{ km}$
5. **(a)** $A = \dfrac{h(b + B)}{2} = \dfrac{(140\text{ m})(180\text{ m} + 130\text{ m})}{2} = 21\,700\text{ m}^2$
   (b) $21\,700\text{ m}^2 \times \dfrac{3\text{ litres}}{100\text{ m}^2} = 651\text{ litres}$
   Thus 651 litres of sealant are needed.
6. The area of the trapezoid is
   $A = \dfrac{(9.2\text{ cm})(12.6\text{ cm} + 19.8\text{ cm})}{2}$
   $= \dfrac{(9.2\text{ cm})(32.4\text{ cm})}{2} = \dfrac{298.08\text{ cm}^2}{2}$
   $= 149.04\text{ cm}^2$.
   The area of the rectangle is
   $A = (8.3\text{ cm})(12.6\text{ cm}) = 104.58\text{ cm}^2$
   Total area $= 149.04\text{ cm}^2 + 104.58\text{ cm}^2 = 253.62\text{ cm}^2$

Section 4 Practice Problems

1. The sum of the measures of the angles in a triangle is $180°$. The two given angles total $125° + 15° = 140°$. Thus $180° - 140° = 40°$. Angle A must measure $40°$.
2. $P = 10.5\text{ m} + 10.5\text{ m} + 8.5\text{ m} = 29.5\text{ m}$
3. $A = \dfrac{bh}{2} = \dfrac{(38\text{ m})(13\text{ m})}{2} = \dfrac{494\text{ m}^2}{2} = 247\text{ m}^2$
4. Area of rectangle $= (11\text{ cm})(24\text{ cm}) = 264\text{ cm}^2$
   Area of triangle $= \dfrac{(11\text{ cm})(7\text{ cm})}{2} = \dfrac{77\text{ cm}^2}{2} = 38.5\text{ cm}^2$
   Total area $= 264\text{ cm}^2 + 38.5\text{ cm}^2 = 302.5\text{ cm}^2$

Section 5 Practice Problems

1. **(a)** $\sqrt{49} = 7$ because $(7)(7) = 49$.
   (b) $\sqrt{169} = 13$ because $(13)(13) = 169$.
2. $\sqrt{49} = 7$ because $(7)(7) = 49$.
   $\sqrt{4} = 2$ because $(2)(2) = 4$.
   Thus $\sqrt{49} - \sqrt{4} = 7 - 2 = 5$.
3. **(a)** Yes. 144 is a perfect square because $(12)(12) = 144$.
   (b) $\sqrt{144} = 12$
4. **(a)** $\sqrt{3} \approx 1.732$ **(b)** $\sqrt{13} \approx 3.606$ **(c)** $\sqrt{5} \approx 2.236$
5. $\sqrt{22\text{ m}^2} \approx 4.690\text{ m}$
   Thus, to the nearest thousandth of a metre, the side measures 4.690 m.

Section 6 Practice Problems

1. Hypotenuse $= \sqrt{(8)^2 + (6)^2}$
   $= \sqrt{64 + 36}$ Square each value first.
   $= \sqrt{100}$ Add together the two values.
   $= 10\text{ m}$ Take the square root.
2. Hypotenuse $= \sqrt{(3)^2 + (7)^2}$
   $= \sqrt{9 + 49}$ Square each value first.
   $= \sqrt{58}\text{ cm}$ Add the two values together.
   Using the square root table or a calculator, we have the hypotenuse ≈ 7.616 cm.
3. Leg $= \sqrt{(17)^2 - (15)^2}$
   $= \sqrt{289 - 225}$ Square each value first.
   $= \sqrt{64}$ Subtract.
   $= 8\text{ m}$ Find the square root.
4. Leg $= \sqrt{(10)^2 - (5)^2}$
   $= \sqrt{100 - 25}$ Square each value first.
   $= \sqrt{75}\text{ m}$ Subtract the two numbers.
   Using a calculator or the square root table, we find that the leg ≈ 8.660 m.
5. 1. ***Understand the problem.***
   We are given a picture.
   The distance between the centres of the holes is the hypotenuse of the triangle.
   2. ***Solve and state the answer.***
   Hypotenuse $= \sqrt{(\text{leg})^2 + (\text{leg})^2}$
   $= \sqrt{(2)^2 + (5)^2}$
   $= \sqrt{4 + 25}$
   $= \sqrt{29}$
   $\sqrt{29} \approx 5.385$
   Rounded to the nearest thousandth, the distance is 5.385 cm.

3. ***Check.***
Work backward to check. Use the Pythagorean Theorem.
$5.385^2 \stackrel{?}{\approx} 2^2 + 5^2$? (We use ≈ because 5.385 is an approximate answer.)
$28.998\,225 \stackrel{?}{\approx} 4 + 25$
$28.998\,225 \approx 29$ ✓

6\. 1. ***Understand the problem.***
We are given a picture.
2. ***Solve and state the answer.***
$$\begin{aligned}\text{Leg} &= \sqrt{(\text{hypotenuse})^2 - (\text{leg})^2}\\ &= \sqrt{(30)^2 - (27)^2}\\ &= \sqrt{900 - 729}\\ &= \sqrt{171}\end{aligned}$$
$\sqrt{171} \approx 13.1$
If we round to the nearest tenth, the kite is 13.1 yd above the rock.

7\. **(a)** In a 30°–60°–90° triangle the side opposite the 30° angle is $\frac{1}{2}$ of the hypotenuse.
$$\frac{1}{2} \times 12 = 6$$
Therefore, $y = 6$ ft.
When we know two sides of a right triangle, we find the third side using the Pythagorean Theorem.
$$\begin{aligned}\text{Leg} &= \sqrt{(\text{hypotenuse})^2 - (\text{leg})^2}\\ &= \sqrt{(12)^2 - (6)^2} = \sqrt{144 - 36}\\ &= \sqrt{108} \approx 10.4\end{aligned}$$
$x = 10.4$ ft rounded to the nearest tenth.
(b) In a 45°–45°–90° triangle we have the following:
$$\begin{aligned}\text{Hypotenuse} &= \sqrt{2} \times \text{leg}\\ &\approx 1.414(8)\\ &= 11.312 \text{ m}\end{aligned}$$
Rounded to the nearest tenth, the hypotenuse = 11.3 m.

Section 7 Practice Problems

1\. $$\begin{aligned}C &= \pi d\\ &= (3.14)(9 \text{ m})\\ &= 28.26 \text{ m}\end{aligned}$$
$C = 28.3$ m rounded to the nearest tenth.

2\. $$\begin{aligned}C &= \pi d\\ &= (3.14)(30 \text{ in.})\\ &= 94.2 \text{ in.}\end{aligned}$$
Change 94.2 in. to feet.
$$94.2 \cancel{\text{in.}} \times \frac{1 \text{ ft}}{12 \cancel{\text{in.}}} = 7.85 \text{ ft}$$
When the wheel makes 2 revolutions, the bicycle travels $7.85 \times 2 = 15.7$ ft.

3\. $$\begin{aligned}A &= \pi r^2\\ &= (3.14)(5 \text{ km})^2\\ &= (3.14)(25 \text{ km}^2)\\ &= 78.5 \text{ km}^2\end{aligned}$$

4\. $r = \frac{d}{2} = \frac{10 \text{ ft}}{2} = 5 \text{ ft}$
$$\begin{aligned}A &= \pi r^2\\ &= (3.14)(5 \text{ ft})^2\\ &= 78.5 \text{ ft}^2\end{aligned}$$
Change 78.5 ft^2 to square yards.
$$78.5 \cancel{\text{ft}^2} \times \frac{1 \text{ yd}^2}{9 \cancel{\text{ft}^2}} \approx 8.7222 \text{ yd}^2$$
Find the cost: $\frac{\$12}{1 \cancel{\text{yd}^2}} \times 8.7222 \cancel{\text{yd}^2} \approx \$104.67.$
The cost of the pool cover is \$104.67.

5\. Area of square − area of circle = shaded area
$$\begin{aligned}A &= s^2\\ &= (5 \text{ m})^2\\ &= 25 \text{ m}^2\\ A &= \pi r^2\\ &= (3.14)(2 \text{ m})^2\\ &= (3.14)(4 \text{ m}^2)\\ &= 12.56 \text{ m}^2\end{aligned}$$
$25 \text{ m}^2 - 12.56 \text{ m}^2 = 12.44 \text{ m}^2$
The area is 12.4 m^2 rounded to the nearest tenth.

6\. $r = \frac{d}{2} = \frac{8 \text{ m}}{2} = 4 \text{ m}$
$$\begin{aligned}A_{\text{semicircle}} &= \frac{\pi r^2}{2}\\ &= \frac{(3.14)(4 \text{ m})^2}{2}\\ &= 25.12 \text{ m}^2\end{aligned}$$
$A_{\text{rectangle}} = lw = (12 \text{ m})(8 \text{ m}) = 96 \text{ m}^2.$
$$\begin{array}{r} 25.12 \text{ m}^2\\ +\ 96.00 \text{ m}^2\\ \hline 121.12 \text{ m}^2\end{array}$$
The total area is approximately 121.1 m^2.

Section 8 Practice Problems

1\. $$\begin{aligned}V &= lwh\\ &= (6 \text{ m})(5 \text{ m})(2 \text{ m})\\ &= (30)(2) \text{ m}^3\\ &= 60 \text{ m}^3\end{aligned}$$

2\. $$\begin{aligned}V &= \pi r^2 h\\ &= (3.14)(2 \text{ in.})^2(5 \text{ in.})\\ &= (3.14)(4 \text{ in.}^2)(5 \text{ in.})\\ &= 62.8 \text{ in.}^3\end{aligned}$$

3\. $V = \frac{4\pi r^3}{3} = \frac{(4)(3.14)(6 \text{ m})^3}{3} = \frac{(4)(3.14)(6)(6)\overset{2}{\cancel{(6)}} \text{ m}^3}{\underset{1}{\cancel{3}}}$
$= (12.56)(36)(2) \text{ m}^3 = 904.32 \text{ m}^3$
The volume is 904.3 m^3 rounded to nearest tenth.

4\. $$\begin{aligned}V &= \frac{\pi r^2 h}{3}\\ &= \frac{(3.14)(5 \text{ m})^2(12 \text{ m})}{3}\\ &= 314.0 \text{ m}^3\end{aligned}$$

5\. $V = \frac{Bh}{3}$
(a) $B = (6 \text{ m})(6 \text{ m}) = 36 \text{ m}^2$
$V = \frac{(36 \text{ m}^2)(10 \text{ m})}{3} = \frac{360 \text{ m}^3}{3} = 120 \text{ m}^3$
(b) $B = (7 \text{ m})(8 \text{ m}) = 56 \text{ m}^2$
$V = \frac{(56 \text{ m}^2)(15 \text{ m})}{3} = \frac{840 \text{ m}^3}{3} = 280 \text{ m}^3$

Section 9 Practice Problems

1\. $$\begin{aligned}\frac{11}{27} &= \frac{15}{n}\\ 11n &= (27)(15)\\ 11n &= 405\\ \frac{11n}{11} &= \frac{405}{11}\\ n &= 36.\overline{81}\end{aligned}$$
$n = 36.8$ metres measured to the nearest tenth.

2. a corresponds to p, b corresponds to m, c corresponds to n

3. $\frac{h}{5} = \frac{20}{2}$
$2h = 100$
$h = 50$
The side wall is 50 feet tall.

4. $\frac{3}{29} = \frac{1.8}{w}$
$3w = (1.8)(29)$
$3w = 52.2$
$\frac{3w}{3} = \frac{52.2}{3}$
$w = 17.4$ The width is 17.4 metres.

Section 10 Practice Problems

Practice Problem 1

1. ***Understand the problem.***

Mathematics Blueprint for Problem Solving

Gather the Facts	What Am I Asked to Do?	How Do I Proceed?	Key Points to Remember
Dharmesh needs to sand three rooms: 24 ft × 13 ft 12 ft × 9 ft 16 ft × 3 ft He can sand 80 ft^2 in 15 min.	Find out how long it will take him to sand all three rooms.	**(a)** Find the total area to be sanded. **(b)** Then find out how long it will take him to sand the total area.	Area = length × width To get the total time, set up a proportion.

2. ***Solve and state the answer:***
$24 \times 13 = 312\text{ ft}^2$ room 1
$12 \times 9 = 108\text{ ft}^2$ room 2
$16 \times 3 = 48\text{ ft}^3$ room 3
Total area $= 468\text{ ft}^2$

$$\frac{80\text{ ft}^2}{15\text{ min}} = \frac{468\text{ ft}^2}{t\text{ min}}$$
$$\frac{80}{15} = \frac{468}{t}$$
$$80t = (15)(468)$$
$$80t = 7020$$
$$\frac{80t}{80} = \frac{7020}{80}$$
$$t = 87.75$$

It will take Dharmesh 87.75 min to sand the rooms.

3. ***Check.*** Estimate to see if the answer is reasonable.

Practice Problem 2

1. ***Understand the problem.***

Mathematics Blueprint for Problem Solving

Gather the Facts	What Am I Asked to Do?	How Do I Proceed?	Key Points to Remember
The trapezoid has a height of 9 m. The bases are 18 m and 12 m. The rectangular portion measures 24 m × 15 m. Roofing costs $24.75 per square metre.	**(a)** Find the area of the roof. **(b)** Find the cost to install new roofing.	**(a)** Find the area of the entire roof. **(b)** Multiply by $24.75.	The area of a trapezoid is $\frac{1}{2}h(b + B)$

2. ***Solve and state the answer:***

(a) Area of trapezoid $= \frac{1}{2}h(b + B)$
$= \frac{1}{2}(9\text{ m})(12\text{ m} + 18\text{ m})$
$= 135\text{ m}^2$
Area of rectangle $= lw$
$= (15\text{ m})(24\text{ m})$
$= 360\text{ m}^2$
Total area $= 135\text{ m}^2 + 360\text{ m}^2 = 495\text{ m}^2$

(b) Cost $= 495\,\cancel{\text{m}^2} \times \frac{\$24.75}{1\,\cancel{\text{m}^2}} = \$12\,251.25$

The cost to install new roofing would be $12 251.25.

3. ***Check.*** Estimate to see if the answers seem reasonable.

Glossary

Adjacent angles (Section 1) Two angles that share a common side and a common vertex.

Altitude of a triangle (Section 4) The height of a triangle.

Angle (Section 1) An angle is made up of two rays that start at a common endpoint.

Area (Section 1) The measure of the surface inside a geometric figure. Area is measured in square units, such as square metres.

Box (Section 8) A three-dimensional object whose every side is a rectangle. Another name for a box is a *rectangular solid.*

Centre of a circle (Section 7) The point in the middle of a circle from which all points on the circle are an equal distance.

Circle (Section 7) A two-dimensional figure for which all points are at an equal distance from a given point.

Circumference of a circle (Section 7) The distance around the rim of a circle.

Cone (Section 8) A three-dimensional object shaped like an ice-cream cone or the sharpened end of a pencil.

Cylinder (Section 8) A three-dimensional object shaped like a tin can.

Degree (Section 1) A unit used to measure an angle. A degree is $\frac{1}{360}$ of a complete revolution. An angle of 32 degrees is written as 32°.

Diameter of a circle (Section 7) A line segment across the circle that passes through the centre of the circle. The diameter of a circle is equal to twice the radius of the circle.

Equilateral triangle (Section 4) A triangle with three equal sides.

Height (Section 3) The distance between two parallel sides in a four-sided figure such as a parallelogram or a trapezoid.

Height of a cone (Section 8) The distance from the vertex of a cone to the base of the cone.

Height of a pyramid (Section 8) The distance from the point on a pyramid to the base of the pyramid.

Height of a triangle (Section 4) The distance of a line drawn from a vertex perpendicular to the other side, or an extension of the other side, of the triangle. This is sometimes called the *altitude of a triangle.*

Hexagon (Section 3) A six-sided figure.

Hypotenuse (Section 6) The side opposite the right angle in a right triangle. The hypotenuse is always the longest side of a right triangle.

Isosceles triangle (Section 4) A triangle with two sides equal.

Legs of a right triangle (Section 6) The two shortest sides of a right triangle.

Length of a rectangle (Section 2) Each of the longer sides of a rectangle.

Line segment (Section 3) A portion of a straight line that has a beginning and an end.

Octagon (Section 3) An eight-sided figure.

Parallel lines (Section 3) Two straight lines that are always the same distance apart.

Parallelogram (Section 3) A four-sided figure with both pairs of opposite sides parallel.

Perfect square (Section 4) When a whole number is multiplied by itself, the number that is obtained is a perfect square. The numbers 1, 4, 9, 16, 25, 36, 49, 64, 81, and 100 are all perfect squares.

Perimeter (Section 2) The distance around a figure.

Perpendicular lines (Section 1) Lines that meet at an angle of 90 degrees.

Pi (Section 7) Pi is an irrational number that we obtain if we divide the circumference of a circle by the diameter of a circle. It is represented by the symbol π. Accurate to eleven decimal places, the value of pi is given by 3.141 592 653 59. For most work in these modules, the value of 3.14 is used to approximate the value of pi.

Pyramid (Section 8) A three-dimensional object made up of a geometric figure for a base and triangular sides that meet at a point. Some pyramids are shaped like the great pyramids of Egypt.

Pythagorean Theorem (Section 6) A statement that for any right triangle the square of the hypotenuse equals the sum of the squares of the two legs of the triangle.

Quadrilateral (Section 3) A four-sided geometric figure.

Radius of a circle (Section 7) A line segment from the centre of a circle to any point on the circle. The radius of a circle is equal to one-half the diameter of the circle.

Ray (Section 1) A part of a line that has only one endpoint and goes on forever in one direction.

Rectangle (Section 2) A four-sided figure that has four right angles.

Regular hexagon (Section 3) A six-sided figure with all sides equal.

Regular octagon (Section 3) An eight-sided figure with all sides equal.

Right angle (Sections 1 and 4) An angle that measures 90 degrees.

Right triangle (Section 4) A triangle with one 90-degree angle.

Semicircle (Section 7) One-half of a circle. The semicircle usually includes the diameter of a circle connected to one-half the circumference of the circle.

Sides of an angle (Section 1) The two line segments that meet to form an angle.

Similar triangles (Section 9) Two triangles that have the same shape but are not necessarily the same size. The corresponding angles of similar triangles are equal. The corresponding sides of similar triangles have the same ratio.

Sphere (Section 8) A three-dimensional object shaped like a perfectly round ball.

Square (Section 2) A rectangle with all four sides equal.

Square root (Section 5) The square root of a number is one of only two identical factors of that number. The square root of 9 is 3. The square root of 121 is 11.

Square root sign (Section 5) The symbol $\sqrt{\ }$. When we want to find the square root of 25, we write $\sqrt{25}$. The answer is 5.

Trapezoid (Section 3) A four-sided figure with at least two parallel sides.

Triangle (Section 4) A three-sided figure.

Vertex of a cone (Section 8) The sharp point of a cone.

Vertex of an angle (Section 1) The point at which two line segments meet to form an angle.

Volume (Section 8) The measure of the space inside a three-dimensional object. Volume is measured in cubic units such as cubic metres.

Width of a rectangle (Section 2) Each of the shorter sides of a rectangle.

Answers to Selected Exercises for Geometry

Answers to Selected Exercises for Geometry

Section 1 Exercises **1.** An acute angle is an angle whose measure is between 0° and 90°. **3.** Complementary angles are two angles whose measures have a sum of 90°. **5.** When two lines intersect, the two angles that are opposite each other are called vertical angles. **7.** A transversal is a line that intersects two or more other lines at different points. **9.** $\angle ABD$, $\angle CBE$ **11.** $\angle ABD$ and $\angle CBE$; $\angle DBC$ and $\angle ABE$ **13.** There are no complementary angles. **15.** 90° **17.** 25° **19.** 110° **21.** 155° **23.** 59° **25.** 53° **27.** 34° **29.** 35° **31.** 25° **33.** $\angle b = 102°$; $\angle c = \angle a = 78°$ **35.** $\angle b = 38°$; $\angle a = \angle c = 142°$ **37.** $\angle a = \angle c = 48°$; $\angle b = 132°$ **39.** $\angle e = \angle d = \angle a = 123°$; $\angle b = \angle c = \angle f = \angle g = 57°$ **41.** 6° **43.** 53° north of east

Quick Quiz 1 **1.** 124° **2.** 56° **3.** 56° **4.** See Instructor

Section 2 Exercises **1.** perpendicular; equal **3.** multiply **5.** 15 km **7.** 23.6 ft **9.** 17.2 in. **11.** 1.92 mm **13.** 17.12 km **15.** 14.4 ft or 172.8 in. **17.** 0.272 mm **19.** 14 cm **21.** 35 cm **23.** 180 cm **25.** 6.25 m^2 **27.** 12 mi^2 **29.** 117 yd^2 or 1053 ft^2 **31. (a)** 294 m^2 **(b)** 78 m **33.** $132 000 **35. (a)** 49 ft^2 **(b)** 28 ft **37. (a)** 1×7, 2×6, 3×5, 4×4 **(b)** 7 m^2, 12 m^2 15 m^2, 16 m^2 **(c)** Square garden measuring 4 m on a side. **39.** $598.22

Quick Quiz 2 **1.** 7.6 cm **2.** 121 km^2 **3.** $1056 **4.** See Instructor

Section 3 Exercises **1.** adding **3.** perpendicular **5.** 40.2 m **7.** 49.6 in. **9.** 354.64 m^2 **11.** 602 m^2 **13.** $P = 48$ m; $A = 72$ m^2 **15.** $P = 9.6$ ft; $A = 3.6$ ft^2 **17.** 82 m **19.** 55 m + 135 m + 80.5 m + 75.5 m = 346 m **21.** 118.8 m^2 **23.** 76 850 m^2 **25. (a)** 718 m^2 **(b)** rectangle **(c)** trapezoid **27. (a)** 357 ft^2 **(b)** parallelogram **(c)** trapezoid **29.** $80 960

Quick Quiz 3 **1.** 50 m **2.** 288 m^2 **3.** 12 cm^2 **4.** See Instructor

Section 4 Exercises **1.** right **3.** Add the measures of the two known angles and subtract that value from 180°. **5.** You could conclude that the lengths of all three sides of the triangle are equal. **7.** true **9.** true **11.** false **13.** false **15.** 70° **17.** 82.9° **19.** 118 m **21.** 116.75 cm **23.** 10 mi **25.** 56.25 $in.^2$ **27.** 83.125 cm^2 **29.** $7\frac{7}{12}$ m^2 **31.** 126.5 cm^2 **33.** 188 m^2 **35.** 1740 ft^2 **37.** $21 060 **39.** 6.25%

Quick Quiz 4 **1.** 81.4 m **2.** 102 cm^2 **3.** 50.9° **4.** See Instructor

Section 5 Exercises **1.** $\sqrt{25} = 5$ because $(5)(5) = 25$ **3.** whole **5.** Use the square root table or a calculator. **7.** 3 **9.** 8 **11.** 12 **13.** 0 **15.** 13 **17.** 10 **19.** 10 **21.** 10 **23.** 3 **25.** 8 **27.** 22 **29. (a)** yes **(b)** 16 **31.** 4.243 **33.** 8.718 **35.** 14.142 **37.** ≈5.831 m **39.** ≈11.662 m **41.** 10.472 **43.** 7.071 **45.** 104.7 ft **47.** 38.8 m **49.** 39.299

Quick Quiz 5 **1.** 8 **2.** 18 **3.** 14 ft **4.** See Instructor

How Am I Doing? Sections 1–5 **1.** 18° (obj. 1.1) **2.** 117° (obj. 1.1) **3.** $\angle b = 136°$; $\angle a = \angle c = 44°$ (obj.1.1) **4.** 18 m (obj.2.1) **5.** 14 m (obj.2.1) **6.** 23.04 cm^2 (obj. 2.3) **7.** 22.62 yd^2 (obj. 2.3) **8.** 25.6 m (obj. 3.1) **9.** 79 ft (obj. 3.2) **10.** 351 cm^2 (obj. 3.1) **11.** 171 cm^2. (obj. 3.2) **12.** 97 m^2 (obj. 3.2) **13.** 56° (obj. 4.1) **14.** 20 in. (obj. 4.2) **15.** 72 m^2 (obj. 4.2) **16. (a)** 592 ft^2 **(b)** 114 ft (obj. 4.2) **17.** 8 (obj. 5.1) **18.** 19 (obj. 5.1) **19.** 13 (obj. 5.1) **20.** 16 (obj. 5.1) **21.** 6.782 (obj. 5.2)

Section 6 Exercises **1.** Square the length of each leg and add those two results. Then take the square root of the remaining number. **3.** 15 m **5.** 15.199 ft **7.** 11.402 m **9.** 14.142 m **11.** 8.660 ft **13.** 9.798 yd **15.** 15 m **17.** 11.619 cm **19.** 13 ft **21.** 9.8 cm **23.** 11.1 yd **25.** 6.9 cm; 4 cm **27.** 8.5 m **29.** 25.5 cm **31.** 7.1 in. **33.** 0.47 mi **35.** 14.866 cm

Quick Quiz 6 **1.** ≈11.18 m **2.** 10 cm **3.** ≈8.54 mi **4.** See Instructor

Section 7 Exercises **1.** circumference **3.** radius **5.** Multiply the radius by 2 and then use $C = \pi d$. **7.** 58 cm **9.** 17 mm **11.** 22.5 m **13.** 16.09 ft **15.** 100.48 cm **17.** 116.18 mm **19.** 41.87 ft **21.** 78.5 m^2 **23.** ≈226.87 $in.^2$ **25.** 803.84 cm^2 **27.** 452.16 ft^2 **29.** 6358.5 mi^2 **31.** 163.28 m^2 **33.** 30.96 m^2 **35.** 189.25 m^2 **37.** $1211.20 **39.** 3.14 m **41.** 141.3 ft **43.** 630.57 revolutions **45. (a)** 25.12 ft **(b)** 50.24 ft^2 **47.** 125 600 km^2 **49. (a)** $1.50 per slice; ≈25.12 $in.^2$ **(b)** ≈$1.33 per slice; ≈18.84 $in.^2$ **(c)** For 12-in.: $0.07 per $in.^2$; for 16-in.: $0.06 per $in.^2$; 16-in.

Quick Quiz 7 **1.** 28.26 in. **2.** 379.94 m^2 **3.** 3.79 cm^2 **4.** See Instructor

Section 8 Exercises **1. (a)** sphere **(b)** $V = \frac{4\pi r^3}{3}$ **3. (a)** cylinder **(b)** $V = \pi r^2 h$ **5. (a)** cone **(b)** $V = \frac{\pi r^2 h}{3}$ **7.** 540 mm^3 **9.** 226.1 m^3 **11.** 6459.0 m^3 **13.** 3052.1 m^3 **15.** 210 ft^3 **17.** 0.216 cm^3 **19.** 65.94 yd^3 **21.** 718.0 m^3 **23.** 937.8 cm^3 **25.** 641.1 ft^3 **27.** 163.3 m^3 **29.** 373.3 m^3 **31.** 12 bags **33.** 1004.8 $in.^3$ **35.** 381 251 976 256 667 mi^3 **37.** 2928 cm^3 **39.** $1130.40 **41.** 413.8 cm^3 **43.** 263 900 m^3

Quick Quiz 8 **1.** 267.95 cm^3 **2.** 112 yd^3 **3.** 367.38 m^3 **4.** See Instructor

Section 9 Exercises **1.** size; shape **3.** sides **5.** $n = 8$ m **7.** $n \approx 2.6$ ft **9.** $n = 3.4$ yd **11.** a corresponds to f, b corresponds to e, c corresponds to d **13.** 3.4 m **15.** 2.5 ft **17.** 67.04 cm **19.** 36 ft **21.** 81 ft **23.** 8.3 ft **25.** 12 cm

Quick Quiz 9 **1.** 85.71 ft **2.** 3.21 m **3.** 21 ft **4.** See Instructor

Section 10 Exercises **1. (a)** 75 km/h **(b)** 76 km/h **(c)** through Woodville and Palermo **3.** 41.88 min **5.** 4006 ft^2 **7.** \$510 **9.** \$795.15 **11. (a)** 40 820 km **(b)** 20 410 km/h **13.** $\approx$50 240 $in.^3$

Quick Quiz 10 **1.** 165.05 m^2 **2.** 638 ft^2 **3.** \$700 **4.** See Instructor

Putting Your Skills to Work **1.** Option A: 2000 litres, Option B: 1111.11 litres, Option C: 869.56 litres **2.** Option A: \$1900, Option B: \$1055.56, Option C: \$826.09 **3.** \$844.44 **4.** 7.83 years **5.** 5 years: \$4222.22, 10 years: \$8444.44 **6.** \$1073.91 **7.** 2.08 years **8.** 5 years: \$5369.55, 10 years: \$10 739.10 **9.** More kilometres per year would increase the litres of gas, money spent on gas, and savings compared with Option A, per year. It would also decrease the number of years necessary to make up the higher cost in purchase price. Fewer kilometres per year would decrease the litres of gas, money spent on gas, and savings compared with Option A, per year. It would also increase the number of years necessary to make up the higher cost in purchase price. More kilometres driven per year makes kilometres per litre an even more critical issue, while fewer kilometres driven per year does the opposite. **10.** Higher gas prices would increase the money spent on gas and savings compared with Option A, per year. This would also decrease the number of years necessary to make up the higher cost in purchase price. Lower gas prices would decrease the money spent on gas and savings compared with Option A, per year. This would also increase the number of years necessary to make up the higher cost in purchase price. Higher gas prices make kilometres per litre an even more critical issue, while lower gas prices do the opposite.

Module Review Problems **1.** 14° **2.** 104° **3.** $\angle b = 146°, \angle a = \angle c = 34°$ **4.** $\angle t = \angle x = \angle y = 65°, \angle s = \angle u = \angle w = \angle z = 115°$ **5.** 23.6 m **6.** 50.8 yd **7.** 16.5 cm^2 **8.** 51.8 $in.^2$ **9.** 38 ft **10.** 58 ft **11.** 68 m^2 **12.** 63.5 m^2 **13.** 105 m **14.** 62 km **15.** 3500 m^2 **16.** 360 m^2 **17.** 422 cm^2 **18.** 357 m^2 **19.** 60 ft **20.** 46.5 ft **21.** 107° **22.** 55° **23.** 52.3 m^2 **24.** 59.4 m^2 **25.** 450 m^2 **26.** 87 m^2 **27.** 9 **28.** 8 **29.** 11 **30.** 16 **31.** 18 **32.** 6.708 **33.** 7.874 **34.** 12.845 **35.** 13.416 **36.** 5 km **37.** 5 yd **38.** 8.72 cm **39.** 9.22 m **40.** 6.4 cm **41.** 18.1 ft **42.** 6.3 ft **43.** 3.6 ft **44.** 106 cm **45.** 63 cm **46.** 62.8 m **47.** 56.5 cm **48.** 254.3 m^2 **49.** 58.06 km^2 **50.** 226.1 $in.^2$ **51.** 201.0 m^2 **52.** 318.5 ft^2 **53.** 126.1 m^2 **54.** 107.4 ft^2 **55.** 80.1 m^2 **56.** 1263.6 ft^3 **57.** 6251.8 cm^3 **58.** 21.2 ft^3 **59.** 575.8 cm^3 **60.** 245 m^3 **61.** 3768 ft^3 **62.** 9074.6 m^3 **63.** 30 m **64.** 3.3 m **65.** 348 cm **66.** 175 ft **67.** 147 m^2 **68.** 2034.7 cm^3, 32 555.2 g **69.** \$736 **70. (a)** 50 km; 100 km/h **(b)** 56 km; 70 km/h **(c)** through Ipswich **71. (a)** $\approx$21 873.2 ft^3 **(b)** $\approx$17 498.6 bushels **72.** 152 454 517.7 m^3 **73.** 6.2 m **74.** 18 000 kg; 18 000 L **75.** 320 000 cm^3 **76.** 314 m **77.** $\approx$106.5 m **78.** 3 spools **79.** 4.6 m **80.** 381 510 m^3 **81.** $\approx$8.8 ft^3 **82.** $\approx$66 gallons **83.** 1662.5 m^2 **84.** \$2493.75

How Am I Doing? Module Test **1.** $\angle b = 52°$; $\angle c = 128°$; $\angle e = 128°$; (obj. 1.1) **2.** 40 yd (obj. 2.1) **3.** 25.2 ft (obj. 2.1) **4.** 20 m (obj. 3.1) **5.** 80 m (obj. 3.2) **6.** 137 m (obj. 4.2) **7.** 180 yd^2 (obj. 2.1) **8.** 104.0 m^2 (obj. 2.1) **9.** 78 m^2 (obj. 3.1) **10.** 144 m^2 (obj. 3.2) **11.** 12 cm^2 (obj. 4.2) **12.** 12 (obj. 5.1) **13.** 13 (obj. 5.1) **14.** 27° (obj. 1.1) **15.** 73° (obj. 1.1) **16.** 84° (obj. 4.1) **17.** 7.348 (obj. 5.2) **18.** 11.619 (obj. 5.2) **19.** 8.602 (obj. 6.2) **20.** 10 (obj. 6.2) **21.** 5.83 cm (obj. 6.3) **22.** 9 ft (obj. 6.3) **23.** 56.52 m (obj. 7.1) **24.** 113.04 ft^2 (obj. 7.1) **25.** 107.4 $in.^2$ (obj. 7.2) **26.** 144.3 cm^2 (obj. 7.2) **27.** 700 m^3 (obj. 8.1) **28.** 803.8 m^3 (obj. 8.4) **29.** 113.0 m^3 (obj. 8.3) **30.** 508.7 ft^3 (obj. 8.2) **31.** 56 m^3 (obj. 8.5) **32.** 46.8 m (obj. 9.1) **33.** 42 ft (obj. 9.1) **34.** 6456 m^2 (obj. 10.1) **35.** \$21 950.40 (obj. 10.1)

Have you ever attended a professional women's basketball game? If so, you were probably amazed at the level of athletic ability of the team players. The Women's National Basketball Association (WNBA) was formed in 1996 as the women's counterpart to the NBA. The fourteen teams play a regular season each year that starts in May and ends in August. Elaborate statistics are maintained for the WNBA just as they are for the NBA. Many of the statistical measurements that are used are studied in this module.

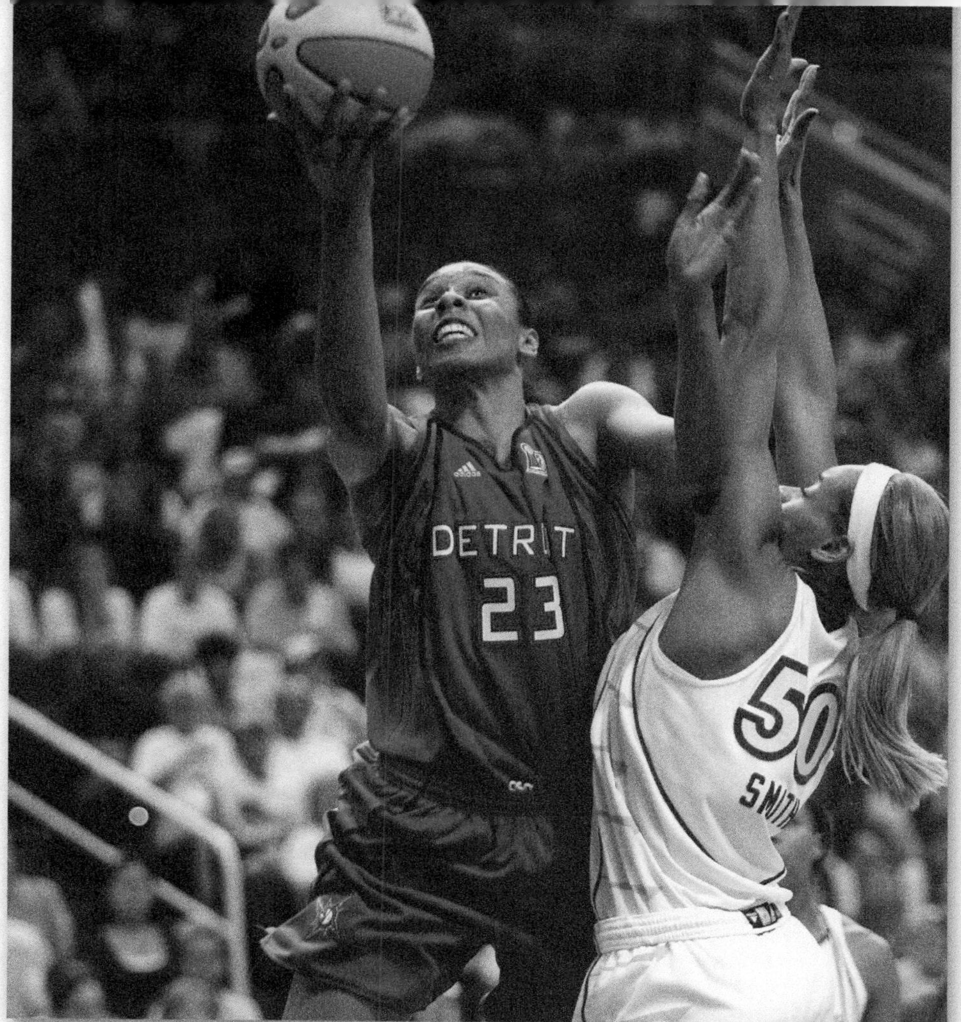

Rick Scuteri/Corbis/Reuters America LLC

Statistics

SECTION 1 CIRCLE GRAPHS

Student Learning Objectives

After studying this section, you will be able to:

1. Read a circle graph with numerical values.
2. Read a circle graph with percentage values.

1 Reading a Circle Graph with Numerical Values

Statistics is that branch of mathematics that collects and studies data. Once the data is collected, it must be organized so that the information is easily readable. We use **graphs** to give a visual representation of the data that is easy to read. Graphs appeal to the eye. Their visual nature allows them to communicate information about the complicated relationships among statistical data. For this reason, newspapers often use graphs to help their readers quickly grasp information.

Circle graphs are especially helpful for showing the relationship of parts to a whole. The entire circle represents 100%; the pie-shaped pieces represent the subcategories. The following circle graph divides the 48 000 students at Algonquin College into four categories.

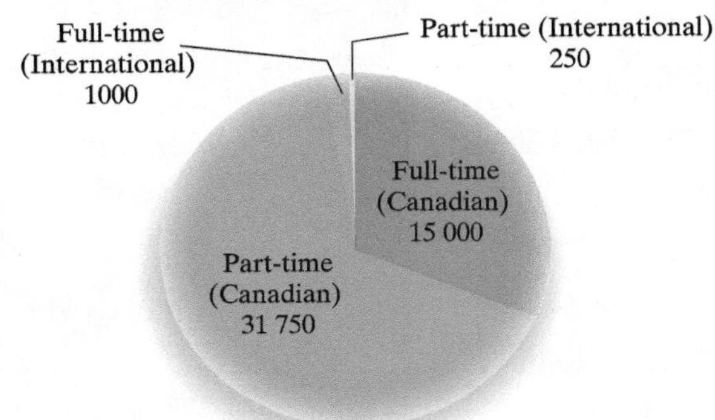

EXAMPLE 1 What is the largest category of students?

Solution The largest pie-shaped section of the circle is labelled "Part-time (Canadian)" Thus the largest category is part-time (Canadian) students.

Practice Problem 1 What is the smallest category of students?

EXAMPLE 2

(a) How many students are full-time (Canadian or international)?
(b) What percent of the students are full-time (Canadian or international)?

Solution

(a) There are 15 000 full-time Canadians and 1000 full-time international students. If we add these two numbers, we have 15 000 + 1000 = 16 000. Thus we see that there are 16 000 students who are full-time (Canadian or international).
(b) 16 000 out of 48 000 are full-time (Canadian or international).

$$\frac{16\,000}{48\,000} = \frac{1}{3} = 33\%$$

NOTE TO STUDENT: Fully worked-out solutions to all of the Practice Problems can be found at the end of the module.

Practice Problem 2

(a) How many students are international (full-time or part-time) students?
(b) What percent of the students are international (full-time or part-time) students?

EXAMPLE 3 What is the ratio of Canadians to internationals?

Solution

Number of Canadians ⟶ 46 750
Number of internationals ⟶ 1250

Thus $\frac{46\ 750}{1250} = \frac{187}{5}$.

The ratio of Canadians to internationals is $\frac{187}{5}$.

Practice Problem 3 What is the ratio of international part-time to international full-time students?

EXAMPLE 4 What is the ratio of Canadians to the total number of students?

Solution There are 46 750 Canadians. We find the total of all the students by adding the number of students in each section of the graph. There are 48 000 students. The ratio of Canadians to the total number of students is

$$\frac{46\ 750}{48\ 000} = \frac{187}{192}.$$

Practice Problem 4 What is the ratio of full-time to part-time students?

Many of the examples in this section will be business or financial examples. Remember that while those fields still often use a comma to separate periods of numerals within large numbers, we will continue to use only spaces as it is the SI and Canadian math classroom standard.

2 Reading a Circle Graph with Percentage Values

Together, the Great Lakes form the largest body of fresh water in the world. The total area of these five lakes is about 244 060 km^2. The percentage of this total area taken up by each of the Great Lakes is shown in the circle graph below.

Percentage of Area Occupied by Each of the Great Lakes

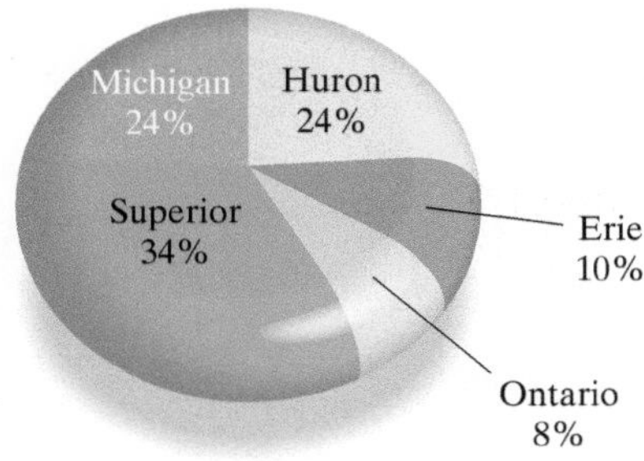

Source: U.S. Department of the Interior

EXAMPLE 5 Which of the Great Lakes occupies the largest area in square kilometres?

Solution The largest percent corresponds to the biggest area, which is occupied by Lake Superior. Lake Superior has the largest area in square kilometres.

Practice Problem 5 Which of the Great Lakes occupies the smallest area in square kilometres?

EXAMPLE 6 What percent of the total area is occupied by Lake Erie or Lake Ontario?

Solution If we add 10% for Lake Erie and 8% for Lake Ontario, we get

$$10\% + 8\% = 18\%.$$

Thus 18% of the area is occupied by Lake Erie or Lake Ontario.

NOTE TO STUDENT: *Fully worked-out solutions to all of the Practice Problems can be found at the end of the module.*

Practice Problem 6 What percent of the total area is occupied by Lake Superior or Lake Michigan?

EXAMPLE 7 How many of the total 244 060 km^2 are occupied by Lake Michigan? Round to the nearest whole number.

Solution Remember that we multiply the percent times the base to obtain the amount. Here, 24% of 244 060 km^2 is occupied by Lake Michigan.

$$(0.24)(244\,060) = n$$
$$58\,574.4 = n$$

Rounded to the nearest whole number, 58 574 km^2 are occupied by Lake Michigan.

Practice Problem 7 How many of the total 244 060 km^2 are occupied by Lake Superior? Round to the nearest whole number.

Sometimes a circle graph is used to investigate the distribution of one part of a larger group. For example, in the 2004–05 academic year there were 134 566 college graduates in the six most popular subject areas in Canada: business, humanities, health sciences, engineering sciences, social sciences, and arts and communications. The circle graph shows how the graduates in these six subject areas were distributed.

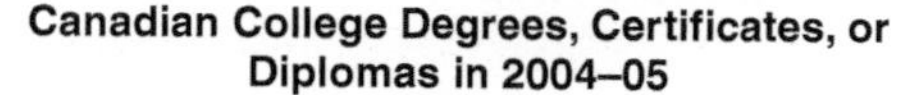

Canadian College Degrees, Certificates, or Diplomas in 2004–05

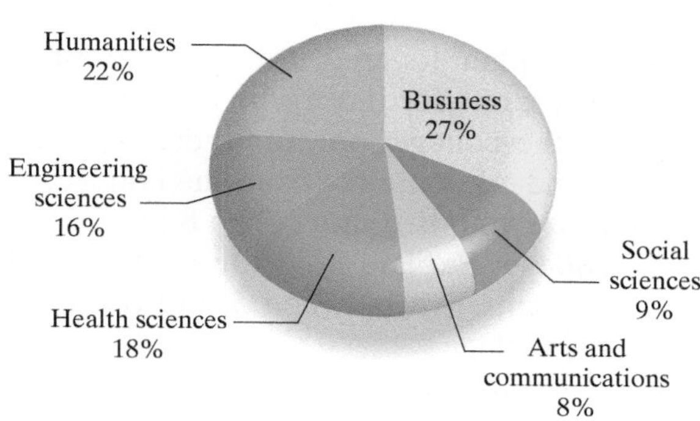

Source: Adapted from Statistics Canada www40.statcan.gc.ca/l01/cst01/educ62a-eng.htm, Oct-09

EXAMPLE 8

(a) What percent of the graduates represented in this circle graph are in the fields of health sciences or business?

(b) Of the 134 566 degrees awarded in these six fields, how many were awarded in the field of engineering?

Solution

(a) We add 27% to 18% to obtain 45%. Thus 45% of the graduates represented by this graph are in the fields of health sciences or business.

(b) We take 16% of the 134 566 people who graduated in these six areas. Thus we have $(0.16)(134\,566) = 21\,530.56$. Approximately 21 531 Canadian college students graduated from engineering sciences in 2005.

Practice Problem 8

(a) What percent of the graduates represented in this circle graph are in the fields of humanities or health sciences?

(b) How many graduates were there in arts and communications in 2005?

Section 1 Exercises

Verbal and Writing Skills *Suppose that you must create a circle graph for 4000 students who attend Lambton College.*

1. If 25% of the students live within 5 kilometres of the college, how would you determine how many students live within 5 kilometres of the college?

2. If 45% of the students live more than 8 kilometres from the college, how would you determine how many students live more than 8 kilometres from the college?

3. How would you construct a pie slice that describes the students who live within 5 kilometres of the college?

4. You plan to create a circle graph with three slices: one for those who live within 5 kilometres of the college, one for those who live between 5 and 8 kilometres from the college, and one for those who live more than 8 kilometres from the college. Explain how you would find how many students live between 5 and 8 kilometres from the college.

Applications

Monthly Budget *The following circle graph displays Bob and Linda McDonald's monthly \$2700 family budget. Use the circle graph to answer exercises 5–14.*

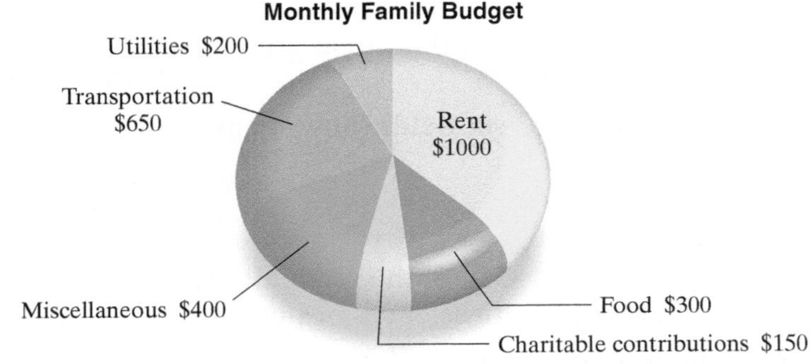

5. What category takes the largest amount of the budget?

6. Which two categories take the least amounts of the budget?

7. How much money is allotted each month for utilities?

8. How much money is allotted each month for transportation (this includes car payments, insurance, and gas)?

9. How much money in total is allotted each month for transportation or charitable contributions?

10. How much money is allotted for food or rent?

11. What is the ratio of money spent for transportation to money spent on utilities?

12. What is the ratio of money spent on rent to money spent on miscellaneous items?

13. What is the ratio of money spent on rent to the total amount of the monthly budget?

14. What is the ratio of money spent on food to the total amount of the monthly budget?

Age Distribution *In July 2008, there were approximately 33 311 400 people living in Canada. The following circle graph shows the age distribution of these people. Use the circle graph to answer exercises 15–24.*

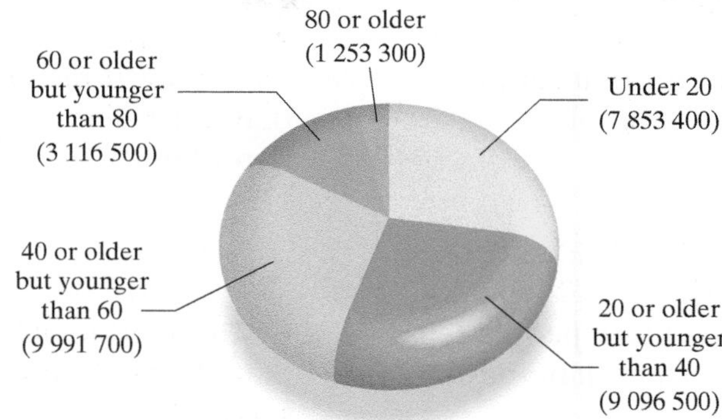

Source: Adapted from Statistics Canada, www40.statcan.gc.ca/l01/cst01/demo10a-eng.htm, Oct-09

15. What age group had the smallest number of people?

16. What age group had the largest number of people?

17. How many people were 60 years old or older but younger than 80?

18. How many people were 20 years old or older but younger than 40?

19. How many people were younger than 60?

20. How many people were 40 or older?

21. What is the ratio of the number of people younger than 40 to the number of people 40 years old or older?

22. What is the ratio of the number of people 20 or older to the number of people under 20?

23. What is the ratio of the number of people under 20 to the total population?

24. What is the ratio of the number of people 80 or older to the total population?

Restaurant Preferences *In a survey, 1010 people were asked which aspect of dining out was most important to them. The results are shown in the circle graph below. Use the graph to answer exercises 25–30. Round all answers to the nearest whole number.*

What Consumers Want Most in a Restaurant

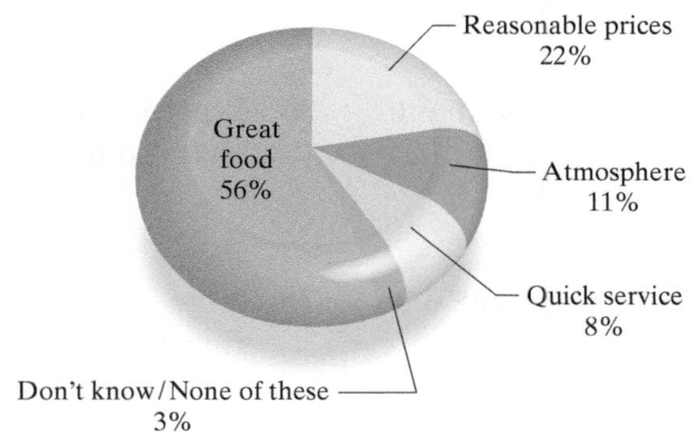

Source: National Restaurant Association

25. What percent of respondents feel atmosphere or quick service is most important?

26. What percent of respondents did not feel that great food was most important?

27. Which two categories together make up approximately three-fourths of the circle graph?

28. Of the 1010 respondents, how many responded that quick service or reasonable prices was most important?

29. Of the 1010 people, how many more people felt that great food was more important than reasonable prices?

30. Of the 1010 people, how many more people felt that atmosphere was more important than quick service?

Vehicle Production *In 2006, the top seven countries for vehicle production were those displayed in the following circle graph. A total of 45 600 000 vehicles were manufactured that year. The approximate percentages of the total, rounded to the nearest tenth, are given for each country. Use the graph to answer exercises 31–38.*

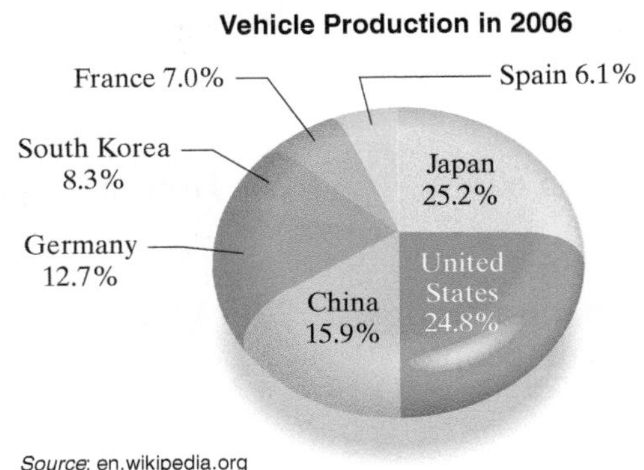

31. Approximately how many vehicles were produced in China?

32. Approximately how many vehicles were produced in the United States?

33. What percentage of the vehicles were produced in Europe (France, Spain, and Germany)?

34. What percentage of the vehicles were produced in Asia (China, Japan, and South Korea)?

35. What percentage of the vehicles were *not* manufactured in Europe?

36. What percentage of the vehicles were *not* manufactured in Asia?

37. How many more vehicles were produced in Asia than in Europe?

38. How many more vehicles were produced in Europe than in the United States?

Quick Quiz 1 Statistics Canada reported the number of passenger and commercial vehicles sold in Ontario in 2008 to be a total of 592 088 vehicles. The estimated distribution by type and manufacturing origin is shown in the circle graph below. Use this graph to answer the following questions.

Sales of Passenger and Commercial Vehicles in Ontario in 2008

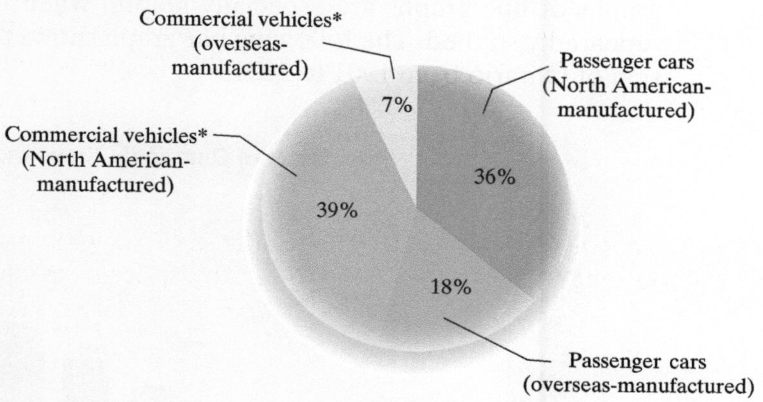

* Includes minivans, sport-utility vehicles, light and heavy trucks, vans, and buses.

Source: Adapted from Statistics Canada, www40.statcan.gc.ca/l01/cst01/trade36f-eng.htm, Oct-09

1. What percent of the vehicles sold were North American-manufactured passenger cars?

2. How many of the vehicles sold were commercial vehicles?

3. How many of the vehicles sold were *not* overseas-manufactured passenger cars?

4. **Concept Check** Explain how you would find the total number of the vehicles sold that were North American-manufactured passenger cars, overseas-manufactured passenger cars, or North American-manufactured commercial vehicles.

SECTION 2 BAR GRAPHS AND LINE GRAPHS

Student Learning Objectives

After studying this section, you will be able to:

1. Read and interpret a bar graph.
2. Read and interpret a double-bar graph.
3. Read and interpret a line graph.
4. Read and interpret a comparison line graph.

1 Reading and Interpreting a Bar Graph

Bar graphs are helpful for seeing changes over a period of time. Bar graphs or line graphs are especially helpful when the same type of data is repeatedly studied. The following bar graph shows the approximate population of Ontario from 1901 to 2001.

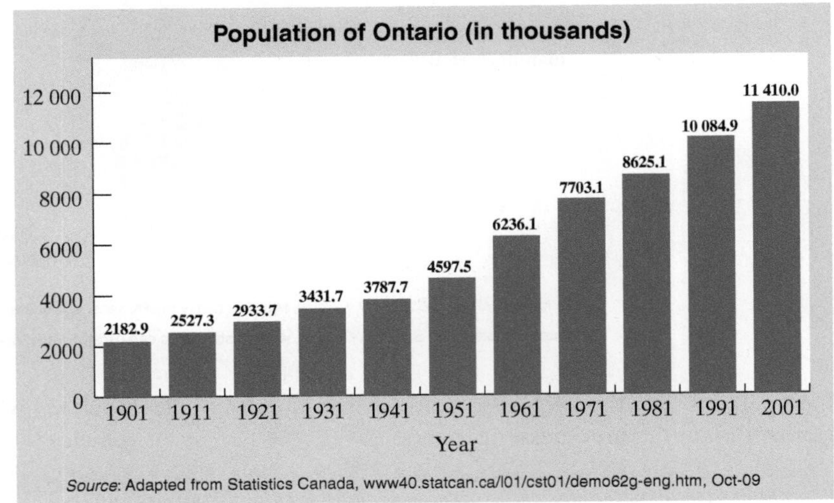

EXAMPLE 1 What was the approximate population of Ontario in 1961?

Solution The bar for 1961 rises to 6236.1. This represents 6236.1 thousand; thus the population was approximately 6 236 100.

Practice Problem 1 What was the approximate population of Ontario in 1911?

EXAMPLE 2 What was the increase in population from 1931 to 1961?

Solution The bar for 1931 rises to 3431.7 or a population of approximately 3 431 700. The bar for 1961 rises to 6236.1 or a population of approximately 6 236 100. To find the increase in population from 1931 to 1961, we subtract.

$$6\,236\,100 - 3\,431\,700 = 2\,804\,400$$

Practice Problem 2 What was the increase in population from 1901 to 2001?

NOTE TO STUDENT: Fully worked-out solutions to all of the Practice Problems can be found at the end of the module.

 Reading and Interpreting a Double-Bar Graph

Double-bar graphs are useful for making comparisons. For example, when a company is analyzing its sales, it may want to compare different years or different quarters. The following double-bar graph illustrates the sales of new cars at a Ford dealership for two different years, 2006 and 2007. The sales are recorded for each quarter of the year.

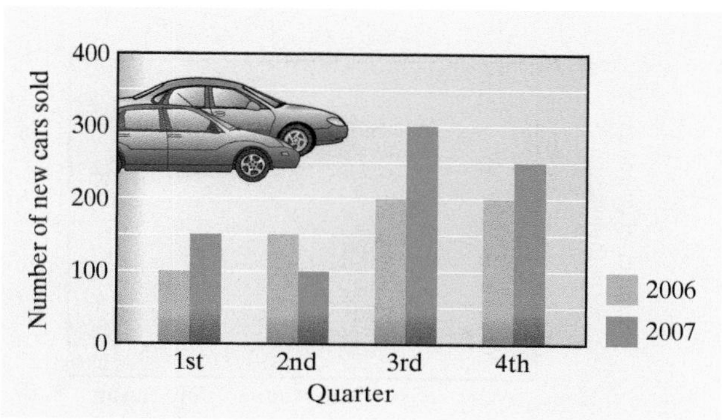

EXAMPLE 3 How many cars were sold in the second quarter of 2006?

Solution The bar rises to 150 for the second quarter of 2006. Therefore, 150 cars were sold.

Practice Problem 3 How many cars were sold in the fourth quarter of 2007?

NOTE TO STUDENT: Fully worked-out solutions to all of the Practice Problems can be found at the end of the module.

EXAMPLE 4 How many more cars were sold in the third quarter of 2007 than in the third quarter of 2006?

Solution From the double-bar graph, we see that 300 cars were sold in the third quarter of 2007 and that 200 cars were sold in the third quarter of 2006.

$$\begin{array}{r} 300 \\ -\,200 \\ \hline 100 \end{array}$$

Thus, 100 more cars were sold.

Practice Problem 4 How many fewer cars were sold in the second quarter of 2007 than in the second quarter of 2006?

3 Reading and Interpreting a Line Graph

A **line graph** is useful for showing trends over a period of time. In a line graph only a few points are actually plotted from measured values. The points are then connected by straight lines to show a trend. The intervening values between points may not lie exactly on the line. The following line graph shows the number of customers per month coming into a restaurant in a vacation community.

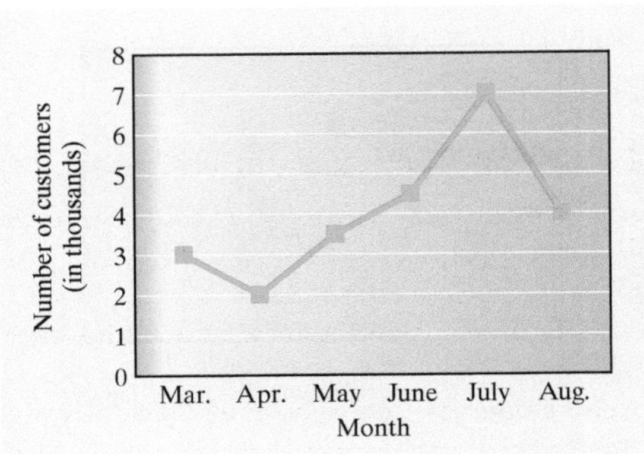

EXAMPLE 5 In which month did the fewest number of customers come into the restaurant?

Solution The lowest point on the graph occurs for the month of April. Thus the fewest number of customers came in April.

Practice Problem 5 In which month did the greatest number of customers come into the restaurant?

EXAMPLE 6

(a) Approximately how many customers came into the restaurant during the month of June?

(b) From May to June, did the number of customers increase or decrease?

Solution

(a) Notice that the dot is halfway between 4 and 5. This represents a value halfway between 4000 and 5000 customers. Thus we would estimate that 4500 customers came during the month of June.

(b) From May to June the line goes up, so the number of customers increased.

Practice Problem 6

(a) Approximately how many customers came into the restaurant during the month of May?

(b) From March to April, did the number of customers increase or decrease?

EXAMPLE 7 Between what two months was the increase in the number of customers the largest?

Solution The line from June to July goes upward at the steepest angle. This represents the largest increase. (You can check this by reading the numbers from the left axis.) Thus the greatest increase in attendance was between June and July.

Practice Problem 7 Between what two months did the biggest decrease occur?

Reading and Interpreting a Comparison Line Graph

Two or more sets of data can be compared by using a **comparison line graph.** A comparison line graph shows two or more line graphs together. A different style for each line distinguishes them. Note that using a blue line and a red line in the following graph makes it easy to read.

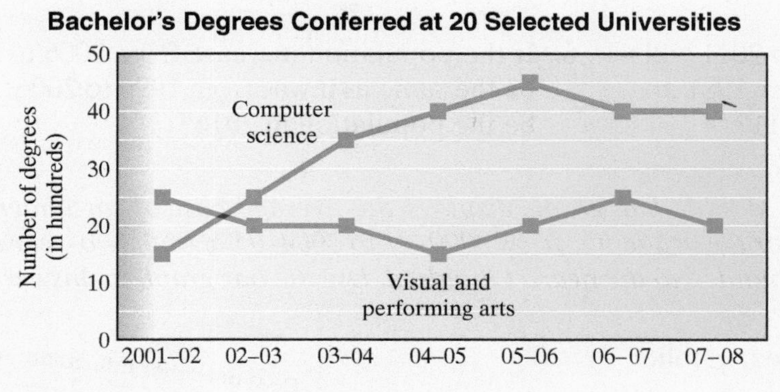

EXAMPLE 8 How many bachelor's degrees in computer science were awarded in the academic year 2007–08?

Solution Because the dot corresponding to 2007–08 is at 40 and the scale is in hundreds, we have $40 \times 100 = 4000$. Thus 4000 degrees were awarded in computer science in 2007–08.

Practice Problem 8 How many bachelor's degrees in visual and performing arts were awarded in the academic year 2007–08?

EXAMPLE 9 In what academic year were more degrees awarded in the visual and performing arts than in computer science?

Solution The only year when more bachelor's degrees were awarded in the visual and performing arts was the academic year 2001–02.

Practice Problem 9 What was the first academic year in which more degrees were awarded in computer science than in the visual and performing arts?

Section 2 Exercises

Applications

Ontario Population *The following bar graph shows the estimated population of Ontario from 1976 to 2006. Use the graph to answer exercises 1–6.*

1. What was the population in 1981?

2. What was the population in 1991?

3. Between what years did the population increase by the largest amount?

4. Between what years did the population decrease by the largest amount?

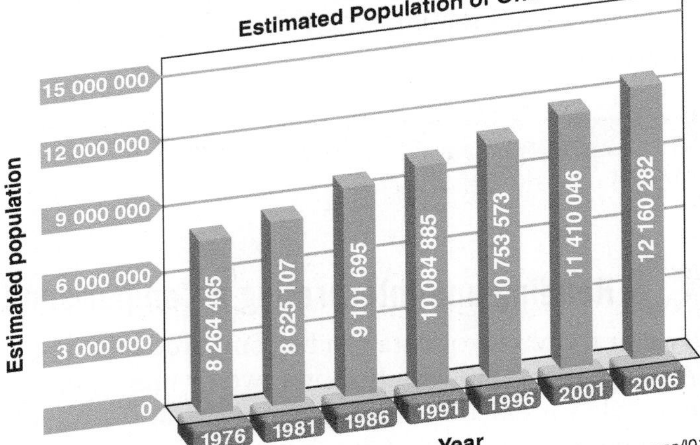

Source: Adapted from Statistics Canada, www40.statcan.ca/l01/cst01/demo62g-eng.htm, Oct-09

5. If the population increase from 2001 to 2011 will be the same as the increase was from 1981 to 1991, what will be the population in 2011?

6. If the population increase from 2006 to 2016 will be the same as it was from 1996 to 2006, what will be the population in 2016?

Cost of Higher Education *The following double-bar graph displays the average cost of an undergraduate student's tuition, fees, and room and board for the academic years 2000–01 to 2004–05 at both two-year and four-year public institutions. Figures have been rounded to the nearest hundred. Use the bar graph to answer exercises 7–18.*

7. What was the average cost at a two-year public institution in 2000–01?

8. What was the average cost at a four-year public institution in 2003–04?

9. How much higher was the average cost at a four-year institution than at a two-year institution in 2001–02?

10. How much less was the average cost at a two-year institution than at a four-year institution in 2003–04?

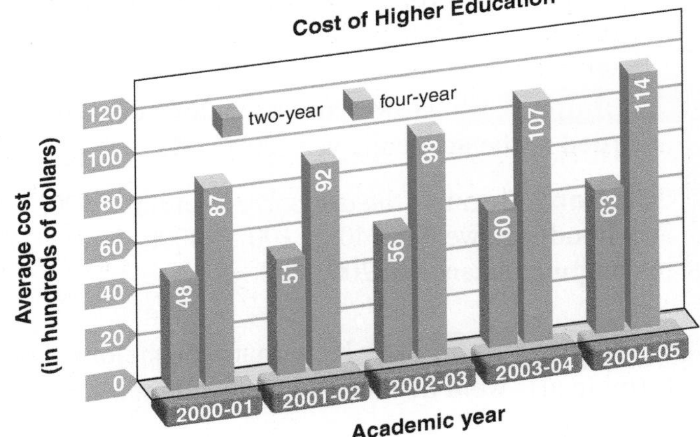

Source: www.informationplease.com

11. In which academic year was there the smallest difference between the average costs at a two-year institution and a four-year institution?

12. In which academic year was there the greatest difference between the average costs at two-year and four-year institutions?

13. By how much did the average cost at a two-year institution increase from 2001–02 to 2002–03?

14. By how much did the average cost at a four-year institution increase from 2002–03 to 2003–04?

15. James decided to attend a two-year college for two years, and then transfer to a four-year college for two years. If he started college in the fall of 2001 and paid the average cost for each of the four years, how much did he spend on his four years of education?

16. Monica attended a two-year community college for two years starting in the fall of 2003, and then transferred to a four-year school. Assuming she paid average costs, how much did she save during the first two years by choosing to start her education at a two-year college?

17. What was the percent increase in the average cost at a public two-year institution from 2000–01 to 2004–05?

18. What was the percent increase in the average cost at a public four-year institution from 2000–01 to 2004–05?

Baseball Players' Salaries *The following line graph shows how the average major league baseball player's salary has increased over a twelve-year period.* Notice the average salary is given for odd-numbered years only. Use the graph to answer exercises 19–24.*

19. What was the average baseball player's salary in 1995?

20. What was the average baseball player's salary in 2005?

21. Which two-year period(s) had the smallest increase?

22. Which two-year period had the largest increase?

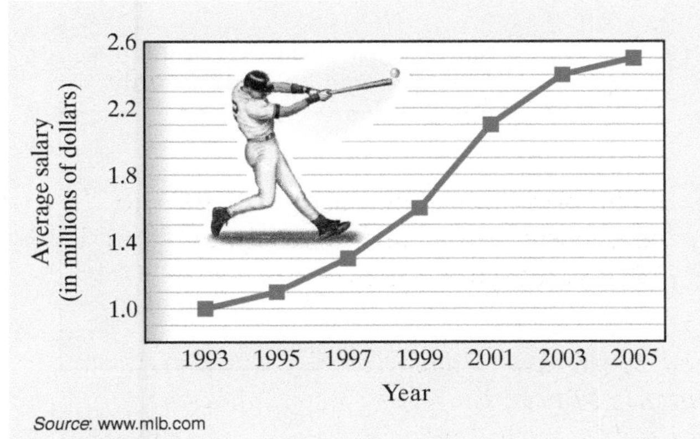

*Figures have been rounded.

23. Compare the average salary in 1999 to the average salary in 2001. By how much did the average salary increase from 1999 to 2001?

24. If the average salary continues to increase by the same amount as from 2003 to 2005, what will the average salary be in 2015?

Ottawa Rainfall *The following comparison line graph indicates the rainfall for six months of two different years in Ottawa. Use the graph to answer exercises 25–30.*

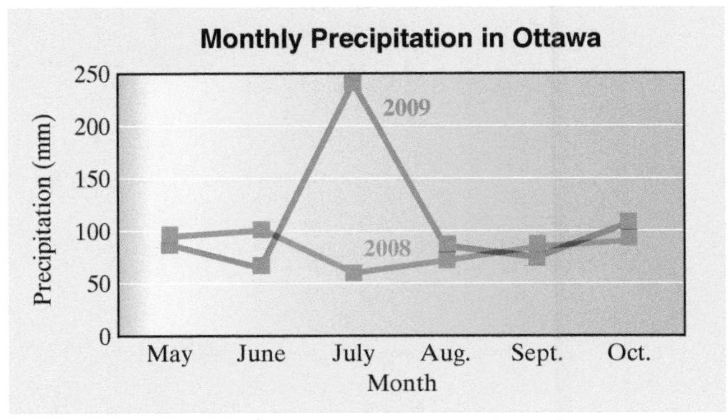

Source: Adapted from WeatherStats, ottawa.weatherstats.ca/1year, Oct-09

25. In September 2009, approximately how many millimetres of precipitation were recorded?

26. In October 2008, approximately how many millimetres of precipitation were recorded?

27. During what months was the precipitation of 2009 less than the precipitation of 2008?

28. During what months was the precipitation of 2009 more than the precipitation of 2008?

29. Approximately how many more millimetres of precipitation fell in July of 2009 than in July of 2008?

30. Approximately how many more millimetres of precipitation fell in July of 2009 than in June 2008?

Quick Quiz 2 The following comparison line graph shows the number of houses and the number of condominiums built in the years 1985 to 2005 in Essex County. Use the graph to answer the problems below.

1. How many condominiums were built in the year 2000?

2. How many more homes were built in 1985 compared to the number of condominiums?

3. During what year was the number of home sales closest to the number of condominium sales?

4. Concept Check If the increase in the number of condominiums from 1995 to 2005 continues at the same rate until 2015, explain how you would find the number of condominiums that will be constructed in 2015.

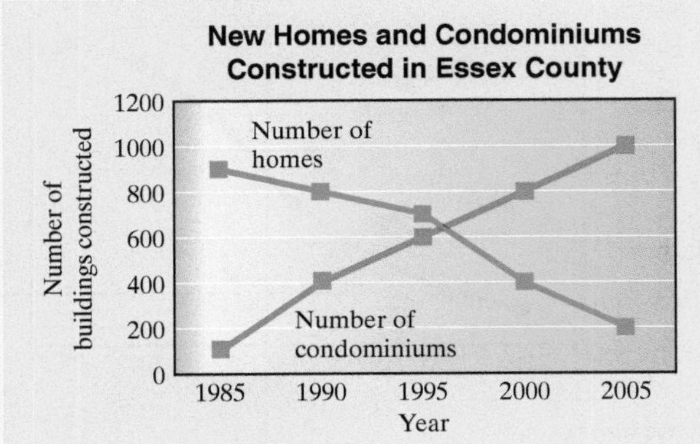

How Am I Doing? Sections 1–2

How are you doing with your homework assignments in Sections 1 and 2? Do you feel you have mastered the material so far? Do you understand the concepts you have covered? Before you go further, take some time to do each of the following problems.

1.

2.

3.

4.

5.

6.

1

In 2008, the top six most-visited Canadian attractions had about 53 700 000 visitors. The circle graph displays the approximate percentages of the total that visited each tourist attraction.

Most-Visited Canadian Tourist Attractions in 2008

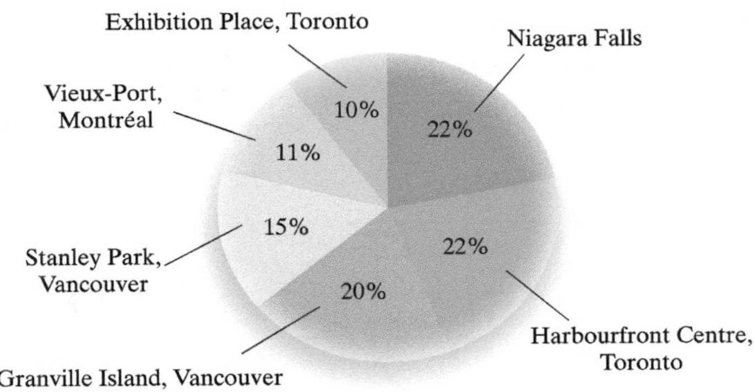

Source: Adapted from Forbes, www.forbestraveler.com/best-lists/canadas-popular-attractions-2009-slide.html, Oct-09

1. What percentage of the visitors went to Exhibition Place, Toronto?
2. To which tourist attraction(s) did the greatest number of visitors go?
3. What percent of the visitors went to Vieux-Port or Granville Island?
4. How many of the 53 700 000 visitors went to Niagara Falls?
5. How many of the 53 700 000 visitors went to Stanley Park or Granville Island?

2

The following double-bar graph indicates the number of new housing starts in Springfield during each quarter of 2006 and 2007.

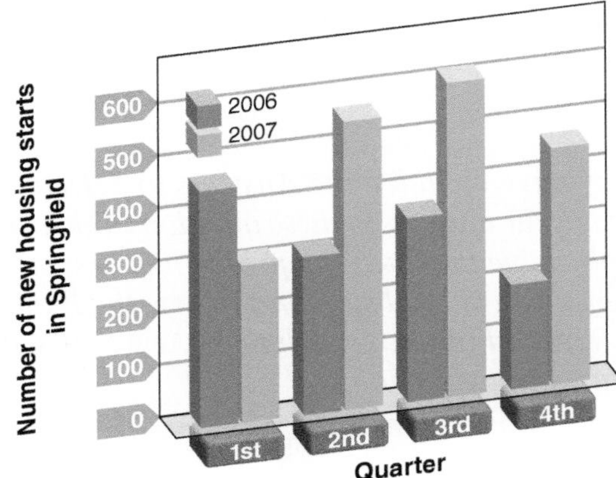

6. How many housing starts were there in Springfield in the first quarter of 2006?

7. ______
8. ______
9. ______
10. ______
11. ______
12. ______
13. ______
14. ______
15. (a) ______
(b) ______

7. How many housing starts were there in Springfield in the second quarter of 2007?

8. When were the fewest number of housing starts in Springfield?

9. When were the greatest number of housing starts in Springfield?

10. How many more housing starts were there in the third quarter of 2007 than in the third quarter of 2006?

11. How many fewer housing starts were there in the first quarter of 2007 than in the first quarter of 2006?

The line graph indicates sales and production of television sets by a major manufacturer during the specified months.

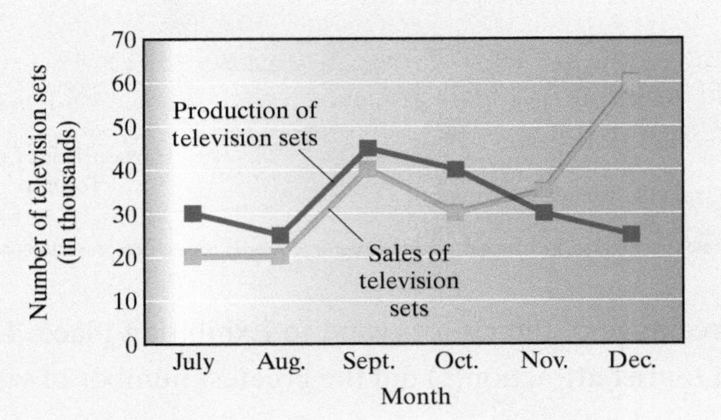

12. During what months were the fewest television sets produced?

13. During what month were the sales of television sets the highest?

14. What was the first month in which the production of television sets was lower than the sales of television sets?

15. **(a)** How many television sets were sold in August?
(b) In November?

Your institution may have included the Answers to Selected Exercises for this module, which contains the answers to these questions. Each answer also includes a reference to the objective in which the problem is first taught. If you missed any of these problems, you should stop and review the Examples and Practice Problems in the referenced objective. A little review now will help you master the material in the upcoming sections.

Section 3 Histograms

Understanding and Interpreting a Histogram

In business or in higher education you are often asked to take data and organize them in some way. This section shows you the technique for making a *histogram*—a type of bar graph.

Suppose that a mathematics professor announced the results of a class test. The 40 students in the class scored between 50 and 99 on the test. The results are displayed in the following chart.

Student Learning Objectives

After studying this section, you will be able to:

 **Understand and interpret a histogram.**

 **Construct a histogram from raw data.**

Scores on the Test	Class Frequency (Number of Students)
50–59	4
60–69	6
70–79	16
80–89	8
90–99	6

The results in the table can be organized in a special type of bar graph known as a **histogram.** In a histogram the width of each bar is the same. The width represents the range of scores on the test. This is called a **class interval.** The height of each bar gives the class frequency of each class interval. The **class frequency** is the number of times a score occurs in a particular class interval. Be sure to notice that the bars touch each other. This is a main difference between the bar graph and the histogram. Use the histogram below to do Examples 1 and 2.

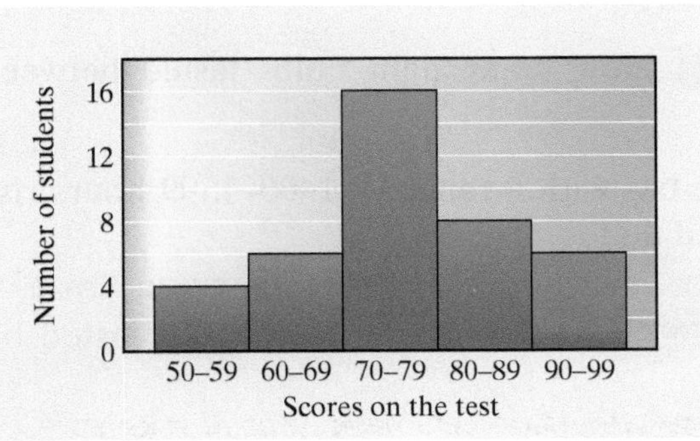

EXAMPLE 1 How many students scored a B on the test if the professor considers a test score of 80–89 a B?

Solution Since the 80–89 bar rises to a height of 8, eight students scored a B on the test.

Practice Problem 1 How many students scored a D on the test if the professor considers a test score of 60–69 a D?

NOTE TO STUDENT: Fully worked-out solutions to all of the Practice Problems can be found at the end of the module.

EXAMPLE 2 How many students scored less than 80 on the test?

Solution From the histogram, we see that there are three different bar heights to be included. Four tests were scored 50–59, six tests were scored 60–69, and 16 tests were scored 70–79. When we combine $4 + 6 + 16 = 26$, we can see that 26 students scored less than 80 on the test.

***NOTE TO STUDENT:** Fully worked-out solutions to all of the Practice Problems can be found at the end of the module.*

Practice Problem 2 How many students scored greater than 69 on the test?

The following histogram tells us about the length of life of 110 new light bulbs tested at a research centre. The number of hours the bulbs lasted is indicated on the horizontal scale. The number of bulbs lasting that long is indicated on the vertical scale. Use this histogram for Examples 3 and 4.

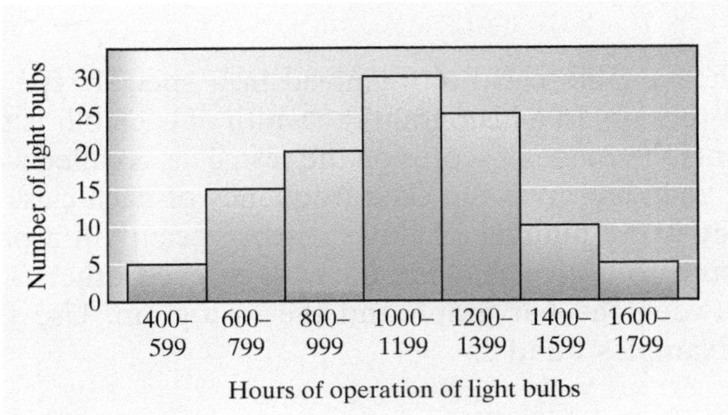

EXAMPLE 3 How many light bulbs lasted between 1400 and 1599 hours?

Solution The bar with a range of 1400–1599 hours rises to 10. Thus 10 light bulbs lasted that long.

Practice Problem 3 How many light bulbs lasted between 800 and 999 hours?

EXAMPLE 4 How many light bulbs lasted less than 1000 hours?

Solution We see that there are three different bar heights to be included. Five bulbs lasted 400–599 hours, 15 bulbs lasted 600–799 hours, and 20 bulbs lasted 800–999 hours. We add $5 + 15 + 20 = 40$. Thus 40 light bulbs lasted less than 1000 hours.

Practice Problem 4 How many light bulbs lasted more than 1199 hours?

 Constructing a Histogram from Raw Data

To construct a histogram, we start with *raw data,* data that have not yet been organized or interpreted. We perform the following steps.

1. Select class intervals of equal width for the data.
2. Make a table with class intervals and a *tally* (count) of how many numbers occur in each interval. Add up the tally to find the class frequency for each class interval.
3. Draw the histogram.

First we will practise making the table. Later we will use the table to draw the histogram.

EXAMPLE 5 Each of the following numbers represents the number of kilowatt-hours of electricity used in a home during a one-month period. Create a set of class intervals for this data and then determine the frequency of each class interval.

770	520	850	900	1100
1200	1150	730	680	900
1160	590	670	1230	980

Solution

1. We select class intervals of equal width for the data. We choose intervals of 200. We might have chosen smaller or larger intervals, but we choose 200 because it gives us a convenient number of intervals to work with, as we will see.
2. We make a table. We write down the class intervals, then count (tally) how many numbers occur within each interval. Then we write the total. This is the class frequency.

Kilowatt-Hours Used (Class Interval)	Tally	Frequency
500–699	||||	4
700–899	|||	3
900–1099	|||	3
1100–1299	~~||||~~	5

Practice Problem 5 Each of the following numbers represents the weight in kilograms of a new truck.

2250	1760	2000	2100	1900
1640	1820	2300	2210	2390
2150	1930	2060	2350	1890

Complete the following table to determine the frequency of each class interval for the preceding data.

Weight in Kilograms (Class Interval)	Tally	Frequency
1600–1799		
1800–1999		
2000–2199		
2200–2399		

NOTE TO STUDENT: Fully worked-out solutions to all of the Practice Problems can be found at the end of the module.

One of the purposes of a histogram is to give you a visual sense of how the data is distributed. For example, if you look at the raw data of Example 5 you may be left with the sense that the home used very different amounts of electricity during a month. For most of us, looking at the raw data does not help us understand the situation. However, once we construct a histogram such as the one in Example 6, we are able to see patterns and trends of electricity use.

EXAMPLE 6 Draw a histogram from the table in Example 5.

Solution

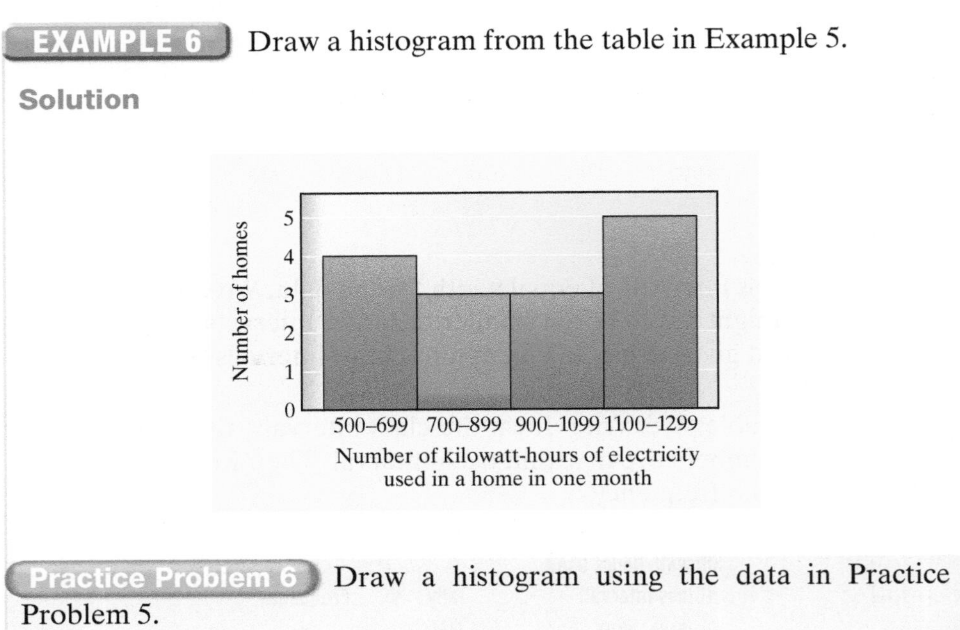

Practice Problem 6 Draw a histogram using the data in Practice Problem 5.

Note: Usually it is desirable for the class intervals to be of equal size. However, sometimes data is collected such that this is not possible. We will see this situation in Example 7. Here government data is displayed with unequal class intervals.

EXAMPLE 7 Draw a histogram for the following table of recent data showing the number of people in Canada, in each of five age categories.

Age Category	Number of People in Canada (2008, in thousands)
19 or younger	7 853.4
20–34	6 786.5
35–54	10 149.3
55–64	3 959.0
65 or older	4 563.1

Source: Adapted from Statistics Canada, www40.statcan.gc.ca/l01/cst01/demo10a-eng.htm, Oct-09

Solution

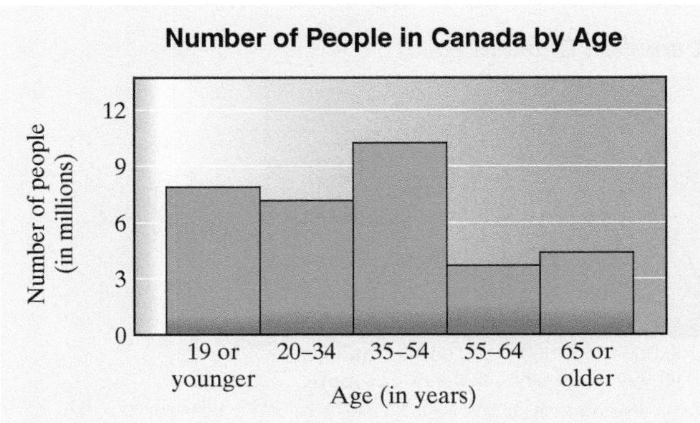

Practice Problem 7 Based on the preceding histogram, between what two age categories is there the greatest difference in population in Canada?

Section 3 Exercises

Verbal and Writing Skills

1. Describe two main differences between the bar graph and the histogram.

2. Suppose you had test data 22, 24, 33, 44, 55, 66, 38, 48, and 60. If you were going to have a histogram with three class intervals, explain how you would pick the intervals.

3. Explain in your own words what is meant by class frequency.

4. Jason made a histogram with the following class intervals: 300–400, 400–500, 500–600, 600–700. Explain why that is not a good choice of class intervals.

Applications

City Population *Recent data showing the number of Canadian cities in 2006 with populations of 75 000 or more is depicted in the following histogram. Use the histogram to answer exercises 5–12.*

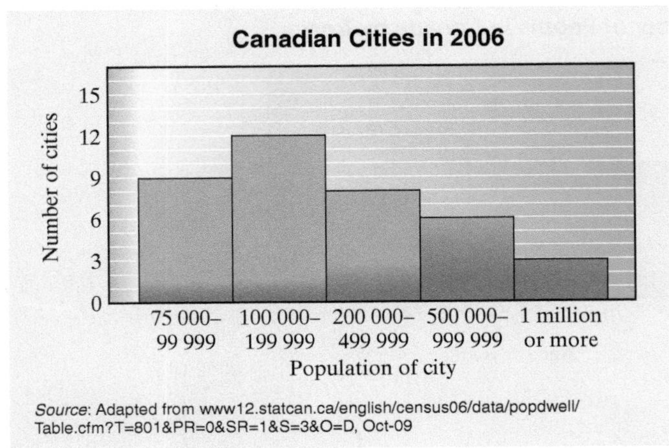

Source: Adapted from www12.statcan.ca/english/census06/data/popdwell/Table.cfm?T=801&PR=0&SR=1&S=3&O=D, Oct-09

5. How many cities have a population of 100 000–199 999?

6. How many cities have a population of 200 000–499 999?

7. How many cities have a population of 1 million or more?

8. How many cities have a population of 75 000–99 999?

9. How many cities have a population of 500 000 or more?

10. How many cities have a population of 75 000 or more?

11. How many cities have between 75 000 and 199 999 people?

12. How many cities have between 100 000 and 999 999 people?

Book Sales *A large company comprising three bookstores studied its yearly report to find out its customers' spending habits. The company sold a total of 70 000 books. The following histogram indicates the number of books sold in certain price ranges. Use the histogram to answer exercises 13–22.*

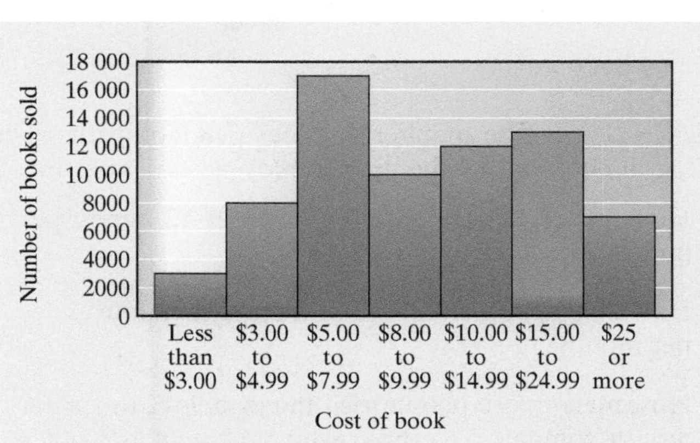

13. How many books priced at $3.00 to $4.99 were sold?

14. How many books priced at $25.00 or more were sold?

15. Which price category of books did the bookstore sell the most of?

16. What price category of books did the bookstore sell the least of?

17. How many books priced at less than $8.00 were sold?

18. How many books priced at more than $9.99 were sold?

19. How many books priced between $5.00 and $24.99 were sold?

20. How many books priced between $3.00 and $9.99 were sold?

21. What percent of the 70 000 books sold were over $14.99?

22. What percent of the 70 000 books sold were under $8.00?

Guelph Temperature *The numbers in the following chart are the daily high temperatures in degrees Celsius in Guelph during February 2008. In exercises 23–30, determine the frequencies of the class intervals for this data.*

–0.5 °C	–0.9 °C	–0.5 °C	1.0 °C	3.9 °C	–0.1 °C	–4.6 °C	–1.3 °C
1.0 °C	–1.8 °C	–11.7 °C	–6.4 °C	–5.5 °C	–1.3 °C	–1.7 °C	–6.3 °C
5.7 °C	6.0 °C	–6.8 °C	–8.5 °C	–7.5 °C	–2.8 °C	–3.3 °C	–0.9 °C
–0.7 °C	0 °C	–9.6 °C	–10.7 °C	0.1 °C			

Source: Adapted From WeatherStats, guelph.weatherstats.ca/temperature, Oct-09

	Temperature (Class Interval)	Tally	Frequency
23.	–12.4° to –10.0°	________	________
24.	–2.4° to 0.0°	________	________
25.	–9.9° to –7.5°	________	________
26.	0.1° to 2.5°	________	________
27.	–7.4° to –5.0°	________	________
28.	2.6° to 5.0°	________	________
29.	–4.9° to –2.5°	________	________
30.	5.1° to 7.5°	________	________

31. Construct a histogram using the table prepared in exercises 23–30.

32. How many days in February was the temperature in Guelph 0.1 °C or greater?

33. How many days in February was the temperature in Guelph –5.0 °C or less?

Quick Quiz 3 The number of times per month that people visit the YMCA gym in Springfield is displayed on the histogram below. Use the histogram to answer questions 1–4 below.

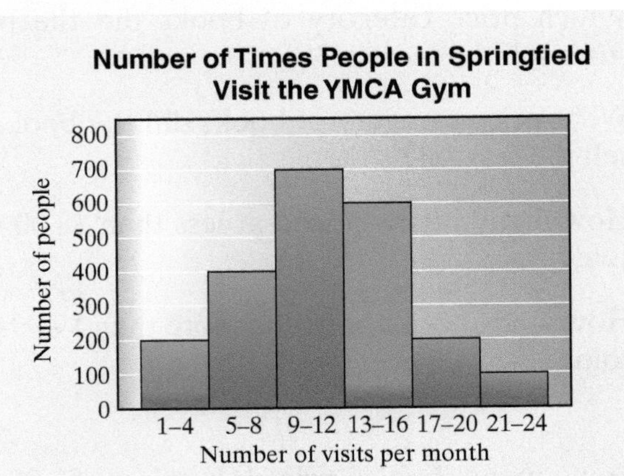

1. How many people visit the gym 9–12 times per month?

2. How many people visit the gym more than four times per month?

3. How many more people visit the gym 9–12 times per month compared to those who visit only 1–4 times per month?

4. Concept Check During a promotion month last summer, nonmembers were allowed to visit the gym for free. The number of people who visited the gym 1–4 times a month tripled. The number of people who visited the gym 5–8 times a month doubled. Explain how you would find how many people visited the gym between one and eight times per month.

SECTION 4 MEAN, MEDIAN, AND MODE

Student Learning Objectives

After studying this section, you will be able to:

1. Find the mean of a set of numbers.
2. Find the median of a set of numbers.
3. Find the mode of a set of numbers.

Finding the Mean of a Set of Numbers

We often want to know the "middle value" of a group of numbers. In this section we learn that, in statistics, there is more than one way of describing this middle value: there is the *mean* of the group of numbers, there is the *median* of the group of numbers, and in most cases there is a *mode* of the group of numbers. In some situations it's more helpful to look at the mean; in others it's more helpful to look at the median; and in yet others, the mode. We'll learn to tell which situations lend themselves to one or the other.

The **mean** of a set of values is the sum of the values divided by the number of values. The mean is often called the **average.**

The mean value is often rounded to a certain decimal-place accuracy.

EXAMPLE 1 Carl recorded the kilometres per litre achieved by his car for the last two months. His results were as follows:

Week	1	2	3	4	5	6	7	8
Kilometres per Litre	16	14	13	15	12	15	14	13

What is the mean kilometres-per-litre figure for the last eight weeks? Round to the nearest whole number.

Solution

$$\begin{array}{ll}\text{Sum of values} \longrightarrow & 16 + 14 + 13 + 15 + 12 + 15 + 14 + 13 \\ \text{Number of values} \longrightarrow & \hline 8\end{array}$$

$$= \frac{112}{8} = 14$$

The mean kilometres-per-litre figure is 14.

Practice Problem 1 Toshi and Yori kept records of their phone bills for the last six months. Their bills were \$39.20, \$43.50, \$81.90, \$34.20, \$51.70, and \$48.10. Find the mean monthly bill. Round to the nearest cent.

NOTE TO STUDENT: Fully worked-out solutions to all of the Practice Problems can be found at the end of the module.

Finding the Median of a Set of Numbers

If a set of numbers is arranged in order from smallest to largest, the **median** is that value that has the same number of values above it as below it.

If the numbers are not arranged in order, then the first step in finding the median is to put the numbers in order.

EXAMPLE 2 Find the median value of the following costs for microwave ovens: \$100, \$60, \$120, \$200, \$190, \$120, \$320, \$290, \$180.

Solution We must arrange the numbers in order from smallest to largest (or largest to smallest).

$$\underbrace{\$60, \$100, \$120, \$120}_{\text{four numbers}} \qquad \underset{\substack{\uparrow \\ \text{middle number}}}{\$180} \qquad \underbrace{\$190, \$200, \$290, \$320}_{\text{four numbers}}$$

Thus \$180 is the median cost.

Practice Problem 2 Find the median value of the following weekly salaries: \$320, \$150, \$400, \$600, \$290, \$150, \$450.

If a list of numbers contains an even number of items, then of course there is no one middle number. In this situation we obtain the median by taking the average of the two middle numbers.

EXAMPLE 3 Find the median of the following numbers: 26, 31, 39, 33, 13, 16, 18, 38.

Solution First we place the numbers in order from smallest to largest.

$$\underbrace{13, 16, 18}_{\text{three numbers}} \qquad \underset{\substack{\uparrow \\ \text{two middle numbers}}}{26, 31} \qquad \underbrace{33, 38, 39}_{\text{three numbers}}$$

The average (mean) of 26 and 31 is

$$\frac{26 + 31}{2} = \frac{57}{2} = 28.5.$$

Thus the median value is 28.5.

Practice Problem 3 Find the median value of the following numbers: 126, 105, 88, 100, 90, 118.

SIDELIGHT

When would someone want to use the mean, and when would someone want to use the median? Which is more helpful?

The mean, or average, is used more frequently. It is most helpful when the data are distributed fairly evenly, that is, when no one value is "much larger" or "much smaller" than the rest.

For example, suppose a company had employees with annual salaries of \$9000, \$11 000, \$14 000, \$15 000, \$17 000, and \$20 000. All the salaries fall within a fairly limited range. The mean salary

$$\frac{\$9000 + \$11\,000 + \$14\,000 + \$15\,000 + \$17\,000 + \$20\,000}{6} \approx \$14\,333.33$$

gives us a reasonable idea of the typical salary.

However, suppose the company had six employees with salaries of \$9000, \$11 000, \$14 000, \$15 000, \$17 000, and \$90 000. Talking about the mean salary, which is $26 000, is deceptive. No one earns a salary very close to the mean salary. The typical worker in that company does not earn around $26 000. In this case, the median value is more appropriate. Here the median is $14 500. See Section 4 Exercises, exercises 43 and 44 for more on this.

Finding the Mode of a Set of Numbers

Another value that is sometimes used to describe a set of data is the mode. The **mode** of a set of data is the number or numbers that occur most often.

EXAMPLE 4 The following numbers are the weights of trucks measured in kilograms:

2345, 2567, 2785, 2967, 3105, 3105, 3245, 3546.

Find the mode of these weights.

Solution The value 3105 occurs twice, whereas each of the other values occurs just once. Thus the mode is 3105 kilograms.

Practice Problem 4 The following numbers are the heights in inches of 10 male students in Stepping It Up Mathematics: 64, 66, 67, 69, 70, 71, 71, 73, 75, 76. Find the mode of these heights.

A set of numbers may have more than one mode.

EXAMPLE 5 The following numbers are finish times for 12 high school students who ran a distance of 1.5 kilometres. The finish times are measured in seconds.

290, 272, 268, 260, 290, 272, 330, 355, 368, 290, 370, 272

Find the mode of these finish times.

Solution First we need to arrange the numbers in order from smallest to largest and include all repeats.

260, 268, 272, 272, 272, 290, 290, 290, 330, 355, 368, 370

Now we can see that the value 272 occurs three times, as does the value 290. Thus the modes for these finish times are 272 seconds and 290 seconds.

Practice Problem 5 The following numbers are distances in kilometres that 16 students travelled to take classes at Confederation College each day.

2, 5, 8, 3, 12, 15, 28, 8, 3, 14, 16, 31, 33, 27, 3, 28

Find the mode of these distances.

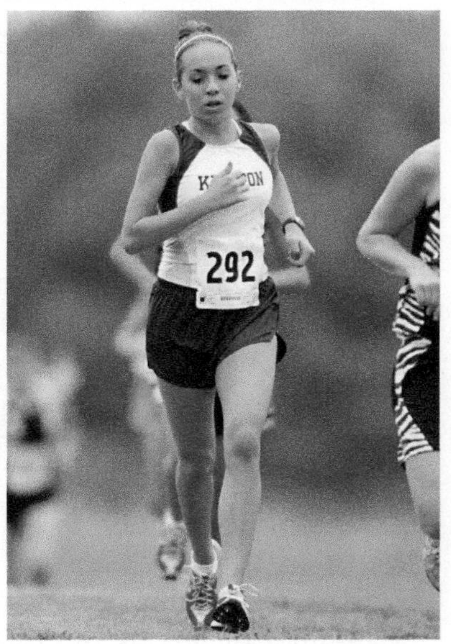

Shutterstock

A set of numbers may have **no mode** at all. For example, the set of numbers 50, 60, 70, 80, 90 has no mode because each number occurs just once. The set of numbers 33, 33, 44, 44, 55, 55 has no mode because each number occurs twice. If all numbers occur the same number of times, there is no mode.

Section 4 Exercises

Verbal and Writing Skills

1. Explain the difference between a median and a mean.

2. Explain why some sets of numbers have one mode, others two modes, and others no modes.

Applications

In exercises 3–12, find the mean. Round to the nearest tenth unless otherwise directed.

3. ***Coffeehouse Customers*** The numbers of customers who were served at Grinders Coffeehouse between 8 A.M. and 9 A.M. in the past seven days were as follows: 30, 29, 28, 35, 34, 37, 31.

4. ***Pizza Delivery*** The numbers of pizzas delivered by Papa John's over the last seven days were as follows: 28, 17, 18, 21, 24, 30, 30.

5. ***Average Rainfall*** The average precipitation for Victoria, British Columbia, for the first six months of 2009 is recorded as follows. Find the mean number of millimetres for these months.

Jan.	Feb.	Mar.	Apr.	May	June
77.54 mm	34.56 mm	54.26 mm	40.04 mm	56.01 mm	6.02 mm

Source: WeatherStats, victoria.weatherstats.ca/precipitation, Oct-09

6. ***Average Temperature*** The average high temperature in Fredericton, New Brunswick, for July through December 2008 is recorded as follows. Find the mean high temperature for these months.

July	Aug.	Sept.	Oct.	Nov.	Dec.
26.7 °C	23.0 °C	20.0 °C	12.7 °C	5.8 °C	0.7 °C

Source: Adapted from WeatherStats, fredericton.weatherstats.ca/temperature, Oct-09

7. ***Baseball*** The captain of the college baseball team achieved the following results:

	Game 1	Game 2	Game 3	Game 4	Game 5
Hits	0	2	3	2	2
Times at Bat	5	4	6	5	4

Find his batting average by dividing his total number of hits by the total times at bat. Round to the nearest thousandth if necessary.

8. ***Bowling*** The captain of the college bowling team had the following results after practice:

	Practice 1	Practice 2	Practice 3	Practice 4
Score (Pins)	541	561	840	422
Number of Games	3	3	4	2

Find her bowling average by dividing the total number of pins scored by the total number of games.

9. ***Population of Guam*** The population on the island of Guam has increased significantly over the last 30 years, and was expected to continue to increase in 2010. Find an approximate value for the mean population for this 40-year period from the following population chart:

1970 Population	1980 Population	1990 Population	2000 Population	2010* Population
86 000	107 000	134 000	152 000	182 000

*estimated

Sources: U.S. Census Bureau, www.brittanica.com

10. ***Population of U.S. Virgin Islands*** The population on the U.S. Virgin Islands went through a significant increase from 1970 to 1990 but since then has stayed relatively unchanged. A slight decrease was projected for 2010. Find the approximate value for the mean population from 1970 to 2010 by using all the values in the following population chart:

1970 Population	1980 Population	1990 Population	2000 Population	2010* Population
63 000	98 000	104 000	109 000	108 000

*estimated

Source: U.S. Census Bureau

11. ***Gas Used on a Trip*** Frank and Wally travelled to the West Coast during the summer. The numbers of kilometres they drove and the numbers of litres of gas they used are recorded in the following chart.

	Day 1	Day 2	Day 3	Day 4
Kilometres Driven	276	350	391	336
Litres of Gas	24	28	34	28

Find the average kilometres per litre achieved by the car on the trip by dividing the total number of kilometres driven by the total number of litres used.

12. ***Gas Used on a Trip*** Cindy and Andrea travelled to Woodstock this fall. The numbers of kilometres they drove and the numbers of litres of gas they used are recorded in the following chart.

	Day 1	Day 2	Day 3	Day 4
Kilometres Driven	260	375	408	416
Litres of Gas	20	30	34	32

Find the average kilometres per litre achieved by the car on the trip by dividing the total number of kilometres driven by the total number of litres used.

In exercises 13–24, find the median value.

13. 126, 232, 180, 195, 229

14. 548, 554, 560, 539, 512

15. 12.4, 11.6, 11.9, 12.1, 12.5, 11.9

16. 8.2, 8.1, 7.8, 8.8, 7.9, 7.5

17. ***Annual Salary*** The annual salaries of six staff members at a local college are \$28 500, \$32 700, \$42 000, \$38 250, \$40 750, and \$35 800.

18. ***Family Income*** The annual incomes of six families are \$24 000, \$60 000, \$32 000, \$18 000, \$29 000, and \$35 000.

19. ***Server Workload*** The numbers of tables Carl waited on at his job the past seven days were 12, 10, 21, 25, 31, 18, 28.

20. ***Swimming Times*** The numbers of minutes Ashley spent swimming the past seven days were 35, 60, 45, 40, 50, 80, and 45.

21. ***Phone Bills*** The phone bills for Dr. Price's cellular phone over the last seven months were as follows: \$109, \$207, \$420, \$218, \$97, \$330, and \$185.

22. ***Compact Disc Prices*** The prices of the same compact disc sold at several different music stores or by mail order were as follows: \$15.99, \$11.99, \$5.99, \$12.99, \$14.99, \$9.99, \$13.99, \$7.99, and \$10.99.

23. ***Grade Point Averages*** The grade point averages (GPA) for eight students were 1.8, 1.9, 3.1, 3.7, 2.0, 3.1, 2.0, and 2.4.

24. ***Food Purchases*** The numbers of pounds of smoked turkey breast purchased at a deli by the last eight customers were 1.2, 2.0, 1.7, 2.5, 2.4, 1.6, 1.5, and 2.3.

25. ***Largest Canadian Businesses*** The table below shows the revenues, in U.S. dollars, of the four largest businesses in Canada for the year 2007. Determine the median revenue based on this data.

Company	Royal Bank of Canada	Manulife Financial	Toronto-Dominion Bank	Bank of Nova Scotia
Revenue, in billions of dollars	$32.13	$28.91	$19.95	$20.04

Source: Forbes, www.forbes.com/lists/2007/18/biz_07forbes2000_The-Global-2000-Canada_10Rank.html, Oct-09

26. ***NBA Leaders*** At the end of the 2006–07 National Basketball Association regular season, the top four scoring leaders with their season point totals were as shown below. The numbers of points per game are also given. Determine the mean number of total points and the mean number of points per game based on this data.

Player	Kobe Bryant (Los Angeles Lakers)	LeBron James (Cleveland Cavaliers)	Vince Carter (New Jersey Nets)	Dirk Nowitzki (Dallas Mavericks)
Total points	2430	2132	2105	2070
Points per game	31.6	27.3	28.4	25.2

Source: www.nba.com

Find the mean. Round to the nearest cent when necessary.

27. ***Business Owners' Salary*** The salaries of eight small business owners in Big Rapids are $30 000, $74 500, $47 890, $89 000, $57 645, $78 090, $110 370, and $65 800.

28. ***Price of Laptop Computer*** The prices of nine laptop computers are $1679, $1902, $1530, $738, $2999, $1105, $1655, $980, and $1430.

In exercises 29 and 30, find the median.

29. 2576, 8764, 3700, 5000, 7200, 4700, 9365, 1987

30. 15.276, 21.375, 18.90, 29.2, 14.77, 19.02

31. ***Holiday Shopping*** It took Jenny five days to complete her holiday shopping. The amounts she spent during these five days were $120.50, $66.74, $80.95, $210.52, and $45.00. Find the mean and the median.

32. ***Property Taxes*** The amounts the Dayton family has paid in property taxes the past five years are $1381, $1405, $1405, $1520, and $1592. Find the mean and the median.

Find the mode.

33. 60, 65, 68, 60, 72, 59, 80

34. 86, 84, 82, 87, 84, 88, 90

35. 121, 150, 116, 150, 121, 181, 117, 123

36. 144, 143, 140, 141, 149, 144, 141, 150

37. ***Bicycle Prices*** The last seven bicycles sold at the Skol Bike shop cost $249, $649, $269, $259, $269, $249, and $269.

38. ***Television Prices*** The last seven televisions sold at the local Future Shop cost $315, $430, $315, $330, $430, $315, and $460.

Mixed Practice

39. ***Life Expectancy*** In 2006, the countries with the highest life expectancies were Andorra: 83.5 years; San Marino: 81.7 years; Singapore: 81.7 years; Japan: 81.2 years; Australia: 80.5 years; Sweden: 80.5 years; Switzerland: 80.5 years. Find the mean, the median, and the mode. (*Source:* www.infoplease.com)

40. ***Commuter Passengers*** The numbers of passengers taking the Toronto to Ottawa train during the last seven days were 568, 388, 588, 688, 750, 900, and 388. Find the mean, the median, and the mode.

41. ***Salary of Employees*** A local travel office has 10 employees. Their monthly salaries are $1500, $1700, $1650, $1300, $1440, $1580, $1820, $1380, $2900, and $6300.

(a) Find the mean.
(b) Find the median.
(c) Find the mode.
(d) Which of these numbers best represents what the typical person earns? Why?

42. ***Track Running Times*** A college track star in Ontario ran the 100-metre event in eight track meets. Her times were 11.7 seconds, 11.6 seconds, 12.0 seconds, 12.1 seconds, 11.9 seconds, 18 seconds, 11.5 seconds, and 12.4 seconds.

(a) Find the mean.
(b) Find the median.
(c) Find the mode.
(d) Which of these numbers represents her typical running time? Why?

43. ***Number of Phone Calls*** Sally made a record of the number of phone calls she received each night this last week.

Day of the Week	Sun.	Mon.	Tues.	Wed.	Thurs.	Fri.	Sat.
Number of Phone Calls	23	3	2	3	7	10	11

(a) Find the mean. Round your answer to the nearest tenth.
(b) Find the median.
(c) Find the mode.
(d) Which of these three measures best represents the number of phone calls Sally receives on a typical night? Why?

44. ***Number of Overnight Business Trips*** David has to travel as a representative for his computer software company. He made a record of the number of nights he had to spend away from home on business travel during the first seven months of the year.

Month of the Year	Jan.	Feb.	Mar.	Apr.	May	June	July
Number of Nights Spent Away from Home on Business	3	7	8	6	9	28	3

(a) Find the mean. Round to the nearest tenth.
(b) Find the median.
(c) Find the mode.
(d) Which of these three measures best represents the number of nights that David has to spend away from home on business? Why?

Quick Quiz 4 Mike Nauth asks his Stepping It Up Mathematics students how many times a year they ordered a pizza. Here are the responses:

1, 3, 8, 35, 16, 8, 5, 17, 24, 15

1. Find the median number of times students ordered a pizza.

2. Find the mean number of times students ordered a pizza.

3. Find the mode of the number of times students ordered a pizza.

4. Concept Check Professor Blair wants to conduct a survey of her students to determine how many times a year they ordered Chinese food. Would you select the mean, the median, or the mode for this survey? Explain your reasoning.

Putting Your Skills to Work: Use Math to Save Money

ADJUST THE THERMOSTAT

Some Helpful Information

Approximately 45% of a typical home utility bill is for heating and/or cooling. We may not have any control over how fuel efficient our home is, but we can control the setting on the thermostat. For every 1 °C change in thermostat, a home will save approximately 3% of the total utility bill. Consider the story of Maria and Josef.

A Specific Example

Maria and Josef use electricity to heat and cool their home, and their electricity bill averages $205 per month. They generally set their thermostat at 22 °C in the cooler months and 26 °C in the warmer months.

Quick Calculations and Facts

1. If Maria and Josef set their thermostat at 20 °C in the colder months, how much per month could they expect to save?
2. If they adjust their thermostat to 29 °C in the warmer months, how much could they expect to save per month?
3. On the average, if Maria and Josef adjusted their thermostat setting 3 °C (either upward in the warmer months or downward in the colder months), how much could they expect to save on their utilities per year?

Making Personal Applications to Your Own Life

4. Where do you have your thermostat set?
5. How much could you save on your utility bill by adjusting the settings either up or down?

HOME HEATING OIL PRICES

In most of Canada, heating by electricity is too expensive, and natural gas or oil is used. Mark lives in Toronto in a house heated by oil. During the winter of 2008, Mark paid $0.65 per litre of heating oil. The price of heating oil has since increased to $1.05 per litre. Looking ahead to the coming winter, Mark wants to budget enough money for his oil bills.

6. The oil company will only deliver 400 litres of heating oil or more. Determine the cost of 400 litres of heating oil in December 2008 and in the coming December. What is the difference in cost?
7. Mark knows he will need a 400-litre oil delivery every month during the winter (November and December of this year and January, February, and March of next year). What can Mark expect to pay in home heating oil costs for the five months of winter from November to March?
8. Mark typically keeps his thermostat set at 22 °C during the winter months. How much money would Mark save on his heating oil costs if he lowered his thermostat to 20 °C for the entire winter?
9. How much money would Mark save if he set his thermostat to 18 °C during the winter?
10. How low would Mark need to set his thermostat for the winter in order to save one month's worth of heating costs ($420)?

Module Organizer

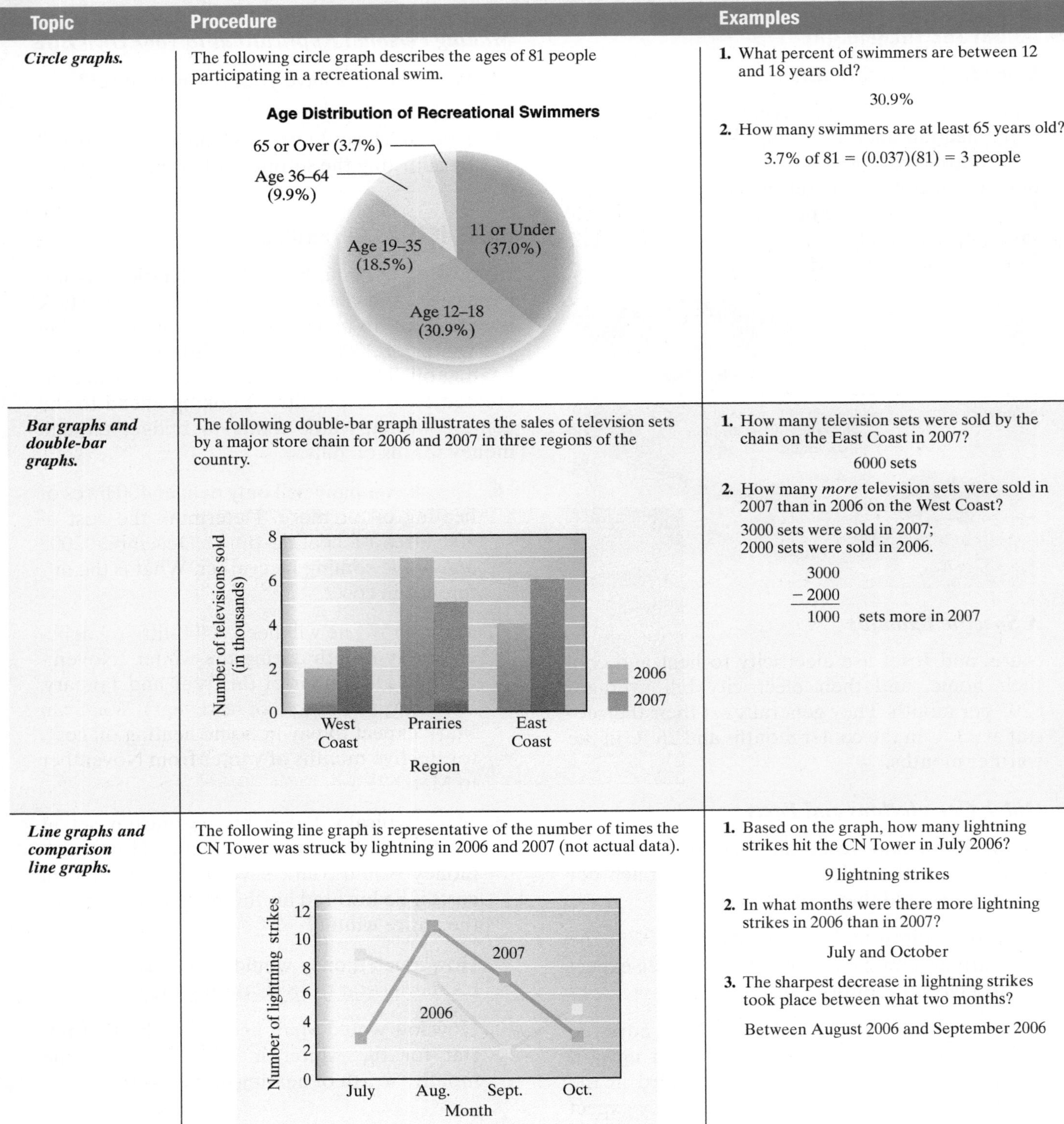

Topic	Procedure	Examples
Circle graphs.	The following circle graph describes the ages of 81 people participating in a recreational swim.	**1.** What percent of swimmers are between 12 and 18 years old? 30.9% **2.** How many swimmers are at least 65 years old? 3.7% of 81 = (0.037)(81) = 3 people
Bar graphs and double-bar graphs.	The following double-bar graph illustrates the sales of television sets by a major store chain for 2006 and 2007 in three regions of the country.	**1.** How many television sets were sold by the chain on the East Coast in 2007? 6000 sets **2.** How many *more* television sets were sold in 2007 than in 2006 on the West Coast? 3000 sets were sold in 2007; 2000 sets were sold in 2006. $\begin{array}{r} 3000 \\ -\,2000 \\ \hline 1000 \end{array}$ sets more in 2007
Line graphs and comparison line graphs.	The following line graph is representative of the number of times the CN Tower was struck by lightning in 2006 and 2007 (not actual data).	**1.** Based on the graph, how many lightning strikes hit the CN Tower in July 2006? 9 lightning strikes **2.** In what months were there more lightning strikes in 2006 than in 2007? July and October **3.** The sharpest decrease in lightning strikes took place between what two months? Between August 2006 and September 2006

Topic	Procedure	Examples
Histograms.	The following histogram indicates the number of students in a math class who scored within each interval on a 15-point quiz. 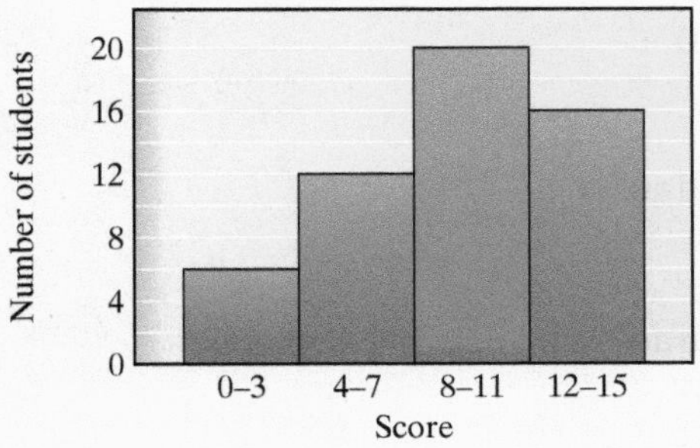 Number of students: 0, 4, 8, 12, 16, 20 Score: 0–3, 4–7, 8–11, 12–15	**1.** How many students had a score between 8 and 11? 20 students **2.** How many students had a score of less than 8? $12 + 6 = 18$ students
Finding the mean.	The *mean* of a set of values is the sum of the values divided by the number of values. The mean is often called the *average*.	Find the mean of 19, 13, 15, 25, and 18. $\frac{19 + 13 + 15 + 25 + 18}{5} = \frac{90}{5} = 18$ The mean is 18.
Finding the median.	If a set of numbers is arranged in order from smallest to largest, the *median* is that value that has the same number of values above it as below it. How do we find the median? **1.** Arrange the numbers in order from smallest to largest. **2.** If there is an odd number of values, the middle value is the median. **3.** If there is an even number of values, the average of the two middle values is the median.	**1.** Find the median of 19, 29, 36, 15, and 20. First we arrange in order from smallest to largest: 15, 19, 20, 29, 36. 15, 19 (two numbers) 20 (middle number) 29, 36 (two numbers) The median is 20. **2.** Find the median of 67, 28, 92, 37, 81, and 75. First we arrange in order from smallest to largest: 28, 37, 67, 75, 81, 92. There is an even number of values. 28, 37, 67, 75 (two middle numbers), 81, 92 $\frac{67 + 75}{2} = \frac{142}{2} = 71$ The median is 71.
Finding the mode.	The *mode* of a set of values is the value that occurs most often. A set of values may have more than one mode or no mode.	**1.** Find the mode of 12, 15, 18, 26, 15, 9, 12, and 27. The modes are 12 and 15. **2.** Find the mode of 4, 8, 15, 21, and 23. There is no mode.

Module Review Problems

Computer Manufacturers *A student found that there were a total of 140 personal computers owned by students in the dormitory. The following circle graph displays the distribution of manufacturers of these computers. Use the graph to answer exercises 1–8.*

1. How many personal computers were manufactured by Lenovo?

2. How many personal computers were manufactured by Apple?

3. How many personal computers were manufactured by Dell or HP?

4. How many personal computers were manufactured by Gateway or Acer?

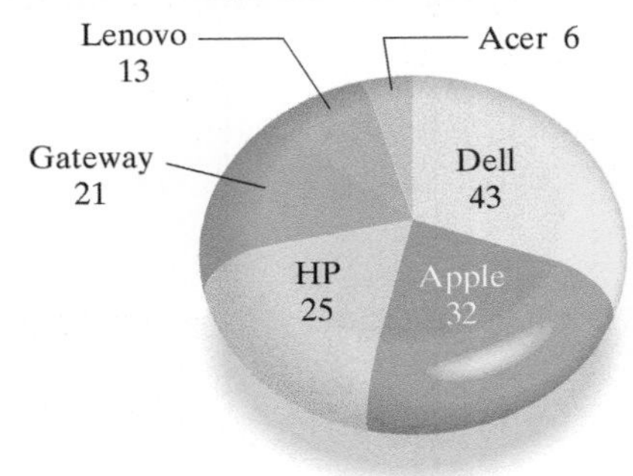

5. What is the ratio of the number of computers manufactured by Lenovo to the number of computers manufactured by Gateway?

6. What is the ratio of the number of computers manufactured by Dell to the number of computers manufactured by Apple?

7. What percent of the 140 computers are manufactured by HP? Round to the nearest tenth.

8. What percent of the computers are manufactured by Apple? Round to the nearest tenth.

College Majors *Bradford College offers majors in six areas: business, science, social science, language arts, education, and art. The distribution by category is displayed in the circle graph below. Use the graph to answer exercises 9–16.*

9. What percent of the students are majoring in business or social science?

10. What percent of the students are majoring in an area other than business?

11. Which area has the least number of students?

12. Which area has the second highest number of students?

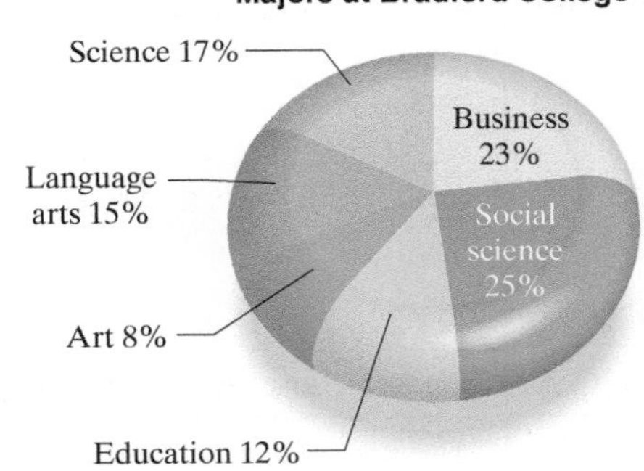

13. Which two areas together make up one-fifth of the graph?

14. If Bradford College has 8000 students, how many of them are majoring in language arts?

15. How many students are majoring in a science (science or social science)?

16. How many more students are majoring in business than education?

Health Expenditures *The following double-bar graph shows the increase of certain health expenditures in Canada from 1975 to 2000. Use the graph to answer exercises 17–24.*

17. How much was spent on drugs in 2000?

18. How much was spent on hospitals in 1980?

19. What was the increase in the amount spent on hospitals from 1985 to 1995?

20. What was the increase in the amount spent on drugs from 1980 to 1990?

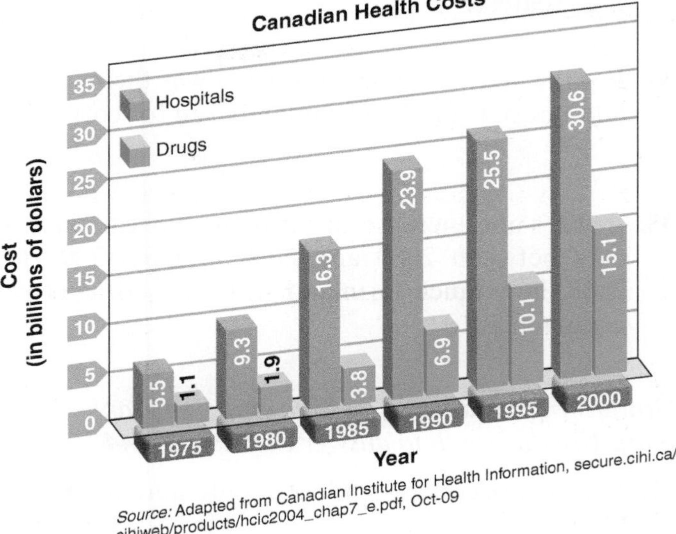

Source: Adapted from Canadian Institute for Health Information, secure.cihi.ca/cihiweb/products/hcic2004_chap7_e.pdf, Oct-09

21. In which five-year period is there the greatest difference in the amount spent on drugs?

22. In which five-year period is there the greatest difference in the amount spent on hospitals?

23. What is the ratio of the amount spent on hospitals to that spent on drugs in 1975?

24. What is the ratio of the amount spent on drugs to that spent on hospitals in 2000?

Crop Production *The following double-bar graph shows the numbers of thousands of hectares of seeded farmland, rounded to the nearest tenth, of canola and corn crops in Canada from 2005 to 2009. Use the bar graph to answer exercises 25–36.*

25. How many hectares were seeded with canola in 2006?

26. How many hectares were seeded with corn in 2008?

27. Between which two years was there the greatest change in farmland for corn?

28. Between which two years was there the greatest change in farmland for canola?

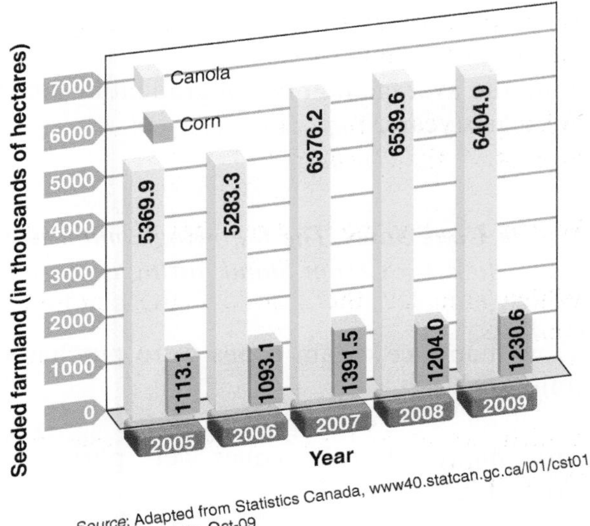

Source: Adapted from Statistics Canada, www40.statcan.gc.ca/l01/cst01/prim11a-eng.htm, Oct-09

29. How many total hectares were seeded with corn or canola in 2007?

30. How many total hectares were seeded with corn or canola in 2009?

31. In which year was the difference between farmland used for corn and farmland used for canola the greatest?

32. In which year was the difference in farmland used for canola and farmland used for corn the smallest?

33. For the years 2005 to 2009, what was the average amount of Canadian farmland used for corn?

34. For the years 2005 to 2009, what was the average amount of Canadian farmland used for canola?

35. If the same increase in farmland for canola occurs between 2009 and 2010 as from 2007 to 2008, how much farmland will be used to grow canola in 2010?

36. If the same decrease in farmland for canola occurs between 2009 and 2010 as from 2008 to 2009, how much farmland will be used to grow canola in 2010?

Graduating Students *The following line graph shows the numbers of graduates of college during the last six years. Use the graph to answer exercises 37–44.*

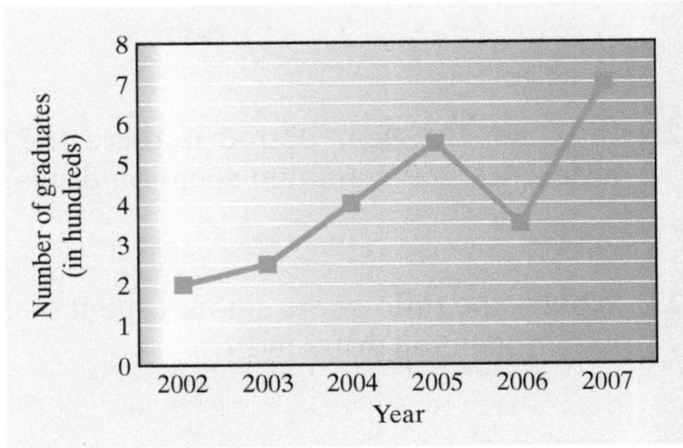

37. How many college students graduated in 2004?

38. How many college students graduated in 2006?

39. How many more college students graduated in 2007 than in 2002?

40. How many fewer college students graduated in 2006 than in 2005?

41. Between what two years was there the smallest increase in the number of graduating students?

42. Between what two years was there a decrease in the number of graduating students?

43. Find the average number of graduating students for all six years.

44. What was the percentage of increase in the number of graduating students from 2004 to 2005?

Ice Cream Cone Sales *The following comparison line graph shows the numbers of ice cream cones purchased at the Junction Ice Cream Stand during a five-month period in 2006 and 2007. Use this graph to answer exercises 45–52.*

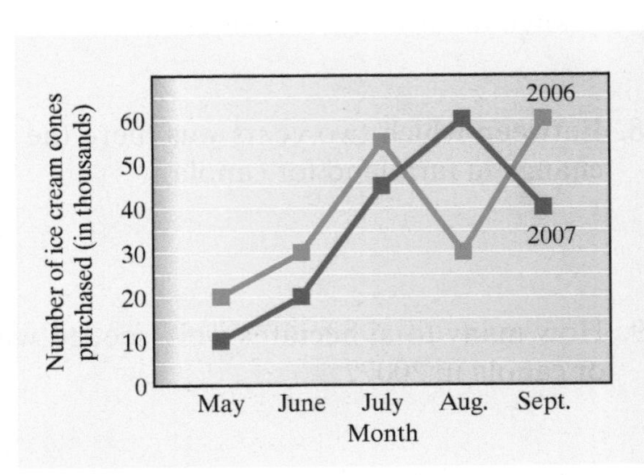

45. How many ice cream cones were purchased in July 2007?

46. How many ice cream cones were purchased in August 2006?

47. How many more ice cream cones were purchased in May 2006 than in May 2007?

48. How many more ice cream cones were purchased in August 2007 than in August 2006?

49. How many total ice cream cones were purchased between May and August of 2006?

50. How many total ice cream cones were purchased between June and September of 2007?

51. At the location of the ice cream stand, July 2006 was warm and sunny, whereas August 2006 was cold and rainy. Describe how the weather might have played a role in the trend shown on the graph from July to August 2006.

52. At the location of the ice cream stand, June 2007 was cold and rainy, whereas July 2007 was warm and sunny. Describe how the weather might have played a role in the trend shown on the graph from June to July 2007.

Doctorate Degrees *The following comparison line graph shows the approximate numbers of doctorate degrees awarded in Canada for humanities and mathematics (including business) for selected years. Use the graph to answer exercises 53–64.*

53. How many humanities doctorate degrees were awarded in 2004?

54. How many mathematics and business doctorate degrees were awarded in 2006?

55. How many more humanities doctorate degrees than mathematics and business doctorate degrees were awarded in 2007?

56. How many fewer humanities doctorate degrees than mathematics and business doctorate degrees were awarded in 2005?

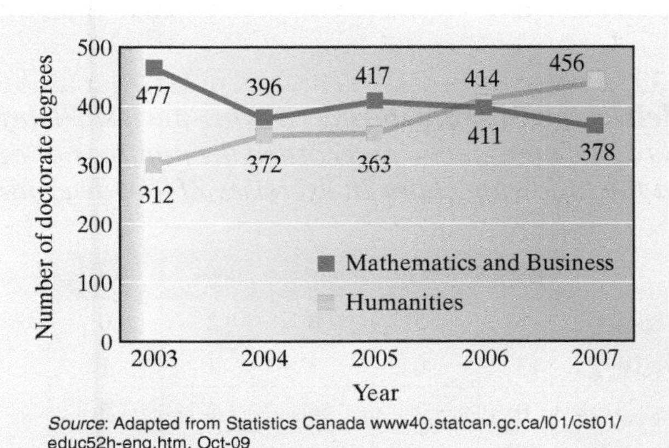

Source: Adapted from Statistics Canada www40.statcan.gc.ca/l01/cst01/educ52h-eng.htm, Oct-09

57. In which years were more humanities than mathematics and business doctorates awarded?

58. In which years were more mathematics and business than humanities doctorates awarded?

59. In which year was approximately the same number of doctorates awarded in each field?

60. Between which years is there the largest decrease in the number of mathematics and business doctorates awarded?

61. Between which years is there the largest increase in the number of humanities doctorates?

62. Where on the graph is there the most dramatic change in any year period?

63. If the number of mathematics and business doctorate degrees increases from 2007 to 2008 the same amount as from 2004 to 2005, how many mathematics and business doctorate degrees will be awarded in 2008?

64. If the same change in the number of humanities doctorate degrees occurs from 2007 to 2009 as from 2004 to 2006, how many humanities doctorate degrees will be awarded in 2009?

Women's Shoe Sales *The following bar graph shows the numbers of pairs of women's shoes sold at the grand opening of a new shoe store. Use the bar graph to answer exercises 65–70.*

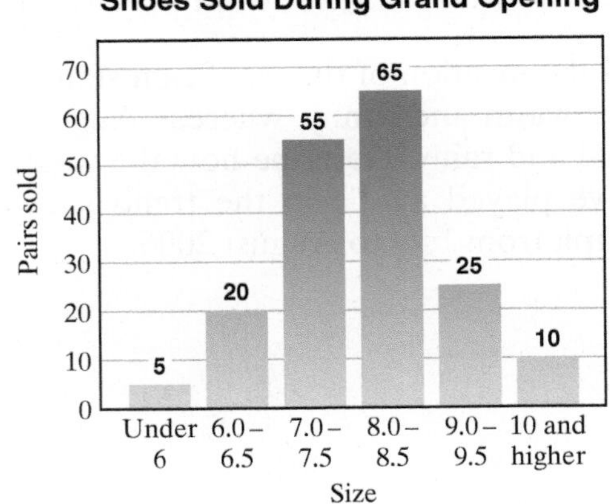

65. How many pairs sold were size 8–8.5?

66. How many pairs sold were size 10 or higher?

67. How many pairs sold were between size 7 and size 9.5?

68. Before the grand opening, the store had 200 pairs of women's shoes. What percent of these were sold during the grand opening?

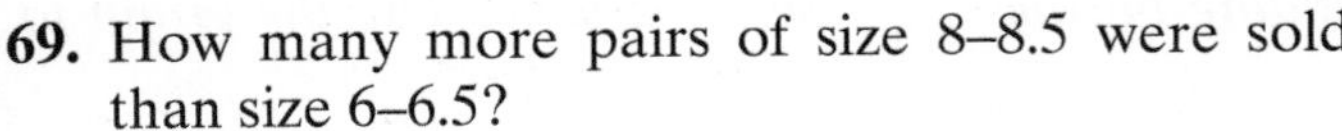

69. How many more pairs of size 8–8.5 were sold than size 6–6.5?

70. What is the ratio of pairs sold of size 9–9.5 to total pairs sold?

Television Manufacturing *During the last 28 days, a major manufacturer produced 400 new television sets each day. The manufacturer recorded the numbers of defective television sets produced each day. The results are shown in the following chart. In exercises 71–75, determine frequencies of the class intervals for this data.*

	Mon.	Tues.	Wed.	Thurs.	Fri.
Week 1	3	5	8	2	0
Week 2	13	6	3	4	1
Week 3	0	2	16	5	7
Week 4	12	10	17	5	4
Week 5	1	7	8	12	13
Week 6	14	0	3	closed	

	Number of Defective Televisions Produced (Class Interval)	Tally	Frequency
71.	0–3	________	______
72.	4–7	________	______
73.	8–11	________	______
74.	12–15	________	______
75.	16–19	________	______

76. Construct a histogram using the table prepared in exercises 71–75.

77. Based on the data of exercises 71–75, how often were between 0 and 7 defective television sets identified in the production?

Find the mean.

78. ***Temperatures in Toronto*** The maximum temperature readings in Toronto for the last seven days in July were: 23 °C, 23 °C, 27 °C, 28 °C, 23 °C, 25 °C, and 28 °C.

79. ***Gas Heating Expenses*** The LeBlanc family's gas bills for January through June were \$145, \$162, \$95, \$67, \$43, and \$26. Round to the nearest cent.

80. ***Visitors at Yellowstone National Park*** The approximate numbers of people who visited Yellowstone National Park from November of 2005 to March of 2006 were: November, 12 000; December, 17 000; January, 24 000; February, 29 000; March, 19 000. Find the mean number of people who visited during a winter month. (*Source:* www.yellowstone-natl-park.com)

81. ***Rental Car Employees*** The numbers of employees throughout the nation employed annually by Freedom Rent a Car for the last six years were 882, 913, 1017, 1592, 1778, and 1936.

Find the median.

82. ***Cost of Trucks*** The costs of eight trucks purchased by the highway department: \$28 500, \$29 300, \$21 690, \$35 000, \$37 000, \$43 600, \$45 300, \$38 600.

83. ***Cost of Houses*** The costs of 10 houses recently purchased at Stillwater: \$98 000, \$150 000, \$120 000, \$139 000, \$170 000, \$156 000, \$135 000, \$144 000, \$154 000, \$126 000.

In exercises 84 and 85, find the median and the mode.

84. ***Toronto Zoo*** The ages of the last 16 people who passed through the entrance of the Toronto Zoo: 28, 30, 15, 54, 77, 79, 10, 8, 43, 38, 28, 31, 4, 7, 34, 35.

85. ***Pizza Deliveries*** The daily numbers of deliveries made by the Northfield House of Pizza: 21, 16, 15, 3, 19, 24, 13, 18, 9, 31, 36, 25, 28, 14, 15, 26.

86. ***Test Scores*** The scores on eight tests taken by Wong Yin in calculus last semester were 96, 98, 88, 100, 31, 89, 94, and 98. Which is a better measure of his usual score, the *mean* or the *median*? Why?

87. ***Sales of Cars*** The 10 salespeople at People's Dodge sold the following numbers of cars last month: 13, 16, 8, 4, 5, 19, 15, 18, 39, 12. Which is a better measure of the usual sales of these salespeople, the *mean* or the *median*? Why?

88. Barbara made a record of the number of hours she uses the computer each day in her apartment.

Day of the Week	Sun.	Mon.	Tues.	Wed.	Thurs.	Fri.	Sat.
Number of Hours Spent on the Computer	2	3	2	4	7	12	5

(a) Find the mean. Round your answer to the nearest tenth if necessary.
(b) Find the median.
(c) Find the mode.
(d) Which of these three measures best represents the number of hours she uses the computer on a typical day? Why?

How Am I Doing? Module Test

A safety commission recently reported the results of inspecting 300 000 automobiles. The following circle graph depicts the percent of automobiles that passed and the percent that had one or more safety violations. Use this graph to answer questions 1–5.

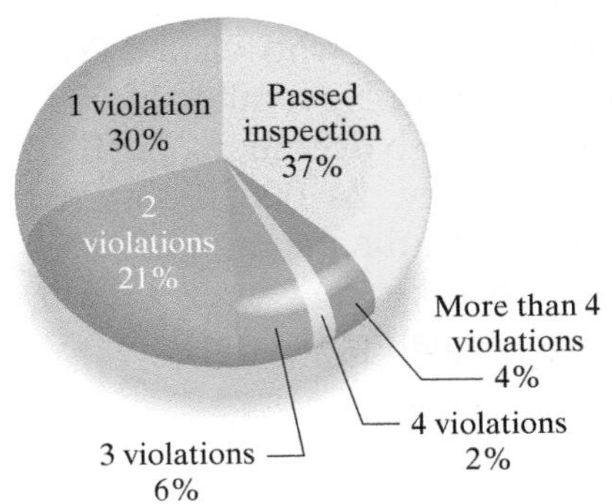

1. What percent of the automobiles passed inspection?

2. What percent of the automobiles had two safety violations?

3. What percent of the automobiles had more than two safety violations?

4. If 300 000 automobiles were inspected, how many of them had one safety violation?

5. If 300 000 automobiles were inspected, how many of them had two violations or three violations?

1. ______

2. ______

3. ______

4. ______

5. ______

The following double-bar graph shows an estimate of how the base college and average university tuition fees have increased per year in Ontario from 1997 to 2001. Use the graph to answer questions 6–11.

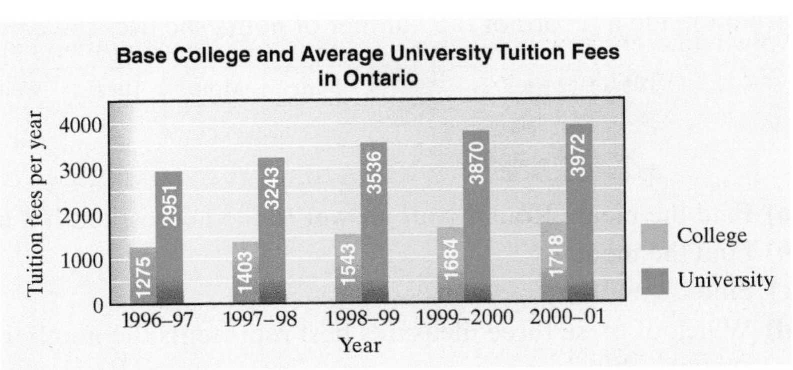

Source: Adapted from The Council On Post Secondary Education, www.copse.mb.ca/en/documents/statistics/ch5_en.pdf, Oct-09

6. What were the tuition fees at an Ontario college in 1997–98?

7. What were the average Ontario university tuition fees in 1999–2000?

8. How much did the average Ontario university tuition fees increase from 1996–97 to 2000–01?

9. How much did the base Ontario college tuition fees increase from 1996–97 to 2000–01?

10. How much more was the tuition at an Ontario university than the tuition at an Ontario college in 1996–97?

11. How much more was the tuition at an Ontario university than the tuition at an Ontario college in 2000–01?

A research study by 10 universities produced the following line graph. Use the graph to answer questions 12–16.

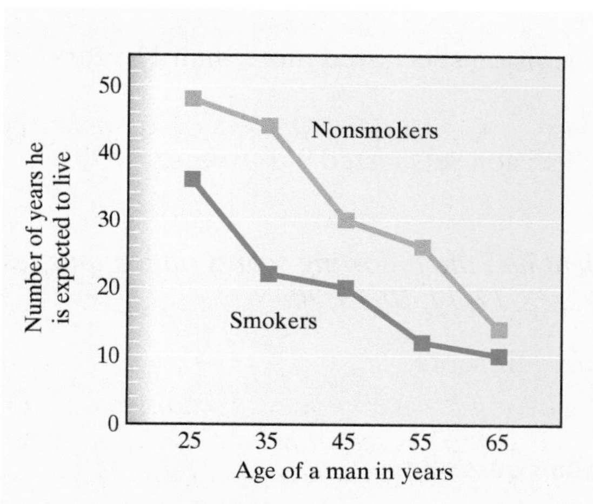

12. Approximately how many more years is a 45-year-old man expected to live if he smokes?

13. Approximately how many more years is a 55-year-old man expected to live if he does not smoke?

14. According to this graph, approximately how much longer is a 25-year-old nonsmoker expected to live than a 25-year-old smoker?

15. According to this graph, at what age is the difference between the life expectancies of a smoker and a nonsmoker the greatest?

6. ______________

7. ______________

8. ______________

9. ______________

10. ______________

11. ______________

12. ______________

13. ______________

14. ______________

15. ______________

16. __________

17. __________

18. __________

19. __________

20. __________

21. __________

22. __________

23. __________

24. __________

16. According to this graph, at what age is the difference between the life expectancies of a smoker and a nonsmoker the smallest?

The following histogram was prepared by a consumer research group. Use the histogram to answer questions 17–20.

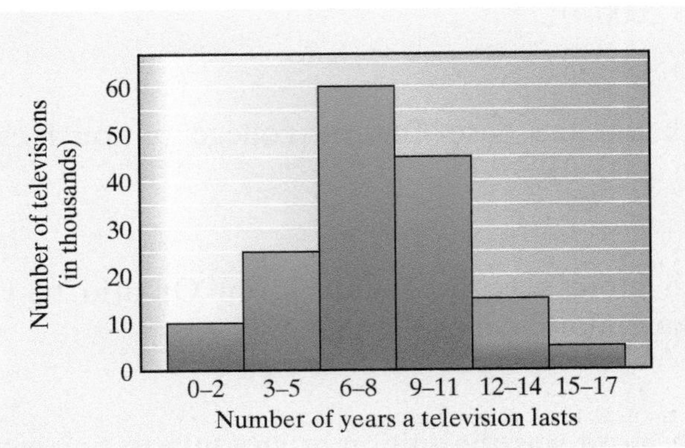

17. How many television sets lasted 6–8 years?

18. How many television sets lasted 3–5 years?

19. How many television sets lasted more than 11 years?

20. How many television sets lasted 9–14 years?

A chemistry student had the following scores on ten quizzes in her chemistry class: 10, 16, 15, 12, 18, 17, 14, 10, 13, 20.

21. Find the mean quiz score.

22. Find the median quiz score.

23. Find the mode quiz score.

24. Which of the values—mean, median, or mode—best represents her typical quiz score?

Solutions to Practice Problems

Section 1 Practice Problems

1. The smallest category of students is part-time international students.
2. **(a)** 1000 full-time + 250 part-time = 1250
   There are 1250 international students
   (b) 1250 out of 48 000 or 2.6% are international students.
   $\frac{1250}{48\,000} = 0.026 = 2.6\%$
3. There are 250 international part-time students and 1000 international full-time students. The ratio of international part-time students to international full-time students is $\frac{250}{1000} = \frac{1}{4}$.
4. The ratio of full-time to part-time students is $\frac{16\,000}{32\,000} = \frac{1}{2}$.
5. Lake Ontario occupies the smallest area with 8%.
6. The percent of the total area occupied by either Lake Superior or Lake Michigan is: 34% + 24% = 58%.
7. Lake Superior has 34% of the area. 34% of 244 060 km^2 is $(0.34)(244\,060 \text{ km}^2) \approx 82\,980 \text{ km}^2$.
8. **(a)** 22% + 18% = 40%
   40% of the graduates represented in the graph are in the fields of health sciences or humanities.
   (b) Take 8% of 134 566.
   (0.08)(134 566) = 10 765
   Approximately 10 765 students graduated from arts and communications programs in 2005.

Section 2 Practice Problems

1. The bar rises to 2527.3. The approximate population was 2 527 300.
2. 11 410 000 − 2 182 900 = 9 227 100. The population increased by 9 227 100.
3. The bar rises to 250. The number of new cars sold in the fourth quarter of 2007 was 250.
4. 150 − 100 = 50. Thus, 50 fewer cars were sold.
5. The greatest number of customers came in July, since the highest point of the graph occurs for July.
6. **(a)** For May, the dot is halfway between 3 and 4, so approximately 3500 customers came during the month of May.
   (b) From March to April, the line goes down, so the number of customers decreased.
7. The line from July to August goes downward at the steepest angle. Thus the greatest decrease occurs between July and August.
8. Because the dot corresponding to 2007–08 is at 20 and the scale is in hundreds, we have 20 × 100 = 2000. Thus, 2000 degrees in visual and performing arts were awarded.
9. The computer science line goes above the visual and performing arts line first in 2002–03. Thus the first academic year with more degrees in computer science was 2002–03.

Section 3 Practice Problems

1. The 60–69 bar rises to a height of 6. Thus six students would have a D grade.
2. From the histogram, 16 tests were 70–79, 8 tests were 80–89, and 6 tests were 90–99. When we combine 16 + 8 + 6 = 30, we can see that 30 students scored greater than 69 on the test.
3. The 800–999 bar rises to a height of 20. Thus 20 light bulbs lasted between 800 and 999 hours.
4. From the histogram, 25 bulbs lasted 1200–1399 hours, 10 lasted 1400–1599 hours, and 5 lasted 1600–1799 hours. When we combine 25 + 10 + 5 = 40, we can see that 40 light bulbs lasted more than 1199 hours.
5. **Weight in Kilograms**

(Class Interval)	Tally	Frequency
1600–1799	||	2
1800–1999	||||	4
2000–2199	||||	4
2200–2399	~~||||~~	5

6.

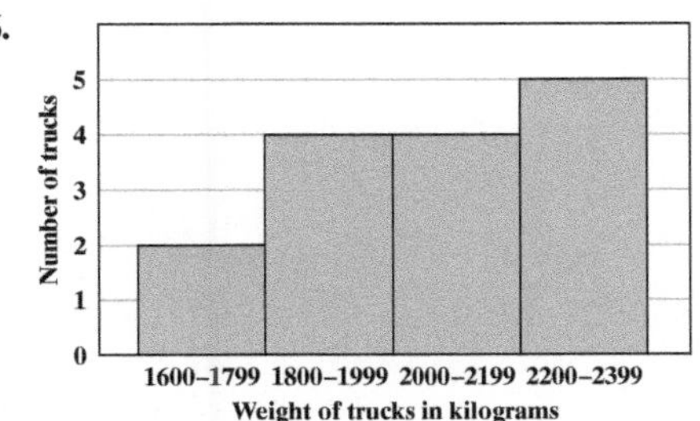

7. The greatest difference occurs between the 35–54 age category and the 55–64 category.

Section 4 Practice Problems

1. $\frac{\$39.20 + \$43.50 + \$81.90 + \$34.20 + \$51.70 + \$48.10}{6} \approx \$49.77$

   The mean monthly phone bill is $49.77.

2. $150, $150, $290 (three numbers) — $320 (middle number) — $400, $450, $600 (three numbers)

   Thus, $320 is the median salary.

3. 88, 90 (two numbers) — 100, 105 (two middle numbers) — 118, 126 (two numbers)

   $\frac{100 + 105}{2} = \frac{205}{2} = 102.5$

   The median is 102.5.

4. The value 71 occurs twice. The mode is 71 inches.
5. Arrange the values in order from smallest to largest.
   2, 3, 3, 3, 5, 8, 8, 12, 14, 15, 16, 27, 28, 28, 31, 33
   The values 3, 8, and 28 repeat. Since the value 3 occurs three times, while 8 and 28 both occur only twice, the mode is 3.

Glossary

Mean (Section 4) The mean of a set of values is the sum of the values divided by the number of values. The mean of the numbers 10, 11, 14, and 15 is 12.5. In everyday language, when people use the word *average,* they are usually referring to the mean.

Median (Section 4) If a set of numbers is arranged in order from smallest to largest, the median is that value that has the same number of values above it as below it. The median of the numbers 3, 7, and 8 is 7. If the list contains an even number of items, we obtain the median by finding the mean of the two middle numbers. The median of the numbers 5, 6, 10, and 11 is 8.

Mode (Section 4) The mode of a set of data is the number or numbers that occur most often.

Answers to Selected Exercises for Statistics

Answers to Selected Exercises for Statistics

Section 1 Exercises **1.** Multiply 25% × 4000, which is 0.25 × 4000 = 1000 students **3.** Divide the circle into quarters by drawing two perpendicular lines. Shade in one quarter of the circle. Label this with the title "Within five kilometres = 1000." **5.** rent **7.** \$200 **9.** \$800 **11.** $\frac{13}{4}$ **13.** $\frac{10}{27}$ **15.** 80 years or older **17.** 3 116 500 people **19.** 26 941 600 people **21.** $\frac{169\,499}{143\,615}$ **23.** $\frac{13\,089}{55\,519}$ **25.** 19% **27.** reasonable prices and great food **29.** 343 people **31.** 7 250 400 vehicles **33.** 25.8% **35.** 74.2% **37.** 10 761 600 vehicles

Quick Quiz 1 **1.** 36% **2.** 272 360 vehicles **3.** 485 512 vehicles **4.** See Instructor

Section 2 Exercises **1.** 8 625 107 people **3.** 1986 and 1991 **5.** 12 869 824 **7.** \$4800 **9.** \$4100 **11.** 2000–01 **13.** \$500 **15.** \$32 800 **17.** 31.25% **19.** \$1.1 million or \$1 100 000 **21.** 1993 to 1995 and 2003 to 2005 **23.** \$0.5 million or \$500 000 **25.** about 80 mm **27.** May, June, and September **29.** about 185 mm

Quick Quiz 2 **1.** 800 condominiums **2.** 800 homes **3.** 1995 **4.** See Instructor

How Am I Doing? Sections 1–2 **1.** 10% (obj. 1.2) **2.** Niagara Falls and Harbourfront Centre, Toronto (obj. 1.2) **3.** 31% (obj. 1.2) **4.** about 11 814 000 visitors (obj. 1.2) **5.** about 18 795 000 visitors (obj. 1.2) **6.** 450 housing starts (obj. 2.2) **7.** 550 housing starts (obj. 2.2) **8.** during the fourth quarter of 2006 (obj. 2.2) **9.** during the third quarter of 2007 (obj. 2.2) **10.** 250 more housing starts (obj. 2.2) **11.** 150 fewer housing starts (obj. 2.2) **12.** Aug. and Dec. (obj. 2.4) **13.** Dec. (obj. 2.4) **14.** Nov. (obj. 2.4) **15. (a)** 20 000 sets (obj. 2.4) **(b)** 35 000 sets (obj. 2.4)

Section 3 Exercises **1.** The horizontal label for each item in a bar graph is usually a single number or a word title. For the histogram it is a class interval. The vertical bars have a space between them in the bar graph. For the histogram, the vertical bars touch each other. **3.** A class frequency is the number of times a score occurs in a particular class interval. **5.** 12 cities **7.** 3 cities **9.** 9 cities **11.** 21 cities **13.** 8000 books **15.** books costing \$5.00–\$7.99 **17.** 28 000 books **19.** 52 000 books **21.** 28.6%

	Tally	Frequency
23.	||	2
25.	|||	3
27.	||||	4
29.	|||	3

31.

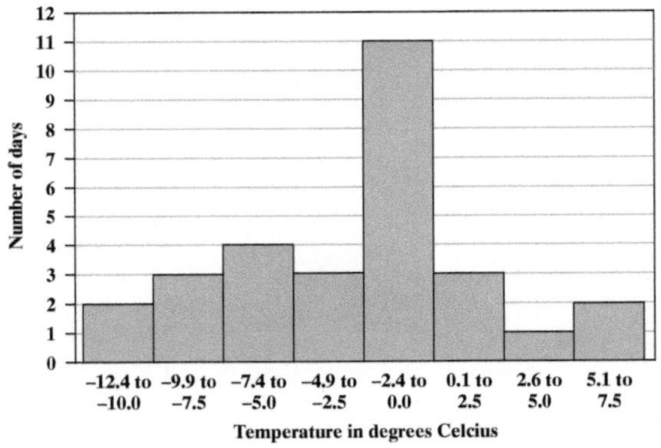

Number of days

0 1 2 3 4 5 6 7 8 9 10 11 12

−12.4 to −10.0 | −9.9 to −7.5 | −7.4 to −5.0 | −4.9 to −2.5 | −2.4 to 0.0 | 0.1 to 2.5 | 2.6 to 5.0 | 5.1 to 7.5

Temperature in degrees Celcius

33. 9 days **34.** m = 138.32 **35.** n = 7 **36.** 615 mi **37.** 13.0 in.

Quick Quiz 3 **1.** 700 people **2.** 2000 people **3.** 500 more people **4.** See Instructor

Section 4 Exercises **1.** The median of a set of numbers when they are arranged in order from smallest to largest is that value that has the same number of values above it as below it. The mean of a set of values is the sum of the values divided by the number of values. The mean is most likely to be not typical of the values you would expect if there are many extremely low values or many extremely high values. The median is more likely to be typical of the value you would expect. **3.** 32 customers **5.** 44.74 mm **7.** 0.375 **9.** 13 200 **11.** 11.9 km/L **13.** 195 **15.** 12 **17.** \$37 025 **19.** 21 **21.** \$207 **23.** 2.2 **25.** \$24.475 billion or \$24 475 000 000 **27.** \$69 161.88 **29.** 4850 **31.** mean ≈ \$104.74; median = \$80.95 **33.** 60 **35.** 121 and 150 **37.** \$269 **39.** mean ≈ 81.4 yr; median = 81.2 yr; mode = 80.5 yr **41. (a)** \$2157 **(b)** \$1615 **(c)** There is no mode. **(d)** The median because the mean is affected by the high amount, \$6300. **43. (a)** 8.4 phone calls **(b)** 7 phone calls **(c)** 3 phone calls **(d)** The median. On three nights she gets more calls than 7. On 3 nights she gets fewer calls than 7. On one night she got 7 calls. The mean is distorted a little because of the very large number of calls on Sunday night. The mode is artificially low because she gets so few calls on Monday and Wednesday and it just happened to be the same number, 3.

Quick Quiz 4 **1.** 11.5 times **2.** 13.2 times **3.** 8 times **4.** See Instructor

Putting Your Skills to Work **1.** \$12.30 **2.** \$18.45 3. \$221.40 **4.** Answers may vary **5.** Answers may vary **6.** \$160 **7.** \$2100 **8.** \$189 **9.** \$378 **10.** about 17.6 °C

Module Review Problems **1.** 13 computers **2.** 32 computers **3.** 68 computers **4.** 27 computers **5.** $\frac{13}{21}$ **6.** $\frac{43}{32}$ **7.** ≈17.9% **8.** ≈22.9% **9.** 48% **10.** 77% **11.** art **12.** business **13.** art and education **14.** 1200 students **15.** 3360 students **16.** 880 students **17.** $15.1 billion or $15 100 000 000 **18.** $9.3 billion or $9 300 000 000 **19.** $9.2 billion or $9 200 000 000 **20.** $5 billion or $5 000 000 000 **21.** 1995 to 2000 **22.** 1985 to 1990 **23.** $\frac{5}{1}$ or 5 **24.** $\frac{151}{306}$ **25.** 5 283 300 hectares **26.** 1 204 000 hectares **27.** 2006 to 2007 **28.** 2006 to 2007 **29.** 7 767 700 hectares **30.** 7 634 600 hectares **31.** 2008 **32.** 2006 **33.** 1 206 460 hectares **34.** 5 994 600 hectares **35.** 6 567 400 hectares **36.** 6 268 400 hectares **37.** 400 students **38.** 350 students **39.** 500 students **40.** 200 students **41.** 2002–03 **42.** 2005–06 **43.** about 408 students **44.** 37.5% **45.** 45 000 cones **46.** 30 000 cones **47.** 10 000 cones **48.** 30 000 cones **49.** 135 000 cones **50.** 165 000 cones **51.** The sharp drop in the number of ice cream cones purchased from July 2006 to August 2006 is probably directly related to the weather. Since August was cold and rainy, significantly fewer people wanted ice cream during August. **52.** The sharp increase in the number of ice cream cones purchased from June 2007 to July 2007 is probably directly related to the weather. Since June was cold and rainy and July was warm and sunny, significantly more people wanted ice cream during July. **53.** 372 degrees **54.** 411 degrees **55.** 78 degrees **56.** 54 degrees **57.** 2006 (barely) and 2007 **58.** 2003, 2004, 2005 **59.** 2006 **60.** 2003 to 2004 **61.** 2003 to 2004 **62.** 2003 to 2004 had the most dramatic changes for both fields **63.** 399 degrees **64.** 498 degrees **65.** 65 pairs **66.** 10 pairs **67.** 145 pairs **68.** 90% **69.** 45 pairs **70.** 5 to 36; or $\frac{5}{36}$

	Number of Defective Televisions (Class Intervals)	Tally	Frequency
71.	0–3	卌 卌	10
72.	4–7	卌 |||	8
73.	8–11	|||	3
74.	12–15	卌	5
75.	16–19	||	2

76.

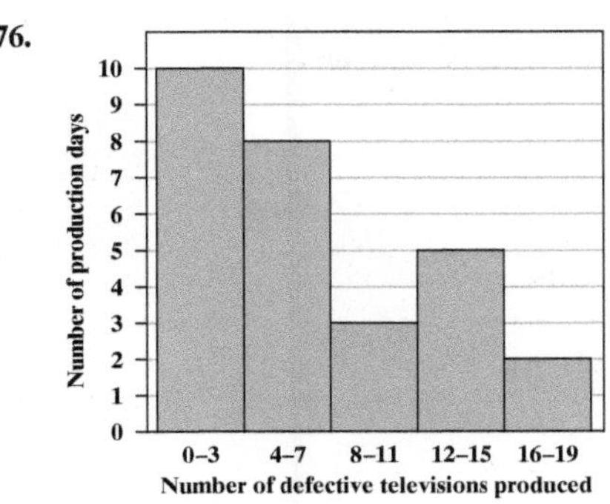

77. 18 times **78.** 25.3 °C **79.** $89.67 **80.** 20 200 people **81.** 1353 employees **82.** $36 000 **83.** $141 500

84. median = 30.5 years; mode = 28 years **85.** median = 18.5 deliveries; mode = 15 deliveries **86.** The median is better because the mean is skewed by the one low score, 31. **87.** The median is better because the mean is skewed by the one high data item, 39. **88. (a)** 5 h **(b)** 4 h **(c)** 2 h **(d)** The mean is the most representative. On three days she uses the computer more than 4 hours and on three days she uses the computer less than 4 hours. One day she used it exactly 7 hours. The mean is distorted a little because of the very large number of hours on Friday. The mode is artificially low because she happened to use the computer only two hours on Sunday and Tuesday. All other days it was more than this.

How Am I Doing? Module Test **1.** 37% (obj. 1.2) **2.** 21% (obj. 1.2) **3.** 12% (obj. 1.2) **4.** 90 000 automobiles (obj. 1.2) **5.** 81 000 automobiles (obj. 1.2) **6.** $1403 (obj. 2.2) **7.** $3870 (obj. 2.2) **8.** $1021 (obj. 2.2) **9.** $443 (obj. 2.2) **10.** $1676 (obj. 2.2) **12.** $2254 (obj. 2.2) **12.** 20 yr (obj. 2.4) **13.** 26 yr (obj. 2.4) **14.** 12 yr (obj. 2.4) **15.** age 35 (obj. 2.4) **16.** age 65 (obj. 2.4) **17.** 60 000 televisions (obj. 3.1) **18.** 25 000 televisions (obj. 3.1) **19.** 20 000 televisions (obj. 3.1) **20.** 60 000 televisions (obj. 3.1) **21.** 14.5 (obj. 4.1) **22.** 14.5 (obj. 4.2) **23.** 10 (obj. 4.3) **24.** mean or median (obj. 4.3)

Signed Numbers

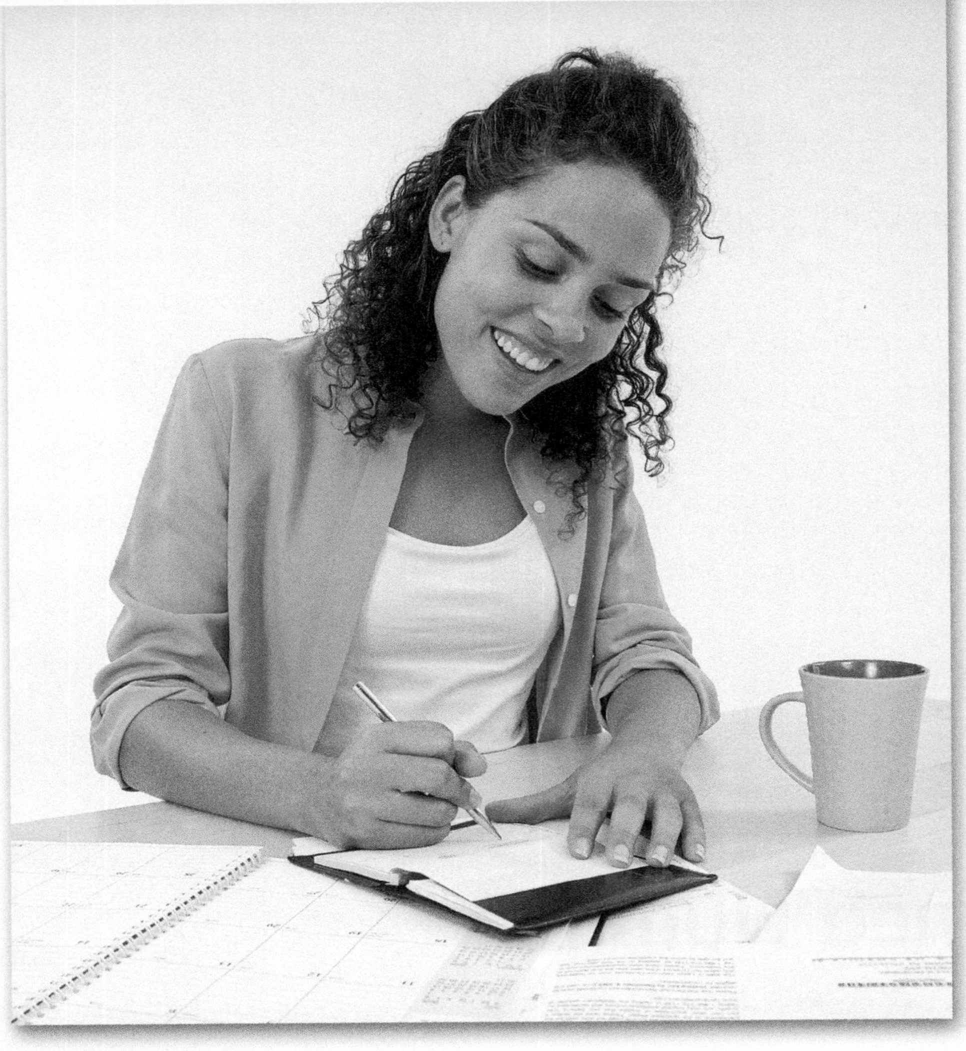

Comstock Complete

Keeping track of positive and negative balances becomes a very important task in the life of anyone who has a bank or investment account. In this module, you will become more proficient in the use of positive and negative numbers. If you master this material, it will save you money and help you avoid costly mistakes in your financial decisions.

Signed Numbers

SECTION 1 ADDING SIGNED NUMBERS

 Adding Two Signed Numbers with the Same Sign

Student Learning Objectives

After studying this section, you will be able to:

 **Add two signed numbers with the same sign.**

 **Add two signed numbers with different signs.**

 **Add three or more signed numbers.**

We have worked with whole numbers, fractions, and decimals. In this module we enlarge the set of numbers we work with to include numbers that are less than zero. Many real-life situations require using numbers that are less than zero. A debt that is owed, a financial loss, temperatures that fall below zero, and elevations that are below sea level can be expressed only in numbers that are less than zero, or negative numbers.

The following is a graph of the financial reports of four small airlines for the year. It shows **positive numbers**—those numbers that rise above zero—and **negative numbers**—those numbers that fall below zero. The positive numbers represent money gained. The negative numbers represent money lost.

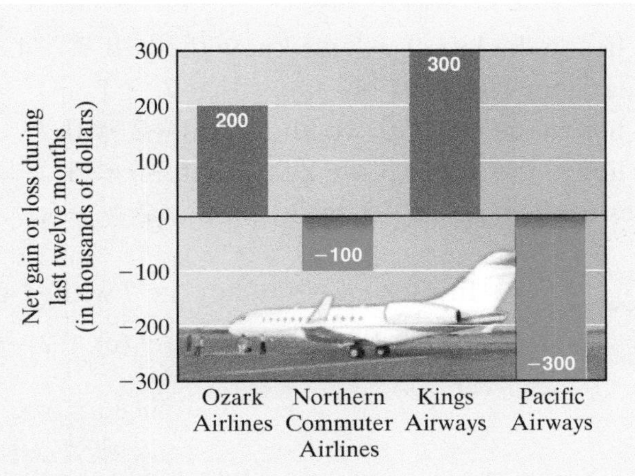

A value of −100 000 is shown for Northern Commuter Airlines. This means that Northern Commuter Airlines lost \$100 000 during the year. A value of −300 000 is recorded for Pacific Airways. What does this mean?

Another way to picture positive and negative numbers is on a number line. A **number line** is a line on which each number is associated with a point. The numbers may be positive or negative, whole numbers, fractions, or decimals. Positive numbers are to the right of zero on the number line. Negative numbers are to the left of zero on the number line. Zero is neither positive nor negative.

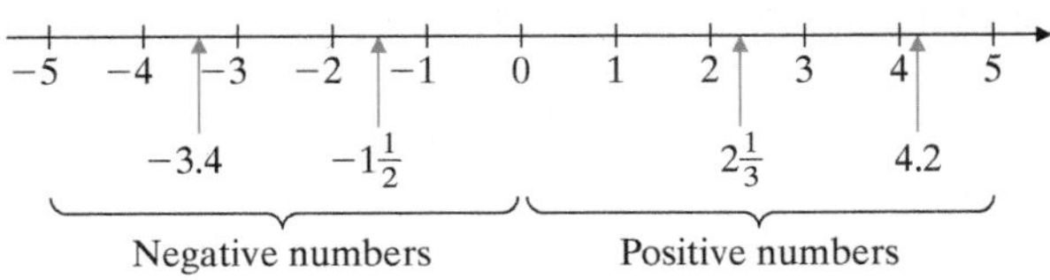

Positive numbers can be written with a plus sign—for example, +2—but this is not usually done. Positive 2 is usually written as 2. It is understood that the *sign* of the number is positive although it is not written. Negative numbers must always have the negative sign so that we know they are negative numbers. Negative 2 is written as −2. The *sign* of the number is negative. The set of positive numbers, negative numbers, and zero is called the set of **signed numbers.**

Order Signed numbers are named in **order** on the number line. Smaller numbers are to the left. Larger numbers are to the right. For any two numbers on the number line, the number on the left is less than the number on the right.

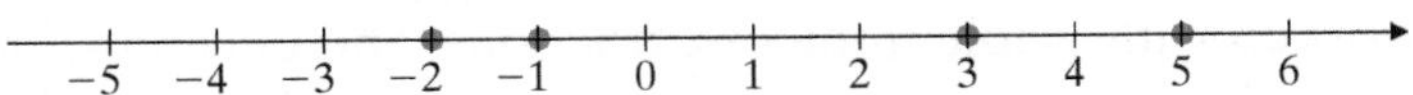

We use the symbol $<$ to mean "is less than." Thus the mathematical sentence $-2 < -1$ means "-2 is less than -1." We use the symbol $>$ to mean "is greater than." Thus the mathematical sentence $5 > 3$ means "5 is greater than 3."

EXAMPLE 1 In each case, replace the ? with $<$ or $>$.

(a) $-8 \ ? -4$ **(b)** $7 \ ? \ 1$ **(c)** $-2 \ ? \ 0$

(d) $-6 \ ? \ 3$ **(e)** $2 \ ? -5$

Solution

(a) Since -8 lies to the left of -4, we know that $-8 < -4$.

(b) Since 7 lies to the right of 1, we know that $7 > 1$.

(c) Since -2 lies to the left of 0, we know that $-2 < 0$.

(d) Since -6 lies to the left of 3, we know that $-6 < 3$.

(e) Since 2 lies to the right of -5, we know that $2 > -5$.

NOTE TO STUDENT: Fully worked-out solutions to all of the Practice Problems can be found at the end of the module.

Practice Problem 1 In each case, replace the ? with $<$ or $>$.

(a) $4 \ ? \ 2$ **(b)** $-5 \ ? -3$ **(c)** $0 \ ? -6$

(d) $-2 \ ? \ 1$ **(e)** $5 \ ? -7$

Absolute Value Sometimes we are only interested in the distance a number is from zero. For example, the distance from 0 to $+3$ is 3. The distance from 0 to -3 is also 3. Notice that distance is always a positive number, regardless of which direction we travel on the number line. This distance is called the *absolute value.*

The **absolute value** of a number is the distance between that number and zero on the number line.

The symbol for absolute value is $| \ |$. When we write $|5|$, we are looking for the distance from 0 to 5 on the number line. Thus $|5| = 5$. This is read, "The absolute value of 5 is 5." $|-5|$ is the distance from 0 to -5 on the number line. Thus $|-5| = 5$. This is read, "The absolute value of -5 is 5."

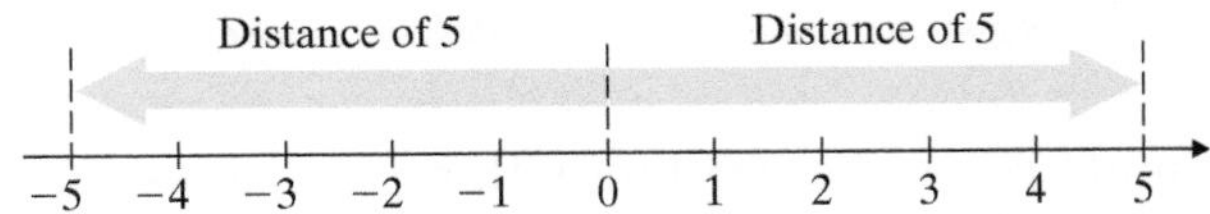

Other examples of absolute value are shown next.

$$|6| = 6 \qquad |-3| = 3$$

$$|7.2| = 7.2 \qquad \left|-\frac{1}{5}\right| = \frac{1}{5}$$

$$|0| = 0 \qquad |-26| = 26$$

When we find the absolute value of any nonzero number, we always get a positive value. We use the concept of absolute value to develop rules for adding signed numbers. We begin by looking at addition of numbers with the same sign. Although you are already familiar with the addition of positive numbers, we will look at an example.

Suppose that we earn \$52 one day and earn \$38 the next day. To learn what our two-day total is, we add the positive numbers. We earn

$$\$52 + \$38 = +\$90.$$

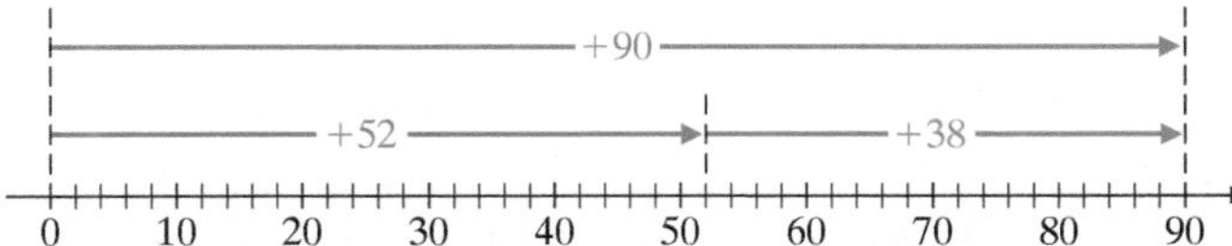

We can show this sum on a number line by drawing an arrow that starts at 0 and points 52 units to the right (because 52 is positive). At the end of this arrow we draw a second arrow that points 38 units to the right. Note that the second arrow ends at the sum, 90.

The money is coming in, and the plus sign records a gain. Notice that we added the numbers and that the sign of the sum is the same as the sign of the addends.

Now let's consider an example of addition of two negative numbers.

Suppose that we consider money spent as negative dollars. If we spend \$52 one day ($-\$52$) and we spend \$38 the next day ($-\$38$), we must add two negative numbers. What is our financial position?

$$-\$52 + (-\$38) = -\$90$$

We have spent \$90. The negative sign tells us the direction of the money: out. Notice that we added the numbers and that the sign of the sum is the same as the sign of the addends.

We can illustrate this sum on a number line by drawing a line that starts at 0 and points 52 units to the left (because -52 is negative). At the end of this arrow we add a second arrow that points 38 units to the left. This second arrow ends at the sum, -90.

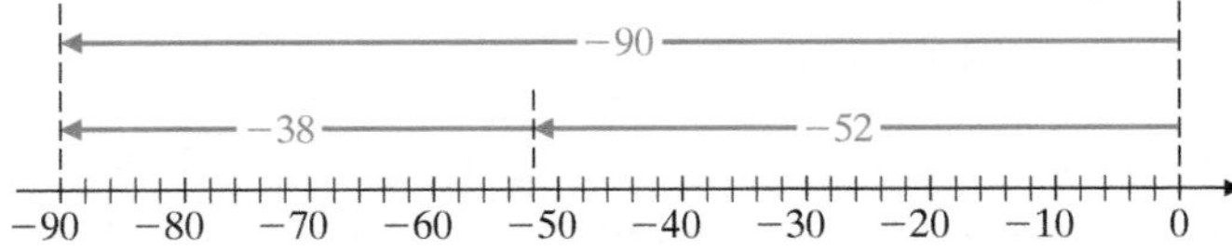

These examples suggest the addition rule for two numbers with the same sign.

ADDITION RULE FOR TWO NUMBERS WITH THE SAME SIGN

To add two numbers with the same sign:

1. Add the absolute values of the numbers.

2. Use the common sign in the answer.

EXAMPLE 2 Add. **(a)** $7 + 5$ **(b)** $-3.2 + (-5.6)$

Solution

(a)
$$\begin{array}{r} 7 \\ +\ 5 \\ \hline 12 \end{array}$$
We add the absolute values of the numbers 7 and 5. The positive sign, although not written, is common to both numbers. The answer is a positive 12. (The + sign is not written.)

(b)
$$\begin{array}{r} -3.2 \\ +\ -5.6 \\ \hline -8.8 \end{array}$$
We add the absolute values of the numbers 3.2 and 5.6.

We use a negative sign in our answer because we added two negative numbers.

NOTE TO STUDENT: Fully worked-out solutions to all of the Practice Problems can be found at the end of the module.

Practice Problem 2 Add. **(a)** $9 + 14$ **(b)** $-4.5 + (-1.9)$

These rules can be applied to fractions as well.

EXAMPLE 3 Add. **(a)** $\frac{5}{18} + \frac{1}{3}$ **(b)** $-\frac{1}{7} + \left(-\frac{3}{5}\right)$

Solution

(a) The LCD = 18. The first fraction already has the LCD.

$$\begin{array}{rcr} \frac{5}{18} & = & \frac{5}{18} \\ +\ \frac{1}{3} \times \frac{6}{6} & = & +\frac{6}{18} \\ \hline & & \frac{11}{18} \end{array}$$

We add two positive numbers, so the answer is positive.

(b) The LCD = 35.

$$\frac{1}{7} \times \frac{5}{5} = \frac{5}{35}$$

Because $\frac{1}{7} = \frac{5}{35}$ it follows that $-\frac{1}{7} = -\frac{5}{35}$.

$$\frac{3}{5} \times \frac{7}{7} = \frac{21}{35}$$

Because $\frac{3}{5} = \frac{21}{35}$ it follows that $-\frac{3}{5} = -\frac{21}{35}$. Thus

$$\begin{array}{r} -\frac{1}{7} \\ +\ -\frac{3}{5} \\ \hline \end{array} \quad \text{is equivalent to} \quad \begin{array}{r} -\frac{5}{35} \\ +\ -\frac{21}{35} \\ \hline -\frac{26}{35} \end{array}$$

We add two negative numbers, so the answer is negative.

It can also be written by adding $\left(\frac{-5}{35}\right) + \left(\frac{-21}{35}\right)$ to get $\frac{-26}{35}$. The negative sign can be placed in the numerator or in front of the fraction bar.

Practice Problem 3 Add.

(a) $\frac{5}{12} + \frac{1}{4}$ **(b)** $-\frac{1}{6} + \left(-\frac{2}{7}\right)$

NOTE TO STUDENT: Fully worked-out solutions to all of the Practice Problems can be found at the end of the module.

It is interesting to see how often negative numbers appear in fiscal budgets. An important comparison is the budget deficit/surplus compared to the gross domestic product (GDP). Observe the data for Canada in the bar graph at the right.

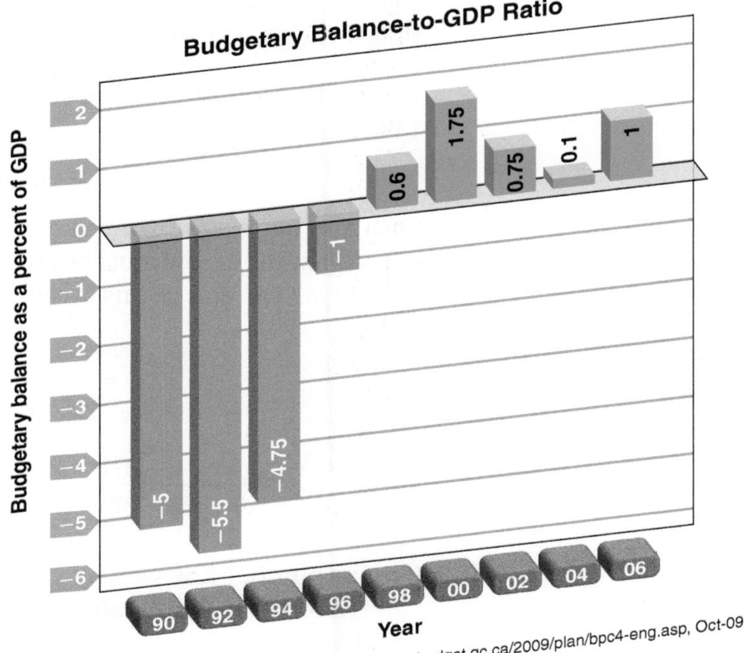

EXAMPLE 4 Find the average percent budgetary balance-to-GDP ratio for 1998 and 2000.

Solution We add 0.6% + 1.75% to obtain 2.35%. We then divide by 2 to get the average of 1.175%.

The average percent budgetary balance-to-GDP ratio for those two years is 1.18%.

Practice Problem 4 Find the total of the percent budgetary balance-to-GDP ratios for the years 1998, 2000, 2002, 2004, and 2006.

2 Adding Two Signed Numbers with Different Signs

Let's look at some real-life situations involving addition of signed numbers with different signs. Suppose that we earn \$52 one day and we spend \$38 the next day. If we combine (add) the two transactions, it would look like

$$\$52 + (-\$38) = +\$14.$$

On a number line we draw an arrow that starts at zero and points 52 units to the right. From the end of this arrow we draw an arrow that points 38 units to the left. (Remember, the arrow points to the left for a negative number.)

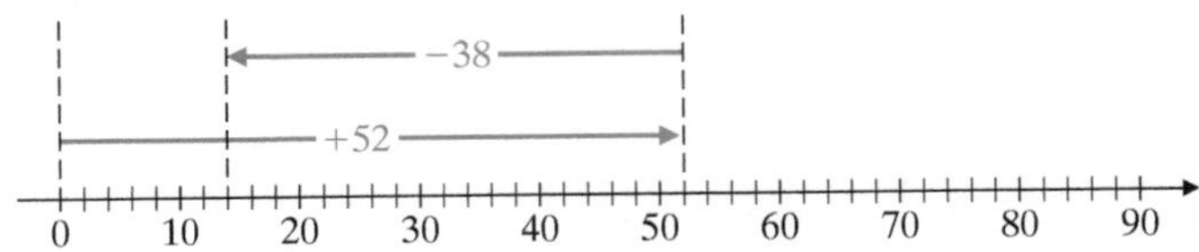

This is a situation with which we are familiar. What we actually do is subtract. That is, we take the difference between \$52 and \$38. Notice that the sign of the larger number is positive and that the sign of the answer is also positive.

Let's look at another situation. Suppose we spend \$52, and we earn \$38. The situation would look like this.

$$(-\$52) + \$38 = -\$14$$

On a number line we draw an arrow that starts at zero and points 52 units to the left. Again the arrow must point to the left to represent a negative number.

From the end of this arrow we draw an arrow that points 38 units to the right.

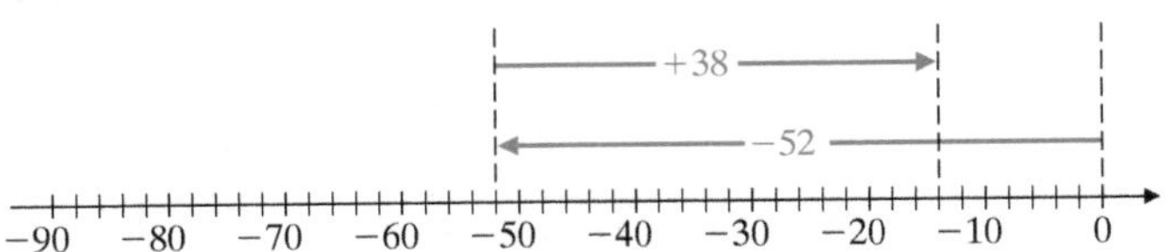

On our number line we end up at −14.

In our real-life situation we end up owing \$14, which is represented by a negative number. To find the sum, we actually find the difference between \$52 and \$38. Notice that if we do not account for sign, the larger number is 52. The sign of that number is negative and the sign of the answer is also negative. This suggests the addition rule for two numbers with different signs.

ADDITION RULE FOR TWO NUMBERS WITH DIFFERENT SIGNS

To add two numbers with different signs:

1. Subtract the absolute values of the numbers.
2. Use the sign of the number with the larger absolute value.

EXAMPLE 5 Add.

(a) $8 + (-10)$ **(b)** $-16.6 + 12.3$ **(c)** $\frac{3}{4} + \left(-\frac{2}{3}\right)$

Solution

(a)

$$\begin{array}{r} 8 \\ + -10 \\ \hline -2 \end{array}$$

−2 ⟵ The signs are different, so we find the difference: $10 - 8 = 2$.

↑ The sign of the number with the larger absolute value is negative, so the answer is negative.

(b)

$$\begin{array}{r} -16.6 \\ +\ \ 12.3 \\ \hline -4.3 \end{array}$$

← The signs are different, so we find the difference.

The sign of the number with the larger absolute value is negative, so the answer is negative.

(c) $\frac{3}{4} + \left(-\frac{2}{3}\right) = \frac{9}{12} + \left(-\frac{8}{12}\right) = \frac{9 + (-8)}{12} = \frac{1}{12}$

The signs are different, so we find the difference. The sign of the number with the larger absolute value is positive, so the answer is positive.

Practice Problem 5 Add.

(a) $7 + (-12)$ **(b)** $-20.8 + 15.2$ **(c)** $\frac{5}{6} + \left(-\frac{3}{4}\right)$

NOTE TO STUDENT: Fully worked-out solutions to all of the Practice Problems can be found at the end of the module.

Notice that in **(b)** of Example 5, the number with the larger absolute value is on top. This makes the numbers easier to subtract. Because addition is commutative, we could have written **(a)** as

$$\begin{array}{r} -10 \\ +\ \ \ 8 \\ \hline \end{array}.$$

This makes the computation easier. If you are adding two numbers with different signs, place the number with the larger absolute value on top so that you can find the difference easily. As noted, the commutative property of addition holds for signed numbers.

COMMUTATIVE PROPERTY OF ADDITION

For any signed numbers a and b,

$$a + b = b + a.$$

EXAMPLE 6 Last night the temperature dropped to −4 °C. From that low, today the temperature rose 16 °C. What was the high temperature today?

Solution We want to add −4 °C and 16 °C. Because addition is commutative, it does not matter whether we add $-4 + 16$ or $16 + (-4)$.

$$\begin{array}{r} 16\ °\text{C} \\ +\ -4\ °\text{C} \\ \hline 12\ °\text{C} \end{array}$$

← The 16 is larger than 4. The difference between 16 and 4 is 12. The number with the larger absolute value is positive, so the answer is positive.

Practice Problem 6 Last night the temperature dropped to −9 °C. From that low, today the temperature rose 13 °C. What was the high temperature today?

Adding Three or More Signed Numbers

We can add three or more numbers using these rules. Since addition is associative, we may group the numbers to be added in reverse order. That is, it does not matter which two numbers are added first.

EXAMPLE 7 Add. $24 + (-16) + (-10)$

Solution We can go from left to right and start with 24, or we can start with -16.

Step 1
$$\begin{array}{r} 24 \\ + \ -16 \\ \hline 8 \end{array}$$
or
Step 1
$$\begin{array}{r} -16 \\ + \ -10 \\ \hline -26 \end{array}$$

Step 2
$$\begin{array}{r} 8 \\ + \ -10 \\ \hline -2 \end{array}$$
Step 2
$$\begin{array}{r} -26 \\ + \ 24 \\ \hline -2 \end{array}$$

Practice Problem 7 Add. $36 + (-21) + (-18)$

ASSOCIATIVE PROPERTY OF ADDITION

For any three real numbers a, b, and c,

$$(a + b) + c = a + (b + c).$$

If there are many numbers to add, it may be easier to add the positive numbers and the negative numbers separately and then combine the results.

EXAMPLE 8 The results of a new company's operations over five months are listed in the following table. What is the company's overall profit or loss over the five-month period?

Net Operations Profit/Loss Statement in Dollars

Month	Profit	Loss
January	30 000	
February		−50 000
March		−10 000
April	20 000	
May	15 000	

Solution First we will add separately the positive numbers and the negative numbers.

$$\begin{array}{r} 30\,000 \\ 20\,000 \\ +\,15\,000 \\ \hline 65\,000 \end{array} \qquad \begin{array}{r} -50\,000 \\ + \ -10\,000 \\ \hline -60\,000 \end{array}$$

Now we add the positive number 65 000 and the negative number −60 000.

$$\begin{array}{r} 65\,000 \\ +\ -60\,000 \\ \hline 5\,000 \end{array}$$

The company had an overall profit of $5000 for the five-month period.

Gary Landsman/Corbis/Stock Market

Practice Problem 8 The results of the next five months of operations for the same company are listed in the following table. What is the overall profit or loss over this five-month period?

Net Operations Profit/Loss Statement in Dollars

Month	Profit	Loss
June		−20 000
July	30 000	
August	40 000	
September		−5 000
October		−35 000

NOTE TO STUDENT: Fully worked-out solutions to all of the Practice Problems can be found at the end of the module.

Section 1 Exercises

Verbal and Writing Skills

1. Explain in your own words how to add two signed numbers if the signs are the same.

2. Explain in your own words how to add two signed numbers if one number is positive and one number is negative.

In each case, replace the ? with < or >.

3. $-9 \,?\, 2$

4. $-8 \,?\, 6$

5. $-3 \,?\, -5$

6. $-7 \,?\, -14$

7. $5 \,?\, -2$

8. $6 \,?\, -3$

9. $-12 \,?\, -10$

10. $-15 \,?\, -13$

Simplify each absolute value expression.

11. $|7|$

12. $|6|$

13. $|-16|$

14. $|-18|$

Add each pair of signed numbers that have the same sign.

15. $-6 + (-11)$

16. $-5 + (-13)$

17. $-4.9 + (-2.1)$

18. $-8.3 + (-3.7)$

19. $8.9 + 7.6$

20. $12.5 + 7.8$

21. $\frac{1}{5} + \frac{2}{7}$

22. $\frac{5}{6} + \frac{1}{4}$

23. $-2\frac{1}{2} + \left(-\frac{1}{2}\right)$

24. $-5\frac{1}{4} + \left(-\frac{3}{4}\right)$

Add each pair of signed numbers that have different signs.

25. $14 + (-5)$

26. $15 + (-6)$

27. $-17 + 12$

28. $-21 + 15$

29. $-36 + 58$

30. $-42 + 57$

31. $-9.3 + 6.05$

32. $-7.2 + 4.04$

33. $\frac{1}{12} + \left(-\frac{3}{4}\right)$

34. $\frac{7}{20} + \left(-\frac{19}{20}\right)$

Mixed Practice *Add.*

35. $\frac{7}{9} + \left(-\frac{2}{9}\right)$

36. $\frac{5}{12} + \left(-\frac{7}{12}\right)$

37. $-18 + (-4)$

38. $-34 + (-2)$

39. $1.48 + (-2.2)$

40. $3.72 + (-4.1)$

41. $-125 + (-238)$

42. $-514 + (-176)$

43. $13 + (-9)$

44. $-18 + 7$

45. $-3\frac{3}{4} + \left(-1\frac{7}{10}\right)$

46. $-5\frac{3}{8} + \left(-3\frac{5}{8}\right)$

47. $-7.56 + 13.8$

48. $-6.89 + 15.9$

49. $-5 + \left(-\frac{1}{2}\right)$

50. $\frac{5}{6} + (-3)$

51. $-20.5 + 18.1 + (-12.3)$

52. $-10.8 + (-14.3) + 12.7$

53. $11 + (-9) + (-10) + 8$

54. $(-13) + 8 + (-12) + 17$

55. $-7 + 6 + (-2) + 5 + (-3) + (-5)$

56. $3 + (-9) + 10 + (-3) + (-15) + 8$

57. $\left(-\frac{1}{5}\right) + \left(-\frac{2}{3}\right) + \left(\frac{4}{25}\right)$

58. $\left(-\frac{1}{7}\right) + \left(-\frac{5}{21}\right) + \left(\frac{3}{14}\right)$

Applications

Profit and Loss Statements *Use signed numbers to represent the total profit or loss for a company after the following reports.*

59. A \$43 000 loss in February followed by a \$51 000 loss in March.

60. A \$16 000 loss in May followed by a \$25 000 loss in June.

61. A \$9500 profit in November followed by a \$17 000 loss in December.

62. An \$11 000 loss in July followed by an \$8400 profit in August.

63. An \$18 500 loss in January, a \$12 300 profit in February, and a \$15 000 profit in March.

64. A \$15 700 profit in April, a \$20 400 loss in May, and a \$9000 profit in June.

Solve.

65. ***Temperature Change*** One night in Juneau, Alaska, the temperature was −5 °F. By the next morning, the temperature had dropped 13 °F. What was the morning temperature?

66. ***Temperature Change*** One morning in Winnipeg, Manitoba, the temperature was −9 °C. By that afternoon, the temperature had risen 15 °C. What was the afternoon temperature?

67. ***Temperature Change*** This morning, the temperature was −5 °C. This evening, the temperature rose 4 °C. What was the new temperature?

68. ***Temperature Change*** Last night the temperature was −7 °C. The temperature dropped 15 °C this afternoon. What was the new temperature?

69. ***Stock Market*** The following list of signed numbers is the daily loss or gain of one share of Kraft Food, Inc. stock for the week of September 22–26, 2003: −0.15, +0.20, +0.21, −0.24, −0.36. What was the net loss or gain for the week?

70. ***Stock Market*** The following list of signed numbers is the daily loss or gain of one share of Coca-Cola Enterprises stock for the week of June 25–29, 2007: −0.15, +0.91, −0.12, +0.32, +0.01. What was the net loss or gain for the week?

71. ***Football*** In three plays of a football game, the quarterback threw passes that lost 8 yards, gained 13 yards, and lost 6 yards. What was the total gain or loss of the three plays?

72. ***Football*** In three plays of a football game, the quarterback threw passes that gained 20 metres, lost 13 metres, and gained 5 metres. What was the total gain or loss of the three plays?

To Think About

73. ***Chequing Accounts*** Bob examined his chequing account register. He thought his balance was $89.50. However, he forgot to subtract an automated teller machine (ATM) withdrawal of $50.00. Since the ATM that he used was at a different bank, he was also charged $2.50 for using the ATM. What was the actual balance in his chequing account?

74. ***Chequing Accounts*** Nancy examined her chequing account register. She thought her balance was $97.40. However, she forgot to subtract a cheque of $95.00 that she had made out the previous week. She also forgot to subtract the monthly $4.50 fee charged by her bank for having a chequing account. What was the actual balance in her chequing account?

Quick Quiz 1 Add the following.

1. $16 + (-3) + 5 + (-12)$

2. $5.9 + (-7.4)$

3. $-4\frac{2}{3} + 1\frac{1}{3}$

4. **Concept Check** In calculating an addition problem such as $4 + (-12) + 23 + (-15)$, some students add from left to right. Other students first add the positive numbers, then add the negative numbers, and then add the two results. Explain which method you prefer and why.

Section 2 Subtracting Signed Numbers

Subtracting One Signed Number from Another

We begin our discussion by defining the word **opposite.** The opposite of a positive number is a negative number with the same absolute value. For example, the opposite of 7 is -7.

The opposite of a negative number is a positive number with the same absolute value. For example, the opposite of -9 is 9. If a number is the opposite of another number, these two numbers are at an equal distance from zero on the number line.

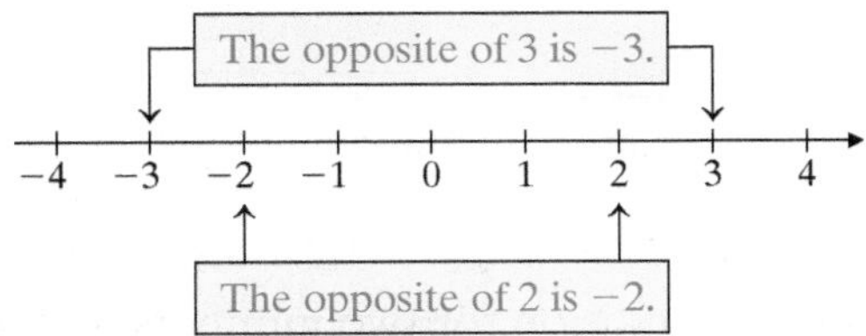

The sum of a number and its opposite is zero.

$$-3 + 3 = 0 \qquad 2 + (-2) = 0$$

We will use the concept of opposite to develop a way to subtract signed numbers.

Let's think about how a chequing account works. Suppose that you deposit \$25 and the bank adds a service charge of \$5 for a new chequebook. Your account looks like this:

$$\$25 + (-\$5) = \$20$$

Suppose instead that you deposit \$25 and the bank adds no charge. The next day, you write a cheque for \$5. The result of these two transactions is

$$\$25 - \$5 = \$20$$

Note that your account has the same amount of money (\$20) in both cases.

We see that adding a negative 5 to 25 is the same as subtracting a positive 5 from 25. That is, $25 + (-5) = 20$ and $25 - 5 = 20$.

Subtracting is equivalent to adding the opposite.

Subtracting	**Adding the Opposite**
$25 - 5 = 20$	$25 + (-5) = 20$
$19 - 6 = 13$	$19 + (-6) = 13$
$7 - 3 = 4$	$7 + (-3) = 4$
$15 - 5 = 10$	$15 + (-5) = 10$

We define a rule for the subtraction of signed numbers.

SUBTRACTION OF SIGNED NUMBERS

To subtract signed numbers, add the opposite of the second number to the first number.

Student Learning Objectives

After studying this section, you will be able to:

1. **Subtract one signed number from another.**
2. **Solve problems involving both addition and subtraction of signed numbers.**
3. **Solve simple applied problems that involve the subtraction of signed numbers.**

Thus, to do a subtraction problem, we first change it to an equivalent addition problem in which the first number does not change but the second number is replaced by its opposite. Then we follow the rules of *addition* for signed numbers.

EXAMPLE 1 Subtract. $-8-(-2)$

Solution

$-8-(-2)$

$-8+2$ ← Write the opposite of −2, which is 2.

↑ Change subtraction to addition.

Now we use the rules of addition for two numbers with opposite signs.

$$-8+2=-6$$

NOTE TO STUDENT: Fully worked-out solutions to all of the Practice Problems can be found at the end of the module.

Practice Problem 1 Subtract. $-10-(-5)$

EXAMPLE 2 Subtract. **(a)** $7-8$ **(b)** $-12-16$

Solution

(a)

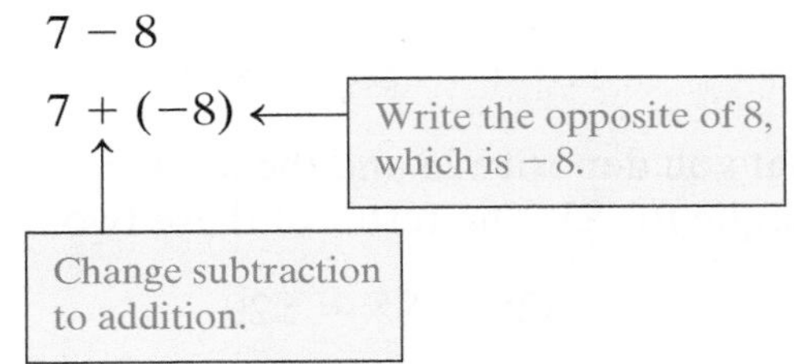

Now we use the rules of addition for two numbers with opposite signs.

$$7+(-8)=-1$$

(b)

$-12-16$

$-12+(-16)$ ← Write the opposite of 16, which is −16.

↑ Change subtraction to addition.

Now we follow the rules of addition of two numbers with the same sign.

$$-12+(-16)=-28$$

Practice Problem 2 Subtract. **(a)** $5-12$ **(b)** $-11-17$

Sometimes the numbers we subtract are fractions or decimals.

EXAMPLE 3 Subtract. **(a)** $5.6 - (-8.1)$ **(b)** $-\frac{6}{11} - \left(-\frac{1}{22}\right)$

Solution

(a) Change the subtraction to adding the opposite. Then add.

$$5.6 - (-8.1) = 5.6 + 8.1$$
$$= 13.7$$

(b) Change the subtraction to adding the opposite. Then add.

$$-\frac{6}{11} - \left(-\frac{1}{22}\right) = -\frac{6}{11} + \frac{1}{22}$$

$$= -\frac{6}{11} \times \frac{2}{2} + \frac{1}{22}$$ We see that the LCD = 22. We change $\frac{6}{11}$ to a fraction with a denominator of 22.

$$= -\frac{12}{22} + \frac{1}{22}$$ Add.

$$= -\frac{11}{22} \text{ or } -\frac{1}{2}$$

Practice Problem 3 Subtract.

(a) $3.6 - (-9.5)$ **(b)** $-\frac{5}{8} - \left(-\frac{5}{24}\right)$

Remember that in performing subtraction of two signed numbers:

1. The first number does not change.
2. The subtraction sign is changed to addition.
3. We write the opposite of the second number.
4. We find the result of this addition problem.

Think of each subtraction problem as a problem of adding the opposite.

If you see $7 - 10$, think $7 + (-10)$.
If you see $-3 - 19$, think $-3 + (-19)$.
If you see $6 - (-3)$, think $6 + (+3)$.

EXAMPLE 4 Subtract.

(a) $6 - (+3)$ **(b)** $-\frac{1}{2} - \left(-\frac{1}{3}\right)$ **(c)** $2.7 - (-5.2)$

Solution

(a) $6 - (+3) = 6 + (-3) = 3$

(b) $-\frac{1}{2} - \left(-\frac{1}{3}\right) = -\frac{1}{2} + \frac{1}{3} = -\frac{3}{6} + \frac{2}{6} = -\frac{1}{6}$

(c) $2.7 - (-5.2) = 2.7 + 5.2 = 7.9$

Practice Problem 4 Subtract.

(a) $20 - (-5)$ **(b)** $-\frac{1}{5} - \left(-\frac{1}{2}\right)$ **(c)** $3.6 - (-5.5)$

Calculator

Negative Numbers

To enter a negative number on most scientific calculators, find the key marked [+/−]. To enter the number −3, press the key 3 and then the key [+/−]. The display should read

[−3]

To find (−32) + (−46), enter

32 [+/−] [+] 46 [+/−] [=]

The display should read

[−78]

Try the following.

(a) $-756 + 184$
(b) $92 + (-51)$
(c) $-618 - (-824)$
(d) $-36 + (-10) - (-15)$

Note: The [+/−] key changes the sign of a number from + to − or − to +.

Solving Problems Involving Both Addition and Subtraction of Signed Numbers

EXAMPLE 5 Perform the following set of operations, working from left to right. $-8 - (-3) + (-5)$

Solution $-8 - (-3) + (-5) = -8 + 3 + (-5)$ First we change subtracting a -3 to adding a 3.

$= -5 + (-5) = -10$

Practice Problem 5 Perform the following set of operations, working from left to right.

$$-5 - (-9) + (-14)$$

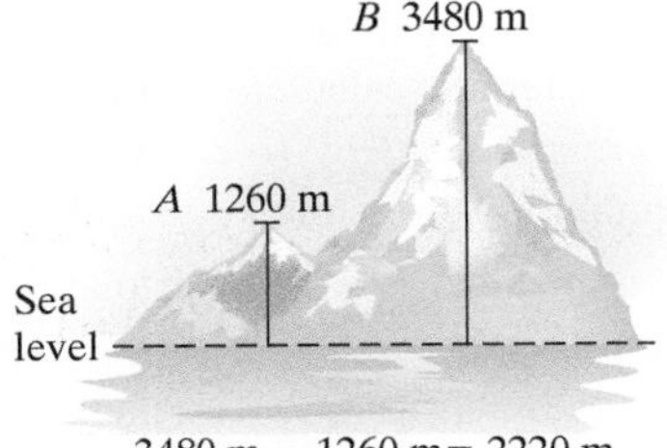

3480 m − 1260 m= 2220 m

Solving Simple Applied Problems That Involve the Subtraction of Signed Numbers

When we want to find the difference in altitude between two mountains, we subtract. We subtract the lower altitude from the higher altitude. Look at the illustration at the left. The difference in altitude between *A* and *B* is 3480 metres − 1260 metres = 2220 metres.

Land that is below sea level is considered to have a negative altitude. The Dead Sea is 400 metres below sea level. Look at the following illustration. The difference in altitude between *C* and *D* is

$$2590 \text{ metres} - (-400 \text{ metres}) = 2990 \text{ metres}.$$

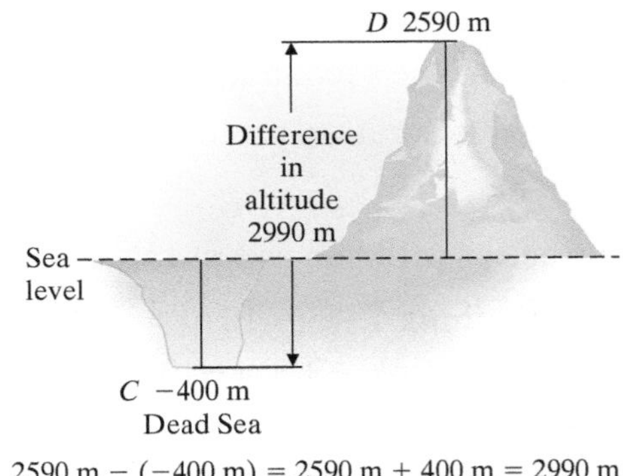

2590 m − (−400 m) = 2590 m + 400 m = 2990 m

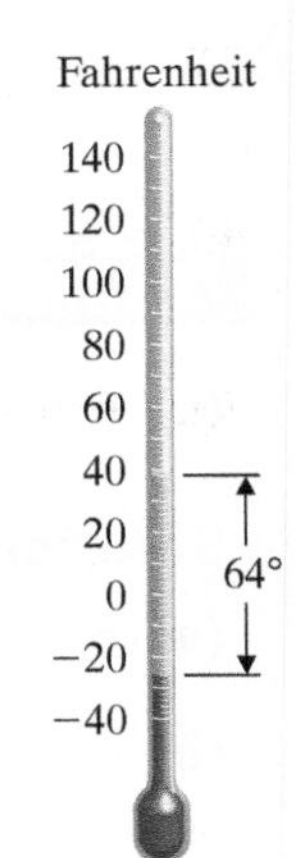

EXAMPLE 6 Find the difference in temperature between 38 °F during the day in Anchorage, Alaska, and −26 °F at night.

Solution We subtract the lower temperature from the higher temperature.

$$38 - (-26) = 38 + 26 = 64$$

The difference is 64 °F.

Practice Problem 6 Find the difference in temperature between 31 °F during the day in Fairbanks, Alaska, and −37 °F at night.

Section 2 Exercises

Subtract the signed numbers by adding the opposite of the second number to the first number.

1. $-9 - (-3)$ **2.** $-7 - (-5)$ **3.** $-12 - (-7)$ **4.** $-10 - (-2)$ **5.** $3 - 9$

6. $5 - 12$ **7.** $-14 - 3$ **8.** $-6 - 18$ **9.** $-16 - (-25)$ **10.** $-12 - (-20)$

11. $46 - (-39)$ **12.** $53 - (-28)$ **13.** $12 - 30$ **14.** $10 - 14$ **15.** $-12 - (-15)$

16. $-17 - (-30)$ **17.** $150 - 210$ **18.** $500 - 150$ **19.** $300 - (-256)$ **20.** $420 - (-300)$

21. $-2.5 - 4.2$ **22.** $-4.1 - 3.9$ **23.** $6.2 - 14.9$ **24.** $8.5 - 19.2$

Mixed Practice *Subtract the signed numbers by adding the opposite of the second number to the first number.*

25. $-10.9 - (-2.3)$ **26.** $-6.8 - (-2.9)$ **27.** $20.23 - (-12.71)$ **28.** $13.92 - (-14.86)$

29. $\frac{1}{4} - \left(-\frac{3}{4}\right)$ **30.** $\frac{5}{7} - \left(-\frac{6}{7}\right)$ **31.** $-\frac{5}{6} - \frac{1}{3}$ **32.** $-\frac{2}{8} - \frac{1}{4}$

33. $-2\frac{3}{10} - \left(-3\frac{5}{6}\right)$ **34.** $-7\frac{5}{8} - \left(-12\frac{2}{3}\right)$ **35.** $\frac{2}{9} - \frac{5}{7}$ **36.** $\frac{3}{5} - \frac{11}{12}$

Perform each set of operations, working from left to right.

37. $2 - (-8) + 5$ **38.** $7 - (-3) + 9$ **39.** $-5 - 6 - (-11)$

40. $-8 - 5 - (-17)$ **41.** $21 - (-15) - (-10)$ **42.** $32 - (-12) - (-18)$

43. $-16 - (-6) - 12$ **44.** $-13 - (-4) - 15$ **45.** $9 - 3 - 2 - 6$

46. $12 - 5 - 4 - 8$ **47.** $-2.4 - 7.1 + 1.3 - (-2.8)$ **48.** $-2.5 + 3.2 - 6.3 - (-5.4)$

Applications *Use your knowledge of signed numbers to answer exercises 49–54.*

49. ***Altitude Change*** The highest point in California is Mt. Whitney at 14 494 feet. The lowest point is −282 feet in Death Valley. How far above Death Valley is Mt. Whitney?

50. ***Altitude Change*** The highest point in Africa is Mount Kilimanjaro at 5895 m. The lowest point is −153 m at Lake Assal. How far above Lake Assal is Mount Kilimanjaro?

51. ***Temperature Change*** Find the difference in temperature in Whitehorse, Yukon, between 23 °C during the day and −19 °C at night.

52. ***Temperature Change*** Find the difference in temperature in Yellowknife, Northwest Territories, between −2 °C during the day and −24 °C at night.

53. ***Temperature Change*** In Thule, Greenland, yesterday, the temperature was −29 °F. Today the temperature rose 16 °F. What is the new temperature?

54. ***Height Change*** Find the difference in height between the top of a mountain 642 metres high and a crack caused by an earthquake 57 metres below sea level.

Profit and Loss Statements *A company's profit and loss statement in dollars for the last five months is shown in the following table.*

Month	Profit	Loss
January	18 700	
February		−34 700
March		−6300
April	43 600	
May		−12 400

55. What is the change in the profit/loss status of the company from the first of January to the end of February?

56. What is the change in the profit/loss status of the company from the first of February to the end of March?

57. What is the change in the profit/loss status of the company from the first of March to the end of May?

58. What is the change in the profit/loss status of the company from the first of January to the end of May?

59. On Monday, the value of one share of a certain stock was $\$15\frac{1}{2}$. During the next three days, the value fell $\$1\frac{1}{2}$, rose $\$2\frac{3}{4}$, and fell $\$3\frac{1}{4}$. What was the value of one share at the end of the three days?

60. On Tuesday, the value of one share of a certain stock was $\$32\frac{1}{4}$. During the next three days, the value rose $\$3\frac{1}{4}$, fell $\$3\frac{3}{4}$, and rose $\$2\frac{3}{4}$. What was the value of one share at the end of these three days?

Quick Quiz 2 Subtract the signed numbers.

1. $\frac{3}{7} - \left(-\frac{9}{14}\right)$

2. $-8.7 - (-3.2)$

3. $-34 - 48$

4. **Concept Check** Explain how you would perform the indicated operations to evaluate $8 - (-13) + (-5)$.

 Multiplying and Dividing Two Signed Numbers

Recall the different ways we can indicate multiplication.

$$3 \times 5 \qquad 3 \cdot 5 \qquad (3)(5) \qquad 3(5)$$

It is common to use parentheses to mean multiplication.

EXAMPLE 1 Evaluate. **(a)** (7)(8) **(b)** 3(12)

Solution

(a) $(7)(8) = 56$ **(b)** $3(12) = 36$

Practice Problem 1 Evaluate.

(a) (6)(9) **(b)** 7(12)

Now suppose we multiply a positive number times a negative number. What will happen? Let us look for a pattern.

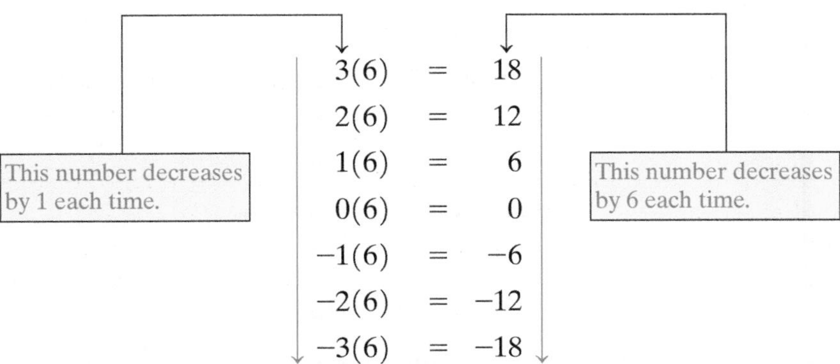

This number decreases by 1 each time.
3(6) = 18
2(6) = 12
1(6) = 6
0(6) = 0
−1(6) = −6
−2(6) = −12
−3(6) = −18
This number decreases by 6 each time.

Our pattern suggests that when we multiply a positive number times a negative number, we get a negative number. Thus we will state the following rule.

MULTIPLICATION RULE FOR TWO NUMBERS WITH DIFFERENT SIGNS

To multiply two numbers with different signs, multiply the absolute values. The result is negative.

EXAMPLE 2 Multiply. **(a)** 2(−8) **(b)** (−3)(25)

Solution In each case, we are multiplying two signed numbers with different signs. We will always get a negative number for an answer.

(a) $2(-8) = -16$ **(b)** $(-3)(25) = -75$

Practice Problem 2 Multiply.

(a) (−8)(5) **(b)** 3(−60)

Student Learning Objectives

After studying this section, you will be able to:

 **Multiply and divide two signed numbers.**

 **Multiply three or more signed numbers.**

A similar rule applies to division of two numbers when the signs are not the same.

DIVISION RULE FOR TWO NUMBERS WITH DIFFERENT SIGNS

To divide two numbers with different signs, divide the absolute values. The result is negative.

EXAMPLE 3 Divide. **(a)** $-20 \div 5$ **(b)** $36 \div (-18)$

Solution

(a) $-20 \div 5 = -4$ **(b)** $36 \div (-18) = -2$

Practice Problem 3 Divide.

(a) $-50 \div 25$ **(b)** $49 \div (-7)$

What happens if we multiply $(-2)(-6)$? What sign will we obtain? Let us once again look for a pattern.

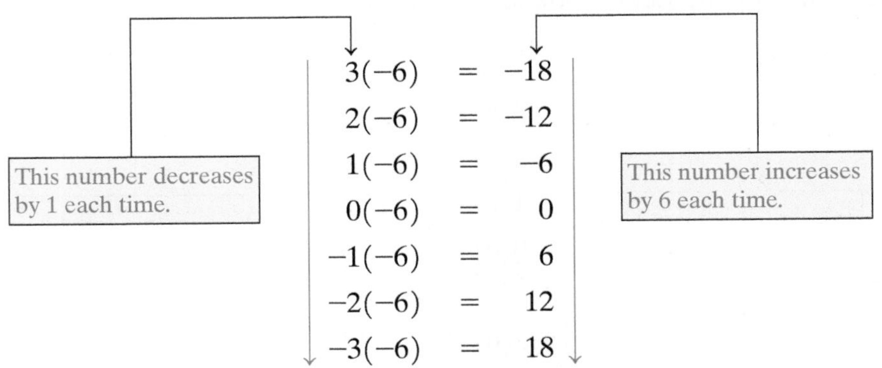

Our pattern suggests that when we multiply a negative number by a negative number, we get a positive number. A similar pattern occurs for division. Thus we are ready to state the following rule.

MULTIPLICATION AND DIVISION RULE FOR TWO NUMBERS WITH THE SAME SIGN

To multiply or divide two numbers with the same sign, multiply or divide the absolute values. The sign of the result is positive.

EXAMPLE 4 Multiply. **(a)** $-5(-6)$ **(b)** $\left(-\frac{1}{2}\right)\left(-\frac{3}{5}\right)$

Solution In each case, we are multiplying two numbers with the same sign. We will always obtain a positive number.

(a) $-5(-6) = 30$ **(b)** $\left(-\frac{1}{2}\right)\left(-\frac{3}{5}\right) = \frac{3}{10}$

Practice Problem 4 Multiply.

(a) $-10(-6)$ **(b)** $\left(-\frac{1}{3}\right)\left(-\frac{2}{7}\right)$

Because division is related to multiplication, we find, just as in multiplication, that whenever we divide two numbers with the same sign, the result is a positive number.

EXAMPLE 5 Divide. **(a)** $(-50) \div (-2)$ **(b)** $(-9.9) \div (-3.0)$

Solution

(a) $(-50) \div (-2) = 25$ **(b)** $(-9.9) \div (-3.0) = 3.3$

Practice Problem 5 Divide.

(a) $-78 \div (-2)$ **(b)** $(-1.2) \div (-0.5)$

 Multiplying Three or More Signed Numbers

When multiplying more than two numbers, multiply any two numbers first, then multiply the result by another number. Continue until each factor has been used.

EXAMPLE 6 Multiply. $5(-2)(-3)$

Solution

$$5(-2)(-3) = -10(-3) \quad \text{First multiply } 5(-2) = -10.$$
$$= 30 \quad \text{Then multiply } -10(-3) = 30.$$

Practice Problem 6 Multiply. $(-6)(3)(-4)$

EXAMPLE 7 Chemists have determined that a phosphate ion has an electrical charge of -3. If 10 phosphate ions are removed from a substance, what is the change in the charge of the remaining substance?

Solution Removing 10 ions from a substance can be represented by the number -10. We can use multiplication to determine the result of removing 10 ions with an electrical charge of -3.

$$(-3)(-10) = 30$$

Thus the change in charge would be $+30$.

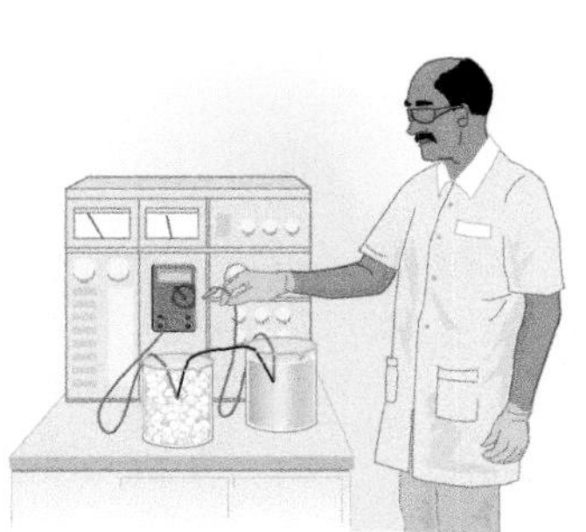

Practice Problem 7 An oxide ion has an electrical charge of -2. If 6 oxide ions are added to a substance, what is the change in the charge of the new substance?

Michael Giannechini/Photo Researchers, Inc.

EXAMPLE 8 Mei-Ling Pak went outside her house to measure the temperature at 4 P.M. for seven days in September in Ellesmere Island, Nunavut. Her temperature readings were −11 °C, −8 °C, −15 °C, −3 °C, −5 °C, −12 °C, and −2 °C. Find the average temperature for this seven-day period.

Solution To find the average, we take the sum of the seven days of temperature readings and divide by seven.

$$\frac{-11 + (-8) + (-15) + (-3) + (-5) + (-12) + (-2)}{7} = \frac{-56}{7} = -8$$

The average temperature was −8 °C.

Practice Problem 8 In March, Tony Erb measured the morning temperature at his house in Ottawa at 8 A.M. each day for six days. He measured the following temperatures: 7 °C, 5 °C, 2 °C, −4 °C, −3 °C, and −1 °C. What was the average temperature at his house over this six-day period?

SECTION 3 EXERCISES

Verbal and Writing Skills

1. In your own words, state the rule for multiplying two signed numbers if the signs are the same.

2. In your own words, state the rule for multiplying two signed numbers if the signs are different.

Multiply.

3. $(12)(3)$ **4.** $(15)(5)$ **5.** $(-20)(-3)$ **6.** $(-30)(-6)$

7. $(-20)(8)$ **8.** $(-15)(12)$ **9.** $(3)(-22)$ **10.** $(4)(-34)$

11. $(2.5)(-0.6)$ **12.** $(8.5)(-0.3)$ **13.** $(-12.5)(-2.25)$ **14.** $(-7.35)(-10.5)$

15. $\left(-\frac{2}{5}\right)\left(\frac{3}{7}\right)$ **16.** $\left(-\frac{5}{12}\right)\left(-\frac{2}{3}\right)$ **17.** $\left(-\frac{6}{5}\right)\left(-\frac{5}{2}\right)$ **18.** $\left(-\frac{9}{4}\right)\left(-\frac{10}{27}\right)$

Divide.

19. $-64 \div 8$ **20.** $-63 \div 7$ **21.** $\frac{48}{-6}$ **22.** $\frac{52}{-13}$

23. $\frac{-150}{-25}$ **24.** $\frac{-180}{-45}$ **25.** $-25 \div (-5)$ **26.** $-36 \div (-4)$

27. $-\frac{4}{9} \div \left(-\frac{16}{27}\right)$ **28.** $-\frac{3}{20} \div \left(-\frac{6}{5}\right)$ **29.** $\dfrac{-\frac{4}{5}}{-\frac{7}{10}}$ **30.** $\dfrac{-\frac{26}{15}}{-\frac{13}{7}}$

31. $50.28 \div (-6)$ **32.** $30.45 \div (-5)$ **33.** $\frac{45.6}{-8}$ **34.** $\frac{66.6}{-9}$

35. $\frac{-21\,000}{-700}$ **36.** $\frac{-320\,000}{-8000}$

Mixed Practice *Multiply or divide.*

37. $5(-9)$ **38.** $6(-11)$ **39.** $(-12)(-4)$ **40.** $(-10)(-7)$

41. $\frac{15}{-3}$ **42.** $\frac{36}{-2}$ **43.** $-30 \div (-3)$ **44.** $-50 \div (-5)$

45. $(-1.4)(2)$ **46.** $(-1.6)(3)$ **47.** $0.028 \div (-1.4)$ **48.** $0.069 \div (-2.3)$

49. $\left(-\frac{3}{5}\right)\left(-\frac{5}{7}\right)$ **50.** $\left(-\frac{4}{9}\right)\left(-\frac{9}{13}\right)$ **51.** $\frac{12}{5} \div \left(-\frac{3}{10}\right)$ **52.** $\frac{11}{4} \div \left(-\frac{33}{6}\right)$

Multiply.

53. $10(-5)(-3)$

54. $5(-4)(-6)$

55. $(-6)(7)(-2)$

56. $(-3)(2)(-9)$

57. $2(-8)(3)\left(-\frac{1}{3}\right)$

58. $7(-2)(-5)\left(\frac{1}{7}\right)$

59. $(-20)(6)(-30)(-5)$

60. $(5)(-40)(-20)(-8)$

61. $8(-3)(-5)(0)(-2)$

62. $9(-6)(-4)(-3)(0)$

Perform each set of operations. Simplify your answer. Work from left to right.

63. $\left(-\frac{2}{3}\right)\left(-\frac{3}{4}\right)\left(-\frac{5}{6}\right)$

64. $\left(-\frac{2}{3}\right) \div \left(-\frac{2}{3}\right)\left(\frac{3}{5}\right)$

Applications

65. ***Stock Market*** Paul owns 70 shares of a stock whose value went up \$2.60 per share. He also owns 120 shares of a stock whose value went down \$0.90 per share. How much did Paul gain or lose?

66. ***Stock Market*** Catalina owns 120 shares of a stock whose value went up \$0.80 per share. She also owns 85 shares of a stock whose value went down \$2.20 per share. How much did Catalina gain or lose?

67. ***Temperature Records*** In Timmins, Ontario, Bob recorded the following temperature readings in degrees Celsius at 7 A.M. each morning for eight days in a row: $-12°, -14°, -3°, -5°, 8°, -1°, -10°$, and $-23°$. What was the average temperature?

68. ***Temperature Records*** In Rhinelander, Wisconsin, Nancy recorded the following temperature readings in degrees Fahrenheit at 9 A.M. each morning for seven days in a row: $-8°, -5°, -18°, -22°, -6°, 3°$, and $7°$. What was the average temperature?

69. ***Underwater Photography*** An underwater photographer made seven sets of underwater shots. He started at the surface, dropped down 5 metres, and shot some pictures. Then he dropped 5 more metres and shot more pictures. He continued this pattern until he had dropped seven times. How far beneath the surface was he at that point?

70. ***Company Losses*** A pharmaceutical company reported losses of \$1.5 million for five quarters in a row. What was the amount of total losses after five quarters?

Electrical Charges *Ions are atoms or groups of atoms with positive or negative electrical charges. The charges of some ions are given in the following box.*

aluminum $+3$	chloride -1	magnesium $+2$
oxide -2	phosphate -3	silver $+1$

In exercises 71–76, find the total charge.

71. 11 aluminum ions

72. 9 phosphate ions

73. 6 magnesium ions and 4 chloride ions (*Hint:* Multiply first, and then add.)

74. 10 oxide ions and 12 silver ions (*Hint:* Multiply first, and then add.)

75. Eight chloride ions are removed from a substance. What is the change in the charge of the remaining substance?

76. Six oxide ions are removed from a substance. What is the change in the charge of the remaining substance?

***Golf** A round of golf is nine holes. Pine Hills Golf Course is a par 3 course. This means that the expected number of strokes it takes to complete each hole is 3. The following table indicates strokes above or below par for each hole. For example, if someone shoots a 5 on one of the holes (that is, takes 5 strokes to complete the hole), this is called a double bogey and is 2 strokes over par.*

Birdie	-1	Bogey	$+1$
Eagle	-2	Double Bogey	$+2$

77. During a round of golf with his friend, Louis got two birdies, one eagle, and two double bogeys. He made par on the rest of the holes. How many strokes above or below par for the entire nine-hole course is this? (*Hint:* Multiply first, and then add.)

78. Judy shot three birdies, two bogeys, and one double bogey. On the other three holes, she made par. How many strokes above or below par for the entire nine-hole course is this? (*Hint:* Multiply first, and then add.)

Quick Quiz 3 Multiply.

1. $(-5)(-9)$

2. $(-2)(3)(-4)(-3)$

Divide.

3. $-156 \div (-4)$

4. Concept Check A student was doing the problem $(-4) + (-8) = -12$ and comparing it to the problem $(-4)(-8) = +32$. The student commented, "In the first problem two negative numbers give you a negative answer. In the second problem two negative numbers give you a positive answer. This is confusing!" Explain how the student could keep from being confused with these two types of problems.

How Am I Doing? Sections 1–3

1. ______
2. ______
3. ______
4. ______
5. ______
6. ______
7. ______
8. ______
9. ______
10. ______
11. ______
12. ______
13. ______
14. ______
15. ______
16. ______
17. ______
18. ______
19. ______
20. ______
21. ______
22. ______
23. ______
24. ______
25. ______
26. ______
27. ______
28. ______
29. ______
30. ______
31. ______
32. ______
33. ______

How are you doing with your homework assignments in Sections 1 to 3? Do you feel you have mastered the material so far? Do you understand the concepts you have covered? Before you go further, take some time to do each of the following problems.

1

Add.

1. $-7 + (-12)$ **2.** $-23 + 19$ **3.** $7.6 + (-3.1)$

4. $8 + (-5) + 6 + (-9)$ **5.** $\frac{8}{9} + \left(-\frac{2}{3}\right)$ **6.** $-\frac{5}{6} + \left(-\frac{1}{3}\right)$

7. $-2.8 + (-4.2)$ **8.** $-3.7 + 5.4$

2

Subtract.

9. $13 - 21$ **10.** $-26 - 15$ **11.** $\frac{5}{17} - \left(-\frac{9}{17}\right)$

12. $-19 - (-7)$ **13.** $-12.5 - 3.8$ **14.** $2.8 - 5.6$

15. $21 - (-21)$ **16.** $\frac{2}{3} - \left(-\frac{3}{5}\right)$

3

Multiply or divide.

17. $(-3)(-8)$ **18.** $-48 \div (-12)$ **19.** $-72 \div 9$

20. $(5)(-4)(2)(-1)\left(-\frac{1}{4}\right)$ **21.** $\frac{72}{-3}$ **22.** $\frac{-\frac{3}{4}}{-\frac{4}{5}}$

23. $(-8)(-2)(-4)$ **24.** $120 \div (-12)$

Mixed Practice

Perform the indicated operations. Simplify your answer.

25. $18 - (-6)$ **26.** $-7(-3)$ **27.** $-15 \div 10$

28. $1.6 + (-1.8) + (-3.4)$ **29.** $2.9 - 3.5$ **30.** $-\frac{1}{3} + \left(-\frac{2}{5}\right)$

31. $\left(-\frac{7}{10}\right)\left(-\frac{2}{7}\right)$ **32.** $2\frac{1}{3} \div \left(-\frac{2}{3}\right)$

33. For six days in December, the temperature in Kenora, Ontario, was 2 °C, −6 °C, −10 °C, −8 °C, −3 °C, and 4 °C. What was the average temperature for these six days?

Your institution may have included the Answers to Selected Exercises for this module, which contains the answers to these questions. Each answer also includes a reference to the objective in which the problem is first taught. If you missed any of these problems, you should stop and review the Examples and Practice Problems in the referenced objective. A little review now will help you master the material in the upcoming sections.

SECTION 4 ORDER OF OPERATIONS WITH SIGNED NUMBERS

Calculating with Signed Numbers Using More Than One Operation

The order of operations we discussed for whole numbers applies to signed numbers as well. The rules that we will use in this module are listed in the following box.

Student Learning Objective

After studying this section, you will be able to:

Calculate with signed numbers using more than one operation.

ORDER OF OPERATIONS FOR SIGNED NUMBERS

With grouping symbols:

Do first
1. Perform operations inside the parentheses.
2. Simplify any expressions with exponents, and find any square roots.
3. Multiply or divide from left to right.
4. Add or subtract from left to right.

Do last

EXAMPLE 1 Perform the indicated operations in the proper order.

$$-6 \div (-2)(5)$$

Solution Multiplication and division are of equal priority. So we work from left to right and divide first.

$$\underbrace{-6 \div (-2)}(5)$$
$$= \quad 3 \quad (5) = 15$$

Practice Problem 1 Perform the indicated operations in the proper order.

$$20 \div (-5)(-3)$$

EXAMPLE 2 Perform the indicated operations in the proper order.

(a) $7 + 6(-2)$ **(b)** $9 \div 3 - 16 \div (-2)$

Solution

(a) Multiplication and division must be done first. We begin with $6(-2)$.

$$7 + \underbrace{6(-2)}$$
$$= 7 + (-12) = -5$$

(b) There is no multiplication, but there is division, and we do that first.

$$\underbrace{9 \div 3} - \underbrace{16 \div (-2)}$$
$$= \quad 3 \quad - \quad (-8) \quad = 3 + 8 \quad \text{Transform subtraction to adding the opposite.}$$
$$= 11$$

Practice Problem 2 Perform the indicated operations in the proper order.

(a) $25 \div (-5) + 16 \div (-8)$ **(b)** $9 + 20 \div (-4)$

If a fraction has operations written in the numerator, in the denominator, or both, these operations must be done first. Then the fraction may be simplified or the division carried out.

EXAMPLE 3 Perform the indicated operations in the proper order.

$$\frac{7(-2) + 4}{8 \div (-2)(5)}$$

Solution

$$\frac{7(-2) + 4}{8 \div (-2)(5)} = \frac{-14 + 4}{(-4)(5)}$$ We perform the multiplication and division first in the numerator and the denominator, respectively.

$$= \frac{-10}{-20}$$ Simplify the fraction.

$$= \frac{1}{2}$$

Note that the answer is positive since a negative number divided by a negative number gives a positive result.

Practice Problem 3 Perform the indicated operations in the proper order.

$$\frac{9(-3) - 5}{2(-4) \div (-2)}$$

Some problems involve both parentheses and exponents and will require additional steps.

EXAMPLE 4 Perform the indicated operations in the proper order.

$$4(6 - 9) + (-2)^3 + 3(-5)$$

Solution

$4(-3) + (-2)^3 + 3(-5)$ First we combine the numbers inside the parentheses.

$= 4(-3) + (-8) + 3(-5)$ Next we simplify the expression with an exponent. We obtain $(-2)^3 = (-2)(-2)(-2) = -8$.

$= -12 + (-8) + (-15)$ Next we perform each multiplication.

$= -35$ Now we add three numbers.

Practice Problem 4 Perform the indicated operations in the proper order.

$$-2(-12 + 15) + (-3)^4 + 2(-6)$$

Be sure to use extra caution with problems involving fractions or decimals. It is easy to make an error in finding a common denominator or in placing a decimal point.

EXAMPLE 5 Perform the indicated operations in the proper order.

$$\left(\frac{1}{2}\right)^3 + 2\left(\frac{3}{4} - \frac{3}{8}\right) \div \left(-\frac{3}{5}\right)$$

Solution

$\left(\frac{1}{2}\right)^3 + 2\left(\frac{6}{8} - \frac{3}{8}\right) \div \left(-\frac{3}{5}\right)$ First find the LCD and write $\frac{3}{4} = \frac{6}{8}$.

$= \left(\frac{1}{2}\right)^3 + 2\left(\frac{3}{8}\right) \div \left(-\frac{3}{5}\right)$ Next we combine the two fractions inside the parentheses.

$= \frac{1}{8} + 2\left(\frac{3}{8}\right) \div \left(-\frac{3}{5}\right)$ Next we simplify $\left(\frac{1}{2}\right)^3 = \left(\frac{1}{2}\right)\left(\frac{1}{2}\right)\left(\frac{1}{2}\right) = \frac{1}{8}$.

$= \frac{1}{8} + \frac{3}{4} \div \left(-\frac{3}{5}\right)$ Next multiply: $\left(\frac{2}{1}\right)\left(\frac{3}{8}\right) = \frac{3}{4}$.

$= \frac{1}{8} + \frac{3}{4} \times \left(-\frac{5}{3}\right)$ To divide two fractions, invert and multiply the second fraction.

$= \frac{1}{8} + \left(-\frac{5}{4}\right)$ Multiply $\left(\frac{3}{4}\right)\left(-\frac{5}{3}\right) = -\frac{5}{4}$.

$= \frac{1}{8} + \left(-\frac{10}{8}\right)$ Change $-\frac{5}{4}$ to the equivalent $-\frac{10}{8}$.

$= -\frac{9}{8}$ Add the two fractions.

Practice Problem 5 Perform the indicated operations in the proper order.

$$\left(\frac{1}{5}\right)^2 + 4\left(\frac{1}{5} - \frac{3}{10}\right) \div \frac{2}{3}$$

***NOTE TO STUDENT:** Fully worked-out solutions to all of the Practice Problems can be found at the end of the module.*

Section 4 Exercises

Perform the indicated operations in the proper order.

1. $-8 \div (-4)(3)$

2. $-20 \div (-5)(6)$

3. $50 \div (-25)(4)$

4. $60 \div (-20)(5)$

5. $16 + 32 \div (-4)$

6. $15 - (-18) \div 3$

7. $24 \div (-3) + 16 \div (-4)$

8. $(-56) \div (-7) + 30 \div (-15)$

9. $3(-4) + 5(-2) - (-3)$

10. $6(-3) + 8(-1) - (-2)$

11. $-4(1.5 - 2.3)$

12. $-10(2.6 - 1.9)$

13. $5 - 30 \div 3$

14. $8 - 70 \div 5$

15. $36 \div 12(-2)$

16. $9(-6) + 6$

17. $3(-4) + 6(-2) - 3$

18. $-6(7) + 8(-3) + 5$

19. $11(-6) - 3(12)$

20. $10(-5) - 4(12)$

21. $16 - 4(8) + 18 \div (-9)$

22. $20 - 3(-2) + (-20) \div (-5)$

In exercises 23–32, simplify the numerator and denominator first, using the proper order of operations. Then reduce the fraction if possible.

23. $\dfrac{8 + 6 - 12}{3 - 6 + 5}$

24. $\dfrac{11 - 3 - 2}{-9 - 5 + 8}$

25. $\dfrac{6(-2) + 4}{6 - 3 - 5}$

26. $\dfrac{12 - 4 + 10}{5(-3) + 9}$

27. $\dfrac{2(8) \div 4 - 5}{-35 \div (-7)}$

28. $\dfrac{-25 \div 5 + (-3)(-4) - 7}{8 - (18 \div 3)}$

29. $\dfrac{24 \div (-3) - (6 - 2)}{-5(4) + 8}$

30. $\dfrac{6(-3) \div (-2) + 5}{32 \div (-8)}$

31. $\dfrac{12 \div 3 + (-2)(2)}{9 - 9 \div (-3)}$

32. $\dfrac{8(-4) - 4}{(-42) \div (-6) + (12 - 10)}$

Perform the operations in the proper order.

33. $3(2 - 6) + 4^2$

34. $-5(8 - 3) + 6^2$

35. $12 \div (-6) + (7 - 2)^3$

36. $-20 \div 2 + (6 - 3)^4$

37. $\left(-1\frac{1}{2}\right)(-4) - 3\frac{1}{4} \div \frac{1}{4}$

38. $(6)\left(-2\frac{1}{2}\right) + 2\frac{1}{3} \div \frac{1}{3}$

39. $\left(\frac{3}{5} - \frac{2}{5}\right)^2 + \left(\frac{3}{2}\right)\left(-\frac{1}{5}\right)$

40. $\left(\frac{5}{8} - \frac{1}{8}\right)^2 - \left(-\frac{5}{6}\right)\left(\frac{8}{5}\right)$

41. $(1.2)^2 - 3.6(-1.5)$

42. $(0.6)^2 - 5.2(-3.4)$

Applications

Temperature Averages *The following chart gives the average monthly high and low temperatures in degrees Fahrenheit for the city of Noril'sk, one of Russia's northernmost cities.*

	Jan.	Feb.	Mar.	Apr.	May	June	July	Aug.	Sept.	Oct.	Nov.	Dec.
High	−13	−11	0	13	29	50	64	59	44	21	−1	−9
Low	−27	−21	−14	−3	17	38	49	46	35	12	−10	−18

Use the chart to solve exercises 43–48. Round to the nearest tenth of a degree when necessary.

43. What is the average low temperature in Noril'sk during December, January, and February?

44. What is the average high temperature in Noril'sk during December, January, and February?

45. What is the average low temperature in Noril'sk from January through June?

46. What is the average high temperature in Noril'sk from October through March?

47. What is the average yearly high temperature in Noril'sk?

48. What is the average yearly low temperature in Noril'sk?

Quick Quiz 4 Perform the indicated operations in the proper order. Simplify all answers.

1. $5(-4) - 6(2 - 5)^2$

2. $-3.2 - 8.5 - (-3.0) + 2(0.4)$

3. $\dfrac{5 + 26 \div (-2)}{-2(3) + 4(-3)}$

4. Concept Check Explain in what order to perform the operations in the expression $4(3 - 9) + 5^2$.

SECTION 5 SCIENTIFIC NOTATION

Student Learning Objectives

After studying this section, you will be able to:

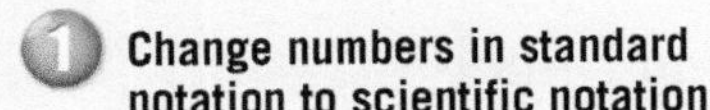

1. Change numbers in standard notation to scientific notation.

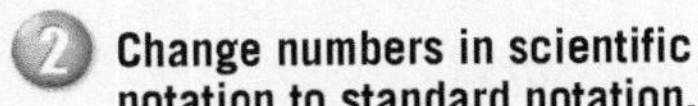

2. Change numbers in scientific notation to standard notation.
3. Add and subtract numbers in scientific notation.

NASA

1 Changing Numbers in Standard Notation to Scientific Notation

Scientists who frequently work with very large or very small measurements use a certain way to write numbers, called *scientific notation*. In our usual way of writing a number, which we call "standard notation" or "ordinary form," we would express the distance to the nearest star, Proxima Centauri, as 39 900 000 000 000 kilometres. In scientific notation, we more conveniently write this as

$$3.99 \times 10^{13} \text{ kilometres.}$$

For a very small number, like two millionths, the standard notation is

$$0.000\,002.$$

The same quantity in scientific notation is

$$2 \times 10^{-6}.$$

Notice that each number in scientific notation has two parts: (1) a number that is 1 or greater but less than 10, which is multiplied by (2) a power of 10. That power is either a whole number or the negative of a whole number. In this section we learn how to go back and forth between standard and scientific notation.

> A positive number is in **scientific notation** if it is in the form $a \times 10^n$, where a is a number greater than (or equal to) 1 and less than 10, and n is an integer.

We begin our investigation of scientific notation by looking at large numbers.

$$10 = 10^1$$
$$100 = 10^2$$
$$1000 = 10^3$$

The number of zeros tells us the number for the exponent. To write a number in scientific notation, we want the first number to be greater than or equal to 1 and less than 10, and the second number to be a power of 10.

Let's see how this can be done. Consider the following.

$$6700 = \underbrace{6.7}_{\text{greater than 1 and less than 10}} \times 1000 = 6.7 \times \underset{\uparrow \text{ a power of 10}}{10^3}$$

Let us look at two more cases.

$$530 = 5.3 \times 100 \qquad\qquad 156\,000 = 1.56 \times 100\,000$$
$$= \underline{5.3 \times 10^2} \qquad\qquad = \underline{1.56 \times 10^5}$$

These numbers are in scientific notation.

Now that we have seen some examples of numbers in scientific notation, let us think through the steps in the next example.

It is important to remember that all numbers *greater than or equal to* 10 always have a positive exponent when expressed in scientific notation.

EXAMPLE 1 Write in scientific notation.

(a) 9826 **(b)** 163 457

Solution

(a)

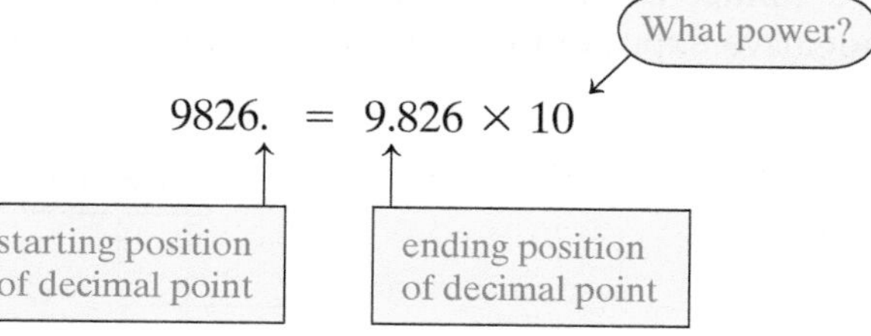

The decimal point moved 3 places to the left. We therefore use 3 for the power of 10.

$$9826 = 9.826 \times 10^3$$

(b)

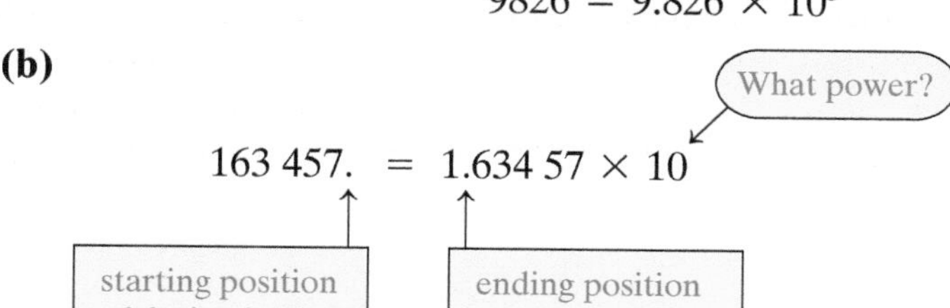

The decimal point moved 5 places to the left. We therefore use 5 for the power of 10.

$$163\,457 = 1.634\,57 \times 10^5$$

Practice Problem 1 Write in scientific notation.

(a) 3729 **(b)** 506 936

When changing to scientific notation, all zeros to the *right* of the final nonzero digit may be eliminated. This does not change the value of your answer.

Now we will look at numbers that are *less than* 1. In the introduction to this section we saw that 0.000 002 can be written as 2×10^{-6}. How is it possible to have a negative exponent? Let's take another look at the powers of 10.

$$10^3 = 1000$$
$$10^2 = 100$$
$$10^1 = 10$$
$$10^0 = 1$$ Recall that any number to the zero power is 1.

Now, following this pattern, what would you expect the next number on the left of the equals sign to be? What would be the next number on the right of the equals sign? Each number on the right is one-tenth the number above it. We continue the pattern.

$$10^{-1} = 0.1$$
$$10^{-2} = 0.01$$
$$10^{-3} = 0.001$$

Calculator

Standard to Scientific

Many calculators have a setting that will display numbers in scientific notation. Consult your manual on how to do this. To convert 154.32 into scientific notation, first change your setting to display in scientific notation. Often this is done by pressing [SCI] or [2nd] [SCI]. Often SCI is then displayed on the calculator. Then enter:

154.32 [=]

Display:

[1.5432 02]

1.5432 02 means

1.5432×10^2.

Note that your calculator display may show the power of 10 in a different manner. Be sure to change your setting back to the regular display when you are done.

Thus you can see how it is possible to have negative exponents. We use negative exponents to write numbers that are less than 1 in scientific notation.

Let's look at 0.76. This number is less than 1. Recall that in our definition for scientific notation the first number must be greater than or equal to 1 and less than 10. To change 0.76 to such a number, we will have to move the decimal point.

$$0.76 = 7.6 \times 10^{-1}$$

The decimal point moves 1 place to the right. We therefore put a -1 for the power of 10. We use a negative exponent because the original number is less than 1. Let's look at two more cases.

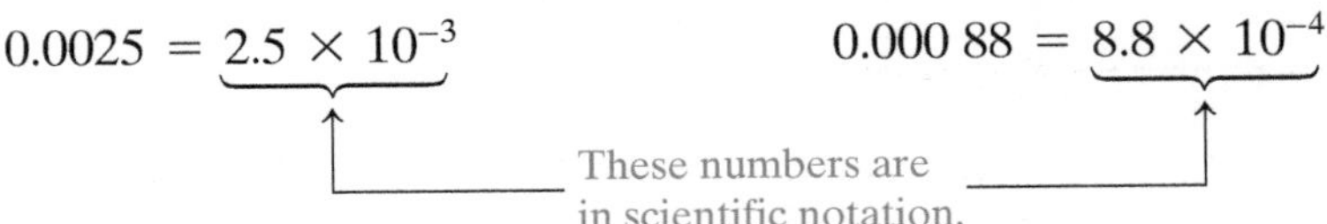

When we start with a positive number that is less than 1 and write it in scientific notation, we will get a result with 10 to a negative power. Think carefully through the steps of the following example.

EXAMPLE 2 Write in scientific notation.

(a) 0.036 **(b)** 0.72

Solution

(a) We change the given number to a number greater than or equal to 1 and less than 10. Thus we change 0.036 to 3.6.

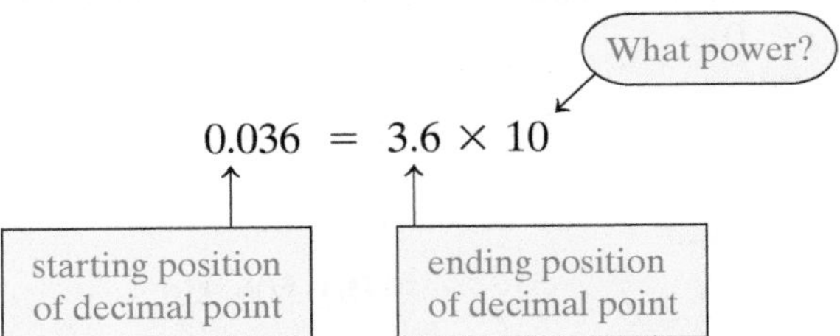

The decimal point moved 2 places to the right. Since the original number is less than 1, we use -2 for the power of 10.

$$0.036 = 3.6 \times 10^{-2}$$

(b)

What power?

$$0.72 = 7.2 \times 10$$

starting position of decimal point

ending position of decimal point

The decimal point moved 1 place to the right. Because the original number is less than 1, we use -1 for the power of 10.

$$0.72 = 7.2 \times 10^{-1}$$

Practice Problem 2 Write in scientific notation.

(a) 0.076 **(b)** 0.982

NOTE TO STUDENT: Fully worked-out solutions to all of the Practice Problems can be found at the end of the module.

It is very helpful when writing numbers in scientific notation to remember these two concepts.

1. A number that is larger than or equal to 10 and written in scientific notation will always have a positive exponent as the power of 10.
2. A positive number that is smaller than 1 and written in scientific notation will always have a negative exponent as the power of 10.

2 Changing Numbers in Scientific Notation to Standard Notation

Often we are given a number in scientific notation and want to write it in standard notation—that is, we want to write it in what we consider "ordinary form." To do this, we reverse the process we've just used. If the number in scientific notation has a positive power of 10, we know the number is greater than 10. Therefore, we move the decimal point to the right to convert to standard notation.

EXAMPLE 3 Write in standard notation.

$$5.8671 \times 10^4$$

Solution

$5.8671 \times 10^4 = 58\,671$ Move the decimal point four places to the right.

Practice Problem 3 Write in standard notation.

$$6.543 \times 10^3$$

NOTE TO STUDENT: Fully worked-out solutions to all of the Practice Problems can be found at the end of the module.

In some cases, we will need to add zeros as we move the decimal point to the right.

EXAMPLE 4 Write in standard notation.

(a) 9.8×10^5 **(b)** 3×10^3

Solution

(a) $9.8 \times 10^5 = 980\,000$ Move the decimal point five places to the right. Add four zeros.

(b) $3 \times 10^3 = 3000$ Move the decimal point three places to the right. Add three zeros.

Practice Problem 4 Write in standard notation.

(a) 4.3×10^5 **(b)** 6×10^4

If the number in scientific notation has a negative power of 10, we know the number is less than 1. Therefore, we move the decimal point to the left to convert to standard notation. In some cases, we need to add zeros as we move the decimal point to the left.

EXAMPLE 5 Write in standard notation.

(a) 2.48×10^{-3} **(b)** 1.2×10^{-4}

Solution

(a) $2.48 \times 10^{-3} = 0.002\,48$ Move the decimal point three places to the left. Add two zeros between the decimal point and 2.

(b) $1.2 \times 10^{-4} = 0.000\,12$ Move the decimal point four places to the left. Add three zeros between the decimal point and 1.

Practice Problem 5 Write in standard notation.

(a) 7.72×10^{-3} **(b)** 2.6×10^{-5}

3 Adding and Subtracting Numbers in Scientific Notation

Scientists calculate with numbers in scientific notation when they study galaxies (the huge) and when they study microbes (the tiny). To add or subtract numbers in scientific notation, the numbers must have the same power of 10.

Numbers in scientific notation may be added or subtracted if they have the same power of 10. We add or subtract the decimal part and leave the power of 10 unchanged.

EXAMPLE 6 Add. 5.89×10^{-20} metres $+ 3.04 \times 10^{-20}$ metres

Solution

$$\begin{array}{r} 5.89 \times 10^{-20} \text{ metres} \\ +3.04 \times 10^{-20} \text{ metres} \\ \hline 8.93 \times 10^{-20} \text{ metres} \end{array}$$

Practice Problem 6 Add.

6.85×10^{22} kilograms $+ 2.09 \times 10^{22}$ kilograms

EXAMPLE 7 Add. $7.2 \times 10^6 + 5.2 \times 10^5$

Solution Note that these two numbers have different powers of ten, so we cannot add them as written. We will change one number from scientific notation to another form.

We can rewrite $5.2 \times 10^5 = 520\,000$ as 0.52×10^6. Now we can add.

$$\begin{array}{r} 7.2 \times 10^6 \\ +0.52 \times 10^6 \\ \hline 7.72 \times 10^6 \end{array}$$

Practice Problem 7 Subtract. $4.36 \times 10^5 - 3.1 \times 10^4$

Section 5 Exercises

Verbal and Writing Skills

1. Why does scientific notation use exponents with base 10?

2. Explain how to write 0.787 in scientific notation.

3. What are the two parts of a number in scientific notation?

4. If $a \times 10^6$ is a number written in scientific notation, what are the possible values of a?

Write in scientific notation.

5. 120

6. 340

7. 1900

8. 5200

9. 26 300

10. 78 100

11. 288 000

12. 238 000

13. 10 000

14. 100 000

15. 12 000 000

16. 28 000 000

17. 0.0931

18. 0.0242

19. 0.002 79

20. 0.006 13

21. 0.82

22. 0.17

23. 0.000 54

24. 0.000 79

25. 0.000 005 31

26. 0.000 001 98

27. 0.000 008

28. 0.000 000 07

Write in standard notation.

29. 5.36×10^4

30. 2.19×10^4

31. 5.334×10^3

32. 8.1215×10^4

33. 4.6×10^{12}

34. 3.8×10^{11}

35. 6.2×10^{-2}

36. 3.5×10^{-2}

37. 8.99×10^{-3}

38. 7.12×10^{-1}

39. 9×10^{11}

40. 2×10^{12}

41. 3.862×10^{-8}

42. 8.139×10^{-9}

Mixed Practice

43. Write in scientific notation. 35 689

44. Write in scientific notation. 76 371

45. Write in standard notation. 3.3×10^{-4}

46. Write in standard notation. 5.7×10^{-2}

47. Write in scientific notation. 0.002 78

48. Write in scientific notation. 0.000 013 4

49. Write in standard notation. 1.88×10^6

50. Write in standard notation. 3.49×10^6

Applications *Write in scientific notation.*

51. ***Light Speed*** In 1 year, light will travel 5 878 000 000 000 miles.

52. ***Forest*** The world's forests total 2 700 000 000 acres of wooded area.

▲ **53.** ***Red Blood Cells*** The average volume of a red blood cell is 0.000 000 000 000 092 litre.

▲ **54.** ***Hydrogen Atom*** The radius of a hydrogen atom is 0.000 000 005 metre.

Write in standard notation.

55. ***Nanosecond*** An electrical signal can travel one foot in one nanosecond, which is 10^{-9} second.

56. ***Femtosecond*** A common measurement used in laser technology is the femtosecond, which is 10^{-15} second.

▲ **57.** ***Human Blood*** The diameter of a red corpuscle of human blood is about 7.5×10^{-5} centimetre.

▲ **58.** ***Mercury Drill*** Recently a tiny hole with an approximate diameter of 3.16×10^{-10} metre was produced by Doctors Heckl and Maddocks using a chemical method involving a mercury drill.

59. ***Volcano Eruption*** During the eruption of the Taupo volcano in New Zealand in 130 A.D., approximately 1.4×10^{10} tons of pumice were carried up in the air.

60. ***National Debt*** In 2001, Canada's federal debt was approximately 5.45×10^{11} dollars.

Add.

61. 3.38×10^7 dollars + 5.63×10^7 dollars

62. 8.17×10^9 atoms + 2.76×10^9 atoms

63. ***Planets*** The mass of Earth is 5.87×10^{21} tons, and the mass of Venus is 4.81×10^{21} tons. What is the total mass of the two planets?

64. ***Celestial bodies*** The masses of Mars, Pluto, and Mercury are 6.34×10^{20} tons, 1.76×10^{20} tons, and 3.21×10^{20} tons, respectively. What is the total mass of the three celestial bodies? (Mars and Mercury are planets, while Pluto is a dwarf planet.)

Subtract.

65. 4×10^8 feet − 3.76×10^7 feet

66. 9×10^{10} metres − 1.26×10^9 metres

▲67. ***Geography*** The two largest continents are Asia and Africa with areas of 1.76×10^7 square miles and 1.16×10^7 square miles, respectively. How much larger is Asia than Africa?

▲68. ***Geography*** Earth's total ocean area is approximately 3.60×10^8 square kilometres and its land area is 1.49×10^8 square kilometres. What is the total area of Earth covered by land or ocean?

To Think About

69. ***Planets*** Recently astronomers have discovered evidence of a planet named Epsilon Eridani b. This planet is in a different solar system and is 10.5 light-years from Earth. A light-year is approximately 9.46 trillion kilometres. Find in scientific notation how many kilometres Epsilon Eridani b is from Earth.

70. ***Planets*** Recently astronomers have discovered evidence of a planet named Cancri c. This planet is in a different solar system and is 41 light-years from Earth. A light-year is approximately 9.46 trillion kilometres. Find in scientific notation how many kilometres Cancri c is from Earth.

Quick Quiz 5

Write in scientific notation.

1. 0.000 345

2. 568 300

Write in standard notation.

3. 8.34×10^{-6}

4. **Concept Check** Explain how to place the zeros and spaces in the correct locations to write the number 5.398×10^8 in standard notation.

Putting Your Skills to Work: Use Math to Save Money

FOOD AND RICE PRICES

If you've noticed an increase in food prices during recent months, you are not alone. Food prices are rising throughout the world. Reasons for this include bad weather that hampered crops, an increased demand for food, particularly in countries throughout Asia, and the global increase in fuel prices.

The average cost of food increases around 1% to 6% per year. Particular foods may drop in price; for example, the price of vegetables dropped 16.5% in Canada in December 2007 as compared to December 2006. (*Source:* www.joconl.com/article/id27266) Other food prices may increase sharply.

In the spring of 2008, Costco moved to limit how much rice customers could buy because of concerns about global supply and demand. The cost of rice in some locations increased by 50% from approximately \$10 to \$15 for a 13.3-kilogram bag.

www.photos.com/Jupiter Images

Food Prices and You

Has the increase in food prices—or the increase in the cost of rice—had an impact on you and your family? How much do you spend on food each week? How about each month? How does that compare with what you were spending on food each month a year ago? Consider the story of Lucy.

Lucy and her family of four enjoy rice as part of their dinner four times a week. They cook approximately $\frac{2}{3}$ cup of raw rice for each of those four meals.

1. How many cups of rice does Lucy prepare per week?

2. If a cup of raw rice weighs approximately 595 grams, how many grams of raw rice does Lucy's family consume each week?

3. There are 1000 grams in a kilogram. Compute the number of kilograms of raw rice Lucy's family eats each week.

4. Last year Lucy bought a 13.3-kilogram bag of rice for \$9.25. She recently purchased a 13.3-kilogram bag of rice for \$15.73.

(a) What is the price increase per kilogram?

(b) What is the percent of increase?

5. Approximately how much in today's prices is the cost per week of the rice consumed by Lucy's family?

6. How much rice do you eat per week? Has the rise in the price of rice influenced your consumption of rice? Why or why not?

7. In what other food prices have you noticed an increase? What are some things you can do as a consumer to keep your costs low?

Module Organizer

Topic	Procedure	Examples
Absolute value.	The absolute value of a number is the distance between the number and zero on a number line.	$\lvert -6 \rvert = 6 \quad \lvert 3 \rvert = 3 \quad \lvert 0 \rvert = 0$
Adding signed numbers with the same sign.	To add two numbers with the same sign: **1.** Add the absolute values of the numbers. **2.** Use the common sign in the answer.	$12 + 5 = 17$ $-6 + (-8) = -14$ $-5.2 + (-3.5) = -8.7$ $-\frac{1}{7} + \left(-\frac{3}{7}\right) = -\frac{4}{7}$
Adding signed numbers with different signs.	To add two numbers with different signs: **1.** Subtract the absolute values of the numbers. **2.** Use the sign of the number with the larger absolute value.	$14 + (-8) = 6$ $-4 + 8 = 4$ $-3.2 + 7.1 = 3.9$ $\frac{5}{13} + \left(-\frac{8}{13}\right) = -\frac{3}{13}$
Subtracting signed numbers.	To subtract signed numbers, add the opposite of the second number to the first number.	$-9 - (-3) = -9 + 3 = -6$ $5 - (-7) = 5 + 7 = 12$ $8 - 12 = 8 + (-12) = -4$ $-4 - 13 = -4 + (-13) = -17$ $-\frac{1}{12} - \left(-\frac{5}{12}\right) = -\frac{1}{12} + \frac{5}{12} = \frac{4}{12} = \frac{1}{3}$
Multiplying or dividing signed numbers with different signs.	To multiply or divide two numbers with different signs, multiply or divide the absolute values. The result is negative.	$7(-3) = -21$ $(-6)(4) = -24$ $(-36) \div 2 = -18$ $\frac{41.6}{-8} = -5.2$
Multiplying or dividing signed numbers with the same sign.	To multiply or divide two numbers with the same sign, multiply or divide the absolute values. The sign of the result is positive.	$(0.5)(0.3) = 0.15$ $(-6)(-2) = 12$ $\frac{-20}{-2} = 10$ $\frac{-\frac{1}{3}}{-\frac{1}{7}} = \left(-\frac{1}{3}\right)\left(-\frac{7}{1}\right) = \frac{7}{3}$
Order of operations for signed numbers.	With grouping symbols: Do first **1.** Perform operations inside the parentheses. ↓ **2.** Simplify any expressions with exponents, and find any square roots. **3.** Multiply or divide from left to right. Do last **4.** Add or subtract from left to right.	Perform the operations in the proper order. $-2(12 - 8) + (-3)^3 + 4(-6)$ $= -2(4) + (-3)^3 + 4(-6)$ $= -2(4) + (-27) + 4(-6)$ $= -8 + (-27) + (-24)$ $= -59$
Simplifying fractions with combined operations in numerator and denominator.	**1.** Perform the operations in the numerator. **2.** Perform the operations in the denominator. **3.** Simplify the fraction.	Perform the operations in the proper order. $\frac{7(-4) - (-2)}{8 - (-5)}$ The numerator is $7(-4) - (-2) = -28 - (-2) = -26.$ The denominator is $8 - (-5) = 8 + 5 = 13.$ Thus the fraction becomes $-\frac{26}{13} = -2.$

(Continued on next page)

Topic	Procedure	Examples
Writing a number in scientific notation.	**1.** Move the decimal point to the position immediately to the right of the first nonzero digit. **2.** Count the number of decimal places you moved the decimal point. **3.** Multiply the result by a power of 10 equal to the number of places moved. If the number you started with is larger than or equal to 10, use a positive exponent. If the number you started with is less than 1, use a negative exponent.	Write in scientific notation. **(a)** 178 **(b)** 25 000 000 **(c)** 0.006 **(d)** 0.000 017 32 **(a)** $178 = 1.78 \times 10^2$ **(b)** $25\ 000\ 000 = 2.5 \times 10^7$ **(c)** $0.006 = 6 \times 10^{-3}$ **(d)** $0.000\ 017\ 32 = 1.732 \times 10^{-5}$
Changing from scientific notation to standard notation.	**1.** If the exponent of 10 is *positive,* move the decimal point to the *right* as many places as the exponent shows. Insert extra zeros as necessary. **2.** If the exponent of 10 is *negative,* move the decimal point to the *left* as many places as the exponent shows. *Note:* Remember that numbers in scientific notation that have positive exponents are always greater than or equal to 10. Numbers in scientific notation that have negative exponents are always less than 1.	Write in standard notation. **(a)** 8×10^6 **(b)** 1.23×10^4 **(c)** 7×10^{-2} **(d)** 8.45×10^{-5} **(a)** $8 \times 10^6 = 8\ 000\ 000$ **(b)** $1.23 \times 10^4 = 12\ 300$ **(c)** $7 \times 10^{-2} = 0.07$ **(d)** $8.45 \times 10^{-5} = 0.000\ 084\ 5$

Module Review Problems

Section 1

Add.

1. $-20 + 5$

2. $-18 + 4$

3. $-3.6 + (-5.2)$

4. $10.4 + (-7.8)$

5. $-\frac{1}{5} + \left(-\frac{1}{3}\right)$

6. $\frac{9}{10} + \left(-\frac{5}{2}\right)$

7. $20 + (-14)$

8. $-95 + 45$

9. $(-82) + 50 + 35 + (-18)$

10. $12 + (-7) + (-8) + 3$

Section 2

Subtract.

11. $25 - 36$

12. $12 - 40$

13. $14.5 - (-6)$

14. $16 - (-2.2)$

15. $-11.4 - 5.8$

16. $-5.2 - 7.1$

17. $-\frac{2}{5} - \left(-\frac{1}{3}\right)$

18. $3\frac{1}{4} - \left(-5\frac{2}{3}\right)$

Perform the indicated operations from left to right.

19. $5 - (-2) - (-6)$ **20.** $-15 - (-3) + 9$ **21.** $9 - 8 - 6 - 4$ **22.** $-7 - 8 - (-3)$

Section 3

Multiply or divide.

23. $\left(-\frac{2}{7}\right)\left(-\frac{1}{5}\right)$ **24.** $\left(-\frac{6}{15}\right)\left(\frac{5}{12}\right)$ **25.** $(5.2)(-1.5)$ **26.** $(-3.6)(-1.2)$

27. $-60 \div (-20)$ **28.** $-18 \div (-3)$ **29.** $\frac{-36}{4}$ **30.** $\frac{70}{-14}$

31. $\frac{-13.2}{-2.2}$ **32.** $\frac{48}{-3.2}$ **33.** $\frac{-\frac{3}{4}}{\frac{1}{6}}$ **34.** $\frac{-\frac{1}{3}}{-\frac{7}{9}}$

35. $3(-5)(-2)$ **36.** $(-2)(3)(-6)(-1)$

Section 4

Perform the indicated operations in the proper order.

37. $10 + 40 \div (-4)$ **38.** $21 - (-9) \div 3$ **39.** $2(-6) + 3(-4) - (-13)$

40. $-49 \div (-7) + 3(-2)$ **41.** $36 \div (-12) + 50 \div (-25)$ **42.** $21 - (-30) \div 15$

43. $50 \div 25(-4)$ **44.** $-3.5 \div (-5) - 1.2$ **45.** $2.5(-2) + 3.8$

In exercises 46–49, simplify the numerator and denominator first, using the proper order of operations. Then reduce the fraction if possible.

46. $\frac{8 - 17 + 1}{6 - 10}$ **47.** $\frac{9 - 3 + 4(-3)}{2 - (-6)}$

48. $\frac{20 \div (-5) - (-6)}{(2)(-2)(-5)}$ **49.** $\frac{(22 - 4) \div (-2)}{-12 - 3(-5)}$

Perform the operations in the proper order.

50. $-3 + 4(2 - 6)^2 \div (-2)$

51. $2(7 - 11)^2 - 4^3$

52. $-50 \div (-10) + (5 - 3)^4$

53. $\frac{2}{3} - \frac{2}{5} \div \left(\frac{1}{3}\right)\left(-\frac{3}{4}\right)$

54. $\left(\frac{2}{3}\right)^2 - \frac{3}{8}\left(\frac{8}{5}\right)$

55. $(1.2)^2 + (2.8)(-0.5)$

56. $1.4(4.7 - 4.9) - 12.8 \div (-0.2)$

Section 5

Write in scientific notation.

57. 4160

58. 3 700 000

59. 200 000

60. 0.007

61. 0.000 021 8

62. 0.000 007 63

Write in standard notation.

63. 1.89×10^4

64. 3.76×10^3

65. 7.52×10^{-2}

66. 6.61×10^{-3}

67. 9×10^{-7}

68. 8×10^{-8}

69. 3.14×10^5

70. 4.89×10^4

Add or subtract. Express your answer in scientific notation.

71. $2.42 \times 10^7 + 5.76 \times 10^7$

72. $6.11 \times 10^{10} + 3.87 \times 10^{10}$

73. $3.42 \times 10^{14} - 1.98 \times 10^{14}$

74. $1.76 \times 10^{26} - 1.08 \times 10^{26}$

75. ***River*** There are 123 120 000 000 000 drops of water in a river 12 kilometres long, 270 metres wide, and 38 metres deep. Write this number in scientific notation.

76. ***Earth Science*** The mass of Earth is approximately 5 983 000 000 000 000 000 000 000 kilograms. Because writing down all of these zeros is not fun, write this number in scientific notation. This can also be characterized as 5983 Yg (yottagrams).

77. ***Astronomy*** The distance from Earth to the sun is approximately 93 000 000 miles. How many feet is that? Write your answer in scientific notation.

78. ***Alpha Centauri*** Alpha Centauri is the closest star system to our own solar system, at approximately 280 000 astronomical units away. One astronomical unit is equal to the distance from Earth to the sun. Using the information given in exercise 77, calculate how many miles Alpha Centauri is from our solar system. Write your answer in scientific notation.

79. ***Atomic Particles*** The mass of a proton is about 1.67 yg (yoctograms), and the mass of an electron is about 0.000 91 yg. If *yocto-* means 0.000 000 000 000 000 000 000 001, write the mass of a proton and that of an electron in grams in scientific notation.

▲ **80.** ***Saturn's Rings*** The rings of Saturn are approximately 2.5×10^8 metres in diameter. Write this number in standard form.

81. ***Moon*** The average distance to the moon is 384.4 Mm (megametres). If a megametre is equal to 10^6 metres, write out the number in metres.

82. ***Football*** In three plays of a football game, the quarterback threw passes that lost 5 yards, gained 6 yards, and lost 7 yards. What was the total gain or loss of the three plays?

83. ***Small Plane*** Fred is 6 feet tall and is standing at the lowest point of Death Valley, California, which is 282 feet below sea level. A small plane flies directly over Fred at an altitude of 2400 feet above sea level. Find the distance from the top of Fred's head to the plane.

84. ***Chequing Account*** Max has overdrawn his chequing account by \$18. His bank charged him \$20 for an overdraft fee. He quickly deposited \$40. What is his current balance?

85. ***Temperature Statistics*** In Toronto, Ontario, the high temperatures in degrees Celsius for five days during January were $-16°$, $-18°$, $-5°$, $3°$, and $-12°$. What was the average high temperature for these five days?

86. ***Golf*** Frank played golf with his friend Samuel. They played nine holes of golf on a special practice course. The expected number of strokes for each hole is 3. A birdie is 1 below par. An eagle is 2 below par. A bogey is 1 above par. A double bogey is 2 above par. Frank played on par for 1 hole and got two birdies, one eagle, four bogeys, and one double bogey on the rest of the course. How many strokes above or below par was Frank on this nine-hole course?

How Am I Doing? Module Test

1. ______
2. ______
3. ______
4. ______
5. ______
6. ______
7. ______
8. ______
9. ______
10. ______
11. ______
12. ______
13. ______
14. ______
15. ______
16. ______
17. ______
18. ______
19. ______
20. ______
21. ______
22. ______

Add.

1. $-26 + 15$

2. $-31 + (-12)$

3. $12.8 + (-8.9)$

4. $-3 + (-6) + 7 + (-4)$

5. $-5\frac{3}{4} + 2\frac{1}{4}$

6. $-\frac{1}{4} + \left(-\frac{5}{8}\right)$

Subtract.

7. $-32 - 6$

8. $23 - 18$

9. $\frac{4}{5} - \left(-\frac{1}{3}\right)$

10. $-50 - (-7)$

11. $-2.5 - (-6.5)$

12. $-8.5 - 2.8$

13. $\frac{1}{12} - \left(-\frac{5}{6}\right)$

14. $-15 - (-15)$

Multiply or divide.

15. $(-20)(-6)$

16. $27 \div \left(-\frac{3}{4}\right)$

17. $-40 \div (-4)$

18. $(-9)(-1)(-2)(4)\left(\frac{1}{4}\right)$

19. $\frac{-39}{-13}$

20. $\frac{-\frac{3}{5}}{\frac{6}{7}}$

21. $(-12)(0.5)(-3)$

22. $96 \div (-3)$

Perform the indicated operations in the proper order.

23. $7 - 2(-5)$

24. $-2.5 - 1.2 \div (-0.4)$

25. $18 \div (-3) + 24 \div (-12)$

26. $-6(-3) - 4(3 - 7)^2$

27. $1.3 - 9.5 - (-2.5) + 3(-0.5)$

28. $-48 \div (-6) - 7(-2)^2$

29. $\dfrac{3 + 8 - 5}{(-4)(6) + (-6)(3)}$

30. $\dfrac{5 + 28 \div (-4)}{7 - (-5)}$

Write in scientific notation.

31. 80 540

32. 0.000 007

Write in standard notation.

33. 9.36×10^{-5}

34. 7.2×10^4

Solve.

35. In Edmonton the high temperatures in degrees Celsius for five days during February were $-14°$, $-8°$, $-5°$, $-7°$, and $-11°$. What was the average high temperature for these five days?

▲ **36.** A rectangular computer chip is 5.8×10^{-5} metre wide and 7.8×10^{-5} metre long. Find the perimeter of the chip and express your answer in scientific notation.

37. The lowest recorded temperature in Antarctica is $-128.6°$F in Vostock II on July 21, 1983. The highest recorded temperature in Antarctica is 58.3°F in Hope Bay on January 5, 1974. What is the difference between these temperatures?

23. ____________

24. ____________

25. ____________

26. ____________

27. ____________

28. ____________

29. ____________

30. ____________

31. ____________

32. ____________

33. ____________

34. ____________

35. ____________

36. ____________

37. ____________

Solutions to Practice Problems

Section 1 Practice Problems

1. (a) 4 lies to the right of 2, so $4 > 2$.
(b) -5 lies to the left of -3, so $-5 < -3$.
(c) 0 lies to the right of -6, so $0 > -6$.
(d) -2 lies to the left of 1, so $-2 < 1$.
(e) 5 lies to the right of -7, so $5 > -7$.

2. (a) $\begin{array}{r} 9 \\ \underline{+14} \\ 23 \end{array}$ **(b)** $\begin{array}{r} -4.5 \\ \underline{+-1.9} \\ -6.4 \end{array}$

3. (a) $\begin{array}{rcl} \frac{5}{12} & = & \frac{5}{12} \\ +\frac{1}{4} \times \frac{3}{3} & = & +\frac{3}{12} \\ \hline & & \frac{8}{12} = \frac{2}{3} \end{array}$

(b) The LCD = 42.
$\frac{1}{6} \times \frac{7}{7} = \frac{7}{42}$
Because $\frac{1}{6} = \frac{7}{42}$ it follows that $-\frac{1}{6} = -\frac{7}{42}$.
$\frac{2}{7} \times \frac{6}{6} = \frac{12}{42}$
Because $\frac{2}{7} = \frac{12}{42}$ it follows that $-\frac{2}{7} = -\frac{12}{42}$.
Thus
$\begin{array}{r} -\frac{1}{6} \\ +-\frac{2}{7} \end{array}$ is equivalent to $\begin{array}{r} -\frac{7}{42} \\ +-\frac{12}{42} \\ \hline -\frac{19}{42} \end{array}$

4. Add $0.60 + 1.75 + 0.75 + 0.10 + 1.00 = 4.20\%$. The total percent for the five years is 4.20%.

5. (a) $\begin{array}{r} 7 \\ \underline{+-12} \\ -5 \end{array}$ **(b)** $\begin{array}{r} -20.8 \\ \underline{+15.2} \\ -5.6 \end{array}$

(c) $\frac{5}{6} + \left(-\frac{3}{4}\right) = \frac{10}{12} + \left(-\frac{9}{12}\right) = \frac{10 + (-9)}{12} = \frac{1}{12}$

6. $\begin{array}{r} 13°\text{C} \\ \underline{+-9°\text{C}} \\ 4°\text{C} \end{array}$

7. $\begin{array}{r} 36 \\ \underline{+-21} \\ 15 \end{array}$ Then we add $\begin{array}{r} 15 \\ \underline{+-18} \\ -3 \end{array}$
Alternatively,
$\begin{array}{r} -21 \\ \underline{+-18} \\ -39 \end{array}$ $\begin{array}{r} -39 \\ \underline{+\ 36} \\ -3 \end{array}$

8. $\begin{array}{r} \$30\,000 \\ \underline{+\$40\,000} \\ \$70\,000 \end{array}$ $\begin{array}{r} -\$20\,000 \\ -\$5\,000 \\ \underline{+-\$35\,000} \\ -\$60\,000 \end{array}$ $\begin{array}{r} \$70\,000 \\ \underline{+-\$60\,000} \\ \$10\,000 \end{array}$

The company had an overall profit of \$10 000 in the five-month period.

Section 2 Practice Problems

1. $-10 - (-5) = -10 + 5 = -5$
2. (a) $5 - 12 = 5 + (-12) = -7$
(b) $-11 - 17 = -11 + (-17) = -28$
3. (a) $3.6 - (-9.5) = 3.6 + 9.5 = 13.1$
(b) $-\frac{5}{8} - \left(-\frac{5}{24}\right) = -\frac{5}{8} + \frac{5}{24}$
$= -\frac{5}{8} \times \frac{3}{3} + \frac{5}{24}$
$= -\frac{15}{24} + \frac{5}{24}$
$= -\frac{10}{24}$ or $-\frac{5}{12}$
4. (a) $20 - (-5) = 20 + 5 = 25$
(b) $-\frac{1}{5} - \left(-\frac{1}{2}\right) = -\frac{1}{5} + \frac{1}{2} = -\frac{2}{10} + \frac{5}{10} = \frac{3}{10}$
(c) $3.6 - (-5.5) = 3.6 + 5.5 = 9.1$
5. $-5 - (-9) + (-14) = -5 + 9 + (-14) = 4 + (-14) = -10$
6. $31 - (-37) = 31 + 37 = 68$ The difference is 68 °F.

Section 3 Practice Problems

1. (a) $(6)(9) = 54$ **(b)** $(7)(12) = 84$
2. (a) $(-8)(5) = -40$ **(b)** $3(-60) = -180$
3. (a) $-50 \div 25 = -2$ **(b)** $49 \div (-7) = -7$
4. (a) $-10(-6) = 60$ **(b)** $\left(-\frac{1}{3}\right)\left(-\frac{2}{7}\right) = \frac{2}{21}$
5. (a) $-78 \div (-2) = 39$ **(b)** $(-1.2) \div (-0.5) = 2.4$
6. $(-6)(3)(-4) = (-18)(-4) = 72$
7. $(-2)(6) = -12$
Thus the change in charge would be -12.
8. $\frac{7 + 5 + 2 + (-4) + (-3) + (-1)}{6} = \frac{6}{6} = 1$
The average temperature was 1 °C.

Section 4 Practice Problems

1. $\underbrace{20 \div (-5)}\,(-3)$
$= (-4)\ (-3)$
$= 12$

2. (a) $\underbrace{25 \div (-5)} + \underbrace{16 \div (-8)}$
$= (-5) + (-2)$
$= -7$

(b) $9 + \underbrace{20 \div (-4)}$
$= 9 + (-5)$
$= 4$

3. $\frac{9(-3) - 5}{2(-4) \div (-2)} = \frac{-27 - 5}{-8 \div (-2)} = \frac{-32}{4} = -8$

4. $-2(-12 + 15) + (-3)^4 + 2(-6)$
$= -2(3) + (-3)^4 + 2(-6)$
$= -2(3) + 81 + 2(-6)$
$= -6 + 81 + (-12)$
$= 75 + (-12)$
$= 63$

5. $\left(\frac{1}{5}\right)^2 + 4\left(\frac{1}{5} - \frac{3}{10}\right) \div \frac{2}{3}$

$= \left(\frac{1}{5}\right)^2 + 4\left(\frac{2}{10} - \frac{3}{10}\right) \div \frac{2}{3}$

$= \left(\frac{1}{5}\right)^2 + 4\left(-\frac{1}{10}\right) \div \frac{2}{3}$

$= \frac{1}{25} + 4\left(-\frac{1}{10}\right) \div \frac{2}{3}$

$= \frac{1}{25} + \left(-\frac{2}{5}\right) \div \frac{2}{3}$

$= \frac{1}{25} + \left(-\frac{2}{5}\right) \times \frac{3}{2}$

$= \frac{1}{25} + \left(-\frac{3}{5}\right)$

$= \frac{1}{25} + \left(-\frac{15}{25}\right)$

$= -\frac{14}{25}$

Section 5 Practice Problems

1. (a) Move the decimal point three places to the left.
$3729 = 3.729 \times 10^3$

(b) Move the decimal point five places to the left.
$506\,936 = 5.069\,36 \times 10^5$

2. (a) Move the decimal point two places to the right.
$0.076 = 7.6 \times 10^{-2}$

(b) Move the decimal point one place to the right.
$0.982 = 9.82 \times 10^{-1}$

3. Move the decimal point three places to the right.
$6.543 \times 10^3 = 6543$

4. (a) Move the decimal point five places to the right. Add four zeros.
$4.3 \times 10^5 = 430\,000$

(b) Move the decimal point four places to the right. Add four zeros.
$6 \times 10^4 = 60\,000$

5. (a) Move the decimal point three places to the left. Add two zeros.
$7.72 \times 10^{-3} = 0.007\,72$

(b) Move the decimal point five places to the left. Add four zeros.
$2.6 \times 10^{-5} = 0.000\,026$

6.
$$\begin{array}{r} 6.85 \times 10^{22} \text{ kilograms} \\ +2.09 \times 10^{22} \text{ kilograms} \\ \hline 8.94 \times 10^{22} \text{ kilograms} \end{array}$$

7. $3.1 \times 10^4 = 31\,000$
But $31\,000 = 0.31 \times 10^5$
$$\begin{array}{r} 4.36 \times 10^5 \\ -0.31 \times 10^5 \\ \hline 4.05 \times 10^5 \end{array}$$

Glossary

Absolute value of a number (Section 1) The absolute value of a number is the distance between that number and zero on the number line. When we find the absolute value of a number, we use the | | notation. To illustrate, $|-4| = 4$, $|6| = 6$, $|-20 - 3| = |-23| = 23$, $|0| = 0$.

Negative numbers (Section 1) All of the numbers to the left of zero on the number line. The numbers -1.5, -16, -200.5, -4500 are all negative numbers. All negative numbers are written with a negative sign in front of the digit(s).

Opposite of a number (Section 2) The opposite of a number is a number that has the same absolute value but the opposite sign. The opposite of -5 is 5. The opposite of 7 is -7.

Positive numbers (Section 1) All of the numbers to the right of zero on the number line. The numbers 5, 6.2, 124.186, 5000 are all positive numbers. A positive number such as $+5$ is usually written without the positive sign.

Scientific notation (Section 5) A positive number is written in scientific notation if it is in the form $a \times 10^n$ where a is a number greater than or equal to 1, but less than 10, and n is an integer. If we write 5678 in scientific notation, we have 5.678×10^3. If we write 0.008 25 in scientific notation, we have 8.25×10^{-3}.

Signed numbers (Section 1) All of the numbers on a number line. Numbers like -33, 2, 5, -4.2, 18.678, -8.432 are all signed numbers. A negative number always has a negative sign in front of the digits. A positive number such as $+3$ is usually written without the positive sign in front of it.

Answers to Selected Exercises for Signed Numbers

Answers to Selected Exercises for Signed Numbers

Section 1 Exercises **1.** First, find the absolute value of each number. Then add those two absolute values. Use the common sign in the answer. **3.** $<$ **5.** $>$ **7.** $>$ **9.** $<$ **11.** 7 **13.** 16 **15.** -17 **17.** -7 **19.** 16.5 **21.** $\frac{17}{35}$ **23.** -3 **25.** 9 **27.** -5 **29.** 22 **31.** -3.25 **33.** $-\frac{2}{3}$ **35.** $\frac{5}{9}$ **37.** -22 **39.** -0.72 **41.** -363 **43.** 4 **45.** $-5\frac{9}{20}$ **47.** 6.24 **49.** $-\frac{11}{2}$ or $-5\frac{1}{2}$ **51.** -14.7 **53.** 0 **55.** -6 **57.** $-\frac{53}{75}$ **59.** $-\$94\,000$ **61.** $-\$7500$ **63.** \$8800 **65.** -18 °F **67.** -1 °C **69.** -0.34 **71.** -1 yd **73.** \$37.00

Quick Quiz 1 **1.** 6 **2.** -1.5 **3.** $-3\frac{1}{3}$ **4.** See Instructor

Section 2 Exercises **1.** -6 **3.** -5 **5.** -6 **7.** -17 **9.** 9 **11.** 85 **13.** -18 **15.** 3 **17.** -60 **19.** 556 **21.** -6.7 **23.** -8.7 **25.** -8.6 **27.** 32.94 **29.** 1 **31.** $-\frac{7}{6}$ or $-1\frac{1}{6}$ **33.** $1\frac{8}{15}$ **35.** $-\frac{31}{63}$ **37.** 15 **39.** 0 **41.** 46 **43.** -22 **45.** -2 **47.** -5.4 **49.** 14 776 ft **51.** 42 °C **53.** -13 °F **55.** $-\$16\,000$ **57.** $+\$24\,900$ **59.** $\$13\frac{1}{2}$ or \$13.50

Quick Quiz 2 **1.** $\frac{15}{14}$ or $1\frac{1}{14}$ **2.** -5.5 **3.** -82 **4.** See Instructor

Section 3 Exercises **1.** To multiply two numbers with the same sign, multiply the absolute values. The sign of the result is positive. **3.** 36 **5.** 60 **7.** -160 **9.** -66 **11.** -1.5 **13.** 28.125 **15.** $-\frac{6}{35}$ **17.** 3 **19.** -8 **21.** -8 **23.** 6 **25.** 5 **27.** $\frac{3}{4}$ **29.** $\frac{8}{7}$ or $1\frac{1}{7}$ **31.** -8.38 **33.** -5.7 **35.** 30 **37.** -45 **39.** 48 **41.** -5 **43.** 10 **45.** -2.8 **47.** -0.02 **49.** $\frac{3}{7}$ **51.** -8 **53.** 150 **55.** 84 **57.** 16 **59.** $-18\,000$ **61.** 0 **63.** $-\frac{5}{12}$ **65.** He gained \$74. **67.** -10.25 °C **69.** 35 m **71.** $+33$ **73.** $+8$ **75.** $+8$ **77.** 0; at par

Quick Quiz 3 **1.** 45 **2.** -72 **3.** 39 **4.** See Instructor

How Am I Doing? Sections 1–3 **1.** -19 (obj. 1.1) **2.** -4 (obj. 1.2) **3.** 4.5 (obj. 1.2) **4.** 0 (obj. 1.3) **5.** $\frac{2}{9}$ (obj. 1.2) **6.** $-\frac{7}{6}$ or $-1\frac{1}{6}$ (obj. 1.1) **7.** -7 (obj. 1.1) **8.** 1.7 (obj. 1.2) **9.** -8 (obj. 2.1) **10.** -41 (obj. 2.1) **11.** $\frac{14}{17}$ (obj. 2.1) **12.** -12 (obj. 2.1) **13.** -16.3 (obj. 2.1) **14.** -2.8 (obj. 2.1) **15.** 42 (obj. 2.1) **16.** $\frac{19}{15}$ or $1\frac{4}{15}$ (obj. 2.1) **17.** 24 (obj. 3.1) **18.** 4 (obj. 3.1) **19.** -8 (obj. 3.1) **20.** -10 (obj. 3.2) **21.** -24 (obj. 3.1) **22.** $\frac{15}{16}$ (obj. 3.1) **23.** -64 (obj. 3.2) **24.** -10 (obj. 3.1) **25.** 24 (obj. 2.1) **26.** 21 (obj. 3.1) **27.** -1.5 (obj. 3.1) **28.** -3.6 (obj. 1.3) **29.** -0.6 (obj. 2.1) **30.** $-\frac{11}{15}$ (obj. 1.1) **31.** $\frac{1}{5}$ (obj. 3.1) **32.** $-3\frac{1}{2}$ (obj. 3.1) **33.** -3.5 °C (obj. 3.2)

Section 4 Exercises **1.** 6 **3.** -8 **5.** 8 **7.** -12 **9.** -19 **11.** 3.2 **13.** -5 **15.** -6 **17.** -27 **19.** -102 **21.** -18 **23.** 1 **25.** 4 **27.** $-\frac{1}{5}$ **29.** 1 **31.** 0 **33.** 4 **35.** 123 **37.** -7 **39.** $-\frac{13}{50}$ **41.** 6.84 **43.** -22 °F **45.** -1.7 °F **47.** 20.5 °F

Quick Quiz 4 **1.** -74 **2.** -7.9 **3.** $\frac{4}{9}$ **4.** See Instructor

Section 5 Exercises **1.** Our number system is structured according to base 10. By making scientific notation also in base 10, the calculations are easier to perform. **3.** The first part is a number greater than or equal to 1 but smaller than 10. It has at least one nonzero digit. The second part is 10 raised to some integer power. **5.** 1.2×10^2 **7.** 1.9×10^3 **9.** 2.63×10^4 **11.** 2.88×10^5 **13.** 1×10^4 **15.** 1.2×10^7 **17.** 9.31×10^{-2} **19.** 2.79×10^{-3} **21.** 8.2×10^{-1} **23.** 5.4×10^{-4} **25.** 5.31×10^{-6} **27.** 8×10^{-6} **29.** 53 600 **31.** 5334 **33.** 4 600 000 000 000 **35.** 0.062 **37.** 0.008 99 **39.** 900 000 000 000 **41.** 0.000 000 038 62 **43.** 3.5689×10^4 **45.** 0.000 33 **47.** 2.78×10^{-3} **49.** 1 880 000 **51.** 5.878×10^{12} mi **53.** 9.2×10^{-14} L **55.** 0.000 000 001 sec **57.** 0.000 075 cm **59.** 14 000 000 000 t **61.** 9.01×10^7 dollars **63.** 1.068×10^{22} t **65.** 3.624×10^8 ft **67.** 6.0×10^6 mi^2 **69.** 9.933×10^{13} km **71.** 2.625 **72.** 0.258 **73.** \$176 **74.** 589 ft

Quick Quiz 5 **1.** 3.45×10^{-4} **2.** 5.683×10^5 **3.** 0.000 008 34 **4.** See Instructor

Putting Your Skills to Work **1.** $\frac{8}{3}$ or $2\frac{2}{3}$ cups **2.** 1586.6 g **3.** 1.5867 kg **4.** **(a)** \$0.49/kg **(b)** 70% **5.** \$1.87 **6.** Answers may vary **7.** Answers may vary

Module Review Problems **1.** −15 **2.** −14 **3.** −8.8 **4.** 2.6 **5.** $-\frac{8}{15}$ **6.** $-\frac{8}{5}$ **7.** 6 **8.** −50 **9.** −15 **10.** 0 **11.** −11 **12.** −28 **13.** 20.5 **14.** 18.2 **15.** −17.2 **16.** −12.3 **17.** $-\frac{1}{15}$ **18.** $\frac{107}{12}$ or $8\frac{11}{12}$ **19.** 13 **20.** −3 **21.** −9 **22.** −12 **23.** $\frac{2}{35}$ **24.** $-\frac{1}{6}$ **25.** −7.8 **26.** 4.32 **27.** 3 **28.** 6 **29.** −9 **30.** −5 **31.** 6 **32.** −15 **33.** $-\frac{9}{2}$ or $-4\frac{1}{2}$ **34.** $\frac{3}{7}$ **35.** 30 **36.** −36 **37.** 0 **38.** 24 **39.** −11 **40.** 1 **41.** −5 **42.** 23 **43.** −8 **44.** −0.5 **45.** −1.2 **46.** 2 **47.** $-\frac{3}{4}$ **48.** $\frac{1}{10}$ **49.** −3 **50.** −35 **51.** −32 **52.** 21 **53.** $\frac{47}{30}$ or $1\frac{17}{30}$ **54.** $-\frac{7}{45}$ **55.** 0.04 **56.** 63.72 **57.** 4.16×10^3 **58.** 3.7×10^6 **59.** 2×10^5 **60.** 7×10^{-3} **61.** 2.18×10^{-5} **62.** 7.63×10^{-6} **63.** 18 900 **64.** 3760 **65.** 0.0752 **66.** 0.006 61 **67.** 0.000 000 9 **68.** 0.000 000 08 **69.** 314 000 **70.** 48 900 **71.** 8.18×10^7 **72.** 9.98×10^{10} **73.** 1.44×10^{14} **74.** 6.8×10^{25} **75.** 1.2312×10^{14} drops **76.** 5.983×10^{24} kg **77.** 4.9104×10^{11} ft **78.** 2.604×10^{13} mi **79.** 1.67×10^{-24} g; 9.1×10^{-28} g **80.** 250 000 000 m **81.** 384 400 000 m **82.** total loss 6 yd **83.** 2676 ft **84.** \$2 **85.** −9.6 °C **86.** 2 strokes above par

How Am I Doing? Module Test **1.** −11 (obj. 1.2) **2.** −43 (obj. 1.1) **3.** 3.9 (obj. 1.2) **4.** −6 (obj. 1.3) **5.** $-3\frac{1}{2}$ (obj. 1.2) **6.** $-\frac{7}{8}$ (obj. 1.1) **7.** −38 (obj. 2.1) **8.** 5 (obj. 2.1) **9.** $\frac{17}{15}$ or $1\frac{2}{15}$ (obj. 2.1) **10.** −43 (obj. 2.1) **11.** 4 (obj. 2.1) **12.** −11.3 (obj. 2.1) **13.** $\frac{11}{12}$ (obj. 2.1) **14.** 0 (obj. 2.1) **15.** 120 (obj. 3.1) **16.** −36 (obj. 3.1) **17.** 10 (obj. 3.1) **18.** −18 (obj. 3.2) **19.** 3 (obj. 3.1) **20.** $-\frac{7}{10}$ (obj. 3.1) **21.** 18 (obj. 3.2) **22.** −32 (obj. 3.1) **23.** 17 (obj. 4.1) **24.** 0.5 (obj. 4.1) **25.** −8 (obj. 4.1) **26.** −46 (obj. 4.1) **27.** −7.2 (obj. 4.1) **28.** −20 (obj. 4.1) **29.** $-\frac{1}{7}$ (obj. 4.1) **30.** $-\frac{1}{6}$ (obj. 4.1) **31.** 8.054×10^4 (obj. 5.1) **32.** 7×10^{-6} (obj. 5.1) **33.** 0.000 093 6 (obj. 5.2) **34.** 72 000 (obj. 5.2) **35.** −9 °C (obj. 2.3) **36.** 2.72×10^{-4} m (obj. 5.3) **37.** 186.9 °F (obj. 2.2)

Introduction to Algebra

Reverie Zurba/U.S. Agency for International Development (USAID)

Introduction to Algebra

An adequate supply of clean drinking water each day is something that we in North America take for granted. However, there are severe water shortages in 80 countries of the world. Children are the most vulnerable, for they are the most susceptible to waterborne diseases. They are the greatest beneficiaries of having new wells drilled that allow all the people of a community to have clean water. Scientists, engineers, and construction workers use the algebra of this module to construct new wells in rural communities that previously did not have clean drinking water.

SECTION 1 VARIABLES AND LIKE TERMS

Student Learning Objectives

After studying this section, you will be able to:

 **Recognize the variable in an equation or a formula.**

 **Combine like terms containing a variable.**

 Recognizing the Variable in an Equation or a Formula

In algebra we reason and solve problems by means of symbols. A **variable** is a symbol, usually a letter of the alphabet, that stands for a number. We can use the variable even though we may not know what number the variable stands for. We can find that number by following a logical order of steps. These are the rules of algebra.

We begin by taking a closer look at variables. In the formula for the area of a circle, the equation $A = \pi r^2$ contains two variables. r represents the value of the radius. A represents the value of the area. π is a known value. We often use the decimal approximation 3.14 for π.

▲ **EXAMPLE 1** Name the variables in each equation.

(a) $A = lw$ **(b)** $V = \dfrac{4\pi r^3}{3}$

Solution

(a) $A = lw$ The variables are A, l, and w.

(b) $V = \dfrac{4\pi r^3}{3}$ The variables are V and r.

▲ **Practice Problem 1** Name the variables.

(a) $A = \dfrac{bh}{2}$ **(b)** $V = lwh$

We have seen various ways to indicate multiplication. For example, 3 times n can be written as $3 \times n$. In algebra we usually do not write the multiplication symbol. We can simply write $3n$ to mean 3 times n. A number just to the left of a variable indicates that the number is multiplied by the variable. Thus $4ab$ means 4 times a times b.

A number just to the left of a set of parentheses also means multiplication. Thus $5(w)$ means $5 \times w$ or $5w$, and $3(n + 8)$ means $3 \times (n + 8)$. So a product can be written with or without a multiplication sign.

▲ **EXAMPLE 2** Write the formula without a multiplication sign.

(a) $V = \dfrac{B \times h}{3}$ **(b)** $A = \dfrac{h \times (B + b)}{2}$

Solution

(a) $V = \dfrac{Bh}{3}$ **(b)** $A = \dfrac{h(B + b)}{2}$

▲ **Practice Problem 2** Write the formula without a multiplication sign.

(a) $P = 2 \times w + 2 \times l$ **(b)** $A = \pi \times r^2$

 Combining Like Terms Containing a Variable

Recall that when we work with measurements we combine like quantities. A carpenter, for example, might perform the following calculations.

$$20 \text{ m} - 3 \text{ m} = 17 \text{ m}$$
$$7 \text{ in.} + 9 \text{ in.} = 16 \text{ in.}$$

We cannot combine quantities that do not have the same units. We cannot add 5 m + 7 L. We cannot subtract 12 kg − 3 cm.

Similarly, when using variables, we can add or subtract only when the same variable is used. For example, we can add $4a + 5a = 9a$, but we cannot add $4a + 5b$.

A **term** is a number, a variable, or a product of a number and one or more variables separated from other terms in an expression by a + sign or a − sign. In the expression $2x + 4y + (-1)$ there are three terms: $2x$, $4y$, and -1. **Like terms** have identical variables and identical exponents, so in the expression $3x + 4y + (-2x)$, the two terms $3x$ and $(-2x)$ are called *like terms*. The terms $2x^2y$ and $5xy$ are not like terms, since the exponents for the variable x are not the same. To combine like terms, you combine the numbers, called the **numerical coefficients,** that are directly in front of the terms by using the rules for adding signed numbers. Then you use this new number as the coefficient of the variable.

EXAMPLE 3 Combine like terms. $5x + 7x$

Solution We add $5 + 7 = 12$. Thus $5x + 7x = 12x$.

Practice Problem 3 Combine like terms. $9x + 2x$

When we combine signed numbers, we try to combine them mentally. Thus to combine $7 - 9$, we think $7 + (-9)$ and we write -2. In a similar way, to combine $7x - 9x$, we think $\boxed{7x + (-9x)}$ and we write $-2x$. Your instructor may ask you to write out this "think" step as part of your work. In the following example we show this extra step inside a $\boxed{}$ box. You should determine from your instructor whether he or she feels it is necessary for you to show this step.

EXAMPLE 4 Combine like terms.

(a) $3x + 7x - 15x$ **(b)** $9x - 12x - 11x$

Solution

(a) $3x + 7x - 15x = \boxed{3x + 7x + (-15x)} = 10x + (-15x) = -5x$

(b) $9x - 12x - 11x = \boxed{9x + (-12x) + (-11x)} = -3x + (-11x)$
$= -14x$

Practice Problem 4 Combine like terms.

(a) $8x - 22x + 5x$ **(b)** $19x - 7x - 12x$

A variable without a numerical coefficient is understood to have a coefficient of 1.

$7x + y$ means $7x + 1y$. $5a - b$ means $5a - 1b$.

EXAMPLE 5 Combine like terms.

(a) $3x - 8x + x$ **(b)** $12x - x - 20.5x$

Solution

(a) $3x - 8x + x = 3x - 8x + 1x = -5x + 1x = -4x$

(b) $12x - x - 20.5x = 12x - 1x - 20.5x = 11.0x - 20.5x = -9.5x$

Practice Problem 5 Combine like terms.

(a) $9x - 12x + x$ **(b)** $5.6x - 8x - x$

Numbers cannot be combined with variable terms.

EXAMPLE 6 Combine like terms.

$$7.8 - 2.3x + 9.6x - 10.8$$

Solution In each case, we combine the numbers separately and the variable terms separately. It may help to use the commutative and associative properties first.

$$\begin{aligned} &7.8 - 2.3x + 9.6x - 10.8 \\ &= 7.8 - 10.8 - 2.3x + 9.6x \\ &= -3 + 7.3x \end{aligned}$$

Practice Problem 6 Combine like terms.

$$17.5 - 6.3x - 8.2x + 10.5$$

There may be more than one variable in a problem. Keep in mind, however, that only like terms may be combined.

EXAMPLE 7 Combine like terms.

(a) $5x + 2y + 8 - 6x + 3y - 4$ **(b)** $\frac{3}{4}x - 12 + \frac{1}{6}x + \frac{2}{3}$

Solution For convenience, we will rearrange the problem to place like terms next to each other. This is an optional step; you do not need to do this.

(a) $5x - 6x + 2y + 3y + 8 - 4 = -1x + 5y + 4 = -x + 5y + 4$

(b) $\frac{3}{4}x + \frac{1}{6}x - 12 + \frac{2}{3} = \frac{9}{12}x + \frac{2}{12}x - \frac{36}{3} + \frac{2}{3}$

$$= \frac{11}{12}x - \frac{34}{3}$$

The order of the terms in an answer is not important in this type of problem. The answer to Example 7(a) could have been $5y + 4 - x$ or $4 + 5y - x$. Often we give the answer with the letters in alphabetical order.

Practice Problem 7 Combine like terms.

(a) $2w + 3z - 12 - 5w - z - 16$ **(b)** $\frac{3}{5}x + 5 - \frac{7}{15}x - \frac{1}{3}$

Section 1 Exercises

Verbal and Writing Skills

1. In your own words, write a definition for the word *variable.*

2. In your own words, define *like terms.*

3. Why is it that you cannot combine like terms with a problem such as $3x^2y + 5xy^2$?

4. Why is it that you cannot combine like terms with a problem such as $7xy + 9x$?

Name the variables in each equation.

5. $G = 5xy$

6. $S = 3\pi r^3$

7. $p = \frac{4ab}{3}$

8. $p = \frac{7ab}{4}$

Write each equation without multiplication signs.

9. $r = 3 \times m + 5 \times n$

▲**10.** $P = 2 \times w + 2 \times l$

11. $H = 2 \times a - 3 \times b$

12. $A = \frac{a \times b + a \times c}{3}$

Combine like terms.

13. $-16x + 26x$

14. $-12x + 40x$

15. $2x - 8x + 5x$

16. $4x - 10x + 3x$

17. $-\frac{1}{2}x + \frac{3}{4}x + \frac{1}{12}x$

18. $\frac{2}{5}x - \frac{2}{3}x + \frac{7}{15}x$

19. $8x - x + 10 - 6$

20. $x + 12x + 11 + 7$

21. $1.3x + 10 - 2.4x - 3.6$

22. $3.8x + 2 - 1.9x - 3.5$

23. $16x + 9y - 11 + 21x$

24. $22x - 13y - 23 - 8x$

Mixed Practice *Combine like terms.*

25. $\left(3\frac{1}{2}\right)x - 32 - \left(1\frac{1}{6}\right)x - 18$

26. $19 - \left(4\frac{1}{4}\right)x + \left(2\frac{3}{8}\right)x - 8$

27. $7a - c + 6b - 3c - 10a$

28. $10b + 3a - 8b - 5c + a$

29. $\frac{1}{2}x + \frac{1}{7}y - \frac{3}{4}x + \frac{5}{21}y$

30. $\frac{1}{4}x + \frac{1}{3}y - \frac{7}{12}x - \frac{1}{2}y$

31. $7.3x + 1.7x + 4 - 6.4x - 5.6x - 10$

32. $3.1x + 2.9x - 8 - 12.8x - 3.2x + 3$

33. $-7.6n + 1.2 + 11.2m - 3.5n - 8.1m$

34. $4.5n - 5.9m + 3.9 - 7.2n + 9m$

To Think About

▲ **35.** **(a)** Find the perimeter of the triangle.
(b) If each side of the triangle is doubled, what is the new perimeter?

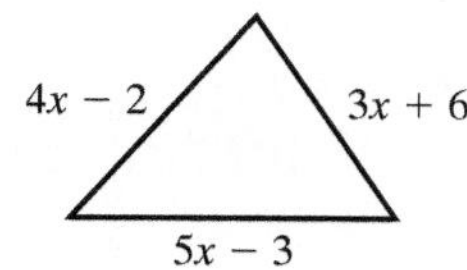

▲ **36.** **(a)** Find the perimeter of this four-sided figure.
(b) If each side is doubled, what is the new perimeter?

2x − 4
x + 5
x + 9
2x + 6

Quick Quiz 1 Combine like terms.

1. $6a - 5b - 3a - 9b$

2. $\frac{1}{3}x - \frac{4}{5}y - \frac{3}{4}x + \frac{3}{25}y$

3. $-12x + 22y - 34 - 6x - 7y - 13$

4. **Concept Check** Explain how you would combine like terms in the following expression without making any sign errors.

$$-8.2x - 3.4y + 6.7z - 3.1x + 5.6y - 9.8z$$

Section 2 The Distributive Property

Student Learning Objectives

After studying this section, you will be able to:

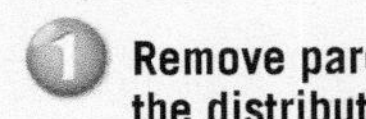

1. **Remove parentheses using the distributive property.**

2. **Simplify expressions by removing parentheses and combining like terms.**

1 Removing Parentheses Using the Distributive Property

What do we mean by the word *property* in mathematics? A **property** is an essential characteristic. A property of addition is an essential characteristic of addition. In this section we learn about the distributive property and how to use this property to simplify expressions.

Sometimes we encounter expressions like $4(x + 3)$. We'd like to be able to simplify the expression so that no parentheses appear. Notice that this expression contains two operations, multiplication and addition. We will use the distributive property to distribute the 4 to both terms in the addition statement. That is,

$$4(x + 3) \quad \text{is equal to} \quad 4(x) + 4(3).$$

The numerical coefficient 4 can be "distributed over" the expression $x + 3$ by multiplying the 4 by each of the terms in the parentheses. The expression $4(x) + 4(3)$ can be simplified to $4x + 12$, which has no parentheses. Thus we can use the distributive property to remove the parentheses.

Using variables, we can write the distributive property two ways.

DISTRIBUTIVE PROPERTIES OF MULTIPLICATION OVER ADDITION

If a, b, and c are signed numbers, then

$$a(b + c) = ab + ac \quad \text{and} \quad (b + c)a = ba + ca.$$

A numerical example shows that the distributive property works.

$$\begin{aligned} 7(4 + 6) &= 7(4) + 7(6) \\ 7(10) &= 28 + 42 \\ 70 &= 70 \end{aligned}$$

When the number is to the left of the parentheses, we use

$$a(b + c) = ab + ac.$$

There is also a distributive property of multiplication over subtraction: $a(b - c) = ab - ac$.

EXAMPLE 1 Simplify.

(a) $8(x + 5)$ **(b)** $-3(x + 3y)$ **(c)** $6(3a - 7b)$

Solution

(a) $8(x + 5) = 8x + 8(5) = 8x + 40$

(b) $-3(x + 3y) = -3x + (-3)(3y) = -3x + (-9y) = -3x - 9y$

(c) $6(3a - 7b) = 6(3a) - 6(7b) = 18a - 42b$

Practice Problem 1 Simplify.

(a) $7(x + 5)$ **(b)** $-4(x + 2y)$ **(c)** $5(6a - 2b)$

Sometimes the number is to the right of the parentheses, so we use

$$(b + c)a = ba + ca.$$

EXAMPLE 2 Simplify. $(5x + y)(2)$

Solution

$$\begin{aligned}(5x + y)(2) &= (5x)(2) + (y)(2)\\ &= 10x + 2y\end{aligned}$$

Notice in Example 2 that we write our final answer with the numerical coefficient to the left of the variable. We would not leave $(y)(2)$ as an answer but would write $2y$.

Practice Problem 2 Simplify. $(x + 3y)(8)$

Sometimes the distributive property is used with three terms within the parentheses. When parentheses are used inside parentheses, the outside ( ) are changed to bracket [ ] notation.

EXAMPLE 3 Simplify.

(a) $-5(x + 2y - 8)$ **(b)** $(1.5x + 3y + 7)(2)$

Solution

(a)
$$\begin{aligned}-5(x + 2y - 8) &= -5[x + 2y + (-8)]\\ &= -5(x) + (-5)(2y) + (-5)(-8)\\ &= -5x + (-10y) + 40\\ &= -5x - 10y + 40\end{aligned}$$

(b)
$$\begin{aligned}(1.5x + 3y + 7)(2) &= (1.5x)(2) + (3y)(2) + (7)(2)\\ &= 3x + 6y + 14\end{aligned}$$

In this example every step is shown in detail. You may find that you do not need to write so many steps.

Practice Problem 3 Simplify.

(a) $-5(x + 4y + 5)$ **(b)** $(2.2x + 5.5y + 6)(3)$

The parentheses may contain four terms. The coefficients may be decimals or fractions.

EXAMPLE 4 Simplify. $\frac{2}{3}\left(x + \frac{1}{2}y - \frac{1}{4}z + \frac{1}{5}\right)$

Solution

$$\begin{aligned}&\frac{2}{3}\left(x + \frac{1}{2}y - \frac{1}{4}z + \frac{1}{5}\right)\\ &= \frac{2}{3}(x) + \frac{2}{3}\left(\frac{1}{2}y\right) + \frac{2}{3}\left(-\frac{1}{4}z\right) + \frac{2}{3}\left(\frac{1}{5}\right)\\ &= \frac{2}{3}x + \frac{1}{3}y - \frac{1}{6}z + \frac{2}{15}\end{aligned}$$

Practice Problem 4 Simplify.

$$\frac{3}{2}\left(\frac{1}{2}x - \frac{1}{3}y + 4z - \frac{1}{2}\right)$$

 Simplifying Expressions by Removing Parentheses and Combining Like Terms

After removing parentheses we may have a chance to combine like terms. The direction "simplify" means remove parentheses, combine like terms, and leave the answer in as simple and correct a form as possible.

EXAMPLE 5 Simplify. $2(x + 3y) + 3(4x + 2y)$

Solution

$$2(x + 3y) + 3(4x + 2y) = 2x + 6y + 12x + 6y$$ Use the distributive property.

$$= 14x + 12y$$ Combine like terms.

Practice Problem 5 Simplify. $3(2x + 4y) + 2(5x + y)$

EXAMPLE 6 Simplify. $2(x - 3y) - 5(2x + 6)$

Solution

$$2(x - 3y) - 5(2x + 6) = 2x - 6y - 10x - 30$$ Use the distributive property.

$$= -8x - 6y - 30$$ Combine like terms.

Notice that in the final step of Example 6 only the x terms could be combined. There are no other like terms.

Practice Problem 6 Simplify. $-4(x - 5) + 3(-1 + 2x)$

SECTION 2 EXERCISES

Verbal and Writing Skills

1. A ______________ is a symbol, usually a letter of the alphabet, that stands for a number.

2. What is the variable in the expression $5x + 9$?

3. Identify the like terms in the expression $3x + 2y - 1 + x - 3y$.

4. Explain the distributive property in your own words. Give an example.

Simplify.

5. $9(3x - 2)$

6. $8(4x - 5)$

7. $(-2)(x + y)$

8. $(-5)(x + y)$

9. $-6(-2.4x + 5y)$

10. $-5(6.2x - 7y)$

11. $(-3x + 7y)(-10)$

12. $(-2x + 8y)(-12)$

13. $(6a - 5b)(8)$

14. $(7a - 11b)(6)$

15. $(-8y - 7z)(-3)$

16. $(-4y - 9z)(-7)$

17. $4(p + 9q - 10)$

18. $6(2p - 7q + 11)$

19. $3\left(\frac{1}{5}x + \frac{2}{3}y - \frac{1}{4}\right)$

20. $4\left(\frac{2}{3}x + \frac{1}{4}y - \frac{3}{8}\right)$

21. $-15(-2a - 3.2b + 4.5)$

22. $-14(-5a + 1.4b - 2.5)$

23. $(8a + 12b - 9c - 5)(4)$

24. $(-7a + 11b - 10c - 9)(7)$

25. $-2(1.3x - 8.5y - 5z + 12)$

26. $-3(1.4x - 7.6y - 9z - 4)$

27. $\frac{1}{2}\left(2x - 3y + 4z - \frac{1}{2}\right)$

28. $\frac{1}{3}\left(-3x + \frac{1}{2}y + 2z - 3\right)$

29. $-\frac{1}{3}(9s - 30t - 63)$

30. $-\frac{1}{6}(-18s + 6t - 24)$

Applications

▲ 31. ***Geometry*** The perimeter of a rectangle is $P = 2(l + w)$. Write this formula without parentheses and without multiplication signs.

▲ 32. ***Geometry*** The surface area of a rectangular solid is $S = 2(lw + lh + wh)$. Write this formula without parentheses and without multiplication signs.

▲ **33.** ***Geometry*** The area of a trapezoid is $A = \dfrac{h(B + b)}{2}$. Write this formula without parentheses and without multiplication signs.

▲ **34.** ***Geometry*** The surface area of a cylinder is $S = 2\pi r(h + r)$. Write this formula without parentheses and without multiplication signs.

Simplify. Be sure to combine like terms.

35. $4(5x - 1) + 7(x - 5)$

36. $8(4x + 3) + 2(x - 15)$

37. $10(4a + 5b) - 8(6a + 2b)$

38. $11(2a - 3b) - 2(a + 5b)$

39. $1.5(x + 2.2y) + 3(2.2x + 1.6y)$

40. $2.4(x + 3.5y) + 2(1.4x + 1.9y)$

41. $2(3b + c - 2a) - 5(a - 2c + 5b)$

42. $3(-4a + c + 4b) - 4(2c + b - 6a)$

To Think About

▲ **43.** Illustrate the distributive property by using the area of two rectangles.

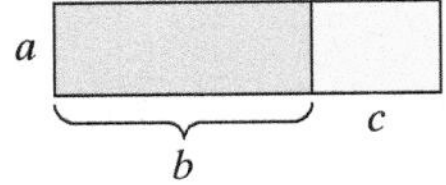

▲ **44.** Show that multiplication is distributive over subtraction by using the area of two rectangles.

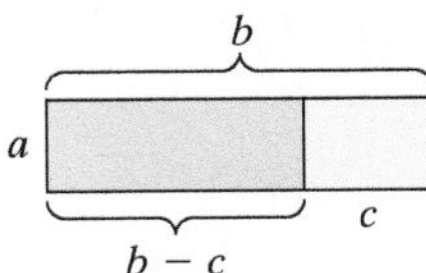

Quick Quiz 2 Simplify.

1. $3\left(\dfrac{5}{6}x - \dfrac{7}{12}y\right)$

2. $-3.5(2x - 3y + z - 4)$

3. $2(-3x + 7y) - 5(2x - 9y)$

4. Concept Check Explain the steps that are needed to simplify $-3(2x + 5y) + 4(5x - 1)$.

Section 3 Solving Equations Using the Addition Property

Solving Equations Using the Addition Property

One of the most important skills in algebra is that of **solving an equation.** Starting from an equation with a variable whose value is unknown, we transform the equation into a simpler, equivalent equation by performing a logical step. In the following sections we'll learn some of the logical steps for solving an equation successfully.

We begin with the concept of an equation. An **equation** is a mathematical statement that says that two expressions are equal. The statement $x + 5 = 13$ means that some number (x) plus 5 equals 13. Experience with the basic addition facts tells us that $x = 8$ since $8 + 5 = 13$. Therefore, 8 is the solution to the equation. The **solution** of an equation is that number which makes the equation true. What if we did not know that $8 + 5 = 13$? How could we find the value of x? Let's look at the first logical step in solving this equation.

The important thing to remember is that an equation is like a balance scale. Whatever you do to one side of the equation, you must do to the other side of the equation to maintain the balance. Our goal is to do this in such a way that we isolate the variable.

Student Learning Objective

After studying this section, you will be able to:

 **Solve equations using the addition property.**

ADDITION PROPERTY OF EQUATIONS

You may add the same number to each side of an equation to obtain an equivalent equation.

Suppose we want to make the equation $x + 5 = 13$ into a simpler equation, such as $x =$ some number. What can we add to each side of the equation so that $x + 5$ becomes simply x? We can add the opposite of $+5$. Let's see what happens when we do this addition.

$$x + 5 = 13$$

$$x + 5 + (-5) = 13 + (-5)$$ Remember to add -5 to both sides of the equation.

$$x + 0 = 8$$

$$x = 8$$

We found the solution to the equation.

Notice that in the second step, the number 5 was removed from the left side of the equation. We know that we may add a number to both sides of the equation. But what number should we choose to add? We always add the opposite of the number we want to remove from one side of the equation.

EXAMPLE 1 Solve. $x - 9 = 3$

Solution We want to isolate the variable x.

$$x - 9 = 3$$ Think: "Add the opposite of -9 to both sides of the equation."

$$x - 9 + 9 = 3 + 9$$

$$x + 0 = 12$$

$$x = 12$$

To check the solution, we substitute 12 for x in the original equation.

$$x - 9 = 3$$
$$12 - 9 \stackrel{?}{=} 3$$
$$3 = 3 \checkmark$$

It is always a good idea to check your solution, especially in more complicated equations.

NOTE TO STUDENT: Fully worked-out solutions to all of the Practice Problems can be found at the end of the module.

Practice Problem 1 Solve. $x + 7 = -8$

When we solve an equation we want to isolate the variable. We do this by performing the same operation on both sides of the equation.

Equations can contain integers, decimals, or fractions.

EXAMPLE 2 Solve. Check your solution.

(a) $x + 1.5 = 4$ **(b)** $\frac{3}{8} = x - \frac{3}{4}$

Solution We use the addition property to solve these equations since each equation involves only addition or subtraction. In each case we want to isolate the variable.

(a) $x + 1.5 = 4$ Think: "Add the opposite of 1.5 to both sides of the equation."

$$x + 1.5 + (-1.5) = 4 + (-1.5)$$
$$x = 2.5$$

Check.

$$x + 1.5 = 4$$ Substitute 2.5 for x in the original equation.
$$2.5 + 1.5 \stackrel{?}{=} 4$$
$$4 = 4 \checkmark$$

(b) $\frac{3}{8} = x - \frac{3}{4}$ Note that here the variable is on the right-hand side.

$$\frac{3}{8} + \frac{3}{4} = x - \frac{3}{4} + \frac{3}{4}$$ Think: "Add the opposite of $-\frac{3}{4}$ to both sides of the equation."

$$\frac{3}{8} + \frac{6}{8} = x + 0$$ We need to change $\frac{3}{4}$ to $\frac{6}{8}$.

$$\frac{9}{8} \text{ or } 1\frac{1}{8} = x$$

Check.

$$\frac{3}{8} = x - \frac{3}{4}$$ Substitute $\frac{9}{8}$ for x in the original equation.
$$\frac{3}{8} \stackrel{?}{=} \frac{9}{8} - \frac{3}{4}$$
$$\frac{3}{8} \stackrel{?}{=} \frac{9}{8} - \frac{6}{8}$$
$$\frac{3}{8} = \frac{3}{8} \checkmark$$

Practice Problem 2 Solve. Check your solution.

(a) $y - 3.2 = 9$ **(b)** $\frac{2}{3} = x + \frac{1}{6}$

NOTE TO STUDENT: Fully worked-out solutions to all of the Practice Problems can be found at the end of the module.

Sometimes you will need to use the addition property twice. If variables and numbers appear on both sides of the equation, you will want to get all of the variables on one side of the equation and all of the numbers on the other side of the equation.

EXAMPLE 3 Solve $2x + 7 = x + 9$. Check your solution.

Solution We want to remove the +7 on the left-hand side of the equation.

$$2x + 7 = x + 9$$
$$2x + 7 + (-7) = x + 9 + (-7)$$ Add −7 to both sides of the equation.
$$2x = x + 2$$ Now we need to remove the x on the right-hand side of the equation.
$$2x + (-x) = x + (-x) + 2$$ Add $-x$ to both sides of the equation.
$$x = 2$$

We would certainly want to check this solution. Solving the equation took several steps and we might have made a mistake along the way. To check, we substitute 2 for x in the original equation.

Check.

$$2x + 7 = x + 9$$
$$2(2) + 7 \stackrel{?}{=} 2 + 9$$
$$4 + 7 \stackrel{?}{=} 2 + 9$$
$$11 = 11 \checkmark$$

Practice Problem 3 Solve $3x - 5 = 2x + 1$. Check your solution.

Section 3 Exercises

Verbal and Writing Skills

1. An ____________ is a mathematical statement that says that two expressions are equal.

2. The ____________ of an equation is that number which makes the equation true.

3. To use the addition property, we add to both sides of the equation the ____________ of the number we want to remove from one side of the equation.

4. To use the addition property to solve the equation $x - 8 = 9$, we add ____________ to both sides of the equation.

Solve for the variable.

5. $y - 12 = 20$

6. $y - 14 = 27$

7. $x + 6 = 15$

8. $x + 8 = 12$

9. $x + 16 = -2$

10. $y + 12 = -8$

11. $14 + x = -11$

12. $10 + y = -9$

13. $-12 + x = 7$

14. $-20 + y = 10$

15. $5.2 = x - 4.6$

16. $3.1 = y - 5.4$

17. $y + 8.2 = -3.4$

18. $x + 7.5 = -9.3$

19. $x - 25.2 = -12$

20. $y - 29.8 = -15$

21. $\frac{4}{5} = x + \frac{2}{5}$

22. $\frac{7}{10} = x + \frac{1}{10}$

23. $x - \frac{3}{5} = \frac{2}{5}$

24. $y - \frac{2}{7} = \frac{6}{7}$

25. $x + \frac{2}{3} = -\frac{5}{6}$

26. $y + \frac{1}{2} = -\frac{3}{4}$

27. $\frac{1}{4} + y = 2\frac{3}{8}$

28. $\frac{1}{3} + y = 4\frac{7}{12}$

Solve for the variable. You may need to use the addition property twice.

29. $3x - 5 = 2x + 9$

30. $5x + 1 = 4x - 3$

31. $5x + 12 = 4x - 1$

32. $8x - 3 = 7x - 12$

33. $7x - 9 = 6x - 7$

34. $10x + 3 = 9x + 11$

35. $18x + 28 = 17x + 19$

36. $14x - 8 = 13x - 10$

Mixed Practice *Solve for the variable.*

37. $y - \frac{1}{2} = 6$

38. $x + 1.2 = -3.8$

39. $5 = z + 13$

40. $-15 = -6 + x$

41. $-5.9 + y = -4.7$

42. $z + \frac{2}{3} = \frac{7}{12}$

43. $2x - 1 = x + 5$

44. $3x - 8 = 2x - 15$

45. $3.6x - 8 = 2.6x + 4$

46. $5.4y + 3 = 4.4y - 1$

47. $6x - 12 = 7x - 5$

48. $9x + 6 = 10x - 9$

To Think About

49. In the equation $x + 9 = 12$, we add -9 to both sides of the equation to solve. What would you do to solve the equation $3x = 12$? Why?

50. In the equation $x - 7 = -12$, we add $+7$ to both sides of the equation to solve. What would you do to solve the equation $4x = -12$? Why?

Quick Quiz 3 Solve for the variable.

1. $x - 8.4 = -10.6$

2. $8x - 15 = 7x + 20$

3. $5 + 6x = 5x - 5$

4. Concept Check Explain the steps that are needed to solve the equation $-7x + 5 = -8x - 13$.

SECTION 4 SOLVING EQUATIONS USING THE DIVISION OR MULTIPLICATION PROPERTY

Student Learning Objectives

After studying this section, you will be able to:

 **Solve equations using the division property.**

 **Solve equations using the multiplication property.**

 Solving Equations Using the Division Property

Recall that when we solve an equation using the addition property, we transform the equation to a simpler one where $x =$ some number. We use the same idea to solve the equation $3n = 75$. Think: "What can we do to the left side of the equation so that n stands alone?" If we divide the left side of the equation by 3, we will obtain $1 \cdot n$. In this way n stands alone, since $\frac{3}{3} \cdot n = 1 \cdot n = n$. Remember, however, that whatever you do to one side of the equation, you must do to the other side of the equation. Our goal once again is to isolate the variable.

$$3n = 75$$
$$\frac{3n}{3} = \frac{75}{3}$$
$$1 \cdot n = 25$$
$$n = 25$$

This is another important procedure used to solve equations.

DIVISION PROPERTY OF EQUATIONS

You may divide each side of an equation by the same nonzero number to obtain an equivalent equation.

EXAMPLE 1 Solve for n. $6n = 72$

Solution

$6n = 72$ The variable n is multiplied by 6.

$\frac{6n}{6} = \frac{72}{6}$ Divide each side by 6.

$1 \cdot n = 12$ We have $72 \div 6 = 12$.

$n = 12$ Since $1 \cdot n = n$

Practice Problem 1 Solve for n. $8n = 104$

Sometimes the coefficient of the variable is a negative number. Therefore, in solving problems of this type, we need to divide each side of the equation by that negative number.

EXAMPLE 2 Solve for the variable. $-3n = 20$

Solution

$-3n = 20$ The coefficient of n is -3.

$\frac{-3n}{-3} = \frac{20}{-3}$ Divide each side of the equation by -3.

$n = -\frac{20}{3}$ Watch your signs!

Practice Problem 2 Solve for the variable.

$$-7n = 30$$

Sometimes the coefficient of the variable is a decimal. In solving problems of this type, we need to divide each side of the equation by that decimal number.

EXAMPLE 3 Solve for the variable. $2.5y = 20$

Solution

$2.5y = 20$ The coefficient of y is 2.5.

$\dfrac{2.5y}{2.5} = \dfrac{20}{2.5}$ Divide each side of the equation by 2.5.

$$2.5_\wedge\overline{)20.0_\wedge}\quad 8$$

$y = 8$

To check, substitute 8 for y in the original equation.

$$2.5(8) \stackrel{?}{=} 20$$
$$20 = 20 \checkmark$$

It is always best to check the solution to equations involving decimals or fractions.

Practice Problem 3 Solve for the variable. Check your solution.

$$3.2x = 16$$

***NOTE TO STUDENT:** Fully worked-out solutions to all of the Practice Problems can be found at the end of the module.*

Solving Equations Using the Multiplication Property

Sometimes the coefficient of the variable is a fraction, as in the equation $\frac{3}{4}x = 6$. Think: "What can we do to the left side of the equation so that x will stand alone?" Recall that when you multiply a fraction by its reciprocal, the product is 1. That is, $\frac{4}{3} \cdot \frac{3}{4} = 1$. We will use this idea to solve the equation. But remember, whatever you do to one side of the equation, you must do to the other side of the equation.

$$\frac{3}{4}x = 6$$

$$\frac{4}{3} \cdot \frac{3}{4}x = 6 \cdot \frac{4}{3}$$

$$1x = \frac{\overset{2}{\cancel{6}}}{1} \cdot \frac{4}{\cancel{3}}$$

$$x = 8$$

MULTIPLICATION PROPERTY OF EQUATIONS

You may multiply each side of an equation by the same nonzero number to obtain an equivalent equation.

EXAMPLE 4 Solve for the variable and check your solution.

(a) $\frac{5}{8}y = 1\frac{1}{4}$ **(b)** $1\frac{1}{2}z = 3$

Solution

(a)

$$\frac{5}{8}y = 1\frac{1}{4}$$

$$\frac{5}{8}y = \frac{5}{4}$$ Change the mixed number to a fraction. It will be easier to work with.

$$\frac{8}{5} \cdot \frac{5}{8}y = \frac{5}{4} \cdot \frac{8}{5}$$ Multiply both sides of the equation by $\frac{8}{5}$ because $\frac{8}{5} \cdot \frac{5}{8} = 1$.

$$1 \cdot y = 2$$

$$y = 2$$

Check.

$$\frac{5}{8}y = 1\frac{1}{4}$$

$$\frac{5}{8}(2) \stackrel{?}{=} 1\frac{1}{4}$$ Substitute 2 for y in the original equation.

$$\frac{10}{8} \stackrel{?}{=} 1\frac{1}{4}$$

$$1\frac{2}{8} \stackrel{?}{=} 1\frac{1}{4}$$

$$1\frac{1}{4} = 1\frac{1}{4} \quad \checkmark$$

(b)

$$1\frac{1}{2}z = 3$$

$$\frac{3}{2}z = 3$$ Change the mixed number to a fraction.

$$\frac{2}{3} \cdot \frac{3}{2}z = 3 \cdot \frac{2}{3}$$ Multiply both sides of the equation by $\frac{2}{3}$. Why?

$$z = 2$$

It is always a good idea to check the solution to an equation involving fractions. We leave the check for this solution up to you.

Practice Problem 4 Solve for the variable and check your solution.

(a) $\frac{1}{6}y = 2\frac{2}{3}$ **(b)** $3\frac{1}{5}z = 4$

Hint: Remember to write all mixed numbers as improper fractions before solving linear equations. An alternative method that may also be used is to convert the mixed number to decimal form. Thus equations like $4\frac{1}{8}x = 12$ can first be written as $4.125x = 12$.

Section 4 Exercises

Verbal and Writing Skills

1. How is an equation similar to a balance scale?

2. The division property states that we may divide each side of an equation by ________________ to obtain an equivalent equation.

3. To change $\frac{3}{4}x = 5$ to a simpler equation, multiply both sides of the equation by __________.

4. Given the equation $1\frac{3}{5}y = 2$, we multiply both sides of the equation by $\frac{5}{8}$ to solve for y. Why?

Solve for the variable.

5. $4x = 36$

6. $8x = 56$

7. $7y = -28$

8. $5y = -45$

9. $-9x = 16$

10. $-7y = 22$

11. $-12x = -144$

12. $-11y = -121$

13. $-64 = -4m$

14. $-88 = -8m$

15. $0.6x = 6$

16. $0.5y = 50$

17. $17.5 = 2.5t$

18. $21.6 = 2.4n$

19. $-0.5x = 6.75$

20. $-0.4y = 6.88$

Solve for the variable.

21. $\frac{5}{8}x = 5$

22. $\frac{3}{4}x = 3$

23. $\frac{2}{5}y = 4$

24. $\frac{5}{6}y = 10$

25. $\frac{3}{5}n = \frac{3}{4}$

26. $\frac{2}{3}z = \frac{1}{3}$

27. $-\frac{2}{9}x = \frac{4}{5}$

28. $-\frac{5}{4}x = \frac{10}{3}$

29. $\frac{1}{2}x = -2\frac{1}{4}$

30. $\frac{3}{4}y = -3\frac{3}{8}$

31. $\left(-3\frac{1}{3}\right)z = -20$

32. $\left(-2\frac{1}{5}\right)z = -33$

Mixed Practice Solve for the variable.

33. $-60 = -10x$

34. $-75 = -15x$

35. $\frac{2}{3}x = -6$

36. $\frac{4}{5}x = -8$

37. $1.5x = 0.045$

38. $1.6x = 0.064$

39. $12 = -\frac{3}{5}x$

40. $20 = -\frac{5}{6}x$

Quick Quiz 4 Solve for the variable.

1. $-4x = 15$

2. $-3.5 = -0.5x$

3. $-\frac{3}{4}x = \frac{9}{2}$

4. Concept Check Explain the steps you would take to solve the equation $12 - 5 = -14x$.

Section 5 Solving Equations Using Two Properties

1 Using Two Properties to Solve an Equation

Student Learning Objectives

After studying this section, you will be able to:

1. **Use two properties to solve an equation.**
2. **Solve equations where the variable is on both sides of the equals sign.**
3. **Solve equations with parentheses.**

To solve an equation, we take logical steps to change the equation to a simpler equivalent equation. The simpler equivalent equation is x = some number. To do this, we use the addition property, the division property, or the multiplication property. In this section you will use more than one property to solve complex equations. Each time you use a property, you take a step toward solving the equation. At each step you try to isolate the variable. That is, you try to get the variable to stand alone.

EXAMPLE 1 Solve $3x + 18 = 27$. Check your solution.

Solution We want only x terms on the left and only numbers on the right. We begin by removing 18 from the left side of the equation.

$$3x + 18 + (-18) = 27 + (-18)$$ Add the opposite of 18 to both sides of the equation so that $3x$ stands alone.

$$3x = 9$$

$$\frac{3x}{3} = \frac{9}{3}$$ Divide both sides of the equation by 3 so that x stands alone.

$$x = 3$$ The solution to the equation is $x = 3$.

Check.

$$3(3) + 18 \stackrel{?}{=} 27$$ Substitute 3 for x in the original equation.

$$9 + 18 \stackrel{?}{=} 27$$

$$27 = 27 \quad \checkmark$$

Practice Problem 1 Solve $5x + 13 = 33$. Check your solution.

Note that the variable is on the right-hand side in the next example.

EXAMPLE 2 Solve $-41 = 9x - 5$. Check your solution.

Solution We begin by removing -5 from the right-hand side of the equals sign.

$$-41 + 5 = 9x - 5 + 5$$ Add the opposite of -5 to both sides of the equation.

$$-36 = 9x$$

$$\frac{-36}{9} = \frac{9x}{9}$$ Divide both sides of the equation by 9.

$$-4 = x$$

The check is left up to you.

Practice Problem 2 Solve $-50 = 7x - 8$. Check your solution.

 Solving Equations Where the Variable Is on Both Sides of the Equals Sign

Sometimes variables appear on both sides of the equation. When this occurs, we need to isolate the variable. This requires us to add a variable term to each side of the equation.

EXAMPLE 3 Solve. $8x = 5x - 21$

Solution We want to remove the $5x$ from the right-hand side of the equation so that all of the variables are on one side of the equation and all of the numbers are on the other side of the equation.

$$8x + (-5x) = 5x + (-5x) - 21$$ Add the opposite of $5x$ to both sides of the equation.

$$3x = -21$$

$$\frac{3x}{3} = \frac{-21}{3}$$ Divide both sides of the equation by 3.

$$x = -7$$

The check is left up to you.

Practice Problem 3 Solve. $4x = -8x + 42$

Suppose there is a variable term and a numerical term on each side of an equation. We want to collect all the variables on one side of the equation and all the numerical terms on the other side of the equation. To do this, we will have to use the addition property twice.

EXAMPLE 4 Solve. $2x + 9 = 5x - 3$

Solution We begin by collecting the numerical terms on the right-hand side of the equation.

$$2x + 9 + (-9) = 5x - 3 + (-9)$$ Add -9 to both sides of the equation.

$$2x = 5x - 12$$

Now we want to collect all the variable terms on the left-hand side of the equation.

$$2x + (-5x) = 5x + (-5x) - 12$$ Add $-5x$ to both sides of the equation.

$$-3x = -12$$

$$\frac{-3x}{-3} = \frac{-12}{-3}$$ Divide both sides of the equation by -3.

$$x = 4$$

Check: $2(4) + 9 \stackrel{?}{=} 5(4) - 3$ Substitute 4 for x in the original equation.

$$8 + 9 \stackrel{?}{=} 20 - 3$$

$$17 = 17 \checkmark$$

Practice Problem 4 Solve. $4x - 7 = 9x + 13$

If there are like terms on one side of the equation, these should be combined first. Then proceed as before.

EXAMPLE 5 Solve for the variable. $-5 + 2y + 8 = 7y + 23$

Solution We begin by combining the like terms on the left-hand side of the equation.

$$-5 + 2y + 8 = 7y + 23$$

$$2y + 3 = 7y + 23 \quad \text{Combine } -5 + 8.$$

$$2y + (-7y) + 3 = 7y + (-7y) + 23 \quad \text{Remove the variables on the right-hand side of the equation.}$$

$$-5y + 3 = 23$$

$$-5y + 3 + (-3) = 23 + (-3) \quad \text{Remove the 3 on the left-hand side of the equation.}$$

$$-5y = 20$$

$$\frac{-5y}{-5} = \frac{20}{-5} \quad \text{Divide both sides of the equation by } -5.$$

$$y = -4$$

Check:

$$-5 + 2(-4) + 8 \stackrel{?}{=} 7(-4) + 23$$

$$-5 + (-8) + 8 \stackrel{?}{=} -28 + 23$$

$$-5 = -5 \checkmark$$

Practice Problem 5 Solve for the variable.

$$4x - 23 = 3x + 7 - 2x$$

NOTE TO STUDENT: Fully worked-out solutions to all of the Practice Problems can be found at the end of the module.

It is wise to check your answer when solving this type of linear equation. The chance of making a simple error with signs is quite high. Checking gives you a chance to detect this type of error.

 3 Solving Equations with Parentheses

PROCEDURE TO SOLVE EQUATIONS

1. Remove any parentheses by using the distributive property.
2. Combine like terms on each side of the equation.
3. Add the appropriate value to both sides of the equation to get all numbers on one side.
4. Add the appropriate term to both sides of the equation to get all variable terms on the other side.
5. Divide both sides of the equation by the numerical coefficient of the variable term.
6. Check by substituting the solution back into the original equation.

You have probably noticed that steps 3 and 4 are interchangeable. You can do step 3 and then step 4, or you can do step 4 and then step 3.

If a problem contains one or more sets of parentheses, remove them using the distributive property. Then combine like terms on each side of the equation. Then solve.

EXAMPLE 6 Isolate the variable on the right-hand side. Then solve for x.

$$7x - 3(x - 4) = 9(x + 2)$$

Solution

$7x - 3x + 12 = 9x + 18$	Remove parentheses by using the distributive property.
$4x + 12 = 9x + 18$	Add like terms.
$4x + 12 + (-18) = 9x + 18 + (-18)$	Add -18 to each side.
$4x + (-6) = 9x$	Simplify.
$4x + (-4x) - 6 = 9x + (-4x)$	Add $-4x$ to each side. This isolates the variable on the right-hand side.
$-6 = 5x$	Simplify.
$\frac{-6}{5} = \frac{5x}{5}$	Divide each side of the equation by 5.
$-\frac{6}{5} = x$	We obtain a solution that is a fraction.

Practice Problem 6 Isolate the variable on the right-hand side. Then solve for x. $8(x - 3) + 5x = 15(x - 2)$

Section 5 Exercises

Verbal and Writing Skills

1. Explain how you would decide what to add to each side of the equation as you begin to solve $-5x - 6 = 29$ for x.

2. Explain how you would decide what to add to each side of the equation as you begin to solve $-11x = 4x - 45$ for x.

Check to see whether the given answer is a solution to the equation.

3. Is $x = 3$ a solution to $2x + 5 = 7 - 4x$?

4. Is $x = 6$ a solution to $5 - 3x = -4x + 1$?

5. Is $x = \frac{1}{2}$ a solution to $8x - 2 = 10 - 16x$?

6. Is $x = \frac{1}{3}$ a solution to $12x - 7 = 3 - 18x$?

Solve.

7. $15x - 10 = 35$

8. $12x - 30 = 6$

9. $6x - 9 = -12$

10. $9x - 3 = -7$

11. $-9x = 3x - 10$

12. $-3x = 7x + 14$

13. $14x - 10 = 18$

14. $11x + 12 = -21$

15. $0.26 = 2x - 0.34$

16. $0.78 = 3x - 0.12$

17. $\frac{2}{3}x - 5 = 17$

18. $\frac{3}{4}x + 2 = -10$

19. $18 - 2x = 4x + 6$

20. $3x + 4 = 7x - 12$

21. $9 - 8x = 3 - 2x$

22. $8 + x = 3x - 6$

23. $5z + 6 = 3z - 2$

24. $2x + 11 = 7x - 4$

25. $1.2 + 0.3x = 0.6x - 2.1$

26. $1.2 + 0.5y = -0.8 - 0.3y$

27. $0.2x + 0.6 = -0.8 - 1.2x$

28. $0.4x + 0.5 = -1.9 - 0.8x$

29. $-10 + 6y + 2 = 3y - 26$

30. $6 - 5x + 2 = 4x + 35$

31. $-y + 7 = 14 + 2y - 6$

32. $-x - 2 = -13 + 3x + 8$

33. $-30 - 12y + 18 = -24y + 13 + 7y$

34. $15 - 18y - 21 = 15y - 22 - 29y$

35. $3(2x - 5) - 5x = 1$

36. $4(2x - 1) - 7x = 9$

37. $5(y - 2) = 2(2y + 3) - 16$

38. $13 + 7(2y - 1) = 5(y + 6)$

39. $8x + 4(4 - x) = 2x - 18$

40. $10x - 3(x - 4) = 9x - 8$

41. $5x + 9 = \frac{1}{3}(3x - 6)$

42. $6x + 5 = \frac{1}{4}(8x - 4)$

43. $-2x - 5(x + 1) = -3(2x + 5)$

44. $-3x - 2(x + 1) = -4(x - 1)$

Quick Quiz 5 Solve for the variable.

1. $0.7 - 0.3x = 0.9x - 4.1$

2. $-6 - 2x + 9 = 12 + 3x + 11$

3. $-4(x + 6) + 9 = 12 + 3(x + 5)$

4. **Concept Check** Explain the steps you would take to solve the equation $7x - 3(x - 6) = 2(x - 3) + 8$.

How Am I Doing? Sections 1–5

How are you doing with your homework assignments in Sections 1 to 5? Do you feel you have mastered the material so far? Do you understand the concepts you have covered? Before you go further, take some time to do each of the following problems.

1

Combine like terms.

1. $23x - 40x$

2. $-8y + 12y - 3y$

3. $6a - 5b - 9a + 7b$

4. $6y - 8 + 3x - 2 + 4y - 5x$

5. $7x - 14 + 5y + 8 - 7y + 9x$

6. $4a - 7b + 3c - 5b$

2

Simplify.

7. $6(7x - 3y)$

8. $-4\left(\frac{1}{2}a - \frac{1}{4}b + 3\right)$

9. $-2(1.5a + 3b - 6c - 5)$

10. $5(2x - y) - 3(3x + y)$

11. $(9x + 4y)(-2)$

12. $(7x - 3y)(-3)$

3

Solve for the variable.

13. $5 + x = 42$

14. $x + 2.5 = 6$

15. $y + \frac{4}{5} = -\frac{3}{10}$

16. $-12 = -20 + x$

4

Solve for the variable.

17. $-9y = -72$

18. $2.7y = 27$

19. $\frac{3}{5}x = \frac{9}{10}$

20. $84 = -7x$

5

Solve for the variable.

21. $-7 + 6m = 25$

22. $-11 + 4m = -5m + 7$

23. $5(x - 1) = 7 - 3(x - 4)$

24. $3x + 7 = 5(5 - x)$

25. $5x - 18 = 2(x + 3)$

26. $8x - 5(x + 2) = -3(x - 5)$

27. $12 + 4y - 7 = 6y - 9$

28. $0.3x + 0.4 = 0.7x - 1.2$

Your institution may have included the Answers to Selected Exercises for this module, which contains the answers to these questions. Each answer also includes a reference to the objective in which the problem is first taught. If you missed any of these problems, you should stop and review the Examples and Practice Problems in the referenced objective. A little review now will help you master the material in the upcoming sections.

1. ________
2. ________
3. ________
4. ________
5. ________
6. ________
7. ________
8. ________
9. ________
10. ________
11. ________
12. ________
13. ________
14. ________
15. ________
16. ________
17. ________
18. ________
19. ________
20. ________
21. ________
22. ________
23. ________
24. ________
25. ________
26. ________
27. ________
28. ________

SECTION 6 TRANSLATING ENGLISH TO ALGEBRA

Student Learning Objectives

After studying this section, you will be able to:

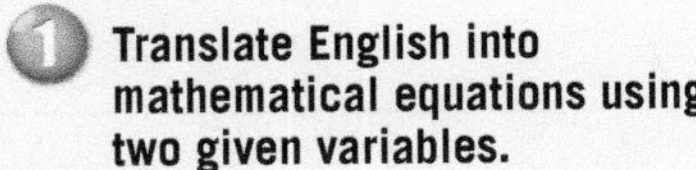

1. **Translate English into mathematical equations using two given variables.**

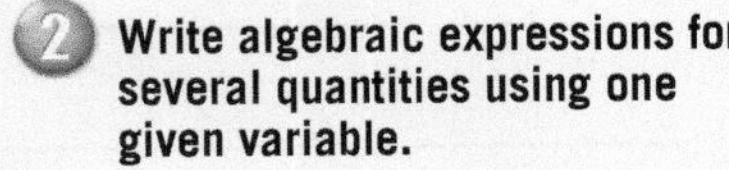

2. **Write algebraic expressions for several quantities using one given variable.**

1 Translating English into Mathematical Equations Using Two Given Variables

In the preceding section you learned how to solve equations. We can use equations to solve applied problems, but before we can do that, we need to know how to write an equation that will represent the situation in a word problem.

In this section we practise *translating* to help you to write your own mathematical equations. That is, we translate English expressions into algebraic expressions. In the next section we'll apply this translation skill to a variety of word problems.

The following chart presents the mathematical symbols generally used in translating English phrases into equations.

The English Phrase:	Is Usually Represented by the Symbol:
greater than increased by more than added to sum of	$+$
less than decreased by smaller than fewer than shorter than difference of	$-$
multiplied by of product of times	$\times$
double	$2 \times$
triple	$3 \times$
divided by ratio of quotient of	$\div$
is was has costs equals represents amounts to	$=$

An English sentence describing the relationship between two or more quantities can often be translated into a short equation using variables. For example, if we say in English "Bob's salary is \$1000 greater than Fred's salary," we can express the mathematical relationship by the equation

$$b = 1000 + f$$

where b represents Bob's salary and f represents Fred's salary.

EXAMPLE 1 Translate the English sentence into an equation using variables. Use r to represent Roberto's weight and j to represent Juan's weight.

Roberto's weight is 42 kilograms more than Juan's weight.

Solution Roberto's weight is 42 kilograms more than Juan's weight.

$$\begin{array}{ccccc} \text{Roberto's weight} & \text{is} & \text{42 kilograms} & \text{more than} & \text{Juan's weight.} \\ \downarrow & \downarrow & \downarrow & \downarrow & \downarrow \\ r & = & 42 & + & j \end{array}$$

The equation $r = 42 + j$ could also be written as

$$r = j + 42.$$

Both are correct translations because addition is commutative.

Practice Problem 1 Translate the English sentence into an equation using variables. Use t to represent Tom's height and a to represent Abdul's height.

Tom's height is 7 centimetres more than Abdul's height.

NOTE TO STUDENT: *Fully worked-out solutions to all of the Practice Problems can be found at the end of the module.*

When translating the phrase "less than" or "fewer than," be sure that the number that appears before the phrase is the value that is subtracted. Words like "costs," "weighs," or "has the value of" are translated into an equals sign (=).

EXAMPLE 2 Translate the English sentence into an equation using variables. Use c to represent the cost of the chair in dollars and s to represent the cost of the sofa in dollars.

The chair costs \$200 less than the sofa.

Solution The chair costs \$200 *less than* the sofa.

$$\begin{array}{ccccc} \text{The chair} & \text{costs} & & \text{\$200 less than} & \text{the sofa.} \\ \downarrow & \downarrow & & & \\ c & = & s & - & 200 \end{array}$$

Note the order of the equation. We subtract 200 from s, so we have $s - 200$. It would be incorrect to write $200 - s$. Do you see why?

Practice Problem 2 Translate the English sentence into an equation using variables. Use n to represent the number of students in the noon class and m to represent the number of students in the morning class.

The noon class has 24 fewer students than the morning class.

In a similar way we can translate the phrases "more than" or "greater than," but since addition is commutative, we find it easier to write the mathematical symbols in the same order as the words in the English sentence.

EXAMPLE 3 Translate the English sentence into an equation using variables. Use f for the cost of a 14-foot truck and e for the cost of an 11-foot truck.

The daily cost of a 14-foot truck is 20 dollars more than the daily cost of an 11-foot truck.

Solution The 14-foot truck cost is 20 more than the 11-foot truck cost.

$$f = 20 + e$$

Practice Problem 3 Translate the English sentence into an equation using variables. Use t to represent the number of boxes carried on Thursday and f to represent the number of boxes carried on Friday.

On Thursday Adrianne carried five more boxes into the dorm than she did on Friday.

EXAMPLE 4 Translate the following English sentence into an equation using the variables indicated. *The length of the rectangle is 3 metres shorter than double the width.* Use l for the length and w for the width of the rectangle.

Solution The length of the rectangle is compared to the width. Therefore, we begin with the width. We have

$$w = \text{the width of the rectangle.}$$

Now the length of the rectangle is 3 metres shorter than double the width. Double the width is $2w$. If it is 3 metres shorter than double the width, we will have to take away 3 from the $2w$. Therefore,

$$2w - 3 = \text{the length of the rectangle.}$$

So we have

$$l = 2w - 3.$$

Practice Problem 4 Translate the following English sentence into an equation using the variables indicated. *The length of the rectangle is 7 metres longer than double the width.* Use l for the length and w for the width of the rectangle.

2 Writing Algebraic Expressions for Several Quantities Using One Given Variable

In each of the examples so far we have used two *different variables*. Now we'll learn how to write algebraic expressions for several quantities using the *same variable*. In the next section we'll use this skill to write and solve equations.

A mathematical expression that contains a variable is often called an **algebraic expression.**

EXAMPLE 5 Write algebraic expressions for Bob's salary and Fred's salary. Fred's salary is \$150 more than Bob's salary. Use the letter b.

Solution

Let b = Bob's salary.

Let $\underbrace{b + 150}_{\text{\$150 more than Bob's salary}}$ = Fred's salary.

Notice that Fred's salary is described in terms of Bob's salary. Thus it is logical to let Bob's salary be b and then to express Fred's salary as \$150 more than Bob's.

Practice Problem 5 Write algebraic expressions for Sally's trip and Melinda's trip. Melinda's trip is 380 kilometres longer than Sally's trip. Use the letter s.

NOTE TO STUDENT: Fully worked-out solutions to all of the Practice Problems can be found at the end of the module.

▲ **EXAMPLE 6** Write algebraic expressions for the size of each of two angles of a triangle. Angle B of the triangle is 34° less than angle A. Use the letter A.

Solution Let A = the number of degrees in angle A.

Let $\underbrace{A - 34}_{\text{34° less than angle } A.}$ = the number of degrees in angle B.

Practice Problem 6 Write algebraic expressions for the height of each of two buildings. Federation Hall is 26 metres shorter than the Mathematics Centre. Use the letter m.

Often in algebra when we write expressions for one or two unknown quantities, we use the letter x.

▲ **EXAMPLE 7** Write algebraic expressions for the length of each of three sides of a triangle. The second side is 4 centimetres longer than the first. The third side is 7 centimetres shorter than triple the length of the first side. Use the letter x.

Solution Since the other two sides are described in terms of the first side, we start by writing an expression for the first side.

Let x = the length of the first side.

Let $x + 4$ = the length of the second side.

Let $3x - 7$ = the length of the third side.

▲ **Practice Problem 7** Write an algebraic expression for the length of each of three sides of a triangle. The second side is double the length of the first side. The third side is 6 centimetres longer than the first side. Use the letter x.

Section 6 Exercises

Verbal and Writing Skills *Translate the English sentence into an equation using the variables indicated.*

1. ***Weight Comparison*** Harry weighs 34 pounds more than Rita. Use h for Harry's weight and r for Rita's weight.

2. ***Cereal Boxes*** The large cereal box contains 7 ounces more than the small box of cereal. Use l for the number of ounces in the large cereal box and s for the number of ounces in the small cereal box.

3. ***Jewellery*** The bracelet costs \$107 less than the necklace. Use b for the cost of the bracelet and n for the cost of the necklace.

4. ***Education*** There were 42 fewer students taking algebra in the fall semester than the spring semester. Use s to represent the number of students registered in spring and f to represent the number of students registered in fall.

5. ***Temperature Comparisons*** The temperature in New Delhi, India, was 14 °C more than the temperature in Athens, Greece. Use n for the temperature in New Delhi and a for the temperature in Athens.

6. ***Temperature Comparisons*** The temperature in Québec City was 21 °C less than the temperature in Rome. Use q for the temperature in Québec City and r for the temperature in Rome.

▲7. ***Geometry*** The length of the rectangle is 7 metres longer than double the width. Use l for the length and w for the width of the rectangle.

▲8. ***Geometry*** The length of the rectangle is 8 metres shorter than double the width. Use l for the length and w for the width of the rectangle.

▲9. ***Geometry*** The length of the rectangle is 2 metres shorter than triple the width. Use l for the length and w for the width of the rectangle.

▲10. ***Geometry*** The length of the parallelogram is 10 ft shorter than double the width. Use l for the length and w for the width of the parallelogram.

11. ***Football*** During a college football game, Hamilton scored 10 points more than triple the number of points scored by Temple. Use h to represent the number of points Hamilton scored and t to represent the number of points Temple scored.

12. ***Soccer*** During a college soccer game, Boréal scored 2 points more than double the number of points scored by Alfred. Use b to represent the number of points Boréal scored and a to represent the number of points Alfred scored.

13. ***Hours Worked*** The combined number of hours Tina and Louise work at Leo's Pizzeria is 32 hours. Use t for the number of hours Tina works and l for the number of hours Louise works.

14. ***High School Play*** The attendance at the high school play was greater on Saturday night than on Friday night. The difference in attendance between the two nights was 138. Use s for the attendance on Saturday and f for the attendance on Friday.

15. ***Hourly Wage*** The product of your hourly wage and the amount of time worked is \$500. Let h = the hourly wage and t = the number of hours worked.

16. ***Education*** The ratio of men to women at Central College is 5 to 3. Let m = the number of men and w = the number of women.

Write algebraic expressions for each quantity using the given variable.

17. ***Airfare*** The airfare from Vancouver to Ottawa was \$135 more than the airfare from Chicago to Toronto. Use the letter p.

18. ***Electronics Cost*** The cost of a Microsoft Zune MP3 player was \$50 more than the cost of an Apple iPod MP3 player. Use the letter c.

▲**19.** ***Geometry*** Angle A of the triangle is 46° less than angle B. Use the letter b.

▲**20.** ***Geometry*** The top of the box is 38 centimetres shorter than the side of the box. Use the letter s.

21. ***Tallest Buildings*** The Burj Tower in the United Arab Emirates is 1190 ft taller than the Sears Tower in Chicago. Use the letter w.

22. ***Largest Lakes*** The two largest lakes in the world are the Caspian Sea and Lake Superior. The maximum depth of the Caspian Sea is 1771 ft more than the maximum depth of Lake Superior. Use the letter d.

23. ***Reading Books*** During the summer, Nina read twice as many books as Aaron. Molly read five more books than Aaron. Use the letter a.

24. ***Tip Salary*** Sam made \$12 more in tips than Lisa one Friday night. Brenda made \$6 less than Lisa. Use the letter l.

▲**25.** ***Geometry*** The length of a box is 5 centimetres longer than its height. The width is triple the height. Use the letter h.

▲**26.** ***Geometry*** The height of a box is 7 centimetres longer than the width. The length is 1 centimetre shorter than double the width. Use the letter w.

▲**27.** ***Triangles*** The measure of the second angle of a triangle is double the measure of the first. The measure of the third angle is 14° smaller than the measure of the first. Use the letter x.

▲**28.** ***Triangles*** The measure of the second angle of a triangle is triple the measure of the first. The measure of the third angle is 36° larger than the measure of the first. Use the letter x.

Quick Quiz 6

Translate the English sentence into an equation using the variables indicated.

1. Charlie's truck gets 12 miles per gallon less than his car gets. Use t to represent the truck's MPG (miles per gallon). Use c to represent the car's MPG.

For questions 2 and 3, write an algebraic expression for each quantity using the given variable.

2. The length of a rectangle is 3 centimetres longer than double the width. Use the letter w.

3. The number of SUVs in the college parking lot is half the number of cars. The number of trucks in the college parking lot is 35 more than the number of cars. Use the variable c.

4. **Concept Check** In Dr. Tobey's Basic Mathematics class, 12 more students have part-time jobs than full-time jobs. The students wanted to describe this relationship with algebraic expressions. One student said let $p =$ the number of students with part-time jobs and let $p - 12 =$ the number of students with full-time jobs. Another student said let $f =$ the number of students with full-time jobs and let $f + 12 =$ the number of students with part-time jobs. Which student is right? Are both right? Explain your answer.

SECTION 7 SOLVING APPLIED PROBLEMS

Solving Problems Involving Comparisons

To solve the following problem, we use the three steps for problem solving with which you are familiar, plus another step: *Write an equation.*

Student Learning Objectives

After studying this section, you will be able to:

 **Solve problems involving comparisons.**

 **Solve problems involving geometric formulas.**

 **Solve problems involving rates and percents.**

EXAMPLE 1 A 12-metre board is cut into two pieces. The longer piece is 3.5 metres longer than the shorter piece. What is the length of each piece?

Solution You may find it helpful to use the Mathematics Blueprint for Problem Solving to organize the data and make a plan for solving.

Mathematics Blueprint for Problem Solving

Gather the Facts	What Am I Asked to Do?	How Do I Proceed?	Key Points to Remember
The board is 12 metres long. It is cut into two pieces. One piece is 3.5 metres longer than the other.	Find the length of each piece.	Let x = length of shorter piece and use x to write an expression for the longer piece.	Make an equation by adding the length of both pieces to get 12 metres.

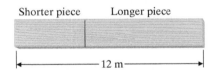

1. ***Understand the problem.***
   Draw a diagram.

   Shorter piece Longer piece

   12 m

   Since the longer piece is described in terms of the shorter piece, we let the variable represent the shorter piece. Let x = the length of the shorter piece. The longer piece is 3.5 metres longer than the shorter piece. Let $x + 3.5$ = the length of the longer piece. The sum of the lengths of the two pieces is 12 metres. We write an equation.

2. ***Write an equation.***

$$x + (x + 3.5) = 12$$

3. ***Solve and state the answer.***

$$x + x + 3.5 = 12$$

$$2x + 3.5 = 12 \qquad \text{Combine like terms.}$$

$$2x + 3.5 + (-3.5) = 12 + (-3.5) \qquad \text{Add } -3.5 \text{ to each side.}$$

$$2x = 8.5 \qquad \text{Combine like terms.}$$

$$\frac{2x}{2} = \frac{8.5}{2} \qquad \text{Divide each side by 2.}$$

$$x = 4.25$$

The shorter piece is 4.25 metres long.

$$x + 3.5 = \text{length of the longer piece}$$

$$4.25 + 3.5 = 7.75$$

The longer piece is 7.75 metres long.

4. ***Check.*** We verify solutions to word problems by making sure that all the calculated values satisfy the original conditions. Do the lengths of the two pieces add up to 12 metres?

$$4.25 + 7.75 \stackrel{?}{=} 12$$
$$12 = 12 \quad ✓$$

Is one piece 3.5 metres longer than the other?

$$7.75 \stackrel{?}{=} 3.5 + 4.25$$
$$7.75 = 7.75 \quad ✓$$

NOTE TO STUDENT: *Fully worked-out solutions to all of the Practice Problems can be found at the end of the module.*

Practice Problem 1 An 6-metre board is cut into two pieces. The longer piece is 1.5 metres longer than the shorter piece. What is the length of each piece?

Sometimes three items are compared. Let a variable represent the quantity to which the other two quantities are compared. Then write an expression for the other two quantities.

EXAMPLE 2 Professor Jones is teaching 332 students in three sections of general psychology this semester. Her noon class has 23 more students than her 8 A.M. class. Her 2 P.M. class has 36 fewer students than her 8 A.M. class. How many students are in each class?

Solution

1. ***Understand the problem.*** Each class enrolment is described in terms of the enrolment in the 8 A.M. class.

Let x = the number of students in the 8 A.M. class.

The noon class has 23 more students than the 8 A.M. class.

Let $x + 23$ = the number of students in the noon class.

The 2 P.M. class has 36 fewer students than the 8 A.M. class.

Let $x - 36$ = the number of students in the 2 P.M. class.

The total enrolment for the three sections is 332.

You can draw a diagram.

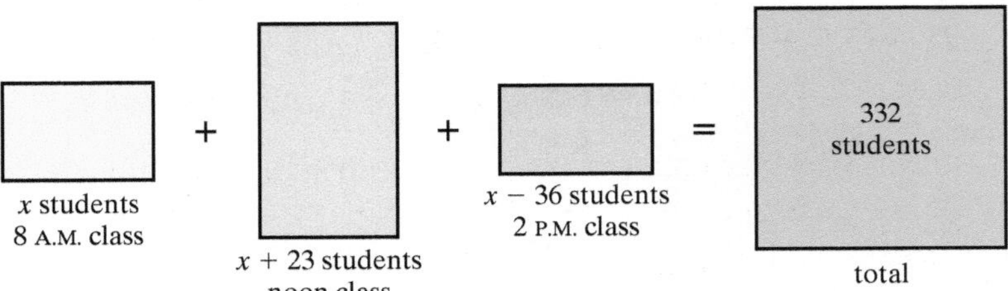

2. ***Write an equation.***

$$x + (x + 23) + (x - 36) = 332$$

3. *Solve and state the answer.*

$$x + x + 23 + x - 36 = 332$$

$$3x - 13 = 332 \quad \text{Combine like terms.}$$

$$3x + (-13) + 13 = 332 + 13 \quad \text{Add 13 to each side.}$$

$$3x = 345 \quad \text{Simplify.}$$

$$\frac{3x}{3} = \frac{345}{3} \quad \text{Divide each side by 3.}$$

$$x = 115 \quad \text{8 A.M. class}$$

$$x + 23 = 115 + 23 = 138 \quad \text{noon class}$$

$$x - 36 = 115 - 36 = 79 \quad \text{2 P.M. class}$$

Thus there are 115 students in the 8 A.M. class, 138 students in the noon class, and 79 students in the 2 P.M. class.

4. *Check.* Do the numbers of students in the classes total 332?

$$115 + 138 + 79 \stackrel{?}{=} 332$$

$$332 = 332 \checkmark$$

Does the noon class have 23 more students than the 8 A.M. class?

$$138 \stackrel{?}{=} 23 + 115$$

$$138 = 138 \checkmark$$

Does the 2 P.M. class have 36 fewer students than the 8 A.M. class?

$$79 \stackrel{?}{=} 115 - 36$$

$$79 = 79 \checkmark$$

Practice Problem 2 The city airport had a total of 349 departures on Monday, Tuesday, and Wednesday. There were 29 more departures on Tuesday than on Monday. There were 16 fewer departures on Wednesday than on Monday. How many departures occurred on each day?

***NOTE TO STUDENT:** Fully worked-out solutions to all of the Practice Problems can be found at the end of the module.*

2 Solving Problems Involving Geometric Formulas

The following applied problems concern the geometric properties of two-dimensional figures. The problems involve perimeter or the measure of the angles in a triangle.

Recall that when we double something, we are multiplying by 2. That is, if something is x units, then double that value is $2x$. Triple that value is $3x$.

 **EXAMPLE 3** A farmer wishes to fence in a rectangular field with 804 metres of fence. The length is to be 3 metres longer than *double the width.* How long and how wide is the field?

Solution

1. *Understand the problem.* The perimeter of a rectangle is given by $P = 2w + 2l$.

Let $w =$ the width.

The length is 3 metres longer than double the width.

$$\text{Length} = 3 + 2w$$

Thus $2w + 3 =$ the length.

You may wish to draw a diagram and label the figures with the given facts.

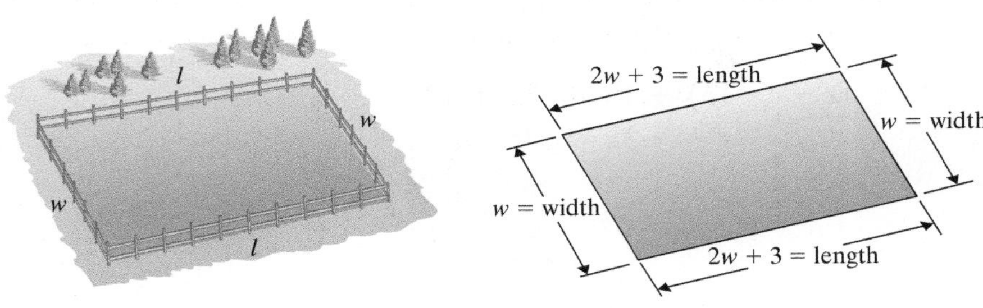

2. ***Write an equation.*** Substitute the given facts into the perimeter formula.

$$2w + 2l = P$$
$$2w + 2(2w + 3) = 804$$

3. ***Solve and state the answer.***

$$2w + 2(2w + 3) = 804$$
$$2w + 4w + 6 = 804 \quad \text{Use the distributive property.}$$
$$6w + 6 = 804 \quad \text{Combine like terms.}$$
$$6w + 6 + (-6) = 804 + (-6) \quad \text{Add } -6 \text{ to each side.}$$
$$6w = 798 \quad \text{Simplify.}$$
$$\frac{6w}{6} = \frac{798}{6} \quad \text{Divide each side by 6.}$$
$$w = 133$$

The width is 133 metres.
The length $= 2w + 3$. When $w = 133$, we have

$$2(133) + 3 = 266 + 3 = 269.$$

Thus the length is 269 metres.

4. ***Check.*** Is the length 3 metres longer than double the width?

$$269 \stackrel{?}{=} 3 + (2)(133)$$
$$269 \stackrel{?}{=} 3 + 266$$
$$269 = 269 \ \checkmark$$

Is the perimeter 804 metres?

$$2(133) + 2(269) \stackrel{?}{=} 804$$
$$266 + 538 \stackrel{?}{=} 804$$
$$804 = 804 \ \checkmark$$

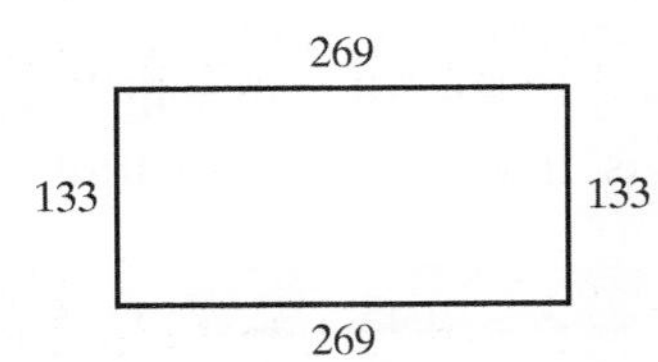

▲ **Practice Problem 3** What are the length and width of a rectangular field that has a perimeter of 772 metres and a length that is 8 metres longer than double the width?

EXAMPLE 4 The perimeter of a triangular rug section is 21 feet. The second side is double the length of the first side. The third side is 3 feet longer than the first side. Find the lengths of the three sides of the rug.

Solution

Let $x =$ the length of the first side.

Let $2x =$ the length of the second side.

Let $x + 3 =$ the length of the third side.

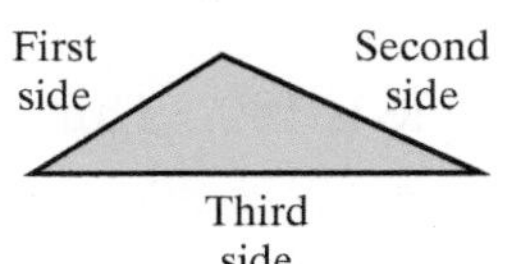

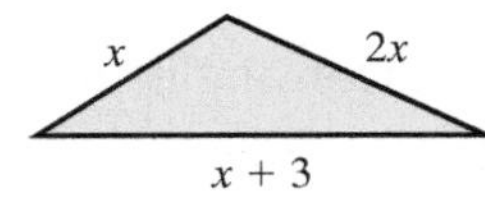

The distance around the three sides totals 21 feet.

Thus

$$x + 2x + (x + 3) = 21 \quad \text{Use the perimeter formula.}$$
$$4x + 3 = 21 \quad \text{Combine like terms.}$$
$$4x + 3 + (-3) = 21 + (-3) \quad \text{Add } -3 \text{ to each side.}$$
$$4x = 18 \quad \text{Simplify.}$$
$$\frac{4x}{4} = \frac{18}{4} \quad \text{Divide each side by 4.}$$
$$x = 4.5$$

The first side is 4.5 feet long.

$$2x = 2(4.5) = 9 \text{ feet}$$

The second side is 9 feet long.

$$x + 3 = 4.5 + 3 = 7.5 \text{ feet}$$

The third side is 7.5 feet long.

Check.

Do the three sides add up to a perimeter of 21 feet?

$$4.5 + 9 + 7.5 \stackrel{?}{=} 21$$
$$21 = 21 \ \checkmark$$

Is the second side double the length of the first side?

$$9 \stackrel{?}{=} 2(4.5)$$
$$9 = 9 \ \checkmark$$

Is the third side 3 feet longer than the first side?

$$7.5 \stackrel{?}{=} 3 + 4.5$$
$$7.5 = 7.5 \ \checkmark$$

Practice Problem 4 The perimeter of a triangle is 36 metres. The second side is double the first side. The third side is 10 metres longer than the first side. Find the length of each side. Check your solutions.

NOTE TO STUDENT: *Fully worked-out solutions to all of the Practice Problems can be found at the end of the module.*

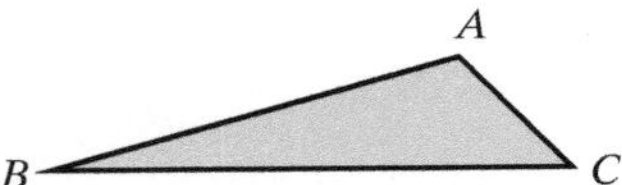

▲ **EXAMPLE 5** A triangle has three angles, A, B, and C. The measure of angle C is triple the measure of angle B. The measure of angle A is 105° larger than the measure of angle B. Find the measure of each angle. Check your answer.

Solution

Let x = the number of degrees in angle B.
Let $3x$ = the number of degrees in angle C.
Let $x + 105$ = the number of degrees in angle A.

The sum of the interior angles of a triangle is 180°. Thus we can write the following.

$$x + 3x + (x + 105) = 180$$
$$5x + 105 = 180$$
$$5x + 105 + (-105) = 180 + (-105)$$
$$5x = 75$$
$$\frac{5x}{5} = \frac{75}{5}$$
$$x = 15$$

Angle B measures 15°.

$$3x = (3)(15) = 45$$

Angle C measures 45°.

$$x + 105 = 15 + 105 = 120$$

Angle A measures 120°.

Check.
Do the angles total 180°?

$$15 + 45 + 120 \stackrel{?}{=} 180$$
$$180 = 180 \quad ✓$$

Is angle C triple angle B?

$$45 \stackrel{?}{=} (3)(15)$$
$$45 = 45 \quad ✓$$

Is angle A 105° larger than angle B?

$$120 \stackrel{?}{=} 105 + 15$$
$$120 = 120 \quad ✓$$

▲ **Practice Problem 5** The measure of angle C of a triangle is triple the measure of angle A. The measure of angle B is 30° less than the measure of angle A. Find the measure of each angle.

 Solving Problems Involving Rates and Percents

You can use equations to solve problems that involve rates and percents. Recall that the commission a salesperson earns is based on the total sales made. For example, a salesperson earns $40 if she gets a 4% commission and she sells $1000 worth of products. That is, 4% of $1000 = $40. Sometimes a salesperson earns a base salary. The commission will then be added to the base salary to determine the total salary. You can find the total salary if you know the amount of sales. How would you find the amount of sales if the salary were known? We will use an equation.

EXAMPLE 6 This month's salary for an appliance salesperson was $3000. This includes her base monthly salary of $1800 plus a 5% commission on total sales. Find her total sales for the month.

Solution

total salary of $3000	=	base salary of $1800	+	5% commission on total sales

Let s = the amount of total sales.
Then $0.05s$ = the amount of commission earned from the sales.

$$3000 = 1800 + 0.05s$$
$$1200 = 0.05s$$
$$\frac{1200}{0.05} = \frac{0.05s}{0.05}$$
$$24\,000 = s$$

She sold $24 000 worth of appliances.

Check.
Does 5% of $24 000 added to $1800 yield a salary of $3000?

$$0.05(24\,000) + 1800 \stackrel{?}{=} 3000$$
$$1200 + 1800 \stackrel{?}{=} 3000$$
$$3000 = 3000 \checkmark$$

Practice Problem 6 A salesperson at a boat dealership earns $1000 a month plus a 3% commission on the total sales of the boats he sells. Last month he earned $3250. What were the total sales of the boats he sold?

NOTE TO STUDENT: Fully worked-out solutions to all of the Practice Problems can be found at the end of the module.

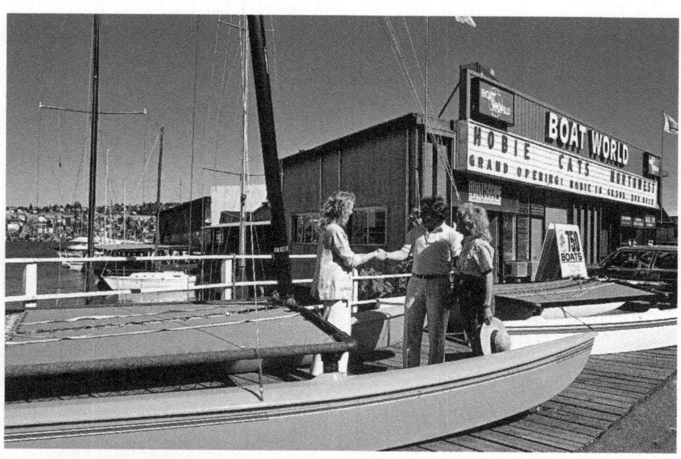

Jeffry W. Myers/Stock Boston

SECTION 7 EXERCISES

Applications *Solve using an equation. Show what you let the variable equal.*

1. ***Carpentry*** A 5-metre board is cut into two pieces. The longer piece is 1.5 metres longer than the shorter piece. What is the length of each piece?

2. ***Carpentry*** A 6.5-metre board is cut into two pieces. The longer piece is 2.5 metres longer than the shorter piece. What is the length of each piece?

3. ***Rugby*** During a rugby game, Japan scored 22 points less than France. A total of 80 points were scored. How many points did each team score?

4. ***Cross-Country*** In a cross-country race, St. Mark's scored 27 points less than Thayer. A total of 63 points were scored. How many points were scored by each team?

5. ***Car Wash*** The Business Club's thrice-yearly car wash serviced 398 cars this year. A total of 84 more cars participated in May than in November. A total of 43 fewer cars were washed in July than in November. How many cars were washed during each month?

6. ***Scrabble*** In the game of Scrabble, wooden tiles with letters on them are placed on a board to spell words. There are three times as many A tiles as there are G tiles. The number of O tiles is two more than twice the number of G tiles. The total number of A, O, and G tiles is 20. How many tiles of each are there?

Solve using an equation. Show what you let the variable equal. Check your answers.

7. ***Furniture*** A 12-foot solid cherry wood tabletop is cut into two pieces to allow for an insert later on. Of the two original pieces, the shorter piece is 4.7 feet shorter than the longer piece. What is the length of each piece?

8. ***Painting*** An artist has created a huge painting 18 feet long. Her goal is to cut the canvas and have two pieces of the same painting. The longer piece of canvas will be 6.5 feet longer than the shorter piece. What will the length of each piece be?

▲ 9. ***Game Board*** The playing board of a new game has a perimeter of 76 centimetres. It was designed so that the length is 4 centimetres shorter than double the width. What are the dimensions of the playing board?

▲ 10. ***New Room*** Marcus and Joannie are having a new family room added on to their home. They have designed the room to have a length 2 metres less than double the width. If the perimeter of the room is 28 metres, find the dimensions of the family room.

▲ 11. ***Triangular Flag*** An unusual triangular wall flag at the United Nations has a perimeter of 199 millimetres. The second side is 20 millimetres longer than the first side. The third side is 4 millimetres shorter than the first side. Find the length of each side.

▲ **12.** ***Alberta Oil Field*** There is a triangular piece of land adjoining an oil field in Alberta, with a perimeter of 271 metres. The length of the second side is double the first side. The length of the third side is 15 metres longer than the first side. Find the length of each side.

▲ **13.** ***Puzzle*** A geometric puzzle has a triangular puzzle piece with a perimeter of 44 centimetres. The length of the second side is double the first side. The length of the third side is 12 centimetres longer than the first side. Find the length of each side.

▲ **14.** ***Triangular Pennant*** An unusual triangular pennant has a perimeter of 63 inches. The length of the first side is twice the length of the second side. The third side is 3 inches longer than twice the second side. Find the length of each side.

▲ **15.** ***Geometry*** A triangle has three angles, A, B, and C. Angle B is triple angle A. Angle C is 40° larger than angle A. Find the measure of each angle.

▲ **16.** ***Geometry*** A triangle has three angles, G, H, and I. Angle H is triple angle I. Angle G is 15° less than angle I. Find the measure of each angle.

17. ***Sales Commission*** A salesperson at a car dealership earns \$1200 per month plus a 5% commission on her total sales. If she earned \$5000 last month, what was the amount of her sales?

18. ***Sales Commission*** A salesperson at a jewellery store earns \$1000 per month plus a 6% commission on his total sales. If he earned \$2200 last month, what was the amount of his sales?

19. ***Real Estate*** A real estate agent charges \$100 to place a rental listing plus 12% of the yearly rent. An apartment in Medicine Hat was rented by the agent for one year. She charged the landowner \$820. How much did the apartment cost to rent for one year?

20. ***Real Estate*** A real estate agent charges \$50 to place a rental listing plus 9% of the yearly rent. An apartment in the city of Orangeville was rented by the agent for one year. He charged the landowner \$482. How much did the apartment cost to rent for one year?

21. ***Mural*** A community in Prince Edward Island has decided to paint a mural. Adults and children each have one section, but since there are more children interested in participating than adults, the children are awarded the larger piece of wall. If the wall is 32 feet long and the children's section is 6.2 feet longer than the adults' section, what is the length of each section of wall?

22. ***Children's Theatre*** The new play at the children's theatre attracted 321 people on opening night. There were 67 more children in attendance than adults. How many children attended? How many adults attended?

To Think About

23. ***Organ Transplants*** In 2006, the combined number of heart, liver, and pancreas transplants performed in the United States was 9238. The number of heart transplants was 273 more than four times the number of pancreas transplants. The number of liver transplants was 295 less than 15 times the number of pancreas transplants. How many transplants of each organ were performed? (*Source:* www.optn.org)

24. ***Vacation Days*** The average number of vacation days per year for nine countries is given in the table below. The numbers for Japan and Korea are missing, but the values are the same for both countries. The average number of vacation days for all nine countries is 29.4. (*Source:* www.infoplease.com) Find the values for Japan and Korea. Round to the nearest whole number.

Italy	42 days
France	37 days
Germany	35 days
Brazil	34 days
United Kingdom	28 days

Canada	26 days
Korea	?
Japan	?
U.S.	13 days

25. ***Workers*** The table below gives the number of U.S. workers, in thousands, for selected occupations in 2005. The numbers are missing for machinists and personal/home care aides, but the values are the same for both occupations. The average number of workers for all eight occupations is 529. (*Source:* www.bls.gov) Find the values for machinists and personal/home care aides. Round to the nearest whole number. (Remember the table gives the number of workers in thousands.)

Child care workers	444
Electricians	747
Firefighters	228
Machinists	?

Personal/home care aides	?
Physicians and surgeons	562
Social workers	602
Waiters and waitresses	848

Quick Quiz 7 Solve using an equation.

1. Melinda earns $125 less per week than Barbara. The combined income of these two people is $437 per week. How much per week does each person earn?

2. At Canadore College, twice as many students work part-time as full-time. The number of students who do not work at all is 1200 less than the number who work part-time. There are 6000 students at the college this semester. How many work part-time? How many work full-time? How many do not work while attending college?

3. A rectangular field has a perimeter of 176 yards. The length is 7 yards longer than double the width. Find the dimensions of the rectangle.

4. **Concept Check** The first angle of a triangle is twice as large as the second angle. The third angle is 10 degrees less than the second angle. Explain how you would write an expression for each of the three angles. How would you set up an equation to find the measures of the angles? Explain how you would solve the equation.

Putting Your Skills to Work: Use Math to Save Money

TIME TO BUDGET

One way to improve your financial situation is to learn to manage the money you have with a budget. A budget can maximize your efforts to ensure you have enough money to cover your fixed expenses (including housing costs, insurance payments, taxes, credit or loan payments, and savings) as well as your variable expenses (including food, education expenses, clothing expenses, and entertainment). Consider the story of Michael.

Going Back to School

Michael is a teacher in Brampton, Ontario. One of Michael's goals is to go back to school to earn his Master's Degree in Education. He knows that this will not only help him further his career, but also provide better financial stability in the long run. His net monthly income, after deductions for items such as taxes and insurance, is currently $2500. So, Michael knows he'll need to put himself on a budget for a period of time in order to save money to go back to school. Michael's research shows that consumer credit counselling services recommend allocating the following percentages for each category of the monthly budget:

Category	Percentage
Housing	25%
Transportation	10%
Savings	5%
Utilities	5%
Medical	5%
Debt Payments	20%
Food	15%
Clothing	5%
Misc.	10%

1. If Michael follows these recommendations, how much will he have saved at the end of one year?

After investigating several schools in his area, Michael chooses to attend a university that offers a one-year program for the degree he wishes to pursue. Michael will need $3000 for tuition and fees the first semester plus $450 for textbooks.

2. What is the total cost for each semester?

3. How much will Michael need to save for two semesters of tuition and fees and textbooks?

4. How many months will it take Michael to save the entire amount needed to complete his degree?

5. How much will Michael need to save per month to have the total tuition cost in two years?

6. Michael decided to cut back on some of his variable monthly expenses such as entertainment so that he could increase his savings to 10% of his net monthly income instead of 5%. How much will he now save per month? How many months will it take Michael to save the entire amount needed for university?

7. Michael's friend told him he could save about 50% on textbook costs if he bought eBooks. If he plans to buy eBooks each semester, how many fewer months would it take him to save the entire amount needed for university?

Once Michael earns his advanced degree, his salary will increase on the following schedule:

Year 1 Michael will earn an additional $4200
Year 2 Michael will earn an additional $4800
Year 3 Michael will earn an additional $5200
Year 4 Michael will earn an additional $5500
Year 5 Michael will earn an additional $5800

8. Over 5 years, how much more money will Michael earn because he went back to school to get an advanced degree?

Making It Personal for You

9. Do you have a budget?

10. How would you adjust Michael's budget to fit your needs?

11. What advice would you give Michael for achieving his goal?

Module Organizer

Topic	Procedure	Examples
Combining like terms.	If the terms are like terms, combine the numerical coefficients directly in front of the variables.	Combine like terms. **(a)** $7x - 8x + 2x = -1x + 2x = x$ **(b)** $3a - 2b - 6a - 5b = -3a - 7b$ **(c)** $a - 2b + 3 - 5a = -4a - 2b + 3$
The distributive properties.	$a(b + c) = ab + ac$ and $(b + c)a = ba + ca$	$5(x - 4y) = 5x - 20y$ $3(a + 2b - 6) = 3a + 6b - 18$ $(-2x + y)(7) = -14x + 7y$
Problems involving parentheses and like terms.	**1.** Remove the parentheses using the distributive property. **2.** Combine like terms.	Simplify. $2(4x - y) - 3(-2x + y) = 8x - 2y + 6x - 3y$ $= 14x - 5y$
Solving equations using the addition property.	**1.** Add the appropriate value to both sides of the equation so that the variable is on one side and a number is on the other side of the equals sign. **2.** Check by substituting your answer back into the original equation.	Solve for x. $x - 2.5 = 7$ $x - 2.5 + 2.5 = 7 + 2.5$ $x + 0 = 9.5$ $x = 9.5$ *Check.* $9.5 - 2.5 \stackrel{?}{=} 7$ $7 = 7$ ✓
Solving equations using the division property.	**1.** Divide both sides of the equation by the numerical coefficient of the variable. **2.** Check by substituting your answer back into the original equation.	Solve for x. $-12x = 60$ $\frac{-12x}{-12} = \frac{60}{-12}$ $x = -5$ *Check.* $(-12)(-5) \stackrel{?}{=} 60$ $60 = 60$ ✓
Solving equations using the multiplication property.	**1.** Multiply both sides of the equation by the reciprocal of the numerical coefficient of the variable. **2.** Check by substituting your answer back into the original equation.	Solve for x. $\frac{3}{4}x = \frac{5}{8}$ $\frac{4}{3} \cdot \frac{3}{4}x = \frac{5}{8} \cdot \frac{4}{3}$ $x = \frac{5}{6}$ *Check.* $\left(\frac{3}{4}\right)\left(\frac{5}{6}\right) \stackrel{?}{=} \frac{5}{8}$ $\frac{5}{8} = \frac{5}{8}$ ✓
Solving equations using more than one step.	**1.** Remove any parentheses by using the distributive property. **2.** Combine like terms on each side of the equation. **3.** Add the appropriate value to both sides of the equation to get all numbers on one side. **4.** Add the appropriate term to both sides of the equation to get all variable terms on the other side. **5.** Divide both sides of the equation by the numerical coefficient of the variable term. **6.** Check by substituting back into the original equation.	Solve for x. $5x - 2(6x - 1) = 3(1 + 2x) + 12$ $5x - 12x + 2 = 3 + 6x + 12$ $-7x + 2 = 15 + 6x$ $-7x + 2 + (-2) = 15 + (-2) + 6x$ $-7x = 13 + 6x$ $-7x + (-6x) = 13 + 6x + (-6x)$ $-13x = 13$ $x = -1$ *Check.* $5(-1) - 2[6(-1) - 1] \stackrel{?}{=} 3[1 + 2(-1)] + 12$ $-5 - 2(-6 - 1) \stackrel{?}{=} 3(1 - 2) + 12$ $-5 - 2(-7) \stackrel{?}{=} 3(-1) + 12$ $9 = 9$ ✓

Topic	Procedure	Examples
Translating an English sentence into an equation.	When translating English into an equation: replace "greater than" by + and "less than" by −. See complete table in objective 6.1.	Translate a comparison in English into an equation using two given variables. Use t to represent Thursday's temperature and w to represent Wednesday's temperature. The temperature Thursday was 12 degrees higher than the temperature on Wednesday. temperature on Thursday → t; was → $=$; 12° → 12; higher than → $+$; temperature on Wednesday → w $t = 12 + w$
Writing algebraic expressions for several quantities.	**1.** Use a variable to describe the quantity that other quantities are described in terms of. **2.** Write an expression in terms of that variable for each of the other quantities.	▲ Write algebraic expressions for the size of each angle of a triangle. The second angle of a triangle is 7° less than the first angle. The third angle of a triangle is double the first angle. Use the letter x. Since two angles are described in terms of the first angle, we let the variable x represent that angle. Let $x =$ the number of degrees in the first angle. Let $x - 7 =$ the number of degrees in the second angle. Let $2x =$ the number of degrees in the third angle.
Solving applied problems using equations.	**1.** *Understand the problem.* **(a)** Draw a sketch. **(b)** Choose a variable. **(c)** Represent other variables in terms of the first variable. **2.** *Write an equation.* **3.** *Solve the equation and state the answer.* **4.** *Check.*	▲ The perimeter of a field is 128 metres. The length of this rectangular field is 4 metres less than triple the width. Find the dimensions of the field. **1.** *Understand the problem.* Let $w =$ the width of the rectangle in metres. Let $3w - 4 =$ the length of the rectangle in metres. **2.** *Write an equation.* Perimeter = 2(width) + 2(length) $128 = 2(w) + 2(3w - 4)$ **3.** *Solve and state the answer.* $128 = 2w + 6w - 8$ $128 = 8w - 8$ $17 = w$ The width is 17 metres. $3w - 4 = 3(17) - 4 = 47$ The length is 47 metres. **4.** *Check.* Is the perimeter 128 metres? Does $17 + 47 + 17 + 47 = 128$? Yes. Is the length 4 less than triple the width? Is $47 = 3(17) - 4$? $47 = 47$ ✓

Module Review Problems

Section 1

Combine like terms.

1. $-8a + 6 - 5a - 3$

2. $\frac{1}{3}x + \frac{1}{3} + \frac{5}{9} + \frac{1}{2}x$

3. $5x + 2y - 7x - 9y$

4. $3x - 7y + 8x + 2y$

5. $5x - 9y - 12 - 6x - 3y + 18$

6. $8a - 11b + 15 - b + 5a - 19$

Section 2

Simplify.

7. $-3(5x + y)$

8. $-4(2x + 3y)$

9. $2(x - 3y + 4)$

10. $5(6a - 8b + 5)$

11. $10\left(-\frac{2}{5}x + \frac{1}{2}y - 3\right)$

12. $-12\left(\frac{3}{4}a - \frac{1}{6}b - 1\right)$

13. $5(1.2x + 3y - 5.5)$

14. $6(1.4x - 2y + 3.4)$

Simplify.

15. $2(x + 3y) - 4(x - 2y)$

16. $2(5x - y) - 3(x + 2y)$

17. $-2(a + b) - 3(2a + 8)$

18. $-4(a - 2b) + 3(5 - a)$

Section 3

Solve for the variable.

19. $x - 3 = 9$

20. $x + 8.3 = 20$

21. $-8 = x - 12$

22. $2.4 = x - 5$

23. $3.1 + x = -9$

24. $7 + x = 5.8$

25. $x - \frac{3}{4} = 2$

26. $x + \frac{1}{2} = 3\frac{3}{4}$

27. $y + \frac{5}{8} = -\frac{1}{8}$

28. $x - \frac{5}{6} = \frac{2}{3}$

29. $2x + 20 = 25 + x$

30. $7y + 12 = 8y + 3$

Section 4

Solve for the variable.

31. $8x = -20$

32. $-12y = 60$

33. $1.5x = 9$

34. $-1.4y = -12.6$

35. $-7.2x = 36$

36. $6x = 1.5$

37. $\frac{3}{4}x = 6$

38. $\frac{2}{9}x = \frac{5}{18}$

Section 5

Solve for the variable.

39. $5x - 3 = 27$

40. $8x - 5 = 19$

41. $10 - x = -3x - 6$

42. $7 - 2x = -4x - 11$

43. $9x - 3x + 18 = 36$

44. $4 + 3x - 8 = 12 + 5x + 4$

45. $-2(3x + 5) = 4x + 8 - x$

46. $2(3x - 4) = 7 - 2x + 5x$

47. $5 + 2y + 5(y - 3) = 6(y + 1)$

48. $5 - (y + 7) = 10 + 3(y - 4)$

Section 6

Translate the English sentence into an equation using the variables indicated.

49. ***Vehicle Weight*** The weight of the truck is 3000 kilograms more than the weight of the car. Use w for the weight of the truck and c for the weight of the car.

50. ***Education*** Professor Garrison's evening psychology class has 12 more students than the afternoon class. Use e for the number of students in the evening class and a for the number of students in the afternoon class.

▲ **51.** ***Geometry*** The number of degrees in angle A is triple the number of degrees in angle B. Use A for the number of degrees in angle A and B for the number of degrees in angle B.

▲ **52.** ***Geometry*** The length of a rectangle is 3 centimetres shorter than double the width of the rectangle. Use w for the width of the rectangle in centimetres and l for the length of the rectangle in centimetres.

Write an algebraic expression for each quantity using the given variable.

53. ***Salary Comparison*** Michael's salary is $2050 more than Roberto's salary. Use the letter r.

▲ **54.** ***Geometry*** The length of the second side of a triangle is double the length of the first side of the triangle. Use the letter x.

55. ***Summer Employment*** During the summer, Carmen worked 12 more days than double the number of days Dennis worked. Use the letter d.

56. ***Book Sale*** The number of fiction books sold at the library's annual sale was 225 more than the number of nonfiction books sold. Use the letter n.

Section 7

Solve using an equation. Show what you let the variable equal.

57. ***Plumbing*** A 14-m length of pipe is divided into two pieces. One piece is 2.5 m longer than the other. Find the length of each piece.

58. ***Salary Comparison*** Two clerks work in a store. The new employee earns $28 less per week than the experienced employee. Together they earn $412 per week. What is the weekly salary of each person?

59. ***Fast-Food Restaurant*** A local fast-food restaurant had twice as many customers in March as in February. It had 3000 more customers in April than in February. Over the three months, 45 200 customers came to the restaurant. How many came each month?

60. ***Trip Distance*** During three days of travel, Anthony drove from Augusta, Maine, to Baltimore, Maryland, a distance of 670 miles. He drove twice as many miles Saturday than on Friday. He drove 30 miles more on Sunday than on Friday. How many miles did he drive each day?

▲ **61.** ***Geometry*** A rectangle has a perimeter of 72 cm. The length is 3 cm less than double the width. Find the dimensions of the rectangle.

▲ **62.** ***Geometry*** A rectangle has a perimeter of 180 m. The length is 2 m more than triple the width. Find the dimensions of the rectangle.

▲ **63.** ***Geometry*** A triangle has three angles, X, Y, and Z. Angle Y is double the measure of angle Z. Angle X is 12 degrees smaller than angle Z. Find the measure of each angle.

▲ **64.** ***Geometry*** A triangle has three angles labelled A, B, and C. Angle C is triple the measure of angle B. Angle A is 74 degrees larger than angle B. Find the measure of each angle.

▲ **65.** ***Football*** A regulation NFL football field is in the shape of a rectangle. The width of the field is 67 yards shorter than the length. The perimeter of the field is 346 yards. Find the width and length of the field.

▲ **66.** ***Basketball*** A regulation NBA basketball court is in the shape of a rectangle. The width of the court is 44 feet shorter than the length. The perimeter of the court is 288 feet. Find the width and length of the court.

67. ***Trip Distance*** Ellen and Laurie drove from Shawinigan, Québec, to St. Catharines, Ontario, a distance of 810 kilometres. It took two days to make the trip. They drove 106 more kilometres on Sunday than on Saturday. How many kilometres did they drive each day?

68. ***Education*** During the second week of July, the Northern College admissions office received 156 more applications than it did during the first week of July. During the third week of July, it received 142 fewer applications than it did during the first week of July. During these three weeks it received 800 applications. How many were received each week?

69. ***Sales Commission*** Wayne receives a 4% commission on the used cars that he sells. Last week his total salary was \$600. His base salary was \$200. What was the cost of the cars he sold last week?

70. ***Sales Commission*** Megan receives an 8% commission on the furniture that she sells. Last month her total salary was \$3050. Her base salary for the month was \$1500. What was the cost of the furniture she sold last month?

How Am I Doing? Module Test

Combine like terms.

1. $5a - 11a$

2. $\frac{1}{3}x + \frac{5}{8}y - \frac{1}{5}x + \frac{1}{2}y$

3. $\frac{1}{4}a - \frac{2}{3}b + \frac{3}{8}a$

4. $6a - 5b - 5a - 3b$

5. $7x - 8y + 2z - 9z + 8y$

6. $x + 5y - 6 - 5x - 7y + 11$

Simplify.

7. $5(12x - 5y)$

8. $4\left(\frac{1}{2}x - \frac{5}{6}y\right)$

9. $-1.5(3a - 2b + c - 8)$

10. $2(-3a + 2b) - 5(a - 2b)$

Solve for the variable.

11. $-5 - 3x = 19$

12. $x - 3.45 = -9.8$

13. $-5x + 9 = -4x - 6$

14. $8x - 2 - x = 3x - 9 - 10x$

15. $0.5x + 0.6 = 0.2x - 0.9$

16. $-\frac{5}{6}x = \frac{7}{12}$

1. ______________________

2. ______________________

3. ______________________

4. ______________________

5. ______________________

6. ______________________

7. ______________________

8. ______________________

9. ______________________

10. ______________________

11. ______________________

12. ______________________

13. ______________________

14. ______________________

15. ______________________

16. ______________________

17. ______

18. ______

19. ______

20. ______

21. ______

22. ______

23. ______

24. ______

Translate the English sentence into an equation using the variables indicated.

17. The second floor of Trabor Laboratory has 15 more classrooms than the first floor. Use s to represent the number of classrooms on the second floor and f to represent the number of classrooms on the first floor.

18. The north field yields 15 000 fewer bushels of wheat than the south field. Use n to represent the number of bushels of wheat in the north field and s to represent the number of bushels of wheat in the south field.

Write an algebraic expression for each quantity using the given variable.

▲**19.** The first angle of a triangle is half the second angle. The third angle of the triangle is twice the second angle. Use the variable s.

▲**20.** The length of a rectangle is 5 centimetres shorter than double the width. Use the letter w.

Solve using an equation.

21. The number of acres of land in the old Smithfield farm is three times the number of acres of land in the Prentice farm. Together the two farms have 348 acres. How many acres of land are there on each farm?

22. Sam earns $1500 less per year than Marcia does. The combined income of the two people is $46 500 per year. How much does each person earn?

23. During the fall semester, 183 students registered for Introduction to Biology. The morning class has 24 fewer students than the afternoon class. The evening class has 12 more students than the afternoon class. How many students registered for each class?

▲**24.** A rectangular field has a perimeter of 118 metres. The width is 8 metres longer than half the length. Find the dimensions of the rectangle.

Solutions to Practice Problems

Section 1 Practice Problems

1. (a) The variables are A, b, and h.
   (b) The variables are V, l, w, and h.
2. (a) $P = 2w + 2l$ (b) $A = \pi r^2$
3. We add $9 + 2 = 11$, therefore $9x + 2x = 11x$.
4. (a) $8x - 22x + 5x = 8x + (-22x) + 5x = -14x + 5x = -9x$
   (b) $19x - 7x - 12x = 19x + (-7x) + (-12x)$
   $= 12x + (-12x) = 0x = 0$
5. (a) $9x - 12x + x = 9x + (-12x) + 1x = -3x + 1x = -2x$
   (b) $5.6x - 8x - x = 5.6x - 8x - 1x = -2.4x - 1x = -3.4x$
6. $17.5 - 6.3x - 8.2x + 10.5$
   $= 17.5 + 10.5 - 6.3x - 8.2x = 28 - 14.5x$
7. (a) $2w + 3z - 12 - 5w - z - 16$
   $= 2w - 5w + 3z - 1z - 12 - 16$
   $= -3w + 2z - 28$
   (b) $\frac{3}{5}x - \frac{7}{15}x + 5 - \frac{1}{3} = \frac{9}{15}x - \frac{7}{15}x + \frac{15}{3} - \frac{1}{3} = \frac{2}{15}x + \frac{14}{3}$

Section 2 Practice Problems

1. (a) $7(x + 5) = 7(x) + 7(5) = 7x + 35$
   (b) $-4(x + 2y) = -4(x) + (-4)(2y) = -4x - 8y$
   (c) $5(6a - 2b) = 5(6a) - 5(2b) = 30a - 10b$
2. $(x + 3y)(8) = (x)(8) + (3y)(8) = 8x + 24y$
3. (a) $-5(x + 4y + 5) = (-5)(1x) + (-5)(4y) + (-5)(5)$
   $= -5x - 20y - 25$
   (b) $(2.2x + 5.5y + 6)(3) = (2.2x)(3) + (5.5y)(3) + (6)(3)$
   $= 6.6x + 16.5y + 18$
4. $\frac{3}{2}\left(\frac{1}{2}x - \frac{1}{3}y + 4z - \frac{1}{2}\right)$
   $= \frac{3}{2}\left(\frac{1}{2}x\right) + \frac{3}{2}\left(-\frac{1}{3}y\right) + \frac{3}{2}(4z) + \frac{3}{2}\left(-\frac{1}{2}\right)$
   $= \frac{3}{4}x - \frac{1}{2}y + 6z - \frac{3}{4}$
5. $3(2x + 4y) + 2(5x + y) = 6x + 12y + 10x + 2y = 16x + 14y$
6. $-4(x - 5) + 3(-1 + 2x)$
   $= -4x + 20 - 3 + 6x$
   $= 2x + 17$

Section 3 Practice Problems

1. $x + 7 = -8$
   $x + 7 + (-7) = -8 + (-7)$
   $x + 0 = -15$
   $x = -15$
2. (a) $y - 3.2 = 9$
   $y - 3.2 + 3.2 = 9.0 + 3.2$
   $y = 12.2$

   Check.
   $y - 3.2 = 9$
   $12.2 - 3.2 \stackrel{?}{=} 9$
   $9 = 9$ ✓

   (b) $\frac{2}{3} = x + \frac{1}{6}$
   $\frac{4}{6} + \left(-\frac{1}{6}\right) = x + \frac{1}{6} + \left(-\frac{1}{6}\right)$
   $\frac{3}{6} = x$
   $\frac{1}{2} = x$

   Check.
   $\frac{2}{3} = x + \frac{1}{6}$
   $\frac{2}{3} \stackrel{?}{=} \frac{1}{2} + \frac{1}{6}$
   $\frac{2}{3} \stackrel{?}{=} \frac{3}{6} + \frac{1}{6}$
   $\frac{2}{3} = \frac{4}{6}$ ✓

3. $3x - 5 = 2x + 1$
   $3x - 5 + 5 = 2x + 1 + 5$
   $3x = 2x + 6$
   $3x + (-2x) = 2x + (-2x) + 6$
   $x = 6$

   Check.
   $3x - 5 = 2x + 1$
   $3(6) - 5 \stackrel{?}{=} 2(6) + 1$
   $18 - 5 \stackrel{?}{=} 12 + 1$
   $13 = 13$ ✓

Section 4 Practice Problems

1. $8n = 104$
   $\frac{8n}{8} = \frac{104}{8}$
   $n = 13$
2. $-7n = 30$
   $\frac{-7n}{-7} = \frac{30}{-7}$
   $n = -\frac{30}{7}$
3. $3.2x = 16$
   $\frac{3.2x}{3.2} = \frac{16}{3.2}$
   $x = 5$

   Check.
   $3.2(5) \stackrel{?}{=} 16$
   $16 = 16$ ✓

4. (a) $\frac{1}{6}y = 2\frac{2}{3}$
   $\frac{1}{6}y = \frac{8}{3}$
   $\frac{6}{1}\cdot\frac{1}{6}y = \frac{8}{3}\cdot\frac{6}{1}$
   $y = 16$

   Check.
   $\frac{1}{6}y = 2\frac{2}{3}$
   $\frac{1}{6}\cdot 16 \stackrel{?}{=} 2\frac{2}{3}$
   $\frac{16}{6} \stackrel{?}{=} \frac{8}{3}$
   $\frac{8}{3} = \frac{8}{3}$ ✓

   (b) $3\frac{1}{5}z = 4$
   $\frac{16}{5}z = 4$
   $\frac{5}{16}\cdot\frac{16}{5}z = 4\cdot\frac{5}{16}$
   $z = \frac{5}{4}$ or $1\frac{1}{4}$

   Check.
   $3\frac{1}{5}z = 4$
   $\frac{16}{5}\cdot\frac{5}{4} \stackrel{?}{=} 4$
   $4 = 4$ ✓

Section 5 Practice Problems

1. $5x + 13 = 33$
   $5x + 13 + (-13) = 33 + (-13)$
   $5x = 20$
   $\frac{5x}{5} = \frac{20}{5}$
   $x = 4$

   Check.
   $5(4) + 13 \stackrel{?}{=} 33$
   $20 + 13 \stackrel{?}{=} 33$
   $33 = 33$ ✓

2. $-50 = 7x - 8$
   $-50 + 8 = 7x - 8 + 8$
   $-42 = 7x$
   $\frac{-42}{7} = \frac{7x}{7}$
   $-6 = x$

   Check.
   $-50 \stackrel{?}{=} 7(-6) - 8$
   $-50 \stackrel{?}{=} -42 - 8$
   $-50 = -50$ ✓

3.
$$\begin{aligned} 4x &= -8x + 42 \\ 4x + 8x &= -8x + 8x + 42 \\ 12x &= 42 \\ \frac{12x}{12} &= \frac{42}{12} \\ x &= \frac{7}{2} \text{ or } 3\frac{1}{2} \end{aligned}$$

4.
$$\begin{aligned} 4x - 7 &= 9x + 13 \\ 4x - 7 + 7 &= 9x + 13 + 7 \\ 4x &= 9x + 20 \\ 4x + (-9x) &= 9x + (-9x) + 20 \\ -5x &= 20 \\ \frac{-5x}{-5} &= \frac{20}{-5} \\ x &= -4 \end{aligned}$$

5.
$$\begin{aligned} 4x - 23 &= 3x + 7 - 2x \\ 4x - 23 &= x + 7 \\ 4x + (-1x) - 23 &= (-1x) + x + 7 \\ 3x - 23 &= 7 \\ 3x - 23 + 23 &= 7 + 23 \\ 3x &= 30 \\ \frac{3x}{3} &= \frac{30}{3} \\ x &= 10 \end{aligned}$$

6.
$$\begin{aligned} 8(x - 3) + 5x &= 15(x - 2) \\ 8x - 24 + 5x &= 15x - 30 \\ 13x - 24 &= 15x - 30 \\ 13x - 24 + 30 &= 15x - 30 + 30 \\ 13x + 6 &= 15x \\ 13x + (-13x) + 6 &= 15x + (-13x) \\ 6 &= 2x \\ \frac{6}{2} &= \frac{2x}{2} \\ 3 &= x \end{aligned}$$

Section 6 Practice Problems

1. Tom's height | is | 7 centimetres | more than | Abdul's height
↓ | ↓ | ↓ | ↓ | ↓
t | $=$ | 7 | $+$ | a

2. The noon class | has | 24 fewer students than | the morning class
↓ | ↓ | ↓ | ↓
n | $=$ | m | $-$ | 24

3. On Thursday she carried 5 more than on Friday. $t = 5 + f$

4. Double the width is $2w$. $l = 2w + 7$

5. Let s = length in kilometres of Sally's trip
$s + 380$ = length in kilometres of Melinda's trip
380 kilometres longer than Sally's trip.

6. Let m = height in metres of the Mathematics Centre
$m - 26$ = height in metres of Federation Hall
126 metres shorter than the Mathematics Centre.

7. Let x = length in centimetres of the first side of the triangle
$2x$ = length in centimetres of the second side of the triangle
$x + 6$ = length in centimetres of the third side of the triangle

Section 7 Practice Problems

1. Let x = length in metres of shorter piece of board
$x + 1.5$ = length in metres of longer piece of board

$$\begin{aligned} x + (x + 1.5) &= 6 \\ x + x + 1.5 &= 6 \\ 2x + 1.5 &= 6 \\ 2x + 1.5 + (-1.5) &= 6 + (-1.5) \\ 2x &= 4.5 \\ \frac{2x}{2} &= \frac{4.5}{2} \\ x &= 2.25 \end{aligned}$$

The shorter piece is 2.25 metres long.
$x + 1.5 = 2.25 + 1.5 = 3.75$
The longer piece is 3.75 metres long.

Check.
$2.25 + 3.75 \stackrel{?}{=} 6$
$6 = 6$ ✓
$3.25 \stackrel{?}{=} 2.25 + 1.5$
$3.75 = 3.75$ ✓

2. Let x = the number of departures on Monday
$x + 29$ = the number of departures on Tuesday
$x - 16$ = the number of departures on Wednesday

$$\begin{aligned} x + (x + 29) + (x - 16) &= 349 \\ x + x + 29 + x - 16 &= 349 \\ 3x + 13 &= 349 \\ 3x + 13 + (-13) &= 349 + (-13) \\ 3x &= 336 \\ \frac{3x}{3} &= \frac{336}{3} \\ x &= 112 \\ x + 29 &= 112 + 29 = 141 \\ x - 16 &= 112 - 16 = 96 \end{aligned}$$

There were 112 departures on Monday, 141 departures on Tuesday, and 96 departures on Wednesday.

Check.
$112 + 141 + 96 \stackrel{?}{=} 349$
$349 = 349$ ✓
$141 \stackrel{?}{=} 112 + 29$
$141 = 141$ ✓
$96 \stackrel{?}{=} 112 - 16$
$96 = 96$ ✓

3. Let w = the width of the field measured in metres
$2w + 8$ = the length of the field measured in metres
2(width) + 2(length) = perimeter

$$\begin{aligned} 2(w) + 2(2w + 8) &= 772 \\ 2w + 4w + 16 &= 772 \\ 6w + 16 &= 772 \\ 6w + 16 + (-16) &= 772 + (-16) \\ 6w &= 756 \\ \frac{6w}{6} &= \frac{756}{6} \\ w &= 126 \end{aligned}$$

The width of the field is 126 metres.
$2w + 8 = 2(126) + 8 = 252 + 8 = 260$
The length of the field is 260 metres.

Check.
$260 \stackrel{?}{=} 2(126) + 8$
$260 \stackrel{?}{=} 252 + 8$
$260 = 260$ ✓
$2(126) + 2(260) \stackrel{?}{=} 772$
$252 + 520 \stackrel{?}{=} 772$
$772 = 772$ ✓

4. Let x = the length in metres of the first side of the triangle
$2x$ = the length in metres of the second side of the triangle
$x + 10$ = the length in metres of the third side of the triangle

$$x + 2x + (x + 10) = 36$$
$$4x + 10 = 36$$
$$4x + 10 + (-10) = 36 + (-10)$$
$$4x = 26$$
$$\frac{4x}{4} = \frac{26}{4}$$
$$x = 6.5$$

The first side of the triangle is 6.5 metres long.
$2x = 2(6.5) = 13$
The second side of the triangle is 13 metres long.
$x + 10 = 6.5 + 10 = 16.5$
The third side of the triangle is 16.5 metres long.

Check.
$6.5 + 13 + 16.5 \stackrel{?}{=} 36$
$36 = 36$ ✓
$13 \stackrel{?}{=} 2(6.5)$
$13 = 13$ ✓
$16.5 \stackrel{?}{=} 10 + 6.5$
$16.5 = 16.5$ ✓

5. Let x = the measure of angle A in degrees
$3x$ = the measure of angle C in degrees
$x - 30$ = the measure of angle B in degrees

$$x + 3x + (x - 30) = 180$$
$$5x - 30 = 180$$
$$5x - 30 + 30 = 180 + 30$$
$$5x = 210$$
$$\frac{5x}{5} = \frac{210}{5}$$
$$x = 42$$

Angle A measures 42°.
$3x = 3(42) = 126$
Angle C measures 126°.
$x - 30 = 42 - 30 = 12$
Angle B measures 12°.

Check.
$42 + 126 + 12 \stackrel{?}{=} 180$
$180 = 180$ ✓
$126 \stackrel{?}{=} 3(42)$
$126 = 126$ ✓
$12 \stackrel{?}{=} 42 - 30$
$12 = 12$ ✓

6. Let s = the total amount of sales of the boats in dollars
$0.03s$ = the amount of the commission earned on sales of s dollars

$$3250 = 1000 + 0.03s$$
$$2250 = 0.03s$$
$$\frac{2250}{0.03} = \frac{0.03s}{0.03}$$
$$75\,000 = s$$

Therefore he sold $75 000 worth of boats for the month.

Check.
$0.03(75\,000) + 1000 \stackrel{?}{=} 3250$
$2250 + 1000 \stackrel{?}{=} 3250$
$3250 = 3250$ ✓

Glossary

Algebraic expression (Section 6) An algebraic expression consists of variables, numerals, and operation signs.

Equations (Section 3) Mathematical statements with variables that say that two expressions are equal, such as $x + 3 = -8$ and $2s + 5s = 34 - 4s$.

Equivalent equations (Section 3) Equations that have the same solution.

Like terms (Section 1) Like terms have identical variables with identical exponents. $-5x$ and $3x$ are like terms. $-7xyz$ and $-12xyz$ are like terms.

Numerical coefficients (Section 1) The numbers in front of the variables in one or more terms. If we look at $-3xy + 12w$, we find that the numerical coefficient of the xy term is -3 while the numerical coefficient of the w term is 12.

Solution of an equation (Section 3) A number is a solution of an equation if replacing the variable by the number makes the equation always true. The solution of $x - 5 = -20$ is the number -15.

Term (Section 1) A number, a variable, or a product of a number and one or more variables. $5x$, $2ab$, and $-43cdef$ are three examples of terms, separated in an expression by a + sign or a − sign.

Variable (Section 1) A letter that is used to represent a number.

Answers to Selected Exercises for Introduction to Algebra

Answers to Selected Exercises for Introduction to Algebra

Section 1 Exercises **1.** A variable is a symbol, usually a letter of the alphabet, that stands for a number. **3.** All the exponents for like terms must be the same. The exponent for x must be the same. The exponent for y must be the same. In this case, x is raised to the second power in the first term but y is raised to the second power in the second term. **5.** G, x, y **7.** p, a, b **9.** $r = 3m + 5n$ **11.** $H = 2a - 3b$ **13.** $10x$ **15.** $-x$ **17.** $\frac{1}{3}x$ **19.** $7x + 4$ **21.** $-1.1x + 6.4$ **23.** $37x + 9y - 11$ **25.** $\left(2\frac{1}{3}\right)x - 50$ or $\frac{7}{3}x - 50$ **27.** $-3a + 6b - 4c$ **29.** $-\frac{1}{4}x + \frac{8}{21}y$ **31.** $-3x - 6$ **33.** $-11.1n + 3.1m + 1.2$ **35. (a)** $12x + 1$ **(b)** It is doubled to obtain $24x + 2$.

Quick Quiz 1 **1.** $3a - 14b$ **2.** $-\frac{5}{12}x - \frac{17}{25}y$ **3.** $-18x + 15y - 47$ **4.** See Instructor

Section 2 Exercises **1.** variable **3.** $3x$ and x; $2y$ and $-3y$ **5.** $27x - 18$ **7.** $-2x - 2y$ **9.** $14.4x - 30y$ **11.** $30x - 70y$ **13.** $48a - 40b$ **15.** $24y + 21z$ **17.** $4p + 36q - 40$ **19.** $\frac{3}{5}x + 2y - \frac{3}{4}$ **21.** $30a + 48b - 67.5$ **23.** $32a + 48b - 36c - 20$ **25.** $-2.6x + 17y + 10z - 24$ **27.** $x - \frac{3}{2}y + 2z - \frac{1}{4}$ **29.** $-3s + 10t + 21$ **31.** $P = 2l + 2w$ **33.** $A = \frac{hB + hb}{2}$ **35.** $27x - 39$ **37.** $-8a + 34b$ **39.** $8.1x + 8.1y$ **41.** $-9a - 19b + 12c$ **43.** $A = a(b + c) = ab + ac$

Quick Quiz 2 **1.** $\frac{5}{2}x - \frac{7}{4}y$ **2.** $-7x + 10.5y - 3.5z + 14$ **3.** $-16x + 59y$ **4.** See Instructor

Section 3 Exercises **1.** equation **3.** opposite **5.** $y = 32$ **7.** $x = 9$ **9.** $x = -18$ **11.** $x = -25$ **13.** $x = 19$ **15.** $9.8 = x$ **17.** $y = -11.6$ **19.** $x = 13.2$ **21.** $x = \frac{2}{5}$ **23.** $x = 1$ **25.** $x = -\frac{3}{2}$ or $-1\frac{1}{2}$ **27.** $y = \frac{17}{8}$ or $2\frac{1}{8}$ **29.** $x = 14$ **31.** $x = -13$ **33.** $x = 2$ **35.** $x = -9$ **37.** $y = \frac{13}{2}$ or $6\frac{1}{2}$ **39.** $-8 = z$ **41.** $y = 1.2$ **43.** $x = 6$ **45.** $x = 12$ **47.** $-7 = x$ **49.** To solve the equation $3x = 12$, divide both sides of the equation by 3 so that x stands alone on one side of the equation.

Quick Quiz 3 **1.** $x = -2.2$ **2.** $x = 35$ **3.** $x = -10$ **4.** See Instructor

Section 4 Exercises **1.** A sample answer is: To maintain the balance, whatever you do to one side of the scale, you need to do the exact same thing to the other side of the scale. **3.** $\frac{4}{3}$ **5.** $x = 9$ **7.** $y = -4$ **9.** $x = -\frac{16}{9}$ **11.** $x = 12$ **13.** $16 = m$ **15.** $x = 10$ **17.** $7 = t$ **19.** $x = -13.5$ **21.** $x = 8$ **23.** $y = 10$ **25.** $n = \frac{5}{4}$ or $1\frac{1}{4}$ **27.** $x = -\frac{18}{5}$ or $-3\frac{3}{5}$ **29.** $x = -\frac{9}{2}$ or $-4\frac{1}{2}$ **31.** $z = 6$ **33.** $6 = x$ **35.** $x = -9$ **37.** $x = 0.03$ **39.** $x = -20$

Quick Quiz 4 **1.** $x = -\frac{15}{4}$ or $-3\frac{3}{4}$ **2.** $7 = x$ **3.** $x = -6$ **4.** See Instructor

Section 5 Exercises **1.** You want to obtain the x-term all by itself on one side of the equation. So you want to remove the -6 from the left side of the equation. Therefore you would add the opposite of -6. This means you would add 6 to each side. **3.** no **5.** yes **7.** $x = 3$ **9.** $x = -\frac{1}{2}$ **11.** $x = \frac{5}{6}$ **13.** $x = 2$ **15.** $x = 0.3$ **17.** $x = 33$ **19.** $x = 2$ **21.** $x = 1$ **23.** $z = -4$ **25.** $x = 11$ **27.** $x = -1$ **29.** $y = -6$ **31.** $y = -\frac{1}{3}$ **33.** $y = 5$ **35.** $x = 16$ **37.** $y = 0$ **39.** $x = -17$ **41.** $x = -\frac{11}{4}$ or $-2\frac{3}{4}$ **43.** $x = 10$

Quick Quiz 5 **1.** $x = 4$ **2.** $x = -4$ **3.** $x = -6$ **4.** See Instructor

How Am I Doing? Sections 1–5 **1.** $-17x$ (obj. 1.2) **2.** y (obj. 1.2) **3.** $-3a + 2b$ (obj. 1.2) **4.** $-2x + 10y - 10$ (obj. 1.2) **5.** $16x - 2y - 6$ (obj. 1.2) **6.** $4a - 12b + 3c$ (obj. 1.2) **7.** $42x - 18y$ (obj. 2.1) **8.** $-2a + b - 12$ (obj. 2.1) **9.** $-3a - 6b + 12c + 10$ (obj. 2.1) **10.** $x - 8y$ (obj. 2.2) **11.** $-18x - 8y$ (obj. 5.1) **12.** $-21x + 9y$ (obj. 2.1) **13.** $x = 37$ (obj. 5.2) **4.** $x = 3.5$ (obj. 3.1) **15.** $y = -\frac{11}{10}$ or $-1\frac{1}{10}$ (obj. 3.1) **16.** $x = 8$ (obj. 3.1) **17.** $y = 8$ (obj. 4.1) **18.** $y = 10$ (obj. 4.1) **19.** $x = \frac{3}{2}$ or $1\frac{1}{2}$ (obj. 4.2) **20.** $x = -12$ (obj. 4.1) **21.** $m = \frac{16}{3}$ or $5\frac{1}{3}$ (obj. 5.1) **22.** $m = 2$ (obj. 5.2) **23.** $x = 3$ (obj. 5.3) **24.** $x = \frac{9}{4}$ or $2\frac{1}{4}$ (obj. 5.3) **25.** $x = 8$ (obj. 5.3) **26.** $x = \frac{25}{6}$ or $4\frac{1}{6}$ (obj. 5.3) **27.** $y = 7$ (obj. 5.2) **28.** $x = 4$ (obj. 5.2)

Section 6 Exercises **1.** $h = 34 + r$ **3.** $b = n - 107$ **5.** $n = a + 14$ **7.** $l = 2w + 7$ **9.** $l = 3w - 2$ **11.** $h = 3t + 10$ **13.** $t + l = 32$ **15.** $ht = 500$ **17.** p = cost of airfare from Vancouver to Ottawa; $p - 135$ = cost of airfare from Chicago to Toronto **19.** b = number of degrees in angle B; $b - 46$ = number of degrees in angle A **21.** w = height of Sears Tower; $w + 1190$ = height of Burj Tower **23.** a = number of books Aaron read; $2a$ = number of books Nina read; $a + 5$ = number of books Molly read **25.** h = height; $h + 5$ = length; $3h$ = width **27.** x = 1st angle; $2x$ = 2nd angle; $x - 14$ = 3rd angle

Quick Quiz 6 **1.** $t = c - 12$ **2.** w = width; $2w + 3$ = length **3.** c = number of cars; $0.5c$ or $\frac{1}{2}c$ or $\frac{c}{2}$ = number of SUVs; $c + 35$ = number of trucks **4.** See Instructor

Section 7 Exercises **1.** x = length of shorter piece; $x + 1.5$ = length of longer piece; 1.75 m; 3.25 m **3.** x = number of points scored by France $x - 22$ = number of points scored by Japan; France scored 51 points, Japan scored 29 points **5.** x = the number of cars in November; $x + 84$ = the number of cars in May; $x - 43$ = the number of cars in July; 119 cars in November; 203 cars in May; 76 cars in July **7.** x = length of shorter piece; $x + 4.7$ = length of the longer piece; the shorter piece is 3.65 feet long; the longer piece is 8.35 feet long **9.** x = width; $2x - 4$ = length; width is 14 cm; length is 24 cm **11.** x = length of the first side; $x + 20$ = length of the second side; $x - 4$ = length of the third side; 61 mm; 81 mm; 57 mm **13.** x = length of the first side; $2x$ = length of the second side; $x + 12$ = length of the third side; 8 cm; 16 cm; 20 cm **15.** x = number of degrees in angle A; $3x$ = number of degrees in angle B; $x + 40$ = number of degrees in angle C; angle A measures 28°; angle B measures 84°; angle C measures 68° **17.** x = total sales; $76,000 **19.** x = yearly rent; $6000

21. x = length of the adults' section; $x + 6.2$ = length of the children's section; adults' section is 12.9 ft; children's section is 19.1 ft

23. 2125 heart transplants; 6650 liver transplants; 463 pancreas transplants **25.** 401 thousand or 401 000

Quick Quiz 7 **1.** Barbara earns $281; Melinda earns $156 **2.** 1440 students work full-time; 2880 students work part-time; 1680 students do not work **3.** width is 27 yd; length is 61 yd

Putting Your Skills to Work **1.** $1500 **2.** $3450 **3.** $6900 **4.** About 55 months, or 4 years and 7 months **5.** About $288 **6.** $250; about 28 months, or 2 years and 4 months **7.** 2 months **8.** $25 500 **9.** Answers may vary **10.** Answers may vary **11.** Answers may vary

Module Review Problems **1.** $-13a + 3$ **2.** $\frac{5}{6}x + \frac{8}{9}$ **3.** $-2x - 7y$ **4.** $11x - 5y$ **5.** $-x - 12y + 6$ **6.** $13a - 12b - 4$ **7.** $-15x - 3y$ **8.** $-8x - 12y$ **9.** $2x - 6y + 8$ **10.** $30a - 40b + 25$ **11.** $-4x + 5y - 30$ **12.** $-9a + 2b + 12$ **13.** $6x + 15y - 27.5$ **14.** $8.4x - 12y + 20.4$ **15.** $-2x + 14y$ **16.** $7x - 8y$ **17.** $-8a - 2b - 24$ **18.** $-7a + 8b + 15$ **19.** $x = 12$ **20.** $x = 11.7$ **21.** $x = 4$ **22.** $x = 7.4$ **23.** $x = -12.1$ **24.** $x = -1.2$ **25.** $x = \frac{11}{4}$ or $2\frac{3}{4}$ **26.** $x = \frac{13}{4}$ or $3\frac{1}{4}$ **27.** $y = -\frac{3}{4}$ **28.** $x = \frac{3}{2}$ or $1\frac{1}{2}$ **29.** $x = 5$ **30.** $9 = y$ **31.** $x = -\frac{5}{2}$ or $-2\frac{1}{2}$ **32.** $y = -5$ **33.** $x = 6$ **34.** $y = 9$ **35.** $x = -5$ **36.** $x = 0.25$ **37.** $x = 8$ **38.** $x = \frac{5}{4}$ or $1\frac{1}{4}$ **39.** $x = 6$ **40.** $x = 3$ **41.** $x = -8$ **42.** $x = -9$ **43.** $x = 3$ **44.** $x = -10$ **45.** $x = -2$ **46.** $x = 5$ **47.** $y = 16$ **48.** $y = 0$ **49.** $w = c + 3000$ **50.** $e = 12 + a$ **51.** $A = 3B$ **52.** $l = 2w - 3$ **53.** r = Roberto's salary; $r + 2050$ = Michael's salary **54.** x = length of first side; $2x$ = length of second side **55.** d = the number of days Dennis worked; $2d + 12$ = the number of days Carmen worked **56.** n = number of nonfiction books; $n + 225$ = number of fiction books **57.** x = length of shorter piece; $x + 2.5$ = length of longer piece; 5.75 m; 8.25 m **58.** x = the experienced employee's salary; $x - 28$ = the new employee's salary; $192; $220 **59.** x = number of customers in February; $2x$ = number of customers in March; $x + 3000$ = number of customers in April; 10 550 in Feb.; 21 000 in Mar.; 13 550 in Apr. **60.** x = miles on Friday; $2x$ = miles on Saturday; $x + 30$ = miles on Sunday; 160 mi on Fri.; 320 mi on Sat.; 190 mi on Sun. **61.** x = width; $2x - 3$ = length; width = 13 cm; length = 23 cm **62.** x = width; $3x + 2$ = length; width = 22 m; length = 68 m **63.** z = measure of angle Z; $2z$ = measure of angle Y; $z - 12$ = measure of angle X; $X = 36°$, $Y = 96°$, $Z = 48°$ **64.** x = measure of angle B; $x + 74$ = measure of angle A; $3x$ = measure of angle C; angle A measures 95.2°; angle B measures 21.2°; angle C measures 63.6° **65.** x = length; $x - 67$ = width; width is 53 yd; length is 120 yd **66.** x = length; $x - 44$ = width; width is 50 ft; length is 94 ft **67.** x = kilometres on Saturday; $x + 106$ = kilometres on Sunday; 352 km on Sat.; 458 km on Sun. **68.** x = number of applications in the first week; $x + 156$ = number of applications in the second week; $x - 142$ = number of applications in the third week; 262 the first week; 418 the second week; 120 the third week **69.** x = total sales; $10 000 **70.** x = total sales; $19 375

How Am I Doing? Module Test **1.** $-6a$ (obj. 1.2) **2.** $\frac{2}{15}x + \frac{9}{8}y$ (obj. 1.2) **3.** $\frac{5}{8}a - \frac{2}{3}b$ (obj. 1.2) **4.** $a - 8b$ (obj. 1.2) **5.** $7x - 7z$ (obj. 1.2) **6.** $-4x - 2y + 5$ (obj. 1.2) **7.** $60x - 25y$ (obj. 2.1) **8.** $2x - \frac{10}{3}y$ (obj. 2.1) **9.** $-4.5a + 3b - 1.5c + 12$ (obj. 2.1) **10.** $-11a + 14b$ (obj. 2.2) **11.** $x = -8$ (obj. 5.1) **12.** $x = -6.35$ (obj. 3.1) **13.** $x = 15$ (obj. 5.1) **14.** $x = -\frac{1}{2}$ (obj. 5.1) **15.** $x = -5$ (obj. 5.1) **16.** $x = -\frac{7}{10}$ (obj. 5.1) **17.** $s = f + 15$ (obj. 6.1) **18.** $n = s - 15\,000$ (obj. 6.1)
19. $\frac{1}{2}s$ = measure of the first angle; s = measure of the second angle; $2s$ = measure of the third angle (obj. 6.2)
20. w = width; $2w - 5$ = length (obj. 6.2) **21.** 87 acres on the Prentice farm; 261 acres on the Smithfield farm (obj. 7.1)
22. Marcia earns $24 000; Sam earns $22 500 (obj. 7.3) **23.** 41 students in the morning class, 65 students in the afternoon class, 77 students in the evening class (obj. 7.1) **24.** width is 25 metres; length is 34 metres (obj. 7.2)

Trigonometry

Janet Foster/Masterfile Corporation

In the 1930s, a *National Geographic* team headed by Brad Washburn used trigonometry, the measurement of triangles, to create a map of the 13 000-square-kilometre region of Yukon. This expedition was a major advance in the way maps are made. Today, trigonometry is used in navigation, building, and engineering.

Trigonometry

SECTION 1 ANGLES AND RADIAN MEASURE

 Recognizing and Using the Vocabulary of Angles

A rotating ray is often a useful means of thinking about angles. Consider the hands on a clock functioning like a ray that rotates from 12 to 2, as in the diagram in the margin. The ray pointing to 12 is the **initial side** and the ray pointing to 2 is the **terminal side**.

When drawing an angle, we use an arc symbol to indicate the amount of rotation from the initial side to the terminal side. Several methods can be used to name an angle. Lowercase Greek letters, such as α (alpha), β (beta), γ (gamma), and θ (theta), are often used when studying trigonometry.

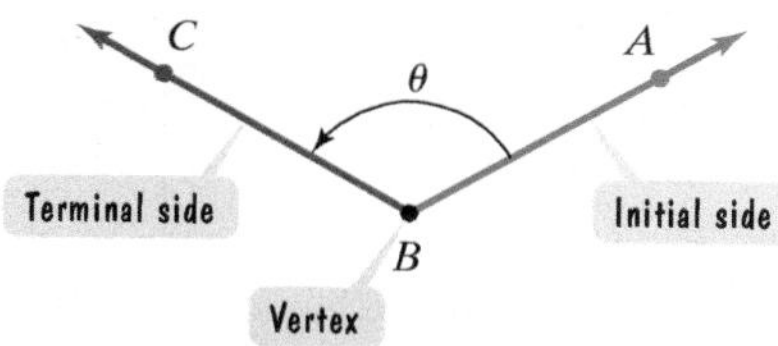

Here are some examples of common types of angles, described using an angle, θ, measured in degrees:

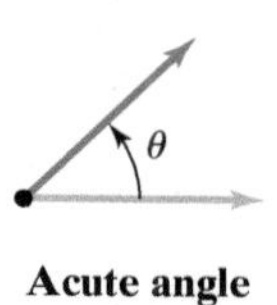

Acute angle
($0° < \theta < 90°$)

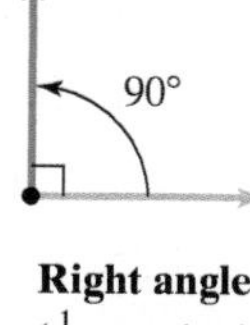

Right angle
($\frac{1}{4}$ rotation)

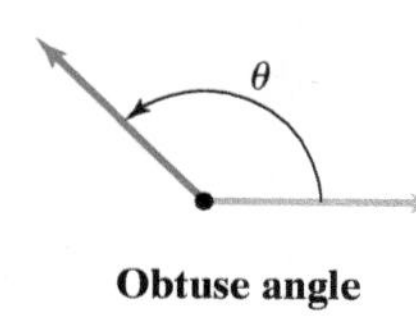

Obtuse angle
($90° < \theta < 180°$)

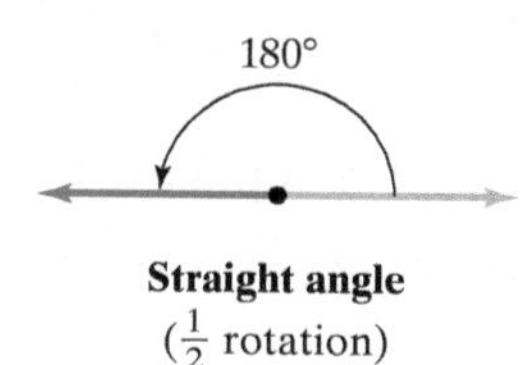

Straight angle
($\frac{1}{2}$ rotation)

Student Learning Objectives

After studying this section, you will be able to:

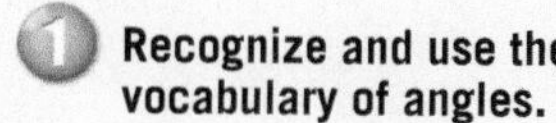

1. **Recognize and use the vocabulary of angles.**

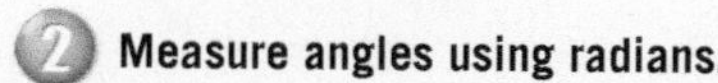

2. **Measure angles using radians.**
3. **Convert between degrees and radians.**

Clock with hands forming an angle

 Measuring Angles Using Radians

Another way to measure angles is in *radians*. Let's first define an angle measuring 1 radian. We use a circle of radius r and construct an angle whose vertex is at the centre of the circle. Such an angle is called a **central angle**.

We will use the term **intercepted arc** to mean the distance along the circumference of a circle between the initial side and the terminal side of a central angle. If the length of this intercepted arc is equal to the circle's radius, then we say the central angle measures **one radian**.

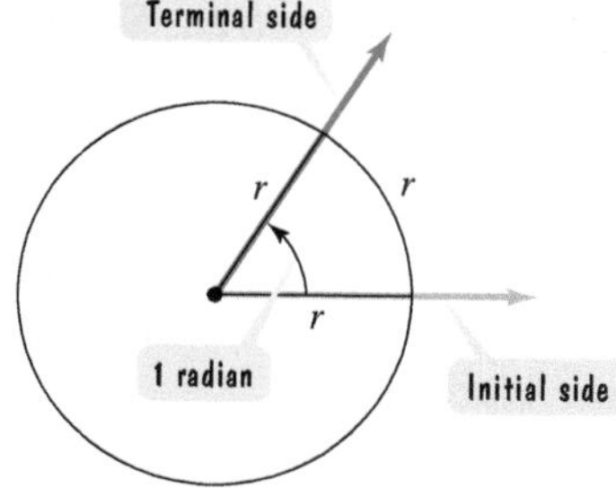

For a 1-radian angle, the intercepted arc and the radius are equal.

The **radian measure** of any central angle is the length of the intercepted arc divided by the circle's radius. For example, the length of the arc intercepted by angle β (shown in the figure below) is double the radius, r. The measure of angle β in radians is:

$$\beta = \frac{\text{length of the intercepted arc}}{\text{radius}} = \frac{2r}{r} = 2 \text{ radians}$$

Angle β measures 2 radians.

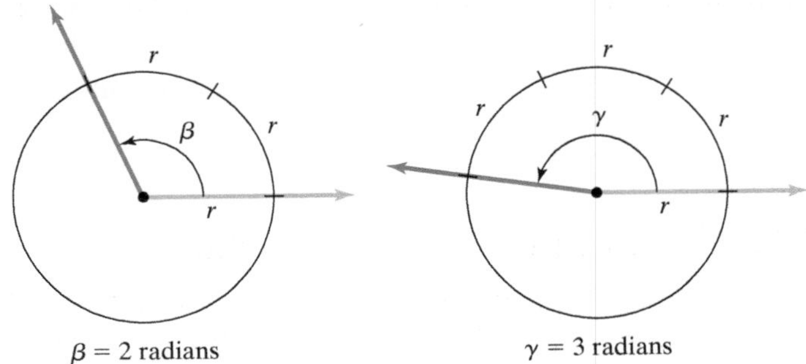

$\beta = 2$ radians $\quad\quad \gamma = 3$ radians

Let us find the measure of angle γ (shown in the figure above):

$$\gamma = \frac{\text{length of the intercepted arc}}{\text{radius}} = \frac{3r}{r} = 3 \text{ radians.}$$

Angle γ measures 3 radians.

RADIAN MEASURE

Let θ be a central angle in a circle of radius r and let s be the length of its intercepted arc. The measure of θ is:

$$\theta = \frac{s}{r} \text{ radians.}$$

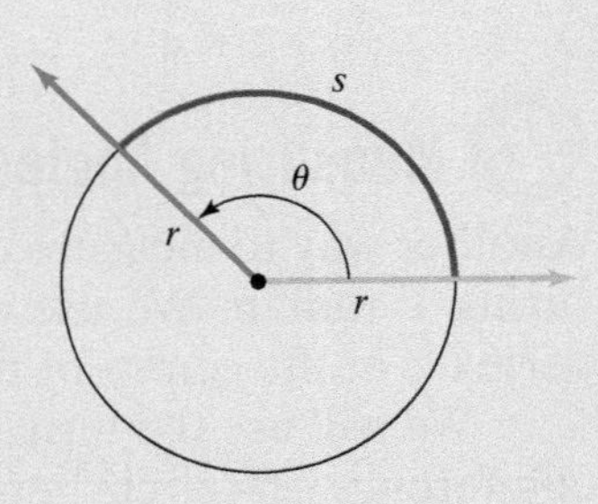

EXAMPLE 1 A central angle, θ, in a circle of radius 6 centimetres intercepts an arc of length 15 centimetres. What is the radian measure of θ?

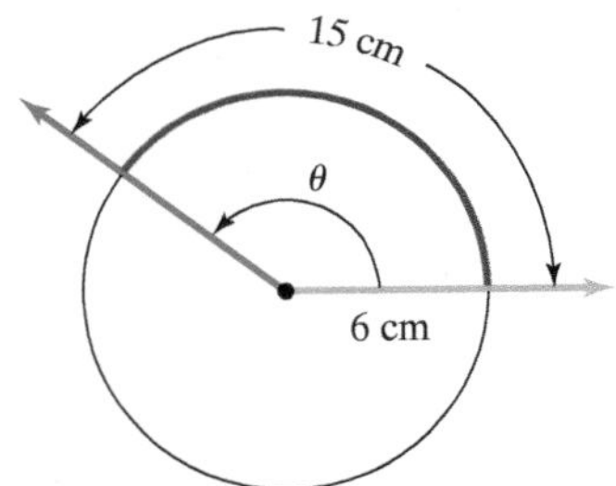

Solution

The length of the intercepted arc is 15 centimetres: $s = 15$ cm. The circle's radius is 6 centimetres: $r = 6$ cm. Now we use the formula for radian measure to find the radian measure of θ.

$$\theta = \frac{s}{r} = \frac{15 \text{ cm}}{6 \text{ cm}} = 2.5$$

The radian measure of θ is 2.5.

In Example 1, notice that the units of r and s are the same (centimetres) and that they cancel when we use the formula for radian measure. We are left with a number with no units. Thus, if an angle θ has a measure of 2.5 radians, we can write $\theta = 2.5$ radians, $\theta = 2.5$ rad, or $\theta = 2.5$. There should be no confusion as to whether radian or degree measure is being used. Why is this so? If θ has a degree measure of, say, $2.5°$, we must include the degree symbol and write $\theta = 2.5°$, and *not* $\theta = 2.5$.

Practice Problem 1 A central angle, θ, in a circle of radius 12 centimetres intercepts an arc of length 42 centimetres. What is the radian measure of θ?

Converting Between Degrees and Radians

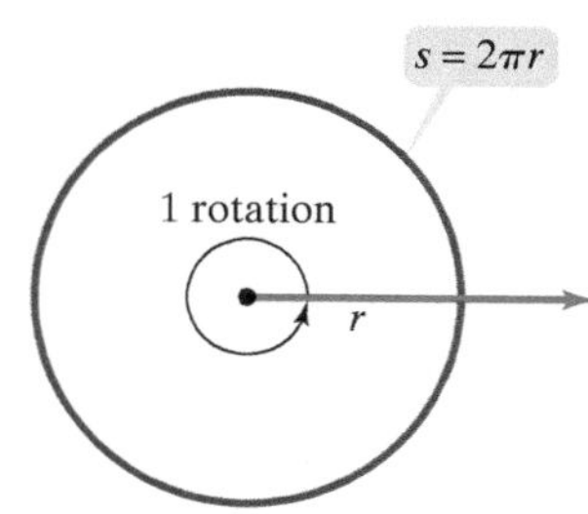

How can we obtain a relationship between degrees and radians? We compare the number of degrees and the number of radians in one complete rotation. We know that 360° is the amount of rotation of a ray back onto itself. The radian measure of this central angle is the circumference of the circle divided by the circle's radius, r. The circle's circumference is $2\pi r$ and the radian measure of the angle is

$$\theta = \frac{s}{r} = \frac{\text{the circle's circumference}}{r} = \frac{2\pi \cancel{r}}{\cancel{r}} = 2\pi \text{ radians}$$

Because one complete rotation measures 360° and 2π radians,

$$360° = 2\pi \text{ radians.}$$

Dividing both sides by 2, we have

$$180° = \pi \text{ radians.}$$

Dividing this last equation by 180° or π gives the following conversion rules:

CONVERSION BETWEEN DEGREES AND RADIANS

Using the basic relationship π radians $= 180°$,

1. To convert degrees to radians, multiply degrees by $\dfrac{\pi \text{ radians}}{180°}$.
2. To convert radians to degrees, multiply radians by $\dfrac{180°}{\pi \text{ radians}}$.

Angles that are fractions of a complete rotation are usually expressed in radian measure as fractional multiples of π, rather than as decimal approximations. For example, we write $\theta = \dfrac{\pi}{2}$ rather than using the decimal approximation $\theta \approx 1.57$.

EXAMPLE 2 Convert each angle in degrees to radians.

(a) $30°$ **(b)** $90°$ **(c)** $-135°$

Solution

To convert degrees to radians, multiply by $\frac{\pi \text{ radians}}{180°}$. Observe how the degree units cancel.

(a) $30° = 30\cancel{°} \cdot \frac{\pi \text{ radians}}{180\cancel{°}} = \frac{30\pi}{180} \text{ radians} = \frac{\pi}{6} \text{ radians}$

(b) $90° = 90\cancel{°} \cdot \frac{\pi \text{ radians}}{180\cancel{°}} = \frac{90\pi}{180} \text{ radians} = \frac{\pi}{2} \text{ radians}$

(c) $-135° = -135\cancel{°} \cdot \frac{\pi \text{ radians}}{180\cancel{°}} = -\frac{135\pi}{180} \text{ radians} = -\frac{3\pi}{4} \text{ radians}$

Divide the numerator and denominator by 45.

Practice Problem 2 Convert each angle in degrees to radians.

(a) $60°$ **(b)** $270°$ **(c)** $-300°$

EXAMPLE 3 Convert each angle in radians to degrees.

(a) $\frac{\pi}{3}$ radians **(b)** $-\frac{5\pi}{3}$ radians **(c)** 1 radian

Solution

To convert radians to degrees, multiply by $\frac{180°}{\pi \text{ radians}}$. Observe how the radian units cancel.

(a) $\frac{\pi}{3} \text{ radians} = \frac{\cancel{\pi \text{ radians}}}{3} \cdot \frac{180°}{\cancel{\pi \text{ radians}}} = \frac{180°}{3} = 60°$

(b) $-\frac{5\pi}{3} \text{ radians} = -\frac{5\cancel{\pi \text{ radians}}}{3} \cdot \frac{180°}{\cancel{\pi \text{ radians}}} = -\frac{5 \cdot 180°}{3} = -300°$

(c) $1 \text{ radian} = 1 \cancel{\text{radian}} \cdot \frac{180°}{\pi \cancel{\text{radians}}} = \frac{180°}{\pi} \approx 57.3°$

Practice Problem 3 Convert each angle in radians to degrees.

(a) $\frac{\pi}{4}$ radians **(b)** $-\frac{4\pi}{3}$ radians **(c)** 6 radians

SECTION 1 EXERCISES

Verbal and Writing Skills

1. Explain what is meant by one radian.

2. Have you ever noticed that we use the vocabulary of angles in everyday speech? Here is an example:

> My opinion about art museums took a 180° turn after visiting the San Francisco Museum of Modern Art.

Explain what this means. Then give another example of the vocabulary of angles in everyday use.

3. Describe how to convert an angle in degrees to radians.

4. Explain how to find the radian measure of a central angle.

In exercises 5–10, the measure of an angle is given. Classify the angle as acute, right, obtuse, or straight.

5. 135°

6. 177°

7. 83.135°

8. 87.177°

9. π

10. $\frac{\pi}{2}$

In exercises 11–15, find the radian measure of the central angle of a circle of radius r that intercepts an arc of length s.

11. $r = 10$ centimetres, $s = 40$ centimetres

12. $r = 5$ centimetres, $s = 30$ centimetres

13. $r = 6$ metres, $s = 8$ metres

14. $r = 8$ metres, $s = 18$ metres

15. $r = 1$ metre, $s = 400$ centimetres

In exercises 16–21, convert each angle in degrees to radians. Express your answer as a multiple of π.

16. 18°

17. 45°

18. 150°

19. 135°

20. −270°

21. 300°

In exercises 22–28, convert each angle in radians to degrees.

22. $\frac{\pi}{9}$

23. $\frac{\pi}{2}$

24. $\frac{3\pi}{4}$

25. $\frac{2\pi}{3}$

26. $\frac{11\pi}{6}$

27. $\frac{7\pi}{6}$

28. -4π

In exercises 29–33, convert each angle in degrees to radians. Round to two decimal places.

29. $18°$ **30.** $76°$ **31.** $-40°$ **32.** $-50°$ **33.** $200°$

In exercises 34–38, convert each angle in radians to degrees. Round to two decimal places.

34. 3 radians **35.** 2 radians **36.** $\frac{\pi}{17}$ radians **37.** $\frac{\pi}{13}$ radians **38.** -5.2 radians

Applications

39. ***Clock Revolutions*** The minute hand of a clock moves from 12 to 2 o'clock, or $\frac{1}{6}$ of a complete revolution. Through how many degrees does it move? Through how many radians does it move?

40. ***Clock Revolutions*** The minute hand of a clock moves from 12 to 4 o'clock, or $\frac{1}{3}$ of a complete revolution. Through how many degrees does it move? Through how many radians does it move?

To Think About

In exercises 41–43, determine whether each statement makes sense or does not make sense, and explain your reasoning.

41. If $\theta = \frac{3}{2}$, is this angle larger or smaller than a right angle?

42. When an angle's measure is given in terms of π, I know that it's measured using radians.

43. When I convert degrees to radians, I multiply by 1, choosing $\frac{\pi}{180°}$ for 1.

Quick Quiz 1

1. Find the radian measure of the central angle of a circle of radius 1 metre that intercepts an arc of length 600 centimetres.

2. Convert $-225°$ to radians. Express your answer as a multiple of π.

3. Convert -3π to degrees

4. Convert $250°$ to radians. Round to two decimal places.

5 Convert -4.8 radians to degrees. Round to two decimal places.

SECTION 2 ANGLES AND THE CARTESIAN PLANE

 Drawing Angles in Standard Position

An angle is in **standard position** on the Cartesian plane or the xy-plane if

- its vertex is at the origin of a rectangular coordinate system and
- its initial side lies along the positive x-axis.

A **positive angle** is generated by a counterclockwise rotation from the initial side to the terminal side. A **negative angle** is generated by a clockwise rotation from the initial side to the terminal side. Here is an example of a positive angle and a negative angle drawn in standard position:

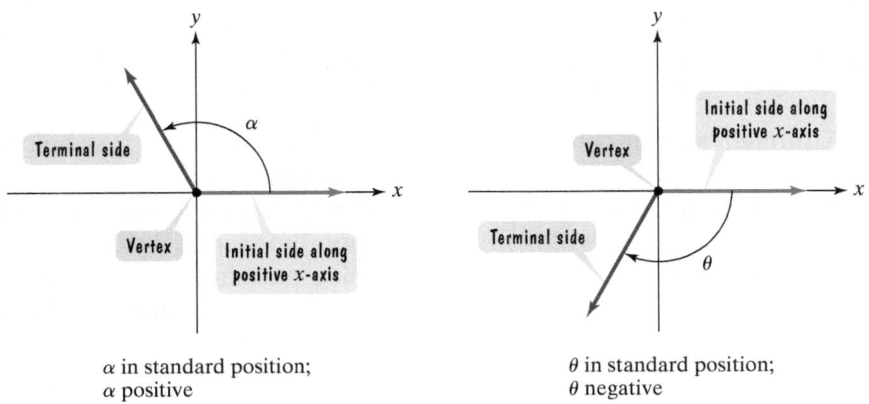

α in standard position; α positive

θ in standard position; θ negative

The xy-plane is divided into four quadrants.

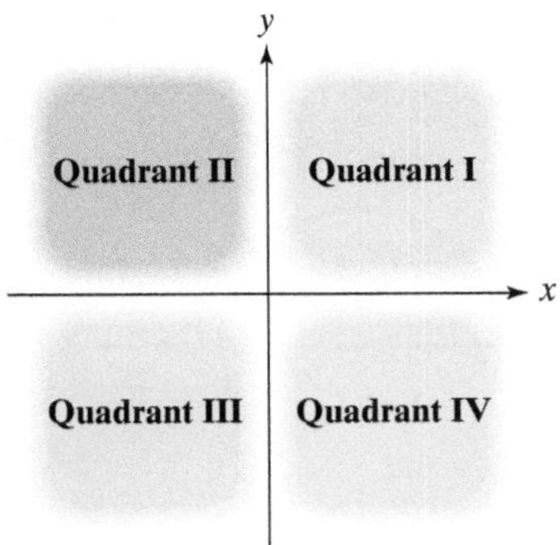

When an angle is in standard position, its terminal side can lie in any of the four quadrants. For example,the terminal side of angle α (shown above) lies in quadrant II. So, angle α lies in quadrant II. By contrast, the terminal side of angle θ (also shown above) lies in quadrant III. So, angle θ lies in quadrant III.

Student Learning Objectives

After studying this section, you will be able to:

 **Draw angles in standard position.**

2 **Find coterminal angles.**

Must all angles in standard position lie in a quadrant? The answer is no. The terminal side can lie on the x-axis or the y-axis and we call such an angle a **quadrantal angle**. Here is an example of a quadrantal angle whose terminal side lies on the negative y-axis:

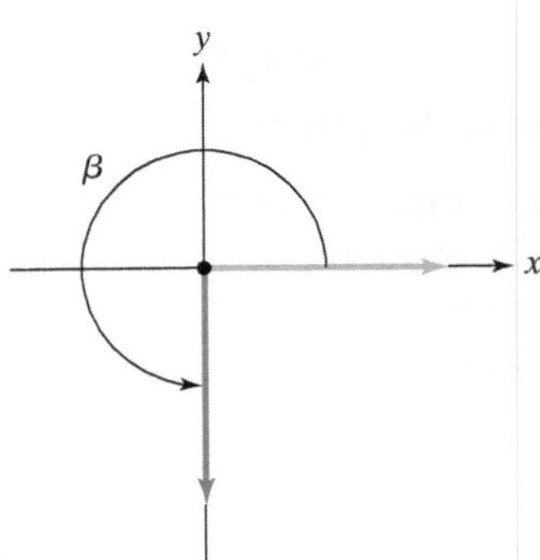

Although we can convert angles in radians to degrees, it is helpful to "think in radians" without having to make this conversion.

We will use quadrantal angles as a starting point for learning to think in radians. The figure below illustrates that when the terminal side makes one full revolution, it forms an angle whose radian measure is 2π or 360°. The figure shows the quadrantal angles formed by $\frac{3}{4}$ of a revolution, $\frac{1}{2}$ of a revolution, and $\frac{1}{4}$ of a revolution.

1 revolution
2π radians
360°

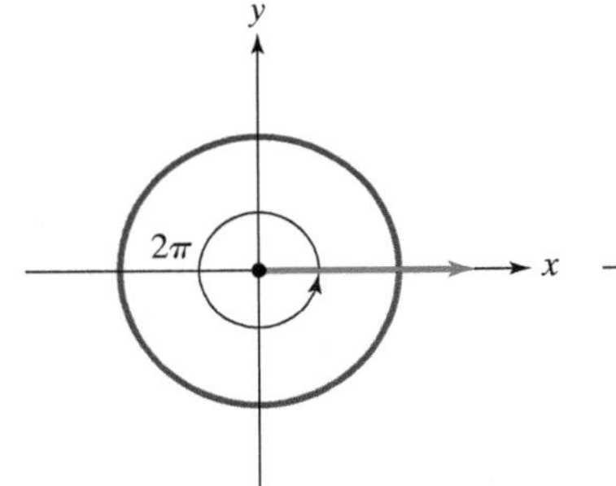

$\frac{3}{4}$ revolution
$\frac{3}{4} \cdot 2\pi = \frac{3\pi}{2}$ radians
$\frac{3}{4} \cdot 360° = 270°$

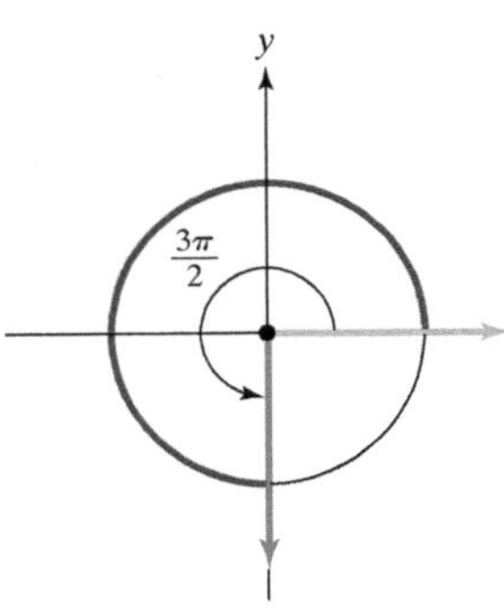

$\frac{1}{2}$ revolution
$\frac{1}{2} \cdot 2\pi = \pi$ radians
$\frac{1}{2} \cdot 360° = 180°$

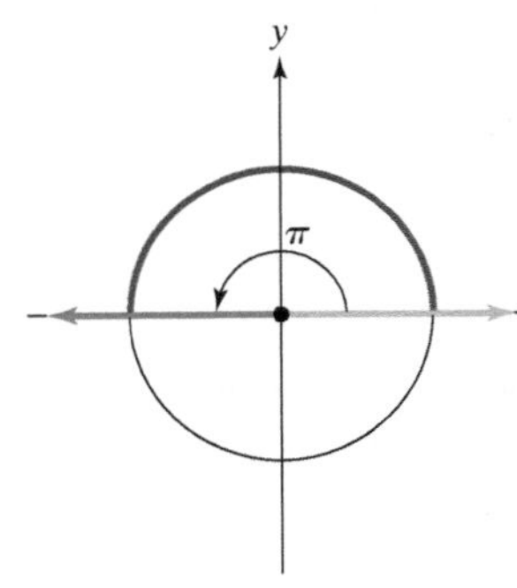

$\frac{1}{4}$ revolution
$\frac{1}{4} \cdot 2\pi = \frac{\pi}{2}$ radians
$\frac{1}{4} \cdot 360° = 90°$

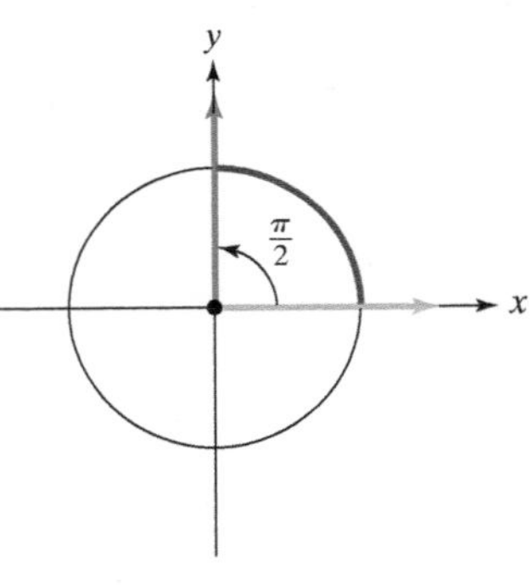

EXAMPLE 1 Draw and label each angle in standard position.

(a) $\theta = \frac{\pi}{4}$ (theta) **(b)** $\alpha = \frac{5\pi}{4}$ (alpha) **(c)** $\beta = -\frac{3\pi}{4}$ (beta) **(d)** $\gamma = \frac{9\pi}{4}$ (gamma)

Solution

Because we are drawing angles in standard position, each vertex is at the origin and each initial side lies along the positive x-axis.

(a) An angle of $\frac{\pi}{4}$ radians is a positive angle. It is obtained by rotating the terminal side counterclockwise. Because 2π is a full-circle revolution, we can express $\frac{\pi}{4}$ as a fractional part of 2π to determine the necessary rotation:

$$\frac{\pi}{4} = \frac{1}{8} \cdot 2\pi.$$

$\frac{\pi}{4}$ is $\frac{1}{8}$ of a complete revolution of 2π radians.

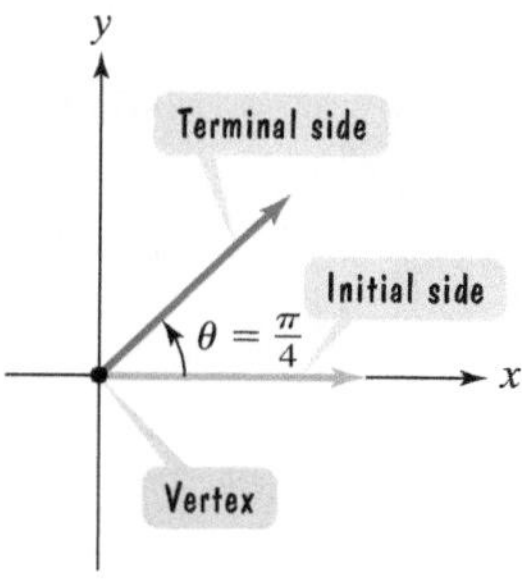

We see that $\theta = \frac{\pi}{4}$ is obtained by rotating the terminal side counterclockwise for $\frac{1}{8}$ of a revolution. The angle lies in quadrant I.

(b) An angle of $\frac{5\pi}{4}$ radians is a positive angle. It is obtained by rotating the terminal side counterclockwise.

$$\frac{5\pi}{4} = \pi + \frac{\pi}{4}.$$

π is a half-circle revolution.

$\frac{\pi}{4}$ is $\frac{1}{8}$ of a complete revolution.

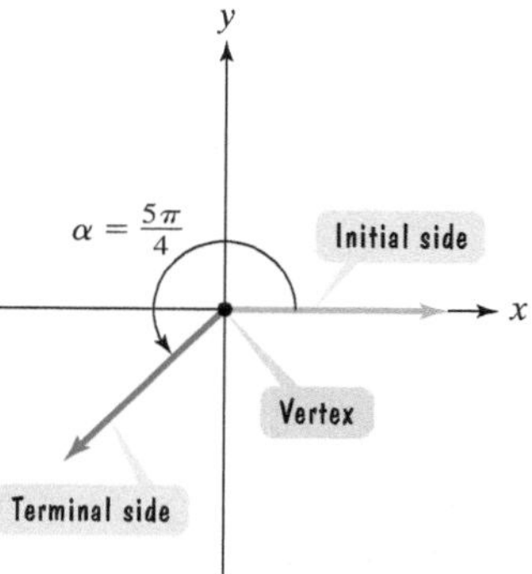

Angle $\alpha = \frac{5\pi}{4}$ is obtained by rotating the terminal side counterclockwise for half of a revolution followed by a counterclockwise rotation of $\frac{1}{8}$ of a revolution. The angle lies in quadrant III.

(c) An angle of $-\frac{3\pi}{4}$ is a negative angle. It is obtained by rotating the terminal side clockwise. We use $\left|-\frac{3\pi}{4}\right|$, or $\frac{3\pi}{4}$, to determine the necessary rotation.

$$\frac{3\pi}{4} = \frac{2\pi}{4} + \frac{\pi}{4} = \frac{\pi}{2} + \frac{\pi}{4}$$

$\frac{\pi}{2}$ is a quarter-circle revolution.

$\frac{\pi}{4}$ is $\frac{1}{8}$ of a complete revolution.

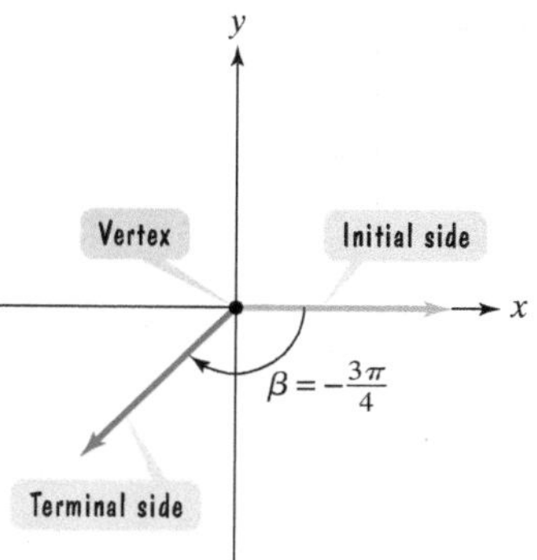

Angle $\beta = -\frac{3\pi}{4}$ is obtained by rotating the terminal side clockwise for $\frac{1}{4}$ of a revolution followed by a clockwise rotation of $\frac{1}{8}$ of a revolution. The angle lies in quadrant III.

(d) An angle of $\frac{9\pi}{4}$ radians is a positive angle. It is obtained by rotating the terminal side counterclockwise.

$$\frac{9\pi}{4} = 2\pi + \frac{\pi}{4}.$$

2π is a full-circle revolution.

$\frac{\pi}{4}$ is $\frac{1}{8}$ of a complete revolution.

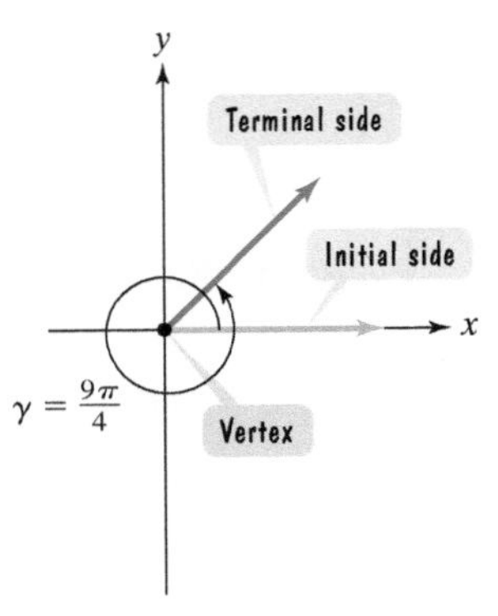

Angle $\gamma = \frac{9\pi}{4}$ is obtained by rotating the terminal side counterclockwise for a full-circle revolution followed by a counterclockwise rotation of $\frac{1}{8}$ of a revolution. The angle lies in quadrant I.

Practice Problem 1 Draw and label each angle in standard position.

(a) $\theta = -\frac{\pi}{4}$ **(b)** $\alpha = \frac{3\pi}{4}$ **(c)** $\beta = -\frac{7\pi}{4}$ **(d)** $\gamma = \frac{13\pi}{4}$

The figure below illustrates the degree and radian measures of angles that you will commonly see in trigonometry. Each angle is in standard position, so that the initial side lies along the positive x-axis. We will be using both degree and radian measure for these angles.

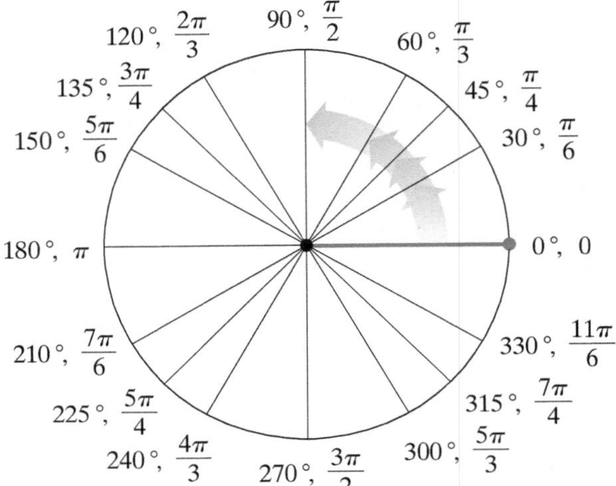

2 Finding Coterminal Angles

Two angles with the same initial and terminal sides but possibly different rotations are called **coterminal angles**.

Every angle has infinitely many coterminal angles. Why? Think of an angle in standard position. If the rotation of the angle is extended by one or more complete rotations of 360° or 2π, clockwise or counterclockwise, the result is an angle with the same initial and terminal sides as the original angle.

COTERMINAL ANGLES MEASURED IN DEGREES

An angle of θ° (an angle measured in degrees) is coterminal with angles of $\theta^\circ + 360^\circ k$, where k is an integer. For example, if $k = 1$ then

$$\theta^\circ + 360^\circ(1) = \theta^\circ + 360^\circ$$

is coterminal with θ°, and if $k = -1$ then

$$\theta^\circ + 360^\circ(-1) = \theta^\circ - 360^\circ$$

is also coterminal with θ°.

COTERMINAL ANGLES MEASURED IN RADIANS

An angle of θ radians (an angle measured in radians) is coterminal with angles of $\theta + 2\pi k$, where k is an integer. For example, if $k = 1$ then

$$\theta + 2\pi(1) = \theta + 2\pi$$

is coterminal with θ, and if $k = -1$ then

$$\theta + 2\pi(-1) = \theta - 2\pi$$

is also coterminal with θ.

Two coterminal angles for an angle of θ° can be found by adding 360° to θ° and subtracting 360° from θ°.

EXAMPLE 2 Assume the following angles are in standard position. Find a positive angle less than 360° that is coterminal with each of the following.

(a) a 420° angle **(b)** a −120° angle

Solution We obtain the coterminal angle by adding or subtracting 360°. The requirement to obtain a positive angle less than 360° determines whether we should add or subtract.

(a) For a 420° angle, subtract 360° to find a positive coterminal angle.

$$420^\circ - 360^\circ = 60^\circ$$

A 60° angle is coterminal with a 420° angle. As seen in the figure, these angles have the same initial and terminal sides.

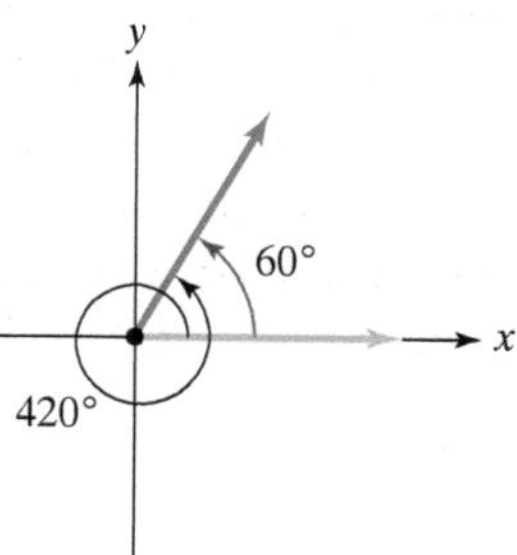

(b) For a −120° angle, add 360° to find a positive coterminal angle.

$$-120^\circ + 360^\circ = 240^\circ$$

A 240° angle is coterminal with a −120° angle. As seen in the figure, these angles have the same initial and terminal sides.

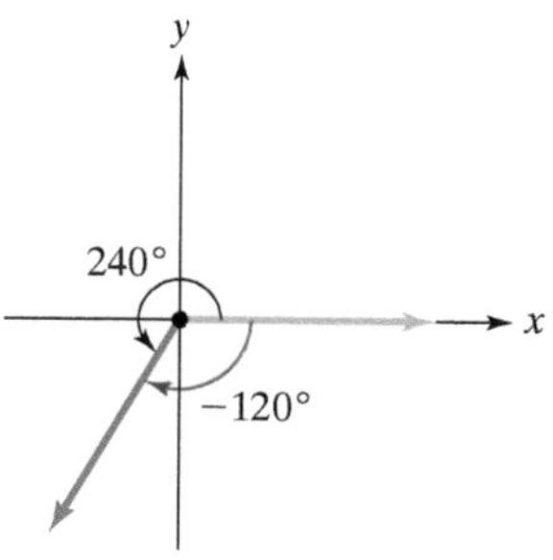

Practice Problem 2 Find a positive angle less than 360° that is coterminal with each of the following.

(a) a 400° angle **(b)** a −135° angle

Two coterminal angles for an angle of θ radians can be found by adding 2π to θ and subtracting 2π from θ.

EXAMPLE 3 Assume the following angles are in standard position. Find a positive angle less than 2π that is coterminal with each of the following.

(a) a $\frac{17\pi}{6}$ angle **(b)** a $-\frac{\pi}{12}$ angle

Solution We obtain the coterminal angle by adding or subtracting 2π. The requirement to obtain a positive angle less than 2π determines whether we should add or subtract.

(a) For a $\frac{17\pi}{6}$, or $2\frac{5}{6}\pi$, angle, subtract 2π to find a positive coterminal angle.

$$\frac{17\pi}{6} - 2\pi = \frac{17\pi}{6} - \frac{12\pi}{6} = \frac{5\pi}{6}$$

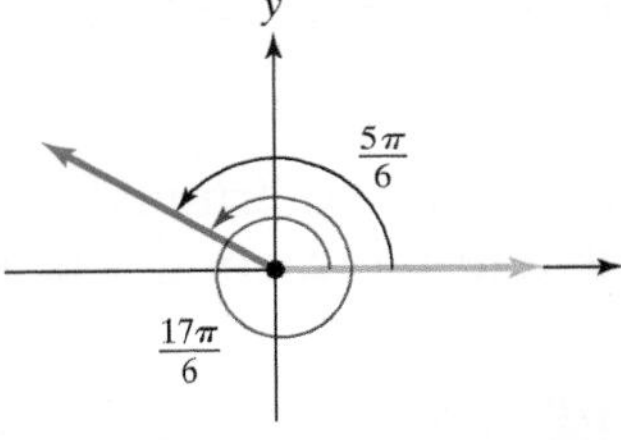

A $\frac{5\pi}{6}$ angle is coterminal with a $\frac{17\pi}{6}$ angle. As seen in the figure, these angles have the same initial and terminal sides.

(b) For a $-\frac{\pi}{12}$ angle, add 2π to find a positive coterminal angle.

$$-\frac{\pi}{12} + 2\pi = -\frac{\pi}{12} + \frac{24\pi}{12} = \frac{23\pi}{12}$$

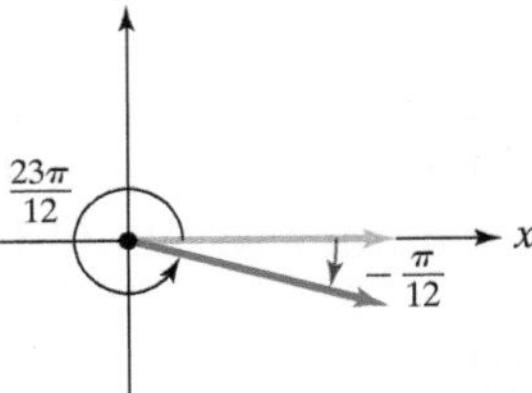

A $\frac{23\pi}{12}$ angle is coterminal with a $-\frac{\pi}{12}$ angle. As seen in the figure, these angles have the same initial and terminal sides.

Practice Problem 3 Find a positive angle less than 2π that is coterminal with each of the following.

(a) a $\frac{13\pi}{5}$ angle **(b)** a $-\frac{\pi}{15}$ angle

SECTION 2 EXERCISES

Verbal and Writing Skills

1. Describe an angle in standard position.

2. Explain the difference between positive and negative angles. What are coterminal angles?

In exercises 3–14, use the circle shown in the rectangular coordinate system to draw each angle in standard position. State the quadrant in which the angle lies. When an angle's measure is given in radians, work the exercise without converting to degrees.

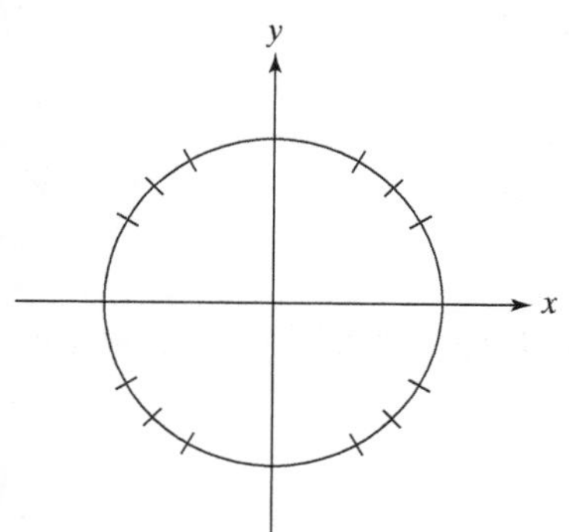

3. $\frac{7\pi}{6}$

4. $\frac{4\pi}{3}$

5. $-\frac{2\pi}{3}$

6. $\frac{7\pi}{4}$

7. $-\frac{5\pi}{4}$

8. $-\frac{5\pi}{6}$

9. $\frac{16\pi}{3}$

10. $-\frac{7\pi}{4}$

11. $150°$

12. $150°$

13. $420°$

14. $-240°$

In exercises 15–26, find a positive angle less than 360° or 2π that is coterminal with the given angle.

15. $395°$

16. $405°$

17. $-150°$

18. $415°$

19. $-765°$

20. $-760°$

21. $\frac{23\pi}{5}$

22. $\frac{17\pi}{5}$

23. $-\frac{\pi}{50}$

24. $\frac{25\pi}{6}$

25. $-\frac{31\pi}{7}$

26. $-\frac{\pi}{40}$

Use the circle shown in the rectangular coordinate system to solve exercises 27–32. Find two angles, in radians, between -2π and 2π such that each angle's terminal side passes through the origin and the given point.

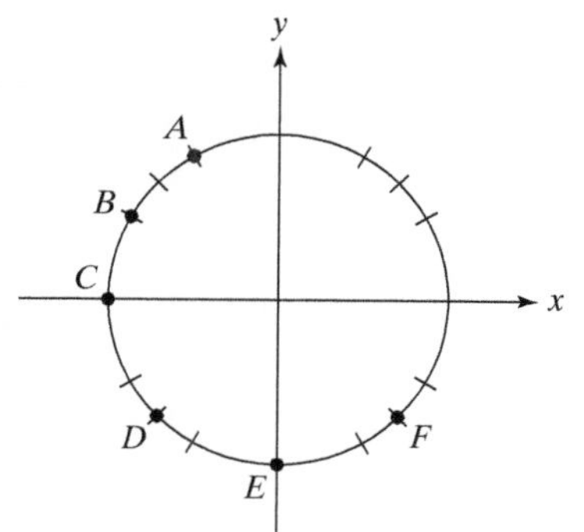

27. *A*

28. *B*

29. *D*

30. *F*

31. *E*

32. *C*

To Think About

In exercises 33–34, determine whether each statement makes sense or does not make sense, and explain your reasoning.

33. I made an error because the angle I drew in standard position exceeded a straight angle.

34. Using radian measure, I can always find a positive angle less than 2π coterminal with a given angle by adding or subtracting 2π.

Quick Quiz 2

In exercises 1–2, use the circle shown in the rectangular coordinate system to draw each angle in standard position. State the quadrant in which the angle lies. When an angle's measure is given in radians, work the exercise without converting to degrees.

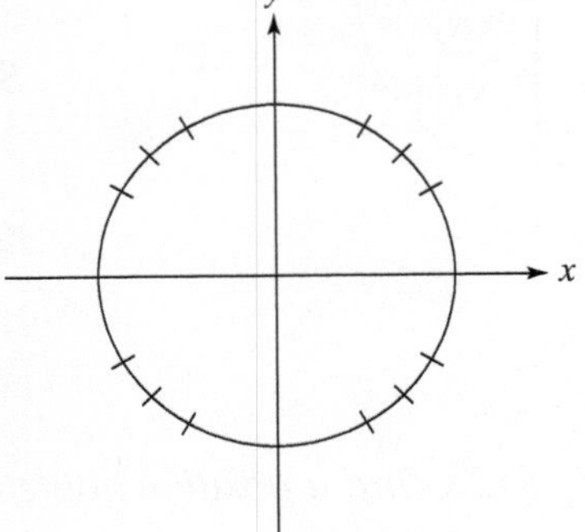

1. $\dfrac{3\pi}{4}$

2. $-210°$

In exercises 3–4, find a positive angle less than 360° or 2π that is coterminal with the given angle.

3. $-160°$

4. $\dfrac{19\pi}{6}$

How Am I Doing? Sections 1–2

How are you doing with your homework assignments in Sections 1 and 2? Do you feel you have mastered the material so far? Do you understand the concepts you have covered? Before you go further, take some time to do each of the following problems.

1

In questions 1–2, find the radian measure of the central angle of a circle of radius r that intercepts an arc of length s.

1. $r = 7$ cm, $s = 28$ cm

2. $r = 1$ m, $s = 300$ cm

Convert each angle in degrees to radians. Express your answer as a multiple of π.

3. $130°$

4. $-45°$

Convert each angle in radians to degrees.

5. $\dfrac{\pi}{6}$

6. $\dfrac{-3\pi}{2}$

Convert each angle in degrees to radians. Round to two decimal places.

7. $-230°$

8. $50°$

Convert each angle in radians to degrees. Round to two decimal places.

9. 5 radians

10. $\dfrac{\pi}{15}$ radians

2

In questions 11–16, draw the given angle in standard position. State the quadrant in which the angle lies. When an angle's measure is given in radians, work the exercise without converting to degrees.

11. $-120°$

12. $30°$

13. $330°$

14. $\dfrac{5\pi}{6}$

15. $-\dfrac{11\pi}{6}$

16. $\dfrac{2\pi}{3}$

1. ________

2. ________

3. ________

4. ________

5. ________

6. ________

7. ________

8. ________

9. ________

10. ________

11. y x

12. y x

13. y x

14. y x

15.

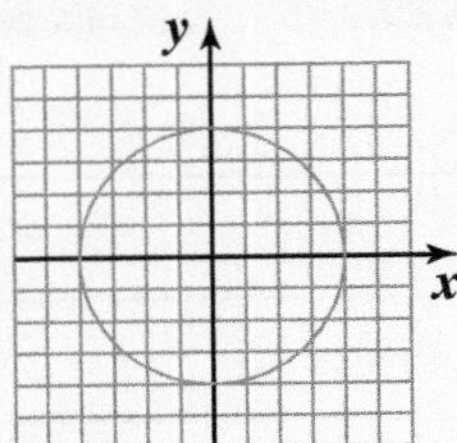

16.

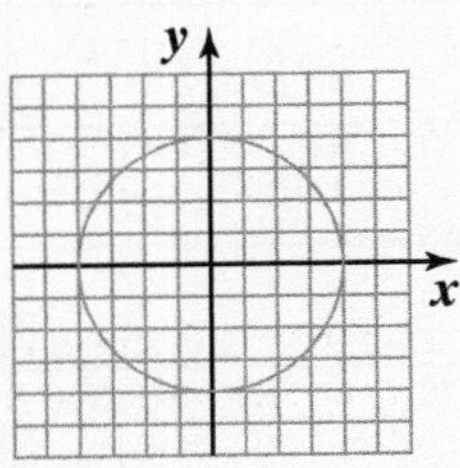

17. ______

18. ______

19. ______

20. ______

Find a positive angle less than 360° or 2π that is coterminal with the given angle.

17. $450°$

18. $-180°$

19. $-\frac{\pi}{25}$

20. $\frac{7\pi}{3}$

Your institution may have included the Answers to Selected Exercises for this module, which contains the answers to these questions. Each answer also includes a reference to the objective in which the problem is first taught. If you missed any of these problems, you should stop and review the Examples and Practice Problems in the referenced objective. A little review now will help you master the material in the upcoming sections.

SECTION 3 RIGHT TRIANGLE TRIGONOMETRY

Labelling a Right Triangle in Standard Form and Applying the Pythagorean Theorem

Using the **standard labelling of a right triangle**, we label its sides and angles so that side a is opposite to angle A, side b is opposite to angle B, and side c is opposite to angle C. Angle C is always taken to be the right angle, making side c the hypotenuse.

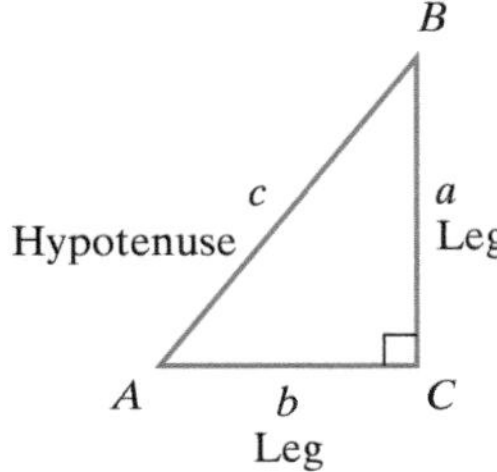

The Pythagorean Theorem in terms of the standard labelling of a right triangle is given by

$$a^2 + b^2 = c^2.$$

EXAMPLE 1 Find the length of the hypotenuse c where $a = 9$ m and $b = 12$ m.

Solution Let $a = 9$ and $b = 12$. Substitute these values into $c^2 = a^2 + b^2$ and solve for c.

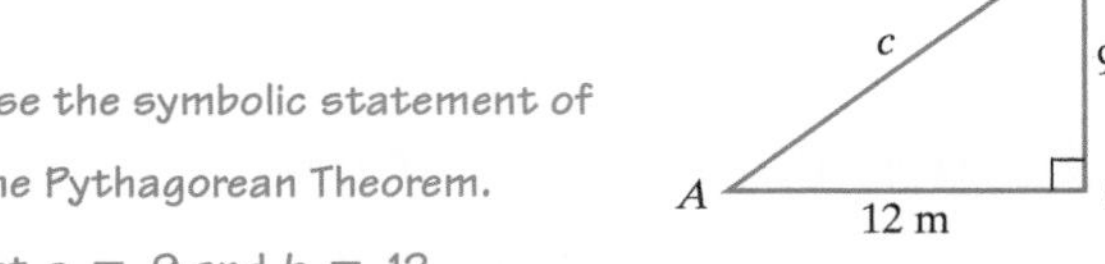

$c^2 = a^2 + b^2$ Use the symbolic statement of the Pythagorean Theorem.

$c^2 = 9^2 + 12^2$ Let $a = 9$ and $b = 12$.

$c^2 = 81 + 144$ $9^2 = 9 \cdot 9 = 81$ and $12^2 = 12 \cdot 12 = 144$.

$c^2 = 225$ Add.

$c = \sqrt{225} = 15$ Solve for c by taking the positive square root of 225.

The length of the hypotenuse is 15 metres.

Practice Problem 1 Find the length of the hypotenuse in a right triangle whose legs have lengths 7 metres and 24 metres.

Student Learning Objectives

After studying this section, you will be able to:

1. **Label a right triangle in standard form and apply the Pythagorean Theorem.**
2. **Use right triangles to evaluate the primary trigonometric ratios.**
3. **Find primary trigonometric ratios for some special angles.**
4. **Evaluate the primary trigonometric ratios using a calculator.**

Using Right Triangles to Evaluate the Primary Trigonometric Ratios

We begin the study of trigonometry by defining the three primary trigonometric ratios—sine, cosine, and tangent. Here are their names, along with their abbreviations.

Name	Abbreviation
sine	sin
cosine	cos
tangent	tan

Consider a right triangle with one of its acute angles labelled θ. The side opposite the right angle, the hypotenuse, has length c. The other sides of the triangle are described by their position relative to the acute angle θ. One side is opposite θ. The length of this side is a. One side is adjacent to θ. The length of this side is b.

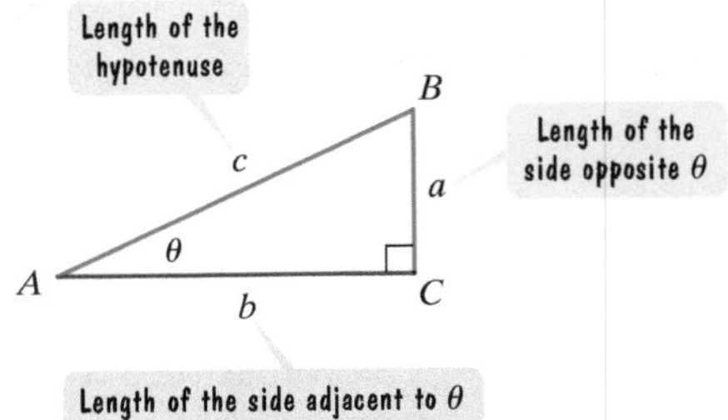

RIGHT TRIANGLE DEFINITIONS OF SINE, COSINE, AND TANGENT

The three **primary trigonometric ratios** of the acute angle θ are defined as follows:

$$\sin\theta = \frac{\text{length of side opposite angle } \theta}{\text{length of hypotenuse}} = \frac{a}{c}$$

$$\cos\theta = \frac{\text{length of side adjacent to angle } \theta}{\text{length of hypotenuse}} = \frac{b}{c}$$

$$\tan\theta = \frac{\text{length of side opposite angle } \theta}{\text{length of side adjacent to angle } \theta} = \frac{a}{b}$$

An understanding of trigonometry depends on applying the concept of similar triangles. The figure below shows four right triangles of varying sizes. In each of the triangles, θ is the same acute angle, measuring approximately 56.3°. All four of these similar triangles have the same shape and the lengths of corresponding sides are in the same ratio. In each triangle, the tangent ratio has the same value for the angle θ: $\tan\theta = \frac{3}{2}$.

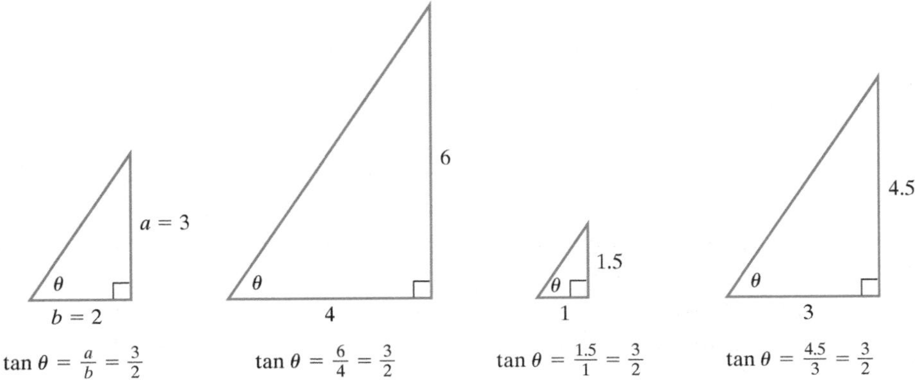

$\tan\theta = \frac{a}{b} = \frac{3}{2}$ $\tan\theta = \frac{6}{4} = \frac{3}{2}$ $\tan\theta = \frac{1.5}{1} = \frac{3}{2}$ $\tan\theta = \frac{4.5}{3} = \frac{3}{2}$

In general, **the values of sine, cosine, and tangent of θ depend only on the size of angle θ and not on the size of the triangle.**

EXAMPLE 2 Find the value of each of the three primary trigonometric ratios of θ.

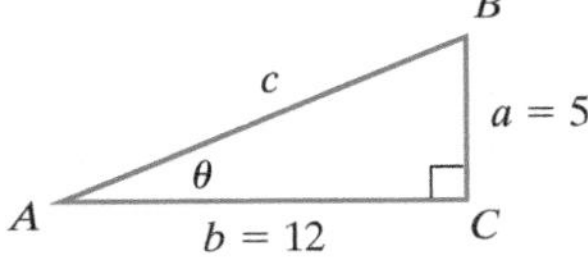

Solution We need to find the values of sine, cosine, and tangent of θ. However, we must first know the lengths of all three sides of the triangle (a, b, and c). The values of a and b are given. We can use the Pythagorean Theorem, $c^2 = a^2 + b^2$, to find c.

$a = 5$ $b = 12$

$$c^2 = a^2 + b^2 = 5^2 + 12^2 = 25 + 144 = 169$$

$$c = \sqrt{169} = 13$$

Note that we take the positive square root of 169 to get the length of the hypotenuse.

Now that we know the lengths of the three sides of the triangle, we apply the definitions of sine, cosine, and tangent of θ. Referring to these lengths as opposite, adjacent, and hypotenuse, we have

$$\sin\theta = \frac{\text{opposite}}{\text{hypotenuse}} = \frac{5}{13}$$

$$\cos\theta = \frac{\text{adjacent}}{\text{hypotenuse}} = \frac{12}{13}$$

$$\tan\theta = \frac{\text{opposite}}{\text{adjacent}} = \frac{5}{12}.$$

Practice Problem 2 Find the values of sine, cosine, and tangent of θ in the figure.

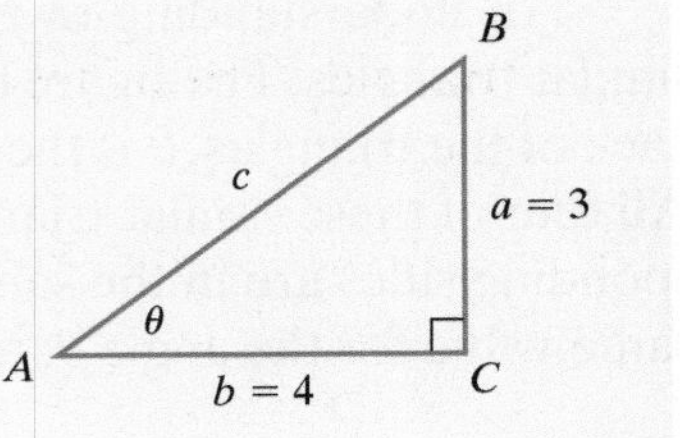

EXAMPLE 3 Find the value of each of the three primary trigonometric ratios of θ .

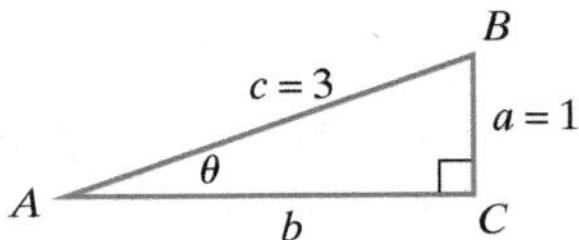

Solution We begin by finding b.

$a^2 + b^2 = c^2$	Use the Pythagorean Theorem.
$1^2 + b^2 = 3^2$	The figure shows that $a = 1$ and $c = 3$.
$1 + b^2 = 9$	$1^2 = 1$ and $3^2 = 9$.
$b^2 = 8$	Subtract 1 from both sides.
$b = \sqrt{8} = 2\sqrt{2}$	Take the positive square root and simplify. $\sqrt{8} = \sqrt{4 \cdot 2} = \sqrt{4}\sqrt{2} = 2\sqrt{2}$

Now that we know the lengths of the three sides of the triangle, we apply the definitions of sine, cosine, and tangent of θ.

$$\sin \theta = \frac{\text{opposite}}{\text{hypotenuse}} = \frac{1}{3}$$

$$\cos \theta = \frac{\text{adjacent}}{\text{hypotenuse}} = \frac{2\sqrt{2}}{3}$$

$$\tan \theta = \frac{\text{opposite}}{\text{adjacent}} = \frac{1}{2\sqrt{2}}$$

Practice Problem 3 Find the sine, cosine, and tangent of θ in the figure.

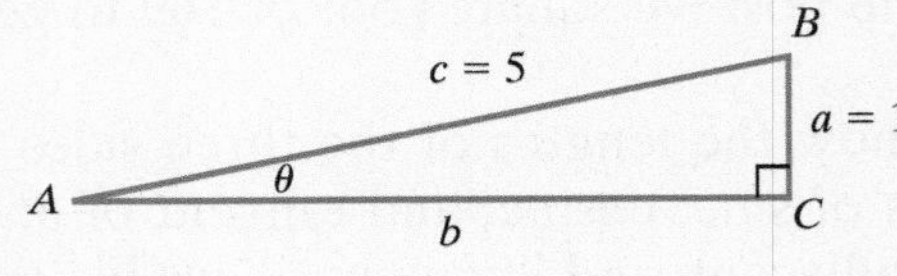

Finding Primary Trigonometric Ratios for Some Special Angles

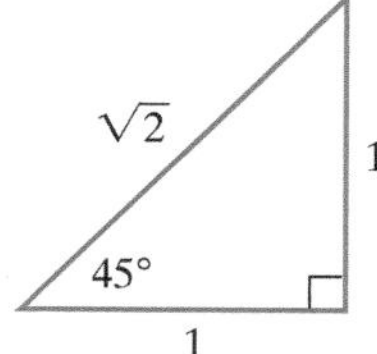

How can we find the values of the trigonometric ratios at $\frac{\pi}{4}$, or 45°, using a right triangle? We construct a right triangle with a 45° angle. The triangle actually has two 45° angles. Thus, the triangle is isosceles—that is, it has two sides of the same length. Assume that each leg of the triangle has a length equal to 1. We can find the length of the hypotenuse using the Pythagorean Theorem.

$$(\text{length of hypotenuse})^2 = 1^2 + 1^2 = 2$$
$$\text{length of hypotenuse} = \sqrt{2}$$

We can then find the values of the three primary trigonometric ratios of 45° by applying the definitions of sine, cosine, and tangent.

$$\sin 45° = \frac{\text{length of side opposite } 45°}{\text{length of hypotenuse}} = \frac{1}{\sqrt{2}}$$

$$\cos 45° = \frac{\text{length of side adjacent to } 45°}{\text{length of hypotenuse}} = \frac{1}{\sqrt{2}}$$

$$\tan 45° = \frac{\text{length of side opposite } 45°}{\text{length of side adjacent to } 45°} = \frac{1}{1} = 1$$

Two other angles that occur frequently in trigonometry are 30°, or $\frac{\pi}{6}$ radians, and 60°, or $\frac{\pi}{3}$ radians. We can find the values of the primary trigonometric ratios of 30° and 60° by using a right triangle. To form this right triangle, draw an equilateral triangle—that is a triangle with all sides the same length. Assume that each side has a length equal to 2. Now take half of the equilateral triangle. We obtain the following right triangle:

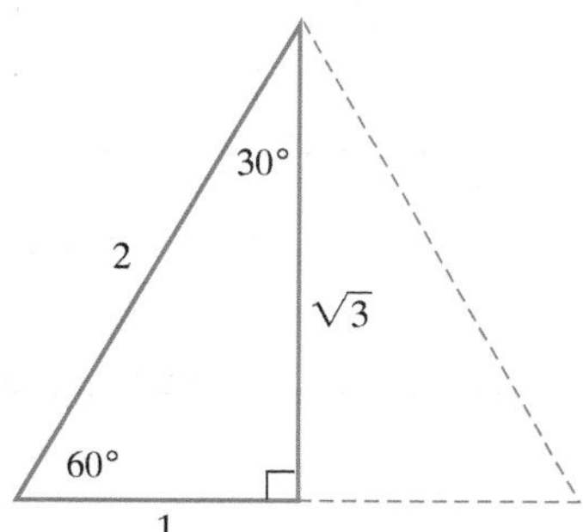

This right triangle has a hypotenuse of length 2 and a leg of length 1. The other leg has length a, which can be found using the Pythagorean Theorem.

$$a^2 + 1^2 = 2^2$$
$$a^2 + 1 = 4$$
$$a^2 = 3$$
$$a = \sqrt{3}$$

We can now determine the primary trigonometric ratios for 30° and 60°.

EXAMPLE 4 Find sin 60°, cos 60°, sin 30°, and cos 30°.

Solution We begin with 60°. Use the angle on the lower left in the figure shown above.

$$\sin 60° = \frac{\text{length of side opposite } 60°}{\text{length of hypotenuse}} = \frac{\sqrt{3}}{2}$$

$$\cos 60° = \frac{\text{length of side adjacent to } 60°}{\text{length of hypotenuse}} = \frac{1}{2}$$

To find sin 30° and cos 30°, use the angle on the upper left in the figure shown above.

$$\sin 30° = \frac{\text{length of side opposite } 30°}{\text{length of hypotenuse}} = \frac{1}{2}$$

$$\cos 30° = \frac{\text{length of side adjacent to } 30°}{\text{length of hypotenuse}} = \frac{\sqrt{3}}{2}$$

Practice Problem 4 Find tan 60° and tan 30°.

Because we will often use the ratio values of 30°, 45°, and 60°, you should learn to construct the right triangles shown in the previous examples.

4 Evaluating the Primary Trigonometric Ratios Using a Calculator

We have been using special angles to find the values of trigonometric ratios for angles of 30, 45, and 60 degrees. These are exact values. We can find approximate values of the trigonometric ratios using a calculator.

The first step in using a calculator is to set the calculator to the correct *mode*, degrees or radians. For the examples given below, we will use the radian mode.

Most calculators have keys marked SIN, COS, and TAN. For example, to find the value of sin 1.2, set the calculator to the radian mode and enter 1.2 SIN on most scientific calculators and SIN 1.2 ENTER on most graphing calculators. Consult the manual for your calculator.

EXAMPLE 5 Use a calculator to find the value to four decimal places.

(a) $\cos \frac{\pi}{4}$ **(b)** tan 1.2

Solution

Scientific Calculator Solution

Function	**Mode**	**Keystrokes**	**Display, rounded to four decimal places**
(a) $\cos \frac{\pi}{4}$	Radian	[π] [÷] 4 [=] [COS]	0.7071
(b) tan 1.2	Radian	1.2 [TAN]	2.572

Graphing Calculator Solution

Function	**Mode**	**Keystrokes**	**Display, rounded to four decimal places**
(a) $\cos \frac{\pi}{4}$	Radian	[COS] [(] [π] [÷] 4 [)] [ENTER]	0.7071
(b) tan 1.2	Radian	[TAN] 1.2 [ENTER]	2.572

Practice Problem 5 Use a calculator to find the value to four decimal places.

(a) $\sin \frac{\pi}{4}$ **(b)** cos 1.25

SECTION 3 EXERCISES

Verbal and Writing Skills

1. If you are given the lengths of the sides of a right triangle, describe how to find the sine of either acute angle.

2. Describe one similarity and one difference between the definitions of $\sin\theta$ and $\cos\theta$, where θ is an acute angle of a right triangle.

3. Describe the triangle used to find the trigonometric ratios of 45°.

4. Describe the triangle used to find the trigonometric ratios of 30° and 60°.

In exercises 5–11, use the Pythagorean Theorem to find the length of the missing side of each right triangle. Then find the value of sine, cosine, and tangent of θ.

5.

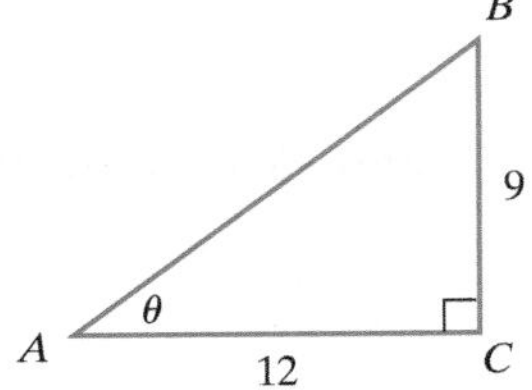

6.

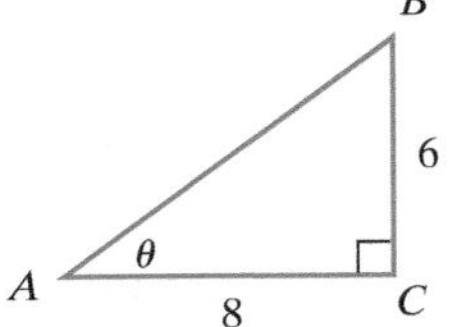

7.

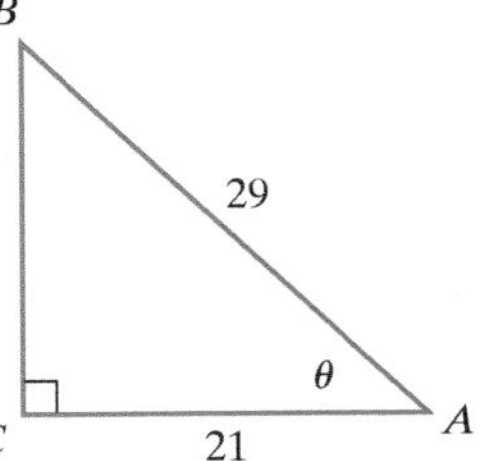

8.

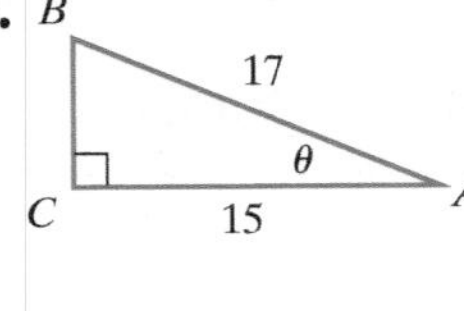

9.

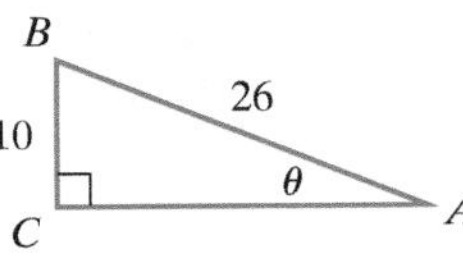

10.

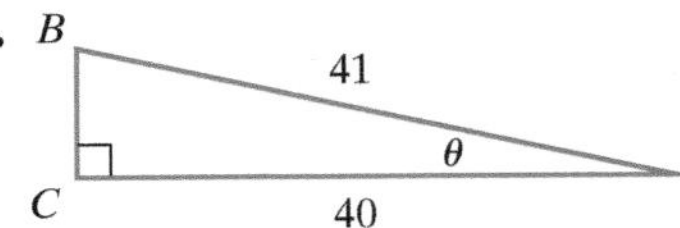

11.

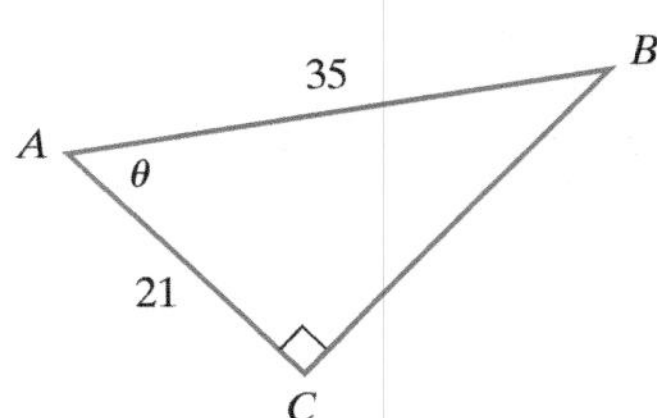

In exercises 12–17, use the given triangles to evaluate each expression.

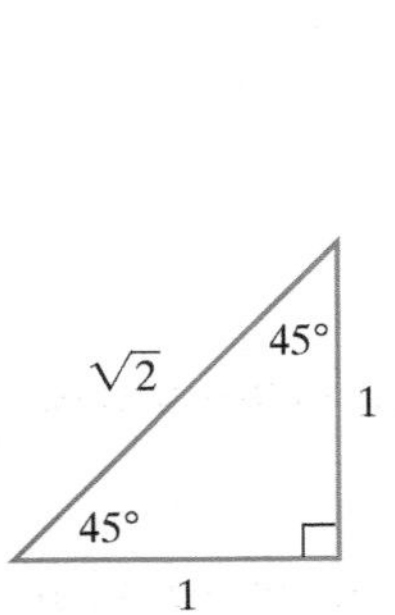

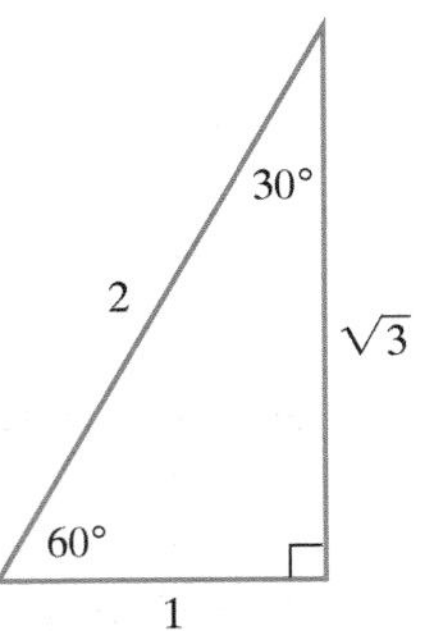

12. $\tan 30°$

13. $\cos 30°$

14. $\tan \frac{\pi}{4}$

15. $\tan \frac{\pi}{3}$

16. $\cos \frac{\pi}{3}$

17. $\sin \frac{\pi}{3} \cos \frac{\pi}{4} - \tan \frac{\pi}{4}$

In exercises 18–22, find the measure of the side of the right triangle whose length is designated by a lowercase letter. Round answers to the nearest whole number.

18.

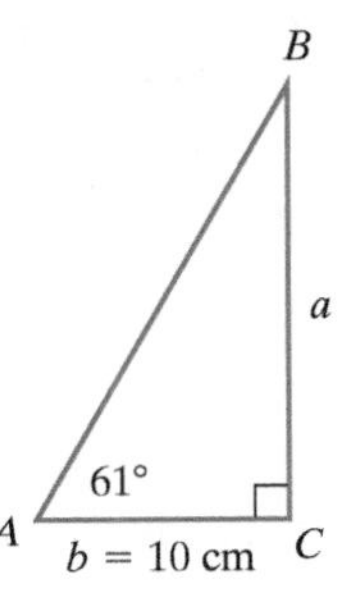

19.

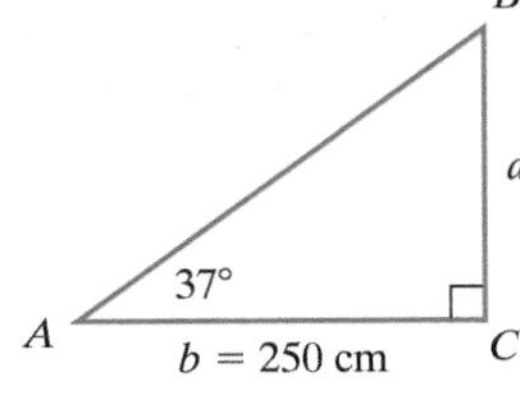

20.

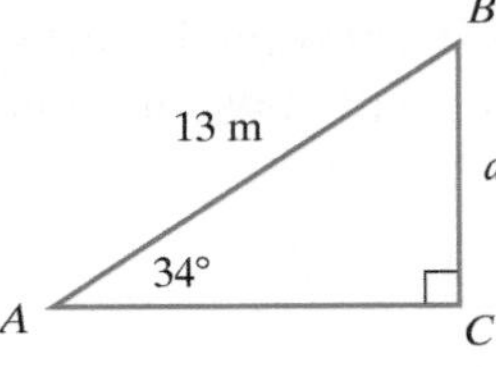

21.

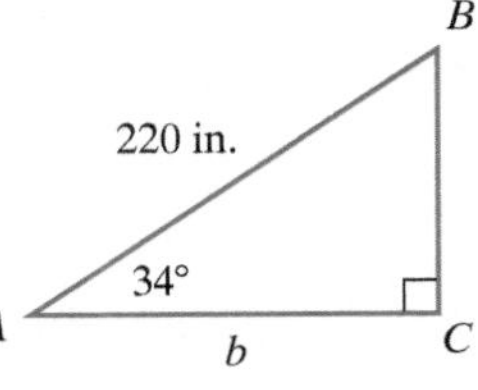

22.

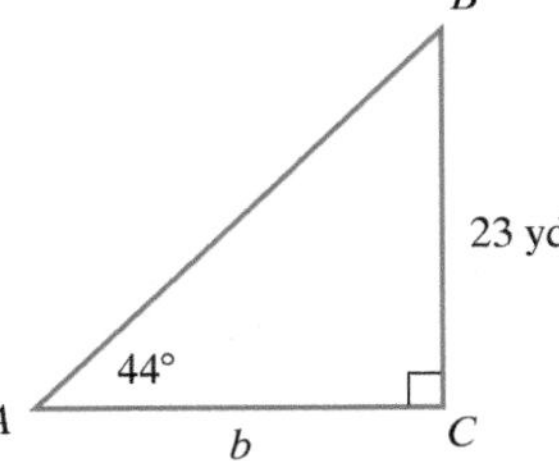

In exercises 23–27, use a calculator to find sine, cosine, or tangent of the given angle. Round to four decimal places.

23. $\sin 0.8$ **24.** $\cos 0.6$ **25.** $\tan 3.4$ **26.** $\sin \frac{3\pi}{10}$ **27.** $\cos \frac{\pi}{10}$

28. Using ideas from special triangles, complete the following chart.

θ	$30° = \frac{\pi}{6}$	$45° = \frac{\pi}{4}$	$60° = \frac{\pi}{3}$
sin θ			
cos θ			
tan θ			

To Think About

In exercises 29–30, determine whether each statement makes sense or does not make sense, and explain your reasoning.

29. Although I can use an isosceles right triangle to determine the exact value of $\sin \frac{\pi}{4}$, I can also use my calculator to obtain this value.

30. For a given angle θ, I found a slight increase in $\sin \theta$ as the size of the triangle increased.

Quick Quiz 3

1. Use the Pythagorean Theorem to find the length of the missing side of the right triangle below. Then find the value of sine, cosine, and tangent of θ.

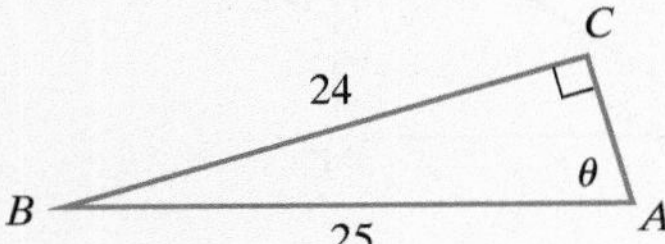

2. Use the given triangles to evaluate $6 \tan \frac{\pi}{4} + \sin \frac{\pi}{3}$.

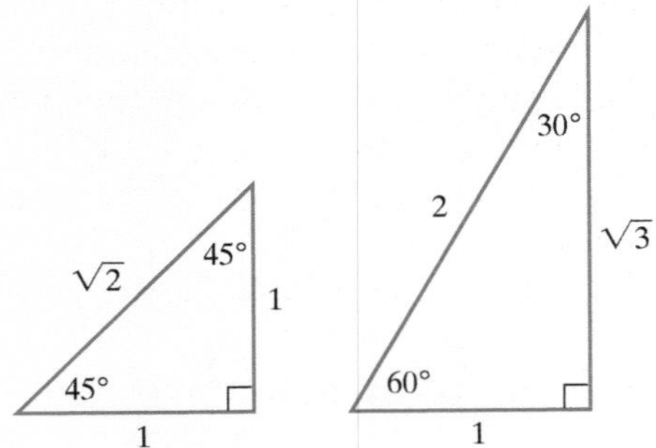

3. Find the measure of c. Round your answer to the nearest whole number.

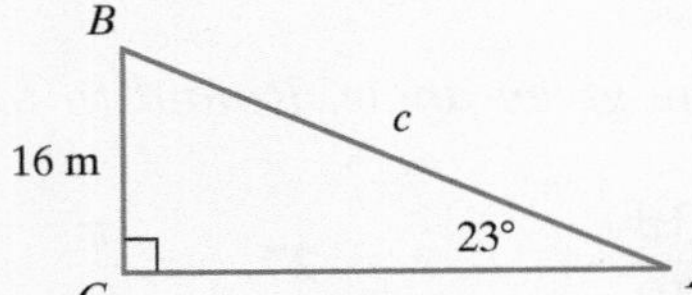

4. Use a calculator to find tan 3.7 to four decimal places.

Section 4 Solving Applied Problems Involving Trigonometry

Solving Right Triangles

Solving a right triangle means finding the missing lengths of its sides and the measurements of its angles. We will label right triangles in the standard way so that side a is opposite angle A, side b is opposite angle B, and side c, the hypotenuse, is opposite right angle C.

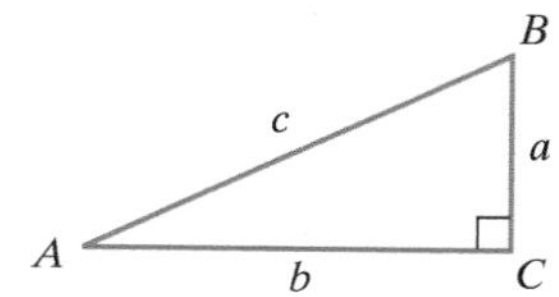

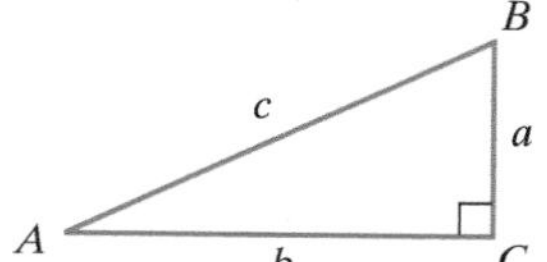

When solving a right triangle, we will use the sine, cosine, and tangent. Example 1 shows how to solve a right triangle when we know the length of a side and the measure of an acute angle.

Student Learning Objectives

After studying this section, you will be able to:

 **Solve a right triangle.**

 **Use right triangle trigonometry to solve applied problems.**

EXAMPLE 1 Solve the right triangle shown in the margin, rounding lengths to two decimal places.

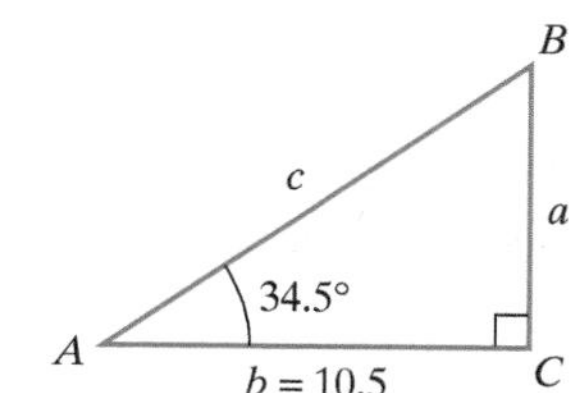

Solution We begin by finding the measure of angle B. We do not need a trigonometric ratio to do so. Because $C = 90°$ and the sum of a triangle's angles is 180°, we see that $A + B = 90°$. Thus,

$$B = 90° - A = 90° - 34.5° = 55.5°.$$

Now we need to find a. Because we have a known angle, an unknown opposite side, and a known adjacent side, we use the tangent ratio.

$$\tan 34.5° = \frac{a}{10.5}$$

Side opposite the 34.5° angle (numerator)
Side adjacent to the 34.5° angle (denominator)

Now we multiply both sides of this equation by 10.5 and solve for a.

$$a = 10.5 \tan 34.5° \approx 7.22$$

Finally, we need to find c. Because we have a known angle, a known adjacent side, and an unknown hypotenuse, we use the cosine ratio.

$$\cos 34.5° = \frac{10.5}{c}$$

Side adjacent to the 34.5° angle (numerator)
Hypotenuse (denominator)

Now we multiply both sides of this equation by c and then solve for c.

$$c \times \cos 34.5° = 10.5 \quad \text{Multiply both sides by } c.$$

$$c = \frac{10.5}{\cos 34.5°} \approx 12.74 \quad \text{Divide both sides by } \cos 34.5° \text{ and solve for } c.$$

In summary, $B = 55.5°$, $a \approx 7.22$, and $c \approx 12.74$.

Practice Problem 1 Using the standard labelling of a right triangle, let $A = 62.7°$ and $a = 8.4$. Solve the right triangle, rounding lengths to two decimal places.

If two sides of a right triangle are known, an appropriate trigonometric ratio can be used to find an acute angle θ in the triangle. To do this, you will need to use an inverse trigonometric key on a calculator. For example, suppose that $\sin\theta = 0.866$. We can find θ in the degree mode by using the secondary *inverse sine* key, usually labelled $\boxed{\text{SIN}^{-1}}$. Here are instructions on how to use the inverse sine key on the calculator:

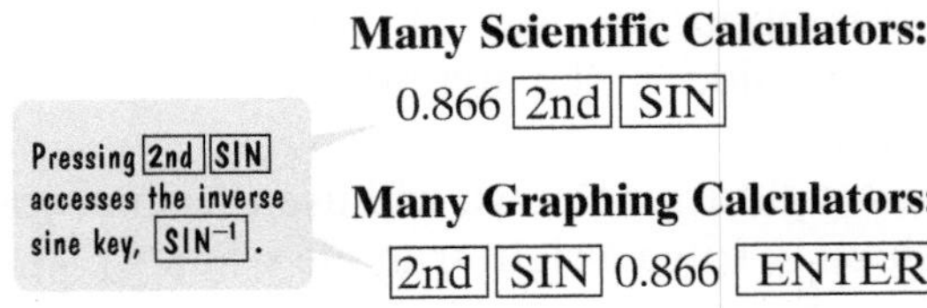

Many Scientific Calculators:
0.866 2nd SIN
Pressing 2nd SIN accesses the inverse sine key, SIN⁻¹.
Many Graphing Calculators:
2nd SIN 0.866 ENTER

The display should show approximately 59.99, which can be rounded to 60. Thus, if $\sin\theta = 0.866$ and θ is acute, then $\theta \approx 60°$.

We can also use the inverse cosine and inverse tangent keys in a similar way. Example 2 shows how to solve a right triangle when we know the lengths of two sides.

EXAMPLE 2 Using the standard labelling of a right triangle, let $b = 21.4$ and $c = 55.3$. Solve the following right triangle, rounding lengths and angles to the nearest tenth.

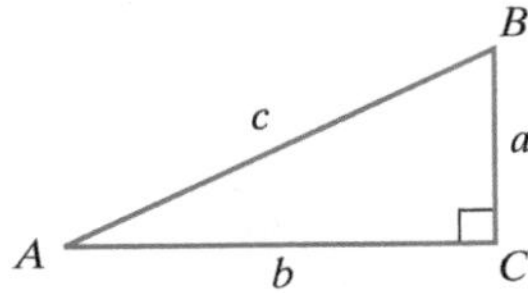

Solution In the right triangle, we have two unknown angles, and one unknown length. We need to use trigonometry to find the value of angle A. We know the side adjacent to angle A and the hypotenuse, therefore we will use cosine to find A.

$$\cos A = \frac{21.4}{55.3}$$

Side adjacent to A

Hypotenuse

$$A = \cos^{-1}\frac{21.4}{55.3} \approx 67.2°$$

Because $C = 90°$ and the sum of a triangle's angles is 180°, we see that $A + B = 90°$. So

$$B = 90° - A = 90° - 67.2° = 22.8°.$$

Now we need to find a. We know angle A, an unknown opposite side a, and a known hypotenuse. Therefore, we use the sine ratio.

$$\sin 67.2° = \frac{a}{55.3}$$

Side adjacent to A

Hypotenuse

Now we multiply both sides of this equation by 55.3 and solve for a.

$$a = 55.3 \sin 67.2° - 67.2° \approx 51.0$$

We have now solved the triangle by finding A, B, and a.

Practice Problem 2 Using the standard labelling of a right triangle, let $a = 19.3$ and $b = 25.1$. Solve the right triangle, rounding lengths and angles to one decimal place.

 Using Right Triangle Trigonometry to Solve Applied Problems

Trigonometry was first developed to measure heights and distances that were inconvenient or impossible to measure directly. In solving application problems, begin by making a sketch involving a right triangle that illustrates the problem's conditions. Then put your knowledge of solving right triangles to work and find the required distance or height.

EXAMPLE 3 From a point on level ground 40 metres from the base of a tower, the angle of elevation is 57.2°. Approximate the height of the tower to the nearest metre.

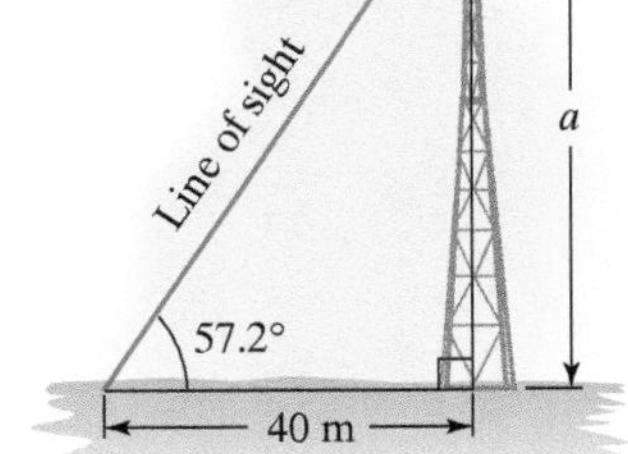

Solution Let a represent the height of the tower. In the right triangle, we have a known angle, an unknown opposite side, and a known adjacent side. Therefore, we use the tangent ratio.

$$\tan 57.2° = \frac{a}{40}$$

Side opposite the 57.2° angle

Side adjacent to the 57.2° angle

Now we multiply both sides of this equation by 40 and solve for a.

$$a = 40 \tan 57.2° \approx 62$$

The tower is approximately 62 metres high.

Practice Problem 3 From a point on level ground 26 metres from the base of the Eiffel Tower, the angle of elevation is 85.4°. Approximate the height of the Eiffel Tower to the nearest metre.

Many applications of right triangle trigonometry involve the angle made with an imaginary horizontal line. An angle formed by a horizontal line and the line of sight to an object that is above the horizontal line is called the **angle of elevation**. The angle formed by a horizontal line and the line of sight to an object that is below the horizontal line is called the **angle of depression**.

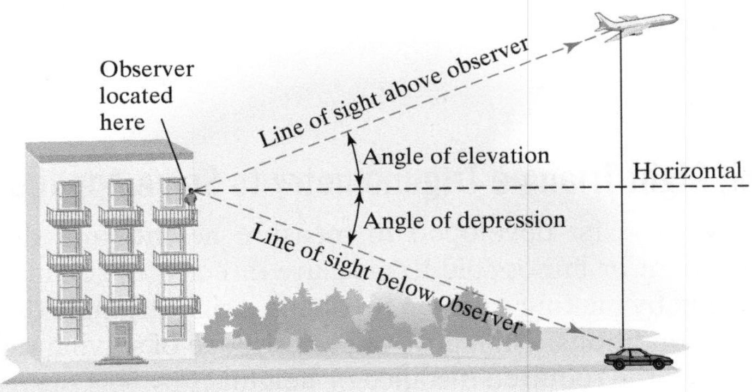

EXAMPLE 4 Sighting the top of a building, a surveyor measured the angle of elevation to be 22°. The transit is 2 metres above the ground and 100 metres from the building. Find the building's height.

Solution Let a be the height of the portion of the building that lies above the transit. The height of the building is the transit's height, 2 metres, plus a. Thus, we need to identify a trigonometric ratio that will make it possible to find a.

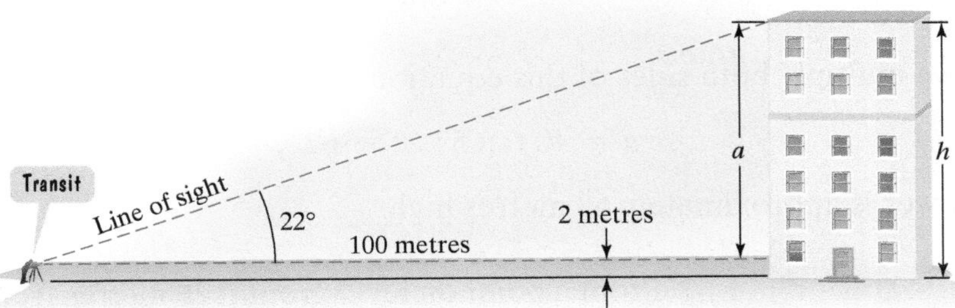

In terms of the 22° angle, we are looking for the side opposite the angle. The transit is 100 metres from the building, so the side adjacent to the 22° angle is 100 metres. Because we have a known angle, an unknown opposite side, and a known adjacent side, we select the tangent ratio.

$$\tan 22° = \frac{a}{100}$$

Length of side opposite the 22° angle

Length of side adjacent to the 22° angle

$a = 100 \tan 22°$ Multiply both sides of the equation by 300.

$a \approx 40$ Use a calculator in the degree mode.

The height of the part of the building above the transit is approximately 40 metres. Thus, the height of the building is determined by adding the transit's height, 2 metres, to 40 metres.

$$h \approx 2 + 40 = 42$$

The building's height is approximately 42 metres.

Practice Problem 4 The irregular blue shape represents a lake. The distance across the lake, a, is unknown. To find this distance, a surveyor took the measurements shown in the figure. What is the distance across the lake?

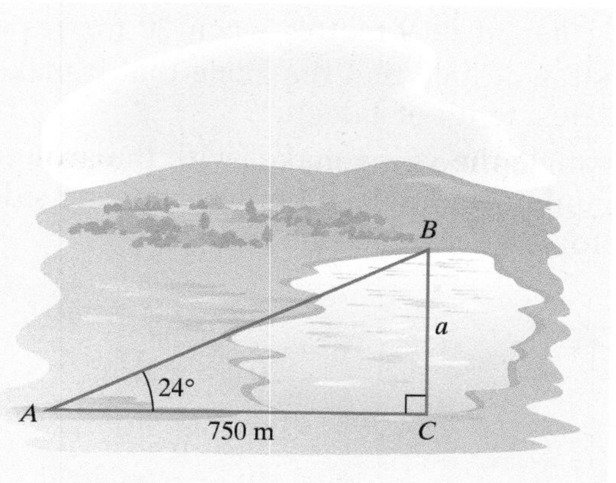

EXAMPLE 5 A building that is 21 metres tall casts a shadow 25 metres long. Find the angle of elevation of the sun to the nearest degree.

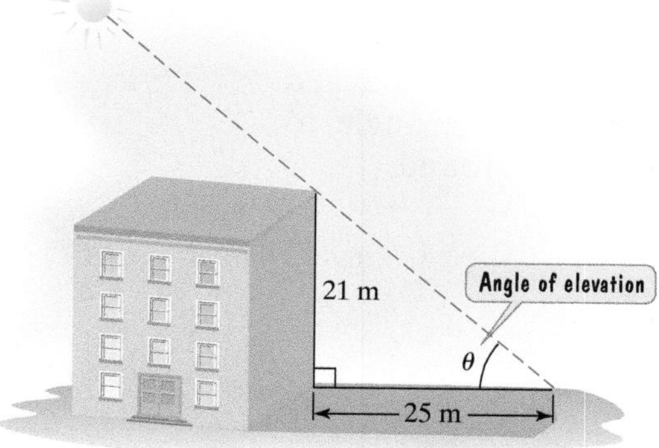

Solution We are asked to find θ. We begin with the tangent ratio.

$$\tan\theta = \frac{\text{side opposite } \theta}{\text{side adjacent to } \theta} = \frac{21}{25}$$

We use a calculator in the degree mode to find θ.

Many Scientific Calculators:

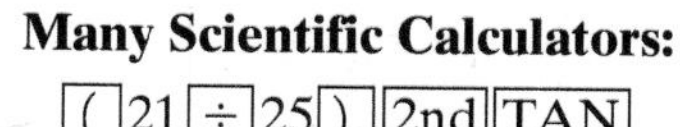

Pressing 2nd TAN accesses the inverse tangent key, TAN^{-1}.

Many Graphing Calculators:

2nd TAN (21 ÷ 25) ENTER

The display should show approximately 40. Thus, the angle of elevation of the sun is approximately 40°.

Practice Problem 5 A flagpole that is 14 metres tall casts a shadow 10 metres long. Find the angle of elevation of the sun to the nearest degree.

EXAMPLE 6 A kite flies at a height of 9 metres when 20 metres of string is out. If the string is in a straight line, find the angle that it makes with the ground. Round to the nearest tenth of a degree.

Solution Let A represents the angle the string makes with the ground. In the right triangle, we have an unknown angle, a known opposite side, and a known hypotenuse. Therefore, we use the sine ratio.

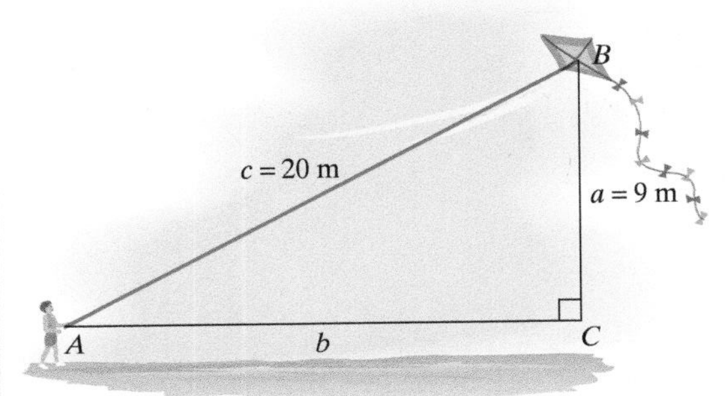

$$\sin A = \frac{9}{20}$$

Side opposite A

Hypotenuse

$$A = \sin^{-1}\frac{9}{20} \approx 26.7°$$

The string makes an angle of approximately 26.7° with the ground.

Practice Problem 6 A guy wire is 13.8 metres long and is attached from the ground to a pole 6.7 metres above the ground. Find the angle, to the nearest tenth of a degree, that the wire makes with the ground.

SECTION 4 EXERCISES

Verbal and Writing Skills

1. What does it mean to solve a right triangle?

2. Explain how to find one of the acute angles of a right triangle if two sides are known.

3. Describe a situation in which a right triangle and a trigonometric ratio are used to measure a height or distance that would otherwise be inconvenient or impossible to measure.

4. Describe what is meant by an angle of elevation and an angle of depression.

5. Stonehenge, the famous "stone circle" in England, was built between 2750 B.C. and 1300 B.C. using solid stone blocks weighing over 45 000 kilograms each. It required 550 people to pull a single stone up a ramp inclined at a 9° angle. Describe how right triangle trigonometry can be used to determine the distance the 550 workers had to drag a stone in order to raise it to a height of 10 metres.

Hugh Sitton/Getty Images Inc.-Stone Allstock

In exercises 6–8, use a calculator to find the value of the acute angle θ to the nearest degree.

6. $\cos\theta = 0.8771$ **7.** $\sin\theta = 0.2974$ **8.** $\tan\theta = 26.0307$ **9.** $\tan\theta = 4.6252$

In exercises 10–13, use a calculator to find the value of the acute angle θ in radians, rounded to three decimal places.

10. $\sin\theta = 0.9499$ **11.** $\cos\theta = 0.4112$ **12.** $\tan\theta = 0.5117$ **13.** $\tan\theta = 0.4169$

In exercises 14–24, solve the right triangle shown in the figure. Round lengths to two decimal places and express angles to the nearest tenth of a degree.

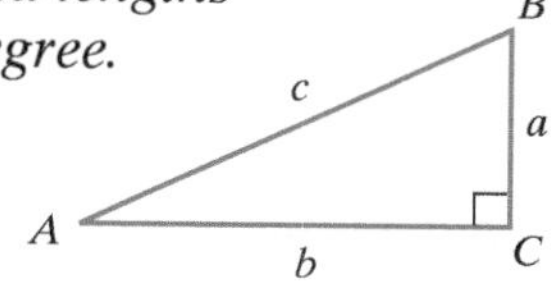

14 $A = 41.5°, b = 20$ **15.** $A = 52.6°, c = 54$ **16.** $A = 54.8°, c = 80$ **17.** $B = 16.8°, b = 30.5$

18. $B = 23.8°, b = 40.5$ **19.** $a = 30.4, c = 50.2$ **20.** $a = 11.2, c = 65.8$ **21.** $a = 10.8, b = 24.7$

22. $a = 15.3, b = 17.6$ **23.** $b = 2, c = 7$ **24.** $b = 4, c = 9$

Applications

25. ***Surveying*** To find the distance across a lake, a surveyor took the measurements shown in the figure. Use these measurements to determine how far it is across the lake. Round to the nearest metre.

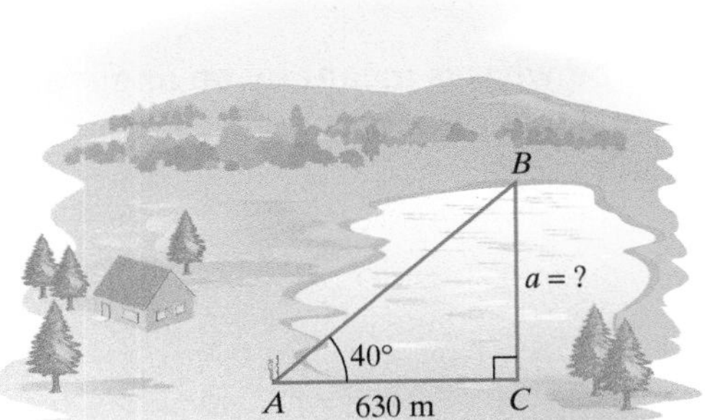

26. ***Tree Height*** At a certain time of day, the angle of elevation of the sun is 40°. To the nearest metre, find the height of a tree whose shadow is 35 metres long.

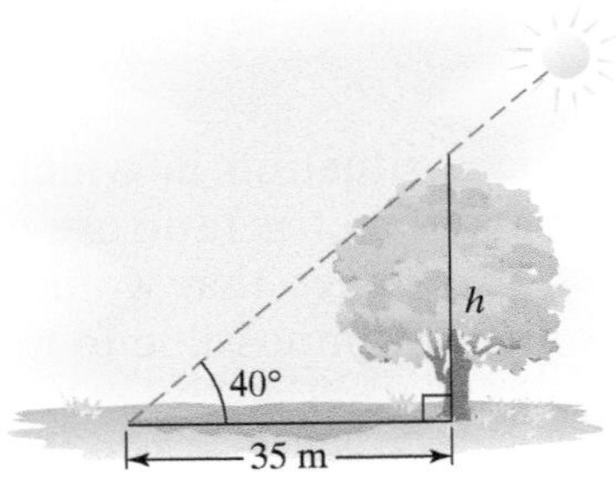

27. ***Sun Angle*** A tower that is 125 metres tall casts a shadow 172 metres long. Find the angle of elevation of the sun to the nearest degree.

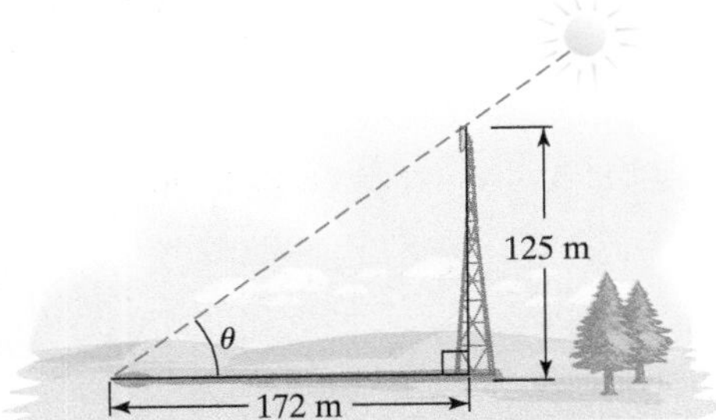

28. ***Elevation Angle*** The Washington Monument is 169 metres high. If you stand 402 metres from the base of the monument and look to the top, find the angle of elevation to the nearest degree.

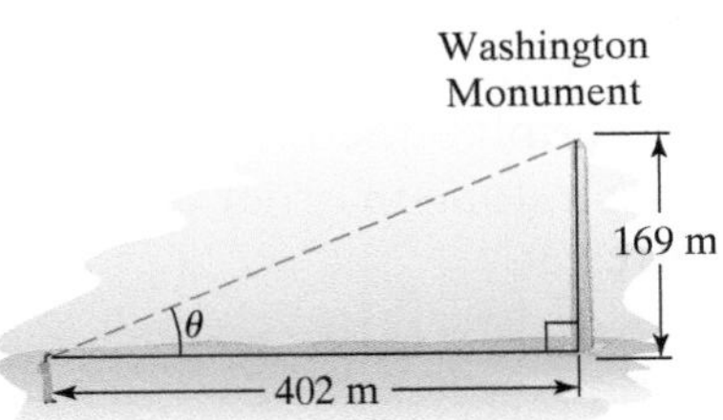

29. ***Flying*** A plane rises from take-off and flies at an angle of 10° with the horizontal runway. When it has gained 500 metres, find the distance, to the nearest metre, the plane has flown.

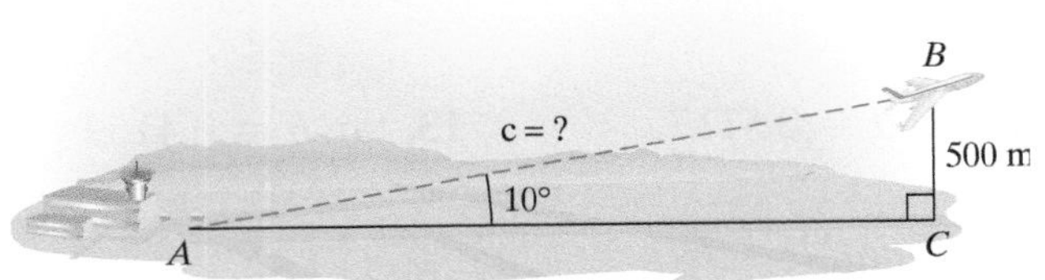

30. ***Distance*** A police helicopter is flying at 245 metres. A stolen car is sighted at an angle of depression of 72°. Find the distance of the stolen car, to the nearest metre, from a point directly below the helicopter.

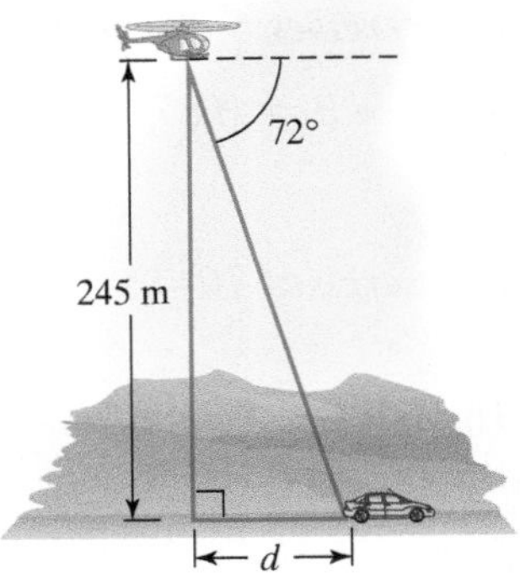

31. ***Angle in Degrees*** A telephone pole is 20 metres tall. A guy wire 23 metres long is attached from the ground to the top of the pole. Find the angle between the wire and the pole to the nearest degree.

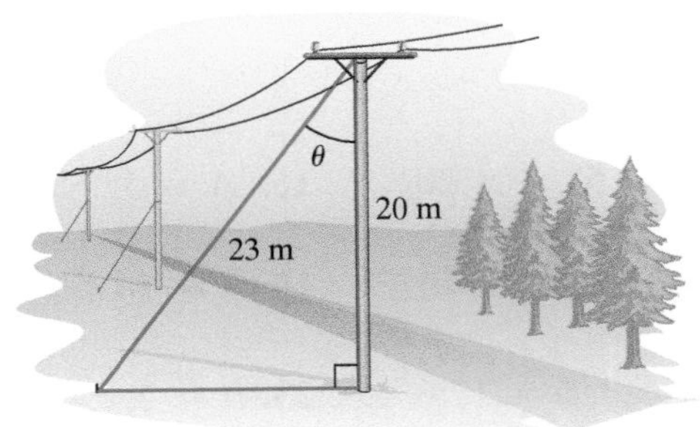

To Think About

32. From the top of an 80-metre lighthouse, a plane is sighted overhead and a ship is observed directly below the plane. The angle of elevation of the plane is 22° and the angle of depression of the ship is 35°. Find **(a)** the distance of the ship from the lighthouse; **(b)** the plane's height above the water. Round to the nearest metre.

33. *Determine whether the following statement makes sense or does not make sense, and explain your reasoning.*

Standing under this arch, I can determine its height by measuring the angle of elevation to the top of the arch and my distance to a point directly under the arch.

Wesley Hitt/Photographer's Choice/ Getty Images Inc. Photographer's Choice

Delicate Arch in Arches National Park, Utah

Quick Quiz 4

1. Solve the right triangle shown in the figure for $A = 23.5°$ and $b = 10$. Round lengths to two decimal places and express angles to the nearest tenth of a degree.

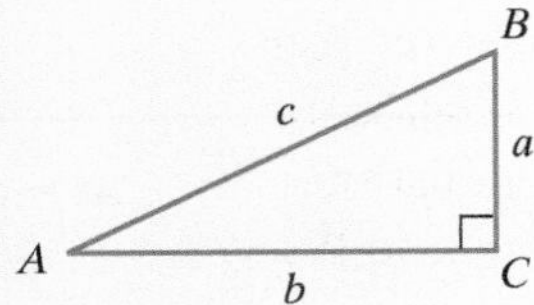

2. A telephone pole is 18 metres tall. A guy wire 26 metres long is attached from the ground to the top of the pole. Find the angle between the wire and the pole to the nearest degree.

Module Organizer

Topic	Procedure	Examples
Components of an angle.	An angle consists of two rays with a common endpoint, the vertex. 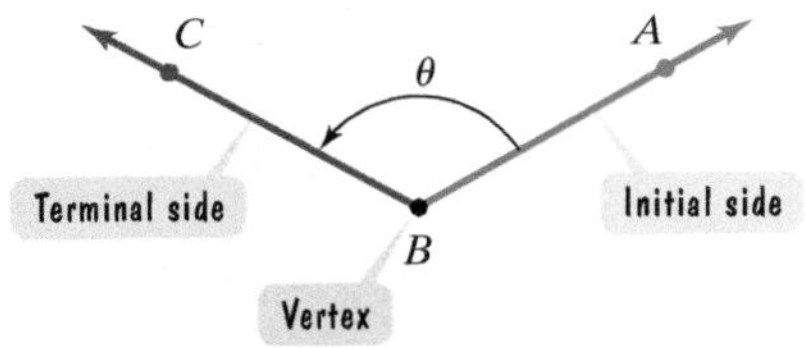	Section 1
Using radians to measure an angle.	Angles can be measured in radians. One radian is the measure of the central angle when the intercepted arc and radius have the same length. 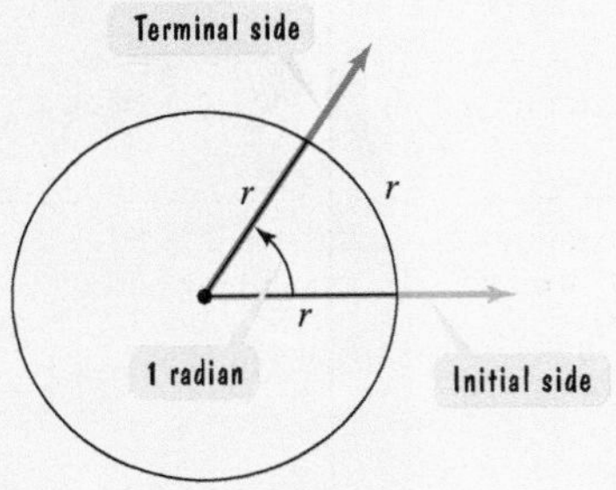	Section 1
Computing an angle measured in radians.	The radian measure of a central angle is the length of the intercepted arc divided by the circle's radius: $\theta = \frac{s}{r}$ 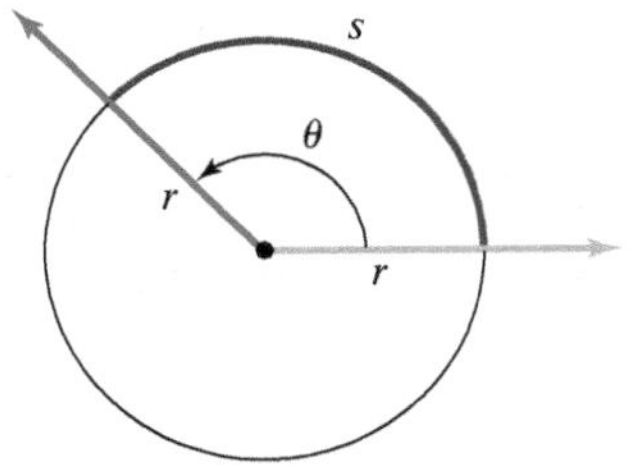 	Section 1 Example 1
Converting from degrees to radians.	Multiply degrees by $\frac{\pi \text{ radians}}{180^\circ}$	Section 1 Example 2
Converting from radians to degrees.	Multiply radians by $\frac{180^\circ}{\pi \text{ radians}}$	Section 1 Example 3
Types of angles.	Acute angles measure more than 0° but less than 90°, right angles 90°, obtuse angles more than 90° but less than 180°, and straight angles 180°.	Section 1

Topic	Procedure	Examples
Angles in standard position.	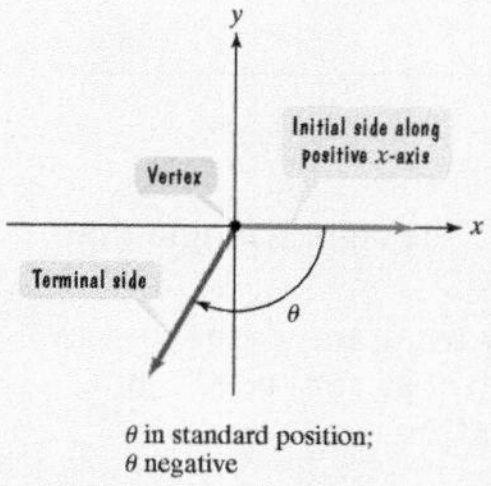 An angle is in standard position if its vertex is at the origin and its initial side lies along the positive x-axis. Positive angles are generated by a counterclockwise rotation and negative angles are generated by a clockwise rotation. 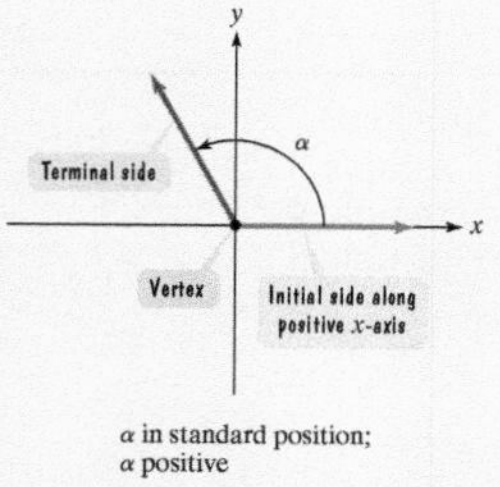 α in standard position; α positive θ in standard position; θ negative	Section 2
Quadrantal angles.	A quadrantal angle is an angle with its terminal side on the x-axis or the y-axis.	Section 2
Drawing angles in standard position.	To draw angles measured in radians in standard position, it is helpful to "think in radians" without having to convert to degrees. 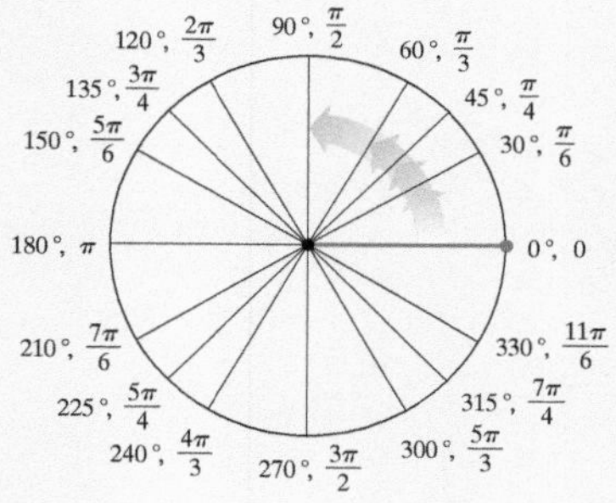	Section 2 Example 1
Coterminal angles.	Two angles with the same initial and terminal sides are called coterminal angles. Increasing or decreasing an angle's measure by integer multiples of 360° or 2π produces coterminal angles.	Section 2 Example 2 Example 3
Applying the Pythagorean Theorem.	The Pythagorean Theorem is used to calculate an unknown side of a right triangle. It states that: $a^2 + b^2 = c^2$ where a, b are the lengths of the legs and c is the length of the hypotenuse.	Section 3 Example 1
Right triangle definitions of sine, cosine, and tangent.	The right triangle definitions of the three primary trigonometric ratios are given in the box in Section 3.	Section 3 Example 2 Example 3
Ratios for special angles.	Ratio values for 30°, 45°, and 60° can be obtained using these special triangles. 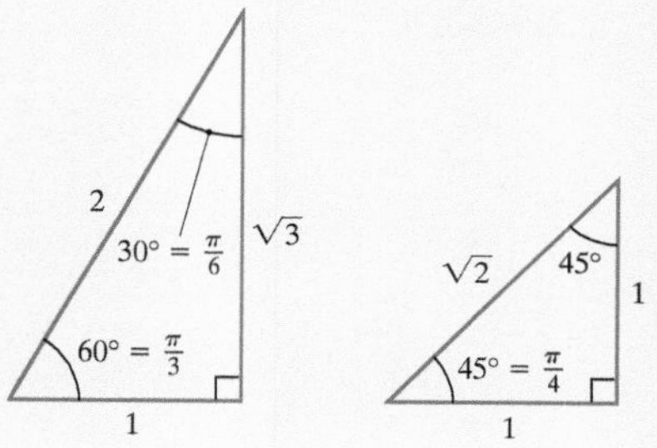	Section 3 Example 4

Topic	Procedure	Examples
Solving a right triangle.	Solving a right triangle means finding the missing lengths of its sides and the measurements of its angles. The methods used in this process are: **1.** The Pythagorean Theorem, **2.** Two acute angles whose sum is 90°, and **3.** Appropriate trigonometric ratios.	Section 4 Example 1 Example 2
Solving applied problems involving trigonometry.	**1.** Read the problem carefully. **2.** Draw a sketch. **3.** Label the sides and angles of the right triangle that are given. **4.** Find the desired quantity by using the Pythagorean Theorem, two acute angles whose sum is 90°, and appropriate trigonometric ratios.	Section 4 Example 3 Example 4 Example 5

Module Review Problems

Section 1

Find the radian measure of the central angle of a circle of radius r that intercepts an arc of length s.

1. $r = 6$ cm; $s = 27$ cm
2. $r = 4$ cm; $s = 16$ cm
3. $r = 5$ cm; $s = 11$ cm
4. $r = 1$ m; $s = 500$ cm

Convert each angle in degrees to radians. Express your answer as a multiple of π.

5. $15°$ **6.** $120°$ **7.** $315°$ **8.** $-45°$

Convert each angle in radians to degrees.

9. $\frac{5\pi}{3}$ **10.** $\frac{7\pi}{5}$ **11.** $-\frac{5\pi}{6}$ **12.** $-\frac{\pi}{4}$

Convert each angle in degrees to radians. Round to two decimal places.

13. $140°$ **14.** $50°$ **15.** $-19°$ **16.** $-230°$

Convert each angle in radians to degrees. Round to two decimal places.

17. 5 radians **18.** $\frac{\pi}{12}$ radians **19.** -4.5 radians **20.** -1.5 radians

Section 2

Draw each angle in standard position.

21. $\frac{5\pi}{6}$ **22.** $-\frac{2\pi}{3}$ **23.** $\frac{8\pi}{3}$ **24.** $190°$ **25.** $-235°$

State the quadrant in which each angle lies.

26. $167°$ **27.** $-30°$ **28.** $-\frac{7\pi}{8}$ **29.** $\frac{5\pi}{4}$ **30.** $\frac{\pi}{6}$

Find a positive angle less than $360°$ or 2π that is coterminal with the given angle.

31. $400°$ **32.** $-445°$ **33.** $\frac{13\pi}{4}$ **34.** $\frac{31\pi}{6}$ **35.** $-\frac{8\pi}{3}$

36. $-\frac{\pi}{4}$ **37.** $\frac{19\pi}{7}$ **38.** $-60°$ **39.** $460°$ **40.** $-215°$

Section 3

In exercises 41–45, use the Pythagorean Theorem to find the missing length in each right triangle. Use your calculator to find square roots, rounding, if necessary, to the nearest tenth.

41.

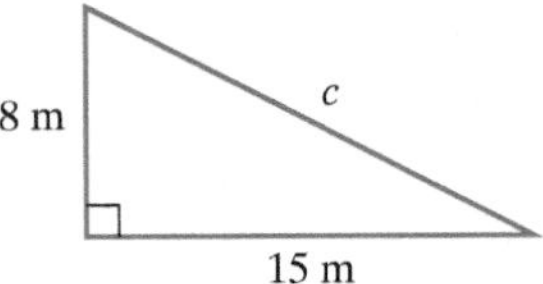

42.

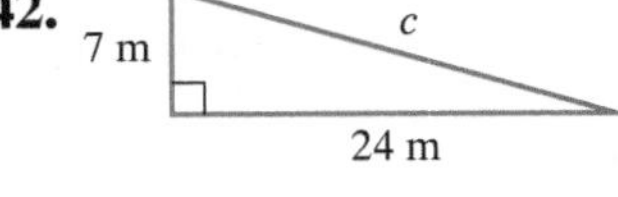

43.

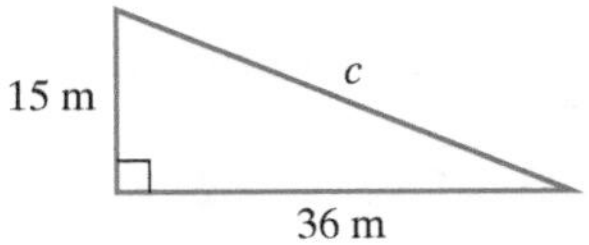

44.

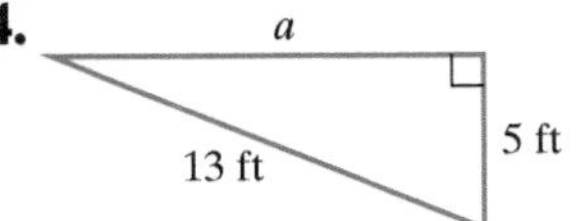

45.

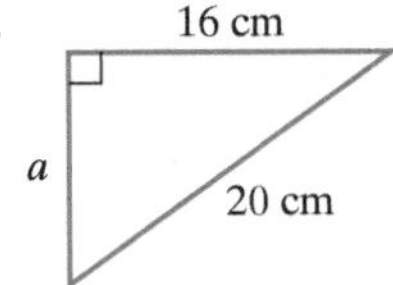

Use the given right triangles to find ratios, in reduced form, for sin B, cos B, and tan B.

46.

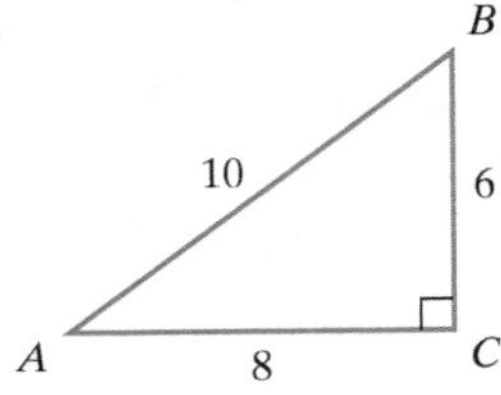

47.

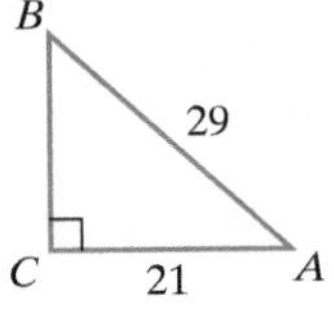

48.

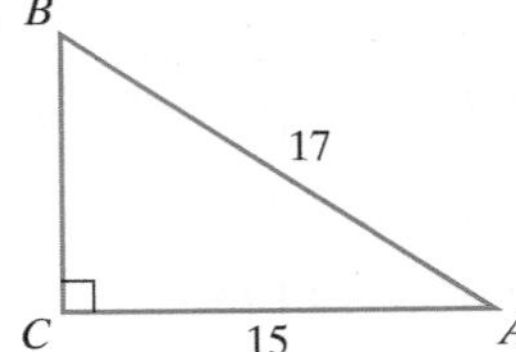

49.

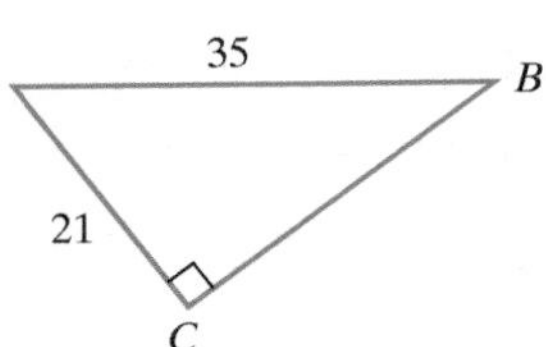

50.

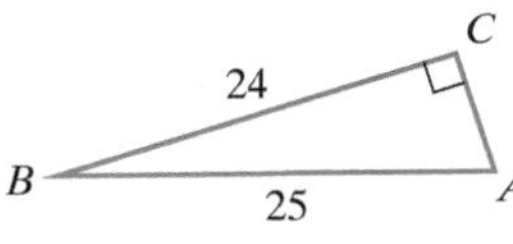

Find the measure of the side of the right triangle whose length is designated by a lowercase letter. Round answers to the nearest whole number.

51.

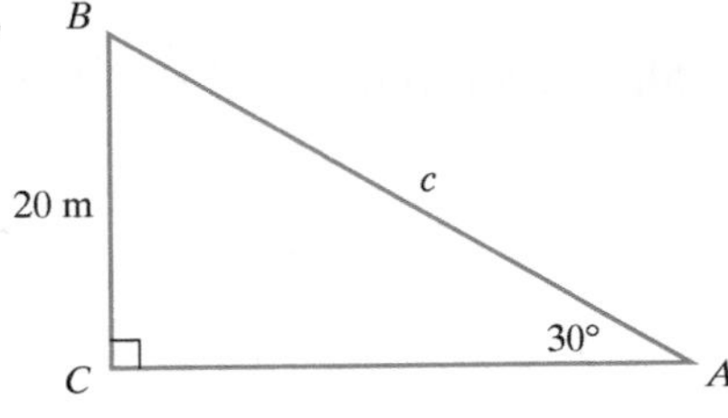

52.

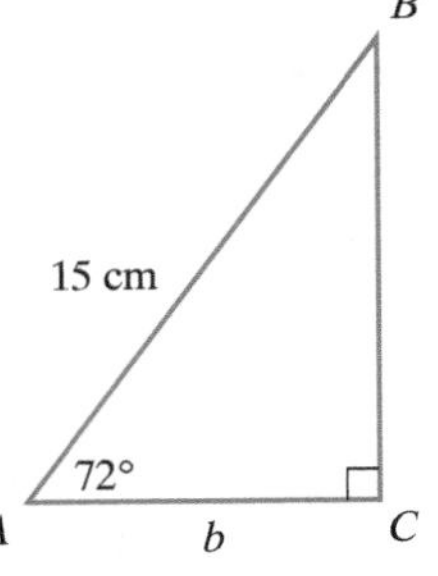

53.

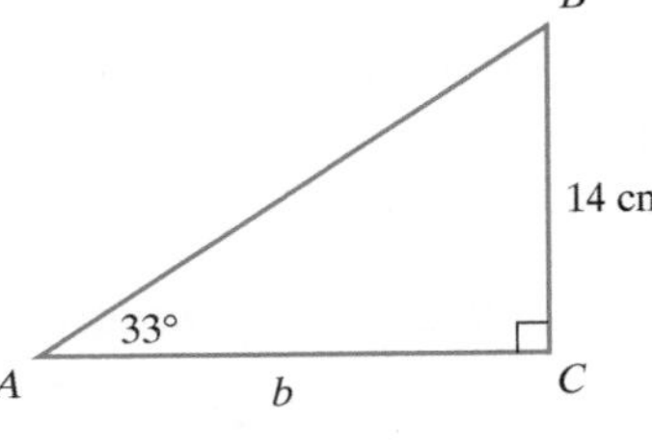

54.

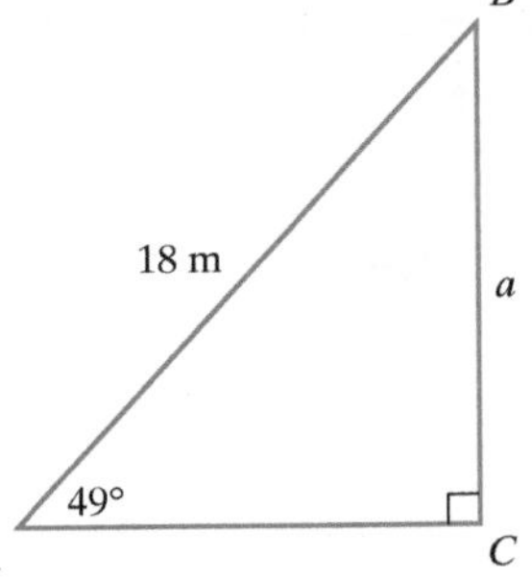

55.

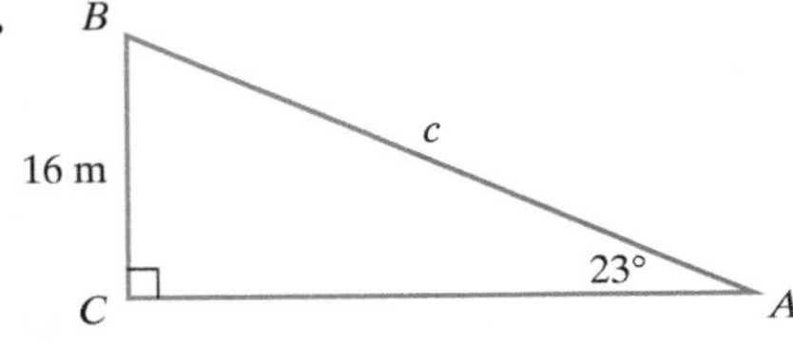

Find the exact value of each expression. Do not use a calculator.

56. $\sin\frac{\pi}{3}$ **57.** $\cos\frac{\pi}{6}$ **58.** $\tan\frac{\pi}{4}$ **59.** $\sin\frac{\pi}{6} - \cos\frac{\pi}{3}$ **60.** $\cos\frac{\pi}{4} + \tan\frac{\pi}{3}$

Use a calculator to find the value of the trigonometric ratio to four decimal places.

61. $\sin 23°$ **62.** $\cos\frac{3\pi}{7}$ **63.** $\tan 5.7$

Use the inverse trigonometric keys on a calculator to find the measure of angle A, rounded to the nearest whole degree.

64.

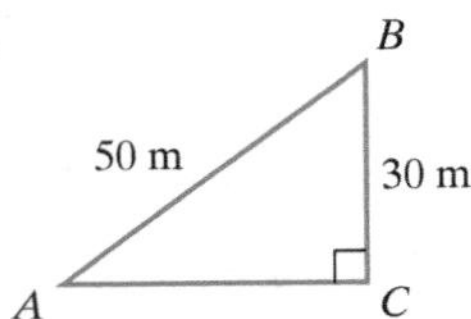

65.

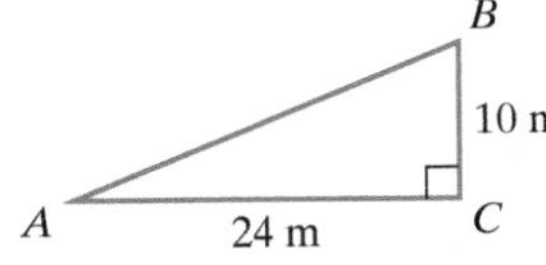

Section 4

In exercises 66–70, solve the right triangle shown in the figure. Round lengths to two decimal places and express angles to the nearest tenth of a degree.

66. $B = 37.4°, b = 6$ **67.** $A = 22.3°, c = 10$

68. $a = 1.4, b = 3.6$ **69.** $a = 2, c = 7$

70. $b = 4, c = 5$

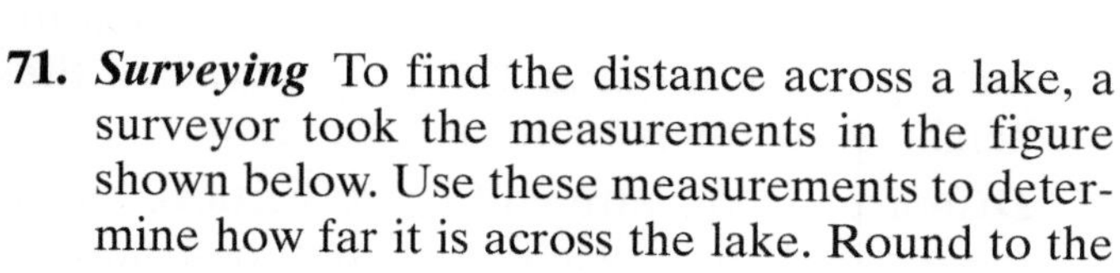

71. ***Surveying*** To find the distance across a lake, a surveyor took the measurements in the figure shown below. Use these measurements to determine how far it is across the lake. Round to the nearest metre.

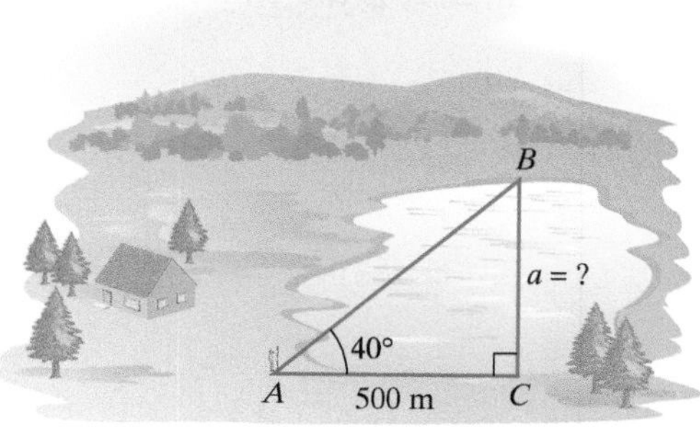

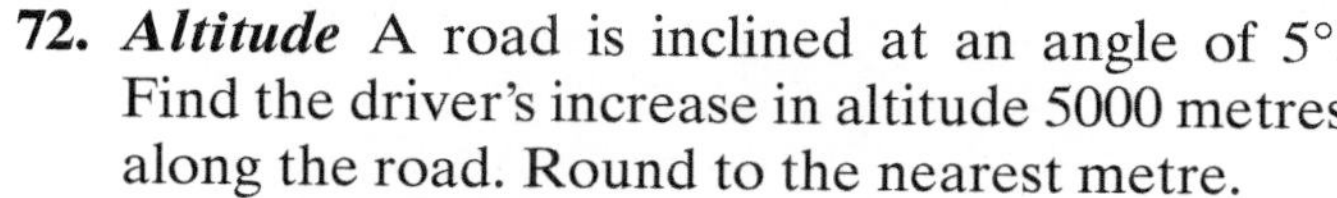

72. ***Altitude*** A road is inclined at an angle of 5°. Find the driver's increase in altitude 5000 metres along the road. Round to the nearest metre.

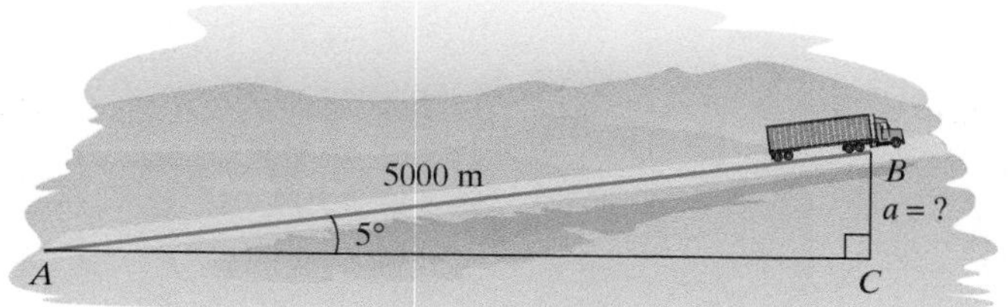

73. ***Tree Height*** At a certain time of day, the angle of elevation of the sun is 35°. To the nearest foot, find the height of a tree whose shadow is 40 feet long.

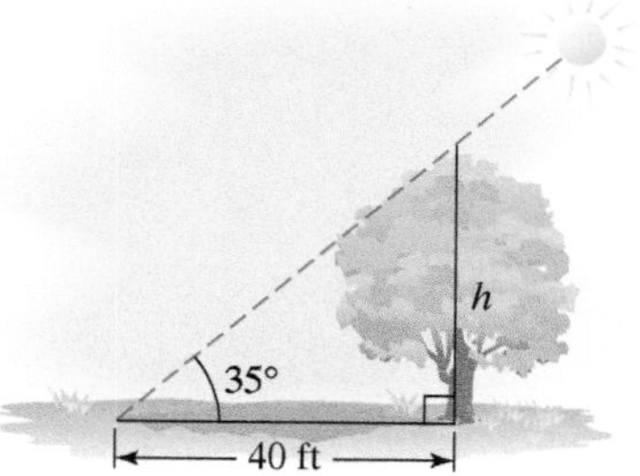

74. ***Hiking*** A hiker climbs for a half kilometre up a slope whose inclination is 17°. How many metres of altitude, to the nearest metre, does the hiker gain?

75. ***Distance*** A helicopter hovers 300 metres above a small island. The figure shows that the angle of depression from the helicopter to point P on the coast is 36°. How far off the coast, to the nearest metre, is the island?

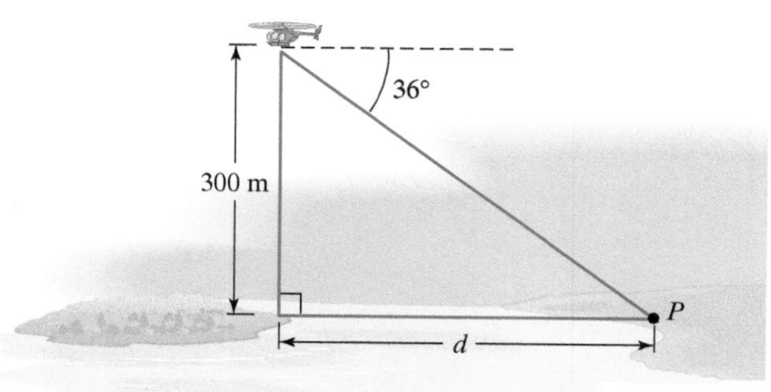

76. ***Sun Angle*** When a six-foot pole casts a four-foot shadow, what is the angle of elevation of the sun? Round to the nearest whole degree.

77. ***Surveying*** To find the distance across a lake, a surveyor took the measurements in the figure shown. What is the distance across the lake? Round to the nearest metre.

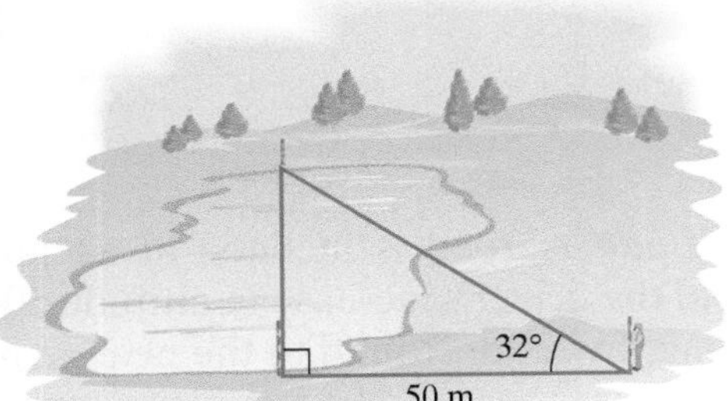

78. ***Building Height*** From a point on level ground 30 metres from the base of a building, the angle of elevation to the top of the building is 38.7°. Approximate the height of the building to the nearest metre.

79. ***Transmitting Tower*** The tallest television transmitting tower in the world is in North Dakota. From a point on level ground 1609 metres from the base of the tower, the angle of elevation to the top of the tower is 21.3°. Approximate the height of the tower to the nearest metre.

80. ***Distance*** A 60-metre cliff drops vertically into the ocean. If the angle of elevation of a ship to the top of the cliff is 22.3°, how far off shore, to the nearest metre, is the ship?

How Am I Doing? Module Test

1. Find the radian measure of the central angle of a circle of radius 3 cm that intercepts an arc of length 6 cm.

Convert each angle in degrees to radians. Express your answer as a multiple of π.

2. 10°

3. -105°

Convert each angle in radians to degrees.

4. $\dfrac{5\pi}{12}$

5. $-\dfrac{13\pi}{20}$

In questions 6–7, draw the given angle in standard position. State the quadrant in which the angle lies. When an angle's measure is given in radians, work the exercise without converting to degrees.

6. $-\dfrac{7\pi}{6}$

7. 120°

Find a positive angle less than 360° or 2π that is coterminal with the given angle.

8. $\dfrac{11\pi}{3}$

9. $-\dfrac{7\pi}{4}$

10. 510°

11. Use the triangle to find sine, cosine, and tangent of θ.

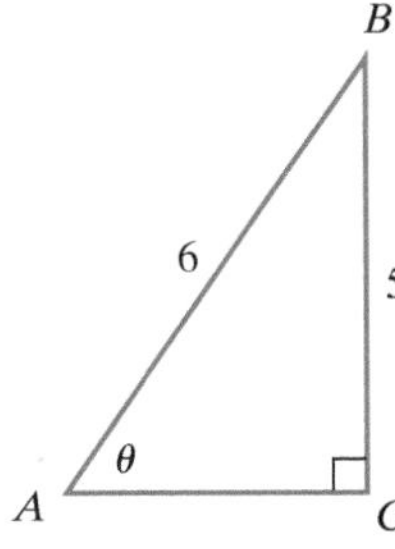

12. Use the triangle to find sine, cosine, and tangent of θ.

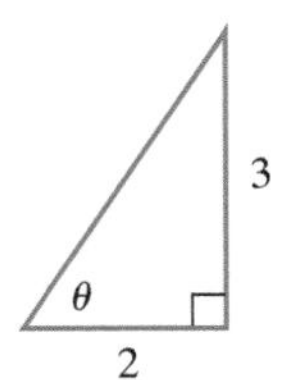

Find the exact value of each expression. Do not use a calculator.

13. $\tan 30^\circ$

14. $\sin\dfrac{\pi}{4} - \cos\dfrac{\pi}{4}$

1. ______
2. ______
3. ______
4. ______
5. ______
6. y, x
7. y, x
8. ______
9. ______
10. ______
11. ______
12. ______
13. ______
14. ______

15. ______________

16. ______________

17. ______________

18. ______________

19. ______________

20. ______________

15. Use a calculator to find the value of $\cos \frac{3\pi}{10}$. Round to four decimal places.

16. Use a calculator to find the value of the acute angle θ to the nearest degree in the equation: $\cos \theta = 0.2974$.

Solve the right triangle shown in the figure. Round lengths to two decimal places and express angles to the nearest tenth of a degree.

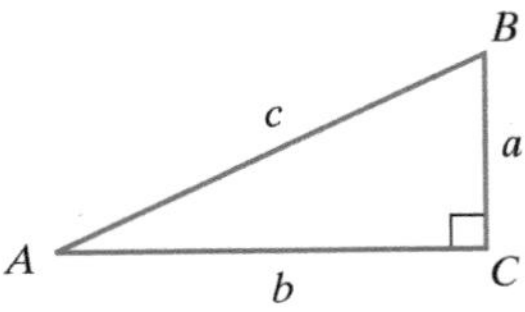

17. $A = 16.8°, a = 30.5$

18. $a = 2, c = 7$

19. A plane takes off at an angle of 6°. After travelling for one kilometre, or 1000 metres, along this flight path, find the plane's height, to the nearest tenth of a metre, above the ground.

20. A tree that is 50 feet tall casts a shadow that is 60 feet long. Find the angle of elevation, to the nearest degree, of the sun.

Solutions to Practice Problems

Section 1 Practice Problems

1. 3.5 radians

2. (a) $\frac{\pi}{3}$ radians **(b)** $\frac{3\pi}{2}$ radians **(c)** $-\frac{5\pi}{3}$ radians

3. (a) 45° **(b)** −240° **(c)** 343.8°

Section 2 Practice Problems

1. (a)

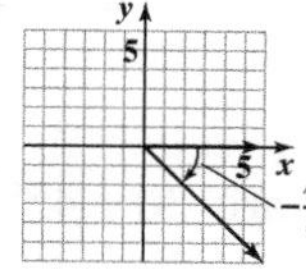

(b)

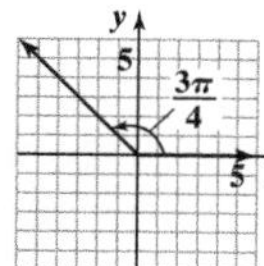

(c)

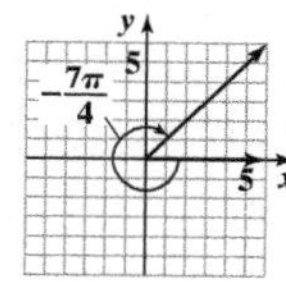

(d)

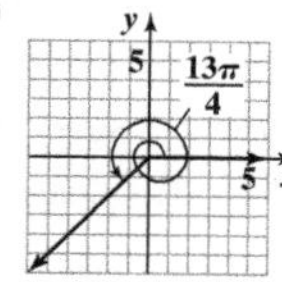

2. (a) 40° **(b)** 225°

3. (a) $\frac{3\pi}{5}$ **(b)** $\frac{29\pi}{15}$

Section 3 Practice Problems

1. 25 m

2. $\sin\theta = \frac{3}{5}$; $\cos\theta = \frac{4}{5}$; $\tan\theta = \frac{3}{4}$

3. $\sin\theta = \frac{1}{5}$; $\cos\theta = \frac{2\sqrt{6}}{5}$; $\tan\theta = \frac{1}{2\sqrt{6}}$

4. $\tan 60° = \sqrt{3}$; $\tan 30° = \frac{1}{\sqrt{3}}$

5. (a) 0.7071 **(b)** 0.3153

Section 4 Practice Problems

1. $B = 27.3°$; $b \approx 4.34$; $c \approx 9.45$

2. $c \approx 31.7$; $A \approx 9.45°$; $B \approx 52.4°$

3. 323 m

4. 333.9 m

5. 54°

6. 29.0°

Glossary

Angle of depression (Section 4) An angle formed by a horizontal line and the line of sight to an object that is below the horizontal line.

Angle of elevation (Section 4) An angle formed by a horizontal line and the line of sight to an object that is above the horizontal line.

Central angle (Section 1) An angle whose vertex is at the centre of the circle.

Coterminal angles (Section 2) Two angles with the same initial and terminal sides but possibly different rotations.

Initial side (Section 1) The line representing the starting position of the ray rotating to form an angle.

Intercepted arc (Section 1) The distance along the circumference of a circle between the initial side and the terminal side of a central angle.

Negative angle (Section 2) An angle generated by a clockwise rotation from the initial side to the terminal side.

One radian (Section 1) A central angle whose intercepted arc has a length equal to the radius of the circle.

Positive angle (Section 2) An angle generated by a counterclockwise rotation from the initial side to the terminal side.

Primary trigonometric ratios (Section 3) The three primary trigonometric ratios are sine, cosine, and tangent.

Quadrantal angles (Section 2) An angle whose terminal side lies on the x-axis or y-axis when drawn in standard position.

Radian measure (Section 1) In any central angle, the length of the intercepted arc divided by the circle's radius.

Solving a right triangle (Section 4) Solving a right triangle means finding the missing lengths of its sides and the measurements of its angles.

Special angles for trigonometric ratios (Section 3) The special angles for trigonometric ratios are 30°, 45°, and 60°.

Standard labelling of a right triangle (Section 3) The standard labelling of a right triangle means to label side a opposite to angle A, side b opposite to angle B, and side c (the hypotenuse) opposite to angle C.

Standard position of an angle (Section 2) An angle is in standard position if its vertex is at the origin of the Cartesian plane (or xy-plane) and its initial side lies along the positive x-axis.

Terminal side (Section 1) The line representing the ending position of the ray rotating to form an angle.

Answers to Selected Exercises for Trigonometry

Answers to Selected Exercises for Trigonometry

Section 1 Exercises **1.** One radian is the central angle of the intercepted arc whose length is equal to the radius of the circle.
3. To convert degrees to radians, multiply the angle (measured in degrees) by $\frac{\pi \text{ radians}}{180°}$. **5.** obtuse **7.** acute **9.** straight
11. 4 radians **13.** $\frac{4}{3}$ radians **15.** 4 radians **17.** $\frac{\pi}{4}$ radians **19.** $\frac{3\pi}{4}$ radians **21.** $\frac{5\pi}{3}$ radians **23.** 90° **25.** 120° **27.** 210°
29. 0.31 radians **31.** −0.70 radians **33.** 3.49 radians **35.** 114.59° **37.** 13.85° **39.** 60°; $\frac{\pi}{3}$ radians **41.** smaller than a right angle
43. makes sense

Quick Quiz 1 **1.** 6 radians **2.** $-\frac{5\pi}{4}$ radians **3.** −540° **4.** 4.36 radians **5.** −275.02°

Section 2 Exercises **1.** An angle is in standard position on the Cartesian plane or the *xy*-plane if its vertex is at the origin, and its initial side lies along the positive *x*-axis.

3. 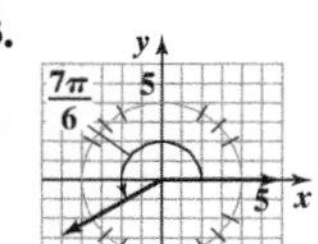

; quadrant III

5. 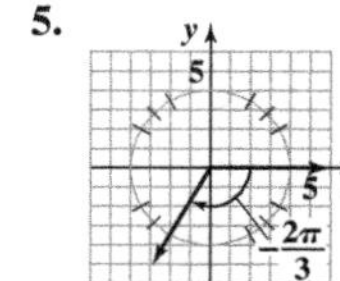

; quadrant III

7. 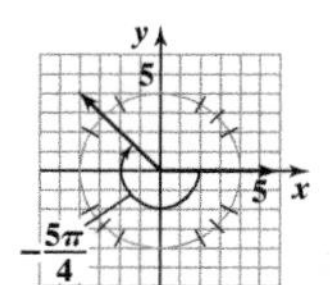

; quadrant II

9. 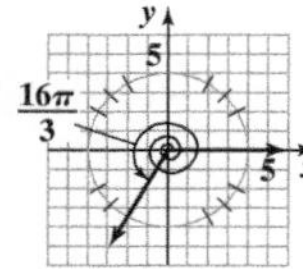

; quadrant III

11. 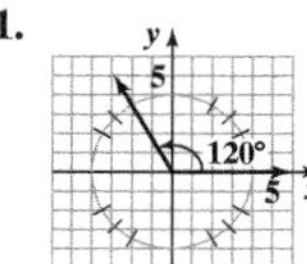

; quadrant II

13. 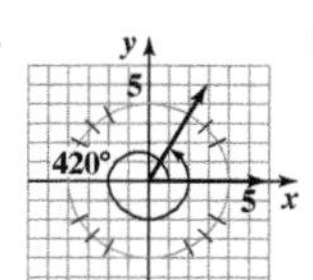

; quadrant I

15. 35° **17.** 210° **19.** 315° **21.** $\frac{3\pi}{5}$ **23.** $\frac{99\pi}{50}$ **25.** $\frac{11\pi}{7}$ **27.** $-\frac{4\pi}{3}$ and $\frac{2\pi}{3}$ **29.** $-\frac{3\pi}{4}$ and $\frac{5\pi}{4}$ **31.** $-\frac{\pi}{2}$ and $\frac{3\pi}{2}$
33. This statement does not make sense because there is no error in drawing an angle in standard position that exceeds a straight line. For example, the angle of 200° when drawn in standard position exceeds a straight line.

Quick Quiz 2 **1.** 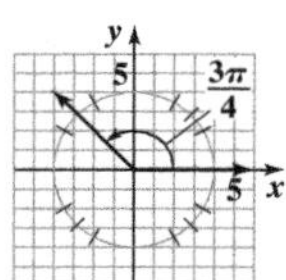

; quadrant II **2.** 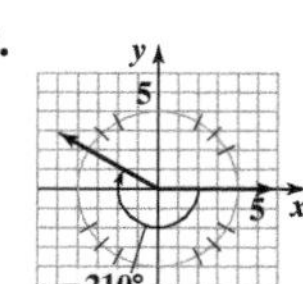

; quadrant II **3.** 200° **4.** $\frac{7\pi}{6}$

How Am I Doing? Sections 1–2 **1.** 4 radians (obj. 1.2) **2.** 3 radians (obj. 1.2) **3.** $\frac{13\pi}{18}$ radians (obj. 1.3) **4.** $-\frac{\pi}{4}$ radians (obj. 1.3)
5. 30° (obj. 1.3) **6.** −270° (obj. 1.3) **7.** −4.01 radians (obj. 1.3) **8.** 0.87 radians (obj. 1.3) **9.** 286.48° (obj. 1.3) **10.** 12.00° (obj. 1.3)

11. 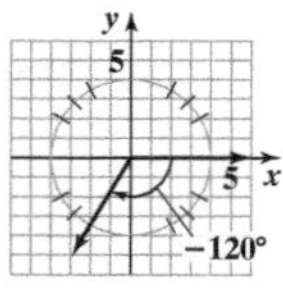

; quadrant III (obj. 2.1) **12.** ; quadrant I (obj. 2.1) **13.** ; quadrant IV obj. 2.1)

14. 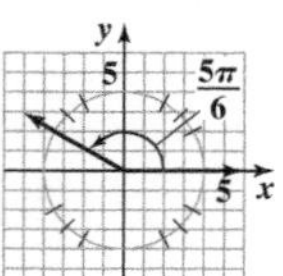

; quadrant II (obj. 2.1) **15.** ; quadrant I (obj. 2.1) **16.** 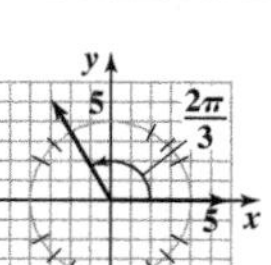

; quadrant II (obj. 2.1)

17. 90° (obj. 2.2) **18.** 180° (obj. 2.2) **19.** $\frac{49\pi}{25}$ radians (obj. 2.2) **20.** $\frac{\pi}{3}$ radians (obj. 2.2)

Section 3 Exercises **1.** The sine of one of the acute angles is the length of the opposite side divided by the length of the hypotenuse. **3.** The legs have length 1 and the hypotenuse has length $\sqrt{2}$. **5.** 15; $\sin\theta = \frac{3}{5}$; $\cos\theta = \frac{4}{5}$; $\tan\theta = \frac{3}{4}$ **7.** 20; $\sin\theta = \frac{20}{29}$; $\cos\theta = \frac{21}{29}$; $\tan\theta = \frac{20}{21}$ **9.** 24; $\sin\theta = \frac{5}{13}$; $\cos\theta = \frac{12}{13}$; $\tan\theta = \frac{5}{12}$ **11.** 28; $\sin\theta = \frac{4}{5}$; $\cos\theta = \frac{3}{5}$; $\tan\theta = \frac{4}{3}$ **13.** $\frac{\sqrt{3}}{2}$ **15.** $\sqrt{3}$ **17.** $\frac{\sqrt{6}-4}{4}$ **19.** 188 cm **21.** 182 in. **23.** 0.7174 **25.** 0.2643 **27.** 0.9511 **29.** This statement does not make sense because when you use your calculator to calculate the value of $\sin\frac{\pi}{4}$ it gives an approximate value. The exact value cannot be calculated with a standard calculator.

Quick Quiz 3 **1.** 7; $\sin\theta = \frac{24}{25}$; $\cos\theta = \frac{7}{25}$; $\tan\theta = \frac{24}{7}$ **2.** $\frac{12+\sqrt{3}}{2}$ **3.** 41 m **4.** 0.6247

Section 4 Exercises **1.** To solve a right triangle means to find the missing lengths of its sides and the measurement of its angles. **3.** The tangent ratio can be used to measure the height of a tree. This would be achieved by creating a right triangle where the three vertices are: the top of the tree, the base of the tree, and a point on the ground a set distance from the tree. **5.** The sine ratio could be used to calculate the length of the ramp (hypotenuse) since the opposite side (the height) and the angle of inclination is known. **7.** 17° **9.** 78° **11.** 1.147 radians **13.** 0.395 radians **15.** $B = 37.4°$; $a \approx 42.90$; $b \approx 32.80$ **17.** $A = 73.2°$; $a \approx 101.02$; $c \approx 105.52$ **19.** $b \approx 39.95$; $A \approx 37.3°$; $B \approx 52.7°$ **21.** $c \approx 26.96$; $A \approx 23.6°$; $B \approx 66.4°$ **23.** $a \approx 6.71$; $B \approx 16.6°$; $A \approx 73.4°$ **25.** 529 m **27.** 36° **29.** 2879 m **31.** 30° **33.** This statement makes sense because the tangent ratio can be used to determine the height of the arch given the angle of elevation and the distance to the base.

Quick Quiz 4 **1.** $B = 66.5°$; $a \approx 4.35$; $c \approx 10.90$ **2.** 46°

Module Review Problems **1.** 4.5 radians **2.** 4 radians **3.** 2.2 radians **4.** 5 radians **5.** $\frac{\pi}{12}$ radians **6.** $\frac{2\pi}{3}$ radians **7.** $\frac{7\pi}{4}$ radians **8.** $-\frac{\pi}{4}$ radians **9.** 300° **10.** 252° **11.** −150° **12.** −45° **13.** 2.44 radians **14.** 0.87 radians **15.** −0.33 radians **16.** −4.01 radians **17.** 286.48° **18.** 15.00° **19.** −257.83° **20.** −85.94°

21. $\frac{5\pi}{6}$ **22.** $-\frac{2\pi}{3}$ **23.** $\frac{8\pi}{3}$ **24.** 190° **25.** −235°

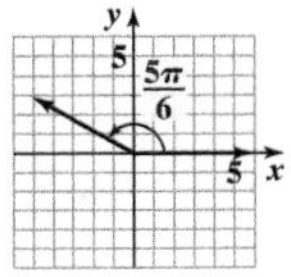

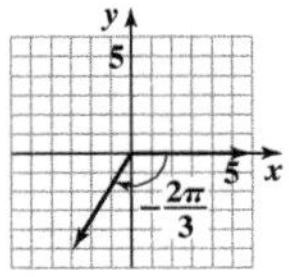

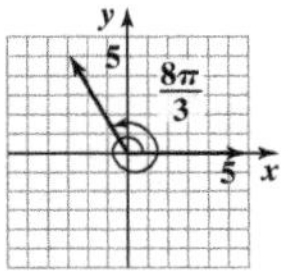

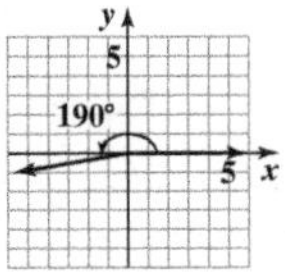

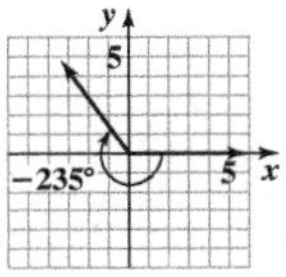

26. quadrant II **27.** quadrant IV **28.** quadrant III **29.** quadrant III **30.** quadrant I **31.** 40° **32.** 275° **33.** $\frac{5\pi}{4}$ radians **34.** $\frac{7\pi}{6}$ radians **35.** $\frac{4\pi}{3}$ radians **36.** $\frac{7\pi}{4}$ radians **37.** $\frac{5\pi}{7}$ radians **38.** 300° **39.** 100° **40.** 145° **41.** $c = 17$ m **42.** $c = 25$ m **43.** $c = 39$ m **44.** $a = 12$ ft **45.** $a = 12$ cm **46.** $\sin B = \frac{4}{5}$; $\cos B = \frac{3}{5}$; $\tan B = \frac{4}{3}$ **47.** $\sin B = \frac{21}{29}$; $\cos B = \frac{20}{29}$; $\tan B = \frac{21}{20}$ **48.** $\sin B = \frac{15}{17}$; $\cos B = \frac{8}{17}$; $\tan B = \frac{15}{8}$ **49.** $\sin B = \frac{3}{5}$; $\cos B = \frac{4}{5}$; $\tan B = \frac{3}{4}$ **50.** $\sin B = \frac{7}{25}$; $\cos B = \frac{24}{25}$; $\tan B = \frac{7}{24}$ **51.** $c = 40$ m **52.** $b = 5$ cm **53.** $b = 22$ cm **54.** $a = 14$ m **55.** $c = 41$ m **56.** $\frac{\sqrt{3}}{2}$ **57.** $\frac{\sqrt{3}}{2}$ **58.** 1 **59.** 0 **60.** $\frac{1+\sqrt{6}}{\sqrt{2}}$ **61.** 0.3907 **62.** 0.2225 **63.** −0.6597 **64.** $A = 37°$ **65.** $A = 23°$ **66.** $A \approx 52.6°$; $a \approx 7.85$; $c \approx 9.88$ **67.** $B \approx 67.7°$; $a \approx 37.9$; $b \approx 9.25$ **68.** $A \approx 21.3°$; $B \approx 68.7°$; $c \approx 3.86$ **69.** $A \approx 16.6°$; $B \approx 73.4°$; $b \approx 6.71$ **70.** $a = 3$; $A \approx 36.9°$; $B \approx 53.1°$ **71.** $a = 420$ m **72.** 436 m **73.** $h = 28$ ft **74.** 146 m **75.** 413 m **76.** 56° **77.** 31 m **78.** 24 m **79.** 627 m **80.** 146 m

How Am I Doing? Module Test **1.** 2 radians (obj. 1.2) **2.** $\frac{\pi}{18}$ radians (obj. 1.3) **3.** $-\frac{7\pi}{12}$ radians (obj. 1.3) **4.** 75° (obj. 1.3) **5.** −117° (obj. 1.3) **6.** $-\frac{7\pi}{6}$; quadrant II (obj. 2.1) **7.** 120°; quadrant II (obj. 2.1) **8.** $\frac{5\pi}{3}$ radians (obj. 2.2) **9.** $\frac{\pi}{4}$ radians (obj. 2.2) **10.** 150° (obj. 2.2) **11.** $\sin\theta = \frac{5}{6}$; $\cos\theta = \frac{\sqrt{11}}{6}$; $\tan\theta = \frac{5}{\sqrt{11}}$ (obj. 3.2) **12.** $\sin\theta = \frac{3}{\sqrt{13}}$; $\cos\theta = \frac{2}{\sqrt{13}}$; $\tan\theta = \frac{3}{2}$ (obj. 3.2) **13.** $\frac{1}{\sqrt{3}}$ (obj. 3.3) **14.** 0 (obj. 3.3) **15.** 0.5878 (obj. 3.4) **16.** 73° (obj. 4.1) **17.** $B \approx 73.2°$; $b \approx 101.02$; $c \approx 105.52$ (obj. 4.1) **18.** $b \approx 6.71$; $A \approx 16.6°$; $B \approx 73.4°$ (obj. 4.1) **19.** 104.5 m (obj. 4.2) **20.** 40° (obj. 4.2)

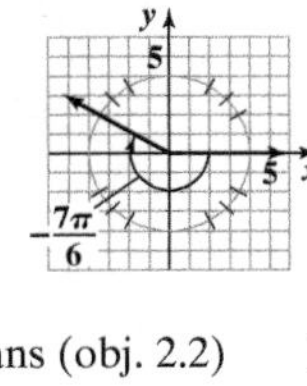

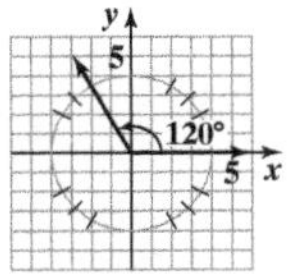

Practice Final Examination

Practice Final Examination

This examination is based on all modules in the textbook. There are 10 questions covering the content of each module.

Whole Numbers

1. Write in words. 82 367

2. Add. $\begin{array}{r} 13\,428 \\ +\ 16\,905 \\ \hline \end{array}$

3. Add. $\begin{array}{r} 19 \\ 23 \\ 16 \\ 45 \\ +\ 70 \\ \hline \end{array}$

4. Subtract. $\begin{array}{r} 89\,071 \\ -\ 54\,968 \\ \hline \end{array}$

Multiply.

5. $\begin{array}{r} 78 \\ \times\ 54 \\ \hline \end{array}$

6. $\begin{array}{r} 2035 \\ \times\ 107 \\ \hline \end{array}$

In questions 7 and 8, divide. (Be sure to indicate the remainder if one exists.)

7. $7\overline{)1106}$

8. $26\overline{)15\,756}$

9. Evaluate. Perform operations in the proper order. $3^4 + 20 \div 4 \times 2 + 5^2$

10. Melinda travelled 256 kilometres in her car. The car used 16 litres of gas on the entire trip. How many kilometres per litre did the car achieve?

Fractions

11. Reduce the fraction. $\frac{14}{30}$

12. Change to an improper fraction. $3\frac{9}{11}$

13. Add. $\frac{1}{10} + \frac{3}{4} + \frac{4}{5}$

14. Add. $2\frac{1}{3} + 3\frac{3}{5}$

15. Subtract. $4\frac{5}{7} - 2\frac{1}{2}$

16. Multiply. $1\frac{1}{4} \times 3\frac{1}{5}$

17. Divide. $\frac{7}{9} \div \frac{5}{18}$

18. Divide. $\dfrac{5\frac{1}{2}}{3\frac{1}{4}}$

19. Lucinda jogged $1\frac{1}{2}$ kilometres on Monday, $3\frac{1}{4}$ kilometres on Tuesday, and $2\frac{1}{10}$ kilometres on Wednesday. How many kilometres in all did she jog over the three-day period?

20. A butcher has $11\frac{2}{3}$ kilograms of steak. She wishes to place them in several equal-size packages. Each package will hold $2\frac{1}{3}$ kilograms of steak. How many packages can be made?

Decimals

21. Express as a decimal. $\dfrac{719}{1000}$

22. Write in reduced fractional notation. 0.86

23. Fill in the blank with <, =, or >. 0.315 _______ 0.309

24. Round to the nearest hundredth. 506.3782

25. Add. $\begin{array}{r} 9.6 \\ 3.82 \\ 1.05 \\ +\ 7.3 \\ \hline \end{array}$

26. Subtract. $\begin{array}{r} 3.61 \\ -\ 2.853 \\ \hline \end{array}$

27. Multiply. $\begin{array}{r} 1.23 \\ \times\ 0.4 \\ \hline \end{array}$

28. Divide. $0.24\overline{)0.8856}$

29. Write as a decimal. $\dfrac{13}{16}$

30. Evaluate by performing operations in proper order.
$0.7 + (0.2)^3 - 0.08(0.03)$

Ratio and Proportion

31. Write a rate in simplest form to compare 7000 students to 215 faculty.

32. Is this a proportion? $\dfrac{12}{15} \stackrel{?}{=} \dfrac{17}{21}$

Solve the proportion. Round to the nearest tenth when necessary.

33. $\dfrac{5}{9} = \dfrac{n}{17}$

34. $\dfrac{3}{n} = \dfrac{7}{18}$

35. $\dfrac{n}{12} = \dfrac{5}{4}$

36. $\dfrac{n}{7} = \dfrac{36}{28}$

Solve using a proportion. Round to the nearest hundredth when necessary.

37. Bob earned \$2000 for painting three houses. How much would he earn for painting five houses?

38. Two cities that are actually 200 miles apart appear 6 inches apart on the map. Two other cities are 325 miles apart. How far apart will they appear on the same map?

39. Roberta earned $68 last week from her part-time job. She had $5 deducted for federal income tax. Last year she earned $4000 from her part-time job. Assuming the same rate, how much was deducted for federal income tax last year?

40. Malaga's recipe feeds 18 people and calls for 1.2 pounds of butter. If she wants to feed 24 people, how many pounds of butter does she need?

Percent

Round to the nearest hundredth when necessary in problems 41–44.

41. Write as a percent. 0.0063

42. Change $\frac{17}{80}$ to a percent.

43. Write as a decimal. 164%

44. What percent of 300 is 52?

Round to the nearest tenth when necessary in problems 45–50.

45. Find 6.3% of 4800.

46. 145 is 58% of what number?

47. 126% of 3400 is what number?

48. Pauline bought a new car. She got an 8% discount. The car listed for $11 800. How much did she pay for the car?

49. A total of 1260 first-year students were admitted to Central College. This is 28% of the student body. How big is the student body?

50. There are 11.28 centimetres of water in the rain gauge this week. Last week the rain gauge held 8.40 centimetres of water. What is the percentage of increase from last week to this week?

Measurement

Convert. Express your answers as a decimal rounded to the nearest hundredth when necessary.

51. 17 quarts = ______ gallons

52. 3.25 tons = ______ pounds

53. 16 feet = ______ inches

54. 5.6 kilometres = ______ metres

55. 69.8 grams = ______ kilogram

56. 2.48 millilitres = ______ litre

57. 12 miles = ______ kilometres

In questions 58 and 59, write in scientific notation.

58. 0.000 631 82

59. 126 400 000 000

60. Two metal sheets are 0.623 centimetre and 0.74 centimetre thick, respectively. An insulating foil is 0.0428 millimetre thick. When all three layers are placed tightly together, what is the total thickness? Express your answer in centimetres.

Geometry

Round to the nearest hundredth when necessary. Use $\pi \approx 3.14$ when necessary.

▲ **61.** Find the perimeter of a rectangle that is 6 metres long and 1.2 metres wide.

▲ **62.** Find the perimeter of a trapezoid with sides of 82 centimetres, 13 centimetres, 98 centimetres, and 13 centimetres.

▲ **63.** Find the area of a triangle with base 6 metres and height 1.8 metres.

▲ **64.** Find the area of a trapezoid with bases of 12 metres and 8 metres and a height of 7.5 metres.

▲ **65.** Find the area of a circle with radius 6 metres.

▲ **66.** Find the circumference of a circle with diameter 18 metres.

▲ **67.** Find the volume of a cone with a radius of 4 centimetres and a height of 10 centimetres.

▲ **68.** Find the volume of a rectangular pyramid with a base of 12 metres by 19 metres and a height of 2.7 metres.

▲ **69.** Find the area of this object, consisting of a square and a triangle.

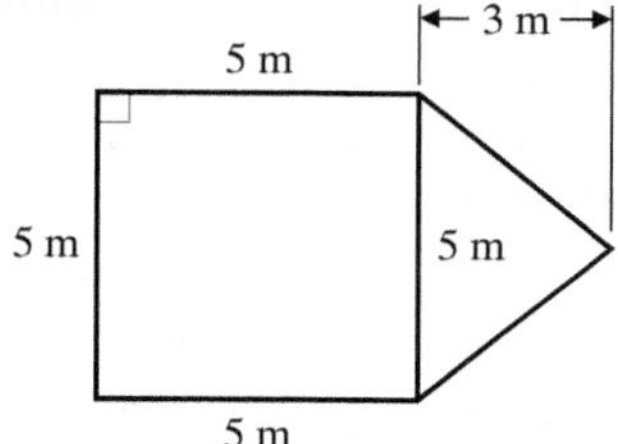

▲ **70.** In the following pair of similar triangles, find n.

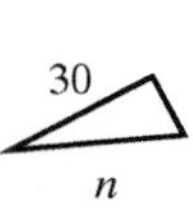

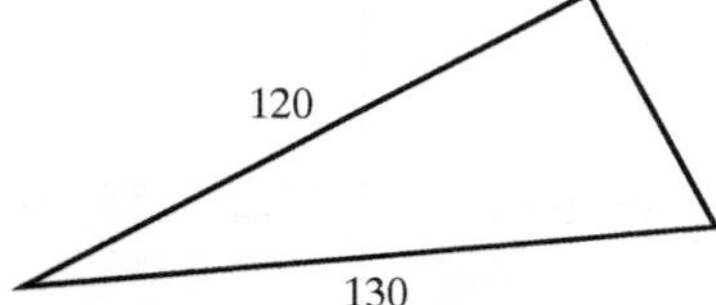

Statistics

The following double-bar graph indicates the quarterly profits for Westar Corporation in 2009 and 2010.

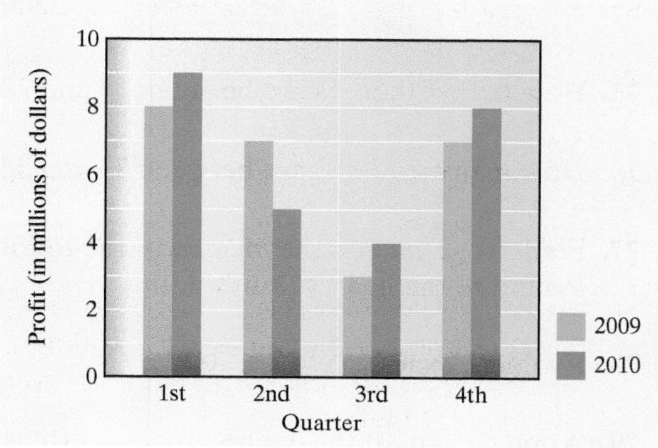

71. What were the profits in the fourth quarter of 2010?

72. How much greater were the profits in the first quarter of 2010 than the profits in the first quarter of 2009?

The following line graph depicts the average annual temperature at West Valley for the years 1960, 1970, 1980, 1990, and 2000.

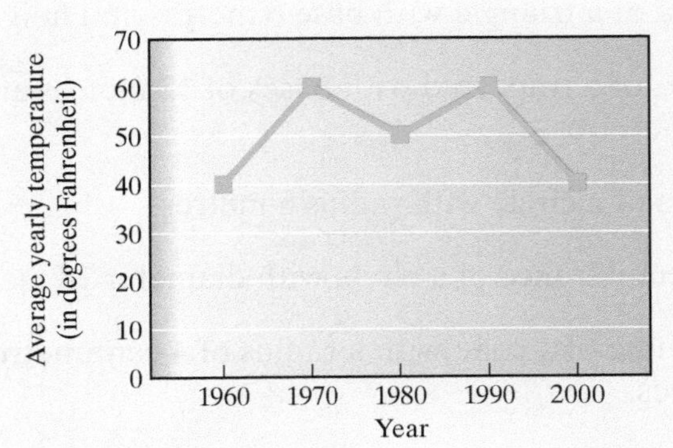

73. What was the average temperature in 1980?

74. In what 10-year period did the average temperature show the greatest decline?

The following histogram shows the number of students in each age category at Centre City College.

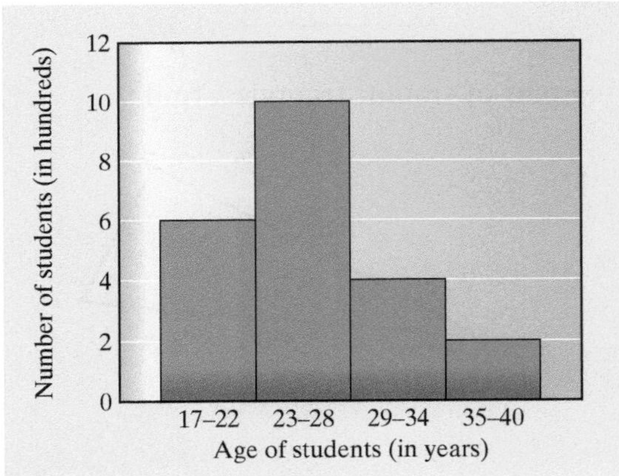

75. How many students are between 17 and 22 years old?

76. How many students are between 23 and 34 years old?

77. Find the *mean* and the *median* of the following. 8, 12, 16, 17, 20, 22. Round to the nearest hundredth.

78. Evaluate exactly. $\sqrt{49} + \sqrt{81}$

79. Approximate to the nearest thousandth using a calculator or the square root table. $\sqrt{123}$

80. Find the unknown side of the right triangle.

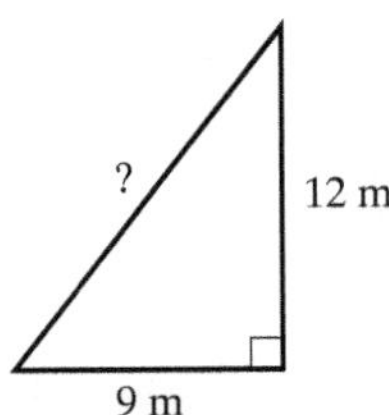

Signed Numbers

Add.

81. $-8 + (-2) + (-3)$

82. $-\frac{1}{4} + \frac{3}{8}$

Subtract.

83. $9 - 12$

84. $-20 - (-3)$

85. Multiply. $(2)(-3)(4)(-1)$

86. Divide. $-\frac{2}{3} \div \frac{1}{4}$

Perform the indicated operations in the proper order.

87. $(-16) \div (-2) + (-4)$

88. $12 - 3(-5)$

89. $7 - (-3) + 12 \div (-6)$

90. $\frac{(-3)(-1) + (-4)(2)}{(0)(6) + (-5)(2)}$

Introduction to Algebra

Combine like terms.

91. $5x - 3y - 8x - 4y$

92. $5 + 2a - 8b - 12 - 6a - 9b$

Simplify.

93. $-2(x - 3y - 5)$

94. $-2(4x + 2) - 3(x + 3y)$

Solve for the variable.

95. $5 - 4x = -3$

96. $5 - 2(x - 3) = 15$

97. $7 - 2x = 10 + 4x$

98. $-3(x + 4) = 2(x - 5)$

Solve using an equation.

99. There are 12 more students taking history than math. There are twice as many students taking psychology as there are students taking math. There are 452 students taking these three subjects. How many are taking history? How many are taking math?

▲ **100.** A rectangle has a perimeter of 106 metres. The length is 5 metres longer than double the width. Find the length and width of the rectangle.

Trigonometry

101. $210° =$ ________ radians

102. $-\frac{7\pi}{5}$ radians $=$ ________ $°$

103. Draw $-\frac{2\pi}{3}$ in standard position and state the quadrant in which the angle lies.

104. Find a positive angle less than $360°$ that is coterminal with $-434°$.

105. Find the exact value of $\cos \frac{\pi}{3}$.

106. Use a calculator to find the value of $\sin 56°$. Round to four decimal places.

In problems 107–108, use the triangle to find the indicated ratios of θ.

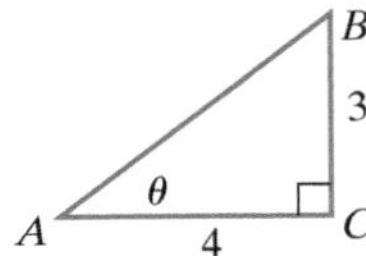

107. $\tan \theta$

108. $\cos \theta$

In problems 109–110, solve the right triangle shown below. Round lengths to one decimal place and express angles to the nearest tenth of a degree.

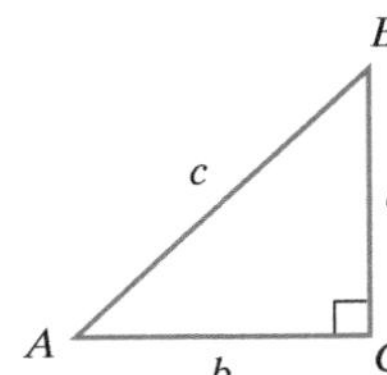

109. $a = 1.5$, $b = 3.4$

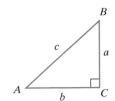

110. The angle of elevation to the top of a building from a point on the ground 30 metres from its base is $37°$. Find the height of the building to the nearest metre.

Answers to Practice Final Examination

Practice Final Examination **1.** eighty-two thousand, three hundred sixty-seven **2.** 30 333 **3.** 173 **4.** 34 103 **5.** 4212 **6.** 217 745 **7.** 158 **8.** 606 **9.** 116 **10.** 16 km/L **11.** $\frac{7}{15}$ **12.** $\frac{42}{11}$ **13.** $\frac{33}{20}$ or $1\frac{13}{20}$ **14.** $\frac{89}{15}$ or $5\frac{14}{15}$ **15.** $\frac{31}{14}$ or $2\frac{3}{14}$ **16.** 4 **17.** $\frac{14}{5}$ or $2\frac{4}{5}$ **18.** $\frac{22}{13}$ or $1\frac{9}{13}$ **19.** $6\frac{17}{20}$ km **20.** 5 packages **21.** 0.719 **22.** $\frac{43}{50}$ **23.** > **24.** 506.38 **25.** 21.77 **26.** 0.757 **27.** 0.492 **28.** 3.69 **29.** 0.8125 **30.** 0.7056 **31.** $\frac{\text{1400 students}}{\text{43 faculty}}$ **32.** no **33.** $n \approx 9.4$ **34.** $n \approx 7.7$ **35.** $n = 15$ **36.** $n = 9$ **37.** \$3333.33 **38.** 9.75 in. **39.** \$294.12 **40.** 1.6 lb **41.** 0.63% **42.** 21.25% **43.** 1.64 **44.** 17.33% **45.** 302.4 **46.** 250 **47.** 4284 **48.** \$10 856 **49.** 4500 students **50.** 34.3% **51.** 4.25 gal **52.** 6500 lb **53.** 192 in. **54.** 5600 m **55.** 0.0698 kg **56.** 0.002 48 L **57.** 19.32 km **58.** 6.3182×10^{-4} **59.** 1.264×10^{11} **60.** 1.367 28 cm **61.** 14.4 m **62.** 206 cm **63.** 5.4 m^2 **64.** 75 m^2 **65.** 113.04 m^2 **66.** 56.52 m **67.** 167.47 cm^3 **68.** 205.2 m^3 **69.** 32.5 m^2 **70.** $n = 32.5$ **71.** \$8 million **72.** \$1 million **73.** 50 °F **74.** from 1990 to 2000 **75.** 600 students **76.** 1400 students **77.** mean $\approx$ 15.83; median = 16.5 **78.** 16 **79.** 11.091 **80.** 15 m **81.** -13 **82.** $\frac{1}{8}$ **83.** -3 **84.** -17 **85.** 24 **86.** $-\frac{8}{3}$ or $-2\frac{2}{3}$ **87.** 4 **88.** 27 **89.** 8 **90.** $\frac{1}{2}$ or 0.5 **91.** $-3x - 7y$ **92.** $-7 - 4a - 17b$ **93.** $-2x + 6y + 10$ **94.** $-11x - 9y - 4$ **95.** $x = 2$ **96.** $x = -2$ **97.** $x = -\frac{1}{2}$ or -0.5 **98.** $x = -\frac{2}{5}$ or -0.4 **99.** 122 students are taking history; 110 students are taking math **100.** length is 37 m.; width is 16 m. **101.** $\frac{7\pi}{6}$ **102.** $-252°$ **103.** , the angle lies in quadrant 3 **104.** 286° **105.** $\frac{1}{2}$ **106.** 0.8290 **107.** $\frac{3}{4}$ **108.** $\frac{4}{5}$ **109.** $c = 3.7; A = 23.8; B = 66.2$ **110.** 23 m

Appendix: Consumer Finance Applications

1 Balancing a Chequing Account

Calculating a Chequebook Balance

If you have a chequing account, you should keep records of the cheques written, ATM withdrawals, deposits, and other transactions on a cheque register. To find the amount of money in a chequing account you subtract debits and add credits to the balance in the account. Debits are cheques written, withdrawals made, or any other amount charged to a chequing account. Credits include deposits made, as well as any other money credited to the account.

Student Learning Objectives

After studying this section, you will be able to:

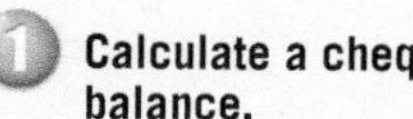

1. **Calculate a chequebook balance.**
2. **Balance a chequebook.**

EXAMPLE 1 Jesse Holm had a balance of $1254.32 in his chequing account before writing five cheques and making a deposit. On September 2, shown here as 9/2, Jesse wrote cheque #243 to the Manor Apartments for $575, cheque #244 to the Electric Company for $23.41, and cheque #245 to the Gas Company for $15.67. Then on 9/3, he wrote cheque #246 to Jack's Market for $125.57, and cheque #247 to Clothing Mart for $35.85, and made a $634.51 deposit. Record the cheques and deposit in Jesse's cheque register and then find Jesse's ending balance.

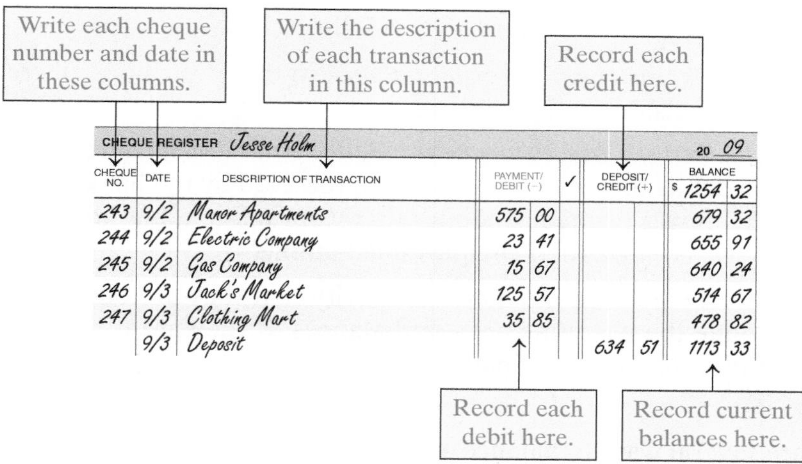

CHEQUE NO.	DATE	DESCRIPTION OF TRANSACTION	PAYMENT/ DEBIT (−)	✓	DEPOSIT/ CREDIT (+)	BALANCE
						$ 1254 32
243	9/2	Manor Apartments	575 00			679 32
244	9/2	Electric Company	23 41			655 91
245	9/2	Gas Company	15 67			640 24
246	9/3	Jack's Market	125 57			514 67
247	9/3	Clothing Mart	35 85			478 82
	9/3	Deposit			634 51	1113 33

Solution To find the ending balance, we subtract each cheque written and add the deposit to the current balance. Then we record these amounts in the cheque register.

$$\begin{array}{r}1254.32\\-\ 575.00\\\hline 679.32\end{array}\quad\begin{array}{r}679.32\\-\ 23.41\\\hline 655.91\end{array}\quad\begin{array}{r}655.91\\-\ 15.67\\\hline 640.24\end{array}\quad\begin{array}{r}640.24\\-\ 125.57\\\hline 514.67\end{array}\quad\begin{array}{r}514.67\\-\ 35.85\\\hline 478.82\end{array}\quad\begin{array}{r}478.82\\+\ 634.51\\\hline 1113.33\end{array}$$

Jesse's balance is 1113.33.

Practice Problem 1 My Chung Nguyen had a balance of $1434.52 in her chequing account before writing three cheques and making a deposit. On 3/1/2009, My Chung wrote cheque #144 to the Leland Mortgage Company for $908 and cheque #145 to the Phone Company for $33.21. Then on 3/2/2009, she wrote cheque #146 to Sam's Food Market for $102.37 and

NOTE TO STUDENT: Fully worked-out solutions to all of the Practice Problems can be found at the end of the module.

made a $524.41 deposit. Record the cheques and deposit in My Chung's cheque register, and then find My Chung's ending balance.

CHEQUE REGISTER *My Chung Nguyen* 20 *09*

CHEQUE NO.	DATE	DESCRIPTION OF TRANSACTION	PAYMENT/ DEBIT (−)	✓	DEPOSIT/ CREDIT (+)	BALANCE $

Balancing a Chequebook

The bank provides customers with a bank statement each month. This statement lists the cheques the bank paid, ATM withdrawals, deposits made, and all other debits and credits made to a chequing account. It is very important to verify that these bank records match ours. We must make sure that we deducted all debits and added all credits in our cheque register. This is called **balancing a chequebook.** Balancing our chequebook allows us to make sure that the balance we think we have in our chequebook is correct. If our chequebook does not balance, we must look for any mistakes.

To balance a chequebook, proceed as follows.

1. First, *adjust the cheque register balance* so that it includes all credits and debits listed on the bank statement.
2. Then, *adjust the bank statement balance* so that it includes all credits and debits that may not have been received by the bank when the statement was printed. Cheques that were written, but not received by the bank, are called **cheques outstanding.**
3. Finally, *compare both balances* to verify that they are equal. If they are equal, the chequing account balances. If they are not equal, we must find the error and make adjustments.

There are several ways to balance a chequebook. Most banks include a form you can fill out to assist you in this process.

EXAMPLE 2 Balance Jesse's chequebook using his cheque register and bank statement.

CHEQUE REGISTER *Jesse Holm* 20 *09*

CHEQUE NO.	DATE	DESCRIPTION OF TRANSACTION	PAYMENT/ DEBIT (−)	✓	DEPOSIT/ CREDIT (+)	BALANCE $ 1254 32
243	9/2	Manor Apartments	575 00	✓		679 32
244	9/2	Electric Company	23 41	✓		655 91
245	9/2	Gas Company	15 67	✓		640 24
246	9/3	Jack's Market	125 57	✓		514 67
247	9/3	Clothing Mart	35 85			478 82
	9/3	Deposit		✓	634 51	1113 33
248	9/12	College Bookstore	168 96	✓		944 37
	9/18	ATM	100 00	✓		844 37
249	9/25	Telephone Company	43 29	✓		801 08
250	9/30	Sports Emporium	40 00			761 08
	10/1	Deposit			530 90	1291 98

Bank Statement: JESSE HOLM 9/1/2009 to 9/30/2009

Beginning Balance $1254.32
Ending Balance $831.68

Cheques cleared by the bank

#243	$575.00	#245	$15.67	#248	$168.96
#244	$23.41	#246*	$125.57	#249*	$43.29

*Indicates that the next cheque in the sequence is outstanding (hasn't cleared).

Deposits

9/3 $634.51

Other withdrawals

9/18 ATM $100.00 Service charge $5.25

Solution Follow steps 1–6 on the Chequing Reconciliation form below.

CHEQUING RECONCILIATION This form is provided to assist you in balancing your chequing account.

List cheques outstanding* not charged to your chequing account

CHEQUE NO.	AMOUNT	
247	35	85
250	40	00
TOTAL	75	85

*and ATM withdrawals

Period ending 9/30, 20 09

1. Cheque Register Balance		$ 1291.98
Subtract any charges listed on the bank statement which you have not previously deducted from your balance.	−	$ 5.25
Adjusted Cheque Register Balance		$ 1286.73
2. **Enter** the ending balance shown on the bank statement.		$ 831.68
3. **Enter** deposits made later than the ending date on the bank statement.	+	$ 530.90
	+	$
	+	$
TOTAL (Step 2 plus Step 3)		$ 1362.58
4. In your cheque register, **check off** all the cheques paid. In the area provided to the left, **list** numbers and amounts of all outstanding cheques and ATM withdrawals.		
5. **Subtract** the total amount in Step 4.	−	$ 75.85
6. This adjusted bank balance should equal the adjusted Cheque Register Balance from Step 1.		$ 1286.73

The balances in steps **1** and **6** are equal, so Jesse's chequebook is balanced.

Practice Problem 2 Balance Anthony's chequebook using his cheque register, his bank statement, and the given Chequing Reconciliation form.

NOTE TO STUDENT: Fully worked-out solutions to all of the Practice Problems can be found at the end of the module.

CHEQUE REGISTER *Anthony Maida* 20 09

CHEQUE NO.	DATE	DESCRIPTION OF TRANSACTION	PAYMENT/ DEBIT (−)		✓	DEPOSIT/ CREDIT (+)		BALANCE $ 1823	00
211	7/2	Apple Apartments	985	00				838	00
	7/9	ATM	101	50				736	50
212	7/10	Leland Groceries	98	87				637	63
213	7/21	The Gas Company	45	56				592	07
	7/21	Deposit				687	10	1279	17
214	7/28	Cellular for Less	59	98				1219	19
215	7/28	The Electric Company	89	75				1129	44
216	7/28	Sports World	129	99				999	45
217	7/28	Leland Groceries	205	99				793	46
	7/30	ATM	141	50				651	96
	8/1	Deposit				398	50	1050	46

Bank Statement: ANTHONY MAIDA 7/1/2009 to 8/1/2009

Beginning Balance $1823.00
Ending Balance $934.95

Cheques cleared by the bank

#211	$985.00	#213	$45.56	#216	$129.99
#212	$98.87	#214*	$59.98		

*Indicates that the next cheque in the sequence is outstanding (hasn't cleared).

Deposits

7/21 $687.10

Other withdrawals

7/9 ATM	$101.50	Service charge	$3.50
7/30 ATM	$141.50	Cheque purchase	$9.25

CHEQUING RECONCILIATION This form is provided to assist you in balancing your chequing account.

List cheques outstanding* not charged to your chequing account

CHEQUE NO.	AMOUNT	
TOTAL		

*and ATM withdrawals

Period ending , 20

1. Cheque Register Balance		$
Subtract any charges listed on the bank statement which you have not previously deducted from your balance.	−	$
Adjusted Cheque Register Balance		$
2. **Enter** the ending balance shown on the bank statement.		$
3. **Enter** deposits made later than the ending date on the bank statement.	+	$
	+	$
	+	$
TOTAL (Step 2 plus Step 3)		$
4. In your cheque register, **check off** all the cheques paid. In the area provided to the left, **list** numbers and amounts of all outstanding cheques and ATM withdrawals.		
5. **Subtract** the total amount in Step 4.	−	$
6. This adjusted bank balance should equal the adjusted Cheque Register Balance from Step 1.		$

Note: To calculate the service charges, we add $3.50 + 9.25 = 12.75$.

EXERCISES

1. Shin Karasuda had a balance of $532 in his chequing account before writing four cheques and making a deposit. On 6/1 he wrote cheque #122 to the Mini Market for $124.95 and cheque #123 to Better Be Dry Cleaners for $41.50. Then on 6/9 he made a $384.10 deposit, wrote cheque #124 to Macy's Department Store for $72.98, and cheque #125 to Costco for $121.55. Record the cheques and deposit in Shin's cheque register, and then find the ending balance.

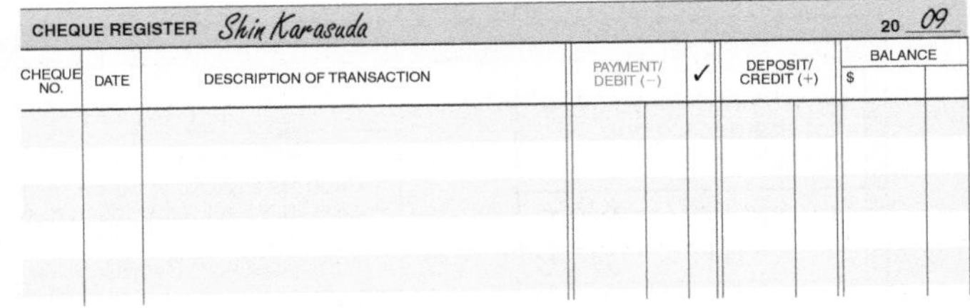

CHEQUE REGISTER *Shin Karasuda* 20 *09*

CHEQUE NO.	DATE	DESCRIPTION OF TRANSACTION	PAYMENT/ DEBIT (−)	✓	DEPOSIT/ CREDIT (+)	BALANCE $

2. Mary Beth O'Brian had a balance of $493 in her chequing account before writing four cheques and making a deposit. On 9/4 she wrote cheque #311 to Ben's Garage for $213.45 and #312 to Food Mart for $132.50. Then on 9/5 she made a $387.50 cheque deposit, wrote cheque #313 to the Shoe Pavilion for $69.98, and cheque #314 to the Electric Company for $92.45. Record the cheques and deposit in Mary Beth's cheque register, and then find the ending balance.

CHEQUE REGISTER *Mary Beth O'Brian* 20 *09*

CHEQUE NO.	DATE	DESCRIPTION OF TRANSACTION	PAYMENT/ DEBIT (−)	✓	DEPOSIT/ CREDIT (+)	BALANCE $

3. The Harbour Beauty Salon had a balance of $2498.90 in its business chequing account on 3/4. The manager made a deposit on the same day for $786 and wrote cheque #734 to the Beauty Supply Factory for $980. Then on 3/9 he wrote cheque #735 to the Water Department for $131.85 and cheque #736 to the Electric Company for $251.50. On 3/19 he made a $2614.10 deposit and wrote two payroll cheques: #737 to Ranik Ghandi for $873 and #738 to Eduardo Gomez for $750. Record the cheques and deposits in the Harbour Beauty Salon's cheque register, and then find the ending balance.

CHEQUE REGISTER *Harbour Beauty Salon* 20 *09*

CHEQUE NO.	DATE	DESCRIPTION OF TRANSACTION	PAYMENT/ DEBIT (−)	✓	DEPOSIT/ CREDIT (+)	BALANCE $

4. Joanna's Coffee Shop had a balance of $1108.50 in its business chequing account on 1/7. The owner made a deposit on the same day for $963 and wrote cheque #527 to the Restaurant Supply Company for $492. Then on 1/11 she wrote cheque #528 to the Gas Company for $122.45 and cheque #529 to the Electric Company for $321.20. Then on 1/12 she made a $1518.20 deposit and wrote two payroll cheques: #530 to Sara O'Conner for $579, and #531 to Nlegan Raskin for $466. Record the cheques and deposits in Joanna's Coffee Shop's cheque register, and then find the ending balance.

CHEQUE REGISTER *Joanna's Coffee Shop* 20 *09*

CHEQUE NO.	DATE	DESCRIPTION OF TRANSACTION	PAYMENT/ DEBIT (−)	✓	DEPOSIT/ CREDIT (+)	BALANCE $

5. On 3/3 Justin Larkin had $321.94 in his chequing account before he withdrew $101.50 at the ATM. On 3/7 he made a $601.90 deposit and wrote cheques to pay the following bills: cheque #114 to the Third Street Apartments for $550, cheque #115 to the Cable Company for $59.50, cheque #116 to the Electric Company for $43.50, and cheque #117 to the Gas Company for $15.90. Does Justin have enough money left in his chequing account to pay $99 for his car insurance?

CHEQUE REGISTER *Justin Larkin* 20 *09*

CHEQUE NO.	DATE	DESCRIPTION OF TRANSACTION	PAYMENT/ DEBIT (–)	✓	DEPOSIT/ CREDIT (+)	BALANCE $

6. On 5/2 Leon Jones had $423.54 in his chequing account when he withdrew $51.50 at the ATM. On 5/9 he made a $601.80 deposit and wrote cheques to pay the following bills: cheque #334 to Fasco Car Finance for $150.25, cheque #335 to A-1 Car Insurance for $89.20, cheque #336 to the Telephone Company for $33.40, and cheque #337 to the Apple Apartments for $615. Does Leon have enough money left in his chequing account to pay $59 for his electric bill?

CHEQUE REGISTER *Leon Jones* 20 *09*

CHEQUE NO.	DATE	DESCRIPTION OF TRANSACTION	PAYMENT/ DEBIT (–)	✓	DEPOSIT/ CREDIT (+)	BALANCE $

7. Balance the monthly statement for the Carson Maid Service on the Chequing Reconciliation form shown below.

CHEQUE REGISTER *Carson Maid Service* 20 *09*

CHEQUE NO.	DATE	DESCRIPTION OF TRANSACTION	PAYMENT/ DEBIT (–)	✓	DEPOSIT/ CREDIT (+)	BALANCE
						$ 1721 50
102	4/3	A&R Cleaning Supplies	422 33			1299 17
103	4/9	Allison De Julio	510 50			788 67
104	4/9	Mai Vu	320 00			468 67
105	4/9	Jon Veldez	320 00			148 67
	4/11	Deposit			1890 00	2038 67
106	4/20	Mobil Gas Company	355 35			1683 32
107	4/25	Peterson Property Mangt. warehouse rent	525 00			1158 32
108	4/29	Jack's Garage	450 10			708 22
	5/2	Deposit			540 00	1248 22

Bank Statement: CARSON MAID SERVICE 4/1/2009 to 4/30/2009

Beginning Balance $1721.50
Ending Balance $1564.82

Cheques cleared by the bank

#102 $422.33 #104 $320.00 #108 $450.10
#103 $510.50 #105* $320.00

*Indicates that the next cheque in the sequence is outstanding (hasn't cleared).

Deposits

4/11 $1890.00

Other withdrawals

Service charge $4.50
Cheque purchase $19.25

CHEQUING RECONCILIATION This form is provided to assist you in balancing your chequing account.

List cheques outstanding* not charged to your chequing account

CHEQUE NO.	AMOUNT
TOTAL	

*and ATM withdrawals

Period ending	, 20
1. Cheque Register Balance	$
Subtract any charges listed on the bank statement which you have not previously deducted from your balance. –	$
Adjusted Cheque Register Balance	$
2. Enter the ending balance shown on the bank statement.	$
3. Enter deposits made later than the ending date on the bank statement. +	$
+	$
+	$
TOTAL (Step 2 plus Step 3)	$
4. In your cheque register, check off all the cheques paid. In the area provided to the left, list numbers and amounts of all outstanding cheques and ATM withdrawals.	
5. Subtract the total amount in Step 4. –	$
6. This adjusted bank balance should equal the adjusted Cheque Register Balance from Step 1.	$

8. Balance the monthly statement for The Flower Shop on the Chequing Reconciliation form shown below.

CHEQUE REGISTER *The Flower Shop* 20 *09*

CHEQUE NO.	DATE	DESCRIPTION OF TRANSACTION	PAYMENT/ DEBIT (−)	✓	DEPOSIT/ CREDIT (+)	BALANCE
						$ 3459.40
502	9/7	Whole Sale Flower Company	733.67			2725.73
503	9/7	Alexsandra Kruse	580.20			2145.53
504	9/7	Jose Sanchez	430.50			1715.03
505	9/7	Kamir Kosedag	601.90			1113.13
	9/11	Deposit			2654.00	3767.13
506	9/21	L&S Pottery	466.84			3300.29
507	9/24	Peterson Property Mangt. (warehouse rent)	985.00			2315.29
508	9/28	Barton Electric Company	525.60			1789.69
	10/2	Deposit			540.00	2329.69

Bank Statement: THE FLOWER SHOP 9/1/2009 to 9/30/2009

Beginning Balance $3459.40
Ending Balance $3220.28

Cheques cleared by the bank

#502 $733.67 #504 $430.50 #508 $525.60
#503 $580.20 #505* $601.90

*Indicates that the next cheque in the sequence is outstanding (hasn't cleared).

Deposits

9/11 $2654.00

Other withdrawals

Service charge $4.75
Cheque purchase $16.50

CHEQUING RECONCILIATION This form is provided to assist you in balancing your chequing account.

List cheques outstanding* not charged to your chequing account

CHEQUE NO.	AMOUNT
TOTAL	

*and ATM withdrawals

Period ending ______, 20

1. Cheque Register Balance	$
Subtract any charges listed on the bank statement which you have not previously deducted from your balance. −	$
Adjusted Cheque Register Balance	$
2. Enter the ending balance shown on the bank statement.	$
3. Enter deposits made later than the ending date on the bank statement. +	$
+	$
+	$
TOTAL (Step 2 plus Step 3)	$
4. In your cheque register, **check off** all the cheques paid. In the area provided to the left, **list** numbers and amounts of all outstanding cheques and ATM withdrawals.	
5. Subtract the total amount in Step 4. −	$
6. This adjusted bank balance should equal the adjusted Cheque Register Balance from Step 1.	$

9. On 2/1 Jeremy Sirk had a balance of $672.10 in his chequing account. On the same day he deposited $735 of his paycheque into his chequing account and wrote cheque #233 to Stanton Sporting Goods for $92.99 and cheque #234 to the Garden Apartments for $680. Then on 2/20 he wrote cheque #235 to the Gas Company for $31.85, cheque #236 to the Cable Company for $51.50, cheque #237 to Ralph's Market for $173.98, and also made an ATM withdrawal for $101.50. Then on 3/1 he made an $814.10 deposit, wrote cheque #238 to State Farm Insurance for $98, and made another ATM withdrawal for $41.50. Record the cheques and deposits in Jeremy's cheque register, and then find the ending balance.

CHEQUE REGISTER *Jeremy Sirk* 20 *09*

CHEQUE NO.	DATE	DESCRIPTION OF TRANSACTION	PAYMENT/ DEBIT (−)	✓	DEPOSIT/ CREDIT (+)	BALANCE
						$

10. On 8/1 Shannon Mending had a balance of $525.90 in her chequing account. Later that same day she deposited $588.23 into her chequing account and wrote cheque #333 to Verizon Telephone Company for $33.20 and cheque #334 to Discount Car Insurance for $332.50. Then on 8/8 she wrote cheque #335 to the Walden Market for $21.35, made an ATM withdrawal for $81.50, and wrote cheque #336 to the Cable Company for $41.50. Then on 9/1 she made a $904.10 deposit, wrote cheque #337 to Next Day Dry Cleaners for $33.50, and cheque #338 to Marty's Dress Shop for $87.99. Record the cheques and deposits in Shannon's cheque register, and then find the ending balance.

CHEQUE REGISTER *Shannon Mending* 20 *09*

CHEQUE NO.	DATE	DESCRIPTION OF TRANSACTION	PAYMENT/ DEBIT (−)	✓	DEPOSIT/ CREDIT (+)	BALANCE $

11. Refer to exercise 9 and use the bank statement and Chequing Reconciliation form below to balance Jeremy's chequing account.

Bank Statement: JEREMY SIRK 2/1/2009 to 2/28/2009

Beginning Balance $672.10
Ending Balance $293.88

Cheques cleared by the bank

#233 $92.99 #236 $51.50
#234* $680.00 #237* $173.98

*Indicates that the next cheque in the sequence is outstanding (hasn't cleared).

Deposits

2/1 $735.00

Other withdrawals

2/20 ATM $101.50 Service charge $3.50
Cheque purchase $9.75

CHEQUING RECONCILIATION This form is provided to assist you in balancing your chequing account.

List cheque outstanding* not charged to your chequing account

CHEQUE NO.	AMOUNT
TOTAL	

*and ATM withdrawals

Period ending , 20

1. Cheque Register Balance $
Subtract any charges listed on the bank statement which you have not previously deducted from your balance. − $
Adjusted Cheque Register Balance $
2. **Enter** the ending balance shown on the bank statement. $
3. **Enter** deposits made later than the ending date on the bank statement. + $ + $ + $
TOTAL (Step 2 plus Step 3) $
4. In your cheque register, **check off** all the cheques paid. In the area provided to the left, **list** numbers and amounts of all outstanding cheques and ATM withdrawals.
5. **Subtract** the total amount in Step 4. − $
6. This adjusted bank balance should equal the adjusted Cheque Register Balance from Step 1. $

12. Refer to exercise 10 and use the bank statement and Chequing Reconciliation form below to balance Shannon's chequing account.

Bank Statement: SHANNON MENDING 8/1/2009 to 8/31/2009

Beginning Balance $525.90
Ending Balance $923.83

Cheques cleared by the bank

#333* $33.20 #336* $41.50
#335 $21.35

*Indicates that the next cheque in the sequence is outstanding (hasn't cleared).

Deposits

8/1 $588.23

Other withdrawals

8/8 ATM $81.50 Service charge $3.25
Cheque purchase $9.50

CHEQUING RECONCILIATION This form is provided to assist you in balancing your chequing account.

List cheques outstanding* not charged to your chequing account

CHEQUE NO.	AMOUNT
TOTAL	

*and ATM withdrawals

Period ending , 20

1. Cheque Register Balance $
Subtract any charges listed on the bank statement which you have not previously deducted from your balance. − $
Adjusted Cheque Register Balance $
2. **Enter** the ending balance shown on the bank statement. $
3. **Enter** deposits made later than the ending date on the bank statement. + $ + $ + $
TOTAL (Step 2 plus Step 3) $
4. In your cheque register, **check off** all the cheques paid. In the area provided to the left, **list** numbers and amounts of all outstanding cheques and ATM withdrawals.
5. **Subtract** the total amount in Step 4. − $
6. This adjusted bank balance should equal the adjusted Cheque Register Balance from Step 1. $

2 Determining the Best Deal When Purchasing a Vehicle

Student Learning Objectives

After studying this section, you will be able to:

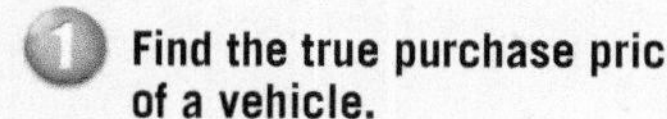

1. **Find the true purchase price of a vehicle.**
2. **Find the total cost of a vehicle to determine the best deal.**

When we buy a car there are several facts to consider in order to determine which car has the best price. The sale price offered by a car dealer or seller is only one factor we must consider—others include the interest rate on the loan, sales tax, licence fee, and sale promotions such as cash rebates or 0% interest. We must also consider the cost of options we choose such as extended warranties, sun roof, tinted glass, etc. In this section we will see how to calculate the total purchase price and determine the best deal when buying a vehicle.

Finding the True Purchase Price of a Vehicle

In most provinces there is a sales tax and a licence or title fee that must be paid on all vehicles purchased. To find the true purchase price for a vehicle, we *add* these extra costs to the sale price. In addition, we must add to the sale price the cost of any extended warranties and extra options or accessories we buy.

purchase price = sale price + sales tax + licence fee + extended warranty (and other accessories)

Sometimes lenders (banks and finance companies) require a **down payment.** The amount of the down payment is usually a percent of the purchase price. We subtract the down payment from the purchase price to find the amount we must finance.

down payment = percent × purchase price

amount financed = purchase price − down payment

EXAMPLE 1 Daniel bought a truck that was on sale for \$28 999 in a city that has a 6% sales tax and a 2% licence fee.

(a) Find the sales tax and licence fee Daniel paid.

(b) Daniel also bought an extended warranty for \$1550. Find the purchase price of the truck.

Solution

(a) sales tax = 6% of sale price
= 0.06 × 28 999
sales tax = \$1739.94

licence fee = 2% of sale price
= 0.02 × 28 999
licence fee = \$579.98

(b) purchase price
= sales price + sales tax + licence fee + extended warranty
= 28 999 + 1739.94 + 579.98 + 1550
purchase price = \$32 868.92

Practice Problem 1 Huy Nguyen bought a van that was on sale for \$24 999 in a city that has a 7% sales tax and a 2% licence fee.

(a) Find the sales tax and licence fee Huy paid.

(b) Huy also bought an extended warranty for \$1275. Find the purchase price of the van.

NOTE TO STUDENT: Fully worked-out solutions to all of the Practice Problems can be found at the end of the module.

EXAMPLE 2 The purchase price of a car Jerome plans to buy is \$19 999. In order to qualify for the loan on the car, Jerome must make a down payment of 20% of the purchase price.

(a) Find the down payment.

(b) Find the amount financed.

Solution

(a) down payment = percent × purchase price

down payment = 20% × 19 999
= 0.20 × 19 999

down payment = \$3999.80

(b) amount financed = purchase price − down payment
= 19 999 − 3999.80

amount financed = \$15 999.20

Practice Problem 2 The purchase price of a Jeep Cheryl plans to buy is \$32 499. In order to qualify for the loan on the Jeep, Cheryl must make a down payment of 15% of the purchase price.

(a) Find the down payment. **(b)** Find the amount financed.

Finding the Total Cost of a Vehicle to Determine the Best Deal

When we borrow money to buy a car, we often pay interest on the loan and we must consider this extra cost when we calculate the **total cost** of the vehicle. If we know the amount of the car payment and the number of months it will take to pay off the loan, we can find the total payments on the car (the amount we borrowed plus interest) by multiplying the monthly payment amount times the number of months of the loan. Then we must add the down payment to that amount.

total cost = (monthly payment × number of months in loan) + down payment

EXAMPLE 3 Marvin went to two dealerships to find the best deal on the truck he plans to purchase. From which dealership should Marvin buy the truck so that the *total cost* of the truck is the least expensive?

Dealership 1	Dealership 2
• Purchase price: \$39 999	• Purchase price: \$36 499
• Financing option: 0% financing with \$5000 down payment	• Financing option: 4% financing with no down payment
• Monthly payments: \$838.52 per month for 48 months	• Monthly payments: \$763.71 per month for 60 months

Solution First, we find the total cost of the truck at Dealership 1.

$$\begin{aligned} \text{total cost} &= (\text{monthly payment} \times \text{number of months in loan}) + \text{down payment} \\ &= (838.52 \times 48) + 5000 \quad \text{We multiply, then add.} \\ &= 45\,248.96 \end{aligned}$$

The total cost of the truck at Dealership 1 is \$45 248.96.

Next, we find the total cost of the truck at Dealership 2.

$$\begin{aligned} \text{total cost} &= (\text{monthly payment} \times \text{number of months in loan}) + \text{down payment} \\ &= (763.71 \times 60) + 0 \quad \text{There is no down payment.} \\ &= 45\,822.60 \end{aligned}$$

The total cost of the truck at Dealership 2 is \$45 822.60.

We see that the best deal on the truck Marvin plans to buy is at Dealership 1.

Practice Problem 3 Phoebe went to two dealerships to find the best deal on the minivan she plans to purchase. From which dealership should Phoebe buy the minivan so that the *total cost* of the minivan is the least expensive?

Dealership 1	Dealership 2
• Purchase price: \$22 999	• Purchase price: \$24 299
• Financing option: 4% financing with no down payment	• Financing option: 0% financing with \$3000 down payment
• Monthly payments: \$453.21 per month for 60 months	• Monthly payments: \$479.17 per month for 48 months

EXERCISES

1. A college student buys a car and pays a 6% sales tax on the $21 599 sale price. How much sales tax did the student pay?

2. A high school teacher buys a minivan and pays a 5% sales tax on the $26 800 sale price. How much sales tax did the teacher pay?

3. Frances is planning to buy a four-door sedan that is on sale for $18 999. She must pay a 2% licence fee. Find the licence fee.

4. Mai Vu saw an ad for a short-bed truck that is on sale for $17 599. If she buys the truck she must pay a 2% licence fee. Find the licence fee.

5. John must make a 10% down payment on the purchase price of the $42 450 sports car he is planning to buy. Find the down payment.

6. Kamir must make a 15% down payment on the purchase price of the $31 500 extended cab truck he is planning to buy. Find the down payment.

7. Tabatha bought a minivan that was on sale for $24 899 in a city that has a 5% sales tax and a 2% licence fee.
   (a) Find the sales tax and licence fee Tabatha paid.
   (b) Tabatha also bought an extended warranty for $1100. Find the purchase price of the minivan.

8. Dante bought a truck that was on sale for $32 499 in a city that has a 7% sales tax and a 2% licence fee.
   (a) Find the sales tax and licence fee Dante paid.
   (b) Dante also bought an extended warranty for $1600. Find the purchase price of the truck.

9. Jeremiah bought a sports car that was on sale for $44 799 in a city that has a 7% sales tax and a 2% licence fee.
   (a) Find the sales tax and licence fee Jeremiah paid.
   (b) Jeremiah also bought an extended warranty for $2100. Find the purchase price of the sports car.

10. Dawn bought a four-door sedan that was on sale for $31 899 in a city that has a 6% sales tax and a 2% licence fee.
    (a) Find the sales tax and licence fee Dawn paid.
    (b) Dawn also bought an extended warranty for $1300. Find the purchase price of the sedan.

11. The purchase price of an SUV that a soccer coach plans to buy is $49 999. In order to qualify for the loan on the SUV, the coach must make a down payment of 15% of the purchase price.
    (a) Find the down payment.
    (b) Find the amount financed.

12. The purchase price of a flat-bed truck a contractor plans to buy is $39 999. In order to qualify for the loan on the truck, the contractor must make a down payment of 10% of the purchase price.
    (a) Find the down payment.
    (b) Find the amount financed.

13. Tammy went to two dealerships to find the best deal on the truck she plans to purchase. From which dealership should Tammy buy the truck so that the *total cost* of the truck is the least expensive?

Dealership 1	Dealership 2
• Purchase price: $35 999	• Purchase price: $32 499
• Financing option: 0% financing with $4000 down payment	• Financing option: 4% financing with $2000 down payment
• Monthly payments: $696.65 per month for 48 months	• Monthly payments: $603.58 per month for 60 months

14. John went to two dealerships to find the best deal on a luxury SUV for his company to purchase. From which dealership should John buy the SUV so that the *total cost* of the SUV is the least expensive?

Dealership 1	Dealership 2
• Purchase price: $49 999	• Purchase price: $46 499
• Financing option: 0% financing with $5000 down payment	• Financing option: 4% financing with no down payment
• Monthly payments: $1010.39 per month for 48 months	• Monthly payments: $916.29 per month for 60 months

To Think About

Natasha went to three car dealerships to check the prices of the same Ford two-door coupe. The city where the dealerships are located has a sales tax of 5% and a licence fee of 2%. All dealerships offer extended warranties that are 3 years/70 000 kilometres. Use the following information gathered by Natasha to answer exercises 15 and 16.

Dealership 1—Ford Coupe	Dealership 2—Ford Coupe	Dealership 3—Ford Coupe
• $24 999 plus $2000 rebate	• $23 799; dealer pays sales tax	• $23 999
• extended warranty $1350	• extended warranty $1450	• free extended warranty

15. **(a)** Which dealership offers the least expensive *purchase price?* State this amount.

(b) Each dealership offers a *different interest rate* on a 60-month loan without a down payment, resulting in the following monthly payments:

Dealership 1	Dealership 2	Dealership 3
$480.65/month	$485.46/month	$496.44/month

From which dealership should Natasha buy the Ford coupe so that the *total cost* of the car is the least expensive? State this amount.

(c) Compare the results of parts **(a)** and **(b)**. What conclusion can you make?

16. **(a)** Which dealership offers the most expensive *purchase price?* State this amount.

(b) Each dealership offers a *different interest rate* on a 48-month loan without a down payment, resulting in the following monthly payments:

Dealership 1	Dealership 2	Dealership 3
$589.27/month	$594.07/month	$603.07/month

From which dealership should Natasha buy the Ford coupe so that the *total cost* of the car is the most expensive? State this amount.

(c) Compare the results of parts **(a)** and **(b)**. What conclusion can you make?

Solutions to Practice Problems

1 Balancing a Chequing Account

Practice Problems

1.

CHEQUE REGISTER *My Chung Nguyen* 20 *09*

CHEQUE NO.	DATE	DESCRIPTION OF TRANSACTION	PAYMENT/ DEBIT (−)	✓	DEPOSIT/ CREDIT (+)	BALANCE
						$ 1434 52
144	3/1	Leland Mortgage Company	908 00			526 52
145	3/1	Phone Company	33 21			493 31
146	3/2	Sam's Food Market	102 37			390 94
	3/2	Deposit			524 41	915 35

To find the ending balance we subtract each cheque written and add the deposit to the current balance. Then we record these amounts in the cheque register.

$$\begin{array}{r}1434.52\\-\ 908.00\\\hline 526.52\end{array}\quad\begin{array}{r}526.52\\-\ 33.21\\\hline 493.31\end{array}\quad\begin{array}{r}493.31\\-\ 102.37\\\hline 390.94\end{array}\quad\begin{array}{r}390.94\\+\ 524.41\\\hline 915.35\end{array}$$

My Chung's balance is $915.35

2.

CHEQUING RECONCILIATION This form is provided to assist you in balancing your chequing account.

List cheques outstanding* not charged to your chequing account

CHEQUE NO.	AMOUNT
215	89 75
217	205 99
TOTAL	295 74

* and ATM withdrawals

Period ending *8/1*, 20 *09*

1. Cheque Register Balance		$ 1050.46
Subtract any charges listed on the bank statement which you have not previously deducted from your balance.	−	$ 12.75
Adjusted Cheque Register Balance		$ 1037.71
2. **Enter** the ending balance shown on the bank statement.		$ 934.95
3. **Enter** deposits made later than the ending date on the bank statement.	+	$ 398.50
	+	$
	+	$
TOTAL (Step 2 plus Step 3)		$ 1333.45
4. In your cheque register, **check off** all the cheques paid. In the area provided to the left, **list** numbers and amounts of all outstanding cheques and ATM withdrawals.		
5. **Subtract** the total amount in Step 4.	−	$ 295.74
6. This adjusted bank balance should equal the adjusted ChequeRegister Balance from Step 1.		$ 1037.71

The balances in steps **1** and **6** are equal, so Anthony's chequebook is balanced.

2 Determining the Best Value When Purchasing a Vehicle

Practice Problems

1. (a) sales tax = 7% of sale price
= 0.07 × 24 999
sales tax = $1749.93
licence fee = 2%of sale price
= 0.02 × 24 999
licence fee = $499.98

(b) purchase price = sales price + sales tax + licence fee + extended warranty
= 24 999 + 1749.93 + 499.98 + 1275
purchase price = $28 523.91

2. (a) down payment = percent × purchase price.
down payment = 15% × 32 499
= 0.15 × 32 499
down payment = $4874.85

(b) amount financed = purchase price − down payment
= 32 499 − 4874.85
amount financed = $27 624.15

3. First, we find the total cost of the minivan at Dealer 1.
total cost = (monthly payment × number of months in loan) + down payment
= (453.21 × 60) + 0 There is no down payment.
= 27 192.60
The total cost of the minivan at Dealership 1 is $27 192.60.

Next, we find the cost of the minivan at Dealer 2.
total cost = (monthly payment × number of months in loan) + down payment
= (479.17 × 48) + 3000 We multiply, then add.
= 26 000.16
The total cost of the minivan at Dealership 2 is $26 000.16.

We see that the best deal on the minivan Phoebe plans to buy is at Dealership 2.

Answers to Selected Exercises for Appendix: Consumer Finance Applications

Exercises Appendix 1 Balancing a Chequing Account

1. $555.12 **3.** $2912.65 **5.** $153.44; Yes, Justin can pay his car insurance. **7.** The account balances. **9.** $949.88 **11.** Jeremy's account balances.

Exercises Appendix 2 Determining the Best Deal When Purchasing a Vehicle

1. $1259.94 **3.** $379.98 **5.** $4245 **7. (a)** $1244.95; $497.98 **(b)** $27 741.93 **9. (a)** $3135.93; $895.98 **(b)** $50 930.91 **11. (a)** $7499.85 **(b)** $42 499.15 **13.** Dealership 1 **15. (a)** Dealership 3; $25 678.93 **(b)** Dealership 1; $28 839 **(c)** The most expensive purchase price does not guarantee the most expensive total cost. Many factors need to be considered to determine the best deal.

Appendix: Tables

Table of Basic Addition Facts

+	0	1	2	3	4	5	6	7	8	9
0	0	1	2	3	4	5	6	7	8	9
1	1	2	3	4	5	6	7	8	9	10
2	2	3	4	5	6	7	8	9	10	11
3	3	4	5	6	7	8	9	10	11	12
4	4	5	6	7	8	9	10	11	12	13
5	5	6	7	8	9	10	11	12	13	14
6	6	7	8	9	10	11	12	13	14	15
7	7	8	9	10	11	12	13	14	15	16
8	8	9	10	11	12	13	14	15	16	17
9	9	10	11	12	13	14	15	16	17	18

Table of Basic Multiplication Facts

×	0	1	2	3	4	5	6	7	8	9	10	11	12
0	0	0	0	0	0	0	0	0	0	0	0	0	0
1	0	1	2	3	4	5	6	7	8	9	10	11	12
2	0	2	4	6	8	10	12	14	16	18	20	22	24
3	0	3	6	9	12	15	18	21	24	27	30	33	36
4	0	4	8	12	16	20	24	28	32	36	40	44	48
5	0	5	10	15	20	25	30	35	40	45	50	55	60
6	0	6	12	18	24	30	36	42	48	54	60	66	72
7	0	7	14	21	28	35	42	49	56	63	70	77	84
8	0	8	16	24	32	40	48	56	64	72	80	88	96
9	0	9	18	27	36	45	54	63	72	81	90	99	108
10	0	10	20	30	40	50	60	70	80	90	100	110	120
11	0	11	22	33	44	55	66	77	88	99	110	121	132
12	0	12	24	36	48	60	72	84	96	108	120	132	144

Table of Prime Factors

Number	Prime Factors
2	prime
3	prime
4	2^2
5	prime
6	2×3
7	prime
8	2^3
9	3^2
10	2×5
11	prime
12	$2^2 \times 3$
13	prime
14	2×7
15	3×5
16	2^4
17	prime
18	2×3^2
19	prime
20	$2^2 \times 5$
21	3×7
22	2×11
23	prime
24	$2^3 \times 3$
25	5^2
26	2×13
27	3^3
28	$2^2 \times 7$
29	prime
30	$2 \times 3 \times 5$
31	prime
32	2^5
33	3×11
34	2×17
35	5×7
36	$2^2 \times 3^2$
37	prime
38	2×19
39	3×13
40	$2^3 \times 5$
41	prime
42	$2 \times 3 \times 7$
43	prime
44	$2^2 \times 11$
45	$3^2 \times 5$
46	2×23
47	prime
48	$2^4 \times 3$
49	7^2
50	2×5^2
51	3×17
52	$2^2 \times 13$
53	prime
54	2×3^3
55	5×11
56	$2^3 \times 7$
57	3×19
58	2×29
59	prime
60	$2^2 \times 3 \times 5$
61	prime
62	2×31
63	$3^2 \times 7$
64	2^6
65	5×13
66	$2 \times 3 \times 11$
67	prime
68	$2^2 \times 17$
69	3×23
70	$2 \times 5 \times 7$
71	prime
72	$2^3 \times 3^2$
73	prime
74	2×37
75	3×5^2
76	$2^2 \times 19$
77	7×11
78	$2 \times 3 \times 13$
79	prime
80	$2^4 \times 5$
81	3^4
82	2×41
83	prime
84	$2^2 \times 3 \times 7$
85	5×17
86	2×43
87	3×29
88	$2^3 \times 11$
89	prime
90	$2 \times 3^2 \times 5$
91	7×13
92	$2^2 \times 23$
93	3×31
94	2×47
95	5×19
96	$2^5 \times 3$
97	prime
98	2×7^2
99	$3^2 \times 11$
100	$2^2 \times 5^2$
101	prime
102	$2 \times 3 \times 17$
103	prime
104	$2^3 \times 13$
105	$3 \times 5 \times 7$
106	2×53
107	prime
108	$2^2 \times 3^3$
109	prime
110	$2 \times 5 \times 11$
111	3×37
112	$2^4 \times 7$
113	prime
114	$2 \times 3 \times 19$
115	5×23
116	$2^2 \times 29$
117	$3^2 \times 13$
118	2×59
119	7×17
120	$2^3 \times 3 \times 5$
121	11^2
122	2×61
123	3×41
124	$2^2 \times 31$
125	5^3
126	$2 \times 3^2 \times 7$
127	prime
128	2^7
129	3×43
130	$2 \times 5 \times 13$
131	prime
132	$2^2 \times 3 \times 11$
133	7×19
134	2×67
135	$3^3 \times 5$
136	$2^3 \times 17$
137	prime
138	$2 \times 3 \times 23$
139	prime
140	$2^2 \times 5 \times 7$
141	3×47
142	2×71
143	11×13
144	$2^4 \times 3^2$
145	5×29
146	2×73
147	3×7^2
148	$2^2 \times 37$
149	prime
150	$2 \times 3 \times 5^2$
151	prime
152	$2^3 \times 19$
153	$3^2 \times 17$
154	$2 \times 7 \times 11$
155	5×31
156	$2^2 \times 3 \times 13$
157	prime
158	2×79
159	3×53
160	$2^5 \times 5$
161	7×23
162	2×3^4
163	prime
164	$2^2 \times 41$
165	$3 \times 5 \times 11$
166	2×83
167	prime
168	$2^3 \times 3 \times 7$
169	13^2
170	$2 \times 5 \times 17$
171	$3^2 \times 19$
172	$2^2 \times 43$
173	prime
174	$2 \times 3 \times 29$
175	$5^2 \times 7$
176	$2^4 \times 11$
177	3×59
178	2×89
179	prime
180	$2^2 \times 3^2 \times 5$
181	prime
182	$2 \times 7 \times 13$
183	3×61
184	$2^3 \times 23$
185	5×37
186	$2 \times 3 \times 31$
187	11×17
188	$2^2 \times 47$
189	$3^3 \times 7$
190	$2 \times 5 \times 19$
191	prime
192	$2^6 \times 3$
193	prime
194	2×97
195	$3 \times 5 \times 13$
196	$2^2 \times 7^2$
197	prime
198	$2 \times 3^2 \times 11$
199	prime
200	$2^3 \times 5^2$

Table of Square Roots

Square Root Values Are Rounded to the Nearest Thousandth

n	$\sqrt{n}$	n	$\sqrt{n}$	n	$\sqrt{n}$	n	$\sqrt{n}$	n	$\sqrt{n}$
1	1.000	**41**	6.403	**81**	9.000	**121**	11.000	**161**	12.689
2	1.414	**42**	6.481	**82**	9.055	**122**	11.045	**162**	12.728
3	1.732	**43**	6.557	**83**	9.110	**123**	11.091	**163**	12.767
4	2.000	**44**	6.633	**84**	9.165	**124**	11.136	**164**	12.806
5	2.236	**45**	6.708	**85**	9.220	**125**	11.180	**165**	12.845
6	2.449	**46**	6.782	**86**	9.274	**126**	11.225	**166**	12.884
7	2.646	**47**	6.856	**87**	9.327	**127**	11.269	**167**	12.923
8	2.828	**48**	6.928	**88**	9.381	**128**	11.314	**168**	12.961
9	3.000	**49**	7.000	**89**	9.434	**129**	11.358	**169**	13.000
10	3.162	**50**	7.071	**90**	9.487	**130**	11.402	**170**	13.038
11	3.317	**51**	7.141	**91**	9.539	**131**	11.446	**171**	13.077
12	3.464	**52**	7.211	**92**	9.592	**132**	11.489	**172**	13.115
13	3.606	**53**	7.280	**93**	9.644	**133**	11.533	**173**	13.153
14	3.742	**54**	7.348	**94**	9.695	**134**	11.576	**174**	13.191
15	3.873	**55**	7.416	**95**	9.747	**135**	11.619	**175**	13.229
16	4.000	**56**	7.483	**96**	9.798	**136**	11.662	**176**	13.266
17	4.123	**57**	7.550	**97**	9.849	**137**	11.705	**177**	13.304
18	4.243	**58**	7.616	**98**	9.899	**138**	11.747	**178**	13.342
19	4.359	**59**	7.681	**99**	9.950	**139**	11.790	**179**	13.379
20	4.472	**60**	7.746	**100**	10.000	**140**	11.832	**180**	13.416
21	4.583	**61**	7.810	**101**	10.050	**141**	11.874	**181**	13.454
22	4.690	**62**	7.874	**102**	10.100	**142**	11.916	**182**	13.491
23	4.796	**63**	7.937	**103**	10.149	**143**	11.958	**183**	13.528
24	4.899	**64**	8.000	**104**	10.198	**144**	12.000	**184**	13.565
25	5.000	**65**	8.062	**105**	10.247	**145**	12.042	**185**	13.601
26	5.099	**66**	8.124	**106**	10.296	**146**	12.083	**186**	13.638
27	5.196	**67**	8.185	**107**	10.344	**147**	12.124	**187**	13.675
28	5.292	**68**	8.246	**108**	10.392	**148**	12.166	**188**	13.711
29	5.385	**69**	8.307	**109**	10.440	**149**	12.207	**189**	13.748
30	5.477	**70**	8.367	**110**	10.488	**150**	12.247	**190**	13.784
31	5.568	**71**	8.426	**111**	10.536	**151**	12.288	**191**	13.820
32	5.657	**72**	8.485	**112**	10.583	**152**	12.329	**192**	13.856
33	5.745	**73**	8.544	**113**	10.630	**153**	12.369	**193**	13.892
34	5.831	**74**	8.602	**114**	10.677	**154**	12.410	**194**	13.928
35	5.916	**75**	8.660	**115**	10.724	**155**	12.450	**195**	13.964
36	6.000	**76**	8.718	**116**	10.770	**156**	12.490	**196**	14.000
37	6.083	**77**	8.775	**117**	10.817	**157**	12.530	**197**	14.036
38	6.164	**78**	8.832	**118**	10.863	**158**	12.570	**198**	14.071
39	6.245	**79**	8.888	**119**	10.909	**159**	12.610	**199**	14.107
40	6.325	**80**	8.944	**120**	10.954	**160**	12.649	**200**	14.142

Appendix: Scientific Calculators

This material *does not require* the use of a calculator. However, you may want to consider the purchase of an inexpensive scientific calculator. It is wise to ask your instructor for advice before you purchase any calculator for this course. It should be stressed that students are asked to avoid using a calculator for any of the exercises in which the calculations can be readily done by hand. The only problems that really demand the use of a scientific calculator are marked with the symbol. Dependence on the use ofthe scientific calculator for regular exercises will only hurt the student in the long run.

The Two Types of Logic Used in Scientific Calculators

Two major types of scientific calculators are popular today. The most common type employs a type of logic known as **algebraic** logic. The calculators manufactured by Casio, Sharp, and Texas Instruments as well as many other companies employ this type of logic. An example of calculation on such a calculator would be the following. To add 14 + 26 on an algebraic logic calculator, the sequence of buttons would be:

$$14 \boxed{+} 26 \boxed{\ =\ }$$

The second type of scientific calculator requires the entry of data in **Reverse Polish Notation (RPN).** Calculators manufactured by Hewlett-Packard and a few other specialized calculators use RPN. To add 14 + 26 on an RPN calculator, the sequence of buttons would be:

$$14 \boxed{\text{enter}} 26 \boxed{+}$$

Graphing scientific calculators such as the TI-83 and TI-84 have a large display for viewing graphs. To perform the calculation on most graphing calculators, the sequence of buttons would be:

$$14 \boxed{+} 26 \boxed{\text{enter}}$$

Mathematicians and scientists do not agree on which type of scientific calculator is superior. However, the clear majority of college students own calculators that employ *algebraic* logic. Therefore this section is explained with reference to the sequence of steps employed by an *algebraic* logic calculator. If you already own or intend to purchase a scientific calculator that uses RPN or a graphing calculator, you are encouraged to study the instruction booklet that comes with the calculator and practise the problems shown in the booklet. After this practice you will be able to solve the calculator problems discussed in this section.

Performing Simple Calculations

The following example will illustrate the use of a scientific calculator in doing basic arithmetic calculations.

EXAMPLE 1 Add. 156 + 298

Solution We first enter the number 156, then press the [+] key, then enter the number 298, and finally press the [=] key.

156 [+] 298 [=] 454

NOTE TO STUDENT: Fully worked-out solutions to all of the Practice Problems can be found at the end of the module.

Practice Problem 1 Add. 3792 + 5896

EXAMPLE 2 Subtract. 1508 − 963

Solution We first enter the number 1508, then press the [−] key, then enter the number 963, and finally press the [=] key.

1508 [−] 963 [=] 545

Practice Problem 2 Subtract. 7930 − 5096

EXAMPLE 3 Multiply. 196 × 358

Solution 196 [×] 358 [=] 70168

Practice Problem 3 Multiply. 896 × 273

EXAMPLE 4 Divide. 2054 ÷ 13

Solution 2054 [÷] 13 [=] 158

Practice Problem 4 Divide. 2352 ÷ 16

Decimal Problems

Problems involving decimals can be readily done on a calculator. Entering numbers with a decimal point is done by pressing the decimal point key, the [·] key, at the appropriate time.

EXAMPLE 5 Calculate. 4.56 × 283

Solution To enter 4.56, we press the [4] key, the decimal point key, then the [5] key, and finally the [6] key.

4.56 [×] 283 [=] 1290.48

The answer is 1290.48. Observe how your calculator displays the decimal point.

Practice Problem 5 Calculate. 72.8 × 197

EXAMPLE 6 Add. 128.6 + 343.7 + 103.4 + 207.5

Solution 128.6 [+] 343.7 [+] 103.4 [+] 207.5 [=] 783.2

The answer is 783.2. Observe how your calculator displays the answer.

Practice Problem 6 Add. 52.98 + 31.74 + 40.37 + 99.82

Combined Operations

You must use extra caution concerning the order of mathematical operations when you are doing a problem on the calculator that involves two or more different operations.

Any scientific calculator with algebraic logic uses a priority system that has a clearly defined order of operations. It is the same order we use in performing arithmetic operations by hand. In either situation, calculations are performed in the following order:

1. First calculations within parentheses are completed.
2. Then numbers are raised to a power or a square root is calculated.
3. Then multiplication and division operations are performed from left to right.
4. Then addition and subtraction operations are performed from left to right.

This order is carefully followed on *scientific calculators* and *graphing calculators*. Small inexpensive calculators that do not have scientific functions often do not follow this order of operations.

The number of digits displayed in the answer varies from calculator to calculator. In the following examples, your calculator may display more or fewer digits than the answer we have listed.

EXAMPLE 7 Evaluate. 5.3 × 1.62 + 1.78 ÷ 3.51

Solution This problem requires that we multiply 5.3 by 1.62 and divide 1.78 by 3.51 first and then add the two results. If the numbers are entered directly into the calculator exactly as the problem is written, the calculator will perform the calculations in the correct order.

5.3 [×] 1.62 [+] 1.78 [÷] 3.51 [=] 9.09312251

Practice Problem 7 Evaluate. 0.0618 × 19.22 − 59.38 ÷ 166.3

The Use of Parentheses

In order to perform some calculations on a calculator, the use of parentheses is helpful. These parentheses may or may not appear in the original problem.

EXAMPLE 8 Evaluate. $5 \times (2.123 + 5.786 - 12.063)$

Solution The problem requires that the numbers in the parentheses be combined first. By entering the parentheses on the calculator this will be accomplished.

5 [×] [(] 2.123 [+] 5.786 [−] 12.063 [)] [=] −20.77

Note: The result is a negative number.

NOTE TO STUDENT: Fully worked-out solutions to all of the Practice Problems can be found at the end of the module.

Practice Problem 8 Evaluate. $3.152 \times (0.1628 + 3.715 - 4.985)$

Negative Numbers

To enter a negative number, enter the number followed by the [+/−] button. Some calculators require a different order. So on some calculators you first use the [+/−] button and then enter the number.

EXAMPLE 9 Evaluate. $(-8.634)(5.821) + (1.634)(-16.082)$

Solution The products will be evaluated first by the calculator. Therefore, parentheses are not needed as we enter the data.

8.634 [+/−] [×] 5.821 [+] 1.634 [×] 16.082 [+/−] [=] −76.536502

Note: The result is negative.

Practice Problem 9 Evaluate. $(0.5618)(-98.3) - (76.31)(-2.98)$

Scientific Notation

If you wish to enter a number in scientific notation, you should use the special scientific notation button. On most calculators it is denoted as [EXP] or [EE].

EXAMPLE 10 Multiply. $(9.32 \times 10^6)(3.52 \times 10^8)$

Solution 9.32 [EXP] 6 [×] 3.52 [EXP] 8 [=] 3.28064 15

This notation means the answer is $3.280\,64 \times 10^{15}$.

Practice Problem 10 Divide. $(3.76 \times 10^{15}) \div (7.76 \times 10^7)$

Raising a Number to a Power

All scientific calculators have a key for finding powers of numbers. It is usually labelled [y^x]. (On a few calculators the notation is [x^y] or sometimes [^].) To raise a number to a power on most scientific calculators, first you enter the base, then push the [y^x] key. Then you enter the exponent, then finally the [=] button.

EXAMPLE 11 Evaluate. $(2.16)^9$

Solution 2.16 [y^x] 9 [=] 1023.490369

Practice Problem 11 Evaluate. $(6.238)^6$

There is a special key to square a number. It is usually labelled [x^2].

EXAMPLE 12 Evaluate. $(76.04)^2$

Solution 76.04 [x^2] 5782.0816

Practice Problem 12 Evaluate. $(132.56)^2$

Finding Square Roots of Numbers

To approximate square roots on a scientific calculator, use the key labelled [$\sqrt{\ }$]. In this example we will need to use parentheses.

EXAMPLE 13 Evaluate. $\sqrt{5618 + 2734 + 3913}$

Solution [( ] 5618 [+] 2734 [+] 3913 [ )] [$\sqrt{\ }$] 110.7474605

Practice Problem 13 Evaluate. $\sqrt{0.0782 - 0.0132 + 0.1364}$

On some calculators, you enter the square root key first and then enter the number. You will need to try this on your own calculator.

Exercises

Use your calculator to complete each of the following. Your answers may vary slightly because of the characteristics of individual calculators.

Complete the table.

To Do This Operation	Use These Keystrokes	Record Your Answer Here
1. 8963 + 2784	8963 [+] 2784 [=]	
2. 15 308 − 7980	15308 [−] 7980 [=]	
3. 2631 × 134	2631 [×] 134 [=]	
4. 70 221 ÷ 89	70221 [÷] 89 [=]	
5. 5.325 − 4.031	5.325 [−] 4.031 [=]	
6. 184.68 + 73.98	184.68 [+] 73.98 [=]	
7. 2004.06 ÷ 7.89	2004.06 [÷] 7.89 [=]	
8. 1.34 × 0.763	1.34 [×] 0.763 [=]	

Write down the answer and then show what problem you have solved.

9. 123.45 [+] 45.9876 [+] 8765.3 [=]

10. 0.0897 [×] 234.56 [×] 2.5428 [=]

11. 34 [÷] 8 [+] 12.56 [=]

12. 458 [÷] 4 [−] 16.897 [=]

Perform each calculation using your calculator.

13. 9.467 + 0.563

14. 0.347 + 23.457

15. 34.89 + 39.6 + 214.897

16. 12.567 + 48.31 + 189.38

17. 412 899 − 34 675

18. 87 456 − 2876

19. 3 567 089 − 2 876 805

20. 8 345 802 − 4 985 004

21. 234 × 4.567

22. 1.9876 × 347

23. 0.456 × 3.48

24. 67 876 × 0.0946

25. 3458 ÷ 2.5

26. 9764 ÷ 8

27. 12.107 524 ÷ 15.86

28. 16.065 13 ÷ 17.98

Perform each calculation using your calculator.

29. $\begin{array}{r} 1.98 \\ 6.34 \\ +\ 7.71 \\ \hline \end{array}$

30. $\begin{array}{r} 8.92 \\ 9.31 \\ +\ 7.79 \\ \hline \end{array}$

31. $\begin{array}{r} \$\ 103.91 \\ 2653.82 \\ +\ 9804.61 \\ \hline \end{array}$

32. $\begin{array}{r} \$3986.21 \\ 4502.89 \\ +\ 989.30 \\ \hline \end{array}$

33. $\begin{array}{r} 368\,781.5 \\ -\ 283\,617.8 \\ \hline \end{array}$

34. $\begin{array}{r} 571\,809.6 \\ -\ 539\,376.8 \\ \hline \end{array}$

35. $\begin{array}{r} \$1\,393\,271.86 \\ -\ 1\,289\,663.21 \\ \hline \end{array}$

36. $\begin{array}{r} \$8\,571\,300.76 \\ -\ 4\,098\,789.39 \\ \hline \end{array}$

37. $\begin{array}{r} 345.34 \\ \times\ \ 45.7 \\ \hline \end{array}$

38. $\begin{array}{r} 8954.34 \\ \times\ \ 425.4 \\ \hline \end{array}$

39. $\begin{array}{r} 0.6314 \\ \times\ \ 3.96 \\ \hline \end{array}$

40. $\begin{array}{r} 0.0789 \\ \times\ \ 12.38 \\ \hline \end{array}$

41. $40.36\overline{)36\,202.92}$

42. $52.98\overline{)172\,608.84}$

43. $0.7613\overline{)17.129\,25}$

44. $0.9854\overline{)3.596\,71}$

Perform the following operations in the proper order using your calculator.

45. $4.567 + 87.89 - 2.45 \times 3.3$

46. $4.891 + 234.5 - 0.98 \times 23.4$

47. $7 \div 8 + 3.56$

48. $9 \div 4.5 + 0.6754$

49. $(9.34)(0.345) + 98.345$

50. $(0.628)(398) + 34.4581$

51. $\dfrac{(95.34)(0.9874)}{381.36}$

52. $\dfrac{(0.8759)(45.87)}{183.48}$

53. $2.56 + 8.98 \times 3.14$

54. $1.62 + 3.81 - 5.23 \times 6.18$

55. $(-4.23)(1.863) - 5.998$

56. $12.34 - (26.314)(-1.856)$

57. $5.62(5 \times 3.16 - 18.12)$

58. $9.356(4.8 - 7.2 - 15.94)$

59. $(3.42 \times 10^8)(0.97 \times 10^{10})$

60. $(6.27 \times 10^{20})(1.35 \times 10^3)$

61. $\dfrac{(2.16 \times 10^3)(1.37 \times 10^{14})}{6.39 \times 10^5}$

62. $\dfrac{(3.84 \times 10^{12})(1.62 \times 10^5)}{7.78 \times 10^8}$

63. $\dfrac{2.3 + 5.8 - 2.6 - 3.9}{5.3 - 8.2}$

64. $\dfrac{(2.6)(-3.2) + (5.8)(-0.9)}{2.614 + 5.832}$

65. $\sqrt{253.12}$

66. $\sqrt{0.0713}$

67. $\sqrt{5.6213 - 3.7214}$

68. $\sqrt{3417.2 - 2216.3}$

69. $(1.78)^3 + 6.342$

70. $(2.26)^8 - 3.1413$

71. $\sqrt{(6.13)^2 + (5.28)^2}$

72. $\sqrt{(0.3614)^2 + (0.9217)^2}$

73. $\sqrt{56 + 83} - \sqrt{12}$

74. $\sqrt{98 + 33} - \sqrt{17}$

Find an approximate value. Round to five decimal places.

75. $\dfrac{7}{18} + \dfrac{9}{13}$

76. $\dfrac{5}{22} + \dfrac{1}{31}$

77. $\dfrac{7}{8} + \dfrac{3}{11}$

78. $\dfrac{9}{14} + \dfrac{5}{19}$

Solutions to Practice Problems

Practice Problems

1. 3792 [+] 5896 [=] 9688
2. 7930 [−] 5096 [=] 2834
3. 896 [×] 273 [=] 244608
4. 2352 [÷] 16 [=] 147
5. 72.8 [×] 197 [=] 14341.6
6. 52.98 [+] 31.74 [+] 40.37 [+] 99.82 [=] 224.91
7. 0.0618 [×] 19.22 [−] 59.38 [÷] 166.3 [=] 0.830730456
8. 3.152 [×] [(] 0.1628 [+] 3.715 [−] 4.985 [)] [=] −3.4898944
9. 0.5618 [×] 98.3 [+/−] [−] 76.31 [×] 2.98 [+/−] [=] 172.17886
10. 3.76 [EXP] 15 [÷] 7.76 [EXP] 7 [=] 48453608.25
11. 6.238 [y^x] 6 [=] 58921.28674
12. 132.56 [x^2] 17572.1536
13. [(] 0.0782 [−] 0.0132 [+] 0.1364 [)] [√] 0.448776113

Answers to Selected Exercises for Appendix: Scientific Calculators

Exercises

1. 11 747 **3.** 352 554 **5.** 1.294 **7.** 254 **9.** 8934.7376; 123.45 + 45.9876 + 8765.3 **11.** 16.81; $\frac{34}{8} + 12.56$ **13.** 10.03 **15.** 289.387 **17.** 378 224 **19.** 690 284 **21.** 1068.678 **23.** 1.586 88 **25.** 1383.2 **27.** 0.7634 **29.** 16.03 **31.** $12 562.34 **33.** 85 163.7 **35.** $103 608.65 **37.** 15 782.038 **39.** 2.500 344 **41.** 897 **43.** 22.5 **45.** 84.372 **47.** 4.435 **49.** 101.5673 **51.** 0.24685 **53.** 30.7572 **55.** −13.878 49 **57.** −13.0384 **59.** 3.3174×10^{18} **61.** $4.630\,985\,915 \times 10^{11}$ **63.** −0.551 724 137 9 **65.** 15.909 745 44 **67.** 1.378 368 601 **69.** 11.981 752 **71.** 8.090 444 982 **73.** 8.325 724 507 **75.** 1.081 20 **77.** 1.147 73

Appendix: Metric and U.S. Customary Measurements

METRIC SYSTEM MEASUREMENTS

Length

1 kilometre	(km)	=	1000 metres
1 hectometre	(hm)	=	100 metres
1 decametre	(dam)	=	10 metres
1 metre	(m)	=	1 metre
1 decimetre	(dm)	=	0.1 metre
1 centimetre	(cm)	=	0.01 metre
1 millimetre	(mm)	=	0.001 metre

Weight

1 tonne	(t)	=	1 000 000 grams
1 kilogram	(kg)	=	1000 grams
1 hectogram	(hg)	=	100 grams
1 decagram	(dag)	=	10 grams
1 gram	(g)	=	1 gram
1 decigram	(dg)	=	0.1 gram
1 centigram	(cg)	=	0.01 gram
1 milligram	(mg)	=	0.001 gram

Volume

1 kilolitre	(kL)	=	1000 litres
1 hectolitre	(hL)	=	100 litres
1 decalitre	(daL)	=	10 litres
1 litre	(L)	=	1 litre
1 decilitre	(dL)	=	0.1 litre
1 centilitre	(cL)	=	0.01 litre
1 millilitre	(mL)	=	0.001 litre

Temperature: Celsius Scale

100 °C = Boiling point of water

–273.15 °C = Absolute zero: coldest possible temperature

0 °C = Freezing point of water

37 °C = Normal human body temperature

U.S. CUSTOMARY SYSTEM MEASUREMENTS

Length

1 mile	(mi)	=	1760 yards (yd)
1 mile	(mi)	=	5280 feet (ft)
1 yard	(yd)	=	3 feet (ft)
1 foot	(ft)	=	12 inches (in.)

Volume

1 gallon	(gal)	=	4 quarts (qt)
1 quart	(qt)	=	2 pints (pt)
1 pint	(pt)	=	2 cups (c)

Weight

1 ton	(T)	=	2000 pounds (lb)
1 pound	(lb)	=	16 ounces (oz)

APPROXIMATE EQUIVALENT MEASURES FOR CONVERSION OF UNITS

	U.S. Customary to Metric	Metric to U.S. Customary
Units of Length	1 mile = 1.61 kilometres 1 yard = 0.914 metre 1 foot = 0.305 metre 1 inch = 2.54 centimetres	1 kilometre = 0.62 mile 1 metre = 3.28 feet 1 metre = 1.09 yards 1 centimetre = 0.394 inch
Units of Volume	1 gallon = 3.79 litres 1 quart = 0.946 litre	1 litre = 0.264 gallon 1 litre = 1.06 quarts
Units of Weight	1 pound = 0.454 kilogram 1 ounce = 28.35 grams	1 kilogram = 2.2 pounds 1 gram = 0.0353 ounce

Appendix: Useful Formulas from Geometry

USEFUL FORMULAS FROM GEOMETRY

Perimeters, Areas, and Volumes

Rectangle

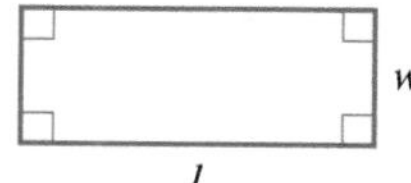

l = length w = width
Perimeter: $P = 2l + 2w$
Area: $A = lw$

Square

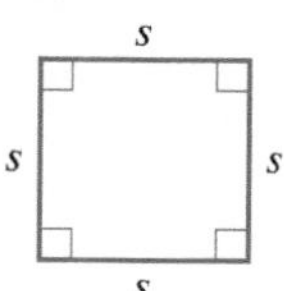

s = length of each side
Perimeter: $P = 4s$
Area: $A = s^2$

Parallelogram

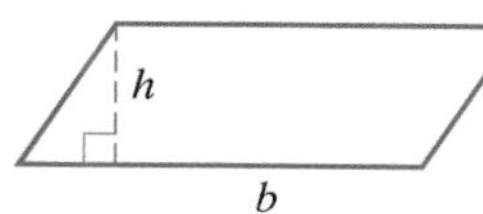

b = base h = height
Perimeter: P = sum of all sides
Area: $A = bh$

Trapezoid

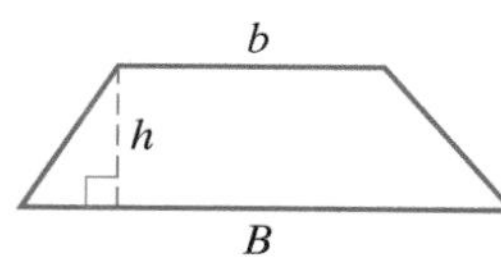

b = shorter base
B = longer base
h = height
Perimeter:
P = sum of all 4 sides
Area: $A = \dfrac{h(b + B)}{2}$

Triangle

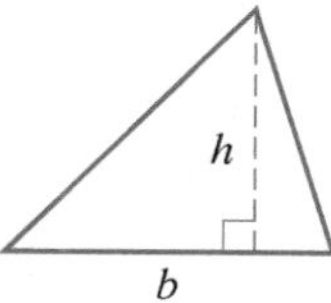

b = base
h = height
Perimeter:
P = sum of all 3 sides
Area: $A = \dfrac{bh}{2}$
Angles: Sum of the measure of all 3 angles of any triangle is 180°

Circle

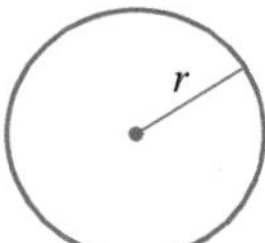

$\pi \approx 3.14$
r = radius
d = diameter
$d = 2r$
Circumference: $C = \pi d = 2\pi r$
Area: $A = \pi r^2$

Rectangular Solid

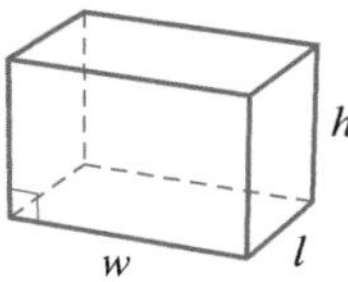

l = length w = width
h = height
Volume: $V = lwh$
Surface Area:
$S = 2lw + 2lh + 2wh$

Cylinder

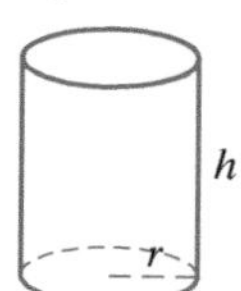

r = radius h = height
$\pi \approx 3.14$
Volume: $V = \pi r^2 h$
Surface Area: $S = 2\pi rh + 2\pi r^2$

Sphere

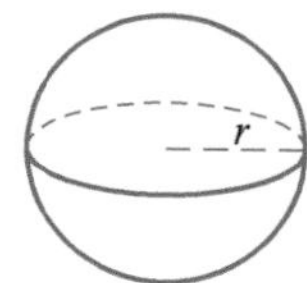

r = radius
$\pi \approx 3.14$
Volume: $V = \dfrac{4\pi r^3}{3}$
Surface Area: $s = 4\pi r^2$

Cone

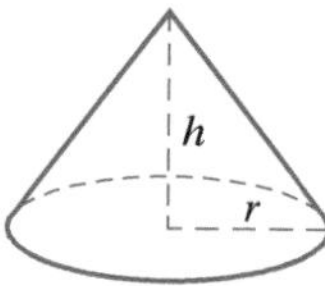

r = radius h = height
$\pi \approx 3.14$
Volume: $V = \dfrac{\pi r^2 h}{3}$
Surface Area:
$S = \pi r\sqrt{r^2 + h^2} + \pi r^2$

Pyramid

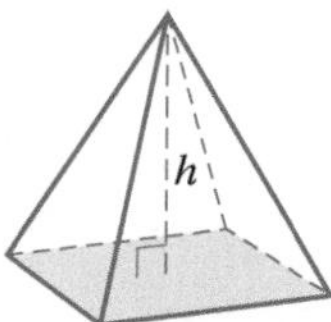

B = Area of the base (shaded)
h = height
Volume: $V = \dfrac{Bh}{3}$

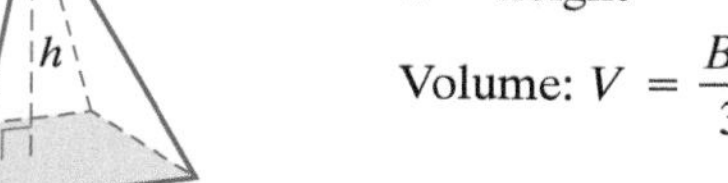

CONVERSION FACTORS

Area	1 square yard	=	9 square feet
	1 square foot	=	144 square inches
	1 square metre	=	10 000 square centimetres
Volume	1 cubic yard	=	27 cubic feet
	1 cubic foot	=	1728 cubic inches
	1 cubic metre	=	1 000 000 cubic centimetres

ndex

'age references followed by "f" indicate illustrated gures or photographs; followed by "t" indicates a able.